Map of the
WESSEX
of the
Novels and Poems

Scale of Miles

Septentrio

Oriens

Meridies

Lumsdon
Christminster

R. Thames

NORTH

The Brown House
Alfredston
Cresscombe
Marygreen

River Thames

M I D

Marlbury
Downs

WESSEX

Gaymead
Kennetbridge

Castle
Royal
Aldbrickham

Batton Castle

Inkpen Beacon

W E S S E X

Stoke Barehills

Quartershot

The Great
Plain

Weydon
Priors

Icenway
House

Stonehenge

U P P E R

ar Head

Melchester

Fernel Hall

Wintoncester

Teddenton
Wingreen
aston
arlott
The Chase
The Slopes
Trantridge Cross
Chaseborough
ourcastle
Knollingwood Hall
Shottsford
Forum
Lornton
Inn
Warborne

Deansleigh
Park

W E S S E X

Southampton

Portsmouth

The Great
Bramshurst
Forest

arrow
mb-Ash
E S S E X
Welland
Chene
Kingsbere
Manor
the
Heath
bothays
Havenpool
ther Mynton
Abury
Sandbourne
Corvsgate
Knollsea

Solentsea

**The
Island**

astle
hip

T h e   C h a n n e l

Emery Walker sc

THE THOMAS HARDY OMNIBUS

THE Thomas Hardy OMNIBUS

FAR FROM THE MADDING CROWD

THE MAYOR OF CASTERBRIDGE

THE WOODLANDERS

WESSEX TALES

TESS OF THE D'URBERVILLES

Introduction by Edward Leeson

M

ISBN: 0 333 24700 0

The dates of first publication of the individual volumes
are as follows: *Far from the Madding Crowd* 1874;
The Mayor of Casterbridge 1886; *The Woodlanders*
1887; *Wessex Tales* 1888; *Tess of the d'Urbervilles* 1891.

The text of this selection is based on that of the
New Wessex Editions, published by
Macmillan London Ltd 1974, 1976.

The title-page illustration is of Blackmore Vale, Dorset,
from Bulbarrow (*K. V. Cooper*), and the illustrations
used to introduce each volume are: *Far from the
Madding Crowd* – a sheep-washing pool (*James and
Gregory Stevens-Cox*); *The Mayor of Casterbridge* –
High East Street, Dorchester ('Casterbridge') (*Robert
Cooke, M.P.*); *The Woodlanders* – Turnworth House
('Hintock House') (*Dorset County Museum,
Dorchester*); *Wessex Tales* – the hangman's cottage,
Dorchester ('Casterbridge') (*Dorset County Museum,
Dorchester*); *Tess of the d'Urbervilles* – Marnhull
('Marlott') with 'The Pure Drop' inn on the right
(*Robert Cooke, M.P.*).

This selection first published 1978 by
MACMILLAN LONDON LIMITED
London and Basingstoke

Associated companies in Auckland, Dallas,
Delhi, Dublin, Hong Kong, Johannesburg,
Lagos, Manzini, Melbourne, Nairobi,
New York, Singapore, Tokyo, Washington
and Zaria

Reprinted 1981

Printed in Great Britain by
THE PITMAN PRESS
Bath

Contents

Major Works with Year of Book Publication

1871 Desperate Remedies
1872 Under the Greenwood Tree
1873 A Pair of Blue Eyes
1874 Far from the Madding Crowd
1876 The Hand of Ethelberta
1878 The Return of the Native
1880 The Trumpet-Major
1881 A Laodicean
1882 Two on a Tower
1886 The Mayor of Casterbridge
1887 The Woodlanders
1888 Wessex Tales
1891 A Group of Noble Dames
1891 Tess of the d'Urbervilles
1894 Life's Little Ironies
1895 Jude the Obscure

1897 The Well-Beloved
1898 Wessex Poems
1902 Poems of the Past and the Present
1904 The Dynasts, pt 1
1906 The Dynasts, pt 2
1908 The Dynasts, pt 3
1909 Time's Laughingstocks
1913 A Changed Man and Other Tales
1914 Satires of Circumstance
1917 Moments of Vision
1922 Late Lyrics and Earlier
1923 The Famous Tragedy of the
       Queen of Cornwall
1925 Human Shows
1928 Winter Words
1952 Our Exploits at West Poley

Introduction

THOMAS HARDY was born on 2 June 1840 in the tiny hamlet of Higher Bockhampton, near Dorchester in Dorset, in the heart of the region he was to immortalise under its old name of Wessex – 'bounded on the north by the Thames, on the south by the English Channel, on the east by a line running from Hayling Island to Windsor Forest, and on the west by the Cornish coast'.

Hardy's father, like his own father before him, was a master-stonemason, and also an enthusiastic player in the local church 'choir' or band. The musicians not only accompanied the hymns in church but also provided music for social gatherings in the neighbourhood, and it was not long before young Thomas Hardy was sufficiently accomplished on the violin to accompany his father to these engagements. He was later to celebrate the musical traditions of his childhood, fast disappearing in the face of modern innovation, in loving detail in his second published novel, *Under the Greenwood Tree*.

However, while Hardy was absorbing local traditions from his father and from his grandmother, who was to provide Hardy with a wealth of local lore and family legend which he was to put to good use throughout his career, his mother was awakening his intellectual life at a precociously early age by giving him such books as Dryden's translation of Virgil's *Aeneid* and Johnson's *Rasselas*. The interplay of the two strands of folk-memory and the intellect was crucial in forming Hardy's literary style.

In 1848 he was sent to the local school in Lower Bockhampton, and a year later was transferred to another school in Dorchester, walking the three miles there and back every day. His schooldays lasted until 1856 when, at the age of sixteen, he was articled to the Dorchester architect John Hicks, at the same time launching himself on a formidable programme of self-education which included rising early each morning to teach himself Greek before walking to work in Dorchester. He had also begun to write poetry.

In 1862 he sought broader experience in London, where he was employed in the office of the architect Arthur Blomfield, and he took full advantage of the cultural riches of the capital. He continued to write poetry, though none of this early work found a publisher. However, he was able to derive some small satisfaction from the fact that in 1864 he won an essay prize offered by the Royal Institute of British Architects. At this time, too, he began his first novel, 'The Poor Man and the Lady'. It was to remain unpublished in its original form; but Hardy allowed little to be wasted, using much of the material in later works.

Inevitably the strain of having a full-time job, educating himself and trying to make a start as a creative writer began to tell, and Hardy was obliged to leave both Blomfield and London and return to Higher Bockhampton to recover his health. Gradually, away from the distractions of London, his condition improved and he resumed work for Hicks – and, after Hicks's death, for his successor Crickmay – in Dorchester, principally on church restoration work.

Church restoration – a dubious practice involving the refurbishing of old churches in the neo-Gothic manner – was to bring about a major event in Hardy's life. In 1870, Crickmay sent Hardy, now thirty years old, to St Juliot in Cornwall to draw up plans for the restoration of the parish church. At the vicarage he was welcomed by Emma Lavinia Gifford, the vicar's sister-in-law. Emma recalled the meeting in her 'Recollections': '. . . the front-door bell rang, and the architect was ushered in. I had to receive him alone, and felt a curious uneasy embarrassment at receiving anyone, especially so necessary a person as the architect. I was immediately arrested by his familiar appearance, as if I had seen him in a dream – his slightly different accent, his soft voice; also I noticed a blue paper sticking out of his pocket. . . . So I met my husband. I thought him much older than he was. He had a beard, and a rather shabby greatcoat, and had quite a business appearance. Afterwards he seemed younger, and by daylight especially so. . . . The blue paper proved to be the MS. of a poem, and not a plan of the church, he informed me, to my surprise.'

This was to be the first of many visits to St Juliot. The two people fell in love and were eventually married in 1874 – by which time Hardy's literary career had blossomed, and the conflict between literature and architecture had been resolved in favour of the former, with his first published novel, *Desperate Remedies* (1871), followed by *Under the Greenwood Tree* (1872), *A Pair of Blue Eyes* (1873) and *Far from the Madding Crowd* (1874).

Far from the Madding Crowd was Hardy's first fully mature novel and has enjoyed continued popularity since it was first published. It has an additional significance in that it was in this novel that Hardy first gave the name 'Wessex' to the stage on which his stories were set. In subsequent works he was to define the region in greater detail; and he was so successful in this regard that before long many of his readers were beginning to explore the 'Hardy country', relating fictional localities to their real-life counterparts – though Hardy advised them that such exact identification was not really possible since he had never hesitated to adjust local geography to suit his requirements.

In the years that followed, the Hardys lived in rented accommodation in various parts of suburban London and in the West Country, and Hardy, who was now an established author, began to play a full part in London literary life.

The Hand of Ethelberta, a slight performance, was published in 1876, to be redeemed in 1878 by *The Return of the Native* – one of Hardy's most powerful novels and a brilliant evocation of the landscape in which he grew up. *The Trumpet-Major* (1880) was Hardy's first full treatment of the Napoleonic era – in particular, how the lives of coastal communities were affected by the constant threat of invasion – and drew heavily on the local tales he had absorbed in childhood. The quality of *A Laodicean* (1881), a long and unconvincing work, was undoubtedly affected by the fact that throughout the winter of 1880–1 Hardy had been immobilised by illness and obliged to dictate almost the whole work. *Two on a Tower*, which despite some fine writing and a striking heroine is only a minor novel, came in 1882.

In 1885 the Hardys moved into Max Gate, the imposing residence just outside Dorchester which Hardy had designed himself. This new-found security seems to have given Hardy fresh confidence, for he now entered a period of intense creativity. *The Mayor of Casterbridge* came in 1886. This is in many ways Hardy's best novel: the fortunes of the hero, Michael Henchard, and his conflict with the 'new man' Donald Farfrae are vividly depicted; Casterbridge is evoked in convincing detail; and the closing pages of the novel are surely among the most moving passages in English fiction.

The Woodlanders was published in 1887 and, although pitched in a lower key than the other major novels, is nevertheless a splendid piece of writing, exploring the conflict between urban sophistication and rural simplicity in a manner which led Arnold Bennett to consider it 'the finest English novel'.

Tess of the d'Urbervilles (1891), the tale of the pure woman Tess Durbeyfield seduced by the wealthy Alec d'Urberville, which is for many Hardy's greatest novel, was to put Hardy at odds with his public for the first time as he tried to approach a sensitive subject directly; but the real trouble was to come with the publication of *Jude the Obscure* in 1895. This novel marks an important point in Hardy's career. Challenging comfortable Victorian attitudes in a forthright manner which impresses the reader even now, *Jude* was to offend many people – including Hardy's wife – and provoke a hostile reaction from reviewers.

This period also saw the emergence of Hardy as a major short-story writer. His first collection, *Wessex Tales*, appeared in 1888. No reader can fail to be struck by the remarkable variety of the stories – from the grim ironies of 'The Three Strangers' and 'The Withered Arm' to the gentle humour of 'The Distracted Preacher'. Two tales – 'A Tradition of Eighteen Hundred and Four' and 'The Melancholy Hussar of the German Legion' – offer revealing sidelights on Hardy's lifelong obsession with the Napoleonic wars, which he treated at greater length in *The Trumpet-Major* and which were ultimately to form the subject of his vast epic-drama, *The Dynasts*.

Further collections were to follow: *A Group of Noble Dames* (1891), a gallery of heroines which owes much to Hardy's knowledge of Dorset local history; *Life's Little Ironies* (1894), which contains 'A Few Crusted Characters', a series of linked stories that amply demonstrate through their range of subject and mood Hardy's astonishing versatility; and *A Changed Man and Other Tales* (1913).

The bitterness of the reception of *Jude the Obscure* prompted Hardy – or, perhaps more accurately, gave him the excuse he needed – to return to poetry, his first love. The transition was made possible by the financial security which his prose writing had brought him; and, apart from publishing an earlier novel, *The Well-Beloved*, in book form in 1897 and a final collection of stories in *A Changed Man*, he devoted the rest of his life to poetry. His first volume, *Wessex Poems*, was published in 1898, and was to be followed by seven more – *Poems of the Past and the Present* (1902), *Time's Laughingstocks* (1909), *Satires of Circumstance* (1914), *Moments of Vision* (1917), *Late Lyrics and Earlier* (1922), *Human Shows* (1925) and the posthumously published *Winter Words* (1928).

Early in the new century Hardy's thoughts turned once again to Napoleon, and he at last set to work on the epic which he had been planning intermittently throughout his career. *The Dynasts*, the last great English verse epic, was published in three parts between 1904 and 1908. Personal reminiscence, family legend and historical research blended to produce a highly distinctive work. Hardy's only other venture into verse drama came in 1923 with *The Famous*

Tragedy of the Queen of Cornwall, a brief play owing much to the mummers' performances that Hardy had seen as a child.

Emma's death in 1912, following a long period of strained relations with her husband, produced in Hardy a profound feeling of remorse. He made a pilgrimage to those places which had meant so much to them in the early days of their love, and from this experience came 'Poems of 1912–13' – one of the finest sequences of love-poems in the English language – included in *Satires of Circumstance*.

In 1914, Hardy married Florence Emily Dugdale, who brought him much-needed companionship for the remaining years of his life – years of undiminished creativity as one substantial volume of poems followed another until old age finally overcame him. He died on the evening of 11 January 1928.

'An hour later', Florence wrote, 'one, going to his bedside yet again, saw on the death-face an expression such as she had never seen before on any being, or indeed on any presentment of the human countenance. It was a look of radiant triumph such as imagination could never have conceived. Later the first radiance passed away, but dignity and peace remained as long as eyes could see the mortal features of Thomas Hardy.

'The dawn of the following day rose in almost unparalleled splendour. Flaming and magnificent the sky stretched its banners over the dark pines that stood sentinel around.'

Hardy's body was cremated and the ashes buried in Westminster Abbey, but his heart was buried in his first wife's grave in Stinsford churchyard, in the depths of the countryside he had celebrated in his novels.

EDWARD LEESON

FAR FROM THE MADDING CROWD

Far from the Madding Crowd

Contents

CHAPTER ONE

Description of Farmer Oak –
An Incident

WHEN Farmer Oak smiled, the corners of his mouth spread till they were within an unimportant distance of his ears, his eyes were reduced to chinks, and diverging wrinkles appeared round them, extending upon his countenance like the rays in a rudimentary sketch of the rising sun.

His Christian name was Gabriel, and on working days he was a young man of sound judgment, easy motions, proper dress, and general good character. On Sundays he was a man of misty views, rather given to postponing, and hampered by his best clothes and umbrella: upon the whole, one who felt himself to occupy morally that vast middle space of Laodicean neutrality which lay between the Communion people of the parish and the drunken section, – that is, he went to church, but yawned privately by the time the congregation reached the Nicene creed, and thought of what there would be for dinner when he meant to be listening to the sermon. Or, to state his character as it stood in the scale of public opinion, when his friends and critics were in tantrums, he was considered rather a bad man; when they were pleased, he was rather a good man; when they were neither, he was a man whose moral colour was a kind of pepper-and-salt mixture.

Since he lived six times as many working days as Sundays, Oak's appearance in his old clothes was most peculiarly his own – the mental picture formed by his neighbours in imagining him being always dressed in that way. He wore a low-crowned felt hat, spread out at the base by tight jamming upon the head for security in high winds, and a coat like Dr Johnson's; his lower extremities being encased in ordinary leather leggings and boots emphatically large, affording to each foot a roomy apartment so constructed that any wearer might stand in a river all day long and know nothing of damp – their maker being a conscientious man who endeavoured to compensate for any weakness in his cut by unstinted dimension and solidity.

Mr Oak carried about him, by way of watch, what may be called a small silver clock; in other words, it was a watch as to shape and intention, and a small clock as to size. This instrument being several years older than Oak's grandfather, had the peculiarity of going either too fast or not at all. The smaller of its hands, too, occasionally slipped round on the pivot, and thus, though the minutes were told with precision, nobody could be quite certain of the hour they belonged to. The stopping peculiarity of his watch Oak remedied by thumps and shakes, and he escaped any evil consequences from the other two defects by constant comparisons with and observations of the sun and stars, and by pressing his face close to the glass of his neighbours' windows, till he could discern the hour marked by the green-faced time-keepers within. It may be mentioned that Oak's fob being difficult of access, by reason of its somewhat high situation in the waistband of his trousers (which also lay at a remote height under his waistcoat), the watch was as a necessity pulled out by throwing the body to one side, compressing the mouth and face to a mere mass of ruddy flesh on account of the exertion, and drawing up the watch by its chain, like a bucket from a well.

But some thoughtful persons, who had seen him walking across one of his fields on a certain December morning – sunny and exceedingly mild – might have regarded Gabriel Oak in other aspects than these. In his face one might notice that many of the hues and curves of youth had tarried on to manhood: there even remained in his remoter crannies some relics of the boy. His height and breadth would have been sufficient to make his presence imposing, had they been exhibited with due consideration. But there is a way some men have, rural and urban alike, for which the mind is more responsible than flesh and sinew: it is a way of curtailing their dimensions by their manner of showing them. And from a quiet modesty that would have become a vestal, which seemed continually to impress upon him that he had no great claim on the world's room, Oak walked unassumingly, and with a faintly perceptible bend, yet distinct from a bowing of the shoulders. This may be said to be a defect in an individual if he depends for his valuation more upon his appearance than upon his capacity to wear well, which Oak did not.

He had just reached the time of life at which 'young' is ceasing to be the prefix of 'man' in speaking of one. He was at the brightest period of masculine growth, for his intellect and his emotions were clearly separated: he had passed the time during which the influence of youth indiscriminately mingles them in the character of impulse, and he had not yet arrived at the stage wherein they become united again, in the character of prejudice, by the influence of a wife and family. In short, he was twenty-eight, and a bachelor.

The field he was in this morning sloped to a ridge called Norcombe Hill. Through a spur of this hill ran the highway between Emminster and Chalk-Newton. Casually glancing over the hedge, Oak saw coming down the incline before him an ornamental spring waggon, painted yellow and gaily marked, drawn by two horses, a waggoner walking alongside bearing a whip perpendicularly. The waggon was laden with household goods and window plants, and on the apex of the whole sat a woman, young and attractive. Gabriel had not beheld the sight for more than half a minute, when the vehicle was brought to a standstill just beneath his eyes.

'The tailboard of the waggon is gone, Miss,' said the waggoner.

'Then I heard it fall,' said the girl, in a soft, though not particularly low voice. 'I heard a noise I could not account for when we were coming up the hill.'

'I'll run back.'

'Do,' she answered.

The sensible horses stood perfectly still, and the waggoner's steps sank fainter and fainter in the distance.

The girl on the summit of the load sat motionless, surrounded by tables and chairs with their legs upwards, backed by an oak settle, and ornamented in front by pots of geraniums, myrtles, and cactuses, together with a caged canary – all probably from the windows of the house just vacated. There was also a cat in a willow basket, from the partly-opened lid of which she gazed with half-closed eyes, and affectionately surveyed the small birds around.

The handsome girl waited for some time idly in her place, and the only sound heard in the stillness was the hopping of the canary up and down the perches of its prison. Then she looked attentively downwards. It was not at the bird, nor at the cat; it was at an oblong package tied in paper, and lying between them. She turned her head to learn if the waggoner were coming. He was not yet in sight; and her eyes crept back to the package, her thoughts seeming to run upon what was inside it. At length she drew the article into her lap, and untied the paper covering; a small swing looking-glass was disclosed, in which she proceeded to survey herself attentively. She parted her lips and smiled.

It was a fine morning, and the sun lighted up to a scarlet glow the crimson jacket she wore, and painted a soft lustre upon her bright face and dark hair. The myrtles, geraniums, and cactuses packed around her were fresh and green, and at such a leafless season they invested the whole concern of horses, waggon, furniture, and girl with a peculiar vernal charm. What possessed her to indulge in such a performance in the sight of the sparrows, blackbirds, and unperceived farmer who were alone its spectators, — whether the smile began as a factitious one, to test her capacity in that art, — nobody knows; it ended certainly in a real smile. She blushed at herself, and seeing her reflection blush, blushed the more.

The change from the customary spot and necessary occasion of such an act — from the dressing hour in a bedroom to a time of travelling out of doors — lent to the idle deed a novelty it did not intrinsically possess. The picture was a delicate one. Woman's prescriptive infirmity had stalked into the sunlight, which had clothed it in the freshness of an originality. A cynical inference was irresistible by Gabriel Oak as he regarded the scene, generous though he fain would have been. There was no necessity whatever for her looking in the glass. She did not adjust her hat, or pat her hair, or press a dimple into shape, or do one thing to signify that any such intention had been her motive in taking up the glass. She simply observed herself as a fair product of Nature in the feminine kind, her thoughts seeming to glide into far-off though likely dramas in which men would play a part — vistas of probable triumphs — the smiles being of a phase suggesting that hearts were imagined as lost and won. Still, this was but conjecture, and the whole series of actions was so idly put forth as to make it rash to assert that intention had any part in them at all.

The waggoner's steps were heard returning. She put the glass in the paper, and the whole again into its place.

When the waggon had passed on, Gabriel withdrew from his point of espial, and descending into the road, followed the vehicle to the turnpike-gate some way beyond the bottom of the hill, where the object of his contemplation now halted for the payment of toll. About twenty steps still remained between him and the gate, when he heard a dispute. It was a difference concerning twopence between the persons with the waggon and the man at the toll-bar.

'Mis'ess's niece is upon the top of the things, and she says that's enough that I've offered ye, you great miser, and she won't pay any more.' These were the waggoner's words.

'Very well; then mis'ess's niece can't pass,' said the turnpike-keeper, closing the gate.

Oak looked from one to the other of the disputants, and fell into a reverie. There was something in the tone of twopence remarkably insignificant. Threepence had a definite value as money – it was an appreciable infringement on a day's wages, and, as such, a higgling matter; but twopence—'Here,' he said, stepping forward and handing twopence to the gatekeeper; 'let the young woman pass.' He looked up at her then; she heard his words, and looked down.

Gabriel's features adhered throughout their form so exactly to the middle line between the beauty of St John and the ugliness of Judas Iscariot, as represented in a window of the church he attended, that not a single lineament could be selected and called worthy either of distinction or notoriety. The red-jacketed and dark-haired maiden seemed to think so too, for she carelessly glanced over him, and told her man to drive on. She might have looked her thanks to Gabriel on a minute scale, but she did not speak them; more probably she felt none, for in gaining her a passage he had lost her her point, and we know how women take a favour of that kind.

The gatekeeper surveyed the retreating vehicle. 'That's a handsome maid,' he said to Oak.

'But she has her faults,' said Gabriel.

'True, farmer.'

'And the greatest of them is – well, what it is always.'

'Beating people down? ay, 'tis so.'

'O no.'

'What, then?'

Gabriel, perhaps a little piqued by the comely traveller's indifference, glanced back to where he had witnessed her performance over the hedge, and said, 'Vanity.'

CHAPTER TWO

Night – The Flock – An Interior –
Another Interior

I T was nearly midnight on the eve of St Thomas's, the shortest day in the year. A desolating wind wandered from the north over the hill whereon Oak had watched the yellow waggon and its occupant in the sunshine of a few days earlier.

Norcombe Hill – not far from lonely Toller-Down – was one of the spots which suggest to a passer-by that he is in the presence of a shape approaching the indestructible as nearly as any to be found on earth. It was a featureless convexity of chalk and soil – an ordinary specimen of those smoothly-outlined pro-tuberances of the globe which may remain undisturbed on some great day of confusion, when far grander heights and dizzy granite precipices topple down.

The hill was covered on its northern side by an ancient and decaying plantation of beeches, whose upper verge formed a line over the crest, fringing its arched curve against the sky, like a mane. To-night these trees sheltered the southern slope from the keenest blasts, which smote the wood and floundered through it with a sound as of grumbling, or gushed over its crowning boughs in a weakened moan. The dry leaves in the ditch simmered and boiled in the same breezes, a tongue of air occasionally ferreting out a few, and sending them spinning across the grass. A group or two of the latest in date amongst the dead multitude had remained till this very mid-winter time on the twigs which bore them, and in falling rattled against the trunks with smart taps.

Between this half-wooded half-naked hill, and the vague still horizon that its summit indistinctly commanded, was a mysterious sheet of fathomless shade — the sounds from which suggested that what it concealed bore some reduced resemblance to features here. The thin grasses, more or less coating the hill, were touched by the wind in breezes of differing powers, and almost of differing natures — one rubbing the blades heavily, another raking them piercingly, another brushing them like a soft broom. The instinctive act of humankind was to stand and listen, and learn how the trees on the right and the trees on the left wailed or chaunted to each other in the regular antiphonies of a cathedral choir; how hedges and other shapes to leeward then caught the note, lowering it to the tenderest sob; and how the hurrying gust then plunged into the south, to be heard no more.

The sky was clear — remarkably clear — and the twinkling of all the stars seemed to be but throbs of one body, timed by a common pulse. The North Star was directly in the wind's eye, and since evening the Bear had swung round it outwardly to the east, till he was now at a right angle with the meridian. A difference of colour in the stars — oftener read of than seen in England — was really perceptible here. The sovereign brilliancy of Sirius pierced the eye with a steely glitter, the star called Capella was yellow, Aldebaran and Betelgueux shone with a fiery red.

To persons standing alone on a hill during a clear midnight such as this, the roll of the world eastward is almost a palpable movement. The sensation may be caused by the panoramic glide of the stars past earthly objects, which is perceptible in a few minutes of stillness, or by the better outlook upon space that a hill affords, or by the wind, or by the solitude; but whatever be its origin the impression of riding along is vivid and abiding. The poetry of motion is a phrase much in use, and to enjoy the epic form of that gratification it is necessary to stand on a hill at a small hour of the night, and, having first expanded with a sense of difference from the mass of civilized mankind, who are dreamwrapt and disregardful of all such proceedings at this time, long and quietly watch your stately progress through the stars. After such a nocturnal reconnoitre it is hard to get back to earth, and to believe that the consciousness of such majestic speeding is derived from a tiny human frame.

Suddenly an unexpected series of sounds began to be heard in this place up against the sky. They had a clearness which was to be found nowhere in the wind, and a sequence which was to be found nowhere in nature. They were the notes of Farmer Oak's flute.

The tune was not floating unhindered into the open air: it seemed muffled in some way, and was altogether too curtailed in power to spread high or wide. It

came from the direction of a small dark object under the plantation hedge – a
shepherd's hut – now presenting an outline to which an uninitiated person might
have been puzzled to attach either meaning or use.

The image as a whole was that of a small Noah's Ark on a small Ararat,
allowing the traditional outlines and general form of the Ark which are
followed by toy-makers – and by these means are established in men's imagin-
ations among their firmest, because earliest impressions – to pass as an
approximate pattern. The hut stood on little wheels, which raised its floor about a
foot from the ground. Such shepherds' huts are dragged into the fields when the
lambing season comes on, to shelter the shepherd in his enforced nightly
attendance.

It was only latterly that people had begun to call Gabriel 'Farmer' Oak.
During the twelvemonth preceding this time he had been enabled by sustained
efforts of industry and chronic good spirits to lease the small sheep-farm of which
Norcombe Hill was a portion, and stock it with two hundred sheep. Previously he
had been a bailiff for a short time, and earlier still a shepherd only, having from
his childhood assisted his father in tending the flocks of large proprietors, till old
Gabriel sank to rest.

This venture, unaided and alone, into the paths of farming as master and not as
man, with an advance of sheep not yet paid for, was a critical juncture with
Gabriel Oak, and he recognized his position clearly. The first movement in his
new progress was the lambing of his ewes, and sheep having been his speciality
from his youth, he wisely refrained from deputing the task of tending them at this
season to a hireling or a novice.

The wind continued to beat about the corners of the hut, but the flute-playing
ceased. A rectangular space of light appeared in the side of the hut, and in the
opening the outline of Farmer Oak's figure. He carried a lantern in his hand, and
closing the door behind him came forward and busied himself about this nook of
the field for nearly twenty minutes, the lantern light appearing and disappearing
here and there, and brightening him or darkening him as he stood before or
behind it.

Oak's motions, though they had a quiet energy, were slow, and their
deliberateness accorded well with his occupation. Fitness being the basis of
beauty, nobody could have denied that his steady swings and turns in and about
the flock had elements of grace. Yet, although if occasion demanded he could do
or think a thing with as mercurial a dash as can the men of towns who are more to
the manner born, his special power, morally, physically, and mentally, was static,
owing little or nothing to momentum as a rule.

A close examination of the ground hereabout, even by the wan starlight only,
revealed how a portion of what would have been casually called a wild slope had
been appropriated by Farmer Oak for his great purpose this winter. Detached
hurdles thatched with straw were stuck into the ground at various scattered
points, amid and under which the whitish forms of his meek ewes moved and
rustled. The ring of the sheep-bell, which had been silent during his absence,
recommenced, in tones that had more mellowness than clearness, owing to an
increasing growth of surrounding wool. This continued till Oak withdrew again
from the flock. He returned to the hut, bringing in his arms a new-born lamb,
consisting of four legs large enough for a full-grown sheep, united by a seemingly

inconsiderable membrane about half the substance of the legs collectively, which constituted the animal's entire body just at present.

The little speck of life he placed on a wisp of hay before the small stove, where a can of milk was simmering. Oak extinguished the lantern by blowing into it and then pinching the snuff, the cot being lighted by a candle suspended by a twisted wire. A rather hard couch, formed of a few corn sacks thrown carelessly down, covered half the floor of this little habitation, and here the young man stretched himself along, loosened his woollen cravat, and closed his eyes. In about the time a person unaccustomed to bodily labour would have decided upon which side to lie, Farmer Oak was asleep.

The inside of the hut, as it now presented itself, was cosy and alluring, and the scarlet handful of fire in addition to the candle, reflecting its own genial colour upon whatever it could reach, flung associations of enjoyment even over utensils and tools. In the corner stood the sheep-crook, and along a shelf at one side were ranged bottles and canisters of the simple preparations pertaining to ovine surgery and physic; spirits of wine, turpentine, tar, magnesia, ginger, and castor-oil being the chief. On a triangular shelf across the corner stood bread, bacon, cheese, and a cup for ale or cider, which was supplied from a flagon beneath. Beside the provisions lay the flute, whose notes had lately been called forth by the lonely watcher to beguile a tedious hour. The house was ventilated by two round holes, like the lights of a ship's cabin, with wood slides.

The lamb, revived by the warmth, began to bleat, and the sound entered Gabriel's ears and brain with an instant meaning, as expected sounds will. Passing from the profoundest sleep to the most alert wakefulness with the same ease that had accompanied the reverse operation, he looked at his watch, found that the hour-hand had shifted again, put on his hat, took the lamb in his arms, and carried it into the darkness. After placing the little creature with its mother he stood and carefully examined the sky, to ascertain the time of night from the altitudes of the stars.

The Dog-star and Aldebaran, pointing to the restless Pleiades, were half-way up the Southern sky, and between them hung Orion, which gorgeous constellation never burnt more vividly than now, as it soared forth above the rim of the landscape. Castor and Pollux with their quiet shine were almost on the meridian: the barren and gloomy Square of Pegasus was creeping round to the north-west; far away through the plantation Vega sparkled like a lamp suspended amid the leafless trees, and Cassiopeia's chair stood daintily poised on the uppermost boughs.

'One o'clock,' said Gabriel.

Being a man not without a frequent consciousness that there was some charm in this life he led, he stood still after looking at the sky as a useful instrument, and regarded it in an appreciative spirit, as a work of art superlatively beautiful. For a moment he seemed impressed with the speaking loneliness of the scene, or rather with the complete abstraction from all its compass of the sights and sounds of man. Human shapes, interferences, troubles, and joys were all as if they were not, and there seemed to be on the shaded hemisphere of the globe no sentient being save himself; he could fancy them all gone round to the sunny side.

Occupied thus, with eyes stretched afar, Oak gradually perceived that what he had previously taken to be a star low down behind the outskirts of the plantation was in reality no such thing. It was an artificial light, almost close at hand.

To find themselves utterly alone at night where company is desirable and expected makes some people fearful; but a case more trying by far to the nerves is to discover some mysterious companionship when intuition, sensation, memory, analogy, testimony, probability, induction – every kind of evidence in the logician's list – have united to persuade consciousness that it is quite in isolation.

Farmer Oak went towards the plantation and pushed through its lower boughs to the windy side. A dim mass under the slope reminded him that a shed occupied a place here, the site being a cutting into the slope of the hill, so that at its back part the roof was almost level with the ground. In front it was formed of boards nailed to posts and covered with tar as a preservative. Through crevices in the roof and side spread streaks and dots of light, a combination of which made the radiance that had attracted him. Oak stepped up behind, where, leaning down upon the roof and putting his eye close to a hole, he could see into the interior clearly.

The place contained two women and two cows. By the side of the latter a steaming bran-mash stood in a bucket. One of the women was past middle age. Her companion was apparently young and graceful: he could form no decided opinion upon her looks, her position being almost beneath his eye, so that he saw her in a bird's-eye view, as Milton's Satan first saw Paradise. She wore no bonnet or hat, but had enveloped herself in a large cloak, which was carelessly flung over her head as a covering.

'There, now we'll go home,' said the elder of the two, resting her knuckles upon her hips, and looking at their goings-on as a whole. 'I do hope Daisy will fetch round again now. I have never been more frightened in my life, but I don't mind breaking my rest if she recovers.'

The young woman, whose eyelids were apparently inclined to fall together on the smallest provocation of silence, yawned without parting her lips to any inconvenient extent, whereupon Gabriel caught the infection and slightly yawned in sympathy.

'I wish we were rich enough to pay a man to do these things,' she said.

'As we are not, we must do them ourselves,' said the other; 'for you must help me if you stay.'

'Well, my hat is gone, however,' continued the younger. 'It went over the hedge, I think. The idea of such a slight wind catching it.'

The cow standing erect was of the Devon breed, and was encased in a tight warm hide of rich Indian red, as absolutely uniform from eyes to tail as if the animal had been dipped in a dye of that colour, her long back being mathematically level. The other was spotted, grey and white. Beside her Oak now noticed a little calf about a day old, looking idiotically at the two women, which showed that it had not long been accustomed to the phenomenon of eyesight, and often turning to the lantern, which it apparently mistook for the moon, inherited instinct having as yet had little time for correction by experience. Between the sheep and the cows Lucina had been busy on Norcombe Hill lately.

'I think we had better send for some oatmeal,' said the elder woman; 'there's no more bran.'

'Yes, aunt; and I'll ride over for it as soon as it is light.'

'But there's no side-saddle.'

'I can ride on the other: trust me.'

Oak, upon hearing these remarks, became more curious to observe her features, but this prospect being denied him by the hooding effect of the cloak, and by his aërial position, he felt himself drawing upon his fancy for their details. In making even horizontal and clear inspections we colour and mould according to the wants within us whatever our eyes bring in. Had Gabriel been able from the first to get a distinct view of her countenance, his estimate of it as very handsome or slightly so would have been as his soul required a divinity at the moment or was ready supplied with one. Having for some time known the want of a satisfactory form to fill an increasing void within him, his position moreover affording the widest scope for his fancy, he painted her a beauty.

By one of those whimsical coincidences in which Nature, like a busy mother, seems to spare a moment from her unremitting labours to turn and make her children smile, the girl now dropped the cloak, and forth tumbled ropes of black hair over a red jacket. Oak knew her instantly as the heroine of the yellow waggon, myrtles, and looking-glass: prosily, as the woman who owed him twopence.

They placed the calf beside its mother again, took up the lantern, and went out, the light sinking down the hill till it was no more than a nebula. Gabriel Oak returned to his flock.

CHAPTER THREE

A Girl on Horseback – Conversation

THE sluggish day began to break. Even its position terrestrially is one of the elements of a new interest, and for no particular reason save that the incident of the night had occurred there Oak went again into the plantation. Lingering and musing here he heard the steps of a horse at the foot of the hill, and soon there appeared in view an auburn pony with a girl on its back, ascending by the path leading past the cattle-shed. She was the young woman of the night before. Gabriel instantly thought of the hat she had mentioned as having lost in the wind; possibly she had come to look for it. He hastily scanned the ditch, and after walking about ten yards along it found the hat among the leaves. Gabriel took it in his hand and returned to his hut. Here he ensconced himself, and peeped through the loophole in the direction of the rider's approach.

She came up and looked around – then on the other side of the hedge. Gabriel was about to advance and restore the missing article, when an unexpected performance induced him to suspend the action for the present. The path, after passing the cowshed, bisected the plantation. It was not a bridle-path – merely a pedestrian's track, and the boughs spread horizontally at a height not greater than seven feet above the ground, which made it impossible to ride erect beneath them. The girl, who wore no riding-habit, looked around for a moment, as if to assure herself that all humanity was out of view, then dexterously dropped backwards flat upon the pony's back, her head over its tail, her feet against its shoulders, and her eyes to the sky. The rapidity of her glide into this position was that of a kingfisher – its noiselessness that of a hawk. Gabriel's eyes had scarcely been able to follow her. The tall lank pony seemed used to such doings, and ambled along unconcerned. Thus she passed under the level boughs.

The performer seemed quite at home anywhere between a horse's head and its tail, and the necessity for this abnormal attitude having ceased with the passage of the plantation, she began to adopt another, even more obviously convenient than the first. She had no side-saddle, and it was very apparent that a firm seat upon the smooth leather beneath her was unattainable sideways. Springing to her accustomed perpendicular like a bowed sapling, and satisfying herself that nobody was in sight, she seated herself in the manner demanded by the saddle, though hardly expected of the woman, and trotted off in the direction of Tewnell Mill.

Oak was amused, perhaps a little astonished, and hanging up the hat in his hut went again among his ewes. An hour passed, the girl returned, properly seated now, with a bag of bran in front of her. On nearing the cattle-shed she was met by a boy bringing a milking-pail, who held the reins of the pony whilst she slid off. The boy led away the horse, leaving the pail with the young woman.

Soon soft spirts alternating with loud spirts came in regular succession from within the shed, the obvious sounds of a person milking a cow. Gabriel took the lost hat in his hand, and waited beside the path she would follow in leaving the hill.

She came, the pail in one hand, hanging against her knee. The left arm was extended as a balance, enough of it being shown bare to make Oak wish that the event had happened in the summer, when the whole would have been revealed. There was a bright air and manner about her now, by which she seemed to imply that the desirability of her existence could not be questioned; and this rather saucy assumption failed in being offensive because a beholder felt it to be, upon the whole, true. Like exceptional emphasis in the tone of a genius, that which would have made mediocrity ridiculous was an addition to recognized power. It was with some surprise that she saw Gabriel's face rising like the moon behind the hedge.

The adjustment of the farmer's hazy conceptions of her charms to the portrait of herself she now presented him with was less a diminution than a difference. The starting-point selected by the judgment was her height. She seemed tall, but the pail was a small one, and the hedge diminutive; hence, making allowance for error by comparison with these, she could have been not above the height to be chosen by women as best. All features of consequence were severe and regular. It may have been observed by persons who go about the shires with eyes for beauty that in Englishwomen a classically-formed face is seldom found to be united with a figure of the same pattern, the highly-finished features being generally too large for the remainder of the frame; that a graceful and proportionate figure of eight heads usually goes off into random facial curves. Without throwing a Nymphean tissue over a milkmaid, let it be said that here criticism checked itself as out of place, and looked at her proportions with a long consciousness of pleasure. From the contours of her figure in its upper part she must have had a beautiful neck and shoulders; but since her infancy nobody had ever seen them. Had she been put into a low dress she would have run and thrust her head into a bush. Yet she was not a shy girl by any means; it was merely her instinct to draw the line dividing the seen from the unseen higher than they do it in towns.

That the girl's thoughts hovered about her face and form as soon as she caught Oak's eyes conning the same page was natural, and almost certain. The self-consciousness shown would have been vanity if a little more pronounced, dignity if a little less. Rays of male vision seem to have a tickling effect upon virgin faces in rural districts; she brushed hers with her hand, as if Gabriel had been irritating its pink surface by actual touch, and the free air of her previous movements was reduced at the same time to a chastened phase of itself. Yet it was the man who blushed, the maid not at all.

'I found a hat,' said Oak.

'It is mine,' said she, and, from a sense of proportion, kept down to a small smile an inclination to laugh distinctly: 'it flew away last night.'

'One o'clock this morning?'

'Well — it was.' She was surprised. 'How did you know?' she said.

'I was here.'

'You are Farmer Oak, are you not?'

'That or thereabouts. I'm lately come to this place.'

'A large farm?' she inquired, casting her eyes round, and swinging back her hair, which was black in the shaded hollows of its mass; but it being now an hour past sunrise the rays touched its prominent curves with a colour of their own.

'No; not large. About a hundred.' (In speaking of farms the word 'acres' is omitted by the natives, by analogy to such old expressions as 'a stag of ten'.)

'I wanted my hat this morning,' she went on. 'I had to ride to Tewnell Mill.'

'Yes, you had.'

'How do you know?'

'I saw you.'

'Where?' she inquired, a misgiving bringing every muscle of her lineaments and frame to a standstill.

'Here — going through the plantation, and all down the hill,' said Farmer Oak, with an aspect excessively knowing with regard to some matter in his mind, as he gazed at a remote point in the direction named, and then turned back to meet his colloquist's eyes.

A perception caused him to withdraw his own eyes from hers as suddenly as if he had been caught in a theft. Recollection of the strange antics she had indulged in when passing through the trees was succeeded in the girl by a nettled palpitation, and that by a hot face. It was a time to see a woman redden who was not given to reddening as a rule; not a point in the milkmaid but was of the deepest rose-colour. From the Maiden's Blush, through all varieties of the Provence down to the Crimson Tuscany the countenance of Oak's acquaintance quickly graduated; whereupon he, in considerateness, turned away his head.

The sympathetic man still looked the other way, and wondered when she would recover coolness sufficient to justify him in facing her again. He heard what seemed to be the flitting of a dead leaf upon the breeze, and looked. She had gone away.

With an air between that of Tragedy and Comedy Gabriel returned to his work.

Five mornings and evenings passed. The young woman came regularly to milk the healthy cow or to attend to the sick one, but never allowed her vision to stray in the direction of Oak's person. His want of tact had deeply offended her – not by seeing what he could not help, but by letting her know that he had seen it. For, as without law there is no sin, without eyes there is no indecorum; and she appeared to feel that Gabriel's espial had made her an indecorous woman without her own connivance. It was food for great regret with him; it was also a *contretemps* which touched into life a latent heat he had experienced in that direction.

The acquaintanceship might, however, have ended in a slow forgetting but for an incident which occurred at the end of the same week. One afternoon it began to freeze, and the frost increased with evening, which drew on like a stealthy tightening of bonds. It was a time when in cottages the breath of the sleepers freezes to the sheets; when round the drawing-room fire of a thick-walled mansion the sitters' backs are cold, even whilst their faces are all aglow. Many a small bird went to bed supperless that night among the bare boughs.

As the milking-hour drew near Oak kept his usual watch upon the cowshed. At last he felt cold, and shaking an extra quantity of bedding round the yeaning ewes he entered the hut and heaped more fuel upon the stove. The wind came in at the bottom of the door, and to prevent it Oak laid a sack there and wheeled the cot round a little more to the south. Then the wind spouted in at a ventilating hole – of which there was one on each side of the hut.

Gabriel had always known that when the fire was lighted and the door closed one of these must be kept open – that chosen being always on the side away from the wind. Closing the slide to windward he turned to open the other; on second thoughts the farmer considered that he would first sit down, leaving both closed for a minute or two, till the temperature of the hut was a little raised. He sat down.

His head began to ache in an unwonted manner and, fancying himself weary by reason of the broken rests of the preceding nights, Oak decided to get up, open the slide, and then allow himself to fall asleep. He fell asleep, however, without having performed the necessary preliminary.

How long he remained unconscious Gabriel never knew. During the first stages of his return to perception peculiar deeds seemed to be in course of enactment. His dog was howling, his head was aching fearfully – somebody was pulling him about, hands were loosening his neckerchief.

On opening his eyes he found that evening had sunk to dusk in a strange manner of unexpectedness. The young girl with the remarkably pleasant lips and white teeth was beside him. More than this – astonishingly more – his head was upon her lap, his face and neck were disagreeably wet, and her fingers were unbuttoning his collar.

'Whatever is the matter?' said Oak vacantly.

She seemed to experience mirth, but of too insignificant a kind to start enjoyment.

'Nothing now,' she answered, 'since you are not dead. It is a wonder you were not suffocated in this hut of yours.'

'Ah, the hut!' murmured Gabriel. 'I gave ten pounds for that hut. But I'll sell it, and sit under thatched hurdles as they did in old times, and curl up to sleep in a lock of straw! It played me nearly the same trick the other day!' Gabriel, by way of emphasis, brought down his fist upon the floor.

'It was not exactly the fault of the hut,' she observed in a tone which showed her to be that novelty among women – one who finished a thought before beginning the sentence which was to convey it. 'You should, I think, have considered, and not have been so foolish as to leave the slides closed.'

'Yes, I suppose I should,' said Oak absently. He was endeavouring to catch and appreciate the sensation of being thus with her, his head upon her dress, before the event passed on into the heap of bygone things. He wished she knew his impressions; but he would as soon have thought of carrying an odour in a net as of attempting to convey the intangibilities of his feeling in the coarse meshes of language. So he remained silent.

She made him sit up, and then Oak began wiping his face and shaking himself like a Samson. 'How can I thank 'ee?' he said at last gratefully, some of the natural, rusty red having returned to his face.

'Oh, never mind that,' said the girl, smiling, and allowing her smile to hold good for Gabriel's next remark, whatever that might prove to be.

'How did you find me?'

'I heard your dog howling and scratching at the door of the hut when I came to the milking (it was so lucky, Daisy's milking is almost over for the season, and I shall not come here after this week or the next). The dog saw me, and jumped over to me, and laid hold of my skirt. I came across and looked round the hut the very first thing to see if the slides were closed. My uncle has a hut like this one, and I have heard him tell his shepherd not to go to sleep without leaving a slide open. I opened the door, and there you were like dead. I threw the milk over you, as there was no water, forgetting it was warm, and no use.'

'I wonder if I should have died?' Gabriel said in a low voice, which was rather meant to travel back to himself than to her.

'O no!' the girl replied. She seemed to prefer a less tragic probability; to have saved a man from death involved talk that should harmonize with the dignity of such a deed – and she shunned it.

'I believe you saved my life, Miss – I don't know your name. I know your aunt's, but not yours.'

'I would just as soon not tell it – rather not. There is no reason either why I should, as you probably will never have much to do with me.'

'Still I should like to know.'

'You can inquire at my aunt's – she will tell you.'

'My name is Gabriel Oak.'

'And mine isn't. You seem fond of yours in speaking it so decisively, Gabriel Oak.'

'You see, it is the only one I shall ever have, and I must make the most of it.'

'I always think mine sounds odd and disagreeable.'

'I should think you might soon get a new one.'

'Mercy! – how many opinions you keep about you concerning other people, Gabriel Oak.'

'Well, Miss – excuse the words – I thought you would like them. But I can't match you, I know, in mapping out my mind upon my tongue. I never was very clever in my inside. But I thank you. Come, give me your hand!'

She hesitated, somewhat disconcerted at Oak's old-fashioned earnest conclusion to a dialogue lightly carried on. 'Very well,' she said, and gave him her hand, compressing her lips to a demure impassivity. He held it but an instant, and in his fear of being too demonstrative, swerved to the opposite extreme, touching her fingers with the lightness of a small-hearted person.

'I am sorry,' he said the instant after.

'What for?'

'Letting your hand go so quick.'

'You may have it again if you like; there it is.' She gave him her hand again.

Oak held it longer this time — indeed, curiously long. 'How soft it is — being winter time, too — not chapped or rough, or anything!' he said.

'There — that's long enough,' said she, though without pulling it away. 'But I suppose you are thinking you would like to kiss it? You may if you want to.'

'I wasn't thinking of any such thing,' said Gabriel simply; 'but I will—'

'That you won't!' She snatched back her hand.

Gabriel felt himself guilty of another want of tact.

'Now find out my name,' she said teasingly; and withdrew.

CHAPTER FOUR

Gabriel's Resolve – The Visit – The Mistake

THE only superiority in women that is tolerable to the rival sex is, as a rule, that of the unconscious kind; but a superiority which recognizes itself may sometimes please by suggesting possibilities of capture to the subordinated man.

This well-favoured and comely girl soon made appreciable inroads upon the emotional constitution of young Farmer Oak.

Love being an extremely exacting usurer (a sense of exorbitant profit, spiritually, by an exchange of hearts, being at the bottom of pure passions, as that of exorbitant profit, bodily or materially, is at the bottom of those of lower atmosphere), every morning Oak's feelings were as sensitive as the money-market in calculations upon his chances. His dog waited for his meals in a way so like that in which Oak waited for the girl's presence that the farmer was quite struck with the resemblance, felt it lowering, and would not look at the dog. However, he continued to watch through the hedge for her regular coming, and thus his sentiments towards her were deepened without any corresponding effect being produced upon herself. Oak had nothing finished and ready to say as yet, and not being able to frame love phrases which end where they begin; passionate tales —

                            − Full of sound and fury
                        − Signifying nothing −

he said no word at all.

By making inquiries he found that the girl's name was Bathsheba Everdene, and that the cow would go dry in about seven days. He dreaded the eighth day.

At last the eighth day came. The cow had ceased to give milk for that year, and Bathsheba Everdene came up the hill no more. Gabriel had reached a pitch of existence he never could have anticipated a short time before. He liked saying 'Bathsheba' as a private enjoyment instead of whistling; turned over his taste to black hair, though he had sworn by brown ever since he was a boy, isolated himself till the space he filled in the public eye was contemptibly small. Love is a possible strength in an actual weakness. Marriage transforms a distraction into a support, the power of which should be, and happily often is, in direct proportion to the degree of imbecility it supplants. Oak began now to see light in this direction, and said to himself, 'I'll make her my wife, or upon my soul I shall be good for nothing!'

All this while he was perplexing himself about an errand on which he might consistently visit the cottage of Bathsheba's aunt.

He found his opportunity in the death of a ewe, mother of a living lamb. On a day which had a summer face and a winter constitution − a fine January morning, when there was just enough blue sky visible to make cheerfully-disposed people wish for more, and an occasional gleam of silvery sunshine, Oak put the lamb into a respectable Sunday basket, and stalked across the fields to the house of Mrs Hurst, the aunt − George, the dog, walking behind, with a countenance of great concern at the serious turn pastoral affairs seemed to be taking.

Gabriel had watched the blue wood-smoke curling from the chimney with strange meditation. At evening he had fancifully traced it down the chimney to the spot of its origin − seen the hearth and Bathsheba beside it − beside it in her out-door dress; for the clothes she had worn on the hill were by association equally with her person included in the compass of his affection; they seemed at this early time of his love a necessary ingredient of the sweet mixture called Bathsheba Everdene.

He had made a toilet of a nicely-adjusted kind − of a nature between the carefully neat and the carelessly ornate − of a degree between fine-market-day and wet-Sunday selection. He thoroughly cleaned his silver watch-chain with whiting, put new lacing straps to his boots, looked to the brass eyelet-holes, went to the inmost heart of the plantation for a new walking-stick, and trimmed it vigorously on his way back; took a new handkerchief from the bottom of his clothes-box, put on the light waistcoat patterned all over with sprigs of an elegant flower uniting the beauties of both rose and lily without the defects of either, and used all the hair-oil he possessed upon his usually dry, sandy, and inextricably curly hair, till he had deepened it to a splendidly novel colour, between that of guano and Roman cement, making it stick to his head like mace round a nutmeg, or wet seaweed round a boulder after the ebb.

Nothing disturbed the stillness of the cottage save the chatter of a knot of sparrows on the eaves; one might fancy scandal and rumour to be no less the

staple topic of these little coteries on roofs than of those under them. It seemed
that the omen was an unpropitious one, for, as the rather untoward commencement of Oak's overtures, just as he arrived by the garden gate he saw a cat inside,
going into various arched shapes and fiendish convulsions at the sight of his dog
George. The dog took no notice, for he had arrived at an age at which all
superfluous barking was cynically avoided as a waste of breath – in fact, he never
barked even at the sheep except to order, when it was done with an absolutely
neutral countenance, as a sort of Commination-service which, though offensive,
had to be gone through once now and then to frighten the flock for their own
good.

A voice came from behind some laurel-bushes into which the cat had run:

'Poor dear! Did a nasty brute of a dog want to kill it; – did he, poor
dear!'

'I beg yer pardon,' said Oak to the voice, 'but George was walking on behind
me with a temper as mild as milk.'

Almost before he had ceased speaking Oak was seized with a misgiving as to
whose ear was the recipient of his answer. Nobody appeared, and he heard the
person retreat among the bushes.

Gabriel meditated, and so deeply that he brought small furrows into his
forehead by sheer force of reverie. Where the issue of an interview is as likely to be
a vast change for the worse as for the better, any initial difference from
expectation causes nipping sensations of failure. Oak went up to the door a little
abashed: his mental rehearsal and the reality had had no common grounds of
opening.

Bathsheba's aunt was indoors. 'Will you tell Miss Everdene that somebody
would be glad to speak to her?' said Mr Oak. (Calling one's self merely
Somebody, without giving a name, is not to be taken as an example of the ill-
breeding of the rural world: it springs from a refined modesty of which
townspeople, with their cards and announcements, have no notion whatever.)

Bathsheba was out. The voice had evidently been hers.

'Will you come in, Mr Oak?'

'Oh, thank 'ee,' said Gabriel, following her to the fireplace. 'I've brought a
lamb for Miss Everdene. I thought she might like one to rear; girls do.'

'She might,' said Mrs Hurst musingly; 'though she's only a visitor here. If you
will wait a minute Bathsheba will be in.'

'Yes, I will wait,' said Gabriel, sitting down. 'The lamb isn't really the business
I came about, Mrs Hurst. In short, I was going to ask her if she'd like to be
married.'

'And were you indeed?'

'Yes. Because if she would I should be very glad to marry her. D'ye know if
she's got any other young man hanging about her at all?'

'Let me think,' said Mrs Hurst, poking the fire superfluously. . . . 'Yes – bless
you, ever so many young men. You see, Farmer Oak, she's so good-looking, and
an excellent scholar besides – she was going to be a governess once, you know,
only she was too wild. Not that her young men ever come here – but, Lord, in the
nature of women, she must have a dozen!'

'That's unfortunate,' said Farmer Oak, contemplating a crack in the stone
floor with sorrow. 'I'm only an every-day sort of man, and my only chance was in

being the first comer. . . . Well, there's no use in my waiting, for that was all I
came about: so I'll take myself off home-along, Mrs Hurst.'

When Gabriel had gone about two hundred yards along the down, he heard a
'hoi-hoi!' uttered behind him, in a piping note of more treble quality than that in
which the exclamation usually embodies itself when shouted across a field. He
looked round, and saw a girl racing after him, waving a white handkerchief.

Oak stood still – and the runner drew nearer. It was Bathsheba Everdene.
Gabriel's colour deepened: hers was already deep, not, as it appeared, from
emotion, but from running.

'Farmer Oak – I—' she said, pausing for want of breath, pulling up in front of
him with a slanted face, and putting her hand to her side.

'I have just called to see you,' said Gabriel pending her further speech.

'Yes – I know that,' she said, panting like a robin, her face red and moist from
her exertions, like a peony petal before the sun dries off the dew. 'I didn't know
you had come to ask to have me, or I should have come in from the garden
instantly. I ran after you to say – that my aunt made a mistake in sending you
away from courting me.'

Gabriel expanded. 'I'm sorry to have made you run so fast, my dear,' he said,
with a grateful sense of favours to come. 'Wait a bit till you've found your
breath.'

' – It was quite a mistake – aunt's telling you I had a young man already,'
Bathsheba went on. 'I haven't a sweetheart at all – and I never had one, and I
thought that, as times go with women, it was *such* a pity to send you away
thinking that I had several.'

'Really and truly I am glad to hear that!' said Farmer Oak, smiling one of his
long special smiles, and blushing with gladness. He held out his hand to take hers,
which, when she had eased her side by pressing it there, was prettily extended
upon her bosom to still her loud-beating heart. Directly he seized it she put it
behind her, so that it slipped through his fingers like an eel.

'I have a nice snug little farm,' said Gabriel, with half a degree less assurance
than when he had seized her hand.

'Yes; you have.'

'A man has advanced me money to begin with, but still, it will soon be paid off,
and though I am only an every-day sort of man I have got on a little since I was a
boy.' Gabriel uttered 'a little' in a tone to show her that it was the complacent
form of 'a great deal'. He continued: 'When we be married, I am quite sure I can
work twice as hard as I do now.'

He went forward and stretched out his arm again. Bathsheba had overtaken
him at a point beside which stood a low stunted holly bush, now laden with red
berries. Seeing his advance take the form of an attitude threatening a possible
enclosure, if not compression, of her person, she edged off round the bush.

'Why, Farmer Oak,' she said over the top, looking at him with rounded eyes, 'I
never said I was going to marry you.'

'Well – that *is* a tale!' said Oak with dismay. 'To run after anybody like this,
and then say you don't want him!'

'What I meant to tell you was only this,' she said eagerly, and yet half conscious
of the absurdity of the position she had made for herself – 'that nobody has got
me yet as a sweetheart, instead of my having a dozen, as my aunt said; I *hate* to be

thought men's property in that way, though possibly I shall be had some day. Why, if I'd wanted you I shouldn't have run after you like this; 'twould have been the *forwardest* thing! But there was no harm in hurrying to correct a piece of false news that had been told you.'

'Oh, no – no harm at all.' But there is such a thing as being too generous in expressing a judgment impulsively, and Oak added with a more appreciative sense of all the circumstances – 'Well, I am not quite certain it was no harm.'

'Indeed, I hadn't time to think before starting whether I wanted to marry or not, for you'd have been gone over the hill.'

'Come,' said Gabriel, freshening again; 'think a minute or two. I'll wait a while, Miss Everdene. Will you marry me? Do, Bathsheba. I love you far more than common!'

'I'll try to think,' she observed rather more timorously; 'if I can think out of doors; my mind spreads away so.'

'But you can give a guess.'

'Then give me time.' Bathsheba looked thoughtfully into the distance, away from the direction in which Gabriel stood.

'I can make you happy,' said he to the back of her head, across the bush. 'You shall have a piano in a year or two – farmers' wives are getting to have pianos now – and I'll practise up the flute right well to play with you in the evenings.'

'Yes; I should like that.'

'And have one of those little ten-pound gigs for market – and nice flowers, and birds – cocks and hens I mean, because they be useful,' continued Gabriel, feeling balanced between poetry and practicality.

'I should like it very much.'

'And a frame for cucumbers – like a gentleman and lady.'

'Yes.'

'And when the wedding was over, we'd have it put in the newspaper list of marriages.'

'Dearly I should like that!'

'And the babies in the births – every man jack of 'em! And at home by the fire, whenever you look up, there I shall be – and whenever I look up, there will be you.'

'Wait, wait, and don't be improper!'

Her countenance fell, and she was silent awhile. He regarded the red berries between them over and over again, to such an extent that holly seemed in his after life to be a cypher signifying a proposal of marriage. Bathsheba decisively turned to him.

'No; 'tis no use,' she said. 'I don't want to marry you.'

'Try.'

'I've tried hard all the time I've been thinking; for a marriage would be very nice in one sense. People would talk about me and think I had won my battle, and I should feel triumphant, and all that. But a husband—'

'Well!'

'Why, he'd always be there, as you say; whenever I looked up, there he'd be.'

'Of course he would – I, that is.'

'Well, what I mean is that I shouldn't mind being a bride at a wedding, if I could be one without having a husband. But since a woman can't show off in that way by herself, I shan't marry – at least yet.'

'That's a terrible wooden story!'

At this criticism of her statement Bathsheba made an addition to her dignity by a slight sweep away from him.

'Upon my heart and soul I don't know what a maid can say stupider than that,' said Oak. 'But dearest,' he continued in a palliative voice, 'don't be like it!' Oak sighed a deep honest sigh – none the less so in that, being like the sigh of a pine plantation, it was rather noticeable as a disturbance of the atmosphere. 'Why won't you have me?' he appealed, creeping round the holly to reach her side.

'I cannot,' she said, retreating.

'But why?' he persisted, standing still at last in despair of ever reaching her, and facing over the bush.

'Because I don't love you.'

'Yes, but—'

She contracted a yawn to an inoffensive smallness, so that it was hardly ill-mannered at all. 'I don't love you,' she said.

'But I love you – and, as for myself, I am content to be liked.'

'O Mr Oak – that's very fine! You'd get to despise me.'

'Never,' said Mr Oak, so earnestly that he seemed to be coming, by the force of his words, straight through the bush and into her arms. 'I shall do one thing in this life – one thing certain – that is, love you, and long for you, and *keep wanting you* till I die.' His voice had a genuine pathos now, and his large brown hands perceptibly trembled.

'It seems dreadfully wrong not to have you when you feel so much!' she said with a little distress, and looking hopelessly around for some means of escape from her moral dilemma. 'How I wish I hadn't run after you!' However, she seemed to have a short cut for getting back to cheerfulness and set her face to signify archness. 'It wouldn't do, Mr Oak. I want somebody to tame me; I am too independent; and you would never be able to, I know.'

Oak cast his eyes down the field in a way implying that it was useless to attempt argument.

'Mr Oak,' she said, with luminous distinctness and common sense, 'you are better off than I. I have hardly a penny in the world – I am staying with my aunt for my bare sustenance. I am better educated than you – and I don't love you a bit: that's my side of the case. Now yours: you are a farmer just beginning, and you ought in common prudence, if you marry at all (which you should certainly not think of doing at present) to marry a woman with money, who would stock a larger farm for you than you have now.'

Gabriel looked at her with a little surprise and much admiration.

'That's the very thing I had been thinking myself!' he naïvely said.

Farmer Oak had one-and-a-half Christian characteristics too many to succeed with Bathsheba: his humility, and a superfluous moiety of honesty. Bathsheba was decidedly disconcerted.

'Well, then, why did you come and disturb me?' she said, almost angrily, if not quite, an enlarging red spot rising in each cheek.

'I can't do what I think would be – would be—'

'Right?'

'No: wise.'

'You have made an admission *now*, Mr Oak,' she exclaimed with even more hauteur, and rocking her head disdainfully. 'After that, do you think I could marry you? Not if I know it.'

He broke in passionately: 'But don't mistake me like that! Because I am open enough to own what every man in my shoes would have thought of, you make your colours come up your face and get crabbed with me. That about you not being good enough for me is nonsense. You speak like a lady – all the parish notice it, and your uncle at Weatherbury is, I've heerd, a large farmer – much larger than ever I shall be. May I call in the evening, or will you walk along with me o' Sundays? I don't want you to make up your mind at once, if you'd rather not.'

'No – no – I cannot. Don't press me any more – don't. I don't love you – so 'twould be ridiculous,' she said, with a laugh.

No man likes to see his emotions the sport of a merry-go-round of skittishness. 'Very well,' said Oak firmly, with the bearing of one who was going to give his days and nights to Ecclesiastes for ever. 'Then I'll ask you no more.'

CHAPTER FIVE

Departure of Bathsheba – A Pastoral Tragedy

T HE news which one day reached Gabriel that Bathsheba Everdene had left the neighbourhood, had an influence upon him which might have surprised any who never suspected that the more emphatic the renunciation the less absolute its character.

It may have been observed that there is no regular path for getting out of love as there is for getting in. Some people look upon marriage as a short cut that way, but it has been known to fail. Separation, which was the means that chance offered to Gabriel Oak by Bathsheba's disappearance, though effectual with people of certain humours, is apt to idealize the removed object with others – notably those whose affection, placid and regular as it may be, flows deep and long. Oak belonged to the even-tempered order of humanity, and felt the secret fusion of himself in Bathsheba to be burning with a finer flame now that she was gone – that was all.

His incipient friendship with her aunt had been nipped by the failure of his suit, and all that Oak learnt of Bathsheba's movements was done indirectly. It appeared that she had gone to a place called Weatherbury, more than twenty miles off, but in what capacity – whether as a visitor or permanently, he could not discover.

Gabriel had two dogs. George, the elder, exhibited an ebony-tipped nose, surrounded by a narrow margin of pink flesh, and a coat marked in random splotches approximating in colour to white and slaty grey; but the grey, after years of sun and rain, had been scorched and washed out of the more prominent locks, leaving them of a reddish-brown, as if the blue component of the grey had faded, like the indigo from the same kind of colour in Turner's pictures. In substance it had originally been hair, but long contact with sheep seemed to be turning it by degrees into wool of a poor quality and staple.

This dog had originally belonged to a shepherd of inferior morals and dreadful temper, and the result was that George knew the exact degrees of condemnation signified by cursing and swearing of all descriptions better than the wickedest old man in the neighbourhood. Long experience had so precisely taught the animal the difference between such exclamations as 'Come in!' and 'D— ye, come in!' that he knew to a hair's breadth the rate of trotting back from the ewes' tails that each call involved, if a staggerer with the sheep-crook was to be escaped. Though old, he was clever and trustworthy still.

The young dog, George's son, might possibly have been the image of his mother, for there was not much resemblance between him and George. He was learning the sheep-keeping business, so as to follow on at the flock when the other should die, but had got no further than the rudiments as yet – still finding an insuperable difficulty in distinguishing between doing a thing well enough and doing it too well. So earnest and yet so wrong-headed was this young dog (he had no name in particular, and answered with perfect readiness to any pleasant interjection) that if sent behind the flock to help them on he did it so thoroughly that he would have chased them across the whole county with the greatest pleasure if not called off, or reminded when to stop by the example of old George.

Thus much for the dogs. On the further side of Norcombe Hill was a chalk-pit, from which chalk had been drawn for generations, and spread over adjacent farms. Two hedges converged upon it in the form of a V, but without quite meeting. The narrow opening left, which was immediately over the brow of the pit, was protected by a rough railing.

One night, when Farmer Oak had returned to his house, believing there would be no further necessity for his attendance on the down, he called as usual to the dogs, previously to shutting them up in the outhouse till next morning. Only one responded – old George; the other could not be found, either in the house, lane, or garden. Gabriel then remembered that he had left the two dogs on the hill eating a dead lamb (a kind of meat he usually kept from them, except when other food ran short), and concluding that the young one had not finished his meal he went indoors to the luxury of a bed, which latterly he had only enjoyed on Sundays.

It was a still, moist night. Just before dawn he was assisted in waking by the abnormal reverberation of familiar music. To the shepherd, the note of the sheep-bell, like the ticking of the clock to other people, is a chronic sound that only makes itself noticed by ceasing or altering in some unusual manner from the well-known idle tinkle which signifies to the accustomed ear, however distant, that all is well in the fold. In the solemn calm of the awakening morn that note was heard by Gabriel, beating with unusual violence and rapidity. This exceptional ringing may be caused in two ways – by the rapid feeding of the sheep bearing the bell, as when the flock breaks into new pasture, which gives it an intermittent rapidity, or by the sheep starting off in a run, when the sound has a regular palpitation. The experienced ear of Oak knew the sound he now heard to be caused by the running of the flock with great velocity.

He jumped out of bed, dressed, tore down the lane through a foggy dawn, and ascended the hill. The forward ewes were kept apart from those among which the fall of lambs would be later, there being two hundred of the latter class in Gabriel's flock. These two hundred seemed to have absolutely vanished from the hill. There were the fifty with their lambs, enclosed at the other end as he had left them, but the rest, forming the bulk of the flock, were nowhere. Gabriel called at the top of his voice the shepherd's call:

'Ovey, ovey, ovey!'[1]

Not a single bleat. He went to the hedge; a gap had been broken through it, and in the gap were the footprints of the sheep. Rather surprised to find them break fence at this season, yet putting it down instantly to their great fondness for ivy in winter-time, of which a great deal grew in the plantation, he followed through the hedge. They were not in the plantation. He called again: the valleys and furthest hills resounded as when the sailors invoked the lost Hylas on the Mysian shore; but no sheep. He passed through the trees and along the ridge of the hill. On the extreme summit, where the ends of the two converging hedges of which we have spoken were stopped short by meeting the brow of the chalk-pit, he saw the younger dog standing against the sky – dark and motionless as Napoleon at St Helena.

A horrible conviction darted through Oak. With a sensation of bodily faintness he advanced: at one point the rails were broken through, and there he saw the footprints of his ewes. The dog came up, licked his hand, and made signs implying that he expected some great reward for signal services rendered. Oak looked over the precipice. The ewes lay dead and dying at its foot – a heap of two hundred mangled carcases, representing in their condition just now at least two hundred more.

Oak was an intensely humane man: indeed, his humanity often tore in pieces any politic intentions of his which bordered on strategy, and carried him on as by gravitation. A shadow in his life had always been that his flock ended in mutton – that a day came and found every shepherd an arrant traitor to his defenceless sheep. His first feeling now was one of pity for the untimely fate of these gentle ewes and their unborn lambs.

It was a second to remember another phase of the matter. The sheep were not insured. All the savings of a frugal life had been dispersed at a blow; his hopes of being an independent farmer were laid low – possibly for ever. Gabriel's energies, patience, and industry had been so severely taxed during the years of his life between eighteen and eight-and-twenty, to reach his present stage of progress, that no more seemed to be left in him. He leant down upon a rail, and covered his face with his hands.

Stupors, however, do not last for ever, and Farmer Oak recovered from his. It was as remarkable as it was characteristic that the one sentence he uttered was in thankfulness: –

---

[1] It is somewhat singular – possibly a survival from the Roman occupation of Britain – that the shepherds of this region should call to their sheep in Latin.

'Thank God I am not married: what would *she* have done in the poverty now coming upon me!'

Oak raised his head, and wondering what he could do, listlessly surveyed the scene. By the outer margin of the pit was an oval pond, and over it hung the attenuated skeleton of a chrome-yellow moon, which had only a few days to last – the morning star dogging her on the left hand. The pool glittered like a dead man's eye, and as the world awoke a breeze blew, shaking and elongating the reflection of the moon without breaking it, and turning the image of the star to a phosphoric streak upon the water. All this Oak saw and remembered.

As far as could be learnt it appeared that the poor young dog, still under the impression that since he was kept for running after sheep, the more he ran after them the better, had at the end of his meal off the dead lamb, which may have given him additional energy and spirits, collected all the ewes into a corner, driven the timid creatures through the hedge, across the upper field, and by main force of worrying had given them momentum enough to break down a portion of the rotten railing, and so hurled them over the edge.

George's son had done his work so thoroughly that he was considered too good a workman to live, and was, in fact, taken and tragically shot at twelve o'clock that same day – another instance of the untoward fate which so often attends dogs and other philosophers who follow out a train of reasoning to its logical conclusion, and attempt perfectly consistent conduct in a world made up so largely of compromise.

Gabriel's farm had been stocked by a dealer – on the strength of Oak's promising look and character – who was receiving a percentage from the farmer till such time as the advance should be cleared off. Oak found that the value of stock, plant, and implements which were really his own would be about sufficient to pay his debts, leaving himself a free man with the clothes he stood up in, and nothing more.

CHAPTER SIX

The Fair – The Journey – The Fire

Two months passed away. We are brought on to a day in February, on which was held the yearly statute or hiring fair in the county-town of Casterbridge.

At one end of the street stood from two to three hundred blithe and hearty labourers waiting upon Chance – all men of the stamp to whom labour suggests nothing worse than a wrestle with gravitation, and pleasure nothing better than a renunciation of the same. Among these, carters and waggoners were distinguished by having a piece of whip-cord twisted round their hats; thatchers wore a fragment of woven straw; shepherds held their sheep-crooks in their hands; and thus the situation required was known to the hirers at a glance.

In the crowd was an athletic young fellow of somewhat superior appearance to the rest – in fact, his superiority was marked enough to lead several ruddy peasants standing by to speak to him inquiringly, as to a farmer, and to use 'Sir' as a finishing word. His answer always was,—

'I am looking for a place myself – a bailiff's. Do ye know of anybody who wants one?'

Gabriel was paler now. His eyes were more meditative, and his expression was more sad. He had passed through an ordeal of wretchedness which had given him more than it had taken away. He had sunk from his modest elevation as pastoral king into the very slime-pits of Siddim; but there was left to him a dignified calm he had never before known, and that indifference to fate which, though it often makes a villain of a man, is the basis of his sublimity when it does not. And thus the abasement had been exaltation, and the loss gain.

In the morning a regiment of cavalry had left the town, and a sergeant and his party had been beating up for recruits through the four streets. As the end of the day drew on, and he found himself not hired, Gabriel almost wished that he had joined them, and gone off to serve his country. Weary of standing in the market-place, and not much minding the kind of work he turned his hand to, he decided to offer himself in some other capacity than that of bailiff.

All the farmers seemed to be wanting shepherds. Sheep-tending was Gabriel's speciality. Turning down an obscure street and entering an obscurer lane, he went up to a smith's shop.

'How long would it take you to make a shepherd's crook?'

'Twenty minutes.'

'How much?'

'Two shillings.'

He sat on a bench and the crook was made, a stem being given him into the bargain.

He then went to a ready-made clothes shop, the owner of which had a large rural connection. As the crook had absorbed most of Gabriel's money, he attempted, and carried out, an exchange of his overcoat for a shepherd's regulation smock-frock.

This transaction having been completed he again hurried off to the centre of the town, and stood on the kerb of the pavement, as a shepherd, crook in hand.

Now that Oak had turned himself into a shepherd it seemed that bailiffs were most in demand. However, two or three farmers noticed him and drew near. Dialogues followed, more or less in the subjoined form: –

'Where do you come from?'

'Norcombe.'

'That's a long way.'

'Fifteen miles.'

'Whose farm were you upon last?'

'My own.'

This reply invariably operated like a rumour of cholera. The inquiring farmer would edge away and shake his head dubiously. Gabriel, like his dog, was too good to be trustworthy, and he never made advance beyond this point.

It is safer to accept any chance that offers itself, and extemporize a procedure to fit it, than to get a good plan matured, and wait for a chance of using it. Gabriel wished he had not nailed up his colours as a shepherd, but had laid himself out for anything in the whole cycle of labour that was required in the fair. It grew dusk. Some merry men were whistling and singing by the corn-exchange. Gabriel's hand, which had lain for some time idle in his smock-frock pocket, touched his flute, which he carried there. Here was an opportunity for putting his dearly bought wisdom into practice

He drew out his flute and began to play 'Jockey to the Fair' in the style of a man who had never known a moment's sorrow. Oak could pipe with Arcadian sweetness, and the sound of the well-known notes cheered his own heart as well as those of the loungers. He played on with spirit, and in half an hour had earned in pence what was a small fortune to a destitute man.

By making inquiries he learnt that there was another fair at Shottsford the next day.

'How far is Shottsford?'

'Ten miles t'other side of Weatherbury.'

Weatherbury! It was where Bathsheba had gone two months before. This information was like coming from night into noon.

'How far is it to Weatherbury?'

'Five or six miles.'

Bathsheba had probably left Weatherbury long before this time, but the place had enough interest attaching to it to lead Oak to choose Shottsford fair as his next field of inquiry, because it lay in the Weatherbury quarter. Moreover, the Weatherbury folk were by no means uninteresting intrinsically. If report spoke truly they were as hardy, merry, thriving, wicked a set as any in the whole county. Oak resolved to sleep at Weatherbury that night on his way to Shottsford, and struck out at once into the high road which had been recommended as the direct route to the village in question.

The road stretched through water-meadows traversed by little brooks, whose quivering surfaces were braided along their centres, and folded into creases at the sides; or, where the flow was more rapid, the stream was pied with spots of white froth, which rode on in undisturbed serenity. On the higher levels the dead and dry carcases of leaves tapped the ground as they bowled along helter-skelter upon the shoulders of the wind, and little birds in the hedges were rustling their feathers and tucking themselves in comfortably for the night, retaining their places if Oak kept moving, but flying away if he stopped to look at them. He passed by Yalbury Wood where the game-birds were rising to their roosts, and heard the crack-voiced cock-pheasants' 'cu-uck, cuck', and the wheezy whistle of the hens.

By the time he had walked three or four miles every shape in the landscape had assumed a uniform hue of blackness. He descended Yalbury Hill and could just discern ahead of him a waggon, drawn up under a great over-hanging tree by the roadside.

On coming close, he found there were no horses attached to it, the spot being apparently quite deserted. The waggon, from its position, seemed to have been left there for the night, for beyond about half a truss of hay which was heaped in the bottom, it was quite empty. Gabriel sat down on the shafts of the vehicle and considered his position. He calculated that he had walked a very fair proportion of the journey; and having been on foot since daybreak, he felt tempted to lie down upon the hay in the waggon instead of pushing on to the village of Weatherbury, and having to pay for a lodging.

Eating his last slices of bread and ham, and drinking from the bottle of cider he had taken the precaution to bring with him, he got into the lonely waggon. Here he spread half of the hay as a bed, and, as well as he could in the darkness, pulled the other half over him by way of bed-clothes, covering himself entirely, and feeling, physically, as comfortable as ever he had been in his life. Inward melancholy it was impossible for a man like Oak, introspective far beyond his neighbours, to banish quite, whilst conning the present untoward page of his history. So, thinking of his misfortunes, amorous and pastoral, he fell asleep, shepherds enjoying, in common with sailors, the privilege of being able to summon the god instead of having to wait for him.

On somewhat suddenly awaking, after a sleep of whose length he had no idea, Oak found that the waggon was in motion. He was being carried along the road at a rate rather considerable for a vehicle without springs, and under circumstances of physical uneasiness, his head being dandled up and down on the bed of the waggon like a kettledrum-stick. He then distinguished voices in conversation, coming from the forepart of the waggon. His concern at this dilemma (which would have been alarm, had he been a thriving man; but misfortune is a fine opiate to personal terror) led him to peer cautiously from the hay, and the first sight he beheld was the stars above him. Charles's Wain was getting towards a right angle with the Pole star, and Gabriel concluded that it must be about nine o'clock—in other words, that he had slept two hours. This small astronomical calculation was made without any positive effort, and whilst he was stealthily turning to discover, if possible, into whose hands he had fallen.

Two figures were dimly visible in front, sitting with their legs outside the waggon, one of whom was driving. Gabriel soon found that this was the waggoner, and it appeared they had come from Casterbridge fair, like himself.

A conversation was in progress, which continued thus: —

'Be as 'twill, she's a fine handsome body as far's looks be concerned. But that's only the skin of the woman, and these dandy cattle be as proud as a lucifer in their insides.'

'Ay—so 'a do seem, Billy Smallbury—so 'a do seem.' This utterance was very shaky by nature, and more so by circumstance, the jolting of the waggon not being without its effect upon the speaker's larynx. It came from the man who held the reins.

'She's a very vain feymell—so 'tis said here and there.'

'Ah, now. If so be 'tis like that, I can't look her in the face. Lord, no: not I— heh-heh-heh! Such a shy man as I be!'

'Yes—she's very vain. 'Tis said that every night at going to bed she looks in the glass to put on her nightcap properly.'

'And not a married woman. Oh, the world!'

'And 'a can play the peanner, so 'tis said. Can play so clever that 'a can make a psalm tune sound as well as the merriest loose song a man can wish for.'

'D'ye tell o't! A happy time for us, and I feel quite a new man! And how do she pay?'

'That I don't know, Master Poorgrass.'

On hearing these and other similar remarks, a wild thought flashed into Gabriel's mind that they might be speaking of Bathsheba. There were, however, no grounds for retaining such a supposition, for the waggon, though going in the direction of Weatherbury, might be going beyond it, and the woman alluded to seemed to be the mistress of some estate. They were now apparently close upon Weatherbury, and not to alarm the speakers unnecessarily Gabriel slipped out of the waggon unseen.

He turned to an opening in the hedge, which he found to be a gate, and mounting thereon he sat meditating whether to seek a cheap lodging in the village, or to ensure a cheaper one by lying under some hay or corn stack. The crunching jangle of the waggon died upon his ear. He was about to walk on, when he noticed on his left hand an unusual light – appearing about half a mile distant. Oak watched it, and the glow increased. Something was on fire.

Gabriel again mounted the gate, and, leaping down on the other side upon what he found to be ploughed soil, made across the field in the exact direction of the fire. The blaze, enlarging in a double ratio by his approach and its own increase, showed him as he drew nearer the outlines of ricks beside it, lighted up to great distinctness. A rick-yard was the source of the fire. His weary face now began to be painted over with a rich orange glow, and the whole front of his smock-front and gaiters was covered with a dancing shadow pattern of thorn-twigs – the light reaching him through a leafless intervening hedge – and the metallic curve of his sheep-crook shone silver-bright in the same abounding rays. He came up to the boundary fence, and stood to regain breath. It seemed as if the spot was unoccupied by a living soul.

The fire was issuing from a long straw-stack, which was so far gone as to preclude a possibility of saving it. A rick burns differently from a house. As the wind blows the fire inwards, the portion in flames completely disappears like melting sugar, and the outline is lost to the eye. However, a hay or a wheat rick, well put together, will resist combustion for a length of time if it begins on the outside.

This before Gabriel's eyes was a rick of straw, loosely put together, and the flames darted into it with lightning swiftness. It glowed on the windward side, rising and falling in intensity like the coal of a cigar. Then a superincumbent bundle rolled down with a whisking noise; flames elongated, and bent themselves about with a quiet roar, but no crackle. Banks of smoke went off horizontally at the back like passing clouds, and behind these burned hidden pyres, illuminating the semi-transparent sheet of smoke to a lustrous yellow uniformity. Individual straws in the foreground were consumed in a creeping movement of ruddy heat, as if they were knots of red worms, and above shone imaginary fiery faces, tongues hanging from lips, glaring eyes, and other impish forms, from which at intervals sparks flew in clusters like birds from a nest.

Oak suddenly ceased from being a mere spectator by discovering the case to be more serious than he had at first imagined. A scroll of smoke blew aside and revealed to him a wheat-rick in startling juxtaposition with the decaying one, and behind this a series of others, composing the main corn produce of the farm; so that instead of the straw-stack standing, as he had imagined, comparatively isolated, there was a regular connection between it and the remaining stacks of the group.

Gabriel leapt over the hedge, and saw that he was not alone. The first man he came to was running about in a great hurry, as if his thoughts were several yards in advance of his body, which they could never drag on fast enough.

'O, man – fire, fire! A good master and a bad servant is fire, fire! – I mane a bad servant and a good master. O Mark Clark – come! And you, Billy Smallbury – and you, Maryann Money – and you, Jan Coggan, and Matthew there!' Other figures now appeared behind this shouting man and among the smoke, and Gabriel found that, far from being alone, he was in a great company – whose shadows danced merrily up and down, timed by the jigging of the flames, and not at all by their owners' movements. The assemblage – belonging to that class of society which casts its thoughts into the form of feeling, and its feelings into the form of commotion – set to work with a remarkable confusion of purpose.

'Stop the draught under the wheat-rick!' cried Gabriel to those nearest to him. The corn stood on stone staddles, and between these, tongues of yellow hue from the burning straw licked and darted playfully. If the fire once got *under* this stack, all would be lost.

'Get a tarpaulin – quick!' said Gabriel.

A rick-cloth was brought, and they hung it like a curtain across the channel. The flames immediately ceased to go under the bottom of the corn-stack, and stood up vertical.

'Stand here with a bucket of water and keep the cloth wet,' said Gabriel again.

The flames, now driven upwards, began to attack the angles of the huge roof covering the wheat-stack.

'A ladder,' cried Gabriel.

'The ladder was against the straw-rick and is burnt to a cinder,' said a spectre-like form in the smoke.

Oak seized the cut ends of the sheaves, as if he were going to engage in the operation of 'reed-drawing', and digging in his feet, and occasionally sticking in the stem of his sheep-crook, he clambered up the beetling face. He at once sat astride the very apex, and began with his crook to beat off the fiery fragments which had lodged thereon, shouting to the others to get him a bough and a ladder, and some water.

Billy Smallbury – one of the men who had been on the waggon – by this time had found a ladder, which Mark Clark ascended, holding on beside Oak upon the thatch. The smoke at this corner was stifling, and Clark, a nimble fellow, having been handed a bucket of water, bathed Oak's face and sprinkled him generally, whilst Gabriel, now with a long beech-bough in one hand, in addition to his crook in the other, kept sweeping the stack and dislodging all fiery particles.

On the ground the groups of villagers were still occupied in doing all they could to keep down the conflagration, which was not much. They were all tinged orange, and backed up by shadows of varying pattern. Round the corner of the largest stack, out of the direct rays of the fire, stood a pony, bearing a young woman on its back. By her side was another woman, on foot. These two seemed to keep at a distance from the fire, that the horse might not become restive.

'He's a shepherd,' said the woman on foot. 'Yes – he is. See how his crook shines as he beats the rick with it. And his smock-frock is burnt in two holes, I declare! A fine young shepherd he is too, ma'am.'

'Whose shepherd is he?' said the equestrian in a clear voice.

'Don't know, ma'am.'

'Don't any of the others know?'

'Nobody at all – I've asked 'em. Quite a stranger, they say.'

The young woman on the pony rode out from the shade and looked anxiously around.

'Do you think the barn is safe?' she said.

'D'ye think the barn is safe, Jan Coggan?' said the second woman, passing on the question to the nearest man in that direction.

'Safe now – leastwise I think so. If this rick had gone the barn would have followed. 'Tis that bold shepherd up there that have done the most good – he sitting on the top o' rick, whizzing his great long arms about like a windmill.'

'He does work hard,' said the young woman on horseback, looking up at Gabriel through her thick woollen veil. 'I wish he was shepherd here. Don't any of you know his name?'

'Never heard the man's name in my life, or seed his form afore.'

The fire began to get worsted, and Gabriel's elevated position being no longer required of him, he made as if to descend.

'Maryann,' said the girl on horseback, 'go to him as he comes down, and say that the farmer wishes to thank him for the great service he has done.'

Maryann stalked off towards the rick and met Oak at the foot of the ladder. She delivered her message.

'Where is your master the farmer?' asked Gabriel, kindling with the idea of getting employment that seemed to strike him now.

' 'Tisn't a master; 'tis a mistress, shepherd.'

'A woman farmer?'

'Ay, 'a b'lieve, and a rich one too!' said a bystander. 'Lately 'a came here from a distance. Took on her uncle's farm, who died suddenly. Used to measure his money in half-pint cups. They say now that she've business in every bank in Casterbridge, and thinks no more of playing pitch-and-toss sovereign than you and I do pitch-halfpenny – not a bit in the world, shepherd.'

'That's she, back there upon the pony,' said Maryann; 'wi' her face a-covered up in that black cloth with holes in it.'

Oak, his features smudged, grimy, and undiscoverable from the smoke and heat, his smock-frock burnt into holes and dripping with water, the ash stem of his sheep-crook charred six inches shorter, advanced with the humility stern adversity had thrust upon him up to the slight female form in the saddle. He lifted his hat with respect, and not without gallantry: stepping close to her hanging feet he said in a hesitating voice, –

'Do you happen to want a shepherd, ma'am?'

She lifted the wool veil tied round her face, and looked all astonishment. Gabriel and his cold-hearted darling, Bathsheba Everdene, were face to face.

Bathsheba did not speak, and he mechanically repeated in an abashed and sad voice, –

'Do you want a shepherd, ma'am?'

CHAPTER SEVEN

Recognition – A Timid Girl

BATHSHEBA withdrew into the shade. She scarcely knew whether most to be amused at the singularity of the meeting, or to be concerned at its awkwardness. There was room for a little pity, also for a very little exultation: the former at his position, the latter at her own. Embarrassed she was not, and she remembered Gabriel's declaration of love to her at Norcombe only to think she had nearly forgotten it.

'Yes,' she murmured, putting on an air of dignity, and turning again to him with a little warmth of cheek; 'I do want a shepherd. But—'

'He's the very man, ma'am,' said one of the villagers, quietly.

Conviction breeds conviction. 'Ay, that 'a is,' said a second, decisively.

'The man, truly!' said a third, with heartiness.

'He's all there!' said number four, fervidly.

'Then will you tell him to speak to the bailiff?' said Bathsheba.

All was practical again now. A summer eve and loneliness would have been necessary to give the meeting its proper fulness of romance.

The bailiff was pointed out to Gabriel, who, checking the palpitation within his breast at discovering that this Ashtoreth of strange report was only a modification of Venus the well known and admired, retired with him to talk over the necessary preliminaries of hiring.

The fire before them wasted away. 'Men,' said Bathsheba, 'you shall take a little refreshment after this extra work. Will you come to the house?'

'We could knock in a bit and a drop a good deal freer, Miss, if so be ye'd send it to Warren's Malthouse,' replied the spokesman.

Bathsheba then rode off into the darkness, and the men straggled on to the village in twos and threes – Oak and the bailiff being left by the rick alone.

'And now,' said the bailiff, finally, 'all is settled, I think, about your coming, and I am going home-along. Good-night to ye, shepherd.'

'Can you get me a lodging?' inquired Gabriel.

'That I can't, indeed,' he said, moving past Oak as a Christian edges past an offertory-plate when he does not mean to contribute. 'If you follow on the road till you come to Warren's Malthouse, where they are all gone to have their snap of victuals, I daresay some of 'em will tell you of a place. Good-night to ye, shepherd.'

The bailiff who showed this nervous dread of loving his neighbour as himself, went up the hill, and Oak walked on to the village, still astonished at the rencounter with Bathsheba, glad of his nearness to her, and perplexed at the rapidity with which the unpractised girl of Norcombe had developed into the supervising and cool woman here. But some women only require an emergency to make them fit for one.

Obliged to some extent to forgo dreaming in order to find the way, he reached the churchyard, and passed round it under the wall where several ancient trees grew. There was a wide margin of grass along here, and Gabriel's footsteps were deadened by its softness, even at this indurating period of the year. When abreast of a trunk which appeared to be the oldest of the old, he became aware that a figure was standing behind it. Gabriel did not pause in his walk, and in another moment he accidentally kicked a loose stone. The noise was enough to disturb the motionless stranger, who started and assumed a careless position.

It was a slim girl, rather thinly clad.

'Good-night to you,' said Gabriel heartily.

'Good-night,' said the girl to Gabriel.

The voice was unexpectedly attractive; it was the low and dulcet note suggestive of romance; common in descriptions, rare in experience.

'I'll thank you to tell me if I'm in the way for Warren's Malthouse?' Gabriel resumed, primarily to gain the information, indirectly to get more of the music.

'Quite right. It's at the bottom of the hill. And do you know—' The girl hesitated and then went on again. 'Do you know how late they keep open the Buck's Head Inn?' She seemed to be won by Gabriel's heartiness, as Gabriel had been won by her modulations.

'I don't know where the Buck's Head is, or anything about it. Do you think of going there to-night?'

'Yes—' The woman again paused. There was no necessity for any continuance of speech, and the fact that she did add more seemed to proceed from an unconscious desire to show unconcern by making a remark, which is noticeable in the ingenuous when they are acting by stealth. 'You are not a Weatherbury man?' she said timorously.

'I am not. I am the new shepherd—just arrived.'

'Only a shepherd—and you seem almost a farmer by your ways.'

'Only a shepherd,' Gabriel repeated, in a dull cadence of finality. His thoughts were directed to the past, his eyes to the feet of the girl; and for the first time he saw lying there a bundle of some sort. She may have perceived the direction of his face, for she said coaxingly, –

'You won't say anything in the parish about having seen me here, will you – at least, not for a day or two?'

'I won't if you wish me not to,' said Oak.

'Thank you, indeed,' the other replied. 'I am rather poor, and I don't want people to know anything about me.' Then she was silent and shivered.

'You ought to have a cloak on such a cold night,' Gabriel observed. 'I would advise 'ee to get indoors.'

'O no! Would you mind going on and leaving me? I thank you much for what you have told me.'

'I will go on,' he said; adding hesitatingly, – 'Since you are not very well off, perhaps you would accept this trifle from me. It is only a shilling, but it is all I have to spare.'

'Yes, I will take it,' said the stranger gratefully.

She extended her hand; Gabriel his. In feeling for each other's palm in the gloom before the money could be passed, a minute incident occurred which told much. Gabriel's fingers alighted on the young woman's wrist. It was beating with a throb of tragic intensity. He had frequently felt the same quick, hard beat in the femoral artery of his lambs when overdriven. It suggested a consumption too great of a vitality which, to judge from her figure and stature, was already too little.

'What is the matter?'

'Nothing.'

'But there is?'

'No, no, no! Let your having seen me be a secret!'

'Very well; I will. Good-night, again.'

'Good-night.'

The young girl remained motionless by the tree, and Gabriel descended into the village of Weatherbury, or Lower Longpuddle as it was sometimes called. He fancied that he had felt himself in the penumbra of a very deep sadness when touching that slight and fragile creature. But wisdom lies in moderating mere impressions, and Gabriel endeavoured to think little of this.

CHAPTER EIGHT

The Malthouse – The Chat – News

WARREN'S Malthouse was enclosed by an old wall inwrapped with ivy, and though not much of the exterior was visible at this hour, the character and purposes of the building were clearly enough shown by its outline upon the sky. From the walls an overhanging thatched roof sloped up to a point in the centre, upon which rose a small wooden lantern, fitted with louvre-boards on all the four sides, and from these openings a mist was dimly perceived to be escaping into the night air. There was no window in front; but a square hole in the door was glazed with a single pane, through which red, comfortable rays now stretched out upon the ivied wall in front. Voices were to be heard inside.

Oak's hand skimmed the surface of the door with fingers extended to an Elymas-the-Sorcerer pattern, till he found a leathern strap, which he pulled. This lifted a wooden latch, and the door swung open.

The room inside was lighted only by the ruddy glow from the kiln mouth, which shone over the floor with the streaming horizontality of the setting sun, and threw upwards the shadows of all facial irregularities in those assembled around. The stone-flag floor was worn into a path from the doorway to the kiln, and into undulations everywhere. A curved settle of unplaned oak stretched along one side, and in a remote corner was a small bed and bedstead, the owner and frequent occupier of which was the maltster.

This aged man was now sitting opposite the fire, his frosty white hair and beard overgrowing his gnarled figure like the grey moss and lichen upon a leafless apple-tree. He wore breeches and the laced-up shoes called ankle-jacks; he kept his eyes fixed upon the fire.

Gabriel's nose was greeted by an atmosphere laden with the sweet smell of new malt. The conversation (which seemed to have been concerning the origin of the fire) immediately ceased, and every one ocularly criticized him to the degree expressed by contracting the flesh of their foreheads and looking at him with narrowed eyelids, as if he had been a light too strong for their sight. Several exclaimed meditatively, after this operation had been completed: –

'Oh, 'tis the new shepherd, 'a b'lieve.'

'We thought we heard a hand pawing about the door for the bobbin, but weren't sure 'twere not a dead leaf blowed across,' said another. 'Come in, shepherd; sure ye be welcome, though we don't know yer name.'

'Gabriel Oak, that's my name, neighbours.'

The ancient maltster sitting in the midst turned at this – his turning being as the turning of a rusty crane.

'That's never Gable Oak's grandson over at Norcombe – never!' he said, as a formula expressive of surprise, which nobody was supposed to take literally.

'My father and my grandfather were old men of the name of Gabriel,' said the shepherd placidly.

'Thought I knowed the man's face as I seed him on the rick! – thought I did! And where be ye trading o't to now, shepherd?'

'I'm thinking of biding here,' said Mr Oak.

'Knowed yer grandfather for years and years!' continued the maltster, the words coming forth of their own accord as if the momentum previously imparted had been sufficient.

'Ah – and did you!'

'Knowed yer grandmother.'

'And her too!'

'Likewise knowed yer father when he was a child. Why, my boy Jacob there and your father were sworn brothers – that they were sure – weren't ye Jacob?'

'Ay, sure,' said his son, a young man about sixty-five, with a semi-bald head and one tooth in the left centre of his upper jaw, which made much of itself by standing prominent, like a milestone in a bank. 'But 'twas Joe had most to do with him. However, my son William must have knowed the very man afore us – didn't ye, Billy, afore ye left Norcombe?'

'No, 'twas Andrew,' said Jacob's son Billy, a child of forty, or thereabouts, who manifested the peculiarity of possessing a cheerful soul in a gloomy body, and whose whiskers were assuming a chinchilla shade here and there.

'I can mind Andrew,' said Oak, 'as being a man in the place when I was quite a child.'

'Ay – the other day I and my youngest daughter, Liddy, were over at my grandson's christening,' continued Billy. 'We were talking about this very family, and 'twas only last Purification Day in this very world, when the use-money is gied away to the second-best poor folk, you know, shepherd, and I can mind the day because they all had to traypse up to the vestry – yes, this very man's family.'

'Come, shepherd, and drink. 'Tis gape and swaller with us – a drap of sommit, but not of much account,' said the maltster, removing from the fire his eyes, which were vermilion-red and bleared by gazing into it for so many years. 'Take up the God-forgive-me, Jacob. See if 'tis warm, Jacob.'

Jacob stooped to the God-forgive-me, which was a two-handled tall mug standing in the ashes, cracked and charred with heat: it was rather furred with extraneous matter about the outside, especially in the crevices of the handles, the innermost curves of which may not have seen daylight for several years by reason of this encrustation thereon – formed of ashes accidentally wetted with cider and baked hard; but to the mind of any sensible drinker the cup was no worse for that, being incontestably clean on the inside and about the rim. It may be observed that such a class of mug is called a God-forgive-me in Weatherbury and its vicinity for uncertain reasons; probably because its size makes any given toper feel ashamed of himself when he sees its bottom in drinking it empty.

Jacob, on receiving the order to see if the liquor was warm enough, placidly dipped his forefinger into it by way of thermometer, and having pronounced it nearly of the proper degree, raised the cup and very civilly attempted to dust some of the ashes from the bottom with the skirt of his smock-frock, because Shepherd Oak was a stranger.

'A clane cup for the shepherd,' said the maltster commandingly.

'No – not at all,' said Gabriel, in a reproving tone of considerateness. 'I never fuss about dirt in its pure state, and when I know what sort it is.' Taking the mug he drank an inch or more from the depth of its contents, and duly passed it to the next man. 'I wouldn't think of giving such trouble to neighbours in washing up when there's so much work to be done in the world already,' continued Oak in a moister tone, after recovering from the stoppage of breath which is occasioned by pulls at large mugs.

'A right sensible man,' said Jacob.

'True, true; it can't be gainsaid!' observed a brisk young man – Mark Clark by name, a genial and pleasant gentleman, whom to meet anywhere in your travels was to know, to know was to drink with, and to drink with was, unfortunately, to pay for.

'And here's a mouthful of bread and bacon that mis'ess have sent, shepherd. The cider will go down better with a bit of victuals. Don't ye chaw quite close, shepherd, for I let the bacon fall in the road outside as I was bringing it along, and may be 'tis rather gritty. There, 'tis clane dirt; and we all know what that is, as you say, and you bain't a particular man we see, shepherd.'

'True, true – not at all,' said the friendly Oak.

'Don't let your teeth quite meet, and you won't feel the sandiness at all. Ah! 'tis wonderful what can be done by contrivance!'

'My own mind exactly, neighbour.'

'Ah, he's his grandfer's own grandson! – his grandfer were just such a nice unparticular man!' said the maltster.

'Drink, Henry Fray – drink,' magnanimously said Jan Coggan, a person who held Saint-Simonian notions of share and share alike where liquor was concerned, as the vessel showed signs of approaching him in its gradual revolution among them.

Having at this moment reached the end of a wistful gaze into mid-air, Henry did not refuse. He was a man of more than middle age, with eyebrows high up in his forehead, who laid it down that the law of the world was bad, with a long-suffering look through his listeners at the world alluded to, as it presented itself to his imagination. He always signed his name 'Henery' – strenuously insisting upon that spelling, and if any passing schoolmaster ventured to remark that the second 'e' was superfluous and old-fashioned, he received the reply that 'H-e-n-e-r-y' was the name he was christened and the name he would stick to — in the tone of one to whom orthographical differences were matters which had a great deal to do with personal character.

Mr Jan Coggan, who had passed the cup to Henery, was a crimson man with a spacious countenance and private glimmer in his eye, whose name had appeared on the marriage register of Weatherbury and neighbouring parishes as best man and chief witness in countless unions of the previous twenty years; he also very frequently filled the post of head godfather in baptisms of the subtly-jovial kind.

'Come, Mark Clark — come. Ther's plenty more in the barrel,' said Jan.

'Ay — that I will; 'tis my only doctor,' replied Mr Clark, who, twenty years younger than Jan Coggan, revolved in the same orbit. He secreted mirth on all occasions for special discharge at popular parties.

'Why, Joseph Poorgrass, ye hadn't had a drop!' said Mr Coggan to a self-conscious man in the background, thrusting the cup towards him.

'Such a modest man as he is!' said Jacob Smallbury. 'Why, ye've hardly had strength of eye enough to look in our young mis'ess's face, so I hear, Joseph?'

All looked at Joseph Poorgrass with pitying reproach.

'No — I've hardly looked at her at all,' simpered Joseph, reducing his body smaller whilst talking, apparently from a meek sense of undue prominence. 'And when I seed her, 'twas nothing but blushes with me!'

'Poor feller,' said Mr Clark.

' 'Tis a curious nature for a man,' said Jan Coggan.

'Yes,' continued Joseph Poorgrass — his shyness, which was so painful as a defect, filling him with a mild complacency now that it was regarded as an interesting study. ' 'Twere blush, blush, blush with me every minute of the time, when she was speaking to me.'

'I believe ye, Joseph Poorgrass, for we all know ye to be a very bashful man.'

' 'Tis a' awkward gift for a man, poor soul,' said the maltster. 'And ye have suffered from it a long time, we know.'

'Ay, ever since I was a boy. Yes — mother was concerned to her heart about it — yes. But 'twas all nought.'

'Did ye ever go into the world to try and stop it, Joseph Poorgrass?'

'Oh ay, tried all sorts o' company. They took me to Greenhill Fair, and into a great gay jerry-go-nimble show, where there were women-folk riding round — standing upon horses, with hardly anything on but their smocks; but it didn't cure me a morsel. And then I was put errand-man at the Women's Skittle Alley at the back of the Tailor's Arms in Casterbridge. 'Twas a horrible sinful situation, and a very curious place for a good man. I had to stand and look ba'dy people in the face from morning till night; but 'twas no use — I was just as bad as ever after all. Blushes hev been in the family for generations. There, 'tis a happy providence that I be no worse.'

'True,' said Jacob Smallbury, deepening his thoughts to a profounder view of the subject. ' 'Tis a thought to look at, that ye might have been worse; but even as you be, 'tis a very bad affliction for 'ee, Joseph. For ye see, shepherd, though 'tis very well for a woman, dang it all, 'tis awkward for a man like him, poor feller?'

' 'Tis — 'tis,' said Gabriel, recovering from a meditation. 'Yes, very awkward for the man.'

'Ay, and he's very timid, too,' observed Jan Coggan. 'Once he had been working late at Yalbury Bottom, and had had a drap of drink, and lost his way as he was coming home-along through Yalbury Wood, didn't ye, Master Poorgrass?'

'No, no, no; not that story!' expostulated the modest man, forcing a laugh to bury his concern.

'– And so 'a lost himself quite,' continued Mr Coggan, with an impassive face, implying that a true narrative, like time and tide, must run its course and would respect no man. 'And as he was coming along in the middle of the night, much afeared, and not able to find his way out of the trees nohow, 'a cried out, "Man-a-lost! man-a-lost!" A owl in a tree happened to be crying "Whoo-whoo-whoo!" as owls do, you know, shepherd' (Gabriel nodded), 'and Joseph, all in a tremble, said, "Joseph Poorgrass, of Weatherbury, sir!"'

'No, no, now – that's too much!' said the timid man, becoming a man of brazen courage all of a sudden. 'I didn't say sir. I'll take my oath I didn't say "Joseph Poorgrass o' Weatherbury, sir." No, no; what's right is right, and I never said sir to the bird, knowing very well that no man of a gentleman's rank would be hollering there at that time o' night. "Joseph Poorgrass of Weatherbury," – that's every word I said, and I shouldn't ha' said that if 't hadn't been for Keeper Day's metheglin. . . . There, 'twas a merciful thing it ended where it did.'

The question of which was right being tacitly waived by the company, Jan went on meditatively: –

'And he's the fearfullest man, bain't ye, Joseph? Ay, another time ye were lost by Lambing-Down Gate, weren't ye, Joseph?'

'I was,' replied Poorgrass, as if there were some conditions too serious even for modesty to remember itself under, this being one.

'Yes; that were the middle of the night, too. The gate would not open, try how he would, and knowing there was the Devil's hand in it, he kneeled down.'

'Ay,' said Joseph, acquiring confidence from the warmth of the fire, the cider, and a perception of the narrative capabilities of the experience alluded to. 'My heart died within me, that time; but I kneeled down and said the Lord's Prayer, and then the Belief right through, and then the Ten Commandments, in earnest prayer. But no, the gate wouldn't open; and then I went on with Dearly Beloved Brethren, and, thinks I, this makes four, and 'tis all I know out of book, and if this don't do it nothing will, and I'm a lost man. Well, when I got to Saying After Me, I rose from my knees and found the gate would open – yes, neighbours, the gate opened the same as ever.'

A meditation on the obvious inference was indulged in by all, and during its continuance each directed his vision into the ashpit, which glowed like a desert in the tropics under a vertical sun, shaping their eyes long and liny, partly because of the light, partly from the depth of the subject discussed.

Gabriel broke the silence. 'What sort of a place is this to live at, and what sort of a mis'ess is she to work under?' Gabriel's bosom thrilled gently as he thus slipped under the notice of the assembly the innermost subject of his heart.

'We d' know little of her – nothing. She only showed herself a few days ago. Her uncle was took bad, and the doctor was called with his world-wide skill; but he couldn't save the man. As I take it, she's going to keep on the farm.'

'That's about the shape o't, 'a b'lieve,' said Jan Coggan. 'Ay, 'tis a very good family. I'd as soon be under 'em as under one here and there. Her uncle was a very fair sort of man. Did ye know en, shepherd – a bachelor-man?'

'Not at all.'

'I used to go to his house a-courting my first wife, Charlotte, who was his dairymaid. Well, a very good-hearted man were Farmer Everdene, and I being a respectable young fellow was allowed to call and see her and drink as much ale as I liked, but not to carry away any – outside my skin I mane, of course.'

'Ay, ay, Jan Coggan; we know yer maning.'

'And so you see 'twas beautiful ale, and I wished to value his kindness as much as I could, and not to be so ill-mannered as to drink only a thimbleful, which would have been insulting the man's generosity –'

'True, Master Coggan, 'twould so,' corroborated Mark Clark.

'– And so I used to eat a lot of salt fish afore going, and then by the time I got there I were as dry as a lime-basket – so thorough dry that that ale would slip down – ah, 'twould slip down sweet! Happy times! heavenly times! Such lovely drunks as I used to have at that house! You can mind, Jacob? You used to go wi' me sometimes.'

'I can – I can,' said Jacob. 'That one, too, that we had at Buck's Head on a White Monday was a pretty tipple.'

' 'Twas. But for a wet of the better class, that brought you no nearer to the horned man than you were afore you begun, there was none like those in Farmer Everdene's kitchen. Not a single damn allowed; no, not a bare poor one, even at the most cheerful moment when all were blindest, though the good old word of sin thrown in here and there at such times is a great relief to a merry soul.'

'True,' said the maltster. 'Nater requires her swearing at the regular times, or she's not herself; and unholy exclamations is a necessity of life.'

'But Charlotte,' continued Coggan – 'not a word of the sort would Charlotte allow, nor the smallest item of taking in vain. . . . Ay, poor Charlotte, I wonder if she had the good fortune to get into Heaven when 'a died! But 'a was never much in luck's way and perhaps 'a went downwards after all, poor soul.'

'And did any of you know Miss Everdene's father and mother?' inquired the shepherd, who found some difficulty in keeping the conversation in the desired channel.

'I knew them a little,' said Jacob Smallbury; 'but they were townsfolk, and didn't live here. They've been dead for years. Father, what sort of people were mis'ess' father and mother?'

'Well,' said the maltster, 'he wasn't much to look at; but she was a lovely woman. He was fond enough of her as his sweetheart.'

'Used to kiss her scores and long-hundreds o' times, so 'twas said,' observed Coggan.

'He was very proud of her, too, when they were married, as I've been told,' said the maltster.

'Ay,' said Coggan. 'He admired her so much that he used to light the candle three times a night to look at her.'

'Boundless love; I shouldn't have supposed it in the universe!' murmured Joseph Poorgrass, who habitually spoke on a large scale in his moral reflections.

'Well, to be sure,' said Gabriel.

'Oh, 'tis true enough. I knowed the man and woman both well. Levi

Everdene — that was the man's name, sure. "Man," saith I in my hurry, but he were of a higher circle of life than that — 'a was a gentleman-tailor really, worth scores of pounds. And he became a very celebrated bankrupt two or three times.'

'Oh, I thought he was quite a common man!' said Joseph.

'O no, no! That man failed for heaps of money; hudreds in gold and silver.'

The maltster being rather short of breath, Mr Coggan, after absently scrutinizing a coal which had fallen among the ashes, took up the narrative, with a private twirl of his eye: —

'Well, now, you'd hardly believe it, but that man — our Miss Everdene's father — was one of the ficklest husbands alive, after a while. Understand, 'a didn't want to be fickle, but he couldn't help it. The poor feller were faithful and true enough to her in his wish, but his heart would rove, do what he would. He spoke to me in real tribulation about it once. "Coggan," he said, "I could never wish for a handsomer woman than I've got, but feeling she's ticketed as my lawful wife, I can't help my wicked heart wandering, do what I will." But at last I believe he cured it by making her take off her wedding-ring and calling her by her maiden name as they sat together after the shop was shut, and so 'a would get to fancy she was only his sweetheart, and not married to him at all. And as soon as he could thoroughly fancy he was doing wrong and committing the seventh, 'a got to like her as well as ever, and they lived on a perfect picture of mutel love.'

'Well, 'twas a most ungodly remedy,' murmured Joseph Poorgrass; 'but we ought to feel deep cheerfulness that a happy Providence kept it from being any worse. You see, he might have gone the bad road and given his eyes to unlawfulness entirely — yes, gross unlawfulness, so to say it.'

'You see,' said Billy Smallbury, 'the man's will was to do right, sure enough, but his heart didn't chime in.'

'He got so much better that he was quite godly in his later years, wasn't he, Jan?' said Joseph Poorgrass. 'He got himself confirmed over again in a more serious way, and took to saying "Amen" almost as loud as the clerk, and he liked to copy comforting verses from the tombstones. He used, too, to hold the money-plate at Let Your Light so Shine, and stand godfather to poor little come-by-chance children; and he kept a missionary box upon his table to nab folks unawares when they called; yes, and he would box the charity-boys' ears, if they laughed in church, till they could hardly stand upright, and do other deeds of piety natural to the saintly inclined.'

'Ay, at that time he thought of nothing but high things,' added Billy Smallbury. 'One day Parson Thirdly met him and said, "Good-morning, Mister Everdene; 'tis a fine day!" "Amen," said Everdene, quite absent-like, thinking only of religion when he seed a parson. Yes, he was a very Christian man.'

'Their daughter was not at all a pretty chiel at that time,' said Henery Fray. 'Never should have thought she'd have growed up such a handsome body as she is.'

' 'Tis to be hoped her temper is as good as her face.'

'Well, yes; but the baily will have most to do with the business and ourselves. Ah!' Henery gazed into the ashpit, and smiled volumes of ironical knowledge.

'A queer Christian, like the Devil's head in a cowl,[1] as the saying is,' volunteered Mark Clark.

'He is,' said Henery, implying that irony must cease at a certain point. 'Between we two, man and man, I believe that man would as soon tell a lie Sundays as working-days – that I do so.'

'Good faith, you do talk!' said Gabriel.

'True enough,' said the man of bitter moods, looking round upon the company with the antithetic laughter that comes from a keener appreciation of the miseries of life than ordinary men are capable of. 'Ah, there's people of one sort, and people of another, but that man – bless your souls!'

Gabriel thought fit to change the subject. 'You must be a very aged man, malter, to have sons growed up so old and ancient,' he remarked.

'Father's so old that 'a can't mind his age, can ye, father?' interposed Jacob. 'And he's growed terrible crooked, too, lately,' Jacob continued, surveying his father's figure, which was rather more bowed than his own. 'Really, one may say that father there is three-double.'

'Crooked folk will last a long while,' said the maltster, grimly, and not in the best humour.

'Shepherd would like to hear the pedigree of yer life, father – wouldn't ye, shepherd?'

'Ay, that I should,' said Gabriel, with the heartiness of a man who had longed to hear it for several months. 'What may your age be, malter?'

The maltster cleared his throat in an exaggerated form for emphasis, and elongating his gaze to the remotest point of the ashpit, said, in the slow speech justifiable when the importance of a subject is so generally felt that any mannerism must be tolerated in getting at it, 'Well, I don't mind the year I were born in, but perhaps I can reckon up the places I've lived at, and so get it that way. I bode at Upper Longpuddle across there' (nodding to the north) 'till I were eleven. I bode seven at Kingsbere' (nodding to the east) 'where I took to malting. I went therefrom to Norcombe, and malted there two-and-twenty years, and two-and-twenty years I was there turnip-hoeing and harvesting. Ah, I knowed that old place, Norcombe, years afore you were thought of, Master Oak' (Oak smiled sincere belief in the fact). 'Then I malted at Durnover four year, and four year turnip-hoeing; and I was fourteen times eleven months at Millpond St Jude's' (nodding north-west-by-north). 'Old Twills wouldn't hire me for more than eleven months at a time, to keep me from being chargeable to the parish if so be I was disabled. Then I was three year at Mellstock, and I've been here one-and-thirty year come Candlemas. How much is that?'

'Hundred and seventeen,' chuckled another old gentleman, given to mental arithmetic and little conversation, who had hitherto sat unobserved in a corner.

'Well, then, that's my age,' said the maltster emphatically.

'O no, father!' said Jacob. 'Your turnip-hoeing were in the summer and your malting in the winter of the same years, and ye don't ought to count both halves father.'

---

[1] This phrase is a conjectural emendation of the unintelligible expression, 'as the Devil said to the Owl', used by the natives.

'Chok' it all! I lived through the summers, didn't I? That's my question. I suppose ye'll say next I be no age at all to speak of?'

'Sure we shan't,' said Gabriel soothingly.

'Ye be a very old aged person, malter,' attested Jan Coggan, also soothingly. 'We all know that, and ye must have a wonderful talented constitution to be able to live so long, mustn't he, neighbours?'

'True, true; ye must, malter, wonderful'; said the meeting unanimously.

The maltster, being now pacified, was even generous enough to voluntarily disparage in a slight degree the virtue of having lived a great many years, by mentioning that the cup they were drinking out of was three years older than he.

While the cup was being examined, the end of Gabriel Oak's flute became visible over his smock-frock pocket, and Henery Fray exclaimed, 'Surely, shepherd, I seed you blowing into a great flute by now at Casterbridge?'

'You did,' said Gabriel, blushing faintly. 'I've been in great trouble, neighbours, and was driven to it. I used not to be so poor as I be now.'

'Never mind, heart!' said Mark Clark. 'You should take it careless-like, shepherd, and your time will come. But we could thank ye for a tune, if ye bain't too tired?'

'Neither drum nor trumpet have I heard since Christmas,' said Jan Coggan. 'Come, raise a tune, Master Oak!'

'That I will,' said Gabriel, pulling out his flute and putting it together. 'A poor tool, neighbours; but such as I can do ye shall have and welcome.'

Oak then struck up 'Jockey to the Fair', and played that sparkling melody three times through, accenting the notes in the third round in a most artistic and lively manner by bending his body in small jerks and tapping with his foot to beat time.

'He can blow the flute very well — that 'a can,' said a young married man, who having no individuality worth mentioning was known as 'Susan Tall's husband'. He continued, 'I'd as lief as not be able to blow into a flute as well as that.'

'He's a clever man, and 'tis a true comfort for us to have such a shepherd,' murmured Joseph Poorgrass, in a soft cadence. 'We ought to feel full o' thanksgiving that he's not a player of ba'dy songs instead of these merry tunes; for 'twould have been just as easy for God to have made the shepherd a loose low man — a man of iniquity, so to speak it — as what he is. Yes, for our wives' and daughters' sakes we should feel real thanksgiving.'

'True, true, — real thanksgiving!' dashed in Mark Clark conclusively, not feeling it to be of any consequence to his opinion that he had only heard about a word and three-quarters of what Joseph had said.

'Yes,' added Joseph, beginning to feel like a man in the Bible; 'for evil do thrive so in these times that ye may be as much deceived in the clanest shaved and whitest shirted man as in the raggedest tramp upon the turnpike, if I may term it so.'

'Ay, I can mind yer face now, shepherd,' said Henery Fray, criticizing Gabriel with misty eyes as he entered upon his second tune. 'Yes — now I see 'ee blowing into the flute I know 'ee to be the same man I see play at Casterbridge, for yer mouth were scrimped up and yer eyes a-staring out like a strangled man's — just as they be now.'

' 'Tis a pity that playing the flute should make a man look such a scarecrow,' observed Mr Mark Clark, with additional criticism of Gabriel's countenance, the latter person jerking out, with the ghastly grimace required by the instrument, the chorus of 'Dame Durden'.

'Twas Moll' and Bet', and Doll' and Kate',
And Dor'-othy Drag'-gle Tail'.

'I hope you don't mind that young man's bad manners in naming your features?' whispered Joseph to Gabriel.

'Not at all,' said Mr Oak.

'For by nature ye be a very handsome man, shepherd,' continued Joseph Poorgrass with winning suavity.

'Ay, that ye be, shepherd,' said the company.

'Thank you very much,' said Oak, in the modest tone good manners demanded, thinking, however, that he would never let Bathsheba see him playing the flute; in this resolve showing a discretion equal to that related of its sagacious inventress, the divine Minerva herself.

'Ah, when I and my wife were married at Norcombe Church,' said the old maltster, not pleased at finding himself left out of the subject, 'we were called the handsomest couple in the neighbourhood – everybody said so.'

'Danged if ye bain't altered now, malter,' said a voice with the vigour natural to the enunciation of a remarkable evident truism. It came from the old man in the background, whose offensiveness and spiteful ways were barely atoned for by the occasional chuckle he contributed to general laughs.

'O no, no,' said Gabriel.

'Don't ye play no more, shepherd,' said Susan Tall's husband, the young married man who had spoken once before. 'I must be moving, and when there's tunes going on I seem as if hung in wires. If I thought after I'd left that music was still playing, and I not there, I should be quite melancholy-like.'

'What's yer hurry then, Laban?' inquired Coggan. 'You used to bide as late as the latest.'

'Well, ye see, neighbours, I was lately married to a woman, and she's my vocation now, and so ye see—' The young man halted lamely.

'New lords new laws, as the saying is, I suppose,' remarked Coggan.

'Ay, 'a b'lieve – ha, ha!' said Susan Tall's husband, in a tone intended to imply his habitual reception of jokes without minding them at all. The young man then wished them good-night and withdrew.

Henery Fray was the first to follow. Then Gabriel arose and went off with Jan Coggan, who had offered him a lodging. A few minutes later, when the remaining ones were on their legs and about to depart, Fray came back again in a hurry. Flourishing his finger ominously he threw a gaze teeming with tidings just where his eye alighted by accident, which happened to be in Joseph Poorgrass's face.

'O – what's the matter, what's the matter, Henery?' said Joseph, starting back.

'What's a-brewing, Henery?' asked Jacob and Mark Clark.

'Baily Pennyways – Baily Pennyways – I said so; yes, I said so!'

'What, found out stealing anything?'

'Stealing it is. The news is, that after Miss Everdene got home she went out again to see all was safe, as she usually do, and coming in found Baily Pennyways creeping down the granary steps with half a bushel of barley. She fleed at him like a cat —never such a tomboy as she is —of course I speak with closed doors?'

'You do —you do, Henery.'

'She fleed at him, and, to cut a long story short, he owned to having carried off five sack altogether, upon her promising not to persecute him. Well, he's turned out neck and crop, and my question is, who's going to be baily now?'

The question was such a profound one that Henery was obliged to drink there and then from the large cup till the bottom was distinctly visible inside. Before he had replaced it on the table, in came the young man, Susan Tall's husband, in a still greater hurry.

'Have ye heard the news that's all over parish?'

'About Baily Pennyways?'

'But besides that?'

'No —not a morsel of it!' they replied, looking into the very midst of Laban Tall as if to meet his words half-way down his throat.

'What a night of horrors!' murmured Joseph Poorgrass, waving his hands spasmodically. 'I've had the news-bell ringing in my left ear quite bad enough for a murder, and I've seen a magpie all alone!'

'Fanny Robin —Miss Everdene's youngest servant —can't be found. They've been wanting to lock up the door these two hours, but she isn't come in. And they don't know what to do about going to bed for fear of locking her out. They wouldn't be so concerned if she hadn't been noticed in such low spirits these last few days, and Maryann d' think the beginning of a crowner's inquest has happened to the poor girl.'

'O —'tis burned —'tis burned!' came from Joseph Poorgrass's dry lips.

'No —'tis drowned!' said Tall.

'Or 'tis her father's razor!' suggested Billy Smallbury with a vivid sense of detail.

'Well —Miss Everdene wants to speak to one or two of us before we go to bed. What with this trouble about the baily, and now about the girl, mis'ess is almost wild.'

They all hastened up the lane to the farmhouse, excepting the old maltster, whom neither news, fire, rain, nor thunder could draw from his hole. There, as the others' footsteps died away, he sat down again, and continued gazing as usual into the furnace with his red, bleared eyes.

From the bedroom window above their heads Bathsheba's head and shoulders, robed in mystic white, were dimly seen extended into the air.

'Are any of my men among you?' she said anxiously.

'Yes, ma'am, several,' said Susan Tall's husband.

'To-morrow morning I wish two or three of you to make inquiries in the villages round if they have seen such a person as Fanny Robin. Do it quietly; there is no reason for alarm as yet. She must have left whilst we were all at the fire.'

'I beg yer pardon, but had she any young man courting her in the parish, ma'am?' asked Jacob Smallbury.

'I don't know,' said Bathsheba.

'I've never heard of any such thing, ma'am,' said two or three.

'It is hardly likely, either,' continued Bathsheba. 'For any lover of hers might have come to the house if he had been a respectable lad. The most mysterious matter connected with her absence — indeed, the only thing which gives me serious alarm — is that she was seen to go out of the house by Maryann with only her indoor working gown on — not even a bonnet.'

'And you mean, ma'am, excusing my words, that a young woman would hardly go to see her young man without dressing up,' said Jacob, turning his mental vision upon past experiences. 'That's true — she would not, ma'am.'

'She had, I think, a bundle, though I couldn't see very well,' said a female voice from another window, which seemed that of Maryann. 'But she had no young man about here. Hers lives in Casterbridge, and I believe he's a soldier.'

'Do you know his name?' Bathsheba said.

'No, mistress; she was very close about it.'

'Perhaps I might be able to find out if I went to Casterbridge barracks,' said William Smallbury.

'Very well; if she doesn't return to-morrow, mind you go there and try to discover which man it is, and see him. I feel more responsible than I should if she had had any friends or relations alive. I do hope she has come to no harm through a man of that kind. . . . And then there's this disgraceful affair of the bailiff — but I can't speak of him now.'

Bathsheba had so many reasons for uneasiness that it seemed she did not think it worth while to dwell upon any particular one. 'Do as I told you, then,' she said in conclusion, closing the casement.

'Ay, ay, mistress; we will,' they replied, and moved away.

That night at Coggan's Gabriel Oak, beneath the screen of closed eyelids, was busy with fancies, and full of movement, like a river flowing rapidly under its ice. Night had always been the time at which he saw Bathsheba most vividly, and through the slow hours of shadow he tenderly regarded her image now. It is rarely that the pleasures of the imagination will compensate for the pain of sleeplessness, but they possibly did with Oak to-night, for the delight of merely seeing her effaced for the time his perception of the great difference between seeing and possessing.

He also thought of plans for fetching his few utensils and books from Norcombe. *The Young Man's Best Companion, The Farrier's Sure Guide, The Veterinary Surgeon, Paradise Lost, The Pilgrim's Progress, Robinson Crusoe*, Ash's *Dictionary*, and Walkingame's *Arithmetic*, constituted his library; and though a limited series, it was one from which he had acquired more sound information by diligent perusal than many a man of opportunities has done from a furlong of laden shelves.

CHAPTER NINE

The Homestead – A Visitor –
Half-Confidences

BY daylight, the bower of Oak's new-found mistress, Bathsheba Everdene, presented itself as a hoary building, of the early stage of Classic Renaissance as regards its architecture, and of a proportion which told at a glance that, as is so frequently the case, it had once been the manorial hall upon a small estate around it, now altogether effaced as a distinct property, and merged in the vast tract of a non-resident landlord, which comprised several such modest demesnes.

Fluted pilasters, worked from the solid stone, decorated its front, and above the roof the chimneys were panelled or columnar, some coped gables with finials and like features still retaining traces of their Gothic extraction. Soft brown mosses, like faded velveteen, formed cushions upon the stone tiling, and tufts of the houseleek or sengreen sprouted from the eaves of the low surrounding buildings. A gravel walk leading from the door to the road in front was encrusted at the sides with more moss – here it was a silver-green variety, the nut-brown of the gravel being visible to the width of only a foot or two in the centre. This circumstance, and the generally sleepy air of the whole prospect here, together with the animated and contrasting state of the reverse façade, suggested to the imagination that on the adaptation of the building for farming purposes the vital principle of the house had turned round inside its body to face the other way. Reversals of this kind, strange deformities, tremendous paralyses, are often seen to be inflicted by trade upon edifices – either individual or in the aggregate as streets and towns – which were originally planned for pleasure alone.

Lively voices were heard this morning in the upper rooms, the main staircase to which was of hard oak, the balusters, heavy as bedposts, being turned and moulded in the quaint fashion of their century, the handrail as stout as a parapet-top, and the stairs themselves continually twisting round like a person trying to look over his shoulder. Going up, the floors above were found to have a very irregular surface, rising to ridges, sinking into valleys; and being just then uncarpeted, the face of the boards was seen to be eaten into innumerable vermiculations. Every window replied by a clang to the opening and shutting of every door, a tremble followed every bustling movement, and a creak accompanied a walker about the house, like a spirit, wherever he went.

In the room from which the conversation proceeded Bathsheba and her servant-companion, Liddy Smallbury, were to be discovered sitting upon the floor, and sorting a complication of papers, books, bottles, and rubbish spread out thereon – remnants from the household stores of the late occupier. Liddy, the maltster's great-granddaughter, was about Bathsheba's equal in age, and her face was a prominent advertisement of the light-hearted English country girl. The beauty her features might have lacked in form was amply made up for by perfection of hue, which at this winter-time was the softened ruddiness on a surface of high rotundity that we meet with in a Terburg or a Gerard Douw; and, like the presentations of those great colourists, it was a face which kept well back from the boundary between comeliness and the ideal. Though elastic in nature she was less daring than Bathsheba, and occasionally showed some earnestness, which consisted half of genuine feeling, and half of mannerliness superadded by way of duty.

Through a partly-opened door the noise of a scrubbing-brush led up to the charwoman, Maryann Money, a person who for a face had a circular disc, furrowed less by age than by long gazes of perplexity at distant objects. To think of her was to get good-humoured; to speak of her was to raise the image of a dried Normandy pippin.

'Stop your scrubbing a moment,' said Bathsheba through the door to her. 'I hear something.'

Maryann suspended the brush.

The tramp of a horse was apparent, approaching the front of the building. The paces slackened, turned in at the wicket, and, what was most unusual, came up the mossy path close to the door. The door was tapped with the end of a crop or stick.

'What impertinence!' said Liddy, in a low voice. 'To ride up the footpath like that! Why didn't he stop at the gate? Lord! 'tis a gentleman! I see the top of his hat.'

'Be quiet!' said Bathsheba.

The further expression of Liddy's concern was continued by aspect instead of narrative.

'Why doesn't Mrs Coggan go to the door?' Bathsheba continued.

Rat-tat-tat-tat resounded more decisively from Bathsheba's oak.

'Maryann, you go!' said she, fluttering under the onset of a crowd of romantic possibilities.

'O ma'am —see, here's a mess!'

The argument was unanswerable after a glance at Maryann.

'Liddy —you must,' said Bathsheba.

Liddy held up her hands and arms, coated with dust from the rubbish they were sorting, and looked imploringly at her mistress.

'There — Mrs Coggan is going!' said Bathsheba, exhaling her relief in the form of a long breath which had lain in her bosom a minute or more.

The door opened, and a deep voice said —

'Is Miss Everdene at home?'

'I'll see, sir,' said Mrs Coggan, and in a minute appeared in the room.

'Dear, what a thirtover place this world is!' continued Mrs Coggan (a wholesome-looking lady who had a voice for each class of remark according to the emotion involved; who could toss a pancake or twirl a mop with the accuracy of pure mathematics, and who at this moment showed hands shaggy with fragments of dough and arms encrusted with flour). 'I am never up to my elbows, Miss, in making a pudding but one of two things do happen —either my nose must needs begin tickling, and I can't live without scratching it, or somebody knocks at the door. Here's Mr Boldwood wanting to see you, Miss Everdene.'

A woman's dress being a part of her countenance, and any disorder in the one being of the same nature with a malformation or wound in the other, Bathsheba said at once –

'I can't see him in this state. Whatever shall I do?'

Not-at-homes were hardly naturalized in Weatherbury farm-houses, so Liddy suggested – 'Say you're a fright with dust, and can't come down.'

'Yes – that sounds very well,' said Mrs Coggan critically.

'Say I can't see him – that will do.'

Mrs Coggan went downstairs, and retured the answer as requested, adding, however, on her own responsibility, 'Miss is dusting bottles, sir, and is quite a object – that's why 'tis.'

'Oh, very well,' said the deep voice indifferently. 'All I wanted to ask was, if anything had been heard of Fanny Robin?'

'Nothing, sir – but we may know to-night. William Smallbury is gone to Casterbridge, where her young man lives, as is supposed, and the other men be inquiring about everywhere.'

The horse's tramp then recommenced and retreated, and the door closed.

'Who is Mr Boldwood?' said Bathsheba.

'A gentleman-farmer at Little Weatherbury.'

'Married?'

'No, miss.'

'How old is he?'

'Forty, I should say – very handsome – rather stern-looking – and rich.'

'What a bother this dusting is! I am always in some unfortunate plight or other,' Bathsheba said complainingly. 'Why should he inquire about Fanny?'

'Oh, because, as she had no friends in her childhood, he took her and put her to school, and got her place here under your uncle. He's a very kind man that way, but Lord – there!'

'What?'

'Never was such a hopeless man for a woman! He's been courted by sixes and sevens – all the girls, gentle and simple, for miles round, have tried him. Jane Perkins worked at him for months like a slave, and the two Miss Taylors spent a year upon him, and he cost Farmer Ives's daughter nights of tears and twenty pounds' worth of new clothes; but Lord – the money might as well have been thrown out of the window.'

A little boy came up at this moment and looked in upon them. This child was one of the Coggans, who, with the Smallburys, were as common among the families of this district as the Avons and Derwents among our rivers. He always had a loosened tooth or a cut finger to show to particular friends, which he did with an air of being thereby elevated above the common herd of afflictionless humanity – to which exhibition people were expected to say 'Poor child!' with a dash of congratulation as well as pity.

'I've got a pen-nee!' said Master Coggan in a scanning measure.

'Well – who gave it you, Teddy?' said Liddy.

'Mis-terr Bold-wood! He gave it to me for opening the gate.'

'What did he say?'

'He said, "Where are you going, my little man?" and I said, "To Miss

Everdene's, please"; and he said, "She is a staid woman, isn't she, my little man?" and I said, "Yes." '

'You naughty child! What did you say that for?'

' 'Cause he gave me the penny!'

'What a pucker everything is in!' said Bathsheba discontentedly, when the child had gone. 'Get away, Maryann, or go on with your scrubbing, or do something! You ought to be married by this time, and not here troubling me!'

'Ay, mistress — so I did. But what between the poor men I won't have, and the rich men who won't have me, I stand as a pelican in the wilderness!'

'Did anybody ever want to marry you, miss?' Liddy ventured to ask when they were again alone. 'Lots of 'em, I daresay?'

Bathsheba paused, as if about to refuse a reply, but the temptation to say yes, since it really was in her power, was irresistible by aspiring virginity, in spite of her spleen at having been published as old.

'A man wanted to once,' she said, in a highly experienced tone, and the image of Gabriel Oak, as the farmer, rose before her.

'How nice it must seem!' said Liddy, with the fixed features of mental realization. 'And you wouldn't have him?'

'He wasn't quite good enough for me.'

'How sweet to be able to disdain, when most of us are glad to say, "Thank you!" I seem I hear it. "No, sir — I'm your better," or "Kiss my foot, sir; my face is for mouths of consequence." And did you love him, miss?'

'Oh, no. But I rather liked him.'

'Do you now?'

'Of course not — what footsteps are those I hear?'

Liddy looked from a back window into the courtyard behind, which was now getting low-toned and dim with the earliest films of night. A crooked file of men was approaching the back door. The whole string of trailing individuals advanced in the completest balance of intention, like the remarkable creatures known as Chain Salpæ, which, distinctly organized in other respects, have one will common to a whole family. Some were, as usual, in snow-white smock-frocks of Russia duck, and some in whitey-brown ones of drabbet — marked on the wrists, breasts, backs, and sleeves with honeycomb-work. Two or three women in pattens brought up the rear.

'The Philistines be upon us,' said Liddy, making her nose white against the glass.

'Oh, very well. Maryann, go down and keep them in the kitchen till I am dressed, and then show them in to me in the hall.'

CHAPTER TEN

Mistress and Men

HALF-AN-HOUR later Bathsheba, in finished dress, and followed by Liddy, entered the upper end of the old hall to find that her men had all deposited themselves on a long form and a settle at the lower extremity. She sat down at a table and opened the time-book, pen in her hand, with a canvas money-bag beside her. From this she poured a small heap of coin. Liddy chose a position at her elbow and began to sew, sometimes pausing and looking round, or, with the air of a privileged person, taking up one of the half-sovereigns lying before her, and surveying it merely as a work of art, while strictly preventing her countenance from expressing any wish to possess it as money.

'Now, before I begin, men,' said Bathsheba, 'I have two matters to speak of. The first is that the bailiff is dismissed for thieving, and that I have formed a resolution to have no bailiff at all, but to manage everything with my own head and hands.'

The men breathed an audible breath of amazement.

'The next matter is, have you heard anything of Fanny?'

'Nothing, ma'am.'

'Have you done anything?'

'I met Farmer Boldwood,' said Jacob Smallbury, 'and I went with him and two of his men, and dragged Newmill Pond, but we found nothing.'

'And the new shepherd have been to Buck's Head, by Yalbury, thinking she had gone there, but nobody had seed her,' said Laban Tall.

'Hasn't William Smallbury been to Casterbridge?'

'Yes, ma'am, but he's not yet come home. He promised to be back by six.'

'It wants a quarter to six at present,' said Bathsheba, looking at her watch. 'I daresay he'll be in directly. Well, now then' – she looked into the book – 'Joseph Poorgrass, are you there?'

'Yes, sir – ma'am I mane,' said the person addressed. 'I be the personal name of Poorgrass.'

'And what are you?'

'Nothing in my own eye. In the eye of other people – well, I don't say it; though public thought will out.'

'What do you do on the farm?'

'I do do carting things all the year, and in seed time I shoots the rooks and sparrows, and helps at pig-killing, sir.'

'How much to you?'

'Please nine and ninepence and a good halfpenny where 'twas a bad one, sir – ma'am I mane.'

'Quite correct. Now here are ten shillings in addition as a small present, as I am a new comer.'

Bathsheba blushed slightly at the sense of being generous in public, and Henery Fray, who had drawn up towards her chair, lifted his eyebrows and fingers to express amazement on a small scale.

'How much do I owe you – that man in the corner – what's your name?' continued Bathsheba.

'Matthew Moon, ma'am,' said a singular framework of clothes with nothing of any consequence inside them, which advanced with the toes in no definite direction forwards, but turned in or out as they chanced to swing.

'Matthew Mark, did you say? – speak out – I shall not hurt you,' inquired the young farmer kindly.

'Matthew Moon, mem,' said Henery Fray, correctingly, from behind her chair, to which point he had edged himself.

'Matthew Moon,' murmured Bathsheba, turning her bright eyes to the book. 'Ten and twopence halfpenny is the sum put down to you, I see?'

'Yes, mis'ess,' said Matthew, as the rustle of wind among dead leaves.

'Here it is, and ten shillings. Now the next – Andrew Randle, you are a new man, I hear. How came you to leave your last farm?'

'P-p-p-p-p-pl-pl-pl-pl-l-l-l-l-ease, ma'am, p-p-p-p-pl-pl-pl-pl-please, ma'am-please'm-please'm—'

''A's a stammering man, mem,' said Henery Fray in an undertone, 'and they turned him away because the only time he ever did speak plain he said his soul was his own, and other iniquities, to the squire. 'A can cuss, mem, as well as you or I, but 'a can't speak a common speech to save his life.'

'Andrew Randle, here's yours – finish thanking me in a day or two. Temperance Miller – oh, here's another, Soberness – both women, I suppose?'

'Yes'm. Here we be, 'a b'lieve,' was echoed in shrill unison.

'What have you been doing?'

'Tending thrashing-machine, and wimbling haybonds, and saying "Hoosh!" to the cocks and hens when they go upon your seeds, and planting Early Flourballs and Thompson's Wonderfuls with a dibble.'

'Yes – I see. Are they satisfactory women?' she inquired softly of Henery Fray.

'O mem – don't ask me! Yielding women – as scarlet a pair as ever was!' groaned Henery under his breath.

'Sit down.'

'Who, mem?'

'Sit down.'

Joseph Poorgrass, in the background, twitched, and his lips became dry with fear of some terrible consequences, as he saw Bathsheba summarily speaking, and Henery slinking off to a corner.

'Now the next. Laban Tall, you'll stay on working for me?'

'For you or anybody that pays me well, ma'am,' replied the young married man.

'True – the man must live!' said a woman in the back quarter, who had just entered with clicking pattens.

'What woman is that?' Bathsheba asked.

'I be his lawful wife!' continued the voice with greater prominence of manner and tone. This lady called herself five-and-twenty, looked thirty, passed as thirty-five, and was forty. She was a woman who never, like some newly married, showed conjugal tenderness in public, perhaps because she had none to show.

'Oh, you are,' said Bathsheba. 'Well, Laban, will you stay on?'

'Yes, he'll stay, ma'am!' said again the shrill tongue of Laban's lawful wife.

'Well, he can speak for himself, I suppose.'

'O Lord, not he, ma'am! A simple tool. Well enough, but a poor gawkhammer mortal,' the wife replied.

'Heh-heh-heh!' laughed the married man, with a hideous effort of appreciation, for he was as irrepressibly good-humoured under ghastly snubs as a parliamentary candidate on the hustings.

The names remaining were called in the same manner.

'Now I think I have done with you,' said Bathsheba, closing the book and shaking back a stray twine of hair. 'Has William Smallbury returned?'

'No, ma'am.'

'The new shepherd will want a man under him,' suggested Henery Fray, trying to make himself official again by a sideway approach towards her chair.

'Oh – he will. Who can he have?'

'Young Cain Ball is a very good lad,' Henery said, 'and Shepherd Oak don't mind his youth?' he added, turning with an apologetic smile to the shepherd, who had just appeared on the scene, and was now leaning against the doorpost with his arms folded.

'No, I don't mind that,' said Gabriel.

'How did Cain come by such a name?' asked Bathsheba.

'Oh you see, mem, his pore mother, not being a Scripture-read woman, made a mistake at his christening, thinking 'twas Abel killed Cain, and called en Cain, meaning Abel all the time. The parson put it right, but 'twas too late, for the name could never be got rid of in the parish. 'Tis very unfortunate for the boy.'

'It is rather unfortunate.'

'Yes. However, we soften it down as much as we can, and call him Cainy. Ah, pore widow-woman! she cried her heart out about it almost. She was brought up by a very heathen father and mother, who never sent her to church or school, and it shows how the sins of the parents are visited upon the children, mem.'

Mr Fray here drew up his features to the mild degree of melancholy required when the persons involved in the given misfortune do not belong to your own family.

'Very well then, Cainy Ball to be under-shepherd. And you quite understand your duties? – you I mean, Gabriel Oak?'

'Quite well, I thank you, Miss Everdene,' said Shepherd Oak from the doorpost. 'If I don't, I'll inquire.' Gabriel was rather staggered by the remarkable coolness of her manner. Certainly nobody without previous information would have dreamt that Oak and the handsome woman before whom he stood had ever been other than strangers. But perhaps her air was the inevitable result of the social rise which had advanced her from a cottage to a large house and fields. The case is not unexampled in high places. When, in the writings of the later poets, Jove and his family are found to have moved from their cramped quarters on the peak of Olympus into the wide sky above it, their words show a proportionate increase of arrogance and reserve.

Footsteps were heard in the passage, combining in their character the qualities both of weight and measure, rather at the expense of velocity.

(All.) 'Here's Billy Smallbury come from Casterbridge.'

'And what's the news?' said Bathsheba, as William, after marching to the middle of the hall, took a handkerchief from his hat and wiped his forehead from its centre to its remoter boundaries.

'I should have been sooner, miss,' he said, 'if it hadn't been for the weather.' He then stamped with each foot severely, and on looking down his boots were perceived to be clogged with snow.

'Come at last, is it?' said Henery.

'Well, what about Fanny?' said Bathsheba.

'Well, ma'am, in round numbers, she's run away with the soldiers,' said William.

'No; not a steady girl like Fanny!'

'I'll tell ye all particulars. When I got to Casterbridge Barracks, they said, "The Eleventh Dragoon Guards be gone away, and new troops have come." The Eleventh left last week for Melchester and onwards. The Route came from Government like a thief in the night, as is his nature to, and afore the Eleventh knew it almost, they were on the march. They passed near here.'

Gabriel had listened with interest. 'I saw them go,' he said.

'Yes,' continued William, 'they pranced down the street playing "The Girl I Left Behind Me", so 'tis said, in glorious notes of triumph. Every looker-on's inside shook with the blows of the great drum to his deepest vitals, and there was not a dry eye throughout the town among the public-house people and the nameless women!'

'But they're not gone to any war?'

'No, ma'am; but they be gone to take the places of them who may, which is very close connected. And so I said to myself, Fanny's young man was one of the regiment, and she's gone after him. There, ma'am, that's it in black and white.'

'Did you find out his name?'

'No; nobody knew it. I believe he was higher in rank than a private.'

Gabriel remained musing and said nothing, for he was in doubt.

'Well, we are not likely to know more to-night, at any rate,' said Bathsheba. 'But one of you had better run across to Farmer Boldwood's and tell him that much.'

She then rose; but before retiring, addressed a few words to them with a pretty dignity, to which her mourning dress added a soberness that was hardly to be found in the words themselves:

'Now mind, you have a mistress instead of a master. I don't yet know my powers or my talents in farming; but I shall do my best, and if you serve me well, so shall I serve you. Don't any unfair ones among you (if there are any such, but I hope not) suppose that because I'm a woman I don't understand the difference between bad goings-on and good.'

(All.) 'No'm!'

(Liddy.) 'Excellent well said.'

'I shall be up before you are awake; I shall be afield before you are up; and I shall have breakfasted before you are afield. In short, I shall astonish you all.'

(All.) 'Yes'm!'

'And so good-night.'

(All.) 'Good-night, ma'am.'

Then this small thesmothete stepped from the table, and surged out of the hall, her black silk dress licking up a few straws and dragging them along with a scratching noise upon the floor. Liddy, elevating her feelings to the occasion from a sense of grandeur, floated off behind Bathsheba with a milder dignity not entirely free from travesty, and the door was closed.

CHAPTER ELEVEN

Outside the Barracks – Snow – A Meeting

F OR dreariness nothing could surpass a prospect in the outskirts of a certain town and military station, many miles north of Weatherbury, at a later hour on this same snowy evening – if that may be called a prospect of which the chief constituent was darkness.

It was a night when sorrow may come to the brightest without causing any great sense of incongruity: when, with impressible persons, love becomes solicitousness, hope sinks to misgiving, and faith to hope: when the exercise of memory does not stir feelings of regret at opportunities for ambition that have been passed by, and anticipation does not prompt to enterprise.

The scene was a public path, bordered on the left hand by a river, behind which rose a high wall. On the right was a tract of land, partly meadow and partly moor, reaching, at its remote verge, to a wide undulating upland.

The changes of the seasons are less obtrusive on spots of this kind than amid woodland scenery. Still, to a close observer, they are just as perceptible; the difference is that their media of manifestation are less trite and familiar than such well-known ones as the bursting of the buds or the fall of the leaf. Many are not so stealthy and gradual as we may be apt to imagine in considering the general torpidity of a moor or waste. Winter, in coming to the country hereabout, advanced in well-marked stages, wherein might have been successively observed the retreat of the snakes, the transformation of the ferns, the filling of the pools, a rising of fogs, the embrowning by frost, the collapse of the fungi, and an obliteration by snow.

This climax of the series had been reached to-night on the aforesaid moor, and for the first time in the season its irregularities were forms without features; suggestive of anything, proclaiming nothing, and without more character than that of being the limit of something else – the lowest layer of a firmament of snow. From this chaotic skyful of crowding flakes the mead and moor momentarily received additional clothing, only to appear momentarily more naked thereby. The vast arch of cloud above was strangely low, and formed as it were the roof of a large dark cavern, gradually sinking in upon its floor; for the instinctive thought was that the snow lining the heavens and that encrusting the earth would soon unite into one mass without any intervening stratum of air at all.

We turn our attention to the left-hand characteristics; which were flatness in respect of the river, verticality in respect of the wall behind it, and darkness as to both. These features made up the mass. If anything could be darker than the sky, it was the wall, and if anything could be gloomier than the wall it was the river beneath. The indistinct summit of the façade was notched and prolonged by chimneys here and there, and upon its face were faintly signified the oblong shapes of windows, though only in the upper part. Below, down to the water's edge, the flat was unbroken by hole or projection.

An indescribable succession of dull blows, perplexing in their regularity, sent their sound with difficulty through the fluffy atmosphere. It was a neighbouring clock striking ten. The bell was in the open air, and being overlaid with several inches of muffling snow, had lost its voice for the time.

About this hour the snow abated: ten flakes fell where twenty had fallen, then one had the room of ten. Not long after a form moved by the brink of the river.

By its outline upon the colourless background a close observer might have seen that it was small. This was all that was positively discoverable, though it seemed human.

The shape went slowly along, but without much exertion, for the snow, though sudden, was not as yet more than two inches deep. At this time some words were spoken aloud: –

'One. Two. Three. Four. Five.'

Between each utterance the little shape advanced about half-a-dozen yards. It was evident now that the windows high in the wall were being counted. The word 'Five' represented the fifth window from the end of the wall.

Here the spot stopped, and dwindled smaller. The figure was stooping. Then a morsel of snow flew across the river towards the fifth window. It smacked against the wall at a point several yards from its mark. The throw was the idea of a man conjoined with the execution of a woman. No man who had ever seen bird, rabbit, or squirrel in his childhood, could possibly have thrown with such utter imbecility as was shown here.

Another attempt, and another; till by degrees the wall must have become pimpled with the adhering lumps of snow. At last one fragment struck the fifth window.

The river would have been seen by day to be of that deep smooth sort which races middle and sides with the same gliding precision, any irregularities of speed being immediately corrected by a small whirlpool. Nothing was heard in reply to the signal but the gurgle and cluck of one of these invisible wheels – together with a few small sounds which a sad man would have called moans, and a happy man laughter – caused by the flapping of the waters against trifling objects in other parts of the stream.

The window was struck again in the same manner.

Then a noise was heard, apparently produced by the opening of the window. This was followed by a voice from the same quarter:

'Who's there?'

The tones were masculine, and not those of surprise. The high wall being that of a barrack, and marriage being looked upon with disfavour in the army, assignations and communications had probably been made across the river before to-night.

'Is it Sergeant Troy?' said the blurred spot in the snow, tremulously.

This person was so much like a mere shade upon the earth, and the other speaker so much a part of the building, that one would have said the wall was holding a conversation with the snow.

'Yes,' came suspiciously from the shadow. 'What girl are you?'

'O, Frank – don't you know me?' said the spot. 'Your wife, Fanny Robin.'

'Fanny!' said the wall, in utter astonishment.

'Yes,' said the girl, with a half-suppressed gasp of emotion.

There was something in the woman's tone which is not that of the wife, and there was a manner in the man which is rarely a husband's. The dialogue went on:

'How did you come here?'

'I asked which was your window. Forgive me!'

'I did not expect you to-night. Indeed, I did not think you would come at all. It was a wonder you found me here. I am orderly tomorrow.'

'You said I was to come.'

'Well – I said that you might.'

'Yes, I mean that I might. You are glad to see me, Frank?'

'O yes – of course.'

'Can you – come to me?'

'My dear Fan, no! The bugle has sounded, the barrack gates are closed, and I have no leave. We are all of us as good as in the county gaol till to-morrow morning.'

'Then I shan't see you till then!' The words were in a faltering tone of disappointment.

'How did you get here from Weatherbury?'

'I walked – some part of the way – the rest by the carriers.'

'I am surprised.'

'Yes – so am I. And Frank, when will it be?'

'What?'

'That you promised.'

'I don't quite recollect.'

'O you do! Don't speak like that. It weighs me to the earth. It makes me say what ought to be said first by you.'

'Never mind – say it.'

'O, must I? – it is, when shall we be married, Frank?'

'Oh, I see. Well – you have to get proper clothes.'

'I have money. Will it be by banns or license?'

'Banns, I should think.'

'And we live in two parishes.'

'Do we? What then?'

'My lodgings are in St Mary's, and this is not. So they will have to be published in both.'

'Is that the law?'

'Yes. O Frank – you think me forward, I am afraid! Don't, dear Frank – will you – for I love you so. And you said lots of times you would marry me, and – and – I – I – I –'

'Don't cry, now! It is foolish. If I said so, of course I will.'
'And shall I put up the banns in my parish, and will you in yours?'
'Yes.'
'To-morrow?'
'Not to-morrow. We'll settle in a few days.'
'You have the permission of the officers?'
'No – not yet.'
'O – how is it? You said you almost had before you left Casterbridge.'
'The fact is, I forgot to ask. Your coming like this is so sudden and unexpected.'
'Yes – yes – it is. It was wrong of me to worry you. I'll go away now. Will you come and see me to-morrow, at Mrs Twills's, in North Street? I don't like to come to the Barracks. There are bad women about, and they think me one.'
'Quite so. I'll come to you, my dear. Good-night.'
'Good-night, Frank – good-night!'
And the noise was again heard of a window closing. The little spot moved away. When she passed the corner a subdued exclamation was heard inside the wall.
'Ho – ho – Sergeant – ho – ho!' An expostulation followed, but it was indistinct; and it became lost amid a low peal of laughter, which was hardly distinguishable from the gurgle of the tiny whirlpools outside.

CHAPTER TWELVE

Farmers – A Rule – An Exception

THE first public evidence of Bathsheba's decision to be a farmer in her own person and by proxy no more was her appearance the following market-day in the cornmarket at Casterbridge.

The low though extensive hall, supported by beams and pillars, and latterly dignified by the name of Corn Exchange, was thronged with hot men who talked among each other in twos and threes, the speaker of the minute looking sideways into his auditor's face and concentrating his argument by a contraction of one eyelid during delivery. The greater number carried in their hands ground-ash saplings, using them partly as walking-sticks and partly for poking up pigs, sheep, neighbours with their backs turned, and restful things in general, which seemed to require such treatment in the course of their peregrinations. During conversations each subjected his sapling to great varieties of usage – bending it round his back, forming an arch of it between his two hands, overweighting it on the ground till it reached nearly a semicircle; or perhaps it was hastily tucked under the arm whilst the sample-bag was pulled forth and a handful of corn poured into the palm, which, after criticism, was flung upon the floor, an issue of events perfectly well known to half-a-dozen acute town-bred fowls which had as usual crept into the building unobserved, and waited the fulfilment of their anticipations with a high-stretched neck and oblique eye.

Among these heavy yeomen a feminine figure glided, the single one of her sex that the room contained. She was prettily and even daintily dressed. She moved between them as a chaise between carts, was heard after them as a romance after sermons, was felt among them like a breeze among furnaces. It had required a little determination – far more than she had at first imagined – to take up a position here, for at her first entry the lumbering dialogues had ceased, nearly every face had been turned towards her, and those that were already turned rigidly fixed there.

Two or three only of the farmers were personally known to Bathsheba, and to these she had made her way. But if she was to be the practical woman she had intended to show herself, business must be carried on, introductions or none, and she ultimately acquired confidence enough to speak and reply boldly to men merely known to her by hearsay. Bathsheba too had her sample-bags, and by degrees adopted the professional pour into the hand – holding up the grains in her narrow palm for inspection, in perfect Casterbridge manner.

Something in the exact arch of her upper unbroken row of teeth, and in the keenly pointed corners of her red mouth when, with parted lips, she somewhat defiantly turned up her face to argue a point with a tall man, suggested that there was a potentiality enough in that lithe slip of humanity for alarming exploits of sex, and daring enough to carry them out. But her eyes had a softness – invariably a softness – which, had they not been dark, would have seemed mistiness; as they were, it lowered an expression that might have been piercing to simple clearness.

Strange to say of a woman in full bloom and vigour, she always allowed her interlocutors to finish their statements before rejoining with hers. In arguing on price she held to her own firmly, as was natural in a dealer, and reduced theirs persistently, as was inevitable in a woman. But there was an elasticity in her firmness which removed it from obstinacy, as there was a *naïveté* in her cheapening which saved it from meanness.

Those of the farmers with whom she had no dealings (by far the greater part) were continually asking each other, 'Who is she?' The reply would be –

'Farmer Everdene's niece; took on Weatherbury Upper Farm; turned away the baily, and swears she'll do everything herself.'

The other man would then shake his head.

'Yes, 'tis a pity she's so headstrong,' the first would say. 'But we ought to be proud of her here – she lightens up the old place. 'Tis such a shapely maid, however, that she'll soon get picked up.'

It would be ungallant to suggest that the novelty of her engagement in such an occupation had almost as much to do with the magnetism as had the beauty of her face and movements. However, the interest was general, and this Saturday's *début* in the forum, whatever it may have been to Bathsheba as the buying and selling farmer, was unquestionably a triumph to her as the maiden. Indeed, the sensation was so pronounced that her instinct on two or three occasions was merely to walk as a queen among these gods of the fallow, like a little sister of a little Jove, and to neglect closing prices altogether.

The numerous evidences of her power to attract were only thrown into greater relief by a marked exception. Women seem to have eyes in their ribbons for such matters as these. Bathsheba, without looking within a right angle of him, was conscious of a black sheep among the flock.

It perplexed her first. If there had been a respectable minority on either side, the case would have been most natural. If nobody had regarded her, she would have taken the matter indifferently – such cases had occurred. If everybody, this man included, she would have taken it as a matter of course – people had done so before. But the smallness of the exception made the mystery.

She soon knew thus much of the recusant's appearance. He was a gentlemanly man, with full and distinctly outlined Roman features, the prominences of which glowed in the sun with a bronze-like richness of tone. He was erect in attitude, and quiet in demeanour. One characteristic pre-eminently marked him – dignity.

Apparently he had some time ago reached that entrance to middle age at which a man's aspect naturally ceases to alter for the term of a dozen years or so; and, artificially, a woman's does likewise. Thirty-five and fifty were his limits of variation – he might have been either, or anywhere between the two.

It may be said that married men of forty are usually ready and generous enough to fling passing glances at any specimen of moderate beauty they may discern by the way. Probably, as with persons playing whist for love, the consciousness of a certain immunity under any circumstances from that worst possible ultimate, the having to pay, makes them unduly speculative. Bathsheba was convinced that this unmoved person was not a married man.

When marketing was over, she rushed off to Liddy, who was waiting for her beside the yellow gig in which they had driven to town. The horse was put in, and on they trotted – Bathsheba's sugar, tea, and drapery parcels being packed behind, and expressing in some indescribable manner, by their colour, shape, and general lineaments, that they were that young lady-farmer's property, and the grocer's and draper's no more.

'I've been through it, Liddy, and it is over. I shan't mind it again, for they will all have grown accustomed to seeing me there; but this morning it was as bad as being married – eyes everywhere!'

'I knowed it would be,' Liddy said. 'Men be such a terrible class of society to look at a body.'

'But there was one man who had more sense than to waste his time upon me.' The information was put in this form that Liddy might not for a moment suppose her mistress was at all piqued. 'A very good-looking man,' she continued, 'upright; about forty, I should think. Do you know at all who he could be?'

Liddy couldn't think.

'Can't you guess at all?' said Bathsheba with some disappointment.

'I haven't a notion; besides, 'tis no difference, since he took less notice of you than any of the rest. Now, if he'd taken more, it would have mattered a great deal.'

Bathsheba was suffering from the reverse feeling just then, and they bowled along in silence. A low carriage, bowling along still more rapidly behind a horse of unimpeachable breed, overtook and passed them.

'Why, there he is!' she said.

Liddy looked. 'That! That's Farmer Boldwood – of course 'tis – the man you couldn't see the other day when he called.'

'Oh, Farmer Boldwood,' murmured Bathsheba, and looked at him as he outstripped them. The farmer had never turned his head once, but with eyes fixed on the most advanced point along the road, passed as unconsciously and abstractedly as if Bathsheba and her charms were thin air.

'He's an interesting man – don't you think so?' she remarked.

'O yes, very. Everybody owns it,' replied Liddy.

'I wonder why he is so wrapt up and indifferent, and seemingly so far away from all he sees around him.'

'It is said – but not known for certain – that he met with some bitter disappointment when he was a young man and merry. A woman jilted him, they say.'

'People always say that – and we know very well women scarcely ever jilt men; 'tis the men who jilt us. I expect it is simply his nature to be so reserved.'

'Simply his nature – I expect so, miss – nothing else in the world.'

'Still, 'tis more romantic to think he has been served cruelly, poor thing! Perhaps, after all, he has.'

'Depend upon it he has. O yes, miss, he has! I feel he must have.'

'However, we are very apt to think extremes of people. I shouldn't wonder after all if it wasn't a little of both – just between the two – rather cruelly used and rather reserved.'

'O dear no, miss – I can't think it between the two!'

'That's most likely.'

'Well, yes, so it is. I am convinced it is most likely. You may take my word, miss, that that's what's the matter with him.'

CHAPTER THIRTEEN

Sortes Sanctorum – The Valentine

IT was Sunday afternoon in the farmhouse, on the thirteenth of February. Dinner being over, Bathsheba, for want of a better companion, had asked Liddy to come and sit with her. The mouldy pile was dreary in winter-time before the candles were lighted and the shutters closed; the atmosphere of the place seemed as old as the walls; every nook behind the furniture had a temperature of its own, for the fire was not kindled in this part of the house early in the day; and Bathsheba's new piano, which was an old one in other annals, looked particularly sloping and out of level on the warped floor before night threw a shade over its less prominent angles and hid the unpleasantness. Liddy, like a little brook, though shallow, was always rippling; her presence had not so much weight as to task thought, and yet enough to exercise it.

On the table lay an old quarto Bible, bound in leather. Liddy looking at it said, –

'Did you ever find out, miss, who you are going to marry by means of the Bible and key?'

'Don't be so foolish, Liddy. As if such things could be.'

'Well, there's a good deal in it, all the same.'

'Nonsense, child.'

'And it makes your heart beat fearful. Some believe in it; some don't; I do.'

'Very well, let's try it,' said Bathsheba, bounding from her seat with that total disregard of consistency which can be indulged in towards a dependant, and entering into the spirit of divination at once. 'Go and get the front door key.'

Liddy fetched it. 'I wish it wasn't Sunday,' she said, on returning. 'Perhaps 'tis wrong.'

'What's right week days is right Sundays,' replied her mistress in a tone which was a proof in itself.

The book was opened — the leaves, drab with age, being quite worn away at much-read verses by the forefingers of unpractised readers in former days, where they were moved along under the line as an aid to the vision. The special verse in the Book of Ruth was sought out by Bathsheba, and the sublime words met her eye. They slightly thrilled and abashed her. It was Wisdom in the abstract facing Folly in the concrete. Folly in the concrete blushed, persisted in her intention, and placed the key on the book. A rusty patch immediately upon the verse, caused by previous pressure of an iron substance thereon, told that this was not the first time the old volume had been used for the purpose.

'Now keep steady, and be silent,' said Bathsheba.

The verse was repeated; the book turned round; Bathsheba blushed guiltily.

'Who did you try?' said Liddy curiously.

'I shall not tell you.'

'Did you notice Mr Boldwood's doings in church this morning, miss?' Liddy continued, adumbrating by the remark the track her thoughts had taken.

'No, indeed,' said Bathsheba, with serene indifference.

'His pew is exactly opposite yours, miss.'

'I know it.'

'And you did not see his goings on!'

'Certainly I did not, I tell you.'

Liddy assumed a smaller physiognomy, and shut her lips decisively.

This more was unexpected, and proportionately disconcerting. 'What did he do?' Bathsheba said perforce.

'Didn't turn his head to look at you once all the service.'

'Why should he?' again demanded her mistress, wearing a nettled look. 'I didn't ask him to.'

'Oh, no. But everybody else was noticing you; and it was odd he didn't. There, 'tis like him. Rich and gentlemanly, what does he care?'

Bathsheba dropped into a silence intended to express that she had opinions on the matter too abstruse for Liddy's comprehension, rather than that she had nothing to say.

'Dear me — I had nearly forgotten the valentine I bought yesterday,' she exclaimed at length.

'Valentine! who for, miss?' said Liddy. 'Farmer Boldwood?'

It was the single name among all possible wrong ones that just at this moment seemed to Bathsheba more pertinent than the right.

'Well, no. It is only for little Teddy Coggan. I have promised him something, and this will be a pretty surprise for him. Liddy, you may as well bring me my desk and I'll direct it at once.'

Bathsheba took from her desk a gorgeously illuminated and embossed design in post-octavo, which had been bought on the previous market-day at the chief stationer's in Casterbridge. In the centre was a small oval enclosure; this was left blank, that the sender might insert tender words more appropriate to the special occasion than any generalities by a printer could possibly be.

'Here's a place for writing,' said Bathsheba. 'What shall I put?'

'Something of this sort, I should think,' returned Liddy promptly: —

> 'The rose is red,
> The violet blue,
> Carnation's sweet,
> And so are you.'

'Yes, that shall be it. It just suits itself to a chubby-faced child like him,' said Bathsheba. She inserted the words in a small though legible handwriting; enclosed the sheet in an envelope, and dipped her pen for the direction.

'What fun it would be to send it to the stupid old Boldwood, and how he would wonder!' said the irrepressible Liddy, lifting her eyebrows, and indulging in an awful mirth on the verge of fear as she thought of the moral and social magnitude of the man contemplated.

Bathsheba paused to regard the idea at full length. Boldwood's had begun to be a troublesome image — a species of Daniel in her kingdom who persisted in kneeling eastward when reason and common sense said that he might just as well follow suit with the rest, and afford her the official glance of admiration which cost nothing at all. She was far from being seriously concerned about his nonconformity. Still, it was faintly depressing that the most dignified and valuable man in the parish should withhold his eyes, and that a girl like Liddy should talk about it. So Liddy's idea was at first rather harassing than piquant.

'No, I won't do that. He wouldn't see any humour in it.'

'He'd worry to death,' said the persistent Liddy.

'Really, I don't care particularly to send it to Teddy,' remarked her mistress. 'He's rather a naughty child sometimes.'

'Yes — that he is.'

'Let's toss, as men do,' said Bathsheba idly. 'Now then, head, Boldwood; tail, Teddy. No, we won't toss money on a Sunday, that would be tempting the devil indeed.'

'Toss this hymn-book; there can't be no sinfulness in that, miss.'

'Very well. Open, Boldwood — shut, Teddy. No; it's more likely to fall open. Open, Teddy — shut, Boldwood.'

The book went fluttering in the air and came down shut.

Bathsheba, a small yawn upon her mouth, took the pen, and with off-hand serenity directed the missive to Boldwood.

'Now light a candle, Liddy. Which seal shall we use? Here's a unicorn's head — there's nothing in that. What's this? — two doves — no. It ought to be something extraordinary, ought it not, Lidd? Here's one with a motto – I remember it is some funny one, but I can't read it. We'll try this, and if it doesn't do we'll have another.'

A large red seal was duly affixed. Bathsheba looked closely at the hot wax to discover the words.

'Capital!' she exclaimed, throwing down the letter frolicsomely. ''Twould upset the solemnity of a parson and clerk too.'

Liddy looked at the words of the seal, and read –

'MARRY ME.'

The same evening the letter was sent, and was duly sorted in Casterbridge post-office that night, to be returned to Weatherbury again in the morning.

So very idly and unreflectingly was this deed done. Of love as a spectacle Bathsheba had a fair knowledge; but of love subjectively she knew nothing.

CHAPTER FOURTEEN

Effect of the Letter – Sunrise

AT dusk on the evening of St Valentine's Day Boldwood sat down to supper as usual, by a beaming fire of aged logs. Upon the mantelshelf before him was a time-piece, surmounted by a spread eagle, and upon the eagle's wings was the letter Bathsheba had sent. Here the bachelor's gaze was continually fastening itself, till the large red seal became as a blot of blood on the retina of his eye; and as he ate and drank he still read in fancy the words theron, although they were too remote for his sight –

'MARRY ME.'

The pert injunction was like those crystal substances, which, colourless themselves, assume the tone of objects about them. Here, in the quiet of Boldwood's parlour, where everything that was not grave was extraneous, and where the atmosphere was that of a Puritan Sunday lasting all the week, the letter and its dictum changed their tenor from the thoughtlessness of their origin to a deep solemnity, imbibed from their accessories now.

Since the receipt of the missive in the morning, Boldwood had felt the symmetry of his existence to be slowly getting distorted in the direction of an ideal passion. The disturbance was as the first floating weed to Columbus – the contemptibly little suggesting possibilities of the infinitely great.

The letter must have had an origin and a motive. That the latter was of the smallest magnitude compatible with its existence at all, Boldwood, of course, did not know. And such an explanation did not strike him as a possibility even. It is foreign to a mystified condition of mind to realize of the mystifier that the processes of approving a course suggested by circumstance, and of striking out a course from inner impulse, would look the same in the result. The vast difference between starting a train of events, and directing into a particular groove a series already started, is rarely apparent to the person confounded by the issue.

When Boldwood went to bed he placed the valentine in the corner of the looking-glass. He was conscious of its presence, even when his back was turned upon it. It was the first time in Boldwood's life that such an event had occurred. The same fascination that caused him to think it an act which had a deliberate motive prevented him from regarding it as an impertinence. He looked again at the direction. The mysterious influences of night invested the writing with the presence of the unknown writer. Somebody's some *woman's* — hand had travelled softly over the paper bearing his name; her unrevealed eyes had watched every curve as she formed it; her brain had seen him in imagination the while. Why should she have imagined him? Her mouth — were the lips red or pale, plump or creased? — had curved itself to a certain expression as the pen went on — the corners had moved with all their natural tremulousness: what had been the expression?

The vision of the woman writing, as a supplement to the words written, had no individuality. She was a misty shape, and well she might be, considering that her original was at that moment sound asleep and oblivious of all love and letter-writing under the sky. Whenever Boldwood dozed she took a form, and comparatively ceased to be a vision: when he awoke there was the letter justifying the dream.

The moon shone to-night, and its light was not of a customary kind. His window admitted only a reflection of its rays, and the pale sheen had that reversed direction which snow gives, coming upward and lighting up his ceiling in an unnatural way, casting shadows in strange places, and putting lights where shadows had used to be.

The substance of the epistle had occupied him but little in comparison with the fact of its arrival. He suddenly wondered if anything more might be found in the envelope than what he had withdrawn. He jumped out of bed in the weird light, took the letter, pulled out the flimsy sheet, shook the envelope — searched it. Nothing more was there. Boldwood looked, as he had a hundred times the preceding day, at the insistent red seal: 'Marry me,' he said aloud.

The solemn and reserved yeoman again closed the letter, and stuck it in the frame of the glass. In doing so he caught sight of his reflected features, wan in expression, and insubstantial in form. He saw how closely compressed was his mouth, and that his eyes were wide-spread and vacant. Feeling uneasy and dissatisfied with himself for this nervous excitability, he returned to bed.

Then the dawn drew on. The full power of the clear heaven was not equal to that of a cloudy sky at noon, when Boldwood arose and dressed himself. He descended the stairs and went out towards the gate of a field to the east, leaning over which he paused and looked around.

It was one of the usual slow sunrises of this time of the year, and the sky, pure violet in the zenith, was leaden to the northward, and murky to the east, where, over the snowy down or ewe-lease on Weatherbury Upper Farm, and apparently resting upon the ridge, the only half of the sun yet visible burnt rayless, like a red and flameless fire shining over a white hearthstone. The whole effect resembled a sunset as childhood resembles age.

In other directions the fields and sky were so much of one colour by the snow that it was difficult in a hasty glance to tell whereabouts the horizon occurred; and in general there was here, too, that before-mentioned preternatural inversion of light and shade which attends the prospect when the garish brightness commonly in the sky is found on the earth, and the shades of earth are in the sky. Over the west hung the wasting moon, now dull and greenish-yellow, like tarnished brass.

Boldwood was listlessly noting how the frost had hardened and glazed the surface of the snow, till it shone in the red eastern light with the polish of marble; how, in some portions of the slope, withered grass-bents, encased in icicles, bristled through the smooth wan coverlet in the twisted and curved shapes of old Venetian glass; and how the footprints of a few birds, which had hopped over the snow whilst it lay in the state of a soft fleece, were now frozen to a short permanency. A half-muffled noise of light wheels interrupted him. Boldwood turned back into the road. It was the mail-cart — a crazy two-wheeled vehicle, hardly heavy enough to resist a puff of wind. The driver held out a letter. Boldwood seized it and opened it, expecting another anonymous one — so greatly are people's ideas of probability a mere sense that precedent will repeat itself.

'I don't think it is for you, sir,' said the man, when he saw Boldwood's action. 'Though there is no name, I think it is for your shepherd.'

Boldwood looked then at the address —

> *To the New Shepherd,*
> *Weatherbury Farm,*
> *Near Casterbridge.*

'Oh — what a mistake! — it is not mine. Nor is it for my shepherd. It is for Miss Everdene's. You had better take it on to him — Gabriel Oak — and say I opened it in mistake.'

At this moment on the ridge, up against the blazing sky, a figure was visible, like the black snuff in the midst of a candle-flame. Then it moved and began to bustle about vigorously from place to place, carrying square skeleton masses, which were riddled by the same rays. A small figure on all fours followed behind. The tall form was that of Gabriel Oak; the small one that of George; the articles in course of transit were hurdles.

'Wait,' said Boldwood. 'That's the man on the hill. I'll take the letter to him myself.'

To Boldwood it was now no longer merely a letter to another man. It was an opportunity. Exhibiting a face pregnant with intention, he entered the snowy field.

Gabriel, at that minute, descended the hill towards the right. The glow stretched down in this direction now, and touched the distant roof of Warren's Malthouse — whither the shepherd was apparently bent. Boldwood followed at a distance.

CHAPTER FIFTEEN

A Morning Meeting – The Letter again

THE scarlet and orange light outside the malthouse did not penetrate to its interior, which was, as usual, lighted by a rival glow of similar hue, radiating from the hearth.

The maltster, after having lain down in his clothes for a few hours, was now sitting beside a three-legged table, breakfasting off bread and bacon. This was eaten on the plateless system, which is performed by placing a slice of bread upon the table, the meat flat upon the bread, a mustard plaster upon the meat, and a pinch of salt upon the whole, then cutting them vertically downwards with a large pocket-knife till wood is reached, when the severed lump is impaled on the knife, elevated, and sent the proper way of food.

The maltster's lack of teeth appeared not to sensibly diminish his powers as a mill. He had been without them for so many years that toothlessness was felt less to be a defect than hard gums an acquisition. Indeed, he seemed to approach the grave as a hyperbolic curve approaches a straight line – less directly as he got nearer, till it was doubtful if he would ever reach it at all.

In the ashpit was a heap of potatoes roasting, and a boiling pipkin of charred bread, called 'coffee', for the benefit of whomsoever should call, for Warren's was a sort of clubhouse, used as an alternative to the inn.

'I say, says I, we get a fine day, and then down comes a snapper at night,' was a remark now suddenly heard spreading into the malthouse from the door, which had been opened the previous moment. The form of Henery Fray advanced to the fire, stamping the snow from his boots when about half-way there. The speech and entry had not seemed to be at all an abrupt beginning to the maltster, introductory matter being often omitted in this neighbourhood, both from word and deed, and the maltster having the same latitude allowed him, did not hurry to reply. He picked up a fragment of cheese by pecking upon it with his knife, as a butcher picks up skewers.

Henery appeared in a drab kerscymere great-coat, buttoned over his smock-frock, the white skirts of the latter being visible to the distance of about a foot below the coat-tails, which, when you got used to the style of dress, looked natural enough, and even ornamental – it certainly was comfortable.

Matthew Moon, Joseph Poorgrass, and other carters and waggoners followed at his heels, with great lanterns dangling from their hands, which showed that they had just come from the cart-horse stables, where they had been busily engaged since four o'clock that morning.

'And how is she getting on without a baily?' the maltster inquired.

Henery shook his head, and smiled one of the bitter smiles, dragging all the flesh of his forehead into a corrugated heap in the centre.

'She'll rue it – surely, surely!' he said. 'Benjy Pennyways were not a true man or an honest baily – as big a betrayer as Joey Iscariot himself. But to think she can carr' on alone!' He allowed his head to swing laterally three or four times in silence. 'Never in all my creeping up – never!'

This was recognized by all as the conclusion of some gloomy speech which had been expressed in thought alone during the shake of the head; Henery meanwhile retained several marks of despair upon his face, to imply that they would be required for use again directly he should go on speaking.

'All will be ruined, and ourselves too, or there's no meat in gentlemen's houses!' said Mark Clark.

'A headstrong maid, that's what she is – and won't listen to no advice at all. Pride and vanity have ruined many a cobbler's dog. Dear, dear, when I think o' it, I sorrows like a man in travel!'

'True, Henery, you do, I've heard ye,' said Joseph Poorgrass, in a voice of thorough attestation, and with a wire-drawn smile of misery.

' 'Twould do a martel man no harm to have what's under her bonnet,' said Billy Smallbury, who had just entered, bearing his one tooth before him. 'She can spaik real language, and must have some sense somewhere. Do ye foller me?'

'I do; but no baily – I deserved that place,' wailed Henery, signifying wasted genius by gazing blankly at visions of a high destiny apparently visible to him on Billy Smallbury's smock-frock. 'There, 'twas to be, I suppose. Your lot is your lot, and Scripture is nothing; for if you do good you don't get rewarded according to your works, but be cheated in some mean way out of your recompense.'

'No, no; I don't agree with'ee there,' said Mark Clark. 'God's a perfect gentleman in that respect.'

'Good works good pay, so to speak it,' attested Joseph Poorgrass.

A short pause ensued, and as a sort of *entr'acte* Henery turned and blew out the lanterns, which the increase of daylight rendered no longer necessary even in the malthouse, with its one pane of glass.

'I wonder what a farmer-woman can want with a harpsichord, dulcimer, pianner, or whatever 'tis they d'call it?' said the maltster. 'Liddy saith she've a new one.'

'Got a pianner?'

'Ay. Seems her old uncle's things were not good enough for her. She've bought all but everything new. There's heavy chairs for the stout, weak and wiry ones for the slender; great watches, getting on to the size of clocks, to stand upon the chimbley-piece.'

'Pictures, for the most part wonderful frames.'

'And long horse-hair settles for the drunk, with horse-hair pillows at each end,' said Mr Clark. 'Likewise looking-glasses for the pretty, and lying books for the wicked.'

A firm loud tread was now heard stamping outside; the door was opened about six inches, and somebody on the other side exclaimed –

'Neighbours, have ye got room for a few new-born lambs?'

'Ay, sure, shepherd,' said the conclave.

The door was flung back till it kicked the wall and trembled from top to bottom with the blow. Mr Oak appeared in the entry with a steaming face, haybands wound about his ankles to keep out the snow, a leather strap round his waist outside the smock-frock, and looking altogether an epitome of the world's health and vigour. Four lambs hung in various embarrassing attitudes over his shoulders, and the dog George, whom Gabriel had contrived to fetch from Norcombe, stalked solemnly behind.

'Well, Shepherd Oak, and how's lambing this year, if I mid say it?' inquired Joseph Poorgrass.

'Terrible trying,' said Oak. 'I've been wet through twice a-day, either in snow or rain, this last fortnight. Cainy and I haven't tined our eyes to-night.'

'A good few twins, too, I hear?'

'Too many by half. Yes; 'tis a very queer lambing this year. We shan't have done by Lady Day.'

'And last year 'twer all over by Sexajessamine Sunday,' Joseph remarked.

'Bring on the rest, Cain,' said Gabriel, 'and then run back to the ewes. I'll follow you soon.'

Cainy Ball — a cheery-faced young lad, with a small circular orifice by way of mouth, advanced and deposited two others, and retired as he was bidden. Oak lowered the lambs from their unnatural elevation, wrapped them in hay, and placed them round the fire.

'We've no lambing-hut here, as I used to have at Norcombe,' said Gabriel, 'and 'tis such a plague to bring the weakly ones to a house. If 'twasn't for your place here, malter, I don't know what I should do, this keen weather. And how is it with you to-day, malter?'

'Oh, neither sick nor sorry, shepherd; but no younger.'

'Ay — I understand.'

'Sit down, Shepherd Oak,' continued the ancient man of malt. 'And how was the old place at Norcombe, when ye went for your dog? I should like to see the old familiar spot; but faith, I shouldn't know a soul there now.'

'I suppose you wouldn't. 'Tis altered very much.'

'Is it true that Dicky Hill's wooden cider-house is pulled down?'

'O yes — years ago, and Dicky's cottage just above it.'

'Well, to be sure!'

'Yes; and Tompkins's old apple-tree is rooted that used to bear two hogsheads of cider, and no help from other trees.'

'Rooted? — you don't say it! Ah! stirring times we live in — stirring times.'

'And you can mind the old well that used to be in the middle of the place? That's turned into a solid iron pump with a large stone trough, and all complete.'

'Dear, dear — how the face of nations alter, and what we live to see nowadays! Yes — and 'tis the same here. They've been talking but now of the mis'ess's strange doings.'

'What have you been saying about her?' inquired Oak, sharply turning to the rest, and getting very warm.

'These middle-aged men have been pulling her over the coals for pride and vanity,' said Mark Clark; 'but I say, let her have rope enough. Bless her pretty face — shouldn't I like to do so — upon her cherry lips!' The gallant Mark Clark here made a peculiar and well-known sound with his own.

'Mark,' said Gabriel sternly, 'now you mind this: none of that dalliance-talk — that smack-and-coddle style of yours — about Miss Everdene. I don't allow it. Do you hear?'

'With all my heart, as I've got no chance,' replied Mr Clark cordially.

'I suppose you've been speaking against her?' said Oak, turning to Joseph Poorgrass with a very grim look.

'No, no — not a word I — 'tis a real joyful thing that she's no worse, that's what I say,' said Joseph, trembling and blushing with terror. 'Matthew just said—'

'Matthew Moon, what have you been saying?' asked Oak.

'I? Why ye know I wouldn't harm a worm — no, not one underground worm?' said Matthew Moon, looking very uneasy.

'Well, somebody has — and look here, neighbours.' Gabriel, though one of the quietest and most gentle men on earth, rose to the occasion, with martial promptness and vigour. 'That's my fist.' Here he placed his fist, rather smaller in size than a common loaf, in the mathematical centre of the maltster's little table, and with it gave a bump or two thereon, as if to ensure that their eyes all throughly took in the idea of fistiness before he went further. 'Now — the first man in the parish that I hear prophesying bad of our mistress, why' (here the fist was raised and let fall, as Thor might have done with his hammer in assaying it) — 'he'll smell and taste that — or I'm a Dutchman.'

All earnestly expressed by their features that their minds did not wander to Holland for a moment on account of this statement, but were deploring the difference which gave rise to the figure; and Mark Clark cried 'Hear, hear; just what I should ha' said.' The dog George looked up at the same time after the shepherd's menace, and, though he understood English but imperfectly, began to growl.

'Now, don't ye take on so, shepherd, and sit down!' said Henery, with a deprecating peacefulness equal to anything of the kind in Christianity.

'We hear that ye be a extraordinary good and clever man, shepherd,' said Joseph Poorgrass with considerable anxiety from behind the maltster's bedstead whither he had retired for safety. ' 'Tis a great thing to be clever, I'm sure,' he added, making movements associated with states of mind rather than body; 'we wish we were, don't we, neighbours?'

'Ay, that we do, sure,' said Matthew Moon, with a small anxious laugh towards Oak, to show how very friendly disposed he was likewise.

'Who's been telling you I'm clever?' said Oak.

' 'Tis blowed about from pillar to post quite common,' said Matthew. 'We hear that ye can tell the time as well by the stars as we can by the sun and moon, shepherd.'

'Yes, I can do a little that way,' said Gabriel, as a man of medium sentiments on the subject.

'And that ye can make sun-dials, and prent folks' names upon their waggons almost like copper-plate, with beautiful flourishes, and great long tails. A excellent fine thing for ye to be such a clever man, shepherd. Joseph Poorgrass used to prent to Farmer James Everdene's waggons before you came, and 'a could never mind which way to turn the J's and E's — could ye, Joseph?' Joseph shook his head to express how absolute was the fact that he couldn't. 'And so you used to do 'em the wrong way, like this, didn't ye, Joseph?' Matthew marked on the dusty floor with his whip-handle

LAMƎS

'And how Farmer James would cuss, and call thee a fool, wouldn't he, Joseph, when 'a seed his name looking so inside-out-like?' continued Matthew Moon, with feeling.

'Ay – 'a would,' said Joseph meekly. 'But, you see, I wasn't so much to blame, for them J's and E's be such trying sons o' witches for the memory to mind whether they face backward or forward; and I always had such a forgetful memory, too.'

''Tis a bad affliction for ye, being such a man of calamities in other ways.'

'Well, 'tis; but a happy Providence ordered that it should be no worse, and I feel my thanks. As to shepherd, there, I'm sure mis'ess ought to have made ye her baily – such a fitting man for't as you be.'

'I don't mind owning that I expected it,' said Oak frankly. 'Indeed, I hoped for the place. At the same time, Miss Everdene has a right to be her own baily if she choose – and to keep me down to be a common shepherd only.' Oak drew a slow breath, looked sadly into the bright ashpit, and seemed lost in thoughts not of the most hopeful hue.

The genial warmth of the fire now began to stimulate the nearly lifeless lambs to bleat and move their limbs briskly upon the hay, and to recognize for the first time the fact that they were born. Their noise increased to a chorus of baas, upon which Oak pulled the milk-can from before the fire, and taking a small tea-pot from the pocket of his smock-frock, filled it with milk, and taught those of the helpless creatures which were not to be restored to their dams how to drink from the spout – a trick they acquired with astonishing aptitude.

'And she don't even let ye have the skins of the dead lambs, I hear?' resumed Joseph Poorgrass, his eyes lingering on the operations of Oak with the necessary melancholy.

'I don't have them,' said Gabriel.

'Ye be very badly used, shepherd,' hazarded Joseph again, in the hope of getting Oak as an ally in lamentation after all. 'I think she's took against ye – that I do.'

'O no – not at all,' replied Gabriel hastily, and a sigh escaped him, which the deprivation of lamb skins could hardly have caused.

Before any further remark had been added a shade darkened the door, and Boldwood entered the malthouse, bestowing upon each a nod of a quality between friendliness and condescension.

'Ah! Oak, I thought you were here,' he said. 'I met the mail-cart ten minutes ago, and a letter was put into my hand, which I opened without reading the address. I believe it is yours. You must excuse the accident, please.'

'O yes – not a bit of difference, Mr Boldwood – not a bit,' said Gabriel readily. He had not a correspondent on earth, nor was there a possible letter coming to him whose contents the whole parish would not have been welcome to peruse.

Oak stepped aside, and read the following in an unknown hand: –

'DEAR FRIEND – I do not know your name, but I think these few lines will reach you, which I write to thank you for your kindness to me the night I left Weatherbury in a reckless way. I also return the money I owe you, which you will excuse my not keeping as a gift. All has ended well, and I am happy to say I am going to be married to the young man who has courted me for some time – Sergeant Troy, of the 11th Dragoon Guards, now quartered in this town. He would, I know, object to my having received anything except as a loan, being a man of great respectability and high honour – indeed, a nobleman by blood.

'I should be much obliged to you if you would keep the contents of this letter a secret for the present, dear friend. We mean to surprise Weatherbury by coming there soon as husband and wife, though I blush to state it to one nearly a stranger. The sergeant grew up in Weatherbury. Thanking you again for your kindness,

I am, your sincere well-wisher,

FANNY ROBIN'

'Have you read it, Mr Boldwood?' said Gabriel; 'if not, you had better do so. I know you are interested in Fanny Robin.'

Boldwood read the letter and looked grieved.

'Fanny – poor Fanny! the end she is so confident of has not yet come, she should remember – and may never come. I see she gives no address.'

'What sort of a man is this Sergeant Troy?' said Gabriel.

'H'm – I'm afraid not one to build much hope upon in such a case as this,' the farmer murmured, 'though he's a clever fellow, and up to everything. A slight romance attaches to him, too. His mother was a French governess, and it seems that a secret attachment existed between her and the late Lord Severn. She was married to a poor medical man, and soon after an infant was born; and while money was forthcoming all went on well. Unfortunately for her boy, his best friends died; and he got then a situation as second clerk at a lawyer's in Casterbridge. He stayed there for some time, and might have worked himself into a dignified position of some sort had he not indulged in the wild freak of enlisting. I have much doubt if ever little Fanny will surprise us in the way she mentions – very much doubt. A silly girl – silly girl!'

The door was hurriedly burst open again, and in came running Cainy Ball out of breath, his mouth red and open, like the bell of a penny trumpet, from which he coughed with noisy vigour and great distension of face.

'Now, Cain Ball,' said Oak sternly, 'why will you run so fast and lose your breath so? I'm always telling you of it.'

'O – I – a puff of mee breath – went – the wrong way, please, Mister Oak, and made me cough – hok – hok!'

'Well – what have you come for?'

'I've run to tell ye,' said the junior shepherd, supporting his exhausted youthful frame against the doorpost, 'that you must come directly. Two more ewes have twinned – that's what's the matter, Shepherd Oak.'

'Oh, that's it,' said Oak, jumping up, and dismissing for the present his thoughts on poor Fanny. 'You are a good boy to run and tell me, Cain, and you shall smell a large plum pudding some day as a treat. But, before we go, Cainy, bring the tarpot, and we'll mark this lot and have done with 'em.'

Oak took from his illimitable pockets a marking iron, dipped it into the pot, and imprinted on the buttocks of the infant sheep the initials of her he delighted to muse on – 'B. E.', which signified to all the region round that henceforth the lambs belonged to Farmer Bathsheba Everdene, and to no one else.

'Now, Cainy, shoulder your two, and off. Good morning, Mr Boldwood.' The shepherd lifted the sixteen large legs and four small bodies he had himself brought, and vanished with them in the direction of the lambing field hard by – their frames being now in a sleek and hopeful state, pleasantly contrasting with their death's-door plight of half an hour before.

Boldwood followed him a little way up the field, hesitated, and turned back. He followed him again with a last resolve, annihilating return. On approaching the nook in which the fold was constructed, the farmer drew out his pocket-book, unfastened it, and allowed it to lie open on his hand. A letter was revealed – Bathsheba's.

'I was going to ask you, Oak,' he said, with unreal carelessness, 'if you know whose writing this is?'

Oak glanced into the book, and replied instantly, with a flushed face, 'Miss Everdene's.'

Oak had coloured simply at the consciousness of sounding her name. He now felt a strangely distressing qualm from a new thought. The letter could of course be no other than anonymous, or the inquiry would not have been necessary.

Boldwood mistook his confusion: sensitive persons are always ready with their 'Is it I?' in preference to objective reasoning.

'The question was perfectly fair,' he returned – and there was something incongruous in the serious earnestness with which he applied himself to an argument on a valentine. 'You know it is always expected that privy inquiries will be made: that's where the – fun lies.' If the word 'fun' had been 'torture', it could not have been uttered with a more constrained and restless countenance than was Boldwood's then.

Soon parting from Gabriel, the lonely and reserved man returned to his house to breakfast – feeling twinges of shame and regret at having so far exposed his mood by those fevered questions to a stranger. He again placed the letter on the mantelpiece, and sat down to think of the circumstances attending it by the light of Gabriel's information.

CHAPTER SIXTEEN

All Saints' and All Souls'

O n a week-day morning a small congregation, consisting mainly of women and girls, rose from its knees in the mouldy nave of a church called All Saints', in the distant barrack-town before-mentioned, at the end of a service without a sermon. They were about to disperse, when a smart footstep, entering the porch and coming up the central passage, arrested their attention. The step echoed with a ring unusual in a church; it was the clink of spurs. Everybody looked. A young cavalry soldier in a red uniform, with the three chevrons of a sergeant upon his sleeve, strode up the aisle, with an embarrassment which was only the more marked by the intense vigour of his step, and by the determination upon his face to show none. A slight flush had mounted his cheek by the time he had run the gauntlet between these women; but, passing on through the chancel arch, he never paused till he came close to the altar railing. Here for a moment he stood alone.

The officiating curate, who had not yet doffed his surplice, perceived the new-comer, and followed him to the communion-space. He whispered to the soldier, and then beckoned to the clerk, who in his turn whispered to an elderly woman, apparently his wife, and they also went up the chancel steps.

''Tis a wedding!' murmured some of the women, brightening. 'Let's wait!'

The majority again sat down.

There was a creaking of machinery behind, and some of the young ones turned their heads. From the interior face of the west wall of the tower projected a little canopy with a quarter-jack and small bell beneath it, the automation being driven by the same clock machinery that struck the large bell in the tower. Between the tower and the church was a close screen, the door of which was kept shut during services, hiding this grotesque clockwork from sight. At present, however, the door was open, and the egress of the jack, the blows on the bell, and the mannikin's retreat into the nook again, were visible to many, and audible throughout the church.

The jack had struck half-past eleven.

'Where's the woman?' whispered some of the spectators.

The young sergeant stood still with the abnormal rigidity of the old pillars around. He faced the south-east, and was as silent as he was still.

The silence grew to be a noticeable thing as the minutes went on, and nobody else appeared, and not a soul moved. The rattle of the quarter-jack again from its niche, its blows for three-quarters, its fussy retreat, were almost painfully abrupt, and caused many of the congregation to start palpably.

'I wonder where the woman is!' a voice whispered again.

There began now that slight shifting of feet, that artificial coughing among several, which betrays a nervous suspense. At length there was a titter. But the soldier never moved. There he stood, his face to the south-east, upright as a column, his cap in his hand.

The clock ticked on. The women threw off their nervousness, and titters and giggling became more frequent. Then came a dead silence. Every one was waiting for the end. Some persons may have noticed how extraordinarily the striking of quarters seems to quicken the flight of time. It was hardly credible that the jack had not got wrong with the minutes when the rattle began again, the puppet emerged, and the four quarters were struck fitfully as before. One could amost be positive that there was a malicious leer upon the hideous creature's face, and a mischievous delight in its twitchings. Then followed the dull and remote resonance of the twelve heavy strokes in the tower above. The women were impressed, and there was no giggle this time.

The clergyman glided into the vestry, and the clerk vanished. The sergeant had not yet turned; every woman in the church was waiting to see his face, and he appeared to know it. At last he did turn, and stalked resolutely down the nave, braving them all, with a compressed lip. Two bowed and toothless old almsmen then looked at each other and chuckled, innocently enough; but the sound had a strange weird effect in that place.

Opposite to the church was a paved square, around which several overhanging wood buildings of old time cast a picturesque shade. The young man on leaving the door went to cross the square, when, in the middle, he met a little woman. The expression of her face, which had been one of intense anxiety, sank at the sight of his nearly to terror.

'Well?' he said, in a suppressed passion, fixedly looking at her.

'O Frank – I made a mistake – I thought that church with the spire was All Saints', and I was at the door at half-past eleven to a minute as you said. I waited till a quarter to twelve, and found then that I was in All Souls'. But I wasn't much frightened, for I thought it could be to-morrow as well.'

'You fool, for so fooling me! But say no more.'

'Shall it be to-morrow, Frank?' she asked blankly.

'To-morrow!' and he gave vent to a hoarse laugh. 'I don't go through that experience again for some time, I warrant you!'

'But after all,' she expostulated in a trembling voice, 'the mistake was not such a terrible thing! Now, dear Frank, when shall it be?'

'Ah, when? God knows!' he said, with a light irony, and turning from her walked rapidly away.

CHAPTER SEVENTEEN

In the Market-place

ON Saturday Boldwood was in Casterbridge market-house as usual, when the disturber of his dreams entered, and became visible to him. Adam had awakened from his deep sleep, and behold! there was Eve. The farmer took courage, and for the first time really looked at her.

Material causes and emotional effects are not to be arranged in regular equation. The result from capital employed in the production of any movement of a mental nature is sometimes as tremendous as the cause itself is absurdly minute. When women are in a freakish mood their usual intuition, either from carelessness or inherent defect, seemingly fails to teach them this, and hence it was that Bathsheba was fated to be astonished to-day.

Boldwood looked at her – not slily, critically, or understandingly, but blankly at gaze, in the way a reaper looks up at a passing train – as something foreign to his element, and but dimly understood. To Boldwood women had been remote phenomena rather than necessary complements – comets of such uncertain aspect, movement, and permanence, that whether their orbits were as geometrical, unchangeable, and as subject to laws as his own, or as absolutely erratic as they superficially appeared, he had not deemed it his duty to consider.

He saw her black hair, her correct facial curves and profile, and the roundness of her chin and throat. He saw then the side of her eyelids, eyes, and lashes, and the shape of her ear. Next he noticed her figure, her skirt, and the very soles of her shoes.

Boldwood thought her beautiful, but wondered whether he was right in his thought, for it seemed impossible that this romance in the flesh, if so sweet as he imagined, could have been going on long without creating a commotion of delight among men, and provoking more inquiry than Bathsheba had done, even though that was not a little. To the best of his judgment neither nature nor art could improve this perfect one of an imperfect many. His heart began to move within him. Boldwood, it must be remembered, though forty years of age, had never before inspected a woman with the very centre and force of his glance; they had struck upon all his senses at wide angles.

Was she really beautiful? He could not assure himself that his opinion was true even now. He furtively said to a neighbour, 'Is Miss Everdene considered handsome?'

'O yes; she was a good deal noticed the first time she came, if you remember. A very handsome girl indeed.'

A man is never more credulous than in receiving favourable opinions on the beauty of a woman he is half, or quite, in love with; a mere child's word on the point has the weight of an R.A.'s. Boldwood was satisfied now.

And this charming woman had in effect said to him, 'Marry me.' Why should she have done that strange thing? Boldwood's blindness to the difference between approving of what circumstances suggest, and originating what they do not suggest, was well matched by Bathsheba's insensibility to the possibly great issues of little beginnings.

She was at this moment coolly dealing with a dashing young farmer, adding up accounts with him as indifferently as if his face had been the pages of a ledger. It was evident that such a nature as his had no attraction for a woman of Bathsheba's taste. But Boldwood grew hot down to his hands with an incipient jealousy; he trod for the first time the threshold of 'the injured lover's hell'. His first impulse was to go and thrust himself between them. This could be done, but only in one way – by asking to see a sample of her corn. Boldwood renounced the idea. He could not make the request; it was debasing loveliness to ask it to buy and sell, and jarred with his conceptions of her.

All this time Bathsheba was conscious of having broken into that dignified stronghold at last. His eyes, she knew, were following her everywhere. This was a triumph; and had it come naturally, such a triumph would have been the sweeter to her for this piquing delay. But it had been brought about by misdirected ingenuity, and she valued it only as she valued an artificial flower or a wax fruit.

Being a woman with some good sense in reasoning on subjects wherein her heart was not involved, Bathsheba genuinely repented that a freak which had owed its existence as much to Liddy as to herself, should ever have been undertaken, to disturb the placidity of a man she respected too highly to deliberately tease.

She that day nearly formed the intention of begging his pardon on the very next occasion of their meeting. The worst features of this arrangement were that, if he thought she ridiculed him, an apology would increase the offence by being disbelieved; and if he thought she wanted him to woo her, it would read like additional evidence of her forwardness.

CHAPTER EIGHTEEN

Boldwood in Meditation — Regret

BOLDWOOD was tenant of what was called Little Weatherbury Farm, and his person was the nearest approach to aristocracy that this remoter quarter of the parish could boast of. Genteel strangers, whose god was their town, who might happen to be compelled to linger about this nook for a day, heard the sound of light wheels, and prayed to see good society, to the degree of a solitary lord, or squire at the very least, but it was only Mr Boldwood going out for the day. They heard the sound of wheels yet once more, and were reanimated to expectancy: it was only Mr Boldwood coming home again.

His house stood recessed from the road, and the stables, which are to a farm what a fireplace is to a room, were behind, their lower portions being lost amid bushes of laurel. Inside the blue door, open half-way down, were to be seen at this time the backs and tails of half-a-dozen warm and contented horses standing in their stalls; and as thus viewed, they presented alternations of roan and bay, in shapes like a Moorish arch, the tail being a streak down the midst of each. Over these, and lost to the eye gazing in from the outer light, the mouths of the same animals could be heard busily sustaining the above-named warmth and plumpness by quantities of oats and hay. The restless and shadowy figure of a colt wandered about a loose-box at the end, whilst the steady grind of all the eaters was occasionally diversified by the rattle of a rope or the stamp of a foot.

Pacing up and down at the heels of the animals was Farmer Boldwood himself. This place was his almonry and cloister in one: here, after looking to the feeding of his four-footed dependants, the celibate would walk and meditate of an evening till the moon's rays streamed in through the cobwebbed windows, or total darkness enveloped the scene.

His square-framed perpendicularity showed more fully now than in the crowd and bustle of the market-house. In this meditative walk his foot met the floor with heel and toe simultaneously, and his fine reddish-fleshed face was bent downwards just enough to render obscure the still mouth and the well-rounded though rather prominent and broad chin. A few clear and thread-like horizontal lines were the only interruption to the otherwise smooth surface of his large forehead.

The phases of Boldwood's life were ordinary enough, but his was not an ordinary nature. That stillness, which struck casual observers more than anything else in his character and habit, and seemed so precisely like the rest of inanition, may have been the perfect balance of enormous antagonistic forces — positives and negatives in fine adjustment. His equilibrium disturbed, he was in extremity at once. If an emotion possessed him at all, it ruled him; a feeling not mastering him was entirely latent. Stagnant or rapid, it was never slow. He was always hit mortally, or he was missed.

He had no light and careless touches in his constitution, either for good or for evil. Stern in the outlines of action, mild in the details, he was serious throughout all. He saw no absurd sides to the follies of life, and thus, though not quite companionable in the eyes of merry men and scoffers, and those to whom all things show life as a jest, he was not intolerable to the earnest and those acquainted with grief. Being a man who read all the dramas of life seriously, if he failed to please when they were comedies, there was no frivolous treatment to reproach him for when they chanced to end tragically.

Bathsheba was far from dreaming that the dark and silent shape upon which she had so carelessly thrown a seed was a hotbed of tropic intensity. Had she known Boldwood's moods her blame would have been fearful, and the stain upon her heart ineradicable. Moreover, had she known her present power for good or evil over this man, she would have trembled at her responsibility. Luckily for her present, unluckily for her future tranquillity, her understanding had not yet told her what Boldwood was. Nobody knew entirely; for though it was possible to form guesses concerning his wild capabilities from old floodmarks faintly visible, he had never been seen at the high tides which caused them.

Farmer Boldwood came to the stable-door and looked forth across the level fields. Beyond the first enclosure was a hedge, and on the other side of this a meadow belonging to Bathsheba's farm.

It was now early spring – the time of going to grass with the sheep, when they have the first feed of the meadows, before these are laid up for mowing. The wind, which had been blowing east for several weeks, had veered to the southward, and the middle of spring had come abruptly – almost without a beginning. It was that period in the vernal quarter when we may suppose the Dryads to be waking for the season. The vegetable world begins to move and swell and the saps to rise, till in the completest silence of lone gardens and trackless plantations, where everything seems helpless and still after the bond and slavery of frost, there are bustlings, strainings, united thrusts, and pulls-all-together, in comparison with which the powerful tugs of cranes and pulleys in a noisy city are but pigmy efforts.

Boldwood, looking into the distant meadows, saw there three figures. They were those of Miss Everdene, Shepherd Oak, and Cainy Ball.

When Bathsheba's figure shone upon the farmer's eyes it lighted him up as the moon lights up a great tower. A man's body is as the shell, or the tablet, of his soul, as he is reserved or ingenuous, overflowing or self-contained. There was a change in Boldwood's exterior from its former impassibleness; and his face showed that he was now living outside his defences for the first time, and with a fearful sense of exposure. It is the usual experience of strong natures when they love.

At last he arrived at a conclusion. It was to go across and inquire boldly of her.

The insulation of his heart by reserve during these many years, without a channel of any kind for disposable emotion, had worked its effect. It has been observed more than once that the causes of love are chiefly subjective, and Boldwood was a living testimony to the truth of the proposition. No mother existed to absorb his devotion, no sister for his tenderness, no idle ties for sense. He became surcharged with the compound, which was genuine lover's love.

He approached the gate of the meadow. Beyond it the ground was melodious with ripples, and the sky with larks; the low bleating of the flock mingling with both. Mistress and man were engaged in the operation of making a lamb 'take', which is performed whenever an ewe has lost her own offspring, one of the twins of another ewe being given her as a substitute. Gabriel had skinned the dead lamb, and was tying the skin over the body of the live lamb in the customary manner, whilst Bathsheba was holding open a little pen of four hurdles, into which the mother and foisted lamb were driven, where they would remain till the old sheep conceived an affection for the young one.

Bathsheba looked up at the completion of the manœuvre and saw the farmer by the gate, where he was overhung by a willow tree in full bloom. Gabriel, to whom her face was as the uncertain glory of an April day, was very regardful of its faintest changes, and instantly discerned thereon the mark of some influence from without, in the form of a keenly self-conscious reddening. He also turned and beheld Boldwood.

At once connecting these signs with the letter Boldwood had shown him, Gabriel suspected her of some coquettish procedure begun by that means, and carried on since, he knew not how.

Farmer Boldwood had read the pantomime denoting that they were aware of his presence, and the perception was as too much light turned upon his new sensibility. He was still in the road, and by moving on he hoped that neither would recognize that he had originally intended to enter the field. He passed by with an utter and overwhelming sensation of ignorance, shyness, and doubt. Perhaps in her manner there were signs that she wished to see him – perhaps not – he could not read a woman. The cabala of this erotic philosophy seemed to consist of the subtlest meanings expressed in misleading ways. Every turn, look, word, and accent contained a mystery quite distinct from its obvious import, and not one had ever been pondered by him until now.

As for Bathsheba, she was not deceived into the belief that Farmer Boldwood had walked by on business or in idleness. She collected the probabilities of the case, and concluded that she was herself responsible for Boldwood's appearance there. It troubled her much to see what a great flame a little wildfire was likely to kindle. Bathsheba was no schemer for marriage, nor was she deliberately a trifler with the affections of men, and a censor's experience on seeing an actual flirt after observing her would have been a feeling of surprise that Bathsheba could be so different from such a one, and yet so like what a flirt is supposed to be.

She resolved never again, by look or by sign, to interrupt the steady flow of this man's life. But a resolution to avoid an evil is seldom framed till the evil is so far advanced as to make avoidance impossible.

CHAPTER NINETEEN

The Sheep-washing — The Offer

BOLDWOOD did eventually call upon her. She was not at home. 'Of course not,' he murmured. In contemplating Bathsheba as a woman, he had forgotten the accidents of her position as an agriculturist — that being as much of a farmer, and as extensive a farmer, as himself, her probable whereabouts was out-of-doors at this time of the year. This, and the other oversights Boldwood was guilty of, were natural to the mood, and still more natural to the circumstances. The great aids to idealization in love were present here: occasional observation of her from a distance, and the absence of social intercourse with her — visual familiarity, oral strangeness. The smaller human elements were kept out of sight; the pettinesses that enter so largely into all earthly living and doing were disguised by the accident of lover and loved-one not being on visiting terms; and there was hardly awakened a thought in Boldwood that sorry household realities appertained to her, or that she, like all others, had moments of commonplace, when to be least plainly seen was to be most prettily remembered. Thus a mild sort of apotheosis took place in his fancy, whilst she still lived and breathed within his own horizon, a troubled creature like himself.

It was the end of May when the farmer determined to be no longer repulsed by trivialities or distracted by suspense. He had by this time grown used to being in love; the passion now startled him less even when it tortured him more, and he felt himself adequate to the situation. On inquiring for her at her house they had told him she was at the sheep-washing, and he went off to seek her there.

The sheep-washing pool was a perfectly circular basin of brick-work in the meadows, full of the clearest water. To birds on the wing its glassy surface, reflecting the light sky, must have been visible for miles around as a glistening Cyclops' eye in a green face. The grass about the margin at this season was a sight to remember long — in a minor sort of way. Its activity in sucking the moisture from the rich damp sod was almost a process observable by the eye. The outskirts of this level water-meadow were diversified by rounded and hollow pastures, where just now every flower that was not a buttercup was a daisy. The river slid along noiselessly as a shade, the swelling reeds and sedge forming a flexible palisade upon its moist brink. To the north of the mead were trees, the leaves of which were new, soft, and moist, not yet having stiffened and darkened under summer sun and drought, their colour being yellow beside a green — green beside a yellow. From the recesses of this knot of foliage the loud notes of three cuckoos were resounding through the still air.

Boldwood went meditating down the slopes with his eyes on his boots, which the yellow pollen from the buttercups had bronzed in artistic gradations. A tributary of the main stream flowed through the basin of the pool by an inlet and outlet at opposite points of its diameter. Shepherd Oak, Jan Coggan, Moon, Poorgrass, Cain Ball, and several others were assembled here, all dripping wet to the very roots of their hair, and Bathsheba was standing by in a new riding-habit – the most elegant she had ever worn – the reins of her horse being looped over her arm. Flagons of cider were rolling about upon the green. The meek sheep were pushed into the pool by Coggan and Matthew Moon, who stood by the lower hatch, immersed to their waists; then Gabriel, who stood on the brink, thrust them under as they swam along, with an instrument like a crutch, formed for the purpose, and also for assisting the exhausted animals when the wool became saturated and they began to sink. They were let out against the stream, and through the upper opening, all impurities flowing away below. Cainy Ball and Joseph, who performed this latter operation, were if possible wetter than the rest; they resembled dolphins under a fountain, every protuberance and angle of their clothes dribbling forth a small rill.

Boldwood came close and bade her good morning with such constraint that she could not but think he had stepped across to the washing for its own sake, hoping not to find her there; more, she fancied his brow severe and his eye slighting. Bathsheba immediately contrived to withdraw, and glided along by the river till she was a stone's throw off. She heard footsteps brushing the grass, and had a consciousness that love was encircling her like a perfume. Instead of turning or waiting, Bathsheba went further among the high sedges, but Boldwood seemed determined, and pressed on till they were completely past the bend of the river. Here, without being seen, they could hear the splashing and shouts of the washers above.

'Miss Everdene!' said the farmer.

She trembled, turned, and said 'Good morning.' His tone was so utterly removed from all she had expected as a beginning. It was lowness and quiet accentuated: an emphasis of deep meanings, their form, at the same time, being scarcely expressed. Silence has sometimes a remarkable power of showing itself as the disembodied soul of feeling wandering without its carcase, and it is then more impressive than speech. In the same way, to say a little is often to tell more than to say a great deal. Boldwood told everything in that word.

As the consciousness expands on learning that what was fancied to be the rumble of wheels is the reverberation of thunder, so did Bathsheba's at her intuitive conviction.

'I feel – almost too much – to think,' he said, with a solemn simplicity. 'I have come to speak to you without preface. My life is not my own since I have beheld you clearly, Miss Everdene – I come to make you an offer of marriage.'

Bathsheba tried to preserve an absolutely neutral countenance, and all the motion she made was that of closing lips which had previously been a little parted.

'I am now forty-one years old,' he went on. 'I may have been called a confirmed bachelor, and I was a confirmed bachelor. I had never any views of myself as a husband in my earlier days, nor have I made any calculation on the subject since I have been older. But we all change, and my change, in this matter, came with seeing you. I have felt lately, more and more, that my present way of living is bad in every respect. Beyond all things, I want you as my wife.'

'I feel, Mr Boldwood, that though I respect you much, I do not feel – what would justify me to – in accepting your offer,' she stammered.

This giving back of dignity for dignity seemed to open the sluices of feeling that Boldwood had as yet kept closed.

'My life is a burden without you,' he exclaimed, in a low voice. 'I want you – I want you to let me say I love you again and again!'

Bathsheba answered nothing, and the mare upon her arm seemed so impressed that instead of cropping the herbage she looked up.

'I think and hope you care enough for me to listen to what I have to tell!'

Bathsheba's momentary impulse at hearing this was to ask why he thought that, till she remembered that, far from being a conceited assumption on Boldwood's part, it was but the natural conclusion of serious reflection based on deceptive premises of her own offering.

'I wish I could say courteous flatteries to you,' the farmer continued in an easier tone, 'and put my rugged feeling into a graceful shape: but I have neither power nor patience to learn such things. I want you for my wife – so wildly that no other feeling can abide in me; but I should not have spoken out had I not been led to hope.'

'The valentine again! O that valentine!' she said to herself, but not a word to him.

'If you can love me say so, Miss Everdene. If not – don't say no!'

'Mr Boldwood, it is painful to have to say I am surprised, so that I don't know how to answer you with propriety and respect – but am only just able to speak out my feeling – I mean my meaning; that I am afraid I can't marry you, much as I respect you. You are too dignified for me to suit you, sir.'

'But, Miss Everdene!'

'I – I didn't – I know I ought never to have dreamt of sending that valentine – forgive me, sir – it was a wanton thing which no woman with any self-respect should have done. If you will only pardon my thoughtlessness, I promise never to—'

'No, no, no. Don't say thoughtlessness! Make me think it was something more – that it was a sort of prophetic instinct – the beginning of a feeling that you would like me. You torture me to say it was done in thoughtlessness – I never thought of it in that light, and I can't endure it. Ah! I wish I knew how to win you! but that I can't do – I can only ask if I have already got you. If I have not, and it is not true that you have come unwittingly to me as I have to you, I can say no more.'

'I have not fallen in love with you, Mr Boldwood – certainly I must say that.' She allowed a very small smile to creep for the first time over her serious face in saying this, and the white row of upper teeth, and keenly-cut lips already noticed, suggested an idea of heartlessness, which was immediately contradicted by the pleasant eyes.

'But you will just think – in kindness and condescension think – if you cannot bear with me as a husband! I fear I am too old for you, but believe me I will take more care of you than would many a man of your own age. I will protect and cherish you with all my strength – I will indeed! You shall have no cares – be worried by no household affairs, and live quite at ease, Miss Everdene. The dairy superintendence shall be done by a man – I can afford it well – you shall never have so much as to look out of doors at haymaking time, or to think of weather in the harvest. I rather cling to the chaise, because it is the same my poor father and mother drove, but if you don't like it I will sell it, and you shall have a pony-carriage of your own. I cannot say how far above every other idea and object on earth you seem to me – nobody knows – God only knows – how much you are to me!'

Bathsheba's heart was young, and it swelled with sympathy for the deep-natured man who spoke so simply.

'Don't say it: don't! I cannot bear you to feel so much, and me to feel nothing. And I am afraid they will notice us, Mr Boldwood. Will you let the matter rest now? I cannot think collectedly. I did not know you were going to say this to me. O, I am wicked to have made you suffer so!' She was frightened as well as agitated at his vehemence.

'Say then, that you don't absolutely refuse. Do not quite refuse?'

'I can do nothing. I cannot answer.'

'I may speak to you again on the subject?'

'Yes.'

'I may think of you?'

'Yes, I suppose you may think of me.'

'And hope to obtain you?'

'No – do not hope! Let us go on.'

'I will call upon you again to-morrow.'

'No – please not. Give me time.'

'Yes – I will give you any time,' he said earnestly and gratefully. 'I am happier now.'

'No – I beg you! Don't he happier if happiness only comes from my agreeing. Be neutral, Mr Boldwood! I must think.'

'I will wait,' he said.

And then she turned away. Boldwood dropped his gaze to the ground, and stood long like a man who did not know where he was. Realities then returned upon him like the pain of a wound received in an excitement which eclipses it, and he, too, then went on.

CHAPTER TWENTY

Perplexity – Grinding the Shears – A Quarrel

'HE is so disinterested and kind to offer me all that I can desire,' Bathsheba mused.

Yet Farmer Boldwood, whether by nature kind or the reverse to kind, did not exercise kindness here. The rarest offerings of the purest loves are but a self-indulgence, and no generosity at all.

Bathsheba, not being the least in love with him, was eventually able to look calmly at his offer. It was one which many women of her own station in the neighbourhood, and not a few of higher rank, would have been wild to accept and proud to publish. In every point of view, ranging from politic to passionate, it was desirable that she, a lonely girl, should marry, and marry this earnest, well-to-do, and respected man. He was close to her doors: his standing was sufficient: his qualities were even supererogatory. Had she felt, which she did not, any wish whatever for the married state in the abstract, she could not reasonably have rejected him, being a woman who frequently appealed to her understanding for deliverance from her whims. Boldwood as a means to marriage was unexceptionable: she esteemed and liked him, yet she did not want him. It appears that ordinary men take wives because possession is not possible without marriage, and that ordinary women accept husbands because marriage is not possible without possession; with totally differing aims the method is the same on both sides. But the understood incentive on the woman's part was wanting here. Besides, Bathsheba's position as absolute mistress of a farm and house was a novel one, and the novelty had not yet begun to wear off.

But a disquiet filled her which was somewhat to her credit, for it would have affected few. Beyond the mentioned reasons with which she combated her objections, she had a strong feeling that, having been the one who began the game, she ought in honesty to accept the consequences. Still the reluctance remained. She said in the same breath that it would be ungenerous not to marry Boldwood, and that she couldn't do it to save her life.

Bathsheba's was an impulsive nature under a deliberative aspect. An Elizabeth in brain and a Mary Stuart in spirit, she often performed actions of the greatest temerity with a manner of extreme discretion. Many of her thoughts were perfect syllogisms; unluckily they always remained thoughts. Only a few were irrational assumptions; but, unfortunately, they were the ones which most frequently grew into deeds.

The next day to that of the declaration she found Gabriel Oak at the bottom of her garden, grinding his shears for the sheep-shearing. All the surrounding cottages were more or less scenes of the same operation; the scurr of whetting spread into the sky from all parts of the village as from an armoury previous to a campaign. Peace and war kiss each other at their hours of preparation — sickles, scythes, shears, and pruning-hooks ranking with swords, bayonets, and lances, in their common necessity for point and edge.

Cainy Ball turned the handle of Gabriel's grindstone, his head performing a melancholy see-saw up and down with each turn of the wheel. Oak stood somewhat as Eros is represented when in the act of sharpening his arrows: his figure slightly bent, the weight of his body thrown over on the shears, and his head balanced sideways, with a critical compression of the lips and contraction of the eyelids to crown the attitude.

His mistress came up and looked upon them in silence for a minute or two; then she said —

'Cain, go to the lower mead and catch the bay mare. I'll turn the winch of the grindstone. I want to speak to you, Gabriel.'

Cain departed, and Bathsheba took the handle. Gabriel had glanced up in intense surprise, quelled its expression, and looked down again. Bathsheba turned the winch, and Gabriel applied the shears.

The peculiar motion involved in turning a wheel has a wonderful tendency to benumb the mind. It is a sort of attenuated variety of Ixion's punishment, and contributes a dismal chapter to the history of gaols. The brain gets muddled, the head grows heavy, and the body's centre of gravity seems to settle by degrees in a leaden lump somewhere between the eyebrows and the crown. Bathsheba felt the unpleasant symptoms after two or three dozen turns.

'Will you turn, Gabriel, and let me hold the shears?' she said. 'My head is in a whirl, and I can't talk.'

Gabriel turned. Bathsheba then began, with some awkwardness, allowing her thoughts to stray occasionally from her story to attend to the shears, which required a little nicety in sharpening.

'I wanted to ask you if the men made any observations on my going behind the sedge with Mr Boldwood yesterday?'

'Yes, they did,' said Gabriel. 'You don't hold the shears right, miss – I knew you wouldn't know the way – hold like this.'

He relinquished the winch, and enclosing her two hands completely in his own (taking each as we sometimes clasp a child's hand in teaching him to write), grasped the shears with her. 'Incline the edge so,' he said.

Hands and shears were inclined to suit the words, and held thus for a peculiarly long time by the instructor as he spoke.

'That will do,' exclaimed Bathsheba. 'Loose my hands. I won't have them held! Turn the winch.'

Gabriel freed her hands quietly, retired to his handle, and the grinding went on.

'Did the men think it odd?' she said again.

'Odd was not the idea, miss.'

'What did they say?'

'That Farmer Boldwood's name and your own were likely to be flung over pulpit together before the year was out.'

'I thought so by the look of them! Why, there's nothing in it. A more foolish remark was never made, and I want you to contradict it: that's what I came for.'

Gabriel looked incredulous and sad, but between his moments of incredulity, relieved.

'They must have heard our conversation,' she continued.

'Well, then, Bathsheba!' said Oak, stopping the handle, and gazing into her face with astonishment.

'Miss Everdene, you mean,' she said with dignity.

'I mean this, that if Mr Boldwood really spoke of marriage, I bain't going to tell a story and say he didn't to please you. I have already tried to please you too much for my own good!'

Bathsheba regarded him with round-eyed perplexity. She did not know whether to pity him for disappointed love of her, or to be angry with him for having got over it – his tone being ambiguous.

'I said I wanted you just to mention that it was not true I was going to be married to him,' she murmured, with a slight decline in her assurance.

'I can say that to them if you wish, Miss Everdene. And I could likewise give an opinion to 'ee on what you have done.'

'I daresay. But I don't want your opinion.'

'I suppose not,' said Gabriel bitterly, and going on with his turning; his words rising and falling in a regular swell and cadence as he stooped or rose with the winch, which directed them, according to his position, perpendicularly into the earth, or horizontally along the garden, his eyes being fixed on a leaf upon the ground.

With Bathsheba a hastened act was a rash act; but, as does not always happen, time gained was prudence ensured. It must be added, however, that time was very seldom gained. At this period the single opinion in the parish on herself and her doings that she valued as sounder than her own was Gabriel Oak's. And the outspoken honesty of his character was such that on any subject, even that of her love for, or marriage with, another man, the same disinterestedness of opinion might be calculated on, and be had for the asking. Thoroughly convinced of the impossibility of his own suit, a high resolve constrained him not to injure that of another. This is a lover's most stoical virtue, as the lack of it is a lover's most venial sin. Knowing he would reply truly she asked the question, painful as she must have known the subject would be. Such is the selfishness of some charming women. Perhaps it was some excuse for her thus torturing honesty to her own advantage, that she had absolutely no other sound judgment within easy reach.

'Well, what is your opinion of my conduct,' she said quietly.

'That it is unworthy of any thoughtful, and meek, and comely woman.'

In an instant Bathsheba's face coloured with the angry crimson of a Danby sunset. But she forbore to utter this feeling, and the reticence of her tongue only made the loquacity of her face the more noticeable.

The next thing Gabriel did was to make a mistake.

'Perhaps you don't like the rudeness of my reprimanding you, for I know it is rudeness; but I thought it would do good.'

She instantly replied sarcastically —

'On the contrary, my opinion of you is so low, that I see in your abuse the praise of discerning people!'

'I am glad you don't mind it, for I said it honestly and with every serious meaning.'

'I see. But, unfortunately, when you try not to speak in jest you are amusing — just as when you wish to avoid seriousness you sometimes say a sensible word.'

It was a hard hit, but Bathsheba had unmistakably lost her temper, and on that account Gabriel had never in his life kept his own better. He said nothing. She then broke out —

'I may ask, I suppose, where in particular my unworthiness lies? In my not marrying you, perhaps!'

'Not by any means,' said Gabriel quietly. 'I have long given up thinking of that matter.'

'Or wishing it, I suppose,' she said; and it was apparent that she expected an unhesitating denial of this supposition.

Whatever Gabriel felt, he coolly echoed her words —

'Or wishing it either.'

A woman may be treated with a bitterness which is sweet to her, and with a rudeness which is not offensive. Bathsheba would have submitted to an indignant chastisement for her levity had Gabriel protested that he was loving her at the same time; the impetuosity of passion unrequited is bearable, even if it stings and anathematizes – there is a triumph in the humiliation, and a tenderness in the strife. This was what she had been expecting, and what she had not got. To be lectured because the lecturer saw her in the cold morning light of open-shuttered disillusion was exasperating. He had not finished, either. He continued in a more agitated voice: –

'My opinion is (since you ask it) that you are greatly to blame for playing pranks upon a man like Mr Boldwood, merely as a pastime. Leading on a man you don't care for is not a praiseworthy action. And even, Miss Everdene, if you seriously inclined towards him, you might have let him find it out in some way of true loving-kindness, and not by sending him a valentine's letter.'

Bathsheba laid down the shears.

'I cannot allow any man to – to criticize my private conduct!' she exclaimed. 'Nor will I for a minute. So you'll please leave the farm at the end of the week!'

It may have been a peculiarity – at any rate it was a fact – that when Bathsheba was swayed by an emotion of an earthly sort her lower lip trembled: when by a refined emotion, her upper or heaven-ward one. Her nether lip quivered now.

'Very well, so I will,' said Gabriel calmly. He had been held to her by a beautiful thread which it pained him to spoil by breaking, rather than by a chain he could not break. 'I should be even better pleased to go at once,' he added.

'Go at once then, in Heaven's name!' said she, her eyes flashing at his, though never meeting them. 'Don't let me see your face any more.'

'Very well, Miss Everdene – so it shall be.'

And he took his shears and went away from her in placid dignity, as Moses left the presence of Pharaoh.

CHAPTER TWENTY-ONE

Troubles in the Fold – A Message

GABRIEL OAK had ceased to feed the Weatherbury flock for about four-and-twenty hours, when on Sunday afternoon the elderly gentlemen Joseph Poorgrass, Matthew Moon, Fray, and half-a-dozen others, came running up to the house of the mistress of the Upper Farm.

'Whatever *is* the matter, men?' she said, meeting them at the door just as she was coming out on her way to church, and ceasing in a moment from the close compression of her two red lips, with which she had accompanied the exertion of pulling on a tight glove.

'Sixty!' said Joseph Poorgrass.

'Seventy!' said Moon.

'Fifty-nine!' said Susan Tall's husband.

'—Sheep have broke fence,' said Fray.

'—And got into a field of young clover,' said Tall.

'—Young clover!' said Moon.

'—Clover!' said Joseph Poorgrass.

'And they be getting blasted,' said Henery Fray.

'That they be,' said Joseph.

'And will all die as dead as nits, if they bain't got out and cured!' said Tall.

Joseph's countenance was drawn into lines and puckers by his concern. Fray's forehead was wrinkled both perpendicularly and crosswise, after the pattern of a portcullis, expressive of a double despair. Laban Tall's lips were thin, and his face rigid. Matthew's jaws sank, and his eyes turned whichever way the strongest muscle happened to pull them.

'Yes,' said Joseph, 'and I was sitting at home looking for Ephesians, and says I to myself, " 'Tis nothing but Corinthians and Thessalonians in this danged Testament," when who should come in but Henery there: "Joseph," he said, "the sheep have blasted theirselves—" '

With Bathsheba it was a moment when thought was speech and speech exclamation. Moreover, she had hardly recovered her equanimity since the disturbance which she had suffered from Oak's remarks.

'That's enough—that's enough!—O you fools!' she cried, throwing the parasol and Prayer-book into the passage, and running out of doors in the direction signified. 'To come to me, and not go and get them out directly! O, the stupid numskulls!'

Her eyes were at their darkest and brightest now. Bathsheba's beauty belonging rather to the demonian than to the angelic school, she never looked so well as when she was angry—and particularly when the effect was heightened by a rather dashing velvet dress, carefully put on before a glass.

All the ancient men ran in a jumbled throng after her to the clover-field, Joseph sinking down in the midst when about half-way, like an individual withering in a world which was more and more insupportable. Having once received the stimulus that her presence always gave them they went round among the sheep with a will. The majority of the afflicted animals were lying down, and could not be stirred. These were bodily lifted out, and the others driven into the adjoining field. Here, after the lapse of a few minutes, several more fell down, and lay helpless and livid as the rest.

Bathsheba, with a sad, bursting heart, looked at these primest specimens of her prime flock as they rolled there—

> Swoln with wind and the rank mist they drew.

Many of them foamed at the mouth, their breathing being quick and short, whilst the bodies of all were fearfully distended.

'O, what can I do, what can I do!' said Bathsheba, helplessly. 'Sheep are such unfortunate animals!—there's always something happening to them! I never knew a flock pass a year without getting into some scrape or other.'

'There's only one way of saving them,' said Tall.

'What way? Tell me quick!'

'They must be pierced in the side with a thing made on purpose.'

'Can you do it? Can I?'

'No, ma'am. We can't, nor you neither. It must be done in a particular spot. If ye go to the right or left but an inch you stab the ewe and kill her. Not even a shepherd can do it, as a rule.'

'Then they must die,' she said, in a resigned tone.

'Only one man in the neighbourhood knows the way,' said Joseph, now just come up. 'He could cure 'em all if he were here.'

'Who is he? Let's get him!'

'Shepherd Oak,' said Matthew. 'Ah, he's a clever man in talents!'

'Ah, that he is so!' said Joseph Poorgrass.

'True – he's the man', said Laban Tall.

'How dare you name that man in my presence!' she said excitedly. 'I told you never to allude to him, nor shall you if you stay with me. Ah!' she added, brightening, 'Farmer Boldwood knows!'

'O no, ma'am,' said Matthew. 'Two of his store ewes got into some vetches t'other day, and were just like these. He sent a man on horseback here post-haste for Gable, and Gable went and saved 'em. Farmer Boldwood hev got the thing they do it with. 'Tis a holler pipe, with a sharp pricker inside. Isn't it, Joseph?'

'Ay – a holler pipe,' echoed Joseph. 'That's what 'tis.'

'Ay, sure – that's the machine,' chimed in Henery Fray reflectively, with an Oriental indifference to the flight of time.

'Well,' burst out Bathsheba, 'don't stand there with your "ayes" and your "sures", talking at me! Get somebody to cure the sheep instantly!'

All then stalked off in consternation, to get somebody as directed, without any idea of who it was to be. In a minute they had vanished through the gate, and she stood alone with the dying flock.

'Never will I send for him – never!' she said firmly.

One of the ewes here contracted its muscles horribly, extended itself, and jumped high into the air. The leap was an astonishing one. The ewe fell heavily, and lay still.

Bathsheba went up to it. The sheep was dead.

'O, what shall I do – what shall I do!' she again exclaimed, wringing her hands. 'I won't send for him. No, I won't!'

The most vigorous expression of a resolution does not always coincide with the greatest vigour of the resolution itself. It is often flung out as a sort of prop to support a decaying conviction which, whilst strong, required no enunciation to prove it so. The 'No, I won't' of Bathsheba meant virtually, 'I think I must.'

She followed her assistants through the gate, and lifted her hand to one of them. Laban answered to her signal.

'Where is Oak staying?'

'Across the valley at Nest Cottage.'

'Jump on the bay mare, and ride across, and say he must return instantly – that I say so.'

Tall scrambled off to the field, and in two minutes was on Poll, the bay, bare-backed, and with only a halter by way of rein. He diminished down the hill.

Bathsheba watched. So did all the rest. Tall cantered along the bridle-path through Sixteen Acres, Sheeplands, Middle Field, The Flats, Cappel's Piece, shrank almost to a point, crossed the bridge, and ascended from the valley through Springmead and Whitepits on the other side. The cottage to which

Gabriel had retired before taking his final departure from the locality was visible as a white spot on the opposite hill, backed by blue firs. Bathsheba walked up and down. The men entered the field and endeavoured to ease the anguish of the dumb creatures by rubbing them. Nothing availed.

Bathsheba continued walking. The horse was seen descending the hill, and the wearisome series had to be repeated in reverse order: Whitepits, Springmead, Cappel's Piece, The Flats, Middle Field, Sheeplands, Sixteen Acres. She hoped Tall had had presence of mind enough to give the mare up to Gabriel, and return himself on foot. The rider neared them. It was Tall.

'O what folly!' said Bathsheba.

Gabriel was not visible anywhere.

'Perhaps he is already gone!' she said.

Tall came into the inclosure, and leapt off, his face tragic as Morton's after the battle of Shrewsbury.

'Well!' said Bathsheba, unwilling to believe that her verbal *lettre-de-cachet* could possibly have miscarried.

'He says *beggars mustn't be choosers*,' replied Laban.

'What!' said the young farmer, opening her eyes and drawing in her breath for an outburst. Joseph Poorgrass retired a few steps behind a hurdle.

'He says he shall not come onless you request en to come civilly and in a proper manner, as becomes any 'ooman begging a favour.'

'Oh, oh, that's his answer! Where does he get his airs? Who am I, then, to be treated like that? Shall I beg to a man who has begged to me?'

Another of the flock sprang into the air, and fell dead.

The men looked grave, as if they suppressed opinion.

Bathsheba turned aside, her eyes full of tears. The strait she was in through pride and shrewishness could not be disguised longer: she burst out crying bitterly; they all saw it; and she attempted no further concealment.

'I wouldn't cry about it, miss,' said William Smallbury compassionately. 'Why not ask him softer like? I'm sure he'd come then. Gable is a true man in that way.'

Bathsheba checked her grief and wiped her eyes. 'O, it is a wicked cruelty to me – it is – it is!' she murmured. 'And he drives me to do what I wouldn't; yes, he does! – Tall, come indoors.'

After this collapse, not very dignified for the head of an establishment, she went into the house, Tall at her heels. Here she sat down and hastily scribbled a note between the small convulsive sobs of convalescence which follow a fit of crying as a ground-swell follows a storm. The note was none the less polite for being written in a hurry. She held it at a distance, was about to fold it, then added these words at the bottom: –

'Do not desert me, Gabriel!'

She looked a little redder in refolding it, and closed her lips, as if thereby to suspend till too late the action of conscience in examining whether such strategy were justifiable. The note was despatched as the message had been, and Bathsheba waited indoors for the result.

It was an anxious quarter of an hour that intervened between the messenger's departure and the sound of the horse's tramp again outside. She could not watch this time, but, leaning over the old bureau at which she had written the letter, closed her eyes, as if to keep out both hope and fear.

The case, however, was a promising one. Gabriel was not angry: he was simply neutral, although her first command had been so haughty. Such imperiousness would have damned a little less beauty; and on the other hand, such beauty would have redeemed a little less imperiousness.

She went out when the horse was heard, and looked up. A mounted figure passed between her and the sky, and drew on towards the field of sheep, the rider turning his face in receding. Gabriel looked at her. It was a moment when a woman's eyes and tongue tell distinctly opposite tales. Bathsheba looked full of gratitude, and she said: —

'O, Gabriel, how could you serve me so unkindly!'

Such a tenderly-shaped reproach for his previous delay was the one speech in the language that he could pardon for not being commendation of his readiness now.

Gabriel murmured a confused reply, and hastened on. She knew from the look which sentence in her note had brought him. Bathsheba followed to the field.

Gabriel was already among the turgid, prostrate forms. He had flung off his coat, rolled up his shirt-sleeves, and taken from his pocket the instrument of salvation. It was a small tube or trochar, with a lance passing down the inside; and Gabriel began to use it with a dexterity that would have graced a hospital-surgeon. Passing his hand over the sheep's left flank, and selecting the proper point, he punctured the skin and rumen with the lance as it stood in the tube; then he suddenly withdrew the lance, retaining the tube in its place. A current of air rushed up the tube, forcible enough to have extinguished a candle held at the orifice.

It has been said that mere ease after torment is delight for a time; and the countenances of these poor creatures expressed it now. Forty-nine operations were successfully performed. Owing to the great hurry necessitated by the far-gone state of some of the flock, Gabriel missed his aim in one case, and in one only — striking wide of the mark, and inflicting a mortal blow at once upon the suffering ewe. Four had died; three recovered without an operation. The total number of sheep which had thus strayed and injured themselves so dangerously was fifty-seven.

When the love-led man had ceased from his labours Bathsheba came and looked him in the face.

'Gabriel, will you stay on with me?' she said, smiling winningly, and not troubling to bring her lips quite together again at the end, because there was going to be another smile soon.

'I will,' said Gabriel.

And she smiled on him again.

CHAPTER TWENTY-TWO

The Great Barn and the Sheep-shearers

M EN thin away to insignificance and oblivion quite as often by not making the most of good spirits when they have them as by lacking good spirits when they are indispensable. Gabriel lately, for the first time since his prostration by misfortune, had been independent in thought and vigorous in action to a marked extent – conditions which, powerless without an opportunity as an opportunity without them is barren, would have given him a sure lift upwards when the favourable conjunction should have occurred. But this incurable loitering beside Bathsheba Everdene stole his time ruinously. The spring tides were going by without floating him off, and the neap might soon come which could not.

It was the first day of June, and the sheep-shearing season culminated, the landscape, even to the leanest pasture, being all health and colour. Every green was young, every pore was open, and every stalk was swollen with racing currents of juice. God was palpably present in the country, and the devil had gone with the world to town. Flossy catkins of the later kinds, fern-sprouts like bishops' croziers, the square-headed moschatel, the odd cuckoo-pint, – like an apoplectic saint in a niche of malachite, – snow-white ladies'-smocks, the toothwort, approximating to human flesh, the enchanter's night-shade, and the black-petaled doleful-bells, were among the quainter objects of the vegetable world in and about Weatherbury at this teeming time; and of the animal, the metamor-phosed figures of Mr Jan Coggan, the master-shearer; the second and third shearers, who travelled in the exercise of their calling, and do not require definition by name; Henery Fray the fourth shearer, Susan Tall's husband the fifth, Joseph Poorgrass the sixth, young Cain Ball as assistant-shearer, and Gabriel Oak as general supervisor. None of these were clothed to any extent worth mentioning, each appearing to have hit in the matter of raiment the decent mean between a high and low caste Hindoo. An angularity of lineament, and a fixity of facial machinery in general, proclaimed that serious work was the order of the day.

They sheared in the great barn, called for the nonce the Shearing-barn, which on ground-plan resembled a church with transepts. It not only emulated the form of the neighbouring church of the parish, but vied with it in antiquity. Whether the barn had ever formed one of a group of conventual buildings nobody seemed to be aware; no trace of such surroundings remained. The vast porches at the sides, lofty enough to admit a waggon laden to its highest with corn in the sheaf, were spanned by heavy-pointed arches of stone, broadly and boldly cut, whose very simplicity was the origin of a grandeur not apparent in erections where more ornament has been attempted. The dusky, filmed, chestnut roof, braced and tied in by huge collars, curves, and diagonals, was far nobler in

93

design, because more wealthy in material, than nine-tenths of those in our modern churches. Along each side wall was a range of striding buttresses, throwing deep shadows on the spaces between them, which were perforated by lancet openings, combining in their proportions the precise requirements both of beauty and ventilation.

One could say about this barn, what could hardly be said of either the church or the castle, akin to it in age and style, that the purpose which had dictated its original erection was the same with that to which it was still applied. Unlike and superior to either of those two typical remnants of mediævalism, the old barn embodied practices which had suffered no mutilation at the hands of time. Here at least the spirit of the ancient builders was at one with the spirit of the modern beholder. Standing before this abraded pile, the eye regarded its present usage, the mind dwelt upon its past history, with a satisfied sense of functional continuity throughout — a feeling almost of gratitude, and quite of pride, at the permanence of the idea which had heaped it up. The fact that four centuries had neither proved it to be founded on a mistake, inspired any hatred of its purpose, nor given rise to any reaction that had battered it down, invested this simple gray effort of old minds with a repose, if not a grandeur, which a too curious reflection was apt to disturb in its ecclesiastical and military compeers. For once mediævalism and modernism had a common standpoint. The lanceolate windows, the time-eaten arch-stones and chamfers, the orientation of the axis, the misty chestnut work of the rafters, referred to no exploded fortifying art or worn-out religious creed. The defence and salvation of the body by daily bread is still a study, a religion, and a desire.

To-day the large side doors were thrown open towards the sun to admit a bountiful light to the immediate spot of the shearers' operations, which was the wood threshing-floor in the centre, formed of thick oak, black with age and polished by the beating of flails for many generations, till it had grown as slippery and as rich in hue as the state-room floors of an Elizabethan mansion. Here the shearers knelt, the sun slanting in upon their bleached shirts, tanned arms, and the polished shears they flourished, causing these to bristle with a thousand rays strong enough to blind a weak-eyed man. Beneath them a captive sheep lay panting, quickening its pants as misgiving merged in terror, till it quivered like the hot landscape outside.

This picture of to-day in its frame of four hundred years ago did not produce that marked contrast between ancient and modern which is implied by the contrast of date. In comparison with cities, Weatherbury was immutable. The citizen's *Then* is the rustic's *Now*. In London, twenty or thirty years ago are old times; in Paris ten years, or five; in Weatherbury three or four score years were included in the mere present, and nothing less than a century set a mark on its face or tone. Five decades hardly modified the cut of a gaiter, the embroidery of a smock-frock, by the breadth of a hair. Ten generations failed to alter the turn of a single phrase. In these Wessex nooks the busy outsider's ancient times are only old; his old times are still new; his present is futurity.

So the barn was natural to the shearers, and the shearers were in harmony with the barn.

The spacious ends of the building, answering ecclesiastically to nave and chancel extremities, were fenced off with hurdles, the sheep being all collected in a crowd within these two enclosures; and in one angle a catching-pen was formed, in which three or four sheep were continuously kept ready for the shearers to seize without loss of time. In the background, mellowed by tawny shade, were the three women, Maryann Money, and Temperance and Soberness Miller, gathering up the fleeces and twisting ropes of wool with a wimble for tying them round. They were indifferently well assisted by the old maltster, who, when the malting season from October to April had passed, made himself useful upon any of the bordering farmsteads.

Behind all was Bathsheba, carefully watching the men to see that there was no cutting or wounding through carelessness, and that the animals were shorn close. Gabriel, who flitted and hovered under her bright eyes like a moth, did not shear continuously, half his time being spent in attending to the others and selecting the sheep for them. At the present moment he was engaged in handing round a mug of mild liquor, supplied from a barrel in the corner, and cut pieces of bread and cheese.

Bathsheba, after throwing a glance here, a caution there, and lecturing one of the younger operators who had allowed his last finished sheep to go off among the flock without re-stamping it with her initials, came again to Gabriel, as he put down the luncheon to drag a frightened ewe to his shear-station, flinging it over upon its back with a dexterous twist of the arm. He lopped off the tresses about its head, and opened up the neck and collar, his mistress quietly looking on.

'She blushes at the insult,' murmured Bathsheba, watching the pink flush which arose and overspread the neck and shoulders of the ewe where they were left bare by the clicking shears – a flush which was enviable, for its delicacy, by many queens of coteries, and would have been creditable, for its promptness, to any woman in the world.

Poor Gabriel's soul was fed with a luxury of content by having her over him, her eyes critically regarding his skilful shears, which apparently were going to gather up a piece of the flesh at every close, and yet never did so. Like Guildenstern, Oak was happy in that he was not over happy. He had no wish to converse with her: that his bright lady and himself formed one group, exclusively their own, and containing no others in the world, was enough.

So the chatter was all on her side. There is a loquacity that tells nothing, which was Bathsheba's; and there is a silence which says much: that was Gabriel's. Full of this dim and temperate bliss he went on to fling the ewe over upon her other side, covering her head with his knee, gradually running the shears line after line round her dewlap, thence about her flank and back, and finishing over the tail.

'Well done, and done quickly!' said Bathsheba, looking at her watch as the last snip resounded.

'How long, miss?' said Gabriel, wiping his brow.

'Three-and-twenty minutes and a half since you took the first lock from its forehead. It is the first time that I have ever seen one done in less than half an hour.'

The clean, sleek creature arose from its fleece – how perfectly like Aphrodite rising from the foam should have been seen to be realized – looking startled and shy at the loss of its garment, which lay on the floor in one soft cloud, united throughout, the portion visible being the inner surface only, which, never before exposed, was white as snow, and without flaw or blemish of the minutest kind.

'Cain Ball!'

'Yes, Mister Oak; here I be!'

Cainy now runs forward with the tar-pot. 'B.E.' is newly stamped upon the shorn skin, and away the simple dam leaps, panting, over the board into the shirtless flock outside. Then up comes Maryann; throws the loose locks into the middle of the fleece, rolls it up, and carries it into the battleground as three-and-a-half pounds of unadulterated warmth for the winter enjoyment of persons unknown and far away, who will, however, never experience the superlative comfort derivable from the wool as it here exists, new and pure – before the unctuousness of its nature whilst in a living state has dried, stiffened, and been washed out – rendering it just now as superior to anything *woollen* as cream is superior to milk-and-water.

But heartless circumstance could not leave entire Gabriel's happiness of this morning. The rams, old ewes, and two-shear ewes had duly undergone their stripping, and the men were proceeding with the shearlings and hogs, when Oak's belief that she was going to stand pleasantly by and time him through another performance was painfully interrupted by Farmer Boldwood's appearance in the extremest corner of the barn. Nobody seemed to have perceived his entry, but there he certainly was. Boldwood always carried with him a social atmosphere of his own, which everybody felt who came near him; and the talk, which Bathsheba's presence had somewhat suppressed, was now totally suspended.

He crossed over towards Bathsheba, who turned to greet him with a carriage of perfect ease. He spoke to her in low tones, and she instinctively modulated her own to the same pitch, and her voice ultimately even caught the inflection of his. She was far from having a wish to appear mysteriously connected with him; but woman at the impressionable age gravitates to the larger body not only in her choice of words, which is apparent every day, but even in her shades of tone and humour when the influence is great.

What they conversed about was not audible to Gabriel, who was too independent to get near, though too concerned to disregard. The issue of their dialogue was the taking of her hand by the courteous farmer to help her over the spreading-board into the bright June sunlight outside. Standing beside the sheep already shorn, they went on talking again. Concerning the flock? Apparently not. Gabriel theorized, not without truth, that in quiet discussion of any matter within reach of the speaker's eyes, these are usually fixed upon it. Bathsheba demurely regarded a contemptible straw lying upon the ground, in a way which suggested less ovine criticism than womanly embarrassment. She became more or less red in the cheek, the blood wavering in uncertain flux and reflux over the sensitive space between ebb and flood. Gabriel sheared on, constrained and sad.

She left Boldwood's side, and he walked up and down alone for nearly a quarter of an hour. Then she reappeared in her new riding-habit of myrtle-green, which fitted her to the waist as a rind fits its fruit; and young Bob Coggan led on her mare, Boldwood fetching his own horse from the tree under which it had been tied.

Oak's eyes could not forsake them; and in endeavouring to continue his shearing at the same time that he watched Boldwood's manner, he snipped the sheep in the groin. The animal plunged; Bathsheba instantly gazed towards it, and saw the blood.

'O Gabriel!' she exclaimed, with severe remonstrance, 'you who are so strict with the other men – see what you are doing yourself!'

To an outsider there was not much to complain of in this remark; but to Oak, who knew Bathsheba to be well aware that she herself was the cause of the poor ewe's wound, because she had wounded the ewe's shearer in a still more vital part, it had a sting which the abiding sense of his inferiority to both herself and Boldwood was not calculated to heal. But a manly resolve to recognize boldly that he had no longer a lover's interest in her, helped him occasionally to conceal a feeling.

'Bottle!' he shouted, in an unmoved voice of routine. Cainy Ball ran up, the would was anointed, and the shearing continued.

Boldwood gently tossed Bathsheba into the saddle, and before they turned away she again spoke out to Oak with the same dominative and tantalizing graciousness.

'I am going now to see Mr Boldwood's Leicesters. Take my place in the barn, Gabriel, and keep the men carefully to their work.'

The horses' heads were put about, and they trotted away.

Boldwood's deep attachment was a matter of great interest among all around him; but, after having been pointed out for so many years as the perfect exemplar of thriving bachelorship, his lapse was an anticlimax somewhat resembling that of St John Long's death by consumption in the midst of his proofs that it was not a fatal disease.

'That means matrimony,' said Temperance Miller, following them out of sight with her eyes.

'I reckon that's the size o't,' said Coggan, working along without looking up.

'Well, better wed over the mixen than over the moor,' said Laban Tall, turning his sheep.

Henery Fray spoke, exhibiting miserable eyes at the same time: 'I don't see why a maid should take a husband when she's bold enough to fight her own battles, and don't want a home; for 'tis keeping another woman out. But let it be, for 'tis a pity he and she should trouble two houses.'

As usual with decided characters, Bathsheba invariably provoked the criticism of individuals like Henery Fray. Her emblazoned fault was to be too pronounced in her objections, and not sufficiently overt in her likings. We learn that it is not the rays which bodies absorb, but those which they reject, that give them the colours they are known by; and in the same way people are specialized by their dislikes and antagonisms, whilst their goodwill is looked upon as no attribute at all.

Henery continued in a more complaisant mood: 'I once hinted my mind to her on a few things, as nearly as a battered frame dared to do so to such a froward piece. You all know, neighbours, what a man I be, and how I come down with my powerful words when my pride is boiling wi' scarn?'

'We do, we do, Henery.'

'So I said, "Miss Everdene, there's places empty, and there's gifted men willing; but the spite" – no, not the spite – I didn't say spite – "but the villainy of the contrarikind," I said (meaning womankind), "keeps 'em out." That wasn't too strong for her, say?'

'Passably well put.'

'Yes; and I would have said it, had death and salvation overtook me for it.
Such is my spirit when I have a mind.'

'A true man, and proud as a lucifer.'

'You see the artfulness? Why, 'twas about being baily really; but I didn't put it
so plain that she could understand my meaning, so I could lay it on all the
stronger. That was my depth! . . . However, let her marry an she will. Perhaps 'tis
high time. I believe Farmer Boldwood kissed her behind the spear-bed at the
sheep-washing t'other day – that I do.'

'What a lie!' said Gabriel.

'Ah, neighbour Oak – how'st know?' said Henery mildly.

'Because she told me all that passed,' said Oak, with a pharisaical sense that he
was not as other shearers in this matter.

'Ye have a right to believe it,' said Henery, with dudgeon; 'a very true right. But
I mid see a little distance into things! To be long-headed enough for a baily's
place is a poor mere trifle – yet a trifle more than nothing. However, I look round
upon life quite cool. Do you heed me, neighbours? My words, though made as
simple as I can, mid be rather deep for some heads.'

'O yes, Henery, we quite heed ye.'

'A strange old piece, goodmen – whirled about from here to yonder, as if I
were nothing! A little warped, too. But I have my depths; ha, and even my great
depths! I might gird at a certain shepherd, brain to brain. But no – O no!'

'A strange old piece, ye say!' interposed the maltster, in a querulous voice. 'At
the same time ye be no old man worth naming – no old man at all. Yer teeth
bain't half gone yet; and what's a old man's standing if so be his teeth bain't
gone? Weren't I stale in wedlock afore ye were out of arms? 'Tis a poor thing to be
sixty, when there's people far past four-score – a boast weak as water.'

It was the unvarying custom in Weatherbury to sink minor differences when
the maltster had to be pacified.

'Weak as water! yes,' said Jan Coggan. 'Malter, we feel ye to be a wonderful
veteran man, and nobody can gainsay it.'

'Nobody,' said Joseph Poorgrass. 'Ye be a very rare old spectacle, malter, and
we all admire ye for that gift.'

'Ay, and as a young man, when my senses were in prosperity, I was likewise
liked by a good-few who knowed me,' said the maltster.

''Ithout doubt you was – 'Ithought doubt.'

The bent and hoary man was satisfied, and so apparently was Henery Fray.
That matters should continue pleasant Maryann spoke, who, what with her
brown complexion, and the working wrapper of rusty linsey, had at present the
mellow hue of an old sketch in oils – notably some of Nicholas Poussin's: –

'Do anybody know of a crooked man, or a lame, or any secondhand fellow at
all that would do for poor me?' said Maryann. 'A perfect one I don't expect to get
at my time of life. If I could hear of such a thing 'twould do me more good than
toast and ale.'

Coggan furnished a suitable reply. Oak went on with his shearing, and said
not another word. Pestilent moods had come, and teased away his quiet.
Bathsheba had shown indications of anointing him above his fellows by
installing him as the bailiff that the farm imperatively required. He did not covet
the post relatively to the farm: in relation to herself, as beloved by him and

unmarried to another, he had coveted it. His readings of her seemed now to be vapoury and indistinct. His lecture to her was, he thought, one of the absurdest mistakes. Far from coquetting with Boldwood, she had trifled with himself in thus feigning that she had trifled with another. He was inwardly convinced that, in accordance with the anticipations of his easy-going and worse-educated comrades, that day would see Boldwood the accepted husband of Miss Everdene. Gabriel at this time of his life had outgrown the instinctive dislike which every Christian boy has for reading the Bible, perusing it now quite frequently, and he inwardly said, ' "I find more bitter than death the woman whose heart is snares and nets!" ' This was mere exclamation – the froth of the storm. He adored Bathsheba just the same.

'We workfolk shall have some lordly junketing to-night,' said Cainy Ball, casting forth his thoughts in a new direction. 'This morning I see 'em making the great puddens in the milking-pails – lumps of fat as big as yer thumb, Mister Oak! I've never seed such splendid large knobs of fat before in the days of my life – they never used to be bigger than a horse-bean. And there was a great black crock upon the brandise with his legs a-sticking out, but I don't know what was in within.'

'And there's two bushels of biffins for apple-pies,' said Maryann.

'Well, I hope to do my duty by it all,' said Joseph Poorgrass, in a pleasant, masticating manner of anticipation. 'Yes; victuals and drink is a cheerful thing, and gives nerves to the nerveless, if the form of words may be used. 'Tis the gospel of the body, without which we perish, so to speak it.'

CHAPTER TWENTY-THREE

Eventide – A Second Declaration

FOR the shearing-supper a long table was placed on the grass-plot beside the house, the end of the table being thrust over the sill of the wide parlour window and a foot or two into the room. Miss Everdene sat inside the window, facing down the table. She was thus at the head without mingling with the men.

This evening Bathsheba was unusually excited, her red cheeks and lips contrasting lustrously with the mazy skeins of her shadowy hair. She seemed to expect assistance, and the seat at the bottom of the table was at her request left vacant until after they had begun the meal. She then asked Gabriel to take the place and the duties appertaining to that end, which he did with great readiness.

At this moment Mr Boldwood came in at the gate, and crossed the green to Bathsheba at the window. He apologized for his lateness: his arrival was evidently by arrangement.

'Gabriel,' said she, 'will you move again, please, and let Mr Boldwood come there?'

Oak moved in silence back to his original seat.

The gentleman-farmer was dressed in cheerful style, in a new coat and white waistcoat, quite contrasting with his usual sober suits of grey. Inwardly, too, he was blithe, and consequently chatty to an exceptional degree. So also was Bathsheba now that he had come, though the uninvited presence of Pennyways, the bailiff who had been dismissed for theft, disturbed her equanimity for a while.

Supper being ended, Coggan began on his own private account, without reference to listeners:

> I've lost my love, and I care not,
> I've lost my love, and I care not;
> I shall soon have another
> That's better than t'other;
> I've lost my love, and I care not.

This lyric, when concluded, was received with a silently appreciative gaze at the table, implying that the performance, like a work by those established authors who are independent of notices in the papers, was a well-known delight which required no applause.

'Now, Master Poorgrass, your song!' said Coggan.

'I be all but in liquor, and the gift is wanting in me,' said Joseph, diminishing himself.

'Nonsense; wou'st never be so ungrateful, Joseph — never!' said Coggan, expressing hurt feelings by an inflection of voice. 'And mistress is looking hard at ye, as much as to say, "Sing at once , Joseph Poorgrass."'

'Faith, so she is; well, I must suffer it! . . . Just eye my features, and see if the tell-tale blood overheats me much, neighbours?'

'No, yer blushes be quite reasonable,' said Coggan.

'I always tries to keep my colours from rising when a beauty's eyes get fixed on me,' said Joseph diffidently; 'but if so be 'tis willed they do, they must.'

'Now, Joseph, your song, please,' said Bathsheba from the window.

'Well, really, ma'am,' he replied in a yielding tone, 'I don't know what to say. It would be a poor plain ballet of my own composure.'

'Hear, hear!' said the supper-party.

Poorgrass, thus assured, trilled forth a flickering yet commendable piece of sentiment, the tune of which consisted of the key-note and another, the latter being the sound chiefly dwelt upon. This was so successful that he rashly plunged into a second in the same breath, after a few false starts: —

> I sow'-ed th'-e . . .
> I sow'-ed . . .
> I sow'-ed the'-e seeds' of' love',
>   I-it was' all' i'-in the'-e spring',
>   I-in A'-pril', Ma'-ay, a'-nd sun'-ny' June',
>   When sma'-all bi'-irds they' do' sing.

'Well put out of hand,' said Coggan, at the end of the verse. '"They do sing" was a very taking paragraph.'

'Ay; and there was a pretty place at "seeds of love", and 'twas well heaved out. Though "love" is a nasty high corner when a man's voice is getting crazed. Next verse, Master Poorgrass.'

But during this rendering young Bob Coggan exhibited one of those anomalies which will afflict little people when other persons are particularly serious: in trying to check his laughter, he pushed down his throat as much of the tablecloth as he could get hold of, when, after continuing hermetically sealed for a short time, his mirth burst out through his nose. Joseph perceived it, and with hectic cheeks of indignation instantly ceased singing. Coggan boxed Bob's ears immediately.

'Go on, Joseph – go on, and never mind the young scamp,' said Coggan. ' 'Tis a very catching ballet. Now then again – the next bar; I'll help ye to flourish up the shrill notes where yer wind is rather wheezy: –

> O the wi′-il-lo′-ow tree′ will′ twist′,
> And the wil′-low′ tre′-ee wi′-ill twine′.'

But the singer could not be set going again. Bob Coggan was sent home for his ill manners, and tranquillity was restored by Jacob Smallbury, who volunteered a ballad as inclusive and interminable as that with which the worthy toper old Silenus amused on a similar occasion the swains Chromis and Mnasylus, and other jolly dogs of his day.

It was still the beaming time of evening, though night was stealthily making itself visible low down upon the ground, the western lines of light raking the earth without alighting upon it to any extent, or illuminating the dead levels at all. The sun had crept round the tree as a last effort before death, and then began to sink, the shearers' lower parts becoming steeped in embrowning twilight, whilst their heads and shoulders were still enjoying day, touched with a yellow of self-sustained brilliancy that seemed inherent rather than acquired.

The sun went down in an ochreous mist; but they sat, and talked on, and grew as merry as the gods in Homer's heaven. Bathsheba still remained enthroned inside the window, and occupied herself in knitting, from which she sometimes looked up to view the fading scene outside. The slow twilight expanded and enveloped them completely before the signs of moving were shown.

Gabriel suddenly missed Farmer Boldwood from his place at the bottom of the table. How long he had been gone Oak did not know; but he had apparently withdrawn into the encircling dusk. Whilst he was thinking of this Liddy brought candles into the back part of the room overlooking the shearers, and their lively new flames shone down the table and over the men, and dispersed among the green shadows behind. Bathsheba's form, still in its original position, was now again distinct between their eyes and the light, which revealed that Boldwood had gone inside the room, and was sitting near her.

Next came the question of the evening. Would Miss Everdene sing to them the song she always sang so charmingly – 'The Banks of Allan Water' – before they went home?

After a moment's consideration Bathsheba assented, beckoning to Gabriel, who hastened up into the coveted atmosphere.

'Have you brought your flute?' she whispered.

'Yes, miss.'

'Play to my singing, then.'

She stood up in the window-opening, facing the men, the candles behind her, Gabriel on her right hand, immediately outside the sash-frame. Boldwood had drawn up on her left, within the room. Her singing was soft and rather tremulous at first, but it soon swelled to a steady clearness. Subsequent events caused one of the verses to be remembered for many months, and even years, by more than one of those who were gathered there: –

> For his bride a soldier sought her,
> And a winning tongue had he:
> On the banks of Allan Water
> None was gay as she!

In addition to the dulcet piping of Gabriel's flute Boldwood supplied a bass in his customary profound voice, uttering his notes so softly, however, as to abstain entirely from making anything like an ordinary duet of the song; they rather formed a rich unexplored shadow, which threw her tones into relief. The shearers reclined against each other as at suppers in the early ages of the world, and so silent and absorbed were they that her breathing could almost be heard between the bars; and at the end of the ballad, when the last tone loitered on to an inexpressible close, there arose that buzz of pleasure which is the attar of applause.

It is scarcely necessary to state that Gabriel could not avoid noting the farmer's bearing to-night towards their entertainer. Yet there was nothing exceptional in his actions beyond what appertained to his time of performing them. It was when the rest were all looking away that Boldwood observed her; when they regarded her he turned aside; when they thanked or praised he was silent; when they were inattentive he murmured his thanks. The meaning lay in the difference between actions none of which had any meaning of itself; and the necessity of being jealous, which lovers are troubled with, did not lead Oak to underestimate these signs.

Bathsheba then wished them good-night, withdrew from the window, and retired to the back part of the room, Boldwood thereupon closing the sash and the shutters, and remaining inside with her. Oak wandered away under the quiet and scented trees. Recovering from the softer impressions produced by Bathsheba's voice, the shearers rose to leave, Coggan turning to Pennyways as he pushed back the bench to pass out: –

'I like to give praise where praise is due, and the man deserves it – that 'a do so,' he remarked, looking at the worthy thief as if he were the masterpiece of some world-renowned artist

'I'm sure I should never have belived it if we hadn't proved it, so to allude,' hiccupped Joseph Poorgrass, 'that every cup, every one of the best knives and forks, and every empty bottle be in their place as perfect now as at the beginning, and not one stole at all.'

'I'm sure I don't deserve half the praise you give me,' said the virtuous thief grimly.

'Well, I'll say this for Pennyways,' added Coggan, 'that whenever he do really make up his mind to do a noble thing in the shape of a good action, as I could see by his face he did to-night afore sitting down, he's generally able to carry it out. Yes, I'm proud to say, neighbours, that he's stole nothing at all.'

'Well, 'tis an honest deed, and we thank ye for it, Pennyways,' said Joseph; to which opinion the remainder of the company subscribed unanimously.

At this time of departure, when nothing more was visible of the inside of the

parlour than a thin and still chink of light between the shutters, a passionate
scene was in course of enactment there.

Miss Everdene and Boldwood were alone. Her cheeks had lost a great deal of
their healthful fire from the very seriousness of her position; but her eye was
bright with the excitement of a triumph – though it was a triumph which had
rather been contemplated than desired.

She was standing behind a low arm-chair, from which she had just risen, and he
was kneeling in it – inclining himself over its back towards her, and holding her
hand in both his own. His body moved restlessly, and it was with what Keats
daintily calls a too happy happiness. This unwonted abstraction by love of all
dignity from a man of whom it had ever seemed the chief component, was, in its
distressing incongruity, a pain to her which quenched much of the pleasure she
derived from the proof that she was idolized.

'I will try to love you,' she was saying, in a trembling voice quite unlike her
usual self-confidence. 'And if I can believe in any way that I shall make you a
good wife I shall indeed be willing to marry you. But, Mr Boldwood, hesitation
on so high a matter is honourable in any woman, and I don't want to give a
solemn promise to-night. I would rather ask you to wait a few weeks till I can see
my situation better.'

'But you have every reason to believe that *then*—'

'I have every reason to hope that at the end of the five or six weeks, between this
time and harvest, that you say you are going to be away from home, I shall be
able to promise to be your wife,' she said firmly. 'But remember this distinctly, I
don't promise yet.'

'It is enough; I don't ask more. I can wait on those dear words. And now, Miss
Everdene, good-night!'

'Good-night,' she said graciously – almost tenderly; and Boldwood withdrew
with a serene smile.

Bathsheba knew more of him now; he had entirely bared his heart before her,
even until he had almost worn in her eyes the sorry look of a grand bird without
the feathers that make it grand. She had been awestruck at her past temerity, and
was struggling to make amends without thinking whether the sin quite deserved
the penalty she was schooling herself to pay. To have brought all this about her
ears was terrible; but after a while the situation was not without a fearful joy. The
facility with which even the most timid women sometimes acquire a relish for the
dreadful when that is amalgamated with a little triumph, is marvellous.

CHAPTER TWENTY-FOUR

The same Night – The Fir Plantation

AMONG the multifarious duties which Bathsheba had voluntarily imposed upon
herself by dispensing with the services of a bailiff, was the particular one of

looking round the homestead before going to bed, to see that all was right and
safe for the night. Gabriel had almost constantly preceded her in this tour every
evening, watching her affairs as carefully as any specially appointed officer of
surveillance could have done; but this tender devotion was to a great extent
unknown to his mistress, and as much as was known was somewhat thanklessly
received. Women are never tired of bewailing man's fickleness in love, but they
only seem to snub his constancy.

As watching is best done invisibly, she usually carried a dark lantern in her
hand, and every now and then turned on the light to examine nooks and corners
with the coolness of a metropolitan policeman. This coolness may have owed its
existence not so much to her fearlessness of expected danger as to her freedom
from the suspicion of any; her worst anticipated discovery being that a horse
might not be well bedded, the fowls not all in, or a door not closed.

This night the buildings were inspected as usual, and she went round to the
farm paddock. Here the only sounds disturbing the stillness were steady
munchings of many mouths, and stentorian breathings from all but invisible
noses, ending in snores and puffs like the blowing of bellows slowly. Then the
munching would recommence, when the lively imagination might assist the eye to
discern a group of pink-white nostrils shaped as caverns, and very clammy and
humid on their surfaces, not exactly pleasant to the touch until one got used to
them; the mouths beneath having a great partiality for closing upon any loose
end of Bathsheba's apparel which came within reach of their tongues. Above
each of these a still keener vision sugested a brown forehead and two staring
though not unfriendly eyes, and above all a pair of whitish crescent-shaped horns
like two particularly new moons, an occasional stolid 'moo!' proclaiming beyond
the shade of a doubt that these phenomena were the features and persons of
Daisy, Whitefoot, Bonny-lass, Jolly-O, Spot, Twinkle-eye, etc., etc. – the
respectable dairy of Devon cows belonging to Bathsheba aforesaid.

Her way back to the house was by a path through a young plantation of
tapering firs, which had been planted some years earlier to shelter the premises
from the north wind. By reason of the density of the interwoven foliage overhead
it was gloomy there at cloudless noontide, twilight in the evening, dark as
midnight at dusk, and black as the ninth plague of Egypt at midnight. To
describe the spot is to call it a vast, low, naturally formed hall, the plumy ceiling
of which was supported by slender pillars of living wood, the floor being covered
with a soft dun carpet of dead spikelets and mildewed cones, with a tuft of grass-
blades here and there.

This bit of the path was always the crux of the night's ramble, though, before
starting, her apprehensions of danger were not vivid enough to lead her to take a
companion. Slipping along here covertly as Time, Bathsheba fancied she could
hear footsteps entering the track at the opposite end. It was certainly a rustle of
footsteps. Her own instantly fell as gently as snowflakes. She reassured herself by
a remembrance that the path was public, and that the traveller was probably
some villager returning home; regretting, at the same time, that the meeting
should be about to occur in the darkest point of her route, even though only just
outside her own door.

The noise approached, came close, and a figure was apparently on the point of
gliding past her when something tugged at her skirt and pinned it forcibly to the

ground. The instantaneous check nearly threw Bathsheba off her balance. In recovering she struck against warm clothes and buttons.

'A rum start, upon my soul!' said a masculine voice, a foot or so above her head. 'Have I hurt you, mate?'

'No,' said Bathsheba, attempting to shrink away.

'We have got hitched together somehow, I think.'

'Yes.'

'Are you a woman?'

'Yes.'

'A lady, I should have said.'

'It doesn't matter.'

'I am a man.'

'Oh!'

Bathsheba softly tugged again, but to no purpose.

'Is that a dark lantern you have? I fancy so,' said the man.

'Yes.'

'If you'll allow me I'll open it, and set you free.'

A hand seized the lantern, the door was opened, the rays burst out from their prison, and Bathsheba beheld her position with astonishment.

The man to whom she was hooked was brilliant in brass and scarlet. He was a soldier. His sudden appearance was to darkness what the sound of a trumpet is to silence. Gloom, the *genius loci* at all times hitherto, was now totally overthrown, less by the lantern-light than by what the lantern lighted. The contrast of this revelation with her anticipations of some sinister figure in sombre garb was so great that it had upon her the effect of a fairy transformation.

It was immediately apparent that the military man's spur had become entangled in the gimp which decorated the skirt of her dress. He caught a view of her face.

'I'll unfasten you in one moment, miss,' he said, with new-born gallantry.

'O no – I can do it, thank you,' she hastily replied, and stooped for the performance.

The unfastening was not such a trifling affair. The rowel of the spur had so wound itself among the gimp cords in those few moments, that separation was likely to be a matter of time.

He too stooped, and the lantern standing on the ground betwixt them threw the gleam from its open side among the fir-tree needles and the blades of long damp grass with the effect of a large glow-worm. It radiated upwards into their faces, and sent over half the plantation gigantic shadows of both man and woman, each dusky shape becoming distorted and mangled upon the tree-trunks till it wasted to nothing.

He looked hard into her eyes when she raised them for a moment; Bathsheba looked down again, for his gaze was too strong to be received point-blank with her own. But she had obliquely noticed that he was young and slim, and that he wore three chevrons upon his sleeve.

Bathsheba pulled again.

'You are a prisoner, miss; it is no use blinking the matter,' said the soldier drily. 'I must cut your dress if you are in such a hurry.'

'Yes – please do!' she exclaimed helplessly.

'It wouldn't be necessary if you could wait a moment'; and he unwound a cord from the little wheel. She withdrew her own hand, but, whether by accident or design, he touched it. Bathsheba was vexed; she hardly knew why.

His unravelling went on, but it nevertheless seemed coming to no end. She looked at him again.

'Thank you for the sight of such a beautiful face!' said the young sergeant, without ceremony.

She coloured with embarrassment. ' 'Twas unwillingly shown,' she replied stiffly, and with as much dignity – which was very little – as she could infuse into a position of captivity.

'I like you the better for that incivility, miss,' he said.

'I should have liked – I wish – you had never shown yourself to me by intruding here!' She pulled again, and the gathers of her dress began to give way like lilliputian musketry.

'I deserve the chastisement your words give me. But why should such a fair and dutiful girl have such an aversion to her father's sex?'

'Go on your way, please.'

'What, Beauty, and drag you after me? Do but look; I never saw such a tangle!'

'O, 'tis shameful of you; you have been making it worse on purpose to keep me here – you have!'

'Indeed, I don't think so,' said the sergeant, with a merry twinkle.

'I tell you you have!' she exclaimed, in high temper. 'I insist upon undoing it. Now, allow me!'

'Certainly, miss; I am not of steel.' He added a sigh which had as much archness in it as a sigh could possess without losing its nature altogether. 'I am thankful for beauty, even when 'tis thrown to me like a bone to a dog. These moments will be over too soon!'

She closed her lips in a determined silence.

Bathsheba was revolving in her mind whether by a bold and desperate rush she could free herself at the risk of leaving her skirt bodily behind her. The thought was too dreadful. The dress – which she had put on to appear stately at the supper – was the head and front of her wardrobe; not another in her stock became her so well. What woman in Bathsheba's position, not naturally timid, and within call of her retainers, would have bought escape from a dashing soldier at so dear a price?

'All in good time; it will soon be done, I perceive,' said her cool friend.

'This trifling provokes, and – and—'

'Not too cruel!'

' – Insults me!'

'It is done in order that I may have the pleasure of apologizing to so charming a woman, which I straightway do most humbly, madam,' he said, bowing low.

Bathsheba really knew not what to say.

'I've seen a good many women in my time,' continued the young man in a murmur, and more thoughtfully than hitherto, critically regarding her bent head at the same time; 'but I've never seen a woman so beautiful as you. Take it or leave it – be offended or like it – I don't care.'

'Who are you, then, who can so well afford to despise opinion?'

'No stranger. Sergeant Troy. I am staying in this place. – There! it is undone at last, you see. Your light fingers were more eager than mine. I wish it had been the knot of knots, which there's no untying!'

This was worse and worse. She started up, and so did he. How to decently get away from him – that was her difficulty now. She sidled off inch by inch, the lantern in her hand, till she could see the redness of his coat no longer.

'Ah, Beauty; good-bye!' he said.

She made no reply, and, reaching a distance of twenty or thirty yards, turned about, and ran indoors.

Liddy had just retired to rest. In ascending to her own chamber, Bathsheba opened the girl's door an inch or two, and, panting, said –

'Liddy, is any soldier staying in the village – sergeant somebody – rather gentlemanly for a sergeant, and good looking – a red coat with blue facings?'

'No, miss. . . . No, I say; but really it might be Sergeant Troy home on furlough, though I have not seen him. He was here once in that way when the regiment was at Casterbridge.'

'Yes; that's the name. Had he a moustache – no whiskers or beard?'

'He had.'

'What kind of a person is he?'

'O! miss – I blush to name it – a gay man! But I know him to be very quick and trim, who might have made his thousands, like a squire. Such a clever young dand as he is! He's a doctor's son by name, which is a great deal; and he's an earl's son by nature!'

'Which is a great deal more. Fancy! Is it true?'

'Yes. And he was brought up so well, and sent to Casterbridge Grammar School for years and years. Learnt all languages while he was there; and it was said he got on so far that he could take down Chinese in shorthand; but that I don't answer for, as it was only reported. However, he wasted his gifted lot, and listed a soldier; but even then he rose to be a sergeant without trying at all Ah! such a blessing it is to be high-born; nobility of blood will shine out even in the ranks and files. And is he really come home, miss?'

'I believe so. Good-night, Liddy.'

After all, how could a cheerful wearer of skirts be permanently offended with the man? There are occasions when girls like Bathsheba will put up with a great deal of unconventional behaviour. When they want to be praised, which is often; when they want to be mastered, which is sometimes; and when they want no nonsense, which is seldom. Just now the first feeling was in the ascendant with Bathsheba, with a dash of the second. Moreover, by chance or by devilry, the ministrant was antecedently made interesting by being a handsome stranger who had evidently seen better days.

So she could not clearly decide whether it was her opinion that he had insulted her or not.

'Was ever anything so odd!' she at last exclaimed to herself, in her own room. 'And was ever anything so meanly done as what I did – to skulk away like that from a man who was only civil and kind!' Clearly she did not think his barefaced praise of her person an insult now.

It was a fatal omission of Boldwood's that he had never once told her she was beautiful.

CHAPTER TWENTY-FIVE

The New Acquaintance described

IDIOSYNCRASY and vicissitude had combined to stamp Sergeant Troy as an exceptional being.

He was a man to whom memories were an incumbrance, and anticipations a superfluity. Simply feeling, considering, and caring for what was before his eyes, he was vulnerable only in the present. His outlook upon time was as a transient flash of the eye now and then: that projection of consciousness into days gone by and to come, which makes the past a synonym for the pathetic and the future a word for circumspection, was foreign to Troy. With him the past was yesterday; the future, to-morrow; never, the day after.

On this account he might, in certain lights, have been regarded as one of the most fortunate of his order. For it may be argued with great plausibility that reminiscence is less an endowment than a disease, and that expectation in its only comfortable form – that of absolute faith – is practically an impossibility; whilst in the form of hope and the secondary compounds, patience, impatience, resolve, curiosity, it is a constant fluctuation between pleasure and pain.

Sergeant Troy, being entirely innocent of the practice of expectation, was never disappointed. To set against this negative gain there may have been some positive losses from a certain narrowing of the higher tastes and sensations which it entailed. But limitation of the capacity is never recognized as a loss by the loser therefrom: in this attribute moral or æsthetic poverty contrasts plausibly with material, since those who suffer do not mind it, whilst those who mind it soon cease to suffer. It is not a denial of anything to have been always without it, and what Troy had never enjoyed he did not miss; but, being fully conscious that what sober people missed he enjoyed, his capacity, though really less, seemed greater than theirs.

He was moderately truthful towards men, but to women lied like a Cretan – a system of ethics above all others calculated to win popularity at the first flush of admission into lively society; and the possibility of the favour gained being transitory had reference only to the future.

He never passed the line which divides the spruce vices from the ugly; and hence, though his morals had hardly been applauded, disapproval of them had frequently been tempered with a smile. This treatment had led to his becoming a sort of regrater of other men's gallantries, to his own aggrandizement as a Corinthian, rather than to the moral profit of his hearers.

His reason and his propensities had seldom any reciprocating influence, having separated by mutual consent long ago: thence it sometimes happened that, while his intentions were as honourable as could be wished, any particular deed formed a dark background which threw them into fine relief. The sergeant's vicious phases being the offspring of impulse, and his virtuous phases of cool meditation, the latter had a modest tendency to be oftener heard of than seen.

Troy was full of activity, but his activities were less of a locomotive than a vegetative nature; and, never being based upon any original choice of foundation or direction, they were exercised on whatever object chance might place in their way. Hence, whilst he sometimes reached the brilliant in speech because that was spontaneous, he fell below the commonplace in action, from inability to guide incipient effort. He had a quick comprehension and considerable force of character; but, being without the power to combine them, the comprehension became engaged with trivialities whilst waiting for the will to direct it, and the force wasted itself in useless grooves through unheeding the comprehension.

He was a fairly well-educated man for one of middle class – exceptionally well educated for a common soldier. He spoke fluently and unceasingly. He could in this way be one thing and seem another; for instance, he could speak of love and think of dinner; call on the husband to look at the wife; be eager to pay and intend to owe.

The wondrous power of flattery in *passados* at woman is a perception so universal as to be remarked upon by many people almost as automatically as they repeat a proverb, or say that they are Christians and the like, without thinking much of the enormous corollaries which spring from the proposition. Still less is it acted upon for the good of the complemental being alluded to. With the majority such an opinion is shelved with all those trite aphorisms which require some catastrophe to bring their tremendous meanings thoroughly home. When expressed with some amount of reflectiveness it seems co-ordinate with a belief that this flattery must be reasonable to be effective. It is to the credit of men that few attempt to settle the question by experiment, and it is for their happiness, perhaps, that accident has never settled it for them. Nevertheless, that a male dissembler who by deluging her with untenable fictions charms the female wisely, may acquire powers reaching to the extremity of perdition, is a truth taught to many by unsought and wringing occurrences. And some profess to have attained to the same knowledge by experiment as aforesaid, and jauntily continue their indulgence in such experiments with terrible effect. Sergeant Troy was one.

He had been known to observe casually that in dealing with womankind the only alternative to flattery was cursing and swearing. There was no third method. 'Treat them fairly, and you are a lost man,' he would say.

This philosopher's public appearance in Weatherbury promptly followed his arrival there. A week or two after the shearing Bathsheba, feeling a nameless relief of spirits on account of Boldwood's absence, approached her hayfields and looked over the hedge towards the haymakers. They consisted in about equal proportions of gnarled and flexuous forms, the former being the men, the latter the women, who wore tilt bonnets covered with nankeen, which hung in a curtain upon their shoulders. Coggan and Mark Clark were mowing in a less forward meadow, Clark humming a tune to the strokes of his scythe, to which Jan made no attempt to keep time with his. In the first mead they were already loading hay, the women raking it into cocks and windrows, and the men tossing it upon the waggon.

From behind the waggon a bright scarlet spot emerged, and went on loading unconcernedly with the rest. It was the gallant sergeant, who had come haymaking for pleasure; and nobody could deny that he was doing the mistress of the farm real knight-service by this voluntary contribution of his labour at a busy time.

As soon as she had entered the field Troy saw her, and sticking his pitchfork into the ground and picking up his crop or cane, he came forward. Bathsheba blushed with half-angry embarrassment, and adjusted her eyes as well as her feet to the direct line of her path.

CHAPTER TWENTY-SIX

Scene on the Verge of the Hay-mead

'A h, Miss Everdene!' said the sergeant, touching his diminutive cap. 'Little did I think it was you I was speaking to the other night. And yet, if I had reflected, the "Queen of the Corn-market" (truth is truth at any hour of the day or night, and I heard you so named in Casterbridge yesterday), the "Queen of the Corn-market", I say, could be no other woman. I step across now to beg your forgiveness a thousand times for having been led by my feelings to express myself too strongly for a stranger. To be sure I am no stranger to the place – I am Sergeant Troy, as I told you, and I have assisted your uncle in these fields no end of times when I was a lad. I have been doing the same for you to-day.'

'I suppose I must thank you for that, Sergeant Troy,' said the Queen of the Corn-market in an indifferently grateful tone.

The sergeant looked hurt and sad. 'Indeed you must not, Miss Everdene,' he said. 'Why could you think such a thing necessary?'

'I am glad it is not.'

'Why? if I may ask without offence.'

'Because I don't much want to thank you for anything.'

'I am afraid I have made a hole in my tongue that my heart will never mend. O these intolerable times: that ill-luck should follow a man for honestly telling a woman she is beautiful! 'Twas the most I said – you must own that; and the least I could say – that I own myself.'

'There is some talk I could do without more easily than money.'

'Indeed. That remark is a sort of digression.'

'No. It means that I would rather have your room than your company.'

'And I would rather have curses from you than kisses from any other woman; so I'll stay here.'

Bathsheba was absolutely speechless. And yet she could not help feeling that the assistance he was rendering forbade a harsh repulse.

'Well,' continued Troy, 'I suppose there is a praise which is rudeness, and that may be mine. At the same time there is a treatment which is injustice, and that may be yours. Because a plain blunt man, who has never been taught concealment, speaks out his mind without exactly intending it, he's to be snapped off like the son of a sinner.'

'Indeed there's no such case between us,' she said, turning away. 'I don't allow strangers to be bold and impudent – even in praise of me.'

'Ah – it is not the fact but the method which offends you,' he said carelessly. 'But I have the sad satisfaction of knowing that my words, whether pleasing or offensive, are unmistakably true. Would you have had me look at you, and tell my acquaintance that you are quite a common-place woman, to save you the embarrassment of being stared at if they come near you? Not I. I couldn't tell any such ridiculous lie about a beauty to encourage a single woman in England in too excessive a modesty.'

'It is all pretence – what you are saying!' exclaimed Bathsheba, laughing in spite of herself at the sergeant's sly method. 'You have a rare invention, Sergeant Troy. Why couldn't you have passed by me that night, and said nothing? – that was all I meant to reproach you for.'

'Because I wasn't going to. Half the pleasure of a feeling lies in being able to express it on the spur of the moment, and I let out mine. It would have been just the same if you had been the reverse person – ugly and old – I should have exclaimed about it in the same way.'

'How long is it since you have been so afflicted with strong feeling, then?'

'Oh, ever since I was big enough to know loveliness from deformity.'

' 'Tis to be hoped your sense of the difference you speak of doesn't stop at faces, but extends to morals as well.'

'I won't speak of morals or religion – my own or anybody else's. Though perhaps I should have been a very good Christian if you pretty women hadn't made me an idolater.'

Bathsheba moved on to hide the irrepressible dimplings of merriment. Troy followed, whirling his crop.

'But – Miss Everdene – you do forgive me?'

'Hardly.'

'Why?'

'You say such things.'

'I said you were beautiful, and I'll say so still, for, by – so you are! The most beautiful ever I saw, or may I fall dead this instant! Why, upon my—'

'Don't – don't! I won't listen to you – you are so profane!' she said, in a restless state between distress at hearing him and a *penchant* to hear more.

'I again say you are a most fascinating woman. There's nothing remarkable in my saying so, is there? I'm sure the fact is evident enough. Miss Everdene, my opinion may be too forcibly let out to please you, and, for the matter of that, too insignificant to convince you, but surely it is honest, and why can't it be excused?'

'Because it – it isn't a correct one,' she femininely murmured.

'O, fie – fie! Am I any worse for breaking the third of that Terrible Ten than you for breaking the ninth?'

'Well, it doesn't seem *quite* true to me that I am fascinating,' she replied evasively.

'Not so to you: then I say with all respect that, if so, it is owing to your modesty, Miss Everdene. But surely you must have been told by everybody of what everybody notices? And you should take their words for it.'

'They don't say so exactly.'

'O yes, they must!'

'Well, I mean to my face, as you do,' she went on, allowing herself to be further lured into a conversation that intention had rigorously forbidden.

'But you know they think so?'

'No — that is — I certainly have heard Liddy say they do, but—' She paused.

Capitulation — that was the purport of the simple reply, guarded as it was — capitulation, unknown to herself. Never did a fragile tailless sentence convey a more perfect meaning. The careless sergeant smiled within himself, and probably too the devil smiled from a loop-hole in Tophet, for the moment was the turning-point of a career. Her tone and mien signified beyond mistake that the seed which was to lift the foundation had taken root in the chink: the remainder was a mere question of time and natural changes.

'There the truth comes out!' said the soldier, in reply. 'Never tell me that a young lady can live in a buzz of admiration without knowing something about it. Ah, well, Miss Everdene, you are — pardon my blunt way — you are rather an injury to our race than otherwise.'

'How — indeed?' she said, opening her eyes.

'O, it is true enough. I may as well be hung for a sheep as a lamb (an old country saying, not of much account, but it will do for a rough soldier), and so I will speak my mind, regardless of your pleasure, and without hoping or intending to get your pardon. Why, Miss Everdene, it is in this manner that your good looks may do more harm than good in the world.' The sergeant looked down the mead in critical abstraction. 'Probably some one man on an average falls in love with each ordinary woman. She can marry him: he is content, and leads a useful life. Such women as you a hundred men always covet — your eyes will bewitch scores on scores into an unavailing fancy for you — you can only marry one of that many. Out of these say twenty will endeavour to drown the bitterness of despised love in drink; twenty more will mope away their lives without a wish or attempt to make a mark in the world, because they have no ambition apart from their attachment to you; twenty more — the susceptible person myself possibly among them — will be always draggling after you, getting where they may just see you, doing desperate things. Men are such constant fools! The rest may try to get over their passion with more or less success. But all these men will be saddened. And not only those ninety-nine men, but the ninety-nine women they might have married are saddened with them. There's my tale. That's why I say that a woman so charming as yourself, Miss Everdene, is hardly a blessing to her race.'

The handsome sergeant's features were during this speech as rigid and stern as John Knox's in addressing his gay young queen.

Seeing she made no reply, he said, 'Do you read French?'

'No; I began, but when I got to the verbs, father died,' she said simply.

'I do — when I have an opportunity, which latterly has not been often (my mother was a Parisienne) — and there's a proverb they have, *Qui aime bien châtie bien* — "He chastens who loves well." Do you understand me?'

'Ah!' she replied, and there was even a little tremulousness in the usually cool girl's voice; 'if you can only fight half as winningly as you can talk, you are able to make a pleasure of a bayonet wound!' And then poor Bathsheba instantly perceived her slip in making this admission: in hastily trying to retrieve it, she went from bad to worse. 'Don't, however, suppose that *I* derive any pleasure from what you tell me.'

'I know you do not – I know it perfectly,' said Troy, with much hearty conviction on the exterior of his face: and altering the expression to moodiness; 'when a dozen men are ready to speak tenderly to you, and give the admiration you deserve without adding the warning you need, it stands to reason that my poor rough-and-ready mixture of praise and blame cannot convey much pleasure. Fool as I may be, I am not so conceited as to suppose that!'

'I think you – are conceited, nevertheless,' said Bathsheba, looking askance at a reed she was fitfully pulling with one hand, having lately grown feverish under the soldier's system of procedure – not because the nature of his cajolery was entirely unperceived, but because its vigour was overwhelming.

'I would not own it to anybody else – nor do I exactly to you. Still, there might have been some self-conceit in my foolish supposition the other night. I knew that what I said in admiration might be an opinion too often forced upon you to give any pleasure, but I certainly did think that the kindness of your nature might prevent you judging an uncontrolled tongue harshly – which you have done – and thinking badly of me and wounding me this morning, when I am working hard to save your hay.'

'Well, you need not think more of that: perhaps you did not mean to be rude to me by speaking out your mind: indeed, I believe you did not,' said the shrewd woman, in painfully innocent earnest. 'And I thank you for giving help here. But – but mind you don't speak to me again in that way, or in any other, unless I speak to you.'

'O Miss Bathsheba! That is too hard!'

'No, it isn't. Why is it?'

'You will never speak to me; for I shall not be here long. I am soon going back again to the miserable monotony of drill – and perhaps our regiment will be ordered out soon. And yet you take away the one little ewe-lamb of pleasure that I have in this dull life of mine. Well, perhaps generosity is not a woman's most marked characteristic.'

'When are you going from here?' she asked with some interest.

'In a month.'

'But how can it give you pleasure to speak to me?'

'Can you ask, Miss Everdene – knowing as you do – what my offence is based on?'

'If you do care so much for a silly trifle of that kind, then, I don't mind doing it,' she uncertainly and doubtingly answered. 'But you can't really care for a word from me? you only say so – I think you only say so.'

'That's unjust – but I won't repeat the remark. I am too gratified to get such a mark of your friendship at any price to cavil at the tone. I *do*, Miss Everdene, care for it. You may think a man foolish to want a mere word – just a good morning. Perhaps he is – I don't know. But you have never been a man looking upon a woman, and that woman yourself.'

'Well.'

'Then you know nothing of what such an experience is like – and Heaven forbid that you ever should!'

'Nonsense, flatterer! What is it like? I am interested in knowing.'

'Put shortly, it is not being able to think, hear, or look in any direction except one without wretchedness, nor there without torture.'

'Ah, sergeant, it won't do – you are pretending!' she said, shaking her head. 'Your words are too dashing to be true.'

'I am not, upon the honour of a soldier.'

'But *why* is it so? – Of course I ask for mere pastime.'

'Because you are so distracting – and I am so distracted.'

'You look like it.'

'I am indeed.'

'Why, you only saw me the other night!'

'That makes no difference. The lightning works instantaneously. I loved you then, at once – as I do now.'

Bathsheba surveyed him curiously, from the feet upward, as high as she liked to venture her glance, which was not quite so high as his eyes.

'You cannot and you don't,' she said demurely. 'There is no such sudden feeling in people. I won't listen to you any longer. Dear me, I wish I knew what o'clock it is – I am going – I have wasted too much time here already!'

The sergeant looked at his watch and told her. 'What, haven't you a watch, miss?' he inquired.

'I have not just at present – I am about to get a new one.'

'No. You shall be given one. Yes – you shall. A gift, Miss Everdene – a gift.'

And before she knew what the young man was intending, a heavy gold watch was in her hand.

'It is an unusually good one for a man like me to possess,' he quietly said. 'That watch has a history. Press the spring and open the back.'

She did so.

'What do you see?'

'A crest and a motto.'

'A coronet with five points, and beneath, *Cedit amor rebus* – "Love yields to circumstance." It's the motto of the Earls of Severn. That watch belonged to the last lord, and was given to my mother's husband, a medical man, for his use till I came of age, when it was to be given to me. It was all the fortune that ever I inherited. That watch has regulated imperial interests in its time – the stately ceremonial, the courtly assignation, pompous travels, and lordly sleeps. Now it is yours.'

'But, Sergeant Troy, I cannot take this – I cannot!' she exclaimed with round-eyed wonder. 'A gold watch! What are you doing? Don't be such a dissembler!'

The sergeant retreated to avoid receiving back his gift, which she held out persistently towards him. Bathsheba followed as he retired.

'Keep it – do, Miss Everdene – keep it!' said the erratic child of impulse. 'The fact of your possessing it makes it worth ten times as much to me. A more plebeian one will answer my purpose just as well, and the pleasure of knowing whose heart my old one beats against – well, I won't speak of that. It is in far worthier hands than ever it has been in before.'

'But indeed I can't have it!' she said, in a perfect simmer of distress. 'O, how can you do such a thing; that is, if you really mean it! Give me your dead father's watch, and such a valuable one! You should not be so reckless, indeed, Sergeant Troy!'

'I loved my father: good; but better, I love you more. That's how I can do it,' said the sergeant with an intonation of such exquisite fidelity to nature that it was evidently not all acted now. Her beauty, which, whilst it had been quiescent, he had praised in jest, had in its animated phases moved him to earnest; and though his seriousness was less than she imagined, it was probably more than he imagined himself.

Bathsheba was brimming with agitated bewilderment, and she said, in half-suspicious accents of feeling, 'Can it be! O, how can it be, that you care for me, and so suddenly! You have seen so little of me: I may not be really so — so nice-looking as I seem to you. Please, do take it; O, do! I cannot and will not have it. Believe me, your generosity is too great. I have never done you a single kindness, and why should you be so kind to me?'

A factitious reply had been again upon his lips, but it was again suspended, and he looked at her with an arrested eye. The truth was, that as she now stood — excited, wild, and honest as the day — her alluring beauty bore out so fully the epithets he had bestowed upon it that he was quite startled at his temerity in advancing them as false. He said mechanically, 'Ah, why?' and continued to look at her.

'And my workfolk see me following you about the field, and are wondering. O, this is dreadful!' she went on, unconscious of the transmutation she was effecting.

'I did not quite mean you to accept it at first, for it was my one poor patent of nobility,' he broke out bluntly; 'but, upon my soul, I wish you would now. Without any shamming, come! Don't deny me the happiness of wearing it for my sake? But you are too lovely even to care to be kind as others are.'

'No, no; don't say so! I have reasons for reserve which I cannot explain.'

'Let it be, then, let it be,' he said, receiving back the watch at last; 'I must be leaving you now. And will you speak to me for these few weeks of my stay?'

'Indeed I will. Yet, I don't know if I will! O, why did you come and disturb me so!'

'Perhaps in setting a gin, I have caught myself. Such things have happened. Well, will you let me work in your fields?' he coaxed.

'Yes, I suppose so; if it is any pleasure to you.'

'Miss Everdene, I thank you.'

'No, no.'

'Good-bye!'

The sergeant brought his hand to the cap on the slope of his head, saluted, and returned to the distant group of haymakers.

Bathsheba could not face the haymakers now. Her heart erratically flitting hither and thither from perplexed excitement, hot, and almost tearful, she retreated homeward, murmuring, 'O, what have I done! What does it mean! I wish I knew how much of it was true!'

CHAPTER TWENTY-SEVEN

Hiving the Bees

T HE Weatherbury bees were late in their swarming this year. It was in the latter part of June, and the day after the interview with Troy in the hayfeld, that Bathsheba was standing in her garden, watching a swarm in the air and guessing their probable settling place. Not only were they late this year, but unruly. Sometimes throughout a whole season all the swarms would alight on the lowest attainable bough – such as part of a currant-bush or espalier apple-tree; next year they would, with just the same unanimity, make straight off to the uppermost member of some tall, gaunt costard, or quarrenden, and there defy all invaders who did not come armed with ladders and staves to take them.

This was the case at present. Bathsheba's eyes, shaded by one hand, were following the ascending multitude against the unexplorable stretch of blue till they ultimately halted by one of the unwieldy trees spoken of. A process somewhat analogous to that of alleged formations of the universe, time and times ago, was observable. The bustling swarm had swept the sky in a scattered and uniform haze, which now thickened to a nebulous centre: this glided on to a bough and grew still denser, till it formed a solid black spot upon the light.

The men and women being all busily engaged in saving the hay – even Liddy had left the house for the purpose of lending a hand – Bathsheba resolved to hive the bees herself, if possible. She had dressed the hive with herbs and honey, fetched a ladder, brush, and crook, made herself impregnable with armour of leather gloves, straw hat, and large gauze veil – once green but now faded to snuff colour – and ascended a dozen rungs of the ladder. At once she heard, not ten yards off, a voice that was beginning to have a strange power in agitating her.

'Miss Everdene, let me assist you; you should not attempt such a thing alone.'

Troy was just opening the garden gate.

Bathsheba flung down the brush, crook, and empty hive, pulled the skirt of her dress tightly round her ankles in a tremendous flurry, and as well as she could slid down the ladder. By the time she reached the bottom Troy was there also, and he stooped to pick up the hive.

'How fortunate I am to have dropped in at this moment!' exclaimed the sergeant.

She found her voice in a minute. 'What! and will you shake them in for me?' she asked, in what, for a defiant girl, was a faltering way; though, for a timid girl, it would have seemed a brave way enough.

'Will I!' said Troy. 'Why of course I will. How blooming you are to-day!' Troy flung down his cane and put his foot on the ladder to ascend.

'But you must have on the veil and gloves, or you'll be stung fearfully!'

'Ah, yes. I must put on the veil and gloves. Will you kindly show me how to fix them properly?'

'And you must have the broad-brimmed hat, too; for your cap has no brim to keep the veil off, and they'd reach your face.'

'The broad-brimmed hat, too, by all means.'

So a whimsical fate ordered that her hat should be taken off – veil and all attached – and placed upon his head, Troy tossing his own into a gooseberry bush. Then the veil had to be tied at its lower edge round his collar and the gloves put on him.

He looked such an extraordinary object in this guise that, flurried as she was, she could not avoid laughing outright. It was the removal of yet another stake from the palisade of cold manners which had kept him off.

Bathsheba looked on from the ground whilst he was busy sweeping and shaking the bees from the tree, holding up the hive with the other hand for them to fall into. She made use of an unobserved minute whilst his attention was absorbed in the operation to arrange her plumes a little. He came down holding the hive at arm's length, behind which trailed a cloud of bees.

'Upon my life,' said Troy, through the veil, 'holding up this hive makes one's arm ache worse than a week of sword-exercise.' When the manœuvre was complete he approached her. 'Would you be good enough to untie me and let me out? I am nearly stifled inside this silk cage.'

To hide her embarrassment during the unwonted process of untying the string about his neck, she said: –

'I have never seen that you spoke of.'

'What?'

'The sword-exercise.'

'Ah! would you like to?' said Troy.

Bathsheba hesitated. She had heard wondrous reports from time to time by dwellers in Weatherbury, who had by chance sojourned awhile in Casterbridge, near the barracks, of this strange and glorious performance, the sword-exercise. Men and boys who had peeped through chinks or over walls into the barrack-yard returned with accounts of its being the most flashing affair conceivable; accoutrements and weapons glistening like stars – here, there, around – yet all by rule and compass. So she said mildly what she felt strongly:

'Yes; I should like to see it very much.'

'And so you shall; you shall see me go through it.'

'No! How?'

'Let me consider.'

'Not with a walking-stick – I don't care to see that. It must be a real sword.'

'Yes, I know; and I have no sword here; but I think I could get one by the evening. Now, will you do this?'

Troy bent over her and murmured some suggestion in a low voice.

'O no, indeed!' said Bathsheba, blushing. 'Thank you very much, but I couldn't on any account.'

'Surely you might? Nobody would know.'

She shook her head, but with a weakened negation. 'If I were to,' she said, 'I must bring Liddy too. Might I not?'

Troy looked far away. 'I don't see why you want to bring her,' he said coldly.

An unconscious look of assent in Bathsheba's eyes betrayed that something more than his coldness had made her also feel that Liddy would be superfluous in the suggested scene. She had felt it, even whilst making the proposal.

'Well, I won't bring Liddy – and I'll come. But only for a very short time,' she added; 'a very short time.'

'It will not take five minutes,' said Troy.

CHAPTER TWENTY-EIGHT

The Hollow amid the Ferns

T HE hill opposite Bathsheba's dwelling extended, a mile off, into an uncultivated tract of land, dotted at this season with tall thickets of brake fern, plump and diaphanous from recent rapid growth, and radiant in hues of clear and untainted green.

At eight o'clock this midsummer evening, whilst the bristling ball of gold in the west still swept the tips of the ferns with its long, luxuriant rays, a soft brushing-by of garments might have been heard among them, and Bathsheba appeared in their midst, their soft, feathery arms caressing her up to her shoulders. She paused, turned, went back over the hill and half-way to her own door, whence she cast a farewell glance upon the spot she had just left, having resolved not to remain near the place after all.

She saw a dim spot of artificial red moving round the shoulder of the rise. It disappeared on the other side.

She waited one minute – two minutes – thought of Troy's disappointment at her non-fulfilment of a promised engagement, till she again ran along the field, clambered over the bank, and followed the original direction. She was now literally trembling and panting at this her temerity in such an errant undertaking; her breath came and went quickly, and her eyes shone with an infrequent light. Yet go she must. She reached the verge of a pit in the middle of the ferns. Troy stood in the bottom, looking up towards her.

'I heard you rustling through the fern before I saw you,' he said, coming up and giving her his hand to help her down the slope.

The pit was a saucer-shaped concave, naturally formed, with a top diameter of about thirty feet, and shallow enough to allow the sunshine to reach their heads. Standing in the centre, the sky overhead was met by a circular horizon of fern: this grew nearly to the bottom of the slope and then abruptly ceased. The middle within the belt of verdure was floored with a thick flossy carpet of moss and grass intermingled, so yielding that the foot was half-buried within it.

'Now,' said Troy, producing the sword, which, as he raised it into the sunlight, gleamed a sort of greeting, like a living thing; 'first, we have four right and four left cuts; four right and four left thrusts. Infantry cuts and guards are more interesting than ours, to my mind; but they are not so swashing. They have seven cuts and three thrusts. So much as a preliminary. Well, next, our cut one is as if you were sowing your corn – so.' Bathsheba saw a sort of rainbow, upside down in the air, and Troy's arm was still again. 'Cut two, as if you were hedging – so. Three, as if you were reaping – so. Four, as if you were threshing – in that way. Then the same on the left. The thrusts are these: one, two, three, four, right; one, two, three, four, left.' He repeated them. 'Have 'em again?' he said. 'One, two—'

She hurriedly interrupted: 'I'd rather not; though I don't mind your twos and fours; but your ones and threes are terrible!'

'Very well. I'll let you off the ones and threes. Next, cuts, points and guards altogether.' Troy duly exhibited them. 'Then there's pursuing practice, in this way.' He gave the movements as before. 'There, those are the stereotyped forms. The infantry have two most diabolical upward cuts, which we are too humane to use. Like this – three, four.'

'How murderous and bloodthirsty!'

'They are rather deathy. Now I'll be more interesting, and let you see some loose play – giving all the cuts and points, infantry and cavalry, quicker than lightning, and as promiscuously – with just enough rule to regulate instinct and yet not to fetter it. You are my antagonist, with this difference from real warfare, that I shall miss you every time by one hair's breadth, or perhaps two. Mind you don't flinch, whatever you do.'

'I'll be sure not to!' she said invincibly.

He pointed to about a yard in front of him.

Bathsheba's adventurous spirit was beginning to find some grains of relish in these highly novel proceedings. She took up her position as directed, facing Troy.

'Now just to learn whether you have pluck enough to let me do what I wish, I'll give you a preliminary test.'

He flourished the sword by way of introduction number two, and the next thing of which she was conscious was that the point and blade of the sword were darting with a gleam towards her left side, just above her hip; then of their reappearance on her right side, emerging as it were from between her ribs, having apparently passed through her body. The third item of consciousness was that of seeing the same sword, perfectly clean and free from blood held vertically in Troy's hand (in the position technically called 'recover swords'). All was as quick as electricity.

'Oh!' she cried out in affright, pressing her hand to her side. 'Have you run me through? – no, you have not! Whatever have you done!'

'I have not touched you,' said Troy quietly. 'It was mere sleight of hand. The sword passed behind you. Now you are not afraid, are you? Because if you are I can't perform. I give my word that I will not only not hurt you, but not once touch you.'

'I don't think I am afraid. You are quite sure you will not hurt me?'

'Quite sure.'

'Is the sword very sharp?'

'O no – only stand as still as a statue. Now!'

In an instant the atmosphere was transformed to Bathsheba's eyes. Beams of light caught from the low sun's rays, above, around, in front of her, well-nigh shut out earth and heaven – all emitted in the marvellous evolutions of Troy's reflecting blade, which seemed everywhere at once, and yet nowhere specially.

These circling gleams were accompanied by a keen rush that was almost a whistling – also springing from all sides of her at once. In short, she was enclosed in a firmament of light, and of sharp hisses, resembling a sky-full of meteors close at hand.

Never since the broadsword became the national weapon had there been more dexterity shown in its management than by the hands of Sergeant Troy, and never had he been in such splendid temper for the performance as now in the evening sunshine among the ferns with Bathsheba. It may safely be asserted with respect to the closeness of his cuts, that had it been possible for the edge of the sword to leave in the air a permanent substance wherever it flew past, the space left untouched would have been almost a mould of Bathsheba's figure.

Behind the luminous streams of this *aurora militaris*, she could see the hue of Troy's sword arm, spread in a scarlet haze over the space covered by its motions, like a twanged harpstring, and behind all Troy himself, mostly facing her; sometimes, to show the rear cuts, half turned away, his eye nevertheless always keenly measuring her breadth and outline, and his lips tightly closed in sustained effort. Next, his movements lapsed slower, and she could see them individually. The hissing of the sword had ceased, and he stopped entirely.

'That outer loose lock of hair wants tidying,' he said, before she had moved or spoken. 'Wait: I'll do it for you.'

An arc of silver shone on her right side: the sword had descended. The lock dropped to the ground.

'Bravely borne!' said Troy. 'You didn't flinch a shade's thickness. Wonderful in a woman!'

'It was because I didn't expect it. O, you have spoilt my hair!'

'Only once more.'

'No – no! I am afraid of you – indeed I am!' she cried.

'I won't touch you at all – not even your hair. I am only going to kill that caterpillar settling on you. Now: still!'

It appeared that a caterpillar had come from the fern and chosen the front of her bodice as his resting place. She saw the point glisten towards her bosom, and seemingly enter it. Bathsheba closed her eyes in the full persuasion that she was killed at last. However, feeling just as usual, she opened them again.

'There it is, look,' said the sergeant, holding his sword before her eyes.

The caterpillar was spitted upon its point.

'Why, it is magic!' said Bathsheba, amazed.

'O no – dexterity. I merely gave point to your bosom where the caterpillar was, and instead of running you through checked the extension a thousandth of an inch short of your surface.'

'But how could you chop off a curl of my hair with a sword that has no edge?'

'No edge! This sword will shave like a razor. Look here.'

He touched the palm of his hand with the blade, and then lifting it, showed her a thin shaving of scarf-skin dangling therefrom.

'But you said before beginning that it was blunt and couldn't cut me!'

'That was to get you to stand still, and so make sure of your safety. The risk of injuring you through your moving was too great not to force me to tell you a fib to escape it.'

She shuddered. 'I have been within an inch of my life, and didn't know it!'

'More precisely speaking, you have been within half an inch of being pared alive two hundred and ninety-five times.'

'Cruel, cruel, 'tis of you!'

'You have been perfectly safe, nevertheless. My sword never errs.' And Troy returned the weapon to the scabbard.

Bathsheba, overcome by a hundred tumultuous feelings resulting from the scene, abstractedly sat down on a tuft of heather.

'I must leave you now,' said Troy softly. 'And I'll venture to take and keep this in remembrance of you.'

She saw him stoop to the grass, pick up the winding lock which he had severed from her manifold tresses, twist it round his fingers, unfasten a button in the breast of his coat, and carefully put it inside. She felt powerless to withstand or deny him. He was altogether too much for her, and Bathsheba seemed as one who, facing a reviving wind, finds it blow so strongly that it stops the breath.

He drew near and said, 'I must be leaving you.' He drew nearer still. A minute later and she saw his scarlet form disappear amid the ferny thicket, almost in a flash, like a brand swiftly waved.

That minute's interval had brought the blood beating into her face, set her stinging as if aflame to the very hollows of her feet, and enlarged emotion to a compass which quite swamped thought. It had brought upon her a stroke resulting, as did that of Moses in Horeb, in a liquid stream – here a stream of tears. She felt like one who has sinned a great sin.

The circumstance had been the gentle dip of Troy's mouth downwards upon her own. He had kissed her.

CHAPTER TWENTY-NINE

Particulars of a Twilight Walk

WE now see the element of folly distinctly mingling with the many varying particulars which made up the character of Bathsheba Everdene. It was almost foreign to her intrinsic nature. Introduced as lymph on the dart of Eros it eventually permeated and coloured her whole constitution. Bathsheba, though she had too much understanding to be entirely governed by her womanliness, had too much womanliness to use her understanding to the best advantage. Perhaps in no minor point does woman astonish her helpmate more than in the strange power she possesses of believing cajoleries that she knows to be false – except, indeed, in that of being utterly sceptical on strictures that she knows to be true.

Bathsheba loved Troy in the way that only self-reliant women love when they abandon their self-reliance. When a strong woman recklessly throws away her strength she is worse than a weak woman who has never had any strength to throw away. One source of her inadequacy is the novelty of the occasion. She has never had practice in making the best of such a condition. Weakness is doubly weak by being new.

Bathsheba was not conscious of guile in this matter. Though in one sense a woman of the world, it was, after all, that world of daylight coteries and green carpets wherein cattle form the passing crowd and winds the busy hum; where a quiet family of rabbits or hares lives on the other side of your party-wall, where your neighbour is everybody in the tything, and where calculation is confined to market-days. Of the fabricated tastes of good fashionable society she knew but little, and of the formulated self-indulgence of bad, nothing at all. Had her utmost thoughts in this direction been distinctly worded (and by herself they never were), they would only have amounted to such a matter as that she felt her impulses to be pleasanter guides than her discretion. Her love was entire as a child's, and though warm as summer it was fresh as spring. Her culpability lay in her making no attempt to control feeling by subtle and careful inquiry into consequences. She could show others the steep and thorny way, but 'reck'd not her own rede'.

And Troy's deformities lay deep down from a woman's vision, whilst his embellishments were upon the very surface; thus contrasting with homely Oak, whose defects were patent to the blindest, and whose virtues were as metals in a mine.

The difference between love and respect was markedly shown in her conduct. Bathsheba had spoken of her interest in Boldwood with the greatest freedom to Liddy, but she had only communed with her own heart concerning Troy.

All this infatuation Gabriel saw, and was troubled thereby from the time of his daily journey a-field to the time of his return, and on to the small hours of many a night. That he was not beloved had hitherto been his great sorrow; that Bathsheba was getting into the toils was now a sorrow greater than the first, and one which nearly obscured it. It was a result which paralleled the oft-quoted observation of Hippocrates concerning physical pains.

That is a noble though perhaps an unpromising love which not even the fear of breeding aversion in the bosom of the one beloved can deter from combating his or her errors. Oak determined to speak to his mistress. He would base his appeal on what he considered her unfair treatment of Farmer Boldwood, now absent from home.

An opportunity occurred one evening when she had gone for a short walk by a path through the neighbouring cornfields. It was dusk when Oak, who had not been far a-field that day, took the same path and met her returning, quite pensively, as he thought.

The wheat was now tall, and the path was narrow; thus the way was quite a sunken groove between the embowing thicket on either side. Two persons could not walk abreast without damaging the crop, and Oak stood aside to let her pass.

'Oh, is it Gabriel?' she said. 'You are taking a walk too. Good-night.'

'I thought I would come to meet you, as it is rather late,' said Oak, turning and following at her heels when she had brushed somewhat quickly by him.

'Thank you, indeed, but I am not very fearful.'

'O no; but there are bad characters about.'

'I never meet them.'

Now Oak, with marvellous ingenuity, had been going to introduce the gallant sergeant through the channel of 'bad characters'. But all at once the scheme broke down, it suddenly occurring to him that this was rather a clumsy way, and too barefaced to begin with. He tried another preamble.

'And as the man who would naturally come to meet you is away from home, too – I mean Farmer Boldwood – why, thinks I, I'll go,' he said.

'Ah, yes.' She walked on without turning her head, and for many steps nothing further was heard from her quarter than the rustle of her dress against the heavy corn-ears. Then she resumed rather tartly –

'I don't quite understand what you meant by saying that Mr Boldwood would naturally come to meet me.'

'I meant on account of the wedding which they say is likely to take place between you and him, miss. Forgive my speaking plainly.'

'They say what is not true,' she returned quickly. 'No marriage is likely to take place between us.'

Gabriel now put forth his unobscured opinion, for the moment had come. 'Well, Miss Everdene,' he said, 'putting aside what people say, I never in my life saw any courting if his is not a courting of you.'

Bathsheba would probably have terminated the conversation there and then by flatly forbidding the subject, had not her conscious weakness of position allured her to palter and argue in endeavours to better it.

'Since this subject has been mentioned,' she said very emphatically, 'I am glad of the opportunity of clearing up a mistake which is very common and very provoking. I didn't definitely promise Mr Boldwood anything. I have never cared for him. I respect him, and he has urged me to marry him. But I have given him no distinct answer. As soon as he returns I shall do so; and the answer will be that I cannot think of marrying him.'

'People are full of mistakes, seemingly.'

'They are.'

'The other day they said you were trifling with him, and you almost proved that you were not; lately they have said that you be not, and you straightway begin to show—'

'That I am, I suppose you mean.'

'Well, I hope they speak the truth.'

'They do, but wrongly applied. I don't trifle with him; but then, I have nothing to do with him.'

Oak was unfortunately led on to speak of Boldwood's rival in a wrong tone to her after all. 'I wish you had never met that young Sergeant Troy, miss,' he sighed.

Bathsheba's steps became faintly spasmodic. 'Why?' she asked.

'He is not good enough for 'ee.'

'Did any one tell you to speak to me like this?'

'Nobody at all.'

'Then it appears to me that Sergeant Troy does not concern us here,' she said intractably. 'Yet I must say that Sergeant Troy is an educated man, and quite worthy of any woman. He is well born.'

'His being higher in learning and birth than the ruck o' soldiers is anything but a proof of his worth. It shows his course to be down'ard.'

'I cannot see what this has to do with our conversation. Mr Troy's course is not by any means downward; and his superiority *is* a proof of his worth!'

'I believe him to have no conscience at all. And I cannot help begging you, miss, to have nothing to do with him. Listen to me this once – only this once! I don't say he's such a bad man as I have fancied – I pray to God he is not. But since we don't exactly know what he is, why not behave as if he *might* be bad, simply for your own safety? Don't trust him, mistress; I ask you not to trust him so.'

'Why, pray?'

'I like soldiers, but this one I do not like,' he said sturdily. 'His cleverness in his calling may have tempted him astray, and what is mirth to the neighbours is ruin to the woman. When he tries to talk to 'ee again, why not turn away with a short "Good day"; and when you see him coming one way, turn the other. When he says anything laughable, fail to see the point and don't smile, and speak of him before those who will report your talk as "that fantastical man", or "that Sergeant What's-his-name". "That man of a family that has come to the dogs." Don't be unmannerly towards en, but harmless-uncivil, and so get rid of the man.'

No Christmas robin detained by a window-pane ever pulsed as did Bathsheba now.

'I say – I say again – that it doesn't become you to talk about him. Why he should be mentioned passes me quite!' she exclaimed desperately. 'I know this, th-th-that he is a thoroughly conscientious man – blunt sometimes even to rudeness – but always speaking his mind about you plain to your face!'

'Oh.'

'He is as good as anybody in this parish! He is very particular, too, about going to church – yes, he is!'

'I am afeard nobody ever saw him there. I never did, certainly.'

'The reason of that is,' she said eagerly, 'that he goes in privately by the old tower door, just when the service commences, and sits at the back of the gallery. He told me so.'

This supreme instance of Troy's goodness fell upon Gabriel's ears like the thirteenth stroke of a crazy clock. It was not only received with utter incredulity as regarded itself, but threw a doubt on all the assurances that had preceded it.

Oak was grieved to find how entirely she trusted him. He brimmed with deep feeling as he replied in a steady voice, the steadiness of which was spoilt by the palpableness of his great effort to keep it so: –

'You know, mistress, that I love you, and shall love you always. I only mention this to bring to your mind that at any rate I would wish to do you no harm: beyond that I put it aside. I have lost in the race for money and good things, and I am not such a fool as to pretend to 'ee now I am poor, and you have got altogether above me. But Bathsheba, dear mistress, this I beg you to consider – that, both to keep yourself well honoured among the workfolk, and in common generosity to an honourable man who loves you as well as I, you should be more discreet in your bearing towards this soldier.'

'Don't, don't, don't!' she exclaimed, in a choking voice.

'Are ye not more to me than my own affairs, and even life!' he went on. 'Come, listen to me! I am six years older than you, and Mr Boldwood is ten years older than I, and consider – I do beg of 'ee to consider before it is too late – how safe you would be in his hands!'

Oak's allusion to his own love for her lessened, to some extent, her anger at his interference; but she could not really forgive him for letting his wish to marry her be eclipsed by his wish to do her good, any more than for his slighting treatment of Troy.

'I wish you to go elsewhere,' she commanded, a paleness of face invisible to the eye being suggested by the trembling words. 'Do not remain on this farm any longer. I don't want you – I beg you to go!'

'That's nonsense,' said Oak calmly. 'This is the second time you have pretended to dismiss me; and what's the use o' it?'

'Pretended! You shall go, sir – your lecturing I will not hear! I am mistress here.'

'Go, indeed – what folly will you say next? Treating me like Dick, Tom and Harry when you know that a short time ago my position was as good as yours! Upon my life, Bathsheba, it is too barefaced. You know, too, that I can't go without putting things in such a strait as you wouldn't get out of I can't tell when. Unless, indeed, you'll promise to have an understanding man as bailiff, or manager, or something. I'll go at once if you'll promise that.'

'I shall have no bailiff; I shall continue to be my own manager,' she said decisively.

'Very well, then; you should be thankful to me for biding. How would the farm go on with nobody to mind it but a woman? But mind this, I don't wish 'ee to feel you owe me anything. Not I. What I do, I do. Sometimes I say I should be as glad as a bird to leave the place – for don't suppose I'm content to be a nobody. I was made for better things. However, I don't like to see your concerns going to ruin, as they must if you keep in this mind. . . . I hate taking my own measure so plain, but, upon my life, your provoking ways make a man say what he wouldn't dream of at other times! I own to being rather interfering. But you know well enough how it is, and who she is that I like too well, and feel too much like a fool about to be civil to her!'

It is more than probable that she privately and unconsciously respected him a little for this grim fidelity, which had been shown in his tone even more than in his words. At any rate she murmured something to the effect that he might stay if he wished. She said more distinctly, 'Will you leave me alone now? I don't order it as a mistress – I ask it as a woman, and I expect you not to be so uncourteous as to refuse.'

'Certainly I will, Miss Everdene,' said Gabriel gently. He wondered that the request should have come at this moment, for the strife was over, and they were on a most desolate hill, far from every human habitation, and the hour was getting late. He stood still and allowed her to get far ahead of him till he could only see her form upon the sky.

A distressing explanation of this anxiety to be rid of him at that point now ensued. A figure apparently rose from the earth beside her. The shape beyond all doubt was Troy's. Oak would not be even a possible listener, and at once turned back till a good two hundred yards were between the lovers and himself.

Gabriel went home by way of the churchyard. In passing the tower he thought of what she had said about the sergeant's virtuous habit of entering the church unperceived at the beginning of service. Believing that the little gallery door alluded to was quite disused, he ascended the external flight of steps at the top of which it stood, and examined it. The pale lustre yet hanging in the north-western heaven was sufficient to show that a sprig of ivy had grown from the wall across the door to a length of more than a foot, delicately tying the panel to the stone jamb. It was a decisive proof that the door had not been opened at least since Troy came back to Weatherbury.

CHAPTER THIRTY

Hot Cheeks and Tearful Eyes

H ALF an hour later Bathsheba entered her own house. There burnt upon her face when she met the light of the candles the flush and excitement which were little less than chronic with her now. The farewell words of Troy, who had accompanied her to the very door, still lingered in her ears. He had bidden her adieu for two days, which were, so he stated, to be spent at Bath in visiting some friends. He had also kissed her a second time.

It is only fair to Bathsheba to explain here a little fact which did not come to light till a long time afterwards: that Troy's presentation of himself so aptly at the roadside this evening was not by any distinctly preconcerted arrangement. He had hinted – she had forbidden; and it was only on the chance of his still coming that she had dismissed Oak, fearing a meeting between them just then.

She now sank down into a chair, wild and perturbed by all these new and fevering sequences. Then she jumped up with a manner of decision, and fetched her desk from a side table.

In three minutes, without pause or modification, she had written a letter to Boldwood, at his address beyond Casterbridge, saying mildly but firmly that she had well considered the whole subject he had brought before her and kindly given her time to decide upon; that her final decision was that she could not marry him. She had expressed to Oak an intention to wait till Boldwood came home before communicating to him her conclusive reply. But Bathsheba found that she could not wait.

It was impossible to send this letter till the next day; yet to quell her uneasiness by getting it out of her hands, and so, as it were, setting the act in motion at once, she arose to take it to any one of the women who might be in the kitchen.

She paused in the passage. A dialogue was going on in the kitchen, and Bathsheba and Troy were the subject of it.

'If he marry her, she'll gie up farming.'

' 'Twill be a gallant life, but may bring some trouble between the mirth – so say I.'

'Well, I wish I had half such a husband.'

Bathsheba had too much sense to mind seriously what her servitors said about her; but too much womanly redundance of speech to leave alone what was said till it died the natural death of unminded things. She burst in upon them.

'Who are you speaking of?' she asked.

There was a pause before anybody replied. At last Liddy said frankly, 'What was passing was a bit of a word about yourself, miss.'

'I thought so! Maryann and Liddy and Temperance – now I forbid you to suppose such things. You know I don't care the least for Mr Troy – not I. Everybody knows how much I hate him. – Yes,' repeated the froward young person, '*hate* him!'

'We know you do, miss,' said Liddy; 'and so do we all.'

'I hate him too,' said Maryann.

'Maryann – O you perjured woman! How can you speak that wicked story!' said Bathsheba excitedly. 'You admired him from your heart only this morning in the very world, you did. Yes, Maryann, you know it!'

'Yes, miss, but so did you. He is a wild scamp now, and you are right to hate him.'

'He's *not* a wild scamp! How dare you to my face! I have no right to hate him, nor you, nor anybody. But I am a silly woman! What is it to me what he is? You know it is nothing. I don't care for him; I don't mean to defend his good name, not I. Mind this, if any of you say a word against him you'll be dismissed instantly!'

She flung down the letter and surged back into the parlour, with a big heart and tearful eyes, Liddy following her.

'O miss!' said mild Liddy, looking pitifully into Bathsheba's face. 'I am sorry we mistook you so! I did think you cared for him; but I see you don't now.'

'Shut the door, Liddy.'

Liddy closed the door, and went on: 'People always say such foolery, miss, I'll make answer hencefor'ard, "Of course a lady like Miss Everdene can't love him"; I'll say it out in plain black and white.'

Bathsheba burst out: 'O Liddy, are you such a simpleton? Can't you read riddles? Can't you see? Are you a woman yourself?'

Liddy's clear eyes rounded with wonderment.

'Yes; you must be a blind thing, Liddy!' she said in reckless abandonment and grief. 'O, I love him to very distraction and misery and agony! Don't be frightened at me, though perhaps I am enough to frighten any innocent woman. Come closer – closer.' She put her arms round Liddy's neck. 'I must let it out to somebody; it is wearing me away! Don't you yet know enough of me to see through that miserable denial of mine? O God, what a lie it was! Heaven and my Love forgive me. And don't you know that a woman who loves at all thinks nothing of perjury when it is balanced against her love? There, go out of the room; I want to be quite alone.'

Liddy went towards the door.

'Liddy, come here. Solemnly swear to me that he's not a fast man; that it is all lies they say about him!'

'But, miss, how can I say he is not if—'

'You graceless girl! How can you have the cruel heart to repeat what they say? Unfeeling thing that you are. . . . But *I'll* see if you or anybody else in the village, or town either, dare do such a thing!' She started off, pacing from fireplace to door, and back again.

'No miss. I don't – I know it is not true!' said Liddy, frightened at Bathsheba's unwonted vehemence.

'I suppose you only agree with me like that to please me. But Liddy, he *cannot be* bad, as is said. Do you hear?'

'Yes, miss, yes.'

'And you don't believe he is?'

'I don't know what to say, miss,' said Liddy, beginning to cry. 'If I say No, you don't believe me; and if I say Yes, you rage at me!'

'Say you don't believe it – say you don't!'

'I don't believe him to be so bad as they make out.'

'He is not bad at all. . . . My poor life and heart, how weak I am!' she moaned, in a relaxed, desultory way, heedless of Liddy's presence. 'O, how I wish I had never seen him! Loving is misery for women always. I shall never forgive God for making me a woman, and dearly am I beginning to pay for the honour of owning a pretty face.' She freshened and turned to Liddy suddenly. 'Mind this, Lydia Smallbury, if you repeat anywhere a single word of what I have said to you inside this closed door, I'll never trust you, or love you, or have you with me a moment longer – not a moment!'

'I don't want to repeat anything,' said Liddy, with womanly dignity of a diminutive order; 'but I don't wish to stay with you. And, if you please, I'll go at the end of the harvest, or this week, or to-day. . . . I don't see that I deserve to be put upon and stormed at for nothing!' concluded the small woman, bigly.

'No, no, Liddy; you must stay!' said Bathsheba, dropping from haughtiness to entreaty with capricious inconsequence. 'You must not notice my being in a taking just now. You are not as a servant – you are a companion to me. Dear, dear – I don't know what I am doing since this miserable ache o' my heart has weighted and worn upon me so! What shall I come to! I suppose I shall get further and further into troubles. I wonder sometimes if I am doomed to die in the Union. I am friendless enough, God knows!'

'I won't notice anything, nor will I leave you!' sobbed Liddy, impulsively putting up her lips to Bathsheba's, and kissing her.

Then Bathsheba kissed Liddy, and all was smooth again.

'I don't often cry, do I, Lidd? but you have made tears come into my eyes,' she said, a smile shining through the moisture. 'Try to think him a good man, won't you, dear Liddy?'

'I will, miss, indeed.'

'He is a sort of steady man in a wild way, you know. That's better than to be as some are, wild in a steady way. I am afraid that's how I am. And promise me to keep my secret – do, Liddy! And do not let them know that I have been crying about him, because it will be dreadful for me, and no good to him, poor thing!'

'Death's head himself shan't wring it from me, mistress, if I've a mind to keep anything; and I'll always be your friend,' replied Liddy emphatically, at the same time bringing a few more tears into her own eyes, not from any particular necessity, but from an artistic sense of making herself in keeping with the remainder of the picture, which seems to influence women at such times. 'I think God likes us to be good friends, don't you?'

'Indeed I do.'

'And, dear miss, you won't harry me and storm at me, will you? because you seem to swell so tall as a lion then, and it frightens me! Do you know, I fancy you would be a match for any man when you are in one o' your takings.'

'Never! do you?' said Bathsheba, slightly laughing, though somewhat seriously alarmed by this Amazonian picture of herself. 'I hope I am not a bold sort of maid – mannish?' she continued with some anxiety.

'O no, not mannish; but so almighty womanish that 'tis getting on that way sometimes. Ah! miss,' she said, after having drawn her breath very sadly in and sent it very sadly out, 'I wish I had half your failing that way. 'Tis a great protection to a poor maid in these illegit'mate days!'

CHAPTER THIRTY-ONE

Blame – Fury

THE next evening Bathsheba, with the idea of getting out of the way of Mr Boldwood in the event of his returning to answer her note in person, proceeded to fulfil an engagement made with Liddy some few hours earlier. Bathsheba's companion, as a gage of their reconciliation, had been granted a week's holiday to visit her sister, who was married to a thriving hurdler and cattle-crib-maker living in a delightful labyrinth of hazel copse not far beyond Yalbury. The arrangement was that Miss Everdene should honour them by coming there for a day or two to inspect some ingenious contrivances which this man of the woods had introduced into his wares.

Leaving her instructions with Gabriel and Maryann, that they were to see everything carefully locked up for the night, she went out of the house just at the close of a timely thunder-shower, which had refined the air, and daintily bathed the coat of the land, though all beneath was dry as ever. Freshness was exhaled in an essence from the varied contours of bank and hollow, as if the earth breathed maiden breath; and the pleased birds were hymning to the scene. Before her, among the clouds, there was a contrast in the shape of lairs of fierce light which showed themselves in the neighbourhood of a hidden sun, lingering on to the farthest north-west corner of the heavens that this midsummer season allowed.

She had walked nearly two miles of her journey, watching how the day was retreating, and thinking how the time of deeds was quietly melting into the time of thought, to give place in its turn to the time of prayer and sleep, when she beheld advancing over Yalbury hill the very man she sought so anxiously to elude. Boldwood was stepping on, not with that quiet tread of reserved strength which was his customary gait, in which he always seemed to be balancing two thoughts. His manner was stunned and sluggish now.

Boldwood had for the first time been awakened to woman's privileges in tergiversation even when it involves another person's possible blight. That

Bathsheba was a firm and positive girl, far less inconsequent than her fellows, had been the very lung of his hope; for he had held that these qualities would lead her to adhere to a straight course for consistency's sake, and accept him, though her fancy might not flood him with the iridescent hues of uncritical love. But the argument now came back as sorry gleams from a broken mirror. The discovery was no less a scourge than a surprise.

He came on looking upon the ground, and did not see Bathsheba till they were less than a stone's throw apart. He looked up at the sound of her pit-pat, and his changed appearance sufficiently denoted to her the depth and strength of the feelings paralysed by her letter.

'Oh; is it you, Mr Boldwood?' she faltered, a guilty warmth pulsing in her face.

Those who have the power of reproaching in silence may find it a means more effective than words. There are accents in the eye which are not on the tongue, and more tales come from pale lips than can enter an ear. It is both the grandeur and the pain of the remoter moods that they avoid the pathway of sound. Boldwood's look was unanswerable.

Seeing she turned a little aside, he said, 'What, are you afraid of me?'

'Why should you say that?' said Bathsheba.

'I fancied you looked so,' said he. 'And it is most strange, because of its contrast with my feeling for you.'

She regained self-possession, fixed her eyes calmly, and waited.

'You know what that feeling is,' continued Boldwood deliberately. 'A thing strong as death. No dismissal by a hasty letter affects that.'

'I wish you did not feel so strongly about me,' she murmured. 'It is generous of you, and more than I deserve, but I must not hear it now.'

'Hear it? What do you think I have to say, then? I am not to marry you, and that's enough. Your letter was excellently plain. I want you to hear nothing – not I.'

Bathsheba was unable to direct her will into any definite groove for freeing herself from this fearfully awkward position. She confusedly said, 'Good evening,' and was moving on. Boldwood walked up to her heavily and dully.

'Bathsheba – darling – is it final indeed?'

'Indeed it is.'

'O Bathsheba – have pity upon me!' Boldwood burst out. 'God's sake, yes – I am come to that low, lowest stage – to ask a woman for pity! Still, she is you – she is you.'

Bathsheba commanded herself well. But she could hardly get a clear voice for what came instinctively to her lips: 'There is little honour to the woman in that speech.' It was only whispered, for something unutterably mournful no less than distressing in this spectacle of a man showing himself to be so entirely the vane of a passion enervated the feminine instinct for punctilios.

'I am beyond myself about this, and am mad,' he said. 'I am no stoic at all to be supplicating here; but I do supplicate to you. I wish you knew what is in me of devotion to you; but it is impossible, that. In bare human mercy to a lonely man, don't throw me off now!'

'I don't throw you off – indeed, how can I? I never had you.' In her noon-clear sense that she had never loved him she forgot for a moment her thoughtless angle on that day in February.

'But there was a time when you turned to me, before I thought of you! I don't reproach you, for even now I feel that the ignorant and cold darkness that I should have lived in if you had not attracted me by that letter — valentine you call it — would have been worse than my knowledge of you, though it has brought this misery. But, I say, there was a time when I knew nothing of you, and cared nothing for you, and yet you drew me on. And if you say you gave me no encouragement, I cannot but contradict you.'

'What you call encouragement was the childish game of an idle minute. I have bitterly repented of it — ay, bitterly, and in tears. Can you still go on reminding me?'

'I don't accuse you of it — I deplore it. I took for earnest what you insist was jest, and now this that I pray to be jest you say is awful, wretched earnest. Our moods meet at wrong places. I wish your feeling was more like mine, or my feeling more like yours! O, could I but have foreseen the torture that trifling trick was going to lead me into, how I should have cursed you; but only having been able to see it since, I cannot do that, for I love you too well! But it is weak, idle drivelling to go on like this. . . . Bathsheba, you are the first woman of any shade or nature that I have ever looked at to love, and it is the having been so near claiming you for my own that makes this denial so hard to bear. How nearly you promised me! But I don't speak now to move your heart, and make you grieve because of my pain; it is no use, that. I must bear it; my pain would get no less by paining you.'

'But I do pity you — deeply — O, so deeply!' she earnestly said.

'Do no such thing — do no such thing. Your dear love, Bathsheba, is such a vast thing beside your pity, that the loss of your pity as well as your love is no great addition to my sorrow, nor does the gain of your pity make it sensibly less. O sweet — how dearly you spoke to me behind the spear-bed at the washing-pool, and in the barn at the shearing, and that dearest last time in the evening at your home! Where are your pleasant words all gone — your earnest hope to be able to love me? Where is your firm conviction that you would get to care for me very much? Really forgotten? — really?'

She checked emotion, looked him quietly and clearly in the face, and said in her low, firm voice, 'Mr Boldwood, I promised you nothing. Would you have had me a woman of clay when you paid me that furthest, highest compliment a man can pay a woman — telling her he loves her? I was bound to show some feeling, if I would not be a graceless shrew. Yet each of those pleasures was just for the day — the day just for the pleasure. How was I to know that what is a pastime to all other men was death to you? Have reason, do, and think more kindly of me!'

'Well, never mind arguing — never mind. One thing is sure: you were all but mine, and now you are not nearly mine. Everything is changed, and that by you alone, remember. You were nothing to me once, and I was contented; you are now nothing to me again, and how different the second nothing is from the first! Would to God you had never taken me up, since it was only to throw me down!'

Bathsheba, in spite of her mettle, began to feel unmistakable signs that she was inherently the weaker vessel. She strove miserably against this femininity which would insist upon supplying unbidden emotions in stronger and stronger current. She had tried to elude agitation by fixing her mind on the trees, sky, any trivial object before her eyes, whilst his reproaches fell, but ingenuity could not save her now.

'I did not take you up — surely I did not!' she answered as heroically as she could. 'But don't be in this mood with me. I can endure being told I am in the wrong, if you will only tell it me gently! O sir, will you not kindly forgive me, and look at it cheerfully?'

'Cheerfully! Can a man fooled to utter heart-burning find a reason for being merry? If I have lost, how can I be as if I had won? Heavens, you must be heartless quite! Had I known what a fearfully bitter sweet this was to be, how I would have avoided you, and never seen you, and been deaf to you. I tell you all this, but what do you care! You don't care.'

She returned silent and weak denials to his charges, and swayed her head desperately, as if to thrust away the words as they came showering about her ears from the lips of the trembling man in the climax of life, with his bronzed Roman face and fine frame.

'Dearest, dearest, I am wavering even now between the two opposites of recklessly renouncing you, and labouring humbly for you again. Forget that you have said No, and let it be as it was! Say, Bathsheba, that you only wrote that refusal to me in fun — come, say it to me!'

'It would be untrue, and painful to both of us. You overrate my capacity for love. I don't possess half the warmth of nature you believe me to have. An unprotected childhood in a cold world has beaten gentleness out of me.'

He immediately said with more resentment: 'That may be true, somewhat; but ah, Miss Everdene, it won't do as a reason! You are not the cold woman you would have me believe. No, no! It isn't because you have no feeling in you that you don't love me. You naturally would have me think so — you would hide from me that you have a burning heart like mine. You have love enough, but it is turned into a new channel. I know where.'

The swift music of her heart became hubbub now, and she throbbed to extremity. He was coming to Troy. He did then know what had occurred! And the name fell from his lips the next moment.

'Why did Troy not leave my treasure alone?' he asked fiercely. 'When I had no thought of injuring him, why did he force himself upon your notice! Before he worried you your inclination was to have me; when next I should have come to you your answer would have been Yes. Can you deny it — I ask, can you deny it?'

She delayed the reply, but was too honest to withhold it. 'I cannot,' she whispered.

'I know you cannot. But he stole in in my absence and robbed me. Why didn't he win you away before, when nobody would have been grieved? — when nobody would have been set tale-bearing. Now the people sneer at me — the very hills and sky seem to laugh at me till I blush shamefully for my folly. I have lost my respect, my good name, my standing — lost it, never to get it again. Go and marry your man — go on!'

'O sir — Mr Boldwood!'

'You may as well. I have no further claim upon you. As for me, I had better go somewhere alone, and hide — and pray. I loved a woman once. I am now ashamed. When I am dead they'll say, Miserable love-sick man that he was.

Heaven – heaven – if I had got jilted secretly, and the dishonour not known, and my position kept! But no matter, it is gone, and the woman not gained. Shame upon him – shame!'

His unreasonable anger terrified her, and she glided from him, without obviously moving, as she said, 'I am only a girl – do not speak to me so!'

'All the time you knew – how very well you knew – that your new freak was my misery. Dazzled by brass and scarlet – O, Bathsheba – this is woman's folly indeed!'

She fired up at once. 'You are taking too much upon yourself!' she said vehemently. 'Everybody is upon me – everybody. It is unmanly to attack a woman so! I have nobody in the world to fight my battles for me; but no mercy is shown. Yet if a thousand of you sneer and say things against me, I *will not* be put down!'

'You'll chatter with him doubtless about me. Say to him, "Boldwood would have died for me." Yes, and you have given way to him, knowing him to be not the man for you. He has kissed you – claimed you as his. Do you hear – he has kissed you. Deny it!'

The most tragic woman is cowed by a tragic man, and although Boldwood was, in vehemence and glow, nearly her own self rendered into another sex, Bathsheba's cheek quivered. She gasped, 'Leave me, sir – leave me! I am nothing to you. Let me go on!'

'Deny that he has kissed you.'

'I shall not.'

'Ha – then he has!' came hoarsely from the farmer.

'He has,' she said slowly, and, in spite of her fear, defiantly. 'I am not ashamed to speak the truth.'

'Then curse him; and curse him!' said Boldwood, breaking into a whispered fury. 'Whilst I would have given worlds to touch your hand, you have let a rake come in without right or ceremony and – kiss you! Heaven's mercy – kiss you! . . . Ah, a time of his life shall come when he will have to repent, and think wretchedly of the pain he has caused another man; and then may he ache, and wish, and curse, and yearn – as I do now!'

'Don't, don't, O, don't pray down evil upon him!' she implored in a miserable cry. 'Anything but that – anything. O, be kind to him, sir, for I love him true!'

Boldwood's ideas had reached that point of fusion at which outline and consistency entirely disappear. The impending night appeared to concentrate in his eye. He did not hear her at all now.

'I'll punish him – by my soul, that will I! I'll meet him, soldier or no, and I'll horsewhip the untimely stripling for this reckless theft of my one delight. If he were a hundred men I'd horsewhip him—' He dropped his voice suddenly and unnaturally. 'Bathsheba, sweet, lost coquette, pardon me! I've been blaming you, threatening you, behaving like a churl to you, when he's the greatest sinner. He stole your dear heart away with his unfathomable lies! . . . It is a fortunate thing for him that he's gone back to his regiment – that he's away up the country, and not here! I hope he may not return here just yet. I pray God he may not come into my sight, for I may be tempted beyond myself. O, Bathsheba, keep him away – yes, keep him away from me!'

For a moment Boldwood stood so inertly after this that his soul seemed to have been entirely exhaled with the breath of his passionate words. He turned his face away, and withdrew, and his form was soon covered over by the twilight as his footsteps mixed in with the low hiss of the leafy trees.

Bathsheba, who had been standing motionless as a model all this latter time, flung her hands to her face, and wildly attempted to ponder on the exhibition which had just passed away. Such astounding wells of fevered feeling in a still man like Mr Boldwood were incomprehensible, dreadful. Instead of being a man trained to repression he was – what she had seen him.

The force of the farmer's threats lay in their relation to a circumstance known at present only to herself: her lover was coming back to Weatherbury in the course of the very next day or two. Troy had not returned to his distant barracks as Boldwood and others supposed, but had merely gone to visit some acquaintance in Bath, and had yet a week or more remaining to his furlough.

She felt wretchedly certain that if he revisited her just at this nick of time, and came into contact with Boldwood, a fierce quarrel would be the consequence. She panted with solicitude when she thought of possible injury to Troy. The least spark would kindle the farmer's swift feelings of rage and jealousy; he would lose his self-mastery as he had this evening; Troy's blitheness might become aggressive; it might take the direction of derision, and Boldwood's anger might then take the direction of revenge.

With almost a morbid dread of being thought a gushing girl, this guideless woman too well concealed from the world under a manner of carelessness the warm depths of her strong emotions. But now there was no reserve. In her distraction, instead of advancing further she walked up and down, beating the air with her fingers, pressing her brow, and sobbing brokenly to herself. Then she sat down on a heap of stones by the wayside to think. There she remained long. Above the dark margin of the earth appeared foreshores and promontories of coppery cloud, bounding a green and pellucid expanse in the western sky. Amaranthine glosses came over them then, and the unresting world wheeled her round to a contrasting prospect eastward, in the shape of indecisive and palpitating stars. She gazed upon their silent throes amid the shades of space, but realized none at all. Her troubled spirit was far away with Troy.

CHAPTER THIRTY-TWO

Night – Horses tramping

THE village of Weatherbury was quiet as the graveyard in its midst, and the living were lying well-nigh as still as the dead. The church clock struck eleven. The air was so empty of other sounds that the whirr of the clock-work immediately before the strokes was distinct, and so was also the click of the same at their close.

The notes flew forth with the usual blind obtuseness of inanimate things — flapping and rebounding among walls, undulating against the scattered clouds, spreading through their interstices into unexplored miles of space.

Bathsheba's crannied and mouldy halls were to-night occupied only by Maryann, Liddy being, as was stated, with her sister, whom Bathsheba had set out to visit. A few minutes after eleven had struck, Maryann turned in her bed with a sense of being disturbed. She was totally unconscious of the nature of the interruption to her sleep. It led to a dream, and the dream to an awakening, with an uneasy sensation that something had happened. She left her bed and looked out of the window. The paddock abutted on this end of the building, and in the paddock she could just discern by the uncertain gray a moving figure approaching the horse that was feeding there. The figure seized the horse by the forelock, and led it to the corner of the field. Here she could see some object which circumstances proved to be a vehicle, for after a few minutes spent apparently in harnessing, she heard the trot of the horse down the road, mingled with the sound of light wheels.

Two varieties only of humanity could have entered the paddock with the ghost-like glide of that mysterious figure. They were a woman and a gipsy man. A woman was out of the question in such an occupation at this hour, and the comer could be no less than a thief, who might probably have known the weakness of the household on this particular night, and have chosen it on that account for his daring attempt. Moreover, to raise suspicion to conviction itself, there were gipsies in Weatherbury Bottom.

Maryann, who had been afraid to shout in the robber's presence, having seen him depart had no fear. She hastily slipped on her clothes, stumped down the disjointed staircase with its hundred creaks, ran to Coggan's, the nearest house, and raised an alarm. Coggan called Gabriel, who now again lodged in his house as at first, and together they went to the paddock. Beyond all doubt the horse was gone.

'Hark!' said Gabriel.

They listened. Distinct upon the stagnant air came the sounds of a trotting horse passing up Longpuddle Lane — just beyond the gipsies' encampment in Weatherbury Bottom.

'That's our Dainty — I'll swear to her step,' said Jan.

'Mighty me! Won't mis'ess storm and call us stupids when she comes back!' moaned Maryann. 'How I wish it had happened when she was at home, and none of us had been answerable!'

'We must ride after,' said Gabriel decisively. 'I'll be responsible to Miss Everdene for what we do. Yes, we'll follow.'

'Faith, I don't see how,' said Coggan, 'All our horses are too heavy for that trick except little Poppet, and what's she between two of us? — If we only had that pair over the hedge we might do something.'

'Which pair?'

'Mr Boldwood's Tidy and Moll.'

'Then wait here till I come hither again,' said Gabriel. He ran down the hill towards Farmer Boldwood's.

'Farmer Boldwood is not at home,' said Maryann.

'All the better,' said Coggan. 'I know what he's gone for.'

Less than five minutes brought up Oak again, running at the same pace, with two halters dangling from his hand.

'Where did you find 'em?' said Coggan, turning round and leaping upon the hedge without waiting for an answer.

'Under the eaves. I knew where they were kept,' said Gabriel, following him.

'Coggan, you can ride bare-backed? there's no time to look for saddles.'

'Like a hero!' said Jan.

'Maryann, you go to bed,' Gabriel shouted to her from the top of the hedge.

Springing down into Boldwood's pastures, each pocketed his halter to hide it from the horses, who, seeing the men empty-handed, docilely allowed themselves to be seized by the mane, when the halters were dexterously slipped on. Having neither bit nor bridle, Oak and Coggan extemporized the former by passing the rope in each case through the animal's mouth and looping it on the other side. Oak vaulted astride, and Coggan clambered up by aid of the bank, when they ascended to the gate and galloped off in the direction taken by Bathsheba's horse and the robber. Whose vehicle the horse had been harnessed to was a matter of some uncertainty.

Weatherbury Bottom was reached in three or four minutes. They scanned the shady green patch by the roadside. The gipsies were gone.

'The villains!' said Gabriel. 'Which way have they gone, I wonder?'

'Straight on, as sure as God made little apples,' said Jan.

'Very well; we are better mounted, and must overtake 'em,' said Oak. 'Now, on at full speed!'

No sound of the rider in their van could now be discovered. The road-metal grew softer and more clayey as Weatherbury was left behind, and the late rain had wetted its surface to a somewhat plastic, but not muddy state. They came to cross-roads. Coggan suddenly pulled up Moll and slipped off.

'What's the matter?' said Gabriel.

'We must try to track 'em, since we can't hear 'em,' said Jan, fumbling in his pockets. He struck a light, and held the match to the ground. The rain had been heavier here, and all foot and horse tracks made previous to the storm had been abraded and blurred by the drops, and they were now so many little scoops of water, which reflected the flame of the match like eyes. One set of tracks was fresh and had no water in them; one pair of ruts was also empty, and not small canals, like the others. The footprints forming this recent impression were full of information as to pace; they were in equidistant pairs, three or four feet apart, the right and left foot of each pair being exactly opposite one another.

'Straight on!' Jan exclaimed. 'Tracks like that mean a stiff gallop. No wonder we don't hear him. And the horse is harnessed – look at the ruts. Ay, that's our mare, sure enough!'

'How do you know?'

'Old Jimmy Harris only shoed her last week, and I'd swear to his make among ten thousand.'

'The rest of the gipsies must ha' gone on earlier, or some other way,' said Oak, 'You saw there were no other tracks?'

'True.' They rode along silently for a long weary time. Coggan carried an old pinchbeck repeater which he had inherited from some genius in his family; and it now struck one. He lighted another match, and examined the ground again.

' 'Tis a canter now,' he said, throwing away the light. 'A twisty, rickety pace for a gig. The fact is, they overdrove her at starting; we shall catch 'em yet.'

Again they hastened on, and entered Blackmore Vale. Coggan's watch struck two. When they looked again the hoof-marks were so spaced as to form a sort of zigzag if united, like the lamps along a street.

'That's a trot, I know,' said Gabriel.

'Only a trot now,' said Coggan cheerfully. 'We shall overtake him in time.'

'They pushed rapidly on for yet two or three miles. 'Ah! a moment,' said Jan. 'Let's see how she was driven up this hill. 'Twill help us.' A light was promptly struck upon his gaiters as before, and the examination made.

'Hurrah!' said Coggan. 'She walked up here – and well she might. We shall get them in two miles, for a crown.'

They rode three, and listened. No sound was to be heard save a mill-pond trickling hoarsely through a hatch, and suggesting gloomy possibilities of drowning by jumping in. Gabriel dismounted when they came to a turning. The tracks were absolutely the only guide as to the direction that they now had, and great caution was necessary to avoid confusing them with some others which had made their appearance lately.

'What does this mean? – though I guess,' said Gabriel, looking up at Coggan as he moved the match over the ground about the turning. Coggan, who, no less than the panting horses, had latterly shown signs of weariness, again scrutinized the mystic characters. This time only three were of the regular horseshoe shape. Every fourth was a dot.

He screwed up his face, and emitted a long 'whew-w-w!'

'Lame,' said Oak.

'Yes. Dainty is lamed; the near-foot-afore,' said Coggan slowly, staring still at the footprints.

'We'll push on,' said Gabriel, remounting his humid steed.

Although the road along its greater part had been as good as any turnpike-road in the country, it was nominally only a byway. The last turning had brought them into the high road leading to Bath. Coggan recollected himself.

'We shall have him now!' he exclaimed.

'Where?'

'Sherton Turnpike. The keeper of that gate is the sleepiest man between here and London – Dan Randall, that's his name – knowed en for years, when he was at Casterbridge gate. Between the lameness and the gate 'tis a done job.'

They now advanced with extreme caution. Nothing was said until, against a shady background of foliage, five white bars were visible, crossing their route a little way ahead.

'Hush – we are almost close!' said Gabriel.

'Amble on upon the grass,' said Coggan.

The white bars were blotted out in the midst by a dark shape in front of them. The silence of this lonely time was pierced by an exclamation from that quarter.

'Hoy-a-hoy! Gate!'

It appeared that there had been a previous call which they had not noticed, for on their close approach the door of the turnpike-house opened, and the keeper came out half-dressed, with a candle in his hand. The rays illumined the whole group.

'Keep the gate close!' shouted Gabriel. 'He has stolen the horse!'

'Who?' said the turnpike-man.

Gabriel looked at the driver of the gig, and saw a woman – Bathsheba, his mistress.

On hearing his voice she had turned her face away from the light. Coggan had, however, caught sight of her in the meanwhile.

'Why, 'tis mistress – I'll take my oath!' he said, amazed.

Bathsheba it certainly was, and she had by this time done the trick she could do so well in crises not of love, namely, mask a surprise by coolness of manner.

'Well, Gabriel,' she inquired quietly, 'where are you going?'

'We thought—' began Gabriel.

'I am driving to Bath,' she said, taking for her own use the assurance that Gabriel lacked. 'An important matter made it necessary for me to give up my visit to Liddy, and go off at once. What, then, were you following me?'

'We thought the horse was stole.'

'Well – what a thing! How very foolish of you not to know that I had taken the trap and horse. I could neither wake Maryann nor get into the house, though I hammered for ten minutes against her window-sill. Fortunately, I could get the key of the coach-house, so I troubled no one further. Didn't you think it might be me?'

'Why should we, miss?'

'Perhaps not. Why, those are never Farmer Boldwood's horses! Goodness mercy! what have you been doing – bringing trouble upon me in this way? What! mustn't a lady move an inch from her door without being dogged like a thief?'

'But how was we to know, if you left no account of your doings?' expostulated Coggan, 'and ladies don't drive at this hours, miss, as a jineral rule of society.'

'I did leave an account – and you would have seen it in the morning. I wrote in chalk on the coach-house doors that I had come back for the horse and gig, and driven off; that I could arouse nobody, and should return soon.'

'But you'll consider, ma'am, that we couldn't see that till it got daylight.'

'True,' she said, and though vexed at first she had too much sense to blame them long or seriously for a devotion to her that was as valuable as it was rare. She added with a very pretty grace, 'Well, I really thank you heartily for taking all this trouble; but I wish you had borrowed anybody's horses but Mr Boldwood's.'

'Dainty is lame, miss,' said Coggan. 'Can ye go on?'

'It was only a stone in her shoe. I got down and pulled it out a hundred yards back. I can manage very well, thank you. I shall be in Bath by daylight. Will you now return, please?'

She turned her head – the gateman's candle shimmering upon her quick, clear eyes as she did so – passed through the gate, and was soon wrapped in the embowering shades of mysterious summer boughs. Coggan and Gabriel put about their horses, and, fanned by the velvety air of this July night, retraced the road by which they had come.

'A strange vagary, this of hers, isn't it, Oak?' said Coggan curiously.

'Yes,' said Gabriel shortly.

'She won't be in Bath by no daylight!'

'Coggan, suppose we keep this night's work as quiet as we can?'

'I am of one and the same mind.'

'Very well. We shall be home by three o'clock or so, and can creep into the parish like lambs.'

Bathsheba's perturbed meditations by the roadside had ultimately evolved a conclusion that there were only two remedies for the present desperate state of affairs. The first was merely to keep Troy away from Weatherbury till Boldwood's indignation had cooled; the second to listen to Oak's entreaties and Boldwood's denunciations, and give up Troy altogether.

Alas! Could she give up this new love – induce him to renounce her by saying she did not like him – could no more speak to him, and beg him, for her good, to end his furlough in Bath, and see her and Weatherbury no more?

It was a picture full of misery, but for a while she contemplated it firmly, allowing herself, nevertheless, as girls will, to dwell upon the happy life she would have enjoyed had Troy been Boldwood, and the path of love the path of duty – inflicting upon herself gratuitous tortures by imagining him the lover of another woman after forgetting her; for she had penetrated Troy's nature so far as to estimate his tendencies pretty accurately, but unfortunately loved him no less in thinking that he might soon cease to love her – indeed, considerably more.

She jumped to her feet. She would see him at once. Yes, she would implore him by word of mouth to assist her in this dilemma. A letter to keep him away could not reach him in time, even if he should be disposed to listen to it.

Was Bathsheba altogether blind to the obvious fact that the support of a lover's arms is not of a kind best calculated to assist a resolve to renounce him? Or was she sophistically sensible, with a thrill of pleasure, that by adopting this course for getting rid of him she was ensuring a meeting with him, at any rate, once more?

It was now dark, and the hour must have been nearly ten. The only way to accomplish her purpose was to give up her idea of visiting Liddy at Yalbury, return to Weatherbury Farm, put the horse into the gig, and drive at once to Bath. The scheme seemed at first impossible: the journey was a fearfully heavy one, even for a strong horse, at her own estimate; and she much underrated the distance. It was most venturesome for a woman, at night, and alone.

But could she go on to Liddy's and leave things to take their course? No, no; anything but that. Bathsheba was full of a stimulating turbulence, beside which caution vainly prayed for a hearing. She turned back towards the village.

Her walk was slow, for she wished not to enter Weatherbury till the cottagers were in bed, and, particularly, till Boldwood was secure. Her plan was now to drive to Bath during the night, see Sergeant Troy in the morning before he set out to come to her, bid him farewell, and dismiss him: then to rest the horse thoroughly (herself to weep the while, she thought), starting early the next morning on her return journey. By this arrangement she could trot Dainty gently all the day, reach Liddy at Yalbury in the evening, and come home to Weatherbury with her whenever they chose – so nobody would know she had been to Bath at all.

Such was Bathsheba's scheme. But in her topographical ignorance as a late comer to the place, she misreckoned the distance of her journey as not much more than half what it really was. Her idea, however, she proceeded to carry out, with what initial success we have already seen.

CHAPTER THIRTY-THREE

In the Sun — A Harbinger

A WEEK passed, and there were no tidings of Bathsheba; nor was there any explanation of her Gilpin's rig.

Then a note came for Maryann, stating that the business which had called her mistress to Bath still detained her there; but that she hoped to return in the course of another week.

Another week passed. The oat-harvest began, and all the men were a-field under a monochromatic Lammas sky, amid the trembling air and short shadows of noon. Indoors nothing was to be heard save the droning of blue-bottle flies; out-of-doors the whetting of scythes and the hiss of tressy oat-ears rubbing together as their perpendicular stalks of amber-yellow fell heavily to each swath. Every drop of moisture not in the men's bottles and flagons in the form of cider was raining as perspiration from their foreheads and cheeks. Drought was everywhere else.

They were about to withdraw for a while into the charitable shade of a tree in the fence, when Coggan saw a figure in a blue coat and brass buttons running to them across the field.

'I wonder who that is?' he said.

'I hope nothing is wrong about mistress,' said Maryann, who with some other women was tying the bundles (oats being always sheafed on this farm), 'but an unlucky token came to me indoors this morning. I went to unlock the door and dropped the key, and it fell upon the stone floor and broke into two pieces. Breaking a key is a dreadful bodement. I wish mis'ess was home.'

''Tis Cain Ball,' said Gabriel, pausing from whetting his reap-hook.

Oak was not bound by his agreement to assist in the corn-field; but the harvest month is an anxious time for a farmer, and the corn was Bathsheba's, so he lent a hand.

'He's dressed up in his best clothes,' said Matthew Moon. 'He hev been away from home for a few days, since he's had that felon upon his finger; for 'a said, since I can't work I'll have a hollerday.'

'A good time for one — a' excellent time,' said Joseph Poorgrass, straightening his back; for he, like some of the others, had a way of resting a while from his labour on such hot days for reasons preternaturally small: of which Cain Ball's advent on a week-day in his Sunday-clothes was one of the first magnitude. ''Twas a bad leg allowed me to read the *Pilgrim's Progress*, and Mark Clark learnt All-Fours in a whitlow.'

'Ay, and my father put his arm out of joint to have time to go courting,' said Jan Coggan, in an eclipsing tone, wiping his face with his shirt-sleeve and thrusting back his hat upon the nape of his neck.

By this time Cainy was nearing the group of harvesters, and was perceived to be carrying a large slice of bread and ham in one hand, from which he took mouthfuls as he ran, the other being wrapped in a bandage. When he came close, his mouth assumed the bell shape, and he began to cough violently.

'Now, Cainy!' said Gabriel sternly. 'How many more times must I tell you to keep from running so fast when you be eating? You'll choke yourself some day, that's what you'll do, Cain Ball.'

'Hok-hok-hok!' replied Cain. 'A crumb of my victual went the wrong way — hok-hok! That's what 'tis, Mister Oak! And I've been visiting to Bath because I had a felon on my thumb; yes, and I've seen — ahok-hok!'

Directly Cain mentioned Bath, they all threw down their hooks and forks and drew round him. Unfortunately the erratic crumb did not improve his narrative powers, and a supplementary hindrance was that of a sneeze, jerking from his pocket his rather large watch, which dangled in front of the young man pendulum-wise.

'Yes,' he continued, directing his thoughts to Bath and letting his eyes follow, 'I've seed the world at last — yes — and I've seed our mis'ess — ahok-hok-hok!'

'Bother the boy!' said Gabriel. 'Something is always going the wrong way down your throat, so that you can't tell what's necessary to be told.'

'Ahok! there! Please, Mister Oak, a gnat have just fleed into my stomach and brought the cough on again!'

'Yes, that's just it. Your mouth is always open, you young rascal!'

' 'Tis terrible bad to have a gnat fly down yer throat, pore boy!' said Matthew Moon.

'Well, at Bath you saw—' prompted Gabriel.

'I saw our mistress,' continued the junior shepherd, 'and a sojer, walking along. And bymeby they got closer and closer, and then they went arm-in-crook, like courting complete — hok-hok! like courting complete — hok! — courting complete—' Losing the thread of his narrative at this point simultaneously with his loss of breath, their informant looked up and down the field apparently for some clue to it. 'Well, I see our mis'ess and a soldier — a-ha-a-wk!'

'Damn the boy!' said Gabriel.

' 'Tis only my manner, Mister Oak, if ye'll excuse it,' said Cain Ball, looking reproachfully at Oak, with eyes drenched in their own dew.

'Here's some cider for him — that'll cure his throat,' said Jan Coggan, lifting a flagon of cider, pulling out the cork, and applying the hole to Cainy's mouth; Joseph Poorgrass in the meantime beginning to think apprehensively of the serious consequences that would follow Cain Ball's strangulation in his cough, and the history of his Bath adventures dying with him.

'For my poor self, I always say "please God" afore I do anything,' said Joseph, in an unboastful voice; 'and so should you, Cain Ball. 'Tis a great safeguard, and might perhaps save you from being choked to death some day.'

Mr Coggan poured the liquor with unstinted liberality at the suffering Cain's circular mouth; half of it running down the side of the flagon, and half of what reached his mouth running down outside his throat, and half of what ran in going the wrong way, and being coughed and sneezed around the persons of the gathered reapers in the form of a cider fog, which for a moment hung in the sunny air like a small exhalation.

'There's a great clumsy sneeze! Why can't ye have better manners, you young dog!' said Coggan, withdrawing the flagon.

'The cider went up my nose!' cried Cainy, as soon as he could speak; 'and now 'tis gone down my neck, and into my poor dumb felon, and over my shiny buttons and all my best cloze!'

'The poor lad's cough is terrible onfortunate,' said Matthew Moon. 'And a great history on hand, too. Bump his back, shepherd.'

' 'Tis my nater,' mourned Cain. 'Mother says I always was so excitable when my feelings were worked up to a point!'

'True, true,' said Joseph Poorgrass. 'The Balls were always a very excitable family. I knowed the boy's grandfather – a truly nervous and modest man, even to genteel refinery. 'Twas blush, blush with him, almost as much as 'tis with me – not but that 'tis a fault in me!'

'Not at all, Master Poorgrass,' said Coggan. ' 'Tis a very noble quality in ye.'

'Hey-heh! well, I wish to noise nothing abroad – nothing at all,' murmured Poorgrass diffidently. 'But we be born to things – that's true. Yet I would rather my trifle were hid; though, perhaps, a high nater is a little high, and at my birth all things were possible to my Maker, and he may have begrudged no gifts. . . . But under your bushel, Joseph! under your bushel with 'ee! A strange desire, neighbours, this desire to hide, and no praise due. Yet there is a Sermon on the Mount with a calendar of the blessed at the head, and certain meek men may be named therein.'

'Cainy's grandfather was a very clever man,' said Matthew Moon. 'Invented a' apple-tree out of his own head, which is called by his name to this day – the Early Ball. You know 'em, Jan? A Quarrenden grafted on a Tom Putt, and a Rathe-ripe upon top o' that again. 'Tis trew 'a used to bide about in a public-house wi' a 'ooman in a way he had no business to by rights, but there – 'a were a clever man in the sense of the term.'

'Now then,' said Gabriel impatiently, 'what did you see, Cain?'

'I seed our mis'ess go into a sort of a park place, where there's seats, and shrubs and flowers, arm-in-crook with a sojer,' continued Cainy firmly, and with a dim sense that his words were very effective as regarded Gabriel's emotions. 'And I think the sojer was Sergeant Troy. And they sat there together for more than half-an-hour, talking moving things, and she once was crying a'most to death. And when they came out her eyes were shining and she was as white as a lily; and they looked into one another's faces, as far gone friendly as a man and woman can be.'

Gabriel's features seemed to get thinner. 'Well, what did you see besides?'

'Oh, all sorts.'

'White as a lily? You are sure 'twas she?'

'Yes.'

'Well, what besides?'

'Great glass windows to the shops, and great clouds in the sky, full of rain, and old wooden trees in the country round.'

'You stun-poll! What will ye say next?' said Coggan.

'Let en alone,' interposed Joseph Poorgrass. 'The boy's maning is that the sky and the earth in the kingdom of Bath is not altogether different from ours here.

'Tis for our good to gain knowledge of strange cities, and as such the boy's words should be suffered, so to speak it.'

'And the people of Bath,' continued Cain, 'never need to light their fires except as a luxury, for the water springs up out of the earth ready boiled for use.'

' 'Tis true as the light,' testified Matthew Moon. 'I've heard other navigators say the same thing.'

'They drink nothing else there,' said Cain, 'and seem to enjoy it, to see how they swaller it down.'

'Well, it seems a barbarian practice enough to us, but I daresay the natives think nothing o' it,' said Matthew.

'And don't victuals spring up as well as drink?' asked Coggan, twirling his eye.

'No – I own to a blot there in Bath – a true blot. God didn't provide 'em with victuals as well as drink, and 'twas a drawback I couldn't get over at all.'

'Well, 'tis a curious place, to say the least,' observed Moon; 'and it must be a curious people that live therein.'

'Miss Everdene and the soldier were walking about together, you say?' said Gabriel, returning to the group.

'Ay, and she wore a beautiful gold-colour silk gown, trimmed with black lace, that would have stood alone 'ithout legs inside if required. 'Twas a very winsome sight; and her hair was brushed splendid. And when the sun shone upon the bright gown and his red coat – my! how handsome they looked. You could see 'em all the length of the street.'

'And what then?' murmured Gabriel.

'And then I went into Griffin's to hae my boots hobbed, and then I went to Riggs's batty-cake shop, and asked 'em for a penneth of the cheapest and nicest stales, that were all but blue-mouldy, but not quite. And whilst I was chawing 'em down I walked on and seed a clock with a face as a big as a baking trendle—'

'But that's nothing to do with mistress!'

'I'm coming to that, if you'll leave me alone, Mister Oak!' remonstrated Cainy. 'If you excites me, perhaps you'll bring on my cough, and then I shan't be able to tell ye nothing.'

'Yes – let him tell it his own way,' said Coggan.

Gabriel settled into a despairing attitude of patience, and Cainy went on: –

'And there were great large houses, and more people all the week long than at Weatherbury club-walking on White Tuesdays. And I went to grand churches and chapels. And how the parson would pray! Yes; he would kneel down and put up his hands together, and make the holy gold rings on his fingers gleam and twinkle in yer eyes, that he'd earned by praying so excellent well! – Ah yes, I wish I lived there.'

'Our poor Parson Thirdly can't get no money to buy such rings,' said Matthew Moon thoughtfully. 'And as good a man as ever walked. I don't believe poor Thirdly have a single one, even of humblest tin or copper. Such a great ornament as they'd be to him on a dull a'ternoon, when he's up in the pulpit lighted by the wax candles! But 'tis impossible, poor man. Ah, to think how unequal things be.'

'Perhaps he's made of different stuff than to wear 'em,' said Gabriel grimly. 'Well, that's enough of this. Go on, Cainy – quick.'

'Oh – and the new style of pa'sons wear moustaches and long beards,' continued the illustrious traveller, 'and look like Moses and Aaron complete, and make we fokes in the congregation feel all over like the children of Israel.'

'A very right feeling – very,' said Joseph Poorgrass.

'And there's two religions going on in the nation now – High Church and High Chapel. And, thinks, I, I'll play fair; so I went to High Church in the morning, and High Chapel in the afternoon.'

'A right and proper boy,' said Joseph Poorgrass.

'Well, at High Church they pray singing, and worship all the colours of the rainbow; and at High Chapel they pray preaching, and worship drab and whitewash only. And then – I didn't see no more of Miss Everdene at all.'

'Why didn't you say so afore, then?' exclaimed Oak, with much disappointment.

'Ah,' said Mathew Moon, 'she'll wish her cake dough if so be she's ever intimate with that man.'

'She's not over intimate with him,' said Gabriel indignantly.

'She would know better,' said Coggan. 'Our mis'ess has too much sense under they knots of black hair to do such a mad thing.'

'You see, he's not a coarse, ignorant man, for he was well brought up,' said Matthew dubiously. ' 'Twas only wildness that made him a soldier, and maids rather like your man of sin.'

'Now, Cain Ball,' said Gabriel restlessly, 'can you swear in the most awful form that the woman you saw was Miss Everdene?'

'Cain Ball, you be no longer a babe and suckling,' said Joseph in the sepulchral tone the circumstances demanded, 'and you know what taking an oath is. 'Tis a horrible testament mind ye, which you say and seal with your blood-stone, and the prophet Matthew tells us that on whomsoever it shall fall it will grind him to powder. Now, before all the work-folk here assembled, can you swear to your words as the shepherd asks ye?'

'Please no, Mister Oak!' said Cainy, looking from one to the other with great uneasiness at the spiritual magnitude of the position. 'I don't mind saying 'tis true, but I don't like to say 'tis damn true, if that's what you mane.'

'Cain, Cain, how can you?' asked Joseph sternly. 'You be asked to swear in a holy manner, and you swear like wicked Shimei, the son of Gera, who cursed as he came. Young man, fie!'

'No, I don't! 'Tis you want to squander a pore boy's soul, Joseph Poorgrass – that's what 'tis!' said Cain, beginning to cry. 'All I mane is that in common truth 'twas Miss Everdene and Sergeant Troy, but in the horrible so-help-me truth that ye want to make of it perhaps 'twas somebody else!'

'There's no getting at the rights of it,' said Gabriel, turning to his work.

'Cain Ball, you'll come to a bit of bread!' groaned Joseph Poorgrass.

Then the reapers' hooks were flourished again, and the old sounds went on. Gabriel, without making any pretence of being lively, did nothing to show that he was particularly dull. However, Coggan knew pretty nearly how the land lay, and when they were in a nook together he said –

'Don't take on about her, Gabriel. What difference does it make whose sweetheart she is, since she can't be yours?'

'That's the very thing I say to myself,' said Gabriel.

CHAPTER THIRTY-FOUR

Home again – A Trickster

THAT same evening at dusk Gabriel was leaning over Coggan's garden-gate, taking an up-and-down survey before retiring to rest.

A vehicle of some kind was softly creeping along the grassy margin of the lane. From it spread the tones of two women talking. The tones were natural and not at all suppressed. Oak instantly knew the voices to be those of Bathsheba and Liddy.

The carriage came opposite and passed by. It was Miss Everdene's gig, and Liddy and her mistress were the only occupants of the seat. Liddy was asking questions about the city of Bath, and her companion was answering them listlessly and unconcernedly. Both Bathsheba and the horse seemed weary.

The exquisite relief of finding that she was here again, safe and sound, overpowered all reflection, and Oak could only luxuriate in the sense of it. All grave reports were forgotten.

He lingered and lingered on, till there was no difference between the eastern and western expanses of sky, and the timid hares began to limp courageously round the dim hillocks. Gabriel might have been there an additional half-hour when a dark form walked slowly by. 'Good-night, Gabriel,' the passer said.

It was Boldwood. 'Good-night, sir,' said Gabriel.

Boldwood likewise vanished up the road, and Oak shortly afterwards turned indoors to bed.

Farmer Boldwood went on towards Miss Everdene's house. He reached the front, and approaching the entrance, saw a light in the parlour. The blind was not drawn down, and inside the room was Bathsheba, looking over some papers or letters. Her back was towards Boldwood. He went to the door, knocked, and waited with tense muscles and an aching brow.

Boldwood had not been outside his garden since his meeting with Bathsheba in the road to Yalbury. Silent and alone, he had remained in moody meditation on woman's ways, deeming as essentials of the whole sex the accidents of the single one of their number he had ever closely beheld. By degrees a more charitable temper had pervaded him, and this was the reason of his sally to-night. He had come to apologize and beg forgiveness of Bathsheba with something like a sense of shame at his violence, having but just now learnt that she had returned – only from a visit to Liddy, as he supposed, the Bath escapade being quite unknown to him.

He inquired for Miss Everdene. Liddy's manner was odd, but he did not notice it. She went in, leaving him standing there, and in her absence the blind of the room containing Bathsheba was pulled down. Boldwood augured ill from that sign. Liddy came out.

'My mistress cannot see you, sir,' she said.

The farmer instantly went out by the gate. He was unforgiven – that was the issue of it all. He had seen her who was to him simultaneously a delight and a torture, sitting in the room he had shared with her as a peculiarly privileged guest only a little earlier in the summer, and she had denied him an entrance there now.

Boldwood did not hurry homeward. It was ten o' clock at least, when, walking deliberately through the lower part of Weatherbury, he heard the carrier's spring van entering the village. The van ran to and from a town in a northern direction, and it was owned and driven by a Weatherbury man, at the door of whose house it now pulled up. The lamp fixed to the head of the hood illuminated a scarlet and gilded form, who was the first to alight.

'Ah!' said Boldwood to himself, 'come to see her again.'

Troy entered the carrier's house, which had been the place of his lodging on his last visit to his native place. Boldwood was moved by a sudden determination. He hastened home. In ten minutes he was back again, and made as if he were going to call upon Troy at the carrier's. But as he approached, some one opened the door and came out. He heard this person say 'Good-night' to the inmates, and the voice was Troy's. This was strange, coming so immediately after his arrival. Boldwood, however, hastened up to him. Troy had what appeared to be a carpet-bag in his hand – the same that he had brought with him. It seemed as if he were going to leave again this very night.

Troy turned up the hill and quickened his pace. Boldwood stepped forward.

'Sergeant Troy?'

'Yes – I 'm Sergeant Troy.'

'Just arrived from up the country, I think?'

'Just arrived from Bath.'

'I am William Boldwood.'

'Indeed.'

The tone in which this word was uttered was all that had been wanted to bring Boldwood to the point.

'I wish to speak a word with you,' he said.

'What about?'

'About her who lives just ahead there – and about a woman you have wronged.'

'I wonder at your impertinence,' said Troy, moving on.

'Now look here,' said Boldwood, standing in front of him, 'wonder or not, you are going to hold a conversation with me.'

Troy heard the dull determination in Boldwood's voice, looked at his stalwart frame, then at the thick cudgel he carried in his hand. He remembered it was past ten o'clock. It seemed worth while to be civil to Boldwood.

'Very well, I'll listen with pleasure,' said Troy, placing his bag on the ground, 'only speak low, for somebody or other may overhear us in the farmhouse there.'

'Well then – I know a good deal concerning your – Fanny Robin's attachment to you. I may say, too, that I believe I am the only person in the village, excepting Gabriel Oak, who does know it. You ought to marry her.'

'I suppose I ought. Indeed, I wish to, but I cannot.'

'Why?'

Troy was about to utter something hastily; he then checked himself and said, 'I am too poor.' His voice was changed. Previously it had had a devil-may-care tone. It was the voice of a trickster now.

Boldwood's present mood was not critical enough to notice tones. He continued, 'I may as well speak plainly; and understand, I don't wish to enter into the questions of right or wrong, woman's honour and shame, or to express any opinion on your conduct. I intend a business transaction with you.'

'I see,' said Troy. 'Suppose we sit down here.'

An old tree trunk lay under the hedge immediately opposite, and they sat down.

'I was engaged to be married to Miss Everdene,' said Boldwood, 'but you came and—'

'Not engaged,' said Troy.

'As good as engaged.'

'If I had not turned up she might have become engaged to you.'

'Hang might!'

'Would, then.'

'If you had not come I should certainly – yes, *certainly* – have been accepted by this time. If you had not seen her you might have been married to Fanny. Well, there's too much difference between Miss Everdene's station and your own for this flirtation with her ever to benefit you by ending in marriage. So all I ask is, don't molest her any more. Marry Fanny. I'll make it worth your while.'

'How will you?'

'I'll pay you well now, I'll settle a sum of money upon her, and I'll see that you don't suffer from poverty in the future. I'll put it clearly. Bathsheba is only playing with you: you are too poor for her as I said; so give up wasting your time about a great match you'll never make for a moderate and rightful match you may make tomorrow; take up your carpet-bag, turn about, leave Weatherbury now, this night, and you shall take fifty pounds with you. Fanny shall have fifty to enable her to prepare for the wedding, when you have told me where she is living, and she shall have five hundred paid down on her wedding-day.'

In making this statement Boldwood's voice revealed only too clearly a consciousness of the weakness of his position, his aims, and his method. His manner had lapsed quite from that of the firm and dignified Boldwood of former times; and such a scheme as he had now engaged in he would have condemned as childishly imbecile only a few months ago. We discern a grand force in the lover which he lacks whilst a free man; but there is a breadth of vision in the free man which in the lover we vainly seek. Where there is much bias there must be some narrowness, and love, though added emotion, is subtracted capacity. Boldwood exemplified this to an abnormal degree: he knew nothing of Fanny Robin's circumstances or whereabouts, he knew nothing of Troy's possibilities, yet that was what he said.

'I like Fanny best,' said Troy; 'and if, as you say, Miss Everdene is out of my reach, why I have all to gain by accepting your money, and marrying Fan. But she's only a servant.'

'Never mind – do you agree to my arrangement?'

'I do.'

'Ah!' said Boldwood, in a more elastic voice. 'O, Troy, if you like her best, why then did you step in here and injure my happiness?'

'I love Fanny best now,' said Troy. 'But Bathsh – Miss Everdene inflamed me, and displaced Fanny for a time. It is over now.'

'Why should it be over so soon? And why then did you come here again?'

'There are weighty reasons. Fifty pounds at once, you said!'

'I did,' said Boldwood, 'and here they are – fifty sovereigns.' He handed Troy a small packet.

'You have everything ready – it seems that you calculated on my accepting them,' said the sergeant, taking the packet.

'I thought you might accept them,' said Boldwood.

'You've only my word that the programme shall be adhered to, whilst I at any rate have fifty pounds.'

'I had thought of that, and I have considered that if I can't appeal to your honour I can trust to your – well, shrewdness we'll call it – not to lose five hundred pounds in prospect, and also make a bitter enemy of a man who is willing to be an extremely useful friend.'

'Stop, listen!' said Troy in a whisper.

A light pit-pat was audible upon the road just above them.

'By George – 'tis she,' he continued. 'I must go on and meet her.'

'She – who?'

'Bathsheba.'

'Bathsheba – out alone at this time o' night!' said Boldwood in amazement, and starting up. 'Why must you meet her?'

'She was expecting me to-night – and I must now speak to her, and wish her good-bye, according to your wish.'

'I don't see the necessity of speaking.'

'It can do no harm – and she'll be wandering about looking for me if I don't. You shall hear all I say to her. It will help you in your love-making when I am gone.'

'Your tone is mocking.'

'O no. And remember this, if she does not know what has become of me, she will think more about me than if I tell her flatly I have come to give her up.'

'Will you confine your words to that one point? – Shall I hear every word you say?'

'Every word. Now sit still there, and hold my carpet bag for me, and mark what you hear.'

The light footstep came closer, halting occasionally, as if the walker listened for a sound. Troy whistled a double note in a soft, fluty tone.

'Come to that, is it!' murmured Boldwood uneasily.

'You promised silence,' said Troy.

'I promise again.'

Troy stepped forward.

'Frank, dearest, is that you?' The tones were Bathsheba's.

'O God!' said Boldwood.

'Yes,' said Troy to her.

'How late you are,' she continued tenderly. 'Did you come by the carrier? I listened and heard his wheels entering the village, but it was some time ago, and I had almost given you up, Frank.'

'I was sure to come,' said Frank. 'You knew I should, did you not?'

'Well, I thought you would,' she said playfully; 'and, Frank, it is so lucky! There's not a soul in my house but me to-night. I've packed them all off, so nobody on earth will know of your visit to your lady's bower. Liddy wanted to go to her grandfather's to tell him about her holiday, and I said she might stay with them till to-morrow – when you'll be gone again.'

'Capital,' said Troy. 'But, dear me, I had better go back for my bag, because my slippers and brush and comb are in it; you run home whilst I fetch it, and I'll promise to be in your parlour in ten minutes.'

'Yes.' She turned and tripped up the hill again.

During the progress of this dialogue there was a nervous twitching of Boldwood's tightly closed lips, and his face became bathed in a clammy dew. He now started forward towards Troy. Troy turned to him and took up the bag.

'Shall I tell her I have come to give her up and cannot marry her?' said the soldier mockingly.

'No, no; wait a minute. I want to say more to you – more to you!' said Boldwood, in a hoarse whisper.

'Now,' said Troy, 'you see my dilemma. Perhaps I am a bad man – the victim of my impulses – led away to do what I ought to leave undone. I can't, however, marry them both. And I have two reasons for choosing Fanny. First, I like her best upon the whole, and second, you make it worth my while.'

At the same instant Boldwood sprang upon him, and held him by the neck. Troy felt Boldwood's grasp slowly tightening. The move was absolutely unexpected.

'A moment,' he gasped. 'You are injuring her you love!'

'Well, what do you mean?' said the farmer.

'Give me breath,' said Troy.

Boldwood loosened his hand, saying, 'By Heaven, I've a mind to kill you!'

'And ruin her.'

'Save her.'

'Oh, how can she be saved now, unless I marry her?'

Boldwood groaned. He reluctantly released the soldier, and flung him back against the hedge. 'Devil, you torture me!' said he.

Troy rebounded like a ball, and was about to make a dash at the farmer; but he checked himself, saying lightly –

'It is not worth while to measure my strength with you. Indeed it is a barbarous way of settling a quarrel. I shall shortly leave the army because of the same conviction. Now after that revelation of how the land lies with Bathsheba, 'twould be a mistake to kill me, would it not?'

' 'Twould be a mistake to kill you,' repeated Boldwood, mechanically, with bowed head.

'Better kill yourself.'

'Far better.'

'I'm glad you see it.'

'Troy, make her your wife, and don't act upon what I arranged just now. The alternative is dreadful, but take Bathsheba; I give her up! She must love you indeed to sell soul and body to you so utterly as she has done. Wretched woman – deluded woman – you are, Bathsheba!'

'But about Fanny?'

'Bathsheba is a woman well to do,' continued Boldwood, in nervous anxiety, 'and, Troy, she will make a good wife; and, indeed, she is worth your hastening on your marriage with her!'

'But she has a will – not to say a temper, and I shall be a mere slave to her. I could do anything with poor Fanny Robin.'

'Troy,' said Boldwood imploringly, 'I'll do anything for you, only don't desert her; pray don't desert her, Troy.'

'Which, poor Fanny?'

'No; Bathsheba Everdene. Love her best! Love her tenderly! How shall I get you to see how advantageous it will be to you to secure her at once?'

'I don't wish to secure her in any new way.'

Boldwood's arm moved spasmodically towards Troy's person again. He repressed the instinct, and his form drooped as with pain.

Troy went on –

'I shall soon purchase my discharge, and then—'

'But I wish you to hasten on this marriage! It will be better for you both. You love each other, and you must let me help you to do it.'

'How?'

'Why, by settling the five hundred on Bathsheba instead of Fanny, to enable you to marry at once. No; she wouldn't have it of me. I'll pay it down to you on the wedding-day.'

Troy paused in secret amazement at Boldwood's wild infatuation. He carelessly said, 'And am I to have anything now?'

'Yes, if you wish to. But I have not much additional money with me. I did not expect this; but all I have is yours.'

Boldwood, more like a somnambulist than a wakeful man, pulled out the large canvas bag he carried by way of a purse, and searched it.

'I have twenty-one pounds more with me,' he said. 'Two notes and a sovereign. But before I leave you I must have a paper signed—'

'Pay me the money, and we'll go straight to her parlour, and make any arrangement you please to secure my compliance with your wishes. But she must know nothing of this cash business.'

'Nothing, nothing,' said Boldwood hastily. 'Here is the sum, and if you'll come to my house we'll write out the agreement for the remainder, and the terms also.'

'First we'll call upon her.'

'But why? Come with me to-night, and go with me to-morrow to the surrogate's.'

'But she must be consulted; at any rate informed.'

'Very well; go on.'

They went up the hill to Bathsheba's house. When they stood at the entrance, Troy said, 'Wait here a moment.' Opening the door, he glided inside, leaving the door ajar.

Boldwood waited. In two minutes a light appeared in the passage. Boldwood then saw that the chain had been fastened across the door. Troy appeared inside carrying a bedroom candlestick.

'What, did you think I should break in?' said Boldwood contemptuously.

'Oh, no; it is merely my humour to secure things. Will you read this a moment? I'll hold the light.'

Troy handed a folded newspaper through the slit between door and door-post, and put the candle close. 'That's the paragraph,' he said, placing his finger on a line.

Boldwood looked and read —

'MARRIAGES

'On the 17th inst., at St Ambrose's Church, Bath, by the Rev. G. Mincing, B.A., Francis Troy, only son of the late Edward Troy, Esq., M.D., of Weatherbury, and sergeant 11th Dragoon Guards, to Bathsheba, only surviving daughter of the late Mr John Everdene, of Casterbridge.'

'This may be called Fort meeting Feeble, hey, Boldwood?' said Troy. A low gurgle of derisive laughter followed the words.

The paper fell from Boldwood's hands. Troy continued —

'Fifty pounds to marry Fanny. Good. Twenty-one pounds not to marry Fanny, but Bathsheba. Good. Finale: already Bathsheba's husband. Now, Boldwood, yours is the ridiculous fate which always attends interference between a man and his wife. And another word. Bad as I am, I am not such a villain at to make the marriage or misery of any woman a matter of huckster and sale. Fanny has long ago left me. I don't know where she is. I have searched everywhere. Another word yet. You say you love Bathsheba; yet on the merest apparent evidence you instantly believe in her dishonour. A fig for such love! Now that I've taught you a lesson, take your money back again.'

'I will not; I will not!' said Boldwood, in a hiss.

'Anyhow I won't have it,' said Troy contemptuously. He wrapped the packet of gold in the notes, and threw the whole into the road.

Boldwood shook his clenched fist at him. 'You juggler of Satan! You black hound! But I'll punish you yet; mark me, I'll punish you yet!'

Another peal of laughter. Troy then closed the door, and locked himself in.

Throughout the whole of that night Boldwood's dark form might have been seen walking about the hills and downs of Weatherbury like an unhappy Shade in the Mournful Fields by Acheron.

CHAPTER THIRTY-FIVE

At an Upper Window

IT was very early the next morning — a time of sun and dew. The confused beginnings of many birds' songs spread into the healthy air, and the wan blue of the heaven was here and there coated with thin webs of incorporeal cloud which were of no effect in obscuring day. All the lights in the scene were yellow as to colour, and all the shadows were attenuated as to form. The creeping plants about the old manor-house were bowed with rows of heavy water drops, which had upon objects behind them the effect of minute lenses of high magnifying power.

Just before the clock struck five Gabriel Oak and Coggan passed the village cross, and went on together to the fields. They were yet barely in view of their mistress's house, when Oak fancied he saw the opening of a casement in one of the upper windows. The two men were at this moment partially screened by an elder bush, now beginning to be enriched with black bunches of fruit, and they paused before emerging from its shade.

A handsome man leaned idly from the lattice. He looked east and then west, in the manner of one who makes a first morning survey. The man was Sergeant Troy. His red jacket was loosely thrown on, but not buttoned, and he had altogether the relaxed bearing of a soldier taking his ease.

Coggan spoke first, looking quietly at the window.

'She has married him!' he said.

Gabriel had previously beheld the sight, and he now stood with his back turned, making no reply.

'I fancied we should know something to-day,' continued Coggan. 'I heard wheels pass my door just after dark – you were out somewhere.' He glanced round upon Gabriel. 'Good heavens above us, Oak, how white your face is; you look like a corpse!'

'Do I?' said Oak, with a faint smile.

'Lean on the gate: I'll wait a bit.'

'All right, all right.'

They stood by the gate awhile, Gabriel listlessly staring at the ground. His mind sped into the future, and saw there enacted in years of leisure the scenes of repentance that would ensue from this work of haste. That they were married he had instantly decided. Why had it been so mysteriously managed? It had become known that she had had a fearful journey to Bath, owing to her miscalculating the distance: that the horse had broken down, and that she had been more than two days getting there. It was not Bathsheba's way to do things furtively. With all her faults she was candour itself. Could she have been entrapped? The union was not only an unutterable grief to him: it amazed him, notwithstanding that he had passed the preceding week in a suspicion that such might be the issue of Troy's meeting her away from home. Her quiet return with Liddy had to some extent dispersed the dread. Just as that imperceptible motion which appears like stillness is infinitely divided in its properties from stillness itself, so had his hope undistinguishable from despair differed from despair indeed.

In a few minutes they moved on again towards the house. The sergeant still looked from the window.

'Morning, comrades!' he shouted, in a cheery voice, when they came up.

Coggan replied to the greeting. 'Bain't ye going to answer the man?' he then said to Gabriel. 'I'd say good morning – you needn't spend a hapeth of meaning upon it, and yet keep the man civil.'

Gabriel soon decided too that, since the deed was done, to put the best face upon the matter would be the greatest kindness to her he loved.

'Good morning, Sergeant Troy,' he returned, in a ghastly voice.

'A rambling, gloomy house this,' said Troy, smiling.

'Why – they *may* not be married!' suggested Coggan. 'Perhaps she's not there.'

Gabriel shook his head. The soldier turned a little towards the east, and the sun kindled his scarlet coat to an orange glow.

'But it is a nice old house,' responded Gabriel.

'Yes – I suppose so; but I feel like new wine in an old bottle here. My notion is that sash-windows should be put throughout, and these old wainscoted walls brightened up a bit; or the oak cleared quite away, and the walls papered.'

'It would be a pity, I think.'

'Well, no. A philosopher once said in my hearing that the old builders, who worked when art was a living thing, had no respect for the work of builders who went before them, but pulled down and altered as they thought fit; and why shouldn't we? "Creation and preservation don't do well together," says he, "and a million of antiquarians can't invent a style." My mind exactly. I am for making this place more modern, that we may be cheerful whilst we can.'

The military man turned and surveyed the interior of the room, to assist his ideas of improvement in this direction. Gabriel and Coggan began to move on.

'Oh, Coggan,' said Troy, as if inspired by a recollection, 'do you know if insanity has ever appeared in Mr Boldwood's family?'

Jan reflected for a moment.

'I once heard that an uncle of his was queer in his head, but I don't know the rights o't,' he said.

'It is of no importance,' said Troy lightly. 'Well, I shall be down in the fields with you some time this week; but I have a few matters to attend to first. So good-day to you. We shall, of course, keep on just as friendly terms as usual. I'm not a proud man: nobody is ever able to say that of Sergeant Troy. However, what is must be, and here's half-a-crown to drink my health, men.'

Troy threw the coin dexterously across the front plot and over the fence towards Gabriel, who shunned it in its fall, his face turning to an angry red. Coggan twirled his eye, edged forward, and caught the money in its ricochet upon the road.

'Very well – you keep it, Coggan,' said Gabriel with disdain, and almost fiercely. 'As for me, I'll do without gifts from him!'

'Don't show it too much,' said Coggan musingly. 'For if he's married to her, mark my words, he'll buy his discharge and be our master here. Therefore 'tis well to say "Friend" outwardly, though you say "Troublehouse" within.'

'Well – perhaps it is best to be silent; but I can't go further than that. I can't flatter, and if my place here is only to be kept by smoothing him down, my place must be lost.'

A horseman, whom they had for some time seen in the distance, now appeared close beside them.

'There's Mr Boldwood,' said Oak. 'I wonder what Troy meant by his question.'

Coggan and Oak nodded respectfully to the farmer, just checked their paces to discover if they were wanted, and finding they were not, stood back to let him pass on.

The only signs of the terrible sorrow Boldwood had been combating through the night, and was combating now, were the want of colour in his well-defined face, the enlarged appearance of the veins in his forehead and temples, and the sharper lines about his mouth. The horse bore him away, and the very step of the animal seemed significant of dogged despair. Gabriel, for a minute, rose above his own grief in noticing Boldwood's. He saw the square figure sitting erect upon the horse, the head turned to neither side, the elbows steady by the hips, the brim of the hat level and undisturbed in its onward glide, until the keen edges of Boldwood's shape sank by degrees over the hill. To one who knew the man and his story there was something more striking in this immobility than in a collapse. The clash of discord between mood and matter here was forced painfully home to the heart; and, as in laughter there are more dreadful phases than in tears, so was there in the steadiness of this agonized man an expression deeper than a cry.

CHAPTER THIRTY-SIX

Wealth in Jeopardy – The Revel

O NE night, at the end of August, when Bathsheba's experiences as a married woman were still new, and when the weather was yet dry and sultry, a man stood motionless in the stackyard of Weatherbury Upper Farm, looking at the moon and sky.

The night had a sinister aspect. A heated breeze from the south slowly fanned the summits of lofty objects, and in the sky dashes of buoyant cloud were sailing in a course at right angles to that of another stratum, neither of them in the direction of the breeze below. The moon, as seen through these films, had a lurid metallic look. The fields were sallow with the impure light, and all were tinged in monochrome, as if beheld through stained glass. The same evening the sheep had trailed homeward head to tail, the behaviour of the rooks had been confused, and the horses had moved with timidity and caution.

Thunder was imminent, and, taking some secondary appearances into consideration, it was likely to be followed by one of the lengthened rains which mark the close of dry weather for the season. Before twelve hours had passed a harvest atmosphere would be a bygone thing.

Oak gazed with misgiving at eight naked and unprotected ricks, massive and heavy with the rich produce of one-half the farm for that year. He went on to the barn.

This was the night which had been selected by Sergeant Troy – ruling now in the room of his wife – for giving the harvest supper and dance. As Oak approached the building the sound of violins and a tambourine, and the regular jigging of many feet, grew more distinct. He came close to the large doors, one of which stood slightly ajar, and looked in.

The central space, together with the recess at one end, was emptied of all incumbrances, and this area, covering about two-thirds of the whole, was appropriated for the gathering, the remaining end, which was piled to the ceiling with oats, being screened off with sail-cloth. Tufts and garlands of green foliage decorated the walls, beams, and extemporized chandeliers, and immediately opposite to Oak a rostrum had been erected, bearing a table and chairs. Here sat three fiddlers, and beside them stood a frantic man with his hair on end, perspiration streaming down his cheeks, and a tambourine quivering in his hand.

The dance ended, and on the black oak floor in the midst a new row of couples formed for another.

'Now, ma'am, and no offence I hope, I ask what dance you would like next?' said the first violin.

'Really, it makes no difference,' said the clear voice of Bathsheba, who stood at the inner end of the building, observing the scene from behind a table covered with cups and viands. Troy was lolling beside her.

'Then,' said the fiddler, 'I'll venture to name that the right and proper thing is "The Soldier's Joy" — there being a gallant soldier married into the farm — hey, my sonnies, and gentlemen all?'

'It shall be "The Soldier's Joy",' exclaimed a chorus.

'Thanks for the compliment,' said the sergeant gaily, taking Bathsheba by the hand and leading her to the top of the dance. 'For though I have purchased my discharge from Her Most Gracious Majesty's regiment of cavalry the 11th Dragoon Guards, to attend to the new duties awaiting me here, I shall continue a soldier in spirit and feeling as long as I live.'

So the dance began. As to the merits of 'The Soldier's Joy', there cannot be, and never were, two opinions. It has been observed in the musical circles of Weatherbury and its vicinity that this melody, at the end of three-quarters of an hour of thunderous footing, still possesses more stimulative properties for the heel and toe than the majority of other dances at their first opening. 'The Soldier's Joy' has, too, an additional charm, in being so admirably adapted to the tambourine aforesaid — no mean instrument in the hands of a performer who understands the proper convulsions, spasms, St Vitus's dances, and fearful frenzies necessary when exhibiting its tones in their highest perfection.

The immortal tune ended, a fine DD rolling forth from the bass-viol with the sonorousness of a cannonade, and Gabriel delayed his entry no longer. He avoided Bathsheba, and got as near as possible to the platform, where Sergeant Troy was now seated, drinking brandy-and-water, though the others drank without exception cider and ale. Gabriel could not easily thrust himself within speaking distance of the sergeant, and he sent a message, asking him to come down for a moment. The sergeant said he could not attend.

'Will you tell him, then,' said Gabriel, 'that I only stepped ath'art to say that a heavy rain is sure to fall soon, and that something should be done to protect the ricks?'

'Mr Troy says it will not rain,' returned the messenger, 'and he cannot stop to talk to you about such fidgets.'

In juxtaposition with Troy, Oak had a melancholy tendency to look like a candle beside gas, and ill at ease he went out again, thinking he would go home; for, under the circumstances, he had no heart for the scene in the barn. At the door he paused for a moment: Troy was speaking.

'Friends, it is not only the harvest home that we are celebrating to-night; but this is also a Wedding Feast. A short time ago I had the happiness to lead to the altar this lady, your mistress, and not until now have we been able to give any public flourish to the event in Weatherbury. That it may be thoroughly well done, and that every man may go happy to bed, I have ordered to be brought here some bottles of brandy and kettles of hot water. A treble-strong goblet will be handed round to each guest.'

Bathsheba put her hand upon his arm, and, with upturned pale face, said imploringly, 'No – don't give it to them – pray don't, Frank! It will only do them harm: they have had enough of everything.'

'True – we don't wish for no more, thank ye,' said one or two.

'Pooh!' said the sergeant contemptuously, and raised his voice as if lighted up by a new idea. 'Friends,' he said, 'we'll send the women-folk home! 'Tis time they were in bed. Then we cockbirds will have a jolly carouse to ourselves! If any of the men show the white feather, let them look elsewhere for a winter's work.'

Bathsheba indignantly left the barn, followed by all the women and children. The musicians, not looking upon themselves as 'company', slipped quietly away to their spring-waggon and put in the horse. Thus Troy and the men on the farm were left sole occupants of the place. Oak, not to appear unnecessarily disagreeable, stayed a little while; then he, too, arose and quietly took his departure, followed by a friendly oath from the sergeant for not staying to a second round of grog.

Gabriel proceeded towards his home. In approaching the door, his toe kicked something which felt and sounded soft, leathery, and distended, like a boxing-glove. It was a large toad humbly travelling across the path. Oak took it up, thinking it might be better to kill the creature to save it from pain; but finding it uninjured, he placed it again among the grass. He knew what this direct message from the Great Mother meant. And soon came another.

When he struck a light indoors there appeared upon the table a thin glistening streak, as if a brush of varnish had been lightly dragged across it. Oak's eyes followed the serpentine sheen to the other side, where it led up to a huge brown garden-slug, which had come indoors to-night for reasons of its own. It was Nature's second way of hinting to him that he was to prepare for foul weather.

Oak sat down meditating for nearly an hour. During this time two black spiders, of the kind common in thatched houses, promenaded the ceiling, ultimately dropping to the floor. This reminded him that if there was one class of manifestation on this matter that he thoroughly understood, it was the instincts of sheep. He left the room, ran across two or three fields towards the flock, got upon a hedge, and looked over among them.

They were crowded close together on the other side around some furze bushes, and the first peculiarity observable was that, on the sudden appearance of Oak's head over the fence, they did not stir or run away. They had now a terror of something greater than their terror of man. But this was not the most noteworthy feature: they were all grouped in such a way that their tails, without a single exception, were towards that half of the horizon from which the storm threatened. There was an inner circle closely huddled, and outside these they radiated wider apart, the pattern formed by the flock as a whole not being unlike a vandyked lace collar, to which the clump of furze-bushes stood in the position of a wearer's neck.

This was enough to re-establish him in his original opinion. He knew now that he was right, and that Troy was wrong. Every voice in nature was unanimous in bespeaking change. But two distinct translations attached to these dumb expressions. Apparently there was to be a thunder-storm, and afterwards a cold continuous rain. The creeping things seemed to know all about the later rain, but little of the interpolated thunder-storm; whilst the sheep knew all about the thunder-storm and nothing of the later rain.

This complication of weathers being uncommon, was all the more to be feared. Oak returned to the stackyard. All was silent here, and the conical tips of the ricks jutted darkly into the sky. There were five wheat-ricks in this yard, and three stacks of barley. The wheat when threshed would average about thirty quarters to each stack; the barley, at least forty. Their value to Bathsheba, and indeed to anybody Oak mentally estimated by the following simple calculation: –

$$5 \times 30 = 150 \text{ quarters} = 500l.$$
$$3 \times 40 = 120 \text{ quarters} = 250l.$$

$$\text{Total} \quad 750l.$$

Seven hundred and fifty pounds in the divinest form that money can wear – that of necessary food for man and beast: should the risk be run of deteriorating this bulk of corn to less than half its value, because of the instability of a woman? 'Never, if I can prevent it!' said Gabriel.

Such was the argument that Oak set outwardly before him. But man, even to himself, is a palimpsest, having an ostensible writing, and another beneath the lines. It is possible that there was this golden legend under the utilitarian one: 'I will help to my last effort the woman I have loved so dearly.'

He went back to the barn to endeavour to obtain assistance for covering the ricks that very night. All was silent within, and he would have passed on in the belief that the party had broken up, had not a dim light, yellow as saffron by contrast with the greenish whiteness outside, streamed through a knot-hole in the folding doors.

Gabriel looked in. An unusual picture met his eye.

The candles suspended among the evergreens had burnt down to their sockets, and in some cases the leaves tied about them were scorched. Many of the lights had quite gone out, others smoked and stank, grease dropping from them upon the floor. Here, under the table, and leaning against forms and chairs in every conceivable attitude except the perpendicular, were the wretched persons of all the work-folk, the hair of their heads at such low levels being suggestive of mops and brooms. In the midst of these shone red and distinct the figure of Sergeant Troy, leaning back in a chair. Coggan was on his back, with his mouth open, buzzing forth snores, as were several others; the united breathings of the horizontal assemblage forming a subdued roar like London from a distance. Joseph Poorgrass was curled round in the fashion of a hedgehog, apparently in attempts to present the least possible portion of his surface to the air; and behind him was dimly visible an unimportant remnant of William Smallbury. The glasses and cups still stood upon the table, a water-jug being overturned, from which a small rill, after tracing its course with marvellous precision down the centre of the long table, fell into the neck of the unconscious Mark Clark, in a steady, monotonous drip, like the dripping of a stalactite in a cave.

Gabriel glanced hopelessly at the group, which, with one or two exceptions, composed all the able-bodied men upon the farm. He saw at once that if the ricks were to be saved that night, or even the next morning, he must save them with his own hands.

A faint 'ting-ting' resounded from under Coggan's waistcoat. It was Coggan's watch striking the hour of two.

Oak went to the recumbent form of Matthew Moon, who usually undertook the rough thatching of the homestead, and shook him. The shaking was without effect.

Gabriel shouted in his ear, 'Where's your thatching-beetle and rick-stick and spars?'

'Under the staddles,' said Moon mechanically, with the unconscious promptness of a medium.

Gabriel let go his head, and it dropped upon the floor like a bowl. He then went to Susan Tall's husband.

'Where's the key of the granary?'

No answer. The question was repeated, with the same result. To be shouted to at night was evidently less of a novelty to Susan Tall's husband than to Matthew Moon. Oak flung down Tall's head into the corner again and turned away.

To be just, the men were not greatly to blame for this painful and demoralizing termination to the evening's entertainment. Sergeant Troy had so strenuously insisted, glass in hand, that drinking should be the bond of their union, that those who wished to refuse hardly liked to be so unmannerly under the circumstances. Having from their youth up been entirely unaccustomed to any liquor stronger than cider or mild ale, it was no wonder that they had succumbed, one and all, with extraordinary uniformity, after the lapse of about an hour.

Gabriel was greatly depressed. This debauch boded ill for that wilful and fascinating mistress whom the faithful man even now felt within him as the embodiment of all that was sweet and bright and hopeless.

He put out the expiring lights, that the barn might not be endangered, closed the door upon the men in their deep oblivious sleep, and went again into the lone night. A hot breeze, as if breathed from the parted lips of some dragon about to swallow the globe, fanned him from the south, while directly opposite in the north rose a grim misshapen body of cloud, in the very teeth of the wind. So unnaturally did it rise that one could fancy it to be lifted by machinery from below. Meanwhile the faint cloudlets had flown back into the south-east corner of the sky, as if in terror of the large cloud, like a young brood gazed in upon by some monster.

Going on to the village, Oak flung a small stone against the window of Laban Tall's bedroom, expecting Susan to open it; but nobody stirred. He went round to the back door, which had been left unfastened for Laban's entry, and passed in to the foot of the staircase.

'Mrs Tall, I've come for the key of the granary, to get at the rick-cloths,' said Oak, in a stentorian voice.

'Is that you?' said Mrs Susan Tall, half awake.

'Yes,' said Gabriel.

'Come along to bed, do, you draw-latching rogue – keeping a body awake like this!'

'It isn't Laban – 'tis Gabriel Oak. I want the key of the granary.'

'Gabriel! What in the name of fortune did you pretend to be Laban for?'

'I didn't. I thought you meant—'

'Yes you did! What do you want here?'

'The key of the granary.'

'Take it then. 'Tis on the nail. People coming disturbing women at this time of night ought—'

Gabriel took the key, without waiting to hear the conclusion of the tirade. Ten minutes later his lonely figure might have been seen dragging four large waterproof coverings across the yard, and soon two of these heaps of treasure in grain were covered snug—two cloths to each. Two hunderd pounds were secured. Three wheat-stacks remained open, and there were no more cloths. Oak looked under the staddles and found a fork. He mounted the third pile of wealth and began operating, adopting the plan of sloping the upper sheaves one over the other; and, in addition, filling the interstices with the material of some untied sheaves.

So far all was well. By this hurried contrivance Bathsheba's property in wheat was safe for at any rate a week or two, provided always that there was not much wind.

Next came the barley. This it was only possible to protect by systematic thatching. Time went on, and the moon vanished not to reappear. It was the farewell of the ambassador previous to war. The night had a haggard look, like a sick thing; and there came finally an utter expiration of air from the whole heaven in the form of a slow breeze, which might have been likened to a death. And now nothing was heard in the yard but the dull thuds of the beetle which drove in the spars, and the rustle of thatch in the intervals.

CHAPTER THIRTY-SEVEN

The Storm — The Two together

A LIGHT flapped over the scene, as if reflected from phosphorescent wings crossing the sky, and a rumble filled the air. It was the first move of the approaching storm.

The second peal was noisy, with comparatively little visible lightning. Gabriel saw a candle shining in Bathsheba's bedroom, and soon a shadow swept to and fro upon the blind.

Then there came a third flash. Manœuvres of a most extraordinary kind were going on in the vast firmamental hollows overhead. The lightning now was the colour of silver, and gleamed in the heavens like a mailed army. Rumbles became rattles. Gabriel from his elevated position could see over the landscape at least half-a-dozen miles in front. Every hedge, bush, and tree was distinct as in a line engraving. In a paddock in the same direction was a herd of heifers, and the forms of these were visible at this moment in the act of galloping about in the wildest and maddest confusion, flinging their heels and tails high into the air, their heads to earth. A poplar in the immediate foreground was like an ink stroke on burnished tin. Then the picture vanished, leaving the darkness so intense that Gabriel worked entirely by feeling with his hands.

He had stuck his ricking-rod, or poniard, as it was indifferently called – a long iron lance, polished by handling – into the stack, used to support the sheaves instead of the support called a groom used on houses. A blue light appeared in the zenith, and in some indescribable manner flickered down near the top of the rod. It was the fourth of the larger flashes. A moment later and there was a smack – smart, clear, and short. Gabriel felt his position to be anything but a safe one, and he resolved to descend.

Not a drop of rain had fallen as yet. He wiped his weary brow, and looked again at the black forms of the unprotected stacks. Was his life so valuable to him after all? What were his prospects that he should be so chary of running risk, when important and urgent labour could not be carried on without such risk? He resolved to stick to the stack. However, he took a precaution. Under the staddles was a long tethering chain, used to prevent the escape of errant horses. This he carried up the ladder, and sticking his rod through the clog at one end, allowed the other end of the chain to trail upon the ground. The spike attached to it he drove in. Under the shadow of this extemporized lightning-conductor he felt himself comparatively safe.

Before Oak had laid his hands upon his tools again out leapt the fifth flash, with the spring of a serpent and the shout of a fiend. It was green as an emerald, and the reverberation was stunning. What was this the light revealed to him? In the open ground before him, as he looked over the ridge of the rick, was a dark and apparently female form. Could it be that of the only venturesome woman in the parish – Bathsheba? The form moved on a step: then he could see no more.

'Is that you, ma'am?' said Gabriel to the darkness.

'Who is there?' said the voice of Bathsheba.

'Gabriel. I am on the rick, thatching.'

'O, Gabriel! – and are you? I have come about them. The weather awoke me, and I thought of the corn. I am so distressed about it – can we save it anyhow? I cannot find my husband. Is he with you?'

'He is not here.'

'Do you know where he is?'

'Asleep in the barn.'

'He promised that the stacks should be seen to, and now they are all neglected! Can I do anything to help? Liddy is afraid to come out. Fancy finding you here at such an hour! Surely I can do something?'

'You can bring up some reed-sheaves to me, one by one, ma'am; if you are not afraid to come up the ladder in the dark,' said Gabriel. 'Every moment is precious now, and that would save a good deal of time. It is not very dark when the lightning has been gone a bit.'

'I'll do anything!' she said resolutely. She instantly took a sheaf upon her shoulder, clambered up close to his heels, placed it behind the rod, and descended for another. At her third ascent the rick suddenly brightened with the brazen glare of shining majolica – every knot in every straw was visible. On the slope in front of him appeared two human shapes, black as jet. The rick lost its sheen –

the shapes vanished. Gabriel turned his head. It had been the sixth flash which had come from the east behind him, and the two dark forms on the slope had been the shadows of himself and Bathsheba.

Then came the peal. It hardly was credible that such a heavenly light could be the parent of such a diabolical sound.

'How terrible!' she exclaimed, and clutched him by the sleeve. Gabriel turned, and steadied her on her aerial perch by holding her arm. At the same moment, while he was still reversed in his attitude, there was more light, and he saw, as it were, a copy of the tall poplar tree on the hill drawn in black on the wall of the barn. It was the shadow of that tree, thrown across by a secondary flash in the west.

The next flare came. Bathsheba was on the ground now, shouldering another sheaf, and she bore its dazzle without flinching – thunder and all – and again ascended with the load. There was then a silence everywhere for four or five minutes, and the crunch of the spars, as Gabriel hastily drove them in, could again be distinctly heard. He thought the crisis of the storm had passed. But there came a burst of light.

'Hold on!' said Gabriel, taking the sheaf from her shoulder, and grasping her arm again.

Heaven opened then, indeed. The flash was almost too novel for its inexpressibly dangerous nature to be at once realized, and they could only comprehend the magnificence of its beauty. It sprang from east, west, north, south, and was a perfect dance of death. The forms of skeletons appeared in the air, shaped with blue fire for bones – dancing, leaping, striding, racing around, and mingling altogether in unparalleled confusion. With these were intertwined undulating snakes of green, and behind these was a broad mass of lesser light. Simultaneously came from every part of the tumbling sky what may be called a shout; since, though no shout ever came near it, it was more of the nature of a shout than of anything else earthly. In the meantime one of the grisly forms had alighted upon the point of Gabriel's rod, to run invisibly down it, down the chain, and into the earth. Gabriel was almost blinded, and he could feel Bathsheba's warm arm tremble in his hand – a sensation novel and thrilling enough; but love, life, everything human, seemed small and trifling in such close juxtaposition with an infuriated universe.

Oak had hardly time to gather up these impressions into a thought, and to see how strangely the red feather of her hat shone in this light, when the tall tree on the hill before mentioned seemed on fire to a white heat, and a new one among these terrible voices mingled with the last crash of those preceding. It was a stupefying blast, harsh and pitiless, and it fell upon their ears in a dead, flat blow, without that reverberation which lends the tones of a drum to more distant thunder. By the lustre reflected from every part of the earth and from the wide domical scoop above it, he saw that the tree was sliced down the whole length of its tall, straight stem, a huge riband of bark being apparently flung off. The other portion remained erect, and revealed the bared surface as a strip of white down the front. The lightning had struck the tree. A sulphurous smell filled the air; then all was silent, and black as a cave in Hinnom.

'We had a narrow escape!' said Gabriel hurriedly. 'You had better go down.'

Bathsheba said nothing; but he could distinctly hear her rhythmical pants, and the recurrent rustle of the sheaf beside her in response to her frightened pulsations. She descended the ladder, and, on second thoughts, he followed her. The darkness was now impenetrable by the sharpest vision. They both stood still at the bottom, side by side. Bathsheba appeared to think only of the weather – Oak thought only of her just then. At last he said –

'The storm seems to have passed now, at any rate.'

'I think so too,' said Bathsheba. 'Though there are multitudes of gleams, look!'

The sky was now filled with an incessant light, frequent repetition melting into complete continuity, as an unbroken sound results from the successive strokes on a gong.

'Nothing serious,' said he. 'I cannot understand no rain falling. But Heaven be praised, it is all the better for us. I am going up again.'

'Gabriel, you are kinder than I deserve! I will stay and help you yet. O, why are not some of the others here!'

'They would have been here if they could,' said Oak, in a hesitating way.

'O, I know it all – all,' she said, adding slowly: 'They are all asleep in the barn, in a drunken sleep, and my husband among them. That's it, is it not? Don't think I am a timid woman and can't endure things.'

'I am not certain,' said Gabriel. 'I will go and see.'

He crossed to the barn, leaving her there alone. He looked through the chinks of the door. All was in total darkness, as he had left it, and there still arose, as at the former time, the steady buzz of many snores.

He felt a zephyr curling about his cheek, and turned. It was Bathsheba's breath – she had followed him, and was looking into the same chink.

He endeavoured to put off the immediate and painful subject of their thoughts by remarking gently, 'If you'll come back again, miss – ma'am, and hand up a few more, it would save much time.'

Then Oak went back again, ascended to the top, stepped off the ladder for greater expedition, and went on thatching. She followed, but without a sheaf.

'Gabriel,' she said, in a strange and impressive voice.

Oak looked up at her. She had not spoken since he left the barn. The soft and continual shimmer of the dying lightning showed a marble face high against the black sky of the opposite quarter. Bathsheba was sitting almost on the apex of the stack, her feet gathered up beneath her, and resting on the top round of the ladder.

'Yes, mistress,' he said.

'I suppose you thought that when I galloped away to Bath that night it was on purpose to be married?'

'I did at last – not at first,' he answered, somewhat surprised at the abruptness with which this new subject was broached.

'And others thought so, too!'

'Yes.'

'And you blamed me for it?'

'Well – a little.'

'I thought so. Now, I care a little for your good opinion, and I want to explain something – I have longed to do it ever since I returned, and you looked so gravely at me. For if I were to die – and I may die soon – it would be dreadful that you should always think mistakenly of me. Now, listen.'

Gabriel ceased his rustling.

'I went to Bath that night in the full intention of breaking off my engagement to Mr Troy. It was owing to circumstances which occurred after I got there that — that we were married. Now, do you see the matter in a new light?'

'I do – somewhat.'

'I must, I suppose, say more, now that I have begun. And perhaps it's no harm, for you are certainly under no delusion that I ever loved you, or that I can have any object in speaking, more than that object I have mentioned. Well, I was alone in a strange city, and the horse was lame. And at last I didn't know what to do. I saw, when it was too late, that scandal might seize hold of me for meeting him alone in that way. But I was coming away, when he suddenly said he had that day seen a woman more beautiful than I, and that his constancy could not be counted on unless I at once became his. . . . And I was grieved and troubled—' She cleared her voice, and waited a moment, as if to gather breath. 'And then, between jealousy and distraction, I married him!' she whispered with desperate impetuosity.

Gabriel made no reply.

'He was not to blame, for it was perfectly true about – about his seeing somebody else,' she quickly added. 'And now I don't wish for a single remark from you upon the subject – indeed, I forbid it. I only wanted you to know that misunderstood bit of my history before a time comes when you could never know it. – You want some more sheaves?'

She went down the ladder, and the work proceeded. Gabriel soon perceived a langour in the movements of his mistress up and down, and he said to her, gently as a mother –

'I think you had better go indoors now, you are tired. I can finish the rest alone. If the wind does not change the rain is likely to keep off.'

'If I am useless I will go,' said Bathsheba, in a flagging cadence. 'But O, if your life should be lost!'

'You are not useless; but I would rather not tire you longer. You have done well.'

'And you better!' she said gratefully. 'Thank you for your devotion, a thousand times, Gabriel! Good-night – I know you are doing your very best for me.'

She diminished in the gloom, and vanished, and he heard the latch of the gate fall as she passed through. He worked in a reverie now, musing upon her story, and upon the contradictoriness of that feminine heart which had caused her to speak more warmly to him to-night than she ever had done whilst unmarried and free to speak as warmly as she chose.

He was disturbed in his meditation by a grating noise from the coach-house. It was the vane on the roof turning round, and this change in the wind was the signal for a disastrous rain.

CHAPTER THIRTY-EIGHT

Rain – One Solitary meets another

I T was now five o'clock, and the dawn was promising to break in hues of drab and ash.

The air changed its temperature and stirred itself more vigorously. Cool breezes coursed in transparent eddies round Oak's face. The wind shifted yet a point or two and blew stronger. In ten minutes every wind of heaven seemed to be roaming at large. Some of the thatching on the wheat-stacks was now whirled fantastically aloft, and had to be replaced and weighted with some rails that lay near at hand. This done, Oak slaved away again at the barley. A huge drop of rain smote his face, the wind snarled round every corner, the trees rocked to the bases of their trunks, and the twigs clashed in strife. Driving in spars at any point and on any system, inch by inch he covered more and more safely from ruin this distracting impersonation of seven hundred pounds. The rain came on in earnest, and Oak soon felt the water to be tracking cold and clammy routes down his back. Ultimately he was reduced well-nigh to a homogeneous sop, and the dyes of his clothes trickled down and stood in a pool at the foot of the ladder. The rain stretched obliquely through the dull atmosphere in liquid spines, unbroken in continuity between their beginnings in the clouds and their points in him.

Oak suddenly remembered that eight months before this time he had been fighting against fire in the same spot as desperately as he was fighting against water now – and for a futile love of the same woman. As for her – But Oak was generous and true, and dismissed his reflections.

It was about seven o'clock in the dark leaden morning when Gabriel came down from the last stack, and thankfully exclaimed, 'It is done!' He was drenched, weary, and sad, and yet not so sad as drenched and weary, for he was cheered by a sense of success in a good cause.

Faint sounds came from the barn, and he looked that way. Figures stepped singly and in pairs through the doors – all walking awkwardly, and abashed, save the foremost, who wore a red jacket, and advanced with his hands in his pockets, whistling. The others shambled after with a conscience-stricken air: the whole procession was not unlike Flaxman's group of the suitors tottering on towards the infernal regions under the conduct of Mercury. The gnarled shapes passed into the village, Troy, their leader, entering the farmhouse. Not a single one of them had turned his face to the ricks, or apparently bestowed one thought upon their condition.

Soon Oak too went homeward, by a different route from theirs. In front of him against the wet glazed surface of the lane he saw a person walking yet more slowly than himself under an umbrella. The man turned and plainly started; he was Boldwood.

'How are you this morning, sir?' said Oak.

'Yes, it is a wet day. – Oh, I am well, very well, I thank you; quite well.'

'I am glad to hear it, sir.'

Boldwood seemed to awake to the present by degrees. 'You look tired and ill, Oak,' he said then, desultorily regarding his companion.

'I am tired. You look strangely altered, sir.'

'I? Not a bit of it: I am well enough. What put that into your head?'

'I thought you didn't look quite so topping as you used to, that was all.'

'Indeed then you are mistaken,' said Boldwood shortly. 'Nothing hurts me. My constitution is an iron one.'

'I've been working hard to get our ricks covered, and was barely in time. Never had such a struggle in my life. . . . Yours of course are safe, sir.'

'O yes.' Boldwood added, after an interval of silence: 'What did you ask, Oak?'

'Your ricks are all covered before this time?'

'No.'

'At any rate, the large ones upon the stone staddles?'

'They are not.'

'Them under the hedge?'

'No. I forgot to tell the thatcher to set about it.'

'Nor the little one by the stile?'

'Nor the little one by the stile. I overlooked the ricks this year.'

'Then not a tenth of your corn will come to measure, sir.'

'Possibly not.'

'Overlooked them,' repeated Gabriel slowly to himself. It is difficult to describe the intensely dramatic effect that announcement had upon Oak at such a moment. All the night he had been feeling that the neglect he was labouring to repair was abnormal and isolated – the only instance of the kind within the circuit of the county. Yet at this very time, within the same parish, a greater waste had been going on, uncomplained of and disregarded. A few months earlier Boldwood's forgetting his husbandry would have been as preposterous an idea as a sailor forgetting he was in a ship. Oak was just thinking that whatever he himself might have suffered from Bathsheba's marriage, here was a man who had suffered more, when Boldwood spoke in a changed voice – that of one who yearned to make a confidence and relieve his heart by an outpouring.

'Oak, you know as well as I that things have gone wrong with me lately. I may as well own it. I was going to get a little settled in life; but in some way my plan has come to nothing.'

'I thought my mistress would have married you,' said Gabriel, not knowing enough of the full depths of Boldwood's love to keep silence on the farmer's account, and determined not to evade discipline by doing so on his own. 'However, it is so sometimes, and nothing happens that we expect,' he added, with the repose of a man whom misfortune had inured rather than subdued.

'I daresay I am a joke about the parish,' said Boldwood, as if the subject came irresistibly to his tongue, and with a miserable lightness meant to express his indifference.

'O no – I don't think that.'

' – But the real truth of the matter is that there was not, as some fancy, any jilting on – her part. No engagement ever existed between me and Miss Everdene.

People say so, but it is untrue: she never promised me!' Boldood stood still now and turned his wild face to Oak. 'O, Gabriel,' he continued, 'I am weak and foolish, and I don't know what, and I can't fend off my miserable grief! . . . I had some faint belief in the mercy of God till I lost that woman. Yes, He prepared a gourd to shade me, and like the prophet I thanked Him and was glad. But the next day He prepared a worm to smite the gourd and wither it; and I feel it is better to die than to live!'

A silence followed. Boldwood aroused himself from the momentary mood of confidence into which he had drifted, and walked on again, resuming his usual reserve.

'No, Gabriel,' he resumed, with a carelessness which was like the smile on the countenance of a skull: 'it was made more of by other people than ever it was by us. I do feel a little regret occasionally, but no woman ever had power over me for any length of time. Well, good morning; I can trust you not to mention to others what has passed between us two here.'

CHAPTER THIRTY-NINE

Coming Home – A Cry

O N the turnpike road, between Casterbridge and Weatherbury, and about three miles from the former place, is Yalbury Hill, one of those steep long ascents which pervade the highways of this undulating part of South Wessex. In returning from market it is usual for the farmers and other gig-gentry to alight at the bottom and walk up.

One Saturday evening in the month of October Bathsheba's vehicle was duly creeping up this incline. She was sitting listlessly in the second seat of the gig, whilst walking beside her in a farmer's marketing suit of unusually fashionable cut was an erect, well-made young man. Though on foot, he held the reins and whip, and occasionally aimed light cuts at the horse's ear with the end of the lash, as a recreation. This man was her husband, formerly Sergeant Troy, who, having bought his discharge with Bathsheba's money, was gradually transforming himself into a farmer of a spirited and very modern school. People of unalterable ideas still insisted upon calling him 'Sergeant' when they met him, which was in some degree owing to his having still retained the well-shaped moustache of his military days, and the soldierly bearing inseparable from his form and training.

'Yes, if it hadn't been for that wretched rain I should have cleared two hundred as easy as looking, my love,' he was saying. 'Don't you see, it altered all the chances? To speak like a book I once read, wet weather is the narrative, and fine days are the episodes, of our country's history; now, isn't that true?'

'But the time of year is come for changeable weather.'

'Well, yes. The fact is, these autumn races are the ruin of everybody. Never did I see such a day as 'twas! 'Tis a wild open place, just out of Budmouth, and a drab sea rolled in towards us like liquid misery. Wind and rain – good Lord! Dark? Why, 'twas as black as my hat before the last race was run. 'Twas five o'clock, and you couldn't see the horses till they were almost in, leave alone colours. The ground was as heavy as lead, and all judgment from a fellow's experience went for nothing. Horses, riders, people, were all blown about like ships at sea. Three booths were blown over, and the wretched folk inside crawled out upon their hands and knees; and in the next field were as many as a dozen hats at one time. Ay, Pimpernel regularly stuck fast, when about sixty yards off, and when I saw Policy stepping on, it did knock my heart against the lining of my ribs, I assure you, my love!'

'And you mean, Frank,' said Bathsheba sadly – her voice was painfully lowered from the fulness and vivacity of the previous summer – 'that you have lost more than a hundred pounds in a month by this dreadful horse-racing? O, Frank, it is cruel; it is foolish of you to take away my money so. We shall have to leave the farm; that will be the end of it!'

'Humbug about cruel. Now, there 'tis again – turn on the water-works; that's just like you.'

'But you'll promise me not to go to Budmouth second meeting, won't you?' she implored. Bathsheba was at the full depth for tears, but she maintained a dry eye.

'I don't see why I should; in fact, if it turns out to be a fine day, I was thinking of taking you.'

'Never, never! I'll go a hundred miles the other way first. I hate the sound of the very word!'

'But the question of going to see the race or staying at home has very little to do with the matter. Bets are all booked safely enough before the race begins, you may depend. Whether it is a bad race for me or a good one, will have very little to do with our going there next Monday.'

'But you don't mean to say that you have risked anything on this one too!' she exclaimed, with an agonized look.

'There now, don't you be a little fool. Wait till you are told. Why, Bathsheba, you have lost all the pluck and sauciness you formerly had, and upon my life if I had known what a chicken-hearted creature you were under all your boldness, I'd never have – I know what.'

A flash of indignation might have been seen in Bathsheba's dark eyes as she looked resolutely ahead after this reply. They moved on without further speech, some early-withered leaves from the trees which hooded the road at this spot occasionally spinning downward across their path to the earth.

A woman appeared on the brow of the hill. The ridge was in a cutting, so that she was very near the husband and wife before she became visible. Troy had turned towards the gig to remount, and whilst putting his foot on the step the woman passed behind him.

Though the overshadowing trees and the approach of eventide enveloped them in gloom, Bathsheba could see plainly enough to discern the extreme poverty of the woman's garb, and the sadness of her face.

'Please, sir, do you know at what time Casterbridge Union-house closes at night?'

The woman said these words to Troy over his shoulder.

Troy started visibly at the sound of the voice; yet he seemed to recover presence of mind sufficient to prevent himself from giving way to his impulse to suddenly turn and face her. He said, slowly –

I don't know.'

The woman, on hearing him speak, quickly looked up, examined the side of his face, and recognized the soldier under the yeoman's garb. Her face was drawn into an expression which had gladness and agony both among its elements. She uttered an hysterical cry, and fell down.

'O, poor thing!' exclaimed Bathsheba, instantly preparing to alight.

'Stay where you are, and attend to the horse!' said Troy peremptorily, throwing her the reins and the whip. 'Walk the horse to the top: I'll see to the woman.'

'But I—'

'Do you hear? Clk – Poppet!'

The horse, gig, and Bathsheba moved on.

'How on earth did you come here? I thought you were miles away, or dead! Why didn't you write to me?' said Troy to the woman, in a strangely gentle, yet hurried voice, as he lifted her up.

'I feared to.'

'Have you any money?'

'None.'

'Good Heaven – I wish I had more to give you! Here's – wretched – the merest trifle. It is every farthing I have left. I have none but what my wife gives me, you know, and I can't ask her now.'

The woman made no answer.

'I have only another moment,' continued Troy; 'and now listen. Where are you going to-night? Casterbridge Union?'

'Yes; I thought to go there.'

'You shan't go there; yet, wait. Yes, perhaps for to-night; I can do nothing better – worse luck! Sleep there to-night, and stay there to-morrow. Monday is the first free day I have; and on Monday morning, at ten exactly, meet me on Grey's Bridge, just out of the town. I'll bring all the money I can muster. You shan't want – I'll see that, Fanny; then I'll get you a lodging somewhere. Good-bye till then. I am a brute – but good-bye!'

After advancing the distance which completed the ascent of the hill, Bathsheba turned her head. The woman was upon her feet, and Bathsheba saw her withdrawing from Troy, and going feebly down the hill by the third milestone from Casterbridge. Troy then came on towards his wife, stepped into the gig, took the reins from her hand, and without making any observation whipped the horse into a trot. He was rather agitated.

'Do you know who that woman was?' said Bathsheba, looking searchingly into his face.

'I do,' he said, looking boldly back into hers.

'I thought you did,' said she, with angry hauteur, and still regarding him. 'Who is she?'

He suddenly seemed to think that frankness would benefit neither of the women.

'Nothing to either of us,' he said. 'I know her by sight.'

'What is her name?'

'How should I know her name?'

'I think you do.'

'Think if you will, and be—' The sentence was completed by a smart cut of the whip round Poppet's flank, which caused the animal to start forward at a wild pace. No more was said.

CHAPTER FORTY

On Casterbridge Highway

FOR a considerable time the woman walked on. Her steps became feebler, and she strained her eyes to look afar upon the naked road, now indistinct amid the penumbræ of night. At length her onward walk dwindled to the merest totter, and she opened a gate within which was a haystack. Underneath this she sat down and presently slept.

When the woman awoke it was to find herself in the depths of a moonless and starless night. A heavy unbroken crust of cloud stretched across the sky, shutting out every speck of heaven; and a distant halo which hung over the town of Casterbridge was visible against the black concave, the luminosity appearing the brighter by its great contrast with the circumscribing darkness. Towards this weak, soft glow the woman turned her eyes.

'If I could only get there!' she said. 'Meet him the day after tomorrow: God help me! Perhaps I shall be in my grave before then.'

A manor-house clock from the far depths of shadow struck the hour, one, in a small, attenuated tone. After midnight the voice of a clock seems to lose in breadth as much as in length, and to diminish its sonorousness to a thin falsetto.

Afterwards a light – two lights – arose from the remote shade, and grew larger. A carriage rolled along the road, and passed the gate. It probably contained some late diners-out. The beams from one lamp shone for a moment upon the crouching woman, and threw her face into vivid relief. The face was young in the ground-work, old in the finish; the general contours were flexuous and childlike, but the finer lineaments had begun to be sharp and thin.

The pedestrian stood up, apparently with a revived determination, and looked around. The road appeared to be familiar to her, and she carefully scanned the fence as she slowly walked along. Presently there became visible a dim white shape; it was another milestone. She drew her fingers across its face to feel the marks.

'Two more!' she said.

She leant against the stone as a means of rest for a short interval, then bestirred herself, and again pursued her way. For a slight distance she bore up bravely, afterwards flagging as before. This was beside a lone copsewood, wherein heaps of white chips strewn upon the leafy ground showed that woodmen had been faggoting and making hurdles during the day. Now there was not a rustle, not a breeze, not the faintest clash of twigs to keep her company. The woman looked over the gate, opened it, and went in. Close to the entrance stood a row of faggots, bound and unbound, together with stakes of all sizes.

For a few seconds the wayfarer stood with that tense stillness which signifies itself to be not the end, but merely the suspension, of a previous motion. Her attitude was that of a person who listens, either to the external world of sound, or to the imagined discourse of thought. A close criticism might have detected signs proving that she was intent on the latter alternative. Moreover, as was shown by what followed, she was oddly exercising the faculty of invention upon the speciality of the clever Jacquet Droz, the designer of automatic substitutes for human limbs.

By the aid of the Casterbridge aurora, and by feeling with her hands, the woman selected two sticks from the heaps. These sticks were nearly straight to the height of three or four feet, where each branched into a fork like the letter Y. She sat down, snapped off the small upper twigs, and carried the remainder with her into the road. She placed one of these forks under each arm as a crutch, tested them, timidly threw her whole weight upon them – so little that it was – and swung herself forward. The girl had made for herself a material aid.

The crutches answered well. The pat of her feet, and the tap of her sticks upon the highway, were all the sounds that came from the traveller now. She had passed the last milestone by a good long distance, and began to look wistfully towards the bank as if calculating upon another milestone soon. The crutches, though so very useful, had their limits of power. Mechanism only transfers labour, being powerless to supersede it, and the original amount of exertion was not cleared away; it was thrown into the body and arms. She was exhausted, and each swing forward became fainter. At last she swayed sideways, and fell.

Here she lay, a shapeless heap, for ten minutes and more. The morning wind began to boom dully over the flats, and to move afresh dead leaves which had lain still since yesterday. The woman desperately turned round upon her knees, and next rose to her feet. Steadying herself by the help of one crutch, she essayed a step, then another, then a third, using the crutches now as walking-sticks only. Thus she progressed till descending Mellstock Hill another milestone appeared, and soon the beginning of an iron-railed fence came into view. She staggered across to the first post, clung to it, and looked around.

The Casterbridge lights were now individually visible. It was getting towards morning, and vehicles might be hoped for, if not expected soon. She listened. There was not a sound of life save that acme and sublimation of all dismal sounds, the bark of a fox, its three hollow notes being rendered at intervals of a minute with the precision of a funeral bell.

'Less than a mile!' the woman murmured. 'No; more,' she added, after a pause. 'The mile is to the county-hall, and my resting-place is on the other side Casterbridge. A little over a mile, and there I am!' After an interval she again spoke. 'Five or six steps to a yard – six perhaps. I have to go seventeen hundred yards. A hundred times six, six hundred. Seventeen times that. O pity me, Lord!'

Holding to the rails, she advanced, thrusting one hand forward upon the rail, then the other, then leaning over it whilst she dragged her feet on beneath.

This woman was not given to soliloquy; but extremity of feeling lessens the individuality of the weak, as it increases that of the strong. She said again in the same tone, 'I'll believe that the end lies five posts forward, and no further, and so get strength to pass them.'

This was a practical application of the principle that a half-feigned and fictitious faith is better than no faith at all.

She passed five posts and held on to the fifth.

'I'll pass five more by believing my longed-for spot is at the next fifth. I can do it.'

She passed five more.

'It lies only five further.'

She passed five more.

'But it is five further.'

She passed them.

'That stone bridge is the end of my journey,' she said, when the bridge over the Froom was in view.

She crawled to the bridge. During the effort each breath of the woman went into the air as if never to return again.

'Now for the truth of the matter,' she said, sitting down. 'the truth is, that I have less than half a mile.' Self-beguilement with what she had known all the time to be false had given her strength to come over half a mile that she would have been powerless to face in the lump. The artifice showed that the woman, by some mysterious intuition, had grasped the paradoxical truth that blindness may operate more vigorously than prescience, and the short-sighted effect more than the far-seeing; that limitation, and not comprehensiveness, is needed for striking a blow.

The half-mile stood now before the sick and weary woman like a stolid Juggernaut. It was an impassive King of her world. The road here ran across Durnover Moor, open to the road on either side. She surveyed the wide space, the lights, herself, sighed, and lay down against a guard-stone of the bridge.

Never was ingenuity exercised so sorely as the traveller here exercised hers. Every conceivable aid, method, stratagem, mechanism, by which these last desperate eight hundred yards could be overpassed by a human being unperceived, was revolved in her busy brain, and dismissed as impracticable. She thought of sticks, wheels, crawling – she even thought of rolling. But the exertion demanded by either of these latter two was greater than to walk erect. The faculty of contrivance was worn out. Hopelessness had come at last.

'No further!' she whispered, and closed her eyes.

From the stripe of shadow on the opposite side of the bridge a portion of shade seemed to detach itself and move into isolation upon the pale white of the road. It glided noiselessly towards the recumbent woman.

She became conscious of something touching her hand; it was softness and it was warmth. She opened her eyes, and the substance touched her face. A dog was licking her cheek.

He was a huge, heavy, and quiet creature, standing darkly against the low horizon, and at least two feet higher than the present position of her eyes. Whether Newfoundland, mastiff, bloodhound, or what not, it was impossible to say. He seemed to be of too strange and mysterious a nature to belong to any variety among those of popular nomenclature. Being thus assignable to no breed, he was the ideal embodiment of canine greatness – a generalization from what was common to all. Night, in its sad, solemn, and benevolent aspect, apart from its stealthy and cruel side, was personified in this form. Darkness endows the small and ordinary ones among mankind with poetical power, and even the suffering woman threw her idea into figure.

In her reclining position she looked up to him just as in earlier times she had, when standing, looked up to a man. The animal, who was as homeless as she, respectfully withdrew a step or two when the woman moved, and, seeing that she did not repulse him, he licked her hand again.

A thought moved within her like lightning. 'Perhaps I can make use of him – I might do it then!'

She pointed in the direction of Casterbridge, and the dog seemed to misunderstand: he trotted on. Then, finding she could not follow, he came back and whined.

The ultimate and saddest singularity of woman's effort and invention was reached when, with a quickened breathing, she rose to a stooping posture, and, resting her two little arms upon the shoulders of the dog, leant firmly thereon, and murmured stimulating words. Whilst she sorrowed in her heart she cheered with her voice, and what was stranger than that the strong should need encouragement from the weak was that cheerfulness should be so well stimulated by such utter dejection. Her friend moved forward slowly, and she with small mincing steps moved forward beside him, half her weight being thrown upon the animal. Sometimes she sank as she had sunk from walking erect, from the crutches, from the rails. The dog, who now thoroughly understood her desire and her incapacity, was frantic in his distress on these occasions; he would tug at her dress and run forward. She always called him back, and it was now to be observed that the woman listened for human sounds only to avoid them. It was evident that she had an object in keeping her presence on the road and her forlorn state unknown.

Their progress was necessarily very slow. They reached the bottom of the town, and the Casterbridge lamps lay before them like fallen Pleiads as they turned to the left into the dense shade of a deserted avenue of chestnuts, and so skirted the borough. Thus the town was passed, and the goal was reached.

On this much-desired spot outside the town rose a picturesque building. Originally it had been a mere case to hold people. The shell had been so thin, so devoid of excrescence, and so closely drawn over the accommodation granted, that the grim character of what was beneath showed through it, as the shape of a body is visible under a winding-sheet.

Then Nature, as if offended, lent a hand. Masses of ivy grew up, completely covering the walls, till the place looked like an abbey; and it was discovered that the view from the front, over the Casterbridge chimneys, was one of the most magnificent in the county. A neighbouring earl once said that he would give up a year's rental to have at his own door the view enjoyed by the inmates from theirs – and very probably the inmates would have given up the view for his year's rental.

This stone edifice consisted of a central mass and two wings, whereon stood as sentinels a few slim chimneys, now gurgling sorrowfully to the slow wind. In the wall was a gate, and by the gate a bell-pull formed of a hanging wire. The woman raised herself as high as possible upon her knees, and could just reach the handle.

She moved it and fell forwards in a bowed attitude, her face upon her bosom.

It was getting on towards six o'clock, and sounds of movement were to be heard inside the building which was the haven of rest to this wearied soul. A little door by the large one was opened, and a man appeared inside. He discerned the panting heap of clothes, went back for a light, and came again. He entered a second time, and returned with two women.

These lifted the prostrate figure and assisted her in through the doorway. The man then closed the door.

'How did she get here?' said one of the women.

'The Lord knows,' said the other.

'There is a dog outside,' murmured the overcome traveller. 'Where is he gone? He helped me.'

'I stoned him away,' said the man.

The little procession then moved forward – the man in front bearing the light, the two bony women next, supporting between them the small and supple one. Thus they entered the house and disappeared.

CHAPTER FORTY-ONE

Suspicion – Fanny is sent for

BATHSHEBA said very little to her husband all that evening of their return from market, and he was not disposed to say much to her. He exhibited the unpleasant combination of a restless condition with a silent tongue. The next day, which was Sunday, passed nearly in the same manner as regarded their taciturnity, Bathsheba going to church both morning and afternoon. This was the day before the Budmouth races. In the evening Troy said, suddenly –

'Bathsheba, could you let me have twenty pounds?'

Her countenance instantly sank. 'Twenty pounds?' she said.

'The fact is, I want it badly.' The anxiety upon Troy's face was unusual and very marked. It was a culmination of the mood he had been in all the day.

'Ah! for those races to-morrow.'

Troy for the moment made no reply. Her mistake had its advantages to a man who shrank from having his mind inspected as he did now. 'Well, suppose I do want it for races?' he said, at last.

'O, Frank!' Bathsheba replied, and there was such a volume of entreaty in the words. 'Only such a few weeks ago you said that I was far sweeter than all your other pleasures put together, and that you would give them all up for me; and now, won't you give up this one, which is more a worry than a pleasure? Do, Frank. Come, let me fascinate you by all I can do – by pretty words and pretty looks, and everything I can think of – to stay at home. Say yes to your wife – say yes!'

The tenderest and softest phases of Bathsheba's nature were prominent now –

advanced impulsively for his acceptance, without any of the disguises and defences which the wariness of her character when she was cool too frequently threw over them. Few men could have resisted the arch yet dignified entreaty of the beautiful face, thrown a little back and sideways in the well-known attitude that expresses more than the words it accompanies, and which seems to have been designed for these special occasions. Had the woman not been his wife, Troy would have succumbed instantly; as it was, he thought he would not deceive her longer.

'The money is not wanted for racing debts at all,' he said.

'What is it for?' she asked. 'You worry me a great deal by these mysterious responsibilities, Frank.'

Troy hesitated. He did not now love her enough to allow himself to be carried too far by her ways. Yet it was necessary to be civil. 'You wrong me by such a suspicious manner,' he said. 'Such straitwaistcoating as you treat me to is not becoming in you at so early a date.'

'I think that I have a right to grumble a little if I pay,' she said, with features between a smile and a pout.

'Exactly; and, the former being done, suppose we proceed to the latter. Bathsheba, fun is all very well, but don't go too far, or you may have cause to regret something.'

She reddened. 'I do that already,' she said quickly.

'What do you regret?'

'That my romance has come to an end.'

'All romances end at marriage.'

'I wish you wouldn't talk like that. You grieve me to my soul by being smart at my expense.'

'You are dull enough at mine. I believe you hate me.'

'Not you – only your faults. I do hate them.'

' 'Twould be much more becoming if you set yourself to cure them. Come, let's strike a balance with the twenty pounds, and be friends.'

She gave a sigh of resignation. 'I have about that sum here for household expenses. If you must have it, take it.'

'Very good. Thank you. I expect I shall have gone away before you are in to breakfast to-morrow.'

'And must you go? Ah! there was a time, Frank, when it would have taken a good many promises to other people to drag you away from me. You used to call me darling, then. But it doesn't matter to you how my days are passed now.'

'I must go, in spite of sentiment.' Troy, as he spoke, looked at his watch, and, apparently actuated by *non lucendo* principles, opened the case at the back, revealing, snugly stowed within it, a small coil of hair.

Bathsheba's eyes had been accidentally lifted at that moment, and she saw the action and saw the hair. She flushed in pain and surprise, and some words escaped her before she had thought whether or not it was wise to utter them. 'A woman's curl of hair!' she said. 'O, Frank, whose is that?'

Troy had instantly closed his watch. He carelessly replied, as one who cloaked some feelings that the sight had stirred: 'Why, yours, of course. Whose should it be? I had quite forgotten that I had it.'

'What a dreadful fib, Frank!'

'I tell you I had forgotten it!' he said loudly.

'I don't mean that – it was yellow hair.'

'Nonsense.'

'That's insulting me. I know it was yellow. Now whose was it? I want to know.'

'Very well – I'll tell you, so make no more ado. It is the hair of a young woman I was going to marry before I knew you.'

'You ought to tell me her name, then.'

'I cannot do that.'

'Is she married yet?'

'No.'

'Is she alive?'

'Yes.'

'Is she pretty?'

'Yes.'

'It is wonderful how she can be, poor thing, under such an awful affliction!'

'Affliction – what affliction?' he inquired quickly.

'Having hair of that dreadful colour.'

'Oh – ho – I like that!' said Troy, recovering himself. 'Why, her hair has been admired by everybody who has seen her since she has worn it loose, which has not been long. It is beautiful hair. People used to turn their heads to look at it, poor girl!'

'Pooh! that's nothing – that's nothing!' she exclaimed, in incipient accents of pique. 'If I cared for your love as much as I used to I could say people had turned to look at mine.'

'Bathsheba, don't be so fitful and jealous. You knew what married life would be like, and shouldn't have entered it if you feared these contingencies.'

Troy had by this time driven her to bitterness: her heart was big in her throat, and the ducts to her eyes were painfully full. Ashamed as she was to show emotion, at last she burst out: –

'This is all I get for loving you so well! Ah! when I married you your life was dearer to me than my own. I would have died for you – how truly I can say that I would have died for you! And now you sneer at my foolishness in marrying you. O! is it kind to me to throw my mistake in my face? Whatever opinion you may have of my wisdom, you should not tell me of it so mercilessly, now that I am in your power.'

'I can't help how things fall out,' said Troy; 'upon my heart, women will be the death of me!'

'Well, you shouldn't keep people's hair. You'll burn it, won't you, Frank?'

Frank went on as if he had not heard her. 'There are considerations even before my consideration for you; reparations to be made – ties you know nothing of. If you repent of marrying, so do I.'

Trembling now, she put her hand upon his arm, saying, in mingled tones of wretchedness and coaxing, 'I only repent it if you don't love me better than any woman in the world! I don't otherwise, Frank. You don't repent because you already love somebody better than you love me, do you?'

'I don't know. Why do you say that?'

'You won't burn that curl. You like the woman who owns that pretty hair –

yes; it is pretty – more beautiful than my miserable black mane! Well, it is no use; I can't help being ugly. You must like her best, if you will!'

'Until to-day, when I took it from a drawer, I have never looked upon that bit of hair for several months – that I am ready to swear.'

'But just now you said "ties"; and then – that woman we met?'

' 'Twas the meeting with her that reminded me of the hair.'

'Is it hers, then?'

'Yes. There, now that you have wormed it out of me, I hope you are content.'

'And what are the ties?'

'Oh! that meant nothing – a mere jest.'

'A mere jest!' she said, in a mournful astonishment. 'Can you jest when I am so wretchedly in earnest? Tell me the truth, Frank, I am not a fool, you know, although I am a woman, and have my woman's moments. Come! treat me fairly,' she said, looking honestly and fearlessly into his face. 'I don't want much; bare justice – that's all! Ah! once I felt I could be content with nothing less than the highest homage from the husband I should choose. Now, anything short of cruelty will content me. Yes! the independent and spirited Bathsheba is come to this!'

'For Heaven's sake don't be so desperate!' Troy said snappishly, rising as he did so, and leaving the room.

Directly he had gone, Bathsheba burst into great sobs – dry-eyed sobs, which cut as they came, without any softening by tears. But she determined to repress all evidences of feeling. She was conquered; but she would never own it as long as she lived. Her pride was indeed brought low by despairing discoveries of her spoliation by marriage with a less pure nature than her own. She chafed to and fro in rebelliousness, like a caged leopard; her whole soul was in arms, and the blood fired her face. Until she had met Troy, Bathsheba had been proud of her position as a woman; it had been a glory to her to know that her lips had been touched by no man's on earth – that her waist had never been encircled by a lover's arm. She hated herself now. In those earlier days she had always nourished a secret contempt for girls who were the slaves of the first good-looking young fellow who should choose to salute them. She had never taken kindly to the idea of marriage in the abstract as did the majority of women she saw about her. In the turmoil of her anxiety for her lover she had agreed to marry him; but the perception that had accompanied her happiest hours on this account was rather that of self-sacrifice than of promotion and honour. Although she scarcely knew the divinity's name, Diana was the goddess whom Bathsheba instinctively adored. That she had never, by look, word, or sign, encouraged a man to approach her – that she had felt herself sufficient to herself, and had in the independence of her girlish heart fancied there was a certain degradation in renouncing the simplicity of a maiden existence to become the humbler half of an indifferent matrimonial whole – were facts now bitterly remembered. O, if she had never stooped to folly of this kind, respectable as it was, and could only stand again, as she had stood on the hill at Norcombe, and dare Troy or any other man to pollute a hair of her head by his interference!

The next morning she rose earlier than usual, and had the horse saddled for her ride round the farm in the customary way. When she came in at half-past eight – their usual hour for breakfasting – she was informed that her husband had risen, taken his breakfast, and driven off to Casterbridge with the gig and Poppet.

After breakfast she was cool and collected – quite herself in fact – and she rambled to the gate, intending to walk to another quarter of the farm, which she still personally superintended as well as her duties in the house would permit, continually, however, finding herself preceded in forethought by Gabriel Oak, for whom she began to entertain the genuine friendship of a sister. Of course, she sometimes thought of him in the light of an old lover, and had momentary imaginings of what life with him as a husband would have been like; also of life with Boldwood under the same conditions. But Bathsheba, though she could feel, was not much given to futile dreaming, and her musings under this head were short and entirely confined to the times when Troy's neglect was more than ordinarily evident.

She saw coming up the road a man like Mr Boldwood. It was Mr Boldwood. Bathsheba blushed painfully, and watched. The farmer stopped when still a long way off, and held up his hand to Gabriel Oak, who was in a footpath across the field. The two men then approached each other and seemed to engage in earnest conversation.

Thus they continued for a long time. Joseph Poorgrass now passed near them, wheeling a barrow of apples up the hill to Bathseba's residence. Boldwood and Gabriel called to him, spoke to him for a few minutes, and then all three parted, Joseph immediately coming up the hill with his barrow.

Bathsheba, who had seen this pantomime with some surprise, experienced great relief when Boldwood turned back again. 'Well, what's the message, Joseph?' she said.

He set down his barrow, and, putting upon himself the refined aspect that a conversation with a lady required, spoke to Bathsheba over the gate.

'You'll never see Fanny Robin no more – use nor principle – ma'am.'

'Why?'

'Because she's dead in the Union.

'Fanny dead – never!'

'Yes, ma'am.'

'What did she die from?'

'I don't know for certain; but I should be inclined to think it was from general neshness of constitution. She was such a limber maid that 'a could stand no hardship, even when I knowed her, and 'a went like a candle-snoff, so 'tis said. She was took bad in the morning, and, being quite feeble and worn out, she died in the evening. She belongs by law to our parish; and Mr Boldwood is going to send a waggon at three this afternoon to fetch her home here and bury her.'

'Indeed I shall not let Mr Boldwood do any such thing – I shall do it! Fanny was my uncle's servant, and, although I only knew her for a couple of days, she belongs to me. How very, very sad this is! – the idea of Fanny being in a workhouse.' Bathsheba had begun to know what suffering was, and she spoke with real feeling. . . . 'Send across to Mr Boldwood's, and say that Mrs Troy will take upon herself the duty of fetching an old servant of the family. . . . We ought not to put her in a waggon; we'll get a hearse.'

'There will hardly be time, ma'am, will there?'

'Perhaps not,' she said, musingly. 'When did you say we must be at the door – three o'clock?'

'Three o'clock this afternoon, ma'am, so to speak it.'

'Very well – you go with it. A pretty waggon is better than an ugly hearse, after all. Joseph, have the new spring waggon with the blue body and red wheels, and wash it very clean. And, Joseph—'

'Yes, ma'am.'

'Carry with you some evergreens and flowers to put upon her coffin – indeed, gather a great many, and completely bury her in them. Get some boughs of laurustinus, and variegated box, and yew, and boy's-love; ay, and some bunches of chrysanthemum. And let old Pleasant draw her, because she knew him so well.'

'I will, ma'am. I ought to have said that the Union, in the form of four labouring men, will meet me when I gets to our churchyard gate, and take her and bury her according to the rites of the Board of Guardians, as by law ordained.'

'Dear me – Casterbridge Union – and is Fanny come to this?' said Bathsheba, musing. 'I wish I had known of it sooner. I thought she was far away. How long has she lived there?'

'On'y been there a day or two.'

'Oh! – then she has not been staying there as a regular inmate?'

'No. She first went to live in a garrison-town t'other side o' Wessex, and since then she's been picking up a living at seampstering in Melchester for several months, at the house of a very respectable widow-woman who takes in work of that sort. She only got handy the Union-house on Sunday morning 'a b'lieve, and 'tis supposed here and there that she had traipsed every step of the way from Melchester. Why she left her place I can't say, for I don't know; and as to a lie, why, I wouldn't tell it. That's the short of the story, ma'am.'

'Ah-h!'

No gem ever flashed from a rosy ray to a white one more rapidly than changed the young wife's countenance whilst this word came from her in a long-drawn breath. 'Did she walk along our turnpike-road?' she said, in a suddenly restless and eager voice.

'I believe she did. . . . Ma'am, shall I call Liddy? You bain't well, ma'am, surely? You look like a lily – so pale and fainty!'

'No; don't call her; it is nothing. When did she pass Weatherbury?'

'Last Saturday night.'

'That will do, Joseph; now you may go.'

'Certainly, ma'am.'

'Joseph, come hither a moment. What was the colour of Fanny Robin's hair?'

'Really, mistress, now that 'tis put to me so judge-and-jury like, I can't call to mind, if ye'll believe me!'

'Never mind; go on and do what I told you. Stop – well, no, go on.'

She turned herself away from him, that he might no longer notice the mood which had set its sign so visibly upon her, and went indoors with a distressing sense of faintness and a beating brow. About an hour after, she heard the noise of the waggon and went out, still with a painful consciousness of her bewildered and troubled look. Joseph, dressed in his best suit of clothes, was putting in the horse to start. The shrubs and flowers were all piled in the waggon, as she had directed. Bathsheba hardly saw them now.

'Whose sweetheart did you say, Joseph?'

'I don't know, ma'am.'

'Are you quite sure?'

'Yes, ma'am, quite sure.'

'Sure of what?'

'I'm sure that all I know is that she arrived in the morning and died in the evening without further parley. What Oak and Mr Boldwood told me was only these few words. "Little Fanny Robin is dead, Joseph," Gabriel said, looking in my face in his steady old way. I was very sorry, and I said, "Ah! —and how did she come to die?" "Well, she's dead in Casterbridge Union," he said; "and perhaps 'tisn't much matter about how she came to die. She reached the Union early Sunday morning, and died in the afternoon —that's clear enough." Then I asked what she'd been doing lately, and Mr Boldwood turned round to me then, and left off spitting a thistle with the end of his stick. He told me about her having lived by seampstering in Melchester, as I mentioned to you, and that she walked therefrom at the end of last week, passing near here Saturday night in the dusk. They then said I had better just name a hent of her death to you, and away they went. Her death might have been brought on by biding in the night wind, you know, ma'am; for people used to say she'd go off in a decline: she used to cough a good deal in winter time. However, 'tisn't much odds to us about that now, for 'tis all over.'

'Have you heard a different story at all?' She looked at him so intently that Joseph's eyes quailed.

'Not a word, mistress, I assure 'ee!' he said. 'Hardly anybody in the parish knows the news yet.'

'I wonder why Gabriel didn't bring the message to me himself. He mostly makes a point of seeing me upon the most trifling errand.' These words were merely murmured, and she was looking upon the ground.

'Perhaps he was busy, ma'am,' Joseph suggested. 'And sometimes he seems to suffer from things upon his mind, connected with the time when he was better off than 'a is now. 'A's rather a curious item, but a very understanding shepherd, and learned in books.'

'Did anything seem upon his mind whilst he was speaking to you about this?'

'I cannot but say that there did, ma'am. He was terrible down, and so was Farmer Boldwood.'

'Thank you, Joseph. That will do. Go on now, or you'll be late.'

Bathsheba, still unhappy, went indoors again. In the course of the afternoon she said to Liddy, who had been informed of the occurrence, 'What was the colour of poor Fanny Robin's hair? Do you know? I cannot recollect —I only saw her for a day or two.'

'It was light, ma'am; but she wore it rather short, and packed away under her cap, so that you would hardly notice it. But I have seen her let it down when she was going to bed, and it looked beautiful then. Real golden hair.'

'Her young man was a soldier, was he not?'

'Yes. In the same regiment as Mr Troy. He says he knew him very well.'

'What, Mr Troy says so? How came he to say that?'

'One day I just named it to him, and asked him if he knew Fanny's young man. He said, "O yes, he knew the young man as well as he knew himself, and that there wasn't a man in the regiment he liked better."'

'Ah! Said that, did he?'

'Yes; and he said there was a strong likeness between himself and the other young man, so that sometimes people mistook them—'

'Liddy, for Heaven's sake stop your talking!' said Bathsheba, with the nervous petulance that comes from worrying perceptions.

CHAPTER FORTY-TWO

Joseph and his Burden — Buck's Head

A WALL bounded the site of Casterbridge Union-house, except along a portion of the end. Here a high gable stood prominent, and it was covered like the front with a mat of ivy. In this gable was no window, chimney, ornament, or protuberance of any kind. The single feature appertaining to it, beyond the expanse of dark green leaves, was a small door.

The situation of the door was peculiar. The sill was three or four feet above the ground, and for a moment one was at a loss for an explanation of this exceptional altitude, till ruts immediately beneath suggested that the door was used solely for the passage of articles and persons to and from the level of a vehicle standing on the outside. Upon the whole, the door seemed to advertise itself as a species of Traitor's Gate translated to another sphere. That entry and exit hereby was only at rare intervals became apparent on noting that tufts of grass were allowed to flourish undisturbed in the chinks of the sill.

As the clock over the South-street Alms-house pointed to five minutes to three, a blue spring waggon, picked out with red, and containing boughs and flowers, passed the end of the street, and up towards this side of the building. Whilst the chimes were yet stammering out a shattered form of 'Malbrook', Joseph Poorgrass rang the bell, and received directions to back his waggon against the high door under the gable. The door then opened, and a plain elm coffin was slowly thrust forth, and laid by two men in fustian along the middle of the vehicle.

One of the men then stepped up beside it, took from his pocket a lump of chalk, and wrote upon the cover the name and a few other words in a large scrawling hand. (We believe that they do these things more tenderly now, and provide a plate). He covered the whole with a black cloth, threadbare, but decent, the tail-board of the waggon was returned to its place, one of the men handed a certificate of registry to Poorgrass, and both entered the door, closing it behind them. Their connection with her, short as it had been, was over for ever.

Joseph then placed the flowers as enjoined, and the evergreens around the flowers, till it was difficult to divine what the waggon contained; he smacked his whip, and the rather pleasing funeral car crept down the hill, and along the road to Weatherbury.

The afternoon drew on apace, and, looking to the right towards the sea as he walked beside the horse, Poorgrass saw strange clouds and scrolls of mist rolling over the long ridges which girt the landscape in that quarter. They came in yet greater volumes, and indolently crept across the intervening valleys, and around the withered papery flags of the moor and river brinks. Then their dank spongy forms closed in upon the sky. It was a sudden overgrowth of atmospheric fungi which had their roots in the neighbouring sea, and by the time that horse, man, and corpse entered Yalbury Great Wood, these silent workings of an invisible hand had reached them, and they were completely enveloped, this being the first arrival of the autumn fogs, and the first fog of the series.

The air was as an eye suddenly struck blind. The waggon and its load rolled no longer on the horizontal division between clearness and opacity, but were imbedded in an elastic body of a monotonous pallor throughout. There was no perceptible motion in the air, not a visible drop of water fell upon a leaf of the beeches, birches, and firs composing the wood on either side. The trees stood in an attitude of intentness, as if they waited longingly for a wind to come and rock them. A startling quiet overhung all surrounding things – so completely, that the crunching of the waggon-wheels was as a great noise, and small rustles, which had never obtained a hearing except by night, were distinctly individualized.

Joseph Poorgrass looked round upon his sad burden as it loomed faintly through the flowering laurustinus, then at the unfathomable gloom amid the high trees on each hand, indistinct, shadowless, and spectre-like in their monochrome of grey. He felt anything but cheerful, and wished he had the company even of a child or dog. Stopping the horse he listened. Not a footstep or wheel was audible anywhere around, and the dead silence was broken only by a heavy particle falling from a tree through the evergreens and alighting with a smart rap upon the coffin of poor Fanny. The fog had by this time saturated the trees, and this was the first dropping of water from the overbrimming leaves. The hollow echo of its fall reminded the waggoner painfully of the grim Leveller. Then hard by came down another drop, then two or three. Presently there was a continual tapping of these heavy drops upon the dead leaves, the road, and the travellers. The nearer boughs were beaded with the mist to the greyness of aged men, and the rusty-red leaves of the beeches were hung with similar drops, like diamonds on auburn hair.

At the roadside hamlet called Roy-Town, just beyond this wood, was the old inn Buck's Head. It was about a mile and a half from Weatherbury, and in the meridian times of stage-coach travelling had been the place where many coaches changed and kept their relays of horses. All the old stabling was now pulled down, and little remained besides the habitable inn itself, which, standing a little way back from the road, signified its existence to people far up and down the highway by a sign hanging from the horizontal bough of an elm on the opposite side of the way.

Travellers – for the variety *tourist* had hardly developed into a distinct species at this date – sometimes said in passing, when they cast their eyes up to the sign-bearing tree, that artists were fond of representing the signboard hanging thus, but that they themselves had never before noticed so perfect an instance in actual working order. It was near this tree that the waggon was standing into which Gabriel Oak crept on his first journey to Weatherbury; but, owing to the darkness, the sign and the inn had been unobserved.

The manners of the inn were of the old-established type. Indeed, in the minds of its frequenters they existed as unalterable formulæ: *e.g.* –

Rap with the bottom of your pint for more liquor.
For tobacco, shout.
In calling for the girl in waiting, say, 'Maid!'
Ditto for the landlady, 'Old Soul!', etc., etc.

It was a relief to Joseph's heart when the friendly signboard came in view, and, stopping his horse immediately beneath it, he proceeded to fulfil an intention made a long time before. His spirits were oozing out of him quite. He turned the horse's head to the green bank, and entered the hostel for a mug of ale.

Going down into the kitchen of the inn, the floor of which was a step below the passage, which in its turn was a step below the road outside, what should Joseph see to gladden his eyes but two copper-coloured discs, in the form of the countenances of Mr Jan Coggan and Mr Mark Clark. These owners of the two most appreciative throats in the neighbourhood, within the pale of respectability, were now sitting face to face over a three-legged circular table, having an iron rim to keep cups and pots from being accidentally elbowed off; they might have been said to resemble the setting sun and the full moon shining *vis-à-vis* across the globe.

'Why, 'tis neighbour Poorgrass!' said Mark Clark. 'I'm sure your face don't praise your mistress's table, Joseph.'

'I've had a very pale companion for the last four miles,' said Joseph, indulging in a shudder toned down by resignation. 'And to speak the truth, 'twas beginning to tell upon me. I assure ye, I ha'n't seed the colour of victuals or drink since breakfast time this morning, and that was no more than a dew-bit afield.'

'Then drink, Joseph, and don't restrain yourself!' said Coggan, handing him a hooped mug three-quarters full.

Joseph drank for a moderately long time, then for a longer time, saying, as he lowered the jug, ''Tis pretty drinking – very pretty drinking, and is more than cheerful on my melancholy errand, so to speak it.'

'True, drink is a pleasant delight,' said Jan, as one who repeated a truism so familiar to his brain that he hardly noticed its passage over his tongue; and, lifting the cup, Coggan tilted his head gradually backwards, with closed eyes, that his expectant soul might not be diverted for one instant from its bliss by irrelevant surroundings.

'Well, I must be on again,' said Poorgrass. 'Not but that I should like another nip with ye; but the parish might lose confidence in me if I was seed here.'

'Where be ye trading o't to to-day, then, Joseph?'

'Back to Weatherbury. I've got poor little Fanny Robin in my waggon outside, and I must be at the churchyard gates at a quarter to five with her.'

'Ay – I've heard of it. And so she's nailed up in parish boards after all, and nobody to pay the bell shilling and the grave half-crown.'

'The parish pays the grave half-crown, but not the bell shilling, because the bell's a luxery: but a' can hardly do without the grave, poor body. However, I expect our mistress will pay all.'

'A pretty maid as ever I see! But what's yer hurry, Joseph? The poor woman's dead, and you can't bring her to life, and you may as well sit down comfortable, and finish another with us.'

'I don't mind taking just the least thimbleful ye can dream of more with ye, sonnies. But only a few minutes, because 'tis as 'tis.'

'Of course, you'll have another drop. A man's twice the man afterwards. You feel so warm and glorious, and you whop and slap at your work without any trouble, and everything goes on like sticks a-breaking. Too much liquor is bad, and leads us to that horned man in the smoky house; but after all, many people haven't the gift of enjoying a wet, and since we be highly favoured with a power that way, we should make the most o't.'

'True,' said Mark Clark. ''Tis a talent the Lord has mercifully bestowed upon us, and we ought not to neglect it. But, what with the parsons and clerks and school-people and serious tea-parties, the merry old ways of good life have gone to the dogs – upon my carcase, they have!'

'Well, really, I must be onward again now,' said Joseph.

'Now, now, Joseph; nonsense! The poor woman is dead, isn't she, and what's your hurry?'

'Well, I hope Providence won't be in a way with me for my doings,' said Joseph, again sitting down. 'I've been troubled with weak moments lately, 'tis true. I've been drinky once this month already, and I did not go to church a-Sunday, and I dropped a curse or two yesterday; so I don't want to go too far for my safety. Your next world is your next world, and not to be squandered off-hand.'

'I believe ye to be a chapel-member, Joseph. That I do.'

'Oh, no, no! I don't go so far as that.'

'For my part,' said Coggan, 'I'm staunch Church of England.'

'Ay, and faith, so be I,' said Mark Clark.

'I won't say much for myself; I don't wish to,' Coggan continued, with that tendency to talk on principles which is characteristic of the barley-corn. 'But I've never changed a single doctrine: I've stuck like a plaster to the old faith I was born in. Yes; there's this to be said for the Church, a man can belong to the Church and bide in his cheerful old inn, and never trouble or worry his mind about doctrines at all. But to be a meetinger, you must go to chapel in all winds and weathers, and make yerself as frantic as a skit. Not but that chapel-members be clever chaps enough in their way. They can lift up beautiful prayers out of their own heads, all about their families and shipwrecks in the newspaper.'

'They can – they can', said Mark Clark, with corroborative feeling; 'but we Churchmen, you see, must have it all printed aforehand, or, dang it all, we should no more know what to say to a great gaffer like the Lord than babes unborn.'

'Chapel-folk be more hand-in-glove with them above than we,' said Joseph thoughtfully.

'Yes,' said Coggan. 'We know very well that if anybody do go to heaven, they will. They've worked hard for it, and they deserve to have it, such as 'tis. I bain't such a fool as to pretend that we who stick to the Church have the same chance as they, because we know we have not. But I hate a feller who'll change his old ancient doctrines for the sake of getting to heaven. I'd as soon turn king's-evidence for the few pounds you get. Why, neighbours, when every one of my taties were frosted, our Pa'son Thirdly were the man who gave me a sack for seed, though he hardly had one for his own use, and no money to buy 'em. If it hadn't been for him, I shouldn't hae had a tatie to put in my garden. D'ye think I'd turn after that? No, I'll stick to my side; and if we be in the wrong, so be it: I'll fall with the fallen!'

'Well said – very well said,' observed Joseph. – 'However, folks, I must be moving now: upon my life I must. Pa'son Thirdly will be waiting at the church gates, and there's the woman a-biding outside in the waggon.'

'Joseph Poorgrass, don't be so miserable! Pa'son Thirdly won't mind. He's a generous man; he's found me in tracts for years, and I've consumed a good many in the course of a long and shady life; but he's never been the man to cry out at the expense. Sit down.'

The longer Joseph Poorgrass remained, the less his spirit was troubled by the duties which devolved upon him this afternoon. The minutes glided by uncounted, until the evening shades began perceptibly to deepen, and the eyes of the three were but sparkling points on the surface of darkness. Coggan's repeater struck six from his pocket in the usual still small tones.

At that moment hasty steps were heard in the entry, and the door opened to admit the figure of Gabriel Oak, followed by the maid of the inn bearing a candle. He stared sternly at the one lengthy and two round faces of the sitters, which confronted him with the expressions of a fiddle and a couple of warming-pans. Joseph Poorgrass blinked, and shrank several inches into the background.

'Upon my soul, I'm ashamed of you; 'tis disgraceful, Joseph, disgraceful!' said Gabriel indignantly. 'Coggan, you call yourself a man, and don't know better than this.'

Coggan looked up indefinitely at Oak, one or other of his eyes occasionally opening and closing of its own accord, as if it were not a member, but a dozy individual with a distinct personality.

'Don't take on so, shepherd!' said Mark Clark, looking reproachfully at the candle, which appeared to possess special features of interest for his eyes.

'Nobody can hurt a dead woman,' at length said Coggan, with the precision of a machine. 'All that could be done for her is done – she's beyond us: and why should a man put himself in a tearing hurry for lifeless clay that can neither feel nor see, and don't know what you do with her at all? If she'd been alive, I would have been the first to help her. If she now wanted victuals and drink, I'd pay for it, money down. But she's dead, and no speed of ours will bring her to life. The woman's past us – time spent upon her is throwed away: why should we hurry to do what's not required? Drink, shepherd, and be friends, for to-morrow we may be like her.'

'We may,' added Mark Clark emphatically, at once drinking himself, to run no further risk of losing his chance by the event alluded to, Jan meanwhile merging his additional thoughts of to-morrow in a song –

> 'To-mor-row, to-mor-row!
> And while peace and plen-ty I find at my board,
> With a heart free from sick-ness and sor-row,
> With my friends will I share what to-day may af-ford,
> And let them spread the ta-ble to-mor-row.
> To-mor-row, to-mor – '

'Do hold thy horning, Jan!' said Oak; and turning upon Poorgrass, 'as for you, Joseph, who do your wicked deeds in such confoundedly holy ways, you are as drunk as you can stand.'

'No, Shepherd Oak, no! Listen to reason, shepherd. All that's the matter with me is the affliction called a multiplying eye, and that's how it is I look double to you – I mean, you look double to me.'

'A multiplying eye is a very bad thing,' said Mark Clark.

'It always comes on when I have been in a public-house a little time,' said Joseph Poorgrass meekly. 'Yes; I see two of every sort, as if I were some holy man living in the times of King Noah and entering into the ark. . . . Y-y-y-yes,' he added, becoming much affected by the picture of himself as a person thrown away, and shedding tears; 'I feel too good for England: I ought to have lived in Genesis by rights, like the other men of sacrifice, and then I shouldn't have b-b-been called a d-d-drunkard in such a way!'

'I wish you'd show yourself a man of spirit, and not sit whining there!'

'Show myself a man of spirit? . . . Ah, well! let me take the name of drunkard humbly – let me be a man of contrite knees – let it be! I know that I always do say "Please God" afore I do anything, from my getting up to my going down of the same, and I be willing to take as much disgrace as there is in that holy act. Hah, yes! . . . But not a man of spirit? Have I ever allowed the toe of pride to be lifted against my hinder parts without groaning manfully that I question the right to do so? I inquire that query boldly?'

'We can't say that you have, Hero Poorgrass,' admitted Jan.

'Never have I allowed such treatment to pass unquestioned! Yet the shepherd says in the face of that rich testimony that I be not a man of spirit! Well, let it pass by, and death is a kind friend!'

Gabriel, seeing that neither of the three was in a fit state to take charge of the waggon for the remainder of the journey, made no reply, but, closing the door again upon them, went across to where the vehicle stood, now getting indistinct in the fog and gloom of this mildewy time. He pulled the horse's head from the large patch of turf it had eaten bare, readjusted the boughs over the coffin, and drove along through the unwholesome night.

It had gradually become rumoured in the village that the body to be brought and buried that day was all that was left of the unfortunate Fanny Robin who had followed the Eleventh from Casterbridge through Melchester and onwards. But, thanks to Boldwood's reticence and Oak's generosity, the lover she had followed had never been individualized as Troy. Gabriel hoped that the whole truth of the matter might not be published till at any rate the girl had been in her grave for a few days, when the interposing barriers of earth and time, and a sense that the events had been somewhat shut into oblivion, would deaden the sting that revelation and invidious remark would have for Bathsheba just now.

By the time that Gabriel reached the old manor-house, her residence, which lay in his way to the church, it was quite dark. A man came from the gate and said through the fog, which hung between them like blown flour –

'Is that Poorgrass with the corpse?'

Gabriel recognized the voice as that of the parson.

'The corpse is here, sir,' said Gabriel.

'I have just been to inquire of Mrs Troy if she could tell me the reason of the delay. I am afraid it is too late now for the funeral to be performed with proper decency. Have you the registrar's certificate?'

'No,' said Gabriel. 'I expect Poorgrass has that; and he's at the Buck's Head. I forgot to ask him for it.'

'Then that settles the matter. We'll put off the funeral till to-morrow morning. The body may be brought on to the church, or it may be left here at the farm and fetched by the bearers in the morning. They waited more than an hour, and have now gone home.'

Gabriel had his reasons for thinking the latter a most objectionable plan, notwithstanding that Fanny had been an inmate of the farm-house for several years in the lifetime of Bathsheba's uncle. Visions of several unhappy contingencies which might arise from this delay flitted before him. But his will was not law, and he went indoors to inquire of his mistress what were her wishes on the subject. He found her in an unusual mood: her eyes as she looked up to him were suspicious and perplexed as with some antecedent thought. Troy had not yet returned. At first Bathsheba assented with a mien of indifference to his proposition that they should go on to the church at once with their burden; but immediately afterwards, following Gabriel to the gate, she swerved to the extreme of solicitousness on Fanny's account, and desired that the girl might be brought into the house. Oak argued upon the convenience of leaving her in the waggon, just as she lay now, with her flowers and green leaves about her, merely wheeling the vehicle into the coach-house till the morning, but to no purpose. 'It is unkind and unchristian,' she said, 'to leave the poor thing in a coach-house all night.'

'Very well, then,' said the parson. 'And I will arrange that the funeral shall take place early to-morrow. Perhaps Mrs Troy is right in feeling that we cannot treat a dead fellow-creature too thoughtfully. We must remember that though she may have erred grievously in leaving her home, she is still our sister; and it is to be believed that God's uncovenanted mercies are extended towards her, and that she is a member of the flock of Christ.'

The parson's words spread into the heavy air with a sad yet unperturbed cadence, and Gabriel shed an honest tear. Bathsheba seemed unmoved. Mr Thirdly then left them, and Gabriel lighted a lantern. Fetching three other men to assist him, they bore the unconscious truant indoors, placing the coffin on two benches in the middle of a little sitting-room next the hall, as Bathsheba directed.

Every one except Gabriel Oak then left the room. He still indecisively lingered beside the body. He was deeply troubled at the wretchedly ironical aspect that circumstances were putting on with regard to Troy's wife, and at his own powerlessness to counteract them. In spite of his careful manœuvring all this day, the very worst event that could in any way have happened in connection with the burial had happened now. Oak imagined a terrible discovery resulting from this afternoon's work that might cast over Bathsheba's life a shade which the interposition of many lapsing years might but indifferently lighten, and which nothing at all might altogether remove.

Suddenly, as in a last attempt to save Bathsheba from, at any rate, immediate anguish, he looked again, as he had looked before, at the chalk writing upon the coffin-lid. The scrawl was this simple one, 'Fanny Robin and child'. Gabriel took his handkerchief and carefully rubbed out the two latter words, leaving visible one inscription 'Fanny Robin' only. He then left the room, and went out quietly by the front door.

CHAPTER FORTY-THREE

Fanny's Revenge

'Do you want me any longer, ma'am?' inquired Liddy, at a later hour the same evening, standing by the door with a chamber candlestick in her hand, and addressing Bathsheba, who sat cheerless and alone in the large parlour beside the first fire of the season.

'No more to-night, Liddy.'

'I'll sit up for master if you like, ma'am. I am not at all afraid of Fanny, if I may sit in my own room and have a candle. She was such a childlike, nesh young thing that her spirit couldn't appear to anybody if it tried, I'm quite sure.'

'O no, no! You go to bed. I'll sit up for him myself till twelve o'clock, and if he has not arrived by that time, I shall give him up and go to bed too.'

'It is half-past ten now.'

'Oh: is it?'

'Why don't you sit upstairs, ma'am?'

'Why don't I?' said Bathsheba desultorily. 'It isn't worth while – there's a fire here, Liddy.' She suddenly exclaimed in an impulsive and excited whisper, 'Have you heard anything strange said of Fanny?' The words had no sooner escaped her than an expression of unutterable regret crossed her face, and she burst into tears.

'No – not a word!' said Liddy, looking at the weeping woman with astonishment. 'What is it makes you cry so, ma'am; has anything hurt you?' She came to Bathsheba's side with a face full of sympathy.

'No, Liddy – I don't want you any more. I can hardly say why I have taken so to crying lately: I never used to cry. Good-night.'

Liddy then left the parlour and closed the door.

Bathsheba was lonely and miserable now; not lonelier actually than she had been before her marriage; but her loneliness then was to that of the present time as the solitude of a mountain is to the solitude of a cave. And within the last day or two had come these disquieting thoughts about her husband's past. Her wayward sentiment that evening concerning Fanny's temporary resting-place had been the result of a strange complication of impulses in Bathsheba's bosom. Perhaps it would be more accurately described as a determined rebellion against her prejudices, a revulsion from a lower instinct of uncharitableness, which would have withheld all sympathy from the dead woman, because in life she had preceded Bathsheba in the attentions of a man whom Bathsheba had by no means ceased from loving, though her love was sick to death just now with the gravity of a further misgiving.

In five or ten minutes there was another tap at the door. Liddy reappeared, and coming in a little way stood hesitating, until at length she said, 'Maryann has just heard something very strange, but I know it isn't true. And we shall be sure to know the rights of it in a day or two.'

'What is it?'

'Oh, nothing connected with you or us, ma'am. It is about Fanny. That same thing you have heard.'

'I have heard nothing.'

'I mean that a wicked story is got to Weatherbury within this last hour – that—' Liddy came close to her mistress and whispered the remainder of the sentence slowly into her ear, inclining her head as she spoke in the direction of the room where Fanny lay.

Bathsheba trembled from head to foot.

'I don't believe it!' she said excitedly. 'And there's only one name written on the coffin-cover.'

'Nor I, ma'am. And a good many others don't; for we should surely have been told more about it if it had been true – don't you think so, ma'am?'

'We might or we might not.'

Bathsheba turned and looked into the fire, that Liddy might not see her face. Finding that her mistress was going to say no more, Liddy glided out, closed the door softly, and went to bed.

Bathsheba's face, as she continued looking into the fire that evening, might have excited solicitousness on her account even among those who loved her least. The sadness of Fanny Robin's fate did not make Bathsheba's glorious, although she was the Esther to this poor Vashti, and their fates might be supposed to stand in some respects as contrasts to each other. When Liddy came into the room a second time the beautiful eyes which met hers had worn a listless, weary look. When she went out after telling the story they had expressed wretchedness in full activity. Her simple country nature, fed on old-fashioned principles, was troubled by that which would have troubled a woman of the world very little, both Fanny and her child, if she had one, being dead.

Bathsheba had grounds for conjecturing a connection between her own history and the dimly suspected tragedy of Fanny's end which Oak and Boldwood never for a moment credited her with possessing. The meeting with the lonely woman on the previous Saturday night had been unwitnessed and unspoken of. Oak may have had the best of intentions in withholding for as many days as possible the details of what had happened to Fanny; but had he known that Bathsheba's perceptions had already been exercised in the matter, he would have done nothing to lengthen the minutes of suspense she was now undergoing, when the certainty which must terminate it would be the worst fact suspected after all.

She suddenly felt a longing to speak to some one stronger than herself, and so get strength to sustain her surmised position with dignity and her carking doubts with stoicism. Where could she find such a friend? nowhere in the house. She was by far the coolest of the women under her roof. Patience and suspension of judgment for a few hours were what she wanted to learn, and there was nobody to teach her. Might she but go to Gabriel Oak! – but that could not be. What a way Oak had, she thought, of enduring things. Boldwood, who seemed so much deeper and higher and stronger in feeling than Gabriel, had not yet learnt, any more than she herself, the simple lesson which Oak showed a mastery of by every turn and look he gave – that among the multitude of interests by which he was surrounded, those which affected his personal well-being were not the most absorbing and important in his eyes. Oak meditatively looked upon the horizon of circumstances without any special regard to his own standpoint in the midst. That was how she would wish to be. But then Oak was not racked by incertitude upon the inmost matter of his bosom, as she was at this moment. Oak knew all about Fanny that she wished to know – she felt convinced of that. If she were to go to him now at once and say no more than these few words, 'What is the truth of the story?' he would feel bound in honour to tell her. It would be an inexpressible relief. No further speech would need to be uttered. He knew her so well that no eccentricity of behaviour in her would alarm him.

She flung a cloak round her, went to the door and opened it. Every blade, every twig was still. The air was yet thick with moisture, though somewhat less dense than during the afternoon, and a steady smack of drops upon the fallen leaves under the boughs was almost musical in its soothing regularity. It seemed better to be out of the house than within it, and Bathsheba closed the door, and walked slowly down the lane till she came opposite to Gabriel's cottage, where he now lived alone, having left Coggan's house through being pinched for room. There was a light in one window only, and that was downstairs. The shutters were not closed, nor was any blind or curtain drawn over the window, neither robbery nor observation being a contingency which could do much injury to the occupant of the domicile. Yes, it was Gabriel himself who was sitting up: he was reading. From her standing-place in the road she could see him plainly, sitting quite still, his light curly head upon his hand, and only occasionally looking up to snuff the candle which stood beside him. At length he looked at the clock, seemed surprised at the lateness of the hour, closed his book, and arose. He was going to bed, she knew, and if she tapped it must be done at once.

Alas for her resolve! She felt she could not do it. Not for worlds now could she give a hint about her misery to him, much less ask him plainly for information on the cause of Fanny's death. She must suspect, and guess, and chafe, and bear it all alone.

Like a homeless wanderer she lingered by the bank, as if lulled and fascinated by the atmosphere of content which seemed to spread from that little dwelling, and was so sadly lacking in her own. Gabriel appeared in an upper room, placed his light in the window-bench, and then – knelt down to pray. The contrast of the picture with her rebellious and agitated existence at this same time was too much for her to bear to look upon longer. It was not for her to make a truce with trouble by any such means. She must tread her giddy distracting measure to its last note, as she had begun it. With a swollen heart she went again up the lane, and entered her own door.

More fevered now by a reaction from the first feelings which Oak's example had raised in her, she paused in the hall, looking at the door of the room wherein Fanny lay. She locked her fingers, threw back her head, and strained her hot hands rigidly across her forehead, saying, with a hysterical sob, 'Would to God you would speak and tell me your secret, Fanny! . . . O, I hope, hope it is not true that there are two of you! . . . If I could only look in upon you for one little minute, I should know all!'

A few moments passed, and she added, slowly, *'And I will.'*

Bathsheba in after times could never gauge the mood which carried her through the actions following this murmured resolution on this memorable evening of her life. She went to the lumber-closet for a screw-driver. At the end of a short though undefined time she found herself in the small room, quivering with emotion, a mist before her eyes, and an excruciating pulsation in her brain, standing beside the uncovered coffin of the girl whose conjectured end had so entirely engrossed her, and saying to herself in a husky voice as she gazed within –

'It was best to know the worst, and I know it now!'

She was conscious of having brought about this situation by a series of actions done as by one in an extravagant dream; of following that idea as to method, which had burst upon her in the hall with glaring obviousness, by gliding to the top of the stairs, assuring herself by listening to the heavy breathing of her maids that they were asleep, gliding down again, turning the handle of the door within which the young girl lay, and deliberately setting herself to do what, if she had anticipated any such undertaking at night and alone, would have horrified her, but which, when done, was not so dreadful as was the conclusive proof of her husband's conduct which came with knowing beyond doubt the last chapter of Fanny's story.

Bathsheba's head sank upon her bosom, and the breath which had been bated in suspense, curiosity, and interest, was exhaled now in the form of a whispered wail: 'Oh-h-h!' she said, and the silent room added length to her moan.

Her tears fell fast beside the unconscious pair in the coffin: tears of a complicated origin, of a nature indescribable, almost indefinable except as other than those of simple sorrow. Assuredly their wonted fires must have lived in Fanny's ashes when events were so shaped as to chariot her hither in this natural, unobtrusive, yet effectual manner. The one feat alone – that of dying – by which a mean condition could be resolved into a grand one, Fanny had achieved. And to that had destiny subjoined this rencounter to-night, which had, in Bathsheba's wild imagining, turned her companion's failure to success, her humiliation to triumph, her lucklessness to ascendency; it had thrown over herself a garish light of mockery, and set upon all things about her an ironical smile.

Fanny's face was framed in by that yellow hair of hers; and there was no longer much room for doubt as to the origin of the curl owned by Troy. In Bathsheba's heated fancy the innocent white countenance expressed a dim triumphant consciousness of the pain she was retaliating for her pain with all the merciless rigour of the Mosaic law: 'Burning for burning; wound for wound; strife for strife.'

Bathsheba indulged in contemplations of escape from her position by immediate death, which, thought she, though it was an inconvenient and awful way, had limits to its inconvenience and awfulness that could not be overpassed; whilst the shames of life were measureless. Yet even this scheme of extinction by death was but tamely copying her rival's method without the reasons which had glorified it in her rival's case. She glided rapidly up and down the room, as was mostly her habit when excited, her hands hanging clasped in front of her, as she thought and in part expressed in broken words: 'O, I hate her, yet I don't mean that I hate her, for it is grievous and wicked; and yet I hate her a little! Yes, my flesh insists upon hating her, whether my spirit is willing or no! . . . If she had only lived, I could have been angry and cruel towards her with some justification; but to be vindictive towards a poor dead woman recoils upon myself. O God, have mercy! I am miserable at all this!'

Bathsheba became at this moment so terrified at her own state of mind that she looked around for some sort of refuge from herself. The vision of Oak kneeling down that night recurred to her, and with the imitative instinct which animates women she seized upon the idea, resolved to kneel, and, if possible, pray. Gabriel had prayed; so would she.

She knelt beside the coffin, covered her face with her hands, and for a time the room was silent as a tomb. Whether from a purely mechanical, or from any other cause, when Bathsheba arose it was with a quieted spirit, and a regret for the antagonistic instincts which had seized upon her just before.

In her desire to make atonement she took flowers from a vase by the window, and began laying them around the dead girl's head. Bathsheba knew no other way of showing kindness to persons departed than by giving them flowers. She knew not how long she remained engaged thus. She forgot time, life, where she was, what she was doing. A slamming together of the coach-house doors in the yard brought her to herself again. An instant after, the front door opened and closed, steps crossed the hall, and her husband appeared at the entrance to the room, looking in upon her.

He beheld it all by degrees, stared in stupefaction at the scene, as if he thought it an illusion raised by some fiendish incantation. Bathsheba, pallid as a corpse on end, gazed back at him in the same wild way.

So little are instinctive guesses the fruit of a legitimate induction that, at this moment, as he stood with the door in his hand, Troy never once thought of Fanny in connection with what he saw. His first confused idea was that somebody in the house had died.

'Well – what?' said Troy blankly.

'I must go! I must go!' said Bathsheba, to herself more than to him. She came with a dilated eye towards the door, to push past him.

'What's the matter, in God's name? who's dead?' said Troy.

'I cannot say; let me go out. I want air!' she continued.

'But no; stay, I insist!' He seized her hand, and then volition seemed to leave her, and she went off into a state of passivity. He, still holding her, came up the room, and thus, hand in hand, Troy and Bathsheba approached the coffin's side.

The candle was standing on a bureau close by them, and the light slanted down, distinctly enkindling the cold features of both mother and babe. Troy looked in, dropped his wife's hand, knowledge of it all come over him in a lurid sheen, and he stood still.

So still he remained that he could be imagined to have left in him no motive power whatever. The clashes of feeling in all directions confounded one another, produced a neutrality, and there was motion in none.

'Do you know her?' said Bathsheba, in a small enclosed echo, as from the interior of a cell.

'I do,' said Troy.

'Is it she?'

'It is.'

He had originally stood erect. And now, in the well-nigh congealed immobility of his frame could be discerned an incipient movement, as in the darkest night may be discerned light after a while. He was gradually sinking forwards. The lines of his features softened, and dismay modulated to illimitable sadness. Bathsheba was regarding him from the other side, still with parted lips and distracted eyes. Capacity for intense feeling is proportionate to the general intensity of the nature, and perhaps in all Fanny's sufferings, much greater relatively to her strength, there never was a time when she suffered in an absolute sense what Bathsheba suffered now.

What Troy did was to sink upon his knees with an indefinable union of remorse and reverence upon his face, and, bending over Fanny Robin, gently kissed her, as one would kiss an infant asleep to avoid awakening it.

At the sight and sound of that, to her, unendurable act, Bathsheba sprang towards him. All the strong feelings which had been scattered over her existence since she knew what feeling was, seemed gathered together into one pulsation now. The revulsion from her indignant mood a little earlier, when she had meditated upon compromised honour, forestalment. eclipse in maternity by another, was violent and entire. All that was forgotten in the simple and still strong attachment of wife to husband. She had sighed for her self-completeness then, and now she cried aloud against the severance of the union she had deplored. She flung her arms round Troy's neck, exclaiming wildly from the deepest deep of her heart –

'Don't – don't kiss them! O, Frank, I can't bear it – I can't! I love you better than she did: kiss me too, Frank – kiss me! *You will, Frank, kiss me too!'*

There was something so abnormal and startling in the childlike pain and simplicity of this appeal from a woman of Bathsheba's calibre and independence, that Troy, loosening her tightly clasped arms from his neck, looked at her in bewilderment. It was such an unexpected revelation of all women being alike at heart, even those so different in their accessories as Fanny and this one beside him, that Troy could hardly seem to believe her to be his proud wife Bathsheba. Fanny's own spirit seemed to be animating her frame. But this was the mood of a few instants only. When the momentary surprise had passed, his expression changed to a silencing imperious gaze.

'I will not kiss you!' he said, pushing her away.

Had the wife now but gone no further. Yet, perhaps, under the harrowing circumstances, to speak out was the one wrong act which can be better understood, if not forgiven in her, than the right and politic one, her rival being now but a corpse. All the feeling she had been betrayed into showing she drew back to herself again by a strenuous effort of self-command.

'What have you to say as your reason?' she asked, her bitter voice being strangely low – quite that of another woman now.

'I have to say that I have been a bad, black-hearted man,' he answered.

'And that this woman is your victim; and I not less than she.'

'Ah! don't taunt me, madam. This woman is more to me, dead as she is, than ever you were, or are, or can be. If Satan had not tempted me with that face of yours, and those cursed coquetries, I should have married her. I never had another thought till you came in my way. Would to God that I had; but it is all too late! I deserve to live in torment for this!' He turned to Fanny then. 'But never mind, darling,' he said; 'in the sight of Heaven you are my very, very wife!'

At these words arose from Bathsheba's lips a long, low cry of measureless despair and indignation, such a wail of anguish as had never before been heard within those old-inhabited walls. It was the Τετελεσται of her union with Troy.

'If she's – that, – what – am I?' she added, as a continuation of the same cry, and sobbing pitifully: and the rarity with her of such abandonment only made the condition more dire.

'You are nothing to me – nothing,' said Troy heartlessly. 'A ceremony before a priest doesn't make a marriage. I am not morally yours.'

A vehement impulse to flee from him, to run from this place, hide, and escape his words at any price, not stopping short of death itself, mastered Bathsheba now. She waited not an instant, but turned to the door and ran out.

CHAPTER FORTY-FOUR

Under a Tree – Reaction

BATHSHEBA went along the dark road, neither knowing nor caring about the direction or issue of her flight. The first time that she definitely noticed her position was when she reached a gate leading into a thicket overhung by some large oak and beech trees. On looking into the place, it occurred to her that she had seen it by daylight on some previous occasion, and that what appeared like an impassable thicket was in reality a brake of fern now withering fast. She could think of nothing better to do with her palpitating self than to go in here and hide; and entering, she lighted on a spot sheltered from the damp fog by a reclining trunk, where she sank down upon a tangled couch of fronds and stems. She mechanically pulled some armfuls round her to keep off the breezes, and closed her eyes.

Whether she slept or not that night Bathsheba was not clearly aware. But it was with a freshened existence and a cooler brain that, a long time afterwards, she became conscious of some interesting proceedings which were going on in the trees above her head and around.

A coarse-throated chatter was the first sound.

It was a sparrow just waking.

Next: 'Chee-weeze-weeze-weeze!' from another retreat.

It was a finch.

Third: 'Tink-tink-tink-tink-a-chink!' from the hedge.

It was a robin.

'Chuck-chuck-chuck!' overhead.

A squirrel.

Then, from the road, 'With my ra-ta-ta, and my rum-tum-tum!'

It was a ploughboy. Presently he came opposite, and she believed from his voice that he was one of the boys on her own farm. He was followed by a shambling tramp of heavy feet, and looking through the ferns Bathsheba could

just discern in the wan light of daybreak a team of her own horses. They stopped
to drink at a pond on the other side of the way. She watched them flouncing into
the pool, drinking, tossing up their heads, drinking again, the water dribbling
from their lips in silver threads. There was another flounce, and they came out of
the pond, and turned back again towards the farm.

She looked further around. Day was just dawning, and beside its cool air and
colours her heated actions and resolves of the night stood out in lurid contrast.
She perceived that in her lap, and clinging to her hair, were red and yellow leaves
which had come down from the tree and settled silently upon her during her
partial sleep. Bathsheba shook her dress to get rid of them, when multitudes of
the same family lying round about her rose and fluttered away in the breeze thus
created, 'like ghosts from an enchanter fleeing'.

There was an opening towards the east, and the glow from the as yet unrisen
sun attracted her eyes thither. From her feet, and between the beautiful yellowing
ferns with their feathery arms, the ground sloped downwards to a hollow, in
which was a species of swamp, dotted with fungi. A morning mist hung over it
now — a noisome yet magnificent silvery veil, full of light from the sun, yet semi-
opaque — the hedge behind it being in some measure hidden by its hazy
luminousness. Up the sides of this depression grew sheaves of the common rush,
and here and there a peculiar species of flag, the blades of which glistened in the
emerging sun, like scythes. But the general aspect of the swamp was malignant.
From its moist and poisonous coat seemed to be exhaled the essences of evil
things in the earth, and in the waters under the earth. The fungi grew in all
manner of positions from rotting leaves and tree stumps, some exhibiting to her
listless gaze their clammy tops, others their oozing gills. Some were marked with
great splotches, red as arterial blood, others were saffron yellow, and others tall
and attenuated, with stems like macaroni. Some were leathery and of richest
browns. The hollow seemed a nursery of pestilences small and great, in the
immediate neighbourhood of comfort and health, and Bathsheba arose with a
tremor at the thought of having passed the night on the brink of so dismal a place.

There were now other footsteps to be heard along the road. Bathsheba's nerves
were still unstrung: she crouched down out of sight again, and the pedestrian
came into view. He was a schoolboy, with a bag slung over his shoulder
containing his dinner, and a book in his hand. He paused by the gate, and,
without looking up, continued murmuring words in tones quite loud enough to
reach her ears.

' "O Lord, O Lord, O Lord, O Lord, O Lord": — that I know out o' book.
"Give us, give us, give us, give us, give us": — that I know. "Grace that, grace
that, grace that, grace that": — that I know.' Other words followed to the same
effect. The boy was of the dunce class apparently; the book was a psalter, and this
was his way of learning the collect. In the worst attacks of trouble there appears
to be always a superficial film of consciousness which is left disengaged and open
to the notice of trifles, and Bathsheba was faintly amused at the boy's method, till
he too passed on.

By this time stupor had given place to anxiety, and anxiety began to make
room for hunger and thirst. A form now appeared upon the rise on the other side
of the swamp, half-hidden by the mist, and came towards Bathsheba. The
woman — for it was a woman — approached with her face askance, as if looking

earnestly on all sides of her. When she got a little further round to the left, and drew nearer, Bathsheba could see the newcomer's profile against the sunny sky, and knew the wavy sweep from forehead to chin, with neither angle nor decisive line anywhere about it, to be the familiar contour of Liddy Smallbury.

Bathsheba's heart bounded with gratitude in the thought that she was not altogether deserted, and she jumped up. 'O, Liddy!' she said, or attempted to say; but the words had only been framed by her lips; there came no sound. She had lost her voice by exposure to the clogged atmosphere all these hours of night.

'O, ma'am! I am so glad I have found you,' said the girl, as soon as she saw Bathsheba.

'You can't come across,' Bathsheba said in a whisper, which she vainly endeavoured to make loud enough to reach Liddy's ears. Liddy, not knowing this, stepped down upon the swamp, saying, as she did so, 'It will bear me up, I think.'

Bathsheba never forgot that transient little picture of Liddy crossing the swamp to her there in the morning light. Iridescent bubbles of dank subterranean breath rose from the sweating sod beside the waiting-maid's feet as she trod, hissing as they burst and expanded away to join the vapoury firmament above. Liddy did not sink, as Bathsheba had anticipated.

She landed safely on the other side, and looked up at the beautiful though pale and weary face of her young mistress.

'Poor thing!' said Liddy, with tears in her eyes. 'Do hearten yourself up a little, ma'am. However did—'

'I can't speak above a whisper—my voice is gone for the present,' said Bathsheba hurriedly. 'I suppose the damp air from that hollow has taken it away. Liddy, don't question me, mind. Who sent you—anybody?'

'Nobody. I thought, when I found you were not at home, that something cruel had happened. I fancy I heard his voice late last night; and so, knowing something was wrong—'

'Is he at home?'

'No; he left just before I came out.'

'Is Fanny taken away?'

'Not yet. She will soon be—at nine o'clock.'

'We won't go home at present, then. Suppose we walk about in this wood?'

Liddy, without exactly understanding everything, or anything, in this episode, assented, and they walked together further among the trees.

'But you had better come in, ma'am, and have something to eat. You will die of a chill!'

'I shall not come indoors yet—perhaps never.'

'Shall I get you something to eat, and something else to put over your head besides that little shawl?'

'If you will, Liddy.'

Liddy vanished, and at the end of twenty minutes returned with a cloak, hat, some slices of bread and butter, a tea-cup, and some hot tea in a little china jug.

'Is Fanny gone?' said Bathsheba.

'No,' said her companion, pouring out the tea.

Bathsheba wrapped herself up and ate and drank sparingly. Her voice was then a little clearer, and a trifling colour returned to her face. 'Now we'll walk about again,' she said.

They wandered about the wood for nearly two hours, Bathsheba replying in monosyllables to Liddy's prattle, for her mind ran on one subject, and one only. She interrupted with –

'I wonder if Fanny is gone by this time?'

'I will go and see.'

She came back with the information that the men were just taking away the corpse; that Bathsheba had been inquired for; that she had replied to the effect that her mistress was unwell and could not be seen.

'Then they think I am in my bedroom?'

'Yes.' Liddy then ventured to add: 'You said when I first found you that you might never go home again – you didn't mean it, ma'am?'

'No; I've altered my mind. It is only women with no pride in them who run away from their husbands. There is one position worse than that of being found dead in your husband's house from his ill-usage, and that is, to be found alive through having gone away to the house of somebody else. I've thought of it all this morning, and I've chosen my course. A runaway wife is an encumbrance to everybody, a burden to herself and a byword – all of which make up a heap of misery greater than any that comes by staying at home – though this may include the trifling items of insult, beating, and starvation. Liddy, if ever you marry – God forbid that you ever should! – you'll find yourself in a fearful situation; but mind this, don't you flinch. Stand your ground, and be cut to pieces. That's what I'm going to do.'

'O, mistress, don't talk so!' said Liddy, taking her hand, 'but I knew you had too much sense to bide away. May I ask what dreadful thing it is that has happened between you and him?'

'You may ask; but I may not tell.'

In about ten minutes they returned to the house by a circuitous route, entering at the rear. Bathsheba glided up the back stairs to a disused attic, and her companion followed.

'Liddy,' she said, with a lighter heart, for youth and hope had begun to reassert themselves; 'you are to be my confidante for the present – somebody must be – and I choose you. Well, I shall take up my abode here for a while. Will you get a fire lighted, put down a piece of carpet, and help me to make the place comfortable? Afterwards, I want you and Maryann to bring up that little stump bedstead in the small room, and the bed belonging to it, and a table, and some other things. . . . What shall I do to pass the heavy time away?'

'Hemming handkerchiefs is a very good thing,' said Liddy.

'O no, no! I hate needlework – I always did.'

'Knitting?'

'And that, too.'

'You might finish your sampler. Only the carnations and peacocks want filling in; and then it could be framed and glazed, and hung beside your aunt's, ma'am.'

'Samplers are out of date – horribly countrified. No, Liddy, I'll read. Bring up some books – not new ones. I haven't heart to read anything new.'

'Some of your uncle's old ones, ma'am?'

'Yes. Some of those we stowed away in boxes.' A faint gleam of humour passed over her face as she said: 'Bring Beaumont and Fletcher's *Maid's Tragedy*; and the *Mourning Bride*; and – let me see – *Night Thoughts*, and the *Vanity of Human Wishes*.'

'And that story of the black man, who murdered his wife Desdemona? It is a nice dismal one that would suit you excellent just now.'

'Now, Lidd, you've been looking into my books, without telling me; and I said you were not to! How do you know it would suit me? It wouldn't suit me at all.'

'But if the others do—'

'No, they don't; and I won't read dismal books. Why should I read dismal books, indeed? Bring me *Love in a Village*, and the *Maid of the Mill*, and *Doctor Syntax*, and some volumes of the *Spectator*.'

All that day Bathsheba and Liddy lived in the attic in a state of barricade; a precaution which proved to be needless as against Troy, for he did not appear in the neighbourhood or trouble them at all. Bathsheba sat at the window till sunset, sometimes attempting to read, at other times watching every movement outside without much purpose, and listening without much interest to every sound.

The sun went down almost blood-red that night, and a livid cloud received its rays in the east. Up against this dark background the west front of the church tower – the only part of the edifice visible from the farm-house windows – rose distinct and lustrous, the vane upon the summit bristling with rays. Hereabouts, at six o'clock, the young men of the village gathered, as was their custom, for a game of Prisoners' base. The spot had been consecrated to this ancient diversion from time immemorial, the old stocks conveniently forming a base facing the boundary of the churchyard, in front of which the ground was trodden hard and bare as a pavement by the players. She could see the brown and black heads of the young lads darting about right and left, their white shirt-sleeves gleaming in the sun; whilst occasionally a shout and a peal of hearty laughter varied the stillness of the evening air. They continued playing for a quarter of an hour or so, when the game concluded abruptly, and the players leapt over the wall and vanished round to the other side behind a yew-tree, which was also half behind a beech, now spreading in one mass of golden foliage, on which the branches traced black lines.

'Why did the base-players finish their game so suddenly?' Bathsheba inquired, the next time that Liddy entered the room.

'I think 'twas because two men came just then from Casterbridge and began putting up a grand carved tombstone,' said Liddy. 'The lads went to see whose it was.'

'Do you know?' Bathsheba asked.

'I don't,' said Liddy.

CHAPTER FORTY-FIVE

Troy's Romanticism

W HEN Troy's wife had left the house at the previous midnight his first act was to cover the dead from sight. This done he ascended the stairs, and throwing himself down upon the bed dressed as he was, he waited miserably for the morning.

Fate had dealt grimly with him through the last four-and-twenty hours. His day had been spent in a way which varied very materially from his intentions regarding it. There is always an inertia to be overcome in striking out a new line of conduct – not more in ourselves, it seems, than in circumscribing events, which appear as if leagued together to allow no novelties in the way of amelioration.

Twenty pounds having been secured from Bathsheba, he had managed to add to the sum every farthing he could muster on his own account, which had been seven pounds ten. With this money, twenty-seven pounds ten in all, he had hastily driven from the gate that morning to keep his appointment with Fanny Robin.

On reaching Casterbridge he left the horse and trap at an inn, and at five minutes before ten came back to the bridge at the lower end of the town, and sat himself upon the parapet. The clocks struck the hour, and no Fanny appeared. In fact, at that moment she was being robed in her grave-clothes by two attendants at the Union poorhouse – the first and last tiring-women the gentle creature had ever been honoured with. The quarter went, the half hour. A rush of recollection came upon Troy as he waited: this was the second time she had broken a serious engagement with him. In anger he vowed it should be the last, and at eleven o'clock, when he had lingered and watched the stones of the bridge till he knew every lichen upon their faces, and heard the chink of the ripples underneath till they oppressed him, he jumped from his seat, went to the inn for his gig, and in a bitter mood of indifference concerning the past, and recklessness about the future, drove on to Budmouth races.

He reached the race-course at two-o'clock, and remained either there or in the town till nine. But Fanny's image, as it had appeared to him in the sombre shadows of that Saturday evening, returned to his mind, backed up by Bathsheba's reproaches. He vowed he would not bet, and he kept his vow, for on leaving the town at nine o'clock in the evening he had diminished his cash only to the extent of a few shillings.

He trotted slowly homeward, and it was now that he was struck for the first time with a thought that Fanny had been really prevented by illness from keeping her promise. This time she could have made no mistake. He regretted that he had not remained in Casterbridge and made inquiries. Reaching home he quietly unharnessed the horse and came indoors, as we have seen, to the fearful shock that awaited him.

As soon as it grew light enough to distinguish objects, Troy arose from the coverlet of the bed, and in a mood of absolute indifference to Bathsheba's whereabouts, and almost oblivious of her existence, he stalked downstairs and left the house by the back door. His walk was towards the churchyard, entering which he searched around till he found a newly dug unoccupied grave – the grave dug the day before for Fanny. The position of this having been marked, he hastened on to Casterbidge, only pausing and musing for a while at the hill whereon he had last seen Fanny alive.

Reaching the town, Troy descended into a side street and entered a pair of gates surmounted by a board bearing the words, 'Lester, stone and marble mason'. Within were lying about stones of all sizes and designs, inscribed as being sacred to the memory of unnamed persons who had not yet died.

Troy was so unlike himself now in look, word, and deed, that the want of likeness was perceptible even to his own consciousness. His method of engaging himself in this business of purchasing a tomb was that of an absolutely unpractised man. He could not bring himself to consider, calculate, or economize. He waywardly wished for something, and he set about obtaining it like a child in a nursery. 'I want a good tomb,' he said to the man who stood in a little office within the yard. 'I want as good a one as you can give me for twenty-seven pounds.'

It was all the money he possessed.

'That sum to include everything?'

'Everything. Cutting the name, carriage to Weatherbury, and erection. And I want it now, at once.'

'We could not get anything special worked this week.'

'I must have it now.'

'If you would like one of these in stock it could be got ready immediately.'

'Very well,' said Troy, impatiently. 'Let's see what you have.'

'The best I have in stock is this one,' said the stone-cutter, going into a shed. 'Here's a marble headstone beautifully crocketed, with medallions beneath of typical subjects; here's the footstone after the same pattern, and here's the coping to enclose the grave. The polishing alone of the set cost me eleven pounds – the slabs are the best of their kind, and I can warrant them to resist rain and frost for a hundred years without flying.'

'And how much?'

'Well, I could add the name, and put it up at Weatherbury for the sum you mention.'

'Get it done to-day, and I'll pay the money now.'

The man agreed, and wondered at such a mood in a visitor who wore not a shred of mourning. Troy then wrote the words which were to form the inscription, settled the account and went away. In the afternoon he came back again, and found that the lettering was almost done. He waited in the yard till the tomb was packed, and saw it placed in the cart and starting on its way to Weatherbury, giving directions to the two men who were to accompany it to inquire of the sexton for the grave of the person named in the inscription.

It was quite dark when Troy came out of Casterbridge. He carried rather a heavy basket upon his arm, with which he strode moodily along the road, resting occasionally at bridges and gates, whereon he deposited his burden for a time.

Midway on his journey he met, returning in the darkness, the men and the waggon which had conveyed the tomb. He merely inquired if the work was done, and, on being assured that it was, passed on again.

Troy entered Weatherbury churchyard about ten o'clock, and went immediately to the corner where he had marked the vacant grave early in the morning. It was on the obscure side of the tower, screened to a great extent from the view of passers along the road – a spot which until lately had been abandoned to heaps of stones and bushes of alder, but now it was cleared and made orderly for interments, by reason of the rapid filling of the ground elsewhere.

Here now stood the tomb as the men had stated, snow-white and shapely in the gloom, consisting of head and foot stone, and enclosing border of marble-work uniting them. In the midst was mould, suitable for plants.

Troy deposited his basket beside the tomb, and vanished for a few minutes. When he returned he carried a spade and a lantern, the light of which he directed for a few moments upon the marble, whilst he read the inscription. He hung his lantern on the lowest bough of the yew-tree, and took from his basket flower-roots of several varieties. There were bundles of snowdrop, hyacinth and crocus bulbs, violets and double daisies, which were to bloom in early spring, and of carnations, pinks, picotees, lilies of the valley, forget-me-not, summer's farewell, meadow-saffron and others, for the later seasons of the year.

Troy laid these out upon the grass, and with an impassive face set to work to plant them. The snowdrops were arranged in a line on the outside of the coping, the remainder within the enclosure of the grave. The crocuses and hyacinths were to grow in rows; some of the summer flowers he placed over her head and feet, the lilies and forget-me-nots over her heart. The remainder were dispersed in the spaces between these.

Troy, in his prostration at this time, had no perception that in the futility of these romantic doings, dictated by a remorseful reaction from previous indifference, there was any element of absurdity. Deriving his idiosyncrasies from both sides of the Channel, he showed at such junctures as the present the inelasticity of the Englishman, together with that blindness to the line where sentiment verges on mawkishness, characteristic of the French.

It was a cloudy, muggy, and very dark night, and the rays from Troy's lantern spread into the two old yews with a strange illuminating power, flickering, as it seemed, up to the black ceiling of cloud above. He felt a large drop of rain upon the back of his hand, and presently one came and entered one of the holes of the lantern, whereupon the candle sputtered and went out. Troy was weary, and it being now not far from midnight, and the rain threatening to increase, he resolved to leave the finishing touches of his labour until the day should break. He groped along the wall and over the graves in the dark till he found himself round at the north side. Here he entered the porch, and, reclining upon the bench within, fell asleep.

CHAPTER FORTY-SIX

The Gurgoyle: its Doings

THE tower of Weatherbury Church was a square erection of fourteenth-century date, having two stone gurgoyles on each of the four faces of its parapet. Of these eight carved protuberances only two at this time continued to serve the purpose of their erection – that of spouting the water from the lead roof within. One mouth in each front had been closed by bygone churchwardens as superfluous, and two others were broken away and choked – a matter not of much consequence to the well-being of the tower, for the two mouths which still remained open and active were gaping enough to do all the work.

It has been sometimes argued that there is no truer criterion of the vitality of any given art-period than the power of the master-spirits of that time in grotesque; and certainly in the instance of Gothic art there is no disputing the proposition. Weatherbury tower was a somewhat early instance of the use of an ornamental parapet in parish as distinct from cathedral churches, and the gurgoyles, which are the necessary correlatives of a parapet, were exceptionally prominent – of the boldest cut that the hand could shape, and of the most original design that a human brain could conceive. There was, so to speak, that symmetry in their distortion which is less the characteristic of British than of Continental grotesques of the period. All the eight were different from each other. A beholder was convinced that nothing on earth could be more hideous than those he saw on the north side until he went round to the south. Of the two on this latter face, only that at the south-eastern corner concerns the story. It was too human to be called like a dragon, too impish to be like a man, too animal to be like a fiend, and not enough like a bird to be called a griffin. This horrible stone entity was fashioned as if covered with a wrinkled hide; it had short, erect ears, eyes starting from their sockets, and its fingers and hands were seizing the corners of its mouth, which they thus seemed to pull open to give free passage to the water it vomited. The lower row of teeth was quite washed away, though the upper still remained. Here and thus, jutting a couple of feet from the wall against which its toes rested as a support, the creature had for four hundred years laughed at the surrounding landscape, voicelessly in dry weather, and in wet with a gurgling and snorting sound.

Troy slept on in the porch, and the rain increased outside. Presently the gurgoyle spat. In due time a small stream began to trickle through the seventy feet of aerial space between its mouth and the ground, which the water-drops smote like duckshot in their accelerated velocity. The stream thickened in substance, and increased in power, gradually spouting further and yet further from the side of the tower. When the rain fell in a steady and ceaseless torrent the stream dashed downward in volumes.

We follow its course to the ground at this point of time. The end of the liquid parabola has come forward from the wall, has advanced over the plinth mouldings, over a heap of stones, over the marble border, into the midst of Fanny Robin's grave.

The force of the stream had, until very lately, been received upon some loose stones spread thereabout, which had acted as a shield to the soil under the onset. These during the summer had been cleared from the ground, and there was now nothing to resist the downfall but the bare earth. For several years the stream had not spouted so far from the tower as it was doing on this night, and such a contingency had been overlooked. Sometimes this obscure corner received no inhabitant for the space of two or three years, and then it was usually but a pauper, a poacher, or other sinner of undignified sins.

The persistent torrent from the gurgoyle's jaws directed all its vengeance into the grave. The rich tawny mould was stirred into motion, and boiled like chocolate. The water accumulated and washed deeper down, and the roar of the pool thus formed spread into the night as the head and chief among other noises of the kind created by the deluging rain. The flowers so carefully planted by Fanny's repentant lover began to move and writhe in their bed. The winter-violets turned slowly upside down, and became a mere mat of mud. Soon the snowdrop and other bulbs danced in the boiling mass like ingredients in a cauldron. Plants of the tufted species were loosened, rose to the surface, and floated off.

Troy did not awake from his comfortless sleep till it was broad day. Not having been in bed for two nights his shoulders felt stiff, his feet tender, and his head heavy. He remembered his position, arose, shivered, took the spade, and again went out.

The rain had quite ceased, and the sun was shining through the green, brown, and yellow leaves, now sparkling and varnished by the raindrops to the brightness of similar effects in the landscapes of Ruysdael and Hobbema, and full of all those infinite beauties that arise from the union of water and colour with high lights. The air was rendered so transparent by the heavy fall of rain that the autumn hues of the middle distance were as rich as those near at hand, and the remote fields intercepted by the angle of the tower appeared in the same plane as the tower itself.

He entered the gravel path which would take him behind the tower. The path, instead of being stony as it had been the night before, was browned over with a thin coating of mud. At one place in the path he saw a tuft of stringy roots washed white and clean as a bundle of tendons. He picked it up — surely it could not be one of the primroses he had planted? He saw a bulb, another, and another as he advanced. Beyond doubt they were the crocuses. With a face of perplexed dismay Troy turned the corner and then beheld the wreck the stream had made.

The pool upon the grave had soaked away into the ground, and in its place was a hollow. The disturbed earth was washed over the grass and pathway in the guise of the brown mud he had already seen, and it spotted the marble tombstone with the same stains. Nearly all the flowers were washed clean out of the ground, and they lay, roots upwards, on the spots whither they had been splashed by the stream.

Troy's brow became heavily contracted. He set his teeth closely, and his compressed lips moved as those of one in great pain. This singular accident, by a strange confluence of emotions in him, was felt as the sharpest sting of all. Troy's face was very expressive, and any observer who had seen him now would hardly have believed him to be a man who had laughed, and sung, and poured love-trifles into a woman's ear. To curse his miserable lot was at first his impulse, but even that lowest stage of rebellion needed an activity whose absence was necessarily antecedent to the existence of the morbid misery which wrung him. The sight, coming as it did, superimposed upon the other dark scenery of the previous days, formed a sort of climax to the whole panorama, and it was more than he could endure. Sanguine by nature, Troy had a power of eluding grief by simply adjourning it. He could put off the consideration of any particular spectre till the matter had become old and softened by time. The planting of flowers on Fanny's grave had been perhaps but a species of elusion of the primary grief, and now it was as if his intention had been known and circumvented.

Almost for the first time in his life Troy, as he stood by this dismantled grave, wished himself another man. It is seldom that a person with much animal spirit does not feel that the fact of his life being his own is the one qualification which singles it out as a more hopeful life than that of others who may actually resemble him in every particular. Troy had felt, in his transient way, hundreds of times, that he could not envy other people their condition, because the possession of that condition would have necessitated a different personality, when he desired no other than his own. He had not minded the peculiarities of his birth, the vicissitudes of his life, the meteor-like uncertainty of all that related to him, because these appertained to the hero of his story, without whom there would have been no story at all for him; and it seemed to be only in the nature of things that matters would right themselves at some proper date and wind up well. This very morning the illusion completed its disappearance, and, as it were, all of a sudden, Troy hated himself. The suddenness was probably more apparent than real. A coral reef which just comes short of the ocean surface is no more to the horizon than if it had never been begun, and the mere finishing stroke is what often appears to create an event which has long been potentially an accomplished thing.

He stood and meditated – a miserable man. Whither should he go? 'He that is accursed, let him be accursed still,' was the pitiless anathema written in this spoliated effort of his new-born solicitousness. A man who has spent his primal strength in journeying in one direction has not much spirit left for reversing his course. Troy had, since yesterday, faintly reversed his; but the merest opposition had disheartened him. To turn about would have been hard enough under the greatest providential encouragement; but to find that Providence, far from helping him into a new course, or showing any wish that he might adopt one, actually jeered his first trembling and critical attempt in that kind, was more than nature could bear.

He slowly withdrew from the grave. He did not attempt to fill up the hole, replace the flowers, or do anything at all. He simply threw up his cards and forswore his game for that time and always. Going out of the churchyard silently and unobserved – none of the villagers having yet risen – he passed down some fields at the back, and emerged just as secretly upon the high road. Shortly afterwards he had gone from the village.

Meanwhile, Bathsheba remained a voluntary prisoner in the attic. The door was kept locked, except during the entries and exits of Liddy, for whom a bed had been arranged in a small adjoining room. The light of Troy's lantern in the churchyard was noticed about ten o'clock by the maid-servant, who casually glanced from the window in that direction whilst taking her supper, and she called Bathsheba's attention to it. They looked curiously at the phenomenon for a time, until Liddy was sent to bed.

Bathsheba did not sleep very heavily that night. When her attendant was unconscious and softly breathing in the next room, the mistress of the house was still looking out of the window at the faint gleam spreading from among the trees – not in a steady shine, but blinking like a revolving coast-light, though this appearance failed to suggest to her that a person was passing and repassing in front of it. Bathsheba sat here till it began to rain, and the light vanished, when she withdrew to lie restlessly in her bed and re-enact in a worn mind the lurid scene of yesternight.

Almost before the first faint sign of dawn appeared she arose again, and opened the window to obtain a full breathing of the new morning air, the panes being now wet with trembling tears left by the night rain, each one rounded with a pale lustre caught from primrose-hued slashes through a cloud low down in the awakening sky. From the trees came the sound of steady dripping upon the drifted leaves under them, and from the direction of the church she could hear another noise – peculiar, and not intermittent like the rest, the purl of water falling into a pool.

Liddy knocked at eight o'clock, and Bathsheba unlocked the door.

'What a heavy rain we've had in the night, ma'am!' said Liddy, when her inquiries about breakfast had been made.

'Yes; very heavy.'

'Did you hear the strange noise from the churchyard?'

'I heard one strange noise. I've been thinking it must have been the water from the tower spouts.'

'Well, that's what the shepherd was saying, ma'am. He's now gone on to see.'

'Oh! Gabriel has been here this morning?'

'Only just looked in in passing – quite in his old way, which I thought he had left off lately. But the tower spouts used to spatter on the stones, and we are puzzled, for this was like the boiling of a pot.'

Not being able to read, think, or work, Bathsheba asked Liddy to stay and breakfast with her. The tongue of the more childish woman still ran upon recent events. 'Are you going across to the church, ma'am?' she asked.

'Not that I know of,' said Bathsheba.

'I thought you might like to go and see where they have put Fanny. The trees hide the place from your window.'

Bathsheba had all sorts of dreads about meeting her husband. 'Has Mr Troy been in to-night?' she said.

'No, ma'am; I think he's gone to Budmouth.'

Budmouth! The sound of the word carried with it a much diminished perspective of him and his deeds; there were thirteen miles interval betwixt them now. She hated questioning Liddy about her husband's movements, and indeed had hitherto sedulously avoided doing so; but now all the house knew that there had been some dreadful disagreement between them, and it was futile to attempt disguise. Bathsheba had reached a stage at which people cease to have any appreciative regard for public opinion.

'What makes you think he has gone there?' she said.

'Laban Tall saw him on the Budmouth road this morning before breakfast.'

Bathsheba was momentarily relieved of that wayward heaviness of the past twenty-four hours which had quenched the vitality of youth in her without substituting the philosophy of maturer years, and she resolved to go out and walk a little way. So when breakfast was over she put on her bonnet, and took a direction towards the church. It was nine o'clock, and the men having returned to work again from their first meal, she was not likely to meet many of them in the road. Knowing that Fanny had been laid in the reprobates' quarter of the graveyard, called in the parish 'behind church', which was invisible from the road, it was impossible to resist the impulse to enter and look upon a spot which, from nameless feelings, she at the same time dreaded to see. She had been unable to overcome an impression that some connection existed between her rival and the light through the trees.

Bathsheba skirted the buttress, and beheld the hole and the tomb, its delicately veined surface splashed and stained just as Troy had seen it and left it two hours earlier. On the other side of the scene stood Gabriel. His eyes, too, were fixed on the tomb, and her arrival having been noiseless, she had not as yet attracted his attention. Bathsheba did not at once perceive that the grand tomb and the disturbed grave were Fanny's, and she looked on both sides and around for some humbler mound, earthed up and clodded in the usual way. Then her eye followed Oak's, and she read the words with which the inscription opened: –

'Erected by Francis Troy in Beloved Memory of
Fanny Robin.'

Oak saw her, and his first act was to gaze inquiringly and learn how she received this knowledge of the authorship of the work, which to himself had caused considerable astonishment. But such discoveries did not much affect her now. Emotional convulsions seemed to have become the commonplaces of her history, and she bade him good morning, and asked him to fill in the hole with the spade which was standing by. Whilst Oak was doing as she desired, Bathsheba collected the flowers, and began planting them with that sympathetic manipulation of roots and leaves which is so conspicuous in a woman's gardening, and which flowers seem to understand and thrive upon. She requested Oak to get the church-wardens to turn the leadwork at the mouth of the gurgoyle that hung gaping down upon them, that by this means the stream might be directed sideways, and a repetition of the accident prevented. Finally, with the superfluous magnanimity of a woman whose narrower instincts have brought down bitterness upon her instead of love, she wiped the mud spots from the tomb as if she rather liked its words than otherwise, and went home again.[1]

---

[1] The local tower and churchyard assumed to be those of 'Weatherbury' do not answer precisely to the foregoing description.

CHAPTER FORTY-SEVEN

Adventures by the Shore

TROY wandered along towards the south. A composite feeling, made up of disgust with the, to him, humdrum tediousness of a farmer's life, gloomy images of her who lay in the churchyard, remorse, and a general averseness to his wife's society, impelled him to seek a home in any place on earth save Weatherbury. The sad accessories of Fanny's end confronted him as vivid pictures which threatened to be indelible, and made life in Bathsheba's house intolerable. At three in the afternoon he found himself at the foot of a slope more than a mile in length, which ran to the ridge of a range of hills lying parallel with the shore, and formed a monotonous barrier between the basin of cultivated country inland and the wilder scenery of the coast. Up the hill stretched a road nearly straight and perfectly white, the two sides approaching each other in a gradual taper till they met the sky at the top about two miles off. Throughout the length of this narrow and irksome inclined plane not a sign of life was visible on this garish afternoon. Troy toiled up the road with a languor and depression greater than any he had experienced for many a day and year before. The air was warm and muggy, and the top seemed to recede as he approached.

At last he reached the summit, and a wide and novel prospect burst upon him with an effect almost like that of the Pacific upon Balboa's gaze. The broad steely sea, marked only by faint lines, which had a semblance of being etched thereon to a degree not deep enough to disturb its general evenness, stretched the whole width of his front and round to the right, where, near the town and port of Budmouth, the sun bristled down upon it, and banished all colour, to substitute in its place a clear oily polish. Nothing moved in sky, land, or sea, except a frill of milkwhite foam along the nearer angles of the shores, shreds of which licked the contiguous stones like tongues.

He descended and came to a small basin of sea enclosed by the cliffs. Troy's nature freshened within him; he thought he would rest and bathe here before going further. He undressed and plunged in. Inside the cove the water was uninteresting to a swimmer, being smooth as a pond, and to get a little of the ocean swell Troy presently swam between the two projecting spurs of rock which formed the pillars of Hercules to this miniature Mediterranean. Unfortunately for Troy a current unknown to him existed outside, which, unimportant to craft of any burden, was awkward for a swimmer who might be taken in it unawares. Troy found himself carried to the left and then round in a swoop out to sea.

He now recollected the place and its sinister character. Many bathers had there prayed for a dry death from time to time, and, like Gonzalo also, had been unanswered; and Troy began to deem it possible that he might be added to their number. Not a boat of any kind was at present within sight, but far in the distance

Budmouth lay upon the sea, as it were quietly regarding his efforts, and beside the town the harbour showed its position by a dim meshwork of ropes and spars. After well-nigh exhausting himself in attempts to get back to the mouth of the cove, in his weakness swimming several inches deeper than was his wont, keeping up his breathing entirely by his nostrils, turning upon his back a dozen times over, swimming *en papillon*, and so on, Troy resolved as a last resource to tread water at a slight incline, and so endeavour to reach the shore at any point, merely giving himself a gentle impetus inwards whilst carried on in the general direction of the tide. This, necessarily a slow process, he found to be not altogether so difficult, and though there was no choice of a landing-place – the objects on shore passing by him in a sad and slow procession – he perceptibly approached the extremity of a spit of land yet further to the right, now well defined against the sunny portion of the horizon. While the swimmer's eyes were fixed upon the spit as his only means of salvation on this side of the Unknown, a moving object broke the outline of the extremity, and immediately a ship's boat appeared, manned with several sailor lads, her bows towards the sea.

All Troy's vigour spasmodically revived to prolong the struggle yet a little further. Swimming with his right arm, he held up his left to hail them, splashing upon the waves, and shouting with all his might. From the position of the setting sun his white form was distinctly visible upon the now deep-hued bosom of the sea to the east of the boat, and the men saw him at once. Backing their oars and putting the boat about, they pulled towards him with a will, and in five or six minutes from the time of his first halloo, two of the sailors hauled him in over the stern.

They formed part of a brig's crew, and had come ashore for sand. Lending him what little clothing they could spare among them as a slight protection against the rapidly cooling air, they agreed to land him in the morning; and without further delay, for it was growing late, they made again towards the roadstead where their vessel lay.

And now night drooped slowly upon the wide watery levels in front; and at no great distance from them, where the shore-line curved round, and formed a long riband of shade upon the horizon, a series of points of yellow light began to start into existence, denoting the spot to be the site of Budmouth, where the lamps were being lighted along the parade. The cluck of their oars was the only sound of any distinctness upon the sea, and as they laboured amid the thickening shades the lamp-lights grew larger, each appearing to send a flaming sword deep down into the waves before it, until there arose, among other dim shapes of the kind, the form of the vessel for which they were bound.

CHAPTER FORTY-EIGHT

Doubts arise – Doubts linger

BATHSHEBA underwent the enlargement of her husband's absence from hours to days with a slight feeling of surprise, and a slight feeling of relief; yet neither sensation rose at any time far above the level commonly designated as indifference. She belonged to him: the certainties of that position were so well defined, and the reasonable probabilities of its issue so bounded, that she could not speculate on contingencies. Taking no further interest in herself as a splendid woman, she acquired the indifferent feelings of an outsider in contemplating her probable fate as a singular wretch; for Bathsheba drew herself and her future in colours that no reality could exceed for darkness. Her original vigorous pride of youth had sickened, and with it had declined all her anxieties about coming years, since anxiety recognizes a better and a worse alternative, and Bathsheba had made up her mind that alternatives on any noteworthy scale had ceased for her. Soon, or later – and that not very late – her husband would be home again. And then the days of their tenancy of the Upper Farm would be numbered. There had originally been shown by the agent to the estate some distrust of Bathsheba's tenure as James Everdene's successor, on the score of her sex, and her youth, and her beauty; but the peculiar nature of her uncle's will, his own frequent testimony before his death to her cleverness in such a pursuit, and her vigorous marshalling of the numerous flocks and herds which came suddenly into her hands before negotiations were concluded, had won confidence in her powers, and no further objections had been raised. She had latterly been in great doubt as to what the legal effects of her marriage would be upon her position; but no notice had been taken as yet of her change of name, and only one point was clear – that in the event of her own or her husband's inability to meet the agent at the forthcoming January rent-day, very little consideration would be shown, and, for that matter, very little would be deserved. Once out of the farm the approach of poverty would be sure.

Hence Bathsheba lived in a perception that her purposes were broken off. She was not a woman who could hope on without good materials for the process, differing thus from the less far-sighted and energetic, though more petted ones of the sex, with whom hope goes on as a sort of clockwork which the merest food and shelter are sufficient to wind up; and perceiving clearly that her mistake had been a fatal one, she accepted her position, and waited coldly for the end.

The first Saturday after Troy's departure she went to Casterbridge alone, a journey she had not taken since her marriage. On this Saturday Bathsheba was passing slowly on foot through the crowd of rural business-men gathered as usual in front of the market-house, who were as usual gazed upon by the burghers with feelings that those healthy lives were dearly paid for by exclusion from possible aldermanship, when a man, who had apparently been following her, said some words to another on her left hand. Bathsheba's ears were keen as those of any wild animal, and she distinctly heard what the speaker said, though her back was towards him.

'I am looking for Mrs Troy. Is that she there?'

'Yes; that's the young lady, I believe,' said the person addressed.

'I have some awkward news to break to her. Her husband is drowned.'

As if endowed with the spirit of prophecy, Bathsheba gasped out, 'No, it is not true; it cannot be true!' Then she said and heard no more. The ice of self-command which had latterly gathered over her was broken, and the currents burst forth again, and overwhelmed her. A darkness came into her eyes, and she fell.

But not to the ground. A gloomy man, who had been observing her from under the portico of the old corn-exchange when she passed through the group without, stepped quickly to her side at the moment of her exclamation, and caught her in his arms as she sank down.

'What is it?' said Boldwood, looking up at the bringer of the big news, as he supported her.

'Her husband was drowned this week while bathing in Lulwind Cove. A coastguardsman found his clothes, and brought them into Budmouth yesterday.'

Thereupon a strange fire lighted up Boldwood's eye, and his face flushed with the suppressed excitement of an unutterable thought. Everybody's glance was now centred upon him and the unconscious Bathsheba. He lifted her bodily off the ground, and smoothed down the folds of her dress as a child might have taken a storm-beaten bird and arranged its ruffled plumes, and bore her along the pavement to the King's Arms inn. Here he passed with her under the archway into a private room; and by the time he had deposited – so lothly – the precious burden upon a sofa, Bathsheba had opened her eyes. Remembering all that had occurred, she murmured, 'I want to go home!'

Boldwood left the room. He stood for a moment in the passage to recover his senses. The experience had been too much for his consciousness to keep up with, and now that he had grasped it it had gone again. For those few heavenly, golden moments she had been in his arms. What did it matter about her not knowing it? She had been close to his breast; he had been close to hers.

He started onward again, and sending a woman to her, went out to ascertain all the facts of the case. These appeared to be limited to what he had already heard. He then ordered her horse to be put into the gig, and when all was ready returned to inform her. He found that, though still pale and unwell, she had in the meantime sent for the Budmouth man who brought the tidings, and learnt from him all there was to know.

Being hardly in a condition to drive home as she had driven to town, Boldwood, with every delicacy of manner and feeling, offered to get her a driver, or to give her a seat in his phaeton, which was more comfortable than her own conveyance. These proposals Bathsheba gently declined, and the farmer at once departed.

About half-an-hour later she invigorated herself by an effort, and took her seat and the reins as usual – in external appearance much as if nothing had happened. She went out of the town by a tortuous back street, and drove slowly along, unconscious of the road and the scene. The first shades of evening were showing themselves when Bathsheba reached home, where, silently alighting and leaving the horse in the hands of the boy, she proceeded at once upstairs. Liddy met her on the landing. The news had preceded Bathsheba to Weatherbury by half-an-hour, and Liddy looked inquiringly into her mistress's face. Bathsheba had nothing to say.

She entered her bedroom and sat by the window, and thought and thought till night enveloped her, and the extreme lines only of her shape were visible. Somebody came to the door, knocked, and opened it.

'Well, what is it, Liddy?' she said.

'I was thinking there must be something got for you to wear,' said Liddy, with hesitation.

'What do you mean?'

'Mourning.'

'No, no, no,' said Bathsheba hurriedly.

'But I suppose there must be something done for poor—'

'Not at present, I think. It is not necessary.'

'Why not, ma'am?'

'Because he's still alive.'

'How do you know that?' said Liddy, amazed.

'I don't know it. But wouldn't it have been different, or shouldn't I have heard more, or wouldn't they have found him, Liddy? – or – I don't know how it is, but death would have been different from how this is. There may be some trick in it. I am perfectly convinced that he is still alive!'

Bathsheba remained firm in this opinion till Monday, when two circumstances conjoined to shake it. The first was a short paragraph in the local newspaper, which, beyond making by a methodizing pen formidable presumptive evidence of Troy's death by drowning, contained the important testimony of a young Mr Barker, M.D., of Budmouth, who spoke to being an eyewitness of the accident, in a letter to the editor. In this he stated that he was passing over the cliff on the remoter side of the cove just as the sun was setting. At that time he saw a bather carried along in the current outside the mouth of the cove, and guessed in an instant that there was but a poor chance for him unless he should be possessed of unusual muscular powers. He drifted behind a projection of the coast, and Mr Barker followed along the shore in the same direction. But by the time that he could reach an elevation sufficiently great to command a view of the sea beyond, dusk had set in, and nothing further was to be seen.

The other circumstances was the arrival of his clothes, when it became necessary for her to examine and identify them – though this had virtually been done long before by those who inspected the letters in his pockets. It was so evident to her in the midst of her agitation that Troy had undressed in the full conviction of dressing again almost immediately, that the notion that anything but death could have prevented him was a perverse one to entertain.

Then Bathsheba said to herself that others were assured in their opinion; strange that she should not be. A strange reflection occurred to her, causing her face to flush. Suppose that Troy had followed Fanny into another world. Had he done this intentionally, yet contrived to make his death appear like an accident?

Nevertheless, this thought of how the apparent might differ from the real – made vivid by her bygone jealousy of Fanny, and the remorse he had shown that night – did not blind her to the perception of a likelier difference, less tragic, but to herself far more disastrous.

When alone late that evening beside a small fire, and much calmed down, Bathsheba took Troy's watch into her hand, which had been restored to her with the rest of the articles belonging to him. She opened the case as he had opened it before her a week ago. There was the little coil of pale hair which had been as the fuze to this great explosion.

'He was hers and she was his; they should be gone together,' she said. 'I am nothing to either of them, and why should I keep her hair?' She took it in her hand, and held it over the fire. 'No – I'll not burn it – I'll keep it in memory of her, poor thing!' she added, snatching back her hand.

CHAPTER FORTY-NINE

Oak's Advancement – A Great Hope

T HE late autumn and the winter drew on apace, and the leaves lay thick upon the turf of the glades and the mosses of the woods. Bathsheba, having previously been living in a state of suspended feeling which was not suspense, now lived in a mood of quietude which was not precisely peacefulness. While she had known him to be alive she could have thought of his death with equanimity; but now that it might be she had lost him, she regretted that he was not hers still. She kept the farm going, raked in her profits without caring keenly about them, and expended money on ventures because she had done so in bygone days, which, though not long gone by, seemed infinitely removed from her present. She looked back upon that past over a great gulf, as if she were now a dead person, having the faculty of meditation still left in her, by means of which, like the mouldering gentlefolk of the poet's story, she could sit and ponder what a gift life used to be.

However, one excellent result of her general apathy was the long-delayed installation of Oak as bailiff; but he having virtually exercised that function for a long time already, the change, beyond the substantial increase of wages it brought, was little more than a nominal one addressed to the outside world.

Boldwood lived secluded and inactive. Much of his wheat and all his barley of that season had been spoilt by the rain. It sprouted, grew into intricate mats, and was ultimately thrown to the pigs in armfuls. The strange neglect which had produced this ruin and waste became the subject of whispered talk among all the people round; and it was elicited from one of Boldwood's men that forgetfulness had nothing to do with it, for he had been reminded of the danger to his corn as many times and as persistently as inferiors dared to do. The sight of the pigs turning in disgust from the rotten ears seemed to arouse Boldwood, and he one evening sent for Oak. Whether it was suggested by Bathsheba's recent act of promotion or not, the farmer proposed at the interview that Gabriel should undertake the superintendence of the Lower Farm as well as of Bathsheba's, because of the necessity Boldwood felt for such aid, and the impossibility of discovering a more trustworthy man. Gabriel's malignant star was assuredly setting fast.

Bathsheba, when she learnt of this proposal – for Oak was obliged to consult her – at first languidly objected. She considered that the two farms together were too extensive for the observation of one man. Boldwood, who was apparently determined by personal rather than commercial reasons, suggested that Oak should be furnished with a horse for his sole use, when the plan would present no difficulty, the two farms lying side by side. Boldwood did not directly communicate with her during these negotiations, only speaking to Oak, who was the go-between throughout. All was harmoniously arranged at last, and we now see Oak mounted on a strong cob, and daily trotting the length and breadth of about two thousand acres in a cheerful spirit of surveillance, as if the crops all belonged to him – the actual mistress of the one-half, and the master of the other, sitting in their respective homes in gloomy and sad seclusion.

Out of this there arose, during the spring succeeding, a talk in the parish that Gabriel Oak was feathering his nest fast.

'Whatever d'ye think?' said Susan Tall, 'Gable Oak is coming it quite the dand. He now wears shining boots with hardly a hob in 'em, two or three times a-week, and a tall hat a-Sundays, and 'a hardly knows the name of smockfrock. When I see people strut enough to be cut up into bantam cocks, I stand dormant with wonder, and says no more!'

It was eventually known that Gabriel, though paid a fixed wage by Bathsheba independent of the fluctuations of agricultural profits, had made an engagement with Boldwood by which Oak was to receive a share of the receipts – a small share certainly, yet it was money of a higher quality than mere wages, and capable of expansion in a way that wages were not. Some were beginning to consider Oak a 'near' man, for though his condition had thus far improved, he lived in no better style than before, occupying the same cottage, paring his own potatoes, mending his stockings, and sometimes even making his bed with his own hands. But as Oak was not only provokingly indifferent to public opinion, but a man who clung persistently to old habits and usages, simply because they were old, there was room for doubt as to his motives.

A great hope had latterly germinated in Boldwood, whose unreasoning devotion to Bathsheba could only be characterized as a fond madness which neither time nor circumstance, evil nor good report, could weaken or destroy. This fevered hope had grown up again like a grain of mustard-seed during the quiet which followed the hasty conjecture that Troy was drowned. He nourished it fearfully, and almost shunned the contemplation of it in earnest, lest facts should reveal the wildness of the dream. Bathsheba having at last been persuaded to wear mourning, her appearance as she entered the church in that guise was in itself a weekly addition to his faith that a time was coming – very far off perhaps, yet surely nearing – when his waiting on events should have its reward. How long he might have to wait he had not yet closely considered. What he would try to recognize was that the severe schooling she had been subjected to had made Bathsheba much more considerate than she had formerly been of the feelings of others, and he trusted that, should she be willing at any time in the future to marry any man at all, that man would be himself. There was a substratum of good feeling in her: her self-reproach for the injury she had thoughtlessly done him might be depended upon now to a much greater extent than before her infatuation and disappointment. It would be possible to approach her by the channel of her good nature, and to suggest a friendly business-like compact between them for fulfilment at some future day, keeping the passionate side of his desire entirely out of her sight. Such was Boldwood's hope.

To the eyes of the middle-aged, Bathsheba was perhaps additionally charming just now. Her exuberance of spirit was pruned down; the original phantom of delight had shown herself to be not too bright for human nature's daily food, and she had been able to enter this second poetical phase without losing much of the first in the process.

Bathsheba's return from a two months' visit to her old aunt at Norcombe afforded the impassioned and yearning farmer a pretext for inquiring directly after her – now possibly in the ninth month of her widowhood – and endeavouring to get a notion of her state of mind regarding him. This occurred in the middle of the haymaking, and Boldwood contrived to be near Liddy, who was assisting in the fields.

'I am glad to see you out of doors, Lydia,' he said pleasantly.

She simpered, and wondered in her heart why he should speak so frankly to her.

'I hope Mrs Troy is quite well after her long absence,' he continued, in a manner expressing that the coldest-hearted neighbour could scarcely say less about her.

'She is quite well, sir.'

'And cheerful, I suppose.'

'Yes, cheerful.'

'Fearful, did you say?'

'O no. I merely said she was cheerful.'

'Tells you all her affairs?'

'No, sir.'

'Some of them?'

'Yes, sir.'

'Mrs Troy puts much confidence in you, Lydia; and very wisely, perhaps.'

'She do, sir. I've been with her all through her troubles, and was with her at the time of Mr Troy's going and all. And if she were to marry again I expect I should bide with her.'

'She promises that you shall – quite natural,' said the strategic lover, throbbing throughout him at the presumption which Liddy's words appeared to warrant – that his darling had thought of remarriage.

'No – she doesn't promise it exactly. I merely judge on my own account.'

'Yes, yes, I understand. When she alludes to the possibility of marrying again, you conclude—'

'She never do allude to it, sir,' said Liddy, thinking how very stupid Mr Boldwood was getting.

'Of course not,' he returned hastily, his hope falling again. 'You needn't take quite such long reaches with your rake, Lydia – short and quick ones are best.

Well, perhaps, as she is absolute mistress again now, it is wise of her to resolve never to give up her freedom.'

'My mistress did certainly once say, though not seriously, that she supposed she might marry again at the end of seven years from last year, if she cared to risk Mr Troy's coming back and claiming her.'

'Ah, six years from the present time. Said that she might. She might marry at once in every reasonable person's opinion, whatever the lawyers may say to the contrary.'

'Have you been to ask them?' said Liddy innocently.

'Not I,' said Boldwood, growing red. 'Liddy, you needn't stay here a minute later than you wish, so Mr Oak says. I am now going on a little further. Good-afternoon.'

He went away vexed with himself, and ashamed of having for this one time in his life done anything which could be called underhand. Poor Boldwood had no more skill in finesse than a battering-ram, and he was uneasy with a sense of having made himself to appear stupid and, what was worse, mean. But he had, after all, lighted upon one fact by way of repayment. It was a singularly fresh and fascinating fact, and though not without its sadness it was pertinent and real. In little more than six years from this time Bathsheba might certainly marry him. There was something definite in that hope, for admitting that there might have been no deep thought in her words to Liddy about marriage, they showed at least her creed on the matter.

This pleasant notion was now continually in his mind. Six years were a long time, but how much shorter than never, the idea he had for so long been obliged to endure! Jacob had served twice seven years for Rachel: what were six for such a woman as this? He tried to like the notion of waiting for her better than that of winning her at once. Boldwood felt his love to be so deep and strong and eternal, that it was possible she had never yet known its full volume, and this patience in delay would afford him an opportunity of giving sweet proof on the point. He would annihilate the six years of his life as if they were minutes – so little did he value his time on earth beside her love. He would let her see, all those six years of intangible ethereal courtship, how little care he had for anything but as it bore upon the consummation.

Meanwhile the early and the late summer brought round the week in which Greenhill Fair was held. This fair was frequently attended by the folk of Weatherbury.

CHAPTER FIFTY

The Sheep Fair —
Troy touches his Wife's Hand

GREENHILL was the Nijni Novgorod of South Wessex; and the busiest, merriest, noisiest day of the whole statute number was the day of the sheep fair. This yearly gathering was upon the summit of a hill which retained in good preservation the remains of an ancient earthwork, consisting of a huge rampart and entrenchment of an oval form encircling the top of the hill, though somewhat broken down here and there. To each of the two chief openings on opposite sides a winding road ascended, and the level green space of ten or fifteen acres enclosed by the bank was the site of the fair. A few permanent erections dotted the spot, but the majority of visitors patronized canvas alone for resting and feeding under during the time of their sojourn here.

Shepherds who attended with their flocks from long distances started from home two or three days, or even a week, before the fair, driving their charges a few miles each day — not more than ten or twelve — and resting them at night in hired fields by the wayside at previously chosen points, where they fed, having fasted since morning. The shepherd of each flock marched behind, a bundle containing his kit for the week strapped upon his shoulders, and in his hand his crook, which he used as the staff of his pilgrimage. Several of the sheep would get worn and lame, and occasionally a lambing occurred on the road. To meet these contingencies, there was frequently provided, to accompany the flocks from the remoter points, a pony and waggon into which the weakly ones were taken for the remainder of the journey.

The Weatherbury Farms, however, were no such long distance from the hill, and those arrangements were not necessary in their case. But the large united flocks of Bathsheba and Farmer Boldwood formed a valuable and imposing multitude which demanded much attention, and on this account Gabriel, in addition to Boldwood's shepherd and Cain Ball, accompanied them along the way, through the decayed old town of Kingsbere, and upward to the plateau, — old George the dog of course behind them.

When the autumn sun slanted over Greenhill this morning and lighted the dewy flat upon its crest, nebulous clouds of dust were to be seen floating between the pairs of hedges which streaked the wide prospect around in all directions. These gradually converged upon the base of the hill, and the flocks became individually visible, climbing the serpentine ways which led to the top. Thus, in a slow procession, they entered the opening to which the roads tended, multitude after multitude, horned and hornless — blue flocks and red flocks, buff flocks and brown flocks, even green and salmon-tinted flocks, according to the fancy of the colourist and custom of the farm. Men were shouting, dogs were barking, with greatest animation, but the thronging travellers in so long a journey had grown nearly indifferent to such terrors, though they still bleated piteously at the unwontedness of their experiences, a tall shepherd rising here and there in the midst of them, like a gigantic idol amid a crowd of prostrate devotees.

The great mass of sheep in the fair consisted of South Downs and the old Wessex horned breeds; to the latter class Bathsheba's and Farmer Boldwood's mainly belonged. These filed in about nine o'clock, their vermiculated horns lopping gracefully on each side of their cheeks in geometrically perfect spirals, a small pink and white ear nestling under each horn. Before and behind came other varieties, perfect leopards as to the full rich substance of their coats, and only lacking the spots. There were also a few of the Oxfordshire breed, whose wool was beginning to curl like a child's flaxen hair, though surpassed in this respect by the effeminate Leicesters, which were in turn less curly than the Cotswolds. But the most picturesque by far was a small flock of Exmoors, which chanced to be there this year. Their pied faces and legs, dark and heavy horns, tresses of wool hanging round their swarthy foreheads, quite relieved the monotony of the flocks in that quarter.

All these bleating, panting, and weary thousands had entered and were penned before the morning had far advanced, the dog belonging to each flock being tied to the corner of the pen containing it. Alleys for pedestrians intersected the pens, which soon became crowded with buyers and sellers from far and near.

In another part of the hill an altogether different scene began to force itself upon the eye towards midday. A circular tent, of exceptional newness and size, was in course of erection here. As the day drew on, the flocks began to change hands, lightening the shepherds' responsibilities; and they turned their attention to this tent and inquired of a man at work there, whose soul seemed concentrated on tying a bothering knot in no time, what was going on.

'The Royal Hippodrome Performance of Turpin's Ride to York and the Death of Black Bess,' replied the man promptly, without turning his eyes or leaving off tying.

As soon as the tent was completed the band struck up highly stimulating harmonies, and the announcement was publicly made, Black Bess standing in a conspicuous position on the outside, as a living proof, if proof were wanted, of the truth of the oracular utterances from the stage over which the people were to enter. These were so convinced by such genuine appeals to heart and understanding both that they soon began to crowd in abundantly, among the foremost being visible Jan Coggan and Joseph Poorgrass, who were holiday keeping here to-day.

'That's the great ruffen pushing me!' screamed a woman in front of Jan over her shoulder at him when the rush was at its fiercest.

'How can I help pushing ye when the folk behind push me?' said Coggan, in a deprecating tone, turning his head towards the aforesaid folk as far as he could without turning his body, which was jammed as in a vice.

There was a silence; then the drums and trumpets again sent forth their echoing notes. The crowd was again ecstasied, and gave another lurch in which Coggan and Poorgrass were again thrust by those behind upon the women in front.

'O that helpless feymels should be at the mercy of such ruffens!' exclaimed one of these ladies again, as she swayed like a reed shaken by the wind.

'Now,' said Coggan, appealing in an earnest voice to the public at large as it stood clustered about his shoulder-blades, 'did ye ever hear such a onreasonable woman as that? Upon my carcase, neighbours, if I could only get out of this cheesewring, the damn women might eat the show for me!'

'Don't ye lose yer temper, Jan!' implored Joseph Poorgrass, in a whisper. 'They might get their men to murder us, for I think by the shine of their eyes that they be a sinful form of womankind.'

Jan held his tongue, as if he had no objection to be pacified to please a friend, and they gradually reached the foot of the ladder, Poorgrass being flattened like a jumping-jack, and the sixpence, for admission, which he had got ready half-an-hour earlier, having become so reeking hot in the tight squeeze of his excited hand that the woman in spangles, brazen rings set with glass diamonds, and with chalked face and shoulders, who took the money of him, hastily dropped it again from a fear that some trick had been played to burn her fingers. So they all entered, and the cloth of the tent, to the eyes of an observer on the outside, became bulged into innumerable pimples such as we observe on a sack of potatoes, caused by the various human heads, backs, and elbows at high pressure within.

At the rear of the large tent there were two small dressing-tents. One of these, allotted to the male performers, was partitioned into halves by a cloth; and in one of the divisions there was sitting on the grass, pulling on a pair of jack-boots, a young man whom we instantly recognize as Sergeant Troy.

Troy's appearance in this position may be briefly accounted 'for. The brig aboard which he was taken in Budmouth Roads was about to start on a voyage, though somewhat short of hands. Troy read the articles and joined, but before they sailed a boat was despatched across the bay to Lulwind Cove; as he had half expected, his clothes were gone. He ultimately worked his passage to the United States, where he made a precarious living in various towns as Professor of Gymnastics, Sword Exercise, Fencing, and Pugilism. A few months were sufficient to give him a distaste for this kind of life. There was a certain animal form of refinement in his nature; and however pleasant a strange condition might be whilst privations were easily warded off, it was disadvantageously coarse when money was short. There was ever present, too, the idea that he could claim a home and its comforts did he but choose to return to England and Weatherbury Farm. Whether Bathsheba thought him dead was a frequent subject of curious conjecture. To England he did return at last; but the fact of drawing nearer to Weatherbury abstracted its fascinations, and his intention to enter his old groove at that place became modified. It was with gloom he considered on landing at Liverpool that if he were to go home his reception would be of a kind very unpleasant to contemplate; for what Troy had in the way of emotion was an occasional fitful sentiment which sometimes caused him as much inconvenience as emotion of a strong and healthy kind. Bathsheba was not a woman to be made a fool of, or a woman to suffer in silence; and how could he endure existence with a spirited wife to whom at first entering he would be beholden for food and lodging? Moreover, it was not at all unlikely that his wife would fail at her farming, if she had not already done so; and he would then become liable for her maintenance: and what a life such a future of poverty with her would be, the spectre of Fanny constantly between them, harrowing his temper and embittering her words! Thus, for reasons touching on distaste, regret, and shame commingled, he put off his return from day to day, and would have decided to put it off altogether if he could have found anywhere else the ready-made establishment which existed for him there.

At this time – the July preceding the September in which we find him at Greenhill Fair – he fell in with a travelling circus which was performing in the outskirts of a northern town. Troy introduced himself to the manager by taming a restive horse of the troupe, hitting a suspended apple with a pistol-bullet fired from the animal's back when in full gallop, and other feats. For his merits in these – all more or less based upon his experiences as a dragoon-guardsman – Troy was taken into the company, and the play of Turpin was prepared with a view to his personation of the chief character. Troy was not greatly elated by the appreciative spirit in which he was undoubtedly treated, but he thought the engagement might afford him a few weeks for consideration. It was thus carelessly, and without having formed any definite plan for the future, that Troy found himself at Greenhill Fair with the rest of the company on this day.

And now the mild autumn sun got lower, and in front of the pavilion the following incident had taken place. Bathsheba – who was driven to the fair that day by her odd man Poorgrass – had, like every one else, read or heard the announcement that Mr Francis, the Great Cosmopolitan Equestrian and Roughrider, would enact the part of Turpin, and she was not yet too old and careworn to be without a little curiosity to see him. This particular show was by far the largest and grandest in the fair, a horde of little shows grouping themselves under its shade like chickens around a hen. The crowd had passed in, and Boldwood, who had been watching all the day for an opportunity of speaking to her, seeing her comparatively isolated, came up to her side.

'I hope the sheep have done well to-day, Mrs Troy?' he said nervously.

'O yes, thank you,' said Bathsheba, colour springing up in the centre of her cheeks. 'I was fortunate enough to sell them all just as we got upon the hill, so we hadn't to pen at all.'

'And now you are entirely at leisure?'

'Yes, except that I have to see one more dealer in two hours' time: otherwise I should be going home. I was looking at this large tent and the announcement. Have you ever seen the play of "Turpin's Ride to York"? Turpin was a real man, was he not?'

'O yes, perfectly true – all of it. Indeed, I think I've heard Jan Coggan say that a relation of his knew Tom King, Turpin's friend, quite well.'

'Coggan is rather given to strange stories connected with his relations, we must remember. I hope they can all be believed.'

'Yes, yes; we know Coggan. But Turpin is true enough. You have never seen it played, I suppose?'

'Never. I was not allowed to go into these places when I was young. Hark! What's that prancing? How they shout!'

'Black Bess just started off, I suppose. Am I right in supposing you would like to see the performance, Mrs Troy? Please excuse my mistake, if it is one; but if you would like to, I'll get a seat for you with pleasure.' Perceiving that she hesitated, he added, 'I myself shall not stay to see it: I've seen it before.'

Now Bathsheba did care a little to see the show, and had only withheld her feet from the ladder because she feared to go in alone. She had been hoping that Oak might appear, whose assistance in such cases was always accepted as an inalienable right, but Oak was nowhere to be seen; and hence it was that she said, 'Then if you will just look in first, to see if there's room, I think I will go in for a minute or two.'

And so a short time after this Bathsheba appeared in the tent with Boldwood at her elbow, who, taking her to a 'reserved' seat, again withdrew.

This feature consisted of one raised bench in a very conspicuous part of the circle, covered with red cloth, and floored with a piece of carpet, and Bathsheba immediately found, to her confusion, that she was the single reserved individual in the tent, the rest of the crowded spectators, one and all, standing on their legs on the borders of the arena, where they got twice as good a view of the performance for half the money. Hence as many eyes were turned upon her, enthroned alone in this place of honour, against a scarlet background, as upon the ponies and clown who were engaged in preliminary exploits in the centre, Turpin not having yet appeared. Once there, Bathsheba was forced to make the best of it and remain: she sat down, spreading her skirts with some dignity over the unoccupied space on each side of her, and giving a new and feminine aspect to the pavilion. In a few minutes she noticed the fat red nape of Coggan's neck among those standing just below her, and Joseph Poorgrass's saintly profile a little further on.

The interior was shadowy with a peculiar shade. The strange luminous semi-opacities of fine autumn afternoons and eves intensified into Rembrandt effects the few yellow sunbeams which came through holes and divisions in the canvas, and spirted like jets of gold-dust across the dusky blue atmosphere of haze pervading the tent, until they alighted on inner surfaces of cloth opposite, and shone like little lamps suspended there.

Troy, on peeping from his dressing-tent through a slit for a reconnoitre before entering, saw his unconscious wife on high before him as described, sitting as queen of the tournament. He started back in utter confusion, for although his disguise effectually concealed his personality, he instantly felt that she would be sure to recognize his voice. He had several times during the day thought of the possibility of some Weatherbury person or other appearing and recognizing him; but he had taken the risk carelessly. If they see me, let them, he had said. But here was Bathsheba in her own person; and the reality of the scene was so much intenser than any of his prefigurings that he felt he had not half enough considered the point.

She looked so charming and fair that his cool mood about Weatherbury people was changed. He had not expected her to exercise this power over him in the twinkling of an eye. Should he go on, and care nothing? He could not bring himself to do that. Beyond a politic wish to remain unknown, there suddenly arose in him now a sense of shame at the possibility that his attractive young wife, who already despised him, should despise him more by discovering him in so mean a condition after so long a time. He actually blushed at the thought, and was vexed beyond measure that his sentiments of dislike towards Weatherbury should have led him to dally about the country in this way.

But Troy was never more clever than when absolutely at his wits' end. He hastily thrust aside the curtain dividing his own little dressing space from that of the manager and proprietor, who now appeared as the individual called Tom King as far down as his waist, and as the aforesaid respectable manager thence to his toes.

'Here's the devil to pay!' said Troy.

'How's that?'

'Why, there's a blackguard creditor in the tent I don't want to see, who'll discover me and nab me as sure as Satan if I open my mouth. What's to be done?'

'You must appear now, I think.'

'I can't.'

'But the play must proceed.'

'Do you give out that Turpin has got a bad cold, and can't speak his part, but that he'll perform it just the same without speaking.'

The proprietor shook his head.

'Anyhow, play or no play, I won't open my mouth,' said Troy firmly.

'Very well, then let me see. I tell you how we'll manage,' said the other, who perhaps felt it would be extremely awkward to offend his leading man just at this time. 'I won't tell 'em anything about your keeping silence; go on with the piece and say nothing, doing what you can by a judicious wink now and then, and a few indomitable nods in the heroic places, you know. They'll never find out that the speeches are omitted.'

This seemed feasible enough, for Turpin's speeches were not many or long, the fascination of the piece lying entirely in the action; and accordingly the play began, and at the appointed time Black Bess leapt into the grassy circle amid the plaudits of the spectators. At the turnpike scene, where Bess and Turpin are hotly pursued at midnight by the officers, and the half-awake gatekeeper in his tasselled nightcap denies that any horseman has passed, Coggan uttered a broad-chested 'Well done!' which could be heard all over the fair above the bleating, and Poorgrass smiled delightedly with a nice sense of dramatic contrast between our hero, who coolly leaps the gate, and halting justice in the form of his enemies, who must needs pull up cumbersomely and wait to be let through. At the death of Tom King, he could not refrain from seizing Coggan by the hand, and whispering, with tears in his eyes, 'Of course he's not really shot, Jan — only seemingly!' And when the last sad scene came on, and the body of the gallant and faithful Bess had to be carried out on a shutter by twelve volunteers from among the spectators, nothing could restrain Poorgrass from lending a hand, exclaiming, as he asked Jan to join him, ''Twill be something to tell of at Warren's in future years, Jan, and hand down to our children.' For many a year in Weatherbury, Joseph told, with the air of a man who had had experiences in his time, that he touched with his own hand the hoof of Bess as she lay upon the board upon his shoulder. If, as some thinkers hold, immortality consists in being enshrined in others' memories, then did Black Bess become immortal that day if she never had done so before.

Meanwhile Troy had added a few touches to his ordinary make-up for the character, the more effectually to disguise himself, and though he had felt faint qualms on first entering, the metamorphosis effected by judiciously 'lining' his face with a wire rendered him safe from the eyes of Bathsheba and her men. Nevertheless, he was relieved when it was got through.

There was a second performance in the evening, and the tent was lighted up. Troy had taken his part very quietly this time, venturing to introduce a few speeches on occasion; and was just concluding it when, whilst standing at the edge of the circle contiguous to the first row of spectators, he observed within a yard of him the eye of a man darted keenly into his side features. Troy hastily shifted his position, after having recognized in the scrutineer the knavish bailiff Pennyways, his wife's sworn enemy, who still hung about the outskirts of Weatherbury.

At first Troy resolved to take no notice and abide by circumstances. That he had been recognized by this man was highly probable; yet there was room for a doubt. Then the great objection he had felt to allowing news of his proximity to precede him to Weatherbury in the event of his return, based on a feeling that knowledge of his present occupation would discredit him still further in his wife's eyes, returned in full force. Moreover, should he resolve not to return at all, a tale of his being alive and being in the neighbourhood would be awkward; and he was anxious to acquire a knowledge of his wife's temporal affairs before deciding which to do.

In this dilemma Troy at once went out to reconnoitre. It occurred to him that to find Pennyways, and make a friend of him if possible, would be a very wise act. He had put on a thick beard borrowed from the establishment, and in this he wandered about the fair-field. It was now almost dark, and respectable people were getting their carts and gigs ready to go home.

The largest refreshment booth in the fair was provided by an innkeeper from a neighbouring town. This was considered an unexceptionable place for obtaining the necessary food and rest: Host Trencher (as he was jauntily called by the local newspaper) being a substantial man of high repute for catering through all the country round. The tent was divided into first- and second-class compartments, and at the end of the first-class division was a yet further enclosure for the most exclusive, fenced off from the body of the tent by a luncheon-bar, behind which the host himself stood, bustling about in white apron and shirt-sleeves, and looking as if he had never lived anywhere but under canvas all his life. In these penetralia were chairs and a table, which, on candles being lighted, made quite a cosy and luxurious show, with an urn, plated tea and coffee pots, china teacups, and plum cakes.

Troy stood at the entrance to the booth, where a gipsy-woman was frying pancakes over a little fire of sticks and selling them at a penny a-piece, and looked over the heads of the people within. He could see nothing of Pennyways, but he soon discerned Bathsheba through an opening into the reserved space at the further end. Troy thereupon retreated, went round the tent into the darkness, and listened. He could hear Bathsheba's voice immediately inside the canvas; she was conversing with a man. A warmth overspread his face: surely she was not so unprincipled as to flirt in a fair! He wondered if, then, she reckoned upon his death as an absolute certainty. To get at the root of the matter, Troy took a penknife from his pocket and softly made two little cuts crosswise in the cloth, which, by folding back the corners, left a hole the size of a wafer. Close to this he placed his face, withdrawing it again in a movement of surprise; for his eye had been within twelve inches of the top of Bathsheba's head. It was too near to be convenient. He made another hole a little to one side and lower down, in a shaded place beside her chair, from which it was easy and safe to survey her by looking horizontally.

Troy took in the scene completely now. She was leaning back, sipping a cup of tea that she held in her hand, and the owner of the male voice was Boldwood, who had apparently just brought the cup to her. Bathsheba, being in a negligent mood, leant so idly against the canvas that it was pressed to the shape of her shoulder, and she was, in fact, as good as in Troy's arms; and he was obliged to keep his breast carefully backward that she might not feel its warmth through the cloth as he gazed in.

Troy found unexpected chords of feeling to be stirred again within him as they had been stirred earlier in the day. She was handsome as ever, and she was his. It was some minutes before he could counteract his sudden wish to go in, and claim her. Then he thought how the proud girl who had always looked down upon him even whilst it was to love him, would hate him on discovering him to be a strolling player. Were he to make himself known, that chapter of his life must at all risks be kept for ever from her and from the Weatherbury people, or his name would be a byword throughout the parish. He would be nicknamed 'Turpin' as long as he lived. Assuredly before he could claim her these few past months of his existence must be entirely blotted out.

'Shall I get you another cup before you start, ma'am?' said Farmer Boldwood.

'Thank you,' said Bathsheba. 'But I must be going at once. It was great neglect in that man to keep me waiting here till so late. I should have gone two hours ago, if it had not been for him. I had no idea of coming in here; but there's nothing so refreshing as a cup of tea, though I should never have got one if you hadn't helped me.'

Troy scrutinized her cheek as lit by the candles, and watched each varying shade thereon, and the white shell-like sinuosities of her little ear. She took out her purse and was insisting to Boldwood on paying for her tea for herself, when at this moment Pennyways entered the tent. Troy trembled: here was his scheme for respectability endangered at once. He was about to leave his hole of espial, attempt to follow Pennyways, and find out if the ex-bailiff had recognized him, when he was arrested by the conversation, and found he was too late.

'Excuse me, ma'am,' said Pennyways; 'I've some private information for your ear alone.'

'I cannot hear it now,' she said coldly. That Bathsheba could not endure this man was evident; in fact, he was continually coming to her with some tale or other, by which he might creep into favour at the expense of persons maligned.

'I'll write it down,' said Pennyways confidently. He stooped over the table, pulled a leaf from a warped pocket-book, and wrote upon the paper, in a round hand —

'Your husband is here. I've seen him. Who's the fool now?'

This he folded small, and handed towards her. Bathsheba would not read it; she would not even put out her hand to take it. Pennyways, then, with a laugh of derision, tossed it into her lap, and, turning away, left her.

From the words and action of Pennyways, Troy, though he had not been able to see what the ex-bailiff wrote, had not a moment's doubt that the note referred to him. Nothing that he could think of could be done to check the exposure. 'Curse my luck!' he whispered, and added imprecations which rustled in the gloom like a pestilent wind. Meanwhile Boldwood said, taking up the note from her lap —

'Don't you wish to read it, Mrs Troy? If not, I'll destroy it.'

'Oh, well,' said Bathsheba carelessly, 'perhaps it is unjust not to read it; but I can guess what it is about. He wants me to recommend him, or it is to tell me of some little scandal or another connected with my work-people. He's always doing that.'

Bathsheba held the note in her right hand. Boldwood handed towards her a plate of cut bread-and-butter; when, in order to take a slice, she put the note into her left hand, where she was still holding the purse, and then allowed her hand to drop beside her close to the canvas. The moment had come for saving his game, and Troy impulsively felt that he would play the card. For yet another time he looked at the fair hand, and saw the pink finger-tips, and the blue veins of the wrist, encircled by a bracelet of coral chippings which she wore: how familiar it all was to him! Then, with the lightning action in which he was such an adept, he noiselessly slipped his hand under the botton of the tent-cloth, which was far from being pinned tightly down, lifted it a little way, keeping his eye to the hole, snatched the note from her fingers, dropped the canvas, and ran away in the gloom towards the bank and ditch, smiling at the scream of astonishment which burst from her. Troy then slid down on the outside of the rampart, hastened round in the bottom of the entrenchment to a distance of a hundred yards, ascended again, and crossed boldly in a slow walk towards the front entrance of the tent. His object was now to get to Pennyways, and prevent a repetition of the announcement until such time as he should choose.

Troy reached the tent door, and standing among the groups there gathered, looked anxiously for Pennyways, evidently not wishing to make himself prominent by inquiring for him. One or two men were speaking of a daring attempt that had just been made to rob a young lady by lifting the canvas of the tent beside her. It was supposed that the rogue had imagined a slip of paper which she held in her hand to be a bank note, for he had seized it, and made off with it, leaving her purse behind. His chagrin and disappointment at discovering its worthlessness would be a good joke, it was said. However, the occurrence seemed to have become known to few, for it had not interrupted a fiddler, who had lately begun playing by the door of the tent, nor the four bowed old men with grim countenances and walking-sticks in hand, who were dancing 'Major Malley's Reel' to the tune. Behind these stood Pennyways. Troy glided up to him, beckoned, and whispered a few words; and with a mutual glance of concurrence the two men went into the night together.

CHAPTER FIFTY-ONE

Bathsheba talks with her Outrider

THE arrangement for getting back again to Weatherbury had been that Oak should take the place of Poorgrass in Bathsheba's conveyance and drive her home, it being discovered late in the afternoon that Joseph was suffering from his old complaint, a multiplying eye, and was, therefore, hardly trustworthy as coachman and protector to a woman. But Oak had found himself so occupied, and was full of so many cares relative to those portions of Boldwood's flocks that were not disposed of, that Bathsheba, without telling Oak or anybody, resolved to drive home herself, as she had many times done from Casterbridge Market, and trust to her good angel for performing the journey unmolested. But having fallen in with Farmer Boldwood accidentally (on her part at least) at the refreshment-tent, she found it impossible to refuse his offer to ride on horseback beside her as escort. It had grown twilight before she was aware, but Boldwood assured her that there was no cause for uneasiness, as the moon would be up in half-an-hour.

Immediately after the incident in the tent she had risen to go – now absolutely alarmed and really grateful for her old lover's protection – though regretting Gabriel's absence, whose company she would have much preferred, as being more proper as well as more pleasant, since he was her own managing-man and servant. This, however, could not be helped; she would not, on any consideration, treat Boldwood harshly, having once already ill-used him, and the moon having risen, and the gig being ready, she drove across the hill-top in the wending ways which led downwards – to oblivious obscurity, as it seemed, for the moon and the hill it flooded with light were in appearance on a level, the rest of the world lying as a vast shady concave between them. Boldwood mounted his horse, and followed in close attendance behind. Thus they descended into the lowlands, and the sounds of those left on the hill came like voices from the sky, and the lights were as those of a camp in heaven. They soon passed the merry stragglers in the immediate vicinity of the hill, traversed Kingsbere, and got upon the high road.

The keen instincts of Bathsheba had perceived that the farmer's staunch devotion to herself was still undiminished, and she sympathized deeply. The sight had quite depressed her this evening; had reminded her of her folly; she wished anew, as she had wished many months ago, for some means of making reparation for her fault. Hence her pity for the man who so persistently loved on to his own injury and permanent gloom had betrayed Bathsheba into an injudicious considerateness of manner, which appeared almost like tenderness, and gave new vigour to the exquisite dream of a Jacob's seven years' service in poor Boldwood's mind.

He soon found an excuse for advancing from his position in the rear, and rode close by her side. They had gone two or three miles in the moonlight, speaking desultorily across the wheel of her gig concerning the fair, farming, Oak's usefulness to them both, and other indifferent subjects, when Boldwood said suddenly and simply –

'Mrs Troy, you will marry again some day?'

This point-blank query unmistakably confused her, and it was not till a minute or more had elapsed that she said, 'I have not seriously thought of any such subject.'

'I quite understand that. Yet your late husband has been dead nearly one year, and—'

'You forget that his death was never absolutely proved, and may not have taken place; so that I may not be really a widow,' she said, catching at the straw of escape that the fact afforded.

'Not absolutely proved, perhaps, but it was proved circumstantially. A man saw him drowning, too. No reasonable person has any doubt of his death; nor have you, ma'am, I should imagine.'

'O yes I have, or I should have acted differently,' she said gently. 'From the first I have had a strange unaccountable feeling that he could not have perished. But I have been able to explain that in several ways since. Even were I half persuaded that I shall see him no more, I am far from thinking of marriage with another. I should be very contemptible to indulge in such a thought.'

They were silent now awhile, and having struck into an unfrequented track across a common, the creaks of Boldwood's saddle and her gig springs were all the sounds to be heard. Boldwood ended the pause.

'Do you remember when I carried you fainting in my arms into the King's Arms, in Casterbridge? Every dog has his day: that was mine.'

'I know – I know it all,' she said, hurriedly.

'I, for one, shall never cease regretting that events so fell out as to deny you to me.'

'I, too, am very sorry,' she said, and then checked herself. 'I mean, you know, I am sorry you thought I—'

'I have always this dreary pleasure in thinking over those past times with you – that I was something to you before *he* was anything, and that you belonged *almost* to me. But of course, that's nothing. You never liked me.'

'I did; and respected you, too.'

'Do you now?'

'Yes.'

'Which?'

'How do you mean which?'

'Do you like me, or do you respect me?'

'I don't know – at least, I cannot tell you. It is difficult for a woman to define her feelings in language which is chiefly made by men to express theirs. My treatment of you was thoughtless, inexcusable, wicked! I shall eternally regret it. If there had been anything I could have done to make amends I would most gladly have done it – there was nothing on earth I so longed to do as to repair the error. But that was not possible.'

'Don't blame yourself – you were not so far in the wrong as you suppose.

Bathsheba, suppose you had real complete proof that you are what, in fact, you are – a widow – would you repair the old wrong to me by marrying me?'

'I cannot say. I shouldn't yet, at any rate.'

'But you might at some future time of your life?'

'O yes, I might at some time.'

'Well, then, do you know that without further proof of any kind you may marry again in about six years from the present – subject to nobody's objection or blame?'

'O yes,' she said, quickly. 'I know all that. But don't talk of it – seven or six years – where may we all be by that time?'

'They will soon glide by, and it will seem an astonishingly short time to look back upon when they are past – much less than to look forward to now.'

'Yes, yes; I have found that in my own experience.'

'Now, listen once more,' Boldwood pleaded. 'If I wait that time, will you marry me? You own that you owe me amends – let that be your way of making them.'

'But, Mr Boldwood – six years—'

'Do you want to be the wife of any other man?'

'No indeed! I mean, that I don't like to talk about this matter now. Perhaps it is not proper, and I ought not to allow it. Let us drop it. My husband may be living, as I said.'

'Of course, I'll drop the subject if you wish. But propriety has nothing to do with reasons. I am a middle-aged man, willing to protect you for the remainder of our lives. On your side, at least, there is no passion or blamable haste – on mine, perhaps, there is. But I can't help seeing that if you choose from a feeling of pity, and, as you say, a wish to make amends, to make a bargain with me for a far-ahead time – an agreement which will set all things right and make me happy, late though it may be – there is no fault to be found with you as a woman. Hadn't I the first place beside you? Haven't you been almost mine once already? Surely you can say to me as much as this, you will have me back again should circumstances permit? Now, pray speak! O Bathsheba, promise – it is only a little promise – that if you marry again, you will marry me!'

His tone was so excited that she almost feared him at this moment, even whilst she sympathized. It was a simple physical fear – the weak of the strong; there was no emotional aversion or inner repugnance. She said, with some distress in her voice, for she remembered vividly his outburst on the Yalbury Road, and shrank from a repetition of his anger: –

'I will never marry another man whilst you wish me to be your wife, whatever comes – but to say more – you have taken me so by surprise—'

'But let it stand in these simple words – that in six years' time you will be my wife? Unexpected accidents we'll not mention, because those, of course, must be given way to. Now, this time I know you will keep your word.'

'That's why I hesitate to give it.'

'But do give it! Remember the past, and be kind.'

She breathed; and then said mournfully: 'O what shall I do? I don't love you, and I much fear that I never shall love you as much as a woman ought to love a husband. If you, sir, know that, and I can yet give you happiness by a mere promise to marry at the end of six years, if my husband should not come back, it is a great honour to me. And if you value such an act of friendship from a woman who doesn't esteem herself as she did, and has little love left, whyI – I will—'

'Promise!'

' – Consider, if I cannot promise soon.'

'But soon is perhaps never?'

'O no, it is not! I mean soon. Christmas, we'll say.'

'Christmas!' He said nothing further till he added: 'Well, I'll say no more to you about it till that time.'

Bathsheba was in a very peculiar state of mind, which showed how entirely the soul is the slave of the body, the ethereal spirit dependent for its quality upon the tangible flesh and blood. It is hardly too much to say that she felt coerced by a force stronger than her own will, not only into the act of promising upon this singularly remote and vague matter, but into the emotion of fancying that she ought to promise. When the weeks intervening between the night of this conversation and Christmas day began perceptibly to diminish, her anxiety and perplexity increased.

One day she was led by an accident into an oddly confidential dialogue with Gabriel about her difficulty. It afforded her a little relief – of a dull and cheerless kind. They were auditing accounts, and something occurred in the course of their labours which led Oak to say, speaking of Boldwood, 'He'll never forget you, ma'am, never.'

Then out came her trouble before she was aware; and she told him how she had again got into the toils; what Boldwood had asked her, and how he was expecting her assent. 'The most mournful reason of all for my agreeing to it,' she said sadly, 'and the true reason why I think to do so for good or for evil, is this – it is a thing I have not breathed to a living soul as yet – I believe that if I don't give my word, he'll go out of his mind.'

'Really, do ye?' said Gabriel, gravely.

'I believe this,' she continued, with reckless frankness; 'and Heaven knows I say it in a spirit the very reverse of vain, for I am grieved and troubled to my soul about it – I believe I hold that man's future in my hand. His career depends entirely upon my treatment of him. O Gabriel, I tremble at my responsibility, for it is terrible!'

'Well, I think this much, ma'am, as I told you years ago,' said Oak, 'that his life is a total blank whenever he isn't hoping for 'ee; but I can't suppose – I hope that nothing so dreadful hangs on to it as you fancy. His natural manner has always been dark and strange, you know. But since the case is so sad and odd-like, why don't ye give the conditional promise? I think I would.'

'But is it right? Some rash acts of my past life have taught me that a watched woman must have very much circumspection to retain only a very little credit, and I do want and long to be discreet in this! And six years – why we may all be in our graves by that time, even if Mr Troy does not come back again, which he may not impossibly do! Such thoughts give a sort of absurdity to the scheme. Now, isn't it preposterous, Gabriel? However he came to dream of it, I cannot think. But is it wrong? You know – you are older than I.'

'Eight years older, ma'am.'

'Yes, eight years – and is it wrong?'

'Perhaps it would be an uncommon agreement for a man and woman to make:

I don't see anything really wrong about it,' said Oak, slowly. 'In fact the very thing that makes it doubtful if you ought to marry en under any condition, that is, your not caring about him – for I may suppose—'

'Yes, you may suppose that love is wanting,' she said shortly. 'Love is an utterly bygone, sorry, worn-out, miserable thing with me – for him or any one else.'

'Well, your want of love seems to me the one thing that takes away harm from such an agreement with him. If wild heat had to do wi' it, making ye long to overcome the awkwardness about your husband's vanishing, it mid be wrong; but a cold-hearted agreement to oblige a man seems different, somehow. The real sin, ma'am, in my mind, lies in thinking of ever wedding wi' a man you don't love honest and true.'

'That I'm willing to pay the penalty of,' said Bathsheba, firmly. 'You know, Gabriel, this is what I cannot get off my conscience – that I once seriously injured him in sheer idleness. If I had never played a trick upon him, he would never have wanted to marry me. O if I could only pay some heavy damages in money to him for the harm I did, and so get the sin off my soul that way! . . . Well, there's the debt, which can only be discharged in one way, and I believe I am bound to do it if it honestly lies in my power, without any consideration of my own future at all. When a rake gambles away his expectations, the fact that it is an inconvenient debt doesn't make him the less liable. I've been a rake, and the single point I ask you is, considering that my own scruples, and the fact that in the eye of the law my husband is only missing, will keep any man from marrying me until seven years have passed – am I free to entertain such an idea, even though 'tis a sort of penance – for it will be that! I *hate* the act of marriage under such circumstances, and the class of women I should seem to belong to by doing it!'

'It seems to me that all depends upon whe'r you think, as everybody else do, that your husband is dead.'

'I shall get to, I suppose because I cannot help feeling what would have brought him back long before this time if he had lived.'

'Well, then, in a religious sense you will be as free to *think* o' marrying again as any real widow of one year's standing. But why don't ye ask Mr Thirdly's advice on how to treat Mr Boldwood?'

'No. When I want a broad-minded opinion for general enlightenment, distinct from special advice, I never go to a man who deals in the subject professionally. So I like the parson's opinion on law, the lawyer's on doctoring, the doctor's on business, and my businessman's – that is, yours – on morals.'

'And on love—'

'My own.'

'I'm afraid there's a hitch in that argument,' said Oak, with a grave smile.

She did not reply at once, and then saying, 'Good evening, Mr Oak,' went away.

She had spoken frankly, and neither asked nor expected any reply from Gabriel more satisfactory than that she had obtained. Yet in the centremost parts of her complicated heart there existed at this minute a little pang of disappointment, for a reason she would not allow herself to recognize. Oak had not once wished her free that he might marry her himself – had not once said, 'I could wait for you as well as he.' That was the insect sting. Not that she would have listened to any such hypothesis. O no — for wasn't she saying all the time that such thoughts of the future were improper, and wasn't Gabriel far too poor a man to speak sentiment to her? Yet he might have just hinted about that old love of his, and asked, in a playful off-hand way, if he might speak of it. It would have seemed pretty and sweet, if no more; and then she would have shown how kind and inoffensive a woman's 'No' can sometimes be. But to give such cool advice — the very advice she had asked for — it ruffled our heroine all the afternoon.

CHAPTER FIFTY-TWO

Converging Courses

I

C HRISTMAS-EVE came, and a party that Boldwood was to give in the evening was the great subject of talk in Weatherbury. It was not that the rarity of Christmas parties in the parish made this one a wonder, but that Boldwood should be the giver. The announcement had had an abnormal and incongruous sound, as if one should hear of croquet-playing in a cathedral aisle, or that some much-respected judge was going upon the stage. That the party was intended to be a truly jovial one there was no room for doubt. A large bough of mistletoe had been brought from the woods that day, and suspended in the hall of the bachelor's home. Holly and ivy had followed in armfuls. From six that morning till past noon the huge wood fire in the kitchen roared and sparkled at its highest, the kettle, the saucepan, and the three-legged pot appearing in the midst of the flames like Shadrach, Meshach, and Abednego; moreover, roasting and basting operations were continually carried on in front of the genial blaze.

As it grew later the fire was made up in the large long hall into which the staircase descended, and all encumbrances were cleared out for dancing. The log which was to form the back-brand of the evening fire was the uncleft trunk of a tree, so unwieldy that it could be neither brought nor rolled to its place; and accordingly two men were to be observed dragging and heaving it in by chains and levers as the hour of assembly drew near.

In spite of all this, the spirit of revelry was wanting in the atmosphere of the house. Such a thing had never been attempted before by its owner, and it was now done as by a wrench. Intended gaieties would insist upon appearing like solemn grandeurs, the organization of the whole effort was carried out coldly by hirelings, and a shadow seemed to move about the rooms, saying that the proceedings were unnatural to the place and the lone man who lived therein, and hence not good.

II

Bathsheba was at this time in her room, dressing for the event. She had called for candles, and Liddy entered and placed one on each side of her mistress's glass.

'Don't go away, Liddy,' said Bathsheba, almost timidly. 'I am foolishly agitated – I cannot tell why. I wish I had not been obliged to go to this dance; but there's no escaping now. I have not spoken to Mr Boldwood since the autumn, when I promised to see him at Christmas on business, but I had no idea there was to be anything of this kind.'

'But I would go now,' said Liddy, who was going with her; for Boldwood had been indiscriminate in his invitations.

'Yes, I shall make my appearance, of course,' said Bathsheba. 'But I am *the cause* of the party, and that upsets me! – Don't tell, Liddy.'

'O no, ma'am. You the cause of it, ma'am?'

'Yes. I am the reason of the party – I. If it had not been for me, there would never have been one. I can't explain any more – there's no more to be explained. I wish I had never seen Weatherbury.'

'That's wicked of you – to wish to be worse off than you are.'

'No, Liddy. I have never been free from trouble since I have lived here, and this party is likely to bring me more. Now, fetch my black silk dress, and see how it sits upon me.'

'But you will leave off that, surely, ma'am? You have been a sort of widow fourteen months, and ought to brighten up a little on such a night as this.'

'Is it necessary? No; I will appear as usual, for if I were to wear any light dress people would say things about me, and I should seem to be rejoicing when I am solemn all the time. The party doesn't suit me a bit; but never mind, stay and help to finish me off.'

III

Boldwood was dressing also at this hour. A tailor from Casterbridge was with him, assisting him in the operation of trying on a new coat that had just been brought home.

Never had Boldwood been so fastidious, unreasonable about the fit, and generally difficult to please. The tailor walked round and round him, tugged at the waist, pulled the sleeve, pressed out the collar, and for the first time in his experience Boldwood was not bored. Times had been when the farmer had exclaimed against all such niceties as childish, but now no philosophic or hasty rebuke whatever was provoked by this man for attaching as much importance to a crease in the coat as to an earthquake in South America. Boldwood at last expressed himself nearly satisfied, and paid the bill, the tailor passing out of the door just as Oak came in to report progress for the day.

'Oh, Oak,' said Boldwood. 'I shall of course see you here to-night. Make yourself merry. I am determined that neither expense nor trouble shall be spared.'

'I'll try to be here, sir, though perhaps it may not be very early,' said Gabriel, quietly. 'I am glad indeed to see such a change in 'ee from what it used to be.'

'Yes – I must own it – I am bright to-night: cheerful and more than cheerful – so much so that I am almost sad again with the sense that all of it is passing away. And sometimes, when I am excessively hopeful and blithe, a trouble is looming in the distance: so that I often get to look upon gloom in me with content, and to fear a happy mood. Still this may be absurd – I feel that it is absurd. Perhaps my day is dawning at last.'

'I hope it 'ill be a long and a fair one.'

'Thank you – thank you. Yet perhaps my cheerfulness rests on a slender hope. And yet I trust my hope. It is faith, not hope. I think this time I reckon with my host. – Oak, my hands are a little shaky, or something: I can't tie this neckerchief properly. Perhaps you will tie it for me. The fact is, I have not been well lately, you know.'

'I am sorry to hear that, sir.'

'Oh, it's nothing. I want it done as well as you can, please. Is there any late knot in fashion, Oak?'

'I don't know, sir,' said Oak. His tone had sunk to sadness.

Boldwood approached Gabriel, and as Oak tied the neckerchief the farmer went on feverishly –

'Does a woman keep her promise, Gabriel?'

'If it is not inconvenient to her she may.'

' – Or rather an implied promise.'

'I won't answer for her implying,' said Oak, with faint bitterness. 'That's a word as full o' holes as a sieve with them.'

'Oak, don't talk like that. You have got quite cynical lately – how is it? We seem to have shifted our positions: I have become the young and hopeful man, and you the old and unbelieving one. However, does a woman keep a promise, not to marry, but to enter on an engagement to marry at some time? Now you know women better than I – tell me.'

'I am afeard you honour my understanding too much. However, she may keep such a promise, if it is made with an honest meaning to repair a wrong.'

'It has not gone far yet, but I think it will soon – yes, I know it will,' he said, in an impulsive whisper. 'I have pressed her upon the subject, and she inclines to be kind to me, and to think of me as a husband at a long future time, and that's enough for me. How can I expect more? She has a notion that a woman should not marry within seven years of her husband's disappearance – that her own self shouldn't, I mean – because his body was not found. It may be merely this legal reason which influences her, or it may be a religious one, but she is reluctant to talk on the point. Yet she has promised – implied – that she will ratify an engagement to-night.'

'Seven years,' murmured Oak.

'No, no – it's no such thing!' he said, with impatience. 'Five years, nine months, and a few days. Fifteen months nearly have passed since he vanished, and is there anything so wonderful in an engagement of little more than five years?'

'It seems long in a forward view. Don't build too much upon such promises, sir. Remember, you have once be'n deceived. Her meaning may be good; but there – she's young yet.'

'Deceived? Never!' said Boldwood, vehemently. 'She never promised me at that first time, and hence she did not break her promise! If she promises me, she'll marry me. Bathsheba is a woman to her word.'

IV

Troy was sitting in a corner of The White Hart tavern at Casterbridge, smoking and drinking a steaming mixture from a glass. A knock was given at the door, and Pennyways entered.

'Well, have you seen him?' Troy inquired, pointing to a chair.

'Boldwood?'

'No – Lawyer Long.'

'He wadn' at home. I went there first, too.'

'That's a nuisance.'

''Tis rather, I suppose.'

'Yet I don't see that, because a man appears to be drowned and was not, he should be liable for anything. I shan't ask any lawyer – not I.'

'But that's not it, exactly. If a man changes his name and so forth, and takes steps to deceive the world and his own wife, he's a cheat, and that in the eye of the law is ayless a rogue, and that is ayless a lammocken vagabond; and that's a punishable situation.'

'Ha-ha! Well done, Pennyways.' Troy had laughed, but it was with some anxiety that he said, 'Now, what I want to know is this, do you think there's really anything going on between her and Boldwood? Upon my soul, I should never have believed it! How she must detest me! Have you found out whether she has encouraged him?'

'I haen't been able to learn. There's a deal of feeling on his side seemingly, but I don't answer for her. I didn't know a word about any such thing till yesterday, and all I heard then was that she was gwine to the party at his house to-night. This is the first time she has ever gone there, they say. And they say that she've not so much as spoke to him since they were at Greenhill Fair: but what can folk believe o't? However, she's not fond of him – quite offish and quite careless, I know.'

'I'm not so sure of that. . . . She's a handsome woman, Pennyways, is she not? Own that you never saw a finer or more splendid creature in your life. Upon my honour, when I set eyes upon her that day I wondered what I could have been made of to be able to leave her by herself so long. And then I was hampered with that bothering show, which I'm free of at last, thank the stars.' He smoked on awhile, and then added, 'How did she look when you passed by yesterday?'

'Oh, she took no great heed of me, ye may well fancy; but she looked well enough, far's I know. Just flashed her haughty eyes upon my poor scram body, and then let them go past me to what was yond, much as if I'd been no more than a leafless tree. She had just got off her mare to look at the last wring-down of cider for the year; she had been riding, and so her colours were up and her breath rather quick, so that her bosom plimmed and fell – plimmed and fell – every time plain to my eye. Ay, and there were the fellers round her wringing down the cheese and bustling about and saying, "Ware o' the pommy, ma'am: 'twill spoil yer gown."'

"Never mind me," says she. Then Gabe brought her some of the new cider, and she must needs go drinking it through a strawmote, and not in a nateral way at all. "Liddy," says she, "bring indoors a few gallons, and I'll make some cider-wine." Sergeant, I was no more to her than a morsel of scroff in the fuel-house!'

'I must go and find her out at once — O yes, I see that — I must go. Oak is head man still, isn't he?'

'Yes, 'a b'lieve. And at Little Weatherbury Farm too. He manages everything.'

''Twill puzzle him to manage her, or any other man of his compass!'

'I don't know about that. She can't do without him, and knowing it well he's pretty independent. And she've a few soft corners to her mind, though I've never been able to get into one, the devil's in't!'

'Ah, baily, she's a notch above you, and you must own it: a higher class of animal — a finer tissue. However, stick to me, and neither this haughty goddess, dashing piece of womanhood, Juno-wife of mine (Juno was a goddess, you know), nor anybody else shall hurt you. But all this wants looking into, I perceive, What with one thing and another, I see that my work is well cut out for me.'

V

'How do I look to-night, Liddy?' said Bathsheba, giving a final adjustment to her dress before leaving the glass.

'I never saw you look so well before. Yes — I'll tell you when you looked like it — that night, a year and a half ago, when you came in so wild-like, and scolded us for making remarks about you and Mr Troy.'

'Everybody will think that I am setting myself to captivate Mr Boldwood, I suppose,' she murmured. 'At least they'll say so. Can't my hair be brushed down a little flatter? I dread going — yet I dread the risk of wounding him by staying away.'

'Anyhow, ma'am, you can't well be dressed plainer than you are, unless you go in sackcloth at once. 'Tis your excitement is what makes you look so noticeable to-night.'

'I don't know what's the matter, I feel wretched at one time, and buoyant at another. I wish I could have continued quite alone as I have been for the last year or so, with no hopes and no fears, and no pleasure and no grief.'

'Now just suppose Mr Boldwood should ask you — only just suppose it — to run away with him, what would you do, ma'am?'

'Liddy — none of that,' said Bathsheba, gravely. 'Mind, I won't hear joking on any such matter. Do you hear?'

'I beg pardon, ma'am. But knowing what rum things we women be, I just said — however, I won't speak of it again.'

'No marrying for me yet for many a year; if ever, 'twill be for reasons very, very different from those you think, or others will believe! Now get my cloak for it is time to go.'

VI

'Oak,' said Boldwood, 'before you go I want to mention what has been passing in my mind lately – that little arrangement we made about your share in the farm I mean. That share is small, too small, considering how little I attend to business now, and how much time and thought you give to it. Well, since the world is brightening for me, I want to show my sense of it by increasing your proportion in the partnership. I'll make a memorandum of the arrangement which struck me as likely to be convenient, for I haven't time to talk about it now; and then we'll discuss it at our leisure. My intention is ultimately to retire from the management altogether, and until you can take all the expenditure upon your shoulders, I'll be a sleeping partner in the stock. Then, if I marry her – and I hope – I feel I shall, why—'

'Pray don't speak of it, sir,' said Oak, hastily. 'We don't know what may happen. So many upsets may befall 'ee. There's many a slip, as they say – and I would advise you – I know you'll pardon me this once – not to be *too sure.*'

'I know, I know. But the feeling I have about increasing your share is on account of what I know of you. Oak, I have learnt a little about your secret: your interest in her is more than that of bailiff for an employer. But you have behaved like a man, and I, as a sort of successful rival – successful partly through your goodness of heart – should like definitely to show my sense of your friendship under what must have been a great pain to you.'

'O that's not necessary, thank 'ee,' said Oak, hurriedly. 'I must get used to such as that; other men have, and so shall I.'

Oak then left him. He was uneasy on Boldwood's account, for he saw anew that this constant passion of the farmer made him not the man he once had been.

As Boldwood continued awhile in his room alone – ready and dressed to receive his company – the mood of anxiety about his appearance seemed to pass away, and to be succeeded by a deep solemnity. He looked out of the window, and regarded the dim outline of the trees upon the sky, and the twilight deepening to darkness.

Then he went to a locked closet, and took from a locked drawer therein a small circular case the size of a pill-box, and was about to put it into his pocket. But he lingered to open the cover and take a momentary glance inside. It contained a woman's finger-ring, set all the way round with small diamonds, and from its appearance had evidently been recently purchased. Boldwood's eyes dwelt upon its many sparkles a long time, though that its material aspect concerned him little was plain from his manner and mien, which were those of a mind following out the presumed thread of that jewel's future history.

The noise of wheels at the front of the house became audible. Boldwood closed the box, stowed it away carefully in his pocket, and went out upon the landing. The old man who was his indoor factotum came at the same moment to the foot of the stairs.

'They be coming, sir – lots of 'em – a-foot and a-driving!'

'I was coming down this moment. Those wheels I heard – is it Mrs Troy?'

'No, sir – 'tis not she yet.'

A reserved and sombre expression had returned to Boldwood's face again, but it poorly cloaked his feelings when he pronounced Bathsheba's name; and his feverish anxiety continued to show its existence by a galloping motion of his fingers upon the side of his thigh as he went down the stairs.

VII

'How does this cover me?' said Troy to Pennyways. 'Nobody would recognize me now, I'm sure.'

He was buttoning on a heavy grey overcoat of Noachian cut, with cape and high collar, the latter being erect and rigid, like a girdling wall, and nearly reaching to the verge of a travelling cap which was pulled down over his ears.

Pennyways snuffed the candle, and then looked up and deliberately inspected Troy.

'You've made up your mind to go then?' he said.

'Made up my mind? Yes; of course I have.'

'Why not write to her? 'Tis a very queer corner that you have got into, sergeant. You see, all these things will come to light if you go back, and they won't sound well at all. Faith, if I was you I'd even bide as you be – a single man of the name of Francis. A good wife is good, but the best wife is not so good as no wife at all. Now that's my outspoke mind, and I've been called a long-headed feller here and there.'

'All nonsense!' said Troy, angrily. 'There she is with plenty of money, and a house and farm, and horses, and comfort, and here am I living from hand to mouth – a needy adventurer. Besides, it is no use talking now; it is too late, and I am glad of it; I've been seen and recognized here this very afternoon. I should have gone back to her the day after the fair, if it hadn't been for you talking about the law, and rubbish about getting a separation; and I don't put it off any longer. What the deuce put it into my head to run away at all, I can't think! Humbugging sentiment – that's what it was. But what man on earth was to know that his wife would be in such a hurry to get rid of his name!'

'I should have known it. She's bad enough for anything.'

'Pennyways, mind who you are talking to.'

'Well, sergeant, all I say is this, that if I were you I'd go abroad again where I came from – 'tisn't too late to do it now. I wouldn't stir up the business and get a bad name for the sake of living with her – for all that about your play-acting is sure to come out, you know, although you think otherwise. My eyes and limbs, there'll be a racket if you go back just now – in the middle of Boldwood's Christmasing!'

'H'm, yes. I expect I shall not be a very welcome guest if he has her there,' said the sergeant, with a slight laugh. 'A sort of Alonzo the Brave; and when I go in the guests will sit in silence and fear, and all laughter and pleasure will be hushed, and the lights in the chamber burn blue, and the worms – Ugh, horrible! – Ring for some more brandy, Pennyways, I felt an awful shudder just then! Well, what is there besides? A stick – I must have a walking-stick.'

Pennyways now felt himself to be in something of a difficulty, for should Bathsheba and Troy become reconciled it would be necessary to regain her good opinion if he would secure the patronage of her husband. 'I sometimes think she likes you yet, and is a good woman at bottom,' he said, as a saving sentence. 'But there's no telling to a certainty from a body's outside. Well, you'll do as you like about going, of course, sergeant, and as for me, I'll do as you tell me.'

'Now, let me see what the time is,' said Troy, after emptying his glass in one draught as he stood. 'Half-past six o'clock. I shall not hurry along the road, and shall be there then before nine.'

CHAPTER FIFTY-THREE

Concurritur — Horæ Momento

O UTSIDE the front of Boldwood's house a group of men stood in the dark, with their faces towards the door, which occasionally opened and closed for the passage of some guest or servant, when a golden rod of light would stripe the ground for the moment and vanish again, leaving nothing outside but the glowworm shine of the pale lamp amid the evergreens over the door.

'He was seen in Casterbridge this afternoon — so the boy said,' one of them remarked in a whisper. 'And I for one believe it. His body was never found, you know.'

''Tis a strange story,' said the next. 'You may depend upon't that she knows nothing about it.'

'Not a word.'

'Perhaps he don't mean that she shall,' said another man.

'If he's alive and here in the neighbourhood, he means mischief,' said the first. 'Poor young thing: I do pity her, if 'tis true. He'll drag her to the dogs.'

'O no; he'll settle down quiet enough,' said one disposed to take a more hopeful view of the case.

'What a fool she must have been ever to have had anything to do with the man! She is so self-willed and independent too, that one is more minded to say it serves her right than pity her.'

'No, no! I don't hold with 'ee there. She was no otherwise than a girl mind, and how could she tell what the man was made of? If 'tis really true, 'tis too hard a punishment, and more than she ought to hae. — Hullo, who's that?' This was to some footsteps that were heard approaching.

'William Smallbury,' said a dim figure in the shades, coming up and joining them. 'Dark as a hedge, to-night, isn't it? I all but missed the plank over the river ath'art there in the bottom — never did such a thing before in my life. Be ye any of Boldwood's workfolk?' He peered into their faces.

'Yes — all o' us. We met here a few minutes ago.'

'Oh, I hear now — that's Sam Samway: thought I knowed the voice, too. Going in?'

'Presently. But I say, William,' Samway whispered, 'have ye heard this strange tale?'

'What – that about Sergeant Troy being seen, d'ye mean, souls?' said Smallbury, also lowering his voice.

'Ay: in Casterbridge.'

'Yes, I have. Laban Tall named a hint of it to me but now – but I don't think it. Hark, here Laban comes himself, 'a b'lieve.' A footstep drew near.

'Laban?'

'Yes, 'tis I,' said Tall.

'Have ye heard any more about that?'

'No,' said Tall, joining the group. 'And I'm inclined to think we'd better keep quiet. If so be 'tis not true, 'twill flurry her, and do her much harm to repeat it; and if so be 'tis true, 'twill do no good to forestall her time o' trouble. God send that it mid be a lie, for though Henery Fray and some of 'em do speak against her, she's never been anything but fair to me. She's hot and hasty, but she's a brave girl who'll never tell a lie however much the truth may harm her, and I've no cause to wish her evil.'

'She never do tell women's little lies, that's true; and 'tis a thing that can be said of very few. Ay, all the harm she thinks she says to yer face: there's nothing underhand wi' her.'

They stood silent then, every man busied with his own thoughts, during which interval sounds of merriment could be heard within. Then the front door again opened, the rays streamed out, the well-known form of Boldwood was seen in the rectangular area of light, the door closed, and Boldwood walked slowly down the path.

''Tis master,' one of the men whispered, as he neared them. 'We'd better stand quiet – he'll go in again directly. He would think it unseemly o' us to be loitering here.'

Boldwood came on, and passed by the men without seeing them, they being under the bushes on the grass. He paused, leant over the gate, and breathed a long breath. They heard low words come from him.

'I hope to God she'll come, or this night will be nothing but misery to me! O my darling, my darling, why do you keep me in suspense like this?'

He said this to himself, and they all distinctly heard it. Boldwood remained silent after that, and the noise from indoors was again just audible, until, a few minutes later, light wheels could be distinguished coming down the hill. They drew nearer, and ceased at the gate. Boldwood hastened back to the door, and opened it; and the light shone upon Bathsheba coming up the path.

Boldwood compressed his emotion to mere welcome: the men marked her light laugh and apology as she met him: he took her into the house; and the door closed again.

'Gracious heaven, I didn't know it was like that with him!' said one of the men. 'I thought that fancy of his was over long ago.'

'You don't know much of master, if you thought that,' said Samway.

'I wouldn't he should know we heard what 'a said for the world,' remarked a third.

'I wish we had told of the report at once,' the first uneasily continued. 'More harm may come of this than we know of. Poor Mr Boldwood, it will be hard upon en. I wish Troy was in— Well, God forgive me for such a wish! A scoundrel to play a poor wife such tricks. Nothing has prospered in Weatherbury since he

came here. And now I've no heart to go in. Let's look into Warren's for a few
minutes first, shall us, neighbours?'

Samway, Tall, and Smallbury agreed to go to Warren's, and went out at the
gate, the remaining ones entering the house. The three soon drew near the malthouse, approaching it from the adjoining orchard, and not by way of the street.
The pane of glass was illuminated as usual. Smallbury was a little in advance of
the rest, when, pausing, he turned suddenly to his companions and said, 'Hist!
See there.'

The light from the pane was now perceived to be shining not upon the ivied
wall as usual, but upon some object close to the glass. It was a human face.

'Let's come closer,' whispered Samway; and they approached on tiptoe. There
was no disbelieving the report any longer. Troy's face was almost close to the
pane, and he was looking in. Not only was he looking in, but he appeared to have
been arrested by a conversation which was in progress in the malt-house, the
voices of the interlocutors being those of Oak and the maltster.

'The spree is all in her honour, isn't it – they?' said the old man. 'Although he
made believe 'tis only keeping up o' Christmas?'

'I cannot say,' replied Oak.

'O 'tis true enough, faith. I cannot understand Farmer Boldwood being such a
fool at his time of life as to ho and hanker after thik woman in the way 'a do, and
she not care a bit about en.'

The men, after recognizing Troy's features, withdrew across the orchard as
quietly as they had come. The air was big with Bathsheba's fortunes to-night:
every word everywhere concerned her. When they were quite out of earshot all by
one instinct paused.

'It gave me quite a turn – his face,' said Tall, breathing.

'And so it did me,' said Samway. 'What's to be done?'

'I don't see that 'tis any business of ours,' Smallbury murmured dubiously.

'But it is! 'Tis a thing which is everybody's business,' said Samway. 'We know
very well that master's on a wrong tack, and that she's quite in the dark, and we
should let 'em know at once. Laban, you know her best – you'd better go and ask
to speak to her.'

'I bain't fit for any such thing,' said Laban, nervously. 'I should think William
ought to do it if anybody. He's oldest.'

'I shall have nothing to do with it,' said Smallbury. '''Tis a ticklish business
altogether. Why, he'll go on to her himself in a few minutes, ye'll see.'

'We don't know that he will. Come, Laban.'

'Very well, if I must I must, I suppose,' Tall reluctantly answered. 'What must I
say?'

'Just ask to see master.'

'O no; I shan't speak to Mr Boldwood. If I tell anybody, 'twill be mistress.'

'Very well,' said Samway.

Laban then went to the door. When he opened it the hum of bustle rolled out as
a wave upon a still strand – the assemblage being immediately inside the hall –
and was deadened to a murmur as he closed it again. Each man waited intently,
and looked around at the dark tree tops gently rocking against the sky and
occasionally shivering in a slight wind, as if he took interest in the scene, which
neither did. One of them began walking up and down, and then came to where he

started from and stopped again, with a sense that walking was a thing not worth doing now.

'I should think Laban must have seen mistress by this time,' said Smallbury, breaking the silence. 'Perhaps she won't come and speak to him.'

The door opened. Tall appeared, and joined them.

'Well?' said both.

'I didn't like to ask for her after all,' Laban faltered out. 'They were all in such a stir, trying to put a little spirit into the party. Somehow the fun seems to hang fire, though everything's there that a heart can desire, and I couldn't for my soul interfere and throw damp upon it – if 'twas to save my life, I couldn't!'

'I suppose we had better all go in together,' said Samway, gloomily. 'Perhaps I may have a chance of saying a word to master.'

So the men entered the hall, which was the room selected and arranged for the gathering because of its size. The younger men and maids were at last just beginning a dance. Bathsheba had been perplexed how to act, for she was not much more than a slim young maid herself, and the weight of stateliness sat heavy upon her. Sometimes she thought she ought not to have come under any circumstances; then she considered what cold unkindness that would have been, and finally resolved upon the middle course of staying for about an hour only, and gliding off unobserved, having from the first made up her mind that she could on no account dance, sing, or take any active part in the proceedings.

Her allotted hour having been passed in chatting and looking on, Bathsheba told Liddy not to hurry herself, and went to the small parlour to prepare for departure, which, like the hall, was decorated with holly and ivy, and well lighted up.

Nobody was in the room, but she had hardly been there a moment when the master of the house entered.

'Mrs Troy – you are not going?' he said. 'We've hardly begun!'

'If you'll excuse me, I should like to go now.' Her manner was restive, for she remembered her promise, and imagined what he was about to say. 'But as it is not late,' she added, 'I can walk home, and leave my man and Liddy to come when they choose.'

'I've been trying to get an opportunity of speaking to you,' said Boldwood. 'You know perhaps what I long to say?'

Bathsheba silently looked on the floor.

'You do give it?' he said eagerly.

'What?' she whispered.

'Now, that's evasion! Why, the promise. I don't want to intrude upon you at all, or to let it become known to anybody. But do give your word! A mere business compact, you know, between two people who are beyond the influence of passion.' Boldwood knew how false this picture was as regarded himself; but he had proved that it was the only tone in which she would allow him to approach her. 'A promise to marry me at the end of five years and three-quarters. You owe it to me!'

'I feel that I do,' said Bathsheba; 'that is, if you demand it. But I am a changed woman – an unhappy woman – and not – not—'

'You are still a very beautiful woman,' said Boldwood. Honesty and pure conviction suggested the remark, unaccompanied by any perception that it might have been adopted by blunt flattery to soothe and win her.

However, it had not much effect now, for she said, in a passionless nurmur which was in itself a proof of her words: 'I have no feeling in the matter at all. And I don't at all know what is right to do in my difficult position, and I have nobody to advise me. But I give my promise, if I must. I give it as the rendering of a debt, conditionally, of course, on my being a widow.'

'You'll marry me between five and six years hence?'

'Don't press me too hard. I'll marry nobody else.'

'But surely you will name the time, or there's nothing in the promise at all?'

'O, I don't know, pray let me go!' she said, her bosom beginning to rise. 'I am afraid what to do! I want to be just to you, and to be that seems to be wronging myself, and perhaps it is breaking the commandments. There is considerable doubt of his death, and then it is dreadful; let me ask a solicitor, Mr Boldwood, if I ought or no!'

'Say the words, dear one, and the subject shall be dismissed; a blissful loving intimacy of six years, and then marriage — O Bathsheba, say them!' he begged in a husky voice, unable to sustain the forms of mere friendship any longer. 'Promise yourself to me; I deserve it, indeed I do, for I have loved you more than anybody in the world! And if I said hasty words and showed uncalled-for heat of manner towards you, believe me, dear, I did not mean to distress you; I was in agony, Bathsheba, and I did not know what I said. You wouldn't let a dog suffer what I have suffered, could you but know it! Sometimes I shrink from your knowing what I have felt for you, and sometimes I am distressed that all of it you never will know. Be gracious, and give up a little to me, when I would give up my life for you!'

The trimmings of her dress, as they quivered against the light, showed how agitated she was, and at last she burst out crying. 'And you'll not — press me — about anything more — if I say in five or six years?' she sobbed, when she had power to frame the words.

'Yes, then I'll leave it to time.'

'Very well. If he does not return, I'll marry you in six years from this day, if we both live,' she said solemnly.

'And you'll take this as a token from me.'

Boldwood had come close to her side, and now he clasped one of her hands in both his own, and lifted it to his breast.

'What is it? Oh I cannot wear a ring!' she exclaimed, on seeing what he held; 'besides, I wouldn't have a soul know that it's an engagement! Perhaps it is improper? Besides, we are not engaged in the usual sense, are we? Don't insist, Mr Boldwood — don't!' In her trouble at not being able to get her hand away from him at once, she stamped passionately on the floor with one foot, and tears crowded to her eyes again.

'It means simply a pledge — no sentiment -- the seal of a practical compact,' he said more quietly, but still retaining her hand in his firm grasp. 'Come, now!' And Boldwood slipped the ring on her finger.

'I cannot wear it,' she said, weeping as if her heart would break. 'You frighten me, almost. So wild a scheme! Please let me go home!'

'Only to-night: wear it just to-night, to please me!'

Bathsheba sat down in a chair, and buried her face in her handkerchief, though Boldwood kept her hand yet. At length she said, in a sort of hopeless whisper –

'Very well, then, I will to-night, if you wish it so earnestly. Now loosen my hand; I will, indeed I will wear it to-night.'

'And it shall be the beginning of a pleasant secret courtship of six years, with a wedding at the end?'

'It must be, I suppose, since you will have it so!' she said, fairly beaten into non-resistance.

Boldwood pressed her hand, and allowed it to drop in her lap. 'I am happy now,' he said. 'God bless you!'

He left the room, and when he thought she might be sufficiently composed sent one of the maids to her. Bathsheba cloaked the effects of the late scene as she best could, followed the girl, and in a few moments came downstairs with her hat and cloak on, ready to go. To get to the door it was necessary to pass through the hall, and before doing so she paused on the bottom of the staircase which descended into one corner, to take a last look at the gathering.

There was no music or dancing in progress just now. At the lower end, which had been arranged for the work-folk specially, a group conversed in whispers, and with clouded looks. Boldwood was standing by the fireplace, and he, too, though so absorbed in visions arising from her promise that he scarcely saw anything, seemed at that moment to have observed their peculiar manner, and their looks askance.

'What is it you are in doubt about, men?' he said.

One of them turned and replied uneasily: 'It was something Laban heard of, that's all, sir.'

'News? Anybody married or engaged, born or dead?' inquired the farmer, gaily. 'Tell it to us, Tall. One would think from your looks and mysterious ways that it was something very dreadful indeed.'

'O no, sir, nobody is dead,' said Tall.

'I wish somebody was,' said Samway, in a whisper.

'What do you say, Samway?' asked Boldwood, somewhat sharply. 'If you have anything to say, speak out; if not, get up another dance.'

'Mrs Troy has come downstairs,' said Samway to Tall. 'If you want to tell her, you had better do it now.'

'Do you know what they mean?' the farmer asked Bathsheba, across the room.

'I don't in the least,' said Bathsheba.

There was a smart rapping at the door. One of the men opened it instantly, and went outside.

'Mrs Troy is wanted,' he said, on returning.

'Quite ready,' said Bathsheba. 'Though I didn't tell them to send.'

'It is a stranger, ma'am,' said the man by the door.

'A stranger?' she said.

'Ask him to come in,' said Boldwood.

The message was given, and Troy, wrapped up to his eyes as we have seen him, stood in the doorway.

There was an unearthly silence, all looking towards the newcomer. Those who had just learnt that he was in the neighbourhood recognized him instantly; those who did not were perplexed. Nobody noted Bathsheba. She was leaning on the stairs. Her brow had heavily contracted; her whole face was pallid, her lips apart, her eyes rigidly staring at their visitor.

Boldwood was among those who did not notice that he was Troy. 'Come in, come in!' he repeated, cheerfully, 'and drain a Christmas beaker with us, stranger!'

Troy next advanced into the middle of the room, took off his cap, turned down his coat-collar, and looked Boldwood in the face. Even then Boldwood did not recognize that the impersonator of Heaven's persistent irony towards him, who had once before broken in upon his bliss, scourged him, and snatched his delight away, had come to do these things a second time. Troy began to laugh a mechanical laugh: Boldwood recognized him now.

Troy turned to Bathsheba. The poor girl's wretchedness at this time was beyond all fancy or narration. She had sunk down on the lowest stair; and there she sat, her mouth blue and dry, and her dark eyes fixed vacantly upon him, as if she wondered whether it were not all a terrible illusion.

Then Troy spoke. 'Bathsheba, I come here for you!'

She made no reply.

'Come home with me: come!'

Bathsheba moved her feet a little, but did not rise.

Troy went across to her.

'Come, madam, do you hear what I say?' he said, peremptorily.

A strange voice came from the fireplace – a voice sounding far off and confined, as if from a dungeon. Hardly a soul in the assembly recognized the thin tones to be those of Boldwood. Sudden despair had transformed him.

'Bathsheba, go with your husband!'

Nevertheless, she did not move. The truth was that Bathsheba was beyond the pale of activity – and yet not in a swoon. She was in a state of mental *gutta serena*; her mind was for the minute totally deprived of light at the same time that no obscuration was apparent from without.

Troy stretched out his hand to pull her towards him, when she quickly shrank back. This visible dread of him seemed to irritate Troy, and he seized her arm and pulled it sharply. Whether his grasp pinched her, or whether his mere touch was the cause, was never known, but at the moment of his seizure she writhed, and gave a quick, low scream.

The scream had been heard but a few seconds when it was followed by a sudden deafening report that echoed through the room and stupefied them all. The oak partition shook with the concussion, and the place was filled with grey smoke.

In bewilderment they turned their eyes to Boldwood. At his back, as he stood before the fireplace, was a gun-rack, as is usual in farmhouses, constructed to hold two guns. When Bathsheba had cried out in her husband's grasp, Boldwood's face of gnashing despair had changed. The veins had swollen, and a frenzied look had gleamed in his eye. He had turned quickly, taken one of the guns, cocked it, and at once discharged it at Troy.

Troy fell. The distance apart of the two men was so small that the charge of shot did not spread in the least, but passed like a bullet into his body. He uttered a long guttural sigh – there was a contraction – an extension – then his muscles relaxed, and he lay still.

Boldwood was seen through the smoke to be now again engaged with the gun. It was double-barrelled, and he had, meanwhile, in some way fastened his handkerchief to the trigger, and with his foot on the other end was in the act of turning the second barrel upon himself. Samway his man was the first to see this, and in the midst of the general horror darted up to him. Boldwood had already twitched the handkerchief, and the gun exploded a second time, sending its contents, by a timely blow from Samway, into the beam which crossed the ceiling.

'Well, it makes no difference!' Boldwood gasped. 'There is another way for me to die.'

Then he broke from Samway, crossed the room to Bathsheba, and kissed her hand. He put on his hat, opened the door, and went into the darkness, nobody thinking of preventing him.

CHAPTER FIFTY-FOUR

After the Shock

BOLDWOOD passed into the high road, and turned in the direction of Casterbridge. Here he walked at an even, steady pace over Yalbury Hill, along the dead level beyond, mounted Mellstock Hill, and between eleven and twelve o'clock crossed the Moor into the town. The stress were nearly deserted now, and the waving lamp-flames only lighted up rows of grey shop-shutters, and strips of white paving upon which his step echoed as he passed along. He turned to the right, and halted before an archway of heavy stone-work, which was closed by an iron-studded pair of doors. This was the entrance to the gaol, and over it a lamp was fixed, the light enabling the wretched traveller to find a bell-pull.

The small wicket at last opened, and a porter appeared. Boldwood stepped forward, and said something in a low tone, when, after a delay, another man came. Boldwood entered, and the door was closed behind him, and he walked the world no more.

Long before this time Weatherbury had been thoroughly aroused, and the wild deed which had terminated Boldwood's merrymaking became known to all. Of those out of the house Oak was one of the first to hear of the catastrophe, and when he entered the room, which was about five minutes after Boldwood's exit, the scene was terrible. All the female guests were huddled aghast against the walls like sheep in a storm, and the men were bewildered as to what to do. As for Bathsheba, she had changed. She was sitting on the floor beside the body of Troy, his head pillowed in her lap, where she had herself lifted it. With one hand she held her handkerchief to his breast and covered the wound, though scarcely a single drop of blood had flowed, and with the other she tightly clasped one of his. The household convulsion had made her herself again. The temporary coma had ceased, and activity had come with the necessity for it. Deeds of endurance which seem ordinary in philosophy are rare in conduct, and Bathsheba was astonishing all around her now, for her philosophy was her conduct, and she seldom thought practicable what she did not practise. She was of the stuff of which great men's mothers are made. She was indispensable to high generation, hated at tea parties, feared in shops, and loved at crises. Troy recumbent in his wife's lap formed now the sole spectacle in the middle of the spacious room.

'Gabriel,' she said, automatically, when he entered, turning up a face of which only the well-known lines remained to tell him it was hers, all else in the picture having faded quite. 'Ride to Casterbridge instantly for a surgeon. It is, I believe, useless, but go. Mr Boldwood has shot my husband.'

Her statement of the fact in such quiet and simple words came with more force than a tragic declamation, and had somewhat the effect of setting the distorted images in each mind present into proper focus. Oak, almost before he had comprehended anything beyond the briefest abstract of the event, hurried out of the room, saddled a horse and rode away. Not till he had ridden more than a mile did it occur to him that he would have done better by sending some other man on this errand, remaining himself in the house. What had become of Boldwood? He should have been looked after. Was he mad – had there been a quarrel? Then how had Troy got there? Where had he come from? How did this remarkable reappearance effect itself when he was supposed by many to be at the bottom of the sea? Oak had in some measure been prepared for the presence of Troy by hearing a rumour of his return just before entering Boldwood's house; but before he had weighed that information, this fatal event had been superimposed. However, it was too late now to think of sending another messenger, and he rode on, in the excitement of these self-inquiries not discerning, when about three miles from Casterbridge, a square-figured pedestrian passing along under the dark hedge in the same direction as his own.

The miles necessary to be traversed, and other hindrances incidental to the lateness of the hour and the darkness of the night, delayed the arrival of Mr Aldritch, the surgeon; and more than three hours passed between the time at which the shot was fired and that of his entering the house. Oak was additionally detained in Casterbridge through having to give notice to the authorities of what had happened; and he then found that Boldwood had also entered the town, and delivered himself up.

In the meantime the surgeon, having hastened into the hall at Boldwood's, found it in darkness and quite deserted. He went on to the back of the house, where he discovered in the kitchen an old man, of whom he made inquiries.

'She's had him took away to her own house, sir,' said his informant.

'Who has?' said the doctor.

'Mrs Troy. 'A was quite dead, sir.'

This was astonishing information. 'She had no right to do that,' said the doctor. 'There will have to be an inquest, and she should have waited to know what to do.'

'Yes, sir; it was hinted to her that she had better wait till the law was known. But she said law was nothing to her, and she wouldn't let her dear husband's corpse bide neglected for folks to stare at for all the crowners in England.'

Mr Aldritch drove at once back again up the hill to Bathsheba's. The first person he met was poor Liddy, who seemed literally to have dwindled smaller in these few latter hours. 'What has been done?' he said.

'I don't know, sir,' said Liddy, with suspended breath. 'My mistress has done it all.'

'Where is she?'

'Upstairs with him, sir. When he was brought home and taken upstairs, she said she wanted no further help from the men. And then she called me, and made me fill the bath, and after that told me I had better go and lie down because I looked so ill. Then she locked herself into the room alone with him, and would not let a nurse come in, or anybody at all. But I thought I'd wait in the next room in case she should want me. I heard her moving about inside for more than an hour, but she only came out once, and that was for more candles, because hers had burnt down into the socket. She said we were to let her know when you or Mr Thirdly came, sir.'

Oak entered with the parson at this moment, and they all went upstairs together, preceded by Liddy Smallbury. Everything was silent as the grave when they paused on the landing. Liddy knocked, and Bathsheba's dress was heard rustling across the room: the key turned in the lock, and she opened the door. Her looks were calm and nearly rigid, like a slightly animated bust of Melpomene.

'Oh, Mr Aldritch, you have come at last,' she murmured from her lips merely, and threw back the door. 'Ah, and Mr Thirdly. Well, all is done, and anybody in the world may see him now.' She then passed by him, crossed the landing, and entered another room.

Looking into the chamber of death she had vacated they saw by the light of the candles which were on the drawers a tall straight shape lying at the further end of the bedroom, wrapped in white. Everything around was quite orderly. The doctor went in, and after a few minutes returned to the landing again, where Oak and the parson still waited.

'It is all done, indeed, as she says,' remarked Mr Aldritch, in a subdued voice. 'The body has been undressed and properly laid out in grave-clothes. Gracious Heaven – this mere girl! She must have the nerve of a stoic!'

'The heart of a wife merely,' floated in a whisper about the ears of the three, and turning they saw Bathsheba in the midst of them. Then, as if at that instant to prove that her fortitude had been more of will than of spontaneity, she silently sank down between them and was a shapeless heap of drapery on the floor. The simple consciousness that superhuman strain was no longer required had at once put a period to her power to continue it.

They took her away into a further room, and the medical attendance which had been useless in Troy's case was invaluable in Bathsheba's, who fell into a series of fainting-fits that had a serious aspect for a time. The sufferer was got to bed, and Oak, finding from the bulletins that nothing really dreadful was to be apprehended on her score, left the house. Liddy kept watch in Bathsheba's chamber, where she heard her mistress moaning in whispers through the dull slow hours of that wretched night: 'O it is my fault – how can I live! O Heaven, how can I live!'

CHAPTER FIFTY-FIVE

The March Following –
'Bathsheba Boldwood'

W E pass rapidly on into the month of March, to a breezy day without sunshine, frost, or dew. On Yalbury Hill, about midway between Weatherbury and Casterbridge, where the turnpike road passes over the crest, a numerous concourse of people had gathered, the eyes of the greater number being frequently stretched afar in a northerly direction. The groups consisted of a throng of idlers, a party of javelin-men, and two trumpeters, and in the midst were carriages, one of which contained the high sheriff. With the idlers, many of whom had mounted to the top of a cutting formed for the road, were several Weatherbury men and boys – among others Poorgrass, Coggan, and Cain Ball.

At the end of half-an-hour a faint dust was seen in the expected quarter, and shortly after a travelling-carriage, bringing one of the two judges on the Western Circuit, came up the hill and halted on the top. The judge changed carriages whilst a flourish was blown by the big-cheeked trumpeters, and a procession being formed of the vehicles and javelin-men, they all proceeded towards the town, excepting the Weatherbury men, who as soon as they had seen the judge move off returned home again to their work.

'Joseph, I zeed you squeezing close to the carriage,' said Coggan, as they walked. 'Did ye notice my lord judge's face?'

'I did,' said Poorgrass, 'I looked hard at en, as if I would read his very soul; and there was mercy in his eyes – or to speak with the exact truth required of us at this solemn time, in the eye that was towards me.'

'Well, I hope for the best,' said Coggan, 'though bad that must be. However, I shan't go to the trial, and I'd advise the rest of ye that bain't wanted to bide away. 'Twill disturb his mind more than anything to see us there staring at him as if he were a show.'

'The very thing I said this morning,' observed Joseph. ' "Justice is come to weigh him in the balances," I said in my reflectious way, "and if he's found wanting, so be it unto him," and a bystander said "Hear, hear! A man who can talk like that ought to be heard." But I don't like dwelling upon it, for my few words are my few words, and not much; though the speech of some men is rumoured abroad as though by nature formed for such.'

'So 'tis, Joseph. And now, neighbours, as I said, every man bide at home.'

The resolution was adhered to; and all waited anxiously for the news next day. Their suspense was diverted, however, by a discovery which was made in the afternoon, throwing more light on Boldwood's conduct and condition than any details which had preceded it.

That he had been from the time of Greenhill Fair until the fatal Christmas Eve in excited and unusual moods was known to those who had been intimate with him; but nobody imagined that there had shown in him unequivocal symptoms of the mental derangement which Bathsheba and Oak, alone of all others and at different times, had momentarily suspected. In a locked closet was now discovered an extraordinary collection of articles. There were several sets of ladies' dresses in the piece, of sundry expensive materials; silks and satins, poplins and velvets, all of colours which from Bathsheba's style of dress might have been judged to be her favourites. There were two muffs, sable and ermine. Above all there was a case of jewellery, containing four heavy gold bracelets and several lockets and rings, all of fine quality and manufacture. These things had been bought in Bath and other towns from time to time, and brought home by stealth. They were all carefully packed in paper, and each package was labelled 'Bathsheba Boldwood', a date being subjoined six years in advance in every instance.

These somewhat pathetic evidences of a mind crazed with care and love were the subject of discourse in Warren's malt-house when Oak entered from Casterbridge with tidings of the sentence. He came in the afternoon, and his face, as the kiln glow shone upon it, told the tale sufficiently well. Boldwood, as every one supposed he would do, had pleaded guilty, and had been sentenced to death.

The conviction that Boldwood had not been morally responsible for his later acts now became general. Facts elicited previous to the trial had pointed strongly in the same direction, but they had not been of sufficient weight to lead to an order for an examination into the state of Boldwood's mind. It was astonishing, now that a presumption of insanity was raised, how many collateral circumstances were remembered to which a condition of mental disease seemed to afford the only explanation – among others, the unprecedented neglect of his corn stacks in the previous summer.

A petition was addressed to the Home Secretary, advancing the circumstances which appeared to justify a request for a reconsideration of the sentence. It was not 'numerously signed' by the inhabitants of Casterbridge, as is usual in such cases, for Boldwood had never made many friends over the counter. The shops thought it very natural that a man who, by importing direct from the producer, had daringly set aside the first great principle of provincial existence, namely, that God made country villages to supply customers to country towns, should have confused ideas about the Decalogue. The prompters were a few merciful men who had perhaps too feelingly considered the facts latterly unearthed, and the result was that evidence was taken which it was hoped might remove the crime, in a moral point of view, out of the category of wilful murder, and lead it to be regarded as a sheer outcome of madness.

The upshot of the petition was waited for in Weatherbury with solicitous interest. The execution had been fixed for eight o'clock on a Saturday morning about a fortnight after the sentence was passed, and up to Friday afternoon no answer had been received. At that time Gabriel came from Casterbridge Gaol, whither he had been to wish Boldwood good-bye, and turned down a by-street to avoid the town. When past the last house he heard a hammering, and lifting his bowed head he looked back for a moment. Over the chimneys he could see the upper part of the gaol entrance, rich and glowing in the afternoon sun, and some figures were there. They were carpenters lifting a post into a vertical position within the parapet. He withdrew his eyes quickly and hastened on.

It was dark when he reached home, and half the village was out to meet him.

'No tidings,' Gabriel said, wearily. 'And I'm afraid there's no hope. I've been with him more than two hours.'

'Do ye think he *really* was out of his mind when he did it?' said Smallbury.

'I can't honestly say that I do,' Oak replied. 'However, that we can talk of another time. Has there been any change in mistress this afternoon?'

'None at all.'

'Is she downstairs?'

'No. And getting on so nicely as she was too. She's but very little better now again than she was at Christmas. She keeps on asking if you be come, and if there's news, till one's wearied out wi' answering her. Shall I go and say you've come?'

'No,' said Oak. 'There's a chance yet; but I couldn't stay in town any longer – after seeing him too. So Laban – Laban is here, isn't he?'

'Yes,' said Tall.

'What I've arranged is, that you shall ride to town the last thing to-night; leave here about nine, and wait a while there, getting home about twelve. If nothing has been received by eleven to-night, they say there's no chance at all.'

'I do so hope his life will be spared,' said Liddy. 'If it is not, she'll go out of her mind too. Poor thing; her sufferings have been dreadful; she deserves anybody's pity.'

'Is she altered much?' said Coggan.

'If you haven't seen poor mistress since Christmas, you wouldn't know her,' said Liddy. 'Her eyes are so miserable that she's not the same woman. Only two years ago she was a romping girl, and now she's this!'

Laban departed as directed, and at eleven o'clock that night several of the villagers strolled along the road to Casterbridge and awaited his arrival – among them Oak, and nearly all the rest of Bathsheba's men. Gabriel's anxiety was great that Boldwood might be saved, even though in his conscience he felt that he ought to die; for there had been qualities in the farmer which Oak loved. At last, when they all were weary the tramp of a horse was heard in the distance –

> First dead, as if on turf it trode,
> Then, clattering, on the village road
> In other pace than forth he yode.

'We shall soon know now, one way or other,' said Coggan, and they all stepped down from the bank on which they had been standing into the road, and the rider pranced into the midst of them.

'Is that you, Laban?' said Gabriel.

'Yes – 'tis come. He's not to die. 'Tis confinement during Her Majesty's pleasure.'

'Hurrah!' said Coggan, with a swelling heart. 'God's above the devil yet!'

CHAPTER FIFTY-SIX

Beauty in Loneliness – After All

BATHSHEBA revived with the spring. The utter prostration that had followed the low fever from which she had suffered diminished perceptibly when all uncertainty upon every subject had come to an end.

But she remained alone now for the greater part of her time, and stayed in the house, or at furthest went into the garden. She shunned every one, even Liddy, and could be brought to make no confidences, and to ask for no sympathy.

As the summer drew on she passed more of her time in the open air, and began to examine into farming matters from sheer necessity, though she never rode out or personally superintended as at former times. One Friday evening in August she walked a little way along the road and entered the the village for the first time since the sombre event of the preceding Christmas. None of the old colour had as yet come to her cheek, and its absolute paleness was heightened by the jet black of her gown, till it appeared preternatural. When she reached a little shop at the other end of the place, which stood nearly opposite to the churchyard, Bathsheba heard singing inside the church, and she knew that the singers were practising. She crossed the road, opened the gate, and entered the graveyard, the high sills of the church windows effectually screening her from the eyes of those gathered within. Her stealthy walk was to the nook wherein Troy had worked at planting flowers upon Fanny Robin's grave, and she came to the marble tombstone.

A motion of satisfaction enlivened her face as she read the complete inscription. First came the words of Troy himself: –

ERECTED BY FRANCIS TROY
IN BELOVED MEMORY OF
FANNY ROBIN,
WHO DIED OCTOBER 9, 18—,
AGED 20 YEARS.

Underneath this was now inscribed in new letters: –

IN THE SAME GRAVE LIE
THE REMAINS OF THE AFORESAID
FRANCIS TROY,
WHO DIED DECEMBER 24TH, 18—,
AGED 26 YEARS.

Whilst she stood and read and meditated the tones of the organ began again in the church, and she went with the same light step round to the porch and listened. The door was closed, and the choir was learning a new hymn. Bathsheba was stirred by emotions which latterly she had assumed to be altogether dead within her. The little attenuated voices of the children brought to her ear in distinct utterance the words they sang without thought or comprehension –

> Lead, kindly Light, amid the encircling gloom,
> Lead Thou me on.

Bathsheba's feeling was always to some extent dependent upon her whim, as is the case with many other women. Something big came into her throat and an uprising to her eyes – and she thought that she would allow the imminent tears to flow if they wished. They did flow and plenteously, and one fell upon the stone bench beside her. Once that she had begun to cry for she hardly knew what, she could not leave off for crowding thoughts she knew too well. She would have given anything in the world to be, as those children were, unconcerned at the meaning of their words, because too innocent to feel the necessity for any such expression. All the impassioned scenes of her brief experience seemed to revive with added emotion at that moment, and those scenes which had been without emotion during enactment had emotion then. Yet grief came to her rather as a luxury than as the scourge of former times.

Owing to Bathsheba's face being buried in her hands she did not notice a form which came quietly into the porch, and on seeing her, first moved as if to retreat, then paused and regarded her. Bathsheba did not raise her head for some time, and when she looked round her face was wet, and her eyes drowned and dim. 'Mr Oak,' exclaimed she, disconcerted, 'how long have you been here?'

'A few minutes, ma'am,' said Oak, respectfully.

'Are you going in?' said Bathsheba; and there came from within the church as from a prompter –

> I loved the garish day, and, spite of fears,
> Pride ruled my will: remember not past years.

'I was,' said Gabriel. 'I am one of the bass singers, you know. I have sung bass for several months.'

'Indeed: I wasn't aware of that. I'll leave you, then.'

> Which I have loved long since, and lost awhile,

sang the children.

'Don't let me drive you away, mistress. I think I won't go in to-night.'

'O no – you don't drive me away.'

Then they stood in a state of some embarrassment, Bathsheba trying to wipe her dreadfully drenched and inflamed face without his noticing her. At length Oak said, 'I've not seen you – I mean spoken to you – since ever so long, have I?' But he feared to bring distressing memories back, and interrupted himself with: 'Were you going into church?'

'No,' she said. 'I came to see the tombstone privately – to see if they had cut the inscription as I wished. Mr Oak, you needn't mind speaking to me, if you wish to, on the matter which is in both our minds at this moment.'

'And have they done it as you wished?' said Oak.

'Yes. Come and see it, if you have not already.'

So together they went and read the tomb. 'Eight months ago!' Gabriel murmured when he saw the date. 'It seems like yesterday to me.'

'And to me as if it were years ago – long years, and I had been dead between. And now I am going home, Mr Oak.'

Oak walked after her. 'I wanted to name a small matter to you as soon as I could,' he said with hesitation. 'Merely about business, and I think I may just mention it now, if you'll allow me.'

'O yes, certainly.'

'It is that I may soon have to give up the management of your farm, Mrs Troy. The fact is, I am thinking of leaving England – not yet, you know – next spring.'

'Leaving England!' she said, in surprise and genuine disappointment. 'Why, Gabriel, what are you going to do that for?'

'Well, I've thought it best,' Oak stammered out. 'California is the spot I've had in my mind to try.'

'But it is understood everywhere that you are going to take poor Mr Boldwood's farm on your own account?'

'I've had the refusal o' it 'tis true; but nothing is settled yet, and I have reasons for gieing up. I shall finish out my year there as manager for the trustees, but no more.'

'And what shall I do without you? Oh, Gabriel, I don't think you ought to go away. You've been with me so long – through bright times and dark times – such old friends as we are – that it seems unkind almost. I had fancied that if you leased the other farm as master, you might still give a helping look across at mine. And now going away!'

'I would have willingly.'

'Yet now that I am more helpless than ever you go away!'

'Yes, that's the ill fortune o' it,' said Gabriel, in a distressed tone. 'And it is because of that very helplessness that I feel bound to go. Good afternoon, ma'am,' he concluded, in evident anxiety to get away, and at once went out of the churchyard by a path she could follow on no pretence whatever.

Bathsheba went home, her mind occupied with a new trouble, which being rather harassing than deadly was calculated to do good by diverting her from the chronic gloom of her life. She was set thinking a great deal about Oak and of his wish to shun her; and there occurred to Bathsheba several incidents of her latter intercourse with him, which, trivial when singly viewed, amounted together to a perceptible disinclination for her society. It broke upon her at length as a great pain that her last old disciple was about to forsake her and flee. He who had believed in her and argued on her side when all the rest of the world was against her, had at last like the others become weary and neglectful of the old cause, and was leaving her to fight her battles alone.

Three weeks went on, and more evidence of his want of interest in her was forthcoming. She noticed that instead of entering the small parlour or office where the farm accounts were kept, and waiting, or leaving a memorandum as he had hitherto done during her seclusion, Oak never came at all when she was likely to be there, only entering at unseasonable hours when her presence in that part of the house was least to be expected. Whenever he wanted directions he sent a message, or note with neither heading nor signature, to which she was obliged to reply in the same off-hand style. Poor Bathsheba began to suffer now from the most torturing sting of all – a sensation that she was despised.

The autumn wore away gloomily enough amid these melancholy conjectures, and Christmas-day came, completing a year of her legal widowhood, and two years and a quarter of her life alone. On examining her heart it appeared beyond measure strange that the subject of which the season might have been supposed suggestive – the event in the hall at Boldwood's – was not agitating her at all; but instead, an agonizing conviction that everybody abjured her – for what she could not tell – and that Oak was the ringleader of the recusants. Coming out of church that day she looked round in hope that Oak, whose bass voice she had heard rolling out from the gallery overhead in a most unconcerned manner, might chance to linger in her path in the old way. There he was, as usual, coming down the path behind her. But on seeing Bathsheba turn, he looked aside, and as soon as he got beyond the gate, and there was the barest excuse for a divergence, he made one, and vanished.

The next morning brought the culminating stroke; she had been expecting it long. It was a formal notice by letter from him that he should not renew his engagement with her for the following Lady-day.

Bathsheba actually sat and cried over this letter most bitterly. She was aggrieved and wounded that the possession of hopeless love from Gabriel, which she had grown to regard as her inalienable right for life, should have been withdrawn just at his own pleasure in this way. She was bewildered too by the prospect of having to rely on her own resources again: it seemed to herself that she never could again acquire energy sufficient to go to market, barter, and sell. Since Troy's death Oak had attended all sales and fairs for her, transacting her business at the same time with his own. What should she do now? Her life was becoming a desolation.

So desolate was Bathsheba this evening, that in an absolute hunger for pity and sympathy, and miserable in that she appeared to have outlived the only true friendship she had ever owned, she put on her bonnet and cloak and went down to Oak's house just after sunset, guided on her way by the pale primrose rays of a crescent moon a few days old.

A lively firelight shone from the window, but nobody was visible in the room. She tapped nervously, and then thought it doubtful if it were right for a single woman to call upon a bachelor who lived alone, although he was her manager, and she might be supposed to call on business without any real impropriety. Gabriel opened the door, and the moon shone upon his forehead.

'Mr Oak,' said Bathsheba faintly.

'Yes; I am Mr Oak,' said Gabriel. 'Who have I the honour – O how stupid of me, not to know you, mistress!'

'I shall not be your mistress much longer, shall I, Gabriel?' she said in pathetic tones.

'Well, no. I suppose – But come in, ma'am. Oh – and I'll get a light,' Oak replied, with some awkwardness.

'No; not on my account.'

'It is so seldom that I get a lady visitor that I'm afraid I haven't proper accommodation. Will you sit down, please? Here's a chair, and there's one, too. I am sorry that my chairs all have wood seats, and are rather hard, but I – was thinking of getting some new ones.' Oak placed two or three for her.

'They are quite easy enough for me.'

So down she sat, and down he sat, the fire dancing in their faces, and upon the old furniture,

> all a-sheenen
> Wi' long years o' handlen,[1]

that formed Oak's array of household possessions, which sent back a dancing reflection in reply. It was very odd to these two persons, who knew each other passing well, that the mere circumstance of their meeting in a new place and in a new way should make them so awkward and constrained. In the fields, or at her house, there had never been any embarrassment; but now that Oak had become the entertainer their lives seemed to be moved back again to the days when they were strangers.

'You'll think it strange that I have come, but—'

'O no; not at all.'

'But I thought – Gabriel, I have been uneasy in the belief that I have offended you, and that you are going away on that account. It grieved me very much, and I couldn't help coming.'

'Offended me! As if you could do that, Bathsheba!'

'Haven't I?' she asked, gladly. 'But, what are you going away for else?'

'I am not going to emigrate, you know; I wasn't aware that you would wish me not to when I told 'ee, or I shouldn't have thought of doing it,' he said, simply. 'I have arranged for Little Weatherbury Farm, and shall have it in my own hands at Lady-day. You know I've had a share in it for some time. Still, that wouldn't prevent my attending to your business as before, hadn't it been that things have been said about us.'

'What?' said Bathsheba in surprise. 'Things said about you and me! What are they?'

'I cannot tell you.'

'It would be wiser if you were to, I think. You have played the part of mentor to me many times, and I don't see why you should fear to do it now.'

'It is nothing that you have done, this time. The top and tail o't is this – that I'm sniffing about here, and waiting for poor Boldwood's farm, with a thought of getting you some day.'

'Getting me! What does that mean?'

'Marrying of 'ee, in plain British. You asked me to tell, so you mustn't blame me.'

Bathsheba did not look quite so alarmed as if a cannon had been discharged by her ear, which was what Oak had expected. 'Marrying me! I didn't know it was that you meant,' she said, quietly. 'Such a thing as that is too absurd – too soon – to think of, by far!'

'Yes; of course, it is too absurd. I don't desire any such thing; I should think that was plain enough by this time. Surely, surely you be the last person in the world I think of marrying. It is too absurd, as you say.'

'"Too – s-s-soon" were the words I used.'

'I must beg your pardon for correcting you, but you said, "too absurd", and so do I.'

---

[1] W. Barnes.

'I beg your pardon too!' she returned, with tears in her eyes. '"Too soon" was what I said. But it doesn't matter a bit – not at all – but I only meant, "too soon". Indeed, I didn't, Mr Oak, and you must believe me!'

Gabriel looked her long in the face, but the firelight being faint there was not much to be seen. 'Bathsheba,' he said, tenderly and in surprise, and coming closer: 'If I only knew one thing – whether you would allow me to love you and win you, and marry you after all – If I only knew that!'

'But you never will know,' she murmured.

'Why?'

'Because you never ask.'

'Oh – Oh!' said Gabriel, with a low laugh of joyousness. 'My own dear—'

'You ought not to have sent me that harsh letter this morning,' she interrupted. 'It shows you didn't care a bit about me, and were ready to desert me like all the rest of them! It was very cruel of you, considering I was the first sweetheart that you ever had, and you were the first I ever had; and I shall not forget it!'

'Now, Bathsheba, was ever anybody so provoking?' he said, laughing. 'You know it was purely that I, as an unmarried man, carrying on a business for you as a very taking young woman, had a proper hard part to play – more particular that people knew I had a sort of feeling for 'ee; and I fancied, from the way we were mentioned together, that it might injure your good name. Nobody knows the heat and fret I have been caused by it.'

'And was that all?'

'All.'

'O, how glad I am I came!' she exclaimed, thankfully, as she rose from her seat. 'I have thought so much more of you since I fancied you did not want even to see me again. But I must be going now, or I shall be missed. Why, Gabriel,' she said, with a slight laugh, as they went to the door, 'it seems exactly as if I had come courting you – how dreadful!'

'And quite right, too,' said Oak. 'I've danced at your skittish heels, my beautiful Bathsheba, for many a long mile, and many a long day; and it is hard to begrudge me this one visit.'

He accompanied her up the hill, explaining to her the details of his forthcoming tenure of the other farm. They spoke very little of their mutual feelings; pretty phrases and warm expressions being probably unnecessary between such tried friends. Theirs was that substantial affection which arises (if any arises at all) when the two who are thrown together begin first by knowing the rougher sides of each other's character, and not the best till further on, the romance growing up in the interstices of a mass of hard prosaic reality. This good-fellowship – camaraderie – usually occurring through similarity of pursuits, is unfortunately seldom superadded to love between the sexes, because men and women associate, not in their labours, but in their pleasures merely. Where, however, happy circumstance permits its development, the compounded feeling proves itself to be the only love which is strong as death – that love which many waters cannot quench, nor the floods drown, beside which the passion usually called by the name is evanescent as steam.

CHAPTER FIFTY-SEVEN

A Foggy Night and Morning – Conclusion

'T HE most private, secret, plainest wedding that it is possible to have.'

Those had been Bathsheba's words to Oak one evening, some time after the event of the preceding chapter, and he meditated a full hour by the clock upon how to carry out her wishes to the letter.

'A license – O yes, it must be a license,' he said to himself at last. 'Very well, then; first, a license.'

On a dark night, a few days later, Oak came with mysterious steps from the surrogate's door in Casterbridge. On the way home he heard a heavy tread in front of him, and, overtaking the man, found him to be Coggan. They walked together into the village until they came to a little lane behind the church, leading down to the cottage of Laban Tall, who had lately been installed as clerk of the parish, and was yet in mortal terror at church on Sundays when he heard his lone voice among certain hard words of the Psalms, whither no man ventured to follow him.

'Well, good-night, Coggan,' said Oak, 'I'm going down this way.'

'Oh!' said Coggan, surprised; 'what's going on to-night, then, make so bold, Mr Oak?'

It seemed rather ungenerous not to tell Coggan, under the circumstances, for Coggan had been true as steel all through the time of Gabriel's unhappiness about Bathsheba, and Gabriel said, 'You can keep a secret, Coggan?'

'You've proved me, and you know.'

'Yes, I have, and I do know. Well, then, mistress and I mean to get married to-morrow morning.'

'Heaven's high tower! And yet I've thought of such a thing from time to time; true, I have. But keeping it so close! Well, there, 'tis no consarn of mine, and I wish 'ee joy o' her.'

'Thank you, Coggan. But I assure 'ee that this great hush is not what I wished for at all, or what either of us would have wished if it hadn't been for certain things that would make a gay wedding seem hardly the thing. Bathsheba has a great wish that all the parish shall not be in church, looking at her – she's shy-like and nervous about it, in fact – so I be doing this to humour her.'

'Ay, I see: quite right, too, I suppose I must say. And you be now going down to the clerk.'

'Yes; you may as well come with me.'

'I am afeard your labour in keeping it close will be throwed away,' said Coggan, as they walked along. 'Labe Tall's old woman will horn it all over parish in half-an-hour.'

'So she will, upon my life; I never thought of that,' said Oak, pausing. 'Yet I must tell him to-night, I suppose, for he's working so far off, and leaves early.'

'I'll tell 'ee how we could tackle her,' said Coggan. 'I'll knock and ask to speak to Laban outside the door, you standing in the background. Then he'll come out, and you can tell yer tale. She'll never guess what I want en for; and I'll make up a few words about the farm-work, as a blind.'

This scheme was considered feasible; and Coggan advanced boldly, and rapped at Mrs Tall's door. Mrs Tall herself opened it.

'I wanted to have a word with Laban.'

'He's not at home, and won't be this side of eleven o'clock. He've been forced to go over to Yalbury since shutting out work. I shall do quite as well.'

'I hardly think you will. Stop a moment'; and Coggan stepped round the corner of the porch to consult Oak.

'Who's t'other man, then?' said Mrs Tall.

'Only a friend,' said Coggan.

'Say he's wanted to meet mistress near church-hatch to-morrow morning at ten,' said Oak, in a whisper. 'That he must come without fail, and wear his best clothes.'

'The clothes will floor us as safe as houses!' said Coggan.

'It can't be helped,' said Oak. 'Tell her.'

So Coggan delivered the message. 'Mind, het or wet, blow or snow, he must come,' added Jan. ''Tis very particular, indeed. The fact is, 'tis to witness her sign some law-work about taking shares wi' another farmer for a long span o' years. There, that's what 'tis, and now I've told 'ee, Mother Tall, in a way I shouldn't ha' done if I hadn't loved 'ee so hopeless well.'

Coggan retired before she could ask any further; and next they called at the vicar's in a manner which excited no curiosity at all. Then Gabriel went home, and prepared for the morrow.

'Liddy,' said Bathsheba, on going to bed that night, 'I want you to call me at seven o'clock to-morrow, in case I shouldn't wake.'

'But you always do wake afore then, ma'am.'

'Yes, but I have something important to do, which I'll tell you of when the time comes, and it's best to make sure.'

Bathsheba, however, awoke voluntarily at four, nor could she by any contrivance get to sleep again. About six, being quite positive that her watch had stopped during the night, she could wait no longer. She went and tapped at Liddy's door, and after some labour awoke her.

'But I thought it was I who had to call you?' said the bewildered Liddy, 'And it isn't six yet.'

'Indeed it is; how can you tell such a story, Liddy! I know it must be ever so much past seven. Come to my room as soon as you can; I want you to give my hair a good brushing.'

When Liddy came to Bathsheba's room her mistress was already waiting. Liddy could not understand this extraordinary promptness. 'Whatever *is* going on, ma'am?' she said.

'Well, I'll tell you,' said Bathsheba, with a mischievous smile in her bright eyes. 'Farmer Oak is coming here to dine with me to-day!'

'Farmer Oak – and nobody else? – you two alone?'

'Yes.'

'But is it safe, ma'am, after what's been said?' asked her companion, dubiously. 'A woman's good name is such a perishable article that—'

Bathsheba laughed with a flushed cheek, and whispered in Liddy's ear, although there was nobody present. Then Liddy stared and exclaimed, 'Souls alive, what news! It makes my heart go quite bumpity-bump!'

'It makes mine rather furious, too,' said Bathsheba. 'However, there's no getting out of it now!'

It was a damp disagreeable morning. Nevertheless, at twenty minutes to ten o'clock, Oak came out of his house, and

> Went up the hill side
> With that sort of stride
> A man puts out when walking in search of a bride,

and knocked at Bathsheba's door. Ten minutes later a large and a smaller umbrella might have been seen moving from the same door, and through the mist along the road to the church. The distance was not more than a quarter of a mile, and these two sensible persons deemed it unnecessary to drive. An observer must have been very close indeed to discover that the forms under the umbrellas were those of Oak and Bathsheba, arm-in-arm for the first time in their lives, Oak in a greatcoat extending to his knees, and Bathsheba in a cloak that reached her clogs. Yet, though so plainly dressed, there was a certain rejuvenated appearance about her: –

> As though a rose should shut and be a bud again.

Repose had again incarnadined her cheeks; and having, at Gabriel's request, arranged her hair this morning as she had worn it years ago on Norcombe Hill, she seemed in his eyes remarkably like the girl of that fascinating dream, which, considering that she was now only three or four-and-twenty, was perhaps not very wonderful. In the church were Tall, Liddy, and the parson, and in a remarkably short space of time the deed was done.

The two sat down very quietly to tea in Bathsheba's parlour in the evening of the same day, for it had been arranged that Farmer Oak should go there to live, since he had as yet neither money, house, nor furniture worthy of the name, though he was on a sure way towards them, whilst Bathsheba was, comparatively, in a plethora of all three.

Just as Bathsheba was pouring out a cup of tea, their ears were greeted by the firing of a cannon, followed by what seemed like a tremendous blowing of trumpets, in the front of the house.

'There!' said Oak, laughing, 'I knew those fellows were up to something, by the look on their faces.'

Oak took up the light and went into the porch, followed by Bathsheba with a shawl over her head. The rays fell upon a group of male figures gathered upon the gravel in front, who, when they saw the newly-married couple in the porch, set up a loud 'Hurrah!' and at the same moment bang again went the cannon in the background, followed by a hideous clang of music from a drum, tambourine, clarionet, serpent, hautboy, tenor-viol, and double-bass – the only remaining relics of the true and original Weatherbury band – venerable worm-eaten instruments, which had celebrated in their own persons the victories of Marlborough, under the fingers of the forefathers of those who played them now. The performers came forward, and marched up to the front.

'Those bright boys, Mark Clark and Jan, are at the bottom of all this,' said Oak. 'Come in, souls, and have something to eat and drink wi' me and my wife.'

'Not to-night,' said Mr Clark, with evident self-denial. 'Thank ye all the same; but we'll call at a more seemly time. However, we couldn't think of letting the day pass without a note of admiration of some sort. If ye could send a drop of som'at down to Warren's, why so it is. Here's long life and happiness to neighbour Oak and his comely bride!'

'Thank ye; thank ye all,' said Gabriel. 'A bit and a drop shall be sent to Warren's for ye at once. I had a thought that we might very likely get a salute of some sort from our old friends, and I was saying so to my wife but now.'

'Faith,' said Coggan, in a critical tone, turning to his companions, 'the man hev learnt to say "my wife" in a wonderful naterel way, considering how very youthful he is in wedlock as yet – hey, neighbours all?'

'I never heerd a skilful old married feller of twenty years' standing pipe "my wife" in a more used note than 'a did,' said Jacob Smallbury. 'It might have been a little more true to nater if 't had been spoke a little chillier, but that wasn't to be expected just now.'

'That improvement will come wi' time,' said Jan, twirling his eye.

Then Oak laughed, and Bathsheba smiled (for she never laughed readily now), and their friends turned to go.

'Yes; I suppose that's the size o't,' said Joseph Poorgrass with a cheerful sigh as they moved away; 'and I wish him joy o' her; though I were once or twice upon saying to-day with holy Hosea, in my scripture manner, which is my second nature, "Ephraim is joined to idols: let him alone." But since 'tis as 'tis, why, it might have been worse, and I feel my thanks accordingly.'

THE MAYOR OF CASTERBRIDGE

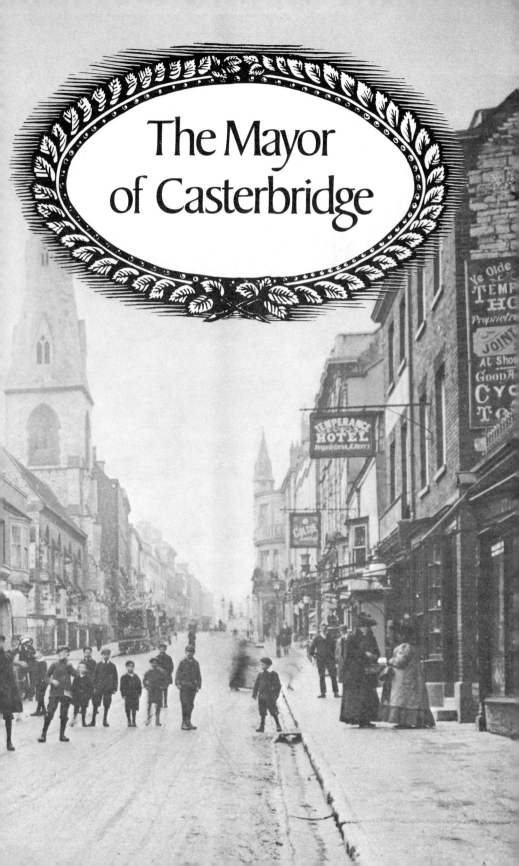

The Mayor of Casterbridge

CHAPTER ONE

O NE evening of late summer, before the nineteenth century had reached one-third of its span, a young man and woman, the latter carrying a child, were approaching the large village of Weydon-Priors, in Upper Wessex, on foot. They were plainly but not ill clad, though the thick hoar of dust which had accumulated on their shoes and garments from an obviously long journey lent a disadvantageous shabbiness to their appearance just now.

The man was of fine figure, swarthy, and stern in aspect; and he showed in profile a facial angle so slightly inclined as to be almost perpendicular. He wore a short jacket of brown corduroy, newer than the remainder of his suit, which was a fustian waistcoat with white horn buttons, breeches of the same, tanned leggings, and a straw hat overlaid with black glazed canvas. At his back he carried by a looped strap a rush basket, from which protruded at one end the crutch of a hay-knife, a wimble for hay-bonds being also visible in the aperture. His measured, springless walk was the walk of the skilled countryman as distinct from the desultory shamble of the general labourer; while in the turn and plant of each foot there was, further, a dogged and cynical indifference personal to himself, showing its presence even in the regularly interchanging fustian folds, now in the left leg, now in the right, as he paced along.

What was really peculiar, however, in this couple's progress, and would have attracted the attention of any casual observer otherwise disposed to overlook them, was the perfect silence they preserved. They walked side by side in such a way as to suggest afar off the low, easy, confidential chat of people full of reciprocity; but on closer view it could be discerned that the man was reading, or pretending to read, a ballad sheet which he kept before his eyes with some difficulty by the hand that was passed through the basket strap. Whether this apparent cause were the real cause, or whether it were an assumed one to escape an intercourse that would have been irksome to him, nobody but himself could have said precisely; but his taciturnity was unbroken, and the woman enjoyed no society whatever from his presence. Virtually she walked the highway alone, save for the child she bore. Sometimes the man's bent elbow almost touched her shoulder, for she kept as close to his side as was possible without actual contact; but she seemed to have no idea of taking his arm, nor he of offering it; and far from exhibiting surprise at his ignoring silence she appeared to receive it as a natural thing. If any word at all were uttered by the little group, it was an occasional whisper of the woman to the child — a tiny girl in short clothes and blue boots of knitted yarn — and the murmured babble of the child in reply.

The chief — almost the only — attraction of the young woman's face was its mobility. When she looked down sideways to the girl she became pretty, and even handsome, particularly that in the action her features caught slantwise the rays of the strongly coloured sun, which made transparencies of her eyelids and nostrils and set fire on her lips. When she plodded on in the shade of the hedge, silently thinking, she had the hard, half-apathetic expression of one who deems anything possible at the hands of Time and Chance except, perhaps, fair play. The first phase was the work of Nature, the second probably of civilization.

That the man and woman were husband and wife, and the parents of the girl in arms, there could be little doubt. No other than such relationship would have accounted for the atmosphere of stale familiarity which the trio carried along with them like a nimbus as they moved down the road.

The wife mostly kept her eyes fixed ahead, though with little interest – the scene for that matter being one that might have been matched at almost any spot in any county in England at this time of the year; a road neither straight nor crooked, neither level nor hilly, bordered by hedges, trees, and other vegetation, which had entered the blackened-green stage of colour that the doomed leaves pass through on their way to dingy, and yellow, and red. The grassy margin of the bank, and the nearest hedgerow boughs, were powdered by the dust that had been stirred over them by hasty vehicles, the same dust as it lay on the road deadening their footfalls like a carpet; and this, with the aforesaid total absence of conversation, allowed every extraneous sound to be heard.

For a long time there was none, beyond the voice of a weak bird singing a trite old evening song that might doubtless have been heard on the hill at the same hour, and with the self-same trills, quavers, and breves, at any sunset of that season for centuries untold. But as they approached the village sundry distant shouts and rattles reached their ears from some elevated spot in that direction, as yet screened from view by foliage. When the outlying houses of Weydon-Priors could just be descried, the family group was met by a turnip-hoer with his hoe on his shoulder, and his dinner-bag suspended from it. The reader promptly glanced up.

'Any trade doing here?' he asked phlegmatically, designating the village in his van by a wave of the broadsheet. And thinking the labourer did not understand him, he added, 'Anything in the hay-trussing line?'

The turnip-hoer had already begun shaking his head. 'Why, save the man, what wisdom's in him that 'a should come to Weydon for a job of that sort this time o' year?'

'Then is there any house to let – a little small new cottage just abuilded, or such like?' asked the other.

The pessimist still maintained a negative. 'Pulling down is more the nater of Weydon. There were five houses cleared away last year, and three this; and the volk nowhere to go – no, not so much as a thatched hurdle; that's the way o' Weydon-Priors.'

The hay-trusser, which he obviously was, nodded with some superciliousness. Looking towards the village, he continued, 'There is something going on here, however, is there not?'

'Ay. 'Tis Fair Day. Though what you hear now is little more than the clatter and scurry of getting away the money o' children and fools, for the real business is done earlier than this. I've been working within sound o't all day, but I didn't go up – not I. 'Twas no business of mine.'

The trusser and his family proceeded on their way, and soon entered the Fairfield, which showed standing-places and pens where many hundreds of horses and sheep had been exhibited and sold in the forenoon, but were now in great part taken away. At present, as their informant had observed, but little real business remained on hand, the chief being the sale by auction of a few inferior animals, that could not otherwise be disposed of, and had been absolutely refused by the better class of traders, who came and went early. Yet the crowd was denser now than during the morning hours, the frivolous contingent of visitors, including journeymen out for a holiday, a stray soldier or two home on furlough, village shop-keepers, and the like, having latterly flocked in; persons whose activities found a congenial field among the peep-shows, toy-stands, waxworks, inspired monsters, disinterested medical men who travelled for the public good, thimble-riggers, nick-nack vendors, and readers of Fate.

Neither of our pedestrians had much heart for these things, and they looked around for a refreshment tent among the many which dotted the down. Two, which stood nearest to them in the ochreous haze of expiring sunlight, seemed almost equally inviting. One was formed of new, milk-hued canvas, and bore red flags on its summit; it announced 'Good Home-brewed Beer, Ale and Cyder'. The other was less new; a little iron stove-pipe came out of it at the back, and in front appeared the placard, 'Good Furmity Sold Hear'. The man mentally weighed the two inscriptions, and inclined to the former tent.

'No – no – the other one,' said the woman. 'I always like furmity; and so does Elizabeth-Jane; and so will you. It is nourishing after a long hard day.'

'I've never tasted it,' said the man. However, he gave way to her representations, and they entered the furmity booth forthwith.

A rather numerous company appeared within, seated at the long narrow tables that ran down the tent on each side. At the upper end stood a stove, containing a charcoal fire, over which hung a large three-legged crock, sufficiently polished round the rim to show that it was made of bell-metal. A haggish creature of about fifty presided, in a white apron, which, as it threw an air of respectability over her as far as it extended, was made so wide as to reach nearly round her waist. She slowly stirred the contents of the pot. The dull scrape of her large spoon was audible throughout the tent as she thus kept from burning the mixture of corn in the grain, flour, milk, raisins, currants, and what not, that composed the antiquated slop in which she dealt. Vessels holding the separate ingredients stood on a white-clothed table of boards and trestles close by.

The young man and woman ordered a basin each of the mixture, steaming hot, and sat down to consume it at leisure. This was very well so far, for furmity, as the woman had said, was nourishing, and as proper a food as could be obtained within the four seas; though, to those not accustomed to it, the grains of wheat swollen as large as lemon-pips, which floated on its surface, might have a deterrent effect at first.

But there was more in that tent than met the cursory glance; and the man, with the instinct of a perverse character, scented it quickly. After a mincing attack on his bowl, he watched the hag's proceedings from the corner of his eye, and saw the game she played. He winked to her, and passed up his basin in reply to her nod; when she took a bottle from under the table, slily measured out a quantity of its contents, and tipped the same into the man's furmity. The liquor poured in was rum. The man as slily sent back money in payment.

He found the concoction, thus strongly laced, much more to his satisfaction than it had been in its natural state. His wife had observed the proceeding with much uneasiness; but he persuaded her to have hers laced also, and she agreed to a milder allowance after some misgiving.

The man finished his basin, and called for another, the rum being signalled for in yet stronger proportion. The effect of it was soon apparent in his manner, and his wife but too sadly perceived that in strenuously steering off the rocks of the licensed liquor-tent she had only got into maelstrom depths here amongst the smugglers.

The child began to prattle impatiently, and the wife more than once said to her husband, 'Michael, how about our lodging? You know we may have trouble in getting it if we don't go soon.'

But he turned a deaf ear to those bird-like chirpings. He talked loud to the company. The child's black eyes, after slow, round, ruminating gazes at the candles when they were lighted, fell together; then they opened, then shut again, and she slept.

At the end of the first basin the man had risen to serenity; at the second he was jovial; at the third, argumentative; at the fourth, the qualities signified by the shape of his face, the occasional clench of his mouth, and the fiery spark of his dark eye, began to tell in his conduct; he was overbearing — even brilliantly quarrelsome.

The conversation took a high turn, as it often does on such occasions. The ruin of good men by bad wives, and, more particularly, the frustration of many a promising youth's high aims and hopes and the extinction of his energies by an early imprudent marriage, was the theme.

'I did for myself that way thoroughly,' said the trusser, with a contemplative bitterness that was well-nigh resentful. 'I married at eighteen, like the fool that I was; and this is the consequence o't.' He pointed at himself and family with a wave of the hand intended to bring out the penuriousness of the exhibition.

The young woman his wife, who seemed accustomed to such remarks, acted as if she did not hear them, and continued her intermittent private words on tender trifles to the sleeping and waking child, who was just big enough to be placed for a moment on the bench beside her when she wished to ease her arms. The man continued —

'I haven't more than fifteen shillings in the world, and yet I am a good experienced hand in my line. I'd challenge England to beat me in the fodder business; and if I were a free man again I'd be worth a thousand pound before I'd done o't. But a fellow never knows these little things till all chance of acting upon 'em is past.'

The auctioneer selling the old horses in the field outside could be heard saying, 'Now this is the last lot — now who'll take the last lot for a song? Shall I say forty shillings? 'Tis a very promising broodmare, a trifle over five years old, and nothing the matter with the hoss at all, except that she's a little holler in the back and had her left eye knocked out by the kick of another, her own sister, coming along the road.'

'For my part I don't see why men who have got wives and don't want 'em, shouldn't get rid of 'em as these gipsy fellows do their old horses,' said the man in the tent. 'Why shouldn't they put 'em up and sell 'em by auction to men who are in need of such articles? Hey? Why, begad, I'd sell mine this minute if anybody would buy her!'

'There's them that would do that,' some of the guests replied, looking at the woman, who was by no means ill-favoured.

'True,' said a smoking gentleman, whose coat had the fine polish about the collar, elbows, seams, and shoulder-blades that long-continued friction with grimy surfaces will produce, and which is usually more desired on furniture than on clothes. From his appearance he had possibly been in former time groom or coachman to some neighbouring county family. 'I've had my breedings in as good circles, I may say, as any man,' he added, 'and I know true cultivation, or nobody do; and I can declare she's got it – in the bone, mind ye, I say – as much as any female in the fair – though it may want a little bringing out.' Then, crossing his legs, he resumed his pipe with a nicely-adjusted gaze at a point in the air.

The fuddled young husband stared for a few seconds at this unexpected praise of his wife, half in doubt of the wisdom of his own attitude towards the possessor of such qualities. But he speedily lapsed into his former conviction, and said harshly –

'Well, then, now is your chance; I am open to an offer for this gem o' creation.'

She turned to her husband and murmured, 'Michael, you have talked this nonsense in public places before. A joke is a joke, but you may make it once too often, mind!'

'I know I've said it before; I meant it. All I want is a buyer.'

At the moment a swallow, one among the last of the season, which had by chance found its way through an opening into the upper part of the tent, flew to and fro in quick curves above their heads, causing all eyes to follow it absently. In watching the bird till it made its escape the assembled company neglected to respond to the workman's offer, and the subject dropped.

But a quarter of an hour later the man, who had gone on lacing his furmity more and more heavily, though he was either so strong-minded or such an intrepid toper that he still appeared fairly sober, recurred to the old strain, as in a musical fantasy the instrument fetches up the original theme. 'Here – I am waiting to know about this offer of mine. The woman is no good to me. Who'll have her?'

The company had by this time decidedly degenerated, and the renewed inquiry was received with a laugh of appreciation. The woman whispered; she was imploring and anxious: 'Come, come, it is getting dark, and this nonsense won't do. If you don't come along, I shall go without you. Come!'

She waited and waited; yet he did not move. In ten minutes the man broke in upon the desultory conversation of the furmity drinkers with, 'I asked this question, and nobody answered to 't. Will any Jack Rag or Tom Straw among ye buy my goods?'

The woman's manner changed, and her face assumed the grim shape and colour of which mention has been made.

'Mike, Mike,' said she; 'this is getting serious. O! – too serious!'

'Will anybody buy her?' said the man.

'I wish somebody would,' said she firmly. 'Her present owner is not at all to her liking!'

'Nor you to mine,' said he. 'So we are agreed about that. Gentlemen, you hear? It's an agreement to part. She shall take the girl if she wants to, and go her ways.

I'll take my tools, and go my ways. 'Tis simple as Scripture history. Now then, stand up, Susan, and show yourself.'

'Don't, my chiel,' whispered a buxom staylace dealer in voluminous petticoats, who sat near the woman; 'yer good man don't know what he's saying.'

The woman, however, did stand up. 'Now, who's auctioneer?' cried the hay-trusser.

'I be,' promptly answered a short man, with a nose resembling a copper knob, a damp voice, and eyes like button-holes. 'Who'll make an offer for this lady?'

The woman looked on the ground, as if she maintained her position by a supreme effort of will.

'Five shillings,' said some one, at which there was a laugh.

'No insults,' said the husband. 'Who'll say a guinea?'

Nobody answered; and the female dealer in staylaces interposed.

'Behave yerself moral, good man, for Heaven's love! Ah, what a cruelty is the poor soul married to! Bed and board is dear at some figures, 'pon my 'vation 'tis!'

'Set it higher, auctioneer,' said the trusser.

'Two guineas!' said the auctioneer; and no one replied.

'If they don't take her for that, in ten seconds they'll have to give more,' said the husband. 'Very well. Now, auctioneer, add another.'

'Three guineas—going for three guineas!' said the rheumy man.

'No bid?' said the husband. 'Good Lord, why she's cost me fifty times the money, if a penny. Go on.'

'Four guineas!' cried the auctioneer.

'I'll tell ye what—I won't sell her for less than five,' said the husband, bringing down his fist so that the basins danced. 'I'll sell her for five guineas to any man that will pay me the money, and treat her well; and he shall have her for ever, and never hear aught o' me. But she shan't go for less. Now then—five guineas—and she's yours. Susan, you agree?'

She bowed her head with absolute indifference.

'Five guineas,' said the auctioneer, 'or she'll be withdrawn. Do anybody give it? The last time. Yes or no?'

'Yes,' said a loud voice from the doorway.

All eyes were turned. Standing in the triangular opening which formed the door of the tent was a sailor, who, unobserved by the rest, had arrived there within the last two or three minutes. A dead silence followed his affirmation.

'You say you do?' asked the husband, staring at him.

'I say so,' replied the sailor.

'Saying is one thing, and paying is another. Where's the money?'

The sailor hesitated a moment, looked anew at the woman, came in, unfolded five crisp pieces of paper, and threw them down upon the table-cloth. They were Bank-of-England notes for five pounds. Upon the face of this he chinked down the shillings severally—one, two, three, four, five.

The sight of real money in full amount, in answer to a challenge for the same till then deemed slightly hypothetical, had a great effect upon the spectators. Their eyes became riveted upon the faces of the chief actors, and then upon the notes as they lay, weighted by the shillings, on the table.

Up to this moment it could not positively have been asserted that the man, in spite of his tantalizing declaration, was really in earnest. The spectators had indeed taken the proceedings throughout as a piece of mirthful irony carried to extremes; and had assumed that, being out of work, he was, as a consequence, out of temper with the world, and society, and his nearest kin. But with the demand and response of real cash the jovial frivolity of the scene departed. A lurid colour seemed to fill the tent, and change the aspect of all therein. The mirth-wrinkles left the listeners' faces, and they waited with parting lips.

'Now,' said the woman, breaking the silence, so that her low dry voice sounded quite loud, 'before you go further, Michael, listen to me. If you touch that money, I and this girl go with the man. Mind, it is a joke no longer.'

'A joke? Of course it is not a joke!' shouted her husband, his resentment rising at her suggestion. 'I take the money: the sailor takes you. That's plain enough. It has been done elsewhere – and why not here?'

''Tis quite on the understanding that the young woman is willing,' said the sailor blandly. 'I wouldn't hurt her feelings for the world.'

'Faith, nor I,' said her husband. 'But she is willing, provided she can have the child. She said so only the other day when I talked o't!'

'That you swear?' said the sailor to her.

'I do,' said she, after glancing at her husband's face and seeing no repentance there.

'Very well, she shall have the child, and the bargain's complete,' said the trusser. He took the sailor's notes and deliberately folded them, and put them with the shillings in a high remote pocket, with an air of finality.

The sailor looked at the woman and smiled. 'Come along!' he said kindly. 'The little one too – the more the merrier!' She paused for an instant, with a close glance at him. Then dropping her eyes again, and saying nothing, she took up the child and followed him as he made towards the door. On reaching it, she turned, and pulling off her wedding-ring, flung it across the booth in the hay-trusser's face.

'Mike,' she said, 'I've lived with thee a couple of years, and had nothing but temper! Now I'm no more to 'ee; I'll try my luck elsewhere. 'Twill be better for me and Elizabeth-Jane, both. So good-bye!'

Seizing the sailor's arm with her right hand, and mounting the little girl on her left, she went out of the tent sobbing bitterly.

A stolid look of concern filled the husband's face, as if, after all, he had not quite anticipated this ending; and some of the guests laughed.

'Is she gone?' he said.

'Faith, ay; she's gone clane enough,' said some rustics near the door.

He rose and walked to the entrance with the careful tread of one conscious of his alcoholic load. Some others followed, and they stood looking into the twilight. The difference between the peacefulness of inferior nature and the wilful hostilities of mankind was very apparent at this place. In contrast with the harshness of the act just ended within the tent was the sight of several horses crossing their necks and rubbing each other lovingly as they waited in patience to be harnessed for the homeward journey. Outside the fair, in the valleys and woods, all was quiet. The sun had recently set, and the west heaven was hung with rosy cloud, which seemed permanent, yet slowly changed. To watch it was like looking at some grand feat of stagery from a darkened auditorium. In presence of this scene after the other there was a natural instinct to abjure man as the blot on an otherwise kindly universe; till it was remembered that all terrestrial conditions were intermittent, and that mankind might some night be innocently sleeping when these quiet objects were raging loud.

'Where do the sailor live?' asked a spectator, when they had vainly gazed around.

'God knows that,' replied the man who had seen high life. 'He's without doubt a stranger here.'

'He came in about five minutes ago,' said the furmity woman, joining the rest with her hands on her hips. 'And then 'a stepped back, and then 'a looked in again. I'm not a penny the better for him.'

'Serves the husband well be-right,' said the staylace vendor. ''A comely respectable body like her – what can a man want more? I glory in the woman's sperrit. I'd ha' done it myself – od send if I wouldn't, if a husband had behaved so to me! I'd go, and 'a might call, and call, till his keacorn was raw; but I'd never come back – no, not till the great trumpet, would I!'

'Well, the woman will be better off,' said another of a more deliberative turn. 'For seafaring natures be very good shelter for shorn lambs, and the man do seem to have plenty of money, which is what she's not been used to lately, by all showings.'

'Mark me – I'll not go after her!' said the trusser, returning doggedly to his seat. 'Let her go! If she's up to such vagaries she must suffer for 'em. She'd no business to take the maid – 'tis my maid; and if it were the doing again she shouldn't have her!'

Perhaps from some little sense of having countenanced an indefensible proceeding, perhaps because it was late, the customers thinned away from the tent shortly after this episode. The man stretched his elbows forward on the table, leant his face upon his arms, and soon began to snore. The furmity seller decided to close for the night, and after seeing the rum-bottles, milk, corn, raisins, etc., that remained on hand, loaded into the cart, came to where the man reclined. She shook him, but could not wake him. As the tent was not to be struck that night, the fair continuing for two or three days, she decided to let the sleeper, who was obviously no tramp, stay where he was, and his basket with him. Extinguishing the last candle, and lowering the flap of the tent, she left it, and drove away.

CHAPTER TWO

THE morning sun was streaming through the crevices of the canvas when the man awoke. A warm glow pervaded the whole atmosphere of the marquee, and a single big blue fly buzzed musically round and round it. Besides the buzz of the fly there was not a sound. He looked about – at the benches – at the table supported by trestles – at his basket of tools – at the stove where the furmity had been boiled – at the empty basins – at some shed grains of wheat – at the corks which dotted the grassy floor. Among the odds and ends he discerned a little shining object, and picked it up. It was his wife's ring.

A confused picture of the events of the previous evening seemed to come back to him, and he thrust his hand into his breast-pocket. A rustling revealed the sailor's bank-notes thrust carelessly in.

This second verification of his dim memories was enough; he knew now they were not dreams. He remained seated, looking on the ground for some time. 'I must get out of this as soon as I can,' he said deliberately at last, with the air of one who could not catch his thoughts without pronouncing them. 'She's gone – to be sure she is – gone with that sailor who bought her, and little Elizabeth-Jane. We walked here, and I had the furmity, and rum in it – and sold her. Yes, that's what's happened, and here am I. Now, what am I to do – am I sober enough to walk, I wonder?' He stood up, found that he was in fairly good condition for progress, unencumbered. Next he shouldered his tool basket, and found he could carry it. Then lifting the tent door he emerged into the open air.

Here the man looked around with gloomy curiosity. The freshness of the September morning inspired and braced him as he stood. He and his family had been weary when they arrived the night before, and they had observed but little of the place; so that he now beheld it as a new thing. It exhibited itself as the top of an open down, bounded on one extreme by a plantation, and approached by a winding road. At the bottom stood the village which lent its name to the upland and the annual fair that was held thereon. The spot stretched downward into valleys, and onward to other uplands, dotted with barrows, and trenched with the remains of prehistoric forts. The whole scene lay under the rays of a newly risen sun, which had not as yet dried a single blade of the heavily dewed grass, whereon the shadows of the yellow and red vans were projected far away, those thrown by the felloe of each wheel being elongated in shape to the orbit of a comet. All the gipsies and showmen who had remained on the ground lay snug within their carts and tents, or wrapped in horse-cloths under them, and were silent and still as death, with the exception of an occasional snore that revealed their presence. But the Seven Sleepers had a dog; and dogs of the mysterious breeds that vagrants own, that are as much like cats as dogs and as much like foxes as cats, also lay about here. A little one started up under one of the carts, barked as a matter of principle, and quickly lay down again. He was the only positive spectator of the hay-trusser's exit from the Weydon Fair-field.

This seemed to accord with his desire. He went on in silent thought, unheeding the yellowhammers which flitted about the hedges with straws in their bills, the crowns of the mushrooms, and the tinkling of local sheep-bells, whose wearers had had the good fortune not to be included in the fair. When he reached a lane, a good mile from the scene of the previous evening, the man pitched his basket and leant upon a gate. A difficult problem or two occupied his mind.

'Did I tell my name to anybody last night, or didn't I tell my name?' he said to himself; and at last concluded that he did not. His general demeanour was enough to show how he was surprised and nettled that his wife had taken him so literally – as much could be seen in his face, and in the way he nibbled a straw which he pulled from the hedge. He knew that she must have been somewhat excited to do this; moreover, she must have believed that there was some sort of binding force in the transaction. On this latter point he felt almost certain, knowing her freedom from levity of character, and the extreme simplicity of her intellect. There may, too, have been enough recklessness and resentment beneath her ordinary placidity to make her stifle any momentary doubts. On a previous occasion when he had declared during a fuddle that he would dispose of her as he had done, she had replied that she would not hear him say that many times more before it happened, in the resigned tones of a fatalist. . . . 'Yet she knows I am not in my senses when I do that!' he exclaimed. 'Well, I must walk about till I find her. . . . Seize her, why didn't she know better than bring me into this disgrace!' he roared out. 'She wasn't queer if I was. 'Tis like Susan to show some idiotic simplicity. Meek – that meekness has done me more harm than the bitterest temper!'

When he was calmer he turned to his original conviction that he must somehow find her and his little Elizabeth-Jane, and put up with the shame as best he could. It was of his own making, and he ought to bear it. But first he resolved to register an oath, a greater oath than he had ever sworn before: and to do it properly he required a fit place and imagery; for there was something fetichistic in this man's beliefs.

He shouldered his basket and moved on, casting his eyes inquisitively round upon the landscape as he walked, and at the distance of three or four miles perceived the roofs of a village and the tower of a church. He instantly made towards the latter object. The village was quite still, it being that motionless hour of rustic daily life which fills the interval between the departure of the field-labourers to their work, and the rising of their wives and daughters to prepare the breakfast for their return. Hence he reached the church without observation, and the door being only latched he entered. The hay-trusser deposited his basket by the font, went up the nave till he reached the altar-rails, and opening the gate entered the sacrarium, where he seemed to feel a sense of the strangeness for a moment; then he knelt upon the foot-pace. Dropping his head upon the clamped book which lay on the Communion-table, he said aloud –

'I, Michael Henchard, on this morning of the sixteenth of September, do take an oath before God here in this solemn place that I will avoid all strong liquors for the space of twenty-one years to come, being a year for every year that I have lived. And this I swear upon the book before me; and may I be strook dumb, blind, and helpless, if I break this my oath!'

When he had said it and kissed the big book, the hay-trusser arose, and seemed relieved at having made a start in a new direction. While standing in the porch a moment he saw a thick jet of wood smoke suddenly start up from the red chimney of a cottage near, and knew that the occupant had just lit her fire. He went round to the door, and the housewife agreed to prepare him some breakfast for a trifling payment, which was done. Then he started on the search for his wife and child.

The perplexing nature of the undertaking became apparent soon enough. Though he examined and inquired, and walked hither and thither day after day, no such characters as those he described had anywhere been seen since the evening of the fair. To add to the difficulty he could gain no sound of the sailor's name. As money was short with him he decided, after some hesitation, to spend the sailor's money in the prosecution of this search; but it was equally in vain. The truth was that a certain shyness of revealing his conduct prevented Michael Henchard from following up the investigation with the loud hue-and-cry such a pursuit demanded to render it effectual; and it was probably for this reason that he obtained no clue, though everything was done by him that did not involve an explanation of the circumstances under which he had lost her.

Weeks counted up to months, and still he searched on, maintaining himself by small jobs of work in the intervals. By this time he had arrived at a seaport, and there he derived intelligence that persons answering somewhat to his description had emigrated a little time before. Then he said he would search no longer, and that he would go and settle in the district which he had had for some time in his mind. Next day he started, journeying south-westward, and did not pause, except for nights' lodgings, till he reached the town of Casterbridge, in a far distant part of Wessex.

CHAPTER THREE

T HE highroad into the village of Weydon-Priors was again carpeted with dust. The trees had put on as of yore their aspect of dingy green, and where the Henchard family of three had once walked along, two persons not unconnected with that family walked now.

The scene in its broad aspect had so much of its previous character, even to the voices and rattle from the neighbouring village down, that it might for that matter have been the afternoon following the previously recorded episode. Change was only to be observed in details; but here it was obvious that a long procession of years had passed by. One of the two who walked the road was she who had figured as the young wife of Henchard on the previous occasion; now her face had lost much of its rotundity; her skin had undergone a textural change; and though her hair had not lost colour it was considerably thinner than heretofore. She was dressed in the mourning clothes of a widow. Her companion, also in black, appeared as a well-formed young woman about eighteen, completely possessed of that ephemeral precious essence youth, which is itself beauty, irrespective of complexion or contour.

A glance was sufficient to inform the eye that this was Susan Henchard's grown-up daughter. While life's middle summer had set its hardening mark on the mother's face, her former spring-like specialities were transferred so dexterously by Time to the second figure, her child, that the absence of certain facts within her mother's knowledge from the girl's mind would have seemed for the moment, to one reflecting on those facts, to be a curious imperfection in Nature's powers of continuity.

They walked with joined hands, and it could be perceived that this was the act of simple affection. The daughter carried in her outer hand a withy basket of old-fashioned make; the mother a blue bundle, which contrasted oddly with her black stuff gown.

Reaching the outskirts of the village they pursued the same track as formerly, and ascended to the fair. Here, too, it was evident that the years had told. Certain mechanical improvements might have been noticed in the roundabouts and highfliers, machines for testing rustic strength and weight, and in the erections devoted to shooting for nuts. But the real business of the fair had considerably dwindled. The new periodical great markets of neighbouring towns were beginning to interfere seriously with the trade carried on here for centuries. The pens for sheep, the tie-ropes for horses, were about half as long as they had been. The stalls of tailors, hosiers, coopers, linen-drapers, and other such trades had almost disappeared, and the vehicles were far less numerous. The mother and daughter threaded the crowd for some little distance, and then stood still.

'Why did we hinder our time by coming in here? I thought you wished to get onward?' said the maiden.

'Yes, my dear Elizabeth-Jane,' explained the other. 'But I had a fancy for looking up here.'

'Why?'

'It was here I first met with Newson – on such a day as this.'

'First met with father here? Yes, you have told me so before. And now he's drowned and gone from us!' As she spoke the girl drew a card from her pocket and looked at it with a sigh. It was edged with black, and inscribed within a design resembling a mural tablet were the words, 'In affectionate memory of Richard Newson, mariner, who was unfortunately lost at sea, in the month of November 184–, aged forty-one years.'

'And it was here,' continued her mother, with more hesitation, 'that I last saw the relation we are going to look for – Mr Michael Henchard.'

'What is his exact kin to us, mother? I have never clearly had it told me.'

'He is, or was – for he may be dead – a connection by marriage,' said her mother deliberately.

'That's exactly what you have said a score of times before!' replied the young woman, looking about her inattentively. 'He's not a near relation, I suppose?'

'Not by any means.'

'He was a hay-trusser, wasn't he, when you last heard of him?'

'He was.'

'I suppose he never knew me?' the girl innocently continued.

Mrs Henchard paused for a moment, and answered uneasily, 'Of course not, Elizabeth-Jane. But come this way.' She moved on to another part of the field.

'It is not much use inquiring here for anybody, I should think,' the daughter observed, as she gazed round about. 'People at fairs change like the leaves of trees; and I daresay you are the only one here to-day who was here all those years ago.'

'I am not so sure of that,' said Mrs Newson, as she now called herself, keenly eyeing something under a green bank a little way off. 'See there.'

The daughter looked in the direction signified. The object pointed out was a tripod of sticks stuck into the earth, from which hung a three-legged crock, kept hot by a smouldering wood fire beneath. Over the pot stooped an old woman, haggard, wrinkled, and almost in rags. She stirred the contents of the pot with a large spoon, and occasionally croaked in a broken voice, 'Good furmity sold here!'

It was indeed the former mistress of the furmity tent – once thriving, cleanly, white-aproned, and chinking with money – now tentless, dirty, owning no tables or benches, and having scarce any customers except two small whity-brown boys, who came up and asked for 'A ha'p'orth, please – good measure', which she served in a couple of chipped yellow basins of commonest clay.

'She was here at that time,' resumed Mrs Newson, making a step as if to draw nearer.

'Don't speak to her – it isn't respectable!' urged the other.

'I will just say a word – you, Elizabeth-Jane, can stay here.'

The girl was not loth, and turned to some stalls of coloured prints while her mother went forward. The old woman begged for the latter's custom as soon as she saw her, and responded to Mrs Henchard-Newson's request for a penny-worth with more alacrity than she had shown in selling sixpennyworths in her younger days. When the *soi-disant* widow had taken the basin of thin poor slop that stood for the rich concoction of the former time, the hag opened a little basket behind the fire, and looking up slily, whispered, 'Just a thought o' rum in it? – smuggled, you know – say two penn'orth – 'twill make it slip down like cordial!'

Her customer smiled bitterly at this survival of the old trick, and shook her head with a meaning the old woman was far from translating. She pretended to eat a little of the furmity with the leaden spoon offered, and as she did so said blandly to the hag, 'You've seen better days?'

'Ah, ma'am – well ye may say it!' responded the old woman, opening the sluices of her heart forthwith. 'I've stood in this fair-ground, maid, wife, and widow, these nine-and-thirty year, and in that time have known what it was to do business with the richest stomachs in the land! Ma'am, you'd hardly believe that I was once the owner of a great pavilion-tent that was the attraction of the fair. Nobody could come, nobody could go, without having a dish of Mrs Goodenough's furmity. I knew the clergy's taste, the dandy gent's taste; I knew the town's taste, the country's taste. I even knowed the taste of the coarse shameless females. But Lord's my life – the world's no memory; straightforward dealings don't bring profit – 'tis the sly and the underhand that get on in these times!'

Mrs Newson glanced round – her daughter was still bending over the distant stalls. 'Can you call to mind,' she said cautiously to the old woman, 'the sale of a wife by her husband in your tent eighteen years ago to-day?'

The hag reflected, and half shook her head. 'If it had been a big thing I should have minded it in a moment,' she said. 'I can mind every serious fight o' married parties, every murder, every manslaughter, even every pocket-picking – least-wise large ones – that 't has been my lot to witness. But a selling? Was it done quiet-like?'

'Well, yes. I think so.'

The furmity woman half shook her head again. 'And yet,' she said, 'I do. At any rate, I can mind a man doing something o' the sort – a man in a cord jacket, with a basket of tools; but, Lord bless ye, we don't gi'e it head-room, we don't, such as that. The only reason why I can mind the man is that he came back here to the next year's fair, and told me quite private-like that if a woman ever asked for him I was to say he had gone to – where? – Casterbridge – yes – to Casterbridge, said he. But, Lord's my life, I shouldn't ha' thought of it again!'

Mrs Newson would have rewarded the old woman as far as her small means afforded had she not discreetly borne in mind that it was by that unscrupulous person's liquor her husband had been degraded. She briefly thanked her informant, and rejoined Elizabeth, who greeted her with, 'Mother, do let's go on – it was hardly respectable for you to buy refreshments there. I see none but the lowest do.'

'I have learned what I wanted, however,' said her mother quietly. 'The last time our relative visited this fair he said he was living at Casterbridge. It is a long, long way from here, and it was many years ago that he said it; but there I think we'll go.'

With this they descended out of the fair, and went onward to the village, where they obtained a night's lodging.

CHAPTER FOUR

H ENCHARD'S wife acted for the best, but she had involved herself in difficulties. A hundred times she had been upon the point of telling her daughter Elizabeth-Jane the true story of her life, the tragical crisis of which had been the transaction at Weydon Fair, when she was not much older than the girl now beside her. But she had refrained. An innocent maiden had thus grown up in the belief that the relations between the genial sailor and her mother were the ordinary ones that they had always appeared to be. The risk of endangering a child's strong affection by disturbing ideas which had grown with her growth was to Mrs Henchard too fearful a thing to contemplate. It had seemed, indeed, folly to think of making Elizabeth-Jane wise.

But Susan Henchard's fear of losing her dearly loved daughter's heart by a revelation had little to do with any sense of wrong-doing on her own part. Her simplicity – the original ground of Henchard's contempt for her – had allowed her to live on in the conviction that Newson had acquired a morally real and justifiable right to her by his purchase – though the exact bearings and legal limits of that right were vague. It may seem strange to sophisticated minds that a sane young matron could believe in the seriousness of such a transfer; and were there not numerous other instances of the same belief the thing might scarcely be credited. But she was by no means the first or last peasant woman who had religiously adhered to her purchaser, as too many rural records show.

The history of Susan Henchard's adventures in the interim can be told in two or three sentences. Absolutely helpless she had been taken off to Canada, where they had lived several years without any great worldly success, though she worked as hard as any woman could to keep their cottage cheerful and well-provided. When Elizabeth-Jane was about twelve years old the three returned to England, and settled at Falmouth, where Newson made a living for a few years as boatman and general handy shoreman.

He then engaged in the Newfoundland trade, and it was during this period that Susan had an awakening. A friend to whom she confided her history ridiculed her grave acceptance of her position; and all was over with her peace of mind. When

Newson came home at the end of one winter he saw that the delusion he had so carefully sustained had vanished for ever.

There was then a time of sadness, in which she told him her doubts if she could live with him longer. Newson left home again on the Newfoundland trade when the season came round. The vague news of his loss at sea a little later on solved a problem which had become torture to her meek conscience. She saw him no more.

Of Henchard they heard nothing. To the liege subjects of Labour, the England of those days was a continent, and a mile a geographical degree.

Elizabeth-Jane developed early into womanliness. One day, a month or so after receiving intelligence of Newson's death off the Bank of Newfoundland, when the girl was about eighteen, she was sitting on a willow chair in the cottage they still occupied, working twine nets for the fishermen. Her mother was in a back corner of the same room, engaged in the same labour; and dropping the heavy wood needle she was filling she surveyed her daughter thoughtfully. The sun shone in at the door upon the young woman's head and hair, which was worn loose, so that the rays streamed into its depths as into a hazel copse. Her face, though somewhat wan and incomplete, possessed the raw materials of beauty in a promising degree. There was an under-handsomeness in it, struggling to reveal itself through the provisional curves of immaturity, and the casual disfigurements that resulted from the straitened circumstances of their lives. She was handsome in the bone, hardly as yet handsome in the flesh. She possibly might never be fully handsome, unless the carking accidents of her daily existence could be evaded before the mobile parts of her countenance had settled to their final mould.

The sight of the girl made her mother sad — not vaguely, but by logical inference. They both were still in that strait-waistcoat of poverty from which she had tried so many times to be delivered for the girl's sake. The woman had long perceived how zealously and constantly the young mind of her companion was struggling for enlargement; and yet now, in her eighteenth year, it still remained but little unfolded. The desire — sober and repressed — of Elizabeth-Jane's heart was indeed to see, to hear, and to understand. How could she become a woman of wider knowledge, higher repute — 'better', as she termed it — this was her constant inquiry of her mother. She sought further into things than other girls in her position ever did, and her mother groaned as she felt she could not aid in the search.

The sailor, drowned or no, was probably now lost to them; and Susan's staunch, religious adherence to him as her husband in principle, till her views had been disturbed by enlightenment, was demanded no more. She asked herself whether the present moment, now that she was a free woman again, were not as opportune a one as she would find in a world where everything had been so inopportune, for making a desperate effort to advance Elizabeth. To pocket her pride and search for the first husband seemed, wisely or not, the best initiatory step. He had possibly drunk himself into his tomb. But he might, on the other hand, have had too much sense to do so; for in her time with him he had been given to bouts only, and was not a habitual drunkard.

At any rate, the propriety of returning to him, if he lived, was unquestionable. The awkwardness of searching for him lay in enlightening Elizabeth, a proceeding which her mother could not endure to contemplate. She finally resolved to undertake the search without confiding to the girl her former relations with Henchard, leaving it to him if they found him to take what steps he might choose to that end. This will account for their conversation at the fair and the half-informed state in which Elizabeth was led onward.

In this attitude they proceeded on their journey, trusting solely to the dim light afforded of Henchard's whereabouts by the furmity woman. The strictest economy was indispensable. Sometimes they might have been seen on foot, sometimes on farmers' waggons, sometimes in carriers' vans; and thus they drew near to Casterbridge. Elizabeth-Jane discovered to her alarm that her mother's health was not what it once had been, and there was ever and anon in her talk that renunciatory tone which showed that, but for the girl, she would not be very sorry to quit a life she was growing thoroughly weary of.

It was on a Friday evening, near the middle of September, and just before dusk, that they reached the summit of a hill within a mile of the place they sought. There were high-banked hedges to the coach-road here, and they mounted upon the green turf within, and sat down. The spot commanded a full view of the town and its environs.

'What an old-fashioned place it seems to be!' said Elizabeth-Jane, while her silent mother mused on other things than topography. 'It is huddled all together; and it is shut in by a square wall of trees, like a plot of garden ground by a box-edging.'

Its squareness was, indeed, the characteristic which most struck the eye in this antiquated borough, the borough of Casterbridge – at that time, recent as it was, untouched by the faintest sprinkle of modernism. It was compact as a box of dominoes. It had no suburbs – in the ordinary sense. Country and town met at a mathematical line.

To birds of the more soaring kind Casterbridge must have appeared on this fine evening as a mosaic-work of subdued reds, browns, greys, and crystals, held together by a rectangular frame of deep green. To the level eye of humanity it stood as an indistinct mass behind a dense stockade of limes and chestnuts, set in the midst of miles of rotund down and concave field. The mass became gradually dissected by the vision into towers, gables, chimneys, and casements, the highest glazings shining bleared and bloodshot with the coppery fire they caught from the belt of sunlit cloud in the west.

From the centre of each side of this tree-bound square ran avenues east, west, and south into the wide expanse of corn-land and coomb to the distance of a mile or so. It was by one of these avenues that the pedestrians were about to enter. Before they had risen to proceed two men passed outside the hedge, engaged in argumentative conversation.

'Why, surely,' said Elizabeth, as they receded, 'those men mentioned the name of Henchard in their talk – the name of our relative?'

'I thought so too,' said Mrs Newson.

'That seems a hint to us that he is still here.'

'Yes.'

'Shall I run after them, and ask them about him—'

'No, no, no! Not for the world just yet. He may be in the workhouse, or in the stocks, for all we know.'

'Dear me – why should you think that, mother?'

' 'Twas just something to say – that's all! But we must make private inquiries.'

Having sufficiently rested they proceeded on their way at evenfall. The dense trees of the avenue rendered the road dark as a tunnel, though the open land on each side was still under a faint daylight; in other words, they passed down a midnight between two gloamings. The features of the town had a keen interest for Elizabeth's mother, now that the human side came to the fore. As soon as they had wandered about they could see that the stockade of gnarled trees which framed in Casterbridge was itself an avenue, standing on a low green bank or escarpment, with a ditch yet visible without. Within the avenue and bank was a wall more or less discontinuous, and within the wall were packed the abodes of the burghers.

Though the two women did not know it these external features were but the ancient defences of the town, planted as a promenade.

The lamplights now glimmered through the engirdling trees, conveying a sense of great snugness and comfort inside, and rendering at the same time the unlighted country without strangely solitary and vacant in aspect, considering its nearness to life. The difference between burgh and champaign was increased, too, by sounds which now reached them above others – the notes of a brass band. The travellers returned into the High Street, where there were timber houses with overhanging stories, whose small-paned lattices were screened by dimity curtains on a drawing-string, and under whose barge-boards old cobwebs waved in the breeze. There were houses of brick-nogging, which derived their chief support from those adjoining. There were slate roofs patched with tiles, and tile roofs patched with slate, with occasionally a roof of thatch.[1]

The agricultural and pastoral character of the people upon whom the town depended for its existence was shown by the class of objects displayed in the shop windows. Scythes, reap-hooks, sheep-shears, bill-hooks, spades, mattocks, and hoes at the ironmonger's; bee-hives, butter-firkins, churns, milking stools and pails, hay-rakes, field-flagons, and seed-lips at the cooper's; cart-ropes and plough-harness at the saddler's; carts, wheel-barrows, and mill-gear at the wheelwright's and machinist's; horse-embrocations at the chemist's; at the glover's and leather-cutter's, hedging-gloves, thatchers' knee-caps, ploughmen's leggings, villagers' pattens and clogs.

They came to a grizzled church, whose massive square tower rose unbroken into the darkening sky, the lower parts being illuminated by the nearest lamp, sufficiently to show how completely the mortar from the joints of the stonework had been nibbled out by time and weather, which had planted in the crevices thus made little tufts of stone-crop and grass almost as far up as the very battlements. From this tower the clock struck eight, and thereupon a bell began to toll with a peremptory clang. The curfew was still rung in Casterbridge, and it was utilized by the inhabitants as a signal for shutting their shops. No sooner did the deep notes of the bell throb between the house-fronts than a clatter of shutters arose from the whole length of the High Street. In a few minutes business at Casterbridge was ended for the day.

[1] Most of these old houses have now been pulled down (1912).

Other clocks struck eight from time to time—one gloomily from the gaol, another from the gable of an almshouse, with a preparative creak of machinery, more audible than the note of the bell; a row of tall, varnished case-clocks from the interior of a clock-maker's shop joined in one after another just as the shutters were enclosing them, like a row of actors delivering their final speeches before the fall of the curtain; then chimes were heard stammering out the Sicilian Mariners' Hymn;[1] so that chronologists of the advanced school were appreciably on their way to the next hour before the whole business of the old one was satisfactorily wound up.

In an open space before the church walked a woman with her gown-sleeves rolled up so high that the edge of her under-linen was visible, and her skirt tucked up through her pocket hole. She carried a loaf under her arm from which she was pulling pieces of bread, and handing them to some other women who walked with her; which pieces they nibbled critically. The sight reminded Mrs Henchard-Newson and her daughter that they had an appetite; and they inquired of the woman for the nearest baker's.

'Ye may as well look for manna-food as good bread in Casterbridge just now,' she said, after directing them. 'They can blare their trumpets and thump their drums, and have their roaring dinners'—waving her hand towards a point further along the street, where the brass band could be seen standing in front of an illuminated building—'but we must needs be put-to for want of a wholesome crust. There's less good bread than good beer in Casterbridge now.'

'And less good beer than swipes,' said a man with his hands in his pockets.

'How does it happen there's no good bread?' asked Mrs Henchard.

'Oh, 'tis the corn-factor—he's the man that our millers and bakers all deal wi', and he has sold 'em growed wheat, which they didn't know was growed, so they *say*, till the dough ran all over the ovens like quicksilver; so that the loaves be as flat as toads, and like suet pudden inside. I've been a wife, and I've been a mother, and I never see such unprincipled bread in Casterbridge as this before.—But you must be a real stranger here not to know what's made all the poor volks' insides plim like blowed bladders this week?'

'I am,' said Elizabeth's mother shyly.

Not wishing to be observed further till she knew more of her future in this place, she withdrew with her daughter from the speaker's side. Getting a couple of biscuits at the shop indicated as a temporary substitute for a meal, they next bent their steps instinctively to where the music was playing.

---

[1] These chimes, like those of other country churches, have been silenced for many years.

CHAPTER FIVE

A few score yards brought them to the spot where the town band was now shaking the window-panes with the strains of 'The Roast Beef of Old England'.

The building before whose doors they had pitched their music-stands was the chief hotel in Casterbridge – namely, the King's Arms. A spacious bow-window projected into the street over the main portico, and from the open sashes came the babble of voices, the jingle of glasses, and the drawing of cords. The blinds, moreover, being left unclosed, the whole interior of this room could be surveyed from the top of a flight of stone steps to the road-waggon office opposite, for which reason a knot of idlers had gathered there.

'We might, perhaps, after all, make a few inquiries about – our relation Mr Henchard,' whispered Mrs Newson who, since her entry into Casterbridge, had seemed strangely weak and agitated, 'And this, I think, would be a good place for trying it – just to ask, you know, how he stands in the town – if he is here, as I think he must be. You, Elizabeth-Jane, had better be the one to do it. I'm too worn out to do anything – pull down your fall first.'

She sat down upon the lowest step, and Elizabeth-Jane obeyed her directions and stood among the idlers.

'What's going on to-night?' asked the girl, after singling out an old man and standing by him long enough to acquire a neighbourly right of converse.

'Well, ye must be a stranger sure,' said the old man, without taking his eyes from the window. 'Why, 'tis a great public dinner of the gentle-people and such like leading volk – wi' the Mayor in the chair. As we plainer fellows bain't invited, they leave the winder-shutters open that we may get jist a sense o't out here. If you mount the steps you can see 'em. That's Mr Henchard, the Mayor, at the end of the table, a facing ye; and that's the Council men right and left. . . . Ah, lots of them when they begun life were no more than I be now!'

'Henchard!' said Elizabeth-Jane, surprised, but by no means suspecting the whole force of the revelation. She ascended to the top of the steps.

Her mother, though her head was bowed, had already caught from the inn-window tones that strangely riveted her attention, before the old man's words, 'Mr Henchard, the Mayor', reached her ears. She arose, and stepped up to her daughter's side as soon as she could do so without showing exceptional eagerness.

The interior of the hotel dining-room was spread out before her, with its tables, and glass, and plate, and inmates. Facing the window, in the chair of dignity, sat a man about forty years of age; of heavy frame, large features, and commanding voice; his general build being rather coarse than compact. He had a rich complexion, which verged on swarthiness, a flashing black eye, and dark, bushy brows and hair. When he indulged in an occasional loud laugh at some remark among the guests, his large mouth parted so far back as to show to the rays of the chandelier a full score or more of the two-and-thirty sound white teeth that he obviously still could boast of.

That laugh was not encouraging to strangers; and hence it may have been well that it was rarely heard. Many theories might have been built upon it. It fell in well with conjectures of a temperament which would have no pity for weakness, but would be ready to yield ungrudging admiration to greatness and strength. Its producer's personal goodness, if he had any, would be of a very fitful cast – an occasional almost oppressive generosity rather than a mild and constant kindness.

Susan Henchard's husband – in law, at least – sat before them, matured in shape, stiffened in line, exaggerated in traits; disciplined, thought-marked – in a word, older. Elizabeth, encumbered with no recollections as her mother was, regarded him with nothing more than the keen curiosity and interest which the discovery of such unexpected social standing in the long-sought relative naturally begot. He was dressed in an old-fashioned evening suit, an expanse of frilled shirt showing on his broad breast; jewelled studs, and a heavy gold chain. Three glasses stood at his right hand; but, to his wife's surprise, the two for wine were empty, while the third, a tumbler, was half full of water.

When last she had seen him he was sitting in a corduroy jacket, fustian waistcoat and breeches, and tanned leather leggings, with a basin of hot furmity before him. Time, the magician, had wrought much here. Watching him, and thus thinking of past days, she became so moved that she shrank back against the jamb of the waggon-office doorway to which the steps gave access, the shadow from it conveniently hiding her features. She forgot her daughter till a touch from Elizabeth-Jane aroused her. 'Have you seen him, mother?' whispered the girl.

'Yes, yes,' answered her companion hastily. 'I have seen him, and it is enough for me! Now I only want to go – pass away – die.'

'Why – O what?' She drew closer, and whispered in her mother's ear, 'Does he seem to you not likely to befriend us? I thought he looked a generous man. What a gentleman he is, isn't he? and how his diamond studs shine! How strange that you should have said he might be in the stocks, or in the workhouse, or dead! Did ever anything go more by contraries! Why do you feel so afraid of him? I am not at all; I'll call upon him – he can but say he don't own such remote kin.'

'I don't know at all – I can't tell what to set about. I feel so down.'

'Don't be that, mother, now we have got here and all! Rest there where you be a little while – I will look on and find out more about him.'

'I don't think I can ever meet Mr Henchard. He is not how I thought he would be – he overpowers me! I don't wish to see him any more.'

'But wait a little time and consider.'

Elizabeth-Jane had never been so much interested in anything in her life as in their present position, partly from the natural elation she felt at discovering herself akin to a coach; and she gazed again at the scene. The younger guests were talking and eating with animation; their elders were searching for titbits, and sniffing and grunting over their plates like sows nuzzling for acorns. Three drinks seemed to be sacred to the company – port, sherry, and rum; outside which old-established trinity few or no palates ranged.

A row of ancient rummers with ground figures on their sides, and each primed with a spoon, was now placed down the table, and these were promptly filled with grog at such high temperatures as to raise serious considerations for the articles exposed to its vapours. But Elizabeth-Jane noticed that, though this filling went on with great promptness up and down the table, nobody filled the Mayor's glass, who still drank large quantities of water from the tumbler behind the clump of crystal vessels intended for wine and spirits.

'They don't fill Mr Henchard's wine-glasses,' she ventured to say to her elbow acquaintance, the old man.

'Ah, no; don't ye know him to be the celebrated abstaining worthy of that name? He scorns all tempting liquors; never touches nothing. O yes, he've strong qualities that way. I have heard tell that he sware a gospel oath in by-gone times, and has bode by it ever since. So they don't press him, knowing it would be unbecoming in the face of that; for yer gospel oath is a serious thing.'

Another elderly man, hearing this discourse, now joined in by inquiring, 'How much longer have he got to suffer from it, Solomon Longways?'

'Another two year, they say. I don't know the why and the wherefore of his fixing such a time, for 'a never has told anybody. But 'tis exactly two calendar years longer, they say. A powerful mind to hold out so long!'

'True. . . . But there's great strength in hope. Knowing that in four-and-twenty months' time ye'll be out of your bondage, and able to make up for all you've suffered, by partaking without stint – why, it keeps a man up, no doubt.'

'No doubt, Christopher Coney, no doubt. And 'a must need such reflections – a lonely widow man,' said Longways.

'When did he lose his wife?' asked Elizabeth.

'I never knowed her. 'Twas afore he came to Casterbridge,' Solomon Longways replied with terminative emphasis, as if the fact of his ignorance of Mrs Henchard were sufficient to deprive her history of all interest. 'But I know that 'a's a banded teetotaller, and that if any of his men be ever so little overtook by a drop he's down upon 'em as stern as the Lord upon the jovial Jews.'

'Has he many men, then?' said Elizabeth-Jane.

'Many! Why, my good maid, he's the powerfullest member of the Town Council, and quite a principal man in the country round besides. Never a big dealing in wheat, barley, oats, hay, roots, and such-like but Henchard's got a hand in it. Ay, and he'll go into other things too; and that's where he makes his mistake. He worked his way up from nothing when 'a came here; and now he's a pillar of the town. Not but what he's been shaken a little to-year about this bad corn he has supplied in his contracts. I've seen the sun rise over Durnover Moor these nine-and-sixty year, and though Mr Henchard has never cussed me unfairly ever since I've worked for'n, seeing I be but a little small man, I must say that I have never before tasted such rough bread as has been made from Henchard's wheat lately. 'Tis that growed out that ye could a'most call it malt, and there's a list at bottom o' the loaf as thick as the sole of one's shoe.'

The band now struck up another melody, and by the time it was ended the dinner was over, and speeches began to be made. The evening being calm, and the windows still open, these orations could be distinctly heard. Henchard's voice arose above the rest; he was telling a story of his hay-dealing experiences, in which he had outwitted a sharper who had been bent upon outwitting him.

'Ha-ha-ha!' responded his audience at the upshot of the story; and hilarity was general till a new voice arose with, 'This is all very well; but how about the bad bread?'

It came from the lower end of the table, where there sat a group of minor tradesmen who, although part of the company, appeared to be a little below the social level of the others; and who seemed to nourish a certain independence of opinion and carry on discussions not quite in harmony with those at the head; just as the west end of a church is sometimes persistently found to sing out of time and tune with the leading spirits in the chancel.

This interruption about the bad bread afforded infinite satisfaction to the loungers outside, several of whom were in the mood which finds its pleasure in others' discomfiture; and hence they echoed pretty freely, 'Hey! How about the bad bread, Mr Mayor?' Moreover, feeling none of the restraints of those who shared the feast, they could afford to add, 'You rather ought to tell the story o' that, sir!'

The interruption was sufficient to compel the Mayor to notice it.

'Well, I admit that the wheat turned out badly,' he said. 'But I was taken in in buying it as much as the bakers who bought it o' me.'

'And the poor folk who had to eat it whether or no,' said the inharmonious man outside the window.

Henchard's face darkened. There was temper under the thin bland surface — the temper which, artificially intensified, had banished a wife nearly a score of years before.

'You must make allowances for the accidents of a large business,' he said. 'You must bear in mind that the weather just at the harvest of that corn was worse than we have known it for years. However, I have mended my arrangements on account o't. Since I have found my business too large to be well looked after by myself alone, I have advertised for a thorough good man as manager of the corn department. When I've got him you will find these mistakes will no longer occur — matters will be better looked into.'

'But what are you going to do to repay us for the past?' inquired the man who had before spoken, and who seemed to be a baker or miller. 'Will you replace the grown flour we've still got by sound grain?'

Henchard's face had become still more stern at these interruptions, and he drank from his tumbler of water as if to calm himself or gain time. Instead of vouchsafing a direct reply, he stiffly observed —

'If anybody will tell me how to turn grown wheat into wholesome wheat I'll take it back with pleasure. But it can't be done.'

Henchard was not to be drawn again. Having said this, he sat down.

CHAPTER SIX

Now the group outside the window had within the last few minutes been reinforced by new arrivals, some of them respectable shop-keepers and their assistants, who had come out for a whiff of air after putting up the shutters for the

night; some of them of a lower class. Distinct from either there appeared a
stranger – a young man of remarkably pleasant aspect – who carried in his hand
a carpet-bag of the smart floral pattern prevalent in such articles at that time.

He was ruddy and of a fair countenance, bright-eyed, and slight in build. He
might possibly have passed by without stopping at all, or at most for half a
minute to glance in at the scene, had not his advent coincided with the discussion
on corn and bread; in which event this history had never been enacted. But the
subject seemed to arrest him, and he whispered some inquiries of the other
bystanders, and remained listening.

When he heard Henchard's closing words, 'It can't be done', he smiled
impulsively, drew out his pocket-book, and wrote down a few words by the aid of
the light in the window. He tore out the leaf, folded and directed it, and seemed
about to throw it in through the open sash upon the dining-table; but, on second
thoughts, edged himself through the loiterers, till he reached the door of the
hotel, where one of the waiters who had been serving inside was now idly leaning
against the door-post.

'Give this to the Mayor at once,' he said, handing in his hasty note.

Elizabeth-Jane had seen his movements and heard the words, which attracted
her both by their subject and by their accent – a strange one for those parts. It
was quaint and northerly.

The waiter took the note, while the young stranger continued –

'And can ye tell me of a respectable hotel that's a little more moderate than
this?'

The waiter glanced indifferently up and down the street.

'They say the Three Mariners, just below here, is a very good place,' he
languidly answered; 'but I have never stayed there myself.'

The Scotchman, as he seemed to be, thanked him, and strolled on in the
direction of the Three Mariners aforesaid, apparently more concerned about the
question of an inn than about the fate of his note, now that the momentary
impulse of writing it was over. While he was disappearing slowly down the street
the waiter left the door, and Elizabeth-Jane saw with some interest the note
brought into the dining-room and handed to the Mayor.

Henchard looked at it carelessly, unfolded it with one hand, and glanced it
through. Thereupon it was curious to note an unexpected effect. The nettled,
clouded aspect which had held possession of his face since the subject of his corn-
dealings had been broached, changed itself into one of arrested attention. He
read the note slowly, and fell into thought, not moody, but fitfully intense, as that
of a man who has been captured by an idea.

By this time toasts and speeches had given place to songs, the wheat subject
being quite forgotten. Men were putting their heads together in twos and threes,
telling good stories, with pantomimic laughter which reached convulsive
grimace. Some were beginning to look as if they did not know how they had come
there, what they had come for, or how they were going to get home again; and
provisionally sat on with a dazed smile. Square-built men showed a tendency to
become hunchbacks; men with a dignified presence lost it in a curious obliquity of
figure, in which their features grew disarranged and one-sided; whilst the heads of
a few who had dined with extreme thoroughness were somehow sinking into their
shoulders, the corners of their mouth and eyes being bent upwards by the

subsidence. Only Henchard did not conform to these flexuous changes; he remained stately and vertical, silently thinking.

The clock struck nine. Elizabeth-Jane turned to her companion. 'The evening is drawing on, mother,' she said. 'What do you propose to do?'

She was surprised to find how irresolute her mother had become. 'We must get a place to lie down in,' she murmured. 'I have seen – Mr Henchard; and that's all I wanted to do.'

'That's enough for to-night, at any rate,' Elizabeth-Jane replied soothingly. 'We can think to-morrow what is best to do about him. The question now is – is it not? – how shall we find a lodging?'

As her mother did not reply Elizabeth-Jane's mind reverted to the words of the waiter, that the Three Mariners was an inn of moderate charges. A recommendation good for one person was probably good for another. 'Let's go where the young man has gone to,' she said. 'He is respectable. What do you say?'

Her mother assented, and down the street they went.

In the meantime the Mayor's thoughtfulness, engendered by the note as stated, continued to hold him in abstraction; till, whispering to his neighbour to take his place, he found opportunity to leave the chair. This was just after the departure of his wife and Elizabeth.

Outside the door of the assembly-room he saw the waiter, and beckoning to him asked who brought the note which had been handed in a quarter of an hour before.

'A young man, sir – a sort of traveller. He was a Scotchman seemingly.'

'Did he say how he had got it?'

'He wrote it himself, sir, as he stood outside the window.'

'Oh – wrote it himself. . . . Is the young man in the hotel?'

'No, sir. He went to the Three Mariners, I believe.'

The Mayor walked up and down the vestibule of the hotel with his hands under his coat tails, as if he were merely seeking a cooler atmosphere than that of the room he had quitted. But there could be no doubt that he was in reality still possessed to the full by the new idea, whatever that might be. At length he went back to the door of the dining-room, paused, and found that the songs, toasts, and conversation were proceeding quite satisfactorily without his presence. The Corporation, private residents, and major and minor tradesmen had, in fact, gone in for comforting beverages to such an extent that they had quite forgotten, not only the Mayor, but all those vast political, religious, and social differences which they felt necessary to maintain in the daytime, and which separated them like iron grills. Seeing this the Mayor took his hat, and when the waiter had helped him on with a thin holland overcoat, went out and stood under the portico.

Very few persons were now in the street; and his eyes, by a sort of attraction, turned and dwelt upon a spot about a hundred yards further down. It was the house to which the writer of the note had gone – the Three Mariners – whose two prominent Elizabethan gables, bow-window, and passage-light could be seen from where he stood. Having kept his eyes on it for a while he strolled in that direction.

This ancient house of accommodation for man and beast, now, unfortunately, pulled down, was built of mellow sandstone, with mullioned windows of the same material, markedly out of perpendicular from the settlement of foundations. The bay window projecting into the street, whose interior was so popular among the frequenters of the inn, was closed with shutters, in each of which appeared a heart-shaped aperture, somewhat more attenuated in the right and left ventricles than is seen in Nature. Inside these illuminated holes, at a distance of about three inches, were ranged at this hour, as every passer knew, the ruddy polls of Billy Wills the glazier, Smart the shoe-maker, Buzzford the general dealer, and others of a secondary set of worthies, of a grade somewhat below that of the diners at the King's Arms, each with his yard of clay.

A four-centred Tudor arch was over the entrance, and over the arch the signboard, now visible in the rays of an opposite lamp. Hereon the Mariners, who had been represented by the artist as persons of two dimensions only – in other words, flat as a shadow – were standing in a row in paralyzed attitudes. Being on the sunny side of the street the three comrades had suffered largely from warping, splitting, fading, and shrinkage, so that they were but a half-invisible film upon the reality of the grain, and knots, and nails, which composed the signboard. As a matter of fact, this state of things was not so much owing to Stannidge the landlord's neglect, as from the lack of a painter in Casterbridge who would undertake to reproduce the features of men so traditional.

A long, narrow, dimly-lit passage gave access to the inn, within which passage the horses going to their stalls at the back, and the coming and departing human guests, rubbed shoulders indiscriminately, the latter running no slight risk of having their toes trodden upon by the animals. The good stabling and the good ale of the Mariners, though somewhat difficult to reach on account of there being but this narrow way to both, were nevertheless perseveringly sought out by the sagacious old heads who knew what was what in Casterbridge.

Henchard stood without the inn for a few instants; then lowering the dignity of his presence as much as possible by buttoning the brown holland coat over his shirt-front, and in other ways toning himself down to his ordinary everyday appearance, he entered the inn door.

CHAPTER SEVEN

ELIZABETH-JANE and her mother had arrived some twenty minutes earlier. Outside the house they had stood and considered whether even this homely place, though recommended as moderate, might not be too serious in its prices for their light pockets. Finally, however, they had found courage to enter, and duly met Stannidge the landlord; a silent man, who drew and carried frothing measures to this room and to that, shoulder to shoulder with his waiting-maids – a stately slowness, however, entering into his ministrations by contrast with theirs, as became one whose service was somewhat optional. It would have been altogether optional but for the orders of the landlady, a person who sat in the bar, corporeally motionless, but with a flitting eye and quick ear, with which she observed and heard through the open door and hatchway the pressing needs of customers whom her husband overlooked though close at hand. Elizabeth and her mother were passively accepted as sojourners, and shown to a small bedroom under one of the gables, where they sat down.

The principle of the inn seemed to be to compensate for the antique awkwardness, crookedness, and obscurity of the passages, floors, and windows, by quantities of clean linen spread about everywhere, and this had a dazzling effect upon the travellers.

''Tis too good for us — we can't meet it!' said the elder woman, looking round the apartment with misgiving as soon as they were left alone.

'I fear it is, too,' said Elizabeth. 'But we must be respectable.'

'We must pay our way even before we must be respectable,' replied her mother. 'Mr Henchard is too high for us to make ourselves known to him, I much fear; so we've only our own pockets to depend on.'

'I know what I'll do,' said Elizabeth-Jane after an interval of waiting, during which their needs seemed quite forgotten under the press of business below. And leaving the room, she descended the stairs and penetrated to the bar.

If there was one good thing more than another which characterized this single-hearted girl it was a willingness to sacrifice her personal comfort and dignity to the common weal.

'As you seem busy here to-night, and mother's not well off, might I take out part of our accommodation by helping?' she asked of the landlady.

The latter, who remained as fixed in the arm-chair as if she had been melted into it when in a liquid state, and could not now be unstuck, looked the girl up and down inquiringly, with her hands on the chair-arms. Such arrangements as the one Elizabeth proposed were not uncommon in country villages; but, though Casterbridge was old-fashioned, the custom was well-nigh obsolete here. The mistress of the house, however, was an easy woman to strangers, and she made no objection. Thereupon Elizabeth, being instructed by nods and motions from the taciturn landlord as to where she could find the different things, trotted up and down stairs with materials for her own and her parent's meal.

While she was doing this the wood partition in the centre of the house thrilled to its centre with the tugging of a bell-pull upstairs. A bell below tinkled a note that was feebler in sound than the twanging of wires and cranks that had produced it.

''Tis the Scotch gentleman,' said the landlady omnisciently; and turning her eyes to Elizabeth, 'Now then, can you go and see if his supper is on the tray? If it is you can take it up to him. The front room over this.'

Elizabeth-Jane, though hungry, willingly postponed serving herself awhile, and applied to the cook in the kitchen, whence she brought forth the tray of supper viands, and proceeded with it upstairs to the apartment indicated. The accommodation of the Three Mariners was far from spacious, despite the fair area of ground it covered. The room demanded by intrusive beams and rafters, partitions, passages, staircases, disused ovens, settles, and four-posters, left comparatively small quarters for human beings. Moreover, this being at a time before home-brewing was abandoned by the smaller victuallers, and a house in which the twelve-bushel strength was still religiously adhered to by the landlord in his ale, the quality of the liquor was the chief attraction of the premises, so that everything had to make way for utensils and operations in connection therewith. Thus Elizabeth found that the Scotchman was located in a room quite close to the small one that had been allotted to herself and her mother.

When she entered nobody was present but the young man himself – the same whom she had seen lingering without the windows of the King's Arms Hotel. He was now idly reading a copy of the local paper, and was hardly conscious of her entry, so that she looked at him quite coolly, and saw how his forehead shone where the light caught it, and how nicely his hair was cut, and the sort of velvet-pile or down that was on the skin at the back of his neck, and how his cheek was so truly curved as to be part of a globe, and how clearly drawn were the lids and lashes which hid his bent eyes.

She set down the tray, spread his supper, and went away without a word. On her arrival below the landlady, who was as kind as she was fat and lazy, saw that Elizabeth-Jane was rather tired, though in her earnestness to be useful she was waiving her own needs altogether. Mrs Stannidge thereupon said with a considerate peremptoriness that she and her mother had better take their own suppers if they meant to have any.

Elizabeth fetched their simple provisions, as she had fetched the Scotchman's, and went up to the little chamber where she had left her mother, noiselessly pushing open the door with the edge of the tray. To her surprise her mother, instead of being reclined on the bed where she had left her, was in an erect position, with lips parted. At Elizabeth's entry she lifted her finger.

The meaning of this was soon apparent. The room allotted to the two women had at one time served as a dressing-room to the Scotchman's chamber, as was evidenced by signs of a door of communication between them – now screwed up and pasted over with the wall paper. But, as is frequently the case with hotels of far higher pretensions than the Three Mariners, every word spoken in either of these rooms was distinctly audible in the other. Such sounds came through now.

Thus silently conjured Elizabeth deposited the tray, and her mother whispered as she drew near, '''Tis he.'

'Who?' said the girl.

'The Mayor.'

The tremors in Susan Henchard's tone might have led any person but one so perfectly unsuspicious of the truth as the girl was, to surmise some closer connection than the admitted simple kinship as a means of accounting for them.

Two men were indeed talking in the adjoining chamber, the young Scotchman and Henchard, who, having entered the inn while Elizabeth-Jane was in the kitchen waiting for the supper, had been deferentially conducted upstairs by host Stannidge himself. The girl noiselessly laid out their little meal, and beckoned to her mother to join her, which Mrs Henchard mechanically did, her attention being fixed on the conversation through the door.

'I merely strolled in on my way home to ask you a question about something that has excited my curiosity,' said the Mayor, with careless geniality. 'But I see you have not finished supper.'

'Ay, but I will be done in a little! Ye needn't go, sir. Take a seat. I've almost done, and it makes no difference at all.'

Henchard seemed to take the seat offered, and in a moment he resumed: 'Well, first I should ask, did you write this?' A rustling of paper followed.

'Yes, I did,' said the Scotchman.

'Then,' said Henchard, 'I am under the impression that we have met by accident while waiting for the morning to keep an appointment with each other?

My name is Henchard; ha'n't you replied to an advertisement for a corn-factor's manager that I put into the paper – ha'n't you come here to see me about it?'

'No,' said the Scotchman, with some surprise.

'Surely you are the man,' went on Henchard insistingly, 'who arranged to come and see me? Joshua, Joshua, Jipp – Jopp – what was his name?'

'You're wrong!' said the young man. 'My name is Donald Farfrae. It is true I am in the corren trade – but I have replied to no advairrtisment, and arranged to see no one. I am on my way to Bristol – from there to the other side of the warrld, to try my fortune in the great wheat-growing districts of the West! I have some inventions useful to the trade, and there is no scope for developing them heere.'

'To America – well, well,' said Henchard, in a tone of disappointment, so strong as to make itself felt like a damp atmosphere. 'And yet I could have sworn you were the man!'

The Scotchman murmured another negative, and there was a silence, till Henchard resumed: 'Then I am truly and sincerely obliged to you for the few words you wrote on that paper.'

'It was nothing, sir.'

'Well, it has a great importance for me just now. This row about my grown wheat, which I declare to Heaven I didn't know to be bad till the people came complaining, has put me to my wits' end. I've some hundreds of quarters of it on hand; and if your renovating process will make it wholesome, why, you can see what a quag 'twould get me out of. I saw in a moment there might be truth in it. But I should like to have it proved; and of course you don't care to tell the steps of the process sufficiently for me to do that, without my paying ye well for't first.'

The young man reflected a moment or two. 'I don't know that I have any objection,' he said. 'I'm going to another country, and curing bad corn is not the line I'll take up there. Yes, I'll tell ye the whole of it – you'll make more out of it heere than I will in a foreign country. Just look heere a minute, sir. I can show ye by a sample in my carpet-bag.'

The click of a lock followed, and there was a sifting and rustling; then a discussion about so many ounces to the bushel, and drying, and refrigerating, and so on.

'These few grains will be sufficient to show ye with,' came in the young fellow's voice; and after a pause, during which some operation seemed to be intently watched by them both, he exclaimed, 'There, now, do you taste that.'

'It's complete! – quite restored, or – well – nearly.'

'Quite enough restored to make good seconds out of it,' said the Scotchman. 'To fetch it back entirely is impossible; Nature won't stand so much as that, but heere you go a great way towards it. Well, sir, that's the process; I don't value it, for it can be but of little use in countries where the weather is more settled than in ours; and I'll be only too glad if it's of service to you.'

'But hearken to me,' pleaded Henchard. 'My business, you know, is in corn and in hay; but I was brought up as a hay-trusser simply, and hay is what I understand best, though I now do more in corn than in the other. If you'll accept the place, you shall manage the corn branch entirely, and receive a commission in addition to salary.'

'You're liberal – very liberal; but no, no – I cannet!' the young man still replied, with some distress in his accents.

'So be it!' said Henchard conclusively. 'Now – to change the subject – one good turn deserves another; don't stay to finish that miserable supper. Come to my house; I can find something better for 'ee than cold ham and ale.'

Donald Farfrae was grateful – said he feared he must decline – that he wished to leave early next day.

'Very well,' said Henchard quickly, 'please yourself. But I tell you, young man, if this holds good for the bulk, as it has done for the sample, you have saved my credit, stranger though you be. What shall I pay you for this knowledge?'

'Nothing at all, nothing at all. It may not prove necessary to ye to use it often, and I don't value it at all. I thought I might just as well let ye know, as you were in a difficulty, and they were harrd upon ye.'

Henchard paused. 'I shan't soon forget this,' he said. 'And from a stranger! . . . I couldn't believe you were not the man I had engaged! Says I to myself "He knows who I am, and recommends himself by this stroke." And yet it turns out, after all, that you are not the man who answered my advertisement, but a stranger!'

'Ay, ay; that's so,' said the young man.

Henchard again suspended his words, and then his voice came thoughtfully: 'Your forehead, Farfrae, is something like my poor brother's – now dead and gone; and the nose, too, isn't unlike his. You must be,' what – five foot nine, I reckon? I am six foot one and a half out of my shoes. But what of that? In my business, 'tis true that strength and bustle build up a firm. But judgment and knowledge are what keep it established. Unluckily, I am bad at science, Farfrae; bad at figures – a rule o' thumb sort of man. You are just the reverse – I can see that. I have been looking for such as you these two year, and yet you are not for me. Well, before I go, let me ask this: Though you are not the young man I thought you were, what's the difference? Can't ye stay just the same? Have you really made up your mind about this American notion? I won't mince matters. I feel you would be invaluable to me – that needn't be said – and if you will bide and be my manager, I will make it worth your while.'

'My plans are fixed,' said the young man, in negative tones. 'I have formed a scheme, and so we need na say any more about it. But will you not drink with me, sir? I find this Casterbridge ale warreming to the stomach.'

'No, no; I fain would, but I can't,' said Henchard gravely, the scraping of his chair informing the listeners that he was rising to leave. 'When I was a young man I went in for that sort of thing too strong – far too strong – and was well-nigh ruined by it! I did a deed on account of it which I shall be ashamed of to my dying day. It made such an impression on me that I swore, there and then, that I'd drink nothing stronger than tea for as many years as I was old that day. I have kept my oath; and though, Farfrae, I am sometimes that dry in the dog days that I could drink a quarter-barrel to the pitching, I think o' my oath, and touch no strong drink at all.'

'I'll no' press ye, sir – I'll no' press ye. I respect your vow.'

'Well, I shall get a manager somewhere, no doubt,' said Henchard, with strong feeling in his tones. 'But it will be long before I see one that would suit me so well!'

The young man appeared much moved by Henchard's warm convictions of his value. He was silent till they reached the door. 'I wish I could stay – sincerely I would like to,' he replied. 'But no – it cannet be! it cannet! I want to see the warrld.'

CHAPTER EIGHT

THUS they parted; and Elizabeth-Jane and her mother remained each in her thoughts over their meal, the mother's face being strangely bright since Henchard's avowal of shame for a past action. The quivering of the partition to its core presently denoted that Donald Farfrae had again rung his bell, no doubt to have his supper removed; for humming a tune, and walking up and down, he seemed to be attracted by the lively bursts of conversation and melody from the general company below. He sauntered out upon the landing, and descended the staircase.

When Elizabeth-Jane had carried down his supper tray, and also that used by her mother and herself, she found the bustle of serving to be at its height below, as it always was at this hour. The young woman shrank from having anything to do with the ground-floor serving, and crept silently about observing the scene – so new to her, fresh from the seclusion of a seaside cottage. In the general sitting-room, which was large, she remarked the two or three dozen strong-backed chairs that stood round against the wall, each fitted with its genial occupant; the sanded floor; the black settle which, projecting endwise from the wall within the door, permitted Elizabeth to be a spectator of all that went on without herself being particularly seen.

The young Scotchman had just joined the guests. These, in addition to the respectable master-tradesmen occupying the seats of privilege in the bow-window and its neighbourhood, included an inferior set at the unlighted end, whose seats were mere benches against the wall, and who drank from cups instead of from glasses. Among the latter she noticed some of those personages who had stood outside the windows of the King's Arms.

Behind their backs was a small window, with a wheel ventilator in one of the panes, which would suddenly start off spinning with a jingling sound, as suddenly stop, and as suddenly start again.

While thus furtively making her survey the opening words of a song greeted her ears from the front of the settle, in a melody and accent of peculiar charm. There had been some singing before she came down; and now the Scotchman had made himself so soon at home that, at the request of some of the master-tradesmen, he, too, was favouring the room with a ditty.

Elizabeth-Jane was fond of music; she could not help pausing to listen; and the longer she listened the more she was enraptured. She had never heard any singing like this; and it was evident that the majority of the audience had not heard such frequently, for they were attentive to a much greater degree than usual. They neither whispered, nor drank, nor dipped their pipe-stems in their ale to moisten them, nor pushed the mug to their neighbours. The singer himself grew emotional, till she could imagine a tear in his eye as the words went on: –

'It's hame, and it's hame, hame fain would I be,
O hame, hame, hame to my ain countree!
There's an eye that ever weeps, and a fair face will be fain,
As I pass through Annan Water with my bonnie bands again;
When the flower is in the bud, and the leaf upon the tree,
The lark shall sing me hame to my ain countree!'

There was a burst of applause, and a deep silence which was even more eloquent than the applause. It was of such a kind that the snapping of a pipe-stem too long for him by old Solomon Longways, who was one of those gathered at the shady end of the room, seemed a harsh and irreverent act. Then the ventilator in the window-pane spasmodically started off for a new spin, and the pathos of Donald's song was temporarily effaced.

''Twas not amiss – not at all amiss!' muttered Christopher Coney, who was also present. And removing his pipe a finger's breadth from his lips, he said aloud, 'Draw on the next verse, young gentleman, please.'

'Yes. Let's have it again, stranger,' said the glazier, a stout, bucket-headed man, with a white apron rolled up round his waist. 'Folks don't lift up their hearts like that in this part of the world.' And turning aside, he said in undertones, 'Who is the young man? – Scotch, d'ye say?'

'Yes, straight from the mountains of Scotland, I believe,' replied Coney.

Young Farfrae repeated the last verse. It was plain that nothing so pathetic had been heard at the Three Mariners for a considerable time. The difference of accent, the excitability of the singer, the intense local feeling, and the seriousness with which he worked himself up to a climax, surprised this set of worthies, who were only too prone to shut up their emotions with caustic words.

'Danged if our country down here is worth singing about like that!' continued the glazier, as the Scotchman again melodized with a dying fall, 'My ain countree!' 'When you take away from among us the fools and the rogues, and the lammigers, and the wanton hussies, and the slatterns, and such like, there's cust few left to ornament a song with in Casterbridge, or the country round.'

'True,' said Buzzford, the dealer, looking at the grain of the table. 'Caster-bridge is a old, hoary place o' wickedness, by all account. 'Tis recorded in history that we rebelled against the King one or two hundred years ago, in the time of the Romans, and that lots of us was hanged on Gallows Hill, and quartered, and our different jints sent about the country like butcher's meat; and for my part I can well believe it.'

'What did ye come away from yer own country for, young maister, if ye be so wownded about it?' inquired Christopher Coney, from the background, with the tone of a man who preferred the original subject. 'Faith, it wasn't worth your while on our account, for, as Maister Billy Wills says, we be bruckle folk here – the best o' us hardly honest sometimes, what with hard winters, and so many mouths to fill, and God-a'mighty sending his little taties so terrible small to fill 'em with. We don't think about flowers and fair faces, not we – except in the shape o' cauliflowers and pigs' chaps.'

'But no!' said Donald Farfrae, gazing round into their faces with earnest concern; 'the best of ye hardly honest – not that surely? None of ye has been stealing what didn't belong to him?'

'Lord! no, no!' said Solomon Longways, smiling grimly. 'That's only his random way o' speaking. 'A was always such a man of under-thoughts.' (And reprovingly towards Christopher): 'Don't ye be so over-familiar with a gentleman that ye know nothing of – and that's travelled a'most from the North Pole.'

Christopher Coney was silenced, and as he could get no public sympathy, he mumbled his feelings to himself: 'Be dazed, if I loved my country half as well as the young feller do, I'd live by claning my neighbour's pigsties afore I'd go away! For my part I've no more love for my country than I have for Botany Bay!'

'Come,' said Longways; 'let the young man draw onward with his ballet, or we shall be here all night.'

'That's all of it,' said the singer apologetically.

'Soul of my body, then we'll have another!' said the general dealer.

'Can you turn a strain to the ladies, sir?' inquired a fat woman with a figured purple apron, the waist-string of which was overhung so far by her sides as to be invisible.

'Let him breathe – let him breathe, Mother Cuxsom. He hain't got his second wind yet,' said the master glazier.

'O yes, but I have!' exclaimed the young man; and he at once rendered 'O Nannie' with faultless modulations, and another or two of the like sentiment, winding up at their earnest request with 'Auld Lang Syne'.

By this time he had completely taken possession of the hearts of the Three Mariners' inmates, including even old Coney. Notwithstanding an occasional odd gravity which awoke their sense of the ludicrous for the moment, they began to view him through a golden haze which the tone of his mind seemed to raise around him. Casterbridge had sentiment – Casterbridge had romance; but this stranger's sentiment was of differing quality. Or rather, perhaps, the difference was mainly superficial; he was to them like the poet of a new school who takes his contemporaries by storm; who is not really new, but is the first to articulate what all his listeners have felt, though but dumbly till then.

The silent landlord came and leant over the settle while the young man sang; and even Mrs Stannidge managed to unstick herself from the framework of her chair in the bar and get as far as the door-post, which movement she accomplished by rolling herself round, as a cask is trundled on the chine by a drayman without losing much of its perpendicular.

'And are you going to bide in Casterbridge, sir?' she asked.

'Ah – no!' said the Scotchman, with melancholy fatality in his voice, 'I'm only passing thirrough! I am on my way to Bristol, and on frae there to foreign parts.'

'We be truly sorry to hear it,' said Solomon Longways. 'We can ill afford to lose tuneful wynd-pipes like yours when they fall among us. And verily, to mak' acquaintance with a man a-come from so far, from the land o' perpetual snow, as we may say, where wolves and wild boars and other dangerous animalcules be as common as blackbirds hereabout – why, 'tis a thing we can't do every day; and there's good sound information for bide-at-homes like we when such a man opens his mouth.'

'Nay, but ye mistake my country,' said the young man, looking round upon them with tragic fixity, till his eye lighted up and his cheek kindled with a sudden enthusiasm to right their errors. 'There are not perpetual snow and wolves at all in it! – except snow in winter, and – well – a little in summer just sometimes, and a "gaberlunzie" or two stalking about here and there, if ye may call them dangerous. Eh, but you should take a summer jarreny to Edinboro', and Arthur's Seat, and all round there, and then go on to the lochs, and all the Highland scenery – in May and June – and you would never say 'tis the land of wolves and perpetual snow!'

'Of course not – it stands to reason,' said Buzzford. ''Tis barren ignorance that leads to such words. He's a simple home-spun man, that never was fit for good company – think nothing of him, sir.'

'And do ye carry your flock bed, and your quilt, and your crock, and your bit of chiney? or do ye go in bare bones, as I may say?' inquired Christopher Coney.

'I've sent on my luggage – though it isn't much; for the voyage is long.' Donald's eyes dropped into a remote gaze as he added: 'But I said to myself, "Never a one of the prizes of life will I come by unless I undertake it!" and I decided to go.'

A general sense of regret, in which Elizabeth-Jane shared not least, made itself apparent in the company. As she looked at Farfrae from the back of the settle she decided that his statements showed him to be no less thoughtful than his fascinating melodies revealed him to be cordial and impassioned. She admired the serious light in which he looked at serious things. He had seen no jest in ambiguities and roguery, as the Casterbridge toss-pots had done; and rightly not – there was none. She disliked those wretched humours of Christopher Coney and his tribe; and he did not appreciate them. He seemed to feel exactly as she felt about life and its surroundings – that they were a tragical rather than a comical thing; that though one could be gay on occasion, moments of gaiety were interludes, and no part of the actual drama. It was extraordinary how similar their views were.

Though it was still early the young Scotchman expressed his wish to retire, whereupon the landlady whispered to Elizabeth to run upstairs and turn down his bed. She took a candlestick and proceeded on her mission, which was the act of a few moments only. When, candle in hand, she reached the top of the stairs on her way down again, Mr Farfrae was at the foot coming up. She could not very well retreat; they met and passed in the turn of the staircase.

She must have appeared interesting in some way – notwithstanding her plain dress – or rather, possibly, in consequence of it, for she was a girl characterized by earnestness and soberness of mien, with which simple drapery accorded well. Her face flushed, too, at the slight awkwardness of the meeting, and she passed him with her eyes bent on the candle-flame that she carried just below her nose. Thus it happened that when confronting her he smiled; and then, with the manner of a temporarily light-hearted man, who has started himself on a flight of song whose momentum he cannot readily check, he softly tuned an old ditty that she seemed to suggest –

> 'As I came in by my bower door,
>   As day was waxin' wearie,
> Oh wha came tripping down the stair
>   But bonnie Peg my dearie.'

Elizabeth-Jane, rather disconcerted, hastened on; and the Scotchman's voice died away, humming more of the same within the closed door of his room.

Here the scene and sentiment ended for the present. When, soon after, the girl rejoined her mother, the latter was still in thought – on quite another matter than a young man's song.

'We've made a mistake,' she whispered (that the Scotchman might not overhear). 'On no account ought ye to have helped serve here to-night. Not because of ourselves, but for the sake of *him*. If he should befriend us, and take us up, and then find out what you did when staying here, 'twould grieve and wound his natural pride as Mayor of the town.'

Elizabeth, who would perhaps have been more alarmed at this than her mother had she known the real relationship, was not much disturbed about it as things stood. Her 'he' was another man than her poor mother's. 'For myself,' she said, 'I didn't at all mind waiting a little upon him. He's so respectable, and educated – far above the rest of 'em in the inn. They thought him very simple not to know their grim broad way of talking about themselves here. But of course he didn't know – he was too refined in his mind to know such things!' Thus she earnestly pleaded.

Meanwhile, the 'he' of her mother was not so far away as even they thought. After leaving the Three Mariners he had sauntered up and down the empty High Street, passing and repassing the inn in his promenade. When the Scotchman sang his voice had reached Henchard's ears through the heart-shaped holes in the window-shutters, and had led him to pause outside them a long while.

'To be sure, to be sure, how that fellow does draw me!' he had said to himself. 'I suppose 'tis because I'm so lonely. I'd have given him a third share in the business to have stayed!'

CHAPTER NINE

W H E N Elizabeth-Jane opened the hinged casement next morning the mellow air brought in the feel of imminent autumn almost as distinctly as if she had been in the remotest hamlet. Casterbridge was the complement of the rural life around; not its urban opposite. Bees and butterflies in the cornfields at the top of the town, who desired to get to the meads at the bottom, took no circuitous course, but flew straight down High Street without any apparent consciousness that they were traversing strange latitudes. And in autumn airy spheres of thistledown floated into the same street, lodged upon the shop fronts, blew into drains, and innumerable tawny and yellow leaves skimmed along the pavement, and stole through people's doorways into their passages with a hesitating scratch on the floor, like the skirts of timid visitors.

Hearing voices, one of which was close at hand, she withdrew her head and glanced from behind the window-curtains. Mr Henchard – now habited no longer as a great personage, but as a thriving man of business – was pausing on his way up the middle of the street, and the Scotchman was looking from the window adjoining her own. Henchard, it appeared, had gone a little way past the inn before he had noticed his acquaintance of the previous evening. He came back a few steps, Donald Farfrae opening the window further.

'And you are off soon, I suppose?' said Henchard upwards.

'Yes – almost this moment, sir,' said the other. 'Maybe I'll walk on till the coach makes up on me.'

'Which way?'

'The way ye are going.'

'Then shall we walk together to the top o' town?'

'If ye'll wait a minute,' said the Scotchman.

In a few minutes the latter emerged, bag in hand. Henchard looked at the bag as at an enemy. It showed there was no mistake about the young man's departure. 'Ah, my lad,' he said, 'you should have been a wise man, and have stayed with me.'

'Yes, yes – it might have been wiser,' said Donald, looking microscopically at the houses that were furthest off. 'It is only telling ye the truth when I say my plans are vague.'

They had by this time passed on from the precincts of the inn, and Elizabeth-Jane heard no more. She saw that they continued in conversation, Henchard turning to the other occasionally, and emphasizing some remark with a gesture. Thus they passed the King's Arms Hotel, the Market House, St Peter's churchyard wall, ascending to the upper end of the long street till they were small as two grains of corn; when they bent suddenly to the right into the Bristol Road, and were out of view.

'He was a good man – and he's gone,' she said to herself. 'I was nothing to him, and there was no reason why he should have wished me good-bye.'

The simple thought, with its latent sense of slight, had moulded itself out of the following little fact: when the Scotchman came out at the door he had by accident glanced up at her; and then he had looked away again without nodding, or smiling, or saying a word.

'You are still thinking, mother,' she said, when she turned inwards.

'Yes; I am thinking of Mr Henchard's sudden liking for that young man. He was always so. Now, surely, if he takes so warmly to people who are not related to him at all, may he not take as warmly to his own kin?'

While they debated this question a procession of five large waggons went past, laden with hay up to the bedroom windows. They came in from the country, and the steaming horses had probably been travelling a great part of the night. To the shaft of each hung a little board, on which was painted in white letters, 'Henchard, corn-factor and hay-merchant'. The spectacle renewed his wife's conviction that, for her daughter's sake, she should strain a point to rejoin him.

The discussion was continued during breakfast, and the end of it was that Mrs Henchard decided, for good or for ill, to send Elizabeth-Jane with a message to Henchard, to the effect that his relative Susan, a sailor's widow, was in the town; leaving it to him to say whether or not he would recognize her. What had brought her to this determination were chiefly two things. He had been described as a lonely widower; and he had expressed shame for a past transaction of his life. There was promise in both.

'If he says no,' she enjoined, as Elizabeth-Jane stood, bonnet on, ready to depart; 'if he thinks it does not become the good position he has reached to in the town, to own – to let us call on him as – his distant kinsfolk, say, "Then, sir, we would rather not intrude; we will leave Casterbridge as quietly as we have come, and go back to our own country." . . . I almost feel that I would rather he did say so, as I have not seen him for so many years, and we are so – little allied to him!'

'And if he say yes?' inquired the more sanguine one.

'In that case,' answered Mrs Henchard cautiously, 'ask him to write me a note, saying when and how he will see us – or *me*.'

Elizabeth-Jane went a few steps towards the landing. 'And tell him,' continued her mother, 'that I fully know I have no claim upon him – that I am glad to find he is thriving; that I hope his life may be long and happy – there, go.' Thus with a half-hearted willingness, a smothered reluctance, did the poor forgiving woman start her unconscious daughter on this errand.

It was about ten o'clock, and market-day, when Elizabeth paced up the High Street, in no great hurry; for to herself her position was only that of a poor relation deputed to hunt up a rich one. The front doors of the private houses were mostly left open at this warm autumn time, no thought of umbrella stealers disturbing the minds of the placid burgesses. Hence, through the long, straight, entrance passages thus unclosed could be seen, as through tunnels, the mossy gardens at the back, glowing with nasturtiums, fuchsias, scarlet geraniums, 'bloody warriors', snapdragons, and dahlias, this floral blaze being backed by crusted grey stone-work remaining from a yet remoter Casterbridge than the venerable one visible in the street. The old-fashioned fronts of these houses, which had older than old-fashioned backs, rose sheer from the pavement, into which the bow-windows protruded like bastions, necessitating a pleasing *chassez-déchassez* movement to the time-pressed pedestrian at every few yards. He was bound also to evolve other Terpsichorean figures in respect of door-steps, scrapers, cellar-hatches, church buttresses, and the overhanging angles of walls which, originally unobtrusive, had become bow-legged and knock-kneed.

In addition to these fixed obstacles which spoke so cheerfully of individual unrestraint as to boundaries, movables occupied the path and roadway to a perplexing extent. First the vans of the carriers in and out of Casterbridge, who hailed from Mellstock, Weatherbury, The Hintocks, Sherton-Abbas, Kingsbere, Overcombe, and many other towns and villages round. Their owners were numerous enough to be regarded as a tribe, and had almost distinctiveness enough to be regarded as a race. Their vans had just arrived, and were drawn up on each side of the street in close file, so as to form at places a wall between the pavement and the roadway. Moreover every shop pitched out half its contents upon trestles and boxes on the kerb, extending the display each week a little further and further into the roadway, despite the expostulations of the two feeble old constables, until there remained but a tortuous defile for carriages down the centre of the street, which afforded fine opportunities for skill with the reins. Over the pavement on the sunny side of the way hung shopblinds so constructed as to give the passenger's hat a smart buffet off his head, as from the unseen hands of Cranstoun's Goblin Page, celebrated in romantic lore.

Horses for sale were tied in rows, their forelegs on the pavement, their hind legs in the street, in which position they occasionally nipped little boys by the shoulder who were passing to school. And any inviting recess in front of a house that had been modestly kept back from the general line was utilized by pig-dealers as a pen for their stock.[1]

The yeomen, farmers, dairymen, and townsfolk, who came to transact business in these ancient streets, spoke in other ways than by articulation. Not to hear the words of your interlocutor in metropolitan centres is to know nothing of his meaning. Here the face, the arms, the hat, the stick, the body throughout spoke equally with the tongue. To express satisfaction the Casterbridge market-man added to his utterance a broadening of the cheeks, a crevicing of the eyes, a throwing back of the shoulders, which was intelligible from the other end of the street. If he wondered, though all Henchard's carts and waggons were rattling past him, you knew it from perceiving the inside of his crimson mouth, and a target-like circling of his eyes. Deliberation caused sundry attacks on the moss of adjoining walls with the end of his stick, a change of his hat from the horizontal to the less so; a sense of tediousness announced itself in a lowering of the person by spreading the knees to a lozenge-shaped aperture and contorting the arms. Chicanery, subterfuge, had hardly a place in the streets of this honest borough to all appearance; and it was said that the lawyers in the Court House hard by occasionally threw in strong arguments for the other side out of pure generosity (though apparently by mischance) when advancing their own.

Thus Casterbridge was in most respects but the pole, focus, or nerve-knot of the surrounding country life; differing from the many manufacturing towns which are as foreign bodies set down, like boulders on a plain, in a green world with which they have nothing in common. Casterbridge lived by agriculture at one remove further from the fountain-head than the adjoining villages – no more. The townsfolk understood every fluctuation in the rustic's condition, for it affected their receipts as much as the labourer's; they entered into the troubles and joys which moved the aristocratic families ten miles round – for the same reason. And even at the dinner-parties of the professional families the subjects of discussion were corn, cattle-disease, sowing and reaping, fencing and planting; while politics were viewed by them less from their own standpoint of burgesses with rights and privileges than from the standpoint of their country neighbours.

All the venerable contrivances and confusions which delighted the eye by their quaintness, and in a measure reasonableness, in this rare old market-town, were metropolitan novelties to the unpractised eyes of Elizabeth-Jane, fresh from netting fish-seines in a seaside cottage. Very little inquiry was necessary to guide her footsteps. Henchard's house was one of the best, faced with dull red-and-grey old brick. The front door was open, and, as in other houses, she could see through the passage to the end of the garden —nearly a quarter of a mile off.

Mr Henchard was not in the house, but in the store-yard. She was conducted into the mossy garden, and through a door in the wall, which was studded with rusty nails speaking of generations of fruit-trees that had been trained there. The door opened upon the yard, and here she was left to find him as she could. It was a place flanked by hay-barns, into which tons of fodder, all in trusses, were being packed from the waggons she had seen pass the inn that morning. On other sides

---

[1] The reader will scarcely need to be reminded that time and progress have obliterated from the town that suggested these descriptions many or most of the old-fashioned features here enumerated.

of the yard were wooden granaries on stone staddles, to which access was given by Flemish ladders, and a store-house several floors high. Wherever the doors of these places were open, a closely packed throng of bursting wheat-sacks could be seen standing inside, with the air of awaiting a famine that would not come.

She wandered about this place, uncomfortably conscious of the impending interview, till she was quite weary of searching; she ventured to inquire of a boy in what quarter Mr Henchard could be found. He directed her to an office which she had not seen before, and knocking at the door she was answered by a cry of 'Come in'.

Elizabeth turned the handle; and there stood before her, bending over some sample-bags on a table, not the corn-merchant, but the young Scotchman Mr Farfrae – in the act of pouring some grains of wheat from one hand to the other. His hat hung on a peg behind him, and the roses of his carpet-bag glowed from the corner of the room.

Having toned her feelings and arranged words on her lips for Mr Henchard, and for him alone, she was for the moment confounded.

'Yes, what is it?' said the Scotchman, like a man who permanently ruled there.

She said she wanted to see Mr Henchard.

'Ah, yes; will you wait a minute? He's engaged just now,' said the young man, apparently not recognizing her as the girl at the inn. He handed her a chair, bade her sit down, and turned to his sample-bags again. While Elizabeth-Jane sits waiting in great amaze at the young man's presence we may briefly explain how he came there.

When the two new acquaintances had passed out of sight that morning towards the Bath and Bristol road they went on silently, except for a few commonplaces, till they had gone down an avenue on the town walls called the Chalk Walk, leading to an angle where the North and West escarpments met. From this high corner of the square earthworks a vast extent of country could be seen. A footpath ran steeply down the green slope, conducting from the shady promenade on the walls to a road at the bottom of the scarp. It was by this path the Scotchman had to descend.

'Well, here's success to 'ee,' said Henchard, holding out his right hand and leaning with his left upon the wicket which protected the descent. In the act there was the inelegance of one whose feelings are nipped and wishes defeated. 'I shall often think of this time, and of how you came at the very moment to throw a light upon my difficulty.'

Still holding the young man's hand he paused, and then added deliberately: 'Now I am not the man to let a cause be lost for want of a word. And before ye are gone for ever I'll speak. Once more, will ye stay? There it is, flat and plain. You can see that it isn't all selfishness that makes me press 'ee; for my business is not quite so scientific as to require an intellect entirely out of the common. Others would do for the place without doubt. Some selfishness perhaps there is, but there is more; it isn't for me to repeat what. Come bide with me – and name your own terms. I'll agree to 'em willingly and 'ithout a word of gainsaying; for, hang it, Farfrae, I like thee well!'

The young man's hand remained steady in Henchard's for a moment or two. He looked over the fertile country that stretched beneath them, then backward along the shaded walk reaching to the top of the town. His face flushed.

'I never expected this – I did not!' he said. 'It's Providence! Should any one go against it? No; I'll not go to America; I'll stay and be your man!'

His hand, which had lain lifeless in Henchard's, returned the latter's grasp.

'Done,' said Henchard.

'Done,' said Donald Farfrae.

The face of Mr Henchard beamed forth a satisfaction that was almost fierce in its strength. 'Now you are my friend!' he exclaimed. 'Come back to my house; let's clinch it at once by clear terms, so as to be comfortable in our minds.' Farfrae caught up his bag and retraced the North-West Avenue in Henchard's company as he had come. Henchard was all confidence now.

'I am the most distant fellow in the world when I don't care for a man,' he said. 'But when a man takes my fancy he takes it strong. Now I am sure you can eat another breakfast? You couldn't have eaten much so early, even if they had anything at that place to gi'e thee, which they hadn't; so come to my house and we will have a solid, staunch tuck-in, and settle terms in black-and-white if you like; though my word's my bond. I can always make a good meal in the morning. I've got a splendid cold pigeon-pie going just now. You can have some home-brewed if you want to, you know.'

'It is too airly in the morning for that,' said Farfrae with a smile.

'Well, of course, I didn't know. I don't drink it because of my oath; but I am obliged to brew for my work-people.'

Thus talking they returned, and entered Henchard's premises by the back way or traffic entrance. Here the matter was settled over the breakfast, at which Henchard heaped the young Scotchman's plate to a prodigal fulness. He would not rest satisfied till Farfrae had written for his luggage from Bristol, and despatched the letter to the post-office. When it was done this man of strong impulses declared that his new friend should take up his abode in his house – at least till some suitable lodgings could be found.

He then took Farfrae round and showed him the place, and the stores of grain, and other stock; and finally entered the offices where the younger of them has already been discovered by Elizabeth.

CHAPTER TEN

WHILE she still sat under the Scotchman's eyes a man came up to the door, reaching it as Henchard opened the door of the inner office to admit Elizabeth. The new-comer stepped forward like the quicker cripple at Bethesda, and entered in her stead. She could hear his words to Henchard: 'Joshua Jopp, sir – by appointment – the new manager.'

'The new manager! – he's in his office,' said Henchard bluntly.

'In his office!' said the man, with a stultified air.

'I mentioned Thursday,' said Henchard; 'and as you did not keep your appointment, I have engaged another manager. At first I thought he must be you. Do you think I can wait when business is in question?'

'You said Thursday or Saturday, sir,' said the new-comer, pulling out a letter.

'Well, you are too late,' said the corn-factor. 'I can say no more.'

'You as good as engaged me,' murmured the man.

'Subject to an interview,' said Henchard. 'I am sorry for you – very sorry indeed. But it can't be helped.'

There was no more to be said, and the man came out, encountering Elizabeth-Jane in his passage. She could see that his mouth twitched with anger, and that bitter disappointment was written in his face everywhere.

Elizabeth-Jane now entered, and stood before the master of the premises. His dark pupils – which always seemed to have a red spark of light in them, though this could hardly be a physical fact – turned indifferently round under his dark brows until they rested on her figure. 'Now then, what is it, my young woman?' he said blandly.

'Can I speak to you – not on business, sir?' said she.

'Yes – I suppose.' He looked at her more thoughtfully.

'I am sent to tell you, sir,' she innocently went on, 'that a distant relative of yours by marriage, Susan Newson, a sailor's widow, is in the town; and to ask whether you would wish to see her.'

The rich *rouge-et-noir* of his countenance underwent a slight change. 'Oh – Susan is – still alive?' he asked with difficulty.

'Yes, sir.'

'Are you her daughter?'

'Yes, sir – her only daughter.'

'What – do you call yourself – your Christian name?'

'Elizabeth-Jane, sir.'

'Newson?'

'Elizabeth-Jane Newson.'

This at once suggested to Henchard that the transaction of his early married life at Weydon Fair was unrecorded in the family history. It was more than he could have expected. His wife had behaved kindly to him in return for his unkindness, and had never proclaimed her wrong to her child or to the world.

'I am – a good deal interested in your news,' he said. 'And as this is not a matter of business, but pleasure, suppose we go indoors.'

It was with a gentle delicacy of manner, surprising to Elizabeth, that he showed her out of the office and through the outer room, where Donald Farfrae was overhauling bins and samples with the inquiring inspection of a beginner in charge. Henchard preceded her through the door in the wall to the suddenly changed scene of the garden and flowers, and onward into the house. The dining-room to which he introduced her still exhibited the remnants of the lavish breakfast laid for Farfrae. It was furnished to profusion with heavy mahogany furniture of the deepest red-Spanish hues. Pembroke tables, with leaves hanging so low that they well-nigh touched the floor, stood against the walls on legs and feet shaped like those of an elephant, and on one lay three huge folio volumes – a Family Bible, a 'Josephus', and a 'Whole Duty of Man'. In the chimney corner was a fire-grate with a fluted semicircular back, having urns and festoons cast in relief thereon; and the chairs were of the kind which, since that day, has cast lustre upon the names of Chippendale and Sheraton, though, in point of fact, their patterns may have been such as those illustrious carpenters never saw or heard of.

'Sit down – Elizabeth-Jane – sit down,' he said, with a shake in his voice as he uttered her name; and sitting down himself he allowed his hands to hang between his knees, while he looked upon the carpet. 'Your mother, then, is quite well?'

'She is rather worn out, sir, with travelling.'

'A sailor's widow – when did he die?'

'Father was lost last spring.'

Henchard winced at the word 'father', thus applied. 'Do you and she come from abroad – America or Australia?' he asked.

'No. We have been in England some years. I was twelve when we came here from Canada.'

'Ah; exactly.' By such conversation he discovered the circumstances which had enveloped his wife and her child in such total obscurity that he had long ago believed them to be in their graves. These things being clear, he returned to the present. 'And where is your mother staying?'

'At the Three Mariners.'

'And you are her daughter Elizabeth-Jane?' repeated Henchard. He arose, came close to her, and glanced in her face. 'I think,' he said, suddenly turning away with a wet eye, 'you shall take a note from me to your mother. I should like to see her. . . . She is not left very well off by her late husband?' His eye fell on Elizabeth's clothes, which, though a respectable suit of black, and her very best, were decidedly old-fashioned even to Casterbridge eyes.

'Not very well,' she said, glad that he had divined this without her being obliged to express it.

He sat down at the table and wrote a few lines; next taking from his pocket-book a five-pound note, which he put in the envelope with the letter, adding to it, as by an after-thought, five shillings. Sealing the whole up carefully, he directed it to 'Mrs Newson, Three Mariners Inn', and handed the packet to Elizabeth.

'Deliver it to her personally, please,' said Henchard. 'Well, I am glad to see you here, Elizabeth-Jane – very glad. We must have a long talk together – but not just now.'

He took her hand at parting, and held it so warmly that she, who had known so little friendship, was much affected, and tears rose to her aerial-grey eyes. The instant that she was gone Henchard's state showed itself more distinctly; having shut the door he sat in his dining-room stiffly erect, gazing at the opposite wall as if he read his history there.

'Begad!' he suddenly exclaimed, jumping up. 'I didn't think of that. Perhaps these are impostors – and Susan and the child dead after all!'

However, a something in Elizabeth-Jane soon assured him that, as regarded her, at least, there could be little doubt. And a few hours would settle the question of her mother's identity; for he had arranged in his note to see her that evening.

'It never rains but it pours!' said Henchard. His keenly excited interest in his new friend the Scotchman was now eclipsed by this event; and Donald Farfrae saw so little of him during the rest of the day that he wondered at the suddenness of his employer's moods.

In the meantime Elizabeth had reached the inn. Her mother, instead of taking the note with the curiosity of a poor woman expecting assistance, was much moved at sight of it. She did not read it at once, asking Elizabeth to describe her reception, and the very words Mr Henchard used. Elizabeth's back was turned when her mother opened the letter. It ran thus: —

'Meet me at eight o'clock this evening, if you can, at the Ring on the Budmouth road. The place is easy to find. I can say no more now. The news upsets me almost. The girl seems to be in ignorance. Keep her so till I have seen you.

M.H.'

He said nothing about the enclosure of five guineas. The amount was significant; it may tacitly have said to her that he bought her back again. She waited restlessly for the close of the day, telling Elizabeth-Jane that she was invited to see Mr Henchard; that she would go alone. But she said nothing to show that the place of meeting was not at his house, nor did she hand the note to Elizabeth.

CHAPTER ELEVEN

T HE Ring at Casterbridge was merely the local name of one of the finest Roman Amphitheatres, if not the very finest, remaining in Britain.

Casterbridge announced old Rome in every street, alley, and precinct. It looked Roman, bespoke the art of Rome, concealed dead men of Rome. It was impossible to dig more than a foot or two deep about the town fields and gardens without coming upon some tall soldier or other of the Empire, who had lain there in his silent unobtrusive rest for a space of fifteen hundred years. He was mostly found lying on his side, in an oval scoop in the chalk, like a chicken in its shell; his knees drawn up to his chest; sometimes with the remains of his spear against his arm; a fibula or brooch of bronze on his breast or forehead; an urn at his knees, a jar at his throat, a bottle at his mouth; and mystified conjecture pouring down upon him from the eyes of Casterbridge street boys and men, who had turned a moment to gaze at the familiar spectacle as they passed by.

Imaginative inhabitants, who would have felt an unpleasantness at the discovery of a comparatively modern skeleton in their gardens, were quite unmoved by these hoary shapes. They had lived so long ago, their time was so unlike the present, their hopes and motives were so widely removed from ours, that between them and the living there seemed to stretch a gulf too wide for even a spirit to pass.

The Amphitheatre was a huge circular enclosure, with a notch at opposite extremities of its diameter north and south. From its sloping internal form it might have been called the spittoon of the Jötuns. It was to Casterbridge what the ruined Coliseum is to modern Rome, and was nearly of the same magnitude. The dusk of evening was the proper hour at which a true impression of this suggestive place could be received. Standing in the middle of the arena at that time there by degrees became apparent its real vastness, which a cursory view from the summit at noon-day was apt to obscure. Melancholy, impressive, lonely, yet accessible from every part of the town, the historic circle was the frequent spot for appointments of a furtive kind. Intrigues were arranged there; tentative meetings were there experimented after divisions and feuds. But one kind of appointment – in itself the most common of any – seldom had place in the Amphitheatre: that of happy lovers.

Why, seeing that it was pre-eminently an airy, accessible, and sequestered spot for interviews, the cheerfullest form of those occurrences never took kindly to the soil of the ruin, would be a curious inquiry. Perhaps it was because its associations had about them something sinister. Its history proved that. Apart from the sanguinary nature of the games originally played therein, such incidents attached to its past as these: that for scores of years the town-gallows had stood at one corner; that in 1705 a woman who had murdered her husband was half-strangled and then burnt there in the presence of ten thousand spectators. Tradition reports that at a certain stage of the burning her heart burst and leapt out of her body, to the terror of them all, and that not one of those ten thousand people ever cared particularly for hot roast after that. In addition to these old tragedies, pugilistic encounters almost to the death had come off down to recent dates in that secluded arena, entirely invisible to the outside world save by climbing to the top of the enclosure, which few townspeople in the daily round of their lives ever took the trouble to do. So that, though close to the turnpike-road, crimes might be perpetrated there unseen at mid-day.

Some boys had latterly tried to impart gaiety to the ruin by using the central arena as a cricket-ground. But the game usually languished for the aforesaid reason – the dismal privacy which the earthen circle enforced, shutting out every appreciative passer's vision, every commendatory remark from outsiders – everything, except the sky; and to play at games in such circumstances was like acting to an empty house. Possibly, too, the boys were timid, for some old people said that at certain moments in the summer time, in broad daylight, persons sitting with a book or dozing in the arena had, on lifting their eyes, beheld the slopes lined with a gazing legion of Hadrian's soldiery as if watching the gladiatorial combat; and had heard the roar of their excited voices; that the scene would remain but a moment, like a lightning flash, and then disappear.

It was related that there still remained under the south entrance excavated cells for the reception of the wild animals and athletes who took part in the games. The arena was still smooth and circular, as if used for its original purpose not so very long ago. The sloping pathways by which spectators had ascended to their seats were pathways yet. But the whole was grown over with grass, which now, at the end of summer, was bearded with withered bents that formed waves under the brush of the wind, returning to the attentive ear Æolian modulations, and detaining for moments the flying globes of thistledown.

Henchard had chosen this spot as being the safest from observation which he could think of for meeting his long-lost wife, and at the same time as one easily to be found by a stranger after nightfall. As Mayor of the town, with a reputation to keep up, he could not invite her to come to his house till some definite course had been decided on.

Just before eight he approached the deserted earthwork, and entered by the south path which descended over the *débris* of the former dens. In a few moments he could discern a female figure creeping in by the great north gap, or public gateway. They met in the middle of the arena. Neither spoke just at first – there was no necessity for speech – and the poor woman leant against Henchard, who supported her in his arms.

'I don't drink' he said in a low, halting, apologetic voice. 'You hear, Susan? – I don't drink now – I haven't since that night.' Those were his first words.

He felt her bow her head in acknowledgment that she understood. After a minute or two he again began:

'If I had known you were living, Susan! But there was every reason to suppose you and the child were dead and gone. I took every possible step to find you – travelled – advertised. My opinion at last was that you had started for some colony with that man, and had been drowned on your voyage out. Why did you keep silent like this?'

'O Michael! because of him – what other reason could there be? I thought I owed him faithfulness to the end of one of our lives – foolishly I believed there was something solemn and binding in the bargain; I thought that even in honour I dared not desert him when he had paid so much for me in good faith. I meet you now only as his widow – I consider myself that, and that I have no claim upon you. Had he not died I should never have come – never! Of that you may be sure.'

'Ts-s-s! How could you be so simple?'

'I don't know. Yet it would have been very wicked – if I had not thought like that!' said Susan, almost crying.

'Yes – yes – so it would. It is only that which makes me feel 'ee an innocent woman. But – to lead me into this!'

'What, Michael?' she asked, alarmed.

'Why, this difficulty about our living together again, and Elizabeth-Jane. She cannot be told all – she would so despise us both that – I could not bear it!'

'That was why she was brought up in ignorance of you. I could not bear it either.'

'Well – we must talk of a plan for keeping her in her present belief, and getting matters straight in spite of it. You have heard I am in a large way of business here – that I am Mayor of the town, and churchwarden, and I don't know what all?'

'Yes,' she murmured.

'These things, as well as the dread of the girl discovering our disgrace, make it necessary to act with extreme caution. So that I don't see how you two can return openly to my house as the wife and daughter I once treated badly, and banished from me; and there's the rub o't.'

'We'll go away at once. I only came to see—'

'No, no, Susan; you are not to go – you mistake me!' he said, with kindly severity. 'I have thought of this plan: that you and Elizabeth take a cottage in the town as the widow Mrs Newson and her daughter; that I meet you, court you, and marry you, Elizabeth-Jane coming to my house as my step-daughter. The thing is so natural and easy that it is half done in thinking o't. This would leave my shady, headstrong, disgraceful life as a young man absolutely unopened; the secret would be yours and mine only; and I should have the pleasure of seeing my own only child under my roof, as well as my wife.'

'I am quite in your hands, Michael,' she said meekly. 'I came here for the sake of Elizabeth; for myself, if you tell me to leave again to-morrow morning, and never come near you more, I am content to go.'

'Now, now; we don't want to hear that,' said Henchard gently. 'Of course you won't leave again. Think over the plan I have proposed for a few hours; and if you can't hit upon a better one we'll adopt it. I have to be away for a day or two on business, unfortunately; but during that time you can get lodgings – the only ones in the town fit for you are those over the china-shop in High Street – and you can also look for a cottage.'

'If the lodgings are in High Street they are dear, I suppose?'

'Never mind – you *must* start genteel if our plan is to be carried out. Look to me for money. Have you enough till I come back?'

'Quite,' said she.

'And are you comfortable at the inn?'

'O yes.'

'And the girl is quite safe from learning the shame of her case and ours? – that's what makes me most anxious of all.'

'You would be surprised to find how unlikely she is to dream of the truth. How could she ever suppose such a thing?'

'True!'

'I like the idea of repeating our marriage,' said Mrs Henchard, after a pause. 'It seems the only right course, after all this. Now I think I must go back to Elizabeth-Jane, and tell her that our kinsman, Mr Henchard, kindly wishes us to stay in the town.'

'Very well – arrange that yourself. I'll go some way with you.'

'No, no. Don't run any risk!' said his wife anxiously. 'I can find my way back – it is not late. Please let me go alone.'

'Right,' said Henchard. 'But just one word. Do you forgive me, Susan?'

She murmured something; but seemed to find it difficult to frame her answer.

'Never mind – all in good time,' said he. 'Judge me by my future works – good-bye!'

He retreated, and stood at the upper side of the Amphitheatre while his wife passed out through the lower way, and descended under the trees to the town. Then Henchard himself went homeward, going so fast that by the time he reached his door he was almost upon the heels of the unconscious woman from whom he had just parted. He watched her up the street, and turned into his house.

CHAPTER TWELVE

On entering his own door after watching his wife out of sight, the Mayor walked on through the tunnel-shaped passage into the garden, and thence by the back door towards the stores and granaries. A light shone from the office-window, and there being no blind to screen the interior Henchard could see Donald Farfrae still seated where he had left him, initiating himself into the managerial work of the house by overhauling the books. Henchard entered, merely observing, 'Don't let me interrupt you, if ye will stay so late.'

He stood behind Farfrae's chair, watching his dexterity in clearing up the numerical fogs which had been allowed to grow so thick in Henchard's books as almost to baffle even the Scotchman's perspicacity. The corn-factor's mien was half admiring, and yet it was not without a dash of pity for the tastes of any one who could care to give his mind to such finnikin details. Henchard himself was mentally and physically unfit for grubbing subtleties from soiled paper; he had in a modern sense received the education of Achilles, and found penmanship a tantalizing art.

'You shall do no more to-night,' he said at length, spreading his great hand over the paper. 'There's time enough to-morrow. Come indoors with me and have some supper. Now you shall! I am determined on't.' He shut the account-books with friendly force.

Donald had wished to get to his lodgings; but he already saw that his friend and employer was a man who knew no moderation in his requests and impulses, and he yielded gracefully. He liked Henchard's warmth, even if it inconvenienced him; the great difference in their characters adding to the liking.

They locked up the office, and the young man followed his companion through the private little door which, admitting directly into Henchard's garden, permitted a passage from the utilitarian to the beautiful at one step. The garden was silent, dewy, and full of perfume. It extended a long way back from the house, first as lawn and flower-beds, then as fruit-garden, where the long-tied espaliers, as old as the old house itself, had grown so stout, and cramped, and gnarled that they had pulled their stakes out of the ground and stood distorted and writhing in vegetable agony, like leafy Laocoöns. The flowers which smelt so sweetly were not discernible; and they passed through them into the house.

The hospitalities of the morning were repeated, and when they were over Henchard said, 'Pull your chair round to the fireplace, my dear fellow, and let's make a blaze — there's nothing I hate like a black grate, even in September.' He applied a light to the laid-in fuel, and a cheerful radiance spread around.

'It is odd,' said Henchard, 'that two men should meet as we have done on a purely business ground, and that at the end of the first day I should wish to speak to 'ee on a family matter. But, damn it all, I am a lonely man, Farfrae: I have nobody else to speak to; and why shouldn't I tell it to 'ee?'

'I'll be glad to hear it, if I can be of any service,' said Donald, allowing his eyes to travel over the intricate wood-carvings of the chimney-piece, representing garlanded lyres, shields, and quivers, on either side of a draped ox-skull, and flanked by heads of Apollo and Diana in low relief.

'I've not been always what I am now,' continued Henchard, his firm deep voice being ever so little shaken. He was plainly under that strange influence which sometimes prompts men to confide to the new-found friend what they will not tell to the old. 'I began life as a working hay-trusser, and when I was eighteen I married on the strength o' my calling. Would you think me a married man?'

'I heard in the town that you were a widower.'

'Ah, yes — you would naturally have heard that. Well, I lost my wife nineteen years ago or so — by my own fault. . . . This is how it came about. One summer evening I was travelling for employment, and she was walking at my side, carrying the baby, our only child. We came to a booth in a country fair. I was a drinking man at that time.'

Henchard paused a moment, threw himself back so that his elbow rested on the table, his forehead being shaded by his hand, which, however, did not hide the marks of introspective inflexibility on his features as he narrated in fullest detail the incidents of the transaction with the sailor. The tinge of indifference which had at first been visible in the Scotchman now disappeared.

Henchard went on to describe his attempts to find his wife; the oath he swore; the solitary life he led during the years which followed. 'I have kept my oath for nineteen years,' he went on; 'I have risen to what you see me now.'

'Ay!'

'Well – no wife could I hear of in all that time; and being by nature something of a woman-hater, I have found it no hardship to keep mostly at a distance from the sex. No wife could I hear of, I say, till this very day. And now – she has come back.'

'Come back, has she!'

'This morning – this very morning. And what's to be done?'

'Can ye no' take her and live with her, and make some amends?'

'That's what I've planned and proposed. But, Farfrae,' said Henchard gloomily, 'by doing right with Susan I wrong another innocent woman.'

'Ye don't say that?'

'In the nature of things, Farfrae, it is almost impossible that a man of my sort should have the good fortune to tide through twenty years o' life without making more blunders than one. It has been my custom for many years to run across to Jersey in the way of business, particularly in the potato and root season. I do a large trade wi' them in that line. Well, one autumn when stopping there I fell quite ill, and in my illness I sank into one of those gloomy fits I sometimes suffer from, on account o' the loneliness of my domestic life, when the world seems to have the blackness of hell, and, like Job, I could curse the day that gave me birth.'

'Ah, no, I never feel like it,' said Farfrae.

'Then pray to God that you never may, young man. While in this state I was taken pity on by a woman – a young lady I should call her, for she was of good family, well bred, and well educated – the daughter of some harum-scarum military officer who had got into difficulties, and had his pay sequestrated. He was dead now, and her mother too, and she was as lonely as I. This young creature was staying at the boarding-house where I happened to have my lodging; and when I was pulled down she took upon herself to nurse me. Heaven knows why, for I wasn't worth it. But being together in the same house, and her feelings warm, we got naturally intimate. I won't go into particulars of what our relations were. It is enough to say that we honestly meant to marry. There arose a scandal, which did me no harm, but was of course ruin to her. Though, Farfrae, between you and me, as man and man, I solemnly declare that philandering with womankind has neither been my vice nor my virtue. She was terribly careless of appearances, and I was perhaps more, because o' my dreary state; and it was through this that the scandal arose. At last I was well and came away. When I was gone she suffered much on my account, and didn't forget to tell me so in letters one after another; till, latterly, I felt I owed her something, and thought that, as I had not heard of Susan for so long, I would make this other one the only return I could make, and ask her if she would run the risk of Susan being alive (very slight as I believed) and marry me, such as I was. She jumped for joy, and we should no doubt soon have been married – but, behold, Susan appears!'

Donald showed his deep concern at a complication so far beyond the degree of his simple experiences.

'Now see what injury a man may cause around him! Even after that wrong-doing at the fair when I was young, if I had never been so selfish as to let this giddy girl devote herself to me over at Jersey, to the injury of her name, all might now be well. Yet, as it stands, I must bitterly disappoint one of these women; and it is the second. My first duty is to Susan – there's no doubt about that.'

'They are both in a very melancholy position, and that's true!' murmured Donald.

'They are! For myself I don't care – 'twill all end one way. But these two.' Henchard paused in reverie. 'I feel I should like to treat the second, no less than the first, as kindly as a man can in such a case.'

'Ah, well, it cannet be helped!' said the other, with philosophic woefulness. 'You mun write to the young lady, and in your letter you must put it plain and honest that it turns out she cannet be your wife, the first having come back; that ye cannet see her more; and that – ye wish her weel.'

'That won't do. 'Od seize it, I must do a little more than that! I must – though she did always brag about her rich uncle or rich aunt, and her expectations from 'em – I must send a useful sum of money to her, I suppose – just as a little recompense, poor girl. . . . Now, will you help me in this, and draw up an explanation to her of all I've told ye, breaking it as gently as you can? I'm so bad at letters.'

'And I will.'

'Now, I haven't told you quite all yet. My wife Susan has my daughter with her – the baby that was in her arms at the fair; and this girl knows nothing of me beyond that I am some sort of relation by marriage. She has grown up in the belief that the sailor to whom I made over her mother, and who is now dead, was her father, and her mother's husband. What her mother has always felt, she and I together feel now – that we can't proclaim our disgrace to the girl by letting her know the truth. Now what would you do? – I want your advice.'

'I think I'd run the risk, and tell her the truth. She'll forgive ye both.'

'Never!' said Henchard. 'I am not going to let her know the truth. Her mother and I be going to marry again; and it will not only help us to keep our child's respect, but it will be more proper. Susan looks upon herself as the sailor's widow, and won't think o' living with me as formerly without another religious ceremony – and she's right.'

Farfrae thereupon said no more. The letter to the young Jersey woman was carefully framed by him, and the interview ended, Henchard saying, as the Scotchman left, 'I feel it a great relief, Farfrae, to tell some friend o' this! You see now that the Mayor of Casterbridge is not so thriving in his mind as it seems he might be from the state of his pocket.'

'I do. And I'm sorry for ye!' said Farfrae.

When he had gone Henchard copied the letter, and, enclosing a cheque, took it to the post-office, from which he walked back thoughtfully.

'Can it be that it will go off so easily!' he said. 'Poor thing – God knows! Now then, to make amends to Susan!'

CHAPTER THIRTEEN

T HE cottage which Michael Henchard hired for his wife Susan under her name of Newson – in pursuance of their plan – was in the upper or western part of the town, near the Roman wall, and the avenue which overshadowed it. The evening sun seemed to shine more yellowly there than anywhere else this autumn – stretching its rays, as the hours grew later, under the lowest sycamore boughs, and steeping the ground-floor of the dwelling, with its green shutters, in a substratum of radiance which the foliage screened from the upper parts. Beneath these sycamores on the town walls could be seen from the sitting-room the tumuli and earth forts of the distant uplands; making it altogether a pleasant spot, with the usual touch of melancholy that a past-marked prospect lends.

As soon as the mother and daughter were comfortably installed, with a white-aproned servant and all complete, Henchard paid them a visit, and remained to tea. During the entertainment Elizabeth was carefully hoodwinked by the very general tone of the conversation that prevailed – a proceeding which seemed to afford some humour to Henchard, though his wife was not particularly happy in it. The visit was repeated again and again with business-like determination by the Mayor, who seemed to have schooled himself into a course of strict mechanical rightness towards this woman of prior claim, at any expense to the later one and to his own sentiments.

One afternoon the daughter was not indoors when Henchard came, and he said drily, 'This is a very good opportunity for me to ask you to name the happy day, Susan.'

The poor woman smiled faintly; she did not enjoy pleasantries on a situation into which she had entered solely for the sake of her girl's reputation. She liked them so little, indeed, that there was room for wonder why she had countenanced deception at all, and had not bravely let the girl know her history. But the flesh is weak; and the true explanation came in due course.

'O Michael!' she said, 'I am afraid all this is taking up your time and giving trouble – when I did not expect any such thing!' And she looked at him and at his dress as a man of affluence, and at the furniture he had provided for the room – ornate and lavish to her eyes.

'Not at all,' said Henchard, in rough benignity. 'This is only a cottage – it costs me next to nothing. And as to taking up my time' – here his red and black visage kindled with satisfaction – 'I've a splendid fellow to superintend my business now – a man whose like I've never been able to lay hands on before. I shall soon be able to leave everything to him, and have more time to call my own than I've had for these last twenty years.'

Henchard's visits here grew so frequent and so regular that it soon became whispered, and then openly discussed, in Casterbridge that the masterful, coercive Mayor of the town was captured and enervated by the genteel widow Mrs Newson. His well-known haughty indifference to the society of womankind, his silent avoidance of converse with the sex, contributed a piquancy to what would otherwise have been an unromantic matter enough. That such a poor fragile woman should be his choice was inexplicable, except on the ground that the engagement was a family affair in which sentimental passion had no place; for it was known that they were related in some way. Mrs Henchard was so pale that the boys called her 'The Ghost'. Sometimes Henchard overheard this epithet when they passed together along the Walks—as the avenues on the walls were named—at which his face would darken with an expression of destructiveness towards the speakers ominous to see; but he said nothing.

He pressed on the preparations for his union, or rather reunion, with this pale creature in a dogged, unflinching spirit which did credit to his conscientiousness. Nobody would have conceived from his outward demeanour that there was no amatory fire or pulse of romance acting as stimulant to the bustle going on in his gaunt, great house; nothing but three large resolves — one, to make amends to his neglected Susan; another, to provide a comfortable home for Elizabeth-Jane under his paternal eye; and a third, to castigate himself with the thorns which these restitutory acts brought in their train; among them the lowering of his dignity in public opinion by marrying so comparatively humble a woman.

Susan Henchard entered a carriage for the first time in her life when she stepped into the plain brougham which drew up at the door on the wedding-day to take her and Elizabeth-Jane to church. It was a windless morning of warm November rain, which floated down like meal, and lay in a powdery form on the nap of hats and coats. Few people had gathered round the church door though they were well packed within. The Scotchman, who assisted as groomsman, was of course the only one present, beyond the chief actors, who knew the true situation of the contracting parties. He, however, was too inexperienced, too thoughtful, too judicial, too strongly conscious of the serious side of the business, to enter into the scene in its dramatic aspect. That required the special genius of Christopher Coney, Solomon Longways, Buzzford, and their fellows. But they knew nothing of the secret; though, as the time for coming out of church drew on, they gathered on the pavement adjoining, and expounded the subject according to their lights.

' 'Tis five-and-forty years since I had my settlement in this here town,' said Coney; 'but daze me if ever I see a man wait so long before to take so little! There's a chance even for thee after this, Nance Mockridge.' The remark was addressed to a woman who stood behind his shoulder—the same who had exhibited Henchard's bad bread in public when Elizabeth and her mother entered Casterbridge.

'Be cust if I'd marry any such as he, or thee either,' replied that lady. 'As for thee, Christopher, we know what ye be, and the less said the better. And as for he—well, there—(lowering her voice) 'tis said 'a was a poor parish 'prentice—I wouldn't say it for all the world—but 'a was a poor parish 'prentice, that began life wi' no more belonging to 'en than a carrion crow.'

'And now he's worth ever so much a minute,' murmured Longways. 'When a man is said to be worth so much a minute, he's a man to be considered!'

Turning, he saw a circular disc reticulated with creases, and recognized the smiling countenance of the fat woman who had asked for another song at the Three Mariners. 'Well, Mother Cuxsom,' he said, 'how's this? Here's Mrs Newson, a mere skellinton, has got another husband to keep her, while a woman of your tonnage have not.'

'I have not. Nor another to beat me. . . . Ah, yes, Cuxsom's gone, and so shall leather breeches!'

'Yes; with the blessing of God leather breeches shall go.'

' 'Tisn't worth my old while to think of another husband,' continued Mrs Cuxsom. 'And yet I'll lay my life I'm as respectable born as she.'

'True; your mother was a very good woman – I can mind her. She were rewarded by the Agricultural Society for having begot the greatest number of healthy children without parish assistance, and other virtuous marvels.'

' 'Twas that that kept us so low upon ground – that great hungry family.'

'Ay. Where the pigs be many the wash runs thin.'

'And dostn't mind how mother would sing, Christopher?' continued Mrs Cuxsom, kindling at the retrospection; 'and how we went with her to the party at Mellstock, do ye mind? – at old Dame Ledlow's, farmer Shiner's aunt, do ye mind? – she we used to call Toad-skin, because her face were so yaller and freckled, do ye mind?'

'I do, hee-hee, I do!' said Christopher Coney.

'And well do I – for I was getting up husband-high at that time – one-half girl, and t'other half woman, as one may say. And canst mind' – she prodded Solomon's shoulder with her finger-tip, while her eyes twinkled between the crevices of their lids – 'canst mind the sherry-wine, and the zilver-snuffers, and how Joan Dummett was took bad when we were coming home, and Jack Griggs was forced to carry her through the mud; and how 'a let her fall in Dairyman Sweetapple's cow-barton, and we had to clane her gown wi' grass – never such a mess as 'a were in?'

'Ay – that I do – hee-hee, such doggery as there was in them ancient days, to be sure! Ah, the miles I used to walk then; and now I can hardly step over a furrow!'

Their reminiscences were cut short by the appearance of the reunited pair – Henchard looking round upon the idlers with that ambiguous gaze of his, which at one moment seemed to mean satisfaction, and at another fiery disdain.

'Well – there's a difference between 'em, though he do call himself a teetotaller,' said Nance Mockridge. 'She'll wish her cake dough afore she's done of him. There's a bluebeardy look about 'en; and 'twill out in time.'

'Stuff – he's well enough! Some folk want their luck buttered. If I had a choice as wide as the ocean sea I wouldn't wish for a better man. A poor twanking woman like her – 'tis a godsend for her, and hardly a pair of jumps or night-rail to her name.'

The plain little brougham drove off in the mist, and the idlers dispersed. 'Well, we hardly know how to look at things in these times!' said Solomon. 'There was a man dropped down dead yesterday, not so very many miles from here; and what wi' that, and this moist weather, 'tis scarce worth one's while to begin any work o' consequence to-day. I'm in such a low key with drinking nothing but small table ninepenny this last week or two that I shall call and warm up at the Mar'ners as I pass along.'

'I don't know but that I may as well go with 'ee, Solomon,' said Christopher; 'I'm as clammy as a cockle-snail.'

CHAPTER FOURTEEN

A MARTINMAS summer of Mrs Henchard's life set in with her entry into her husband's large house and respectable social orbit; and it was as bright as such summers well can be. Lest she should pine for deeper affection than he could give he made a point of showing some semblance of it in external action. Among other things he had the iron railings, that had smiled sadly in dull rust for the last eighty years, painted a bright green, and the heavy-barred, small-paned Georgian sash windows enlivened with three coats of white. He was as kind to her as a man, mayor, and churchwarden could possibly be. The house was large, the rooms lofty, and the landings wide; and the two unassuming women scarcely made a perceptible addition to its contents.

To Elizabeth-Jane the time was a most triumphant one. The freedom she experienced, the indulgence with which she was treated, went beyond her expectations. The reposeful, easy, affluent life to which her mother's marriage had introduced her was, in truth, the beginning of a great change in Elizabeth. She found she could have nice personal possessions and ornaments for the asking, and, as the mediæval saying puts it, 'Take, have, and keep, are pleasant words.' With peace of mind came development, and with development beauty. Knowledge – the result of great natural insight – she did not lack; learning, accomplishments – those, alas, she had not; but as the winter and spring passed by her thin face and figure filled out in rounder and softer curves; the lines and contractions upon her young brow went away; the muddiness of skin which she had looked upon as her lot by nature departed with a change to abundance of good things, and a bloom came upon her cheek. Perhaps, too, her grey, thoughtful eyes revealed an arch gaiety sometimes; but this was infrequent; the sort of wisdom which looked from their pupils did not readily keep company with these lighter moods. Like all people who have known rough times, light-heartedness seemed to her too irrational and inconsequent to be indulged in except as a reckless dram now and then; for she had been too early habituated to anxious reasoning to drop the habit suddenly. She felt none of those ups and downs of spirit which beset so many people without cause; never – to paraphrase a recent poet – never a gloom in Elizabeth-Jane's soul but she well knew how it came there; and her present cheerfulness was fairly proportionate to her solid guarantees for the same.

It might have been supposed that, given a girl rapidly becoming good-looking, comfortably circumstanced, and for the first time in her life commanding ready money, she would go and make a fool of herself by dress. But no. The reasonableness of almost everything that Elizabeth did was nowhere more conspicuous than in this question of clothes. To keep in the rear of opportunity in matters of indulgence is as valuable a habit as to keep abreast of opportunity in matters of enterprise. This unsophisticated girl did it by an innate perceptiveness that was almost genius. Thus she refrained from bursting out like a water-flower that spring, and clothing herself in puffings and knick-knacks, as most of the Casterbridge girls would have done in her circumstances. Her triumph was tempered by circumspection; she had still that fieldmouse fear of the coulter of destiny despite fair promise, which is common among the thoughtful who have suffered early from poverty and oppression.

'I won't be too gay on any account,' she would say to herself. 'It would be tempting Providence to hurl mother and me down, and afflict us again as He used to do.'

We now see her in a black silk bonnet, velvet mantle or silk spencer, dark dress, and carrying a sunshade. In this latter article she drew the line at fringe, and had it plain edged, with a little ivory ring for keeping it closed. It was odd about the necessity for that sunshade. She discovered that with the clarification of her complexion and the birth of pink cheeks her skin had grown more sensitive to the sun's rays. She protected those cheeks forthwith, deeming spotlessness part of womanliness.

Henchard had become very fond of her, and she went out with him more frequently than with her mother now. Her appearance one day was so attractive that he looked at her critically.

'I happened to have the ribbon by me, so I made it up,' she faltered, thinking him perhaps dissatisfied with some rather bright trimming she had donned for the first time.

'Ay – of course – to be sure,' he replied in his leonine way. 'Do as you like – or rather as your mother advises ye. 'Od send – I've nothing to say to't!'

Indoors she appeared with her hair divided by a parting that arched like a white rainbow from ear to ear. All in front of this line was covered with a thick encampment of curls; all behind was dressed smoothly, and drawn to a knob.

The three members of the family were sitting at breakfast one day, and Henchard was looking silently, as he often did, at this head of hair, which in colour was brown – rather light than dark. 'I thought Elizabeth-Jane's hair – didn't you tell me that Elizabeth-Jane's hair promised to be black when she was a baby?' he said to his wife.

She looked startled, jerked her foot warningly, and murmured, 'Did I?'

As soon as Elizabeth was gone to her own room Henchard resumed. 'Begad, I nearly forgot myself just now! What I meant was that the girl's hair certainly looked as if it would be darker, when she was a baby.'

'It did; but they alter so,' replied Susan.

'Their hair gets darker, I know – but I wasn't aware it lightened ever?'

'O yes.' And the same uneasy expression came out on her face, to which the future held the key. It passed as Henchard went on:

'Well, so much the better. Now, Susan, I want to have her called Miss Henchard – not Miss Newson. Lots o' people do it already in carelessness – it is her legal name – so it may as well be made her usual name – I don't like t'other name at all for my own flesh and blood. I'll advertise it in the Casterbridge paper – that's the way they do it. She won't object.'

'No. O no. But—'

'Well, then, I shall do it,' said he, peremptorily. 'Surely, if she's willing, you must wish it as much as I?'

'O yes – if she agrees let us do it by all means,' she replied.

Then Mrs Henchard acted somewhat inconsistently; it might have been called falsely, but that her manner was emotional and full of the earnestness of one who wishes to do right at great hazard. She went to Elizabeth-Jane, whom she found sewing in her own sitting-room upstairs, and told her what had been proposed about her surname. 'Can you agree – is it not a slight upon Newson – now he's dead and gone?'

Elizabeth reflected. 'I'll think of it, mother,' she answered.

When, later in the day, she saw Henchard, she adverted to the matter at once, in a way which showed that the line of feeling started by her mother had been persevered in. 'Do you wish this change so very much, sir?' she asked.

'Wish it? Why, my blessed fathers, what an ado you women make about a trifle! I proposed it – that's all. Now, 'Lizabeth-Jane, just please yourself. Curse me if I care what you do. Now, you understand, don't 'ee go agreeing to it to please me.'

Here the subject dropped, and nothing more was said, and nothing was done, and Elizabeth still passed as Miss Newson, and not by her legal name.

Meanwhile the great corn and hay traffic conducted by Henchard throve under the management of Donald Farfrae as it had never thriven before. It had formerly moved in jolts; now it went on oiled castors. The old crude *vivâ voce* system of Henchard, in which everything depended upon his memory, and bargains were made by the tongue alone, was swept away. Letters and ledgers took the place of 'I'll do't', and 'you shall hae't'; and, as in all such cases of advance, the rugged picturesqueness of the old method disappeared with its inconveniences.

The position of Elizabeth-Jane's room – rather high in the house, so that it commanded a view of the hay-stores and granaries across the garden – afforded her opportunity for accurate observation of what went on there. She saw that Donald and Mr Henchard were inseparables. When walking together Henchard would lay his arm familiarly on his manager's shoulder, as if Farfrae were a younger brother, bearing so heavily that his slight figure bent under the weight. Occasionally she would hear a perfect cannonade of laughter from Henchard, arising from something Donald had said, the latter looking quite innocent and not laughing at all. In Henchard's somewhat lonely life he evidently found the young man as desirable for comradeship as he was useful for consultations. Donald's brightness of intellect maintained in the corn-factor the admiration it had won at the first hour of their meeting. The poor opinion, and but ill-concealed, that he entertained of the slim Farfrae's physical girth, strength, and dash was more than counterbalanced by the immense respect he had for his brains.

Her quiet eye discerned that Henchard's tigerish affection for the younger man, his constant liking to have Farfrae near him, now and then resulted in a tendency to domineer, which, however, was checked in a moment when Donald exhibited marks of real offence. One day, looking down on their figures from on high, she heard the latter remark, as they stood in the doorway between the garden and yard, that their habit of walking and driving about together rather neutralized Farfrae's value as a second pair of eyes, which should be used in places where the principal was not. ' 'Od damn it,' cried Henchard, 'what's all the world! I like a fellow to talk to. Now come along and hae some supper, and don't take too much thought about things, or ye'll drive me crazy.'

When she walked with her mother, on the other hand, she often beheld the Scotchman looking at them with a curious interest. The fact that he had met her at the Three Mariners was insufficient to account for it, since on the occasions on which she had entered his room he had never raised his eyes. Besides, it was at her mother more particularly than at herself that he looked, to Elizabeth-Jane's half-conscious, simple-minded, perhaps pardonable, disappointment. Thus she could not account for this interest by her own attractiveness, and she decided that it might be apparent only – a way of turning his eyes that Mr Farfrae had.

She did not divine the ample explanation of his manner, without personal vanity, that was afforded by the fact of Donald being the depositary of Henchard's confidence in respect of his past treatment of the pale, chastened mother who walked by her side. Her conjectures on that past never went further than faint ones based on things casually heard and seen – mere guesses that Henchard and her mother might have been lovers in their younger days, who had quarrelled and parted.

Casterbridge, as has been hinted, was a place deposited in the block upon a corn-field. There was no suburb in the modern sense, or transitional intermixture of town and down. It stood, with regard to the wide fertile land adjoining, clean-cut and distinct, like a chess-board on a green table-cloth. The farmer's boy could sit under his barley-mow and pitch a stone into the office-window of the town-clerk; reapers at work among the sheaves nodded to acquaintances standing on the pavement-corner; the red-robed judge, when he condemned a sheep-stealer, pronounced sentence to the tune of Baa, that floated in at the window from the remainder of the flock browsing hard by; and at executions the waiting crowd stood in a meadow immediately before the drop, out of which the cows had been temporarily driven to give the spectators room.

The corn grown on the uplands side of the borough was garnered by farmers who lived in an eastern purlieu called Durnover. Here wheat-ricks overhung the old Roman street, and thrust their eaves against the church tower; green-thatched barns, with doorways as high as the gates of Solomon's temple, opened directly upon the main thoroughfare. Barns indeed were so numerous as to alternate with every half-dozen houses along the way. Here lived burgesses who daily walked the fallow; shepherds in an intra-mural squeeze. A street of farmers' homesteads – a street ruled by a mayor and corporation, yet echoing with the thump of the flail, the flutter of the winnowing-fan, and the purr of the milk into the pails – a street which had nothing urban in it whatever – this was the Durnover end of Casterbridge.

Henchard, as was natural, dealt largely with this nursery or bed of small farmers close at hand – and his waggons were often down that way. One day, when arrangements were in progress for getting home corn from one of the aforesaid farms, Elizabeth-Jane received a note by hand, asking her to oblige the writer by coming at once to a granary on Durnover Hill. As this was the granary whose contents Henchard was removing, she thought the request had something to do with his business, and proceeded thither as soon as she had put on her bonnet. The granary was just within the farm-yard, and stood on stone staddles, high enough for persons to walk under. The gates were open, but nobody was within. However, she entered and waited. Presently she saw a figure approaching the gate – that of Donald Farfrae. He looked up at the church clock, and came in. By some unaccountable shyness, some wish not to meet him there alone, she quickly ascended the step-ladder leading to the granary door, and entered it before he had seen her. Farfrae advanced, imagining himself in solitude; and a few drops of rain beginning to fall he moved and stood under the shelter where she had just been standing. Here he leant against one of the staddles, and gave himself up to patience. He, too, was plainly expecting some one; could it be herself? if so, why? In a few minutes he looked at his watch, and then pulled out a note, a duplicate of the one she had herself received.

The situation began to be very awkward, and the longer she waited the more awkward it became. To emerge from a door just above his head and descend the ladder, and show she had been in hiding there, would look so very foolish that she still waited on. A winnowing machine stood close beside her, and to relieve her suspense she gently moved the handle; whereupon a cloud of wheat husks flew out into her face, and covered her clothes and bonnet, and stuck into the fur of her victorine. He must have heard the slight movement for he looked up, and then ascended the steps.

'Ah – it's Miss Newson,' he said as soon as he could see into the granary. 'I didn't know you were there. I have kept the appointment, and am at your service.'

'O Mr Farfrae,' she faltered; 'so have I. But I didn't know it was you who wished to see me, otherwise I—'

'I wished to see you? O no – at least, that is, I am afraid there may be a mistake.'

'Didn't you ask me to come here? Didn't you write this?' Elizabeth held out her note.

'No. Indeed, at no hand would I have thought of it! And for you – didn't you ask me? This is not your writing?' And he held up his.

'By no means.'

'And is that really so! Then it's somebody wanting to see us both. Perhaps we would do well to wait a little longer.'

Acting on this consideration they lingered, Elizabeth-Jane's face being arranged to an expression of preternatural composure, and the young Scot, at every footstep in the street without, looking from under the granary to see if the passer were about to enter and declare himself their summoner. They watched individual drops of rain creeping down the thatch of the opposite rick – straw after straw – till they reached the bottom; but nobody came, and the granary roof began to drip.

'The person is not likely to be coming,' said Farfrae. 'It's a trick perhaps, and if so, it's a great pity to waste our time like this, and so much to be done.'

' 'Tis a great liberty,' said Elizabeth.

'It's true, Miss Newson. We'll hear news of this some day, depend on't, and who it was that did it. I wouldn't stand for it hindering myself; but you, Miss Newson—'

'I don't mind – much,' she replied.

'Neither do I.'

They lapsed again into silence. 'You are anxious to get back to Scotland, I suppose, Mr Farfrae?' she inquired.

'O no, Miss Newson. Why would I be?'

'I only supposed you might be from the song you sang at the Three Mariners – about Scotland and home, I mean – which you seemed to feel so deep down in your heart; so that we all felt for you.'

'Ay – and I did sing there – I did – But, Miss Newson' – and Donald's voice musically undulated between two semitones, as it always did when he became earnest – 'it's well you feel a song for a few minutes, and your eyes they get quite tearful; but you finish it, and for all you felt you don't mind it or think of it again for a long while. O no, I don't want to go back! Yet I'll sing the song to you wi' pleasure whenever you like. I could sing it now, and not mind at all?'

'Thank you, indeed. But I fear I must go – rain or no.'

'Ay! Then, Miss Newson, ye had better say nothing about this hoax, and take no heed of it. And if the person should say anything to you, be civil to him or her, as if you did not mind it – so you'll take the clever person's laugh away.' In speaking his eyes became fixed upon her dress, still sown with wheat husks. 'There's husks and dust on you. Perhaps you don't know it?' he said, in tones of extreme delicacy. 'And it's very bad to let rain come upon clothes when there's chaff on them. It washes in and spoils them. Let me help you – blowing is the best.'

As Elizabeth neither assented nor dissented Donald Farfrae began blowing her back hair, and her side hair, and her neck, and the crown of her bonnet, and the fur of her victorine, Elizabeth saying, 'O, thank you,' at every puff. At last she was fairly clean, though Farfrae, having got over his first concern at the situation, seemed in no manner of hurry to be gone.

'Ah – now I'll go and get ye an umbrella,' he said.

She declined the offer, stepped out and was gone. Farfrae walked slowly after, looking thoughtfully at her diminishing figure, and whistling in undertones, 'As I came down through Cannobie'.

CHAPTER FIFTEEN

A T first Miss Newson's budding beauty was not regarded with much interest by anybody in Casterbridge. Donald Farfrae's gaze, it is true, was now attracted by the Mayor's so-called step-daughter, but he was only one. The truth is that she was but a poor illustrative instance of the prophet Baruch's sly definition: 'The virgin that loveth to go gay'.

When she walked abroad she seemed to be occupied with an inner chamber of ideas, and to have slight need for visible objects. She formed curious resolves on checking gay fancies in the matter of clothes, because it was inconsistent with her past life to blossom gaudily the moment she had become possessed of money. But nothing is more insidious than the evolution of wishes from mere fancies, and of wants from mere wishes. Henchard gave Elizabeth-Jane a box of delicately-tinted gloves one spring day. She wanted to wear them to show her appreciation of his kindness, but she had no bonnet that would harmonize. As an artistic indulgence she thought she would have such a bonnet. When she had a bonnet that would go with the gloves she had no dress that would go with the bonnet. It was now absolutely necessary to finish; she ordered the requisite article, and found that she had no sunshade to go with the dress. In for a penny in for a pound; she bought the sunshade, and the whole structure was at last complete.

Everybody was attracted, and some said that her bygone simplicity was the art that conceals art, the 'delicate imposition' of Rochefoucauld; she had produced an effect, a contrast, and it had been done on purpose. As a matter of fact this was not true, but it had its result; for as soon as Casterbridge thought her artful it thought her worth notice. 'It is the first time in my life that I have been so much admired,' she said to herself; 'though perhaps it is by those whose admiration is not worth having.'

But Donald Farfrae admired her, too; and altogether the time was an exciting one; sex had never before asserted itself in her so strongly, for in former days she had perhaps been too impersonally human to be distinctively feminine. After an unprecedented success one day she came indoors, went upstairs, and leant upon her bed face downwards, quite forgetting the possible creasing and damage. 'Good Heaven,' she whispered, 'can it be? Here am I setting up as the town beauty!'

When she had thought it over, her usual fear of exaggerating appearances engendered a deep sadness. 'There is something wrong in all this,' she mused. 'If they only knew what an unfinished girl I am – that I can't talk Italian, or use globes, or show any of the accomplishments they learn at boarding-schools, how they would despise me! Better sell all this finery and buy myself grammar-books and dictionaries and a history of all the philosophies!'

She looked from the window and saw Henchard and Farfrae in the hay-yard talking, with that impetuous cordiality on the Mayor's part, and genial modesty on the younger man's, that was now so generally observable in their intercourse. Friendship between man and man; what a rugged strength there was in it, as evinced by these two. And yet the seed that was to lift the foundation of this friendship was at that moment taking root in a chink of its structure.

It was about six o'clock; the men were dropping off homeward one by one. The last to leave was a round shouldered, blinking young man of nineteen or twenty, whose mouth fell ajar on the slightest provocation, seemingly because there was no chin to support it. Henchard called aloud to him as he went out of the gate. 'Here – Abel Whittle!'

Whittle turned, and ran back a few steps. 'Yes, sir,' he said, in breathless deprecation, as if he knew what was coming next.

'Once more – be in time to-morrow morning. You see what's to be done, and you hear what I say, and you know I'm not going to be trifled with any longer.'

'Yes, sir.' Then Abel Whittle left, and Henchard and Farfrae; and Elizabeth saw no more of them.

Now there was good reason for this command on Henchard's part. Poor Abel, as he was called, had an inveterate habit of over-sleeping himself and coming late to his work. His anxious will was to be among the earliest; but if his comrades omitted to pull the string that he always tied round his great toe and left hanging out of the window for that purpose, his will was as wind. He did not arrive in time.

As he was often second hand at the hay-weighing, or at the crane which lifted the sacks, or was one of those who had to accompany the waggons into the country to fetch away stacks that had been purchased, this affliction of Abel's was productive of much inconvenience. For two mornings in the present week he had kept the others waiting nearly an hour; hence Henchard's threat. It now remained to be seen what would happen to-morrow.

Six o'clock struck, and there was no Whittle. At half-past six Henchard entered the yard; the waggon was horsed that Abel was to accompany; and the other man had been waiting twenty minutes. Then Henchard swore, and Whittle coming up breathless at that instant, the corn-factor turned on him, and declared with an oath that this was the last time; that if he were behind once more, by God, he would come and drag him out o' bed.

'There is sommit wrong in my make, your worshipful!' said Abel, 'especially in the inside, whereas my poor dumb brain gets as dead as a clot afore I've said my few scrags of prayers. Yes – it came on as a stripling, just afore I'd got man's wages, whereas I never enjoy my bed at all, for no sooner do I lie down than I be asleep, and afore I be awake I be up. I've fretted my gizzard green about it, maister, but what can I do? Now last night, afore I went to bed, I only had a scantling o' cheese and—'

'I don't want to hear it!' roared Henchard. 'To-morrow the waggons must start at four, and if you're not here, stand clear. I'll mortify thy flesh for thee!'

'But let me clear up my points, your worshipful—'

Henchard turned away.

'He asked me and he questioned me, and then 'a wouldn't hear my points!' said Abel, to the yard in general. 'Now, I shall twitch like a moment-hand all night to-night for fear o' him!'

The journey to be taken by the waggons next day was a long one into Blackmoor Vale, and at four o'clock lanterns were moving about the yard. But Abel was missing. Before either of the other men could run to Abel's and warn him, Henchard appeared in the garden doorway. 'Where's Abel Whittle? Not come after all I've said? Now I'll carry out my word, by my blessed fathers – nothing else will do him any good! I'm going up that way.'

Henchard went off, entered Abel's house, a little cottage in Back Street, the door of which was never locked because the inmates had nothing to lose. Reaching Whittle's bedside the corn-factor shouted a bass note so vigorously that Abel started up instantly, and beholding Henchard standing over him, was galvanized into spasmodic movements which had not much relation to getting on his clothes.

'Out of bed, sir, and off to the granary, or you leave my employ to-day! 'Tis to teach ye a lesson. March on; never mind your breeches!'

The unhappy Whittle threw on his sleeve waistcoat, and managed to get into his boots at the bottom of the stairs, while Henchard thrust his hat over his head. Whittle then trotted on down Back Street, Henchard walking sternly behind.

Just at this time Farfrae, who had been to Henchard's house to look for him, came out of the back gate, and saw something white fluttering in the morning gloom, which he soon perceived to be the part of Abel's shirt that showed below his waistcoat.

'For maircy's sake, what object's this?' said Farfrae, following Abel into the yard, Henchard being some way in the rear by this time.

'Ye see, Mr Farfrae,' gibbered Abel with a resigned smile of terror, 'he said he'd mortify my flesh if so be I didn't get up sooner, and now he's a-doing on't! Ye see it can't be helped, Mr Farfrae; things do happen queer sometimes! Yes — I'll go to Blackmoor Vale half naked as I be, since he do command; but I shall kill myself afterwards; I can't outlive the disgrace; for the women-folk will be looking out of their winders at my mortification all the way along, and laughing me to scorn as a man 'ithout breeches! You know how I feel such things, Maister Farfrae, and how forlorn thoughts get hold upon me. Yes — I shall do myself harm — I feel it coming on!'

'Get back home, and slip on your breeches, and come to wark like a man! If ye go not, you'll ha'e your death standing there!'

'I'm afeard I mustn't! Mr Henchard said—'

'I don't care what Mr Henchard said, nor anybody else! 'Tis simple foolishness to do this. Go and dress yourself instantly, Whittle.'

'Hullo, hullo!' said Henchard, coming up behind. 'Who's sending him back?'

All the men looked toward Farfrae.

'I am,' said Donald. 'I say this joke has been carried far enough.'

'And I say it hasn't! Get up in the waggon, Whittle.'

'Not if I am manager,' said Farfrae. 'He either goes home, or I march out of this yard for good.'

Henchard looked at him with a face stern and red. But he paused for a moment, and their eyes met. Donald went up to him, for he saw in Henchard's look that he began to regret this.

'Come,' said Donald quietly, 'a man o' your position should ken better, sir! It is tyrannical and no worthy of you.'

''Tis not tyrannical!' murmured Henchard, like a sullen boy. 'It is to make him remember!' He presently added, in a tone of one bitterly hurt: 'Why did you speak to me before them like that, Farfrae? You might have stopped till we were alone. Ah — I know why! I've told ye the secret o' my life — fool that I was to do't — and you take advantage of me!'

'I had forgot it,' said Farfrae simply.

Henchard looked on the ground, said nothing more, and turned away. During the day Farfrae learnt from the men that Henchard had kept Abel's old mother in coals and snuff all the previous winter, which made him less antagonistic to the corn-factor. But Henchard continued moody and silent, and when one of the men inquired of him if some oats should be hoisted to an upper floor or not, he said shortly, 'Ask Mr Farfrae. He's master here!'

Morally he was; there could be no doubt of it. Henchard, who had hitherto been the most admired man in his circle, was the most admired no longer. One day the daughters of a deceased farmer in Durnover wanted an opinion on the value of their haystack, and sent a messenger to ask Mr Farfrae to oblige them with one. The messenger, who was a child, met in the yard not Farfrae, but Henchard.

'Very well,' he said. 'I'll come.'

'But please will Mr Farfrae come?' said the child.

'I am going that way. . . . Why Mr Farfrae?' said Henchard, with the fixed look of thought. 'Why do people always want Mr Farfrae?'

'I suppose because they like him so – that's what they say.'

'Oh – I see – that's what they say – hey? They like him because he's cleverer than Mr Henchard, and because he knows more; and in short, Mr Henchard can't hold a candle to him – hey?'

'Yes – that's just it, sir – some of it.'

'Oh, there's more? Of course there's more! What besides? Come, here's sixpence for a fairing.'

'"And he's better-tempered, and Henchard's a fool to him," they say. And when some of the women were a-walking home they said, "He's a diment – he's a chap o' wax – he's the best – he's the horse for my money," says they. And they said, "He's the most understanding man o' them two by long chalks. I wish he was the master instead of Henchard," they said.'

'They'll talk any nonsense,' Henchard replied with covered gloom. 'Well, you can go now. And *I* am coming to value the hay, d'ye hear? – I.' The boy departed, and Henchard murmured, 'Wish he were master here, do they?'

He went towards Durnover. On his way he overtook Farfrae. They walked on together, Henchard looking mostly on the ground.

'You're no yoursel' the day?' Donald inquired.

'Yes, I am very well,' said Henchard.

'But ye are a bit down – surely ye are down? Why, there's nothing to be angry about! 'Tis splendid stuff that we've got from Blackmoor Vale. By the by, the people in Durnover want their hay valued.'

'Yes. I am going there.'

'I'll go with ye.'

As Henchard did not reply Donald practised a piece of music *sotto voce*, till, getting near the bereaved people's door, he stopped himself with –

'Ah, as their father is dead I won't go on with such as that. How could I forget?'

'Do you care so very much about hurting folks' feelings?' observed Henchard with a half sneer. 'You do, I know – especially mine!'

'I am sorry if I have hurt yours, sir,' replied Donald, standing still, with a second expression of the same sentiment in the regretfulness of his face. 'Why should you say it – think it?'

The cloud lifted from Henchard's brow, and as Donald finished the corn-merchant turned to him, regarding his breast rather than his face.

'I have been hearing things that vexed me,' he said. ' 'Twas that made me short in my manner – made me overlook what you really are. Now, I don't want to go in here about this hay – Farfrae, you can do it better than I. They sent for 'ee, too. I have to attend a meeting of the Town Council at eleven, and 'tis drawing on for't.'

They parted thus in renewed friendship, Donald forbearing to ask Henchard for meanings that were not very plain to him. On Henchard's part there was now again repose; and yet, whenever he thought of Farfrae, it was with a dim dread; and he often regretted that he had told the young man his whole heart, and confided to him the secrets of his life.

CHAPTER SIXTEEN

ON this account Henchard's manner towards Farfrae insensibly became more reserved. He was courteous – too courteous – and Farfrae was quite surprised at the good breeding which now for the first time showed itself among the qualities of a man he had hitherto thought undisciplined, if warm and sincere. The corn-factor seldom or never again put his arm upon the young man's shoulder so as to nearly weigh him down with the pressure of mechanized friendship. He left off coming to Donald's lodgings and shouting into the passage, 'Hoy, Farfrae, boy, come and have some dinner with us! Don't sit here in solitary confinement!' But in the daily routine of their business there was little change.

Thus their lives rolled on till a day of public rejoicing was suggested to the country at large in celebration of a national event that had recently taken place.

For some time Casterbridge, by nature slow, made no response. Then one day Donald Farfrae broached the subject to Henchard by asking if he would have any objection to lend some rick-cloths to himself and a few others, who contemplated getting up an entertainment of some sort on the day named, and required a shelter for the same, to which they might charge admission at the rate of so much a head.

'Have as many cloths as you like,' Henchard replied.

When his manager had gone about the business Henchard was fired with emulation. It certainly had been very remiss of him, as Mayor, he thought, to call no meeting ere this, to discuss what should be done on this holiday. But Farfrae had been so cursed quick in his movements as to give old-fashioned people in authority no chance of the initiative. However, it was not too late; and on second thoughts he determined to take upon his own shoulders the responsibility of organizing some amusements, if the other Councilmen would leave the matter in his hands. To this they quite readily agreed, the majority being fine old crusted characters who had a decided taste for living without worry.

So Henchard set about his preparations for a really brilliant thing – such as should be worthy of the venerable town. As for Farfrae's little affair, Henchard nearly forgot it; except once now and then when, on it coming into his mind, he said to himself, 'Charge admission at so much a head – just like a Scotchman! – who is going to pay anything a head?' The diversions which the Mayor intended to provide were to be entirely free.

He had grown so dependent upon Donald that he could scarcely resist calling him in to consult. But by sheer self-coercion he refrained. No, he thought, Farfrae would be suggesting such improvements in his damned luminous way that in spite of himself he, Henchard, would sink to the position of second fiddle, and only scrape harmonies to his manager's talents.

Everybody applauded the Mayor's proposed entertainment, especially when it became known that he meant to pay for it all himself.

Close to the town was an elevated green spot surrounded by an ancient square earthwork — earthworks square, and not square, were as common as blackberries hereabout — a spot whereon the Casterbridge people usually held any kind of merry-making, meeting, or sheep-fair that required more space than the streets would afford. On one side it sloped to the river Froom, and from any point a view was obtained of the country round for many miles. This pleasant upland was to be the scene of Henchard's exploit.

He advertised about the town, in long posters of a pink colour, that games of all sorts would take place here; and set to work a little battalion of men under his own eye. They erected greasy-poles for climbing, with smoked hams and local cheeses at the top. They placed hurdles in rows for jumping over; across the river they laid a slippery pole, with a live pig of the neighbourhood tied at the other end, to become the property of the man who could walk over and get it. There were also provided wheelbarrows for racing, donkeys for the same, a stage for boxing, wrestling, and drawing blood generally; sacks for jumping in. Moreover, not forgetting his principles, Henchard provided a mammoth tea, of which everybody who lived in the borough was invited to partake without payment. The tables were laid parallel with the inner slope of the rampart, and awnings were stretched overhead.

Passing to and fro the Mayor beheld the unattractive exterior of Farfrae's erection in the West Walk, rick-cloths of different sizes and colours being hung up to the arching trees without any regard to appearance. He was easy in his mind now, for his own preparations far transcended these.

The morning came. The sky, which had been remarkably clear down to within a day or two, was overcast, and the weather threatening, the wind having an unmistakable hint of water in it. Henchard wished he had not been quite so sure about the continuance of a fair season. But it was too late to modify or postpone, and the proceedings went on. At twelve o'clock the rain began to fall, small and steady, commencing and increasing so insensibly that it was difficult to state exactly when dry weather ended or wet established itself. In an hour the slight moisture resolved itself into a monotonous smiting of earth by heaven, in torrents to which no end could be prognosticated.

A number of people had heroically gathered in the field, but by three o'clock Henchard discerned that his project was doomed to end in failure. The hams at the top of the poles dripped watered smoke in the form of a brown liquor, the pig shivered in the wind, the grain of the deal tables showed through the sticking tablecloths, for the awning allowed the rain to drift under at its will, and to enclose the sides at this hour seemed a useless undertaking. The landscape over the river disappeared; the wind played on the tentcords in Æolian improvisations; and at length rose to such a pitch that the whole erection slanted to the ground, those who had taken shelter within it having to crawl out on their hands and knees.

But towards six the storm abated, and a drier breeze shook the moisture from the grass bents. It seemed possible to carry out the programme after all. The awning was set up again; the band was called out from its shelter, and ordered to begin, and where the tables had stood a place was cleared for dancing.

'But where are the folk?' said Henchard, after the lapse of half-an-hour, during which time only two men and a woman had stood up to dance. 'The shops are all shut. Why don't they come?'

'They are at Farfrae's affair in the West Walk,' answered a Council-man who stood in the field with the Mayor.

'A few, I suppose. But where are the body o' 'em?'

'All out of doors are there.'

'Then the more fools they!'

Henchard walked away moodily. One or two young fellows gallantly came to climb the poles, to save the hams from being wasted; but as there were no spectators, and the whole scene presented the most melancholy appearance, Henchard gave orders that the proceedings were to be suspended, and the entertainment closed, the food to be distributed among the poor people of the town. In a short time nothing was left in the field but a few hurdles, the tents, and the poles.

Henchard returned to his house, had tea with his wife and daughter, and then walked out. It was now dusk. He soon saw that the tendency of all promenaders was towards a particular spot in the Walks, and eventually proceeded thither himself. The notes of a stringed band came from the enclosure that Farfrae had erected – the pavilion as he called it – and when the Mayor reached it he perceived that a gigantic tent had been ingeniously constructed without poles or ropes. The densest point of the avenue of sycamores had been selected, where the boughs made a closely interlaced vault overhead; to these boughs the canvas had been hung, and a barrel roof was the result. The end towards the wind was enclosed, the other end was open. Henchard went round and saw the interior.

In form it was like the nave of a cathedral with one gable removed, but the scene within was anything but devotional. A reel or fling of some sort was in progress; and the usually sedate Farfrae was in the midst of the other dancers in the costume of a wild Highlander, flinging himself about and spinning to the tune. For a moment Henchard could not help laughing. Then he perceived the immense admiration for the Scotchman that revealed itself in the women's faces; and when this exhibition was over, and a new dance proposed, and Donald had disappeared for a time to return in his natural garments, he had an unlimited choice of partners, every girl being in a coming-on disposition towards one who so thoroughly understood the poetry of motion as he.

All the town crowded to the Walk, such a delightful idea of a ballroom never having occurred to the inhabitants before. Among the rest of the onlookers were Elizabeth and her mother – the former thoughtful yet much interested, her eyes beaming with a longing lingering light, as if Nature had been advised by Correggio in their creation. The dancing progressed with unabated spirit, and Henchard walked and waited till his wife should be disposed to go home. He did not care to keep in the light, and when he went into the dark it was worse, for there he heard remarks of a kind which were becoming too frequent:

'Mr Henchard's rejoicings couldn't say good morning to this,' said one. 'A man must be a headstrong stunpoll to think folk would go up to that bleak place to-day.'

The other answered that people said it was not only in such things as those that the Mayor was wanting. 'Where would his business be if it were not for this young fellow? 'Twas verily Fortune sent him to Henchard. His accounts were like a bramblewood when Mr Farfrae came. He used to reckon his sacks by chalk strokes all in a row like garden-palings, measure his ricks by stretching with his arms, weigh his trusses by a lift, judge his hay by a chaw, and settle the price with a curse. But now this accomplished young man does it all by ciphering and mensuration. Then the wheat – that sometimes used to taste so strong o' mice when made into bread that people could fairly tell the breed – Farfrae has a plan for purifying, so that nobody would dream the smallest four-legged beast had walked over it once. O yes, everybody is full of him, and the care Mr Henchard has to keep him, to be sure!' concluded this gentleman.

'But he won't do it for long, good-now,' said the other.

'No!' said Henchard to himself behind the tree. 'Or if he do, he'll be honeycombed clean out of all the character and standing that he's built up in these eighteen year!'

He went back to the dancing pavilion. Farfrae was footing a quaint little dance with Elizabeth-Jane – an old country thing, the only one she knew, and though he considerately toned down his movements to suit her demurer gait, the pattern of the shining little nails in the soles of his boots became familiar to the eyes of every bystander. The tune had enticed her into it; being a tune of a busy, vaulting, leaping sort – some low notes on the silver string of each fiddle, then a skipping on the small, like running up and down ladders – 'Miss M'Leod of Ayr' was its name, so Mr Farfrae had said, and that it was very popular in his own country.

It was soon over, and the girl looked at Henchard for approval; but he did not give it. He seemed not to see her. 'Look here, Farfrae,' he said, like one whose mind was elsewhere, 'I'll go to Port-Bredy Great Market to-morrow myself. You can stay and put things right in your clothes-box, and recover strength to your knees after your vagaries.' He planted on Donald an antagonistic glare that had begun as a smile.

Some other townsmen came up, and Donald drew aside. 'What's this, Henchard,' said Alderman Tubber, applying his thumb to the corn-factor like a cheese-taster. 'An opposition randy to yours, eh? Jack's as good as his master, eh? Cut ye out quite, hasn't he?'

'You see, Mr Henchard,' said the lawyer, another good-natured friend, 'where you made the mistake was in going so far afield. You should have taken a leaf out of his book, and have had your sports in a sheltered place like this. But you didn't think of it, you see; and he did, and that's where he's beat you.'

'He'll be top-sawyer soon of you two, and carry all afore him,' added jocular Mr Tubber.

'No,' said Henchard gloomily. 'He won't be that, because he's shortly going to leave me.' He looked towards Donald, who had again come near. 'Mr Farfrae's time as my manager is drawing to a close – isn't it, Farfrae?'

The young man, who could now read the lines and folds of Henchard's strongly-traced face as if they were clear verbal inscriptions, quietly assented; and when people deplored the fact, and asked why it was, he simply replied that Mr Henchard no longer required his help.

Henchard went home, apparently satisfied. But in the morning, when his jealous temper had passed away, his heart sank within him at what he had said and done. He was the more disturbed when he found that this time Farfrae was determined to take him at his word.

CHAPTER SEVENTEEN

ELIZABETH-JANE had perceived from Henchard's manner that in assenting to dance she had made a mistake of some kind. In her simplicity she did not know what it was till a hint from a nodding acquaintance enlightened her. As the Mayor's step-daughter, she learnt, she had not been quite in her place in treading a measure amid such a mixed throng as filled the dancing pavilion.

Thereupon her ears, cheeks, and chin glowed like live coals at the dawning of the idea that her tastes were not good enough for her position, and would bring her into disgrace.

This made her very miserable, and she looked about for her mother; but Mrs Henchard, who had less idea of conventionality than Elizabeth herself, had gone away, leaving her daughter to return at her own pleasure. The latter moved on into the dark dense old avenues, or rather vaults of living woodwork, which ran along the town boundary, and stood reflecting.

A man followed in a few minutes, and her face being towards the shine from the tent he recognized her. It was Farfrae — just come from the dialogue with Henchard which had signified his dismissal.

'And it's you, Miss Newson? — and I've been looking for ye everywhere!' he said, overcoming a sadness imparted by the estrangement with the corn-merchant. 'May I walk on with you as far as your street-corner?'

She thought there might be something wrong in this, but did not utter any objection. So together they went on, first down the West Walk, and then into the Bowling Walk, till Farfrae said, 'It's like that I'm going to leave you soon.'

She faltered 'Why?'

'Oh — as a mere matter of business — nothing more. But we'll not concern ourselves about it — it is for the best. I hoped to have another dance with you.'

She said she could not dance — in any proper way.

'Nay, but you do! It's the feeling for it rather than the learning of steps that makes pleasant dancers. . . . I fear I offend your father by getting up this! And now, perhaps, I'll have to go to another part o' the warrld altogether!'

This seemed such a melancholy prospect that Elizabeth-Jane breathed a sigh — letting it off in fragments that he might not hear her. But darkness makes people truthful, and the Scotchman went on impulsively — perhaps he had heard her after all:

'I wish I was richer, Miss Newson; and your stepfather had not been offended; I would ask you something in a short time — yes, I would ask you to-night. But that's not for me!'

What he would have asked her he did not say, and instead of encouraging him she remained incompetently silent. Thus afraid one of another they continued their promenade along the walls till they got near the bottom of the Bowling Walk; twenty steps further and the trees would end, and the street-corner and lamps appear. In consciousness of this they stopped.

'I never found out who it was that sent us to Durnover granary on a fool's errand that day,' said Donald, in his undulating tones. 'Did ye ever know yourself, Miss Newson?'

'Never,' said she.

'I wonder why they did it!'

'For fun, perhaps.'

'Perhaps it was not for fun. It might have been that they thought they would like us to stay waiting there, talking to one another? Ay, well! I hope you Casterbridge folk will not forget me if I go.'

'That I'm sure we won't!' she said earnestly. 'I — wish you wouldn't go at all.'

They had got into the lamplight. 'Now, I'll think over that,' said Donald Farfrae. 'And I'll not come up to your door; but part from you here; lest it make your father more angry still.'

They parted, Farfrae returning into the dark Bowling Walk, and Elizabeth-Jane going up the street. Without any consciousness of what she was doing she started running with all her might till she reached her father's door. 'O dear me — what am I at?' she thought, as she pulled up breathless.

Indoors she fell to conjecturing the meaning of Farfrae's enigmatic words about not daring to ask her what he fain would. Elizabeth, that silent observing woman, had long noted how he was rising in favour among the townspeople; and knowing Henchard's nature now she had feared that Farfrae's days as manager were numbered; so that the announcement gave her little surprise. Would Mr Farfrae stay in Casterbridge despite his words and her father's dismissal? His occult breathings to her might be solvable by his course in that respect.

The next day was windy — so windy that walking in the garden she picked up a portion of the draft of a letter on business in Donald Farfrae's writing, which had flown over the wall from the office. The useless scrap she took indoors, and began to copy the caligraphy, which she much admired. The letter began 'Dear Sir', and presently writing on a loose slip 'Elizabeth-Jane', she laid the latter over 'Sir', making the phrase 'Dear Elizabeth-Jane'. When she saw the effect a quick red ran up her face and warmed her through, though nobody was there to see what she had done. She quickly tore up the slip, and threw it away. After this she grew cool and laughed at herself, walked about the room, and laughed again; not joyfully, but distressfully rather.

It was quickly known in Casterbridge that Farfrae and Henchard had decided to dispense with each other. Elizabeth-Jane's anxiety to know if Farfrae were going away from the town reached a pitch that disturbed her, for she could no longer conceal from herself the cause. At length the news reached her that he was not going to leave the place. A man following the same trade as Henchard, but on a very small scale, had sold his business to Farfrae, who was forthwith about to start as corn and hay merchant on his own account.

Her heart fluttered when she heard of this step of Donald's, proving that he meant to remain; and yet, would a man who cared one little bit for her have endangered his suit by setting up a business in opposition to Mr Henchard's? Surely not; and it must have been a passing impulse only which had led him to address her so softly.

To solve the problem whether her appearance on the evening of the dance were such as to inspire a fleeting love at first sight, she dressed herself up exactly as she had dressed then – the muslin, the spencer, the sandals, the parasol – and looked in the mirror. The picture glassed back was, in her opinion, precisely of such a kind as to inspire that fleeting regard, and no more – 'just enough to make him silly, and not enough to keep him so,' she said luminously; and Elizabeth thought, in a much lower key, that by this time he had discovered how plain and homely was the informing spirit of that pretty outside.

Hence, when she felt her heart going out to him, she would say to herself with a mock pleasantry that carried an ache with it, 'No, no, Elizabeth-Jane – such dreams are not for you!' She tried to prevent herself from seeing him, and thinking of him; succeeding fairly well in the former attempt, in the latter not so completely.

Henchard, who had been hurt at finding that Farfrae did not mean to put up with his temper any longer, was incensed beyond measure when he learnt what the young man had done as an alternative. It was in the town-hall, after a council meeting, that he first became aware of Farfrae's *coup* for establishing himself independently in the town; and his voice might have been heard as far as the town-pump expressing his feelings to his fellow councilmen. Those tones showed that, though under a long reign of self-control he had become Mayor and churchwarden and what not, there was still the same unruly volcanic stuff beneath the rind of Michael Henchard as when he had sold his wife at Weydon Fair.

'Well, he's a friend of mine, and I'm a friend of his – or if we are not, what are we? 'Od send, if I've not been his friend, who has, I should like to know? Didn't he come here without a sound shoe to his voot? Didn't I keep him here –help him to a living? Didn't I help him to money, or whatever he wanted? I stuck out for no terms – I said "Name your own price." I'd have shared my last crust with that young fellow at one time, I liked him so well. And now he's defied me! But damn him, I'll have a tussle with him now – at fair buying and selling, mind – at fair buying and selling! And if I can't overbid such a stripling as he, then I'm not wo'th a varden! We'll show that we know our business as well as one here and there!'

His friends of the Corporation did not specially respond. Henchard was less popular now than he had been when, nearly two years before, they had voted him to the chief magistracy on account of his amazing energy. While they had collectively profited by this quality of the corn-factor's they had been made to wince individually on more than one occasion. So he went out of the hall and down the street alone.

Reaching home he seemed to recollect something with a sour satisfaction. He called Elizabeth-Jane. Seeing how he looked when she entered she appeared alarmed.

'Nothing to find fault,' he said, observing her concern. 'Only I want to caution you, my dear. That man, Farfrae – it is about him. I've seen him talking to you two or three times – he danced with 'ee at the rejoicings, and came home with 'ee. Now, now, no blame to you. But just hearken: Have you made him any foolish promise? Gone the least bit beyond sniff and snaff at all?'

'No. I have promised him nothing.'

'Good. All's well that ends well. I particularly wish you not to see him again.'

'Very well, sir.'

'You promise?'

She hesitated for a moment, and then said —

'Yes, if you much wish it.'

'I do. He's an enemy to our house!'

When she had gone he sat down, and wrote in a heavy hand to Farfrae thus: —

Sir, — I make request that henceforth you and my step-daughter be as strangers to each other. She on her part has promised to welcome no more addresses from you; and I trust, therefore, you will not attempt to force them upon her.

M. Henchard

One would almost have supposed Henchard to have had policy to see that no better *modus vivendi* could be arrived at with Farfrae than by encouraging him to become his son-in-law. But such a scheme for buying over a rival had nothing to recommend it to the Mayor's headstrong faculties. With all domestic *finesse* of that kind he was hopelessly at variance. Loving a man or hating him, his diplomacy was as wrongheaded as a buffalo's; and his wife had not ventured to suggest the course which she, for many reasons, would have welcomed gladly.

Meanwhile Donald Farfrae had opened the gates of commerce on his own account at a spot on Durnover Hill — as far as possible from Henchard's stores, and with every intention of keeping clear of his former friend and employer's customers. There was, it seemed to the younger man, room for both of them and to spare. The town was small, but the corn and hay-trade was proportionately large, and with his native sagacity he saw opportunity for a share of it.

So determined was he to do nothing which should seem like trade-antagonism to the Mayor that he refused his first customer — a large farmer of good repute — because Henchard and this man had dealt together within the preceding three months.

'He was once my friend,' said Farfrae, 'and it's not for me to take business from him. I am sorry to disappoint you, but I cannot hurt the trade of a man who's been so kind to me.'

In spite of this praiseworthy course the Scotchman's trade increased. Whether it were that his northern energy was an overmastering force among the easy-going Wessex worthies, or whether it was sheer luck, the fact remained that whatever he touched he prospered in. Like Jacob in Padan-Aram, he would no sooner humbly limit himself to the ringstraked-and-spotted exceptions of trade than the ringstraked-and-spotted would multiply and prevail.

But most probably luck had little to do with it. Character is Fate, said Novalis, and Farfrae's character was just the reverse of Henchard's, who might not inaptly be described as Faust has been described — as a vehement gloomy being who had quitted the ways of vulgar men, without light to guide him on a better way.

Farfrae duly received the request to discontinue attentions to Elizabeth-Jane. His acts of that kind had been so slight that the request was almost superfluous. Yet he had felt a considerable interest in her, and after some cogitation he decided that it would be as well to enact no Romeo part just then — for the young girl's sake no less than his own. Thus the incipient attachment was stifled down.

A time came when, avoid collision with his former friend as he might, Farfrae was compelled, in sheer self-defence, to close with Henchard in mortal commercial combat. He could no longer parry the fierce attacks of the latter by simple avoidance. As soon as their war of prices began everybody was interested, and some few guessed the end. It was, in some degree, Northern insight matched against Southron doggedness – the dirk against the cudgel – and Henchard's weapon was one which, if it did not deal ruin at the first or second stroke, left him afterwards well-nigh at his antagonist's mercy.

Almost every Saturday they encountered each other amid the crowd of farmers which thronged about the market-place in the weekly course of their business. Donald was always ready, and even anxious, to say a few friendly words; but the Mayor invariably gazed stormfully past him, like one who had endured and lost on his account, and could in no sense forgive the wrong; nor did Farfrae's snubbed manner of perplexity at all appease him. The large farmers, corn-merchants, millers, auctioneers, and others had each an official stall in the corn-market room, with their names painted thereon; and when to the familiar series of 'Henchard', 'Everdene', 'Shiner', 'Darton', and so on, was added one inscribed 'Farfrae', in staring new letters, Henchard was stung into bitterness; like Bellerophon, he wandered away from the crowd, cankered in soul.

From that day Donald Farfrae's name was seldom mentioned in Henchard's house. If at breakfast or dinner Elizabeth-Jane's mother inadvertently alluded to her favourite's movements, the girl would implore her by a look to be silent; and her husband would say, 'What – are you, too, my enemy?'

CHAPTER EIGHTEEN

THERE came a shock which had been foreseen for some time by Elizabeth, as the box passenger foresees the approaching jerk from some channel across the highway.

Her mother was ill – too unwell to leave her room. Henchard, who treated her kindly, except in moments of irritation, sent at once for the richest, busiest doctor, whom he supposed to be the best. Bedtime came, and they burnt a light all night. In a day or two she rallied.

Elizabeth, who had been staying up, did not appear at breakfast on the second morning, and Henchard sat down alone. He was startled to see a letter for him from Jersey in a writing he knew too well, and had expected least to behold again. He took it up in his hands and looked at it as at a picture, a vision, a vista of past enactments; and then he read it as an unimportant finale to conjecture.

The writer said that she at length perceived how impossible it would be for any further communications to proceed between them now that his re-marriage had taken place. That such re-union had been the only straightforward course open to him she was bound to admit.

'On calm reflection, therefore,' she went on, 'I quite forgive you for landing me in such a dilemma, remembering that you concealed nothing before our ill-advised acquaintance;

and that you really did set before me in your grim way the fact of there being a certain risk in intimacy with you, slight as it seemed to be after fifteen or sixteen years of silence on your wife's part. I thus look upon the whole as a misfortune of mine, and not a fault of yours.

'So that, Michael, I must ask you to overlook those letters with which I pestered you day after day in the heat of my feelings. They were written whilst I thought your conduct to me cruel; but now I know more particulars of the position you were in I see how inconsiderate my reproaches were.

'Now you will, I am sure, perceive that the one condition which will make any future happiness possible for me is that the past connection between our lives be kept secret outside this isle. Speak of it I know you will not; and I can trust you not to write of it. One safeguard more remains to be mentioned – that no writings of mine, or trifling articles belonging to me, should be left in your possession through neglect or forgetfulness. To this end may I request you to return to me any such you may have, particularly the letters written in the first abandonment of feeling.

'For the handsome sum you forwarded to me as a plaster to the wound I heartily thank you.

'I am now on my way to Bristol, to see my only relative. She is rich, and I hope will do something for me. I shall return through Casterbridge and Budmouth, where I shall take the packet-boat. Can you meet me with the letters and other trifles? I shall be in the coach which changes horses at the Antelope Hotel at half-past five Wednesday evening; I shall be wearing a Paisley shawl with a red centre, and thus may easily be found. I should prefer this plan of receiving them to having them sent. – I remain still, yours ever,

'LUCETTA'

Henchard breathed heavily. 'Poor thing – better you had not known me! Upon my heart and soul, if ever I should be left in a position to carry out that marriage with thee, I *ought* to do it – I ought to do it, indeed!'

The contingency that he had in his mind was, of course, the death of Mrs Henchard.

As requested, he sealed up Lucetta's letters, and put the parcel aside till the day she had appointed; this play of returning them by hand being apparently a little *ruse* of the young lady for exchanging a word or two with him on past times. He would have preferred not to see her; but deeming that there could be no great harm in acquiescing thus far, he went at dusk and stood opposite the coach-office.

The evening was chilly, and the coach was late. Henchard crossed over to it while the horses were being changed; but there was no Lucetta inside or out. Concluding that something had happened to modify her arrangements he gave the matter up and went home, not without a sense of relief.

Meanwhile Mrs Henchard was weakening visibly. She could not go out of doors any more. One day, after much thinking which seemed to distress her, she said she wanted to write something. A desk was put upon her bed with pen and paper, and at her request she was left alone. She remained writing for a short time, folded her paper carefully, called Elizabeth-Jane to bring a taper and wax, and then, still refusing assistance, sealed up the sheet, directed it, and locked it in her desk. She had directed it in these words: –

'Mr Michael Henchard. Not to be opened till Elizabeth-Jane's wedding-day.'

The latter sat up with her mother to the utmost of her strength night after night. To learn to take the universe seriously there is no quicker way than to watch – to be a 'waker', as the country-people call it. Between the hours at which the last toss-pot went by and the first sparrow shook himself, the silence in Casterbridge – barring the rare sound of the watchman – was broken in Elizabeth's ear only by the time-piece in the bedroom ticking frantically against the clock on the stairs; ticking harder and harder till it seemed to clang like a gong; and all this while the subtle-souled girl asking herself why she was born, why sitting in a room, and blinking at the candle; why things around her had taken the shape they wore in preference to every other possible shape. Why they stared at her so helplessly, as if waiting for the touch of some wand that should release them from terrestrial constraint; what that chaos called consciousness, which spun in her at this moment like a top, tended to, and began in. Her eyes fell together; she was awake, yet she was asleep.

A word from her mother roused her. Without preface, and as the continuation of a scene already progressing in her mind, Mrs Henchard said: 'You remember the note sent to you and Mr Farfrae – asking you to meet some one in Durnover Barton – and that you thought it was a trick to make fools of you?'

'Yes.'

'It was not to make fools of you – it was done to bring you together. 'Twas I did it.'

'Why?' said Elizabeth, with a start.

'I – wanted you to marry Mr Farfrae.'

'O mother!' Elizabeth-Jane bent down her head so much that she looked quite into her own lap. But as her mother did not go on, she said, 'What reason?'

'Well, I had a reason. 'Twill out one day. I wish it could have been in my time! But there – nothing is as you wish it! Henchard hates him.'

'Perhaps they'll be friends again,' murmured the girl.

'I don't know – I don't know.' After this her mother was silent, and dozed; and she spoke on the subject no more.

Some little time later on Farfrae was passing Henchard's house on a Sunday morning, when he observed that the blinds were all down. He rang the bell so softly that it only sounded a single full note and a small one; and then he was informed that Mrs Henchard was dead – just dead – that very hour.

At the town-pump there were gathered when he passed a few old inhabitants, who came there for water whenever they had, as at present, spare time to fetch it, because it was purer from that original fount than from their own wells. Mrs Cuxsom, who had been standing there for an indefinite time with her pitcher, was describing the incidents of Mrs Henchard's death, as she had learnt them from the nurse.

'And she was as white as marble-stone,' said Mrs Cuxsom. 'And likewise such a thoughtful woman, too – ah, poor soul – that a' minded every little thing that wanted tending. "Yes," says she, "when I'm gone, and my last breath's blowed, look in the top drawer o' the chest in the back room by the window, and you'll find all my coffin clothes; a piece of flannel – that's to put under me, and the little piece is to put under my head; and my new stockings for my feet – they are folded alongside, and all my other things. And there's four ounce pennies, the heaviest I could find, a-tied up in bits of linen, for weights – two for my right eye and two for my left," she said. "And when you've used 'em, and my eyes don't open no more, bury the pennies, good souls, and don't ye go spending 'em, for I shouldn't like it. And open the windows as soon as I am carried out, and make it as cheerful as you can for Elizabeth-Jane." '

'Ah, poor heart!'

'Well, and Martha did it, and buried the ounce pennies in the garden. But if ye'll believe words, that man, Christopher Coney, went and dug 'em up, and spent 'em at the Three Mariners. "Faith," he said, "why should death rob life o' fourpence? Death's not of such good report that we should respect 'en to that extent," says he.'

''Twas a cannibal deed!' deprecated her listeners.

'Gad, then, I won't quite ha'e it,' said Solomon Longways. 'I say it to-day, and 'tis a Sunday morning, and I wouldn't speak wrongfully for a zilver zixpence at such a time. I don't see noo harm in it. To respect the dead is sound doxology; and I wouldn't sell skellintons – leastwise respectable skellintons – to be varnished for 'natomies, except I were out o' work. But money is scarce, and throats get dry. Why *should* death rob life o' fourpence? I say there was no treason in it.'

'Well, poor soul; she's helpless to hinder that or anything now,' answered Mother Cuxsom. 'And all her shining keys will be took from her, and her cupboards opened; and little things a' didn't wish seen, anybody will see; and her wishes and ways will all be as nothing!'

CHAPTER NINETEEN

HENCHARD and Elizabeth sat conversing by the fire. It was three weeks after Mrs Henchard's funeral; the candles were not lighted, and a restless, acrobatic flame, poised on a coal, called from the shady walls the smiles of all shapes that could respond – the old pier-glass, with gilt columns and huge entablature, the picture-frames, sundry knobs and handles, and the brass rosette at the bottom of each riband bell-pull on either side of the chimney-piece.

'Elizabeth, do you think much of old times?' said Henchard.

'Yes, sir; often,' said she.

'Who do you put in your pictures of 'em?'

'Mother and father – nobody else hardly.'

Henchard always looked like one bent on resisting pain when Elizabeth-Jane spoke of Richard Newson as 'father'. 'Ah! I am out of all that, am I not?' he said. . . . 'Was Newson a kind father?'

'Yes, sir; very.'

Henchard's face settled into an expression of stolid loneliness which gradually modulated into something softer. 'Suppose I had been your real father?' he said. 'Would you have cared for me as much as you cared for Richard Newson?'

'I can't think it,' she said quickly. 'I can think of no other as my father, except my father.'

Henchard's wife was dissevered from him by death; his friend and helper Farfrae by estrangement; Elizabeth-Jane by ignorance. It seemed to him that only one of them could possibly be recalled, and that was the girl. His mind began vibrating between the wish to reveal himself to her and the policy of leaving well alone, till he could no longer sit still. He walked up and down, and then he came and stood behind her chair, looking down upon the top of her head. He could no longer restrain his impulse. 'What did your mother tell you about me – my history?' he asked.

'That you were related by marriage.'

'She should have told more – before you knew me! Then my task would not have been such a hard one. . . . Elizabeth, it is I who am your father, and not Richard Newson. Shame alone prevented your wretched parents from owning this to you while both of 'em were alive.'

The back of Elizabeth's head remained still, and her shoulders did not denote even the movements of breathing. Henchard went on: 'I'd rather have your scorn, your fear, anything than your ignorance; 'tis that I hate. Your mother and I were man and wife when we were young. What you saw was our second marriage. Your mother was too honest. We had thought each other dead – and – Newson became her husband.'

This was the nearest approach Henchard could make to the full truth. As far as he personally was concerned he would have screened nothing; but he showed a respect for the young girl's sex and years worthy of a better man.

When he had gone on to give details which a whole series of slight and unregarded incidents in her past life strangely corroborated; when, in short, she believed his story to be true, she became greatly agitated, and turning round to the table flung her face upon it weeping.

'Don't cry – don't cry!' said Henchard, with vehement pathos, 'I can't bear it, I won't bear it. I am your father; why should you cry? Am I so dreadful, so hateful to 'ee? Don't take against me, Elizabeth-Jane!' he cried, grasping her wet hand. 'Don't take against me – though I was a drinking man once, and used your mother roughly – I'll be kinder to you than *he* was! I'll do anything, if you will only look upon me as your father!'

She tried to stand up and confront him trustfully; but she could not; she was troubled at his presence, like the brethren at the avowal of Joseph.

'I don't want you to come to me all of a sudden,' said Henchard in jerks, and moving like a great tree in a wind. 'No, Elizabeth, I don't. I'll go away and not see you till to-morrow, or when you like; and then I'll show 'ee papers to prove my words. There, I am gone, and won't disturb you any more. . . . 'Twas I that chose your name, my daughter; your mother wanted it Susan. There, don't forget 'twas I gave you your name!' He went out at the door and shut her softly in, and she heard him go away into the garden. But he had not done. Before she had moved, or in any way recovered from the effect of his disclosure, he reappeared.

'One word more, Elizabeth,' he said. 'You'll take my surname now – hey? Your mother was against it; but it will be much more pleasant to me. 'Tis legally yours, you know. But nobody need know that. You shall take it as if by choice. I'll talk to my lawyer – I don't know the law of it exactly; but will you do this – let me put a few lines into the newspaper that such is to be your name?'

'If it is my name I must have it, mustn't I?' she asked.

'Well, well; usage is everything in these matters.'

'I wonder why mother didn't wish it?'

'Oh, some whim of the poor soul's. Now get a bit of paper and draw up a paragraph as I shall tell you. But let's have a light.'

'I can see by the firelight,' she answered. 'Yes – I'd rather.'

'Very well.'

She got a piece of paper, and bending over the fender wrote at his dictation words which he had evidently got by heart from some advertisement or other – words to the effect that she, the writer, hitherto known as Elizabeth-Jane Newson, was going to call herself Elizabeth-Jane Henchard forthwith. It was done, and fastened up, and directed to the office of the *Casterbridge Chronicle*.

'Now,' said Henchard, with the blaze of satisfaction that he always emitted when he had carried his point – though tenderness softened it this time – 'I'll go upstairs and hunt for some documents that will prove it all to you. But I won't trouble you with them till tomorrow. Good-night, my Elizabeth-Jane!'

He was gone before the bewildered girl could realize what it all meant, or adjust her filial sense to the new centre of gravity. She was thankful that he had left her to herself for the evening, and sat down over the fire. Here she remained in silence, and wept – not for her mother now, but for the genial sailor Richard Newson, to whom she seemed doing a wrong.

Henchard in the meantime had gone upstairs. Papers of a domestic nature he kept in a drawer in his bedroom, and this he unlocked. Before turning them over he leant back and indulged in reposeful thought. Elizabeth was his at last, and she was a girl of such good sense and kind heart that she would be sure to like him. He was the kind of man to whom some human object for pouring out his heat upon – were it emotive or were it choleric – was almost a necessity. The craving of his heart for the re-establishment of this tenderest human tie had been great during his wife's lifetime, and now he had submitted to its mastery without reluctance and without fear. He bent over the drawer again, and proceeded in his search.

Among the other papers had been placed the contents of his wife's little desk, the keys of which had been handed to him at her request. Here was the letter addressed to him with the restriction, *'Not to be opened till Elizabeth-Jane's wedding-day.'*

Mrs Henchard, though more patient than her husband, had been no practical hand at anything. In sealing up the sheet, which was folded and tucked in without an envelope, in the old-fashioned way, she had overlaid the junction with a large mass of wax without the requisite under-touch of the same. The seal had cracked, and the letter was open. Henchard had no reason to suppose the restriction one of serious weight, and his feeling for his late wife had not been of the nature of deep respect. 'Some trifling fancy or other of poor Susan's, I suppose,' he said; and without curiosity he allowed his eyes to scan the letter: –

M Y DEAR M ICHAEL, – For the good of all three of us I have kept one thing a secret from you till now. I hope you will understand why; I think you will; though perhaps you may not forgive me. But, dear Michael, I have done it for the best. I shall be in my grave when you read this, and Elizabeth-Jane will have a home. Don't curse me, Mike – think of how I was situated. I can hardly write it, but here it is. Elizabeth-Jane is not your Elizabeth-Jane – the child who was in my arms when you sold me. No; she died three months after that, and this living one is my other husband's. I christened her by the same name we had given to the first, and she filled up the ache I felt at the other's loss. Michael, I am dying, and I might have held my tongue; but I could not. Tell her husband of this or not, as you may judge; and forgive, if you can, a woman you once deeply wronged, as she forgives you.

SUSAN HENCHARD

Her husband regarded the paper as if it were a window-pane through which he saw for miles. His lip twitched, and he seemed to compress his frame, as if to bear better. His usual habit was not to consider whether destiny were hard upon him or not – the shape of his ideas in cases of affliction being simply a moody 'I am to suffer, I perceive.' 'This much scourging, then, is it for me?' But now through his passionate head there stormed this thought – that the blasting disclosure was what he had deserved.

His wife's extreme reluctance to have the girl's name altered from Newson to Henchard was now accounted for fully. It furnished another illustration of that honesty in dishonesty which had characterized her in other things.

He remained unnerved and purposeless for near a couple of hours; till he suddenly said, 'Ah – I wonder if it is true!'

He jumped up in an impulse, kicked off his slippers, and went with a candle to the door of Elizabeth-Jane's room, where he put his ear to the keyhole and listened. She was breathing profoundly. Henchard softly turned the handle, entered, and shading the light, approached the bedside. Gradually bringing the light from behind a screening curtain he held it in such manner that it fell slantwise on her face without shining on her eyes. He steadfastly regarded her features.

They were fair: his were dark. But this was an unimportant preliminary. In sleep there come to the surface buried genealogical facts, ancestral curves, dead men's traits, which the mobility of daytime animation screens and overwhelms. In the present statuesque repose of the young girl's countenance Richard Newson's was unmistakably reflected. He could not endure the sight of her, and hastened away.

Misery taught him nothing more than defiant endurance of it. His wife was dead, and the first impulse for revenge died with the thought that she was beyond him. He looked out at the night as at a fiend. Henchard, like all his kind, was superstitious, and he could not help thinking that the concatenation of events this evening had produced was the scheme of some sinister intelligence bent on punishing him. Yet they had developed naturally. If he had not revealed his past history to Elizabeth he would not have searched the drawer for papers, and so on. The mockery was, that he should have no sooner taught a girl to claim the shelter of his paternity than he discovered her to have no kinship with him.

This ironical sequence of things angered him like an impish trick from a fellow-creature. Like Prester John's, his table had been spread, and infernal harpies had snatched up the food. He went out of the house, and moved sullenly onward down the pavement till he came to the bridge at the bottom of the High Street. Here he turned in upon a bypath on the river bank, skirting the north-eastern limits of the town.

These precincts embodied the mournful phases of Casterbridge life, as the south avenues embodied its cheerful moods. The whole way along here was sunless, even in summer time; in spring, white frosts lingered here when other places were steaming with warmth; while in winter it was the seed-field of all the aches, rheumatisms, and torturing cramps of the year. The Casterbridge doctors must have pined away for want of sufficient nourishment but for the configuration of the landscape on the north-eastern side.

The river – slow, noiseless, and dark – the Schwarzwasser of Casterbridge – ran beneath a low cliff, the two together forming a defence which had rendered walls and artificial earthworks on this side unnecessary. Here were ruins of a Franciscan priory, and a mill attached to the same, the water of which roared down a back-hatch like the voice of desolation. Above the cliff, and behind the river, rose a pile of buildings, and in the front of the pile a square mass cut into the sky. It was like a pedestal lacking its statue. This missing feature, without which the design remained incomplete, was, in truth, the corpse of a man; for the square mass formed the base of the gallows, the extensive buildings at the back being the county goal. In the meadow where Henchard now walked the mob were wont to gather whenever an execution took place, and there to the tune of the roaring weir they stood and watched the spectacle.

The exaggeration which darkness imparted to the glooms of this region impressed Henchard more than he had expected. The lugubrious harmony of the spot with his domestic situation was too perfect for him, impatient of effects, scenes, and adumbrations. It reduced his heartburning to melancholy, and he exclaimed, 'Why the deuce did I come here!' He went on past the cottage in which the old local hangman had lived and died, in times before that calling was monopolized over all England by a singlegentleman; and climbed up by a steep back lane into the town.

For the sufferings of that night, engendered by his bitter disappointment, he might well have been pitied. He was like one who had half fainted, and could neither recover nor complete the swoon. In words he could blame his wife, but not in his heart; and had he obeyed the wise directions outside her letter this pain would have been spared him for long – possibly for ever, Elizabeth-Jane seeming to show no ambition to quit her safe and secluded maiden courses for the speculative path of matrimony.

The morning came after this night of unrest, and with it the necessity for a plan. He was far too self-willed to recede from a position, especially as it would involve humiliation. His daughter he had asserted her to be, and his daughter she should always think herself, no matter what hypocrisy it involved.

But he was ill-prepared for the first step in this new situation. The moment he came into the breakfast-room Elizabeth advanced with open confidence to him and took him by the arm.

'I have thought and thought all night of it,' she said frankly. 'And I see that everything must be as you say. And I am going to look upon you as the father that you are, and not to call you Mr Henchard any more. It is so plain to me now. Indeed, father, it is. For, of course, you would not have done half the things you have done for me, and let me have my own way so entirely, and bought me presents, if I had only been your stepdaughter! He – Mr Newson – whom my poor mother married by such a strange mistake' (Henchard was glad that he had disguised matters here), 'was very kind – O so kind!' (she spoke with tears in her eyes); 'but that is not the same thing as being one's real father after all. Now, father, breakfast is ready!' said she cheerfully.

Henchard bent and kissed her cheek. The moment and the act he had prefigured for weeks with a thrill of pleasure; yet it was no less than a miserable insipidity to him now that it had come. His reinstation of her mother had been chiefly for the girl's sake, and the fruition of the whole scheme was such dust and ashes as this.

CHAPTER TWENTY

OF all the enigmas which ever confronted a girl there can have been seldom one like that which followed Henchard's announcement of himself to Elizabeth as her father. He had done it in an ardour and an agitation which had half carried the point of affection with her; yet, behold, from the next morning onwards his manner was constrained as she had never seen it before.

The coldness soon broke out into open chiding. One grievous failing of Elizabeth's was her occasional pretty and picturesque use of dialect words – those terrible marks of the beast to the truly genteel.

It was dinner-time – they never met except at meals – and she happened to say when he was rising from table, wishing to show him something, 'If you'll bide where you be a minute, father, I'll get it.'

' "Bide where you be," ' he echoed sharply. 'Good God, are you only fit to carry wash to a pig-trough, that ye use such words as those?'

She reddened with shame and sadness.

'I meant "Stay where you are", father,' she said, in a low, humble voice. 'I ought to have been more careful.'

He made no reply, and went out of the room.

The sharp reprimand was not lost upon her, and in time it came to pass that for 'fay' she said 'succeed'; that she no longer spoke of 'dumbledores' but of 'humble bees'; no longer said of young men and women that they 'walked together', but that they were 'engaged'; that she grew to talk of 'greggles' as 'wild hyacinths'; that when she had not slept she did not quaintly tell the servants next morning that she had been 'hag-rid', but that she had 'suffered from indigestion'.

These improvements, however, are somewhat in advance of the story. Henchard, being uncultivated himself, was the bitterest critic the fair girl could possibly have had of her own lapses – really slight now, for she read omnivorously. A gratuitous ordeal was in store for her in the matter of her handwriting. She was passing the dining-room door one evening, and had occasion to go in for something. It was not till she had opened the door that she knew the Mayor was there in the company of a man with whom he transacted business.

'Here, Elizabeth-Jane,' he said, looking round at her, 'just write down what I tell you – a few words of an agreement for me and this gentleman to sign. I am a poor tool with a pen.'

'Be jowned, and so be I,' said the gentleman.

She brought forward blotting-book, paper, and ink, and sat down.

'Now then – "An agreement entered into this sixteenth day of October" – write that first.'

She started the pen in an elephantine march across the sheet. It was a splendid round, bold hand of her own conception, a style that would have stamped a woman as Minerva's own in more recent days. But other ideas reigned then: Henchard's creed was that proper young girls wrote ladies'-hand — nay, he believed that bristling characters were as innate and inseparable a part of refined womanhood as sex itself. Hence when, instead of scribbling, like the Princess Ida, —

'In such a hand as when a field of corn
Bows all its ears before the roaring East,'

Elizabeth-Jane produced a line of chain-shot and sand-bags, he reddened in angry shame for her, and, peremptorily saying, 'Never mind — I'll finish it,' dismissed her there and then.

Her considerate disposition became a pitfall to her now. She was, it must be admitted, sometimes provokingly and unnecessarily willing to saddle herself with manual labours. She would go to the kitchen instead of ringing, 'Not to make Phœbe come up twice.' She went down on her knees, shovel in hand, when the cat overturned the coal-scuttle; moreover, she would persistently thank the parlour-maid for everything, till one day, as soon as the girl was gone from the room, Henchard broke out with, 'Good God, why dostn't leave off thanking that girl as if she were a goddess-born! Don't I pay her a dozen pound a year to do things for 'ee?' Elizabeth shrank so visibly at the exclamation that he became sorry a few minutes after, and said that he did not mean to be rough.

These domestic exhibitions were the small protruding needle-rocks which suggested rather than revealed what was underneath. But his passion had less terror for her than his coldness. The increasing frequency of the latter mood told her the sad news that he disliked her with a growing dislike. The more interesting that her appearance and manners became under the softening influences which she could now command, and in her wisdom did command, the more she seemed to estrange him. Sometimes she caught him looking at her with a louring invidiousness that she could hardly bear. Not knowing his secret it was a cruel mockery that she should for the first time excite his animosity when she had taken his surname.

But the most terrible ordeal was to come. Elizabeth had latterly been accustomed of an afternoon to present a cup of cider or ale and bread-and-cheese to Nance Mockridge, who worked in the yard wimbling hay-bonds. Nance accepted this offering thankfully at first; afterwards as a matter of course. On a day when Henchard was on the premises he saw his stepdaughter enter the hay-barn on this errand; and, as there was no clear spot on which to deposit the provisions, she at once set to work arranging two trusses of hay as a table, Mockridge meanwhile standing with her hands on her hips, easefully looking at the preparations on her behalf.

'Elizabeth, come here!' said Henchard; and she obeyed.

'Why do you lower yourself so confoundedly?' he said with suppressed passion. 'Haven't I told you o't fifty times? Hey? Making yourself a drudge for a common workwoman of such a character as hers! Why, ye'll disgrace me to the dust!'

Now these words were uttered loud enough to reach Nance inside the barn door, who fired up immediately at the slur upon her personal character. Coming to the door she cried, regardless of consequences, 'Come to that, Mr Michael Henchard, I can let 'ee know she've waited on worse!'

'Then she must have had more charity than sense,' said Henchard.

'O no, she hadn't. 'Twere not for charity but for hire; and at a public-house in this town!'

'It is not true!' cried Henchard indignantly.

'Just ask her,' said Nance, folding her naked arms in such a manner that she could comfortably scratch her elbows.

Henchard glanced at Elizabeth-Jane, whose complexion, now pink and white from confinement, lost nearly all of the former colour. 'What does this mean?' he said to her. 'Anything or nothing?'

'It is true,' said Elizabeth-Jane. 'But it was only—'

'Did you do it, or didn't you? Where was it?'

'At the Three Mariners; one evening for a little while, when we were staying there.'

Nance glanced triumphantly at Henchard, and sailed into the barn; for assuming that she was to be discharged on the instant she had resolved to make the most of her victory. Henchard, however, said nothing about discharging her. Unduly sensitive on such points by reason of his own past, he had the look of one completely ground down to the last indignity. Elizabeth followed him to the house like a culprit; but when she got inside she could not see him. Nor did she see him again that day.

Convinced of the scathing damage to his local repute and position that must have been caused by such a fact, though it had never before reached his own ears, Henchard showed a positive distaste for the presence of this girl not his own, whenever he encountered her. He mostly dined with the farmers at the market-room of one of the two chief hotels, leaving her in utter solitude. Could he have seen how she made use of those silent hours he might have found reason to reverse his judgment on her quality. She read and took notes incessantly, mastering facts with painful laboriousness, but never flinching from her self-imposed task. She began the study of Latin, incited by the Roman characteristics of the town she lived in. 'If I am not well-informed it shall be by no fault of my own,' she would say to herself through the tears that would occasionally glide down her peachy cheeks when she was fairly baffled by the portentous obscurity of many of these educational works.

Thus she lived on, a dumb, deep-feeling, great-eyed creature, construed by not a single contiguous being; quenching with patient fortitude her incipient interest in Farfrae, because it seemed to be one-sided, unmaidenly, and unwise. True, that for reasons best known to herself, she had, since Farfrae's dismissal, shifted her quarters from the back room affording a view of the yard (which she had occupied with such zest) to a front chamber overlooking the street; but as for the young man, whenever he passed the house he seldom or never turned his head.

Winter had almost come, and unsettled weather made her still more dependent upon indoor resources. But there were certain early winter days in Casterbridge – days of firmamental exhaustion which followed angry south-westerly tempests – when, if the sun shone, the air was like velvet. She seized on these days for her periodical visits to the spot where her mother lay buried – the still-used burial-ground of the old Roman-British city, whose curious feature was this, its continuity as a place of sepulture. Mrs Henchard's dust mingled with the dust of women who lay ornamented with glass hair-pins and amber necklaces, and men who held in their mouths coins of Hadrian, Posthumus, and the Constantines.

Half-past ten in the morning was about her hour for seeking this spot – a time when the town avenues were deserted as the avenues of Karnac. Business had long since passed down them into its daily cells, and Leisure had not arrived there. So Elizabeth-Jane walked and read, or looked over the edge of the book to think, and thus reached the churchyard.

There, approaching her mother's grave she saw a solitary dark figure in the middle of the gravel-walk. This figure, too, was reading; but not from a book: the words which engrossed it being the inscription on Mrs Henchard's tombstone. The personage was in mourning like herself, was about her age and size, and might have been her wraith or double, but for the fact that it was a lady much more beautifully dressed than she. Indeed, comparatively indifferent as Elizabeth-Jane was to dress, unless for some temporary whim or purpose, her eyes were arrested by the artistic perfection of the lady's appearance. Her gait, too, had a flexuousness about it, which seemed to avoid angularity of movement less from choice than from predisposition. It was a revelation to Elizabeth that human beings could reach this stage of external development – she had never suspected it. She felt all the freshness and grace to be stolen from herself on the instant by the neighbourhood of such a stranger. And this was in face of the fact that Elizabeth could now have been writ handsome, while the young lady was simply pretty.

Had she been envious she might have hated the woman; but she did not do that – she allowed herself the pleasure of feeling fascinated. She wondered where the lady had come from. The stumpy and practical walk of honest homeliness which mostly prevailed there, the two styles of dress thereabout, the simple and the mistaken, equally avouched that this figure was no Casterbridge woman's, even if a book in her hand resembling a guide-book had not also suggested it.

The stranger presently moved from the tombstone of Mrs Henchard, and vanished behind the corner of the wall. Elizabeth went to the tomb herself; beside it were two footprints distinct in the soil, signifying that the lady had stood there a long time. She returned homeward, musing on what she had seen, as she might have mused on a rainbow or the Northern Lights, a rare butterfly or a cameo.

Interesting as things had been out of doors, at home it turned out to be one of her bad days. Henchard, whose two years' mayoralty was ending, had been made aware that he was not to be chosen to fill a vacancy in the list of aldermen; and that Farfrae was likely to become one of the Council. This caused the unfortunate discovery that she had played the waiting-maid in the town of which he was Mayor to rankle in his mind yet more poisonously. He had learnt by personal inquiry at the time that it was to Donald Farfrae – that treacherous upstart – that she had thus humiliated herself. And though Mrs Stannidge seemed to attach no great importance to the incident – the cheerful souls at the Three Mariners having exhausted its aspects long ago – such was Henchard's haughty spirit that the simple thrifty deed was regarded as little less than a social catastrophe by him.

Ever since the evening of his wife's arrival with her daughter there had been something in the air which had changed his luck. That dinner at the King's Arms with his friends had been Henchard's Austerlitz: he had had his successes since, but his course had not been upward. He was not to be numbered among the aldermen – that Peerage of burghers – as he had expected to be, and the consciousness of this soured him to-day.

'Well, where have you been?' he said to her with off-hand laconism.

'I've been strolling in the Walks and churchyard, father, till I feel quite leery.' She clapped her hand to her mouth, but too late.

This was just enough to incense Henchard after the other crosses of the day. 'I *won't* have you talk like that!' he thundered. ' "Leery", indeed. One would think you worked upon a farm! One day I learn that you lend a hand in public-houses. Then I hear you talk like a clodhopper. I'm burned, if it goes on, this house can't hold us two.'

The only way of getting a single pleasant thought to go to sleep upon after this was by recalling the lady she had seen that day, and hoping she might see her again.

Meanwhile Henchard was sitting up, thinking over his jealous folly in forbidding Farfrae to pay his addresses to this girl who did not belong to him, when if he had allowed them to go on he might not have been encumbered with her. At last he said to himself with satisfaction as he jumped up and went to the writing-table: 'Ah! he'll think it means peace, and a marriage portion – not that I don't want my house to be troubled with her, and no portion at all!' He wrote as follows: –

Sir, – On consideration, I don't wish to interfere with your courtship of Elizabeth-Jane, if you care for her. I therefore withdraw my objection; excepting in this – that the business be not carried on in my house. – Yours,

Mr Farfrae

M. HENCHARD

The morrow, being fairly fine, found Elizabeth-Jane again in the churchyard; but while looking for the lady she was startled by the apparition of Farfrae, who passed outside the gate. He glanced up for a moment from a pocket-book in which he appeared to be making figures as he went; whether or not he saw her he took no notice, and disappeared.

Unduly depressed by a sense of her own superfluity she thought he probably scorned her; and quite broken in spirit sat down on a bench. She fell into painful thought on her position, which ended with her saying quite loud, 'O, I wish I was dead with dear mother!'

Behind the bench was a little promenade under the wall where people sometimes walked instead of on the gravel. The bench seemed to be touched by something; she looked round, and a face was bending over her, veiled, but still distinct, the face of the young woman she had seen yesterday.

Elizabeth-Jane looked confounded for a moment, knowing she had been overheard, though there was pleasure in her confusion. 'Yes, I heard you,' said the lady, in a vivacious voice, answering her look. 'What can have happened?'

'I don't – I can't tell you,' said Elizabeth, putting her hand to her face to hide a quick flush that had come.

There was no movement or word for a few seconds; then the girl felt that the young lady was sitting down beside her.

'I guess how it is with you,' said the latter. 'That was your mother.' She waved her hand towards the tombstone. Elizabeth looked up at her as if inquiring of herself whether there should be confidence. The lady's manner was so desirous, so anxious, that the girl decided there should be confidence. 'It was my mother,' she said, 'my only friend.'

'But your father, Mr Henchard. He is living?'

'Yes, he is living,' said Elizabeth-Jane.

'Is he not kind to you?'

'I've no wish to complain of him.'

'There has been a disagreement?'

'A little.'

'Perhaps you were to blame,' suggested the stranger.

'I was – in many ways,' sighed the meek Elizabeth. 'I swept up the coals when the servant ought to have done it; and I said I was leery; – and he was angry with me.'

The lady seemed to warm towards her for that reply. 'Do you know the impression your words give me?' she said ingenuously. 'That he is a hot-tempered man – a little proud – perhaps ambitious; but not a bad man.' Her anxiety not to condemn Henchard while siding with Elizabeth was curious.

'O no; certainly not *bad*,' agreed the honest girl. 'And he has not even been unkind to me till lately – since mother died. But it has been very much to bear while it has lasted. All is owing to my defects, I daresay; and my defects are owing to my history.'

'What is your history?'

Elizabeth-Jane looked wistfully at her questioner. She found that her questioner was looking at her; turned her eyes down; and then seemed compelled to look back again. 'My history is not gay or attractive,' she said. 'And yet I can tell it, if you really want to know.'

The lady assured her that she did want to know; whereupon Elizabeth-Jane told the tale of her life as she understood it, which was in general the true one, except that the sale at the fair had no part therein.

Contrary to the girl's expectation her new friend was not shocked. This cheered her; and it was not till she thought of returning to that home in which she had been treated so roughly of late that her spirits fell.

'I don't know how to return,' she murmured. 'I think of going away. But what can I do? Where can I go?'

'Perhaps it will be better soon,' said her friend gently. 'So I would not go far. Now what do you think of this: I shall soon want somebody to live in my house, partly as housekeeper, partly as companion; would you mind coming to me? But perhaps—'

'O yes,' cried Elizabeth, with tears in her eyes. 'I would, indeed – I would do anything to be independent; for then perhaps my father might get to love me. But, ah!'

'What?'

'I am no accomplished person. And a companion to *you* must be that.'

'O, not necessarily.'

'Not? But I can't help using rural words, sometimes, when I don't mean to.'

'Never mind, I shall like to know them.'

'And – O, I know I shan't do!' – she cried with a distressful laugh. 'I accidentally learned to write round hand instead of ladies'-hand. And, of course, you want some one who can write that?'

'Well, no.'

'What, not necessary to write ladies'-hand?' cried the joyous Elizabeth.

'Not at all.'

'But where do you live?'

'In Casterbridge, or rather I shall be living here after twelve o' clock to-day.'

Elizabeth expressed her astonishment.

'I have been staying at Budmouth for a few days while my house was getting ready. The house I am going into is that one they call High-Place Hall – the old stone one looking down the lane to the Market. Two or three rooms are fit for occupation, though not all: I sleep there to-night for the first time. Now will you think over my proposal, and meet me here the first fine day next week, and say if you are still in the same mind?'

Elizabeth, her eyes shining at this prospect of a change from an unbearable position, joyfully assented; and the two parted at the gate of the churchyard.

CHAPTER TWENTY-ONE

As a maxim glibly repeated from childhood remains practically unmarked till some mature experience enforces it, so did this High-Place Hall now for the first time really show itself to Elizabeth-Jane, though her ears had heard its name on a hundred occasions.

Her mind dwelt upon nothing else but the stranger, and the house, and her own chance of living there, all the rest of the day. In the afternoon she had occasion to pay a few bills in the town and do a little shopping, when she learnt that what was a new discovery to herself had become a common topic about the streets. High-Place Hall was undergoing repair; a lady was coming there to live shortly; all the shop-people knew it, and had already discounted the chance of her being a customer.

Elizabeth-Jane could, however, add a capping touch to information so new to her in the bulk. The lady, she said, had arrived that day.

When the lamps were lighted, and it was yet not so dark as to render chimneys, attics, and roofs invisible, Elizabeth, almost with a lover's feeling, thought she would like to look at the outside of High-Place Hall. She went up the street in that direction.

The Hall, with its grey *façade* and parapet, was the only residence of its sort so near the centre of the town. It had, in the first place, the characteristics of a country mansion – birds' nests in its chimneys, damp nooks where fungi grew, and irregularities of surface direct from Nature's trowel. At night the forms of passengers were patterned by the lamps in black shadows upon the pale walls.

This evening motes of straw lay around, and other signs of the premises having been in that lawless condition which accompanies the entry of a new tenant. The house was entirely of stone, and formed an example of dignity without great size. It was not altogether aristocratic, still less consequential, yet the old-fashioned stranger instinctively said, 'Blood built it, and Wealth enjoys it,' however vague his opinions of those accessories might be.

Yet as regards the enjoying it the stranger would have been wrong, for until this very evening, when the new lady had arrived, the house had been empty for a year or two, while before that interval its occupancy had been irregular. The reason of its unpopularity was soon made manifest. Some of its rooms overlooked the market-place; and such a prospect from such a house was not considered desirable or seemly by its would-be occupiers.

Elizabeth's eyes sought the upper rooms, and saw lights there. The lady had obviously arrived. The impression that this woman of comparatively practised manner had made upon the studious girl's mind was so deep that she enjoyed standing under an opposite archway merely to think that the charming lady was inside the confronting walls, and to wonder what she was doing. Her admiration for the architecture of that front was entirely on account of the inmate it screened. Though for that matter the architecture deserved admiration, or at least study, on its own account. It was Palladian, and like most architecture erected since the Gothic age was a compilation rather than a design. But its reasonableness made it impressive. It was not rich, but rich enough. A timely consciousness of the ultimate vanity of human architecture, no less than of other human things, had prevented artistic superfluity.

Men had till quite recently been going in and out with parcels and packing-cases, rendering the door and hall within like a public thoroughfare. Elizabeth trotted through the open door in the dusk, but becoming alarmed at her own temerity she went quickly out again by another which stood open in the lofty wall of the back court. To her surprise she found herself in one of the little-used alleys of the town. Looking round at the door which had given her egress, by the light of the solitary lamp fixed in the alley, she saw that it was arched and old – older even than the house itself. The door was studded, and the keystone of the arch was a mask. Originally the mask had exhibited a comic leer, as could still be discerned; but generations of Casterbridge boys had thrown stones at the mask, aiming at its open mouth; and the blows thereon had chipped off the lips and jaws as if they had been eaten away by disease. The appearance was so ghastly by the weakly lamp-glimmer that she could not bear to look at it – the first unpleasant feature of her visit.

The position of the queer old door and the odd presence of the leering mask suggested one thing above all others as appertaining to the mansion's past history – intrigue. By the alley it had been possible to come unseen from all sorts of quarters in the town – the old play-house, the old bull-stake, the old cock-pit, the pool wherein nameless infants had been used to disappear. High-Place Hall could boast of its conveniences undoubtedly.

She turned to come away in the nearest direction homeward, which was down the alley, but hearing footsteps approaching in that quarter, and having no great wish to be found in such a place at such a time she quickly retreated. There being no other way out she stood behind a brick pier till the intruder should have gone his ways.

Had she watched she would have been surprised. She would have seen that the pedestrian on coming up made straight for the arched doorway: that as he paused with his hand upon the latch the lamp-light fell upon the face of Henchard.

But Elizabeth-Jane clung so closely to her nook that she discerned nothing of this. Henchard passed in, as ignorant of her presence as she was ignorant of his identity, and disappeared in the darkness. Elizabeth came out a second time into the alley, and made the best of her way home.

Henchard's chiding, by begetting in her a nervous fear of doing anything definable as unlady-like, had operated thus curiously in keeping them unknown to each other at a critical moment. Much might have resulted from recognition – at the least a query on either side in one and the self-same form: What could he or she possibly be doing there?

Henchard, whatever his business at the lady's house, reached his own home only a few minutes later than Elizabeth-Jane. Her plan was to broach the question of leaving his roof this evening; the events of the day had urged her to the course. But its execution depended upon his mood, and she anxiously awaited his manner towards her. She found that it had changed. He showed no further tendency to be angry; he showed something worse. Absolute indifference had taken the place of irritability; and his coldness was such that it encouraged her to departure, even more than hot temper could have done.

'Father, have you any objection to my going away?' she asked.

'Going away! No – none whatever. Where are you going?'

She thought it undesirable and unnecessary to say anything at present about her destination to one who took so little interest in her. He would know that soon enough. 'I have heard of an opportunity of getting more cultivated and finished, and being less idle,' she answered, with hesitation. 'A chance of a place in a household where I can have advantages of study, and seeing refined life.'

'Then make the best of it, in Heaven's name – if you can't get cultivated where you are.'

'You don't object?'

'Object – I? Ho – no! Not at all.' After a pause he said, 'But you won't have enough money for this lively scheme without help, you know? If you like I should be willing to make you an allowance, so that you be not bound to live upon the starvation wages refined folk are likely to pay 'ee.'

She thanked him for this offer.

'It had better be done properly,' he added after a pause. 'A small annuity is what I should like you to have – so as to be independent of me – and so that I may be independent of you. Would that please ye?'

'Certainly.'

'Then I'll see about it this very day.' He seemed relieved to get her off his hands by this arrangement, and as far as they were concerned the matter was settled. She now simply waited to see the lady again.

The day and the hour came; but a drizzling rain fell. Elizabeth-Jane, having now changed her orbit from one of gay independence to laborious self-help, thought the weather good enough for such declined glory as hers, if her friend would only face it – a matter of doubt. She went to the boot-room where her pattens had hung ever since her apotheosis, took them down, had their mildewed leathers blacked, and put them on as she had done in old times. Thus mounted, and with cloak and umbrella, she went off to the place of appointment – intending, if the lady were not there, to call at the house.

One side of the churchyard – the side towards the weather – was sheltered by an ancient thatched mud wall whose eaves overhung as much as one or two feet. At the back of the wall was a corn-yard with its granary and barns – the place wherein she had met Farfrae many months earlier. Under the projection of the thatch she saw a figure. The young lady had come.

Her presence so exceptionally substantiated the girl's utmost hopes that she almost feared her good fortune. Fancies find room in the strongest minds. Here, in a churchyard old as civilization, in the worst of weathers, was a strange woman of curious fascinations never seen elsewhere: there might be some devilry about her presence. However, Elizabeth went on to the church tower, on whose summit the rope of a flag-staff rattled in the wind; and thus she came to the wall.

The lady had such a cheerful aspect in the drizzle that Elizabeth forgot her fancy. 'Well,' said the lady, a little of the whiteness of her teeth appearing with the word through the black fleece that protected her face, 'have you decided?'

'Yes, quite,' said the other eagerly.

'Your father is willing?'

'Yes.'

'Then come along.'

'When?'

'Now – as soon as you like. I had a good mind to send to you to come to my house, thinking you might not venture up here in the wind. But as I like getting out of doors, I thought I would come and see first.'

'It was my own thought.'

'That shows we shall agree. Then can you come to-day? My house is so hollow and dismal that I want some living thing there.'

'I think I might be able to,' said the girl, reflecting.

Voices were borne over to them at that instant on the wind and raindrops from the other side of the wall. There came such words as 'sacks', 'quarters', 'threshing', 'tailing', 'next Saturday's market', each sentence being disorganized by the gusts like a face in a cracked mirror. Both the women listened.

'Who are those?' said the lady.

'One is my father. He rents that yard and barn.'

The lady seemed to forget the immediate business in listening to the technicalities of the corn trade. At last she said suddenly, 'Did you tell him where you were going to?'

'No.'

'O – how was that?'

'I thought it safer to get away first – as he is so uncertain in his temper.'

'Perhaps you are right. . . . Besides, I have never told you my name. It is Miss Templeman. . . . Are they gone – on the other side?'

'No. They are only gone up into the granary.'

'Well, it is getting damp here. I shall expect you to-day – this evening, say, at six.'

'Which way shall I come, ma'am?'

'The front way – round by the gate. There is no other that I have noticed.' Elizabeth-Jane had been thinking of the door in the alley.

'Perhaps, as you have not mentioned your destination, you may as well keep silent upon it till you are clear off. Who knows but that he may alter his mind?'

Elizabeth-Jane shook her head. 'On consideration I don't fear it,' she said sadly. 'He has grown quite cold to me.'

'Very well. Six o'clock then.'

When they had emerged upon the open road and parted, they found enough to do in holding their bowed umbrellas to the wind. Nevertheless the lady looked in at the corn-yard gates as she passed them, and paused on one foot for a moment. But nothing was visible there save the ricks, and the humpbacked barn cushioned with moss, and the granary rising against the church-tower behind, where the smacking of the rope against the flag-staff still went on.

Now Henchard had not the slightest suspicion that Elizabeth-Jane's movement was to be so prompt. Hence when, just before six, he reached home and saw a fly at the door from the King's Arms, and his stepdaughter, with all her little bags and boxes, getting into it, he was taken by surprise.

'But you said I might go, father?' she explained through the carriage window.

'Said! – yes. But I thought you meant next month, or next year. 'Od, seize it – you take time by the forelock! This, then, is how you be going to treat me for all my trouble about ye?'

'O father! how can you speak like that? It is unjust of you!' she said with spirit.

'Well, well, have your own way,' he replied. He entered the house, and, seeing that all her things had not yet been brought down, went up to her room to look on. He had never been there since she had occupied it. Evidences of her care, of her endeavours for improvement, were visible all around, in the form of books, sketches, maps, and little arrangements for tasteful effects. Henchard had known nothing of these efforts. He gazed at them, turned suddenly about, and came down to the door.

'Look here,' he said, in an altered voice – he never called her by name now – 'don't 'ee go away from me. It may be I've spoke roughly to you – but I've been grieved beyond everything by you – there's something that caused it.'

'By me?' she said, with deep concern. 'What have I done?'

'I can't tell you now. But if you'll stop, and go on living as my daughter, I'll tell you all in time.'

But the proposal had come ten minutes too late. She was in the fly – was already, in imagination, at the house of the lady whose manner had such charms for her. 'Father,' she said, as considerately as she could, 'I think it best for us that I go on now. I need not stay long; I shall not be far away; and if you want me badly I can soon come back again.'

He nodded ever so slightly, as a receipt of her decision and no more. 'You are not going far, you say. What will be your address, in case I wish to write to you? Or am I not to know?'

'Oh yes – certainly. It is only in the town – High-Place Hall.'

'Where?' said Henchard, his face stilling.

She repeated the words. He neither moved nor spoke, and waving her hand to him in utmost friendliness she signified to the flyman to drive up the street.

CHAPTER TWENTY-TWO

We go back for a moment to the preceding night, to account for Henchard's attitude.

At the hour when Elizabeth-Jane was contemplating her stealthy reconnoitring excursion to the abode of the lady of her fancy, he had been not a little amazed at receiving a letter by hand in Lucetta's well-known characters. The self-repression, the resignation of her previous communication had vanished from her mood; she wrote with some of the natural lightness which had marked her in their early acquaintance.

High-Place Hall

My dear Mr Henchard, – Don't be surprised. It is for your good and mine, as I hope, that I have come to live at Casterbridge – for how long I cannot tell. That depends upon another; and he is a man, and a merchant, and a Mayor, and one who has the first right to my affections.

Seriously, *mon ami*, I am not so light-hearted as I may seem to be from this. I have come here in consequence of hearing of the death of your wife – whom you used to think of as dead so many years before! Poor woman, she seems to have been a sufferer, though uncomplaining, and though weak in intellect not an imbecile. I am glad you acted fairly by her. As soon as I knew she was no more, it was brought home to me very forcibly by my conscience that I ought to endeavour to disperse the shade which my *étourderie* flung over my name, by asking you to carry out your promise to me. I hope you are of the same mind, and that you will take steps to this end. As, however, I did not know how you were situated, or what had happened since our separation, I decided to come and establish myself here before communicating with you.

You probably feel as I do about this. I shall be able to see you in a day or two. Till then, farewell. – Yours,

Lucetta

P.S. – I was unable to keep my appointment to meet you for a moment or two in passing through Casterbridge the other day. My plans were altered by a family event, which it will surprise you to hear of.

Henchard had already heard that High-Place Hall was being prepared for a tenant. He said with a puzzled air to the first person he encountered, 'Who is coming to live at the Hall?'

'A lady of the name of Templeman, I believe, sir,' said his informant.

Henchard thought it over. 'Lucetta is related to her, I suppose,' he said to himself. 'Yes, I must put her in her proper position, undoubtedly.'

It was by no means with the oppression that would once have accompanied the thought that he regarded the moral necessity now; it was, indeed, with interest, if not warmth. His bitter disappointment at finding Elizabeth-Jane to be none of his, and himself a childless man, had left an emotional void in Henchard that he unconsciously craved to fill. In this frame of mind, though without strong feeling, he had strolled up the alley and into High-Place Hall by the postern at which Elizabeth had so nearly encountered him. He had gone on thence into the court, and inquired of a man whom he saw unpacking china from a crate if Miss Le Sueur was living there. Miss Le Sueur had been the name under which he had known Lucetta – or 'Lucette', as she had called herself at that time.

The man replied in the negative; that Miss Templeman only had come. Henchard went away, concluding that Lucetta had not as yet settled in.

He was in this interested stage of the inquiry when he witnessed Elizabeth-Jane's departure the next day. On hearing her announce the address there suddenly took possession of him the strange thought that Lucetta and Miss Templeman were one and the same person, for he could recall that in her season of intimacy with him the name of the rich relative whom he had deemed somewhat a mythical personage had been given as Templeman. Though he was not a fortune-hunter, the possibility that Lucetta had been sublimed into a lady of means by some munificent testament on the part of this relative lent a charm to her image which it might not otherwise have acquired. He was getting on towards the dead level of middle age, when material things increasingly possess the mind.

But Henchard was not left long in suspense. Lucetta was rather addicted to scribbling, as had been shown by the torrent of letters after the *fiasco* in their marriage arrangements, and hardly had Elizabeth gone away when another note came to the Mayor's house from High-Place Hall.

'I am in residence,' she said, 'and comfortable, though getting here has been a wearisome undertaking. You probably know what I am going to tell you, or do you not? My good Aunt Templeman, the banker's widow, whose very existence you used to doubt, much more her affluence, has lately died, and bequeathed some of her property to me. I will not enter into details except to say that I have taken her name – as a means of escape from mine, and its wrongs.

'I am now my own mistress, and have chosen to reside in Casterbridge – to be tenant of High-Place Hall, that at least you may be put to no trouble if you wish to see me. My first intention was to keep you in ignorance of the changes in my life till you should meet me in the street; but I have thought better of this.

'You probably are aware of my arrangement with your daughter, and have doubtless laughed at the – what shall I call it? – practical joke (in all affection) of my getting her to live with me. But my first meeting with her was purely an accident. Do you see, Michael, partly why I have done it? – why, to give you an excuse for coming here as if to visit *her*, and thus to form my acquaintance naturally. She is a dear, good girl, and she thinks you have treated her with undue severity. You may have done so in your haste, but not deliberately, I am sure. As the result has been to bring her to me I am not disposed to upbraid you. – In haste, yours always,

LUCETTA'

The excitement which these announcements produced in Henchard's gloomy soul was to him most pleasurable. He sat over his dining-table long and dreamily, and by an almost mechanical transfer the sentiments which had run to waste since his estrangement from Elizabeth-Jane and Donald Farfrae gathered around Lucetta before they had grown dry. She was plainly in a very coming-on disposition for marriage. But what else could a poor woman be who had given her time and heart to him so thoughtlessly, at that former time, as to lose her credit by it? Probably conscience no less than affection had brought her here. On the whole he did not blame her.

'The artful little woman!' he said, smiling (with reference to Lucetta's adroit and pleasant manœuvre with Elizabeth-Jane).

To feel that he would like to see Lucetta was with Henchard to start for her house. He put on his hat and went. It was between eight and nine o'clock when he reached her door. The answer brought him was that Miss Templeman was engaged for that evening; but that she would be happy to see him the next day.

'That's rather like giving herself airs!' he thought. 'And considering what we—' But after all, she plainly had not expected him, and he took the refusal quietly. Nevertheless he resolved not to go next day. 'These cursed women – there's not an inch of straight grain in 'em!' he said.

Let us follow the track of Mr Henchard's thought as if it were a clue line, and view the interior of High-Place Hall on this particular evening.

On Elizabeth-Jane's arrival she had been phlegmatically asked by an elderly woman to go upstairs and take off her things. She had replied with great earnestness that she would not think of giving that trouble, and on the instant divested herself of her bonnet and cloak in the passage. She was then conducted to the first door on the landing, and left to find her way further alone.

The room disclosed was prettily furnished as a boudoir or small drawing-room, and on a sofa with two cylindrical pillows reclined a dark-haired, large-eyed, pretty woman, of unmistakably French extraction on one side or the other. She was probably some years older than Elizabeth, and had a sparkling light in her eye. In front of the sofa was a small table, with a pack of cards scattered upon it faces upward.

The attitude had been so full of abandonment that she bounded up like a spring on hearing the door open.

Perceiving that it was Elizabeth she lapsed into ease, and came across to her with a reckless skip that innate grace only prevented from being boisterous.

'Why, you are late,' she said, taking hold of Elizabeth-Jane's hands.

'There were so many little things to put up.'

'And you seem dead-alive and tired. Let me try to enliven you by some wonderful tricks I have learnt, to kill time. Sit there and don't move.' She gathered up the pack of cards, pulled the table in front of her, and began to deal them rapidly, telling Elizabeth to choose some.

'Well, have you chosen?' she asked, flinging down the last card.

'No,' stammered Elizabeth, arousing herself from a reverie. 'I quite forgot, I was thinking of – you, and me – and how strange it is that I am here.'

Miss Templeman looked at Elizabeth-Jane with interest, and laid down the cards. 'Ah! never mind,' she said. 'I'll lie here while you sit by me; and we'll talk.'

Elizabeth drew up silently to the head of the sofa, but with obvious pleasure. It could be seen that though in years she was younger than her entertainer in manner and general vision she seemed more of the sage. Miss Templeman deposited herself on the sofa in her former flexuous position, and throwing her arm above her brow – somewhat in the pose of a well-known conception of Titian's – talked up at Elizabeth-Jane invertedly across her forehead and arm.

'I must tell you something,' she said. 'I wonder if you have suspected it. I have only been mistress of a large house and a fortune a little while.'

'Oh – only a little while?' murmured Elizabeth-Jane, her countenance slightly falling.

'As a girl I lived about in garrison towns and elsewhere with my father, till I was quite flighty and unsettled. He was an officer in the army. I should not have mentioned this had I not thought it best you should know the truth.'

'Yes, yes.' She looked thoughtfully round the room – at the little square piano with brass inlayings, at the window-curtains, at the lamp, at the fair and dark kings and queens on the card-table, and finally at the inverted face of Lucetta Templeman, whose large lustrous eyes had such an odd effect upside down.

Elizabeth's mind ran on acquirements to an almost morbid degree. 'You speak French and Italian fluently, no doubt,' she said. 'I have not been able to get beyond a wretched bit of Latin yet.'

'Well, for that matter, in my native isle speaking French does not go for much. It is rather the other way.'

'Where is your native isle?'

It was with rather more reluctance that Miss Templeman said, 'Jersey. There they speak French on one side of the street and English on the other, and a mixed tongue in the middle of the road. But it is a long time since I was there. Bath is where my people really belong to, though my ancestors in Jersey were as good as anybody in England. They were the Le Sueurs, an old family who have done great things in their time. I went back and lived there after my father's death. But I don't value such past matters, and am quite an English person in my feelings and tastes.'

Lucetta's tongue had for a moment outrun her discretion. She had arrived at Casterbridge as a Bath lady, and there were obvious reasons why Jersey should drop out of her life. But Elizabeth had tempted her to make free, and a deliberately formed resolve had been broken.

It could not, however, have been broken in safer company. Lucetta's words went no further, and after this day she was so much upon her guard that there appeared no chance of her identification with the young Jersey woman who had been Henchard's dear comrade at a critical time. Not the least amusing of her safeguards was her resolute avoidance of a French word if one by accident came to her tongue more readily than its English equivalent. She shirked it with the suddenness of the weak Apostle at the accusation, 'Thy speech bewrayeth thee!'

Expectancy sat visibly upon Lucetta the next morning. She dressed herself for Mr Henchard, and restlessly awaited his call before mid-day; as he did not come she waited on through the afternoon. But she did not tell Elizabeth that the person expected was the girl's stepfather.

They sat in adjoining windows of the same room in Lucetta's great stone mansion, netting, and looking out upon the market, which formed an animated scene. Elizabeth could see the crown of her stepfather's hat among the rest beneath, and was not aware that Lucetta watched the same object with yet intenser interest. He moved about amid the throng, at this point lively as an anthill; elsewhere more reposeful, and broken up by stalls of fruit and vegetables. The farmers as a rule preferred the open *carrefour* for their transactions, despite its inconvenient jostlings and the danger from crossing vehicles, to the gloomy sheltered market-room provided for them. Here they surged on this one day of the week, forming a little world of leggings, switches, and sample-bags; men of extensive stomachs, sloping like mountain sides; men whose heads in walking swayed as the trees in November gales; who in conversing varied their attitudes much, lowering themselves by spreading their knees, and thrusting their hands into the pockets of remote inner jackets. Their faces radiated tropical warmth; for though when at home their countenances varied with the seasons, their market-faces all the year round were glowing little fires.

All over-clothes here were worn as if they were an inconvenience, a hampering necessity. Some men were well-dressed; but the majority were careless in that respect, appearing in suits which were historical records of their wearer's deeds, sun-scorchings, and daily struggles for many years past. Yet many carried ruffled cheque-books in their pockets which regulated at the bank hard by a balance of never less than four figures. In fact, what these gibbous human shapes specially represented was ready money — money insistently ready — not ready next year like a nobleman's — often not merely ready at the bank like a professional man's, but ready in their large plump hands.

It happened that to-day there rose in the midst of them all two or three tall apple-trees standing as if they grew on the spot; till it was perceived that they were held by men from the cider-districts who came here to sell them, bringing the clay of their county on their boots. Elizabeth-Jane, who had often observed them, said, 'I wonder if the same trees come every week?'

'What trees?' said Lucetta, absorbed in watching for Henchard.

Elizabeth replied vaguely, for an incident checked her. Behind one of the trees stood Farfrae, briskly discussing a sample-bag with a farmer. Henchard had come up, accidentally encountering the young man, whose face seemed to inquire, 'Do we speak to each other?'

She saw her stepfather throw a shine into his eye which answered 'No!' Elizabeth-Jane sighed.

'Are you particularly interested in anybody out there?' said Lucetta.

'O no,' said her companion, a quick red shooting over her face.

Luckily Farfrae's figure was immediately covered by the apple-tree.

Lucetta looked hard at her. 'Quite sure?' she said.

'O yes,' said Elizabeth-Jane.

Again Lucetta looked out. 'They are all farmers, I suppose?' she said.

'No. There's Mr Bulge — he's a wine merchant; there's Benjamin Brownlet — a horse dealer; and Kitson, the pig breeder; and Yopper, the auctioneer; besides maltsters, and millers — and so on.' Farfrae stood out quite distinctly now; but she did not mention him.

The Saturday afternoon slipped on thus desultorily. The market changed from the sample-showing hour to the idle hour before starting homewards, when tales were told. Henchard had not called on Lucetta though he had stood so near. He must have been too busy, she thought. He would come on Sunday or Monday.

The days came but not the visitor, though Lucetta repeated her dressing with scrupulous care. She was disheartened. It may at once be declared that Lucetta no longer bore towards Henchard all that warm allegiance which had characterized her in their first acquaintance; the then unfortunate issue of things had chilled pure love considerably. But there remained a conscientious wish to bring about her union with him, now that there was nothing to hinder it — to right her position — which in itself was a happiness to sigh for. With strong social reasons on her side why their marriage should take place there had ceased to be any worldly reason on his why it should be postponed, since she had succeeded to fortune.

Tuesday was the great Candlemas fair. At breakfast she said to Elizabeth-Jane quite coolly: 'I imagine your father may call to see you to-day. I suppose he stands close by in the market-place with the rest of the corn-dealers?'

She shook her head. 'He won't come.'

'Why?'

'He has taken against me,' she said in a husky voice.

'You have quarrelled more deeply than I know of.'

Elizabeth, wishing to shield the man she believed to be her father from any charge of unnatural dislike, said 'Yes.'

'Then where you are is, of all places, the one he will avoid?'

Elizabeth nodded sadly.

Lucetta looked blank, twitched up her lovely eyebrows and lips, and burst into hysterical sobs. Here was a disaster – her ingenious scheme completely stultified.

'O, my dear Miss Templeman – what's the matter?' cried her companion.

'I like your company much!' said Lucetta, as soon as she could speak.

'Yes, yes – and so do I yours!' Elizabeth chimed in soothingly.

'But – but –' She could not finish the sentence, which was, naturally, that if Henchard had such a rooted dislike for the girl as now seemed to be the case, Elizabeth-Jane would have to be got rid of – a disagreeable necessity.

A provisional resource suggested itself. 'Miss Henchard – will you go on an errand for me as soon as breakfast is over? – Ah, that's very good of you. Will you go and order –' Here she enumerated several commissions at sundry shops, which would occupy Elizabeth's time for the next hour or two, at least.

'And have you ever seen the Museum?'

Elizabeth-Jane had not.

'Then you should do so at once. You can finish the morning by going there. It is an old house in a back street – I forget where – but you'll find out – and there are crowds of interesting things – skeletons, teeth, old pots and pans, ancient boots and shoes, birds' eggs – all charmingly instructive. You'll be sure to stay till you get quite hungry.'

Elizabeth hastily put on her things and departed. 'I wonder why she wants to get rid of me to-day!' she said sorrowfully as she went. That her absence, rather than her services or instruction, was in request, had been readily apparent to Elizabeth-Jane, simple as she seemed, and difficult as it was to attribute a motive for the desire.

She had not been gone ten minutes when one of Lucetta's servants was sent to Henchard's with a note. The contents were briefly: –

DEAR MICHAEL, – You will be standing in view of my house to-day for two or three hours in the course of your business, so do please call and see me. I am sadly disappointed that you have not come before, for can I help anxiety about my own equivocal relation to you? – especially now my aunt's fortune has brought me more prominently before society? Your daughter's presence here may be the cause of your neglect; and I have therefore sent her away for the morning. Say you come on business – I shall be quite alone.

LUCETTA

When the messenger returned her mistress gave directions that if a gentleman called he was to be admitted at once, and sat down to await results.

Sentimentally she did not much care to see him – his delays had wearied her; but it was necessary; and with a sigh she arranged herself picturesquely in the chair; first this way, then that; next so that the light fell over her head. Next she flung herself on the couch in the cyma-recta curve which so became her, and with her arm over her brow looked towards the door. This, she decided, was the best position after all; and thus she remained till a man's step was heard on the stairs. Whereupon Lucetta, forgetting her curve (for Nature was too strong for Art as yet), jumped up and ran and hid herself behind one of the window-curtains in a freak of timidity. In spite of the waning of passion the situation was an agitating one – she had not seen Henchard since his (supposed) temporary parting from her in Jersey.

She could hear the servant showing the visitor into the room, shutting the door upon him, and leaving as if to go and look for her mistress. Lucetta flung back the curtain with a nervous greeting. The man before her was not Henchard.

CHAPTER TWENTY-THREE

A CONJECTURE that her visitor might be some other person had, indeed, flashed through Lucetta's mind when she was on the point of bursting out; but it was just too late to recede.

He was years younger than the Mayor of Casterbridge; fair, fresh, and slenderly handsome. He wore genteel cloth leggings with white buttons, polished boots with infinite lace holes, light cord breeches under a black velveteen coat and waistcoat; and he had a silver-topped switch in his hand. Lucetta blushed, and said with a curious mixture of pout and laugh on her face – 'O, I've made a mistake!'

The visitor, on the contrary, did not laugh half a wrinkle.

'But I'm very sorry!' he said, in deprecating tones. 'I came and I inquired for Miss Henchard, and they showed me up heere, and in no case would I have caught ye so unmannerly if I had known!'

'I was the unmannerly one,' said she.

'But is it that I have come to the wrong house, madam?' said Mr Farfrae, blinking a little in his bewilderment and nervously tapping his legging with his switch.

'O no, sir, – sit down. You must come and sit down now you are here,' replied Lucetta kindly, to relieve his embarrassment. 'Miss Henchard will be here directly.'

Now this was not strictly true; but that something about the young man – that hyperborean crispness, stringency, and charm, as of a well-braced musical instrument, which had awakened the interest of Henchard, and of Elizabeth-Jane, and of the Three Mariners' jovial crew, at sight, made his unexpected presence here attractive to Lucetta. He hesitated, looked at the chair, thought there was no danger in it (though there was), and sat down.

Farfrae's sudden entry was simply the result of Henchard's permission to him to see Elizabeth if he were minded to woo her. At first he had taken no notice of Henchard's brusque letter; but an exceptionally fortunate business transaction put him on good terms with everybody, and revealed to him that he could undeniably marry if he chose. Then who so pleasing, thrifty, and satisfactory in every way as Elizabeth-Jane? Apart from her personal recommendations a reconciliation with his former friend Henchard would, in the natural course of things, flow from such a union. He therefore forgave the Mayor his curtness; and this morning on his way to the fair he had called at her house, where he learnt that she was staying at Miss Templeman's. A little stimulated at not finding her ready and waiting – so fanciful are men! – he hastened on to High-Place Hall to encounter no Elizabeth but its mistress herself.

'The fair to-day seems a large one,' she said when, by a natural deviation, their eyes sought the busy scene without. 'Your numerous fairs and markets keep me interested. How many things I think of while I watch from here!'

He seemed in doubt how to answer, and the babble without reached them as they sat – voices as of wavelets on a lopping sea, one ever and anon rising above the rest. 'Do you look out often?' he asked.

'Yes – very often.'

'Do you look for any one you know?'

Why should she have answered as she did?

'I look as at a picture merely. But,' she went on, turning pleasantly to him, 'I may do so now – I may look for you. You are always there, are you not? Ah – I don't mean it seriously! But it is amusing to look for somebody one knows in a crowd, even if one does not want him. It takes off the terrible oppressiveness of being surrounded by a throng, and having no point of junction with it through a single individual.'

'Ay! Maybe you'll be very lonely, ma'am?'

'Nobody knows how lonely.'

'But you are rich, they say?'

'If so, I don't know how to enjoy my riches. I came to Casterbridge thinking I should like to live here. But I wonder if I shall.'

'Where did ye come from, ma'am?'

'The neighbourhood of Bath.'

'And I from near Edinboro',' he murmured. 'It's better to stay at home, and that's true; but a man must live where his money is made. It is a great pity, but it's always so! Yet I've done very well this year. O yes,' he went on with ingenuous enthusiasm. 'You see that man with the drab kerseymere coat? I bought largely of him in the autumn when wheat was down, and then afterwards when it rose a little I sold off all I had! It brought only a small profit to me; while the farmers kept theirs, expecting higher figures – yes, though the rats were gnawing the ricks hollow. Just when I sold the markets went lower, and I bought up the corn of those who had been holding back at less price than my first purchases. And then,' cried Farfrae impetuously, his face alight, 'I sold it a few weeks after, when it happened to go up again! And so, by contenting mysel' with small profits frequently repeated, I soon made five hundred pounds – yes!' – (bringing down his hand upon the table, and quite forgetting where he was) – 'while the others by keeping theirs in hand made nothing at all!'

Lucetta regarded him with a critical interest. He was quite a new type of person to her. At last his eye fell upon the lady's and their glances met.

'Ay, now, I'm wearying you!' he exclaimed.

She said, 'No, indeed,' colouring a shade.

'What then?'

'Quite otherwise. You are most interesting.'

It was now Farfrae who showed the modest pink.

'I mean all you Scotchmen,' she added in hasty correction. 'So free from Southern extremes. We common people are all one way or the other – warm or cold, passionate or frigid. You have both temperatures going on in you at the same time.'

'But how do you mean that? Ye were best to explain clearly, ma'am.'

'You are animated – then you are thinking of getting on. You are sad the next moment – then you are thinking of Scotland and friends.'

'Yes. I think of home sometimes!' he said simply.

'So do I – as far as I can. But it was an old house where I was born, and they pulled it down for improvements, so I seem hardly to have any home to think of now.'

Lucetta did not add, as she might have done, that the house was in St Helier, and not in Bath.

'But the mountains, and the mists and the rocks, they are there! And don't they seem like home?'

She shook her head.

'They do to me – they do to me,' he murmured. And his mind could be seen flying away northwards. Whether its origin were national or personal, it was quite true what Lucetta had said, that the curious double strands in Farfrae's thread of life – the commercial and the romantic – were very distinct at times. Like the colours in a variegated cord those contrasts could be seen intertwisted, yet not mingling.

'You are wishing you were back again,' said she.

'Ah, no, ma'am,' said Farfrae, suddenly recalling himself.

The fair without the windows was now raging thick and loud. It was the chief hiring fair of the year, and differed quite from the market of a few days earlier. In substance it was a whitey-brown crowd flecked with white – this being the body of labourers waiting for places. The long bonnets of the women, like waggon-tilts, their cotton gowns and checked shawls, mixed with the carters' smock-frocks; for they, too, entered into the hiring. Among the rest, at the corner of the pavement, stood an old shepherd, who attracted the eyes of Lucetta and Farfrae by his stillness. He was evidently a chastened man. The battle of life had been a sharp one with him, for, to begin with, he was a man of small frame. He was now so bowed by hard work and years that, approaching from behind, a person could hardly see his head. He had planted the stem of his crook in the gutter and was resting upon the bow, which was polished to silver brightness by the long friction of his hands. He had quite forgotten where he was, and what he had come for, his eyes being bent on the ground. A little way off negotiations were proceeding which had reference to him; but he did not hear them, and there seemed to be passing through his mind pleasant visions of the hiring successes of his prime, when his skill laid open to him any farm for the asking.

The negotiations were between a farmer from a distant county and the old man's son. In these there was a difficulty. The farmer would not take the crust without the crumb of the bargain, in other words, the old man without the younger; and the son had a sweetheart on his present farm, who stood by, waiting the issue with pale lips.

'I'm sorry to leave ye, Nelly,' said the young man with emotion. 'But, you see, I can't starve father, and he's out o' work at Lady-day. 'Tis only thirty-five mile.'

The girl's lips quivered. 'Thirty-five mile!' she murmured. 'Ah! 'tis enough! I shall never see 'ee again!' It was, indeed, a hopeless length of traction for Dan Cupid's magnet; for young men were young men at Casterbridge as elsewhere.

'O! no, no – I never shall,' she insisted, when he pressed her hand; and she turned her face to Lucetta's wall to hide her weeping. The farmer said he would give the young man half-an-hour for his answer, and went away, leaving the group sorrowing.

Lucetta's eyes, full of tears, met Farfrae's. His, too, to her surprise, were moist at the scene.

'It is very hard,' she said with strong feelings. 'Lovers ought not to be parted like that! O, if I had my wish, I'd let people live and love at their pleasure!'

'Maybe I can manage that they'll not be parted,' said Farfrae. 'I want a young carter; and perhaps I'll take the old man too – yes; he'll not be very expensive, and doubtless he will answer my pairrpose somehow.'

'O, you are so good!' she cried, delighted. 'Go and tell them, and let me know if you have succeeded!'

Farfrae went out, and she saw him speak to the group. The eyes of all brightened; the bargain was soon struck. Farfrae returned to her immediately it was concluded.

'It is kind-hearted of you, indeed,' said Lucetta. 'For my part, I have resolved that all my servants shall have lovers if they want them! Do make the same resolve!'

Farfrae looked more serious, waving his head a half turn. 'I must be a little stricter than that,' he said.

'Why?'

'You are a – a thriving woman; and I am a struggling hay-and-corn merchant.'

'I am a very ambitious woman.'

'Ah, well, I cannet explain. I don't know how to talk to ladies, ambitious or no; and that's true,' said Donald with grave regret. 'I try to be civil to a' folk – no more!'

'I see you are as you say,' replied she, sensibly getting the upper hand in these exchanges of sentiment. Under this revelation of insight Farfrae again looked out of the window into the thick of the fair.

Two farmers met and shook hands, and being quite near the window their remarks could be heard as others' had been.

'Have you seen young Mr Farfrae this morning?' asked one. 'He promised to meet me here at the stroke of twelve; but I've gone athwart and about the fair half-a-dozen times, and never a sign of him: though he's mostly a man to his word.'

'I quite forgot the engagement,' murmured Farfrae.

'Now you must go,' said she; 'must you not?'

'Yes,' he replied. But he still remained.

'You had better go,' she urged. 'You will lose a customer.'

'Now, Miss Templeman, you will make me angry,' exclaimed Farfrae.

'Then suppose you don't go; but stay a little longer?'

He looked anxiously at the farmer who was seeking him, and who just then ominously walked across to where Henchard was standing, and he looked into the room and at her. 'I like staying; but I fear I must go!' he said. 'Business ought not to be neglected, ought it?'

'Not for a single minute.'

'It's true. I'll come another time – if I may, ma'am?'

'Certainly,' she said. 'What has happened to us to-day is very curious.'

'Something to think over when we are alone, it's like to be?'

'Oh, I don't know that. It is commonplace after all.'

'No, I'll not say that. O no!'

'Well, whatever it has been, it is now over; and the market calls you to be gone.'

'Yes, yes. Market – business! I wish there were no business in the warrld.'

Lucetta almost laughed – she would quite have laughed – but that there was a little emotion going in her at the time. 'How you change!' she said. 'You should not change like this.'

'I have never wished such things before,' said the Scotchman, with a simple, shamed, apologetic look for his weakness. 'It is only since coming here and seeing you!'

'If that's the case, you had better not look at me any longer. Dear me, I feel I have quite demoralized you!'

'But look or look not, I will see you in my thoughts. Well, I'll go – thank you for the pleasure of this visit.'

'Thank you for staying.'

'Maybe I'll get into my market-mind when I've been out a few minutes,' he murmured. 'But I don't know – I don't know!'

As he went she said eagerly, 'You may hear them speak of me in Casterbridge as time goes on. If they tell you I'm a coquette, which some may, because of the incidents of my life, don't believe it, for I am not.'

'I swear I will not!' he said fervidly.

Thus the two. She had enkindled the young man's enthusiasm till he was quite brimming with sentiment; while he, from merely affording her a new form of idleness had gone on to wake her serious solicitude. Why was this? They could not have told.

Lucetta as a young girl would hardly have looked at a tradesman. But her ups and downs, capped by her indiscretions with Henchard, had made her uncritical as to station. In her poverty she had met with repulse from the society to which she had belonged, and she had no great zest for renewing an attempt upon it now. Her heart longed for some ark into which it could fly and be at rest. Rough or smooth she did not care so long as it was warm.

Farfrae was shown out, it having entirely escaped him that he had called to see Elizabeth. Lucetta at the window watched him threading the maze of farmers and farmers' men. She could see by his gait that he was conscious of her eyes, and her heart went out to him for his modesty – pleaded with her sense of his unfitness that he might be allowed to come again. He entered the market-house, and she could see him no more.

Three minutes later, when she had left the window, knocks, not of multitude but of strength, sounded through the house, and the waiting-maid tripped up.

'The Mayor,' she said.

Lucetta had reclined herself, and was looking dreamily through her fingers. She did not answer at once, and the maid repeated the information with the addition, 'And he's afraid he hasn't much time to spare, he says.'

'Oh! Then tell him that as I have a headache I won't detain him to-day.'

The message was taken down, and she heard the door close.

Lucetta had come to Casterbridge to quicken Henchard's feelings with regard to her. She had quickened them, and now she was indifferent to the achievement.

Her morning view of Elizabeth-Jane as a disturbing element changed, and she no longer felt strongly the necessity of getting rid of the girl for her stepfather's sake. When the young woman came in, sweetly unconscious of the turn in the tide, Lucetta went up to her, and said quite sincerely –

'I'm so glad you've come. You'll live with me a long time, won't you?'

Elizabeth as a watch-dog to keep her father off – what a new idea. Yet it was not unpleasing. Henchard had neglected her all these days, after compromising her indescribably in the past. The least he could have done when he found himself free, and herself affluent, would have been to respond heartily and promptly to her invitation.

Her emotions rose, fell, undulated, filled her with wild surmise at their suddenness; and so passed Lucetta's experiences of that day.

CHAPTER TWENTY-FOUR

POOR Elizabeth-Jane, little thinking what her malignant star had done to blast the budding attentions she had won from Donald Farfrae, was glad to hear Lucetta's words about remaining.

For in addition to Lucetta's house being a home, that raking view of the market-place which it afforded had as much attraction for her as for Lucetta. The *carrefour* was like the regulation Open Place in spectacular dramas, where the incidents that occur always happen to bear on the lives of the adjoining residents. Farmers, merchants, dairymen, quacks, hawkers, appeared there from week to week, and disappeared as the afternoon wasted away. It was the node of all orbits.

From Saturday to Saturday was as from day to day with the two young women now. In an emotional sense they did not live at all during the intervals. Wherever they might go wandering on other days, on market-day they were sure to be at home. Both stole sly glances out of the window at Farfrae's shoulders and poll. His face they seldom saw, for, either through shyness, or not to disturb his mercantile mood, he avoided looking towards their quarters.

Thus things went on, till a certain market-morning brought a new sensation. Elizabeth and Lucetta were sitting at breakfast when a parcel containing two dresses arrived for the latter from London. She called Elizabeth from her breakfast, and entering her friend's bedroom Elizabeth saw the gowns spread out on the bed, one of a deep cherry colour, the other lighter – a glove lying at the end of each sleeve, a bonnet at the top of each neck, and parasols across the gloves, Lucetta standing beside the suggested human figures in an attitude of contemplation.

'I wouldn't think so hard about it,' said Elizabeth, marking the intensity with which Lucetta was alternating the question whether this or that would suit best.

'But settling upon new clothes is so trying,' said Lucetta. 'You are that person' (pointing to one of the arrangements), 'or you are *that* totally different person' (pointing to the other), 'for the whole of the coming spring: and one of the two, you don't know which, may turn out to be very objectionable.'

It was finally decided by Miss Templeman that she would be the cherry-coloured person at all hazards. The dress was pronounced to be a fit, and Lucetta walked with it into the front room, Elizabeth following her.

The morning was exceptionally bright for the time of year. The sun fell so flat on the houses and pavement opposite Lucetta's residence that they poured their brightness into her rooms. Suddenly, after a rumbling of wheels, there were added to this steady light a fantastic series of circling irradiations upon the ceiling, and the companions turned to the window. Immediately opposite a vehicle of strange description had come to a standstill, as if it had been placed there for exhibition.

It was the new-fashioned agricultural implement called a horse-drill, till then unknown, in its modern shape, in this part of the country, where the venerable seed-lip was still used for sowing as in the days of the Heptarchy. Its arrival created about as much sensation in the corn-market as a flying machine would create at Charing Cross. The farmers crowded round it, women drew near it, children crept under and into it. The machine was painted in bright hues of green, yellow, and red, and it resembled as a whole a compound of hornet, grasshopper, and shrimp, magnified enormously. Or it might have been likened to an upright musical instrument with the front gone. That was how it struck Lucetta. 'Why, it is a sort of agricultural piano,' she said.

'It has something to do with corn,' said Elizabeth.

'I wonder who thought of introducing it here?'

Donald Farfrae was in the minds of both as the innovator, for though not a farmer he was closely leagued with farming operations. And as if in response to their thought he came up at that moment, looked at the machine, walked round it, and handled it as if he knew something about its make. The two watchers had inwardly started at his coming, and Elizabeth left the window, went to the back of the room, and stood as if absorbed in the panelling of the wall. She hardly knew that she had done this till Lucetta, animated by the conjunction of her new attire with the sight of Farfrae, spoke out: 'Let us go and look at the instrument, whatever it is.'

Elizabeth-Jane's bonnet and shawl were pitchforked on in a moment, and they went out. Among all the agriculturists gathering round the only appropriate possessor of the new machine seemed to be Lucetta, because she alone rivalled it in colour.

They examined it curiously; observing the rows of trumpet-shaped tubes one within the other, the little scoops, like revolving salt-spoons, which tossed the seed into the upper ends of the tubes that conducted it to the ground; till somebody said, 'Good morning, Elizabeth-Jane.' She looked up, and there was her stepfather.

His greeting had been somewhat dry and thunderous, and Elizabeth-Jane, embarrassed out of her equanimity, stammered at random, 'This is the lady I live with, father – Miss Templeman.'

Henchard put his hand to his hat, which he brought down with a great wave till it met his body at the knee. Miss Templeman bowed. 'I am happy to become acquainted with you, Mr Henchard,' she said. 'This is a curious machine.'

'Yes,' Henchard replied; and he proceeded to explain it, and still more forcibly to ridicule it.

'Who brought it here?' said Lucetta.

'Oh, don't ask me, ma'am!' said Henchard. 'The thing – why 'tis impossible it should act. 'Twas brought here by one of our machinists on the recommendation of a jumped-up jackanapes of a fellow who thinks—' His eye caught Elizabeth-Jane's imploring face, and he stopped, probably thinking that the suit might be progressing.

He turned to go away. Then something seemed to occur which his stepdaughter fancied must really be a hallucination of hers. A murmur apparently came from Henchard's lips in which she detected the words, 'You refused to see me!' reproachfully addressed to Lucetta. She could not believe that they had been uttered by her stepfather; unless, indeed, they might have been spoken to one of the yellow-gaitered farmers near them. Yet Lucetta seemed silent; and then all thought of the incident was dissipated by the humming of a song, which sounded as though from the interior of the machine. Henchard had by this time vanished into the market-house, and both the women glanced towards the corn-drill. They could see behind it the bent back of a man who was pushing his head into the internal works to master their simple secrets. The hummed song went on –

> ''Tw—s on a s—m—r aftern—n,
> A wee be—re the s—n w—nt d—n,
> When Kitty wi' a braw n—w g—wn
> C—me ow're the h—lls to Gowrie.'

Elizabeth-Jane had apprehended the singer in a moment, and looked guilty of she did not know what. Lucetta next recognized him, and more mistress of herself said archly, 'The "Lass of Gowrie" from the inside of a seed-drill – what a phenomenon!'

Satisfied at last with his investigation the young man stood upright, and met their eyes across the summit.

'We are looking at the wonderful new drill,' Miss Templeman said. 'But practically it is a stupid thing – is it not?' she added, on the strength of Henchard's information.

'Stupid? O no!' said Farfrae gravely. 'It will revolutionize sowing heerabout! No more sowers flinging their seed about broadcast, so that some falls by the wayside and some among thorns, and all that. Each grain will go straight to its intended place, and nowhere else whatever!'

'Then the romance of the sower is gone for good,' observed Elizabeth-Jane, who felt herself at one with Farfrae in Bible-reading at least. ' "He that observeth the wind shall not sow," so the Preacher said; but his words will not be to the point any more. How things change!'

'Ay; ay. . . . It must be so!' Donald admitted, his gaze fixing itself on a blank point far away. 'But the machines are already very common in the East and North of England,' he added apologetically.

Lucetta seemed to be outside this train of sentiment, her acquaintance with the Scriptures being somewhat limited. 'Is the machine yours?' she asked of Farfrae.

'O no, madam,' said he, becoming embarrassed and deferential at the sound of her voice, though with Elizabeth-Jane he was quite at his ease. 'No, no — I merely recommended that it should be got.'

In the silence which followed Farfrae appeared only conscious of her; to have passed from perception of Elizabeth into a brighter sphere of existence than she appertained to. Lucetta, discerning that he was much mixed that day, partly in his mercantile mood and partly in his romantic one, said gaily to him —

'Well, don't forsake the machine for us,' and went indoors with her companion.

The latter felt that she had been in the way, though why was unaccountable to her. Lucetta explained the matter somewhat by saying when they were again in the sitting-room —

'I had occasion to speak to Mr Farfrae the other day, and so I knew him this morning.'

Lucetta was very kind towards Elizabeth that day. Together they saw the market thicken, and in course of time thin away with the slow decline of the sun towards the upper end of the town, its rays taking the street endways and enfilading the long thoroughfare from top to bottom. The gigs and vans disappeared one by one till there was not a vehicle in the street. The time of the riding world was over; the pedestrian world held sway. Field labourers and their wives and children trooped in from the villages for their weekly shopping, and instead of a rattle of wheels and a tramp of horses ruling the sound as earlier, there was nothing but the shuffle of many feet. All the implements were gone; all the farmers; all the moneyed class. The character of the town's trading had changed from bulk to multiplicity, and pence were handled now as pounds had been handled earlier in the day.

Lucetta and Elizabeth looked out upon this, for though it was night and the street lamps were lighted, they had kept their shutters unclosed. In the faint blink of the fire they spoke more freely.

'Your father was distant with you,' said Lucetta.

'Yes.' And having forgotten the momentary mystery of Henchard's seeming speech to Lucetta she continued, 'It is because he does not think I am respectable. I have tried to be so more than you can imagine, but in vain! My mother's separation from my father was unfortunate for me. You don't know what it is to have shadows like that upon your life.'

Lucetta seemed to wince. 'I do not — of that kind precisely,' she said, 'but you may feel a — sense of disgrace — shame — in other ways.'

'Have you ever had any such feeling?' said the younger innocently.

'O no,' said Lucetta quickly. 'I was thinking of — what happens sometimes when women get themselves in strange positions in the eyes of the world from no fault of their own.'

'It must make them very unhappy afterwards.'

'It makes them anxious; for might not other women despise them?'

'Not altogether despise them. Yet not quite like or respect them.'

Lucetta winced again Her past was by no means secure from investigation, even in Casterbridge. For one thing Henchard had never returned to her the cloud of letters she had written and sent him in her first excitement. Possibly they were destroyed; but she could have wished that they had never been written.

The rencounter with Farfrae and his bearing towards Lucetta had made the reflective Elizabeth more observant of her brilliant and amiable companion. A few days afterwards, when her eyes met Lucetta's as the latter was going out, she somehow knew that Miss Templeman was nourishing a hope of seeing the attractive Scotchman. The fact was printed large all over Lucetta's cheeks and eyes to any one who could read her as Elizabeth-Jane was beginning to do. Lucetta passed on and closed the street door.

A seer's spirit took possession of Elizabeth, impelling her to sit down by the fire and divine events so surely from data already her own that they could be held as witnessed. She followed Lucetta thus mentally—saw her encounter Donald somewhere as if by chance—saw him wear his special look when meeting women, with an added intensity because this one was Lucetta. She depicted his impassioned manner; beheld the indecision of both between their lothness to separate and their desire not to be observed; depicted their shaking of hands; how they probably parted with frigidity in their general contour and movements, only in the smaller features showing the spark of passion, thus invisible to all but themselves. This discerning silent witch had not done thinking of these things when Lucetta came noiselessly behind her and made her start.

It was all true as she had pictured—she could have sworn it. Lucetta had a heightened luminousness in her eye over and above the advanced colour of her cheeks.

'You've seen Mr Farfrae,' said Elizabeth demurely.

'Yes,' said Lucetta. 'How did you know?'

She knelt down on the hearth and took her friend's hands excitedly in her own. But after all she did not say when or how she had seen him or what he had said.

That night she became restless; in the morning she was feverish; and at breakfast-time she told her companion that she had something on her mind — something which concerned a person in whom she was interested much. Elizabeth was earnest to listen and sympathize.

'This person—a lady—once admired a man much—very much,' she said tentatively.

'Ah,' said Elizabeth-Jane.

'They were intimate—rather. He did not think so deeply of her as she did of him. But in an impulsive moment, purely out of reparation, he proposed to make her his wife. She agreed. But there was an unexpected hitch in the proceedings; though she had been so far compromised with him that she felt she could never belong to another man, as a pure matter of conscience, even if she should wish to. After that they were much apart, heard nothing of each other for a long time, and she felt her life quite closed up for her.'

'Ah—poor girl!'

'She suffered much on account of him; though I should add that he could not altogether be blamed for what had happened. At last the obstacle which separated them was providentially removed; and he came to marry her.'

'How delightful!'

'But in the interval she – my poor friend – had seen a man she liked better than him. Now comes the point: Could she in honour dismiss the first?'

'A new man she liked better – that's bad!'

'Yes,' said Lucetta, looking pained at a boy who was swinging the town pump-handle. 'It is bad! Though you must remember that she was forced into an equivocal position with the first man by an accident – that he was not so well educated or refined as the second, and that she had discovered some qualities in the first that rendered him less desirable as a husband than she had at first thought him to be.'

'I cannot answer,' said Elizabeth-Jane thoughtfully. 'It is so difficult. It wants a Pope to settle that!'

'You prefer not to, perhaps?' Lucetta showed in her appealing tone how much she leant on Elizabeth's judgment.

'Yes, Miss Templeman,' admitted Elizabeth. 'I would rather not say.'

Nevertheless, Lucetta seemed relieved by the simple fact of having opened out the situation a little, and was slowly convalescent of her headache. 'Bring me a looking-glass. How do I appear to people?' she said languidly.

'Well – a little worn,' answered Elizabeth, eyeing her as a critic eyes a doubtful painting; fetching the glass she enabled Lucetta to survey herself in it, which Lucetta anxiously did.

'I wonder if I wear well, as times go!' she observed after a while.

'Yes – fairly.'

'Where am I worst?'

'Under your eyes – I notice a little brownness there.'

'Yes. That is my worst place, I know. How many years more do you think I shall last before I get hopelessly plain?'

There was something curious in the way in which Elizabeth, though the younger, had come to play the part of experienced sage in these discussions. 'It may be five years,' she said judicially. 'Or, with a quiet life, as many as ten. With no love you might calculate on ten.'

Lucetta seemed to reflect on this as on an unalterable, impartial verdict. She told Elizabeth-Jane no more of the past attachment she had roughly adumbrated as the experiences of a third person; and Elizabeth, who in spite of her philosophy was very tender-hearted, sighed that night in bed at the thought that her pretty, rich Lucetta did not treat her to the full confidence of names and dates in her confessions. For by the 'she' of Lucetta's story Elizabeth had not been beguiled.

CHAPTER TWENTY-FIVE

THE next phase of the supersession of Henchard in Lucetta's heart was an experiment in calling on her performed by Farfrae with some apparent trepidation. Conventionally speaking he conversed with both Miss Templeman and her companion; but in fact it was rather that Elizabeth sat invisible in the room. Donald appeared not to see her at all, and answered her wise little remarks with curtly indifferent monosyllables, his looks and faculties hanging on the woman who could boast of a more Protean variety in her phases, moods, opinions, and also principles, than could Elizabeth. Lucetta had persisted in dragging her into the circle; but she had remained like an awkward third point which that circle would not touch.

Susan Henchard's daughter bore up against the frosty ache of the treatment, as she had borne up under worse things, and contrived as soon as possible to get out of the inharmonious room without being missed. The Scotchman seemed hardly the same Farfrae who had danced with her and walked with her in a delicate poise between love and friendship – that period in the history of a love when alone it can be said to be unalloyed with pain.

She stoically looked from her bedroom window, and contemplated her fate as if it were written on the top of the church-tower hard by. 'Yes,' she said at last, bringing down her palm upon the sill with a pat: '*He* is the second man of that story she told me!'

All this time Henchard's smouldering sentiments towards Lucetta had been fanned into higher and higher inflammation by the circumstances of the case. He was discovering that the young woman for whom he once felt a pitying warmth which had been almost chilled out of him by reflection, was, when now qualified with a slight inaccessibility and a more matured beauty, the very being to make him satisfied with life. Day after day proved to him, by her silence, that it was no use to think of bringing her round by holding aloof; so he gave in, and called upon her again, Elizabeth-Jane being absent.

He crossed the room to her with a heavy tread of some awkwardness, his strong, warm gaze upon her – like the sun beside the moon in comparison with Farfrae's modest look – and with something of a hail-fellow bearing, as, indeed, was not unnatural. But she seemed so transubstantiated by her change of position, and held out her hand to him in such cool friendship, that he became deferential, and sat down with a perceptible loss of power. He understood but little of fashion in dress, yet enough to feel himself inadequate in appearance beside her whom he had hitherto been dreaming of as almost his property. She said something very polite about his being good enough to call. This caused him to recover balance. He looked her oddly in the face, losing his awe.

'Why, of course I have called, Lucetta,' he said. 'What does that nonsense mean? You know I couldn't have helped myself if I had wished – that is, if I had any kindness at all. I've called to say that I am ready, as soon as custom will permit, to give you my name in return for your devotion, and what you lost by it in thinking too little of yourself and too much of me; to say that you can fix the day or month, with my full consent, whenever in your opinion it would be seemly: you know more of these things than I.'

'It is full early yet,' she said evasively.

'Yes, yes; I suppose it is. But you know, Lucetta, I felt directly my poor ill-used Susan died, and when I could not bear the idea of marrying again, that after what had happened between us it was my duty not to let any unnecessary delay occur before putting things to rights. Still, I wouldn't call in a hurry, because – well, you can guess how this money you've come into made me feel.' His voice slowly fell; he was conscious that in this room his accents and manner wore a roughness not observable in the street. He looked about the room at the novel hangings and ingenious furniture with which she had surrounded herself.

'Upon my life I didn't know such furniture as this could be bought in Casterbridge,' he said.

'Nor can it be,' said she. 'Nor will it till fifty years more of civilization have passed over the town. It took a waggon and four horses to get it here.'

'H'm. It looks as if you were living on capital.'

'O no, I am not.'

'So much the better. But the fact is, your setting up like this makes my bearing towards you rather awkward.'

'Why?'

An answer was not really needed, and he did not furnish one. 'Well,' he went on, 'there's nobody in the world I would have wished to see enter into this wealth before you, Lucetta, and nobody, I am sure, who will become it more.' He turned to her with congratulatory admiration so fervid that she shrank somewhat, notwithstanding that she knew him so well.

'I am greatly obliged to you for all that,' said she, rather with an air of speaking ritual. The stint of reciprocal feeling was perceived, and Henchard showed chagrin at once – nobody was more quick to show that than he.

'You may be obliged or not for't. Though the things I say may not have the polish of what you've lately learnt to expect for the first time in your life, they are real, my lady Lucetta.'

'That's rather a rude way of speaking to me,' pouted Lucetta, with stormy eyes.

'Not at all!' replied Henchard hotly. 'But there, there, I don't wish to quarrel with 'ee. I come with an honest proposal for silencing your Jersey enemies, and you ought to be thankful.'

'How can you speak so!' she answered, firing quickly. 'Knowing that my only crime was the indulging in a foolish girl's passion for you with too little regard for correctness, and that I was what *I* call innocent all the time they called me guilty, you ought not to be so cutting! I suffered enough at that worrying time, when you wrote to tell me of your wife's return and my consequent dismissal, and if I am a little independent now, surely the privilege is due to me!'

'Yes, it is,' he said. 'But it is not by what is, in this life, but by what appears, that you are judged; and I therefore think you ought to accept me – for your own good name's sake. What is known in your native Jersey may get known here.'

'How you keep on about Jersey! I am English!'

'Yes, yes. Well, what do you say to my proposal?'

For the first time in their acquaintance Lucetta had the move; and yet she was backward. 'For the present let things be,' she said with some embarrassment. 'Treat me as an acquaintance; and I'll treat you as one. Time will—' she stopped; and he said nothing to fill the gap for awhile, there being no pressure of half acquaintance to drive them into speech if they were not minded for it.

'That's the way the wind blows, is it?' he said at last grimly, nodding an affirmative to his own thoughts.

A yellow flood of reflected sunlight filled the room for a few instants. It was produced by the passing of a load of newly trussed hay from the country, in a waggon marked with Farfrae's name. Beside it rode Farfrae himself on horseback. Lucetta's face became – as a woman's face becomes when the man she loves rises upon her gaze like an apparition.

A turn of the eye by Henchard, a glance from the window, and the secret of her inaccessibility would have been revealed. But Henchard in estimating her tone was looking down so plumb-straight that he did not note the warm consciousness upon Lucetta's face.

'I shouldn't have thought it – I shouldn't have thought it of women!' he said emphatically by-and-by, rising and shaking himself into activity; while Lucetta was so anxious to divert him from any suspicion of the truth that she asked him to be in no hurry. Bringing him some apples she insisted upon paring one for him.

He would not take it. 'No, no; such is not for me,' he said drily, and moved to the door. At going out he turned his eye upon her.

'You came to live in Casterbridge entirely on my account,' he said. 'Yet now you are here you won't have anything to say to my offer!'

He had hardly gone down the staircase when she dropped upon the sofa and jumped up again in a fit of desperation. 'I *will* love him!' she cried passionately; 'as for *him* – he's hot-tempered and stern, and it would be madness to bind myself to him knowing that. I won't be a slave to the past – I'll love where I choose!'

Yet having decided to break away from Henchard one might have supposed her capable of aiming higher than Farfrae. But Lucetta reasoned nothing: she feared hard words from the people with whom she had been earlier associated; she had no relatives left; and with native lightness of heart took kindly to what fate offered.

Elizabeth-Jane, surveying the position of Lucetta between her two lovers from the crystalline sphere of a straightforward mind, did not fail to perceive that her father, as she called him, and Donald Farfrae became more desperately enamoured of her friend every day. On Farfrae's side it was the unforced passion of youth. On Henchard's the artificially stimulated coveting of maturer age.

The pain she experienced from the almost absolute obliviousness to her existence that was shown by the pair of them became at times half dissipated by her sense of its humorousness. When Lucetta had pricked her finger they were as deeply concerned as if she were dying; when she herself had been seriously sick or in danger they uttered a conventional word of sympathy at the news, and forgot all about it immediately. But, as regarded Henchard, this perception of hers also caused her some filial grief; she could not help asking what she had done to be neglected so, after the professions of solicitude he had made. As regarded Farfrae, she thought, after honest reflection, that it was quite natural. What was she beside Lucetta? – as one of the 'meaner beauties of the night', when the moon had risen in the skies.

She had learnt the lesson of renunciation, and was as familiar with the wreck of each day's wishes as with the diurnal setting of the sun. If her earthly career had taught her few book philosophies it had at least well practised her in this. Yet her experience had consisted less in a series of pure disappointments than in a series of substitutions. Continually it had happened that what she had desired had not been granted her, and that what had been granted her she had not desired. So she viewed with an approach to equanimity the now cancelled days when Donald had been her undeclared lover, and wondered what unwished-for thing Heaven might send her in place of him.

CHAPTER TWENTY-SIX

I T chanced that on a fine spring morning Henchard and Farfrae met in the chestnut-walk which ran along the south wall of the town. Each had just come out from his early breakfast, and there was not another soul near. Henchard was reading a letter from Lucetta, sent in answer to a note from him, in which she made some excuse for not immediately granting him a second interview that he had desired.

Donald had no wish to enter into conversation with his former friend on their present constrained terms; neither would he pass him in scowling silence. He nodded, and Henchard did the same. They had receded from each other several paces when a voice cried 'Farfrae!' It was Henchard's, who stood regarding him.

'Do you remember,' said Henchard, as if it were the presence of the thought and not of the man which made him speak, 'do you remember my story of that second woman – who suffered for her thoughtless intimacy with me?'

'I do,' said Farfrae.

'Do you remember my telling 'ee how it all began and how it ended?'

'Yes.'

'Well, I have offered to marry her now that I can; but she won't marry me. Now what would you think of her – I put it to you?'

'Well, ye owe her nothing more now,' said Farfrae heartily.

'It is true,' said Henchard, and went on.

That he had looked up from a letter to ask his questions completely shut out from Farfrae's mind all vision of Lucetta as the culprit. Indeed, her present position was so different from that of the young woman of Henchard's story as of itself to be sufficient to blind him absolutely to her identity. As for Henchard, he was reassured by Farfrae's words and manner against a suspicion which had crossed his mind. They were not those of a conscious rival.

Yet that there was rivalry by some one he was firmly persuaded. He could feel it in the air around Lucetta, see it in the turn of her pen. There was an antagonistic force in exercise, so that when he had tried to hang near her he seemed standing in a refluent current. That it was not innate caprice he was more and more certain. Her windows gleamed as if they did not want him; her curtains seemed to hang slily, as if they screened an ousting presence. To discover whose presence that was – whether really Farfrae's after all, or another's – he exerted himself to the utmost to see her again; and at length succeeded.

At the interview, when she offered him tea, he made it a point to launch a cautious inquiry if she knew Mr Farfrae.

O yes, she knew him, she declared; she could not help knowing almost everybody in Casterbridge, living in such a gazebo over the centre and arena of the town.

'Pleasant young fellow,' said Henchard.

'Yes,' said Lucetta.

'We both know him,' said kind Elizabeth-Jane, to relieve her companion's divined embarrassment.

There was a knock at the door; literally, three full knocks and a little one at the end.

'That kind of knock means half-and-half — somebody between gentle and simple,' said the corn-merchant to himself. 'I shouldn't wonder therefore if it is he.' In a few seconds surely enough Donald walked in.

Lucetta was full of little fidgets and flutters, which increased Henchard's suspicions without affording any special proof of their correctness. He was well-nigh ferocious at the sense of the queer situation in which he stood towards this woman. One who had reproached him for deserting her when calumniated, who had urged claims upon his consideration on that account, who had lived waiting for him, who at the first decent moment had come to ask him to rectify, by making her his, the false position into which she had placed herself for his sake; such she had been. And now he sat at her tea-table eager to gain her attention, and in his amatory rage feeling the other man present to be a villain, just as any young fool of a lover might feel.

They sat stiffly side by side at the darkening table, like some Tuscan painting of the two disciples supping at Emmaus. Lucetta, forming the third and haloed figure, was opposite them; Elizabeth-Jane, being out of the game, and out of the group, could observe all from afar, like the evangelist who had to write it down: that there were long spaces of taciturnity, when all exterior circumstance was subdued to the touch of spoons and china, the click of a heel on the pavement under the window, the passing of a wheel-barrow or cart, the whistling of the carter, the gush of water into householders' buckets at the town-pump opposite; the exchange of greetings among their neighbours, and the rattle of the yokes by which they carried off their evening supply.

'More bread-and-butter?' said Lucetta to Henchard and Farfrae equally, holding out between them a plateful of long slices. Henchard took a slice by one end and Donald by the other; each feeling certain he was the man meant; neither let go, and the slice came in two.

'Oh — I am so sorry!' cried Lucetta, with a nervous titter. Farfrae tried to laugh; but he was too much in love to see the incident in any but a tragic light.

'How ridiculous of all three of them!' said Elizabeth to herself.

Henchard left the house with a ton of conjecture, though without a grain of proof, that the counter-attraction was Farfrae; and therefore he would not make up his mind. Yet to Elizabeth-Jane it was plain as the town-pump that Donald and Lucetta were incipient lovers. More than once, in spite of her care, Lucetta had been unable to restrain her glance from flitting across into Farfrae's eyes like a bird to its nest. But Henchard was constructed upon too large a scale to discern such minutiæ as these by any evening light, which to him were as the notes of an insect that lie above the compass of the human ear.

But he was disturbed. And the sense of occult rivalry in suitorship was so much superadded to the palpable rivalry of their business lives. To the coarse materiality of that rivalry it added an inflaming soul.

The thus vitalized antagonism took the form of action by Henchard sending for Jopp, the manager originally displaced by Farfrae's arrival. Henchard had frequently met this man about the streets, observed that his clothing spoke of neediness, heard that he lived in Mixen Lane — a back slum of the town, the *pis aller* of Casterbridge domiciliation — itself almost a proof that a man had reached a stage when he would not stick at trifles.

Jopp came after dark, by the gates of the store-yard, and felt his way through the hay and straw to the office where Henchard sat in solitude awaiting him.

'I am again out of a foreman,' said the corn-factor. 'Are you in a place?'

'Not so much as a beggar's, sir.'

'How much do you ask?'

Jopp named his price, which was very moderate.

'When can you come?'

'At this hour and moment, sir,' said Jopp, who, standing hands-pocketed at the street corner till the sun had faded the shoulders of his coat to scarecrow green, had regularly watched Henchard in the market-place, measured him, and learnt him, by virtue of the power which the still man has in his stillness of knowing the busy one better than he knows himself. Jopp, too, had had a convenient experience; he was the only one in Casterbridge besides Henchard and the close-lipped Elizabeth who knew that Lucetta came truly from Jersey, and but proximately from Bath. 'I know Jersey, too, sir,' he said. 'Was living there when you used to do business that way. O yes — have often seen ye there.'

'Indeed! Very good. Then the thing is settled. The testimonials you showed me when you first tried for't are sufficient.'

That characters deteriorate in time of need possibly did not occur to Henchard. Jopp said, 'Thank you,' and stood more firmly, in the consciousness that at last he officially belonged to that spot.

'Now,' said Henchard, digging his strong eyes into Jopp's face, 'one thing is necessary to me, as the biggest corn-and-hay-dealer in these parts. The Scotchman, who's taking the town trade so bold into his hands, must be cut out. D'ye hear? We two can't live side by side — that's clear and certain.'

'I've seen it all,' said Jopp.

'By fair competition I mean, of course,' Henchard continued. 'But as hard, keen, and unflinching as fair — rather more so. By such a desperate bid against him for the farmers' custom as will grind him into the ground — starve him out. I've capital, mind ye, and I can do it.'

'I'm all that way of thinking,' said the new foreman. Jopp's dislike of Farfrae as the man who had once usurped his place, while it made him a willing tool, made him, at the same time, commercially as unsafe a colleague as Henchard could have chosen.

'I sometimes think,' he added, 'that he must have some glass that he sees next year in. He has such a knack of making everything bring him fortune.'

'He's deep beyond all honest men's discerning; but we must make him shallower. We'll under-sell him, and over-buy him, and so snuff him out.'

They then entered into specific details of the process by which this would be accomplished, and parted at a late hour.

Elizabeth-Jane heard by accident that Jopp had been engaged by her stepfather. She was so fully convinced that he was not the right man for the place that, at the risk of making Henchard angry, she expressed her apprehension to him when they met. But it was done to no purpose. Henchard shut up her argument with a sharp rebuff.

The season's weather seemed to favour their scheme. The time was in the years immediately before foreign competition had revolutionized the trade in grain; when still, as from the earliest ages, the wheat quotations from month to month depended entirely upon the home harvest. A bad harvest, or the prospect of one, would double the price of corn in a few weeks; and the promise of a good yield would lower it as rapidly. Prices were like the roads of the period, steep in gradient, reflecting in their phases the local conditions, without engineering, levellings, or averages.

The farmer's income was ruled by the wheat-crop within his own horizon, and the wheat-crop by the weather. Thus, in person, he became a sort of flesh-barometer, with feelers always directed to the sky and wind around him. The local atmosphere was everything to him; the atmospheres of other countries a matter of indifference. The people, too, who were not farmers, the rural multitude, saw in the god of the weather a more important personage than they do now. Indeed, the feeling of the peasantry in this matter was so intense as to be almost unrealizable in these equable days. Their impulse was well-nigh to prostrate themselves in lamentation before untimely rains and tempests, which came as the Alastor of those households whose crime it was to be poor.

After midsummer they watched the weather-cocks as men waiting in antechambers watch the lackey. Sun elated them; quiet rain sobered them; weeks of watery tempest stupefied them. That aspect of the sky which they now regard as disagreeable they then beheld as maleficent.

It was June, and the weather was very unfavourable. Casterbridge, being as it were the bell-board on which all the adjacent hamlets and villages sounded their notes, was decidedly dull. Instead of new articles in the shop-windows those that had been rejected in the foregoing summer were brought out again; superseded reap-hooks, badly-shaped rakes, shop-worn leggings, and time-stiffened water-tights reappeared, furbished up as near to new as possible.

Henchard, backed by Jopp, read a disastrous garnering, and resolved to base his strategy against Farfrae upon that reading. But before acting he wished — what so many have wished — that he could know for certain what was at present only strong probability. He was superstitious — as such headstrong natures often are — and he nourished in his mind an idea bearing on the matter; an idea he shrank from disclosing even to Jopp.

In a lonely hamlet a few miles from the town — so lonely that what are called lonely villages were teeming by comparison — there lived a man of curious repute as a forecaster or weather-prophet. The way to his house was crooked and miry — even difficult in the present unpropitious season. One evening when it was raining so heavily that ivy and laurel resounded like distant musketry, and an out-door man could be excused for shrouding himself to his ears and eyes, such a shrouded figure on foot might have been perceived travelling in the direction of the hazel-copse which dripped over the prophet's cot. The turnpike-road became a lane, the lane a cart-track, the cart-track a bridle-path, the bridle-path a footway, the foot-way overgrown. The solitary walker slipped here and there, and stumbled over the natural springes formed by the brambles, till at length he reached the house, which, with its garden, was surrounded with a high, dense hedge. The cottage, comparatively a large one, had been built of mud by the occupier's own hands, and thatched also by himself. Here he had always lived, and here it was assumed he would die.

He existed on unseen supplies; for it was an anomalous thing that while there was hardly a soul in the neighbourhood but affected to laugh at this man's assertions, uttering the formula, 'There's nothing in 'em', with full assurance on the surface of their faces, very few of them were unbelievers in their secret hearts. Whenever they consulted him they did it 'for a fancy'. When they paid him they said, 'Just a trifle for Christmas', or 'Candlemas', as the case might be.

He would have preferred more honesty in his clients, and less sham ridicule; but fundamental belief consoled him for superficial irony. As stated, he was enabled to live; people supported him with their backs turned. He was sometimes astonished that men could profess so little and believe so much at his house, when at church they professed so much and believed so little.

Behind his back he was called 'Wide-oh', on account of his reputation; to his face 'Mr' Fall.

The hedge of his garden formed an arch over the entrance, and a door was inserted as in a wall. Outside the door the tall traveller stopped, bandaged his face with a handkerchief as if he were suffering from toothache, and went up the path. The window shutters were not closed, and he could see the prophet within, preparing his supper.

In answer to the knock Fall came to the door, candle in hand. The visitor stepped back a little from the light, and said, 'Can I speak to 'ee?' in significant tones. The other's invitation to come in was responded to by the country formula, 'This will do, thank 'ee', after which the householder has no alternative but to come out. He placed the candle on the corner of the dresser, took his hat from a nail, and joined the stranger in the porch, shutting the door behind him.

'I've long heard that you can — do things of a sort?' began the other, repressing his individuality as much as he could.

'Maybe so, Mr Henchard,' said the weather-caster.

'Ah — why do you call me that?' asked the visitor with a start.

'Because it's your name. Feeling you'd come I've waited for 'ee; and thinking you might be leery from your walk I laid two supper plates — look ye here.' He threw open the door and disclosed the supper-table, at which appeared a second chair, knife and fork, plate and mug, as he had declared.

Henchard felt like Saul at his reception by Samuel; he remained in silence for a few moments, then throwing off the disguise of frigidity which he had hitherto preserved, he said, 'Then I have not come in vain. . . . Now, for instance, can ye charm away warts?'

'Without trouble.'

'Cure the evil?'

'That I've done — with consideration — if they will wear the toad-bag by night as well as by day.'

'Forecast the weather?'

'With labour and time.'

'Then take this,' said Henchard. ' 'Tis a crown-piece. Now, what is the harvest fortnight to be? When can I know?'

'I've worked it out already, and you can know at once.' (The fact was that five farmers had already been there on the same errand from different parts of the country.) 'By the sun, moon, and stars, by the clouds, the winds, the trees, and grass, the candleflame and swallows, the smell of the herbs; likewise by the cats' eyes, the ravens, the leeches, the spiders, and the dungmixen, the last fortnight in August will be – rain and tempest.'

'You are not certain, of course?'

'As one can be in a world where all's unsure. 'Twill be more like living in Revelations this autumn than in England. Shall I sketch it out for 'ee in a scheme?'

'O no, no,' said Henchard. 'I don't altogether believe in forecasts, come to second thoughts on such. But I—'

'You don't – you don't – 'tis quite understood,' said Wide-oh, without a sound of scorn. 'You have given me a crown because you've one too many. But won't you join me at supper, now 'tis waiting and all?'

Henchard would gladly have joined; for the savour of the stew had floated from the cottage into the porch with such appetizing distinctness that the meat, the onions, the pepper, and the herbs could be severally recognized by his nose. But as sitting down to hob-and-nob there would have seemed to mark him too implicitly as the weather-caster's apostle, he declined, and went his way.

The next Saturday Henchard bought grain to such an enormous extent that there was quite a talk about his purchases among his neighbours the lawyer, the wine merchant, and the doctor; also on the next, and on all available days. When his granaries were full to choking, all the weathercocks of Casterbridge creaked and set their faces in another direction, as if tired of the south-west. The weather changed; the sunlight, which had been like tin for weeks, assumed the hues of topaz. The temperament of the welkin passed from the phlegmatic to the sanguine; an excellent harvest was almost a certainty; and as a consequence prices rushed down.

All these transformations, lovely to the outsider, to the wrong-headed corn-dealer were terrible. He was reminded of what he had well known before, that a man might gamble upon the square green areas of fields as readily as upon those of a card-room.

Henchard had backed bad weather, and apparently lost. He had mistaken the turn of the flood for the turn of the ebb. His dealings had been so extensive that settlement could not long be postponed, and to settle he was obliged to sell off corn that he had bought only a few weeks before at figures higher by many shillings a quarter. Much of the corn he had never seen; it had not even been moved from the ricks in which it lay stacked miles away. Thus he lost heavily.

In the blaze of an early August day he met Farfrae in the market-place. Farfrae knew of his dealings (though he did not guess their intended bearing on himself) and commiserated him; for since their exchange of words in the South Walk they had been on stiffly speaking terms. Henchard for the moment appeared to resent the sympathy; but he suddenly took a careless turn.

'Ho, no no! – nothing serious, man!' he cried with fierce gaiety. 'These things always happen, don't they? I know it has been said that figures have touched me tight lately; but is that anything rare? The case is not so bad as folk make out perhaps. And dammy, a man must be a fool to mind the common hazards of trade!'

But he had to enter the Casterbridge Bank that day for reasons which had never before sent him there – and to sit a long time in the partners' room with a constrained bearing. It was rumoured soon after that much real property as well as vast stores of produce, which had stood in Henchard's name in the town and neighbourhood, was actually the possession of his bankers.

Coming down the steps of the bank he encountered Jopp. The gloomy transactions just completed within had added fever to the original sting of Farfrae's sympathy that morning, which Henchard fancied might be satire disguised, so that Jopp met with anything but a bland reception. The latter was in the act of taking off his hat to wipe his forehead, and saying, 'A fine hot day,' to an acquaintance.

'You can wipe and wipe, and say, "A fine hot day," can ye!' cried Henchard in a savage undertone, imprisoning Jopp between himself and the bank wall. 'If it hadn't been for your blasted advice it might have been a fine day enough! Why did ye let me go on, hey? – when a word of doubt from you or anybody would have made me think twice! For you can never be sure of weather till 'tis past.'

'My advice, sir, was to do what you thought best.'

'A useful fellow! And the sooner you help somebody else in that way the better!' Henchard continued his address to Jopp in similar terms till it ended in Jopp's dismissal there and then, Henchard turning upon his heel and leaving him.

'You shall be sorry for this, sir; sorry as a man can be!' said Jopp, standing pale, and looking after the corn-merchant as he disappeared in the crowd of market-men hard by.

CHAPTER TWENTY-SEVEN

It was the eve of harvest. Prices being low Farfrae was buying. As was usual, after reckoning too surely on famine weather the local farmers had flown to the other extreme, and (in Farfrae's opinion) were selling off too recklessly – calculating with just a trifle too much certainty upon an abundant yield. So he went on buying old corn at its comparatively ridiculous price: for the produce of the previous year, though not large, had been of excellent quality.

When Henchard had squared his affairs in a disastrous way, and got rid of his burdensome purchases at a monstrous loss, the harvest began. There were three days of excellent weather, and then – 'What if that curst conjuror should be right after all!' said Henchard.

The fact was, that no sooner had the sickles begun to play than the atmosphere suddenly felt as if cress would grow in it without other nourishment. It rubbed people's cheeks like damp flannel when they walked abroad. There was a gusty, high, warm wind; isolated raindrops starred the window-panes at remote distances: the sunlight would flap out like a quickly opened fan, throw the pattern of the window upon the floor of the room in a milky, colourless shine, and withdraw as suddenly as it had appeared.

From that day and hour it was clear that there was not to be so successful an ingathering after all. If Henchard had only waited long enough he might at least have avoided loss though he had not made a profit. But the momentum of his character knew no patience. At this turn of the scales he remained silent. The movements of his mind seemed to tend to the thought that some power was working against him.

'I wonder,' he asked himself with eerie misgiving; 'I wonder if it can be that somebody has been roasting a waxen image of me, or stirring an unholy brew to confound me! I don't believe in such power; and yet — what if they should ha' been doing it!' Even he could not admit that the perpetrator, if any, might be Farfrae. These isolated hours of superstition came to Henchard in time of moody depression, when all his practical largeness of view had oozed out of him.

Meanwhile Donald Farfrae prospered. He had purchased in so depressed a market that the present moderate stiffness of prices was sufficient to pile for him a large heap of gold where a little one had been.

'Why, he'll soon be Mayor!' said Henchard. It was indeed hard that the speaker should, of all others, have to follow the triumphal chariot of this man to the Capitol.

The rivalry of the masters was taken up by the men.

September-night shades had fallen upon Casterbridge; the clocks had struck half-past eight, and the moon had risen. The streets of the town were curiously silent for such a comparatively early hour. A sound of jangling horse-bells and heavy wheels passed up the street. These were followed by angry voices outside Lucetta's house, which led her and Elizabeth-Jane to run to the windows, and pull up the blinds.

The neighbouring Market House and Town Hall abutted against its next neighbour the Church except in the lower storey, where an arched thoroughfare gave admittance to a large square called Bull Stake, A stone post rose in the midst, to which the oxen had formerly been tied for baiting with dogs to make them tender before they were killed in the adjoining shambles. In a corner stood the stocks.

The thoroughfare leading to this spot was now blocked by two four-horse waggons and horses, one laden with hay-trusses, the leaders having already passed each other, and become entangled head to tail. The passage of the vehicles might have been practicable if empty; but built up with hay to the bedroom windows as one was, it was impossible.

'You must have done it a' purpose!' said Farfrae's waggoner. 'You can hear my horses' bells half-a-mile such a night as this!'

'If ye'd been minding your business instead of zwailing along in such a gawk-hammer way, you would have zeed me!' retorted the worthy representative of Henchard.

However, according to the strict rule of the road it appeared that Henchard's man was most in the wrong; he therefore attempted to back into the High Street. In doing this the near hind-wheel rose against the churchyard wall, and the whole mountainous load went over, two of the four wheels rising in the air, and the legs of the thill horse.

Instead of considering how to gather up the load the two men closed in a fight with their fists. Before the first round was quite over Henchard came upon the spot, somebody having run for him.

Henchard sent the two men staggering in contrary directions by collaring one with each hand, turned to the horse that was down, and extricated him after some trouble. He then inquired into the circumstances; and seeing the state of his waggon and its load began hotly rating Farfrae's man.

Lucetta and Elizabeth-Jane had by this time run down to the street corner, whence they watched the bright heap of new hay lying in the moon's rays, and passed and re-passed by the forms of Henchard and the waggoners. The women had witnessed what nobody else had seen – the origin of the mishap; and Lucetta spoke.

'I saw it all, Mr Henchard,' she cried; 'and your man was most in the wrong!'

Henchard paused in his harangue and turned. 'Oh, I didn't notice you, Miss Templeman,' said he. 'My man in the wrong? Ah, to be sure; to be sure! But I beg your pardon notwithstanding. The other's is the empty waggon, and he must have been most to blame for coming on.'

'No; I saw it, too,' said Elizabeth-Jane. 'And I can assure you he couldn't help it.'

'You can't trust *their* senses!' murmured Henchard's man.

'Why not?' asked Henchard sharply.

'Why, you see, sir, all the women side with Farfrae – being a damn young dand – of the sort that he is – one that creeps into a maid's heart like the giddying worm into a sheep's brain – making crooked seem straight to their eyes!'

'But do you know who that lady is you talk about in such a fashion? Do you know that I pay my attentions to her, and have for some time? Just be careful!'

'Not I. I know nothing, sir, outside eight shillings a week.'

'And that Mr Farfrae is well aware of it? He's sharp in trade, but he wouldn't do anything so underhand as what you hint at.'

Whether because Lucetta heard this low dialogue, or not, her white figure disappeared from her doorway inward, and the door was shut before Henchard could reach it to converse with her further. This disappointed him, for he had been sufficiently disturbed by what the man had said to wish to speak to her more closely. While pausing the old constable came up.

'Just see that nobody drives against that hay and waggon to-night, Stubberd,' said the corn-merchant. 'It must bide till the morning, for all hands are in the fields still. And if any coach or road-waggon wants to come along, tell 'em they must go round by the back street, and be hanged to 'em. . . . Any case to-morrow up in Hall?'

'Yes, sir. One in number, sir.'

'Oh, what's that?'

'An old flagrant female, sir, swearing and committing a nuisance in a horrible profane manner against the church wall, sir, as if 'twere no more than a pot-house! That's all, sir.'

'Oh. The Mayor's out o' town, isn't he?'

'He is, sir.'

'Very well, then I'll be there. Don't forget to keep an eye on that hay. Good night t' 'ee.'

During those moments Henchard had determined to follow up Lucetta notwithstanding her elusiveness, and he knocked for admission.

The answer he received was an expression of Miss Templeman's sorrow at being unable to see him again that evening because she had an engagement to go out.

Henchard walked away from the door to the opposite side of the street, and stood by his hay in a lonely reverie, the constable having strolled elsewhere, and the horses being removed. Though the moon was not bright as yet there were no lamps lighted, and he entered the shadow of one of the projecting jambs which formed the thoroughfare to Bull Stake; here he watched Lucetta's door.

Candle-lights were flitting in and out of her bedroom, and it was obvious that she was dressing for the appointment, whatever the nature of that might be at such an hour. The lights disappeared, the clock struck nine, and almost at the moment Farfrae came round the opposite corner and knocked. That she had been waiting just inside for him was certain, for she instantly opened the door herself. They went together by the way of a back lane westward, avoiding the front street; guessing where they were going he determined to follow.

The harvest had been so delayed by the capricious weather that whenever a fine day occurred all sinews were strained to save what could be saved of the damaged crops. On account of the rapid shortening of the days the harvesters worked by moonlight. Hence to-night the wheat-fields abutting on the two sides of the square formed by Casterbridge town were animated by the gathering hands. Their shouts and laughter had reached Henchard at the Market House, while he stood there waiting, and he had little doubt from the turn which Farfrae and Lucetta had taken that they were bound for the spot.

Nearly the whole town had gone into the fields. The Casterbridge populace still retained the primitive habit of helping one another in time of need; and thus, though the corn belonged to the farming section of the little community – that inhabiting the Durnover quarter – the remainder was no less interested in the labour of getting it home.

Reaching the top of the lane Henchard crossed the shaded avenue on the walls, slid down the green rampart, and stood amongst the stubble. The 'stitches' or shocks rose like tents about the yellow expanse, those in the distance becoming lost in the moonlit hazes.

He had entered at a point removed from the scene of immediate operations; but two others had entered at that place, and he could see them winding among the shocks. They were paying no regard to the direction of their walk, whose vague serpentining soon began to bear down towards Henchard. A meeting promised to be awkward, and he therefore stepped into the hollow of the nearest shock, and sat down.

'You have my leave,' Lucetta was saying gaily. 'Speak what you like.'

'Well, then,' replied Farfrae, with the unmistakable inflection of the lover pure, which Henchard had never heard in full resonance on his lips before, 'you are sure to be much sought after for your position, wealth, talents, and beauty. But will ye resist the temptation to be one of those ladies with lots of admirers – ay – and be content to have only a homely one?'

'And he the speaker?' said she, laughing. 'Very well, sir, what next?'

'Ah! I'm afraid that what I feel will make me forget my manners!'

'Then I hope you'll never have any, if you lack them only for that cause.' After some broken words which Henchard lost she added, 'Are you sure you won't be jealous?'

Farfrae seemed to assure her that he would not, by taking her hand.

'You are convinced, Donald, that I love nobody else,' she presently said. 'But I should wish to have my own way in some things.'

'In everything! What special thing did you mean?'

'If I wished not to live always in Casterbridge, for instance, upon finding that I should not be happy here?'

Henchard did not hear the reply; he might have done so and much more, but he did not care to play the eavesdropper. They went on towards the scene of activity, where the sheaves were being handed, a dozen a minute, upon the carts and waggons which carried them away.

Lucetta insisted on parting from Farfrae when they drew near the workpeople. He had some business with them and, though he entreated her to wait a few minutes, she was inexorable, and tripped off homeward alone.

Henchard thereupon left the field and followed her. His state of mind was such that on reaching Lucetta's door he did not knock but opened it, and walked straight up to her sitting-room, expecting to find her there. But the room was empty, and he perceived that in his haste he had somehow passed her on the way hither. He had not to wait many minutes, however, for he soon heard her dress rustling in the hall, followed by a soft closing of the door. In a moment she appeared.

The light was so low that she did not notice Henchard at first. As soon as she saw him she uttered a little cry, almost of terror.

'How can you frighten me so?' she exclaimed, with a flushed face. 'It is past ten o'clock, and you have no right to surprise me here at such a time.'

'I don't know that I've not the right. At any rate I have the excuse. Is it so necessary that I should stop to think of manners and customs?'

'It is too late for propriety, and might injure me.'

'I called an hour ago, and you would not see me, and I thought you were in when I called now. It is you, Lucetta, who are doing wrong. It is not proper in 'ee to throw me over like this. I have a little matter to remind you of, which you seem to forget.'

She sank into a chair, and turned pale.

'I don't want to hear it — I don't want to hear it!' she said through her hands, as he, standing close to the edge of her gown, began to allude to the Jersey days.

'But you ought to hear it,' said he.

'It came to nothing; and through you. Then why not leave me the freedom that I gained with such sorrow! Had I found that you proposed to marry me for pure love I might have felt bound now. But I soon learnt that you had planned it out of mere charity — almost as an unpleasant duty — because I had nursed you, and compromised myself, and you thought you must repay me. After that I did not care for you so deeply as before.'

'Why did you come here to find me, then?'

'I thought I ought to marry you for conscience' sake, since you were free, even though I — did not like you so well.'

'And why then don't you think so now?'

She was silent. It was only too obvious that conscience had ruled well enough till new love had intervened and usurped that rule. In feeling this she herself forgot for the moment her partially justifying argument – that having discovered Henchard's infirmities of temper, she had some excuse for not risking her happiness in his hands after once escaping them. The only thing she could say was, 'I was a poor girl then; and now my circumstances have altered, so I am hardly the same person.'

'That's true. And it makes the case awkward for me. But I don't want to touch your money. I am quite willing that every penny of your property shall remain to your personal use. Besides, that argument has nothing in it. The man you are thinking of is no better than I.'

'If you were as good as he you would leave me!' she cried passionately.

This unluckily aroused Henchard. 'You cannot in honour refuse me,' he said. 'And unless you give me your promise this very night to be my wife, before a witness, I'll reveal our intimacy – in common fairness to other men!'

A look of resignation settled upon her. Henchard saw its bitterness; and had Lucetta's heart been given to any other man in the world than Farfrae he would probably have had pity upon her at that moment. But the supplanter was the upstart (as Henchard called him) who had mounted into prominence upon his shoulders, and he could bring himself to show no mercy.

Without another word she rang the bell, and directed that Elizabeth-Jane should be fetched from her room. The latter appeared, surprised in the midst of her lucubrations. As soon as she saw Henchard she went across to him dutifully.

'Elizabeth-Jane,' he said, taking her hand, 'I want you to hear this.' And turning to Lucetta: 'Will you, or will you not, marry me?'

'If you – wish it, I must agree!'

'You say yes?'

'I do.'

No sooner had she given the promise than she fell back in a fainting state.

'What dreadful thing drives her to say this, father, when it is such a pain to her?' asked Elizabeth, kneeling down by Lucetta. 'Don't compel her to do anything against her will! I have lived with her, and know that she cannot bear much.'

'Don't be a no'thern simpleton!' said Henchard drily. 'This promise will leave him free for you, if you want him, won't it?'

At this Lucetta seemed to wake from her swoon with a start.

'Him? Who are you talking about?' she said wildly.

'Nobody, as far as I am concerned,' said Elizabeth firmly.

'Oh – well. Then it is my mistake,' said Henchard. 'But the business is between me and Miss Templeman. She agrees to be my wife.'

'But don't dwell on it just now,' entreated Elizabeth, holding Lucetta's hand.

'I don't wish to, if she promises,' said Henchard.

'I have, I have,' groaned Lucetta, her limbs hanging like flails, from very misery and faintness. 'Michael, please don't argue it any more!'

'I will not,' he said. And taking up his hat he went away.

Elizabeth-Jane continued to kneel by Lucetta. 'What is this?' she said. 'You called my father "Michael" as if you knew him well? And how is it he has got this power over you, that you promise to marry him against your will? Ah – you have many many secrets from me!'

'Perhaps you have some from me,' Lucetta murmured with closed eyes, little thinking, however, so unsuspicious was she, that the secret of Elizabeth's heart concerned the young man who had caused this damage to her own.

'I would not – do anything against you at all!' stammered Elizabeth, keeping in all signs of emotion till she was ready to burst. 'I cannot understand how my father can command you so; I don't sympathize with him in it at all. I'll go to him and ask him to release you.'

'No, no,' said Lucetta. 'Let it all be.'

CHAPTER TWENTY-EIGHT

THE next morning Henchard went to the Town Hall below Lucetta's house, to attend Petty Sessions, being still a magistrate for the year by virtue of his late position as Mayor. In passing he looked up at her windows, but nothing of her was to be seen.

Henchard as a Justice of the Peace may at first seem to be an even greater incongruity than Shallow and Silence themselves. But his rough and ready perceptions, his sledge-hammer directness, had often served him better than nice legal knowledge in despatching such simple business as fell to his hands in this Court. To-day Dr Chalkfield, the Mayor for the year, being absent, the corn-merchant took the big chair, his eyes still abstractedly stretching out of the window to the ashlar front of High-Place Hall.

There was one case only, and the offender stood before him. She was an old woman of mottled countenance, attired in a shawl of that nameless tertiary hue which comes, but cannot be made – a hue neither tawny, russet, hazel, nor ash; a sticky black bonnet that seemed to have been worn in the country of the Psalmist where the clouds drop fatness; and an apron that had been white in times so comparatively recent as still to contrast visibly with the rest of her clothes. The steeped aspect of the woman as a whole showed her to be no native of the country-side or even of a country-town.

She looked cursorily at Henchard and the second magistrate, and Henchard looked at her, with a momentary pause, as if she had reminded him indistinctly of somebody or something which passed from his mind as quickly as it had come. 'Well, and what has she been doing?' he said, looking down at the charge-sheet.

'She is charged, sir, with the offence of disorderly female and nuisance,' whispered Stubberd.

'Where did she do that?' said the other magistrate.

'By the church, sir, of all the horrible places in the world! – I caught her in the act, your worship.'

'Stand back then,' said Henchard, 'and let's hear what you've got to say.'

Stubberd was sworn, the magistrate's clerk dipped his pen, Henchard being no note-taker himself, and the constable began –

'Hearing a' illegal noise I went down the street at twenty-five minutes past eleven p.m. on the night of the fifth instinct, Hannah Dominy. When I had—'

'Don't got on so fast, Stubberd,' said the clerk.

The constable waited, with his eyes on the clerk's pen, till the latter stopped scratching and said, 'yes.' Stubberd continued: 'When I had proceeded to the spot I saw defendant at another spot, namely, the gutter.' He paused, watching the point of the clerk's pen again.

'Gutter, yes, Stubberd.'

'Spot measuring twelve feet nine inches or thereabouts, from where I—' Still careful not to outrun the clerk's penmanship Stubberd pulled up again; for having got his evidence by heart it was immaterial to him whereabouts he broke off.

'I object to that,' spoke up the old woman, ' "spot measuring twelve feet nine or thereabouts from where I," is not sound testimony!'

The magistrates consulted, and the second one said that the bench was of opinion that twelve feet nine inches from a man on his oath was admissible.

Stubberd, with a suppressed gaze of victorious rectitude at the old woman, continued: 'Was standing myself. She was wambling about quite dangerous to the thoroughfare, and when I approached to draw near she committed the nuisance, and insulted me.'

' "Insulted me." . . . Yes, what did she say?'

'She said, "Put away that dee lantern," she says.'

'Yes.'

'Says she, "Dost hear, old turmit-head? Put away that dee lantern. I have floored fellows a dee sight finer-looking than a dee fool like thee, you son of a bee, dee me if I haint," she says.'

'I object to that conversation!' interposed the old woman. 'I was not capable enough to hear what I said, and what is said out of my hearing is not evidence.'

There was another stoppage for consultation, a book was referred to, and finally Stubberd was allowed to go on again. The truth was that the old woman had appeared in court so many more times than the magistrates themselves, that they were obliged to keep a sharp look-out upon their procedure. However, when Stubberd had rambled on a little further Henchard broke out impatiently, 'Come – we don't want to hear any more of them cust dees and bees! Say the words out like a man, and don't be so modest, Stubberd; or else leave it alone!' Turning to the woman, 'Now then, have you any questions to ask him, or anything to say?'

'Yes,' she replied with a twinkle in her eye; and the clerk dipped his pen.

'Twenty years ago or thereabout I was selling of furmity in a tent at Weydon Fair—'

' "Twenty years ago" – well, that's beginning at the beginning; suppose you go back to the Creation!' said the clerk, not without satire.

But Henchard stared, and quite forgot what was evidence and what was not.

'A man and a woman with a little child came into my tent,' the woman continued. 'They sat down and had a basin apiece. Ah, Lord's my life! I was of a more respectable station in the world then than I am now, being a land smuggler in a large way of business; and I used to season my furmity with rum for them who asked fo't. I did it for the man; and then he had more and more; till at last he quarrelled with his wife, and offered to sell her to the highest bidder. A sailor came in and bid five guineas, and paid the money, and led her away. And the man who sold his wife in that fashion is the man sitting there in the great big chair.' The speaker concluded by nodding her head at Henchard and folding her arms.

Everybody looked at Henchard. His face seemed strange, and in tint as if it had been powdered over with ashes. 'We don't want to hear your life and adventures,' said the second magistrate sharply, filling the pause which followed. 'You've been asked if you've anything to say bearing on the case.'

'That bears on the case. It proves that he's no better than I, and has no right to sit there in judgment upon me.'

' 'Tis a concocted story,' said the clerk. 'So hold your tongue!'

'No – 'tis true.' The words came from Henchard. ' 'Tis as true as the light,' he said slowly. 'And upon my soul it does prove that I'm no better than she! And to keep out of any temptation to treat her hard for her revenge, I'll leave her to you.'

The sensation in the court was indescribably great. Henchard left the chair, and came out, passing through a group of people on the steps and outside that was much larger than usual; for it seemed that the old furmity dealer had mysteriously hinted to the denizens of the lane in which she had been lodging since her arrival, that she knew a queer thing or two about their great local man Mr Henchard, if she chose to tell it. This had brought them hither.

'Why are there so many idlers round the Town-Hall to-day?' said Lucetta to her servant when the case was over. She had risen late, and had just looked out of the window.

'Oh, please, ma'am, 'tis this larry about Mr Henchard. A woman has proved that before he became a gentleman he sold his wife for five guineas in a booth at a fair.'

In all the accounts which Henchard had given her of the separation from his wife Susan for so many years, of his belief in her death, and so on, he had never clearly explained the actual and immediate cause of that separation. The story she now heard for the first time.

A gradual misery overspread Lucetta's face as she dwelt upon the promise wrung from her the night before. At bottom, then, Henchard was this. How terrible a contingency for a woman who should commit herself to his care.

During the day she went out to the Ring and to other places, not coming in till nearly dusk. As soon as she saw Elizabeth-Jane after her return indoors she told her that she had resolved to go away from home to the seaside for a few days – to Port-Bredy; Casterbridge was so gloomy.

Elizabeth, seeing that she looked wan and disturbed, encouraged her in the idea, thinking a change would afford her reflief. She could not help suspecting that the gloom which seemed to have come over Casterbridge in Lucetta's eyes might be partially owing to the fact that Farfrae was away from home.

Elizabeth saw her friend depart for Port-Bredy, and took charge of High-Place Hall till her return. After two or three days of solitude and incessant rain Henchard called at the house. He seemed disappointed to hear of Lucetta's absence, and though he nodded with outward indifference he went away handling his beard with a nettled mien.

The next day he called again. 'Is she come now?' he asked.

'Yes. She returned this morning,' replied his stepdaughter. 'But she is not indoors. She has gone for a walk along the turnpike-road to Port-Bredy. She will be home by dusk.'

After a few words, which only served to reveal his restless impatience, he left the house again.

CHAPTER TWENTY-NINE

AT this hour Lucetta was bounding along the road to Port-Bredy just as Elizabeth had announced. That she had chosen for her afternoon walk the road along which she had returned to Casterbridge three hours earlier in a carriage was curious – if anything should be called curious in concatenations of phenomena wherein each is known to have its accounting cause. It was the day of the chief market – Saturday – and Farfrae for once had been missed from his corn-stand in the dealers' room. Nevertheless, it was known that he would be home that night – 'for Sunday', as Casterbridge expressed it.

Lucetta, in continuing her walk, had at length reached the end of the ranked trees which bordered the highway in this and other directions out of the town. This end marked a mile; and here she stopped.

The spot was a vale between two gentle acclivities, and the road, still adhering to its Roman foundation, stretched onward straight as a surveyor's line till lost to sight on the most distant ridge. There was neither hedge nor tree in the prospect now, the road clinging to the stubbly expanse of corn-land like a stripe to an undulating garment. Near her was a barn – the single building of any kind within her horizon.

She strained her eyes up the lessening road, but nothing appeared thereon – not so much as a speck. She sighed one word – 'Donald!' and turned her face to the town for retreat.

Here the case was different. A single figure was approaching her – Elizabeth-Jane's.

Lucetta, in spite of her loneliness, seemed a little vexed. Elizabeth's face, as soon as she recognized her friend, shaped itself into affectionate lines while yet beyond speaking distance. 'I suddenly thought I would come and meet you,' she said, smiling.

Lucetta's reply was taken from her lips by an unexpected diversion. A by-road on her right hand descended from the fields into the highway at the point where she stood, and down the track a bull was rambling uncertainly towards her and Elizabeth, who, facing the other way, did not observe him.

In the latter quarter of each year cattle were at once the mainstay and the terror of families about Casterbridge and its neighbourhood, where breeding was carried on with Abrahamic success. The head of stock driven into and out of the town at this season to be sold by the local auctioneer was very large; and all these horned beasts, in travelling to and fro, sent women and children to shelter as nothing else could do. In the main the animals would have walked along quietly enough; but the Casterbridge tradition was that to drive stock it was indispensable that hideous cries, coupled with Yahoo antics and gestures, should be used, large sticks flourished, stray dogs called in, and in general everything done that was likely to infuriate the viciously disposed and terrify the mild. Nothing was commoner than for a householder on going out of his parlour to find his hall or passage full of little children, nursemaids, aged women, or a ladies' school, who apologized for their presence by saying, 'A bull passing down street from the sale.'

Lucetta and Elizabeth regarded the animal in doubt, he meanwhile drawing vaguely towards them. It was a large specimen of the breed, in colour rich dun, though disfigured at present by splotches of mud about his seamy sides. His horns were thick and tipped with brass; his two nostrils like the Thames Tunnel as seen in the perspective toys of yore. Between them, through the gristle of his nose, was a stout copper ring, welded on, and irremovable as Gurth's collar of brass. To the ring was attached an ash staff about a yard long, which the bull with the motions of his head flung about like a flail.

It was not till they observed this dangling stick that the young women were really alarmed; for it revealed to them that the bull was an old one, too savage to be driven, which had in some way escaped, the staff being the means by which the drover controlled him and kept his horns at arms' length.

They looked round for some shelter or hiding-place, and thought of the barn hard by. As long as they had kept their eyes on the bull he had shown some deference in his manner of approach; but no sooner did they turn their backs to seek the barn than he tossed his head and decided to thoroughly terrify them. This caused the two helpless girls to run wildly, whereupon the bull advanced in a deliberate charge.

The barn stood behind a green slimy pond, and it was closed save as to one of the usual pair of doors facing them, which had been propped open by a hurdle-stake, and for this opening they made. The interior had been cleared by a recent bout of threshing except at one end, where there was a stack of dry clover. Elizabeth-Jane took in the situation. 'We must climb up there,' she said.

But before they had even approached it they heard the bull scampering through the pond without, and in a second he dashed into the barn, knocking down the hurdle-stake in passing; the heavy door slammed behind him; and all three were imprisoned in the barn together. The mistaken creature saw them, and stalked towards the end of the barn into which they had fled. The girls doubled so adroitly that their pursuer was against the wall when the fugitives were already half way to the other end. By the time that his length would allow him to turn and follow them thither they had crossed over; thus the pursuit went on, the hot air from his nostrils blowing over them like a sirocco, and not a moment being attainable by Elizabeth or Lucetta in which to open the door. What might have happened had their situation continued cannot be said; but in a few moments a rattling of the door distracted their adversary's attention, and a man appeared. He ran forward towards the leading-staff, seized it, and wrenched the animal's head as if he would snap it off. The wrench was in reality so violent that the thick neck seemed to have lost its stiffness and to become half-paralysed, whilst the nose dropped blood. The premeditated human contrivance of the nose-ring was too cunning for impulsive brute force, and the creature flinched.

The man was seen in the partial gloom to be large-framed and unhesitating. He led the bull to the door, and the light revealed Henchard. He made the bull fast without, and re-entered to the succour of Lucetta; for he had not perceived Elizabeth, who had climbed on to the clover-heap. Lucetta was hysterical, and Henchard took her in his arms and carried her to the door.

'You – have saved me!' she cried, as soon as she could speak.

'I have returned your kindness,' he responded tenderly. 'You once saved me.'

'How – comes it to be you – you?' she asked, not heeding his reply.

'I came out here to look for you. I have been wanting to tell you something these two or three days; but you have been away, and I could not. Perhaps you cannot talk now?'

'Oh – no! Where is Elizabeth?'

'Here am I!' cried the missing one cheerfully; and without waiting for the ladder to be placed she slid down the face of the clover-stack to the floor.

Henchard supporting Lucetta on one side, and Elizabeth-Jane on the other, they went slowly along the rising road. They had reached the top and were descending again when Lucetta, now much recovered, recollected that she had dropped her muff in the barn.

'I'll run back,' said Elizabeth-Jane. 'I don't mind it at all, as I am not tired as you are.' She thereupon hastened down again to the barn, the others pursuing their way.

Elizabeth soon found the muff, such an article being by no means small at that time. Coming out she paused to look for a moment at the bull, now rather to be pitied with his bleeding nose, having perhaps rather intended a practical joke than a murder. Henchard had secured him by jamming the staff into the hinge of the barn-door, and wedging it there with a stake. At length she turned to hasten onward after her contemplation, when she saw a green-and-black gig approaching from the contrary direction, the vehicle being driven by Farfrae.

His presence here seemed to explain Lucetta's walk that way. Donald saw her, drew up, and was hastily made acquainted with what had occurred. At Elizabeth-Jane mentioning how greatly Lucetta had been jeopardized, he exhibited an agitation different in kind no less than in intensity from any she had seen in him before. He became so absorbed in the circumstance that he scarcely had sufficient knowledge of what he was doing to think of helping her up beside him.

'She has gone on with Mr Henchard, you say?' he inquired at last.

'Yes. He is taking her home. They are almost there by this time.'

'And you are sure she can get home?'

Elizabeth-Jane was quite sure.

'Your stepfather saved her?'

'Entirely.'

Farfrae checked his horse's pace: she guessed why. He was thinking that it would be best not to intrude on the other two just now. Henchard had saved Lucetta, and to provoke a possible exhibition of her deeper affection for himself was as ungenerous as it was unwise.

The immediate subject of their talk being exhausted she felt more embarrassed at sitting thus beside her past lover; but soon the two figures of the others were visible at the entrance to the town. The face of the woman was frequently turned back, but Farfrae did not whip on the horse. When these reached the town walls Henchard and his companion had disappeared down the street; Farfrae set down

Elizabeth-Jane on her expressing a particular wish to alight there, and drove round to the stables at the back of his lodgings.

On this account he entered the house through his garden, and going up to his apartments found them in a particularly disturbed state, his boxes being hauled out upon the landing, and his bookcase standing in three pieces. These phenomena, however, seemed to cause him not the least surprise. 'When will everything be sent up?' he said to the mistress of the house, who was superintending.

'I am afraid not before eight, sir,' said she. 'You see we wasn't aware till this morning that you were going to move, or we could have been forwarder.'

'A – well, never mind, never mind!' said Farfrae cheerily. 'Eight o'clock will do well enough if it be not later. Now, don't ye be standing here talking, or it will be twelve, I doubt.' Thus speaking he went out by the front door and up the street.

During this interval Henchard and Lucetta had had experiences of a different kind. After Elizabeth's departure for the muff the corn-merchant opened himself frankly, holding her hand within his arm, though she would fain have withdrawn it. 'Dear Lucetta, I have been very, very anxious to see you these two or three days,' he said; 'ever since I saw you last! I have thought over the way I got your promise that night. You said to me, "If I were a man I should not insist." That cut me deep. I felt that there was some truth in it. I don't want to make you wretched; and to marry me just now would do that as nothing else could – it is but too plain. Therefore I agree to an indefinite engagement – to put off all thought of marriage for a year or two.'

'But – but – can I do nothing of a different kind?' said Lucetta. 'I am full of gratitude to you – you have saved my life. And your care of me is like coals of fire on my head! I am a monied person now. Surely I can do something in return for your goodness – something practical?'

Henchard remained in thought. He had evidently not expected this. 'There is one thing you might do, Lucetta,' he said. 'But not exactly of that kind.'

'Then of what kind is it?' she asked with renewed misgiving.

'I must tell you a secret to ask it. – You may have heard that I have been unlucky this year! I did what I have never done before – speculated rashly; and I lost. That's just put me in a strait.'

'And you would wish me to advance some money?'

'No, no!' said Henchard, almost in anger. 'I'm not the man to sponge on a woman, even though she may be so nearly my own as you. No, Lucetta; what you can do is this; and it would save me. My great creditor is Grower, and it is at his hands I shall suffer if at anybody's; while a fortnight's forbearance on his part would be enough to allow me to pull through. This may be got out of him in one way – that you would let it be known to him that you are my intended – that we are to be quietly married in the next fortnight.— Now stop, you haven't heard all! Let him have this story, without, of course, any prejudice to the fact that the actual engagement between us is to be a long one. Nobody else need know: you could go with me to Mr Grower and just let me speak to 'ee before him as if we were on such terms. We'll ask him to keep it secret. He will willingly wait then. At the fortnight's end I shall be able to face him; and I can coolly tell him all is postponed between us for a year or two. Not a soul in the town need know how you've helped me. Since you wish to be of use, there's your way.'

It being now what the people called the 'pinking in' of the day, that is, the quarter-hour just before dusk, he did not at first observe the result of his own words upon her.

'If it were anything else,' she began, and the dryness of her lips was represented in her voice.

'But it is such a little thing!' he said, with a deep reproach. 'Less than you have offered – just the beginning of what you have so lately promised! I could have told him as much myself, but he would not have believed me.'

'It is not because I won't – it is because I absolutely can't,' she said, with rising distress.

'You are provoking!' he burst out. 'It is enough to make me force you to carry out at once what you have promised.'

'I cannot!' she insisted desperately.

'Why? When I have only within these few minutes released you from your promise to do the thing off-hand.'

'Because – he was a witness!'

'Witness? Of what?'

'If I must tell you—. Don't, don't upbraid me!'

'Well! Let's hear what you mean?'

'Witness of my marriage – Mr Grower was!'

'Marriage?'

'Yes. With Mr Farfrae. O Michael! I am already his wife. We were married this week at Port-Bredy. There were reasons against our doing it here. Mr Grower was a witness because he happened to be at Port-Bredy at the time.'

Henchard stood as if idiotized. She was so alarmed at his silence that she murmured something about lending him sufficient money to tide over the perilous fortnight.

'Married him?' said Henchard at length. 'My good – what married him whilst – bound to marry me?'

'It was like this,' she explained, with tears in her eyes and quavers in her voice; 'don't – don't be cruel! I loved him so much, and I thought you might tell him of the past – and that grieved me! And then, when I had promised you, I learnt of the rumour that you had – sold your first wife at a fair like a horse or cow! How could I keep my promise after hearing that? I could not risk myself in your hands; it would have been letting myself down to take your name after such a scandal. But I knew I should lose Donald if I did not secure him at once – for you would carry out your threat of telling him of our former acquaintance, as long as there was a chance of keeping me for yourself by doing so. But you will not do so now, will you, Michael? for it is too late to separate us.'

The notes of St Peter's bells in full peal had been wafted to them while she spoke; and now the genial thumping of the town band, renowned for its unstinted use of the drum-stick, throbbed down the street.

'Then this racket they are making is on account of it, I suppose?' said he.

'Yes – I think he has told them, or else Mr Grower has. . . . May I leave you now? My – he was detained at Port-Bredy to-day, and sent me on a few hours before him.'

'Then it is *his wife's* life I have saved this afternoon.'

'Yes – and he will be for ever grateful to you.'

'I am much obliged to him. . . . O you false woman!' burst from Henchard. 'You promised me!'

'Yes, yes! But it was under compulsion, and I did not know all your past—'

'And now I've a mind to punish you as you deserve! One word to this bran-new husband of how you courted me, and your precious happiness is blown to atoms!'

'Michael — pity me, and be generous!'

'You don't deserve pity! You did; but you don't now.'

'I'll help you to pay off your debt.'

'A pensioner of Farfrae's wife — not I! Don't stay with me longer — I shall say something worse. Go home!'

She disappeared under the trees of the south walk as the band came round the corner, awaking the echoes of every stock and stone in celebration of her happiness. Lucetta took no heed, but ran up the back street and reached her own home unperceived.

CHAPTER THIRTY

FARFRAE'S words to his landlady had referred to the removal of his boxes and other effects from his late lodgings to Lucetta's house. The work was not heavy, but it had been much hindered on account of the frequent pauses necessitated by exclamations of surprise at the event, of which the good woman had been briefly informed by letter a few hours earlier.

At the last moment of leaving Port-Bredy, Farfrae, like John Gilpin, had been detained by important customers, whom, even in the exceptional circumstances, he was not the man to neglect. Moreover, there was a convenience in Lucetta arriving first at her house. Nobody there as yet knew what had happened; and she was best in a position to break the news to the inmates, and give directions for her husband's accommodation. He had, therefore, sent on his two-days' bride in a hired brougham, whilst he went across the country to a certain group of wheat and barley ricks a few miles off, telling her the hour at which he might be expected the same evening. This accounted for her trotting out to meet him after their separation of four hours.

By a strenuous effort, after leaving Henchard she calmed herself in readiness to receive Donald at High-Place Hall when he came on from his lodgings. One supreme fact empowered her to this, the sense that, come what would, she had secured him. Half-an-hour after her arrival he walked in, and she met him with a relieved gladness, which a month's perilous absence could not have intensified.

'There is one thing I have not done; and yet it is important,' she said earnestly, when she had finished talking about the adventure with the bull. 'That is, broken the news of our marriage to my dear Elizabeth-Jane.'

'Ah, and you have not?' he said thoughtfully. 'I gave her a lift from the barn homewards; but I did not tell her either; for I thought she might have heard of it in the town, and was keeping back her congratulations from shyness, and all that.'

'She can hardly have heard of it. But I'll find out; I'll go to her now. And, Donald, you don't mind her living on with me just the same as before? She is so quiet and unassuming.'

'O no, indeed I don't,' Farfrae answered with, perhaps, a faint awkwardness. 'But I wonder if she would care to?'

'O yes!' said Lucetta eagerly. 'I am sure she would like to. Besides, poor thing, she has no other home.'

Farfrae looked at her and saw that she did not suspect the secret of her more reserved friend. He liked her all the better for the blindness. 'Arrange as you like with her by all means,' he said. 'It is I who have come to your house, not you to mine.'

'I'll run and speak to her,' said Lucetta.

When she got upstairs to Elizabeth-Jane's room the latter had taken off her out-door things, and was resting over a book. Lucetta found in a moment that she had not yet learnt the news.

'I did not come down to you, Miss Templeman,' she said simply. 'I was coming to ask if you had quite recovered from your fright, but I found you had a visitor. What are the bells ringing for, I wonder? And the band, too, is playing. Somebody must be married; or else they are practising for Christmas.'

Lucetta uttered a vague 'Yes', and seating herself by the other young woman looked musingly at her. 'What a lonely creature you are,' she presently said; 'never knowing what's going on, or what people are talking about everywhere with keen interest. You should get out, and gossip about as other women do, and then you wouldn't be obliged to ask me a question of that kind. Well, now, I have something to tell you.'

Elizabeth-Jane said she was so glad, and made herself receptive.

'I must go rather a long way back,' said Lucetta, the difficulty of explaining herself satisfactorily to the pondering one beside her growing more apparent at each syllable. 'You remember that trying case of conscience I told you of some time ago – about the first lover and the second lover?' She let out in jerky phrases a leading word or two of the story she had told.

'O yes – I remember; the story of *your friend*,' said Elizabeth drily, regarding the irises of Lucetta's eyes as though to catch their exact shade. 'The two lovers – the old and the new: how she wanted to marry the second, but felt she ought to marry the first; so that she neglected the better course to follow the evil, like the poet Ovid I've just been construing: "Video meliora proboque, deteriora sequor." '

'Oh no; she didn't follow evil exactly!' said Lucetta hastily.

'But you said that she – or as I may say *you*' – answered Elizabeth, dropping the mask, 'were in honour and conscience bound to marry the first?'

Lucetta's blush at being seen through came and went again before she replied anxiously, 'You will never breathe this, will you, Elizabeth-Jane?'

'Certainly not, if you say not.'

'Then I will tell you that the case is more complicated – worse, in fact – than it seemed in my story. I and the first man were thrown together in a strange way, and felt that we ought to be united, as the world had talked of us. He was a widower, as he supposed. He had not heard of his first wife for many years. But the wife returned, and we parted. She is now dead; and the husband comes paying me addresses again, saying, "Now we'll complete our purpose." But, Elizabeth-Jane, all this amounts to a new courtship of me by him; I was absolved from all vows by the return of the other woman.'

'Have you not lately renewed your promise?' said the younger with quiet surmise. She had divined Man Number One.

'That was wrung from me by a threat.'

'Yes, it was. But I think when any one gets coupled up with a man in the past so unfortunately as you have done, she ought to become his wife if she can, even if she were not the sinning party.'

Lucetta's countenance lost its sparkle. 'He turned out to be a man I should be afraid to marry,' she pleaded. 'Really afraid! And it was not till after my renewed promise that I knew it.'

'Then there is only one course left to honesty. You must remain a single woman.'

'But think again! Do consider—'

'I am certain,' interrupted her companion hardily. 'I have guessed very well who the man is. My father; and I say it is him or nobody for you.'

Any suspicion of impropriety was to Elizabeth-Jane like a red rag to a bull. Her craving for correctness of procedure was, indeed, almost vicious. Owing to her early troubles with regard to her mother a semblance of irregularity had terrors for her which those whose names are safeguarded from suspicion know nothing of. 'You ought to marry Mr Henchard or nobody – certainly not another man!' she went on with a quivering lip in whose movement two passions shared.

'I don't admit that!' said Lucetta passionately.

'Admit it or not, it is true!'

Lucetta covered her eyes with her right hand, as if she could plead no more, holding out her left to Elizabeth-Jane.

'Why, you *have* married him!' cried the latter, jumping up with pleasure after a glance at Lucetta's fingers. 'When did you do it? Why did you not tell me, instead of teasing me like this? How very honourable of you! He did treat my mother badly once, it seems, in a moment of intoxication. And it is true that he is stern sometimes. But you will rule him entirely, I am sure, with your beauty and wealth and accomplishments. You are the woman he will adore, and we shall all three be happy together now!'

'O, my Elizabeth-Jane!' cried Lucetta distressfully. ''Tis somebody else that I have married! I was so desperate – so afraid of being forced to anything else – so afraid of revelations that would quench his love for me, that I resolved to do it off-hand, come what might, and purchase a week of happiness at any cost!'

'You – have – married Mr Farfrae!' cried Elizabeth-Jane, in Nathan tones.

Lucetta bowed. She had recovered herself.

'The bells are ringing on that account,' she said. 'My husband is downstairs. He will live here till a more suitable house is ready for us; and I have told him that I want you to stay with me just as before.'

'Let me think of it alone,' the girl quickly replied, corking up the turmoil of her feeling with grand control.

'You shall. I am sure we shall be happy together.'

Lucetta departed to join Donald below, a vague uneasiness floating over joy at seeing him quite at home there. Not on account of her friend Elizabeth did she feel it: for of the bearings of Elizabeth-Jane's emotions she had not the least suspicion; but on Henchard's alone.

Now the instant decision of Susan Henchard's daughter was to dwell in that house no more. Apart from her estimate of the propriety of Lucetta's conduct, Farfrae had been so nearly her avowed lover that she felt she could not abide there.

It was still early in the evening when she hastily put on her things and went out. In a few minutes, knowing the ground, she had found a suitable lodging, and arranged to enter it that night. Returning and entering noiselessly she took off her pretty dress and arrayed herself in a plain one, packing up the other to keep as her best; for she would have to be very economical now. She wrote a note to leave for Lucetta, who was closely shut up in the drawing-room with Farfrae; and then Elizabeth-Jane called a man with a wheelbarrow; and seeing her boxes put into it she trotted off down the street to her rooms. They were in the street in which Henchard lived, and almost opposite his door.

Here she sat down and considered the means of subsistence. The little annual sum settled on her by her stepfather would keep body and soul together. A wonderful skill in netting of all sorts – acquired in childhood by making seines in Newson's home – might serve her in good stead; and her studies, which were pursued unremittingly, might serve her in still better.

By this time the marriage that had taken place was known throughout Casterbridge; had been discussed noisily on kerbstones, confidentially behind counters, and jovially at the Three Mariners. Whether Farfrae would sell his business and set up for a gentleman on his wife's money, or whether he would show independence enough to stick to his trade in spite of his brilliant alliance, was a great point of interest.

CHAPTER THIRTY-ONE

T HE retort of the furmity-woman before the magistrates had spread; and in four-and-twenty hours there was not a person in Casterbridge who remained unacquainted with the story of Henchard's mad freak at Weydon-Priors Fair, long years before. The amends he had made in after life were lost sight of in the dramatic glare of the original act. Had the incident been well known of old and always, it might by this time have grown to be lightly regarded as the rather tall wild oat, but well-nigh the single one, of a young man with whom the steady and mature (if somewhat headstrong) burgher of to-day had scarcely a point in common. But the act having lain as dead and buried ever since, the interspace of years was unperceived; and the black spot of his youth wore the aspect of a recent crime.

Small as the police-court incident had been in itself, it formed the edge or turn in the incline of Henchard's fortunes. On that day – almost at that minute – he passed the ridge of prosperity and honour, and began to descend rapidly on the other side. It was strange how soon he sank in esteem. Socially he had received a startling fillip downwards; and, having already lost commercial buoyancy from rash transactions, the velocity of his descent in both aspects became accelerated every hour.

He now gazed more at the pavements and less at the house-fronts when he walked about; more at the feet and leggings of men, and less into the pupils of their eyes with the blazing regard which formerly had made them blink.

· New events combined to undo him. It had been a bad year for others besides himself, and the heavy failure of a debtor whom he had trusted generously completed the overthrow of his tottering credit. And now, in his desperation, he failed to preserve that strict correspondence between bulk and sample which is the soul of commerce in grain. For this, one of his men was mainly to blame; that worthy, in his great unwisdom, having picked over the sample of an enormous quantity of second-rate corn which Henchard had in hand, and removed the pinched, blasted, and smutted grains in great numbers. The produce if honestly offered would have created no scandal; but the blunder of misrepresentation, coming at such a moment, dragged Henchard's name into the ditch.

The details of his failure were of the ordinary kind. One day Elizabeth-Jane was passing the King's Arms, when she saw people bustling in and out more than usual when there was no market. A bystander informed her, with some surprise at her ignorance, that it was a meeting of the Commissioners under Mr Henchard's bankruptcy. She felt quite tearful, and when she heard that he was present in the hotel she wished to go in and see him, but was advised not to intrude that day.

The room in which debtor and creditors had assembled was a front one, and Henchard looking out of the window, had caught sight of Elizabeth-Jane through the wire blind. His examination had closed, and the creditors were leaving. The appearance of Elizabeth threw him into a reverie; till, turning his face from the window, and towering above all the rest, he called their attention for a moment more. His countenance had somewhat changed from its flush of prosperity; the black hair and whiskers were the same as ever, but a film of ash was over the rest.

'Gentlemen,' he said, 'over and above the assets that we've been talking about, and that appear on the balance-sheet, there be these. It all belongs to ye, as much as everything else I've got, and I don't wish to keep it from you, not I.' Saying this, he took his gold watch from his pocket and laid it on the table; then his purse – the yellow canvas money-bag, such as was carried by all farmers and dealers – untying it, and shaking the money out upon the table beside the watch. The latter he drew back quickly for an instant, to remove the hair-guard made and given him by Lucetta. 'There, now you have all I've got in the world,' he said. 'And I wish for your sakes 'twas more.'

The creditors, farmers almost to a man, looked at the watch, and at the money, and into the street; when Farmer James Everdene of Weatherbury spoke.

'No, no, Henchard,' he said warmly. 'We don't want that. 'Tis honourable in ye; but keep it. What do you say, neighbours – do ye agree?'

'Ay, sure: we don't wish it at all,' said Grower, another creditor.

'Let him keep it, of course,' murmured another in the background – a silent, reserved young man named Boldwood; and the rest responded unanimously.

'Well,' said the senior Commissioner, addressing Henchard, 'though the case is a desperate one, I am bound to admit that I have never met a debtor who behaved more fairly. I've proved the balance-sheet to be as honestly made out as it could possibly be; we have had no trouble; there have been no evasions and no concealments. The rashness of dealing which led to this unhappy situation is obvious enough; but as far as I can see every attempt has been made to avoid wronging anybody.'

Henchard was more affected by this than he cared to let them perceive, and he turned aside to the window again. A general murmur of agreement followed the Commissioner's words; and the meeting dispersed. When they were gone Henchard regarded the watch they had returned to him. '''Tisn't mine by rights,' he said to himself. 'Why the devil didn't they take it? – I don't want what don't belong to me!' Moved by a recollection he took the watch to the maker's just opposite, sold it there and then for what the tradesman offered, and went with the proceeds to one among the smaller of his creditors, a cottager of Durnover in straitened circumstances, to whom he handed the money.

When everything was ticketed that Henchard had owned, and the auctions were in progress, there was quite a sympathetic reaction in the town, which till then for some time past had done nothing but condemn him. Now that Henchard's whole career was pictured distinctly to his neighbours, and they could see how admirably he had used his one talent of energy to create a position of affluence out of absolutely nothing – which was really all he could show when he came to the town as a journeyman hay-trusser, with his wimble and knife in his basket – they wondered and regretted his fall.

Try as she might, Elizabeth could never meet with him. She believed in him still, though nobody else did; and she wanted to be allowed to forgive him for his roughness to her, and to help him in his trouble.

She wrote to him; he did not reply. She then went to his house – the great house she had lived in so happily for a time – with its front of dun brick, vitrified here and there, and its heavy sash-bars – but Henchard was to be found there no more. The ex-Mayor had left the house of his prosperity, and gone into Jopp s cottage by the Priory Mill – the sad purlieu to which he had wandered on the night of his discovery that she was not his daughter. Thither she went.

Elizabeth thought it odd that he had fixed on this spot to retire to, but assumed that necessity had no choice. Trees which seemed old enough to have been planted by the friars still stood around, and the back hatch of the original mill yet formed a cascade which had raised its terrific roar for centuries. The cottage itself was built of old stones from the long dismantled Priory, scraps of tracery, moulded window-jambs, and arch-labels, being mixed in with the rubble of the walls.

In this cottage he occupied a couple of rooms, Jopp, whom Henchard had employed, abused, cajoled, and dismissed by turns, being the householder. But even here her stepfather could not be seen.

'Not by his daughter?' pleaded Elizabeth.

'By nobody – at present: that's his order,' she was informed.

Afterwards she was passing by the corn-stores and hay-barns which had been the headquarters of his business. She knew that he ruled there no longer; but it was with amazement that she regarded the familiar gateway. A smear of decisive lead-coloured paint had been laid on to obliterate Henchard's name, though its letters dimly loomed through like ships in a fog. Over these, in fresh white, spread the name of Farfrae.

Abel Whittle was edging his skeleton in at the wicket, and she said, 'Mr Farfrae is master here?'

'Yaas, Miss Henchet,' he said, 'Mr Farfrae have bought the concern and all of we work-folk with it; and 'tis better for us than 'twas – though I shouldn't say that to you as a daughter-law. We work harder, but we bain't made afeard now. It was fear made my few poor hairs so thin! No busting out, no slamming of doors, no meddling with yer eternal soul and all that; and though 'tis a shilling a week less I'm the richer man; for what's all the world if yer mind is always in a larry, Miss Henchet?'

The intelligence was in a general sense true; and Henchard's stores, which had remained in a paralyzed condition during the settlement of his bankruptcy, were stirred into activity again when the new tenant had possession. Thenceforward the full sacks, looped with the shining chain, went scurrying up and down under the cat-head, hairy arms were thrust out from the different door-ways, and the grain was hauled in; trusses of hay were tossed anew in and out of the barns, and the wimbles creaked; while the scales and steel-yards began to be busy where guess-work had formerly been the rule.

CHAPTER THIRTY-TWO

Two bridges stood near the lower part of Casterbridge town. The first, of weather-stained brick, was immediately at the end of High Street, where a diverging branch from that thoroughfare ran round to the low-lying Durnover lanes; so that the precincts of the bridge formed the merging point of respectability and indigence. The second bridge, of stone, was further out on the highway – in fact, fairly in the meadows, though still within the town boundary.

These bridges had speaking countenances. Every projection in each was worn down to obtuseness, partly by weather, more by friction from generations of loungers, whose toes and heels had from year to year made restless movements against these parapets, as they had stood there meditating on the aspect of affairs. In the case of the more friable bricks and stones even the flat faces were worn into hollows by the same mixed mechanism. The masonry of the top was clamped with iron at each joint; since it had been no uncommon thing for desperate men to wrench the coping off and throw it down the river, in reckless defiance of the magistrates.

For to this pair of bridges gravitated all the failures of the town; those who had failed in business, in love, in sobriety, in crime. Why the unhappy hereabout usually chose the bridges for their meditations in preference to a railing, a gate, or a stile, was not so clear.

There was a marked difference of quality between the personages who haunted the near bridge of brick and the personages who haunted the far one of stone. Those of lowest character preferred the former, adjoining the town; they did not mind the glare of the public eye. They had been of comparatively no account during their successes; and, though they might feel dispirited, they had no particular sense of shame in their ruin. Their hands were mostly kept in their pockets; they wore a leather strap round their hips or knees, and boots that required a great deal of lacing, but seemed never to get any. Instead of sighing at their adversities they spat, and instead of saying the iron had entered into their souls they said they were down on their luck. Jopp in his times of distress had often stood here; so had Mother Cuxsom, Christopher Coney, and poor Abel Whittle.

The *misérables* who would pause on the remoter bridge were of a politer stamp. They included bankrupts, hypochondriacs, persons who were what is called 'out of a situation' from fault or lucklessness, the inefficient of the professional class – shabby-genteel men, who did not know how to get rid of the weary time between breakfast and dinner, and the yet more weary time between dinner and dark. The eyes of this species were mostly directed over the parapet upon the running water below. A man seen there looking thus fixedly into the river was pretty sure to be one whom the world did not treat kindly for some reason or other. While one in straits on the townward bridge did not mind who saw him so, and kept his back to the parapet to survey the passers-by, one in straits on this never faced the road, never turned his head at coming footsteps, but, sensitive to his own condition, watched the current whenever a stranger approached, as if some strange fish interested him, though every finned thing had been poached out of the river years before.

There and thus they would muse; if their grief were the grief of oppression they would wish themselves kings; if their grief were poverty, wish themselves millionaires; if sin, they would wish they were saints or angels; if despised love, that they were some much-courted Adonis of county fame. Some had been known to stand and think so long with this fixed gaze downward that eventually they had allowed their poor carcases to follow that gaze; and they were discovered the next morning out of reach of their troubles, either here or in the deep pool called Blackwater, a little higher up the river.

To this bridge came Henchard, as other unfortunates had come before him, his way thither being by the riverside path on the chilly edge of the town. Here he was standing one windy afternoon when Durnover church clock struck five. While the gusts were bringing the notes to his ears across the damp intervening flat a man passed behind him and greeted Henchard by name. Henchard turned slightly and saw that the comer was Jopp, his old foreman, now employed elsewhere, to whom, though he hated him, he had gone for lodgings because Jopp was the one man in Casterbridge whose observation and opinion the fallen corn-merchant despised to the point of indifference.

Henchard returned him a scarcely perceptible nod, and Jopp stopped.

'He and she are gone into their new house to-day,' said Jopp.

'Oh,' said Henchard absently. 'Which house is that?'

'Your old one.'

'Gone into my house?' And starting up Henchard added, '*My* house of all others in the town!'

'Well, as somebody was sure to live there, and you couldn't, it can do 'ee no harm that he's the man.'

It was quite true: he felt that it was doing him no harm. Farfrae, who had already taken the yards and stores, had acquired possession of the house for the obvious convenience of its contiguity. And yet this act of his taking up residence within those roomy chambers while he, their former tenant, lived in a cottage, galled Henchard indescribably.

Jopp continued: 'And you heard of that fellow who bought all the best furniture at your sale? He was bidding for no other than Farfrae all the while! It has never been moved out of the house, as he'd already got the lease.'

'My furniture too! Surely he'll buy my body and soul likewise!'

'There's no saying he won't, if you be willing to sell.' And having planted these wounds in the heart of his once imperious master Jopp went on his way; while Henchard stared and stared into the racing river till the bridge seemed moving backward with him.

The low land grew blacker, and the sky a deeper grey. When the landscape looked like a picture blotted in with ink, another traveller approached the great stone bridge. He was driving a gig, his direction being also townwards. On the round of the middle of the arch the gig stopped. 'Mr Henchard?' came from it in the voice of Farfrae. Henchard turned his face.

Finding that he had guessed rightly Farfrae told the man who accompanied him to drive home; while he alighted and went up to his former friend.

'I have heard that you think of emigrating, Mr Henchard,' he said. 'Is it true? I have a real reason for asking.'

Henchard withheld his answer for several instants, and then said, 'Yes; it is true. I am going where you were going to a few years ago, when I prevented you and got you to bide here. 'Tis turn and turn about, isn't it! Do ye mind how we stood like this in the Chalk Walk when I persuaded 'ee to stay? You then stood without a chattel to your name, and I was the master of the house in Corn Street. But now I stand without a stick or a rag, and the master of that house is you.'

'Yes, yes; that's so! It's the way o' the warrld,' said Farfrae.

'Ha, ha, true!' cried Henchard, throwing himself into a mood of jocularity. 'Up and down! I'm used to it. What's the odds after all!'

'Now listen to me, if it's no taking up your time,' said Farfrae, 'just as I listened to you. Don't go. Stay at home.'

'But I can do nothing else, man!' said Henchard scornfully. 'The little money I have will just keep body and soul together for a few weeks, and no more. I have not felt inclined to go back to journey-work yet; but I can't stay doing nothing, and my best chance is elsewhere.'

'No; but what I propose is this—if ye will listen. Come and live in your old house. We can spare some rooms very well—I am sure my wife would not mind it at all—until there's an opening for ye.'

Henchard started. Probably the picture drawn by the unsuspecting Donald of himself under the same roof with Lucetta was too striking to be received with equanimity. 'No, no,' he said gruffly; 'we should quarrel.'

'You should hae a part to yourself,' said Farfrae; 'and nobody to interfere wi' you. It will be a deal healthier than down there by the river where you live now.'

Still Henchard refused. 'You don't know what you ask,' he said. 'However, I can do no less than thank 'ee.'

They walked into the town together side by side, as they had done when Henchard persuaded the young Scotchman to remain. 'Will you come in and have some supper?' said Farfrae when they reached the middle of the town, where their paths diverged right and left.

'No, no.'

'By-the-bye, I had nearly forgot. I bought a good deal of your furniture.'

'So I have heard.'

'Well, it was no that I wanted it so very much for myself; but I wish ye to pick out all that you care to have – such things as may be endeared to ye by associations, or particularly suited to your use. And take them to your own house – it will not be depriving me; we can do with less very well, and I will have plenty of opportunities of getting more.'

'What – give it to me for nothing?' said Henchard. 'But you paid the creditors for it!'

'Ah, yes; but maybe it's worth more to you than it is to me.'

Henchard was a little moved. 'I – sometimes think I've wronged 'ee!' he said, in tones which showed the disquietude that the night shades hid in his face. He shook Farfrae abruptly by the hand, and hastened away as if unwilling to betray himself further. Farfrae saw him turn through the thoroughfare into Bull Stake and vanish down towards the Priory Mill.

Meanwhile Elizabeth-Jane, in an upper room no larger than the Prophet's chamber, and with the silk attire of her palmy days packed away in a box, was netting with great industry between the hours which she devoted to studying such books as she could get hold of.

Her lodgings being nearly opposite her stepfather's former residence, now Farfrae's, she could see Donald and Lucetta speeding in and out of their door with all the bounding enthusiasm of their situation. She avoided looking that way as much as possible, but it was hardly in human nature to keep the eyes averted when the door slammed.

While living on thus quietly she heard the news that Henchard had caught cold and was confined to his room – possibly a result of standing about the meads in damp weather. She went off to his house at once. This time she was determined not to be denied admittance, and made her way upstairs. He was sitting up in the bed with a greatcoat round him, and at first resented her intrusion. 'Go away – go away,' he said. 'I don't like to see 'ee!'

'But, father—'

'I don't like to see 'ee,' he repeated.

However, the ice was broken, and she remained. She made the room more comfortable, gave directions to the people below, and by the time she went away had reconciled her stepfather to her visiting him.

The effect, either of her ministrations or of her mere presence, was a rapid recovery. He soon was well enough to go out; and now things seemed to wear a new colour in his eyes. He no longer thought of emigration, and thought more of Elizabeth. The having nothing to do made him more dreary than any other circumstance; and one day, with better views of Farfrae than he had held for some time, and a sense that honest work was not a thing to be ashamed of, he stoically went down to Farfrae's yard and asked to be taken on as a journeyman hay-trusser. He was engaged at once. This hiring of Henchard was done through a foreman, Farfrae feeling that it was undesirable to come personally in contact with the ex-corn-factor more than was absolutely necessary. While anxious to help him he was well aware by this time of his uncertain temper, and thought reserved relations best. For the same reason his orders to Henchard to proceed to this and that country farm trussing in the usual way were always given through a third person.

For a time these arrangements worked well, it being the custom to truss in the respective stack-yards, before bringing it away, the hay bought at the different farms about the neighbourhood; so that Henchard was often absent at such places the whole week long. When this was all done, and Henchard had become in a measure broken in, he came to work daily on the home premises like the rest. And thus the once flourishing merchant and Mayor and what not stood as a day-labourer in the barns and granaries he formerly had owned.

'I have worked as a journeyman before now, ha'n't I?' he would say in his defiant way; 'and why shouldn't I do it again?' But he looked a far different journeyman from the one he had been in his earlier days. Then he had worn clean, suitable clothes, light and cheerful in hue; leggings yellow as marigolds, corduroys immaculate as new flax, and a neckerchief like a flower-garden. Now he wore the remains of an old blue cloth suit of his gentlemanly times, a rusty silk hat, and a once black satin stock, soiled and shabby. Clad thus he went to and fro, still comparatively an active man – for he was not much over forty – and saw with the other men in the yard Donald Farfrae going in and out of the green door that led to the garden, and the big house, and Lucetta.

At the beginning of the winter it was rumoured about Casterbridge that Mr Farfrae, already in the Town Council, was to be proposed for Mayor in a year or two.

'Yes; she was wise, she was wise in her generation!' said Henchard to himself when he heard of this one day on his way to Farfrae's hay-barn. He thought it over as he wimbled his bonds, and the piece of news acted as a reviviscent breath to that old view of his – of Donald Farfrae as his triumphant rival who rode rough-shod over him.

'A fellow of his age going to be Mayor, indeed!' he murmured with a corner-drawn smile on his mouth. 'But 'tis her money that floats en upward. Ha-ha – how cust odd it is! Here be I, his former master, working for him as man, and he the man standing as master, with my house and my furniture and my what-you-may-call wife all his own.'

He repeated these things a hundred times a day. During the whole period of his acquaintance with Lucetta he had never wished to claim her as his own so desperately as he now regretted her loss. It was no mercenary hankering after her fortune that moved him; though that fortune had been the means of making her so much the more desired by giving her the air of independence and sauciness which attracts men of his composition. It had given her servants, house, and fine clothing – a setting that invested Lucetta with a startling novelty in the eyes of him who had known her in her narrow days.

He accordingly lapsed into moodiness, and at every allusion to the possibility of Farfrae's near election to the municipal chair his former hatred of the

Scotchman returned. Concurrently with this he underwent a moral change. It resulted in his significantly saying every now and then, in tones of recklessness, 'Only a fortnight more!' – 'Only a dozen days!' and so forth, lessening his figures day by day.

'Why d'ye say only a dozen days?' asked Solomon Longways as he worked beside Henchard in the granary weighing oats.

'Because in twelve days I shall be released from my oath.'

'What oath?'

'The oath to drink no spirituous liquid. In twelve days it will be twenty-one years since I swore it, and then I mean to enjoy myself, please God!'

Elizabeth-Jane sat at her window one Sunday, and while there she heard in the street below a conversation which introduced Henchard's name. She was wondering what was the matter, when a third person who was passing by asked the question in her mind.

'Michael Henchard have busted out drinking after taking nothing for twenty-one years!'

Elizabeth-Jane jumped up, put on her things, and went out.

CHAPTER THIRTY-THREE

At this date there prevailed in Casterbridge a convivial custom – scarcely recognized as such, yet none the less established. On the afternoon of every Sunday a large contingent of the Casterbridge journeymen – steady church-goers and sedate characters – having attended service, filed from the church doors across the way to the Three Mariners inn. The rear was usually brought up by the choir, with their bass-viols, fiddles, and flutes under their arms.

The great point, the point of honour, on these sacred occasions was for each man to strictly limit himself to half-a-pint of liquor. This scrupulosity was so well understood by the landlord that the whole company was served in cups of that measure. They were all exactly alike – straight-sided, with two leafless lime-trees done in eel-brown on the sides – one towards the drinker's lips, the other confronting his comrade. To wonder how many of these cups the landlord possessed altogether was a favourite exercise of children in the marvellous. Forty at least might have been seen at these times in the large room, forming a ring round the margin of the great sixteen-legged oak table, like the monolithic circle at Stonehenge in its pristine days. Outside and above the forty cups came a circle of forty smoke-jets from forty clay pipes; outside the pipes the countenances of the forty church-goers, supported at the back by a circle of forty chairs.

The conversation was not the conversation of weekdays, but a thing altogether finer in point and higher in tone. They invariably discussed the sermon, dissecting it, weighing it, as above or below the average – the general tendency being to regard it as a scientific feat or performance which had no relation to their own lives, except as between critics and the thing criticized. The bass-viol player and the clerk usually spoke with more authority than the rest on account of their official connection with the preacher.

Now the Three Mariners was the inn chosen by Henchard as the place for closing his long term of dramless years. He had so timed his entry as to be well established in the large room by the time the forty church-goers entered to their customary cups. The flush upon his face proclaimed at once that the vow of twenty-one years had lapsed, and the era of recklessness begun anew. He was seated on a small table, drawn up to the side of the massive oak board reserved for the churchmen, a few of whom nodded to him as they took their places and said, 'How be ye, Mr Henchard! Quite a stranger here.'

Henchard did not take the trouble to reply for a few moments, and his eyes rested on his stretched-out legs and boots. 'Yes,' he said at length; 'that's true. I've been down in spirit for weeks; some of ye know the cause. I am better now; but not quite serene. I want you fellows of the choir to strike up a tune; and what with that and this brew of Stannidge's, I am in hopes of getting altogether out of my minor key.'

'With all my heart,' said the first fiddle. 'We've let back our strings, that's true; but we can soon pull 'em up again. Sound A, neighbours, and give the man a stave.'

'I don't care a curse what the words be,' said Henchard. 'Hymns, ballets, or rantipole rubbish; the Rogue's March or the cherubim's warble — 'tis all the same to me if 'tis good harmony, and well put out.'

'Well — heh, heh — it may be we can do that, and not a man among us that have sat in the gallery less than twenty year,' said the leader of the band. 'As 'tis Sunday, neighbours, suppose we raise the Fourth Psa'am, to Samuel Wakely's tune, as improved by me?'

'Hang Samuel Wakely's tune, as improved by thee!' said Henchard. 'Chuck across one of your psalters — old Wiltshire is the only tune worth singing — the psalm-tune that would make my blood ebb and flow like the sea when I was a steady chap. I'll find some words to fit en.' He took one of the psalters and began turning over the leaves.

Chancing to look out of the window at that moment he saw a flock of people passing by, and perceived them to be the congregation of the upper church, now just dismissed, their sermon having been a longer one than that the lower parish was favoured with. Among the rest of the leading inhabitants walked Mr Councillor Farfrae with Lucetta upon his arm, the observed and imitated of all the smaller tradesmen's womankind. Henchard's mouth changed a little, and he continued to turn over the leaves.

'Now then,' he said, 'Psalm the Hundred-and-Ninth, to the tune of Wiltshire: verses ten to fifteen. I gi'e ye the words:

> 'His seed shall orphans be, his wife
>   A widow plunged in grief;
> His vagrant children beg their bread
>   Where none can give relief.
>
> His ill-got riches shall be made
>   To usurers a prey;
> The fruit of all his toil shall be
>   By strangers borne away.

> None shall be found that to his wants
>   Their mercy will extend,
> Or to his helpless orphan seed
>   The least assistance lend.
>
> A swift destruction soon shall seize
>   On his unhappy race;
> And the next age his hated name
>   Shall utterly deface.'

'I know the Psa'am – I know the Psa'am!' said the leader hastily; 'but I would as lief not sing it. 'Twasn't made for singing. We chose it once when the gipsy stole the pa'son's mare, thinking to please him, but pa'son was quite upset. Whatever Servant David were thinking about when he made a Psalm that nobody can sing without disgracing himself, I can't fathom! Now then, the Fourth Psalm, to Samuel Wakely's tune, as improved by me.'

''Od seize your sauce – I tell ye to sing the Hundred-and-Ninth to Wiltshire, and sing it you shall!' roared Henchard. 'Not a single one of all the droning crew of ye goes out of this room till that Psalm is sung!' He slipped off the table, seized the poker, and going to the door placed his back against it. 'Now then, go ahead, if you don't wish to have your cust pates broke!'

'Don't 'ee, don't 'ee take on so! – As 'tis the Sabbath-day, and 'tis Servant David's words and not ours, perhaps we don't mind for once, hey?' said one of the terrified choir, looking round upon the rest. So the instruments were tuned and the comminatory verses sung.

'Thank ye, thank ye,' said Henchard in a softened voice, his eyes growing downcast, and his manner that of a man much moved by the strains. 'Don't you blame David,' he went on in low tones, shaking his head without raising his eyes. 'He knew what he was about when he wrote that! . . . If I could afford it, be hanged if I wouldn't keep a church at my own expense to play and sing to me at these low, dark times of my life. But the bitter thing is, that when I was rich I didn't need what I could have, and now I be poor I can't have what I need!'

While they paused, Lucetta and Farfrae passed again, this time homeward, it being their custom to take, like others, a short walk out on the highway and back, between church and tea-time. 'There's the man we've been singing about,' said Henchard.

The players and singers turned their heads and saw his meaning. 'Heaven forbid!' said the bass-player.

''Tis the man,' repeated Henchard doggedly.

'Then if I'd known,' said the performer on the clarionet solemnly, 'that 'twas meant for a living man, nothing should have drawn out of my wynd-pipe the breath for that Psalm, so help me!'

'Nor from mine,' said the first singer. 'But, thought I, as it was made so long ago perhaps there isn't much in it, so I'll oblige a neighbour; for there's nothing to be said against the tune.'

'Ah, my boys, you've sung it,' said Henchard triumphantly. 'As for him, it was partly by his songs that he got over me, and heaved me out. . . . I could double him up like that – and yet I don't.' He laid the poker across his knee, bent it as if it were a twig, flung it down, and came away from the door.

It was at this time that Elizabeth-Jane, having heard where her stepfather was, entered the room with a pale and agonized countenance. The choir and the rest of the company moved off, in accordance with their half-pint regulation. Elizabeth-Jane went up to Henchard, and entreated him to accompany her home.

By this hour the volcanic fires of his nature had burnt down, and having drunk no great quantity as yet he was inclined to acquiesce. She took his arm, and together they went on. Henchard walked blankly, like a blind man, repeating to himself the last words of the singers –

> 'And the next age his hated name
> Shall utterly deface.'

At length he said to her, 'I am a man to my word. I have kept my oath for twenty-one years; and now I can drink with a good conscience. . . . If I don't do for him – well, I am a fearful practical joker when I choose! He has taken away everything from me, and by heavens, if I meet him I won't answer for my deeds!'

These half-uttered words alarmed Elizabeth – all the more by reason of the still determination of Henchard's mien.

'What will you do?' she asked cautiously, while trembling with disquietude, and guessing Henchard's allusion only too well.

Henchard did not answer, and they went on till they had reached his cottage. 'May I come in?' she said.

'No, no; not to-day,' said Henchard; and she went away; feeling that to caution Farfrae was almost her duty, as it was certainly her strong desire.

As on the Sunday, so on the week-days, Farfrae and Lucetta might have been seen flitting about the town like two butterflies – or rather like a bee and a butterfly in league for life. She seemed to take no pleasure in going anywhere except in her husband's company; and hence when business would not permit him to waste an afternoon she remained indoors waiting for the time to pass till his return, her face being visible to Elizabeth-Jane from her window aloft. The latter, however, did not say to herself that Farfrae should be thankful for such devotion, but, full of her reading, she cited Rosalind's exclamation: 'Mistress, know yourself; down on your knees and thank Heaven fasting for a good man's love.'

She kept her eye upon Henchard also. One day he answered her inquiry for his health by saying that he could not endure Abel Whittle's pitying eyes upon him while they worked together in the yard. 'He is such a fool,' said Henchard, 'that he can never get out of his mind the time when I was master there.'

'I'll come and wimble for you instead of him, if you will allow me,' said she. Her motive on going to the yard was to get an opportunity of observing the general position of affairs on Farfrae's premises now that her stepfather was a workman there. Henchard's threats had alarmed her so much that she wished to see his behaviour when the two were face to face.

For two or three days after her arrival Donald did not make any appearance. Then one afternoon the green door opened, and through came, first Farfrae, and at his heels Lucetta. Donald brought his wife forward without hesitation, it being obvious that he had no suspicion whatever of any antecedents in common between her and the now journeyman hay-trusser.

Henchard did not turn his eyes toward either of the pair, keeping them fixed on the bond he twisted, as if that alone absorbed him. A feeling of delicacy, which ever prompted Farfrae to avoid anything that might seem like triumphing over a fallen rival, led him to keep away from the hay-barn where Henchard and his daughter were working, and to go on to the corn department. Meanwhile Lucetta, never having been informed that Henchard had entered her husband's service, rambled straight on to the barn, where she came suddenly upon Henchard, and gave vent to a little 'Oh!' which the happy and busy Donald was too far off to hear. Henchard, with withering humility of demeanour, touched the brim of his hat to her as Whittle and the rest had done, to which she breathed a dead-alive 'Good afternoon'.

'I beg your pardon, ma'am?' said Henchard, as if he had not heard.

'I said good afternoon,' she faltered.

'O yes, good afternoon, ma'am,' he replied, touching his hat again. 'I am glad to see you, ma'am.' Lucetta looked embarrassed, and Henchard continued: 'For we humble workmen here feel it a great honour that a lady should look in and take an interest in us.'

She glanced at him entreatingly; the sarcasm was too bitter, too unendurable.

'Can you tell me the time, ma'am?' he asked.

'Yes,' she said hastily; 'half-past four.'

'Thank 'ee. An hour and a half longer before we are released from work. Ah, ma'am, we of the lower classes know nothing of the gay leisure that such as you enjoy!'

As soon as she could do so Lucetta left him, nodded and smiled to Elizabeth-Jane, and joined her husband at the other end of the enclosure, where she could be seen leading him away by the outer gates, so as to avoid passing Henchard again. That she had been taken by surprise was obvious. The result of this casual rencounter was that the next morning a note was put into Henchard's hand by the postman.

'Will you,' said Lucetta, with as much bitterness as she could put into a small communication, 'will you kindly undertake not to speak to me in the biting undertones you used to-day, if I walk through the yard at any time? I bear you no ill-will, and I am only too glad that you should have employment of my dear husband; but in common fairness treat me as his wife, and do not try to make me wretched by covert sneers. I have committed no crime, and done you no injury.'

'Poor fool!' said Henchard with fond savagery, holding out the note. 'To know no better than commit herself in writing like this! Why, if I were to show that to her dear husband – pooh!' He threw the letter into the fire.

Lucetta took care not to come again among the hay and corn. She would rather have died than run the risk of encountering Henchard at such close quarters a second time. The gulf between them was growing wider every day. Farfrae was always considerate to his fallen acquaintance; but it was impossible that he should not, by degrees, cease to regard the ex-corn-merchant as more than one of his other workmen. Henchard saw this, and concealed his feelings under a cover of stolidity, fortifying his heart by drinking more freely at the Three Mariners every evening.

Often did Elizabeth-Jane, in her endeavours to prevent his taking other liquor, carry tea to him in a little basket at five o'clock. Arriving one day on this errand she found her stepfather was measuring up clover-seed and rape-seed in the corn-stores on the top floor, and she ascended to him. Each floor had a door opening into the air under a cat-head, from which a chain dangled for hoisting the sacks.

When Elizabeth's head rose through the trap she perceived that the upper door was open, and that her stepfather and Farfrae stood just within it in conversation, Farfrae being nearest the dizzy edge, and Henchard a little way behind. Not to interrupt them she remained on the steps without raising her head any higher. While waiting thus she saw — or fancied she saw, for she had a terror of feeling certain — her stepfather slowly raise his hand to a level behind Farfrae's shoulders, a curious expression taking possession of his face. The young man was quite unconscious of the action, which was so indirect that, if Farfrae had observed it, he might almost have regarded it as an idle outstretching of the arm. But it would have been possible, by a comparatively light touch, to push Farfrae off his balance, and send him head over heels into the air.

Elizabeth felt quite sick at heart on thinking of what this *might* have meant. As soon as they turned she mechanically took the tea to Henchard, left it, and went away. Reflecting, she endeavoured to assure herself that the movement was an idle eccentricity, and no more. Yet, on the other hand, his subordinate position in an establishment where he once had been master might be acting on him like an irritant poison; and she finally resolved to caution Donald.

CHAPTER THIRTY-FOUR

NEXT morning, accordingly, she rose at five o'clock and went into the street. It was not yet light; a dense fog prevailed, and the town was as silent as it was dark, except that from the rectangular avenues which framed in the borough there came a chorus of tiny rappings, caused by the fall of water-drops condensed on the boughs; now it was wafted from the West Walk, now from the South Walk; and then from both quarters simultaneously. She moved on to the bottom of Corn Street, and, knowing his time well, waited only a few minutes before she heard the familiar bang of his door, and then his quick walk towards her. She met him at the point where the last tree of the engirding avenue flanked the last house in the street.

He could hardly discern her till, glancing inquiringly, he said, 'What — Miss Henchard — and are ye up so airly?'

She asked him to pardon her for waylaying him at such an unseemly time. 'But I am anxious to mention something,' she said. 'And I wished not to alarm Mrs Farfrae by calling.'

'Yes?' said he, with the cheeriness of a superior. 'And what may it be? It's very kind of ye, I'm sure.'

She now felt the difficulty of conveying to his mind the exact aspect of possibilities in her own. But she somehow began, and introduced Henchard's name. 'I sometimes fear,' she said with an effort, 'that he may be betrayed into some attempt to — insult you, sir.'

'But we are the best of friends?'

'Or to play some practical joke upon you, sir. Remember that he has been hardly used.'

'But we are quite friendly?'

'Or to do something – that would injure you – hurt you – wound you.' Every word cost her twice its length of pain. And she could see that Farfrae was still incredulous. Henchard, a poor man in his employ, was not to Farfrae's view the Henchard who had ruled him. Yet he was not only the same man, but that man with his sinister qualities, formerly latent, quickened into life by his buffetings.

Farfrae, happy, and thinking no evil, persisted in making light of her fears. Thus they parted, and she went homeward, journeymen now being in the street, waggoners going to the harness-makers for articles left to be repaired, farm-horses going to the shoeing-smiths, and the sons of labour showing themselves generally on the move. Elizabeth entered her lodging unhappily, thinking she had done no good, and only made herself appear foolish by her weak note of warning.

But Donald Farfrae was one of those men upon whom an incident is never absolutely lost. He revised impressions from a subsequent point of view, and the impulsive judgment of the moment was not always his permanent one. The vision of Elizabeth's earnest face in the rimy dawn came back to him several times during the day. Knowing the solidity of her character he did not treat her hints altogether as idle sounds.

But he did not desist from a kindly scheme on Henchard's account that engaged him just then; and when he met Lawyer Joyce, the town-clerk, later in the day, he spoke of it as if nothing had occurred to damp it.

'About that little seedsman's shop,' he said; 'the shop overlooking the churchyard, which is to let. It is not for myself I want it but for our unlucky fellow-townsman Henchard. It would be a new beginning for him, if a small one; and I have told the Council that I would head a private subscription among them to set him up in it – that I would be fifty pounds, if they would make up the other fifty among them.'

'Yes, yes; so I've heard; and there's nothing to say against it for that matter,' the town-clerk replied, in his plain, frank way. 'But, Farfrae, others see what you don't. Henchard hates 'ee – ay, hates 'ee; and 'tis right that you should know it. To my knowledge he was at the Three Mariners last night, saying in public that about you which a man ought not to say about another.'

'Is that so – ah, is that so?' said Farfrae, looking down. 'Why should he do it?' added the young man bitterly; 'what harm have I done him that he should try to wrong me?'

'God only knows,' said Joyce, lifting his eyebrows. 'It shows much long-suffering in you to put up with him, and keep him in your employ.'

'But I cannet discharge a man who was once a good friend to me? How can I forget that when I came here 'twas he enabled me to make a footing for mysel'? No, no. As long as I've a day's wark to offer he shall do it if he chooses. 'Tis not I who will deny him such a little as that. But I'll drop the idea of establishing him in a shop till I can think more about it.'

It grieved Farfrae much to give up this scheme. But a damp having been thrown over it by these and other voices in the air, he went and countermanded his orders. The then occupier of the shop was in it when Farfrae spoke to him, and feeling it necessary to give some explanation of his withdrawal from the negotiation Donald mentioned Henchard's name, and stated that the intentions of the Council had been changed.

The occupier was much disappointed, and straightway informed Henchard, as soon as he saw him, that a scheme of the Council for setting him up in a shop had been knocked on the head by Farfrae. And thus out of error enmity grew.

When Farfrae got indoors that evening the tea-kettle was singing on the high hob of the semi-egg-shaped grate. Lucetta, light as a sylph, ran forward and seized his hands, whereupon Farfrae duly kissed her.

'Oh!' she cried playfully, turning to the window. 'See – the blinds are not drawn down, and the people can look in – what a scandal!'

When the candles were lighted, the curtains drawn, and the twain sat at tea, she noticed that he looked serious. Without directly inquiring why she let her eyes linger solicitously on his face.

'Who has called?' he absently asked. 'Any folk for me?'

'No,' said Lucetta. 'What's the matter, Donald?'

'Well – nothing worth talking of,' he responded sadly.

'Then, never mind it. You will get through it. Scotchmen are always lucky.'

'No – not always!' he said, shaking his head gloomily as he contemplated a crumb on the table. 'I know many who have not been so! There was Sandy Macfarlane, who started to America to try his fortune, and he was drowned; and Archibald Leith, he was murdered! And poor Willie Dunbleeze and Maitland Macfreeze – they fell into bad courses, and went the way of all such!'

'Why – you old goosey – I was only speaking in a general sense, of course! You are always so literal. Now when we have finished tea, sing me that funny song about high-heeled shoon and siller tags, and the one-and-forty wooers.'

'No, no. I couldna sing to-night! It's Henchard – he hates me; so that I may not be his friend if I would. I would understand why there should be a wee bit envy; but I cannet see a reason for the whole intensity of what he feels. Now, can you, Lucetta? It is more like old-fashioned rivalry in love than just a bit of rivalry in trade.'

Lucetta had grown somewhat wan. 'No,' she replied.

'I give him employment – I cannet refuse it. But neither can I blind myself to the fact that with a man of passions such as his, there is no safeguard for conduct!'

'What have you heard – O Donald, dearest?' said Lucetta in alarm. The words on her lips were 'anything about me?' – but she did not utter them. She could not, however, suppress her agitation, and her eyes filled with tears.

'No, no – it is not so serious as ye fancy,' declared Farfrae soothingly; though he did not know its seriousness so well as she.

'I wish you would do what we have talked of,' mournfully remarked Lucetta. 'Give up business, and go away from here. We have plenty of money, and why should we stay?'

Farfrae seemed seriously disposed to discuss this move, and they talked thereon till a visitor was announced. Their neighbour Alderman Vatt came in.

'You've heard, I suppose, of poor Doctor Chalkfield's death? Yes – died this afternoon at five,' said Mr Vatt. Chalkfield was the Councilman who had succeeded to the Mayoralty in the preceding November.

Farfrae was sorry at the intelligence, and Mr Vatt continued: 'Well, we know he's been going some days, and as his family is well provided for we must take it all as it is. Now I have called to ask 'ee this – quite privately. If I should nominate 'ee to succeed him, and there should be no particular opposition, will 'ee accept the chair?'

'But there are folk whose turn is before mine; and I'm over young, and may be thought pushing!' said Farfrae after a pause.

'Not at all. I don't speak for myself only, several have named it. You won't refuse?'

'We thought of going away,' interposed Lucetta, looking at Farfrae anxiously.

'It was only a fancy,' Farfrae murmured. 'I woundna refuse if it is the wish of a respectable majority in the Council.'

'Very well, then, look upon yourself as elected. We have had older men long enough.'

When he was gone Farfrae said musingly, 'See now how it's ourselves that are ruled by the powers above us! We plan this, but we do that. If they want to make me Mayor I will stay, and Henchard must rave as he will.'

From this evening onward Lucetta was very uneasy. If she had not been imprudence incarnate she would not have acted as she did when she met Henchard by accident a day or two later. It was in the bustle of the market, when no one could readily notice their discourse.

'Michael,' said she, 'I must again ask you what I asked you months ago – to return me any letters or papers of mine that you may have – unless you have destroyed them? You must see how desirable it is that the times at Jersey should be blotted out, for the good of all parties.'

'Why, bless the woman! – I packed up every scrap of your handwriting to give you in the coach – but you never appeared.'

She explained how the death of her aunt had prevented her taking the journey on that day. 'And what became of the parcel then?' she asked.

He could not say – he would consider. When she was gone he recollected that he had left a heap of useless papers in his former dining-room safe – built up in the wall of his old house – now occupied by Farfrae. The letters might have been amongst them.

A grotesque grin shaped itself on Henchard's face. Had that safe been opened?

On the very evening which followed this there was a great ringing of bells in Casterbridge, and the combined brass, wood, catgut, and leather bands played round the town with more prodigality of percussion-notes than ever. Farfrae was Mayor – the two-hundredth odd of a series forming an elective dynasty dating back to the days of Charles I – and the fair Lucetta was the courted of the town. . . . But, ah! that worm i' the bud – Henchard; what he could tell!

He, in the meantime, festering with indignation at some erroneous intelligence of Farfrae's opposition to the scheme for installing him in the little seed-shop, was greeted with the news of the municipal election (which, by reason of Farfrae's comparative youth and his Scottish nativity – a thing unprecedented in the case – had an interest far beyond the ordinary). The bell-ringing and the band-playing, loud as Tamerlane's trumpet, goaded the downfallen Henchard indescribably: the ousting now seemed to him to be complete.

The next morning he went to the corn-yard as usual, and about eleven o'clock Donald entered through the green door, with no trace of the worshipful about him. The yet more emphatic change of places between him and Henchard which this election had established renewed a slight embarrassment in the manner of the modest younger man; but Henchard showed the front of one who had overlooked all this; and Farfrae met his amenities half-way at once.

'I was going to ask you,' said Henchard, 'about a packet that I may possibly have left in my old safe in the dining-room.' He added particulars.

'If so, it is there now,' said Farfrae. 'I have never opened the safe at all as yet; for I keep ma papers at the bank, to sleep easy o' nights.'

'It was not of much consequence – to me,' said Henchard. 'But I'll call for it this evening, if you don't mind?'

It was quite late when he fulfilled his promise. He had primed himself with grog, as he did very frequently now, and a curl of sardonic humour hung on his lip as he approached the house, as though he were contemplating some terrible form of amusement. Whatever it was, the incident of his entry did not diminish its force, this being his first visit to the house since he had lived there as owner. The ring of the bell spoke to him like the voice of a familiar drudge who had been bribed to forsake him; the movements of the doors were revivals of dead days.

Farfrae invited him into the dining-room, where he at once unlocked the iron safe built into the wall, *his*, Henchard's safe, made by an ingenious locksmith under his direction. Farfrae drew thence the parcel, and other papers, with apologies for not having returned them.

'Never mind,' said Henchard drily. 'The fact is they are letters mostly. . . . Yes,' he went on, sitting down and unfolding Lucetta's passionate bundle, 'here they be. That ever I should see 'em again! I hope Mrs Farfrae is well after her exertions of yesterday?'

'She has felt a bit weary; and has gone to bed airly on that account.'

Henchard returned to the letters, sorting them over with interest, Farfrae being seated at the other end of the dining-table. 'You don't forget, of course,' he resumed, 'that curious chapter in the history of my past which I told you of, and that you gave me some assistance in? These letters are, in fact, related to that unhappy business. Though, thank God, it is all over now.'

'What became of the poor woman?' asked Farfrae.

'Luckily she married, and married well,' said Henchard. 'So that these reproaches she poured out on me do not now cause me any twinges, as they might otherwise have done. . . . Just listen to what an angry woman will say!'

Farfrae, willing to humour Henchard, though quite uninterested, and bursting with yawns, gave well mannered attention.

' "For me," ' Henchard read, ' "there is practically no future. A creature too unconventionally devoted to you – who feels it impossible that she can be wife of any other man; and who is yet no more to you than the first woman you meet in the street – such am I. I quite acquit you of any intention to wrong me, yet you are the door through which wrong has come to me. That in the event of your present wife's death you will place me in her position is a consolation so far as it goes – but how far does it go? Thus I sit here, forsaken by my few acquaintance, and forsaken by you!" '

'That's how she went on to me,' said Henchard, 'acres of words like that, when what had happened was what I could not cure.'

'Yes,' said Farfrae absently, 'it is the way wi' women.' But the fact was that he knew very little of the sex; yet detecting a sort of resemblance in style between the effusions of the woman he worshipped and those of the supposed stranger, he concluded that Aphrodite ever spoke thus, whosesoever the personality she assumed.

Henchard unfolded another letter, and read it through likewise, stopping at the subscription as before. 'Her name I don't give,' he said blandly. 'As I didn't marry her, and another man did, I can scarcely do that in fairness to her.'

'Tr-rue, tr-rue,' said Farfrae. 'But why didn't you marry her when your wife Susan died?' Farfrae asked this and the other questions in the comfortably indifferent tone of one whom the matter very remotely concerned.

'Ah – well you may ask that!' said Henchard, the new-moon-shaped grin adumbrating itself again upon his mouth. 'In spite of all her protestations, when I came forward to do so, as in generosity bound, she was not the woman for me.'

'She had already married another – maybe?'

Henchard seemed to think it would be sailing too near the wind to descend further into particulars, and he answered 'Yes.'

'The young lady must have had a heart that bore transplanting very readily!'

'She had, she had,' said Henchard emphatically.

He opened a third and fourth letter, and read. This time he approached the conclusion as if the signature were indeed coming with the rest. But again he stopped short. The truth was that, as may be divined, he had quite intended to effect a grand catastrophe at the end of this drama by reading out the name; he had come to the house with no other thought. But sitting here in cold blood he could not do it. Such a wrecking of hearts appalled even him. His quality was such that he could have annihilated them both in the heat of action; but to accomplish the deed by oral poison was beyond the nerve of his enmity.

CHAPTER THIRTY-FIVE

As Donald stated, Lucetta had retired early to her room because of fatigue. She had, however, not gone to rest, but sat in the bedside chair reading and thinking over the events of the day. At the ringing of the door-bell by Henchard she wondered who it should be that would call at that comparatively late hour. The dining-room was almost under her bedroom; she could hear that somebody was admitted there, and presently the indistinct murmur of a person reading became audible.

The usual time for Donald's arrival upstairs came and passed, yet still the reading and conversation went on. This was very singular. She could think of nothing but that some extraordinary crime had been committed, and that the visitor, whoever he might be, was reading an account of it from a special edition of the *Casterbridge Chronicle*. At last she left the room, and descended the stairs. The dining-room door was ajar, and in the silence of the resting household the voice and the words were recognizable before she reached the lower flight. She stood transfixed. Her own words greeted her in Henchard's voice, like spirits from the grave.

Lucetta leant upon the banister with her cheek against the hand-rail, as if she would make a friend of it in her misery. Rigid in this position, more and more words fell successively upon her ear. But what amazed her most was the tone of her husband. He spoke merely in the accents of a man who made a present of his time.

'One word,' he was saying, as the crackling of paper denoted that Henchard was unfolding yet another sheet. 'Is it quite fair to this young woman's memory to read at such length to a stranger what was intended for your eye alone?'

'Well, yes,' said Henchard. 'By not giving her name I make it an example of all womankind, and not a scandal to one.'

'If I were you I would destroy them,' said Farfrae, giving more thought to the letters than he had hitherto done. 'As another man's wife it would injure the woman if it were known.'

'No, I shall not destroy them,' murmured Henchard, putting the letters away. Then he arose, and Lucetta heard no more.

She went back to her bedroom in a semi-paralyzed state. For very fear she could not undress, but sat on the edge of the bed, waiting. Would Henchard let out the secret in his parting words? Her suspense was terrible. Had she confessed all to Donald in their early acquaintance he might possibly have got over it, and married her just the same – unlikely as it had once seemed; but for her or any one else to tell him now would be fatal.

The door slammed; she could hear her husband bolting it. After looking round in his customary way he came leisurely up the stairs. The spark in her eyes well-nigh went out when he appeared round the bedroom door. Her gaze hung doubtful for a moment, then to her joyous amazement she saw that he looked at her with the rallying smile of one who had just been relieved of a scene that was irksome. She could hold out no longer, and sobbed hysterically.

When he had restored her Farfrae naturally enough spoke of Henchard. 'Of all men he was the least desirable as a visitor,' he said; 'but it is my belief that he's just a bit crazed. He has been reading to me a long lot of letters relating to his past life; and I could do no less than indulge him by listening.'

This was sufficient. Henchard, then, had not told. Henchard's last words to Farfrae, in short, as he stood on the door-step, had been these: 'Well – I'm much obliged to 'ee for listening. I may tell more about her some day.'

Finding this, she was much perplexed as to Henchard's motives in opening the matter at all; for in such cases we attribute to an enemy a power of consistent action which we never find in ourselves or in our friends; and forget that abortive efforts from want of heart are as possible to revenge as to generosity.

Next morning Lucetta remained in bed, meditating how to parry this incipient attack. The bold stroke of telling Donald the truth, dimly conceived, was yet too bold; for she dreaded lest in doing so he, like the rest of the world, should believe that the episode was rather her fault than her misfortune. She decided to employ persuasion – not with Donald, but with the enemy himself. It seemed the only practicable weapon left her as a woman. Having laid her plan she rose, and wrote to him who kept her on these tenterhooks: –

'I overheard your interview with my husband last night, and saw the drift of your revenge. The very thought of it crushes me! Have pity on a distressed woman! If you could see me you would relent. You do not know how anxiety has told upon me lately. I will be at the Ring at the time you leave work – just before the sun goes down. Please come that way. I cannot rest till I have seen you face to face, and heard from your mouth that you will carry this horse-play no further.'

To herself she said, on closing up this appeal: 'If ever tears and pleadings have served the weak to fight the strong, let them do so now!'

With this view she made a toilette which differed from all she had ever attempted before. To heighten her natural attractions had hitherto been the unvarying endeavour of her adult life, and one in which she was no novice. But now she neglected this, and even proceeded to impair the natural presentation. Beyond a natural reason for her slightly drawn look, she had not slept all the previous night, and this had produced upon her pretty though slightly worn features the aspect of a countenance ageing prematurely from extreme sorrow. She selected – as much from want of spirit as design – her poorest, plainest, and longest discarded attire.

To avoid the contingency of being recognized she veiled herself, and slipped out of the house quickly. The sun was resting on the hill like a drop of blood on an eyelid by the time she had got up the road opposite the amphitheatre, which she speedily entered. The interior was shadowy, and emphatic of the absence of every living thing.

She was not disappointed in the fearful hope with which she awaited him. Henchard came over the top, descended, and Lucetta waited breathlessly. But having reached the arena she saw a change in his bearing: he stood still at a little distance from her; she could not think why.

Nor could any one else have known. The truth was that in appointing this spot, and this hour, for the rendezvous, Lucetta had unwittingly backed up her entreaty by the strongest argument she could have used outside words, with this man of moods, glooms, and superstitions. Her figure in the midst of the huge enclosure, the unusual plainness of her dress, her attitude of hope and appeal, so strongly revived in his soul the memory of another ill-used woman who had stood there and thus in bygone days, and had now passed away into her rest, that he was unmanned, and his heart smote him for having attempted reprisals on one of a sex so weak. When he approached her, and before she had spoken a word, her point was half gained.

His manner as he had come down had been one of cynical carelessness; but he now put away his grim half-smile, and said in a kindly subdued tone, 'Good-night t'ye. Of course I'm glad to come if you want me.'

'O, thank you,' she said apprehensively.

'I am sorry to see 'ee looking so ill,' he stammered with unconcealed compunction.

She shook her head. 'How can you be sorry,' she asked, 'when you deliberately cause it?'

'What!' said Henchard uneasily. 'Is it anything I have done that has pulled you down like that?'

'It is all your doing,' said she. 'I have no other grief. My happiness would be secure enough but for your threats. O Michael! don't wreck me like this! You might think that you have done enough! When I came here I was a young woman; now I am rapidly becoming an old one. Neither my husband nor any other man will regard me with interest long.'

Henchard was disarmed. His old feeling of supercilious pity for womankind in general was intensified by this suppliant appearing here as the double of the first. Moreover, that thoughtless want of foresight which had led to all her trouble remained with poor Lucetta still; she had come to meet him here in this compromising way without perceiving the risk. Such a woman was very small deer to hunt; he felt ashamed, lost all zest and desire to humiliate Lucetta there and then, and no longer envied Farfrae his bargain. He had married money, but nothing more. Henchard was anxious to wash his hands of the game.

'Well, what do you want me to do?' he said gently. 'I am sure I shall be very willing. My reading of those letters was only a sort of practical joke, and I revealed nothing.'

'To give me back the letters and any papers you may have that breathe of matrimony or worse.'

'So be it. Every scrap shall be yours. . . . But, between you and me, Lucetta, he is sure to find out something of the matter, sooner or later.'

'Ah!' she said with eager tremulousness; 'but not till I have proved myself a faithful and deserving wife to him, and then he may forgive me everything!'

Henchard silently looked at her: he almost envied Farfrae such love as that, even now. 'H'm – I hope so,' he said. 'But you shall have the letters without fail. And your secret shall be kept. I swear it.'

'How good you are! – how shall I get them?'

He reflected, and said he would send them the next morning. 'Now don't doubt me,' he added. 'I can keep my word.'

CHAPTER THIRTY-SIX

RETURNING from her appointment Lucetta saw a man waiting by the lamp nearest to her own door. When she stopped to go in he came and spoke to her. It was Jopp.

He begged her pardon for addressing her. But he had heard that Mr Farfrae had been applied to by a neighbouring corn-merchant to recommend a working partner; if so, he wished to offer himself. He could give good security, and had stated as much to Mr Farfrae in a letter; but he would feel much obliged if Lucetta would say a word in his favour to her husband.

'It is a thing I know nothing about,' said Lucetta coldly.

'But you can testify to my trustworthiness better than anybody, ma'am,' said Jopp. 'I was in Jersey several years, and knew you there by sight.'

'Indeed,' she replied. 'But I knew nothing of you.'

'I think, ma'am, that a word or two from you would secure for me what I covet very much,' he persisted.

She steadily refused to have anything to do with the affair, and cutting him short, because of her anxiety to get indoors before her husband should miss her, left him on the pavement.

He watched her till she had vanished, and then went home. When he got there he sat down in the fireless chimney corner looking at the iron dogs, and the wood laid across them for heating the morning kettle. A movement upstairs disturbed him, and Henchard came down from his bedroom, where he seemed to have been rummaging boxes.

'I wish,' said Henchard, 'you would do me a service, Jopp, now – to-night, I mean, if you can. Leave this at Mrs Farfrae's for her. I should take it myself, of course, but I don't wish to be seen there.'

He handed a package in brown paper, sealed. Henchard had been as good as his word. Immediately on coming indoors he had searched over his few belongings; and every scrap of Lucetta's writing that he possessed was here. Jopp indifferently expressed his willingness.

'Well, how have ye got on to-day?' his lodger asked. 'Any prospect of an opening?'

'I am afraid not,' said Jopp, who had not told the other of his application to Farfrae.

'There never will be in Casterbridge,' declared Henchard decisively. 'You must roam further afield.' He said good-night to Jopp, and returned to his own part of the house.

Jopp sat on till his eyes were attracted by the shadow of the candle-snuff on the wall, and looking at the original he found that it had formed itself into a head like a red-hot cauliflower. Henchard's packet next met his gaze. He knew there had been something of the nature of wooing between Henchard and the now Mrs Farfrae; and his vague ideas on the subject narrowed themselves down to these: Henchard had a parcel belonging to Mrs Farfrae, and he had reasons for not returning that parcel to her in person. What could be inside it? So he went on and on till, animated by resentment at Lucetta's haughtiness, as he thought it, and curiosity to learn if there were any weak sides to this transaction with Henchard, he examined the package. The pen and all its relations being awkward tools in Henchard's hands he had affixed the seals without an impression, it never occurring to him that the efficacy of such a fastening depended on this. Jopp was far less of a tyro; he lifted one of the seals with his penknife, peeped in at the end thus opened, saw that the bundle consisted of letters; and, having satisfied himself thus far, sealed up the end again by simply softening the wax with the candle, and went off with the parcel as requested.

His path was by the river-side at the foot of the town. Coming into the light at the bridge which stood at the end of High Street he beheld lounging thereon Mother Cuxsom and Nance Mockridge.

'We be just going down Mixen Lane way, to look into Peter's Finger afore creeping to bed,' said Mrs Cuxsom. 'There's a fiddle and tambourine going on there. Lord, what's all the world – do ye come along too, Jopp – 'twon't hinder ye five minutes.'

Jopp had mostly kept himself out of this company, but present circumstance made him somewhat more reckless than usual, and without many words he decided to go to his destination that way.

*

Though the upper part of Durnover was mainly composed of a curious congeries of barns and farmsteads, there was a less picturesque side to the parish. This was Mixen Lane, now in great part pulled down.

Mixen Lane was the Adullam of all the surrounding villages. It was the hiding-place of those who were in distress, and in debt, and trouble of every kind. Farm-labourers and other peasants, who combined a little poaching with their farming, and a little brawling and bibbing with their poaching, found themselves sooner or later in Mixen Lane. Rural mechanics too idle to mechanize, rural servants too rebellious to serve, drifted or were forced into Mixen Lane.

The lane and its surrounding thicket of thatched cottages stretched out like a spit into the moist and misty lowland. Much that was sad, much that was low, some things that were baneful, could be seen in Mixen Lane. Vice ran freely in and out certain of the doors of the neighbourhood; recklessness dwelt under the roof with the crooked chimney; shame in some bow-windows; theft (in times of privation) in the thatched and mud-walled houses by the sallows. Even slaughter had not been altogether unknown here. In a block of cottages up an alley there might have been erected an altar to disease in years gone by. Such was Mixen Lane in the times when Henchard and Farfrae were Mayors.

Yet this mildewed leaf in the sturdy and flourishing Casterbridge plant lay close to the open country; not a hundred yards from a row of noble elms, and commanding a view across the moor of airy uplands and corn-fields, and mansions of the great. A brook divided the moor from the tenements, and to outward view there was no way across it – no way to the houses but round about by the road. But under every householder's stairs there was kept a mysterious plank nine inches wide; which plank was a secret bridge.

If you, as one of those refugee householders, came in from business after dark – and this was the business time here – you stealthily crossed the moor, approached the border of the aforesaid brook, and whistled opposite the house to which you belonged. A shape thereupon made its appearance on the other side bearing the bridge on end against the sky; it was lowered; you crossed, and a hand helped you to land yourself, together with the pheasants and hares gathered from neighbouring manors. You sold them slily the next morning, and the day after you stood before the magistrates with the eyes of all your sympathizing neighbours concentrated on your back. You disappeared for a time; then you were again found quietly living in Mixen Lane.

Walking along the lane at dusk the stranger was struck by two or three peculiar features therein. One was an intermittent rumbling from the back premises of the inn half-way up; this meant a skittle alley. Another was the extensive prevalence of whistling in the various domiciles – a piped note of some kind coming from nearly every open door. Another was the frequency of white aprons over dingy gowns among the women around the doorways. A white apron is a suspicious vesture in situations where spotlessness is difficult; moreover, the industry and cleanliness which the white apron expressed were belied by the postures and gaits of the women who wore it – their knuckles being mostly on their hips (an attitude which lent them the aspect of two-handled mugs), and their shoulders against door-posts; while there was a curious alacrity in the turn of each honest woman's head upon her neck and in the twirl of her honest eyes, at any noise resembling a masculine footfall along the lane.

Yet amid so much that was bad needy respectability also found a home. Under some of the roofs abode pure and virtuous souls whose presence there was due to the iron hand of necessity, and to that alone. Families from decayed villages — families of that once bulky, but now nearly extinct, section of village society called 'liviers', or lifeholders — copyholders and others, whose roof-trees had fallen for some reason or other, compelling them to quit the rural spot that had been their home for generations — came here, unless they chose to lie under a hedge by the wayside.

The inn called Peter's Finger was the church of Mixen Lane.

It was centrally situate, as such places should be, and bore about the same social relation to the Three Mariners as the latter bore to the King's Arms. At first sight the inn was so respectable as to be puzzling. The front door was kept shut, and the step was so clean that evidently but few persons entered over its sanded surface. But at the corner of the public-house was an alley, a mere slit, dividing it from the next building. Half-way up the alley was a narrow door, shiny and paintless from the rub of infinite hands and shoulders. This was the actual entrance to the inn.

A pedestrian would be seen abstractedly passing along Mixen Lane; and then, in a moment, he would vanish, causing the gazer to blink like Ashton at the disappearance of Ravenswood. That abstracted pedestrian had edged into the slit by the adroit fillip of his person sideways; from the slit he edged into the tavern by a similar exercise of skill.

The company at the Three Mariners were persons of quality in comparison with the company which gathered here; though it must be admitted that the lowest fringe of the Mariners' party touched the crest of Peter's at points. Waifs and strays of all sorts loitered about here. The landlady was a virtuous woman who years ago had been unjustly sent to gaol as an accessory to something or other after the fact. She underwent her twelvemonth, and had worn a martyr's countenance ever since, except at times of meeting the constable who apprehended her, when she winked her eye.

To this house Jopp and his acquaintances had arrived. The settles on which they sat down were thin and tall, their tops being guyed by pieces of twine to hooks in the ceiling; for when the guests grew boisterous the settles would rock and overturn without some such security. The thunder of bowls echoed from the backyard; swingels hung behind the blower of the chimney; and ex-poachers and ex-gamekeepers, whom squires had persecuted without a cause, sat elbowing each other — men who in past times had met in fights under the moon, till lapse of sentences on the one part, and loss of favour and expulsion from service on the other, brought them here together to a common level, where they sat calmly discussing old times.

'Dos't mind how you could jerk a trout ashore with a bramble, and not ruffle the stream, Charl?' a deposed keeper was saying. ' 'Twas at that I caught 'ee once, if you can mind?'

'That can I. But the worst larry for me was that pheasant business at Yalbury Wood. Your wife swore false that time, Joe — O, by Gad, she did — there's no denying it.'

'How was that?' asked Jopp.

'Why — Joe closed wi' me, and we rolled down together, close to his garden hedge. Hearing the noise, out ran his wife with the oven pyle, and it being dark under the trees she couldn't see which was uppermost. "Where beest thee, Joe, under or top?" she screeched. "O – under, by Gad!" says he. She then began to rap down upon my skull, back, and ribs with the pyle till we'd roll over again. "Where beest now, dear Joe, under or top?" she'd scream again. By George, 'twas through her I was took! And then when we got up in hall she sware that the cock pheasant was one of her rearing, when 'twas not your bird at all, Joe; 'twas Squire Brown's bird – that's whose 'twas – one that we'd picked off as we passed his wood, an hour afore. It did hurt my feelings to be so wronged! . . . Ah well – 'tis over now.'

'I might have had 'ee days afore that,' said the keeper. 'I was within a few yards of 'ee dozens of times, with a sight more of birds than that poor one.'

'Yes – 'tis not our greatest doings that the world gets wind of,' said the furmity-woman, who, lately settled in this purlieu, sat among the rest. Having travelled a great deal in her time she spoke with cosmopolitan largeness of idea. It was she who presently asked Jopp what was the parcel he kept so snugly under his arm.

'Ah, therein lies a grand secret,' said Jopp. 'It is the passion of love. To think that a woman should love one man so well, and hate another so unmercifully.'

'Who's the object of your meditation, sir?'

'One that stands high in this town. I'd like to shame her! Upon my life, 'twould be as good as a play to read her love-letters, the proud piece of silk and wax-work! For 'tis her love-letters that I've got here.'

'Love-letters? then let's hear 'em, good soul,' said Mother Cuxsom. 'Lord, do ye mind, Richard, what fools we used to be when we were younger? Getting a schoolboy to write ours for us; and giving him a penny, do ye mind, not to tell other folks what he'd put inside, do ye mind?'

By this time Jopp had pushed his finger under the seals, and unfastened the letters, tumbling them over and picking up one here and there at random, which he read aloud. These passages soon began to uncover the secret which Lucetta had so earnestly hoped to keep buried, though the epistles, being allusive only, did not make it altogether plain.

'Mrs Farfrae wrote that!' said Nance Mockridge. ' 'Tis a humbling thing for us, as respectable women, that one of the same sex could do it. And now she's vowed herself to another man!'

'So much the better for her,' said the aged furmity-woman. 'Ah, I saved her from a real bad marriage, and she's never been the one to thank me.'

'I say, what a good foundation for a skimmity-ride,' said Nance.

'True,' said Mrs Cuxson, reflecting. ' 'Tis as good a ground for a skimmity-ride as ever I knowed; and it ought not to be wasted. The last one seen in Casterbridge must have been ten years ago, if a day.'

At this moment there was a shrill whistle, and the landlady said to the man who had been called Charl, ' 'Tis Jim coming in. Would ye go and let down the bridge for me?'

Without replying Charl and his comrade Joe rose, and receiving a lantern from her went out at the back door and down the garden-path, which ended abruptly at the edge of the stream already mentioned. Beyond the stream was the open moor, from which a clammy breeze smote upon their faces as they advanced.

Taking up the board that had lain in readiness one of them lowered it across the water, and the instant its further end touched the ground footsteps entered upon it, and there appeared from the shade a stalwart man with straps round his knees, a double-barrelled gun under his arm and some birds slung up behind him. They asked him if he had had much luck.

'Not much,' he said indifferently. 'All safe inside?'

Receiving a reply in the affirmative he went on inwards, the others withdrawing the bridge and beginning to retreat in his rear. Before, however, they had entered the house a cry of 'Ahoy' from the moor led them to pause.

The cry was repeated. They pushed the lantern into an outhouse, and went back to the brink of the stream.

'Ahoy – is this the way to Casterbridge?' said some one from the other side.

'Not in particular,' said Charl. 'There's a river afore 'ee.'

'I don't care – here's for through it!' said the man in the moor. 'I've had travelling enough for to-day.'

'Stop a minute, then,' said Charl, finding that the man was no enemy. 'Joe, bring the plank and lantern; here's somebody that's lost his way. You should have kept along the turnpike road, friend, and not have strook across here.'

'I should – as I see now. But I saw a light here, and says I to myself, that's an outlying house, depend on't.'

The plank was now lowered; and the stranger's form shaped itself from the darkness. He was a middle-aged man, with hair and whiskers prematurely grey, and a broad and genial face. He had crossed on the plank without hesitation, and seemed to see nothing odd in the transit. He thanked them, and walked between them up the garden. 'What place is this?' he asked, when they reached the door.

'A public-house.'

'Ah. Perhaps it will suit me to put up at. Now then, come in and wet your whistle at my expense for the lift over you have given me.'

They followed him into the inn, where the increased light exhibited him as one who would stand higher in an estimate by the eye than in one by the ear. He was dressed with a certain clumsy richness – his coat being furred, and his head covered by a cap of seal-skin, which, though the nights were chilly, must have been warm for the daytime, spring being somewhat advanced. In his hand he carried a small mahogany case, strapped, and clamped with brass.

Apparently surprised at the kind of company which confronted him through the kitchen door, he at once abandoned his idea of putting up at the house; but taking the situation lightly, he called for glasses of the best, paid for them as he stood in the passage, and turned to proceed on his way by the front door. This was barred, and while the landlady was unfastening it the conversation about the skimmington was continued in the sitting-room, and reached his ears.

'What do they mean by a "skimmity-ride"?' he asked.

'O, sir!' said the landlady, swinging her long earrings with deprecating modesty; ' 'tis a' old foolish thing they do in these parts when a man's wife is – well, not too particularly his own. But as a respectable householder I don't encourage it.'

'Still, are they going to do it shortly? It is a good sight to see, I suppose?'

'Well, sir!' she simpered. And then, bursting into naturalness, and glancing from the corner of her eye, ' 'Tis the funniest thing under the sun! And it costs money.'

'Ah! I remember hearing of some such thing. Now I shall be in Casterbridge for two or three weeks to come, and should not mind seeing the performance. Wait a moment.' He turned back, entered the sitting-room, and said, 'Here, good folks; I should like to see the old custom you are talking of, and I don't mind being something towards it – take that.' He threw a sovereign on the table and returned to the landlady at the door, of whom, having inquired the way into the town, he took his leave.

'There were more where that one came from,' said Charl, when the sovereign had been taken up and handed to the landlady for safe keeping. 'By George! we ought to have got a few more while we had him here.'

'No, no,' answered the landlady. 'This is a respectable house, thank God! And I'll have nothing done but what's honourable.'

'Well,' said Jopp; 'now we'll consider the business begun, and will soon get it in train.'

'We will!' said Nance. 'A good laugh warms my heart more than a cordial, and that's the truth on't.'

Jopp gathered up the letters, and it being now somewhat late he did not attempt to call at Farfrae's with them that night. He reached home, sealed them up as before, and delivered the parcel at its address next morning. Within an hour its contents were reduced to ashes by Lucetta, who, poor soul! was inclined to fall down on her knees in thankfulness that at last no evidence remained of the unlucky episode with Henchard in her past. For though hers had been rather the laxity of inadvertence than of intention, that episode, if known, was not the less likely to operate fatally between herself and her husband.

CHAPTER THIRTY-SEVEN

S UCH was the state of things when the current affairs of Casterbridge were interrupted by an event of such magnitude that its influence reached to the lowest social stratum there, stirring the depths of its society simultaneously with the preparations for the skimmington. It was one of those excitements which, when they move a country town, leave a permanent mark upon its chronicles, as a warm summer permanently marks the ring in the tree-trunk corresponding to its date.

A Royal Personage was about to pass through the borough on his course further west, to inaugurate an immense engineering work out that way. He had consented to halt half-an-hour or so in the town, and to receive an address from the corporation of Casterbridge, which, as a representative centre of husbandry, wished thus to express its sense of the great services he had rendered to agricultural science and economics, by his zealous promotion of designs for placing the art of farming on a more scientific footing.

Royalty had not been seen in Casterbridge since the days of the third King

George, and then only by candlelight for a few minutes, when that monarch, on a night-journey, had stopped to change horses at the King's Arms. The inhabitants therefore decided to make a thorough *fête carillonnée* of the unwonted occasion. Half-an-hour's pause was not long, it is true; but much might be done in it by a judicious grouping of incidents, above all, if the weather were fine.

The address was prepared on parchment by an artist who was handy at ornamental lettering, and was laid on with the best gold-leaf and colours that the sign-painter had in his shop. The Council met on the Tuesday before the appointed day, to arrange the details of the procedure. While they were sitting, the door of the Council Chamber standing open, they heard a heavy footstep coming up the stairs. It advanced along the passage, and Henchard entered the room, in clothes of frayed and threadbare shabbiness, the very clothes which he had used to wear in the primal days when he had sat among them.

'I have a feeling,' he said, advancing to the table and laying his hand upon the green cloth, 'that I should like to join ye in this reception of our illustrious visitor. I suppose I could walk with the rest?'

Embarrassed glances were exchanged by the Council, and Grower nearly ate the end of his quillpen off, so gnawed he it during the silence. Farfrae the young Mayor, who by virtue of his office sat in the large chair, intuitively caught the sense of the meeting, and as spokesman was obliged to utter it, glad as he would have been that the duty should have fallen to another tongue.

'I hardly see that it would be proper, Mr Henchard,' said he. 'The Council are the Council, and as ye are no longer one of the body, there would be an irregularity in the proceeding. If ye were included, why not others?'

'I have a particular reason for wishing to assist at the ceremony.'

Farfrae looked round. 'I think I have expressed the feeling of the Council,' he said.

'Yes, yes,' from Dr Bath, Lawyer Long, Alderman Tubber, and several more.

'Then I am not to be allowed to have anything to do with it officially?'

'I am afraid so; it is out of the question indeed. But of course you can see the doings full well, such as they are to be, like the rest of the spectators.'

Henchard did not reply to that very obvious suggestion, and turning on his heel, went away.

It had been only a passing fancy of his, but opposition crystallized it into a determination. 'I'll welcome his Royal Highness, or nobody shall!' he went about saying. 'I am not going to be sat upon by Farfrae, or any of the rest of the paltry crew! You shall see.'

The eventful morning was bright, a full-faced sun confronting early window-gazers eastward, and all perceived (for they were practised in weather-lore) that there was permanence in the glow. Visitors soon began to flock in from county houses, villages, remote copses, and lonely uplands, the latter in oiled boots and tilt bonnets, to see the reception, or if not to see it, at any rate to be near it. There was hardly a workman in the town who did not put a clean shirt on. Solomon Longways, Christopher Coney, Buzzford, and the rest of that fraternity, showed their sense of the occasion by advancing their customary eleven o'clock pint to half-past ten; from which they found a difficulty in getting back to the proper hour for several days.

Henchard had determined to do no work that day. He primed himself in the morning with a glass of rum, and walking down the street met Elizabeth-Jane, whom he had not seen for a week. 'It was lucky,' he said to her, 'my twenty-one years had expired before this came on, or I should never have had the nerve to carry it out.'

'Carry out what?' said she, alarmed.

'This welcome I am going to give our Royal visitor.'

She was perplexed. 'Shall we go and see it together?' she said.

'See it! I have other fish to fry. You see it. It will be worth seeing!'

She could do nothing to elucidate this, and decked herself out with a heavy heart. As the appointed time drew near she got sight again of her stepfather. She thought he was going to the Three Mariners; but no, he elbowed his way through the gay throng to the shop of Woolfrey, the draper. She waited in the crowd without.

In a few minutes he emerged, wearing, to her surprise, a brilliant rosette, while more surprising still, in his hand he carried a flag of somewhat homely construction, formed by tacking one of the small Union Jacks, which abounded in the town to-day, to the end of a deal wand – probably the roller from a piece of calico. Henchard rolled up his flag on the doorstep, put it under his arm, and went down the street.

Suddenly the taller members of the crowd turned their heads, and the shorter stood on tiptoe. It was said that the Royal *cortège* approached. The railway had stretched out an arm towards Casterbridge at this time, but had not reached it by several miles as yet; so that the intervening distance, as well as the remainder of the journey, was to be traversed by road in the old fashion. People thus waited – the county families in their carriages, the masses on foot – and watched the far-stretching London highway to the ringing of bells and chatter of tongues.

From the background Elizabeth-Jane watched the scene. Some seats has been arranged from which ladies could witness the spectacle, and the front seat was occupied by Lucetta, the Mayor's wife, just at present. In the road under her eyes stood Henchard. She appeared so bright and pretty that, as it seemed, he was experiencing the momentary weakness of wishing for her notice. But he was far from attractive to a woman's eye, ruled as that is so largely by the superficies of things. He was not only a journeyman, unable to appear as he formerly had appeared, but he disdained to appear as well as he might. Everybody else, from the Mayor to the washer-woman, shone in new vesture according to means; but Henchard had doggedly retained the fretted and weather-beaten garments of bygone years.

Hence, alas, this occurred: Lucetta's eyes slid over him to this side and to that without anchoring on his features – as gaily dressed women's eyes will too often do on such occasions. Her manner signified quite plainly that she meant to know him in public no more.

But she was never tired of watching Donald, as he stood in animated converse with his friends a few yards off, wearing round his young neck the official gold chain with great square links, like that round the Royal unicorn. Every trifling emotion that her husband showed as he talked had its reflex on her face and lips, which moved in little duplicates to his. She was living his part rather than her own, and cared for no one's situation but Farfrae's that day.

At length a man stationed at the furthest turn of the high road, namely, on the second bridge of which mention has been made, gave a signal; and the Corporation in their robes proceeded from the front of the Town Hall to the archway erected at the entrance of the town. The carriages containing the Royal visitor and his suite arrived at the spot in a cloud of dust, a procession was formed, and the whole came on to the Town Hall at a walking pace.

This spot was the centre of interest. There were a few clear yards in front of the Royal carriage, sanded; and into this space a man stepped before any one could prevent him. It was Henchard. He had unrolled his private flag, and removing his hat he staggered to the side of the slowing vehicle, waving the Union Jack to and fro with his left hand, while he blandly held out his right to the Illustrious Personage.

All the ladies said with bated breath, 'O, look there!' and Lucetta was ready to faint. Elizabeth-Jane peeped through the shoulders of those in front, saw what it was, and was terrified; and then her interest in the spectacle as a strange phenomenon got the better of her fear.

Farfrae, with Mayoral authority, immediately rose to the occasion. He seized Henchard by the shoulder, dragged him back, and told him roughly to be off. Henchard's eyes met his, and Farfrae observed the fierce light in them despite his excitement and irritation. For a moment Henchard stood his ground rigidly; then by an unaccountable impulse gave way and retired. Farfrae glanced to the ladies' gallery, and saw that his Calphurnia's cheek was pale.

'Why – it is your husband's old patron!' said Mrs Blowbody, a lady of the neighbourhood who sat beside Lucetta.

'Patron!' said Donald's wife with quick indignation.

'Do you say the man is an acquaintance of Mr Farfrae's?' observed Mrs Bath, the physician's wife, a new-comer to the town through her recent marriage with the doctor.

'He works for my husband,' said Lucetta.

'Oh – is that all? They have been saying to me that it was through him your husband first got a footing in Casterbridge. What stories people will tell!'

'They will indeed. It was not so at all. Donald's genius would have enabled him to get a footing anywhere, without anybody's help! He would have been just the same if there had been no Henchard in the world!'

It was partly Lucetta's ignorance of the circumstances of Donald's arrival which led her to speak thus; partly the sensation that everybody seemed bent on snubbing her at this triumphant time. The incident had occupied but a few moments, but it was necessarily witnessed by the Royal Personage, who, however, with practised tact, affected not to have noticed anything unusual. He alighted, the Mayor advanced, the address was read; the Illustrious Personage replied, then said a few words to Farfrae, and shook hands with Lucetta as the Mayor's wife. The ceremony occupied but a few minutes, and the carriages rattled heavily as Pharaoh's chariots down Corn Street and out upon the Budmouth Road, in continuation of the journey coastward.

In the crowd stood Coney, Buzzford, and Longways. 'Some difference between him now and when he zung at the Dree Mariners,' said the first. ' 'Tis wonderful how he could get a lady of her quality to go snacks wi' en in such quick time.'

'True. Yet how folk do worship fine clothes! Now there's a better-looking woman than she that nobody notices at all, because she's akin to that hontish fellow Henchard.'

'I could worship ye, Buzz, for saying that,' remarked Nance Mockridge. 'I do like to see the trimming pulled off such Christmas candles. I am quite unequal to the part of villain myself, or I'd gi'e all my small silver to see that lady toppered. . . . And perhaps I shall soon,' she added significantly.

'That's not a noble passiont for a 'oman to keep up,' said Longways.

Nance did not reply, but every one knew what she meant. The ideas diffused by the reading of Lucetta's letters at Peter's Finger had condensed into a scandal, which was spreading like a miasmatic fog through Mixen Lane, and thence up the back streets of Casterbridge.

This mixed assemblage of idlers known to each other presently fell apart into two bands by a process of natural selection, the frequenters of Peter's Finger going off Mixen Lane-wards, where most of them lived, while Coney, Buzzford, Longways, and that connection remained in the street.

'You know what's brewing down there, I suppose?' said Buzzford mysteriously to the others.

Coney looked at him – 'Not the skimmity-ride?'

Buzzford nodded.

'I have my doubts if it will be carried out,' said Longways. 'If they are getting it up they are keeping it mighty close.'

'I heard they were thinking of it a fortnight ago, at all events.'

'If I were sure o't I'd lay information,' said Longways emphatically. ' 'Tis too rough a joke, and apt to wake riots in towns. We know that the Scotchman is a right enough man, and that his lady has been a right enough 'oman since she came here, and if there was anything wrong about her afore, that's their business, not ours.'

Coney reflected. Farfrae was still liked in the community; but it must be owned that, as the Mayor and man of money, engrossed with affairs and ambitions, he had lost in the eyes of the poorer inhabitants something of that wondrous charm which he had had for them as a light-hearted penniless young man, who sang ditties as readily as the birds in the trees. Hence the anxiety to keep him from annoyance showed not quite the ardour that would have animated it in former days.

'Suppose we make inquiration into it, Christopher,' continued Longways; 'and if we find there's really anything in it, drop a letter to them most concerned, and advise 'em to keep out of the way?'

This course was decided on, and the group separated, Buzzford saying to Coney, 'Come, my ancient friend; let's move on. There's nothing more to see here.'

These well-intentioned ones would have been surprised had they known how ripe the great jocular plot really was. 'Yes, to-night,' Jopp had said to the Peter's party at the corner of Mixen Lane. 'As a wind-up to the Royal visit the hit will be all the more pat by reason of their great elevation to-day.'

To him, at least, it was not a joke, but a retaliation.

CHAPTER THIRTY-EIGHT

T HE proceedings had been brief – too brief – to Lucetta, whom an intoxicating *Weltlust* had fairly mastered; but they had brought her a great triumph nevertheless. The shake of the Royal hand still lingered in her fingers; and the chit-chat she had overheard, that her husband might possibly receive the honour of knighthood, though idle to a degree, seemed not the wildest vision; stranger things had occurred to men so good and captivating as her Scotchman was.

After the collision with the Mayor, Henchard had withdrawn behind the ladies' stand; and there he stood, regarding with a stare of abstraction the spot on the lappel of his coat where Farfrae's hand had seized it. He put his own hand there, as if he could hardly realize such an outrage from one whom it had once been his wont to treat with ardent generosity. While pausing in this half-stupefied state the conversation of Lucetta with the other ladies reached his ears; and he distinctly heard her deny him – deny that he had assisted Donald, that he was anything more than a common journeyman.

He moved on homeward, and met Jopp in the archway to the Bull Stake. 'So you've had a snub,' said Jopp.

'And what if I have?' answered Henchard sternly.

'Why, I've had one too, so we are both under the same cold shade.' He briefly related his attempt to win Lucetta's intercession.

Henchard merely heard this story, without taking it deeply in. His own relation to Farfrae and Lucetta overshadowed all kindred ones. He went on saying brokenly to himself, 'She has supplicated to me in her time; and now her tongue won't own me nor her eyes see me! . . . And he – how angry he looked. He drove me back as if I were a bull breaking fence. . . . I took it like a lamb, for I saw it could not be settled there. He can rub brine on a green wound! . . . But he shall pay for it, and she shall be sorry. It must come to a tussle – face to face; and then we'll see how a coxcomb can front a man!'

Without further reflection the fallen merchant, bent on some wild purpose, ate a hasty dinner and went forth to find Farfrae. After being injured by him as a rival, and snubbed by him as a journeyman, the crowning degradation had been reserved for this day – that he should be shaken at the collar by him as a vagabond in the face of the whole town.

The crowds had dispersed. But for the green arches which still stood as they were erected Casterbridge life had resumed its ordinary shape. Henchard went down Corn Street till he came to Farfrae's house, where he knocked, and left a message that he would be glad to see his employer at the granaries as soon as he conveniently could come there. Having done this he proceeded round to the back and entered the yard.

Nobody was present, for, as he had been aware, the labourers and carters were enjoying a half-holiday on account of the events of the morning – though the carters would have to return for a short time later on, to feed and litter down the

424

horses. He had reached the granary steps and was about to ascend, when he said to himself aloud, 'I'm stronger than he.'

Henchard returned to a shed, where he selected a short piece of rope from several pieces that were lying about; hitching one end of this to a nail, he took the other in his right hand and turned himself bodily round, while keeping his arm against his side; by this contrivance he pinioned the arm effectively. He now went up the ladders to the top floor of the corn-stores.

It was empty except of a few sacks, and at the further end was the door often mentioned, opening under the cathead and chain that hoisted the sacks. He fixed the door open and looked over the sill. There was a depth of thirty or forty feet to the ground; here was the spot on which he had been standing with Farfrae when Elizabeth-Jane had seen him lift his arm, with many misgivings as to what the movement portended.

He retired a few steps into the loft and waited. From this elevated perch his eye could sweep the roofs round about, the upper parts of the luxurious chestnut trees, now delicate in leaves of a week's age, and the drooping boughs of the limes; Farfrae's garden and the green door leading therefrom. In course of time – he could not say how long – that green door opened and Farfrae came through. He was dressed as if for a journey. The low light of the nearing evening caught his head and face when he emerged from the shadow of the wall, warming them to a complexion of flame-colour. Henchard watched him with his mouth firmly set, the squareness of his jaw and the verticality of his profile being unduly marked.

Farfrae came on with one hand in his pocket, and humming a tune in a way which told that the words were most in his mind. They were those of the song he had sung when he arrived years before at the Three Mariners, a poor young man, adventuring for life and fortune, and scarcely knowing whitherward:-

> 'And here's a hand, my trusty fiere,
> And gie's a hand o' thine.'

Nothing moved Henchard like an old melody. He sank back. 'No; I can't do it!' he gasped. 'Why does the infernal fool begin that now!'

At length Farfrae was silent, and Henchard looked out of the loft door. 'Will ye come up here?' he said.

'Ay, man,' said Farfrae. 'I couldn't see ye. What's wrang?'

A minute later Henchard heard his feet on the lowest ladder. He heard him land on the first floor, ascend and land on the second, begin the ascent to the third. And then his head rose through the trap behind.

'What are you doing up here at this time?' he asked, coming forward. 'Why didn't ye take your holiday like the rest of the men?' He spoke in a tone which had just severity enough in it to show that he remembered the untoward event of the forenoon, and his conviction that Henchard had been drinking.

Henchard said nothing; but going back he closed the stair hatch-way, and stamped upon it so that it went tight into its frame; he next turned to the wondering young man, who by this time observed that one of Henchard's arms was bound to his side.

'Now,' said Henchard quietly, 'we stand face to face – man and man. Your money and your fine wife no longer lift 'ee above me as they did but now, and my poverty does not press me down.'

'What does it all mean?' asked Farfrae simply.

'Wait a bit, my lad. You should ha' thought twice before you affronted to extremes a man who had nothing to lose. I've stood your rivalry, which ruined me, and your snubbing, which humbled me; but your hustling, that disgraced me, I won't stand!'

Farfrae warmed a little at this. 'Ye'd no business there,' he said.

'As much as any one among ye! What, you forward stripling, tell a man of my age he'd no business there!' The anger-vein swelled in his forehead as he spoke.

'You insulted Royalty, Henchard; and 'twas my duty, as the chief magistrate, to stop you.'

'Royalty be damned,' said Henchard. 'I am as loyal as you, come to that!'

'I am not here to argue. Wait till you cool doon, wait till you cool; and you will see things the same way as I do.'

'You may be the one to cool first,' said Henchard grimly. 'Now this is the case. Here be we, in this four-square loft, to finish out that little wrestle you began this morning. There's the door, forty foot above ground. One of us two puts the other out by that door – the master stays inside. If he likes he may go down afterwards and give the alarm that the other has fallen out by accident – or he may tell the truth – that's his business. As the strongest man I've tied one arm to take no advantage of 'ee. D'ye understand? Then here's at 'ee!'

There was no time for Farfrae to do aught but one thing, to close with Henchard, for the latter had come on at once. It was a wrestling match, the object of each being to give his antagonist a back fall; and on Henchard's part, unquestionably, that it should be through the door.

At the outset Henchard's hold by his only free hand, the right, was on the left side of Farfrae's collar, which he firmly grappled, the latter holding Henchard by his collar with the contrary hand. With his right he endeavoured to get hold of his antagonist's left arm, which, however, he could not do, so adroitly did Henchard keep it in the rear as he gazed upon the lowered eyes of his fair and slim antagonist.

Henchard planted the first toe forward, Farfrae crossing him with his; and thus far the struggle had very much the appearance of the ordinary wrestling of those parts. Several minutes were passed by them in this attitude, the pair rocking and writhing like trees in a gale, both preserving an absolute silence. By this time their breathing could be heard. Then Farfrae tried to get hold of the other side of Henchard's collar, which was resisted by the larger man exerting all his force in a wrenching movement, and this part of the struggle ended by his forcing Farfrae down on his knees by sheer pressure of one of his muscular arms. Hampered as he was, however, he could not keep him there, and Farfrae finding his feet again the struggle proceeded as before.

By a whirl Henchard brought Donald dangerously near the precipice; seeing his position the Scotchman for the first time locked himself to his adversary, and all the efforts of that infuriated Prince of Darkness – as he might have been called from his appearance just now – were inadequate to lift or loosen Farfrae for a time. By an extraordinary effort he succeeded at last, though not until they had got far back again from the fatal door. In doing so Henchard contrived to turn Farfrae a complete somersault. Had Henchard's other arm been free it would have been all over with Farfrae then. But again he regained his feet, wrenching

Henchard's arm considerably, and causing him sharp pain, as could be seen from the twitching of his face. He instantly delivered the younger man an annihilating turn by the left fore-hip, as it used to be expressed, and following up his advantage thrust him towards the door, never loosening his hold till Farfrae's fair head was hanging over the window-sill, and his arm dangling down outside the wall.

'Now,' said Henchard between his gasps, 'this is the end of what you began this morning. Your life is in my hands.'

'Then take it, take it!' said Farfrae. 'Ye've wished to long enough!'

Henchard looked down upon him in silence, and their eyes met. 'O Farfrae! – that's not true!' he said bitterly. 'God is my witness that no man ever loved another as I did thee at one time. . . . And now – though I came here to kill 'ee, I cannot hurt thee! Go and give me in charge – do what you will – I care nothing for what comes of me!'

He withdrew to the back part of the loft, loosened his arm, and flung himself into a corner upon some sacks, in the abandonment of remorse. Farfrae regarded him in silence; then went to the hatch and descended through it. Henchard would fain have recalled him; but his tongue failed in its task, and the young man's steps died on his ear.

Henchard took his full measure of shame and self-reproach. The scenes of his first acquaintance with Farfrae rushed back upon him – that time when the curious mixture of romance and thrift in the young man's composition so commanded his heart that Farfrae could play upon him as on an instrument. So thoroughly subdued was he that he remained on the sacks in a crouching attitude, unusual for a man, and for such a man. Its womanliness sat tragically on the figure of so stern a piece of virility. He heard a conversation below, the opening of the coach-house door, and the putting in of a horse, but took no notice.

Here he stayed till the thin shades thickened to opaque obscurity, and the loft-door became an oblong of gray light – the only visible shape around. At length he arose, shook the dust from his clothes wearily, felt his way to the hatch, and gropingly descended the steps till he stood in the yard.

'He thought highly of me once,' he murmured. 'Now he'll hate me and despise me for ever!'

He became possessed by an overpowering wish to see Farfrae again that night, and by some desperate pleading to attempt the well-nigh impossible task of winning pardon for his late mad attack. But as he walked towards Farfrae's door he recalled the unheeded doings in the yard while he had lain above in a sort of stupor. Farfrae he remembered had gone to the stable and put the horse into the gig; while doing so Whittle had brought him a letter; Farfrae had then said that he would not go towards Budmouth as he had intended – that he was unexpectedly summoned to Weatherbury, and meant to call at Mellstock on his way thither, that place lying but one or two miles out of his course.

He must have come prepared for a journey when he first arrived in the yard, unsuspecting enmity; and he must have driven off (though in a changed direction) without saying a word to any one on what had occurred between themselves.

It would therefore be useless to call at Farfrae's house till very late.

There was no help for it but to wait till his return, though waiting was almost torture to his restless and self-accusing soul. He walked about the streets and outskirts of the town, lingering here and there till he reached the stone bridge of which mention has been made, an accustomed halting-place with him now. Here he spent a long time, the purl of waters through the weirs meeting his ear, and the Casterbridge lights glimmering at no great distance off.

While leaning thus upon the parapet his listless attention was awakened by sounds of an unaccustomed kind from the town quarter. They were a confusion of rhythmical noises, to which the streets added yet more confusion by encumbering them with echoes. His first incurious thought that the clangour arose from the town band, engaged in an attempt to round off a memorable day by a burst of evening harmony, was contradicted by certain peculiarities of reverberation. But inexplicability did not rouse him to more than a cursory heed; his sense of degradation was too strong for the admission of foreign ideas; and he leant against the parapet as before.

CHAPTER THIRTY-NINE

WHEN Farfrae descended out of the loft breathless from his encounter with Henchard, he paused at the bottom to recover himself. He arrived at the yard with the intention of putting the horse into the gig himself (all the men having a holiday), and driving to a village on the Budmouth Road. Despite the fearful struggle he decided still to persevere in his journey, so as to recover himself before going indoors and meeting the eyes of Lucetta. He wished to consider his course in a case so serious.

When he was just on the point of driving off Whittle arrived with a note badly addressed, and bearing the word 'immediate' upon the outside. On opening it he was surprised to see that it was unsigned. In contained a brief request that he would go to Weatherbury that evening about some business which he was conducting there. Farfrae knew nothing that could make it pressing; but as he was bent upon going out he yielded to the anonymous request, particularly as he had a call to make at Mellstock which could be included in the same tour. Thereupon he told Whittle of his change of direction, in words which Henchard had overheard; and set out on his way. Farfrae had not directed his man to take the message indoors, and Whittle had not been supposed to do so on his own responsibility.

Now the anonymous letter was a well-intentioned but clumsy contrivance of Longways and other of Farfrae's men to get him out of the way for the evening, in order that the satirical mummery should fall flat, if it were attempted. By giving open information they would have brought down upon their heads the vengeance of those among their comrades who enjoyed these boisterous old games; and therefore the plan of sending a letter recommended itself by its indirectness.

For poor Lucetta they took no protective measure, believing with the majority there was some truth in the scandal, which she would have to bear as she best might.

It was about eight o'clock, and Lucetta was sitting in the drawing-room alone. Night had set in for more than half an hour, but she had not had the candles lighted, for when Farfrae was away she preferred waiting for him by the firelight, and, if it were not too cold, keeping one of the window-sashes a little way open that the sound of his wheels might reach her ears early. She was leaning back in her chair, in a more hopeful mood than she had enjoyed since her marriage. The day had been such a success; and the temporary uneasiness which Henchard's show of effrontery had wrought in her disappeared with the quiet disappearance of Henchard himself under her husband's reproof. The floating evidences of her absurd passion for him, and its consequences, had been destroyed, and she really seemed to have no cause for fear.

The reverie in which these and other subjects mingled was disturbed by a hubbub in the distance, that increased moment by moment. It did not greatly surprise her, the afternoon having been given up to recreation by a majority of the populace since the passage of the Royal equipages. But her attention was at once riveted to the matter by the voice of a maid-servant next door, who spoke from an upper window across the street to some other maid even more elevated than she.

'Which way be they going now?' inquired the first with interest.

'I can't be sure for a moment,' said the second, 'because of the malter's chimbley. O yes — I can see 'em. Well, I declare, I declare!'

'What, what?' from the first, more enthusiastically.

'They are coming up Corn Street after all! They sit back to back!'

'What — two of 'em — are there two figures?'

'Yes. Two images on a donkey, back to back, their elbows tied to one another's! She's facing the head, and he's facing the tail.'

'Is it meant for anybody particular?'

'Well — it mid be. The man has got on a blue coat and kerseymere leggings; he has black whiskers, and a reddish face. 'Tis a stuffed figure, with a falseface.'

The din was increasing now — then it lessened a little.

'There — I shan't see, after all!' cried the disappointed first maid.

'They have gone into a back street — that's all,' said the one who occupied the enviable position in the attic. 'There — now I have got 'em all endways nicely!'

'What's the woman like? Just say, and I can tell in a moment if 'tis meant for one I've in mind.'

'My — why — 'tis dressed just as *she* was dressed when she sat in the front seat at the time the play-actors came to the Town Hall!'

Lucetta started to her feet; and almost at the instant the door of the room was quickly and softly opened. Elizabeth-Jane advanced into the firelight.

'I have come to see you,' she said breathlessly. 'I did not stop to knock — forgive me! I see you have not shut your shutters, and the window is open.'

Without waiting for Lucetta's reply she crossed quickly to the window and pulled out one of the shutters. Lucetta glided to her side. 'Let it be — hush!' she said peremptorily, in a dry voice, while she seized Elizabeth-Jane by the hand, and held up her finger. Their intercourse had been so low and hurried that not a word had been lost of the conversation without; which had thus proceeded: —

'Her neck is uncovered, and her hair in bands, and her back-comb in place; she's got on a puce silk, and white stockings, and coloured shoes.'

Again Elizabeth-Jane attempted to close the window, but Lucetta held her by main force.

' 'Tis me!' she said, with a face pale as death. 'A procession – a scandal – an effigy of me, and him!'

The look of Elizabeth betrayed that the latter knew it already.

'Let us shut it out,' coaxed Elizabeth-Jane, noting that the rigid wildness of Lucetta's features was growing yet more rigid and wild with the nearing of the noise and laughter. 'Let us shut it out!'

'It is no use!' she shrieked out. 'He will see it, won't he? Donald will see it! He is just coming home – and it will break his heart – he will never love me any more – and O, it will kill me – kill me!'

Elizabeth-Jane was frantic now. 'O, can't something be done to stop it?' she cried. 'Is there nobody to do it – not one?'

She relinquished Lucetta's hands, and ran to the door. Lucetta herself, saying recklessly 'I will see it!' turned to the window, threw up the sash, and went out upon the balcony. Elizabeth immediately followed her, and put her arm round her to pull her in. Lucetta's eyes were straight upon the spectacle of the uncanny revel, now advancing rapidly. The numerous lights around the two effigies threw them up into lurid distinctness; it was impossible to mistake the pair for other than the intended victims. 'Come in, come in,' implored Elizabeth; 'and let me shut the window!'

'She's me – she's me – even to the parasol – my green parasol!' cried Lucetta with a wild laugh as she stepped in. She stood motionless for one second – then fell heavily to the floor.

Almost at the instant of her fall the rude music of the skimmington ceased. The roars of sarcastic laughter went off in ripples, and the trampling died out like the rustle of a spent wind. Elizabeth was only indirectly conscious of this; she had rung the bell, and was bending over Lucetta, who remained convulsed on the carpet in the paroxysms of an epileptic seizure. She rang again and again, in vain; the probability being that the servants had all run out of the house to see more of the Dæmonic Sabbath than they could see within.

At last Farfrae's man, who had been agape on the door-step, came up; then the cook. The shutters, hastily pushed to by Elizabeth, were quite closed, a light was obtained, Lucetta carried to her room, and the man sent off for a doctor. While Elizabeth was undressing her she recovered consciousness; but as soon as she remembered what had passed the fit returned.

The doctor arrived with unhoped-for promptitude; he had been standing at his door, like others, wondering what the uproar meant. As soon as he saw the unhappy sufferer he said, in answer to Elizabeth's mute appeal, 'This is serious.'

'It is a fit,' Elizabeth said.

'Yes. But a fit in the present state of her health means mischief. You must send at once for Mr Farfrae. Where is he?'

'He has driven into the country, sir,' said the parlour-maid; 'to some place on the Budmouth Road. He's likely to be back soon.'

'Never mind; he must be sent for, in case he should not hurry.' The doctor returned to the bedside again. The man was despatched, and they soon heard him clattering out of the yard at the back.

Meanwhile Mr Benjamin Grower, that prominent burgess of whom mention has been already made, hearing the din of cleavers, tongs, tambourines, kits, crouds, humstrums, serpents, rams'-horns, and other historical kinds of music as he sat indoors in the High Street, had put on his hat and gone out to learn the cause. He came to the corner above Farfrae's, and soon guessed the nature of the proceedings; for being a native of the town he had witnessed such rough jests before. His first move was to search hither and thither for the constables; there were two in the town, shrivelled men whom he ultimately found in hiding up an alley yet more shrivelled than usual, having some not ungrounded fears that they might be roughly handled if seen.

'What can we two poor lammigers do against such a multitude!' expostulated Stubberd, in answer to Mr Grower's chiding. ' 'Tis tempting 'em to commit *felo de se* upon us, and that would be the death of the perpetrator; and we wouldn't be the cause of a fellow-creature's death on no account, not we!'

'Get some help, then! Here, I'll come with you. We'll see what a few words of authority can do. Quick now; have you got your staves?'

'We didn't want the folk to notice us as law officers, being so short-handed, sir; so we pushed our Gover'ment staves up this water-pipe.'

'Out with 'em, and come along, for Heaven's sake! Ah, here's Mr Blowbody; that's lucky.' (Blowbody was the third of the three borough magistrates.)

'Well, what's the row?' said Blowbody. 'Got their names – hey?'

'No. Now,' said Grower to one of the constables, 'you go with Mr Blowbody round by the Old Walk and come up the street; and I'll go with Stubberd straight forward. By this plan we shall have 'em between us. Get their names only: no attack or interruption.'

Thus they started. But as Stubberd with Mr Grower advanced into Corn Street, whence the sounds had proceeded, they were surprised that no procession could be seen. They passed Farfrae's, and looked to the end of the street. The lamp flames waved, the Walk trees soughed, a few loungers stood about with their hands in their pockets. Everything was as usual.

'Have you seen a motley crowd making a disturbance?' Grower said magisterially to one of these in a fustian jacket, who smoked a short pipe and wore straps round his knees.

'Beg yer pardon, sir?' blandly said the person addressed, who was no other than Charl, of Peter's Finger. Mr Grower repeated the words.

Charl shook his head to the zero of childlike ignorance, 'No; we haven't seen anything; have we, Joe? And you was here afore I.'

Joseph was quite as blank as the other in his reply.

'H'm – that's odd,' said Mr Grower. 'Ah – here's a respectable man coming that I know by sight. Have you,' he inquired, addressing the nearing shape of Jopp, 'have you seen any gang of fellows making a devil of a noise – skimmington riding, or something of the sort?'

'O no – nothing, sir,' Jopp replied, as if receiving the most singular news. 'But I've not been far to-night, so perhaps—'

'Oh, 'twas here – just here,' said the magistrate.

'Now I've noticed, come to think o't, that the wind in the Walk trees makes a peculiar poetical-like murmur to-night, sir; more than common; so perhaps 'twas that?' Jopp suggested, as he rearranged his hand in his greatcoat pocket (where it ingeniously supported a pair of kitchen tongs and a cow's horn, thrust up under his waist-coat).

'No, no, no, – d'ye think I'm a fool? Constable, come this way. They must have gone into the back street.'

Neither in back street nor in front street, however, could the disturbers be perceived; and Blowbody and the second constable, who came up at this time, brought similar intelligence. Effigies, donkey, lanterns, band, all had disappeared like the crew of *Comus*.

'Now,' said Mr Grower, 'there's only one thing more we can do. Get ye half-a-dozen helpers, and go in a body to Mixen Lane, and into Peter's Finger. I'm much mistaken if you don't find a clue to the perpetrators there.'

The rusty-jointed executors of the law mustered assistance as soon as they could, and the whole party marched off to the lane of notoriety. It was no rapid matter to get there at night, not a lamp or glimmer of any sort offering itself to light the way, except an occasional pale radiance through some window-curtain, or through the chink of some door which could not be closed because of the smoky chimney within. At last they entered the inn boldly, by the till then bolted front-door, after a prolonged knocking of loudness commensurate with the importance of their standing.

In the settles of the large room, guyed to the ceiling by cords as usual for stability, an ordinary group sat drinking and smoking with statuesque quiet of demeanour. The landlady looked mildly at the invaders, saying in honest accents, 'Good evening, gentlemen; there's plenty of room. I hope there's nothing amiss?'

They looked round the room. 'Surely,' said Stubberd to one of the men, 'I saw you by now in Corn Street – Mr Grower spoke to 'ee?'

The man, who was Charl, shook his head absently. 'I've been here this last hour, hain't I, Nance?' he said to the woman who meditatively sipped her ale near him.

'Faith, that you have. I came in for my quiet supper-time half-pint, and you was here then, as was all the rest.'

The other constable was facing the clock-case, where he saw reflected in the glass a quick motion by the landlady. Turning sharply, he caught her closing the oven-door.

'Something curious about that oven, ma'am!' he observed advancing, opening it, and drawing out a tambourine.

'Ah,' she said apologetically, 'that's what we keep here to use when there's a little quiet dancing. You see damp weather spoils it, so I put it there to keep it dry.'

The constable nodded knowingly; but what he knew was nothing. Nohow could anything be elicited from this mute and inoffensive assembly. In a few minutes the investigators went out, and joining those of their auxiliaries who had been left at the door they pursued their way elsewhither.

CHAPTER FORTY

L ONG before this time Henchard, weary of his ruminations on the bridge, had repaired towards the town. When he stood at the bottom of the street a procession burst upon his view, in the act of turning out of an alley just above him. The lanterns, horns, and multitude startled him; he saw the mounted images, and knew what it all meant.

They crossed the way, entered another street, and disappeared. He turned back a few steps and was lost in grave reflection, finally wending his way homeward by the obscure river-side path. Unable to rest there he went to his stepdaughter's lodging, and was told that Elizabeth-Jane had gone to Mrs Farfrae's. Like one acting in obedience to a charm, and with a nameless apprehension, he followed in the same direction in the hope of meeting her, the roysterers having vanished. Disappointed in this he gave the gentlest of pulls to the door-bell, and then learnt particulars of what had occurred, together with the doctor's imperative orders that Farfrae should be brought home, and how they had set out to meet him on the Budmouth Road.

'But he has gone to Mellstock and Weatherbury!' exclaimed Henchard, now unspeakably grieved. 'Not Budmouth way at all.'

But, alas! for Henchard; he had lost his good name. They would not believe him, taking his words but as the frothy utterances of recklessness. Though Lucetta's life seemed at that moment to depend upon her husband's return (she being in great mental agony lest he should never know the unexaggerated truth of her past relations with Henchard), no messenger was despatched towards Weatherbury. Henchard, in a state of bitter anxiety and contrition, determined to seek Farfrae himself.

To this end he hastened down the town, ran along the eastern road over Durnover moor, up the hill beyond, and thus onward in the moderate darkness of this spring night till he had reached a second and almost a third hill about three miles distant. In Yalbury Bottom, or Plain, at the foot of the hill, he listened. At first nothing, beyond his own heart-throbs, was to be heard but the slow wind making its moan among the masses of spruce and larch of Yalbury Wood which clothed the heights on either hand; but presently there came the sound of light wheels whetting their felloes against the newly stoned patches of road, accompanied by the distant glimmer of lights.

He knew it was Farfrae's gig descending the hill from an indescribable personality in its noise, the vehicle having been his own till bought by the Scotchman at the sale of his effects. Henchard thereupon retraced his steps along Yalbury Plain, the gig coming up with him as its driver slackened speed between two plantations.

It was a point in the highway near which the road to Mellstock branched off from the homeward direction. By diverging to that village, as he had intended to do, Farfrae might probably delay his return by a couple of hours. It soon

433

appeared that his intention was to do so still, the light swerving towards Cuckoo Lane, the by-road aforesaid. Farfrae's off gig-lamp flashed in Henchard's face. At the same time, Farfrae discerned his late antagonist.

'Farfrae – Mr Farfrae!' cried the breathless Henchard, holding up his hand.

Farfrae allowed the horse to turn several steps into the branch lane before he pulled up. He then drew rein, and said 'Yes?' over his shoulder, as one would towards a pronounced enemy.

'Come back to Casterbridge at once!' Henchard said. 'There's something wrong at your house – requiring your return. I've run all the way here on purpose to tell ye.'

Farfrae was silent, and at his silence Henchard's soul sank within him. Why had he not, before this, thought of what was only too obvious? He who, four hours earlier, had enticed Farfrae into a deadly wrestle stood now in the darkness of late night-time on a lonely road, inviting him to come a particular way, where an assailant might have confederates, instead of going his purposed way, where there might be a better opportunity of guarding himself from attack. Henchard could almost feel this view of things in course of passage through Farfrae's mind.

'I have to go to Mellstock,' said Farfrae coldly, as he loosened his rein to move on.

'But,' implored Henchard, 'the matter is more serious than your business at Mellstock. It is – your wife! She is ill. I can tell you particulars as we go along.'

The very agitation and abruptness of Henchard increased Farfrae's suspicion that this was a *ruse* to decoy him on to the next wood, where might be effectually compassed what, from policy or want of nerve, Henchard had failed to do earlier in the day. He started the horse.

'I know what you think,' deprecated Henchard running after, almost bowed down with despair as he perceived the image of unscrupulous villainy that he assumed in his former friend's eyes. 'But I am not what you think!' he cried hoarsely. 'Believe me, Farfrae; I have come entirely on your own and your wife's account. She is in danger. I know no more; and they want you to come. Your man has gone the other way in a mistake. O Farfrae! don't mistrust me – I am a wretched man; but my heart is true to you still!'

Farfrae, however, did distrust him utterly. He knew his wife was with child, but he had left her not long ago in perfect health; and Henchard's treachery was more credible than his story. He had in his time heard bitter ironies from Henchard's lips, and there might be ironies now. He quickened the horse's pace, and had soon risen into the high country lying between there and Mellstock, Henchard's spasmodic run after him lending yet more substance to his thought of evil purposes.

The gig and its driver lessened against the sky in Henchard's eyes; his exertions for Farfrae's good had been in vain. Over this repentant sinner, at least, there was to be no joy in heaven. He cursed himself like a less scrupulous Job, as a vehement man will do when he loses self-respect, the last mental prop under poverty. To this he had come after a time of emotional darkness of which the adjoining woodland shade afforded inadequate illustration. Presently he began to walk back again along the way by which he had arrived. Farfrae should at all events have no reason for delay upon the road by seeing him there when he took his journey homeward later on.

Arriving at Casterbridge Henchard went again to Farfrae's house to make inquiries. As soon as the door opened anxious faces confronted his from the staircase, hall, and landing; and they all said in grievous disappointment, 'O – it is not he!' The manservant, finding his mistake, had long since returned, and all hopes had been centred upon Henchard.

'But haven't you found him?' said the doctor.

'Yes. . . . I cannot tell 'ee!' Henchard replied as he sank down on a chair within the entrance. 'He can't be home for two hours.'

'H'm,' said the surgeon, returning upstairs.

'How is she?' asked Henchard of Elizabeth, who formed one of the group.

'In great danger, father. Her anxiety to see her husband makes her fearfully restless. Poor woman – I fear they have killed her!'

Henchard regarded the sympathetic speaker for a few instants as if she struck him in a new light; then, without further remark, went out of the door and onward to his lonely cottage. So much for man's rivalry, he thought. Death was to have the oyster, and Farfrae and himself the shells. But about Elizabeth-Jane; in the midst of his gloom she seemed to him as a pin-point of light. He had liked the look of her face as she answered him from the stairs. There had been affection in it, and above all things what he desired now was affection from anything that was good and pure. She was not his own; yet, for the first time, he had a faint dream that he might get to like her as his own, – if she would only continue to love him.

Jopp was just going to bed when Henchard got home. As the latter entered the door Jopp said, 'This is rather bad about Mrs Farfrae's illness.'

'Yes,' said Henchard shortly, though little dreaming of Jopp's complicity in the night's harlequinade, and rising his eyes just sufficiently to observe that Jopp's face was lined with anxiety.

'Somebody has called for you,' continued Jopp, when Henchard was shutting himself into his own apartment. 'A kind of traveller, or sea-captain of some sort.'

'Oh? – who could he be?'

'He seemed a well-be-doing man – had grey hair and a broadish face; but he gave no name, and no message.'

'Nor do I gi'e him any attention.' And, saying this, Henchard closed his door.

The divergence to Mellstock delayed Farfrae's return very nearly the two hours of Henchard's estimate. Among the other urgent reasons for his presence had been the need of his authority to send to Budmouth for a second physician; and when at length Farfrae did come back he was in a state bordering on distraction at his misconception of Henchard's motives.

A messenger was despatched to Budmouth, late as it had grown; the night wore on, and the other doctor came in the small hours. Lucetta had been much soothed by Donald's arrival; he seldom or never left her side; and when, immediately after his entry, she had tried to lisp out to him the secret which so oppressed her, he checked her feeble words, lest talking should be dangerous, assuring her there was plenty of time to tell him everything.

Up to this time he knew nothing of the skimmington-ride. The dangerous illness and miscarriage of Mrs Farfrae was soon rumoured through the town, and an apprehensive guess having been given as to its cause by the leaders in the exploit, compunction and fear threw a dead silence over all particulars of their orgie; while those immediately around Lucetta would not venture to add to her husband's distress by alluding to the subject.

What, and how much, Farfrae's wife ultimately explained to him of her past entanglement with Henchard, when they were alone in the solitude of that sad night, cannot be told. That she informed him of the bare facts of her peculiar intimacy with the corn-merchant became plain from Farfrae's own statements. But in respect of her subsequent conduct – her motive in coming to Casterbridge to unite herself with Henchard – her assumed justification in abandoning him when she discovered reasons for fearing him (though in truth her inconsequent passion for another man at first sight had most to do with that abandonment) – her method of reconciling to her conscience a marriage with the second when she was in a measure committed to the first: to what extent she spoke of these things remained Farfrae's secret alone.

Besides the watchman who called the hours and weather in Casterbridge that night there walked a figure up and down Corn Street hardly less frequently. It was Henchard's, whose retiring to rest had proved itself a futility as soon as attempted; and he gave it up to go hither and thither, and make inquiries about the patient every now and then. He called as much on Farfrae's account as on Lucetta's, and on Elizabeth-Jane's even more than on either's. Shorn one by one of all other interests, his life seemed centring on the personality of the stepdaughter whose presence but recently he could not endure. To see her on each occasion of his inquiry at Lucetta's was a comfort to him.

The last of his calls was made about four o'clock in the morning, in the steely light of dawn. Lucifer was fading into day across Durnover Moor, the sparrows were just alighting into the street, and the hens had begun to cackle from the outhouses. When within a few yards of Farfrae's he saw the door gently opened, and a servant raise her hand to the knocker, to untie the piece of cloth which had muffled it. He went across, the sparrows in his way scarcely flying up from the road-litter, so little did they believe in human aggression at so early a time.

'Why do you take off that?' said Henchard.

She turned in some surprise at his presence, and did not answer for an instant or two. Recognizing him, she said, 'Because they may knock as loud as they will; she will never hear it any more.'

CHAPTER FORTY-ONE

HENCHARD went home. The morning having now fully broke he lit his fire, and sat abstractedly beside it. He had not sat there long when a gentle footstep approached the house and entered the passage, a finger tapping lightly at the door. Henchard's face brightened, for he knew the motions to be Elizabeth's. She came into his room, looking wan and sad.

'Have you heard?' she asked. 'Mrs Farfrae! She is – dead! Yes, indeed – about an hour ago!'

'I know it,' said Henchard. 'I have but lately come in from there. It is so very good of 'ee, Elizabeth, to come and tell me. You must be so tired out, too, with sitting up. Now do you bide here with me this morning. You can go and rest in the other room; and I will call 'ee when breakfast is ready.'

To please him, and herself – for his recent kindliness was winning a surprised gratitude from the lonely girl – she did as he bade her, and lay down on a sort of couch which Henchard had rigged up out of a settle in the adjoining room. She could hear him moving about in his preparations; but her mind ran most strongly on Lucetta, whose death in such fulness of life and amid such cheerful hopes of maternity was appallingly unexpected. Presently she fell asleep.

Meanwhile her stepfather in the outer room had set the breakfast in readiness; but finding that she dozed he would not call her; he waited on, looking into the fire and keeping the kettle boiling with housewifely care, as if it were an honour to have her in his house. In truth, a great change had come over him with regard to her, and he was developing the dream of a future lit by her filial presence, as though that way alone could happiness lie.

He was disturbed by another knock at the door, and rose to open it, rather deprecating a call from anybody just then. A stoutly built man stood on the doorstep, with an alien, unfamiliar air about his figure and bearing – an air which might have been called colonial by people of cosmopolitan experience. It was the man who had asked the way at Peter's Finger. Henchard nodded, and looked inquiry.

'Good morning, good morning,' said the stranger with profuse heartiness. 'Is it Mr Henchard I am talking to?'

'My name is Henchard.'

'Then I've caught 'ee at home – that's right. Morning's the time for business, says I. Can I have a few words with you?'

'By all means,' Henchard answered, showing the way in.

'You may remember me?' said his visitor, seating himself.

Henchard observed him indifferently, and shook his head.

'Well – perhaps you may not. My name is Newson.'

Henchard's face and eyes seemed to die. The other did not notice it. 'I know the name well,' Henchard said at last, looking on the floor.

'I make no doubt of that. Well, the fact is, I've been looking for 'ee this fortnight past. I landed at Havenpool and went through Casterbridge on my way to Falmouth, and when I got there, they told me you had some years before been living at Casterbridge. Back came I again, and by long and by late I got here by coach, ten minutes ago. "He lives down by the mill," says they. So here I am. Now – that transaction between us some twenty years agone – 'tis that I've called about. 'Twas a curious business. I was younger then than I am now, and perhaps the less said about it, in one sense, the better.'

'Curious business! 'Twas worse than curious. I cannot even allow that I'm the man you met then. I was not in my senses, and a man's senses are himself.'

'We were young and thoughtless,' said Newson. 'However, I've come to mend matters rather than open arguments. Poor Susan – hers was a strange experience.'

'It was.'

'She was a warm-hearted, home-spun woman. She was not what they call shrewd or sharp at all – better she had been.'

'She was not.'

'As you in all likelihood know, she was simple-minded enough to think that the sale was in a way binding. She was as guiltless o' wrong-doing in that particular as a saint in the clouds.'

'I know it, I know it. I found it out directly,' said Henchard, still with averted eyes. 'There lay the sting o't to me. If she had seen it as what it was she would never have left me. Never! But how should she be expected to know? What advantages had she? None. She could write her own name, and no more.'

'Well, it was not in my heart to undeceive her when the deed was done,' said the sailor of former days. 'I thought, and there was not much vanity in thinking it, that she would be happier with me. She was fairly happy, and I never would have undeceived her till the day of her death. Your child died; she had another, and all went well. But a time came – mind me, a time always does come. A time came – it was some while after she and I and the child returned from America – when somebody she had confided her history to, told her my claim to her was a mockery, and made a jest of her belief in my right. After that she was never happy with me. She pined and pined, and socked and sighed. She said she must leave me, and then came the question of our child. Then a man advised me how to act, and I did it, for I thought it was best. I left her at Falmouth, and went off to sea. When I got to the other side of the Atlantic there was a storm, and it was supposed that a lot of us, including myself, had been washed overboard. I got ashore at Newfoundland, and then I asked myself what I should do. "Since I'm here, here I'll bide," I thought to myself; "'twill be most kindness to her, now she's taken against me, to let her believe me lost; for," I thought, "while she supposes us both alive she'll be miserable; but if she thinks me dead she'll go back to him, and the child will have a home." I've never returned to this country till a month ago, and I found that, as I had supposed, she went to you, and my daughter with her. They told me in Falmouth that Susan was dead. But my Elizabeth-Jane – where is she?'

'Dead likewise,' said Henchard doggedly. 'Surely you learnt that too?'

The sailor started up, and took an enervated pace or two down the room. 'Dead!' he said, in a low voice. 'Then what's the use of my money to me?'

Henchard, without answering, shook his head as if that were rather a question for Newson himself than for him.

'Where is she buried?' the traveller inquired.

'Beside her mother,' said Henchard, in the same stolid tones.

'When did she die?'

'A year ago and more,' replied the other without hesitation.

The sailor continued standing. Henchard never looked up from the floor. At last Newson said: 'My journey hither has been for nothing! I may as well go as I came! It has served me right. I'll trouble you no longer.'

Henchard heard the retreating footsteps of Newson upon the sanded floor, the mechanical lifting of the latch, the slow opening and closing of the door that was natural to a baulked or dejected man; but he did not turn his head. Newson's shadow passed the window. He was gone.

Then Henchard, scarcely believing the evidence of his senses, rose from his seat amazed at what he had done. It had been the impulse of a moment. The regard he had lately acquired for Elizabeth, the new-sprung hope of his loneliness that she would be to him a daughter of whom he could feel as proud as of the actual daughter she still believed herself to be, had been stimulated by the unexpected coming of Newson to a greedy exclusiveness in relation to her; so that the sudden prospect of her loss had caused him to speak mad lies like a child, in pure mockery of consequences. He had expected questions to close in round him, and unmask his fabrication in five minutes; yet such questioning had not come. But surely they would come; Newson's departure could be but momentary; he would learn all by inquiries in the town; and return to curse him, and carry his last treasure away!

He hastily put on his hat, and went out in the direction that Newson had taken. Newson's back was soon visible up the road, crossing Bull-stake. Henchard followed; and saw his visitor stop at the King's Arms, where the morning coach which had brought him waited half-an-hour for another coach which crossed there. The coach Newson had come by was now about to move again. Newson mounted; his luggage was put in, and in a few minutes the vehicle disappeared with him.

He had not so much as turned his head. It was an act of simple faith in Henchard's words — faith so simple as to be almost sublime. The young sailor who had taken Susan Henchard on the spur of the moment and on the faith of a glance at her face, more than twenty years before, was still living and acting under the form of the grizzled traveller who had taken Henchard's words on trust so absolute as to shame him as he stood.

Was Elizabeth-Jane to remain his by virtue of this hardy invention of a moment? 'Perhaps not for long,' said he. Newson might converse with his fellow-travellers, some of whom might be Casterbridge people; and the trick would be discovered.

This probability threw Henchard into a defensive attitude, and instead of considering how best to right the wrong, and acquaint Elizabeth's father with truth at once, he bethought himself of ways to keep the position he had accidentally won. Towards the young woman herself his affection grew more jealously strong with each new hazard to which his claim to her was exposed.

He watched the distant highway expecting to see Newson return on foot, enlightened and indignant, to claim his child. But no figure appeared. Possibly he had spoken to nobody on the coach, but buried his grief in his own heart.

His grief! — what was it, after all, to that which he, Henchard, would feel at the loss of her? Newson's affection, cooled by years, could not equal his who had been constantly in her presence. And thus his jealous soul speciously argued to excuse the separation of father and child.

He returned to the house half expecting that she would have vanished. No; there she was — just coming out from the inner room, the marks of sleep upon her eyelids, and exhibiting a generally refreshed air.

'O father!' she said, smiling. 'I had no sooner lain down than I napped, though I did not mean to. I wonder I did not dream about poor Mrs Farfrae, after thinking of her so; but I did not. How strange it is that we do not often dream of latest events, absorbing as they may be.'

'I am glad you have been able to sleep,' he said, taking her hand with anxious proprietorship – an act which gave her a pleasant surprise.

They sat down to breakfast, and Elizabeth-Jane's thoughts reverted to Lucetta. Their sadness added charm to a countenance whose beauty had ever lain in its meditative soberness.

'Father,' she said, as soon as she recalled herself to the outspread meal, 'it is so kind of you to get this nice breakfast with your own hands, and I idly asleep the while.'

'I do it every day,' he replied. 'You have left me; everybody has left me; how should I live but by my own hands.'

'You are very lonely, are you not?'

'Ay, child – to a degree that you know nothing of! It is my own fault. You are the only one who has been near me for weeks. And you will come no more.'

'Why do you say that? Indeed I will, if you would like to see me.'

Henchard signified dubiousness. Though he had so lately hoped that Elizabeth-Jane might again live in his house as daughter, he would not ask her to do so now. Newson might return at any moment, and what Elizabeth would think of him for his deception it were best to bear apart from her.

When they had breakfasted his stepdaughter still lingered, till the moment arrived at which Henchard was accustomed to go to his daily work. Then she arose, and with assurances of coming again soon went up the hill in the morning sunlight.

'At this moment her heart is as warm towards me as mine is towards her; she would live with me here in this humble cottage for the asking! Yet before the evening probably he will have come; and then she will scorn me!'

This reflection, constantly repeated by Henchard to himself, accompanied him everywhere through the day. His mood was no longer that of the rebellious, ironical, reckless misadventurer; but the leaden gloom of one who has lost all that can make life interesting, or even tolerable. There would remain nobody for him to be proud of, nobody to fortify him; for Elizabeth-Jane would soon be but as a stranger, and worse. Susan, Farfrae, Lucetta, Elizabeth – all had gone from him, one after one, either by his fault or by his misfortune.

In place of them he had no interest, hobby, or desire. If he could have summoned music to his aid his existence might even now have been borne; for with Henchard music was of regal power. The merest trumpet or organ tone was enough to move him, and high harmonies transubstantiated him. But hard fate had ordained that he should be unable to call up this Divine spirit in his need.

The whole land ahead of him was as darkness itself; there was nothing to come, nothing to wait for. Yet in the natural course of life he might possibly have to linger on earth another thirty or forty years – scoffed at; at best pitied.

The thought of it was unendurable.

To the east of Casterbridge lay moors and meadows through which much water flowed. The wanderer in this direction who should stand still for a few moments on a quiet night, might hear singular symphonies from these waters, as from a lampless orchestra, all playing in their sundry tones from near and far parts of the moor. At a hole in a rotten weir they executed a recitative; where a tributary brook fell over a stone breastwork they trilled cheerily; under an arch they performed a metallic cymballing; and at Durnover Hole they hissed. The spot at which their instrumentation rose loudest was a place called Ten Hatches, whence during high springs there proceeded a very fugue of sounds.

The river here was deep and strong at all times, and the hatches on this account were raised and lowered by cogs and a winch. A path led from the second bridge over the highway (so often mentioned) to these Hatches, crossing the stream at their head by a narrow plank-bridge. But after night-fall human beings were seldom found going that way, the path leading only to a deep reach of the stream called Blackwater, and the passage being dangerous.

Henchard, however, leaving the town by the east road, proceeded to the second, or stone bridge, and thence struck into this path of solitude, following its course beside the stream till the dark shapes of the Ten Hatches cut the sheen thrown upon the river by the weak lustre that still lingered in the west. In a second or two he stood beside the weir-hole where the water was at its deepest. He looked backwards and forwards, and no creature appeared in view. He then took off his coat and hat, and stood on the brink of the stream with his hands clasped in front of him.

While his eyes were bent on the water beneath there slowly became visible a something floating in the circular pool formed by the wash of centuries; the pool he was intending to make his death-bed. At first it was indistinct by reason of the shadow from the bank; but it emerged thence and took shape, which was that of a human body, lying stiff and stark upon the surface of the stream.

In the circular current imparted by the central flow the form was brought forward, till it passed under his eyes; and then he perceived with a sense of horror that it was *himself*. Not a man somewhat resembling him, but one in all respects his counterpart, his actual double, was floating as if dead in Ten Hatches Hole.

The sense of the supernatural was strong in this unhappy man, and he turned away as one might have done in the actual presence of an appalling miracle. He covered his eyes and bowed his head. Without looking again into the stream he took his coat and hat, and went slowly away.

Presently he found himself by the door of his own dwelling. To his surprise Elizabeth-Jane was standing there. She came forward, spoke, called him 'father' just as before. Newson, then, had not even yet returned.

'I thought you seemed very sad this morning,' she said, 'so I have come again to see you. Not that I am anything but sad myself. But everybody and everything seem against you so; and I know you must be suffering.'

How this woman divined things! Yet she had not divined their whole extremity.

He said to her, 'Are miracles still worked, do ye think, Elizabeth? I am not a read man. I don't know so much as I could wish. I have tried to peruse and learn all my life; but the more I try to know the more ignorant I seem.'

'I don't quite think there are any miracles nowadays,' she said.

'No interference in the case of desperate intentions, for instance? Well, perhaps not, in a direct way. Perhaps not. But will you come and walk with me, and I will show 'ee what I mean?'

She agreed willingly, and he took her over the highway, and by the lonely path to Ten Hatches. He walked restlessly, as if some haunting shade, unseen of her, hovered round him and troubled his glance. She would gladly have talked of Lucetta, but feared to disturb him. When they got near the weir he stood still, and asked her to go forward and look into the pool, and tell him what she saw.

She went, and soon returned to him. 'Nothing,' she said.

'Go again,' said Henchard, 'and look narrowly.'

She proceeded to the river brink a second time. On her return, after some delay, she told him that she saw something floating round and round there; but what it was she could not discern. It seemed to be a bundle of old clothes.

'Are they like mine?' asked Henchard.

'Well – they are. Dear me – I wonder if— Father, let us go away!'

'Go and look once more; and then we will get home.'

She went back, and he could see her stoop till her head was close to the margin of the pool. She started up, and hastened back to his side.

'Well,' said Henchard; 'what do you say now?'

'Let us go home.'

'But tell me – do – what is it floating there?'

'The effigy,' she answered hastily. 'They must have thrown it into the river higher up amongst the willows at Blackwater, to get rid of it in their alarm at discovery by the magistrates; and it must have floated down here.'

'Ah – to be sure – the image o' me! But where is the other? Why that one only? . . . That performance of theirs killed her, but kept me alive!'

Elizabeth-Jane thought and thought of these words 'kept me alive', as they slowly retraced their way to the town, and at length guessed their meaning. 'Father! – I will not leave you alone like this!' she cried. 'May I live with you, and tend upon you as I used to do? I do not mind your being poor. I would have agreed to come this morning, but you did not ask me.'

'May you come to me?' he cried bitterly. 'Elizabeth, don't mock me! If you only would come!'

'I will,' said she.

'How will you forgive all my roughness in former days? You cannot!'

'I have forgotten it. Talk of that no more.'

Thus she assured him, and arranged their plans for reunion; and at length each went home. Then Henchard shaved for the first time during many days, and put on clean linen, and combed his hair; and was as a man resuscitated thenceforward.

The next morning the fact turned out to be as Elizabeth-Jane had stated; the effigy was discovered by a cowherd, and that of Lucetta a little higher up in the same stream. But as little as possible was said of the matter, and the figures were privately destroyed.

Despite this natural solution of the mystery Henchard no less regarded it as an intervention that the figure should have been floating there. Elizabeth-Jane heard him say, 'Who is such a reprobate as I! And yet it seems that even I be in Somebody's hand!'

CHAPTER FORTY-TWO

B ut the emotional conviction that he was in Somebody's hand began to die out of Henchard's breast as time slowly removed into distance the event which had given that feeling birth. The apparition of Newson haunted him. He would surely return.

Yet Newson did not arrive. Lucetta had been borne along the churchyard path; Casterbridge had for the last time turned its regard upon her, before proceeding to its work as if she had never lived. But Elizabeth remained undisturbed in the belief of her relationship to Henchard, and now shared his home. Perhaps, after all, Newson was gone for ever.

In due time the bereaved Farfrae had learnt the, at least, proximate cause of Lucetta's illness and death; and his first impulse was naturally enough to wreak vengeance in the name of the law upon the perpetrators of the mischief. He resolved to wait till the funeral was over ere he moved in the matter. The time having come he reflected. Disastrous as the result had been, it was obviously in no way foreseen or intended by the thoughtless crew who arranged the motley procession. The tempting prospect of putting to the blush people who stand at the head of affairs — that supreme and piquant enjoyment of those who writhe under the heel of the same — had alone animated them, so far as he could see; for he knew nothing of Jopp's incitements. Other considerations were also involved. Lucetta had confessed everything to him before her death, and it was not altogether desirable to make much ado about her history, alike for her sake, for Henchard's, and for his own. To regard the event as an untoward accident seemed, to Farfrae, truest consideration for the dead one's memory, as well as best philosophy.

Henchard and himself mutually forbore to meet. For Elizabeth's sake the former had fettered his pride sufficiently to accept the small seed and root business which some of the Town Council, headed by Farfrae, had purchased to afford him a new opening. Had he been only personally concerned Henchard, without doubt, would have declined assistance even remotely brought about by the man whom he had so fiercely assailed. But the sympathy of the girl seemed necessary to his very existence; and on her account pride itself wore the garments of humility.

Here they settled themselves; and on each day of their lives Henchard anticipated her every wish with a watchfulness in which paternal regard was heightened by a burning jealous dread of rivalry. Yet that Newson would ever now return to Casterbridge to claim her as a daughter there was little reason to suppose. He was a wanderer and a stranger, almost an alien; he had not seen his daughter for several years; his affection for her could not in the nature of things be keen; other interests would probably soon obscure his recollections of her, and prevent any such renewal of inquiry into the past as would lead to a discovery that she was still a creature of the present. To satisfy his conscience somewhat

Henchard repeated to himself that the lie which had retained for him the coveted treasure had not been deliberately told to that end, but had come from him as the last defiant word of a despair which took no thought of consequences. Furthermore he pleaded within himself that no Newson could love her as he loved her, or would tend her to his life's extremity as he was prepared to do cheerfully.

Thus they lived on in the shop overlooking the churchyard, and nothing occurred to mark their days during the remainder of the year. Going out but seldom, and never on a market-day, they saw Donald Farfrae only at rarest intervals, and then mostly as a transitoɪy object in the distance of the street. Yet he was pursuing his ordinary avocations, smiling mechanically to fellow-tradesmen, and arguing with bargainers – as bereaved men do after a while.

Time, 'in his own grey style', taught Farfrae how to estimate his experience of Lucetta – all that it was, and all that it was not. There are men whose hearts insist upon a dogged fidelity to some image or cause thrown by chance into their keeping, long after their judgment has pronounced it no rarity – even the reverse, indeed; and without them the band of the worthy is incomplete. But Farfrae was not of those. It was inevitable that the insight, briskness, and rapidity of his nature should take him out of the dead blank which his loss threw about him. He could not but perceive that by the death of Lucetta he had exchanged a looming misery for a simple sorrow. After that revelation of her history, which must have come sooner or later in any circumstances, it was hard to believe that life with her would have been productive of further happiness.

But as a memory, notwithstanding such conditions, Lucetta's image still lived on with him, her weaknesses provoking only the gentlest criticism, and her sufferings attenuating wrath at her concealments to a momentary spark now and then.

By the end of a year Henchard's little retail seed and grain shop, not much larger than a cupboard, had developed its trade considerably, and the stepfather and daughter enjoyed much serenity in the pleasant, sunny corner in which it stood. The quiet bearing of one who brimmed with an inner activity characte-rized Elizabeth-Jane at this period. She took long walks into the country two or three times a week, mostly in the direction of Budmouth. Sometimes it occurred to him that when she sat with him in the evening after these invigorating walks she was civil rather than affectionate; and he was troubled; one more bitter regret being added to those he had already experienced at having, by his severe censorship, frozen up her precious affection when originally offered.

She had her own way in everything now. In going and coming, in buying and selling, her word was law.

'You have got a new muff, Elizabeth,' he said to her one day quite humbly.

'Yes; I bought it,' she said.

He looked at it again as it lay on an adjoining table. The fur was of a glossy brown, and, though he was no judge of such articles, he thought it seemed an unusually good one for her to possess.

'Rather costly, I suppose, my dear, was it not?' he hazarded.

'It was rather above my figure,' she said quietly. 'But it is not showy.'

'O no,' said the netted lion, anxious not to pique her in the least.

Some little time after, when the year had advanced into another spring, he paused opposite her empty bedroom in passing it. He thought of the time when she had cleared out of his then large and handsome house in Corn Street, in consequence of his dislike and harshness, and he had looked into her chamber in just the same way. The present room was much humbler, but what struck him about it was the abundance of books lying everywhere. Their number and quality made the meagre furniture that supported them seem absurdly disproportionate. Some, indeed many, must have been recently purchased; and though he encouraged her to buy in reason, he had no notion that she indulged her innate passion so extensively in proportion to the narrowness of their income. For the first time he felt a little hurt by what he thought her extravagance, and resolved to say a word to her about it. But, before he had found the courage to speak, an event happened which set his thoughts flying in quite another direction.

The busy time of the seed trade was over; and the quiet weeks that preceded the hay-season had come – setting their special stamp upon Casterbridge by thronging the market with wood rakes, new waggons in yellow, green, and red, formidable scythes, and pitchforks of prong sufficient to skewer up a small family. Henchard, contrary to his wont, went out one Saturday afternoon towards the market-place, from a curious feeling that he would like to pass a few minutes on the spot of his former triumphs. Farfrae, to whom he was still a comparative stranger, stood a few steps below the Corn Exchange door – a usual position with him at this hour – and he appeared lost in thought about something he was looking at a little way off.

Henchard's eyes followed Farfrae's, and he saw that the object of his gaze was no sample-showing farmer, but his own stepdaughter, who had just come out of a shop over the way. She, on her part, was quite unconscious of his attention, and in this was less fortunate than those young women whose very plumes, like those of Juno's bird, are set with Argus eyes whenever possible admirers are within ken.

Henchard went away, thinking that perhaps there was nothing significant after all in Farfrae's look at Elizabeth-Jane at that juncture. Yet he could not forget that the Scotchman had once shown a tender interest in her, of a fleeting kind. Thereupon promptly came to the surface that idiosyncrasy of Henchard's which had ruled his courses from the beginning and had mainly made him what he was. Instead of thinking that a union between his cherished stepdaughter and the energetic thriving Donald was a thing to be desired for her good and his own, he hated the very possibility.

Time had been when such instinctive opposition would have taken shape in action. But he was not now the Henchard of former days. He schooled himself to accept her will, in this as in other matters, as absolute and unquestionable. He dreaded lest an antagonistic word should lose for him such regard as he had regained from her by his devotion, feeling that to retain this under separation was better than to incur her dislike by keeping her near.

But the mere thought of such separation fevered his spirit much, and in the evening he said, with the stillness of suspense: 'Have you seen Mr Farfrae to-day, Elizabeth?'

Elizabeth-Jane started at the question; and it was with some confusion that she replied 'No.'

'Oh – that's right – that's right. . . . It was only that I saw him in the street when we both were there.' He was wondering if her embarrassment justified him in a new suspicion – that the long walks which she had latterly been taking, that the new books which had so surprised him, had anything to do with the young man. She did not enlighten him, and lest silence should allow her to shape thoughts unfavourable to their present friendly relations, he diverted the discourse into another channel.

Henchard was, by original make, the last man to act stealthily, for good or for evil. But the *solicitus timor* of his love – the dependence upon Elizabeth's regard into which he had declined (or, in another sense, to which he had advanced) – denaturalized him. He would often weigh and consider for hours together the meaning of such and such a deed or phrase of hers, when a blunt settling question would formerly have been his first instinct. And now, uneasy at the thought of a passion for Farfrae which should entirely displace her mild filial sympathy with himself, he observed her going and coming more narrowly.

There was nothing secret in Elizabeth-Jane's movements beyond what habitual reserve induced; and it may at once be owned on her account that she was guilty of occasional conversations with Donald when they chanced to meet. Whatever the origin of her walks on the Budmouth Road, her return from those walks was often coincident with Farfrae's emergence from Corn Street for a twenty minutes' blow on that rather windy highway – just to winnow the seeds and chaff out of him before sitting down to tea, as he said. Henchard became aware of this by going to the Ring, and, screened by its enclosure, keeping his eye upon the road till he saw them meet. His face assumed an expression of extreme anguish.

'Of her, too, he means to rob me!' he whispered. 'But he has the right. I do not wish to interfere.'

The meeting, in truth, was of a .very innocent kind, and matters were by no means so far advanced between the young people as Henchard's jealous grief inferred. Could he have heard such conversation as passed he would have been enlightened thus much: –

He. – 'You like walking this way, Miss Henchard – and is it not so?' (uttered in his undulatory accents, and with an appraising, pondering gaze at her).

She. – 'O yes. I have chosen this road latterly. I have no great reason for it.'

He. – 'But that may make a reason for others.'

She (reddening). – 'I don't know that. My reason, however, such as it is, is that I wish to get a glimpse of the sea every day.'

He. – 'Is it a secret why?'

She (reluctantly). – 'Yes.'

He (with the pathos of one of his native ballads). – 'Ah, I doubt there will be any good in secrets! A secret cast a deep shadow over my life. And well you know what it was.'

Elizabeth admitted that she did, but she refrained from confessing why the sea attracted her. She could not herself account for it fully, not knowing the secret possibly to be that, in addition to early marine associations, her blood was a sailor's.

'Thank you for those new books, Mr Farfrae,' she added shyly. 'I wonder if I ought to accept so many!'

'Ay! why not? It gives me more pleasure to get them for you, than you to have them!'

'It cannot!'

They proceeded along the road together till they reached the town, and their paths diverged.

Henchard vowed that he would leave them to their own devices, put nothing in the way of their courses, whatever they might mean. If he were doomed to be bereft of her, so it must be. In the situation which their marriage would create he could see no *locus standi* for himself at all. Farfrae would never recognize him more than superciliously; his poverty ensured that, no less than his past conduct. And so Elizabeth would grow to be a stranger to him, and the end of his life would be friendless solitude.

With such a possibility impending he could not help watchfulness. Indeed, within certain lines, he had the right to keep an eye upon her as his charge. The meetings seemed to become matters of course with them on special days of the week.

At last full proof was given him. He was standing behind a wall close to the place at which Farfrae encountered her. He heard the young man address her as 'Dearest Elizabeth-Jane', and then kiss her, the girl looking quickly round to assure herself that nobody was near.

When they were gone their way Henchard came out from the wall, and mournfully followed them to Casterbridge. The chief looming trouble in this engagement had not decreased. Both Farfrae and Elizabeth-Jane, unlike the rest of the people, must suppose Elizabeth to be his actual daughter, from his own assertion while he himself had the same belief; and though Farfrae must have so far forgiven him as to have no objection to own him as a father-in-law, intimate they could never be. Thus would the girl, who was his only friend, be withdrawn from him by degrees through her husband's influence, and learn to despise him.

Had she lost her heart to any other man in the world than the one he had rivalled, cursed, wrestled with for life in days before his spirit was broken, Henchard would have said, 'I am content.' But content with the prospect as now depicted was hard to acquire.

There is an outer chamber of the brain in which thoughts unowned, unsolicited, and of noxious kind, are sometimes allowed to wander for a moment prior to being sent off whence they came. One of these thoughts sailed into Henchard's ken now.

Suppose he were to communicate to Farfrae the fact that his betrothed was not the child of Michael Henchard at all — legally, nobody's child; how would that correct and leading townsman receive the information? He might possibly forsake Elizabeth-Jane, and then she would be her stepsire's own again.

Henchard shuddered, and exclaimed, 'God forbid such a thing! Why should I still be subject to these visitations of the devil, when I try so hard to keep him away?'

CHAPTER FORTY-THREE

W HAT Henchard saw thus early was, naturally enough, seen at a little later date by other people. That Mr Farfrae 'walked with that bankrupt Henchard's stepdaughter, of all women,' became a common topic in the town, the simple perambulating term being used hereabout to signify a wooing; and the nineteen superior young ladies of Casterbridge, who had each looked upon herself as the only woman capable of making the merchant Councilman happy, indignantly left off going to the church Farfrae attended, left off conscious mannerisms, left off putting him in their prayers at night amongst their blood relations; in short, reverted to their natural courses.

Perhaps the only inhabitants of the town to whom this looming choice of the Scotchman's gave unmixed satisfaction were the members of the philosophic party, which included Longways, Christopher Coney, Billy Wills, Mr Buzzford, and the like. The Three Mariners having been, years before, the house in which they had witnessed the young man and woman's first and humble appearance on the Casterbridge stage, they took a kindly interest in their career, not unconnected, perhaps, with visions of festive treatment at their hands hereafter. Mrs Stannidge, having rolled into the large parlour one evening and said that it was a wonder such a man as Mr Farfrae, 'a pillow of the town', who might have chosen one of the daughters of the professional men or private residents, should stoop so low, Coney ventured to disagree with her.

'No, ma'am, no wonder at all. 'Tis she that's a stooping to he – that's my opinion. A widow man – whose first wife was no credit to him – what is it for a young perusing woman that's her own mistress and well liked? But as a neat patching up of things I see much good in it. When a man have put up a tomb of best marble-stone to the other one, as he've done, and weeped his fill, and thought it all over, and said to hisself, "T'other took me in; I knowed this one first; she's a sensible piece for a partner, and there's no faithful woman in high life now"; – well, he may do worse than not to take her, if she's tender-inclined.'

Thus they talked at the Mariners. But we must guard against a too liberal use of the conventional declaration that a great sensation was caused by the prospective event, that all the gossips' tongues were set wagging thereby, and so on, even though such a declaration might lend some *éclat* to the career of our poor only heroine. When all has been said about busy rumourers, a superficial and temporary thing is the interest of anybody in affairs which do not directly touch them. It would be a truer representation to say that Casterbridge (ever excepting the nineteen young ladies) looked up for a moment at the news, and withdrawing its attention, went on labouring and victualling, bringing up its children, and burying its dead, without caring a tittle for Farfrae's domestic plans.

Not a hint of the matter was thrown out to her stepfather by Elizabeth herself or by Farfrae either. Reasoning on the cause of their reticence he concluded that, estimating him by his past, the throbbing pair were afraid to broach the subject, and looked upon him as an irksome obstacle whom they would be heartily glad to get out of the way. Embittered as he was against society, this moody view of himself took deeper and deeper hold of Henchard, till the daily necessity of facing mankind, and of them particularly Elizabeth-Jane, became well-nigh more than he could endure. His health declined; he became morbidly sensitive. He wished he could escape those who did not want him, and hide his head for ever.

But what if he were mistaken in his views, and there were no necessity that his own absolute separation from her should be involved in the incident of her marriage?

He proceeded to draw a picture of the alternative – himself living like a fangless lion about the back rooms of a house in which his stepdaughter was mistress; an inoffensive old man, tenderly smiled on by Elizabeth, and good-naturedly tolerated by her husband. It was terrible to his pride to think of descending so low; and yet, for the girl's sake he might put up with anything; even from Farfrae; even snubbings and masterful tongue-scourgings. The privilege of being in the house she occupied would almost outweigh the personal humiliation.

Whether this were a dim possibility or the reverse, the courtship – which it evidently now was – had an absorbing interest for him.

Elizabeth, as has been said, often took her walks on the Budmouth Road, and Farfrae as often made it convenient to create an accidental meeting with her there. Two miles out, a quarter of a mile from the highway, was the prehistoric fort called Mai Dun, of huge dimensions and many ramparts, within or upon whose enclosures a human being, as seen from the road, was but an insignificant speck. Hitherward Henchard often resorted, glass in hand, and scanned the hedgeless *Via* – for it was the original track laid out by the legions of the Empire – to a distance of two or three miles, his object being to read the progress of affairs between Farfrae and his charmer.

One day Henchard was at this spot when a masculine figure came along the road from Budmouth, and lingered. Applying his telescope to his eye Henchard expected that Farfrae's features would be disclosed as usual. But the lenses revealed that to-day the man was not Elizabeth-Jane's lover.

It was one clothed as a merchant captain; and as he turned in his scrutiny of the road he revealed his face. Henchard lived a lifetime the moment he saw it. The face was Newson's.

Henchard dropped the glass, and for some seconds made no other movement. Newson waited, and Henchard waited – if that could be called a waiting which was a transfixture. But Elizabeth-Jane did not come. Something or other had caused her to neglect her customary walk that day. Perhaps Farfrae and she had chosen another road for variety's sake. But what did that amount to? She might be here to-morrow, and in any case Newson, if bent on a private meeting and a revelation of the truth to her, would soon make his opportunity.

Then he would tell her not only of his paternity, but of the ruse by which he had been once sent away. Elizabeth's strict nature would cause her for the first time to despise her stepfather, would root out his image as that of an arch-deceiver, and Newson would reign in her heart in his stead.

But Newson did not see anything of her that morning. Having stood still awhile he at last retraced his steps, and Henchard felt like a condemned man who has a few hours' respite. When he reached his own house he found her there.

'O father!' she said innocently, 'I have had a letter – a strange one – not signed. Somebody has asked me to meet him, either on the Budmouth Road at noon to-day, or in the evening at Mr Farfrae's. He says he came to see me some time ago, but a trick was played him, so that he did not see me. I don't understand it; but between you and me I think Donald is at the bottom of the mystery, and that it is a relation of his who wants to pass an opinion on his choice. But I did not like to go till I had seen you. Shall I go?'

Henchard replied heavily, 'Yes; go.'

The question of his remaining in Casterbridge was for ever disposed of by this closing in of Newson on the scene. Henchard was not the man to stand the certainty of condemnation on a matter so near his heart. And being an old hand at bearing anguish in silence, and haughty withal, he resolved to make as light as he could of his intention, while immediately taking his measures.

He surprised the young woman whom he had looked upon as his all in this world by saying to her, as if he did not care about her more: 'I am going to leave Casterbridge, Elizabeth-Jane.'

'Leave Casterbridge!' she cried, 'and leave – me?'

'Yes, this little shop can be managed by you alone as well as by us both; I don't care about shops and streets and folk – I would rather get into the country by myself, out of sight, and follow my own ways, and leave you to yours.'

She looked down and her tears fell silently. It seemed to her that this resolve of his had come on account of her attachment and its probable result. She showed her devotion to Farfrae, however, by mastering her emotion and speaking out.

'I am sorry you have decided on this,' she said with difficult firmness. 'For I thought it probable – possible – that I might marry Mr Farfrae some little time hence, and I did not know that you disapproved of the step!'

'I approve of anything you desire to do, Izzy,' said Henchard huskily. 'If I did not approve it would be no matter! I wish to go away. My presence might make things awkward in the future; and, in short, it is best that I go.'

Nothing that her affection could urge would induce him to reconsider his determination; for she could not urge what she did not know – that when she should learn he was not related to her other than as a step-parent she would refrain from despising him, and that when she knew what he had done to keep her in ignorance she would refrain from hating him. It was his conviction that she would not so refrain; and there existed as yet neither word nor event which could argue it away.

'Then,' she said at last, 'you will not be able to come to my wedding; and that is not as it ought to be.'

'I don't want to see it – I don't want to see it!' he exclaimed; adding more softly, 'but think of me sometimes in your future life – you'll do that, Izzy? – think of me when you are living as the wife of the richest, the foremost man in the town, and don't let my sins, *when you know them all*, cause 'ee to quite forget that though I loved 'ee late I loved 'ee well.'

'It is because of Donald!' she sobbed.

'I don't forbid you to marry him,' said Henchard. 'Promise not to quite forget me when—' He meant when Newson should come.

She promised mechanically, in her agitation; and the same evening at dusk

Henchard left the town, to whose development he had been one of the chief stimulants for many years. During the day he had bought a new tool-basket, cleaned up his old hay-knife and wimble, set himself up in fresh leggings, knee-naps and corduroys, and in other ways gone back to the working clothes of his young manhood, discarding for ever the shabby-genteel suit of cloth and rusty silk hat that since his decline had characterized him in the Casterbridge street as a man who had seen better days.

He went secretly and alone, not a soul of the many who had known him being aware of his departure. Elizabeth-Jane accompanied him as far as the second bridge on the highway – for the hour of her appointment with the unguessed visitor at Farfrae's had not yet arrived – and parted from him with unfeigned wonder and sorrow, keeping him back a minute or two before finally letting him go. She watched his form diminish across the moor, the yellow rush-basket at his back moving up and down with each tread, and the creases behind his knees coming and going alternately till she could no longer see them. Though she did not know it Henchard formed at this moment much the same picture as he had presented when entering Casterbridge for the first time nearly a quarter of a century before; except, to be sure, that the serious addition to his years had considerably lessened the spring of his stride, that his state of hopelessness had weakened him, and imparted to his shoulders, as weighted by the basket, a perceptible bend.

He went on till he came to the first milestone, which stood in the bank, half way up a steep hill. He rested his basket on the top of the stone, placed his elbows on it, and gave way to a convulsive twitch, which was worse than a sob, because it was so hard and so dry.

'If I had only got her with me – if I only had!' he said. 'Hard work would be nothing to me then! But that was not to be. I – Cain – go alone as I deserve – an outcast and a vagabond. But my punishment is *not* greater than I can bear!'

He sternly subdued his anguish, shouldered his basket, and went on.

Elizabeth, in the meantime, had breathed him a sigh, recovered her equanimity, and turned her face to Casterbridge. Before she had reached the first house she was met in her walk by Donald Farfrae. This was evidently not their first meeting that day; they joined hands without ceremony, and Farfrae anxiously asked, 'And is he gone – and did you tell him? – I mean of the other matter – not of ours.'

'He is gone; and I told him all I knew of your friend. Donald, who is he?'

'Well, well, dearie; you will know soon about that. And Mr Henchard will hear of it if he does not go far.'

'He will go far – he's bent upon getting out of sight and sound!'

She walked beside her lover, and when they reached the Crossways, or Bow, turned with him into Corn Street instead of going straight on to her own door. At Farfrae's house they stopped and went in.

Farfrae flung open the door of the ground-floor sitting-room, saying, 'There he is waiting for you,' and Elizabeth entered. In the arm-chair sat the broad-faced genial man who had called on Henchard on a memorable morning between one and two years before this time, and whom the latter had seen mount the coach and depart within half-an-hour of his arrival. It was Richard Newson. The meeting with the light-hearted father from whom she had been separated half-a-dozen years, as if by death, need hardly be detailed. It was an affecting one, apart from the question of paternity. Henchard's departure was in a moment explained. When the true facts came to be handled the difficulty of restoring her to her old belief in Newson was not so great as might have seemed likely, for Henchard's conduct itself was a proof that those facts were true. Moreover, she had grown up under Newson's paternal care; and even had Henchard been her father in nature, this father in early domiciliation might almost have carried the point against him, when the incidents of her parting with Henchard had a little worn off.

Newson's pride in what she had grown up to be was more than he could express. He kissed her again and again.

'I've saved you the trouble to come and meet me – ha-ha!' said Newson. 'The fact is that Mr Farfrae here, he said, "Come up and stop with me for a day or two, Captain Newson, and I'll bring her round." "Faith," says I, "so I will"; and here I am.'

'Well, Henchard is gone,' said Farfrae, shutting the door. 'He has done it all voluntarily, and, as I gather from Elizabeth, he has been very nice with her. I was got rather uneasy; but all is as it should be, and we will have no more deefficulties at all.'

'Now, that's very much as I thought,' said Newson, looking into the face of each by turns. 'I said to myself, ay, a hundred times, when I tried to get a peep at her unknown to herself – "Depend upon it, 'tis best that I should live on quiet for a few days like this till something turns up for the better." I now know you are all right, and what can I wish for more?'

'Well, Captain Newson, I will be glad to see ye here every day now, since it can do no harm,' said Farfrae. 'And what I've been thinking is that the wedding may as well be kept under my own roof, the house being large, and you being in lodgings by yourself – so that a great deal of trouble and expense would be saved ye? – and 'tis a convenience when a couple's married not to hae far to go to get home!'

'With all my heart,' said Captain Newson; 'since, as ye say, it can do no harm, now poor Henchard's gone; though I wouldn't have done it otherwise, or put myself in his way at all; for I've already in my lifetime been an intruder into his family quite as far as politeness can be expected to put up with. But what do the young woman say herself about it? Elizabeth, my child, come and hearken to what we be talking about, and not bide staring out o' the window as if ye didn't hear.'

'Donald and you must settle it,' murmured Elizabeth, still keeping up a scrutinizing gaze at some small object in the street.

'Well, then,' continued Newson, turning anew to Farfrae with a face expressing thorough entry into the subject, 'that's how we'll have it. And, Mr Farfrae, as you provide so much, and houseroom, and all that, I'll do my part in the drinkables, and see to the rum and schiedam – maybe a dozen jars will be sufficient? – as many of the folk will be ladies, and perhaps they won't drink hard enough to make a high average in the reckoning? But you know best. I've provided for men and shipmates times enough, but I'm as ignorant as a child how many glasses of grog a woman, that's not a drinking woman, is expected to consume at these ceremonies?'

'Oh, none — we'll no want much of that — O no!' said Farfrae, shaking his head with appalled gravity. 'Do you leave all to me.'

When they had gone a little further in these particulars Newson, leaning back in his chair and smiling reflectively at the ceiling, said, 'I've never told ye, or have I, Mr Farfrae, how Henchard put me off the scent that time?'

He expressed ignorance of what the Captain alluded to.

'Ah, I thought I hadn't. I resolved that I would not, I remember, not to hurt the man's name. But now he's gone I can tell ye. Why, I came to Casterbridge nine or ten months before that day last week that I found ye out. I had been here twice before then. The first time I passed through the town on my way westward, not knowing Elizabeth lived here. Then hearing at some place — I forget where — that a man of the name of Henchard had been mayor here, I came back, and called at his house one morning. The old rascal! — he said Elizabeth-Jane had died years ago.'

Elizabeth now gave earnest heed to his story.

'Now, it never crossed my mind that the man was selling me a packet,' continued Newson. 'And, if you'll believe me, I was that upset, that I went back to the coach that had brought me, and took passage onward without lying in the town half-an-hour. Ha-ha! — 'twas a good joke, and well carried out, and I give the man credit for't!'

Elizabeth-Jane was amazed at the intelligence. 'A joke? — O no!' she cried. 'Then he kept you from me, father, all those months, when you might have been here?'

The father admitted that such was the case.

'He ought not to have done it!' said Farfrae.

Elizabeth sighed. 'I said I would never forget him. But O! I think I ought to forget him now!'

Newson, like a good many rovers and sojourners among strange men and strange moralities, failed to perceive the enormity of Henchard's crime, notwithstanding that he himself had been the chief sufferer therefrom. Indeed, the attack upon the absent culprit waxing serious, he began to take Henchard's part.

'Well, 'twas not ten words that he said, after all,' Newson pleaded. 'And how could he know that I should be such a simpleton as to believe him? 'Twas as much my fault as his, poor fellow!'

'No,' said Elizabeth-Jane firmly, in her revulsion of feeling. 'He knew your disposition — you always were so trusting, father; I've heard my mother say so hundreds of times — and he did it to wrong you. After weaning me from you these five years by saying he was my father, he should not have done this.'

Thus they conversed; and there was nobody to set before Elizabeth any extenuation of the absent one's deceit. Even had he been present Henchard might scarce have pleaded it, so little did he value himself or his good name.

'Well, well — never mind — it is all over and past,' said Newson good-naturedly. 'Now, about this wedding again.'

CHAPTER FORTY-FOUR

MEANWHILE, the man of their talk had pursued his solitary way eastward till weariness overtook him, and he looked about for a place of rest. His heart was so exacerbated at parting from the girl that he could not face an inn, or even a household of the most humble kind; and entering a field he lay down under a wheatrick, feeling no want of food. The very heaviness of his soul caused him to sleep profoundly.

The bright autumn sun shining into his eyes across the stubble awoke him the next morning early. He opened his basket and ate for his breakfast what he had packed for his supper; and in doing so overhauled the remainder of his kit. Although everything he brought necessitated carriage at his own back, he had secreted among his tools a few of Elizabeth-Jane's cast-off belongings, in the shape of gloves, shoes, a scrap of her handwriting, and the like; and in his pocket he carried a curl of her hair. Having looked at these things he closed them up again, and went onward.

During five consecutive days Henchard's rush basket rode along upon his shoulder between the highway hedges, the new yellow of the rushes catching the eye of an occasional field-labourer as he glanced through the quickset, together with the wayfarer's hat and head, and down-turned face, over which the twig shadows moved in endless procession. It now became apparent that the direction of his journey was Weydon-Priors, which he reached on the afternoon of the sixth day.

The renowned hill whereon the annual fair had been held for so many generations was now bare of human beings, and almost of aught besides. A few sheep grazed thereabout, but these ran off when Henchard halted upon the summit. He deposited his basket upon the turf, and looked about with sad curiosity; till he discovered the road by which his wife and himself had entered on the upland so memorable to both, five-and-twenty years before.

'Yes, we came up that way,' he said, after ascertaining his bearings. 'She was carrying the baby, and I was reading a ballet-sheet. Then we crossed about here – she so sad and weary, and I speaking to her hardly at all, because of my cursed pride and mortification at being poor. Then we saw the tent – that must have stood more this way.' He walked to another spot; it was not really where the tent had stood, but it seemed so to him. 'Here we went in, and here we sat down. I faced this way. Then I drank, and committed my crime. It must have been just on that very pixy-ring that she was standing when she said her last words to me before going off with him; I can hear their sound now, and the sound of her sobs: "O Mike! I've lived with thee all this while, and had nothing but temper. Now I'm no more to 'ee – I'll try my luck elsewhere." '

He experienced not only the bitterness of a man who finds, in looking back upon an ambitious course, that what he has sacrificed in sentiment was worth as much as what he has gained in substance; but the superadded bitterness of seeing

454

his very recantation nullified. He had been sorry for all this long ago; but his attempts to replace ambition by love had been as fully foiled as his ambition itself. His wronged wife had foiled them by a fraud so grandly simple as to be almost a virtue. It was an odd sequence that out of all this tampering with social law came that flower of Nature, Elizabeth. Part of his wish to wash his hands of life arose from his perception of its contrarious inconsistencies – of Nature's jaunty readiness to support unorthodox social principles.

He intended to go on from this place – visited as an act of penance – into another part of the country altogether. But he could not help thinking of Elizabeth, and the quarter of the horizon in which she lived. Out of this it happened that the centrifugal tendency imparted by weariness of the world was counteracted by the centripetal influence of his love for his stepdaughter. As a consequence, instead of following a straight course yet further away from Casterbridge, Henchard gradually, almost unconsciously, deflected from that right line of his first intention; till, by degrees, his wandering, like that of the Canadian woodsman, became part of a circle of which Casterbridge formed the centre. In ascending any particular hill he ascertained the bearings as nearly as he could by means of the sun, moon, or stars, and settled in his mind the exact direction in which Casterbridge and Elizabeth-Jane lay. Sneering at himself for his weakness he yet every hour – nay, every few minutes – conjectured her actions for the time being – her sitting down and rising up, her goings and comings, till thought of Newson's and Farfrae's counter-influence would pass like a cold blast over a pool, and efface her image. And then he would say of himself, 'O you fool! All this about a daughter who is no daughter of thine!'

At length he obtained employment at his own occupation of hay-trusser, work of that sort being in demand at this autumn time. The scene of his hiring was a pastoral farm near the old western highway, whose course was the channel of all such communications as passed between the busy centres of novelty and the remote Wessex boroughs. He had chosen the neighbourhood of this artery from a sense that, situated here, though at a distance of fifty miles, he was virtually nearer to her whose welfare was so dear than he would be at a roadless spot only half as remote.

And thus Henchard found himself again on the precise standing which he had occupied a quarter of a century before. Externally there was nothing to hinder his making another start on the upward slope, and by his new lights achieving higher things than his soul in its half-formed state had been able to accomplish. But the ingenious machinery contrived by the Gods for reducing human possibilities of amelioration to a minimum – which arrange that wisdom to do shall come *pari passu* with the departure of zest for doing – stood in the way of all that. He had no wish to make an arena a second time of a world that had become a mere painted scene to him.

Very often, as his hay-knife crunched down among the sweet-smelling grassy stems, he would survey mankind and say to himself: 'Here and everywhere be folk dying before their time like frosted leaves, though wanted by their families, the country, and the world; while I, an outcast, and encumberer of the ground, wanted by nobody, and despised by all, live on against my will!'

He often kept an eager ear upon the conversation of those who passed along the road – not from a general curiosity by any means – but in the hope that among these travellers between Casterbridge and London some would, sooner or later, speak of the former place. The distance, however, was too great to lend much probability to his desire; and the highest result of his attention to wayside words was that he did indeed hear the name 'Casterbridge' uttered one day by the driver of a road-waggon. Henchard ran to the gate of the field he worked in, and hailed the speaker, who was a stranger.

'Yes – I've come from there, maister,' he said, in answer to Henchard's inquiry. 'I trade up and down, ye know; though, what with this travelling without horses that's getting so common, my work will soon be done.'

'Anything moving in the old place, mid I ask?'

'All the same as usual.'

'I've heard that Mr Farfrae, the late mayor, is thinking of getting married. Now is that true or not?'

'I couldn't say for the life o' me. O no, I should think not.'

'But yes John – you forget,' said a woman inside the waggon-tilt. 'What were them packages we carr'd there at the beginning o' the week? Surely they said a wedding was coming off soon – on Martin's Day?'

The man declared he remembered nothing about it; and the waggon went on jangling over the hill.

Henchard was convinced that the woman's memory served her well. The date was an extremely probable one, there being no reason for delay on either side. He might, for that matter, write and inquire of Elizabeth; but his instinct for sequestration had made the course difficult. Yet before he left her she had said that for him to be absent from her wedding was not as she wished it to be.

The remembrance would continually revive in him now that it was not Elizabeth and Farfrae who had driven him away from them, but his own haughty sense that his presence was no longer desired. He had assumed the return of Newson without absolute proof that the Captain meant to return; still less that Elizabeth-Jane would welcome him; and with no proof whatever that if he did return he would stay. What if he had been mistaken in his views; if there had been no necessity that his own absolute separation from her he loved should be involved in these untoward incidents? To make one more attempt to be near her: to go back; to see her, to plead his cause before her, to ask forgiveness for his fraud, to endeavour strenuously to hold his own in her love; it was worth the risk of repulse, ay, of life itself.

But how to initiate this reversal of all his former resolves without causing husband and wife to despise him for his inconsistency was a question which made him tremble and brood.

He cut and cut his trusses two days more, and then he concluded his hesitancies by a sudden reckless determination to go to the wedding festivity. Neither writing nor message would be expected of him. She had regretted his decision to be absent – his unanticipated presence would fill the little unsatisfied corner that would probably have place in her just heart without him.

To intrude as little of his personality as possible upon a gay event with which that personality could show nothing in keeping, he decided not to make his appearance till evening – when stiffness would have worn off, and a gentle wish to let bygones be bygones would exercise its sway in all hearts.

He started on foot, two mornings before St Martin's-tide, allowing himself about sixteen miles to perform for each of the three days' journey, reckoning the wedding-day as one. There were only two towns, Melchester and Shottsford, of any importance along his course, and at the latter he stopped on the second night, not only to rest, but prepare himself for the next evening.

Possessing no clothes but the working suit he stood in – now stained and distorted by their two months of hard usage, he entered a shop to make some purchases which should put him, externally at any rate, a little in harmony with the prevailing tone of the morrow. A rough yet respectable coat and hat, a new shirt and neck-cloth, were the chief of these; and having satisfied himself that in appearance at least he would not now offend her, he proceeded to the more interesting particular of buying her some present.

What should that present be? He walked up and down the street, regarding dubiously the display in the shop windows, from a gloomy sense that what he might most like to give her would be beyond his miserable pocket. At length a caged goldfinch met his eye. The cage was a plain and small one, the shop humble, and on inquiry he concluded he could afford the modest sum asked. A sheet of newspaper was tied round the little creature's wire prison, and with the wrapped up cage in his hand Henchard sought a lodging for the night.

Next day he set out upon the last stage, and was soon within the district which had been his dealing ground in bygone years. Part of the distance he travelled by carrier, seating himself in the darkest corner at the back of that trader's van; and as the other passengers, mainly women going short journeys, mounted and alighted in front of Henchard, they talked over much local news, not the least portion of this being the wedding then in course of celebration at the town they were nearing. It appeared from their accounts that the town band had been hired for the evening party, and, lest the convivial instincts of that body should get the better of their skill, the further step had been taken of engaging the string band from Budmouth, so that there would be a reserve of harmony to fall back upon in case of need.

He heard, however, but few particulars beyond those known to him already, the incident of the deepest interest on the journey being the soft pealing of the Casterbridge bells, which reached the travellers' ears while the van paused on the top of Yalbury Hill to have the drag lowered. The time was just after twelve o'clock.

Those notes were a signal that all had gone well; that there had been no slip 'twixt cup and lip in this case; that Elizabeth-Jane and Donald Farfrae were man and wife.

Henchard did not care to ride any further with his chattering companions after hearing this sound. Indeed, it quite unmanned him; and in pursuance of his plan of not showing himself in Casterbridge street till evening, lest he should mortify Farfrae and his bride, he alighted here, with his bundle and bird-cage, and was soon left as a lonely figure on the broad white highway.

It was the hill near which he had waited to meet Farfrae, almost two years earlier, to tell him of the serious illness of his wife Lucetta. The place was unchanged; the same larches sighed the same notes; but Farfrae had another wife – and, as Henchard knew, a better one. He only hoped that Elizabeth-Jane had obtained a better home than had been hers at the former time.

He passed the remainder of the afternoon in a curious high-strung condition, unable to do much but think of the approaching meeting with her, and sadly satirize himself for his emotions thereon, as a Samson shorn. Such an innovation on Casterbridge customs as a flitting of bridegroom and bride from the town immediately after the ceremony, was not likely, but if it should have taken place he would wait till their return. To assure himself on this point he asked a market-man when near the borough if the newly-married couple had gone away, and was promptly informed that they had not; they were at that hour, according to all accounts, entertaining a houseful of guests at their home in Corn Street.

Henchard dusted his boots, washed his hands at the river-side, and proceeded up the town under the feeble lamps. He need have made no inquiries beforehand, for on drawing near Farfrae's residence it was plain to the least observant that festivity prevailed within, and that Donald himself shared it, his voice being distinctly audible in the street, giving strong expression to a song of his dear native country that he loved so well as never to have revisited it. Idlers were standing on the pavement in front; and wishing to escape the notice of these Henchard passed quickly on to the door.

It was wide open; the hall was lighted extravagantly, and people were going up and down the stairs. His courage failed him; to enter footsore, laden, and poorly dressed in to the midst of such resplendency was to bring needless humiliation upon her he loved, if not to court repulse from her husband. Accordingly he went round into the street at the back that he knew so well, entered the garden, and came quietly into the house through the kitchen, temporarily depositing the bird and cage under a bush outside, to lessen the awkwardness of his arrival.

Solitude and sadness had so emolliated Henchard that he now feared circumstances he would formerly have scorned, and he began to wish that he had not taken upon himself to arrive at such a juncture. However, his progress was made unexpectedly easy by his discovering alone in the kitchen an elderly woman who seemed to be acting as provisional housekeeper during the convulsions from which Farfrae's establishment was just then suffering. She was one of those people whom nothing surprises, and though to her, a total stranger, his request must have seemed odd, she willingly volunteered to go up and inform the master and mistress of the house that 'a humble old friend' had come.

On second thoughts she said that he had better not wait in the kitchen, but come up into the little back-parlour, which was empty. He thereupon followed her thither, and she left him. Just as she had got across the landing to the door of the best parlour a dance was struck up, and she returned to say that she would wait till that was over before announcing him – Mr and Mrs Farfrae having both joined in the figure.

The door of the front room had been taken off its hinges to give more space, and that of the room Henchard sat in being ajar, he could see fractional parts of the dancers whenever their gyrations brought them near the doorway, chiefly in the shape of the skirts of dresses and streaming curls of hair; together with about three-fifths of the band in profile, including the restless shadow of a fiddler's elbow, and the tip of the bass-viol bow.

The gaiety jarred upon Henchard's spirits; and he could not quite understand why Farfrae, a much-sobered man, and a widower, who had had his trials, should have cared for it all, notwithstanding the fact that he was quite a young man still, and quickly kindled to enthusiasm by dance and song. That the quiet Elizabeth, who had long ago appraised life at a moderate value, and who knew in spite of her maidenhood that marriage was as a rule no dancing matter, should have had zest for this revelry surprised him still more. However, young people could not be quite old people, he concluded, and custom was omnipotent.

With the progress of the dance the performers spread out somewhat, and then for the first time he caught a glimpse of the once despised daughter who had mastered him, and made his heart ache. She was in a dress of white silk or satin, he was not near enough to say which – snowy white, without a tinge of milk or cream; and the expression of her face was one of nervous pleasure rather than of gaiety. Presently Farfrae came round, his exuberant Scotch movement making him conspicuous in a moment. The pair were not dancing together, but Henchard could discern that whenever the changes of the figure made them the partners of a moment their emotions breathed a much subtler essence than at other times.

By degrees Henchard became aware that the measure was trod by some one who out-Farfraed Farfrae in saltatory intenseness. This was strange, and it was stranger to find that the eclipsing personage was Elizabeth-Jane's partner. The first time that Henchard saw him he was sweeping grandly round, his head quivering and low down, his legs in the form of an X and his back towards the door. The next time he came round in the other direction, his white waistcoat preceding his face, and his toes preceding his white waistcoat. That happy face – Henchard's complete discomfiture lay in it. It was Newson's, who had indeed come and supplanted him.

Henchard pushed to the door, and for some seconds made no other movement. He rose to his feet, and stood like a dark ruin, obscured by 'the shade from his own soul upthrown'.

But he was no longer the man to stand these reverses unmoved. His agitation was great, and he would fain have been gone, but before he could leave the dance had ended, the housekeeper had informed Elizabeth-Jane of the stranger who awaited her, and she entered the room immediately.

'Oh – it is – Mr Henchard!' she said, starting back.

'What; Elizabeth?' he cried, as he seized her hand. 'What do you say? – Mr Henchard? Don't, don't scourge me like that! Call me worthless old Henchard – anything – but don't 'ee be so cold as this! O my maid – I see you have another – a real father in my place. Then you know all; but don't give all your thought to him! Do ye save a little room for me!'

She flushed up, and gently drew her hand away. 'I could have loved you always – I would have, gladly,' said she. 'But how can I when I know you have deceived me so – so bitterly deceived me! You persuaded me that my father was not my father – allowed me to live on in ignorance of the truth for years; and then when he, my warm-hearted real father, came to find me, cruelly sent him away with a wicked invention of my death, which nearly broke his heart. O how can I love as I once did a man who has served us like this!'

Henchard's lips half parted to begin an explanation. But he shut them up like a vice, and uttered not a sound. How should he, there and then, set before her with any effect the palliatives of his great faults – that he had himself been deceived in her identity at first, till informed by her mother's letter that his own child had died; that, in the second accusation, his lie had been the last desperate throw of a gamester who loved her affection better than his own honour? Among the many hindrances to such a pleading not the least was this, that he did not sufficiently value himself to lessen his sufferings by strenuous appeal or elaborate argument.

Waiving, therefore, his privilege of self-defence, he regarded only her discomposure. 'Don't ye distress yourself on my account,' he said, with proud superiority. 'I would not wish it – at such a time, too, as this. I have done wrong in coming to 'ee – I see my error. But it is only for once, so forgive it. I'll never trouble 'ee again, Elizabeth-Jane – no, not to my dying day! Good-night. Good-bye!'

Then, before she could collect her thoughts, Henchard went out from her rooms, and departed from the house by the back way as he had come; and she saw him no more.

CHAPTER FORTY-FIVE

I T was about a month after the day which closed as in the last chapter. Elizabeth-Jane had grown accustomed to the novelty of her situation, and the only difference between Donald's movements now and formerly was that he hastened indoors rather more quickly after business hours than he had been in the habit of doing for some time.

Newson had stayed in Casterbridge three days after the wedding party (whose gaiety, as might have been surmised, was of his making rather than of the married couple's), and was stared at and honoured as became the returned Crusoe of the hour. But whether or not because Casterbridge was difficult to excite by dramatic returns and disappearances, through having been for centuries an assize town, in which sensational exits from the world, antipodean absences, and such like, were half-yearly occurrences, the inhabitants did not altogether lose their equanimity on his account. On the fourth morning he was discovered disconsolately climbing a hill, in his craving to get a glimpse of the sea from somewhere or other. The contiguity of salt water proved to be such a necessity of his existence that he preferred Budmouth as a place of residence, notwithstanding the society of his daughter in the other town. Thither he went, and settled in lodgings in a green-shuttered cottage which had a bow-window, jutting out sufficiently to afford glimpses of a vertical strip of blue sea to any one opening the sash, and leaning forward far enough to look through a narrow lane of tall intervening houses.

Elizabeth-Jane was standing in the middle of her upstairs parlour, critically surveying some re-arrangement of articles with her head to one side, when the housemaid came in with the announcement, 'Oh, please ma'am, we know now how that bird-cage came there.'

In exploring her new domain during the first week of residence, gazing with critical satisfaction on this cheerful room and that, penetrating cautiously into dark cellars, sallying forth with gingerly tread to the garden, now leaf-strewn by autumn winds, and thus, like a wise field-marshal, estimating the capabilities of the site whereon she was about to open her house-keeping campaign – Mrs

Donald Farfrae had discovered in a screened corner a new bird-cage, shrouded in newspaper, and at the bottom of the cage a little ball of feathers – the dead body of a goldfinch. Nobody could tell her how the bird and cage had come there; though that the poor little songster had been starved to death was evident. The sadness of the incident had made an impression on her. She had not been able to forget it for days, despite Farfrae's tender banter; and now when the matter had been nearly forgotten it was again revived.

'Oh, please ma'am, we know how that bird-cage came there. That farmer's man who called on the evening of the wedding – he was seen wi' it in his hand as he came up the street; and 'tis thought that he put it down while he came in with his message, and then went away forgetting where he had left it.'

This was enough to set Elizabeth thinking, and in thinking she seized hold of the idea, at one feminine bound, that the caged bird had been brought by Henchard for her as a wedding gift and token of repentance. He had not expressed to her any regrets or excuses for what he had done in the past; but it was a part of his nature to extenuate nothing, and live on as one of his own worst accusers. She went out, looked at the cage, buried the starved little singer, and from that hour her heart softened towards the self-alienated man.

When her husband came in she told him her solution of the bird-cage mystery; and begged Donald to help her in finding out, as soon as possible, whither Henchard had banished himself, that she might make her peace with him; try to do something to render his life less that of an outcast, and more tolerable to him. Although Farfrae had never so passionately liked Henchard as Henchard had liked him, he had, on the other hand, never so passionately hated in the same direction as his former friend had done; and he was therefore not the least indisposed to assist Elizabeth-Jane in her laudable plan.

But it was by no means easy to set about discovering Henchard. He had apparently sunk into the earth on leaving Mr and Mrs Farfrae's door. Elizabeth-Jane remembered what he had once attempted; and trembled.

But though she did not know it Henchard had become a changed man since then – as far, that is, as change of emotional basis can justify such a radical phrase; and she needed not to fear. In a few days Farfrae's inquiries elicited that Henchard had been seen by one who knew him walking steadily along the Melchester highway eastward, at twelve o'clock at night – in other words, retracing his steps on the road by which he had come.

This was enough; and the next morning Farfrae might have been discovered driving his gig out of Casterbridge in that direction., Elizabeth-Jane sitting beside him, wrapped in a thick flat fur – the victorine of the period – her complexion somewhat richer than formerly, and an incipient matronly dignity, which the serene Minerva-eyes of one 'whose gestures beamed with mind' made becoming, settling on her face. Having herself arrived at a promising haven from at least the grosser troubles of her life, her object was to place Henchard in some similar quietude before he should sink into that lower stage of existence which was only too possible to him now.

After driving along the highway for a few miles they made further inquiries, and learnt of a road-mender, who had been working thereabouts for weeks, that he had observed such a man at the time mentioned; he had left the Melchester coach-road at Weatherbury by a forking highway which skirted the north of

Egdon Heath. Into this road they directed the horse's head, and soon were bowling across that ancient country whose surface never had been stirred to a finger's depth, save by the scratchings of rabbits, since brushed by the feet of the earliest tribes. The tumuli these had left behind, dun and shagged with heather, jutted roundly into the sky from the uplands, as though they were the full breasts of Diana Multimammia supinely extended there.

They searched Egdon, but found no Henchard. Farfrae drove onward, and by the afternoon reached the neighbourhood of some extension of the heath to the north of Anglebury, a prominent feature of which, in the form of a blasted clump of firs on the summit of a hill, they soon passed under. That the road they were following had, up to this point, been Henchard's track on foot they were pretty certain; but the ramifications which now began to reveal themselves in the route made further progress in the right direction a matter of pure guess-work, and Donald strongly advised his wife to give up the search in person, and trust to other means for obtaining news of her stepfather. They were now a score of miles at least from home, but, by resting the horse for a couple of hours at a village they had just traversed, it would be possible to get back to Casterbridge that same day; while to go much further afield would reduce them to the necessity of camping out for the night; 'and that will make a hole in a sovereign,' said Farfrae. She pondered the position, and agreed with him.

He accordingly drew rein, but before reversing their direction paused a moment and looked vaguely round upon the wide country which the elevated position disclosed. While they looked a solitary human form came from under the clump of trees, and crossed ahead of them. The person was some labourer; his gait was shambling, his regard fixed in front of him as absolutely as if he wore blinkers; and in his hand he carried a few sticks. Having crossed the road he descended into a ravine, where a cottage revealed itself, which he entered.

'If it were not so far away from Casterbridge I should say that must be poor Whittle. 'Tis just like him,' observed Elizabeth-Jane.

'And it may be Whittle, for he's never been to the yard these three weeks, going away without saying any word at all; and I owing him for two days' work, without knowing who to pay it to.'

The possibility led them to alight, and at least make an inquiry at the cottage. Farfrae hitched the reins to the gate-post, and they approached what was of humble dwellings surely the humblest. The walls, built of kneaded clay originally faced with a trowel, had been worn by years of rain-washings to a lumpy crumbling surface, channelled and sunken from its plane, its gray rents held together here and there by a leafy strap of ivy which could scarcely find substance enough for the purpose. The rafters were sunken, and the thatch of the roof in ragged holes. Leaves from the fence had been blown into the corners of the doorway, and lay there undisturbed. The door was ajar; Farfrae knocked; and he who stood before them was Whittle, as they had conjectured.

His face showed marks of deep sadness, his eyes lighting on them with an unfocused gaze; and he still held in his hand the few sticks he had been out to gather. As soon as he recognized them he started.

'What, Abel Whittle; is it that ye are heere?' said Farfrae.

'Ay, yes, sir! You see he was kind-like to mother when she wer here below, though 'a was rough to me.'

'Who are you talking of?'

'O sir – Mr Henchet! Didn't ye know it? He's just gone – about half-an-hour ago, by the sun; for I've got no watch to my name.'

'Not – dead?' faltered Elizabeth-Jane.

'Yes, ma'am, he's gone! He was kind-like to mother when she wer here below, sending her the best ship-coal, and hardly any ashes from it at all; and taties, and such-like that were very needful to her. I seed en go down street on the night of your worshipful's wedding to the lady at yer side, and I thought he looked low and faltering. And I followed en over Grey's Bridge, and he turned and zeed me, and said, "You go back!" But I followed, and he turned again, and said, "Do you hear, sir? Go back!" But I zeed that he was low, and I followed on still. Then 'a said, "Whittle, what do ye follow me for when I've told ye to go back all these times?" And I said, "Because, sir, I see things be bad with 'ee, and ye wer kind-like to mother if ye were rough to me, and I would fain be kind-like to you." Then he walked on, and I followed; and he never complained at me no more. We walked on like that all night; and in the blue o' the morning, when 'twas hardly day, I looked ahead o' me, and I zeed that he wambled, and could hardly drag along. By that time we had got past here, but I had seen that this house was empty as I went by, and I got him to come back; and I took down the boards from the windows, and helped him inside. "What, Whittle," he said, "and can ye really be such a poor fond fool as to care for such a wretch as I!" Then I went on further, and some neighbourly woodmen lent me a bed, and a chair, and a few other traps, and we brought 'em here, and made him as comfortable as we could. But he didn't gain strength, for you see, ma'am, he couldn't eat – no, no appetite at all – and he got weaker; and to-day he died. One of the neighbours have gone to get a man to measure him.'

'Dear me – is that so!' said Farfrae.

As for Elizabeth, she said nothing.

'Upon the head of his bed he pinned a piece of paper, with some writing upon it,' continued Abel Whittle. 'But not being a man o' letters, I can't read writing; so I don't know what it is. I can get it and show ye.'

They stood in silence while he ran into the cottage; returning in a moment with a crumpled scrap of paper. On it there was pencilled as follows: –

'MICHAEL HENCHARD'S WILL

'That Elizabeth-Jane Farfrae be not told of my death, or made to grieve on account of me.

'& that I be not bury'd in consecrated ground.

'& that no sexton be asked to toll the bell.

'& that nobody is wished to see my dead body.

'& that no murners walk behind me at my funeral.

'& that no flours be planted on my grave.

'& that no man remember me.

'To this I put my name.

'MICHAEL HENCHARD'

'What are we to do?' said Donald, when he had handed the paper to her.

She could not answer distinctly. 'O Donald!' she said at last through her tears, 'what bitterness lies there! O I would not have minded so much if it had not been for my unkindness at that last parting! . . . But there's no altering – so it must be.'

What Henchard had written in the anguish of his dying was respected as far as practicable by Elizabeth-Jane, though less from a sense of the sacredness of last words, as such, than from her independent knowledge that the man who wrote them meant what he said. She knew the directions to be a piece of the same stuff that his whole life was made of, and hence were not to be tampered with to give herself a mournful pleasure, or her husband credit for large-heartedness.

All was over at last, even her regrets for having misunderstood him on his last visit, for not having searched him out sooner, though these were deep and sharp for a good while. From this time forward Elizabeth-Jane found herself in a latitude of calm weather, kindly and grateful in itself, and doubly so after the Capharnaum in which some of her preceding years had been spent. As the lively and sparkling emotions of her early married life cohered into an equable serenity, the finer movements of her nature found scope in discovering to the narrow-lived ones around her the secret (as she had once learnt it) of making limited opportunities endurable; which she deemed to consist in the cunning enlargement, by a species of microscopic treatment, of those minute forms of satisfaction that offer themselves to everybody not in positive pain; which, thus handled, have much of the same inspiriting effect upon life as wider interests cursorily embraced.

Her teaching had a reflex action upon herself, insomuch that she thought she could perceive no great personal difference between being respected in the nether parts of Casterbridge and glorified at the uppermost end of the social world. Her position was, indeed, to a marked degree one that, in the common phrase, afforded much to be thankful for. That she was not demonstratively thankful was no fault of hers. Her experience had been of a kind to teach her, rightly or wrongly, that the doubtful honour of a brief transit through a sorry world hardly called for effusiveness, even when the path was suddenly irradiated at some half-way point by daybeams rich as hers. But her strong sense that neither she nor any human being deserved less than was given, did not blind her to the fact that there were others receiving less who had deserved much more. And in being forced to class herself among the fortunate she did not cease to wonder at the persistence of the unforseen, when the one to whom such unbroken tranquillity had been accorded in the adult stage was she whose youth had seemed to teach that happiness was but the occasional episode in a general drama of pain.

THE WOODLANDERS

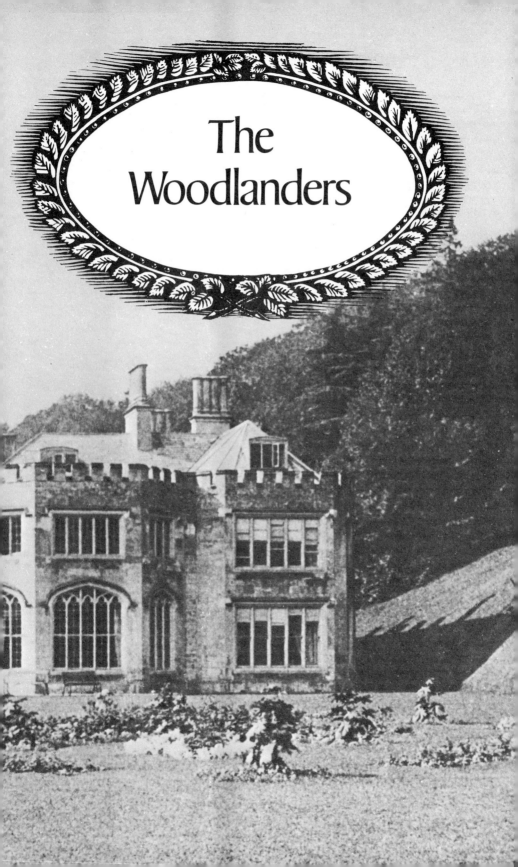

The Woodlanders

CHAPTER ONE

THE rambler who, for old association's sake, should trace the forsaken coach-road running almost in a meridional line from Bristol to the south shore of England, would find himself during the latter half of his journey in the vicinity of some extensive woodlands, interspersed with apple-orchards. Here the trees, timber or fruit-bearing as the case may be, make the wayside hedges ragged by their drip and shade, their lower limbs stretching in level repose over the road, as though reclining on the insubstantial air. At one place, on the skirts of Blackmoor Vale, where the bold brow of High-Stoy Hill is seen two or three miles ahead, the leaves lie so thick in autumn as to completely bury the track. The spot is lonely, and when the days are darkening the many gay charioteers now perished who have rolled along the way, the blistered soles that have trodden it, and the tears that have wetted it, return upon the mind of the loiterer.

The physiognomy of a deserted highway expresses solitude to a degree that is not reached by mere dales or downs, and bespeaks a tomb-like stillness more emphatic than that of glades and pools. The contrast of what is with what might be, probably accounts for this. To step, for instance, at the place under notice, from the edge of the plantation into the adjoining thoroughfare, and pause amid its emptiness for a moment, was to exchange by the act of a single stride the simple absence of human companionship for an incubus of the forlorn.

At this spot, on the louring evening of a bygone winter's day, there stood a man who had thus indirectly entered upon the scene from a stile hard by, and was temporarily influenced by some such feeling of being suddenly more alone than before he had emerged upon the highway.

It could be seen by a glance at his rather finical style of dress that he did not belong to the country proper; and from his air, after a while, that though there might be a sombre beauty in the scenery, music in the breeze, and a wan procession of coaching ghosts in the sentiment of this old turnpike-road, he was mainly puzzled about the way.

He looked north and south, and mechanically prodded the ground with his cane.

At first not a soul appeared who could enlighten him as he desired, or seemed likely to appear that night. But presently a slight noise of labouring wheels, and the steady dig of a horse's shoe-tips became audible; and there loomed in the notch of sky and plantation a carrier's van drawn by a single horse.

The vehicle was half full of passengers, mostly women. He held up his stick at its approach, and the woman who was driving drew rein.

'I've been trying to find a short way to Little Hintock this last half-hour, Mrs Dollery,' he said. 'But though I've been to Great Hintock and Hintock House half a dozen times, on business with the dashing lady there, I am at fault about the small village. You can help me, I dare say?'

She assured him that she could – that as she went to Abbot's Cernel her van passed near it – that it was only up the lane branching out of the road she followed. 'Though,' continued Mrs Dollery, ''tis such a little small place that, as a town gentleman, you'd need have a candle and lantern to find it if ye don't know where 'tis. Bedad! I wouldn't live there if they'd pay me to. Now at Abbot's Cernel you do see the world a bit.'

He mounted and sat beside her, with his feet outwards, where they were ever and anon brushed over by the horse's tail.

This van was rather a movable attachment of the roadway than an extraneous object, to those who knew it well. The old horse, whose hair was of the roughness and colour of heather, whose leg-joints, shoulders, and hoofs were distorted by harness and drudgery from colthood – though if all had their rights he ought, symmetrical in outline, to have been picking the herbage of some Eastern plain instead of tugging here – had trodden this road almost daily for twenty years. Even his subjection was not made congruous throughout, for, the harness being too short, his tail was not drawn through the crupper, and the breeching slipped awkwardly to one side. He knew every subtle incline of the ten miles of ground between Abbot's Cernel and Sherton – the market town to which he journeyed – as accurately as any surveyor could have learnt it by a Dumpy level.

The vehicle had a square black tilt which nodded with the motion of the wheels, and at a point in it over the driver's head was a hook to which the reins were hitched at times, forming a catenary curve from the horse's shoulders. Somewhere about the axles was a loose chain, whose only known function was to clink as it went. Mrs Dollery, having to hop up and down many times in the service of her passengers, wore, especially in windy weather, short leggings under her gown for modesty's sake; and instead of a bonnet a felt hat tied down with a handkerchief, to guard against an ear-ache to which she was frequently subject. In the rear of the van was a glass window, which she cleaned with her pocket-handkerchief every market-day before starting. Looking at the van from the back the spectator could thus see, through its interior, a square piece of the same sky and landscape that he saw without, but intruded on by the profiles of the seated passengers, who, as they rumbled onward, their lips moving and heads nodding in animated private converse, remained in cheerful unconsciousness that their mannerisms and facial peculiarities were sharply defined to the public eye.

This hour of coming home from market was the happy one, if not the happiest, of the week for them. Snugly ensconced under the tilt they could forget the sorrows of the world without, and survey life and discuss the incidents of the day with placid smiles.

The passengers in the back part formed a group to themselves, and while the newcomer spoke to the proprietress they indulged in a confidential chat about him, which the noise of the van rendered inaudible to himself and Mrs Dollery sitting forward.

''Tis Barber Percomb – he that's got the waxen woman in his window,' said one. 'What business can bring him out here at this time, and not a journeyman haircutter, but a master-barber that's left off his pole because 'tis not genteel?'

The barber, though he had nodded and spoken genially, seemed indisposed to gratify the curiosity that he had aroused; and the unrestrained flow of ideas which had animated the inside of the van before his arrival was checked thenceforward.

Thus they rode on, and High-Stoy Hill grew larger ahead. At length could be discerned in the dusk, about half a mile to one side, gardens and orchards sunk in a concave, and, as it were, snipped out of the woodland. From this self-contained place rose in stealthy silence tall stems of smoke, which the eye of imagination could trace downward to their root on quiet hearthstones, festooned overhead with hams and flitches. It was one of those sequestered spots outside the gates of the world where may usually be found more meditation than action, and more listlessness than meditation; where reasoning proceeds on narrow premises, and results in inferences wildly imaginative; yet where, from time to time, dramas of a grandeur and unity truly Sophoclean are enacted in the real, by virtue of the concentrated passions and closely-knit interdependence of the lives therein.

This place was the Little Hintock of the master-barber's search. The coming night gradually obscured the smoke of the chimneys, but the position of the wood-environed community could still be distinguished by a few faint lights, winking more or less ineffectually through the leafless boughs and the undiscernible songsters they bore, in the form of balls of feathers, at roost among them.

At the corner of the lane which branched to the hamlet the barber alighted, Mrs Dollery's van going onward to the larger place, whose superiority to the despised smaller one as an exemplar of the world's movements was not particularly apparent in its means of approach.

'A very clever and learned young doctor lives in the place you be going to – not because there's anybody for'n to cure there, but because they say he is in league with the devil.'

The observation was flung at the barber by one of the women at parting, as a last attempt to get at his errand that way.

But he made no reply and without further pause plunged towards the umbrageous nook, and paced cautiously over the dead leaves which nearly buried the road or street of the hamlet. As very few people except themselves passed this way after dark, a majority of the denizens of Little Hintock deemed window curtains unnecessary; and on this account their visitor made it his business to stop opposite the casements of each cottage that he came to, with a demeanour which showed that he was endeavouring to conjecture, from the persons and things he observed within, the whereabouts of somebody or other who resided here.

Only the smaller dwellings interested him; one or two houses whose size, antiquity, and rambling appurtenances signified that notwithstanding their remoteness they must formerly have been, if they were not still, inhabited by people of a certain social standing, being neglected by him entirely. Smells of pomace, and the hiss of fermenting cider, which reached him from the back quarters of other tenements, revealed the recent occupation of some of the inhabitants, and joined with the scent of decay from the perishing leaves underfoot.

Half a dozen dwellings were passed without result. The next, which stood opposite a tall tree, was in an exceptional state of radiance, the flickering brightness from the inside shining up the chimney and making a luminous mist of the emerging smoke. The interior, as seen through the window, caused him to draw up with a terminative air and watch. The house was rather large for a cottage, and the door, which opened immediately into the living-room, stood ajar, so that a riband of light fell through the opening into the dark atmosphere without. Every now and then a moth, decrepit from the late season, would flit for a moment across the outcoming rays and disappear again into the night.

CHAPTER TWO

I n the room from which this cheerful blaze proceeded he beheld a girl seated on a willow chair, and busily working by the light of the fire, which was ample and of wood. With a bill-hook in one hand and a leather glove much too large for her on the other, she was making spars, such as are used by thatchers, with great rapidity. She wore a leather apron for this purpose, which was also much too large for her figure. On her left hand lay a bundle of the straight, smooth hazel rods called spar-gads – the raw material of her manufacture; on her right a heap of chips and ends – the refuse – with which the fire was maintained; in front a pile of the finished articles. To produce them she took up each gad, looked critically at it from end to end, cut it to length, split it into four, and sharpened each of the quarters with dexterous blows, which brought it to a triangular point precisely resembling that of a bayonet.

Beside her, in case she might require more light, a brass candle-stick stood on a little round table curiously formed of an old coffin-stool, with a deal top nailed on, the white surface of the latter contrasting oddly with the black carved oak of the sub-structure. The social position of the household in the past was almost as definitively shown by the presence of this article as that of an esquire or nobleman by his old helmets or shields. It had been customary for every well-to-do villager, whose tenure was by copy of court-roll, or in any way more permanent than that of the mere cotter, to keep a pair of these stools for the use of his own dead; but changes had led to the discontinuance of the custom, and the stools were frequently made use of in the manner described.

The young woman laid down the bill-hook for a moment and examined the palm of her right hand which, unlike the other, was ungloved, and showed little hardness or roughness about it. The palm was red and blistering, as if her present occupation were as yet too recent to have subdued it to what it worked in. As with so many right hands born to manual labour, there was nothing in its fundamental shape to bear out the physiological conventionalism that gradations of birth show themselves primarily in the form of this member. Nothing but a cast of the die of destiny had decided that the girl should handle the tool; and the fingers which clasped the heavy ash haft might have skilfully guided the pencil or swept the string, had they only been set to do it in good time.

Her face had the usual fulness of expression which is developed by a life of solitude. Where the eyes of a multitude continuously beat like waves upon a countenance they seem to wear away its mobile power; but in the still water of privacy every feeling and sentiment unfolds in visible luxuriance, to be interpreted as readily as a printed word by an intruder. In years she was no more than nineteen or twenty, but the necessity of taking thought at a too early period of life had forced the provisional curves of her childhood's face to a premature finality. Thus she had but little pretension to beauty, save in one prominent particular – her hair.

Its abundance made it almost unmanageable; its colour was, roughly speaking, and as seen here by firelight, brown; but careful notice, or an observation by day, would have revealed that its true shade was a rare and beautiful approximation to chestnut.

On this one bright gift of Time to the particular victim of his now before us the newcomer's eyes were fixed; meanwhile the fingers of his right hand mechanically played over something sticking up from his waistcoat pocket – the bows of a pair of scissors, whose polish made them feebly responsive to the light from within the house. In her present beholder's mind the scene formed by the girlish spar-maker composed itself into an impression-picture of extremest type, wherein the girl's hair alone, as the focus of observation, was depicted with intensity and distinctness, while her face, shoulders, hands, and figure in general were a blurred mass of unimportant detail lost in haze and obscurity.

He hesitated no longer, but tapped at the door and entered. The young woman turned at the crunch of his boots on the sanded floor, and exclaiming, 'O, Mr Percomb, how you frightened me!' quite lost her colour for a moment.

He replied, 'You should shut your door – then you'd hear folk open it.'

'I can't,' she said; 'the chimney smokes so. Mr Percomb, you look as unnatural away from your wigs as a canary in a thorn hedge. Surely you have not come out here on my account – for—'

'Yes – to have your answer about this.' He touched her hair with his cane, and she winced. 'Do you agree?' he continued. 'It is necessary that I should know at once, as the lady is soon going away, and it takes time to make up.'

'Don't press me – it worries me. I was in hopes you had thought no more of it. I can *not* part with it – so there!'

'Now look here, Marty,' said the other, sitting down on the coffin-stool table. 'How much do you get for making these spars?'

'Hush – father's upstairs awake, and he don't know that I am doing his work.'

'Well, now tell me,' said the man more softly. 'How much do you get?'

'Eighteenpence a thousand,' she said reluctantly.

'Who are you making them for?'

'Mr Melbury, the timber-dealer, just below here.'

'And how many can you make in a day?'

'In a day and half the night, three bundles – that's a thousand and a half.'

'Two and threepence.' Her visitor paused. 'Well, look here,' he continued, with the remains of a computation in his tone, which reckoning had been to fix the probable sum of money necessary to outweigh her present resources and her woman's love of comeliness; 'here's a sovereign – a gold sovereign, almost new.' He held it out between his finger and thumb. 'That's as much as you'd earn in a week and a half at that rough man's-work, and it's yours for just letting me snip off what you've got too much of.'

The girl's bosom moved a very little. 'Why can't the lady send to some other girl who don't value her hair – not to me?' she exclaimed.

'Why, simpleton, because yours is the exact shade of her own, and 'tis a shade you can't match by dyeing. But you are not going to refuse me now I've come all the way from Sherton on purpose?'

'I say I won't sell it – to you or anybody.'

'Now listen,' and he drew up a little closer beside her. 'The lady is very rich, and won't be particular to a few shillings; so I will advance to this on my own responsibility – I'll make the one sovereign two, rather than go back empty-handed.'

'No, no, no!' she cried, beginning to be much agitated. 'You are tempting me. You go on like the Devil to Doctor Faustus in the penny book. But I don't want your money, and won't agree. Why did you come? I said when you got me into your shop and urged me so much that I didn't mean to sell my hair!'

'Marty, now hearken. The lady that wants it wants it badly. And, between you and me, you'd better let her have it. 'Twill be bad for you if you don't.'

'Bad for me? Who is she, then?'

The wig-maker held his tongue, and the girl repeated the question.

'I am not at liberty to tell you. And as she is going abroad soon it makes no difference who she is at all.'

'She wants it to go abroad wi'?'

He assented by a nod.

The girl regarded him reflectively. 'Now, Mr Percomb,' she said, 'I know who 'tis. 'Tis she at the House – Mrs Charmond!'

'That's my secret. However, if you agree to let me have it I'll tell you in confidence.'

'I'll certainly not let you have it unless you tell me the truth. Is it Mrs Charmond?'

The man dropped his voice. 'Well – it is. You sat in front of her in church the other day, and she noticed how exactly your hair matches her own. Ever since then she's been hankering for it, to help out hers, and at last decided to get it. As she won't wear it till she goes off abroad she knows nobody will recognize the change. I'm commissioned to get it for her, and then it is to be made up. I shouldn't have vamped all these miles for any less important employer. Now, mind – 'tis as much as my business with her is worth if it should be known that I've let out her name; but honour between us two, Marty, and you'll say nothing that would injure me?'

'I don't wish to tell upon her,' said Marty coolly. 'But my hair is my own, and I'm going to keep it.'

'Now that's not fair, after what I've told you,' said the nettled emissary. 'You see, Marty, as you are in the same parish, and in one of this lady's cottages, and your father is ill, and wouldn't like to turn out, it would be as well to oblige her. I say that as a friend. But I won't press you to make up your mind to-night. You'll be coming to market to-morrow, I dare say, and you can call then. If you think it over you'll be inclined to bring what I want, I know.'

'I've nothing more to say,' she answered.

Her companion saw from her manner that it was useless to urge her further by speech. 'As you are a trusty young woman,' he said, 'I'll put these sovereigns up here for ornament, that you may see how handsome they are. Bring the article tomorrow, or return the sovereigns.' He stuck them edgewise into the frame of a small mantel looking-glass. 'I hope you'll bring it; for your sake and mine. I should have thought she could have suited herself elsewhere; but as it's her fancy it must be indulged if possible. If you cut it off yourself, mind how you do it so as to keep all the locks one way.' He showed her how this was to be done.

'But I shan't,' she replied with laconic indifference. 'I value my looks too much to spoil 'em. She wants my curls to get another lover with; though if stories are true she's broke the heart of many a noble gentleman already.'

'Lord, it's wonderful how you guess things, Marty,' said the barber. 'I've had it from those that know that there certainly is some foreign gentleman in her eye. However, mind what I ask.'

'She's not going to get him through me.'

Percomb had retired as far as the door; he came back, planted his cane on the coffin-stool, and looked her in the face. 'Marty South,' he said with deliberate emphasis, '*you've got a lover yourself*, and that's why you won't let it go!'

She reddened so intensely as to pass the mild blush that suffices to heighten beauty; she put the yellow leather glove on one hand, took up the hook with the other, and sat down doggedly to her work without turning her face to him again. He regarded her head for a moment, went to the door, and with one look back at her departed on his way homeward.

Marty pursued her occupation for a few minutes, then suddenly laying down the bill-hook she jumped up and went to the back of the room, where she opened a door which disclosed a staircase so whitely scrubbed that the grain of the wood was wellnigh sodden away by cleansing. At the top she gently approached a bedroom, and without entering said, 'Father, do you want anything?'

A weak voice inside answered in the negative; adding, 'I should be all right by to-morrow if it were not for the tree!'

'The tree again—always the tree! O, father, don't worry so about that. You know it can do you no harm.'

'Who have ye had talking to 'ee downstairs?'

'A Sherton man called—nothing to trouble about,' she said soothingly. 'Father,' she went on, 'can Mrs Charmond turn us out of our house if she's minded to?'

'Turn us out? No. Nobody can turn us out till my poor soul is turned out of my body. 'Tis lifehold, like Giles Winterborne's. But when my life drops 'twill be hers—not till then.' His words on this subject so far had been rational and firm enough. But now he lapsed into his moaning strain: 'And the tree will do it—that tree will soon be the death of me.'

'Nonsense, you know better. How can it be?' She refrained from further speech, and descended to the ground floor again.

'Thank Heaven then,' she said to herself, 'what belongs to me I keep.'

CHAPTER THREE

T HE lights in the village went out, house after house, till there only remained two in the darkness. One of these came from a residence on the hill-side — that of the young medical gentleman in league with the devil, of whom there is something to be said later on; the other shone from the window of Marty South. Precisely the same extinguished effect was produced here, however, by her rising when the clock struck ten and hanging up a thick cloth curtain. The door it was necessary to keep ajar in hers as in most cottages because of the smoke; but she obviated the effect of the riband of light through the chink by hanging a cloth over that also. She was one of these people who, if they have to work harder than their neighbours, prefer to keep the necessity a secret as far as possible; and, but for the slight sounds of wood-splintering which came from within, no wayfarer would have perceived that here the cottager did not sleep as elsewhere.

Eleven, twelve, one o'clock struck; the heap of spars grew higher, and the pile of chips and ends more bulky. Even the light on the hill had now been extinguished; but still she worked on. When the temperature of the night without had fallen so low as to make her chilly she opened a large blue umbrella to ward off the draught from the door. The two sovereigns confronted her from the looking-glass in such a manner as to suggest a pair of jaundiced eyes on the watch for an opportunity. Whenever she sighed for weariness she lifted her gaze towards them, but withdrew it quickly, stroking her tresses for a moment as if to convince herself that they were still secure. When the clock struck three she arose and tied up the spars she had last made in a bundle resembling those that lay against the wall.

She wrapped round her a long red woollen cravat and opened the door. The night in all its fulness met her flatly on the threshold, like the very brink of an absolute void, or the ante-mundane Ginnung-Gap believed in by her Teuton forefathers. For her eyes were fresh from the blaze, and here there was no street lamp or lantern to form a kindly transition between the inner glare and the outer dark. A lingering wind brought to her ear the creaking sound of two overcrowded branches in the neighbouring wood, which were rubbing each other into wounds, and other vocalized sorrows of the trees, together with the screech of owls, and the fluttering tumble of some awkward wood-pigeon ill-balanced on its roosting-bough.

But the pupils of her young eyes soon expanded, and she could see well enough for her purpose. Taking a bundle of spars under each arm, and guided by the serrated line of tree-tops against the sky, she went some hundred yards or more down the lane till she reached a long open shed, carpeted around with the dead leaves that lay about everywhere. Night, that strange personality which within walls brings ominous introspectiveness and self-distrust, but under the open sky banishes such subjective anxieties as too trivial for thought, gave to Marty South a less perturbed and brisker manner now. She laid the spars on the ground within

the shed and returned for more, going to and fro till her whole manufactured stock was deposited here.

This erection was the waggon-house of the chief man of business hereabout, Mr George Melbury, the timber, bark, and copse-ware merchant for whom Marty's father did work of this sort by the piece. It formed one of the many rambling outhouses which surrounded his dwelling, an equally irregular block of building whose immense chimneys could just be discerned even now. The four huge waggons under the shed were built on those ancient lines whose proportions have been ousted by modern patterns, their shapes bulging and curving at the base and ends like Trafalgar line-of-battle ships, with which venerable hulks, indeed, these vehicles evidenced a constructive spirit curiously in harmony. One was laden with sheep-cribs, another with hurdles, another with ash poles, and the fourth, at the foot of which she had placed her thatching-spars, was half full of similar bundles.

She was pausing a moment with that easeful sense of accomplishment which follows work done that has been a hard struggle in the doing, when she heard a woman's voice on the other side of the hedge say anxiously, 'George!'

In a moment the name was repeated, with 'Do come indoors! What are you doing there?'

The cart-house adjoined the garden, and before Marty had moved she saw enter the latter from the timber-merchant's back door an elderly woman sheltering a candle with her hand, the light from which cast a moving thorn-pattern of shade on Marty's face. Its rays soon fell upon a man whose clothes were carelessly thrown on, standing in advance of the speaker. He was a thin, slightly stooping figure, with a small, nervous mouth, and a face cleanly shaven; and he walked along the path with his eyes bent on the ground. In the pair Marty South recognized her employer Melbury and his wife. She was the second Mrs Melbury, the first having died shortly after the birth of the timber-merchant's only child.

''Tis no use to stay in bed!' he said, as soon as she came up to where he was pacing restlessly about. 'I can't sleep. I keep thinking of things.'

'What things?'

He did not answer.

'The lady at the Great House?'

'No.'

'The turnpike bonds?'

'No. Though I wish I hadn't got 'em.'

'The ghosts of the Two Brothers?'

He shook his head.

'Not about Grace again?'

'Yes. 'Tis she.'

(Grace was the speaker's only daughter.)

'Why worry about her always?'

'First, I cannot think why she doesn't answer my letter. She must be ill.'

'No, no. Things only appear so gloomy in the night-time.'

'Second, I have not invested any money specially for her, to put her out of the reach of poverty if my affairs fail.'

'They are safe. Besides, she is sure to marry well.'

'You are wrong. That's my third trouble. I have, as I have hinted to you a dozen times, that plan in my head about her, and according to my plan she won't marry well.'

'Why won't it be marrying well?' said his wife.

'Because it is a plan for her to marry that particular person, Giles Winterborne, and he is poor.'

'Well, it is all right. Love will make up for his want of money. He adores the very ground she walks on.'

(Marty South started, and could not tear herself away.)

'Yes,' said the timber-merchant; 'I know that well. There will be no lack of that with him. But since I have educated her so well, and so long, and so far above the level of the daughters hereabout, it is *wasting her* to give her to a man of no higher standing than he.'

'Then why do it?' she asked.

'Why, as you must surely see, it is in obedience to that solemn resolve I made. . . . I made it because I did his father a terrible wrong; and it has been a weight on my conscience ever since that time, till this scheme of making amends occurred to me through seeing that Giles liked her.'   •

'Wronged his father?' asked Mrs Melbury.

'Yes, grievously wronged him,' said her husband. 'I have spoken of it to you.'

'Well, don't think of it to-night,' she urged. 'Come indoors.'

'No, no; the air cools my head. I shall not stay long.'

He was silent awhile; then he reminded her that his first wife, his daughter's mother, was first the promised of Winterborne's father, who loved her tenderly, till he, the speaker, won her away from him by a trick, because he wanted to marry her himself. He went on to say that the other man's happiness was ruined by it; that though he married Winterborne's mother it was but a half-hearted business with him. Thus much Marty had heard before. Melbury added that he was afterwards very miserable at what he had done; but that as time went on, and the children grew up, and seemed to be attached to each other, he determined to do all he could to right the wrong by letting his daughter marry the lad; not only that, but to give her the best education he could afford, so as to make the gift as valuable a one as it lay in his power to bestow. 'I still mean to do it,' said Melbury.

'Then do,' said she.

'But all these things trouble me,' said he; 'for I feel I am sacrificing her for my own sin; and I think of her, and often come down here to look at this. I have come to-night to do so once more.'

He took the candle from her hand, held it to the ground, and removed a tile which lay in the garden-path. ''Tis the track of her shoe that she made when she ran down here the day before she went away all those months ago. I covered it up when she was gone; and when I come here to look at it, I ask myself again, why should she be sacrificed to a poor man?'

'It is not altogether a sacrifice,' said the woman. 'He is in love with her, and he's honest and upright. If she encourages him, what can you wish for more?'

'I wish for nothing definite. But there's a lot of things possible for her. Why, Mrs Charmond is wanting some refined young lady, I hear, to go abroad with her – as companion or something of the kind. She'd jump at Grace.'

'That's all uncertain. Better stick to what's sure.'

'True, true,' said Melbury; 'and I hope it will be for the best. Yes, let me get 'em married up as soon as I can, so as to have it over and done with.' He continued looking at the imprint while he added, 'Suppose she should be dying, and never make a track on this path any more?'

'She'll write soon, depend upon't. Come, 'tis wrong to stay here and brood so.'

He admitted it, but said he could not help it. 'Whether she write or no, I shall fetch her in a few days.' And thus speaking he covered the shoe-track, and preceded his wife indoors.

Melbury perhaps was an unlucky man in having the sentiment which could make him wander out in the night to regard the imprint of a daughter's footstep. Nature does not carry on her government with a view to such feelings; and when advancing years render the opened hearts of those that possess them less dexterous than formerly in shutting against the blast, they must inevitably, like little celandines, suffer 'buffeting at will by rain and storm'.

But her own existence, and not Mr Melbury's, was the centre of Marty's consciousness, and it was in relation to this that the matter struck her as she slowly withdrew.

'That, then, is the secret of it all,' she said. 'I had half thought so. And Giles Winterborne is not for me!'

She returned to her cottage. The sovereigns were staring at her from the looking-glass as she had left them. With a preoccupied countenance, and with tears in her eyes, she got a pair of scissors and began mercilessly cutting off the long locks of her hair, arranging and tying them with their points all one way as the barber had directed. Upon the pale scrubbed deal of the coffin-stool table they stretched like waving and ropy weeds over the washed white bed of a stream.

She would not turn again to the little looking-glass out of humanity to herself, knowing what a deflowered visage would look back at her and almost break her heart; she dreaded it as much as did her own ancestral goddess the reflection in the pool after the rape of her locks by Loke the Malicious. She steadily stuck to business, wrapped the hair in a parcel, and sealed it up; after which she raked out the fire and went to bed, having first set up an alarum made of a candle and piece of thread with a stone attached.

But such a reminder was unnecessary to-night. Having tossed about till five o'clock Marty heard the sparrows walking down their long holes in the thatch above her sloping ceiling to their exits at the eaves; whereupon she also arose and descended to the ground floor.

It was still dark, but she began moving about the house in those automatic initiatory acts and touches which represent among house-wives the installation of another day. While thus engaged she heard the rumbling of Mr Melbury's waggons, and knew that there, too, the day's toil had begun.

An armful of gads thrown on the still hot embers caused them to blaze up cheerfully, and bring her diminished headgear into sudden prominence as a shadow. At this a step approached the door.

'Are folk astir here yet?' inquired a voice she knew well.

'Yes, Mr Winterborne,' said Marty, throwing on a tilt bonnet, which completely hid the recent ravages of the scissors. 'Come in!'

The door was flung back, and there stepped in upon the mat a man not particularly young for a lover, nor particularly mature for a person of affairs —

each of which functions he in some degree discharged. There was reserve in his glance, and restraint upon his mouth. He carried a perforated lantern which hung upon a swivel and, wheeling as it dangled, marked grotesque shapes upon the shadier part of the walls and ceiling.

He said that he had looked in on his way down to tell her that they did not expect her father to make up his contract if he was not well. Mr Melbury would give him another week, and they would go their journey with a short load that day.

'They are done,' said Marty, 'and lying in the cart-house.'

'Done?' he repeated. 'Your father has not been too ill to work after all, then?'

She made some evasive reply. 'I'll show you where they be, if you are going down,' she added.

They went out and walked together, the pattern of the air-holes in the top of the lantern rising now to the mist overhead, where they appeared of giant size, as if reaching the tent-shaped sky. They had no remarks to make to each other, and they uttered none. Hardly anything could be more isolated or more self-contained than the lives of these two walking here in the lonely hour before day, when grey shades, material and mental, are so very grey. And yet their lonely courses formed no detached design at all, but were part of the pattern in the great web of human doings then weaving in both hemispheres from the White Sea to Cape Horn.

The shed was reached, and she pointed out the spars. Winterborne regarded them silently; then looked at her.

'Now, Marty, I believe—' he said, and shook his head.

'What?'

'That you've done the work yourself!'

'Don't you tell anybody, will you, Mr Winterborne?' she pleaded by way of answer. 'Because I am afraid Mr Melbury may refuse the work if he knows it is mine.'

'But how could you learn to do it? 'Tis a trade!'

'Trade!' said she. 'I'd be bound to learn it in two hours.'

'O no, you wouldn't, Miss Marty.' Winterborne held down his lantern, and examined the cleanly split hazels as they lay. 'Marty,' he said with dry admiration, 'your father with his forty years of practice never made a spar better than that. They are too good for the thatching of houses; they are good enough for the furniture. But I won't tell. Let me look at your hands – your poor hands!'

He had a kindly manner of quietly severe tone; and when she seemed reluctant to show her hands he took hold of one and examined it as if it were his own. Her fingers were blistered.

'They'll get harder in time,' she said. 'For if father continues ill I shall have to go on wi' it. Now I'll help put 'em up in waggon.'

Winterborne without speaking set down his lantern, lifted her like a baby as she was about to stoop over the bundles, dumped her down behind him, and began throwing up the bundles himself. 'Rather than you should do it I will,' he said. 'But the men will be here directly. Why, Marty – whatever has happened to your head? Lord, it has shrunk to nothing – it looks like an apple upon a gate-post!'

Her heart swelled, and she could not speak. At length she managed to groan, looking on the ground, 'I've made myself ugly – and hateful – that's what I've done!'

'No, no,' he answered. 'You've only cut your hair – I see now.'

'Then why must you needs say that about apples and gate-posts?'

'Let me see!' He moved to lift her bonnet.

But she ran off into the gloom of the sluggish dawn. He did not attempt to follow her. When she reached her father's door she stood on the step and looked back. Mr Melbury's men had arrived and were loading up the spars; and their foggy lanterns appeared from the distance at which she stood to have wan circles round them, like eyes weary with watching. She observed them for a few seconds as they set about harnessing the horses, and then went indoors.

CHAPTER FOUR

T HERE was now a distinct manifestation of morning in the air, and presently the bleared white visage of a sunless winter day emerged like a dead-born child. The woodlanders everywhere had already bestirred themselves, rising this month of the year at the far less dreary time of absolute darkness. It had been above an hour earlier, before a single bird had untucked his head, that twenty lights were struck in as many bedrooms, twenty pairs of shutters opened, and twenty pairs of eyes stretched to the sky to forecast the weather for the day.

Owls that had been catching mice in the outhouses, rabbits that had been eating the winter-greens in the gardens, and stoats that had been sucking the blood of the rabbits, discerning that their human neighbours were on the move discreetly withdrew from publicity, and were seen and heard no more till nightfall.

The daylight revealed the whole of Mr Melbury's homestead, of which the waggon-sheds had been an outlying erection. It formed three sides of an open quadrangle, and consisted of all sorts of buildings, the largest and central one being the dwelling itself. The fourth side of the quadrangle was the public road.

It was a dwelling-house of respectable, roomy, almost dignified aspect; which, taken with the fact that there were the remains of other such buildings hereabout, indicated that Little Hintock had at some time or other been of greater importance than now. The house was of no marked antiquity, yet of a well-advanced age; older than a stale novelty, but no canonized antique; faded, not hoary; looking at you from the still distinct middle-distance of the early Georgian time, and awakening on that account the instincts of reminiscence more decidedly than the remoter, and far grander, memorials which have to speak from the misty reaches of mediævalism. The faces, dress, passions, gratitudes, and revenges of the great-great-grandfathers and grandmothers who had been the first to gaze from those rectangular windows, and had stood under that keystoned doorway, could be divined and measured by homely standards of to-day. It was a house in whose reverberations queer old personal tales were yet audible if properly listened for; and not, as with those of the castle and cloister, silent beyond the possibility of echo.

The garden-front remained much as it had always been, and there was a porch and entrance that way. But the principal house-door opened on the square yard or quadrangle towards the road, formerly a regular carriage entrance, though the middle of the area was now made use of for stacking timber, faggots, hurdles, and other products of the wood. It was divided from the lane by a lichen-coated wall, in which hung a pair of gates, flanked by piers out of the perpendicular, with a round white ball on the top of each.

The building on the left of the inclosure was a long-backed erection, now used for spar-making, sawing, crib-framing, and copse-ware manufacture in general. Opposite were the waggon-sheds where Marty had deposited her spars.

Here Winterborne had remained after the girl's abrupt departure, to see that the loads were properly made up. Winterborne was connected with the Melbury family in various ways. In addition to the sentimental relationship which arose from his father having been the first Mrs Melbury's lover, Winterborne's aunt had married and emigrated with the brother of the timber-merchant many years before – an alliance that was sufficient to place Winterborne, though the poorer, on a footing of social intimacy with the Melburys. As in most villages so secluded as this, intermarriages were of Hapsburgian frequency among the inhabitants, and there were hardly two houses in Little Hintock unrelated by some matrimonial tie or other.

For this reason a curious kind of partnership existed between Melbury and the younger man – a partnership based upon an unwritten code, by which each acted in the way he thought fair towards the other, on a give-and-take principle. Melbury, with his timber and copse-ware business, found that the weight of his labour came in winter and spring. Winterborne was in the apple and cider trade, and his requirements in cartage and other work came in the autumn of each year. Hence horses, waggons, and in some degree men, were handed over to him when the apples began to fall; he, in return, lending his assistance to Melbury in the busiest wood-cutting season, as now.

Before he had left the shed a boy came from the house to ask him to remain till Mr Melbury had seen him. Winterborne thereupon crossed over to the spar-house where some journeymen were already at work, two of them being travelling spar-makers from Stagfoot Lane, who, when the fall of the leaf began, made their appearance regularly, and when winter was over disappeared in silence till the season came again.

Firewood was the one thing abundant in Little Hintock; and a blaze of gad-ends made the outhouse gay with its light, which vied with that of the day as yet. In the hollow shades of the roof could be seen dangling and etiolated arms of ivy which had crept through the joints of the tiles and were groping in vain for some support, their leaves being dwarfed and sickly for want of sunlight; others were pushing in with such force at the eaves as to lift from their supports the shelves that were fixed there.

Besides the itinerant journey-workers there were also present John Upjohn, Melbury's regular man; a neighbour engaged in the hollow-turnery trade; old Timothy Tangs and young Timothy Tangs, top and bottom sawyers at work in Mr Melbury's pit outside; Farmer Cawtree, who kept the cider-house, and

Robert Creedle, an old man who worked for Winterborne, and stood warming his hands; these latter having been enticed in by the ruddy blaze, though they had no particular business there. None of them calls for any remark, except perhaps Creedle. To have completely described him it would have been necessary to write a military memoir, for he wore under his smock-frock a cast-off soldier's jacket that had seen hot service, its collar showing just above the flap of the frock; also a hunting memoir, to include the top-boots that he had picked up by chance; also chronicles of voyaging and shipwreck, for his pocket-knife had been given him by a weather-beaten sailor. But Creedle carried about with him on his uneventful rounds these silent testimonies of war, sport, and adventure, and thought nothing of their associations or their stories.

Copse-work, as it was called, being an occupation which the secondary intelligence of the hands and arms could carry on without the sovereign attention of the head, allowed the minds of its professors to wander considerably from the objects before them; hence the tales, chronicles, and ramifications of family history which were recounted here were of a very exhaustive kind.

Winterborne, seeing that Melbury had not arrived, stepped back again outside the door; and the conversation interrupted by his momentary presence flowed anew, reaching his ears as an accompaniment to the regular dripping of the fog from the plantation boughs around.

The topic at present handled was a highly popular and frequent one – the personal character of Mrs Charmond, the owner of the surrounding glades and groves.

'My brother-in-law told me, and I have no reason to doubt it,' said Creedle, 'that she'll sit down to her dinner with a gown hardly higher than her elbows. "O, you wicked woman!" he said to hisself when he first see her, "you go to the Table o' Sundays, and kneel, as if your knee-jints were greased with very saint's anointment, and tell off your hear-us-good-Lords as pat as a business-man counting money; and yet you can eat your victuals a-stript to such a wanton figure as that!" Whether she's a reformed character by this time I can't say; but I don't care who the man is, that's how she went on when my brother-in-law lived there.'

'Did she do it in her husband's time?'

'That I don't know – hardly, I should think, considering his temper. Ah—!' Here Creedle threw grieved remembrances into physical form by resigning his head to obliquity and letting his eyes water. 'That man! "Not if the angels of heaven come down, Creedle," he said, "shall you do another day's work for me!" Yes – he would as soon take a winged angel's name in vain as yours or mine! Well, now I must get these spars home-along, and to-morrow, thank God, I must see about using 'em.'

An old woman now entered upon the scene. She was Mr Melbury's servant, and passed a great part of her time in crossing the yard between the house-door and the spar-shed, whither she had come now for fuel. She had two facial aspects – one, of a soft and flexible kind, which she used indoors; the other, with stiff lines and corners, which she assumed when addressing the men outside.

'Ah, Grammer Oliver,' said John Upjohn, 'it do do my heart good to see a old woman like you so dapper and stirring, when I bear in mind that, after fifty, one year counts as two did afore! But your smoke didn't rise this morning till twenty minutes past seven by my beater; and that's late, Grammer Oliver.'

'If you was a full-sized man, John, I might take notice of your scornful meanings. But really a woman couldn't feel hurt if such smallness were to spit fire and brimstone itself at her. Here,' she added, holding out a spar-gad to one of the workmen, from which dangled a long black-pudding, 'here's something for thy breakfast, and if you want tea you must fetch it from indoors.'

'Mr Melbury is late this morning,' said the bottom-sawyer.

'Yes. 'Twas a dark dawn,' said Mrs Oliver. 'Even when I opened the door, so late as I was, you couldn't have told poor men from gentlemen, or John from a reasonable-sized object. And I don't think maister's slept at all well to-night. He's anxious about his daughter; and I know what that is, for I've cried bucketfuls for my own.'

When the old woman had gone Creedle said –

'He'll fret his gizzard green if he don't soon hear from that maid of his. Well, learning is better than houses and lands. But to keep a maid at school till she is taller out of pattens than her mother was in 'em – 'tis a tempting o' Providence.'

'It seems no time ago that she was a little playward girl,' said young Timothy Tangs.

'I can mind her mother,' said the hollow-turner. 'Alway a teuny, delicate piece; her touch upon your hand was like the passing of wind. She was inoculated for the small-pox and had it beautiful fine, just about the time that I was out of my apprenticeship – ay, and a long apprenticeship 'twas. I served that master of mine six years and three hundred and fourteen days.'

The hollow-turner pronounced the days with emphasis, as if, considering their number, they were a rather more remarkable fact than the years.

'Mr Winterborne's father walked with her at one time,' said old Timothy Tangs; 'but Mr Melbury won her. She was a child of a woman, and would cry like rain if so be he huffed her. Whenever she and her husband came to a puddle in their walks together he'd take her up like a half-penny doll and put her over without dirting her a speck. And if he keeps the daughter so long at boarding-school he'll make her as nesh as her mother was. But here he comes.'

Just before this moment Winterborne had seen Melbury crossing the court from his door. He was carrying an open letter in his hand, and came straight to Winterborne. His gloom of the preceding night had quite gone.

'I'd no sooner made up my mind, Giles, to go and see why Grace didn't come or write than I get a letter from her. "My dear father," says she, "I'm coming home to-morrow (that's to-day), but I didn't think it worth while to write long beforehand." The little rascal, and didn't she! Now, Giles, as you are going to Sherton market to-day with your apple-trees, why not join me and Grace there, and we'll drive home all together?'

He made the proposal with cheerful energy; he was hardly the same man as the man of the small dark hours. Even among the moodiest the tendency to be cheered is stronger than the tendency to be cast down; and a soul's specific gravity constantly re-asserts itself as less than that of the sea of troubles into which it is thrown.

Winterborne, though not demonstrative, replied to this suggestion with alacrity. There was not much doubt that Marty's grounds for cutting off her hair were substantial enough, if this man's eyes had been a reason for keeping it on. As for the timber-merchant, his invitation had been given solely in pursuance of his scheme for uniting the pair. He had made up his mind to the course as a duty, and was strenuously bent upon following it out.

Accompanied by Winterborne he now turned towards the door of the spar-house, when his footsteps were heard by the men as aforesaid.

'Well, John, and Robert,' he said, nodding as he entered. 'A rimy morning.'

''Tis, sir!' said Creedle energetically, for not having as yet been able to summon force sufficient to go away and begin work he felt the necessity of throwing some into his speech. 'I don't care who the man is, 'tis the rimiest morning we've had this fall.'

'I heard you wondering why I've kept my daughter so long at boarding-school,' said Mr Melbury, looking up from the letter which he was reading anew by the fire, and turning to them with the suddenness that was a trait in him. 'Hey?' he asked with affected shrewdness. 'But you did, you know. Well now, though it is my own business more than anybody else's, I'll tell ye. When I was a boy, another boy – the pa'son's son – along with a lot of others, asked me "Who dragged Whom round the walls of What?" and I said, "Sam Barret, who dragged his wife in a wheeled chair round the tower when she went to be churched." They laughed at me so much that I went home and couldn't sleep for shame; and I cried that night till my pillow was wet; till I thought to myself – "They may laugh at me for my ignorance, but that was father's fault, and none o' my making, and I must bear it. But they shall never laugh at my children, if I have any; I'll starve first!" Thank God I've been able to keep her at school at the figure of near a hundred a year; and her scholarship is such that she has stayed on as governess for a time. Let 'em laugh now if they can: Mrs Charmond herself is not better informed than my girl Grace.'

There was something between high indifference and humble emotion in his delivery, which made it difficult for them to reply. Winterborne's interest was of a kind which did not show itself in words; listening, he stood by the fire, mechanically stirring the embers with a spar-gad.

'You'll be ready, then, Giles?' Melbury continued, awaking from a reverie. 'Well, what was the latest news at Shottsford yesterday, Mr Cawtree?'

'Oh, well Shottsford is Shottsford still – you can't victual your carcase there unless you've got money; and you can't buy a cup of genuine there, whether or no. . . . But as the saying is, "Go abroad and you'll hear news of home." It seems that our new neighbour, this young Doctor What's-his-name, is a strange, deep, perusing gentleman; and there's good reason for supposing he has sold his soul to the wicked one.'

''Od name it all,' murmured the timber-merchant, unimpressed by the news but reminded of other things by the subject of it; 'I've got to meet a gentleman this very morning, and yet I've planned to go to Sherton Abbas for the maid.'

'I won't praise the doctor's wisdom till I hear what sort of bargain he's made,' said the top-sawyer.

''Tis only an old woman's tale,' said Cawtree. 'But it seems that he wanted certain books on some mysterious black art, and in order that the people hereabout should not know anything about them he ordered 'em direct from

London, and not from the Sherton book-seller. The parcel was delivered by mistake at the pa'son's, and as he wasn't at home his wife opened it, and went into hysterics when she read 'em, thinking her husband had turned heathen, and 'twould be the ruin of the children. But when he came he knew no more about 'em than she; and found they were this Mr Fitzpiers's property. So he wrote "Beware!" outside, and sent 'em on by the sexton.'

'He must be a curious young man,' mused the hollow-turner.

'He must,' said Timothy Tangs.

'Nonsense,' said Mr Melbury; 'he's only a gentleman fond of science and philosophy, and poetry, and, in fact, every kind of knowledge; and being lonely here he passes his time in making such matters his hobby.'

'Well,' said old Timothy, ''tis a strange thing about doctors that the worse they be the better they be. I mean that if you hear anything of this sort about 'em ten to one they can cure 'ee as nobody else can.'

'True,' said Cawtree emphatically. 'And for my part I shall take my custom from old Jones and go to this one directly I've anything the matter inside me. That last medicine old Jones gave me had no taste in it at all.'

Mr Melbury, as became a well-informed man, did not listen to these recitals, being moreover preoccupied with the business appointment which had come into his head. He walked up and down looking on the floor – his usual custom when undecided. That stiffness about the arm, hip, and knee-joint, which was apparent when he walked, was the net product of the divers sprains and over-exertions that had been required of him in handling trees and timber when a young man, for he was of the sort called self-made, and had worked hard. He knew the origin of every one of these cramps; that in his left shoulder had come of carrying a pollard, unassisted, from Tutcombe Bottom home; that in one leg was caused by the crash of an elm against it when they were felling; that in the other was from lifting a bole. On many a morrow, after wearying himself by these prodigious muscular efforts, he had risen from his bed fresh as usual; and confident in the recuperative power of his youth he had repeated the strains anew. But treacherous Time had been only hiding ill-results when they could be guarded against for greater effect when they could not. Now in his declining years the store had been unfolded in the form of rheumatisms, pricks, and spasms, in every one of which Melbury recognized some act which, had its consequences been contemporaneously made known, he would wisely have abstained from repeating.

On a summons by Grammer Oliver to breakfast he went to the kitchen, where the family breakfasted in winter to save house-labour; and sitting down by the fire looked a long time at the pair of dancing shadows cast by each fire-iron and dog-knob on the white-washed chimney corner – a yellow one from the window, and a blue one from the fire.

'I don't quite know what to do to-day,' he said to his wife at last. 'I've recollected that I promised to meet Mrs Charmond's steward in Round Wood at twelve o'clock, and yet I want to go for Grace.'

'Why not let Giles fetch her by himself? 'Twill bring 'em together all the quicker.'

'I could do that – but I always have gone, without fail, every time hitherto; and perhaps she'll be disappointed if I stay away.'

'You may be disappointed, but I don't think she will, if you send Giles,' said Mrs Melbury dryly.

'Very well – I'll send him.'

Melbury was often persuaded by the quiet of his wife's words when strenuous argument would have had no effect. This second Mrs Melbury was a placid woman who had been nurse to his child Grace after her mother's death. Little Grace had clung to the nurse with much affection; and ultimately Melbury, in dread lest the only woman who cared for the girl should be induced to leave her, persuaded the mild Lucy to marry him. The arrangement – for it was little more – had worked satisfactorily enough; Grace had thriven, and Melbury had not repented.

He returned to the spar-house and found Giles near at hand, to whom he explained the change of plan. 'As she won't arrive till five o'clock you can get your business very well over in time to receive her,' said Melbury. 'The green gig will do for her; you'll spin along quicker with that, and won't be late upon the road. Her boxes can be called for by one of the waggons.'

Winterborne, knowing nothing of the timber-merchant's restitutory aims, quietly thought this to be a kindly chance. Wishing, even more than her father, to despatch his apple-tree business in the market before Grace's arrival, he prepared to start at once.

Melbury was careful that the turn-out should be seemly. The gig-wheels, for instance, were not always washed during winter-time before a journey, the muddy roads rendering that labour useless; but they were washed to-day. The harness was polished, and when the grey horse had been put in, and Winterborne was in his seat ready to start, Mr Melbury stepped out with a blacking-brush and with his own hands touched over the yellow hoofs of the animal.

'You see, Giles,' he said as he blacked, 'coming from a fashionable school she might feel shocked at the homeliness of home; and 'tis these little things that catch a dainty woman's eye if they are neglected. We, living here alone, don't notice how the whitey-brown creeps out of the earth over us; but she, fresh from a city – why, she'll notice everything!'

'That she will,' said Giles.

'And scorn us if we don't mind.'

'Not scorn us.'

'No, no, no – that's only words. She's too good a girl to do that. But when we consider what she knows, and what she has seen since she last saw us, 'tis as well to meet her views. Why, 'tis a year since she was in this old place, owing to her going abroad in the summer; and naturally we shall look small, just at first – I only say just at first.'

Mr Melbury's tone evinced a certain exultation in the very sense of that inferiority he affected to deplore; for this advanced and refined being, was she not his own all the time? Not so Giles; he felt doubtful. He looked at his clothes with misgiving; but said nothing.

It was his custom during the planting season to carry a specimen apple-tree to market with him as an advertisement of what he dealt in. This had been tied across the gig; and mounting in front he drove away, the twigs nodding with each step of the horse. Melbury went indoors. Before the gig had passed out of sight Mr Melbury reappeared and shouted after –

'Here, Giles,' he said, breathlessly following with some wraps, 'it may be very chilly to-night, and she may want something extra about her. And Giles,' he added, when the young man put the horse in motion once more, 'tell her that I should have come myself, but I had particular business with Mrs Charmond's agent which prevented me. Don't forget.'

He watched Winterborne out of sight under the boughs, where cobwebs glistened in the now clearing air, lengthening and shortening their shine like elastic needles; he saw the wood-pigeons rise as Giles drove past them; and said to himself with a jerk – a shape into which emotion with him often resolved itself – 'There now, I hope the two will bring it to a point, and have done with it! 'Tis a pity to let such a girl throw herself away upon him – a thousand pities! . . . And yet 'tis my duty, for his father's sake.'

CHAPTER FIVE

WINTERBORNE sped on his way to Sherton Abbas without elation and without discomposure. Had he regarded his inner self spectacularly, as lovers are now daily more wont to do, he might have felt pride in the discernment of a somewhat rare power in him – that of keeping not only judgment but emotion suspended in difficult cases. But he noted it not.

Arrived at the entrance to a long flat lane, which had taken the spirit out of many a pedestrian in times when, with the majority, to travel meant to walk, he saw before him the trim figure of a young woman in pattens, journeying with that steadfast concentration which means purpose and not pleasure. He was soon near enough to see that she was Marty South. Click click, click went the pattens; and she did not turn her head.

Yet she had seen him, and shrank from being overtaken by him thus; but as it was inevitable she braced herself up for his inspection by closing her lips so as to make her mouth quite unemotional, and by throwing an additional firmness into her tread.

'Why do you wear pattens, Marty? The turnpike is clean enough although the lanes are muddy.'

'They save my boots.'

'But twelve miles in pattens – 'twill twist your feet off. Come, get up and ride with me.'

She hesitated, removed her pattens, knocked the gravel out of them against the wheel, and mounted in front of the nodding specimen apple-tree. She had so arranged her bonnet with a full border and trimmings that her lack of long hair did not much injure her appearance; though Giles of course saw that it was gone, and may have guessed her motive in parting with it; such sales, though infrequent, being not unheard-of in that locality.

But nature's adornment was still hard by – in fact, within two feet of him. In Marty's basket was a brown-paper packet, and in the packet the chestnut locks which, by reason of the barber's request for secrecy, she had not ventured to intrust to other hands.

Giles asked, with some hesitation, how her father was getting on.

He was better, she said; he would be able to work in a day or two; he would be quite well but for his craze about the tree falling on him.

'You know why I don't ask for him so often as I might, I suppose?' said Winterborne. 'Or don't you know?'

'I think I do.'

'Because of the houses?'

She nodded.

'Yes. I am afraid it may seem that my anxiety is about those houses which I should lose by his death, more than about him. Marty, I do feel anxious about the houses, since half my income depends upon them; but I do likewise care for him; and it almost seems wrong that houses should be leased for lives, so as to lead to such mixed feelings.'

'After father's death they will be Mrs Charmond's?'

'They'll be hers.'

'They are going to keep company with my hair,' she thought.

Thus talking they reached the ancient town of Sherton Abbas. By no pressure would she ride up the street with him. 'That's the right of another woman,' she said with playful malice as she put on her pattens. 'I wonder what you are thinking of! Thank you for the lift in that handsome gig. Good-bye.'

He blushed a little, shook his head at her, and drove on ahead into the streets; the churches, the abbey, and other mediæval buildings on this clear bright morning having the linear distinctness of architectural drawings, as if the original dream and vision of the conceiving master-mason were for a brief hour flashed down through the centuries to an unappreciative age. Giles saw their eloquent look on this day of transparency, but could not construe it. He turned into the inn-yard.

Marty, following the same track, marched promptly to the hair-dresser's. Percomb was the chief of his trade in Sherton Abbas. He had the patronage of such county off-shoots as had been obliged to seek the shelter of small houses in that venerable town, of the local clergy, and so on; for some of whom he had made wigs, while others among them had compensated for neglecting him in their lifetime by patronizing him when they were dead, and letting him shave their corpses. On the strength of all this he had taken down his pole and called himself 'Perruquier to the aristocracy'.

Nevertheless, this sort of support did not quite fill his children's mouths, and they had to be filled. So behind his house there was a little yard, reached by a passage from the back street, and in that yard was a pole, and under the pole a shop of quite another description than the ornamental one in the front street. Here on Saturday nights from seven till ten he took an almost innumerable succession of twopences from the farm-labourers who flocked thither in crowds from the country. And thus he lived.

Marty, of course, went to the front shop, and handed her packet to him silently.

'Thank you,' said the barber quite joyfully. 'I hardly expected it after what you said last night.'

She turned aside, while a tear welled up in each eye at this reminder.

'Nothing of what I told you,' he whispered. 'But I can trust you, I see.'

She had now reached the end of this distressing business, and went listlessly along the street to attend to other errands. These occupied her till four o'clock, at which time she recrossed the market-place. It was impossible to avoid rediscovering Winterborne every time she passed that way, for standing, as he always did at this season of the year, with his specimen apple-tree in the midst, the boughs rose above the heads of the farmers, and brought a delightful suggestion of orchards into the heart of the town.

When her eye fell upon him for the last time he was standing somewhat apart, holding the tree like an ensign, and looking on the ground instead of pushing his produce as he ought to have been doing. He was, in fact, not a very successful seller either of his trees or of his cider, his habit of speaking his mind when he spoke at all militating against this branch of his business.

While she regarded him he lifted his eyes in a direction away from Marty, and his face kindled with recognition and surprise. She followed his gaze and saw walking across to him a flexible young creature in whom she perceived the features of her she had known as Miss Grace Melbury, but now looking glorified and refined to much above her former level. Winterborne, being fixed to the spot by his apple-tree, could not advance to meet her: he held out his spare hand with his hat in it, and with some embarrassment beheld her coming on tip-toe through the mud to the middle of the square where he stood.

Miss Melbury, as Marty could see, had not been expected by Giles so early. Indeed, her father had named five o'clock as her probable time, for which reason that hour had been looming out all the day in his forward perspective like an important edifice on a dull plain. Now here she was come, he knew not how, and his arranged welcome stultified.

His face became gloomy at her necessity for stepping into the road, and more still at the little look of shamefacedness she showed at having to perform the meeting with him under an apple-tree ten feet high in the middle of the market-place. Having had occasion to take off the new gloves she had bought to come home in she held out to him a hand graduating from pink at the tips of the fingers to white at the palm; and the reception formed a scene, with the tree over their heads, which was not by any means an ordinary one in town streets.

The greeting in her looks and on her lips had a restrained shape, which perhaps was not unnatural. For true it was that Giles Winterborne, though well-attired and well-mannered for a yeoman, looked rough beside her. It had sometimes dimly occurred to him, in his ruminating silences at Little Hintock, that external phenomena – such as the lowness or height or colour of a hat, the fold of a coat, the make of a boot, or the chance attitude of a limb at the instant of view – may have a great influence upon feminine opinion of a man's worth, so frequently founded on non-essentials; but a certain causticity of mental tone towards himself and the world in general had prevented to-day, as always, any enthusiastic action on the strength of that reflection; and her momentary instinct of reserve at first sight of him was the penalty he paid for his laxness.

He gave away the tree to a bystander as soon as he could find one who would accept the cumbersome gift, and the twain moved on towards the inn at which he had put up. Marty made as if to step forward for the pleasure of being recognized by Miss Melbury; but abruptly checking herself she glided behind a carrier's van, saying dryly, 'No; I bain't wanted there'; and critically regarded Winterborne's companion.

It would have been difficult to describe Grace Melbury with precision, either then or at any time. Nay, from the highest point of view, to precisely describe a human being, the focus of a universe, how impossible! But apart from transcendentalism, there never probably lived a person who was in herself more completely a *reductio ad absurdum* of attempts to appraise a woman, even externally, by items of face and figure.

Speaking generally it may be said that she was sometimes beautiful, at other times not beautiful, according to the state of her health and spirits.

In simple corporeal presentment she was of a fair and clear complexion, rather pale than pink, slim in build and elastic in movement. Her look expressed a tendency to wait for others' thoughts before uttering her own; possibly also to wait for others' deeds before her own doings. In her small, delicate mouth, which had hardly settled down to its matured curves, there was a gentleness that might hinder sufficient self-assertion for her own good. She had well-formed eyebrows which, had her portrait been painted, would probably have been done in Prouts's or Vandyke brown.

There was nothing remarkable in her dress just now beyond a natural fitness, and a style that was recent for the streets of Sherton. But had it been quite striking it would have meant just as little. For there can be hardly anything less connected with a woman's personality than drapery which she has neither designed, manufactured, cut, sewed, nor even seen, except by a glance of approval when told that such and such a shape and colour must be had because it has been decided by others as imperative at that particular time.

What people therefore saw of her in a cursory view was very little; in truth, mainly something that was not she. The woman herself was a conjectural creature who had little to do with the outlines presented to Sherton eyes; a shape in the gloom, whose true quality could only be approximated by putting together a movement now and a glance then, in that patient attention which nothing but watchful loving-kindness ever troubles itself to give.

There was a little delay in their setting out from the town, and Marty South took advantage of it to hasten forward with the view of escaping them on the way, lest they should feel compelled to spoil their *tête-à-tête* by asking her to ride. She walked fast, and one-third of the journey was done, and the evening rapidly darkening, before she perceived any sign of them behind her. Then, while ascending a hill, she dimly saw their vehicle drawing near the lowest part of the incline, their heads slightly bent towards each other; drawn together, no doubt, by their souls; as the heads of a pair of horses well in hand are drawn in by the rein. She walked still faster.

But between these and herself there was a carriage, apparently a brougham, coming in the same direction, with lighted lamps. When it overtook her — which was not soon on account of her pace — the scene was much darker, and the lights glared in her eyes sufficiently to hide the details of the equipage.

It occurred to Marty that she might take hold behind this carriage and so keep along with it, to save herself from the patronage of being overtaken and picked up for pity's sake by the coming pair. Accordingly, as the carriage drew abreast of her in climbing the long ascent, she walked close to the wheels, the rays of the nearest lamp penetrating her very pores. She had only just dropped behind when the carriage stopped, and to her surprise the coachman asked her, over his shoulder, if she would ride. What made the question more surprising was that it came in obedience to an order from the interior of the vehicle.

Marty gladly assented, for she was weary, very weary, after working all night and keeping afoot all day. She mounted beside the coachman, wondering why this good fortune had happened to her. He was rather a great man in aspect, and she did not like to inquire of him for some time.

At last she said, 'Who has been so kind as to ask me to ride?'

'Mrs Charmond,' replied her statuesque companion.

Marty was stirred at the name, so closely connected with her last night's experiences. 'Is this her carriage?' she whispered.

'Yes; she's inside.'

Marty reflected, and perceived that Mrs Charmond must have recognized her plodding up the hill under the blaze of the lamp: recognized, probably, her stubbly poll (since she had kept away her face), and thought that those stubbles were the result of her own desire.

Marty South was not so very far wrong. Inside the carriage a pair of deep eyes looked from a ripely handsome face, and though behind those deep eyes was a mind of unfathomed mysteries, beneath them there beat a heart capable of quick, extempore warmth – a heart which could indeed be passionately and im-prudently warm on certain occasions. At present, after recognizing the girl, she had acted on impulse, possibly feeling gratified at the denuded appearance which signified the success of her agent in obtaining what she had required.

' 'Tis wonderful that she should ask 'ee,' observed the majestic coachman presently. 'I have never known her do it before, for as a rule she takes no interest in the village folk at all.'

Marty said no more, but occasionally turned her head to see if she could get a glimpse of the Olympian creature who, as the coach-man had truly observed, hardly ever descended from her clouds into the Tempe-vale of the parishioners. But she could discern nothing of the lady. She also looked for Miss Melbury and Winterborne. The nose of their horse sometimes came quite near the back of Mrs Charmond's carriage. But they never attempted to pass it till the latter conveyance turned towards the park gate, when they sped by. Here the carriage drew up that the gate might be opened; and in the momentary silence Marty heard a gentle oral sound, soft as a breeze.

'What's that?' she whispered.

'Mis'ess yawning.'

'Why should she yawn?'

'Oh, because she's been used to such wonderful good life, and finds it dull here. She'll soon be off again on account of it.'

'So rich and so powerful, and yet to yawn!' the girl murmured. 'Then things don't fay with her any more than with we!'

Marty now alighted; the lamp again shone upon her, and as the carriage rolled on a voice said to her from the interior, 'Good night.'

'Good night, ma'am,' said Marty, dropping a curtsey. But she had not been able to see the woman who began so greatly to interest her – the second person of her own sex who had operated strongly on her mind that day.

CHAPTER SIX

MEANWHILE Winterborne and Grace Melbury had also undergone their little experiences.

As he drove off with her out of the town the glances of people fell upon them, the younger thinking that Mr Winterborne was in a pleasant place, and wondering in what relation he stood towards her. Winterborne himself was unconscious of this. Occupied solely with the idea of having her in charge he did not notice much with outward eye.

Their conversation was in briefest phrase for some time, Grace being somewhat disconcerted through not having understood till they were about to start that Giles was to be her sole conductor, in place of her father. When they had left Sherton Park and Castle nearly out of sight and were in the open country, he spoke.

'Don't Brownley's farm-buildings look strange to you, now they have been moved bodily from the hollow where the old ones stood to the top of the hill?'

She admitted that they did, though she should not have seen any difference in them if he had not pointed it out.

'They had a good crop of bitter-sweets; they couldn't grind them all.' He nodded towards an orchard where some heaps of apples had been left lying ever since the ingathering.

She said 'Yes', but looking at another orchard.

'Why, you are looking at John-apple trees! You know bitter-sweets – you used to well enough?'

'I am afraid I have forgotten, and it is getting too dark to distinguish.'

Winterborne did not continue. It seemed as if the knowledge and interests which had formerly moved Grace's mind had quite died away from her. He wondered whether the special attributes of his image in the past had evaporated like these other things.

However that might be, the fact at present was merely this, that where he was seeing John-apples and farm-buildings she was beholding a much contrasting scene: a broad lawn in the fashionable suburb of a fast city, the evergreen leaves shining in the evening sun, amid which bounding girls, gracefully clad in artistic arrangements of blue, brown, red, and white, were playing at games with laughter and chat in all the pride of life, the notes of piano and harp trembling in the air from the open windows adjoining. Moreover they were girls – and this was a fact which Grace Melbury's delicate femininity could not lose sight of – whose parents Giles would have addressed with a deferential Sir or Madam. Beside this visioned scene the homely farmsteads did not quite hold their own from her present twenty-year point of survey. For all his woodland sequestration

Giles knew the primitive simplicity of the subject he had started, and now sounded a deeper note.

' 'Twas very odd what we said to each other years ago; I often think of it. I mean our saying that if we still liked each other when you were twenty and I twenty-five, we'd—'

'It was child's tattle.'

'H'm?' said Giles suddenly.

'I mean we were young,' said she more considerately. That abrupt manner of his in making inquiries reminded her that he was unaltered.

'Yes . . . I beg your pardon, Miss Melbury; your father *sent* me to meet you to-day.'

'I know it, and I am glad of it.' And she looked at him affectionately.

He seemed satisfied with her and went on – 'At that time you were sitting beside me at the back of your father's covered car when we were coming home from gipsying, all the party being squeezed in together as tight as sheep in an auction-pen. It got darker and darker and I said – I forget the exact words – but I put my arm round your waist, and there you let it stay till your father, sitting in front, suddenly stopped telling his story to Farmer Bollen, to light his pipe. The flash shone into the car, and showed us all up distinctly; my arm flew from your waist like lightning, yet not so quickly but that some of 'em had seen and laughed at us. Yet your father, to our amazement, instead of being angry, was mild as milk, and seemed quite pleased. Have you forgot all that, or haven't you?'

She owned that she remembered it very well, now that he mentioned the circumstances. 'But I must have been in short frocks,' she said slyly.

'Come now, Miss Melbury, that won't do! Short frocks indeed! You know better as well as I.'

Grace thereupon declared that she would not argue with an old friend she valued so highly as she valued him, but if it were as he said, then she was virtually no less than an old woman now, so far did the time seem removed from her present.

'But old feelings come to life again in some people,' she added softly.

'And in others they have never died!' said he.

'Ah – they are Love's very *ownest* and best, I suppose! I don't pretend to rank so high as they.'

'It's not a they – it's a he.'

Grace sighed. 'Shall I tell you all about Brighton or Cheltenham, or places on the Continent that I visited last summer?' she said.

'With all my heart.'

She then described places and persons, avoiding, however, what he most wished to hear – everything specially appertaining to her own inner existence. When she had done she said gaily, 'Now do you tell me in return what has happened in Hintock since I have been away.'

'Anything to keep the conversation away from her and me,' said Giles within him.

It was true; cultivation had so far advanced in the soil of Miss Melbury's mind as to lead her to talk of anything save of that she knew well, and had the greatest interest in developing: herself. She had fallen from the good old Hintock ways.

He had not proceeded far with his somewhat bald narration when they drew near a carriage that had been preceding them for some time in the dusk. Miss Melbury inquired if he knew whose carriage it was.

Winterborne, although he had seen it, had not taken it into account. On examination he said it was Mrs Charmond's.

Grace watched the vehicle and its easy roll, and seemed to feel more nearly akin to it than to the one she was in.

'Pooh—we can polish off the mileage as well as they, come to that,' said Winterborne, reading her mind; and rising to emulation at what it bespoke he whipped on the horse. This it was which had brought the nose of Mr Melbury's grey close to the back of Mrs Charmond's much eclipsing vehicle.

'There's Marty South sitting up with the coachman,' said he, discerning her by her dress.

'Ah, poor Marty! I must ask her to come to see me this very evening. How does she happen to be riding there?'

'I don't know. It is very singular.'

Thus these people with converging destinies went along the road together, till the track of the carriage and that of Winterborne parted, and he turned into Little Hintock, where almost the first house was the timber-merchant's. Pencils of light streamed out of the windows sufficiently to show the white laurustinus flowers, and glance against the polished leaves of laurel. The interior of the rooms could be seen distinctly, warmed up by the fire-flames, which in the parlour were reflected from picture and book-case, and in the kitchen from the utensils and ware.

'Let us look at the dear place for a moment before we call them,' she said.

In the kitchen dinner was preparing; for though Melbury dined at one o'clock at other times to-day the meal had been kept back for Grace. A rickety old spit was in motion, its end being fixed in the fire-dog, and the whole kept going by means of a cord conveyed over pulleys along the ceiling to a large stone suspended in a corner of the room. Old Grammer Oliver came and wound it up with a rattle like that of a mill.

In the parlour a colossal shade of Mrs Melbury's head fell on the wall and ceiling; but before the girl had regarded this room many moments their presence was discovered, and her father and step-mother came out to welcome her.

The character of the Melbury family was of that kind which evinces some shyness in showing strong emotion among each other; a trait frequent in rural households, and one curiously inverse to most of the peculiarities distinguishing villagers from the people of towns. Thus hiding their warmer feelings under commonplace talk all round, Grace's reception produced no extraordinary demonstrations. But that more was felt than was enacted appeared from the fact that her father, in taking her indoors, quite forgot the presence of Giles without, as did also Grace herself.

He said nothing; but took the gig round to the yard and called out from the spar-house the man who attended to these matters when there was no conversation among the spar-makers to particularly engage him. Winterborne then returned to the door with the intention of entering the house.

The family had gone into the parlour, and were still absorbed in themselves. The fire was as before the only light, and it irradiated Grace's face and hands so as to make them look wondrously smooth and fair beside those of the two elders;

shining also through the loose hair about her temples as sunlight through a brake. Her father was surveying her in a dazed conjecture, so much had she developed and progressed in manner and in stature since he last had set eyes on her.

Observing these things Winterborne remained dubious by the door, mechanically tracing with his fingers certain timeworn letters carved in the jambs – initials of bygone generations of householders who had lived and died there.

No, he declared to himself, he would not enter and join the family; they had forgotten him, and it was enough for to-day that he had brought her home. Still, he was a little surprised that her father's eagerness to send him for Grace should have resulted in such indifference as this.

He walked softly away into the lane towards his own house, looking back when he reached the turning from which he could get a last glimpse of the timber-merchant's roof. He hazarded guesses as to what Grace was saying just at that moment, and murmured, with some self-derision, 'nothing about me!' He looked also in the other direction, and saw against the sky the thatched hip and solitary chimney of Marty's cottage, and thought of her too, struggling bravely along under that humble shelter, among her spar-gads and pots and skimmers.

At the timber-merchant's, in the meantime, conversation flowed; and as Giles Winterborne had rightly enough deemed, on subjects in which he had no share. Among the excluding matters there was, as chief, the effect upon Mr Melbury of the womanly mien and manners of his daughter, which took him so much unawares that it thrust back the image of her conductor homeward into quite the obscurest cellarage of his brain.

Another was his interview with Mrs Charmond's agent that morning, at which the lady herself had been present for a few minutes. Melbury had purchased some standing timber from her a long time before, and now that the date had come for felling it he was left to pursue almost his own course. This is what the household were actually talking of during Giles's cogitation without.

'So thoroughly does she trust me,' said Melbury, 'that I might fell, top, or lop, on my own judgment, any stick o' timber whatever in her wood, and fix the price o't, and settle the matter. But name it all, I wouldn't do such a thing. However, it may be useful to have this good understanding with her. . . . I wish she took more interest in the place and stayed here all the year round.'

'I am afraid 'tis not her regard for you, but her dislike of Hintock, that makes her so easy about the trees,' said Mrs Melbury.

When dinner was over Grace took a candle and began to ramble pleasurably through the rooms of her old home, from which she had latterly become well-nigh an alien. Each nook and each object revived a memory, and simultaneously modified it. The chambers seemed lower than they had appeared on any previous occasion of her return, the surfaces of both walls and ceilings standing in such near relations to the eye that it could not avoid taking microscopic note of their irregularities and old fashion. Her own bedroom wore at once a look more familiar than when she had left it, and yet a face estranged. The world of little things therein gazed at her in helpless stationariness, as though they had tried and been unable to make any progress without her presence. Over the place where her candle had been accustomed to stand, when she had used to read in bed till the midnight hour, there was still the brown spot of smoke. She did not know that her father had taken especial care to keep it from being cleaned off.

Having concluded her perambulation of this now uselessly commodious edifice, Grace began to feel that she had come a long journey since the morning; and when her father had been up himself, as well as his wife, to see that her room was comfortable and the fire burning, she prepared to retire for the night.

No sooner, however, had she extinguished her candle than her momentary sleepiness took itself off, and she wished she had stayed up longer. She amused herself by listening to the old familiar noises that she could hear to be still going on downstairs, and by looking towards the window as she lay. The blind had been drawn up as she used to have it when a girl, and she could just discern the dim tree-tops against the sky on the neighbouring hill. Beneath this meeting-line of light and shade nothing was visible save one solitary point of light, which blinked as the tree-twigs waved to and fro before its beams.

From its position it seemed to radiate from the window of a house on the hill-side. The house had been empty when she was last at home, and she wondered who inhabited the place now.

Her conjectures, however, were not intently carried on, and she was watching the light quite idly when it gradually changed colour, and at length shone blue as sapphire. Thus it remained several minutes, and then it passed through violet to red.

Her curiosity was so widely awakened by the phenomenon that she sat up in bed, and stared steadily at the shine. An appearance of this sort, sufficient to excite attention anywhere, was no less than a marvel in Hintock, as Grace had known the hamlet. Almost every diurnal and nocturnal effect in that woodland place had hitherto been the direct result of the regular terrestrial roll which produced the season's changes; but here was something dissociated from these normal sequences, and foreign to local knowledge.

It was about this moment that Grace heard the household below preparing to retire, the most emphatic noise in the proceeding being that of her father bolting the doors. Then the stairs creaked, and her father and mother passed her chamber. The last to come was Grammer Oliver.

Grace slid out of bed, ran across the room, and lifting the latch said, 'I am not asleep, Grammer. Come in and talk to me.'

Before the old woman had entered Grace was again under the bedclothes. Grammer set down her candlestick, and seated herself on the edge of Miss Melbury's coverlet.

'I want you to tell me what light that is I see on the hill-side,' said Grace.

Mrs Oliver looked across. 'Oh, that,' she said, 'is from the young doctor's. He's often doing things of that sort. Perhaps you don't know that we've a doctor living here now – Mr Fitzpiers by name?'

Grace admitted that she had not heard of him.

'Well, then, miss, he's come here to get up a practice. Though he belongs to the oldest, ancientest family in the country, he's stooped to make hisself useful like any common man. I know him very well, through going there to help 'em scrub sometimes, which your father said I might do if I wanted to in my spare time. Being a bachelor-man he've only lodgings. O yes, I know him very well. Sometimes he'll talk to me as if I were his own mother.'

'Indeed.'

'Yes. "Grammer," he said one day when I asked him why he came here where there's hardly anybody living, "I'll tell you why I came here. I took a map, and I marked on it where Dr Jones's practice ends to the north of this district, and where Mr Taylor's ends on the south, and little Jemmy Green's on the east, and somebody else's to the west. Then I took a pair of compasses, and found the exact middle of the country that was left between these bounds, and that middle was Little Hintock; so here I am." . . . But, Lord, there: poor young man!'

'Why?'

'He said, "Grammer Oliver, I've been here three months, and although there are a good many people in the Hintocks and the villages round, and a scattered practice is often a very good one, I don't seem to get many patients; and I'm not rich. And there's no society at all; and I'm pretty near melancholy mad," he said, with a great yawn. "I should be quite if it were not for my books, and my lab – laboratory, and what not. Grammer, I was made for higher things!" And then he'd yawn and yawn again.'

'Was he really made for higher things, do you think? Is he clever?'

'Well, no. How can he be clever? He may be able to jine up a broken man or woman after a fashion, and put his finger upon an ache if you tell him nearly where 'tis; but these young men – they should live to my time of life, and then they'd see how clever they were at five-and-twenty! And yet he's a projick, a real projick, and says the oddest of rozums. "Ah, Grammer," he said at another time, "let me tell you that Everything is Nothing. There's only Me and Not Me in the whole world." And he told me that no man's hands could help what they did, any more than the hands of a clock. . . . Yes, he's a man of strange meditations, and his eyes seem to see as far as the north star.'

'He will soon go away, no doubt.'

'I don't think so.'

Grace did not say 'Why?' and Grammer hesitated. At last she went on, 'Don't tell your father or mother, miss, if I let you know a secret?'

Grace gave the required promise.

'Well, he talks of buying me; so he won't go away just yet.'

'Buying you – how?'

'Not my soul – my body, when I'm dead! One day when I was there cleaning, he said, "Grammer, you've a large brain – a very large organ of brain," he said. "A woman's is usually four ounces less than a man's; but yours is man's size." Well, then – hee, hee! – after he'd flattered me a bit like that, he said he'd give me ten pounds to have my head as a natomy after my death. Well, knowing I'd no chick nor chiel left, and nobody with any interest in me, I thought, faith if I can be of any use to my fellow-creatures after I'm gone they are welcome to me; so I said I'd think it over, and would most likely agree and take the ten pounds. Now this is a secret, miss, between us two. The money would be very useful to me; and I see no harm in it.'

'Of course there's no harm. But O, Grammer – how can you think to do it? I wish you hadn't told me.'

'I wish I hadn't – if you don't like to know it, miss. But you needn't mind. Lord, hee! hee! I shall keep him waiting many a year yet, bless ye!'

'I hope you will, I am sure.'

The girl thereupon fell into such deep reflection that conversation languished, and Grammer Oliver taking her candle wished Miss Melbury good-night.

The latter's eyes rested on the distant glimmer, around which she allowed her reasoning fancy to play in vague eddies that shaped the doings of the philosopher behind that light on the lines of intelligence just received. It was strange to her to come back from the world to Little Hintock and find in one of its nooks, like a tropical plant in a hedgerow, a nucleus of advanced ideas and practices which had nothing in common with the life around. Chemical experiments, anatomical projects, and metaphysical conceptions had found a strange home here.

Thus she remained thinking, the imagined pursuits of the man behind the light intermingling with conjectural sketches of his personality; till her eyelids fell together with their own heaviness, and she slept.

CHAPTER SEVEN

KALEIDOSCOPIC dreams of a weird alchemist-surgeon, Grammer Oliver's skeleton, and the face of Giles Winterborne, brought Grace Melbury to the morning of the next day. It was fine. A north wind was blowing – that not unacceptable compromise between the atmospheric cutlery of the eastern blast and the spongy gales of the west quarter. She looked from her window in the direction of the light of the previous evening, and could just discern through the trees the shape of the surgeon's house. Somehow, in the broad, practical daylight, that unknown and lonely gentleman seemed to be shorn of much of the interest which had invested his personality and pursuits in the hours of darkness, and as Grace's dressing proceeded he faded from her mind.

Meanwhile Winterborne, though half-assured of her father's favour, was rendered a little restless by Miss Melbury's own behaviour. Despite his shy self-control he could not help looking continually from his own door towards the timber-merchant's, in the probability of somebody's emergence there-from.

His attention was at length justified by the appearance of two figures, that of Mr Melbury himself, and Grace beside him. They stepped out in a direction towards the densest quarter of the wood, and Winterborne walked contemplatively behind till all three were soon under the trees.

Although the time of bare boughs had now set in there were sheltered hollows amid the Hintock plantations and copses in which a more tardy leave-taking than on windy summits was the rule with the foliage. This caused here and there an apparent mixture of the seasons; so that in some of the dells they passed by holly-berries in full red growing beside oak and hazel whose leaves were as yet not far removed from green, and brambles whose verdure was rich and deep as in the month of August. To Grace these well-known peculiarities were as an old painting restored.

Now could be beheld that change from the handsome to the curious which the features of a wood undergo at the ingress of the winter months. Angles were taking the place of curves, and reticulations of surfaces – a change constituting a sudden lapse from the ornate to the primitive on Nature's canvas, and comparable to a retrogressive step from the art of an advanced school of painting to that of the Pacific Islander.

Winterborne followed and kept his eye upon the two figures as they threaded their way through these sylvan masses. Mr Melbury's long legs, his gaiters drawn in to the bone at the ankles, his slight stoop, his habit of getting lost in thought and arousing himself with an exclamation of 'Hah!' accompanied with an upward jerk of the head, composed a personage recognizable by his neighbours as far as he could be seen. It seemed as if the squirrels and birds knew him. One of the former would occasionally run from the path to hide behind the arm of some tree, which the little animal carefully edged round *pari passu* with Melbury and his daughter's movement onward, assuming a mock manner as though he were saying, 'Ho, ho! you are only a timber-merchant, and carry no gun!'

They went noiselessly over mats of starry moss, rustled through interspersed tracts of leaves, skirted trunks with spreading roots whose mossed rinds made them like hands wearing green gloves; elbowed old elms and ashes with great forks, in which stood pools of water that overflowed on rainy days and ran down their stems in green cascades. On older trees still than these huge lobes of fungi grew like lungs. Here, as everywhere, the Unfulfilled Intention, which makes life what it is, was as obvious as it could be among the depraved crowds of a city slum. The leaf was deformed, the curve was crippled, the taper was interrupted; the lichen ate the vigour of the stalk, and the ivy slowly strangled to death the promising sapling.

They dived amid beeches under which nothing grew, the younger boughs still retaining their hectic leaves, that rustled in the breeze with a sound almost metallic, like the sheet-iron foliage of the fabled Jarnvid wood. Some flecks of white in Grace's drapery had enabled Giles to keep her and her father in view till this time; but now he lost sight of them and was obliged to follow by ear – no difficult matter, for on the line of their course every wood-pigeon rose from its perch with a continued clash, dashing its wings against the branches with well-nigh force enough to break every quill. By taking the track of this noise he soon came to a stile.

Was it worth while to go further? He examined the doughy soil at the foot of the stile, and saw amongst the large sole-and-heel tracks an impression of a slighter kind from a boot that was obviously not local. The mud-picture was enough to make him swing himself over and proceed.

The character of the woodland now changed. The bases of the smaller trees were nibbled bare by rabbits, and at divers points heaps of fresh-made chips, and the newly cut stool of a tree, stared white through the undergrowth. There had been a large fall of timber this year, which explained the meaning of some sounds that soon reached him.

A voice was shouting intermittently in a sort of human bark, reminding Giles that there was a sale of trees and faggots that very day. Melbury would naturally be present. Winterborne decided that he himself wanted a few faggots, and entered upon the scene.

A large group of buyers stood round the auctioneer, or followed him when, between his pauses, he wandered on from one lot of plantation-produce to another, like some philosopher of the Peripatetic school delivering his lectures in the shady groves of the Lyceum. His companions were timber-dealers, yeomen, farmers, villagers, and others; mostly woodland men, who on that account could afford to be curious in their walking-sticks, which consequently exhibited various monstrosities of vegetation, the chief being corkscrew shapes in black and white thorn, brought to that pattern by the slow torture of an encircling woodbine during their growth, as the Chinese have been said to mould human beings into grotesque toys by continued compression in infancy. Two women wearing men's jackets on their gowns conducted in the rear of the halting procession a pony-cart containing bread and cheese, with a barrel of strong ale for the select, and cider in milking-pails into which anybody dipped who chose.

The auctioneer adjusted himself to circumstances by using his walking-stick as a hammer, and knocked down the lot on any convenient object that took his fancy, such as the crown of a little boy's head, or the shoulders of a bystander who had no business there except to taste the brew; a proceeding which would have been deemed humorous but for the air of stern rigidity which the auctioneer's face preserved, tending to show that the eccentricity was a result of that absence of mind which is engendered by the press of affairs, and no freak of fancy at all.

Mr Melbury stood slightly apart from the rest of the Peripatetics, and Grace beside him, clinging closely to his arm; her modern attire looking almost odd where everything else was old-fashioned, and throwing over the familiar garniture of the trees a homeliness that seemed to demand improvement by the addition of a few contemporary novelties also. Grace seemed to regard the selling with the interest which attaches to memories revived after an interval of obliviousness.

Winterborne went and stood close to them; the timber-merchant spoke, and continued his buying; Grace merely smiled. To justify his presence there Winterborne began bidding for timber and faggots that he did not want, pursuing the occupation in an abstracted mood in which the auctioneer's voice seemed to become one of the natural sounds of the woodland.

A few flakes of snow descended, at the sight of which a robin, alarmed at these signs of imminent winter, and seeing that no offence was meant by the human invasion, came and perched on the tip of the faggots that were being sold, and looked into the auctioneer's face whilst waiting for some chance crumb from the bread-basket. Standing a little behind Grace, Winterborne observed how one flake would sail downward and settle on a curl of her hair, and how another would choose her shoulder, and another the edge of her bonnet, which took up so much of his attention that his biddings proceeded incoherently; and when the auctioneer said every now and then, with a nod towards him, 'Yours, Mr Winterborne,' he had no idea whether he had bought faggots, poles, or log-wood.

He regretted that her father should show such inequalities of temperament as to keep Grace tightly on his arm to-day, when he had quite lately seemed anxious to recognize their betrothal as a fact. And thus musing, and joining in no conversation with other buyers except when directly addressed, he followed the assemblage hither and thither till the end of the auction, when Giles for the first time realized what his purchases had been. Hundreds of faggots, and divers lots of timber, had been set down to him, when all he had required had been a few bundles of spray for his man Robert Creedle's use in baking and lighting fires.

Business being over, he turned to speak to the timber-merchant. But Melbury's manner was short and distant; and Grace too looked vexed and reproachful. Winterborne then discovered that he had been unwittingly bidding against her father, and picking up his favourite lots in spite of him. With a very few words they left the spot, and pursued their way homeward.

Giles was extremely blank at what he had done, and remained standing under the trees, all the other men having strayed silently away. He saw Melbury and his daughter pass down a glade without looking back. While they moved slowly through it a lady appeared on horseback in the middle distance, the line of her progress converging upon that of Melbury's. They met, Melbury took off his hat, and she reined in her horse. A conversation was evidently in progress between Grace and her father and this equestrian, in whom he was almost sure that he recognized Mrs Charmond, less by her outline than by the livery of the groom who had halted some yards off.

The interlocutors did not part till after a prolonged pause, during which much seemed to be said. When Melbury and Grace resumed their walk it was with something of a lighter tread than before.

Winterborne pursued his own course homeward. He was unwilling to let coldness grow up between himself and the Melburys for any trivial reason, and in the evening he went to their house. On drawing near the gate his attention was attracted by the sight of one of the bedrooms blinking into a state of illumination. In it stood Grace lighting several candles, her right hand elevating the taper, her left hand on her bosom, her face thoughtfully fixed on each wick as it kindled, as if she saw in every flame's growth the rise of a life to maturity. He wondered what such unusual brilliance could mean to-night.

On getting indoors he found her father and stepmother in a state of suppressed excitement which he could not comprehend.

'I am sorry about my biddings to-day,' said Giles. 'I don't know what I was doing. I have come to say that any of the lots you may require are yours.'

'Oh, never mind – never mind,' replied the timber-merchant with a slight wave of his hand. 'I have so much else to think of that I nearly had forgot it. Just now, too, there are matters of a different kind from trade to attend to, so don't let it concern 'ee.'

As the timber-merchant spoke, as it were, down to him from a higher plane than his own, Giles turned to Mrs Melbury.

'Grace is going to the House to-morrow,' she said quietly. 'She is looking out her things now. I dare say she is wanting me this minute to assist her.' Thereupon Mrs Melbury left the room.

Nothing is more remarkable than the independent personality of the tongue now and then. Mr Melbury knew that his words had been a sort of boast. He decried boasting, particularly to Giles; yet whenever the subject was Grace his judgment resigned the ministry of speech in spite of him.

Winterborne felt surprise, pleasure, and also a little apprehension at the news. He repeated Mrs Melbury's words.

'Yes,' said paternal pride, not sorry to have dragged out of him what he could not in any circumstances have kept in. 'Coming home from the woods this afternoon we met Mrs Charmond out for a ride. She spoke to me on a little matter of business, and then got acquainted with Grace. 'Twas wonderful how she took to Grace in a few minutes; that free-masonry of education made 'em close at once. Naturally enough she was amazed that such an article – ha-ha! – could come out of my house. At last it led on to Mis'ess Grace being asked to the House. So she's busy hunting up her frills and furbelows to go in.' As Giles remained in thought without responding, Melbury continued: 'But I'll call her downstairs.'

'No, no; don't do that, since she's busy,' said Winterborne.

Melbury, feeling from the young man's manner that his own talk had been too much at Giles and too little to him, repented at once. His face changed, and he said, in lower tones, with an effort: 'She's yours, Giles, as far as I am concerned.'

'Thanks – my best thanks, sir. But I think since it is all right between us about the biddings, that I'll not interrupt her now. I'll step homeward, and call another time.'

On leaving the house he looked up at the bedroom again. Grace, surrounded by a sufficient number of candles to answer all purposes of self-criticism, was standing before a cheval glass that her father had lately bought expressly for her use; she was bonneted, cloaked, and gloved, and glanced over her shoulder into the mirror, estimating her aspect. Her face was lit with the natural elation of a young girl hoping to inaugurate on the morrow an intimate acquaintance with a new, interesting, and influential friend.

CHAPTER EIGHT

THE inspiriting appointment which had led Grace Melbury to indulge in a six-candle illumination for the arrangement of her attire carried her over the ground the next morning with a springy tread. Her sense of being properly appreciated on her own native soil charged her heart with expansive gratitude. She moved along, a vessel of emotion, going to empty itself on she knew not what.

Twenty minutes' walking through copses, over a stile, and along an upland lawn, brought her to the verge of a deep glen, in which Hintock House appeared immediately beneath her eye. To describe it as standing in a hollow would not express the situation of the manor-house; it stood in a hole. But the hole was full of beauty. From the spot which Grace had reached a stone could easily have been thrown over or into the birds'-nested chimneys of the mansion. Its walls were surmounted by a battlemented parapet; but the grey lead roofs were quite visible behind it, with their gutters, laps, rolls, and skylights, together with letterings and shoe-patterns cut by idlers thereon.

The front of the house was an ordinary manorial presentation of Elizabethan windows, mullioned and hooded, worked in rich snuff-coloured freestone from Ham-hill quarries. The ashlar of the walls, where not overgrown with ivy and other creepers, was coated with lichen of every shade, intensifying its luxuriance with its nearness to the ground till, below the plinth, it merged in moss.

Above the house to the back was a dense plantation, the roots of whose trees were above the level of the chimneys. The corresponding high ground on which Grace stood was richly grassed, with only an old tree here and there. A few sheep lay about, which as they ruminated looked quietly into the bedroom windows.

The situation of the house, prejudicial to humanity, was a stimulus to vegetation, on which account an endless shearing of the heavy-armed ivy went on, and a continual lopping of trees and shrubs. It was an edifice built in times when human constitutions were damp-proof, when shelter from the boisterous was all that men thought of in choosing a dwelling-place, the insidious being beneath their notice; and its hollow site was an ocular reminder by its unfitness for modern lives of the fragility to which these have declined.

The highest architectural cunning could have done nothing to make Little Hintock House dry and salubrious; and ruthless ignorance could have done little to make it unpicturesque. It was vegetable nature's own home; a spot to inspire the painter and poet of still life – if they did not suffer too much from the relaxing atmosphere – and to draw groans from the gregariously disposed.

Grace descended the green escarpment by a zigzag path into the drive, which swept round beneath the slope. The exterior of the house had been familiar to her from her childhood, but she had never been inside, and the first step to knowing an old thing in a new way was a lively experience.

It was with a little flutter that she was shown in; but she recollected that Mrs Charmond would probably be alone. Up to a few days before this time that lady had been accompanied in her comings, stayings, and goings by a relative, believed to be her aunt; latterly, however, the two had separated, owing, it was supposed, to a quarrel; and Mrs Charmond had been left desolate. Being presumably a woman who did not care for solitude this deprivation might account for her sudden interest in Grace.

Mrs Charmond was at the end of a gallery opening from the hall when Miss Melbury was announced, and saw her through the glass doors between them. She came forward with a smile on her face, and told the young girl it was good of her to come.

'Ah! you have noticed those,' she said, seeing that Grace's eyes were attracted by some curious objects against the walls. 'They are man-traps. My husband was a connoisseur in man-traps and spring-guns and such articles, collecting them from all his neighbours. He knew the histories of all these – which gin had broken a man's leg, which gun had killed a man. I don't like them here; but I've never yet given directions for them to be taken away.' She added playfully, 'Man-traps are of rather ominous significance where a person of our sex lives, are they not?'

Grace was bound to smile; but that side of womanliness was one which her inexperience felt no great zest in contemplating.

'They are interesting, no doubt, as relics of a barbarous time happily past,' she said, looking thoughtfully at the varied designs of the instruments.

'Well, we must not take them too seriously,' said Mrs Charmond with an indolent turn of her head, and they moved on inwards.

When she had shown her visitor different articles in cabinets that she deemed likely to interest her, some tapestries, wood carvings, ivories, miniatures, and so on – always with a mien of listlessness which might either have been constitutional, or partly owing to the situation of the place – they sat down to an early cup of tea.

'Will you pour it out, please? Do,' she said, leaning back in her chair, and placing her hand above her forehead, while her almond eyes – those long eyes so common to the angelic legions of early Italian art – became longer, and her voice more languishing. She showed that oblique-mannered softness which is perhaps seen oftenest in women of darker complexion and more lymphatic temperament than Mrs Charmond's; women who lingeringly smile their meanings to men rather than speak them, who inveigle rather than prompt, and take advantage of currents rather than steer.

'I am the most inactive woman when I am here,' she said. 'I think sometimes I was born to live and do nothing, nothing, nothing but float about, as we fancy we do sometimes in dreams. But that cannot be really my destiny, and I must struggle against such fancies.'

'I am so sorry you do not enjoy exertion – it is quite sad! I wish I could tend you and make you very happy.'

There was always something so sympathetic, so responsive in Grace's voice, that it impelled people to overstep their customary reservations in talking to her. 'It is tender and kind of you to feel that!' said Mrs Charmond. 'Perhaps I have given you the notion that my languor is more than it really is. But this place oppresses me, and I have a plan of going abroad a good deal. I used to go with a relation, but that arrangement has dropped through.'

Regarding Grace with a final glance of criticism she seemed to make up her mind to consider the young girl satisfactory, and continued:

'Now, I am often impelled to record my impressions of times and places. I have often thought of writing a new *Sentimental Journey*. But I cannot find energy enough to do it alone. When I am at different places in the south of Europe I feel a crowd of ideas and fancies thronging upon me continually; but to unfold writing materials, take up a cold steel pen, and put these impressions down systematically on cold smooth paper – that I cannot do. So I have thought that if I always could have somebody at my elbow with whom I am in sympathy, I might dictate any ideas that come into my head. And directly I had made your acquaintance the other day it struck me that you would suit me so well. Would you like to undertake it? You might read to me, too, if desirable. Will you think it over, and ask your parents if they are willing?'

'O yes,' said Grace. 'I am almost sure they would be very glad.'

'You are so accomplished, I hear; I should be quite honoured by such intellectual company.'

Grace, modestly blushing, deprecated any such idea.

'Do you keep up your lucubrations at Little Hintock?' the lady went on.

'O no. . . . Lucubrations are not unknown at Little Hintock; but they are not carried on by me.'

'What – another student in that retreat?'

'There is a surgeon lately come, and I have heard that he reads a great deal – I see his light sometimes through the trees late at night.'

'O yes – a doctor – I believe I was told of him. It is a strange place for him to settle in.'

'It is a convenient centre for a practice, they say. But he does not confine his studies to medicine, it seems. He investigates theology, and metaphysics and all sorts of subjects.'

'What is his name?'

'Fitzpiers. He represents a very old family, I believe, the Fitzpierses of Oakbury-Fitzpiers – not a great many miles from here.'

'I am not sufficiently local to know the history of the family. I was never in the county till my husband brought me here.'

Mrs Charmond did not care to pursue this line of investigation. Whatever mysterious merit might attach to family antiquity, it was one which her adaptable, wandering, *weltbürgerliche* nature had grown tired of caring about – a peculiarity that made her a piquant contrast to her neighbours.

'It is of rather more importance to know what the man is himself than what his family is,' she said, 'if he is going to practise upon us as a surgeon. Heaven send him skill! Have you seen him?'

Grace had not. 'I think he is not a very old man,' she added.

'Has he a wife?'

'I am not aware that he has.'

'Well, I hope he will be useful here. I must get to know him when I come back. It will be very convenient to have a medical man – if he is clever – in one's own parish. I get dreadfully nervous sometimes, living in such an outlandish place; and Sherton is so far to send to. No doubt you feel Little Hintock to be a great change after watering-place life.'

'I do. But it is home. It has its advantages and its disadvantages.' Grace was thinking less of the solitude than of the attendant circumstances.

They chatted on for some time, Grace being set quite at her ease by her entertainer. Mrs Charmond was far too well-practised a woman not to know that to show anything like patronage towards a sensitive young girl who would probably be very quick to discern it was to demolish her dignity rather than to establish it in that young girl's eyes. So being violently possessed with her idea of making use of this gentle acquaintance, ready and waiting at her own door, she took great pains to win her confidence at starting.

Just before Grace's departure the two chanced to pause before a mirror which reflected their faces in immediate juxtaposition, bringing into prominence their resemblances and their contrasts. Both looked attractive as glassed back by the faithful reflector; but Grace's countenance had the effect of making Mrs Charmond appear more than her full age. There are complexions which set off each other to great advantage, and there are those which antagonize, one of such killing or damaging its neighbour unmercifully.

This was unhappily the case here. Mrs Charmond fell into a meditation, and replied abstractedly to a cursory remark of her companion's. However, she parted from her young friend in the kindliest tones, promising to send and let her know as soon as her mind was made up on the arrangement she had suggested.

When Grace had ascended nearly to the top of the adjoining slope she looked back, and saw that Mrs Charmond still stood at the door meditatively regarding her.

Often during the previous night, after his call on the Melburys, Winterborne's thoughts had run upon Grace's announced visit to Hintock House. Why had he not proposed to walk with her part of the way? Something told him that she might not, on such an occasion, have cared for his company.

He was still more of that opinion when, standing in his garden next day, he saw her go past on the journey with such a pretty pride in the event. He questioned if her father's ambition, which had purchased for her the means of intellectual light and culture far beyond those of any other native of the village, would not operate to the flight of her future interests above and away from the local life which was once to her the movement of the world.

Nevertheless, he had her father's permission to win her if he could; and to this end it became desirable to bring matters soon to a crisis. If she should think herself too good for him he must let her go, and make the best of his loss. The question was how to quicken events towards an issue.

He thought and thought, and at last decided that as good a way as any would be to give a Christmas party, and ask Grace and her parents to come as chief guests.

These ruminations were occupying him when there became audible a slight knocking at his front door. He descended the path, and looked out, and beheld Marty South, dressed for out-door work.

'Why didn't you come, Mr Winterborne?' she said; 'I've been waiting there hours and hours, and at last I thought I must try to find you!'

'Bless my soul, I'd quite forgot!' said Giles.

What he had forgotten was that there were a thousand young fir trees to be planted in a neighbouring spot which had been cleared by the wood-cutters, and that he had arranged to plant them with his own hands. He had a marvellous power of making trees grow. Although he would seem to shovel in the earth quite carelessly there was a sort of sympathy between himself and the fir, oak, or beech that he was operating on; so that the roots took hold of the soil in a few days. When, on the other hand, any of the journeymen planted, although they seemed to go through an identically similar process, one quarter of the trees would die away during the ensuing August.

Hence Winterborne found delight in the work even when, as at present, he contracted to do it on portions of the woodland in which he had no personal interest. Marty, who turned her hand to anything, was usually the one who performed the part of keeping the trees in a perpendicular position whilst he threw in the mould.

He accompanied her towards the spot, being inclined yet further to proceed with the work by the knowledge that the ground was close to the roadside along which Grace must pass on her way from Hintock House.

'You've a cold in the head, Marty,' he said as they walked. 'That comes of cutting off your hair.'

'I suppose it do. Yes; I've three headaches going on in my head at the same time.'

'Three headaches!'

'Yes, Mr Winterborne: a rheumatic headache in my poll, a sick headache over my eyes, and a misery headache in the middle of my brain. However, I came out, for I thought you might be waiting and grumbling like anything if I was not there.'

The holes were already dug, and they set to work. Winterborne's fingers were endowed with a gentle conjurer's touch in spreading the roots of each little tree, resulting in a sort of caress under which the delicate fibres all laid themselves out in their proper directions for growth. He put most of these roots towards the south-west; for, he said, in forty years' time, when some great gale is blowing from that quarter, the trees will require the strongest holdfast on that side to stand against it and not fall.

'How they sigh directly we put 'em upright, though while they are lying down they don't sigh at all,' said Marty.

'Do they?' said Giles. 'I've never noticed it.'

She erected one of the young pines into its hole, and held up her finger; the soft musical breathing instantly set in which was not to cease night or day till the grown tree should be felled – probably long after the two planters had been felled themselves.

'It seems to me,' the girl continued, 'as if they sigh because they are very sorry to begin life in earnest – just as we be.'

'Just as we be?' He looked critically at her. 'You ought not to feel like that, Marty.'

Her only reply was turning to take up the next tree; and they planted on through a great part of the day, almost without another word. Winterborne's mind ran on his contemplated evening-party, his abstraction being such that he hardly was conscious of Marty's presence beside him.

From the nature of their employment, in which he handled the spade and she merely held the tree, it followed that he got good exercise and she got none. But she was a heroic girl, and though her outstretched hand was chill as a stone, and her cheeks blue, and her cold worse than ever, she would not complain whilst he was disposed to continue work. But when he paused she said, 'Mr Winterborne, can I run down the lane and back to warm my feet?'

'Why, yes, of course,' he said, awakening to her existence. 'Though I was just thinking what a mild day it is for the season. Now I warrant that cold of yours is twice as bad as it was. You had no business to chop that hair off, Marty; it serves you almost right. Look here, cut off home at once.'

'A run down the lane will be quite enough.'

'No, it won't. You ought not to have come out to-day at all.'

'But I should like to finish the—'

'Marty, I tell you to go home!' said he peremptorily. 'I can manage to keep the rest of them upright with a forked stick or something.'

She went away without saying any more. When she had gone down the orchard a little distance she looked back. Giles suddenly went after her.

'Marty, it was for your good that I was rough, you know. But warm yourself in your own way; I don't care.' He took her hand kindly a moment, and then let her go.

When she had run off he fancied he discerned a woman's dress through the holly bushes which divided the coppice from the road. It was Grace at last, on her way back from the interview with Mrs Charmond. He threw down the tree he was planting, and was about to break through the belt of holly when he suddenly became aware of the presence of another man, who was looking over the hedge on the opposite side of the way upon the figure of the unconscious Grace.

The stranger appeared as a handsome and gentlemanly personage of six or eight and twenty, and he was quizzing her through an eyeglass. Seeing that Winterborne was noticing him he let his glass drop with a click upon the rail which protected the hedge, and walked away in the opposite direction.

Giles knew in a moment that this must be Mr Fitzpiers. When he was gone Winterborne pushed through the holly, and emerged close beside the interesting object of their contemplation.

CHAPTER NINE

'I HEARD the bushes move long before I saw you,' she began. 'I said first, "It is some terrible beast"; next, "It is a poacher"; next, "It is a friend!"'

He regarded her with a slight smile, weighing, not her speech, but the question whether he should tell her that she had been flatteringly watched by a gentleman. He decided in the negative.

'You have been to the House?' he said. 'But I need not ask.' The fact was that there shone upon Miss Melbury's face a species of exaltation which saw no environing details; not even Giles's occupation, only his bare presence.

'Why need you not ask?'

'Your face is like the face of Moses when he came down from the Mount.'

She reddened a little and said, 'How can you be so profane, Giles Winterborne!'

'How can you think so much of that class of people! Well, I beg pardon, I didn't mean to speak so freely. How do you like her house and her?'

'Exceedingly. I had not been near the place since I was a child, when it used to be let to strangers, before Mrs Charmond's late husband bought the property. She is *so* nice!' And Grace fell into such an abstracted gaze at the mental image of Mrs Charmond and her niceness that it almost conjured up a vision of that lady to Giles himself.

'She has only been here a month or two it seems, and cannot stay much longer, because she finds it so lonely and damp in winter. She is going abroad. Only think, she would like me to go with her!'

Giles's features stiffened a little at the news. 'Indeed: what for? But I won't keep you standing here. Hoi, Robert!' he cried to a swaying collection of old clothes in the distance, which composed the figure of Creedle, his man, who was looking for him. 'Go on filling in there till I come back.'

'I'm a-coming, sir; I'm a-coming.'

'Well, the reason is this,' continued she as they went on together. 'Mrs Charmond has a delightful side to her character — a desire to record her impressions of travel, like Alexandre Dumas, and Méry, and Sterne, and others.

But she cannot find energy enough to do it herself.' And Grace proceeded to explain Mrs Charmond's proposal at large. 'My notion is that Méry's style will suit her best, because he writes in that soft, emotional, luxurious way she has,' Grace said musingly.

'Indeed!' said Winterborne, sighing. 'Suppose you talk over my head a little longer, Miss Grace Melbury.'

'O, I didn't mean it!' she said repentantly, looking into his eyes. 'And as for myself, I hate French books. And I love dear old Hintock, *and the people in it*, fifty times better than all the Continent! But the scheme; I think it an enchanting notion, don't you, Giles?'

'It is well enough in one sense, but it will take you away,' said he, mollified.

'Only for a short time; we should return in May.'

'Well, Miss Melbury; it is a question for your father.'

Winterborne walked with her nearly to her house. He had awaited her coming mainly with the view of mentioning to her his proposal to have a Christmas party; but homely Christmas gatherings in the jovial Hintock style seemed so primitive and uncouth beside the lofty matters of her conversation that he refrained.

As soon as she was gone he turned back towards the scene of his planting, and could not help saying to himself as he walked that this engagement of his was a very unpromising business. Her outing to-day had not improved it. A woman who could go to Hintock House, and be friendly with its mistress; enter into the views of its mistress, talk like her, and dress not much unlike her: why, she would hardly be contented with him, a yeoman, immersed in tree planting, even though he planted them well. 'And yet she's a true-hearted girl,' he said, thinking of her words about Hintock. 'I must bring matters to a point, and there's an end of it.'

When he reached the place of work he found that Marty had come back, and dismissing Creedle he went on planting silently with the girl as before.

'Suppose, Marty,' he said after a while, looking at her extended arm, upon which old scratches from briars showed themselves purple in the cold wind, 'suppose you know a person, and want to bring that person to a good understanding with you, do you think a Christmas party of some sort is a warming-up thing, and likely to be useful in hastening on the matter?'

'Is there to be dancing?'

'There might be, certainly.'

'Will He dance with Her?'

'Well, yes.'

'Then it might bring things to a head, one way or the other, I won't be the maid to say which.'

'It shall be done,' said Winterborne, not to her, though he spoke the words quite loudly. And as the day was nearly ended, he added, 'Here, Marty, I'll send up a man to plant the rest to-morrow. I've other things to think of just now.'

She did not inquire what other things, for she had seen him walking with Grace Melbury. She looked towards the western sky, which was now aglow like some vast foundry wherein new worlds were being cast. Across it the bare bough of a tree stretched horizontally, revealing every twig against the evening fire, and showing in dark profile every beck and movement of three pheasants that were settling themselves down on it in a row to roost.

'It will be fine to-morrow,' said Marty, observing them with the vermilion light of the sun in the pupils of her eyes, 'for they are a-croupied down nearly at the end of the bough. If it were going to be stormy they'd squeeze close to the trunk. The weather is almost all they have to think of, isn't it, Mr Winterborne? And so they must be lighter-hearted than we.'

'I dare say they are,' said Winterborne.

Before taking a single step in the preparations, Winterborne, with no great hopes, went across that evening to the timber-merchant's to ascertain if Grace and her parents would honour him with their presence. Having first to set his nightly gins in the garden to catch the rabbits that ate his winter-greens, his call was delayed till just after the rising of the moon, whose rays reached the Hintock houses but fitfully as yet, on account of the trees. Melbury was crossing his yard on his way to call on some one at the larger village, but he readily turned and walked up and down with the young man.

Giles, in his self-deprecatory sense of living on a much smaller scale than the Melburys did, would not for the world imply that his invitation was to a gathering of any importance. So he put it in the mild form of 'Can you come in for an hour when you have done business, the day after to-morrow; and Mrs and Miss Melbury, if they have nothing more pressing to do?'

Melbury would give no answer at once. 'No, I can't tell you to-day,' he said. 'I must talk it over with the women. As far as I am concerned, my dear Giles, you know I'll come with pleasure. But how do I know what Grace's notions may be? You see, she has been away amongst cultivated folks a good while; and now this acquaintance with Mrs Charmond – well, I'll ask her. I can say no more.'

When Winterborne was gone the timber-merchant went on his way. He knew very well that Grace, whatever her own feelings, would either go or not go, according as he suggested; and his instinct was, for the moment, to suggest staying at home. His errand took him near the church, and the way to his destination was equally easy across the churchyard or outside it. For some reason or other he chose the former way.

The moon was faintly lighting up the gravestones, and the path, and the front of the building. Suddenly Mr Melbury paused, turned in upon the grass, and approached a particular headstone, where he read, 'In memory of John Winterborne,' with the subjoined date and age. It was the grave of Giles's father.

The timber-merchant laid his hand upon the stone, and was humanized. 'Jack, my wronged friend!' he said, 'I'll be faithful to my plan of making amends to thee.'

When he reached home that evening he said to Grace and Mrs Melbury, who were working at a little table by the fire, 'Giles wants us to go down and spend an hour with him the day after to-morrow; and I'm thinking, that as 'tis Giles who asks us, we'll go.'

They assented without demur; and the timber-merchant sent Giles the next morning an answer in the affirmative.

Winterborne, in his modesty, had mentioned no particular hour in his invitation to the Melburys, though he had to the inferior guests; therefore Mr Melbury and his family, expecting no other people, chose their own time, which chanced to be rather early in the afternoon, by reason of the somewhat quicker despatch than usual of the timber-merchant's business that day.

They showed their sense of the unimportance of the occasion by walking quite slowly to the house, as if they were merely out for a ramble, and going to nothing special at all; or at most intending to pay a casual call and take a cup of tea.

At this hour stir and bustle pervaded the interior of Winterborne's domicile from cellar to apple-loft. He had planned an elaborate high tea for six o'clock or thereabouts, and a good roaring supper to come on about eleven. Being a bachelor of rather retiring habits the whole of the preparations devolved upon himself and his trusty man and familiar Robert Creedle, who did everything that required doing, from making Giles's bed to catching moles in his field. He was a survival from the days when Giles's father held the homestead and Giles was a playing boy.

These two, with a certain dilatoriness which appertained to both, were now in the heat of preparation in the bakehouse, expecting nobody before six o'clock. Winterborne was standing in front of the brick oven in his shirt-sleeves, tossing in thorn-sprays, and stirring about the blazing mass with a long-handled, three-pronged Beelzebub kind of fork, the heat shining out upon his streaming face and making his eyes like furnaces; the thorns crackling and sputtering; while Creedle, having ranged the pastry dishes in a row on the table till the oven should be ready, was pressing out the crust of a final apple-pie with a rolling-pin. A great pot boiled on the fire: and through the open door of the back-kitchen a boy was seen seated on the fender, emptying the snuffers and scouring the candle-sticks, a row of the latter standing upside down on the hob to melt out the grease.

Looking up from the rolling-pin Creedle saw passing the window first the timber-merchant, in his second best suit, next Mrs Melbury in her best silk, and behind them Grace in the fashionable attire which, lately brought home with her from the Continent, she had worn on her visit to Mrs Charmond's. The eyes of the three had been attracted through the window to the proceedings within by the fierce illumination which the oven threw out upon the operators and their utensils.

'Lord, lord! if they bain't come a'ready!' said Creedle.

'No – hey?' said Giles, looking round aghast; while the boy in the background waved a reeking candlestick in his delight.

As there was no help for it Winterborne hastily rolled down his shirt-sleeves and went to meet them in the doorway.

'My dear Giles, I see we have made a mistake in the time,' said the timber-merchant's wife, her face lengthening with concern.

'Oh, it is not much difference. I hope you'll come in.'

'But this means a regular randyvoo!' Mr Melbury accusingly glanced round and pointed towards the viands in the bakehouse with his stick.

'Well, yes,' said Giles.

'And – not Great Hintock band, and dancing, surely?'

'I told three of 'em they might drop in if they'd nothing else to do,' Giles mildly admitted.

'Now why the name didn't ye tell us afore that 'twas going to be a bouncing kind of thing? How should I know what folk mean if they don't say? Now, shall we come in, or shall we go home, and come back-along in a couple of hours?'

'I hope you'll stay, if you'll be so good as not to mind, now you are here! I shall have it all right and tidy in a very little time. I ought not to have been so backward; but Creedle is rather slow.'

Giles spoke quite anxiously for one of his undemonstrative temperament; for he feared that if the Melburys once were back in their own house they would not be disposed to turn out again.

' 'Tis we ought not to have been so forward; that's what 'tis,' said Mr Melbury testily. 'Don't keep us here in your best sitting-room; lead on to the bakehouse, man. Now we are here we'll help ye get ready for the rest. Here, mis'ess, take off your things, and help him out in his baking, or he won't get done to-night. I'll finish heating the oven, and set you free to go and skiver up them ducks.' His eye had passed with pitiless directness of criticism into yet remoter recesses of Winterborne's awkwardly built premises, where the aforesaid birds were hanging.

'And I'll help finish the tarts,' said Grace cheerfully.

'I don't know about that,' said her father. ' 'Tisn't quite so much in your line as it is in your step-mother's and mine.'

'Of course I couldn't let you, Grace!' said Giles, with distress.

'I'll do it, of course,' said Mrs Melbury, taking off her silk train, hanging it up to a nail, carefully rolling back her sleeves, pinning them to her shoulders, and stripping Giles of his apron for her own use.

So Grace pottered idly about while her father and his wife helped on the preparations. A kindly pity of his household management, which Winterborne saw in her eyes whenever he caught them, depressed him much more than her contempt would have done.

Creedle met Giles at the pump after a while, when each of the others was absorbed in the difficulties of a *cuisine* based on utensils, cupboards, and provisions that were strange to them. He groaned to the young man in a whisper, 'This is a bruckle het, maister, I'm much afeard! Who'd ha' thought they'd ha' come so soon!'

The bitter placidity of Winterborne's look hinted the misgivings he did not care to express. 'Have you got the celery ready?' he asked quickly.

'Now, that's a thing I never could mind; no, not if you'd pay me in silver and gold!' said Creedle. 'And I don't care who the man is, I says that a stick of celery that isn't scrubbed with the scrubbing-brush is not clean.'

'*Very* well, very well! I'll attend to it. You go and get 'em comfortable in-doors.'

He hastened to the garden, and soon returned, tossing the stalks to Creedle, who was still in a tragic mood. 'If ye'd ha' married, d'ye see, maister,' he murmured, 'this calamity couldn't have happened to us!'

Everything being at last under way, the oven set, and all done that could insure the supper turning up ready at some time or other, Giles and his friends entered the parlour, where the Melburys again dropped into position as guests, though the room was not nearly so warm and cheerful as the blazing bakehouse. Others now arrived, among them Farmer Cawtree and the hollow-turner, and tea went off very well.

Grace's disposition to make the best of everything, and to wink at deficiencies in Winterborne's way of living, was so uniform and persistent that he suspected her of seeing even more deficiencies than he was aware of. That suppressed sympathy which had showed in her face ever since her arrival told him as much too plainly.

'This muddling style of housekeeping is what you've not lately been used to, I suppose?' he said when they were a little apart.

'No; but I like it; it reminds me so pleasantly that everything here in dear old Hintock is just as it used to be. The oil is — not quite nice; but everything else is.'

'The oil?'

'On the chairs, I mean; because it gets on one's dress. Still, mine is not a new one.'

Giles found that the boy, in his zeal to make things look bright, had smeared the chairs with some greasy furniture-polish, and refrained from rubbing it dry in order not to diminish the mirror-like effect that the mixture produced as laid on. Giles apologized and scolded the boy; but he felt that the fates were against him.

CHAPTER TEN

SUPPER-TIME came, and with it the hot-baked meats from the oven, laid on a snowy cloth fresh from the press, and reticulated with folds as in Flemish Last-Suppers. Creedle and the boy fetched and carried with amazing alacrity; the latter, to mollify his superior, and make things pleasant, expressing his admiration of Creedle's cleverness when they were alone.

'I s'pose the time when you learnt all these knowing things, Mr Creedle, was when you was in the militia?'

'Well, yes. I seed the world that year somewhat, certainly, and mastered many arts of strange, dashing life. Not but that Giles has worked hard in helping me to bring things to such perfection to-day. "Giles," says I, though he's maister. Not that I should call 'n maister by rights, for his father growed up side by side with me, as if one mother had twinned us and been our nourishing.'

'I s'pose your memory can reach a long way back into history, Mr Creedle?'

'O yes. Ancient days, when there was battles, and famines, and hang-fairs, and other pomps, seem to me as yesterday. Ah, many's the patriarch I've seed come and go in this parish! There, he's calling for more plates. Lord, why can't 'em turn their plates bottom upward for pudding, as we bucks used to do in former days!'

Meanwhile in the adjoining room Giles was presiding in a half-unconscious state. He could not get over the initial failures in his scheme for advancing his suit; and hence he did not know that he was eating mouthfuls of bread and nothing else, and continually snuffing the two candles next him till he had reduced them to mere glimmers drowned in their own grease. Creedle now appeared with a specially prepared stew, which he served by elevating the little three-legged crock that contained it and tilting the contents into a platter on the table, exclaiming simultaneously, 'Draw back, gentlemen and ladies, please!'

A splash followed. Grace gave a quick involuntary nod and blink, and put her handkerchief to her face.

'Good heavens! what did you do that for, Creedle?' said Giles sternly, jumping up.

' 'Tis how I do it when they bain't here, maister,' mildly expostulated Creedle, in an aside audible to all the company.

'Well, yes – but—' replied Giles. He went over to Grace, and hoped none of it had gone into her eye.

'O no,' she said. 'Only a sprinkle on my face. It was nothing.'

'Kiss it and make it well,' gallantly observed Mr Cawtree.

Miss Melbury blushed.

The timber-merchant replied quickly, 'O, it is nothing! She must bear these little mishaps.' But there could be discerned in his face something which said, 'I ought to have foreseen all this, and kept her away.'

Giles himself, since the untoward beginning of the feast, had not quite liked to see Grace present. He wished he had not asked such people as Cawtree and the hollow-turner. He had done it, in dearth of other friends, that the room might not appear empty. In his mind's eye, before the event, they had been the mere background or padding of the scene; but somehow in the reality they were the most prominent personages there.

After supper they sat down to cards; Cawtree and the hollow-turner monopolizing the new packs for an interminable game of langterloo, in which a lump of chalk was incessantly used – a game those two always played wherever they were, taking a solitary candle and going to a private table in a corner with the mien of persons bent on weighty matters. The rest of the company on this account were obliged to put up with old packs for their round game, that had been lying by in a drawer ever since the time that Giles's grandmother was alive. Each card had a great stain in the middle of its back, produced by the touch of generations of damp and excited thumbs, now fleshless in the grave; and the kings and queens wore a decayed expression of feature, as if they were rather an impecunious dethroned dynasty hiding in obscure slums than real regal characters. Every now and then the comparatively few remarks of the players at the round game were harshly intruded on by the langterloo jingle of Farmer Cawtree and the hollow-turner from the back of the room:

'And I' will hold' a wa'-ger with you'
That all' these marks' are thirt' -y two!'

accompanied by rapping strokes with the chalk on the table: then an exclamation, an argument, a dealing of the cards; then the commencement of the rhymes anew.

The timber-merchant showed his feelings by talking with a reserved weight in his words, and by praising the party in a patronizing tone, when Winterborne expressed his fear that he and his were not enjoying themselves.

'O yes, yes; pretty much. What handsome glasses those are! I didn't know you had such glasses in the house. Now, Lucy [to his wife], you ought to get some like them for ourselves.' And when they had abandoned cards, and Winterborne was talking to Melbury by the fire, it was the timber-merchant who stood with his back to the mantel in a proprietary attitude; from which post of vantage he critically regarded Giles's person, rather as a superficies than as a solid with ideas and feelings inside it; saying, 'What a splendid coat that one is you have on, Giles. I can't get such coats. You dress better than I.'

After supper there was a dance, the bandsmen from Great Hintock having arrived some time before. Grace had been away from home so long, and was so drilled in new dances, that she had forgotten the old figures, and hence did not join in the movement. Then Giles felt that all was over. As for her, she was thinking, as she watched the gyrations, of a very different measure that she had been accustomed to tread with a bevy of sylph-like creatures in muslin in the music-room of a large house, most of whom were now moving in scenes widely removed from this, both as regarded place and character.

A woman she did not know came and offered to tell her fortune with the abandoned cards. Grace assented to the proposal, and the woman told her tale unskilfully, for want of practice, as she declared.

Mr Melbury was standing by, and exclaimed contemptuously, 'Tell her fortune indeed! Her fortune has been told by men of science – what do you call 'em? Phrenologists. You can't teach her anything new. She's been too far among the wise ones to be astonished at anything she can hear among us folks in Hintock.'

At last the time came for breaking up, Melbury and his family being the earliest to leave, the two card-players still pursuing their game doggedly in the corner, where they had completely covered Giles's mahogany table with chalk scratches. The Melburys walked home, the distance being short and the night clear.

'Well, Giles is a very good fellow,' said Mr Melbury, as they struck down the lane under boughs which formed a black filigree in which the stars seemed set.

'Certainly he is.' Grace spoke quickly, and in such a tone as to show that he stood no lower, if no higher, in her regard than he had stood before.

When they were opposite an opening through which, by day, the doctor's house could be seen, they observed a light in one of his rooms, although it was now about two o'clock.

'The doctor is not abed yet,' said Mrs Melbury.

'Hard study, no doubt,' said her husband.

'One would think that, as he seems to have nothing to do about here by day, he could at least afford to go to bed early at night. 'Tis astonishing how little we see of him.'

Melbury's mind seemed to turn with much relief to the contemplation of Mr Fitzpiers after the scenes of the evening. 'It is natural enough,' he replied. 'What can a man of that sort find to interest him in Hintock? I don't expect he'll stay here long.'

His thoughts then reverted to Giles's party, and when they were nearly home he spoke again, his daughter being a few steps in advance: 'It is hardly the line of life for a girl like Grace, after what she's been accustomed to. I didn't foresee that, in sending her to boarding-school and letting her travel and what not, to make her a good bargain for Giles, I should be really spoiling her for him. Ah, 'tis a thousand pities! But he ought to have her – he ought!'

At this moment the two chalk-marking, langterloo men, having at last really finished their play, could be heard coming along in the rear, vociferously singing a song to march-time, and keeping vigorous step to the same in far-reaching strides –

> '. . . said she,
> "A maid again I never shall be,
> Till apples grow on an orange tree!"'

The timber-merchant turned indignantly to Mrs Melbury. 'That's the sort of society we've been asked to meet!' he said. 'For us old folk it didn't matter; but for Grace – Giles should have known better!'

Meanwhile, in the empty house from which the guests had just cleared out, the subject of their discourse was walking from room to room surveying the general displacement of furniture with no ecstatic feeling; rather the reverse indeed. At last he entered the bakehouse, and found there Robert Creedle sitting over the embers, also lost in contemplation. Winterborne sat down beside him.

'Well, Robert, you must be tired. You'd better get on to bed.'

'Ay, ay, Giles – what do I call ye? Maister, I would say. But 'tis well to think the day *is* done, when 'tis done.'

Winterborne had abstractedly taken the poker, and with a wrinkled forehead was ploughing abroad the wood-embers on the wide hearth, till it was like a vast scorching Sahara, with red-hot boulders lying about everywhere. 'Do you think it went off well, Creedle?' he asked.

'The victuals did; that I know. And the drink did; that I steadfastly believe, from the holler sound of the barrels. Good honest drink 'twere, the headiest drink I ever brewed; and the best wine that berries could rise to; and the briskest Horner-and-Cleeves cider ever wrung down, leaving out the spice and sperrits I put into it, while that egg-flip would ha' passed through muslin, so little criddled 'twere. 'Twas good enough to make any king's heart merry – ay, to make his whole carcase smile! Still, I don't deny I'm afeard some things didn't go well with He and his.' Creedle nodded in a direction which signified where the Melburys lived.

'I'm afraid, too, that it was a failure there.'

'If so, 'twere doomed to be so. Not but what that slug might as well have come upon anybody else's plate as hers.'

'What slug?'

'Well, maister, there was a little small one upon the edge of her plate when I brought it out, and so it must have been in her few leaves of wintergreen.'

'How the deuce did a slug get there?'

'That I don't know no more than the dead; but there my gentleman was.'

'But, Robert, of all places, that was where he shouldn't have been!'

'Well, 'twas his native home, come to that; and where else could we expect him to be? I don't care who the man is, slugs and caterpillars always will lurk in close to the stump of cabbages in that tantalizing way.'

'He wasn't alive, I suppose?' said Giles, with a shudder on Grace's account.

'O no. He was well boiled. I warrant him well boiled. God forbid that a *live* slug should be seed on any plate of victuals that's served by Robert Creedle. . . . But Lord, there; I don't mind 'em myself – them green ones; for they were born on cabbage, and they've lived on cabbage, so they must be made of cabbage. But she, the close-mouthed little lady, she didn't say a word about it; though 'twould have made good small conversation as to the nater of such creatures; especially as wit ran short among us sometimes.'

'O yes – 'tis all over!' murmured Giles to himself, shaking his head over the glooming plain of embers, and lining his forehead more than ever. 'Do you know, Robert,' he said, 'that she's been accustomed to servants and everything superfine these many years? How, then, could she stand our ways?'

'Well, all I can say is, then, that she ought to hob-and-nob elsewhere. They shouldn't have schooled her so monstrous high, or else bachelor-men shouldn't give randys, or if they do give 'em, only to their own race.'

'Perhaps that's true,' said Winterborne rising, and yawning a sigh.

CHAPTER ELEVEN

''Tis a pity – a thousand pities!' her father kept saying next morning at breakfast, Grace being still in her bedroom.

Here was the fact which could not be disguised: since seeing what an immense change her last twelve months of absence had produced in his daughter, after the heavy sum per annum that he had been spending for several years upon her education, he was reluctant to let her marry Giles Winterborne, indefinitely occupied as woodsman, cider-merchant, apple-farmer, and what not, even were she willing to marry him herself.

But how could he, with any self-respect, obstruct Winterborne's suit at this stage, and nullify a scheme he had laboured to promote – was, indeed, mechanically promoting at this moment? A crisis was approaching, mainly as a result of his contrivances; and it would have to be met.

'She will be his wife, if you don't upset her notion that she's bound to accept him as an understood thing,' said Mrs Melbury. 'Bless you, she'll soon shake down here in Hintock, and be content with Giles's way of living, which he'll improve with what money she'll have from you. 'Tis the strangeness after her genteel life that makes her feel uncomfortable at first. Why, when *I* saw Hintock the first time I thought I never could like it. But things gradually get familiar, and stone floors seem not so very cold and hard, and the hooting of owls not so very dreadful, and loneliness not so very lonely after a while.'

'Yes, I believe 'ee. That's just it. I *know* Grace will gradually sink down to our level again, and catch our manners and way of speaking, and feel a drowsy content in being Giles's wife. But I can't bear the thought of dragging down to that old level as promising a piece of maidenhood as ever lived – fit to ornament a palace wi', that I've taken so much trouble to lift up. Fancy her white hands getting redder every day, and her tongue losing its pretty up-country curl in talking, and her bounding walk becoming the regular Hintock shail-and-wamble.'

'She may shail; but she'll never wamble,' replied his wife decisively.

When Grace came downstairs he complained of her lying in bed so late; not so much moved by a particular objection to that form of indulgence as discomposed by these other reflections.

The corners of her pretty mouth dropped a little down. 'You used to complain with justice when I was a girl,' she said. 'But I am a woman now, and can judge for myself. . . . But it is not that: it is something else!' Instead of sitting down she went outside the door.

He was sorry. The petulance that relatives show towards each other is in truth directed against that intangible Cause which has shaped the situation no less for the offenders than the offended, but is too elusive to be discerned and cornered by poor humanity in irritated mood. Melbury followed her. She had rambled on to the paddock, where the white frost lay, making the grass rustle like paper-shavings under their feet, and where starlings in flocks of twenties and thirties were walking about, watched by a comfortable family of sparrows perched in a line along the string-course of the chimney, and preening themselves in the rays of the sun.

'Come in to breakfast, my girl!' he said. 'And as to Giles, use your own mind. Whatever pleases you will please me.'

'I am promised to him, father; and I cannot help thinking that in honour I ought to marry him, whenever I do marry.'

He had a strong suspicion that somewhere in the bottom of her heart there pulsed an old simple indigenous feeling favourable to Giles, though it had become overlaid with implanted tastes. 'Very well,' he said. 'But I hope I shan't lose you yet. Come in to breakfast. What did you think of the inside of Hintock House the other day?'

'I liked it much.'

'Different from friend Winterborne's?'

She said nothing; but he who knew her was aware that she meant by her silence to reproach him with drawing cruel comparisons.

'Mrs Charmond has asked you to come again – when, did you say?'

'She thought Tuesday; but would send the day before to let me know if it suited her.' And with this subject upon their lips they entered to breakfast.

Tuesday came, but no message from Mrs Charmond. Nor was there any on Wednesday. In brief, a fortnight slipped by without a sign, and it looked suspiciously as if Mrs Charmond was not going further in the direction of 'taking up' Grace at present.

Her father reasoned thereon. Immediately after his daughter's two indubitable successes with Mrs Charmond – the interview in the wood and the visit to the House – she had attended Winterborne's party. No doubt the out-and-out joviality of that gathering had made it a topic in the neighbourhood, and that every one present as guests had been widely spoken of – Grace, with her exceptional qualities, above all. What then so natural as that Mrs Charmond should have heard the village news, and become quite disappointed in her expectations of Grace at finding she kept such company?

Full of this *post hoc* argument Mr Melbury overlooked the infinite throng of other possible reasons and unreasons for a woman changing her mind. For instance, while knowing that his Grace was attractive he quite forgot that Mrs Charmond had also great pretensions to beauty.

So it was settled in his mind that her sudden mingling with the villagers at the unlucky Winterborne's was the cause of her most grievous loss, as he deemed it, in the direction of Hintock House.

''Tis a great sacrifice!' he would repeat to himself. 'I am ruining her for conscience' sake!'

It was one morning later on, while these things were agitating his mind, that something darkened the window just as they finished breakfast. Looking up they saw Giles in person, mounted on horse-back, and straining his neck forward, as he had been doing for some time, to catch their attention through the window. Grace had been the first to see him, and involuntarily exclaimed, 'There he is — and a new horse!'

On their faces, as they regarded Giles, were written their suspended thoughts and compound feelings concerning him, could he have read them through those old panes. But he saw nothing: his features just now were, for a wonder, lit up with a red smile at some other idea. So they rose from breakfast and went to the door, Grace with an anxious, wistful manner, her father in a reverie, Mrs Melbury placid and inquiring.

'We have come out to look at your horse,' she said.

It could be seen that he was pleased at their attention, and explained that he had ridden a mile or two to try the animal's paces. 'I bought her,' he added, with warmth so severely repressed as to seem indifference, 'because she has been used to carry a lady.'

Still Mr Melbury did not brighten. Mrs Melbury said, 'And is she quiet?'

Winterborne assured her that there was no doubt of it. 'I took care of that. She's twenty-one, and very clever for her age.'

'Well, get off and come in,' said Melbury brusquely; and Giles dismounted accordingly.

This event was the concrete result of Winterborne's thoughts during the past week or two. The want of success with his evening party he had accepted in as philosophic a mood as he was capable of; but there had been enthusiasm enough left in him one day at Sherton Abbas market to purchase the mare, which had belonged to a neighbouring parson with several daughters, and was offered him to carry either a gentleman or a lady, and to do odd jobs of carting and agriculture at a pinch. This obliging quadruped seemed to furnish Giles with means of reinstating himself in Melbury's good opinion as a man of considerateness, by throwing out equestrian possibilities to Grace if she became his wife.

The latter looked at him with intensified interest this morning, in the mood which is altogether peculiar to woman's nature, and which, when reduced into plain words, seems as impossible as the penetrability of matter — that of entertaining a tender pity for the object of her own unnecessary coldness. The imperturbable poise which marked Winterborne in general was enlivened now by a freshness and animation that set a brightness in his eye and on his cheek. Mrs

Melbury asked him to have some breakfast, and he pleasurably replied that he would join them, not perceiving that they had all finished the meal, and that the tune piped by the kettle denoted it to be nearly empty; so that fresh water had to be brought in, and a general renovation of the table carried out. Neither did he know, so full was he of his tender ulterior object in buying that horse, how the morning was slipping away, nor how he was keeping the family from dispersing about their duties.

Then he told throughout the humorous story of the horse's purchase, looking particularly grim at some fixed object in the room, a way he always looked when he narrated anything that amused him. While he was still thinking of the scene he had described Grace rose and said, 'I have to go and help my mother now, Mr Winterborne.'

'H'm?' he ejaculated, turning his eyes suddenly upon her.

She repeated her words with a slight blush of awkwardness; whereupon Giles, becoming suddenly conscious, too conscious, jumped up, saying, 'To be sure, to be sure!' and wished them quickly good-morning.

Nevertheless he had upon the whole strengthened his position, with her at least. Time, too, was on his side, for (as her father saw with regret) already the homeliness of Hintock life was fast becoming lost to her observation as a singularity; as the momentary strangeness of a face from which we have for years been separated insensibly passes off with renewed intercourse, and tones itself down into identity with the lineaments of the past.

Thus Mr Melbury went out of the house still unreconciled to the sacrifice of the gem he had been at such pains in mounting. He fain could hope, in the secret nether chamber of his mind, that something would happen before the balance of her feeling had quite turned in Winterborne's favour, to relieve his conscience and at the same time preserve her on her elevated plane.

CHAPTER TWELVE

It was a day of rather bright weather for the season. Miss Melbury went out for a morning walk, and her ever-regardful father, having an hour's leisure, offered to walk with her.

The breeze was fresh and quite steady, filtering itself through the denuded mass of twigs without swaying them, but making the point of each ivy-leaf on the trunks scratch its underlying neighbour restlessly. Grace's lips sucked in this native air of hers like milk. They soon reached a place where the wood ran down into a corner, and they went outside it towards comparatively open ground. Having looked round they were intending to re-enter the copse when a panting fox emerged with a dragging brush, trotted past them tamely as a domestic cat, and disappeared amid some dead fern. They walked on, her father merely observing after watching the animal, 'They are hunting somewhere near.'

Further up they saw in the mid-distance the hounds running hither and thither, as if the scent lay cold that day. Soon members of the hunt appeared on the scene, and it was evident that the chase had been stultified by general puzzle-headedness as to the whereabouts of the intended victim. In a minute a gentleman-farmer, panting with Actæonic excitement, rode up to the two pedestrians, and Grace being a few steps in advance he asked her if she had seen the fox.

'Yes,' said she. 'I saw him some time ago – just out there.'

'Did you cry Halloo?'

'I said nothing.'

'Then why the devil didn't you, or get the old buffer to do it for you?' said the man as he cantered away.

She looked rather disconcerted, and observing her father's face saw that it was quite red.

'He ought not to have spoken to 'ee like that!' said the old man in the tone of one whose heart was bruised, though it was not by the epithet applied to himself. 'And he wouldn't if he had been a gentleman. 'Twas not the language to use to a woman of any niceness. You so well read and cultivated – how could he expect ye to go shouting a view-halloo like a farm tomboy! Hasn't it cost me near a hundred a year to lift you out of all that, so as to show an example to the neighbourhood of what a woman can be? Grace, shall I tell you the secret of it? 'Twas because *I* was in your company. If a black-coated squire or pa'son had been walking with you instead of me he wouldn't have spoken so.'

'No, no, father; there's nothing in you rough or ill-mannered!'

'I tell you it is that! I've noticed, and I've noticed it many times, that a woman takes her colour from the man she's walking with. The woman who looks an unquestionable lady when she's with a polished-up fellow, looks a tawdry imitation article when she's hobbing and nobbing with a homely blade. You shan't be treated like that for long, or at least your children shan't. You shall have somebody to walk with you who looks more of a dandy than I – please God you shall!'

'But, my dear father,' she said much distressed, 'I don't mind at all. I don't wish for more honour than I already have!'

'A perplexing and ticklish possession is a daughter', according to the Greek poet, and to nobody was one ever more so than to Melbury. As for Grace, she began to feel troubled; she did not perhaps wish, there and then, to devote her life unambitiously to Giles Winterborne, but she was more and more uneasy at being the social hope of the family.

'You would like to have more honour, if it pleases me?' asked her father, in continuation of the subject.

Despite her feeling she assented to this. His reasoning had not been without weight upon her.

'Grace,' he said, just before they had reached the house, 'if it costs me my life you shall marry well! To-day has shown me that whatever a young woman's niceness she stands for nothing alone. You shall marry well.'

He breathed heavily, and his breathing was caught up by the breeze, which seemed to sigh a soft remonstrance.

She looked calmly at him. 'And how about Mr Winterborne?' she asked. 'I mention it, father, not as a matter of sentiment, but as a question of keeping faith.'

The timber-merchant's eyes fell for a moment. 'I don't know – I don't know,' he said. ' 'Tis a trying strait. Well, well; there's no hurry. We'll wait and see how he gets on.'

That evening he called her into his room, a snug little apartment behind the large parlour. It had at one time been part of the bakehouse, with the ordinary oval brick oven in the wall; but Mr Melbury in turning it into an office had built into the cavity an iron safe, which he used for holding his private papers. The door of the safe was now open, and his keys were hanging from it.

'Sit down, Grace, and keep me company,' he said. 'You may amuse yourself by looking over these.' He threw out a heap of papers before her.

'What are they?' she asked.

'Securities of various sorts.' He unfolded them one by one. 'Papers worth so much money each. Now here's a lot of turnpike bonds, for one thing. Would you think that each of these pieces of paper is worth two hundred pounds?'

'No, indeed, if you didn't say so.'

' 'Tis so then. Now here are papers of another sort. They are for different sums in the three per cents. Now these are Port-Bredy Harbour bonds. We have a great stake in that harbour, you know, because I send off timber there. Open the rest at your pleasure. They'll interest 'ee.'

'Yes, I will, some day,' said she, rising.

'Nonsense, open them now. You ought to learn a little of such matters. A young lady of education should not be ignorant of money affairs altogether. Suppose you should be left a widow some day, with your husband's title-deeds and investments thrown upon your hands—'

'Don't say that, father. Title-deeds; it sounds so vain!'

'It does not. Come to that, I have title-deeds myself. There, that piece of parchment represents houses in Sherton Abbas.'

'Yes, but—' She hesitated, looked at the fire, and went on in a low voice, 'If what has been arranged about me should come to anything, my sphere will be quite a middling one.'

'Your sphere ought not to be middling,' he exclaimed. 'You said you never felt more at home, more in your element, anywhere than you did that afternoon with Mrs Charmond, when she showed you her house, and all her knick-knacks, and made you stay to tea so nicely in her drawing-room, surely you did!'

'Yes, I did say so,' admitted Grace.

'Was it true?'

'Yes, I felt so at the time. The feeling is less strong now, perhaps.'

'Ah! Now, though you don't see it, your feeling at the time was the right one, because your mind and body were just in full and fresh cultivation, so that going there with her was like meeting like. Since then you've been staying with us, and have fallen back a little, and so you don't feel your place so strongly. Now, do as I tell you, and look over these papers, and see what you'll be worth some day. For they'll all be yours, you know; who have I got to leave 'em to but you? Perhaps when your education is backed up by what these papers represent, and that backed up by another such a set and their owner, men such as that fellow was this morning may think you a little more than a buffer's girl.'

So she did as commanded, and opened each of the folded representatives of hard cash that her father put before her. To sow in her heart cravings for social position was obviously his strong desire, though in direct antagonism to a better feeling which had hitherto prevailed with him, and had, indeed, only succumbed that morning during the ramble.

She wished that she was not his worldly hope; the responsibility of such a position was too great. She had made it for herself mainly by her appearance and attractive behaviour to him since her return. 'If I had only come home in a shabby dress, and tried to speak roughly, this might not have happened,' she thought. She deplored less the fact, however, than the contingencies.

Her father then insisted upon her looking over his cheque-book and reading the counterfoils. This also she obediently did, and at last came to two or three which had been drawn to defray some of the late expenses of her clothes, board, and education.

'I, too, cost a good deal, like the horses and waggons and corn!' she said, looking up sorrily.

'I didn't want you to look at those; I merely meant to give you an idea of my investment transactions. But if you do cost as much as they, never mind. You'll yield a better return.'

'Don't think of me like that!' she begged. 'A mere chattel.'

'A what? Oh, a dictionary word. Well, as that's in your line I don't forbid it, even if it tells against me,' he said good-humouredly. And he looked her proudly up and down.

A few minutes later Grammer Oliver came to tell them that supper was ready, and in giving the information she added incidentally, 'So we shall soon lose the mistress of Hintock House for some time, I hear, Maister Melbury. Yes, she is going off to foreign parts to-morrow, for the rest of the winter months; and be-chok'd if I don't wish I could do the same, for my wind-pipe is furred like a flue.'

When the old woman had left the room Melbury turned to his daughter and said, 'So, Grace, you've lost your new friend, and your chance of keeping her company and writing her travels is quite gone from 'ee!'

Grace said nothing.

'Now,' he went on emphatically, ' 'tis Winterborne's affair has done this. O yes, 'tis! So let me say one word. Promise me that you will not meet him again without my knowledge.'

'I never do meet him, father, either without your knowledge or with it.'

'So much the better. I don't like the look of this at all. And I say it not out of harshness to him, poor fellow, but out of tenderness to you. For how could a woman, brought up delicately as you have been, bear the roughness of a life with him?'

She sighed; it was a sigh of sympathy with Giles, complicated by a sense of the intractability of circumstances.

At that same hour, and almost at that same minute, there was a conversation about Winterborne in progress in the village lane, opposite Mr Melbury's gates, where Timothy Tangs the elder and Robert Creedle had accidentally met.

The sawyer was asking Creedle if he had heard what was all over the parish, the skin of his face being toned towards brightness in respect of it as news, and towards concern in respect of its bearings.

'Why, that poor little lonesome thing, Marty South, is likely to lose her father.

He was almost well, but is much worse again; a man all skin and grief he ever were; and if he leave Little Hintock for a better land, won't it make some difference to your good man Winterborne, neighbour Creedle?'

'Can I be a prophet in Hintock?' said Creedle. 'I was only shaping of such a thing yesterday in my poor long-seeing way! It is upon John South's life that all Mr Winterborne's houses hang. If so be South die and so make his decease, thereupon the law ordains that the houses fall without the least chance of saving 'em into Her hands at the House. I told him so; but the words of the faithful be only as wind!'

CHAPTER THIRTEEN

THE news was true. The life – the one fragile life – that had been used as a measuring-tape of time by law, was in danger of being frayed away. It was the last of a group of lives which had served this purpose, at the end of whose breathings the small homestead occupied by South himself, the larger one of Giles Winterborne, and half a dozen others that had been in the possession of various Hintock village families for the previous hundred years, and were now Winterborne's, would fall in and become part of the encompassing estate.

Winterborne walked up and down his garden next day thinking of the contingency. The sense that the paths he was pacing, the cabbage-plots, the apple-trees, his dwelling, cider-cellar, wring-house, stables, weathercock, were all slipping away over his head and beneath his feet as if they were painted on a magic-lantern slide, was curious. In spite of John South's late indisposition he had not anticipated danger.

Whilst he was here in the garden somebody came to fetch him. It was Marty herself, and she showed her distress by her unconsciousness of a cropped poll. 'Father is still so much troubled in his mind about that tree,' she said. 'You know the tree I mean, Mr Winterborne? the tall one in front of the house that he thinks will blow down and kill us. Can you come and see if you can persuade him out of his notion? I can do nothing.'

He accompanied her to the cottage, and she conducted him upstairs. John South was pillowed up in a chair between the bed and the window, exactly opposite the latter, towards which his face was turned.

'Ah, neighbour Winterborne,' he said. 'I wouldn't have minded if my life had only been my own to lose; I don't vallie it in much of itself, and can let it go if 'tis required of me. But to think what 'tis worth to you, a young man rising in life, that do trouble me! It seems a trick of dishonesty towards ye to go off at fifty-five! I could bear up, I know I could, if it were not for the tree – yes, the tree 'tis that's killing me. There he stands, threatening my life every minute that the wind do blow. He'll come down upon us, and squat us dead; and what will ye do when the life on your property is taken away!'

'Never you mind me – that's of no consequence,' said Giles. 'Think of yourself alone.'

He looked out of the window in the direction of the woodman's gaze. The tree was a tall elm, familiar to him from childhood, which stood at a distance of two-thirds its own height from the front of South's dwelling. Whenever the wind blew, as it did now, the tree rocked, naturally enough; and the sight of its motion, and sound of its sighs, had gradually bred the terrifying illusion in the woodman's mind. Thus he would sit all day, in spite of persuasion, watching its every sway, and listening to the melancholy Gregorian melodies which the air wrung out of it. This fear it apparently was, rather than any organic disease, which was eating away the health of John South.

As the tree waved South waved his head, making it his fugleman with abject obedience. 'Ah, when it was quite a small tree,' he said, 'and I was a little boy, I thought one day of chopping it off with my hook to make a clothes-line prop with. But I put off doing it, and then I again thought that I would; but I forgot and didn't. And at last it got too big, and now 'tis my enemy, and will be the death of me. Little did I think, when I let that sapling stay, that a time would come when it would torment me, and dash me into my grave.'

'No, no,' said Winterborne and Marty soothingly. But they thought it possible that it might hasten him into his grave, though in another way than by falling.

'I tell you what,' added Winterborne; 'I'll climb up this afternoon, and shroud off the lower boughs, and then it won't be so heavy, and the wind won't affect it so.'

'She won't allow it – a strange woman come from nobody knows where – she won't have it done.'

'You mean Mrs Charmond? Oh, she doesn't know there's such a tree on her estate. Besides, shrouding is not felling, and I'll risk that much.'

He went out, and when afternoon came he returned, took a bill-hook from the shed, and with a ladder climbed into the lower part of the tree, where he began lopping off – 'shrouding' as they called it at Hintock – the lowest boughs. Each of these quivered under his attack, bent, cracked, and fell into the hedge. Having cut away the lowest tier he stepped off the ladder, climbed a few steps higher, and attacked those at the next level. Thus as ascended with the progress of his work far above the top of the ladder, cutting away his perches as he went, and leaving nothing but a bare stem below him.

The work was troublesome, for the tree was large. The afternoon wore on, turning dark and misty about four o'clock. From time to time Giles cast his eyes across towards the bedroom-window of South, where, by the flickering fire in the chamber, he could see the old man watching him, sitting motionless with a hand upon each arm of the chair. Beside him sat Marty, also straining her eyes towards the skyey field of his operations.

A curious question suddenly occurred to Winterborne, and he stopped his chopping. He was operating on another person's property to prolong the years of a lease by whose termination that person would considerably benefit. In that aspect of the case he doubted if he ought to go on. On the other hand he was working to save a man's life, and this seemed to empower him to adopt arbitrary measures.

The wind had died down to a calm, and while he was weighing the circumstances he saw coming along the road through the increasing mist a figure which, indistinct as it was, he knew well. Grace Melbury was on her way out from the house, probably for a short evening walk before dark. He arranged himself for a greeting from her, since she could hardly avoid passing immediately beneath the tree.

But Grace, though she looked up and saw him, was just at that time too full of the words of her father to give him any encouragement. The years-long regard that she had had for him was not kindled by her return into a flame of sufficient brilliancy to make her rebellious. Thinking that she might not see him, he cried, 'Miss Melbury, here I am.'

She turned up her head again. She was near enough to see the expression of his face, and the nails in his soles, silver-bright with constant walking. But she did not reply; and dropping her glance anew went on.

Winterborne's face grew strange; he mused, and proceeded automatically with his work. Grace meanwhile had not gone far. She had reached a gate, whereon she had leant sadly and whispered to herself, 'What shall I do?'

A sudden fog came on, and she curtailed her walk, passing under the tree again on her return. Again he addressed her. 'Grace,' he said, when she was close to the trunk, 'speak to me.' She gazed straight up, shook her head without stopping, and went on to a little distance, where she stood observing him from behind the hedge.

Her coldness had been kindly meant. If it was to be done, she had said to herself, it should be begun at once. While she stood out of observation Giles seemed to recognize her meaning; with a sudden start he worked on, climbing higher into the sky, and cutting himself off more and more from all intercourse with the sublunary world. At last he had worked himself so high up the elm, and the mist had so thickened, that he could only just be discerned as a dark grey spot on the light grey zenith; he would have been altogether out of notice but for the stroke of his bill-hook, and the flight of a bough downward, and its crash upon the hedge at intervals.

It was not to be done thus, after all: plainness and candour were best. She went back a third time; he did not see her now, and she lingeringly gazed up at his unconscious figure, loth to put an end to any kind of hope that might live on in him still.

'Giles – Mr Winterborne,' she said.

His work so rustled the boughs that he did not hear.

'Mr Winterborne!' she cried again, and this time he stopped, looked down, and replied.

'My silence just now was not accident,' she said in an unequal voice. 'My father says it is better for us not to think too much of that – engagement, or understanding, between us, that you know of. I, too, think that upon the whole he is right. But we are friends, you know, Giles, and almost relations.'

'Very well,' he answered in an enfeebled voice which barely reached down the tree. 'I have nothing to say, Grace – I cannot say anything till I've thought a while!'

She added with emotion in her tone, 'For myself I would have married you – some day – I think. But I give way, for I am assured it would be unwise.'

He made no reply, but sat back upon a bough, placed his elbow in a fork, and rested his head upon his hand. Thus he remained till the fog and the night had completely inclosed him from her view.

Grace heaved a divided sigh with a tense pause between, and moved onward, her heart feeling uncomfortably big and heavy, and her eyes wet. Had Giles, instead of remaining still, immediately come down from the tree to her, would she have continued in that filial, acquiescent frame of mind which she had announced to him as final? If it be true, as women themselves have declared, that one of their sex is never so much inclined to throw in her lot with a man for good and all as five minutes after she has told him such a thing cannot be, the probabilities are that something might have been done by the appearance of Winterborne on the ground beside Grace. But he continued motionless and silent in that gloomy Niflheim or fogland which involved him, and she proceeded on her way.

The spot seemed now to be quite deserted. The light from South's window made rays on the fog, but did not reach the tree. A quarter of an hour passed, and all was blackness overhead. Giles had not yet come down.

Then the tree seemed to shiver, then to heave a sigh: a movement was audible, and Winterborne dropped almost noiselessly to the ground. He had thought the matter out; and having returned the ladder and bill-hook to their places pursued his way homeward. He would not allow this incident to affect his outer conduct any more than the danger to his leaseholds had done, and went to bed as usual.

Two simultaneous troubles do not always make a double trouble; and thus it came to pass that Giles's practical anxiety about his houses, which would have been enough to keep him awake half the night at any other time, was displaced and not reinforced by his sentimental trouble about Grace Melbury. This severance was in truth more like a burial of her than a rupture with her, but he did not realize so much at present; even when he arose in the morning he felt quite moody and stern; as yet the second note in the gamut of such emotions, a distracting regret for his loss, had not made itself heard.

A load of oak timber was to be sent away before dawn that morning to a builder whose works were in a town many miles off. The trunks were chained down to a heavy timber carriage with enormous red wheels, and four of the most powerful of Melbury's horses were harnessed in front to draw them.

The horses wore their bells that day. There were sixteen to the team, carried on a frame above each animal's shoulders, and tuned to scale, so as to form two octaves, running from the highest note on the right or off-side of the leader to the lowest on the left or nearside of the shaft-horse. Melbury was among the last to retain horse-bells in that neighbourhood; for living at Little Hintock, where the lanes yet remained as narrow as before the days of turnpike roads, these sound-signals were still as useful to him and his neighbours as they had ever been in former times. Much backing was saved in the course of a year by the warning notes they cast ahead; moreover, the tones of all the teams in the district being known to the carters of each, they could tell a long way off on a dark night whether they were about to encounter friends or strangers.

The fog of the previous evening still lingered so heavily over the woods that the morning could not penetrate the trees. The load being a ponderous one, the lane crooked, and the air so thick, Winterborne set out, as he often did, to accompany the team as far as the corner, where it would turn into a wider road.

So they rumbled on, shaking the foundations of the roadside cottages by the weight of their progress, the sixteen bells chiming harmoniously over all, till they had risen out of the valley, and were descending towards the more open route, sparks rising from their creaking skid as if they would set fire to the dead leaves alongside.

Then occurred one of the very incidents against which the bells were an endeavour to guard. Suddenly there beamed into their eyes, quite close to them, the two lamps of a carriage, haloed by the fog. Its approach had been quite unheard by reason of their own noise. The carriage was a covered one, while behind it could be discerned another vehicle laden with luggage.

Winterborne went to the head of the team, and heard the coachman telling the carter that he must turn back. The carter declared that this was impossible.

'You can turn if you unhitch your string-horses,' said the coachman.

'It is much easier for you to turn than for us,' said Winterborne. 'We've five ton of timber on these wheels if we've an ounce.'

'But I've another carriage with luggage at my back.'

Winterborne admitted the strength of the argument. 'But even with that,' he said, 'you can back better than we. And you ought to, for you could hear our bells half a mile off.'

'And you could see our lights.'

'We couldn't, because of the fog.'

'Well, our time's precious,' said the coachman haughtily. 'You are only going to some trumpery little village or other in the neighbourhood, while we are going straight to Italy.'

'Driving all the way, I suppose?' said Winterborne sarcastically.

The contention continued in these terms till a voice from the interior of the carriage inquired what was the matter. It was a lady's.

She was informed of the timber people's obstinacy; and then Giles could hear her telling the footman to direct the timber people to turn their horses' heads.

The message was brought, and Winterborne sent the bearer back to say that he begged the lady's pardon, but that he could not do as she requested; that though he would not assert it to be impossible, it was impossible by comparison with the slight difficulty to her party to back their light carriages. As fate would have it, the incident with Grace Melbury on the previous day made Giles less gentle than he might otherwise have shown himself, his confidence in the sex being rudely shaken.

In fine, nothing could move him, and the carriages were compelled on back till they reached one of the sidings or turn-outs constructed in the bank for the purpose. Then the team came on ponderously, and the clanging of its sixteen bells as it passed the discomfited carriages tilted up against the bank, lent a particularly triumphant tone to the team's progress – a tone which, in point of fact, did not at all attach to its conductor's feelings.

Giles walked behind the timber, and just as he had got past the yet stationary carriages he heard a lofty voice say, 'Who is that rude man? Not Melbury?' The sex of the speaker was so prominent in the tones that Winterborne felt a pang of regret.

'No, ma'am. A younger man, in a smaller way of business in Little Hintock. Winterborne is his name.'

Thus they parted company. 'Why, Mr Winterborne,' said the waggoner when they were out of hearing, 'that was she – Mrs Charmond! Who'd ha' thought it? What in the world can a woman that does nothing be cock-watching out here at this time o' day for? Oh, going to Italy – yes, to be sure, I heard she was going abroad. She can't endure the winter here.'

Winterborne was vexed at the incident; the more so that he knew Mr Melbury, in his adoration of Hintock House, would be the first to blame him if it became known. He accompanied the load to the end of the lane, and then turned back with an intention to call at South's to learn the result of the experiment of the preceding evening.

It chanced that a few minutes before this time Grace Melbury, who now rose soon enough to breakfast with her father, in spite of the unwontedness of the hour, had been commissioned by him to make the same inquiry at South's. Marty had been standing at the door when Miss Melbury arrived. Almost before the latter had spoken Mrs Charmond's carriages, released from the obstruction up the lane, came bowling along, and the two girls turned to regard the spectacle.

Mrs Charmond did not see them, but there was sufficient light for them to discern her outline between the carriage windows. A noticeable feature in her *tournure* was a magnificent mass of braided locks.

'How well she looks this morning!' said Grace, forgetting Mrs Charmond's slight in her generous admiration. 'Her hair so becomes her worn that way. I have never seen any more beautiful!'

'Nor have I, miss,' said Marty drily, and unconsciously stroking her crown.

Grace watched the carriages with lingering regret till they were out of sight. She then learnt of Marty that South was no better. Before she had come away Winterborne approached the house, but seeing that one of the two girls standing on the doorstep was Grace he turned back again, and sought the shelter of his own home till she should have gone away.

CHAPTER FOURTEEN

THE encounter with the carriages forced Winterborne's mind back again to the houses of his which would fall into Mrs Charmond's possession in the event of South's death. He marvelled, as many have done since, what could have induced his ancestors at Hintock, and other village people, to exchange their old copyholds for lifeleases. And he was much struck with his father's negligence in not insuring South's life.

After breakfast he went upstairs, turned over his bed, and drew out a flat canvas bag which lay between the mattress and the sacking. In this he kept his leases, which had remained there unopened ever since his father's death. It was the usual hiding-place among rural lifeholders for such documents. Winterborne sat down on the bed and looked them over. They were ordinary leases for three lives, which a member of the South family, some fifty years before this time, had accepted of the lord of the manor in lieu of certain copyholds and other rights, in consideration of having the dilapidated houses rebuilt by the said lord. They had come into his father's possession chiefly through his mother, who was a South.

Pinned to the corner of one of the indentures was a letter which Winterborne had never seen before. It bore a remote date, the handwriting being that of some solicitor or agent, and the signature the landholder's. It was to the effect that, at any time before the last of the stated lives should drop, Mr John Winterborne, or his representative, should have the privilege of adding his own and his son's life to the life remaining on payment of a merely nominal fine; the concession being in consequence of the elder Winterborne's consent to demolish one of the houses and relinquish its site, which stood at an awkward corner of the lane, and impeded the way.

The house had been pulled down years before. Why Giles's father had not taken advantage of his privilege to insert his own and his son's lives it was impossible to say. In all likelihood death alone had hindered him in the execution of that project, the elder Winterborne having been a man who took much pleasure in dealing with house property in his small way.

Since one of the Souths still survived there was not much doubt that Giles could do what his father had left undone, as far as his own life was concerned. This possibility cheered him much; for by those houses hung many things. Melbury's doubt of the young man's fitness to be the husband of Grace had been based not a little on the precariousness of his holdings in Little and Great Hintock. He resolved to attend to the business at once, the fine for renewal being a sum that he could easily muster.

His scheme, however, could not be carried out in a day; and meanwhile he would run up to South's as he had intended to do, to learn the result of the experiment with the tree.

Marty met him at the door. 'Well, Marty,' he said; and was surprised to read in her face that the case was not so hopeful as he had imagined.

'I am sorry for your labour,' she said. 'It is all lost. He says the tree seems taller than ever.'

Winterborne looked around at it. Taller the tree certainly did seem, the gauntness of its now naked stem being more marked than before.

'It quite terrified him when he first saw what you had done to it this morning,' she added. 'He declares it will come down upon us and cleave us, like "the sword of the Lord and of Gideon".'

'Well; can I do anything else?' asked he.

'The doctor says the tree ought to be cut down.'

'O, you've had the doctor?'

'I didn't send for him. Mrs Charmond before she left heard that father was ill, and told him to attend him at her expense.'

'That was very good of her. And he says it ought to be cut down. We mustn't cut it down without her knowledge, I suppose.'

He went upstairs. There the old man sat, staring at the now gaunt tree as if his gaze were frozen on to its trunk. Unluckily the tree waved afresh by this time, a wind having sprung up and blown the fog away; and his eyes turned with its wavings.

They heard footsteps – a man's, but of a lighter weight than usual. 'There is Dr Fitzpiers again,' she said, and descended. Presently his tread was heard on the naked stairs.

Mr Fitzpiers entered the sick chamber as a doctor is wont to do on such occasions, and pre-eminently when the room is that of the humble cottager;

looking round towards the patient with a pre-occupied gaze which so plainly reveals that he has well-nigh forgotten all about the case and the circumstances since he dismissed them from his mind at his last exit from the same apartment. He nodded to Winterborne, who had not seen him since his peep over the hedge at Grace, recalled the case to his thoughts, and went leisurely on to where South sat.

Edred Fitzpiers was, on the whole, a finely formed, handsome man. His eyes were dark and impressive, and beamed with the light either of energy or of susceptivity – it was difficult to say which; it might have been chiefly the latter. That quick, glittering, empirical eye, sharp for the surface of things if for nothing beneath, he had not. But whether his apparent depth of vision were real, or only an artistic accident of his corporeal moulding, nothing but his deeds could reveal.

His face was rather soft than stern, charming than grand, pale than flushed; his nose – if a sketch of his features be *de rigueur* for a person of his pretensions – was artistically beautiful enough to have been worth modelling by any sculptor not over busy, and was hence devoid of those knotty irregularities which often mean power; while the classical curve of his mouth was not without a looseness in its close. Either from his readily appreciative mien, or his reflective manner, his presence bespoke the philosopher rather than the dandy – an effect which was helped by the absence of trinkets or other trivialities from his attire, though this was more finished and up to date than is usually the case among rural practitioners.

Strict people of the highly respectable class, knowing a little about him by report, said that he seemed likely to err rather in the possession of too many ideas than too few; to be a dreamy 'ist of some sort, or too deeply steeped in some false kind of 'ism. However this may be, it will be seen that he was undoubtedly a somewhat rare kind of gentleman and doctor to have descended, as from the clouds, upon Little Hintock.

'This is an extraordinary case,' he said at last to Winterborne, after examining South by conversation, looks, and touch, and learning that the craze about the elm was stronger than ever. 'Come downstairs, and I'll tell you what I think.'

They accordingly descended, and the doctor continued, 'The tree must be cut down; or I won't answer for his life.'

' 'Tis Mrs Charmond's tree; and I suppose we must get permission?' said Giles.

'O, never mind whose tree it is – what's a tree beside a life! Cut it down. I have not the honour of knowing Mrs Charmond as yet; but I am disposed to risk that much with her.'

' 'Tis timber,' rejoined Giles. 'They never fell a stick about here without its being marked first, either by her or the agent.'

'Then we'll inaugurate a new era forthwith. How long has he complained of the tree?' asked the doctor of Marty.

'Weeks and weeks, sir. The shape of it seems to haunt him like an evil spirit. He says that it is exactly his own age, that it has got human sense, and sprouted up when he was born on purpose to rule him, and keep him as its slave. Others have been like it afore in Hintock.'

They could hear South's voice upstairs. 'O, he's rocking this way; he must come! And then my poor life, that's worth houses upon houses, will be squashed out o' me. O! O!'

'That's how he goes on,' she added. 'And he'll never look anywhere else but out of the window, and scarcely have the curtains drawn.'

'Down with it, then, and hang Mrs Charmond,' said Mr Fitzpiers. 'The best plan will be to wait till the evening, when it is dark, or early in the morning before he is awake, so that he doesn't see it fall, for that would terrify him worse than ever. Keep the blind down till I come, and then I'll assure him, and show him that his trouble is over.'

The doctor departed, and they waited till the evening. When it was dusk, and the curtains drawn, Winterborne directed a couple of woodmen to bring a cross-cut saw; and the tall threatening tree was soon nearly off at its base. Next morning, before South was awake, they went and lowered it cautiously, in a direction away from the cottage. It was a business difficult to do quite silently; but it was done at last, and the elm of the same birth-year as the woodman's lay stretched upon the ground. The weakest idler that passed could now set foot on marks formerly made in the upper forks by the shoes of adventurous climbers only; once inaccessible nests could be examined microscopically; and on swaying extremities where birds alone had perched the bystanders sat down.

As soon as it was broad daylight the doctor came, and Winterborne entered the house with him. Marty said that her father was wrapped up and ready, as usual, to be put into his chair. They ascended the stairs, and soon seated him. He began at once to complain of the tree, and the danger to his life and Winterborne's house property in consequence.

The doctor signalled to Giles, who went and drew back the dimity curtains. 'It is gone, see,' said Mr Fitzpiers.

As soon as the old man saw the vacant patch of sky in place of the branched column so familiar to his gaze, he sprang up, speechless; his eyes rose from their hollows till the whites showed all round, he fell back, and a bluish whiteness overspread him.

Greatly alarmed they put him on the bed. As soon as he came a little out of his fit he gasped, 'O, it is gone! – where – where?'

His whole system seemed paralysed by amazement. They were thunderstruck at the result of the experiment, and did all they could. Nothing seemed to avail. Giles and Fitzpiers went and came, but uselessly. He lingered through the day, and died that evening as the sun went down.

'Damned if my remedy hasn't killed him!' murmured the doctor.

Dismissing the subject he went downstairs. When going out of the house he turned suddenly to Giles and said, 'Who was that young lady we looked at over the hedge the other day?'

Giles shook his head, as if he did not remember.

CHAPTER FIFTEEN

WHEN Melbury heard what had happened he seemed much moved, and walked thoughtfully about the premises. On South's own account he was genuinely

sorry; and on Winterborne's he was the more grieved in that this catastrophe had
so closely followed the somewhat harsh suggestion to Giles to draw off from his
daughter.

He was quite angry with circumstances for so heedlessly inflicting on Giles a
second trouble when the needful one inflicted by himself was all that the proper
order of events demanded. 'I told Giles's father when he came into those houses
not to spend too much money on lifehold property held neither for his own life
nor his sons's,' he exclaimed; 'but he wouldn't listen to me. And now Giles has to
suffer for it.'

'Poor Giles!' murmured Grace.

'Now, Grace, between us two, it is very, very remarkable. It is almost as if I had
foreseen this; and I am thankful for your escape, though I am sincerely sorry for
Giles. Had we not dismissed him already we could hardly have found it in our
hearts to dismiss him now. So I say, be thankful. I'll do all I can for him as a
friend; but as a pretender to the position of my son-in-law, that can never be
thought of more.'

And yet at that very moment the impracticability to which poor Winterborne's
suit had been reduced was touching Grace's heart to a warmer sentiment in his
behalf than she had felt for years concerning him.

He, meanwhile, was sitting down alone in the familiar house which had ceased
to be his; taking a calm if somewhat dismal survey of affairs. The pendulum of the
clock bumped every now and then against one side of the case in which it swung,
as the muffled drum to his worldly march. Looking out of the window he could
perceive that a paralysis had come over Creedle's occupation of manuring the
garden, owing, obviously, to a conviction that they might not be living there long
enough to profit by next season's crop.

He looked at the leases again and the letter attached. There was no doubt that
he had lost his houses and was left practically penniless by an accident which
might easily have been circumvented if he had known the true conditions of his
holding. The time for performance had now lapsed in strict law; but why should
not the intention be considered by the landholder when she became aware of the
circumstances, and his moral right to retain the holdings for the term of his life be
conceded?

His heart sank within him when he perceived that, despite all the legal
reciprocities and safeguards prepared and written, the upshot of the matter was
that it depended upon the mere caprice of the woman he had met the day before,
in such an unfortunate way, whether he was to possess his houses for life or no.

While he was sitting and thinking a step came to the door, and Melbury
appeared, looking very sorry for his position. Winterborne welcomed him by a
word and a nod, and went on with his examination of the parchments. His visitor
sat down.

'Giles,' he said, 'this is very awkward, and I am sorry for it. What are you going
to do?'

Giles informed him of the real state of affairs, and how barely he had missed
availing himself of his chance of renewal.

'What a misfortune! Why was this neglected? Well, the best thing you can do is
to write and tell her all about it, and throw yourself upon her generosity.'

'I would rather not,' murmured Giles.

'But you must,' said Melbury. 'Much depends on it.'

In short, he argued so cogently that Giles allowed himself to be persuaded, firmly believing it to be a last blow for Grace. The letter to Mrs Charmond was written and sent to Hintock House, whence, as he knew, it would at once be forwarded to her.

Melbury, feeling that he had done so good an action in coming as to extenuate his previous arbitrary conduct, went home; and Giles was left alone to the suspense of waiting for a reply from the divinity who shaped the ends of the Hintock population. By this time all the villagers knew of the circumstances, and being well-nigh like one family a keen interest was the result all round.

Everybody thought of Giles; nobody thought of Marty. Had any of them looked in upon her during those moonlight nights which preceded the burial of her father they would have seen the girl absolutely alone in the house with the dead man. Her own chamber being nearest the stair-top, the coffin had been placed there for convenience; and at a certain hour of the night, when the moon arrived opposite the window, its beams streamed across the still profile of South, sublimed by the august presence of death, and onward a few feet further upon the face of his daughter, lying in her little bed in the silence of a repose almost as dignified as that of her companion – the repose of a guileless soul that had nothing more left on earth to lose, except a life which she did not over-value.

South was buried, and a week passed, and Winterborne watched for a reply from Mrs Charmond. Melbury was very sanguine as to its tenor; but Winterborne had not told him of the encounter with her carriage, when, if ever he had heard an affronted tone on a woman's lips, he had heard it on hers.

The postman's time for passing was just after Melbury's men had assembled in the spar-house; and Winterborne, who when not busy on his own account would lend assistance there, used to go out into the lane every morning and meet the postman at the end of one of the green rides through the hazel-copse, in the straight stretch of which his laden figure could be seen a long way off. Grace also was very anxious; more anxious than her father, more perhaps than Winterborne himself. This anxiety led her into the spar-house on some pretext or other almost every morning whilst they were awaiting the answer.

Eleven times had Winterborne gone to that corner of the ride, and looked up its long straight slope through the wet greys of winter dawn. But though the postman's bowed figure loomed in view pretty regularly, he brought nothing for Giles. On the twelfth day the man of missives, while yet in the extreme distance, held up his hand, and Winterborne saw a letter in it. He took it into the spar-house before he broke the seal, and those who were there gathered round him while he read, Grace looking in at the door.

The letter was not from Mrs Charmond herself, but from her agent at Sherton. Winterborne glanced it over and looked up.

'It's all over,' he said.

'Ah!' said they all together.

'Her lawyer is instructed to say that Mrs Charmond sees no reason for disturbing the natural course of things, particularly as she contemplates pulling the houses down,' he said quietly.

'Only think of that!' said several. 'Pulling down is always the game.'

Winterborne had turned away, and said vehemently to himself, 'Then let her pull 'em down, and be damned to her!'

Creedle looked at him with a face of seven sorrows, saying, 'Ah 'twas that sperrit that lost 'em for ye, maister!'

Winterborne subdued his feelings, and from that hour, whatever they were, kept them entirely to himself. Yet assuming the value of taciturnity to a man among strangers, it is apt to express more than talkativeness when he dwells among friends. The countryman who is obliged to judge the time of day from changes in external nature sees a thousand successive tints and traits in the landscape which are never discerned by him who hears the regular chime of a clock, because they are never in request. In like manner do we use our eyes on our taciturn comrade. The infinitesimal movement of muscle, curve, hair, and wrinkle, which when accompanied by a voice goes unregarded, is watched and translated in the lack of it, till virtually the whole surrounding circle of familiars is charged with the reserved one's moods and meanings.

So with Winterborne and his neighbours after his stroke of ill-luck. He held his tongue; and they observed him, and knew that he was discomposed.

Encountering Melbury one day his manner was that of a man who abandoned all claims. 'I am glad to meet 'ee, Mr Melbury,' he said in a low voice whose quality he endeavoured to make as practical as possible. 'I am afraid I shall not after this be able to keep that mare I bought for the use of – a possible wife, and as I don't care to sell her, I should like, if you don't object, to give her to Miss Melbury. The horse is very quiet, and would be quite safe for her.'

Mr Melbury was rather affected at this. 'You sha'n't hurt your pocket like that on our account, Giles. Grace shall have the horse, but I'll pay you what you gave for her, and any expense you may have been put to for her keep.'

He would not hear of any other terms, and thus it was arranged. They were now opposite Melbury's house, and the timber-merchant pressed Winterborne to enter, Grace being out of the way.

'Pull round the settle, Giles,' said the timber-merchant as soon as they were within. 'I should like to have a serious talk with you.'

Thereupon he put the case to Winterborne frankly, and in quite a friendly way. He declared that he did not like to be hard on a man when he was in difficulty; but he really did not see how Winterborne could marry his daughter now without even a house to take her to.

Giles quite acquiesced in the awkwardness of his situation, but from a momentary gasp of hope – a feeling that he would like to know Grace's mind from her own lips – he did not speak out positively even then. He accordingly departed somewhat abruptly, and went home to consider whether he would seek to bring about a meeting with her.

In the evening while he sat pondering he fancied that he heard a scraping on the wall outside his house. The boughs of a monthly rose which grew there made such a noise sometimes, but as no wind was stirring he knew that it could not be the rose-tree. He took up the candle and went out. Nobody was near. As he turned the light flickered on the whitewashed rough-cast of the front, and he saw words written thereon in charcoal, which he read as follows: –

'O Giles, you've lost your dwelling-place,
And therefore, Giles, you'll lose your grace.'

Giles went indoors. He had his suspicions as to the scrawler of those lines, but he could not be sure. What filled his heart far more than curiosity about their authorship was a terrible belief that they were turning out to be true, try to regain Grace as he might. They decided the question for him. He sat down and wrote a formal note to Melbury, stating that he shared to the full Melbury's view of his own and his daughter's promise made some years before; he wished that it should be considered as cancelled, and they themselves quite released from any obligation on account of it.

Having fastened up this their plenary absolution he determined to get it out of his hands and have done with it; to which end he went off to Melbury's at once. It was now so late that the family had all retired; he crept up to the house, thrust the note under the door, and stole away as silently as he had come.

Melbury himself was the first to rise the next morning, and when he had read the letter his relief was great, for he knew that Giles could have made matters unpleasant if he had chosen to work upon Grace. 'Very honourable of Giles, very honourable,' he kept saying to himself. 'I shall not forget him. Now to keep her up to her own true level.'

It happened that Grace went out for an early ramble that morning, and to go in her customary direction she could not avoid passing Winterborne's house. The morning sun was shining flat upon its white surface, and the words, which still remained, were immediately visible to her. She read them. Her face flushed to crimson. She could see Giles and Creedle talking together at the back; the charred spar-gad with which the lines had been written lay on the ground beneath the wall. Feeling pretty sure that Winterborne would observe her action she quickly went up to the wall, rubbed out 'lose' and inserted 'keep' in its stead. Then she made the best of her way home without looking behind her. Giles could draw an inference now if he chose.

There could not be the least doubt that gentle Grace was warming to more sympathy with, and interest in, Winterborne than ever she had done while he was her promised lover; that since his misfortune those social shortcomings of his, which contrasted so awkwardly with her later experiences of life, had become obscured by the generous revival of an old romantic attachment to him. Though mentally trained and tilled into foreignness of view, as compared with her youthful time, Grace was not an ambitious girl, and might, if left to herself, have declined upon Winterborne without much discontent. Her feelings just now were so far from latent that the writing on the wall had quickened her to an unusual rashness.

Having returned from her walk she sat at breakfast silently. When her stepmother had left the room she said to her father, 'I have made up my mind that I should like my engagement to Giles to continue.'

Melbury looked much surprised.

'Nonsense,' he said sharply. 'You don't know what you are talking about. Look here.'

He handed across to her the letter received from Giles.

She read it and said no more. Could he have seen her write on the wall? She did not know. Fate, it seemed, would have it this way, and there was nothing to do but to acquiesce.

It was a few hours after this that Winterborne who, curiously enough, had *not* perceived Grace writing, was clearing away the tree from the front of South's late dwelling. He saw Marty standing in her doorway, a slim figure in meagre black, almost without womanly contours as yet. He went up to her and said:

'Marty, why did you write that on my wall last night? It *was* you, you know.'

'Because it was the truth.'

'Having prophesied one thing, why did you alter it to another? Your predictions can't be worth much.'

'I have not altered it.'

'But you have.'

'No.'

'It is altered. Go and see.'

She went, and read that in spite of losing his dwelling-place he would *keep* his Grace. Marty came back surprised.

'Well,' she said. 'Who can have made such nonsense of it?'

'Who indeed?' said he.

'I have rubbed it all out, as the point of it is quite gone.'

'You'd no business to rub it out; I meant to let it stay a little longer.'

'Some idle boy altered it, no doubt,' she murmured.

As this seemed very probable Winterborne said no more, and dismissed the matter from his mind.

From this day of his life onward for a considerable time Winterborne, though not absolutely out of his house as yet, retired into the background of human life and action thereabout – a feat not particularly difficult of performance anywhere when the doer has the assistance of a lost prestige. Grace, thinking that Winterborne saw her write, made no further sign, and the frail barque of fidelity that she had thus timidly launched was stranded and lost.

CHAPTER SIXTEEN

D R F ITZPIERS lived on the slope of the hill, in a house of much less pretension both as to architecture and as to magnitude than the timber-merchant's. The latter had without doubt been once the manorial residence appertaining to the snug and modest domain of Little Hintock, of which the boundaries were now lost by its absorption into the adjoining estate of Mrs Charmond. Though the Melburys themselves were unaware of the fact there was every reason to believe – at least so the parson said – that the owners of that little manor had been Melbury's own ancestors, the family name occurring in numerous documents relating to transfers of land about the time of the civil wars.

Mr Fitzpiers's dwelling, on the contrary, was small, box-like, and comparatively modern. It had been occupied, and was in part occupied still, by a retired farmer and his wife, who, on the surgeon's arrival in quest of a home, had accommodated him by receding from their front rooms into the kitchen quarter, whence they administered to his wants, and emerged at regular intervals to receive from him a not unwelcome addition to their income.

The cottage and its garden were so regular in their plan that they might have been laid out by a Dutch designer of the time of William and Mary. In a low, dense hedge was a door, over which the hedge formed an arch, and from the inside of the door a straight path, bordered with clipped box, ran up the slope of the garden to the porch, which was exactly in the middle of the house-front, with two windows on each side. Right and left of the path were first a bed of gooseberry-bushes; next of currant; next of raspberry; next of strawberry; next of old-fashioned flowers; at the corners opposite the porch being spheres of box resembling a pair of school globes. Over the roof of the house could be seen the orchard on yet higher ground, and behind the orchard the forest-trees, reaching up to the crest of the hill.

Opposite the garden door into the lane, and visible from the parlour window, was a swing-gate leading to a field, across which there ran a footpath. The swing-gate had just been repainted, and on one fine afternoon, before the paint was dry, and while gnats stuck dying thereon, the surgeon was standing in his room abstractedly looking out at an occasional pedestrian who passed along that route. Being of a philosophical stamp he perceived that the character of each of these travellers exhibited itself in a somewhat amusing manner by his or her method of handling the gate.

In the men there was not much variety: they gave the gate a kick and passed through. The women were more contrasting. To them the sticky woodwork was a barricade, a disgust, a menace, a treachery, as the case might be.

The first that he noticed was a bouncing young woman with her skirts tucked up and her hair wild. Fitzpiers knew her as Suke Damson. She grasped the gate without looking, giving it a supplementary push with her shoulder, when the white imprint drew from her an exclamation in language not too refined. She went to the green bank and sat down and rubbed herself in the grass, cursing the while.

'Ha! ha! ha!' laughed the doctor.

The next was a girl with her hair cropped short, in whom the surgeon recognized the daughter of his late patient, the woodman South. Moreover, a black gown that she wore by way of mourning unpleasantly reminded him that he had ordered a tree-felling which had caused her parent's death. She walked in thought, and not recklessly; but her pre-occupation led her to grasp without suspicion the bar of the gate, and touch it with her arm. Fitzpiers felt sorry that she should have soiled that new black frock, poor as it was, for it was probably her only one. She looked at her hand and arm, seemed but little surprised, wiped off the disfigurement with an unmoved face and as if without abandoning her original thoughts. Thus she went on her way.

Then there came over the green quite a different sort of personage. She walked as delicately as if she had been bred in town, and as firmly as if she had been bred in the country; she seemed one who dimly knew her appearance to be attractive, but who retained some of the charm of ignorance by forgetting self in a general pensiveness. She approached the gate.

To let such a creature touch it even with the tip of her glove was to Fitzpiers almost like letting her proceed to tragical self-destruction. He jumped up and looked for his hat, but was unable to find the right one; glancing again out of the window he saw that his assistance was unnecessary. Having come up she looked at the gate, picked up a little stick, and using it as a bayonet pushed open the obstacle without touching it at all.

He steadily watched her out of sight, recognizing her as the very young lady whom he had seen once before and been unable to identify. Whose could that emotional face be? All the others he had seen in Hintock as yet oppressed him with their crude rusticity; the contrast offered by this suggested that she hailed from elsewhere.

Precisely these thoughts had occurred to him at the first time of seeing her; but he now went a little further with them, and considered that as there had been no carriage lately in that spot she could not have come a very long distance. She must be somebody staying at Hintock House – probably Mrs Charmond, of whom he had heard so much; and this probability was sufficient to set a mild radiance in the surgeon's somewhat dull sky.

Fitzpiers sat down to the book he had been perusing. It happened to be that of a German metaphysician, for the doctor was not a practical man, except by fits, and much preferred the ideal world to the real, and the discovery of principles to their application. The young lady remained in his thoughts. He might have followed her; but he was not constitutionally active, and preferred a conjectural pursuit. However, when he went out for a ramble just before dusk he insensibly took the direction of Hintock House, which was the way Grace had been walking, her mind having run on Mrs Charmond that day; though Grace had returned long since by another route.

Fitzpiers reached the edge of the glen overlooking the manor-house. The shutters were shut, and only one chimney smoked. The mere aspect of the place was enough to inform him that Mrs Charmond had gone away, and that nobody else was staying there. Fitzpiers felt a vague disappointment that the young lady was not Mrs Charmond; and without pausing longer to gaze at a carcase from which the spirit had flown he bent his steps homeward.

Later in the evening Fitzpiers was summoned to visit a cottage-patient about five miles distant. Like the majority of young practitioners in his vicinity he was far from having assumed the dignity of being driven his rounds by a servant in a brougham that flashed the sunlight like a mirror; his way of getting about was by means of a gig which he drove himself, hitching the rein of the horse to the gate-post, shutter-hook, or garden-paling of the domicile under visitation, or giving pennies to little boys to hold the animal during his stay – pennies which were well earned when the cases to be attended were of a certain cheerful kind that wore out the patience of the little boys.

On this account of travelling alone the night-journeys which Fitzpiers had frequently to take were dismal enough, an apparent perversity in nature ruling that whenever there was to be a birth in a particularly inaccessible and lonely place that event should occur in the night. The surgeon, having been of late years a town man, hated the solitary midnight woodland. He was not altogether skilful with the reins, and it often occurred to his mind that if in some remote depths of the trees an accident were to happen, his being alone might be the death of him. Hence he made a practice of picking up any countryman or lad whom he chanced to pass by, and under the disguise of treating him to a nice drive obtained his companionship on the journey, and his convenient assistance in opening gates.

The doctor had started on his way out of the village on the night in question when the light of his lamps fell upon the musing form of Winterborne, walking leisurely along as if he had no object in life. Winterborne was a better class of companion than the doctor usually could get, and he at once pulled up and asked him if he would like a drive through the wood that fine night.

Giles seemed rather surprised at the doctor's friendliness, but said that he had no objection, and accordingly mounted beside Mr Fitzpiers.

They drove along under the black boughs which formed a tracery upon the stars. Looking up as they passed under a horizontal limb they sometimes saw objects like large tadpoles lodged diametrically across it, which Giles explained to be pheasants at roost; and they sometimes heard the report of a gun, which reminded him that others knew what those tadpole shapes represented as well as he.

Presently the doctor said what he had been going to say for some time:

'Is there a young lady staying in this neighbourhood – a very attractive girl – with a little white boa round her neck, and white fur round her gloves?'

Winterborne, of course, knew in a moment that Grace, whom he had caught the doctor peering at, was represented by these accessories. With a wary grimness induced by the circumstances he evaded an answer by saying, 'I saw a young lady talking to Mrs Charmond the other day; perhaps it was she.'

'It might have been,' said Fitzpiers. 'She is quite a gentlewoman – the one I mean. She cannot be a permanent resident in Hintock, or I should have seen her before. Nor does she look like one.'

'She is not staying at Hintock House?'

'No; it is closed.'

'Then perhaps she is staying at one of the cottages, or farmhouses?'

'O no – you mistake. She was a different sort of woman altogether.' As Giles was nobody Fitzpiers treated him accordingly, and rhapsodized to the night in continuation:

'She moved upon this earth a shape of brightness,
A power, that from its objects scarcely drew
One impulse of her being – in her lightness
Most like some radiant cloud of morning dew
Which wanders through the waste air's pathless blue
To nourish some far desert: she did seem
Beside me, gathering beauty as she grew,
Like the bright shade of some immortal dream
Which walks, when tempest sleeps, the wave of life's dark stream.'

The charm of the lines seemed to Winterborne to be somehow the result of his lost love's charms upon Fitzpiers.

'You seem to be mightily in love with her, sir,' he said, with a sensation of heart-sickness, and more than ever resolved not to mention Grace by name.

'O no – I am not that, Winterborne; people living insulated, as I do by the solitude of this place, get charged with emotive fluid like a Leyden jar with electric, for want of some conductor at hand to disperse it. Human love is a subjective thing – the essence itself of man, as that great thinker Spinoza says – *ipsa hominis essentia* – it is joy accompanied by an idea which we project against any suitable object in the line of our vision, just as the rainbow iris is projected against an oak, ash, or elm tree indifferently. So that if any other young lady had appeared instead of the one who did appear, I should have felt just the same interest in her, and have quoted precisely the same lines from Shelley about her, as about this one I saw. Such miserable creatures of circumstances are we all!'

'Well, it is what we call being in love down in these parts, whether or no,' said Winterborne.

'You are right enough if you admit that I am in love with something in my own head, and no thing-in-itself outside it at all.'

'Is it part of a country doctor's duties to learn that view of things, may I ask, sir?' said Winterborne, adopting the Socratic $\epsilon\iota\rho\omega\nu\epsilon\iota\alpha$ with such well-assumed simplicity that Fitzpiers answered readily —

'O no. The real truth is, Winterborne, that medical practice in places like this is a very rule of thumb matter: a bottle of bitter stuff for this and that old woman — the bitterer the better — compounded from a few simple stereotyped pre-scriptions; occasional attendance at births, where mere presence is almost sufficient, so healthy and strong are the people; and a lance for an abscess now and then. Investigation and experiment cannot be carried on without more appliances than one has here — though I have attempted a little.'

Giles did not enter into this view of the case; what he had been struck with was the curious parallelism between Mr Fitzpiers's manner and Grace's, as shown by the fact of both of them straying into a subject of discourse so engrossing to themselves that it made them forget it was foreign to him.

Nothing further passed between himself and the doctor in relation to Grace till they were on their way back. They had stopped at a wayside inn for a glass of brandy-and-cider hot, and when they were again in motion Fitzpiers, possibly a little warmed by the liquor, resumed the subject by saying, 'I should like very much to know who that young lady was.'

'What difference can it make, if she's only the tree your rainbow falls on?'

'Ha, ha! True.'

'You have no wife, sir?'

'I have no wife; and no idea of one. I hope to do better things than marry and settle in Hintock. Not but that it is well for a medical man to be married; and sometimes, begad, 'twould be pleasant enough in this place, with the wind roaring round the house, and the rain and the boughs beating against it. I hear that you lost your lifeholds by the death of South?'

'I did. I lost by that in more ways than one.'

They had reached the top of Hintock Lane or Street, if it could be called such where three-quarters of the roadside consisted of copse and orchard. One of the first houses to be passed was Melbury's. A light was shining from a bedroom window facing lengthwise of the lane. Winterborne glanced at it, and saw what was coming. He had withheld an answer to the doctor's inquiry, to hinder his knowledge of Grace. But 'who hath gathered the wind in his fists? who hath bound the waters in a garment?' — he could not hinder what was doomed to arrive, and might just as well have been outspoken. As they came up to the house Grace's figure was distinctly visible, drawing the two white curtains together which were used here instead of blinds.

'Why, there she is!' said Fitzpiers. 'How in the name of Heaven does she come there?'

'In the most natural way in the world. It is her home. Mr Melbury is her father.'

'Indeed – indeed – indeed! How comes he to have a daughter of that sort?'

Winterborne laughed coldly. 'Won't money do anything,' he said, 'if you've promising material to work upon? Why shouldn't a Hintock girl, taken early from home and put under proper instruction, become as finished as any other young lady if she's got brains and good looks to begin with?'

'No reason at all why she shouldn't,' murmured the surgeon with reflective disappointment. 'Only I didn't anticipate quite that kind of origin for her.'

'And you think an inch or two less of her now.' There was a little tremor in Winterborne's voice as he spoke.

'Well,' said the doctor with recovered warmth, 'I am not so sure that I think less of her. At first it was a sort of blow; but, dammy, I'll stick up for her. She's charming, every inch of her!'

'So she is,' said Winterborne. . . . 'But not for me!'

From this ambiguous expression of the reticent woodlander Dr Fitzpiers inferred that Giles disliked Miss Melbury, possibly for some haughtiness in her bearing towards him, and had, on that account, withheld her name. The supposition did not tend to diminish his admiration for her.

CHAPTER SEVENTEEN

GRACE's exhibition of herself in the act of pulling-to the window curtains had been the result of an unfortunate incident in the house that day – nothing less than the illness of Grammer Oliver, a woman who had never, till now, lain down for such a reason in her life. Like others to whom an unbroken career of health has made the idea of keeping their bed almost as repugnant as death itself, she had continued on foot till she literally fell on the floor; and though she had, as yet, been scarcely a day off duty, she had sickened into quite a different personage from the independent Grammer of the yard and spar-house. Ill as she was, on one point she was firm. On no account would she see a doctor; in other words, Fitzpiers.

The room in which Grace had been discerned was not her own but the old woman's. On the girl's way to bed she had received a message from Grammer to the effect that she would much like to speak to her that night.

Grace entered and set the candle on a low chair beside the bed, so that the profile of Grammer, as she lay, cast itself in a coal-black shadow upon the whitened wall, her large head being still further magnified by an enormous turban, which was really her petticoat wound in a wreath round her temples. Grace put the room a little in order, and approaching the sick woman said –

'I am come, Grammer, as you wish. Do let us send for the doctor before it gets later?'

''Ch woll not have him!' said Grammer Oliver decisively.

'Then somebody to sit up with you?'

'Can't abear it! No. I wanted to see you, Miss Grace, because 'ch have something on my mind. Dear Miss Grace, *I took that money of the doctor, after all!'*

'What money?'

'The ten pounds.'

Grace did not quite understand.

'The ten pounds er offered me for my head, because I've a large organ of brain. I signed a paper when I took the money, not feeling concerned about it at all. I have not liked to tell 'ee that it was really settled with him, because you showed such horror at the notion. Well, having thought it over more at length, I wish I hadn't done it; and it weighs upon my mind. John South's death of fear about the tree makes me think I shall die of this. . . . 'Ch have been going to ask him again to let me off, but I hadn't the face.'

'Why?'

'I've spent some of the money — more'n two pounds o't! It do wherrit me terribly; and I shall die o' the thought of that paper I signed with my holy cross, as South died of his trouble!'

'If you ask him to burn the paper he will, I'm sure, and think no more of it.'

''Ch have done it once already, miss. But er laughed cruel-like. "Yours is such a fine brain, Grammer," er said, "that science couldn't afford to lose you. Besides, you've taken my money." . . . Don't let your father know of this, please, on no account whatever!'

'No, no. I will let you have the money to return to him.'

Grammer rolled the head in question negatively upon the pillow. 'Even if I should be well enough to take it to him he won't like it. Though why he should so particular want to look into the works of a poor old woman's headpiece like mine, when there's so many other folks about, I don't know. I know how he'll answer me: "A lonely person like you, Grammer," er woll say; "what difference is it to you what becomes of 'ee when the breath's out of your body?" O, it do trouble me! If you only knew how he do chevy me round the chimmer in my dreams you'd pity me. How I could do it I can't think! But 'ch was always so rackless! . . . If I only had anybody to plead for me!'

'Mrs Melbury would, I am sure.'

'Ay, but he wouldn't hearken to she! It wants a younger face than hers to work upon such as he.'

Grace started with comprehension. 'You don't think he would do it for me?' she said.

'O, wouldn't he!'

'I couldn't go to him, Grammer, on any account. I don't know him at all.'

'Ah, if I were a young lady,' said the artful Grammer, 'and could save a poor old woman's skellington from a heathen's chopper, to rest in a Christian grave, I would do it, and be glad to. But nobody will do anything for a poor old woman but push her out of the way!'

'You are very ungrateful, Grammer, to say that. But you are ill, I know, and that's why you speak so. Now believe me, you are not going to die yet. Remember you told me yourself that you meant to keep him waiting many a year.'

'Ay, one can joke when one is well, even in old age; but in sickness one's gaiety falters; and that which seemed small looks large; and the far-off seems near.'

Grace's eyes had tears in them. 'I don't like to go to him on such an errand, Grammer,' she said. 'But I will, if I must, to ease your mind!'

It was with extreme reluctance that Grace cloaked herself next morning for the undertaking. She was all the more indisposed to the journey by reason of Grammer's allusion to the effect of a pretty face upon Dr Fitzpiers; and hence she most illogically did that which, had the doctor never seen her, would have operated to stultify the sole motive of her journey; that is to say, she put on a woollen veil which hid all her face except an occasional spark of her eyes.

Her own wish that nothing should be known of this strange and gruesome proceeding, no less than Grammer Oliver's own desire, led Grace to take every precaution against being discovered. She went out by the garden-door as the safest way, all the household having occupations at the other side. The morning looked forbidding enough when she stealthily edged forth. The battle between snow and thaw was continuing in mid-air: the trees dripped on the garden plots, where no vegetables would grow for the dripping, though they were planted year after year with that curious mechanical regularity of country people in the face of hopelessness; the moss which covered the once broad gravel terrace was swamped; and Grace stood irresolute. Then she thought of poor Grammer, and her dreams of the doctor running after her, scalpel in hand, and the possibility of a case so curiously similar to South's ending in the same way; thereupon she stepped out into the drizzle.

The nature of her errand, and Grammer Oliver's account of the post-mortem compact she had made, lent a fascinating horror to Grace's conception of Fitzpiers. She knew that he was a young man; but her single object in seeking an interview with him put all considerations of his age and social aspect from her mind. Standing as she stood in Grammer Oliver's shoes, he was simply a remorseless Jehovah of the sciences, who would not have mercy, and would have sacrifice; a man whom, save for this, she would have preferred to avoid knowing. But since, in such a small village, it was improbable that any long time could pass without their meeting, there was not much to deplore in her having to meet him now.

But, as need hardly be said, Miss Melbury's view of the doctor as a merciless, unwavering, irresistible scientist was not quite in accordance with fact. The real Dr Fitzpiers was a man of too many hobbies to show likelihood of rising to any great eminence in the profession he had chosen, or even to acquire any wide practice in the rural district he had marked out as his field of survey for the present. In the course of a year his mind was accustomed to pass in a grand solar sweep throughout the zodiac of the intellectual heaven. Sometimes it was in the Ram, sometimes in the Bull; one month he would be immersed in alchemy, another in poesy; one month in the Twins of astrology and astronomy; then in the Crab of German literature and metaphysics. In justice to him it must be stated that he took such studies as were immediately related to his own profession in turn with the rest, and it had been in a month of anatomical ardour without the possibility of a subject that he had proposed to Grammer Oliver the terms she had mentioned to her mistress.

As may be inferred from the tone of his conversation with Winterborne he had lately plunged into abstract philosophy with much zest; perhaps his keenly appreciative, modern, unpractical mind found this a realm more in his taste than any other. Though his aims were desultory Fitzpiers's mental constitution was not without its creditable side; a real inquirer he honestly was at times; even if the midnight rays of his lamp, visible so far through the trees of Hintock, lighted rank literatures of emotion and passion as often as, or oftener than, the books and *matériel* of science.

But whether he meditated the Muses or the philosophers, the loneliness of Hintock life was beginning to tell upon his impressionable nature. Winter in a solitary house in the country, without society, is tolerable, nay even enjoyable and delightful, given certain conditions; but these are not the conditions which attach to the life of a professional man who drops down into such a place by mere accident. They were present to the lives of Winterborne, Melbury, and Grace; but not to the doctor's. They are old association – an almost exhaustive biographical or historical acquaintance with every object, animate and inanimate, within the observer's horizon. He must know all about those invisible ones of the days gone by, whose feet have traversed the fields which look so grey from his windows; recall whose creaking plough has turned those sods from time to time; whose hands planted the trees that form a crest to the opposite hill; whose horses and hounds have torn through that underwood; what birds affect that particular brake; what bygone domestic dramas of love, jealousy, revenge, or disappointment have been enacted in the cottages, the mansion, the street or on the green. The spot may have beauty, grandeur, salubrity, convenience; but if it lack memories it will ultimately pall upon him who settles there without opportunity of intercourse with his kind.

In such circumstances, maybe, an old man dreams of an ideal friend, till he throws himself into the arms of any imposter who chooses to wear that title on his face. A young man may dream of an ideal friend likewise, but some humour of the blood will probably lead him to think rather of an ideal mistress, and at length the rustle of a woman's dress, the sound of her voice, or the transit of her form across the field of his vision, will enkindle his soul with a flame that blinds his eyes.

The discovery of the attractive Grace's name and family would have been enough in other circumstances to lead the doctor, if not to put her personality out of his head, to change the character of his interest in her. Instead of treasuring her image as a rarity he would at most have played with her as a toy. He was that kind of man. But situated here he could not go so far as amative cruelty. He dismissed all deferential thought about her, but he could not help taking her somewhat seriously.

He went on to imagine the impossible. So far, indeed, did he go in this futile direction that, as others are wont to do, he constructed dialogues and scenes in which Grace had turned out to be the mistress of Hintock manor-house, the mysterious Mrs Charmond, particularly ready and willing to be wooed by himself and nobody else.

'Well, she isn't that,' he said finally. 'But she's a very sweet, nice, exceptional girl.'

The next morning he breakfasted alone as usual. It was snowing with a fine-flaked desultoriness just sufficient to make the woodland grey without ever achieving whiteness. There was not a single letter for Fitzpiers, only a medical circular and a weekly newspaper.

To sit before a large fire on such mornings and read, and gradually acquire energy till the evening came, and then, with lamp alight and feeling full of vigour, to pursue some engrossing subject or other till the small hours, had hitherto been his practice since arriving here. But to-day he could not settle into his chair. That self-contained position he had lately occupied, in which his whole attention was given to objects of the inner eye, all outer regard being quite disdainful, seemed to have been taken by insidious stratagem, and for the first time he had an interest without the house. He walked from one window to another, and became aware that the most irksome of solitudes is not the solitude of remoteness, but that which is just outside desirable company.

The breakfast hour went by heavily enough, and the next followed in the same half-snowy, half-rainy style, the weather now being the inevitable relapse which sooner or later succeeds a time too radiant for the season, such as they had enjoyed in the late mid-winter at Hintock. To people at home there these changeful tricks had their interests; the strange mistakes that some of the more sanguine trees had made in budding before their month, to be incontinently glued up by frozen thawings now; the similar sanguine errors of impulsive birds in framing nests that were swamped by snow-water, and other such incidents, prevented any sense of wearisomeness in the minds of the natives. But these were features of a world not familiar to Fitzpiers, and the inner visions to which he had almost exclusively attended having suddenly failed in their power to absorb him, he felt unutterably dreary.

He wondered how long Miss Melbury was going to stay in Hintock. The season was unpropitious for accidental encounters with her out of doors, and except by accident he saw not how they were to become acquainted. One thing was clear – any acquaintance with her could only, with a due regard to his future, be casual, at most of the nature of a mild flirtation; for he had high aims, and they would some day lead him into other spheres than this.

Thus desultorily thinking he flung himself down upon the couch, which, as in many draughty old country houses, was constructed with a hood, being in fact a legitimate development from the settle. He tried to read as he reclined, but having sat up till three o'clock that morning the book slipped from his hand and he fell asleep.

CHAPTER EIGHTEEN

GRACE approached the house. Her knock, always soft in virtue of her nature, was softer to-day by reason of her strange errand. However, it was heard by the farmer's wife who kept the house, and Grace was admitted. Opening the door of the doctor's room the housewife glanced in, and imagining Fitzpiers absent asked Miss Melbury to enter and wait a few minutes whilst she should go and find him, believing him to be somewhere on the premises. Grace acquiesced, went in, and sat down close to the door.

As soon as the door was shut upon her she looked round the room, and started at perceiving a handsome man snugly ensconced on the couch, like a recumbent figure within some canopied mural tomb of the fifteenth century, except that his hands were not exactly clasped in prayer. She had no doubt that this was the surgeon.

Awaken him herself she could not, and her immediate impulse was to go and pull the broad riband with a brass rosette which hung at one side of the fireplace. But expecting the landlady to re-enter in a moment she abandoned this intention, and stood gazing in great embarrassment at the reclining philosopher.

The windows of Fitzpiers's soul being at present shuttered he probably appeared less impressive than in his hours of animation; but the light abstracted from his material features by sleep was more than counterbalanced by the mysterious influence of that state, in a stranger, upon the consciousness of a beholder so sensitive. So far as she could criticize at all she became aware that she had encountered a specimen of creation altogether unusual in that locality. The occasions on which Grace had observed men of this stamp were when she had been far away from Hintock, and even then such examples as had met her eye were at a distance, and mainly of commoner fibre than the one who now confronted her.

She nervously wondered why the woman had not discovered her mistake and returned, and went again towards the bell-pull. Approaching the chimney her back was to Fitzpiers, but she could see him in the glass. An indescribable thrill passed through her as she perceived that the eyes of the reflected image were open gazing wonderingly at her. Under the curious unexpectedness of the sight she became as if spell-bound, almost powerless to turn her head and regard the original. However, by an effort she did turn, when there he lay asleep the same as before.

Her startled perplexity as to what he could be meaning was sufficient to lead her to abandon her errand precipitately. She crossed quickly to the door, opened and closed it noiselessly, and went out of the house unobserved. By the time that she had gone down the path and through the garden-door into the lane she had recovered her equanimity. Here, screened by the hedge, she stood and considered a while.

Drip, drip, drip, fell the rain upon her umbrella and around; she had come out on such a morning because of the seriousness of the matter in hand; yet now she had allowed her mission to be stultified by a momentary tremulousness concerning an incident which perhaps had meant nothing after all.

In the meantime her departure from the room, stealthy as it had been, had roused Fitzpiers; and he sat up. In the reflection from the mirror which Grace had beheld there was no mystery; he had opened his eyes for a few moments, but had immediately relapsed into unconsciousness, if indeed he had ever been positively awake. That somebody had just left the room he was certain, and that the lovely form which seemed to have visited him in a dream was no less than the real presentation of the person departed he could hardly doubt.

Looking out of the window a few minutes later, down the box-edged gravel-path which led to the bottom, he saw the garden-door open and through it enter the young girl of his thoughts, Grace having just at this juncture determined to return and attempt the interview a second time. That he saw her coming instead of going made him ask himself if his first impression of her were not a dream indeed. She came hesitatingly along, carrying her umbrella so low over her head that he could hardly see her face. When she reached the point where the raspberry-bushes ended and the strawberry-bed began she made a little pause.

Fitzpiers feared that she might not be coming to him even now, and hastily quitting the room he ran down the path to meet her. The nature of her errand he could not divine, but he was prepared to give her any amount of encouragement.

'I beg pardon, Miss Melbury,' he said. 'I saw you from the window, and fancied you might imagine that I was not at home — if it is I you were coming for?'

'I was coming to speak one word to you, nothing more,' she replied. 'And I can say it here.'

'No, no. Please do come in. Well then, if you will not come into the house, come so far as the porch!'

Thus pressed she went on to the porch, and they stood together inside it, Fitzpiers closing her umbrella for her.

'I have merely a request or petition to make,' she said. 'My father's servant is ill — a woman you know — and her illness is serious.'

'I am sorry to hear it. I will come and see her at once.'

'But I particularly wish you not to come.'

'O indeed.'

'Yes; and she wishes the same. It would make her seriously worse if you were to come. It would almost kill her. . . . My errand is of a peculiar and awkward nature. It is concerning a subject which weighs on her mind — that unfortunate arrangement she made with you, that you might have her skull after death.'

'O, Grammer Oliver, the old woman with the fine head. Seriously ill, is she?'

'And *so* disturbed by her rash compact! I have brought the money back — will you please return to her the agreement she signed?' Grace held out to him a couple of five-pound notes which she had kept ready tucked in her glove.

Without replying or considering the notes Fitzpiers allowed his thoughts to follow his eyes and dwell upon Grace's personality, and the sudden close relation in which he stood to her. The porch was narrow; the rain increased. It ran off the porch and dripped on the creepers, and from the creepers upon the edge of Grace's cloak and skirts.

'The rain is wetting your dress; please do come in,' he said. 'It really makes my heart ache to let you stay here.'

Immediately inside the front door was the door of his sitting-room; he flung it open, and stood in a coaxing attitude. Try how she would Grace could not resist the supplicatory mandate written in the face and manner of this man, and distressful resignation sat on her as she glided past him into the room — brushing his coat with her elbow because of the narrowness.

He followed her, shut the door — which she somehow had hoped he would leave open — and placing a chair for her sat down.

The concern which Grace felt at the development of these commonplace incidents was, of course, mainly owing to the strange effect upon her nerves of that view of him in the mirror gazing at her with open eyes when she had thought him sleeping, which made her fancy that his slumber might have been a feint based on inexplicable reasons.

She again proffered the notes; he awoke from looking at her as at a piece of live statuary and listened deferentially as she said, 'Will you then reconsider, and cancel the bond which poor Grammer Oliver so foolishly gave?'

'I'll cancel it without reconsideration. Though you will allow me to have my own opinion about her foolishness. Grammer is a very wise woman, and she was as wise in that as in other things. You think there was something very fiendish in the compact, do you not, Miss Melbury? But remember that the most eminent of our surgeons in past times have entered into such agreements.'

'Not fiendish – strange.'

'Yes, that may be, since strangeness is not in the nature of a thing, but in its relation to something extrinsic – in this case an unessential observer.'

He went to his desk, and searching a while found a paper which he unfolded and brought to her. A thick cross appeared in ink at the bottom – evidently from the hand of Grammer. Grace put the paper in her pocket with a look of much relief.

As Fitzpiers did not take up the money (half of which had come from Grace's own purse) she pushed it a little nearer to him. 'No, no. I shall not take it from the old woman,' he said. 'It is more strange than the fact of a surgeon arranging to obtain a subject for dissection that our acquaintance should be formed out of it.'

'I am afraid you think me uncivil in showing my dislike to the notion. But I did not mean to be.'

'O no, no.'

He looked at her, as he had done before, with puzzled interest. 'I cannot think, I cannot think,' he murmured. 'Something bewilders me greatly.' He still reflected and hesitated. 'Last night I sat up very late,' he at last went on, 'and on that account I fell into a little nap on that couch about half-an-hour ago. And during my few minutes of unconsciousness I dreamt – what do you think? – that you stood in the room.'

Should she tell? She merely blushed.

'You may imagine,' Fitzpiers continued, now persuaded that it had indeed been a dream, 'that I should not have dreamt of you without considerable thinking about you first.'

He could not be acting; of that she felt assured.

'I fancied in my vision that you stood there,' he said, pointing to where she had paused. 'I did not see you directly, but reflected in the glass. I thought, what a lovely creature! The design is for once carried out. Nature has at last recovered her lost union with the Idea! My thoughts ran in that direction because I had been reading the work of a transcendental philosopher last night; and I dare say it was the dose of Idealism that I received from it that made me scarcely able to distinguish between reality and fancy. I almost wept when I awoke, and found that you had appeared to me in Time, but not in Space, alas!'

At moments there was something theatrical in the delivery of Fitzpiers's effusion; yet it would have been inexact to say that it was intrinsically theatrical. It often happens that in situations of unrestraint, where there is no thought of the eye of criticism, real feeling glides into a mode of manifestation not easily distinguishable from rodomontade. A veneer of affectation overlies a bulk of truth, with the evil consequence, if perceived, that the substance is estimated by the superficies, and the whole rejected.

Grace, however, was no specialist in men's manners, and she admired the sentiment without thinking of the form. And she was embarrassed; 'lovely creature' made explanation awkward to her gentle modesty.

'But can it be,' said he suddenly, 'that you really were here?'

'I have to confess that I have been in the room once before,' faltered she. 'The woman showed me in, and went away to fetch you; but as she did not return, I left.'

'And you saw me asleep,' he murmured, with the faintest show of humiliation.

'Yes – *if* you were asleep, and did not deceive me.'

'Why do you say if?'

'I saw your eyes open in the glass, but as they were closed when I looked round upon you I thought you were perhaps deceiving me.'

'Never,' said Fitzpiers fervently. 'Never could I deceive you.'

Foreknowledge to the distance of a year or so, in either of them, might have spoilt the effect of that pretty speech. Never deceive her! But they knew nothing, and the phrase had its day.

Grace began now to be anxious to terminate the interview, but the compelling power of Fitzpiers's atmosphere still held her there. She was like an inexperienced actress who, having at last taken up her position on the boards and spoken her speeches, does not know how to move off. The thought of Grammer occurred to her. 'I'll go at once and tell poor Grammer of your generosity,' she said. 'It will relieve her at once.'

'Grammer's is a nervous disease, too – how singular,' he answered, accompanying her to the door. 'One moment: look at this – it is something which may interest you.'

He had thrown open the door on the other side of the passage, and she saw a microscope on the table of the confronting room. 'Look into it, please; you'll be interested,' he repeated.

She applied her eye, and saw the usual circle of light patterned all over with a cellular tissue of some indescribable sort. 'What do you think that is?' said Fitzpiers.

She did not know.

'That's a fragment of old John South's brain, which I am investigating.'

She started back, not exactly with aversion, but with wonder as to how it should have got there. Fitzpiers laughed.

'Here am I,' he said, 'endeavouring to carry on simultaneously the study of physiology and transcendental philosophy, the material world and the ideal, so as to discover if possible a point of contact between them; and your finer sense is quite offended!'

'O no, Mr Fitzpiers,' said Grace earnestly; 'it is not so at all. I know from seeing your light at night how deeply you meditate and work. Instead of condemning you for your studies I admire you very much!'

Her face, upturned from the microscope, was so sweet, sincere, and self-forgetful in its aspect that the susceptible Fitzpiers more than wished to annihilate the lineal yard which separated it from his own. Whether anything of the kind showed in his eyes or not, Grace remained no longer at the microscope, but quickly went her way into the falling mixture of rain and snow.

CHAPTER NINETEEN

INSTEAD of resuming his investigation of South's brain Fitzpiers reclined and ruminated on the interview. Grace's curious susceptibility to his presence – though it was as if the currents of her life were disturbed rather than attracted by him – added a special interest to her general charm.

Fitzpiers was in a distinct degree scientific, being ready and zealous to interrogate all physical manifestations; but primarily he was an idealist. He believed that behind the imperfect lay the perfect; that rare things were to be discovered amidst a bulk of commonplace; that results in a new and untried case might be different from those in other cases where the material conditions had been precisely similar. Regarding his own personality as one of unbounded possibilities, because it was his own (notwithstanding that the factors of his life had worked out a sorry product for thousands), he saw a grand speciality in his discovery at Hintock of an altogether exceptional being of the other sex.

One habit of Fitzpiers, commoner in dreamers of more advanced age than in men of his years, was that of talking to himself. He paced round his room with a selective tread upon the more prominent blooms of the carpet and murmured: 'This phenomenal girl will be the light of my life while I am at Hintock; and the special beauty of the situation is that our attitude and relations to each other will be purely casual. Socially we can never be intimate. Anything like matrimonial intentions towards her, charming as she is, would be absurd. They would spoil the recreative character of such acquaintance. And, indeed, I have other aims on the practical side of my life.'

Fitzpiers bestowed a regulation thought on the advantageous marriage he was bound to make with a woman of family as good as his own, and of purse much longer. But as an object of contemplation for the present Grace Melbury would serve to keep his soul alive, and to relieve the monotony of his days.

His first lax notion (acquired from the mere sight of her without converse) – that of a vulgar intimacy with a timber-merchant's pretty daughter, grated painfully upon him now that he had found what Grace intrinsically was. Personal intercourse with such as she could take no lower form than seemly communion, mutual explorations of the world of fancy. Since he could not call at her father's, having no practical views, cursory encounters in the lane, in the wood, coming and going to and from church, or in passing her dwelling, were what the acquaintance would have to feed on.

Such anticipated glimpses of her realized themselves in the event. Rencounters of not more than a minute's duration, frequently repeated, will build up mutual interest, even warm confidence, in a lonely place. Theirs grew as imperceptibly as the twigs budded on the trees. There never was a particular moment at which it could be said they became friends; yet a delicate understanding now existed between two who in the winter had been strangers.

Spring weather came on rather suddenly, the unsealing of buds that had long been swollen accomplishing itself in the space of one warm night. The rush of sap in the veins of the trees could almost be heard. The flowers of late April took up a position unseen, and looked as if they had been blooming a long while, though there had been no trace of them the day before yesterday; birds began not to mind getting wet. In-door people said they had heard the nightingale, to which out-door people replied contemptuously that they had heard him a fortnight before.

The young doctor's practice being scarcely so large as a London surgeon's he frequently walked in the wood. Indeed, such practice as he had he did not follow up with the assiduity that would have been necessary for developing it to exceptional proportions.

One day, book in hand, he went to a part of the wood where the trees were mainly oaks. It was a calm afternoon, and there was everywhere around that sign of great undertakings on the part of vegetable nature which is apt to fill reflective human beings who are not undertaking much themselves with a sudden uneasiness at the contrast. He heard in the distance a curious sound, something like the quack of ducks, which though it was common enough here about this time was not common to him.

Looking through the trees Fitzpiers soon perceived the origin of the noise. The barking season had just commenced, and what he had heard was the tear of the ripping-tool as it ploughed its way along the sticky parting between the trunk and the rind. Melbury did a large business in bark, and as he was Grace's father, and possibly might be found on the spot, Fitzpiers was attracted to the scene even more than he might have been by its intrinsic interest. When he got nearer he recognized among the workmen John Upjohn, the two Timothys, and Robert Creedle, who probably had been 'lent' by Winterborne; Marty South also assisted. A milking-pail of cider stood near, a half-pint cup floating on it, with which they dipped and drank whenever they passed the pail.

Each tree doomed to the flaying process was first attacked by Upjohn. With a small bill-hook he carefully freed the collar of the tree from twigs and patches of moss which encrusted it to a height of a foot or two above the ground, an operation comparable to the 'little toilette' of the executioner's victim. After this it was barked in its erect position to a point as high as a man could reach. If a fine product of vegetable nature could ever be said to look ridiculous it was the case now, when the oak stood naked-legged, and as if ashamed, till the axe-man came and cut a ring round it, and the two Timothys finished the work with the cross-cut saw.

As soon as it had fallen the barkers attacked it like locusts, and in a short time not a particle of rind was left on the trunk and larger limbs. Marty South was an adept at peeling the upper parts; and there she stood encaged amid the mass of twigs and buds like a great bird, running her ripping-tool into the smallest branches, beyond the furthest points to which the skill and patience of the men enabled them to proceed — branches which, in their lifetime, had swayed high above the bulk of the wood, and caught the earliest rays of the sun and moon while the lower part of the forest was still in darkness.

'You seem to have a better instrument than they, Marty,' said Fitzpiers.

'No, sir,' she said, holding up the tool, a horse's leg-bone fitted into a handle and filed to an edge; ''tis only that they've less patience with the twigs, because their time is worth more than mine.'

A little shed had been constructed on the spot, of thatched hurdles and boughs, and in front of it was a fire, over which a kettle sang. Fitzpiers sat down inside the shelter and went on with his reading, except when he looked up to observe the scene and the actors.

The thought that he might settle here and become welded in with this sylvan life by marrying Grace Melbury crossed his mind for a moment. Why should he go further into the world than where he was? The secret of happiness lay in limiting the aspirations; these men's thoughts were conterminous with the margin of the Hintock woodlands, and why should not his be likewise limited – a small practice among the people around him being the bound of his desires?

Presently Marty South discontinued her operations upon the quivering boughs, came out from the reclining oak, and prepared tea. When it was ready the men were called; and Fitzpiers, being in a mood to join, sat down with them.

The latent reason of his lingering here so long revealed itself when the faint creaking of the joints of a vehicle became audible, and one of the men said, 'Here's he.' Turning their heads they saw Melbury's gig approaching, the wheels muffled by the yielding moss.

The timber-merchant was leading the horse past the tree-stumps, looking back at every few steps to warn his daughter, who kept her seat, where and how to duck her head so as to avoid overhanging branches. They stopped at the spot where the bark-ripping had been temporarily suspended; Melbury cursorily examined the heaps of bark, and drawing near to where the workmen were sitting down accepted their shouted invitation to have a dish of tea, for which purpose he hitched the horse to a bough.

Grace declined to take any of their beverage, and remained in her place in the vehicle, looking dreamily at the sunlight that came in thin threads through the hollies with which the oaks were interspersed.

When Melbury stepped up close to the shelter he for the first time perceived that the doctor was present, and warmly appreciated Fitzpiers's invitation to sit down on the log beside him.

'Bless my heart, who would have thought of finding you here,' he said, obviously much pleased at the circumstance. 'I wonder now if my daughter knows you are so nigh at hand? I don't expect she do.'

He looked out towards the gig wherein Grace sat, her face still turned sunward in the opposite direction.

'She doesn't see us,' said Melbury. 'Well, never mind; let her be.'

Grace was indeed quite unconscious of Fitzpiers's propinquity. She was thinking of something which had little connection with the scene before her – thinking of her friend, lost as soon as found, Mrs Charmond; of her capricious conduct, and of the contrasting scenes she was possibly enjoying at that very moment in other climes, to which Grace herself had hoped to be introduced by her friend's means. She wondered if this patronizing lady would return to Hintock during the summer, and whether the acquaintance which had been nipped on the last occasion of her residence there would develop on the next.

Melbury told ancient timber-stories as he sat, relating them directly to Fitzpiers and obliquely to the men, who had heard them often before. Marty, who poured out tea, was just saying, 'I think I'll take out a cup to Miss Grace,' when they heard a clashing of the gig-harness and turning round Melbury saw that the horse had become restless, and was jerking about the vehicle in a way which alarmed its occupant, though she refrained from screaming. Melbury jumped up immediately, but not more quickly than Fitzpiers; and while her father ran to the horse's head and speedily began to control him, Fitzpiers was alongside the gig assisting Grace to descend.

Her surprise at his appearance was so great that, far from making a calm and independent descent, she was very nearly lifted down in his arms. He relinquished her when she touched ground, and hoped she was not frightened.

'O no, not much,' she managed to say. 'There was no danger – unless the horse had run under the trees where the boughs are low enough to hit my head.'

'Which was by no means impossible, and justifies any amount of alarm.'

He referred to what he thought he saw written in her face, and she could not tell him that this had little to do with the horse, but much with himself. His contiguity had, in fact, the same effect upon her as on those former occasions when he had come closer to her than usual – that of producing in her an unaccountable tendency to tearfulness. Melbury soon put the horse to rights, and seeing that Grace was safe turned again to the work-people.

His daughter's nervous distress had passed off in a few moments, and she said quite gaily to Fitzpiers as she walked with him towards the group, 'There's destiny in it, you see. I was doomed to join in your picnic, although I did not intend to do so.'

Marty prepared her a comfortable place and she sat down in the circle, and listened to Fitzpiers while he drew from her father and the bark-rippers sundry narratives of their fathers', their grandfathers', and their own adventures in these woods; of the mysterious sights they had seen – only to be accounted for by supernatural agency; of white witches and black witches: and the standard story of the spirits of the Two Brothers who had fought and fallen, and had haunted King's Hintock Court a few miles off till they were exorcised by the priest, and compelled to retreat to a swamp, whence they were returning to their old quarters at the Court at the rate of a cock's stride every New Year's Day, Old Style; hence the local saying, 'On new-year's tide, a cock's stride.'

It was a pleasant time. The smoke from the little fire of peeled sticks rose between the sitters and the sunlight, and behind its blue films stretched the naked arms of the prostrate trees. The smell of the uncovered sap mingled with the smell of the burning wood, and the sticky inner surface of the scattered bark glistened as it revealed its pale madder hues to the eye. Melbury was so highly satisfied at having Fitzpiers as a sort of guest that he would have sat on for any length of time, but Grace, on whom Fitzpiers's eyes only too frequently alighted, seemed to think it incumbent upon her to make a show of going; and her father thereupon accompanied her to the gig.

As the doctor had helped her out of it he appeared to think that he had excellent reasons for helping her in, and performed the attention lingeringly enough.

'What were you almost in tears about just now?' he asked softly.

'I don't know,' she said; and the words were strictly true.

Melbury mounted on the other side, and they drove on out of the grove, their wheels silently crushing delicate-patterned mosses, hyacinths, primroses, lords-and-ladies, and other strange and common plants, and cracking up little sticks that lay across the track. Their way homeward ran along the western flank of the

Vale, whence afar they beheld a wide district differing somewhat in feature and atmosphere from the Hintock precincts. It was the cider country more especially, which met the woodland district some way off. There the air was blue as sapphire — such a blue as outside that apple-region was never seen. Under the blue the orchards were in a blaze of pink bloom, some of the richly flowered trees running almost up to where they drove along. At a gate, which opened down an incline, a man leant on his arms regarding this fair promise so intently that he did not observe their passing.

'That was Giles,' said Melbury, when they had gone by.

'Was it? Poor Giles,' said she.

'All that apple-blooth means heavy autumn work for him and his hands. If no blight happens before the setting the cider yield will be such as we have not had for years.'

Meanwhile, in the wood they had come from, the men had sat on so long that they were indisposed to begin work again that evening; they were paid by the ton, and their time for labour was as they chose. They placed the last gatherings of bark in rows for the curers, which led them further and further away from the shed; and thus they gradually withdrew homeward as the sun went down.

Fitzpiers lingered yet. He had opened his book again, though he could hardly see a word in it, and sat before the dying fire scarcely knowing of the men's departure. He dreamed and mused till his consciousness seemed to occupy the whole space of the woodland round, so little was there of jarring sight or sound to hinder perfect mental unity with the sentiment of the place. The idea returned upon him of sacrificing all practical aims to live in calm contentment here, and instead of going on elaborating new conceptions with infinite pains, to accept quiet domesticity according to oldest and homeliest notions. These reflections detained him till the wood was embrowned with the coming night, and the shy little bird of this dusky time had begun to pour out all the intensity of his eloquence from a bush not very far off.

Fitzpiers's eyes commanded as much of the ground in front as was open. Entering upon this he saw a figure whose direction of movement was towards the spot where he sat. The surgeon was quite shrouded from observation by the recessed shadow of the hurdle-screen, and there was no reason why he should move till the stranger had passed by.

The shape resolved itself into a woman's; she was looking on the ground and walking slowly, as if searching for something that had been lost, her course being precisely that of Mr Melbury's gig. Fitzpiers, by a sort of divination, jumped to the idea that the figure was Grace's; her nearer approach made the guess a certainty.

Yes, she was looking for something; and she came round by the prostrate trees that would have been invisible but for their white nakedness, which enabled her to avoid them easily. Thus she approached the heap of ashes, and acting upon what was suggested by a still shining ember or two she took a stick and stirred the heap, which thereupon burst into a flame. On looking around by the light thus obtained she for the first time saw the illumined face of Fitzpiers precisely in the spot where she had left him.

Grace gave a start and a scream; she had not the least expected to find him there still. Fitzpiers lost not a moment in rising and going to her side.

'I frightened you dreadfully, I know,' he said. 'I ought to have spoken; but I did not at first expect it to be you. I have been sitting here ever since.'

He was actually supporting her with his arm as though under the impression that she was quite overcome and in danger of falling. As soon as she could collect her ideas she gently withdrew from his grasp and explained what she had returned for: in getting up or down from the gig, or when sitting by the hut fire, she had dropped her purse.

'Now we will find it,' said Fitzpiers.

He threw an armful of last year's leaves on to the fire, which made the flame leap higher, and the encompassing shades to weave themselves into a blacker contrast, turning eve into night in a moment. By this radiance they groped about on their hands and knees, till Fitzpiers rested on his elbow, and looked at Grace.

'We almost always meet in odd circumstances,' he said; 'and this is one of the oddest. I wonder if it means anything?'

'O no, I'm sure it doesn't,' said Grace in haste, quickly assuming an erect posture. 'Pray don't say it any more.'

'I hope there was not much money in the purse,' said Fitzpiers, rising to his feet more slowly, and brushing the leaves from his trousers.

'Scarcely any. I cared most about the purse itself, because it was given me. Indeed, money is of little more use at Hintock than on Crusoe's island: there's hardly any way of spending it.'

They had given up the search when Fitzpiers discerned something by his foot. 'Here it is!' he said. 'So that your father, mother, friend, or *admirer* will not have his or her feelings hurt by a sense of your negligence after all.'

'O, he knows nothing of what I do now.'

'The admirer?' said Fitzpiers slyly.

'I don't know if you would call him that,' said Grace with simplicity. 'The admirer is a superficial, conditional creature, and this person is quite different.'

'He has all the cardinal virtues?'

'Perhaps — though I don't know them precisely.'

'You unconsciously practise them, Miss Melbury, which is better. According to Schleiermacher they are Self-control, Perseverance, Wisdom, and Love; and his is the best list that I know.'

'I am afraid poor—' She was going to say that she feared Winterborne, the giver of the purse years before, had not much perseverance, though he had all the other three; but she determined to go no further in this direction, and was silent.

These half-revelations made a perceptible difference in Fitzpiers. His sense of personal superiority wasted away, and Grace assumed in his eyes the true aspect of a mistress in her lover's regard.

'Miss Melbury,' he said suddenly; 'I divine that this virtuous man you mention has been refused by you?'

She could do no otherwise than admit it.

'I did not inquire without good reason. God forbid that I should kneel in another's place at any shrine unfairly. But, my dear Miss Melbury, now that he is gone from the temple, may I draw near?'

'I — I can't say anything about that!' she cried quickly. 'Because when a man has been refused you feel pity for him, and like him more than you did before.'

This increasing complication added still more value to Grace in the surgeon's eyes: it rendered her adorable. 'But cannot you say?' he pleaded distractedly.

'I'd rather not – I think I must go home at once.'

'O yes,' said Fitzpiers.

But as he did not move she felt it awkward to walk straight away from him; and so they stood silently together. A diversion was created by the accident of two large birds, that had either been roosting above their heads or nesting there, tumbling one over the other into the hot ashes at their feet, apparently engrossed in a desperate quarrel that prevented the use of their wings. They speedily parted, however, and flew up with a singed smell, and were seen no more.

'That's the end of what is called love,' said some one.

The speaker was neither Grace nor Fitzpiers, but Marty South, who approached with her face turned up to the sky in her endeavour to trace the birds. Suddenly perceiving Grace she exclaimed, 'O – Miss Melbury! – I have been looking at they pigeons, and didn't see you. And here's Mr Winterborne!' she continued shyly, as she looked towards Fitzpiers, who stood in the background.

'Marty,' Grace interrupted; 'I want you to walk home with me – will you? Come along.' And without lingering longer she took hold of Marty's arm and led her away.

They went between the spectral arms of the peeled trees as they lay, and onward among the growing ones by a path where there were no oaks, and no barking, and no Fitzpiers – nothing but copse-wood, between which the primroses could be discerned in. pale bunches.

'I – didn't know Mr Winterborne was there,' said Marty, breaking the silence when they had nearly reached Grace's door.

'Nor was he,' said Grace.

'But, Miss Melbury – I saw him.'

'No,' said Grace. 'It was somebody else. Giles Winterborne is nothing to me.'

CHAPTER TWENTY

T HE leaves over Hintock unrolled their creased tissues, and the woodland seemed to change from an open filigree to a solid opaque body of infinitely larger shape and importance. The boughs cast green shades, which disagreed with the complexion of the girls who walked there; and a fringe of the same boughs which overhung Mr Melbury's garden dripped on his seed-plots when it rained, pitting their surface all over as with pock-marks, till Melbury declared that gardens in such a place were no good at all. The two trees that had creaked all the winter left off creaking, the whirr of the night-hawk, however, forming a very satisfactory continuation of uncanny music from that quarter. Except at midday the sun was not seen complete by the Hintock people, but rather in the form of numerous little stars staring through the leaves.

Such an appearance it had on Midsummer eve of this year, and as the hour grew later, and nine o'clock drew on, the irradiation of the day-time became broken up by the weird shadows and ghostly nooks of indistinctness. Imagination could trace amid the trunks and boughs swarthy faces and funereal figures. This was before the moon rose. Later on, when that planet was getting command of the upper heaven, and consequently shining with an unbroken face into such open glades as there were in the neighbourhood of the hamlet, it became apparent that the margin of the wood which approached the timbermerchant's premises was not to be left to the customary stillness of that reposeful time.

Fitzpiers having heard a voice or voices was looking over his garden gate (where he now looked more frequently than into his books) fancying that Grace might be abroad with some friends. He was irretrievably committed in heart to Grace Melbury, though he was by no means sure that she was so far committed to him. That the Idea had for once completely fulfilled itself in the objective substance (which he had hitherto deemed an impossibility) he was enchanted enough to fancy must be the case at last.

It was not Grace who had passed, however, but several of the ordinary village girls in a group; some steadily walking, some in a mood of wild gaiety. He quietly asked his landlady, who was also in the garden, what these girls were intending, and she informed him that it being old Midsummer eve they were about to attempt some spell or enchantment which would afford them a glimpse of their future partners for life. She declared it to be an ungodly performance, and one that she for her part would never countenance; saying which she entered her house and retired to bed.

The young man lit a cigar, and followed the bevy of maidens slowly up the road. They had turned into the wood at an opening between Melbury's and Marty South's; but Fitzpiers could easily track them by their voices, low as they endeavoured to keep their tones.

In the meantime other inhabitants of Little Hintock had become aware of the nocturnal experiment about to be tried, and were also sauntering stealthily after the frisky maidens. Miss Melbury had been informed by Marty South during the day of the proposed peep into futurity, and, being only a girl like the rest, she was sufficiently interested to wish to see the issue. The moon was so bright and the night so calm that she had no difficulty in persuading Mrs Melbury to accompany her; and thus, joined by Marty, these went onward in the same direction.

Passing Winterborne's house they heard a noise of hammering. Marty explained it. This was the last night on which his paternal roof would shelter him, the days of grace since it fell into hand having expired; and late as it was Giles was taking down his cupboards and bedsteads with a view to an early exit next morning. His encounter with Mrs Charmond had cost him dearly.

When they had proceeded a little further Marty was joined by Grammer Oliver (who was as young as the youngest in such matters), and Grace and Mrs Melbury went on by themselves till they had arrived at the spot chosen by the village daughters, whose primary intention of keeping their expedition a secret had been quite defeated. Grace and her stepmother paused by a holly tree; and at a little distance stood Fitzpiers under the shade of a young oak, intently observing Grace; who was in the full rays of the moon.

He watched her without speaking, and unperceived by any but Marty and Grammer, who had drawn up on the dark side of the same holly which sheltered

Mrs and Miss Melbury on its bright side. The two former conversed in low tones.

'If they two come up in wood *next* Midsummer night they'll come as one,' said Grammer, signifying Fitzpiers and Grace. 'Instead of my skellinton he'll carry home her living carcase before long. But though she's a lady in herself, and worthy of any such as he, it do seem to me that he ought to marry somebody more of the sort of Mrs Charmond, and that Miss Grace should make the best of Winterborne.'

Marty returned no comment; and at that minute the girls, some of whom were from Great Hintock, were seen advancing to work the incantation, it being now about midnight.

'Directly we see anything we'll run home as fast as we can,' said one, whose courage had begun to fail her. To this the rest assented, not knowing that a dozen neighbours lurked in the bushes around.

'I wish we had not thought of trying this,' said another, 'but had contented ourselves with the hole-digging to-morrow at twelve, and hearing our husbands' trades. It is too much like having dealings with the evil one to try to raise their forms.'

However, they had gone too far to recede, and slowly began to march forward in a skirmishing line through the trees, each intending to plunge alone into a deep recess of the wood. As far as the listeners could gather, the particular form of black art to be practised on this occasion was one connected with the sowing of hempseed, a handful of which was carried by each girl.

At the moment of their advance they looked back, and discerned the figure of Miss Melbury who, alone of all the observers, stood in the full face of the moonlight, deeply engrossed in the proceedings. By contrast with her life of late years they made her feel as if she had receded a couple of centuries in the world's history. She was rendered doubly conspicuous by her light dress, and after a few whispered words one of the girls (a bouncing maiden called Suke, plighted to young Timothy Tangs) asked her if she would join in. Grace with some excitement said that she would, and moved on a little in the rear of the rest.

Soon the listeners could hear nothing of their proceedings beyond the faintest occasional rustle of leaves. Grammer whispered again to Marty: 'Why didn't ye go and try your luck with the rest of the maids?'

'I don't believe in it!' said Marty shortly. 'And they've spoilt it by letting people know.'

'Yes, half the parish is here; the silly hussies should have kept it quiet. I see Mr Winterborne through the leaves, just come up with Robert Creedle. Marty, we ought to act the part o' Providence sometimes. Do go and tell him that if he stands just behind the bush at the bottom of the slope, Miss Grace must pass down it when she comes back, and she will most likely rush into his arms; for as soon as the clock strikes they'll bundle back home-along like hares. I've seen such larries before.'

'Do you think I'd better?' said Marty reluctantly.

'O yes, he'll bless ye for it.'

'I don't want that kind of blessing!'

But after a moment's thought she went and delivered the information; and Grammer had the satisfaction of seeing Giles walk slowly to the bend in the leafy defile along which Grace would have to return.

Meanwhile Mrs Melbury, deserted by Grace, had perceived Fitzpiers and Winterborne, and also the move of the latter. An improvement on Grammer's idea entered the mind of Mrs Melbury, for she had lately discerned what her husband had not, that Grace was rapidly fascinating the surgeon. She therefore drew near to Fitzpiers.

'You should be where Mr Winterborne is standing,' she said to him significantly. 'She will run down through that opening much faster than she went up it, if she is like the rest of the girls.'

Fitzpiers did not require to be told twice. He went across to Winterborne, and stood beside him. Each knew the probable purpose of the other in standing there, and neither spoke, Fitzpiers scorning to look upon Winterborne as a rival, and Winterborne adhering to the off-hand manner of indifference which had grown upon him since his dismissal.

Neither Grammer nor Marty South had seen the surgeon's manœuvre, and still to help Winterborne, as she supposed, the old woman suggested to the wood-girl that she should walk forward at the heels of Grace, and 'tole' her down the required way if she showed a tendency to run in another direction. Poor Marty, always doomed to sacrifice desire to obligation, walked forward accordingly, and waited as a beacon, still and silent, for the retreat of Grace and her giddy companions, now quite out of hearing.

The first sound to break the silence was the distant note of Great Hintock clock striking the significant hour. About a minute later that quarter of the wood to which the girls had wandered resounded with the flapping of disturbed birds; then two or three hares and rabbits bounded down the glade from the same direction, and after these the rustling and crackling of leaves and dead twigs denoted the hurried approach of the adventurers, whose fluttering gowns soon became visible.

Miss Melbury having gone forward quite in the rear of the rest was one of the first to return, and the excitement being contagious she ran laughing towards Marty, who still stood as a hand-post to guide her; then, passing on, she flew round the fatal bush where the undergrowth narrowed to a gorge. Marty arrived at her heels just in time to see the result. Fitzpiers had quickly stepped forward in front of Winterborne, who disdaining to shift his position had turned on his heel, and then the surgeon did what he would not have thought of doing but for Mrs Melbury's encouragement and the sentiment of an eve which effaced conventionality. Stretching out his arms as the white figure burst upon him he captured her in a moment, as if she had been a bird.

'O!' cried Grace in her fright.

'You are in my arms, dearest,' said Fitzpiers; 'and I am going to claim you, and keep you there all our two lives!'

She rested on him like one utterly mastered; and it was several seconds before she recovered from this helplessness. Subdued screams and struggles audible from neighbouring brakes revealed that there had been other lurkers thereabout for a similar purpose. Grace, unlike most of these companions of hers, instead of giggling and writhing, said in a trembling voice, 'Mr Fitzpiers, will you let me go?'

'Certainly,' he said, laughing; 'as soon as you have recovered.'

She waited another few moments, then quietly and firmly pushed him aside and glided on her path, the moon whitening her hot blush away. But it had been enough: new relations between them had begun.

The case of the other girls was different, as has been said. They wrestled and tittered, only escaping after a desperate struggle. Fitzpiers could hear these enactments still going on after Grace had left him, and he remained on the spot where he had caught her, Winterborne having gone away. On a sudden another girl came bounding down the same descent that had been followed by Grace; a fine-framed young woman, with bare arms. Seeing Fitzpiers standing there she said with playful effrontery: 'May'st kiss me if 'canst catch me, Tim!'

Fitzpiers recognized her as Suke Damson, a hoydenish maiden of the hamlet – the girl whom he had heard swear to herself when she got soiled by the newly painted gate. She was plainly mistaking him for her lover. He was impulsively disposed to profit by her error, and as soon as she began racing away he started in pursuit.

On she went under the boughs, now in light, now in shade, looking over her shoulder at him every few moments and kissing her hand; but so cunningly dodging about among the trees and moon-shades that she never allowed him to get dangerously near her. Thus they ran and doubled, Fitzpiers warming with the chase, till the sound of their companions had quite died away.

He began to lose hope of ever overtaking her, when all at once, by way of encouragement, she turned to a fence in which there was a stile, and leapt over it. Outside, the scene was a changed one; a meadow, where the half-made hay lay about in heaps, in the uninterrupted shine of the now high moon.

Fitzpiers saw in a moment that having taken to open ground she had placed herself at his mercy, and he promptly vaulted over after her. She flitted a little way down the mead, when all at once her elusive form disappeared, as if it had sunk into the earth. She had buried herself in one of the hay-cocks.

Fitzpiers, now thoroughly excited, was not going to let her escape him thus. He approached, and set about turning over the heaps one by one. As soon as he paused, tantalized and puzzled, he was directed anew by an imitative kiss which came from her hiding-place under the hay, and by snatches of a local ballad, in the smallest voice she could assume –

'O come in from the foggy, foggy dew.'

In a minute or two he uncovered her.

'O – 'tis not Tim!' said she with a laugh, and burying her face.

Fitzpiers, however, disregarded her resistance by reason of its mildness, stooped, and imprinted the purposed kiss; then sank down on the same hay-cock, panting with his race.

'Whom do you mean by Tim?' he asked presently.

'My young man, Tim Tangs,' said she.

'Now honour bright, did you really think it was he?'

'I did at first.'

'But you didn't at last.'

'No. I didn't at last.'

'Do you much mind that it is not?'

'No,' she answered slyly.

Fitzpiers kissed her again, and pressed her close to him.

He did not pursue his questioning. In the moonlight Suke looked very beautiful, the scratches and blemishes incidental to her outdoor occupation being invisible under these pale rays. While they remained silent on the hay the coarse whirr of the eternal night-hawk burst sarcastically from the top of a tree at the nearest corner of the wood. Besides this not a sound of any kind reached their ears, the time of nightingales being now past, and Hintock lying at a distance of two miles at least. In the opposite direction the hay-field stretched away into remoteness till it was lost to the eye in a soft mist.

It was daybreak before Fitzpiers and Suke Damson re-entered Little Hintock.

CHAPTER TWENTY-ONE

WHEN the general stampede occurred Winterborne had also been looking on, and encountering one of the girls had asked her what caused them all to fly.

She said with solemn breathlessness that they had seen something very different from what they had hoped to see, and that she for one would never attempt such unholy ceremonies again. 'We saw Satan pursuing us with his hour-glass. It was terrible!'

This account being a little mixed Giles went forward towards the spot whence the girls had retreated. After listening there a few minutes he heard slow footsteps rustling over the leaves, and, looking through a tangled screen of honeysuckle which hung from a bough, he saw in the open space beyond a short stout man in evening dress, carrying on one arm a light overcoat and also his hat, so awkwardly arranged as possibly to have suggested the 'hour-glass' to his timid observers – if this were the person whom the girls had seen. With the other hand he silently gesticulated, and the moonlight falling upon his bare brow showed him to have dark hair and a high forehead of the shape seen oftener in old prints and paintings than in real life. His curious and altogether alien aspect, his strange gestures, like those of one who is rehearsing a scene to himself, and the unusual place and hour, were sufficient to account for any trepidation among the Hintock daughters at encountering him.

He paused and looked round, as if he had forgotten where he was; not observing Giles, who was of the colour of his environment. The latter advanced into the light. The gentleman held up his hand and came towards Giles, the two meeting half way.

'I have lost my track,' said the stranger. 'Perhaps you can put me in the path again.' He wiped his forehead with the air of one suffering under an agitation more than that of simple fatigue.

'The turnpike-road is over there,' said Giles.

'I don't want the turnpike-road,' said the gentleman impatiently. 'I came from that. I want Hintock House. Is there not a path to it across here?'

'Well, yes, a sort of path. But it is hard to find from this point. I'll show you the way, sir, with pleasure.'

'Thanks, my good friend. The truth is that I decided to walk across the country after dinner from the hotel at Sherton, where I am staying for a day or two. But I did not know it was so far.'

'It is about a mile to the house from here.'

They walked on together. As there was no path Giles occasionally stepped in front and bent aside the under-boughs of the trees to give his companion a passage, saying every now and then when the twigs, on being released, flew back like whips, 'Mind your eyes, sir.' To which the stranger replied, 'Yes, yes,' in a preoccupied tone.

So they went on, the leaf-shadows running in their usual quick succession over the forms of the pedestrians, till the stranger said –

'Is it far?'

'Not much further,' said Winterborne. 'The plantation runs up into a corner here, close behind the house.' He added with hesitation, 'You know, I suppose, sir, that Mrs Charmond is not at home?'

'You mistake,' said the other shortly. 'Mrs Charmond has been away for some time, but she's at home now.'

Giles did not contradict him, though he felt sure that the gentleman was wrong.

'You are a native of this place?' the stranger said.

'Yes.'

'You are happy in having a home.'

'I hope you are too, sir.'

'It is what I don't possess.'

'You came from far, seemingly?'

'I come now from the south of Europe.'

'O indeed, sir. You are an Italian, or Spanish, or French gentleman, perhaps?'

'I am not either.'

Giles did not fill the pause which ensued, and the gentleman, who seemed of an emotional nature, unable to resist friendship, at length answered the question.

'I am an Italianized American; a South Carolinian by birth,' he said. 'I left my native country on the failure of the Southern cause, and have never returned to it since.'

He spoke no more about himself, and they came to the verge of the wood. Here, striding over the fence out upon the upland sward, they could at once see the chimneys of the house in the gorge immediately beneath their position, silent, still, and pale.

'Can you tell me the time?' the gentleman asked. 'My watch has stopped.'

'It is between twelve and one,' said Giles.

His companion expressed his astonishment. 'I thought it between nine and ten at latest! My! My!'

He now begged Giles to return and offered him a gold coin, which looked like a sovereign, for the assistance rendered. Giles declined to accept anything, to the surprise of the stranger, who on putting the money back into his pocket said awkwardly, 'I thought it was the custom here. I offered it because I want you to utter no word about this meeting with me. Will you promise?'

Winterborne promised readily. He stood still whilst the other descended the slope. At the bottom the stranger looked back mistrustfully. Giles would no longer remain when he was so evidently desired to leave, and returned through the boughs to Little Hintock.

He suspected that this man, who seemed so distressed and melancholy, might be that lover and persistent wooer of Mrs Charmond whom he had heard so frequently spoken of, and whom it was said she had treated cavalierly. But he received no confirmation of his suspicion beyond a report which reached him a few days later that a gentleman had called up the servants who were taking care of Hintock House at an hour past midnight; and on learning that Mrs Charmond, though returned from abroad, was as yet in London, he had sworn bitterly, and gone away without leaving a card or any trace of himself.

The girls who related the story added that he sighed three times before he swore, and seemed wandering in his mind, but this part of the narrative was not corroborated. Anyhow such a gentleman drove away from Sherton next day in a carriage hired at the inn.

CHAPTER TWENTY-TWO

THE sunny, leafy week which followed the tender doings of Midsummer Eve brought a visitor to Fitzpiers's door; a voice that he knew sounded in the passage. Mr Melbury had called.

At first he had a particular objection to enter the parlour because his boots were dusty, but as the surgeon insisted he waived the point and came in.

Looking neither to the right nor to the left, hardly at Fitzpiers himself, he put his hat under his chair and with a preoccupied gaze at the floor said, 'I have called to ask you, doctor, quite privately, a question that troubles me. I've a daughter, Grace, an only daughter as you may have heard. Well, she's been out in the dew; on Midsummer Eve in particular she went out in thin slippers to watch some vagary of the Hintock maids; and she's got a cough, a distinct hemming and hacking, that makes me uneasy. Now I have decided to send her away to some seaside place for a change—'

'Send her away!' Fitzpiers's countenance had fallen.

'Yes. And the question is, where would you advise me to send her?'

The timber-merchant had happened to call at a moment when Fitzpiers was at the spring-tide of a sentiment that Grace was a necessity of his existence. The sudden pressure of her form upon his breast as she came headlong round the bush had never ceased to linger with him since he adopted the manœuvre for which the hour and the moonlight and the occasion had been the only excuse. Now she was to be sent away.

Ambition?—it could be postponed. Family?—a common culture and reciprocity of tastes had taken the place of family considerations nowadays. He allowed himself to be carried forward on the wave of his desire.

'How strange, how very strange it is,' he said, 'that you should have come to me about her just now. I have been thinking every day of coming to you on the very same errand.'

'Ah? You have noticed, too, that her health—'

'I have noticed nothing the matter with her health, because there is nothing. But, Mr Melbury, I have seen your daughter several times by accident. I have admired her infinitely, and I was coming to ask you if I may become better acquainted with her – pay my addresses to her?'

Melbury was looking down as he listened, and did not see the air of half-misgiving at his own rashness that spread over Fitzpiers's face as he made this declaration.

'You have – got to know her?' said Melbury, a spell of dead silence having preceded his utterance, during which his emotion rose with almost visible effect.

'Yes,' said Fitzpiers.

'And you wish to become better acquainted with her? You mean with a view to marrying o' her – is that what you mean?'

'Yes,' said the young man. 'I mean, get acquainted with her, with a view to being her accepted lover; and if we suited each other, what would naturally follow.'

The timber-dealer was much surprised, and fairly agitated; his hand trembled as he laid by his walking-stick.

'This takes me unawares,' said he, his voice well-nigh breaking down. 'I don't mean that there is anything unexpected in a gentleman being attracted by her; but it did not occur to me that it would be you. I always said,' continued he, with a lump in his throat, 'that my Grace would make a mark at her own level some day. That was why I educated her. I said to myself, "I'll do it, cost what it may"; though her stepmother was pretty frightened at my paying out so much money year after year. I knew it would tell in the end. "Where you've not good material to work on, such doings would be waste and vanity," I said. "But where you have that material, it is sure to be worth while."'

'I am glad you don't object,' said Fitzpiers, almost wishing that Grace had not been quite so cheap for him.

'If she is willing I don't object, certainly. Indeed,' added the honest man, 'it would be deceit if I were to pretend to feel anything else than highly honoured by your wish; and it is a great credit to her to have drawn to her a man of such good professional station and venerable old family. That huntsman-fellow little thought how wrong he was about her! Take her and welcome, sir.'

'I'll endeavour to ascertain her mind.'

'Yes, yes. But she will be agreeable, I think. She ought to be.'

'I hope she may. Well, now you'll expect to see me frequently?'

'O yes. But, name it all – about her cough, and her going away? I had quite forgot that that was what I came about.'

'I assure you,' said the surgeon, 'that her cough can only be the result of a slight cold, and it is not necessary to banish her to any seaside place at all.'

Melbury looked unconvinced, doubting whether he ought to take Fitzpiers's professional opinion in circumstances which naturally led him to wish to keep her by him. The doctor saw this, and honestly dreading to lose sight of her he said eagerly, 'Between ourselves, if I am successful with her I will take her away myself for a month or two, as soon as we are married, which I hope will be before the chilly weather comes on. This will be so very much better than letting her go now.'

The proposal pleased Melbury much. There could be hardly any danger in postponing desirable change of air as long as the warm weather lasted, and for such a reason.

Suddenly recollecting himself he said, 'Your time must be precious, doctor. I'll get home-along. I am much obliged to 'ee. As you will see her often you'll discover for yourself if anything serious is the matter.'

'I can assure you it is nothing,' said Fitzpiers, who had seen Grace much oftener already than her father knew of.

When he was gone Fitzpiers paused, silent, registering his sensations like a man who has made a plunge for a pearl into a medium of which he knows neither the density nor temperature. But he had done it, and Grace was the sweetest girl alive.

As for the departed visitor, his own last words lingered in Melbury's ears as he walked homeward; he felt that what he had said in the emotion of the moment was very stupid, ungenteel, and unsuited to a duologue with an educated gentleman, the smallness of whose practice was more than compensated by the former greatness of his family. He had uttered thoughts before they were weighed, and almost before they were shaped. They had expressed in a certain sense his feeling at Fitzpiers's news, but yet they were not right. Looking on the ground, and planting his stick at each tread as if it were a flagstaff, he reached his own precincts where, as he passed through the court, he automatically stopped to look at the men working in the shed and around. One of them asked him a question about waggon-spokes.

'Hey?' said Melbury, looking hard at him. The man repeated the words.

Melbury stood; then turning suddenly away without answering he went up the court and entered the house.

As time was no concern with the journeymen, except as a thing to get passed, they leisurely surveyed the door through which he had disappeared.

'What maggot has the gaffer got in his head now?' said Tangs the elder. 'Sommit to do with that chiel of his! When you've got a maid of yer own, John Upjohn, that costs 'ee what she costs him, that will take the squeak out of your Sunday shoes, John! But you'll never be man enough to accomplish such as she; and 'tis a lucky thing for 'ee, John, as things be. Well, he ought to have a dozen – that would bring him to reason. I see 'em walking together last Sunday, and when they came to a puddle he lifted her over like a waxen figure. He ought to have a dozen; he'd let 'em walk through puddles for themselves then.'

Meanwhile Melbury had entered the house with the eye of a man who sees a vision before him. His wife was in the room. Without taking off his hat he sat down at random.

'Luce – we've done it!' he said. 'Yes – the thing is as I expected. The spell, that I foresaw might be worked, has worked. She's done it, and done it well. Where is she – Grace, I mean?'

'Up in her room: what has happened?'

Mr Melbury explained the circumstances as coherently as he could. 'I told you so,' he said. 'A maid like her couldn't stay hid long, even in a place like this. But where is Grace? Let's have her down. Here – Gra-a-ce!'

She appeared after a reasonable interval, for she was sufficiently spoilt by this father of hers not to put herself in a hurry, however impatient his tones. 'What is it, father?' said she, with a smile.

'Why, you scamp, what's this you've been doing? Not home here more than six months, yet instead of confining yourself to your father's rank making havoc in the upper classes!'

Though accustomed to show herself instantly appreciative of her father's meanings Grace was fairly unable to look anyhow but at a loss now.

'No, no; of course you don't know what I mean, or you pretend you don't. Though for my part I believe women can see these things through a double hedge. But I suppose I must tell 'ee. Why, you've flung your grapnel over the doctor, and he's coming courting forthwith.'

'Only think of that, my dear! Don't you feel it a triumph?' said Mrs Melbury.

'Coming courting – I've done nothing to make him!' Grace exclaimed.

''Twasn't necessary that you should; 'tis voluntary that rules in these things. Well, he has behaved very honourably, and asked my consent. You'll know what to do when he gets here, I dare say. I needn't tell you to make it all smooth for him.'

'You mean, to lead him on to marry me?'

'I do. Haven't I educated you for it?'

Grace looked out of the window, and at the fireplace, with no animation in her face. 'Why is it settled off-hand in this way?' said she pettishly. 'You'll wait till you hear what I think of him, I suppose?'

'O yes, of course. But you see what a good thing it will be.'

She weighed the statement without speaking.

'You will be restored to the society you've been taken away from,' continued her father; 'for I don't suppose he'll stay here long.'

She shyly admitted the advantage; but it was plain that though Fitzpiers when he was present exercised a certain fascination over her – or even more, an almost psychic influence, as it is called – and though his impulsive act in the wood had stirred her feelings indescribably, she had never regarded him in the light of a destined husband. 'I don't know what to answer,' she said. 'I have learnt that he is very clever.'

'He's all right, and he's coming here to see you.'

A premonition that she could not resist him if he came strangely moved her. 'Of course, father, you remember that it is only lately that Giles—'

'You know that you can't think of him. He has given up all claim to you.'

She could not explain the subtleties of her feeling as clearly as he could state his opinion, even though she had skill in speech, and her father had none. That Fitzpiers acted upon her like a dram, exciting her, throwing her into a novel atmosphere which biassed her doings until the influence was over, when she felt something of the nature of regret for the mood she had experienced – could not be told to this worthy couple in words.

It so happened that on this very day Fitzpiers was called away from Hintock by an engagement to attend some medical meetings, and his visits therefore did not begin at once. A note, however, arrived from him addressed to Grace, deploring his enforced absence. As a material object this note was pretty and superfine, a note of a sort that she had been unaccustomed to see since her return to Hintock, except when a school friend wrote to her – a rare instance, for the girls were respecters of persons, and many cooled down towards the timber-dealer's daughter when she was out of sight. Thus the receipt of it pleased her, and she afterwards walked about with a reflective air.

In the evening her father, who knew that the note had come, said, 'Why be ye not sitting down to answer your letter? That's what young folks did in my time.'

She replied that it did not require an answer.

'O, you know best,' he said. Nevertheless he went about his business doubting if she were right in not replying; possibly she might be so mismanaging matters as to risk the loss of an alliance which would bring her much happiness.

Melbury's respect for Fitzpiers was based less on his professional position, which was not much, than on the standing of his family in the county in bygone days. That touching faith in members of long-established families as such, irrespective of their personal condition or character, which is still found among old-fashioned people in the rural districts, reached its full perfection in Melbury. His daughter's suitor was descended from a line he had heard of in his grandfather's time as being once among the greatest, a family which had conferred its name upon a neighbouring village; how then could anything be amiss in this betrothal?

'I must keep her up to this,' he said to his wife. 'She sees it is for her happiness; but still she's young, and may want a little prompting from an older tongue.'

CHAPTER TWENTY-THREE

WITH this in view Melbury took her out for a walk, a custom of his when he wished to say anything specially impressive. Their way was towards that lofty ridge bordering their woodland and the western extremity of the Vale of Blackmoor, the ridge culminating further on in Highstoy Hill. They could look back over the outskirts of the cider district, where they had in the spring beheld the miles of apple-trees in bloom. All was now deep green.

The spot recalled to Grace's mind the last occasion of her sight of it, and she said, 'The promise of an enormous apple-crop is fulfilling itself, is it not? I suppose Giles is getting his mills and presses ready.'

This was just what her father had not come there to talk about. Without replying he raised his arm and moved his finger till he fixed it at a point round to the right.

'There,' he said. 'You see that hill rising out of the level like a great whale, and just behind the hill a particularly green sheltered bottom? That's where Mr Fitzpiers's family were lords of the manor for I don't know how many hundred years, and there stands the village of Oakbury Fitzpiers. A wonderful property 'twas — wonderful!'

'But they are not lords of the manor there now.'

'Why, no. But good and great folk fall as well as humble and foolish. The only ones representing the family now, I believe, are our doctor and a maiden lady living I don't know where. You can't help being happy, Grace, in allying yourself with such a romantical family. Why, on the mother's side he's connected with the long line of the Lords Baxby of Sherton. You'll feel as if you've stepped into history.'

'We've been at Hintock as long as they were at Oakbury; is it not so? You say our name occurs in old deeds continually.'

'O yes — as yeomen, copyholders, and such like. But think how much better this will be for 'ee. You'll be living a high, perusing life, such as has now become natural to you; and though the doctor's practice is small here he'll no doubt go to a dashing town when he's got his hand in, and keep a stylish carriage, and you'll be brought to know a good many ladies of excellent society. If you should ever meet me then, Grace, you can drive past me, looking the other way. I shouldn't expect you to speak to me, or wish such a thing — unless it happened to be in some lonely private place where 'twouldn't lower 'ee at all. Don't think such men as neighbour Giles your equal. He and I shall be good friends enough, but he's not for the like of you. He's lived our rough and homely life here, and his wife's life must be rough and homely likewise.'

So much pressure could not but produce some displacement. As Grace was left very much to herself she took advantage of one fine day before Fitzpiers's return to drive into the aforesaid vale where stood the village of Oakbury Fitzpiers. On another day she drove to the ruins of Sherton Castle, the original stronghold of the Lords Baxby, Fitzpiers's maternal ancestors.

The remains were few, and consisted mostly of remnants of the lower vaulting, supported on low stout columns surmounted by the *crochet* capital of the period. The two or three arches of these vaults that were still in position had been utilized by the adjoining farmer as shelter for his calves, the floor being spread with straw, amid which the young creatures rustled, cooling their thirsty tongues by licking the quaint Norman carving, which glistened with the moisture. It was a degradation of even such a rude form of art as this to be treated so grossly, she thought, and for the first time the aspect of Fitzpiers assumed in her imagination the hues of a melancholy romanticism.

She traversed the distance home with a preoccupied mind. The idea of so modern a man in science and æsthetics as the young surgeon springing out of relics so ancient was a kind of novelty she had never before experienced. The combination lent him a social and intellectual interest which she dreaded, so much weight did it add to the strange influence he exercised upon her whenever he came near her.

In an excitement which was not love, not ambition, rather a fearful consciousness of hazard in the air, she awaited his return.

Meanwhile her father was awaiting him also. In his house there was an old work on medicine, published towards the end of the eighteenth century, and to put himself in harmony with events Melbury spread this work on his knees when he had done his day's business, and read about Galen, Hippocrates, and Herophilus, of the dogmatic, the empiric, the hermetical, and other sects of practitioners that have arisen in history; and thence proceeded to study the classification of maladies and the rules for their treatment by copious bleeding, as laid down in this valuable book with absolute precision. Melbury regretted that the treatise was so old, fearing that he might in consequence be unable to hold as complete a conversation as he could wish with Mr Fitzpiers, primed, no doubt, with more recent discoveries.

The day of Fitzpiers's return arrived, and he sent to say that he would call immediately. In the little time that was afforded for putting the house in order the sweeping of Melbury's parlour was as the sweeping of the parlour at the Interpreter's which well-nigh choked the Pilgrim. Motes stood in the sunbeams, which sloped visibly into the room. At the end of it Mrs Melbury sat down, folded her hands and lips, and waited. Her husband restlessly walked in and out from the timber-yard, stared at the interior of the room, jerked out 'Ay,' and retreated again.

Between four and five Fitzpiers arrived, hitching his horse to the hook under the uppingstock outside the door.

As soon as he had walked in and perceived that Grace was not in the parlour he seemed to have a misgiving. Nothing less than her actual presence could long keep him to the level of this impassioned enterprise; that lacking he appeared as one who wished to retrace his steps.

He mechanically talked at what he considered a woodland matron's level of thought till a rustling was heard on the stairs, and Grace came in. Fitzpiers was for once as agitated as she. Over and above the genuine emotion which she raised in his heart there hung the sense that he was casting a die by impulse which he might not have thrown by judgment.

Mr Melbury was not in the room at the moment. Having to attend to matters in the yard he had delayed putting on his afternoon coat and waistcoat till the doctor's appearance, when, not wishing to be backward in receiving him, he entered the parlour hastily buttoning up those garments. Grace's fastidiousness was a little distressed that Fitzpiers should see by this action the strain his visit was putting upon her father; and to make matters worse for her just then, old Grammer seemed to have a passion for incessantly pumping in the back kitchen, leaving the doors open so that the banging and splashing were distinct above the parlour conversation.

Whenever the chat over the tea sank into pleasant desultoriness Mr Melbury broke in with speeches of laboured precision on very remote topics, as if he feared to let Fitzpiers's mind dwell critically on the subject nearest the hearts of all. In truth a constrained manner was natural enough in Melbury just now, for the greatest interest of his life was reaching its crisis. Could the real have been beheld instead of the corporeal merely, the corner of the room in which he sat would have been filled with a form typical of anxious suspense, large-eyed, tight-lipped, awaiting the issue. That paternal hopes and fears so intense should be bound up in the person of one child so peculiarly circumstanced, and not have dispersed themselves over the larger field of a whole family, involved dangerous risks to his own future happiness.

Fitzpiers did not stay more than an hour, but that time had apparently advanced his sentiments towards Grace, once and for all, from a vaguely liquescent to an organic shape. She would not have accompanied him to the door, in response to his whispered 'Come!' if her mother had not said in a matter-of-fact way, 'Of course, Grace; go to the door with Mr Fitzpiers.' Accordingly Grace went, both her parents remaining in the room.

When the young pair were in the great brick-floored hall the lover took the girl's hand in his, drew it under his arm, and thus led her on to the front door, where he stealthily put his lips to her own.

She broke from him trembling, blushed, and turned aside, hardly knowing how things had advanced to this. Fitzpiers drove off kissing his hand to her, and waving it to Melbury, who was visible through the window. Her father returned the surgeon's action with a great flourish of his own hand, and a satisfied smile.

The intoxication that Fitzpiers had, as usual, produced in Grace's brain during the visit passed off somewhat with his withdrawal. She felt like a woman who did not know what she had been doing for the previous hour; but supposed with trepidation that the afternoon's proceedings, though vague, had amounted to an engagement between herself and the handsome, coercive, irresistible Fitzpiers.

This visit was a type of many which followed it during the long summer days of that year. Grace was borne along upon a stream of reasonings, arguments, and persuasions, supplemented, it must be added, by inclinations of her own at times. No woman is without aspirations, which may be innocent enough within limits; and Grace had been so trained socially, and educated intellectually, as to see clearly enough a pleasure in the position of wife to such a man as Fitzpiers. His material standing of itself, either present or future, had little in it to feed her ambition, but the possibilities of a refined and cultivated inner life, of subtle psychological intercourse, had their charm. It was this rather than any vulgar idea of marrying well which caused her to float with the current, and to yield to the immense influence which Fitzpiers exercised over her whenever she shared his society.

Any observer would shrewdly have prophesied that whether or not she loved him as yet in the ordinary sense, she was pretty sure to do so in time.

One evening just before dusk they had taken a rather long walk together, and for a short cut homeward passed through the shrubberies of Hintock House — still deserted, and still blankly confronting with its sightless shuttered windows the surrounding foliage and slopes.

Grace was tired, and they approached the wall, and sat together on one of the stone sills — still warm with the sun that had been pouring its rays upon them all the afternoon.

'This place would just do for us, would it not, dearest?' said her betrothed, as they sat, turning and looking idly at the old facade.

'O yes,' said Grace, plainly showing that no such fancy had ever crossed her mind. 'She is away from home still,' Grace added in a minute rather sadly, for she could not forget that she had somehow lost the valuable friendship of the lady of this bower.

'Who is? —O, you mean Mrs Charmond. Do you know, dear, at one time I thought *you* lived here?'

'Indeed,' said Grace. 'How was that?'

He explained, as far as he could do so without mentioning his disappointment at finding it was otherwise; and then went on: 'Well, never mind that. Now I want to ask you something. There is one detail of our wedding which I am sure you will leave to me. My inclination is not to be married at the horrid little church here, with all the yokels staring round at us, and a droning parson reading.'

'Where then can it be? At a church in town?'

'No. Not at a church at all. At a registry office. It is a quieter, snugger, and more convenient place in every way.'

'O,' said she with real distress. 'How can I be married except at church, and with all my dear friends round me!'

'Yeoman Winterborne among them.'

'Yes — why not? You know there was nothing serious between him and me.'

'You see, dear, a noisy, bell-ringing marriage at church has this objection in our case: it would be a thing of report a long way round. Now I would gently, as gently as possible, indicate to you how inadvisable such publicity would be if we leave Hintock, and I purchase the practice that I contemplate purchasing at Budmouth — barely twenty miles off. Forgive my saying that it will be far better if nobody there knows much of where you come from, nor anything about your parents. Your beauty and knowledge and manners will carry you anywhere if you are not hampered by such retrospective criticism.'

'But could it not be a quiet ceremony, even at church?' she pleaded.

'I don't see the necessity of going there!' he said, a trifle impatiently. 'Marriage is a civil contract, and the shorter and simpler it is made the better. People don't go to church when they take a house, or even when they make a will.'

'O Edred — I don't like to hear you speak like that.'

'Well, well — I didn't mean to. But I have mentioned as much to your father, who has made no objection; and why should you?'

She deemed the point one on which she ought to allow sentiment to give way to policy — if there were indeed policy in his plan. But she was indefinably depressed as they walked homeward.

CHAPTER TWENTY-FOUR

H E left her at the door of her father's house. As he receded and was clasped out of sight by the filmy shades he impressed Grace as a man who hardly appertained to her existence at all. Cleverer, greater than herself, one outside her mental orbit, as she considered him, he seemed to be her ruler rather than her equal, protector, and dear familiar friend.

The disappointment she had experienced at his wish, the shock given to her girlish sensibilities by his irreverent views of marriage, together with the sure and near approach of the day fixed for committing her future to his keeping, made her so restless that she could scarcely sleep at all that night. She rose when the sparrows began to creep out of the roof-holes, sat on the floor of her room in the dim light, and by and by peeped out behind the window curtains.

It was even now day out of doors, though the tones of morning were feeble and wan, and it was long before the sun would be perceptible in this over-shadowed vale. Not a sound came from any of the out-houses as yet. The tree-trunks, the road, the out-buildings, the garden, every object, wore that aspect of mesmeric passivity which the quietude of daybreak lends to such scenes. Helpless immobility seemed to be combined with intense consciousness; a meditative inertness possessed all things, oppressively contrasting with her own active emotions. Beyond the road were some cottage roofs and orchards; over these roofs and over the apple-trees behind, high up the slope, and backed by the plantation on the crest, was the house yet occupied by her future husband, the rough-cast front showing whitely through its creepers. The window-shutters were closed, the bedroom curtains closely drawn, and not the thinnest coil of smoke rose from the rugged chimneys.

Something broke the stillness. The front-door of the house she was gazing at opened softly, and there came out into the porch a female figure, wrapped in a large cloak, beneath which was visible the white skirt of a long loose garment like a night-dress. A grey arm, stretching from within the porch, adjusted the cloak over the woman's shoulders; it was withdrawn and disappeared, the door closing behind her.

The woman went quickly down the box-edged path between the raspberries and currants, and as she walked her well-developed form and gait betrayed her individuality. It was Suke Damson, the affianced one of simple young Tim Tangs. At the bottom of the garden she entered the shelter of the tall hedge, and only the top of her head could be seen hastening in the direction of her own dwelling.

Grace had recognized, or thought she recognized, in the grey arm stretching from the porch, the sleeve of a dressing-gown which Mr Fitzpiers had been wearing on her own memorable visit to him. Her face fired red. She had just before thought of dressing herself and taking a lonely walk under the trees, so coolly green this early morning; but she now sat down on her bed and fell into reverie.

It seemed as if hardly any time had passed when she heard the household moving briskly about, and breakfast preparing downstairs; though, on rousing herself to robe and descend, she found that the sun was throwing his rays completely over the tree-tops, a progress in the world's diurnal turn denoting that at least three hours had elapsed since she last looked out of the window.

When attired she searched about the house for her father; she found him at last in the garden, stooping to examine the potatoes for signs of disease. Hearing her rustle he stood up and stretched his back and arms, saying, 'Morning t'ye, Gracie. I congratulate 'ee. It is only a month to-day to the time!'

She did not answer, but, without lifting her dress, waded between the dewy rows of tall potato-green into the middle of the plot where he was.

'I have been thinking very much about my position this morning – ever since it was light,' she began excitedly, and trembling so that she could hardly stand. 'And I feel it is a false one. I wish not to marry Mr Fitzpiers. I wish not to marry anybody; but I'll marry Giles Winterborne if you say I must as an alternative.'

Her father's face settled into rigidity, he turned pale, and came deliberately out of the plot before he answered her. She had never seen him look so incensed before.

'Now, hearken to me,' he said. 'There's a time for a woman to alter her mind; and there's a time when she can no longer alter it, if she has any right eye to her parents' honour and the seemliness of things. That time has come. I won't say to 'ee, you *shall* marry him. But I will say, that if you refuse, I shall for ever be ashamed and aweary of 'ee as a daughter, and shall look upon you as the hope of my life no more. What do you know about life and what it can bring forth, and how you ought to act to lead up to best ends? O, you are an ungrateful maid, Grace; you've seen that fellow Giles, and he has got over 'ee; that's where the secret lies, I'll warrant me!'

'No, father, no! It is not Giles – it is something I cannot tell you of—'

'Well, make fools of us all; make us laughing-stocks; break it off; have your own way!'

'But who knows of the engagement as yet; how can breaking it disgrace you?'

Melbury then by degrees admitted that he had mentioned the engagement to this acquaintance and to that, till she perceived that in his restlessness and pride he had published it everywhere. She went dismally away to a bower of laurel at the top of the garden. Her father followed her.

'It is that Giles Winterborne!' he said with an upbraiding gaze at her.

'No, it is not; though for that matter you encouraged him once!' she said, troubled to the verge of despair. 'It is not Giles, it is Mr Fitzpiers.'

'You've had a tiff – a lovers' tiff – that's all, I suppose?'

'It is some woman—'

'Ay, ay; you are jealous. The old story. Don't tell me. Now do you bide here. I'll send Fitzpiers to you. I saw him smoking in front of his house but a minute bygone.'

He went off hastily out of the garden-gate and up the lane. But she would not stay where she was; and edging through a slit in the garden fence walked away into the wood.

Just about here the trees were large and wide apart, and there was no undergrowth, so that she could be seen to some distance; a sylph-like greenish-white creature, as toned by the sunlight and leafage. She heard a footfall crushing dead leaves behind her, and turning hastily found herself reconnoitred by Fitzpiers himself, approaching gay and fresh as the morning around them.

His remote gaze at her had been one of mild interest rather than of rapture. But she looked so lovely in the green world about her; her pink cheeks, her simple white dress, and the delicate flexibility of her movements acquired such rarity from their wildwood setting that his eyes kindled as he drew near.

'My darling, what is it? Your father says you are in the pouts, and jealous, and I don't know what. Ha! ha! ha! as if there were any rival to you except vegetable nature, in this home of recluses. We know better.'

'Jealous; O no, it is not so,' said she gravely. 'That's a mistake of his and yours, sir. I spoke to him so closely about the question of marriage with you that he did not apprehend my state of mind.'

'But there's something wrong – eh?' he asked, eyeing her narrowly, and bending to kiss her.

She shrank away, and his purposed kiss miscarried.

'What is it?' he said, more seriously for this little defeat.

She made no answer beyond, 'Mr Fitzpiers, I have had no breakfast, I must go in.'

'Come,' he insisted, fixing his eyes upon her. 'Tell me at once, I say.'

It was the greater strength against the smaller, but she was mastered less by his manner than by her own sense of the unfairness of silence.

'I looked out of the window,' she said with hesitation. 'I'll tell you by and by. I must go indoors. I have had no breakfast.'

By a sort of divination his conjecture went straight to the fact. 'Nor I,' said he lightly. 'Indeed, I rose late to-day. I have had a broken night, or rather morning. A girl of the village – I don't know her name – came and rang at my bell as soon as it was light – between four and five I should think it was – perfectly maddened with an aching tooth. As nobody heard her ring she threw some gravel at my window, till at last I heard her and slipped on my dressing-gown and went down. The poor thing had come half-dressed to beg me, with tears in her eyes, to take out her tormentor if I dragged her head off. Down she sat and out it came; a lovely molar, not a speck upon it; and off she went with it in her handkerchief, much contented, though it would have done good work for her for fifty years to come.'

It was all so plausible – so completely explained. Knowing nothing of the intimacy established in the hayfield on old Midsummer Eve, Grace felt that her suspicions were unworthy and absurd, and with the readiness of an honest heart she jumped at the opportunity of honouring his word. At the moment of her mental liberation the bushes about the garden had moved, and her father emerged into the shady glade.

'Well, I hope it is made up?' he said cheerily.

'O yes,' said Fitzpiers, with his eyes fixed on Grace, whose eyes were shyly bent downwards.

'Now,' said her father, 'tell me, the pair of ye, that you still mean to take one another for good and all; and on the strength o't you shall have another couple of hundred paid down. I swear it by the Name.'

Fitzpiers took her hand. 'We declare it, do we not, my dear Grace?' said he.

Relieved of her doubt, somewhat overawed, and ever anxious to please, she was disposed to settle the matter. Yet, woman-like, she would not relinquish her opportunity of asking a concession of some sort. 'If our wedding can be at church, I say yes,' she answered in a measured voice. 'If not, I say no.'

Fitzpiers was generous in his turn. 'It shall be so,' he rejoined gracefully. 'To holy church we'll go – and much good may it do us.'

They returned through the bushes indoors, Grace walking full of thought between the other two, somewhat comforted both by Fitzpiers's ingenious explanation and by the sense that she was not to be deprived of a religious ceremony. 'So let it be,' she said to herself. 'Pray God it is for the best.'

From this hour there was no serious recalcitration on her part. Fitzpiers kept himself continually near her, dominating any rebellious impulse, and shaping her will into passive concurrence with all his desires. Apart from his lover-like anxiety to possess her the few golden hundreds of the timber-dealer, ready to hand, formed a warm background to Grace's lovely face, and went some way to remove his uneasiness at the prospect of endangering his professional and social chances by an alliance with the family of a simple country-man.

The interim closed up its perspective surely and silently. Whenever Grace had any doubts of her position the sense of contracting time was like a shortening chamber: at other moments she was comparatively blithe.

Day after day waxed and waned; the one or two woodmen who sawed, shaped, or spokeshaved on her father's premises at this inactive season of the year, regularly came and unlocked the doors in the morning, locked them in the evening, supped, leant over their garden-gates for a whiff of evening air, and to catch any last and furthest throb of news from the outer world, which entered and expired at Little Hintock like the exhausted swell of a wave in some innermost cavern of some innermost creek of an embayed sea; yet no news interfered with the nuptial purpose at their neighbour's house.

The sappy green twig-tips of the season's growth would not, she thought, be appreciably woodier on the day she became a wife, so near was the time; the tints of the foliage would hardly have changed. Everything was so much as usual that no itinerant stranger would have supposed a woman's fate to be hanging in the balance at that summer's decline.

But there were preparations, imaginable enough by those who had special knowledge. In the remote and fashionable city of Exonbury something was growing up under the hands of several persons who had never seen Grace Melbury, never would see her, or care anything about her at all; though their creation had such interesting relation to her life that it would enclose her very heart at a moment when that heart would beat, if not with more emotional ardour, at least with more emotional turbulence than at any previous time.

Why did Mrs Dollery's van on its return from Sherton, instead of passing along the highway to Abbot's Cernel direct, turn one Saturday night into Little Hintock Lane, and never pull up till it reached Mr Melbury's gates? The gilding sheen of evening fell upon a large flat box, not less than a yard square and safely tied with cord, as it was handed out from under the tilt with a great deal of care. But it was not heavy for its size; Mrs Dollery herself carried it into the house. Tim Tangs, the hollow-turner, Cawtree, Suke Damson, and others, looked knowing and made remarks to each other as they watched its entrance. Melbury stood at the door of the timber-shed in the attitude of a man to whom such an arrival was a trifling domestic detail with which he did not condescend to be concerned. Yet he well divined the contents of that box, and was in truth all the while in a pleasant exaltation at the proof that thus far, at any rate, no disappointment had supervened. While Mrs Dollery remained – which was rather long, from her sense of the importance of her errand – he went into the outhouse; but as soon as she had had her say, been paid, and had rumbled away, he entered the dwelling, to find there what he knew he should find – his wife and daughter in a flutter of excitement over the wedding-gown, just arrived from the leading dressmaker of Exonbury city aforesaid.

During these weeks Giles Winterborne was nowhere to be seen or heard of. At the close of his tenure in Hintock he had sold some of his furniture, packed up the rest – a few pieces endeared by associations, or necessary to his occupation – in the house of a friendly neighbour, and gone away. People said that a certain laxity had crept into his life; that he had never gone near a church latterly, and had been sometimes seen on Sundays with unblacked boots, lying on his elbow under a tree, with a cynical gaze at surrounding objects. He was likely to return to Hintock when the cider-making season came round, his apparatus being stored there, and travel with his mill and press from village to village.

The narrow interval that stood before the day diminished yet. There was in Grace's mind sometimes a certain anticipative satisfaction, the satisfaction of feeling that she would be the heroine of an hour; moreover, she was proud, as a cultivated woman, to be the wife of a cultivated man. It was an opportunity denied very frequently to young women in her position, nowadays not a few; those in whom parental discovery of the value of education has implanted tastes which parental circles fail to gratify. But what an attenuation this cold pride was of the dream of her youth, in which she had pictured herself walking in state towards the altar, flushed by the purple light and bloom of her own passion, without a single misgiving as to the sealing of the bond, and fervently receiving as her due

> 'The homage of a thousand hearts; the fond deep love of one.'

Everything had been clear then, in imagination; now something was undefined. She had little carking anxieties; a curious fatefulness seemed to rule her, and she experienced a mournful want of some one to confide in.

The day loomed so big and nigh that her prophetic ear could in fancy catch the noise of it, hear the murmur of the villagers as she came out of church, imagine the jangle of the three thin-toned Hintock bells. The dialogues seemed to grow louder, and the ding-ding-dong of those crazed bells more persistent. She awoke: the morning had come.

Five hours later she was the wife of Fitzpiers.

CHAPTER TWENTY-FIVE

THE chief hotel at Sherton Abbas was the 'Earl of Wessex' — a substantial inn of Ham-hill stone with a yawning back yard into which vehicles were driven by coachmen to stabling of wonderful commodiousness. The windows to the street were mullioned into narrow lights, and only commanded a view of the opposite houses; hence, perhaps, it arose that the best and most luxurious private sitting-room that the inn could afford overlooked the lateral parts of the establishment, where beyond the yard were to be seen gardens and orchards now bossed, nay encrusted, with scarlet and gold fruit, stretching to infinite distance under a luminous lavender mist. The time was early autumn,

> 'When the fair apples, red as evening sky,
> Do bend the tree unto the fruitful ground,
> When juicy pears, and berries of black dye
> Do dance in air, and call the eyes around.'

The landscape confronting the window might indeed have been part of the identical stretch of country which the 'marvellous boy' had in his mind when he penned those lines.

In this room sat she who had been the maiden Grace Melbury till the finger of fate touched her and turned her to a wife. It was two months after the wedding, and she was alone. Fitzpiers had walked out to see the abbey by the light of sunset, but she had been too fatigued to accompany him. They had reached the last stage of a long eight-weeks' tour, and were going on to Little Hintock that night.

In the yard between Grace and the orchards there progressed a scene natural to the locality at this time of the year. An apple-mill and press had been erected on the spot, to which some men were bringing fruit from divers points in mawn-baskets, while others were grinding them, and others wringing down the pomace, whose sweet juice gushed forth into tubs and pails. The superintendent of these proceedings, to whom the others spoke as master, was a young yeoman of prepossessing manner and aspect, whose form she recognized in a moment. He had hung his coat to a nail of the outhouse wall, and wore his shirt-sleeves rolled up beyond his elbows, to keep them unstained while he rammed the pomace into the bags of horsehair. Fragments of apple-rind had alighted upon the brim of his hat – probably from the bursting of a bag – while brown pips of the same fruit were sticking among the down upon his fine round arms, and in his beard.

She realized in a moment how he had come there. Down in the heart of the apple-country nearly every farmer kept a cider-making apparatus and wring-house for his own use, building up the pomace in great straw 'cheeses', as they were called; but here, on the margin of Pomona's plain, was a debatable land neither orchard nor sylvan exclusively, where the apple-produce was hardly sufficient to warrant each proprietor in keeping a mill of his own. This was the field of the travelling cider-maker. His press and mill were fixed to wheels instead of being set up in a cider-house; and with a couple of horses, buckets, tubs, strainers, and an assistant or two, he wandered from place to place, deriving very satisfactory returns for his trouble in such a prolific season as the present.

The outskirts of the town were just now abounding with apple-gatherings. They stood in the yards in carts, baskets, and loose heaps; and the blue stagnant air of autumn which hung over everything was heavy with a sweet cidery smell. Cakes of pomace lay against the walls in the yellow sun, where they were drying to be used as fuel. Yet it was not the great make of the year as yet; before the standard crop came in there accumulated, in abundant times like this, a large superfluity of early apples, and windfalls from the trees of later harvest, which would not keep long. Thus in the baskets, and quivering in the hopper of the mill, she saw specimens of mixed dates, including the mellow countenances of streaked-jacks, codlins, costards, stubbards, ratheripes, and other well-known friends of the ravenous youth.

Grace watched the head man with interest. The slightest sigh escaped her. Perhaps she thought of the day – not so far distant – when that friend of her childhood had met her by her father's arrangement in this same town, warm with hope, though diffident, and trusting in a promise rather implied than given. Or she might have thought of days earlier yet – days of childhood – when her mouth was somewhat more ready to receive a kiss from his than was his to bestow one. However, all that was over. She had felt superior to him then, and she felt superior to him now.

She wondered why he never looked towards her open window. She did not know that in the slight commotion caused by their arrival at the inn that afternoon Winterborne had caught sight of her through the archway, had turned red, and was continuing his work with more concentrated attention on the very account of his discovery. Robert Creedle, too, who travelled with Giles, had been incidentally informed by the ostler that Dr Fitzpiers and his young wife were in the hotel; after which news Creedle kept shaking his head and saying to himself, 'Ah!' very audibly, between his thrusts at the screw of the cider-press.

'Why the deuce do you sigh like that, Robert?' asked Winterborne at last.

'Ah, maister, – 'tis my thoughts – 'tis my thoughts! . . . Yes, ye've lost a hundred load o' timber well seasoned; ye've lost five hundred pound in good money; ye've lost the stone-windered house that's big enough to hold a dozen families; ye've lost your share of half-a-dozen good waggons and their horses; – all lost! – through your letting slip she that was once yer own!'

'Good God, Creedle! you'll drive me mad!' said Giles sternly. 'Don't speak of that any more!'

Thus the subject had ended in the yard. Meanwhile the passive cause of all this loss still regarded the scene. She was beautifully dressed; she was seated in the most comfortable room that the inn afforded; her long journey had been full of variety, and almost luxuriously performed, for Fitzpiers did not study economy where pleasure was in question. Hence it perhaps arose that Giles and all his belongings seemed sorry and common to her for the moment – moving in a groove so far removed from her own of late that she could scarcely believe she had ever found congruity therein.

'No – I could never have married him!' she said, gently shaking her head. 'Dear father was right. It would have been too rough a life for me.' And she looked at the rings of sapphire and opal upon her white and slender fingers that had been gifts from Fitzpiers.

Seeing that Giles still kept his back turned, and with a little of the above-described pride of life – easily to be understood, possibly excused, in a young inexperienced woman who thought she had married well – she opened the window wider and cried with a smile on her lips, 'Mr Winterborne!'

He appeared to take no heed, and she said a second time, 'Mr Winterborne!'

Even now he seemed not to hear, though a person close enough to him to see the expression of his face might have doubted it; and she said a third time, with a timid loudness, 'Mr Winterborne! What, have you forgotten my voice?' She remained with her lips parted in a welcoming smile.

He turned without surprise and came deliberately towards the window.

'Why do you call me?' he said, with a sternness that took her completely unawares, his face being now pale. 'Is it not enough that you see me here moiling and muddling for my daily bread while you are sitting there in your success, that you can't refrain from opening old wounds by calling out my name?'

She flushed, and was struck dumb for some moments; but she forgave his unreasoning anger, knowing so well in what it had its root.

'I am sorry I offended you by speaking, Giles,' she replied. 'Believe me, I did not intend to do that. I could hardly sit here so near you without a word of recognition.'

Winterborne's heart had swollen big and his eyes grown moist by this time, so much had the gentle answer of that familiar voice moved him. He assured her hurriedly, and without looking at her, that he was not angry. He then managed to ask her, in a clumsy constrained way, if she had had a pleasant journey, and seen many interesting sights. She spoke of a few places that she had visited, and so the time passed till he withdrew to take his place at one of the levers which pulled round the screw.

Forgotten her voice! Indeed, he had not forgotten her voice, as his bitterness showed. But though in the heat of the moment he had reproached her keenly, his second mood was a far more tender one – that which could regard her renunciation of such as he as her glory and her privilege, his own fidelity notwithstanding. He could have declared with a contemporary poet –

> 'If I forget,
> The salt creek may forget the ocean;
>   If I forget
> The heart whence flowed my heart's bright motion,
> May I sink meanlier than the worst,
> Abandoned, outcast, crushed, accurst, –
>   If I forget.
>
>   Though you forget,
> No word of mine shall mar your pleasure;
>   Though you forget, –
> You filled my barren life with treasure;
> You may withdraw the gift you gave,
> You still are queen, I still am slave,
>   Though you forget.'

She had tears in her eyes at the thought that she could not remind him of what he ought to have remembered; that not herself but the pressure of events had dissipated the dreams of their early youth.

Grace was thus unexpectedly worsted in her encounter with her old friend. She had opened the window with a faint sense of triumph, but he had turned it into sadness; she did not quite comprehend the reason why. In truth it was because she was not cruel enough in her cruelty. If you have to use the knife, use it, say the great surgeons; and for her own peace Grace should have handled Winterborne thoroughly or not at all. As it was, on closing the window an indescribable – some might have said dangerous – pity quavered in her bosom for him.

Presently her husband entered the room and told her what a wonderful sunset there was to be seen.

'I have not noticed it. But I have seen somebody out there that we know,' she replied, looking into the court.

Fitzpiers followed the direction of her eyes and said he did not recognize anybody.

'Why, Mr Winterborne – there he is cider-making. He combines that with his other business, you know.'

'O – that fellow,' said Fitzpiers, his curiosity becoming extinct.

She, reproachfully: 'What, call Mr Winterborne a fellow, Edred! It is true I was just saying to myself that I never could have married him; but I have much regard for him, and always shall.'

'Well, do by all means, my dear one. I dare say I am inhuman, and supercilious, and contemptibly proud of my poor old ramshackle family; but I do honestly confess to you that I feel as if I belonged to a different species from the people who are working in that yard.'

'And from me, too, then. For my blood is no better than theirs.'

He looked at her with a droll sort of awakening. It was, indeed, a startling anomaly that this woman of the tribe without should be standing there beside him as his wife, if his sentiments were as he had said. In their travels together she had ranged so unerringly at his level in ideas, tastes, and habits, that he had almost forgotten how his heart had played havoc with his ambition in taking her to him.

'Ah, *you* – you are refined and educated into something quite different,' he said self-assuringly.

'I don't quite like to think that,' she murmured with regret. 'And I think you under-estimate Giles Winterborne. Remember I was brought up with him till I was sent away to school, so I cannot be radically different. At any rate I don't feel so. That is no doubt my fault, and a great blemish in me. But I hope you will put up with it, Edred.'

Fitzpiers said that he would endeavour to do so, and as it was now getting on for dusk they prepared to perform the last stage of their journey, so as to arrive at Hintock before it grew very late.

In less than half-an-hour they started, the cider-makers in the yard having ceased their labours and gone away, so that the only sounds audible there now were the trickling of the juice from the tightly screwed press, and the buzz of a single wasp, which had drunk itself so tipsy that it was unconscious of nightfall.

Grace was very cheerful at the thought of being soon in her sylvan home; but Fitzpiers sat beside her almost silent. An indescribable oppressiveness had overtaken him with the near approach of the journey's end and the realities of life that lay there. It was two months since he married her.

'You don't say a word, Edred,' she observed. 'Aren't you glad to get back? I am.'

'You have friends here. I have none.'

'But my friends are yours.'

'O yes – in that sense.'

The conversation languished, and they drew near the end of Hintock Lane. It had been decided that they should, at least for a time, take up their abode in her father's roomy house, one wing of which was quite at their service, being almost disused by the Melburys. Workmen had been painting, papering, and white-washing this set of rooms in the wedded pair's absence; and so scrupulous had been the timber-dealer that there should occur no hitch or disappointment on their arrival that not the smallest detail remained undone. To make it all complete a ground-floor room had been fitted up as a surgery, with an independent outer door, to which Fitzpiers's brass plate was screwed – for mere ornament, such a sign being quite superfluous where everybody knew the latitude and longitude of his neighbours for miles round.

Melbury and his wife welcomed the twain with affection, and all the house showed them deference. They went up to explore their rooms, that opened from a passage on the left hand of the staircase, the entrance to which could be shut off on the landing by a door that Melbury had hung for the purpose. A friendly fire was burning in the grate although it was not cold. Fitzpiers said it was too soon for any sort of meal, they having dined but shortly before leaving Sherton Abbas; he would walk across to his old lodging to learn how his deputy had got on in his absence.

In leaving Melbury's door he looked back at the house. There was economy in living under that roof – and economy was desirable; but in some way he was dissatisfied with the arrangement; it immersed him so deeply in son-in-lawship to Melbury. He went on to his former residence; his *locum tenens* was out, and Fitzpiers fell into conversation with his old landlady.

'Well, Mrs Cox, what's the best news?' he asked of her with cheery weariness.

She was a little soured at losing by his marriage so profitable a tenant as the surgeon had proved to be during his residence under her roof; and the more so in there being hardly the remotest chance of her getting such another settler in the Hintock solitudes. ''Tis what I don't wish to repeat, sir; least of all to you,' she mumbled.

'Never mind me, Mrs Cox; go ahead.'

'It is what people say about your hasty marrying, Dr Fitzpiers. Whereas they won't believe you know such clever doctrines in physic as they once supposed of 'ee, seeing as you could marry into Mr Melbury's family, which is only Hintock-born such as I be meself.'

'They are kindly welcome to their opinion,' said Fitzpiers, not allowing himself to recognize that he winced. 'Anything else?'

'Yes; *she's* come home at last.'

'Who's she?'

'Mrs Charmond.'

'O indeed,' said Fitzpiers, with but slight interest. 'I've never seen her.'

'She has seen you, sir, whether or no.'

'Never.'

'Yes. She saw you in some hotel or street for a minute or two whilst you were away travelling, and accidentally heard your name; and when she made some remark about you, Miss Ellis – that's her maid – told her you was on your wedding-tour with Mr Melbury's daughter; and she said, "He ought to have done better than that. I fear he has spoilt his chances," she says.'

Fitzpiers did not talk much longer to this cheering housewife, and walked home with no very brisk step. He entered the door quietly, and went straight upstairs to the drawing-room extemporized for their use by Melbury in his and his bride's absence, expecting to find her there as he had left her.

The fire was burning still but there were no lights; he looked into the next apartment fitted up as a dining-room, but no supper was laid. He went to the top of the stairs and heard a chorus of voices in the timber-merchant's parlour below, Grace's being occasionally intermingled.

Descending, and looking into the room from the doorway, he found quite a large gathering of neighbours and other acquaintances, praising and congratulating Mrs Fitzpiers on her return, among them being the dairyman, Farmer Cawtree, and the relieving officer from Great Hintock; also the road-contractor, the master-tanner, the exciseman, and some others with their wives. Grace – girl that she was – had quite forgotten her new dignity and her husband's; she was in the midst of them, blushing and receiving their compliments with all the pleasures of old comradeship.

Fitzpiers experienced a profound distaste for the situation. Melbury was nowhere in the room, but Melbury's wife, perceiving the doctor, came to him.

'We thought, Grace and I,' she said, 'that as they have called, hearing you were come, we could do no less than ask them to supper; and then Grace proposed that we should all sup together as it is the first night of your return.'

By this time Grace had come round to him. 'Is it not good of them to welcome me so warmly?' she exclaimed with tears of friendship in her eyes. 'After so much good feeling I could not think of our shutting ourselves up away from them in our own dining-room.'

'Certainly not — certainly not,' said Fitzpiers. And he entered the room with the heroic smile of a martyr.

As soon as they sat down to table Melbury came in, and seemed to see at once that Fitzpiers would much rather have received no such demonstrative reception. He thereupon privately chid his wife for her forwardness in the matter. Mrs Melbury declared that it was as much Grace's doing as hers, after which there was no more to be said by that young woman's tender father.

By this time Fitzpiers was making the best of his position among the wide-elbowed and genial company who sat eating and drinking, laughing and joking around him; and, getting warmed himself by the good cheer, he was obliged to admit that, after all, the supper was not the least enjoyable he had ever known.

At times, however, the words about his having spoiled his opportunities, repeated to him as coming from Mrs Charmond, haunted him like a handwriting on the wall. Then his manner would become suddenly abstracted. At one moment he would mentally put an indignant query why Mrs Charmond or any other woman should make it her business to have opinions about his opportunities: at another he thought that he could hardly be angry with her for taking an interest in the doctor of her own parish. Then he would drink a glass of grog and so get rid of the misgiving.

These hitches and quaffings were soon perceived by Grace as well as by her father; and hence both of them were much relieved when the first of the guests to discover that the hour was growing late rose and declared that he must think of moving homewards. At the words Melbury rose as alertly as if lifted by a spring; and in ten minutes they were gone.

'Now, Grace,' said her husband as soon as he found himself alone with her in their private apartments, 'we've had a very pleasant evening, and everybody has been very kind. But we must come to an understanding about our way of living here. If we continue in these rooms there must be no mixing in with your people below. I can't stand it, and that's the truth.'

She had been sadly surprised at the suddenness of his distaste for those old-fashioned woodland forms of life which in his courtship he had professed to regard with so much interest. But she assented in a moment.

'We must be simply your father's tenants,' he continued, 'and our goings and comings must be as independent as if we lived elsewhere.'

'Certainly, Edred — I quite see that it must be so.'

'But you joined in with all those people in my absence, without knowing whether I should approve or disapprove. When I came I couldn't help myself at all.'

She, sighing: 'Yes — I see I ought to have waited; though they came un-expectedly, and I thought I had acted for the best.'

Thus the discussion ended, and the next day Fitzpiers went on his old rounds as usual. But it was easy for so supersubtle an eye as his to discern, or to think he discerned, that he was no longer regarded as an extrinsic, unfathomed gentleman of limitless potentiality, scientific and social; but as Mr Melbury's compeer, and therefore in a degree only one of themselves. The Hintock woodlanders held with all the strength of inherited conviction to the aristocratic principle, and as soon as they had discovered that Fitzpiers was one of the old Oakbury Fitzpierses they had accorded to him for nothing a touching of hat-brims, promptness of service, and deference of approach, which Melbury had to do without though he paid for it over and over. But now, having proved a traitor to his own cause by this marriage, Fitzpiers was believed in no more as a superior hedged by his own divinity; while as doctor he began to be rated no higher than old Jones, whom they had so long despised.

His few patients seemed in his two months' absence to have dwindled considerably in number, and no sooner had he returned than there came to him from the Board of Guardians a complaint that a pauper had been neglected by his substitute. In a fit of pride Fitzpiers resigned his appointment as one of the surgeons to the Union, which had been the nucleus of his practice here.

At the end of a fortnight he came indoors one evening to Grace more briskly than usual. 'They have written to me again about that practice in Budmouth that I once negotiated for,' he said to her. 'The premium asked is eight hundred pounds, and I think that between your father and myself it ought to be raised. Then we can get away from this place for ever.'

The question had been mooted between them before, and she was not unprepared to consider it. They had not proceeded far with the discussion when a knock came to the door, and in a minute Grammer ran up to say that a message had arrived from Hintock House requesting Dr Fitzpiers to attend there at once. Mrs Charmond had met with a slight accident through the overturning of her carriage.

'This is something, anyhow,' said Fitzpiers, rising with an interest which he could not have defined. 'I have had a presentiment that this mysterious woman and I were to be better acquainted.'

The latter words were murmured to himself alone.

'Good-night,' said Grace as soon as he was ready. 'I shall be asleep probably when you return.'

'Good-night,' he replied inattentively, and went downstairs. It was the first time since their marriage that he had left her without a kiss.

CHAPTER TWENTY-SIX

WINTERBORNE had given up his house. On this account his face was seen but fitfully in Hintock; and he would probably have disappeared from the place altogether but for his slight business connection with Melbury, on whose premises Giles kept his cider-making apparatus now that he had no place of his own to stow it in.

Coming here one afternoon on his way to a hut beyond the wood, where he now slept, he noticed that the familiar brown-thatched pinion of his paternal roof had vanished from its site, and that the walls were levelled, according to the landlords' principle at this date of getting rid of cottages whenever possible. In present circumstances he had a feeling for the spot that might have been called morbid, and when he had supped in the hut aforesaid he made use of the spare hour before bedtime to return to Little Hintock in the twilight, and ramble over the patch of ground on which he had first seen the day.

He repeated this evening visit on several like occasions. Even in the gloom he could trace where the different rooms had stood; could mark the shape of the kitchen chimney-corner in which he had roasted apples and potatoes in his boyhood, cast his bullets, and burnt his initials on articles that did and did not belong to him. The apple-trees still remained to show where the garden had been, the oldest of them even now retaining the crippled slant to north-east given them by the great November gale of 1824, which carried a brig bodily over the Chesil Bank. They were at present bent to still greater obliquity by the heaviness of their produce. Apples bobbed against his head, and in the grass beneath he crunched scores of them as he walked. There was nobody to gather them now.

It was on the evening under notice that, half-sitting, half-leaning against one of these inclined trunks, Winterborne became lost in his thoughts as usual, till one little star after another had taken up a position in the piece of sky which now confronted him where his walls and chimneys had formerly raised their outlines. The house had jutted awkwardly into the road and the opening caused by its absence was very distinct.

In the silence the trot of horses and the spin of carriage wheels became audible; the vehicle soon shaped itself against the blank sky, bearing down upon him with the bend in the lane which here occurred, and of which the house had been the cause. He could discern the figure of a woman high up on the driving-seat of a phaeton, a groom being just visible behind.

Presently there was a slight scrape, then a scream. Winterborne went across to the spot, and found the phaeton half overturned, its driver sitting on the heap of rubbish which had once been his dwelling, and the man seizing the horses' heads. The equipage was Mrs Charmond's and the unseated charioteer that lady herself.

To his inquiry if she were hurt she made some incoherent reply to the effect that she did not know. The damage in other respects was little or none; the phaeton was righted, Mrs Charmond placed in it, and the reins given to the servant. It appeared that she had been deceived by the removal of the house, imagining the gap caused by the demolition to be the opening of the road, so that she turned in upon the ruins instead of at the bend, a few yards further on.

'Drive home – drive home!' she cried impatiently; and they started on their way.

They had not however gone many paces when, the air being still, Winterborne heard her say, 'Stop; tell that man to call the doctor – Mr Fitzpiers – and send him on to the House. I find I am hurt more seriously than I thought.'

The seriousness seemed ludicrous to Winterborne; but he took the message from the groom, and proceeded to the doctor's at once. Having delivered it he stepped back into the darkness, and waited till he had seen Fitzpiers leave the door. He stood for a few minutes looking at the window which, by its light, revealed the room where Grace was sitting; and went away under the gloomy trees.

*

Fitzpiers duly arrived at Hintock House, whose doors he now saw open for the first time. Contrary to his expectation there was visible no sign of that confusion or alarm which a grave accident to the mistress of the abode would have occasioned. He was shown into a room at the top of the staircase, cosily and femininely draped, where by the light of the shaded lamp he saw a woman of elegant figure reclining upon a couch in such a position as not to disturb a pile of magnificent hair on the crown of her head. A deep purple dressing-gown formed an admirable foil to the peculiarly rich brown of her hair-plaits; her left arm, which was naked nearly up to the shoulder, was thrown upwards, and between the fingers of her right hand she held a cigarette, while she idly breathed from her delicately curled lips a thin stream of smoke towards the ceiling.

The doctor's first feeling was a sense of his exaggerated prevision in having brought appliances for a serious case; the next, something more curious. While the scene and the moment were new to him and unanticipated, the sentiment and essence of the moment were indescribably familiar. What could be the cause of it? Probably a dream.

Mrs Charmond did not move more than to raise her eyes to him, and he came and stood by her. She glanced up at his face across her brows and forehead, and then he observed a blush creep slowly over her decidedly handsome cheeks. Her eyes, which had lingered upon him with an inquiring, conscious expression, were hastily withdrawn, and she mechanically applied the cigarette again to her lips.

For a moment he forgot his errand, till suddenly arousing himself he addressed her, formally condoled with her, and made the usual professional inquiries about what had happened to her, and where she was hurt.

'That's what I want you to tell me,' she murmured in tones of indefinable reserve. 'I quite believe in you, for I know you are very accomplished, because you study so hard.'

'I'll do my best to justify your good opinion,' said the young man, bowing. 'And none the less that I am happy to find the accident has not been serious.'

'I am very much shaken,' she said.

'O yes,' he replied; and completed his examination, which convinced him that there was really nothing the matter with her, and more than ever puzzled him as to why he had been summoned, since she did not appear to be a timid woman. 'You must rest a while; and I'll send something,' he said.

'O, I forgot,' she returned. 'Look here.' And she showed him a little scrape on her arm – the full round arm that was exposed. 'Put some court-plaster on that, please.'

He obeyed. 'And now, doctor,' she said, 'before you go I want to put a question to you. Sit round there in front of me, on that low chair, and bring the candles, or one, to the little table. Do you smoke? Yes? That's right – I am learning. Take one of these; and here's a light.' She threw a match-box across.

Fitzpiers caught it, and having lit up regarded her from his new position, which, with the shifting of the candles, for the first time afforded him a full view of her face.

'How many years have passed since first we met?' she resumed, in a voice which she endeavoured to maintain at its former pitch of composure, and eyeing him with daring bashfulness.

'*We* met, do you say?'

She nodded. 'I saw you recently at an hotel in London, when you were passing through, I suppose, with your bride, and I recognized you as one I had met in my girlhood. Do you remember, when you were studying at Heidelberg, an English family that was staying there, who used to walk—'

'And the young lady who wore a long tail of rare-coloured hair – ah, I see it before my eyes! – who lost her handkerchief on the Great Terrace – who was going back in the dusk to find it – to whom I said, "I'll go for it," and who answered, "O, it is not worth coming all the way up again for." I *do* remember, and how very long we stayed talking there: I went next morning, whilst the dew was on the grass: there it lay – a little morsel of damp lacework, with "Felice" marked in one corner. I see it now! I picked it up, and then. . . .'

'Well?'

'I kissed it,' he rejoined, rather shamefacedly.

'But you had hardly ever seen me except in the dusk?'

'Never mind. I was young then, and I kissed it. I wondered how I could make the most of my *trouvaille*, and decided that I would call at your hotel with it that afternoon. It rained, and I waited till next day. I called, and you were gone.'

'Yes,' answered she with dry melancholy. 'My mother, knowing my face was my only fortune, said she had no wish for such a chit as me to go falling in love with an impecunious student, and spirited me away to Baden. As it is all over and past I'll tell you one thing; I should have sent you a line had I known your name. That name I never knew till my maid said as you passed up the hotel stairs a month ago, "There's Dr Fitzpiers." '

'Good God,' said Fitzpiers musingly. 'How the time comes back to me! The evening, the morning, the dew, the spot. When I found that you really were gone it was as if a cold iron had been passed down my back. I went up to where you had stood when I last saw you – I flung myself on the grass, and – being not much more than a boy – my eyes were literally blinded with tears. Nameless, unknown to me as you were, I couldn't forget your voice!'

'For how long?'

'O – ever so long. Days and days.'

'Days and days! *Only* days and days? O, the heart of a man! Days and days!'

'But, my dear madam, I had not known you more than a day or two. It was not a full-blown love – it was the merest bud – red, fresh, vivid, but small. It was a colossal passion in embryo. It never matured.'

'So much the better perhaps.'

'Perhaps. But see how powerless is the human will against predestination! We were prevented meeting; we have met. One feature of the case remains the same amid many changes. While you have grown rich, I am still poor. Better than that, you have (judging by your last remark) outgrown the foolish impulsive passions of your early girlhood. I have not outgrown mine.'

'I beg your pardon,' said she with vibrations of feeling in her words. 'I have been placed in a position which hinders such outgrowings. Besides, I don't believe that the genuine subjects of emotion do outgrow them; I believe that the older such people get the worse they are. Possibly at ninety or a hundred they may feel they are cured: but a mere threescore and ten won't do it – at least for me, if I live so long.'

He gazed at her in undisguised admiration. Here was a soul of souls!

'You speak truly,' he exclaimed. 'But you speak sadly as well. Why is that?'

'I always am sad when I come here,' she said, dropping to a low tone with a sense of having been too demonstrative.

'Then may I inquire why you came?'

'A man brought me. Women are always carried about like corks upon the waves of masculine desires. . . . I hope I have not alarmed you; but Hintock has the curious effect of bottling up the emotions till one can no longer hold them; I am often obliged to fly away and discharge my sentiments somewhere, or I should die outright.'

'There is very good society in the county, I suppose, for those who have the privilege of entering it.'

'Perhaps so. But the misery of remote country life is that your neighbours have no toleration for difference of opinion and habit. My neighbours think I am an atheist, except those who think I am a Roman Catholic; and when I speak disrespectfully of the weather or the crops they think I am a blasphemer.'

'You don't wish me to stay any longer?' he inquired, when he found that she remained musing.

'No – I think not.'

'Then tell me that I am to be gone.'

'Why? cannot you go without?'

'I may consult my own feelings only, if left to myself.'

'Well, if you do, what then? Do you suppose you'll be in my way?'

'I feared it might be so.'

'Then fear no more. But good-night. Come to-morrow and see if I am going on right. This renewal of acquaintance touches me. I have already a friendship for you.'

'If it depends upon myself it shall last for ever.'

'My best hopes that it may!'

Fitzpiers went down the stairs absolutely unable to decide whether she had sent for him in the natural alarm which might have followed her mishap, or with the single view of making herself known to him as she had done, for which the capsize had afforded excellent opportunity.

Outside the house he mused over the spot under the light of the stars. It seemed very strange that he should have come there more than once when its inhabitant was absent, and observed the house with a nameless interest; that he should have assumed off-hand before he knew Grace that it was here she lived; that, in short, at sundry times and seasons the individuality of Hintock House should have forced itself upon him as appertaining to some existence with which he was concerned.

The intersection of his temporal orbit with Mrs Charmond's for a day or two in the past had created a sentimental interest in her at the time, but it had been so evanescent that in the ordinary onward roll of affairs he would scarce ever have recalled it again. To find her here, however, in these somewhat romantic circumstances, magnified that bygone and transitory tenderness to indescribable proportions.

On entering Little Hintock he found himself regarding that hamlet in a new way – from the Hintock House point of view rather than from his own and the Melburys'. The household had all gone to bed. As he went upstairs he heard the snore of the timber-merchant from his quarter of the building, and turned into the passage communicating with his own rooms in a strange access of sadness.

A light was burning for him in the chamber; but Grace, though in bed, was not asleep. In a moment her sympathetic voice came from behind the curtains.

'Edred, is she very seriously hurt?'

Fitzpiers had so entirely lost sight of Mrs Charmond as a patient that he was not on the instant ready with a reply.

'O no,' he said. 'There are no bones broken, but she is shaken. I am going again to-morrow.'

Another inquiry or two, and Grace said –

'Did she ask for me?'

'Well, I think she did – I don't quite remember; but I am under the impression that she spoke of you.'

'Cannot you recollect at all what she said?'

'I cannot, just this minute.'

'At any rate, she did not talk much about me?' said Grace with disappointment.

'O no.'

'But you did, perhaps,' she added, innocently fishing for a compliment.

'O yes – you may depend upon that!' replied he warmly, though scarcely thinking of what he was saying, so vividly was there present to his mind the personality of Mrs Charmond.

CHAPTER TWENTY-SEVEN

THE doctor's professional visit to Hintock House was promptly repeated the next day and the next. He always found Mrs Charmond reclining on a sofa, and behaving generally as became a patient who was in no great hurry to lose that title. On each occasion he looked gravely at the little scratch on her arm, as if it had been a serious wound.

He had also, to his further satisfaction, found a slight scar on her temple, and it was very convenient to put a piece of black plaster on this conspicuous part of her person in preference to gold-beater's skin, so that it might catch the eyes of the servants and make his presence appear decidedly necessary, in case there should be any doubt of the fact.

'O – you hurt me!' she exclaimed one day.

He was peeling off the bit of plaster on her arm, under which the scrape had turned the colour of an unripe blackberry previous to vanishing altogether.

'Wait a moment then – I'll damp it,' said Fitzpiers. He put his lips to the place and kept them there, without any objecting on her part, till the plaster came off easily. 'It was at your request I put it on,' said he.

'I know it,' she replied. 'Is that blue vein still in my temple that used to show there? The scar must be just upon it. If the cut had been a little deeper it would have spilt my hot blood indeed!'

Fitzpiers examined so closely that his breath touched her tenderly, at which their eyes rose to an encounter – hers showing themselves as deep and mysterious as interstellar space. She turned her face away.

'Ah! none of that! none of that – I cannot coquet with you!' she cried. 'Don't suppose I consent to for one moment. Our poor, brief, youthful hour of love-making was too long ago to bear continuing now. It is as well that we should understand each other on that point before we go further.'

'Coquet! Nor I with you. As it was when I found the historic handkerchief, so it is now. I might have been and may be foolish; but I am no trifler. I naturally cannot forget that little space in which I flitted across the field of your vision in those days of the past, and the recollection opens up all sorts of imaginings.'

'Suppose my mother had not taken me away?' she murmured, her dreamy eyes resting on the swaying tip of a distant tree.

'I should have seen you again.'

'And then?'

'Then the fire would have burnt higher and higher. What would have immediately followed I know not, but sorrow and sickness of heart at last.'

'Why?'

'Well – that's the end of all love, according to Nature's law. I can give no other reason.'

'O, don't speak like that!' she exclaimed. 'Since we are only picturing the possibilities of that time, don't for pity's sake spoil the picture.' Her voice sank almost to a whisper as she added with an incipient pout upon her lips, 'Let me think at least that if you had really loved me at all seriously you would have loved me for ever and ever!'

'You are right – think it with all your heart,' said he. 'It is a pleasant thought, and costs nothing.'

She weighed that remark in silence a while. 'Did you ever hear anything of me from then till now?' she inquired.

'Not a word.'

'So much the better. I had to fight the battle of life as well as you. I may tell you about it some day. But don't ever ask me to do it, and particularly do not press me to tell you now.'

Thus the two or three days that they had spent in tender acquaintance on the romantic slopes above the Neckar were stretched out in retrospect to the length and importance of years; made to form a canvas for infinite fancies, idle dreams, luxurious melancholies, and pretty, alluring assertions which could neither be proved nor disproved.

Grace was never mentioned between them, but a rumour of his contemplated removal from the neighbourhood somehow reached Mrs Charmond's ears.

'Doctor, you are going away!' she exclaimed, confronting him with accusatory reproach in her large dark eyes no less than in her cooing voice. 'O yes, you are,' she went on, springing to her feet with an air which might almost have been called passionate. 'It is no use denying it! You have bought a practice at Budmouth. I don't blame you. Nobody can live at Hintock – least of all a professional man who wants to keep abreast of recent discovery. And there is nobody here to induce such a one to stay for other reasons. That's right, that's right – go away!'

'But no – I have not actually bought the practice as yet, though I am indeed in treaty for it. And, my dear friend, if I continue to feel about the business as I feel at this moment – perhaps I may conclude never to go at all.'

'But you hate Hintock, and everything and everybody in it that you don't mean to take away with you!'

Fitzpiers contradicted this idea in his most vibratory tones, and she lapsed into the frivolous archness under which she hid passions of no mean strength – strange, smouldering, erratic passions, kept down like a stifled conflagration, but bursting out now here, now there – the only certain element in their direction being its unexpectedness.

If one word could have expressed Felice Charmond it would have been Inconsequence. She was a woman of perversities, delighting in piquant contrasts. She liked mystery, in her life, in her love, in her history. To be fair to her, there was nothing in these which she had any great reason to be ashamed of, and many things of which she might have been proud; but her past had never been fathomed by the honest minds of Hintock, and she rarely volunteered her experiences. As for her capricious nature the people on her estates grew accustomed to it, and with that marvellous subtlety of contrivance in steering round odd tempers that is found in sons of the soil and dependents generally, they managed to get along under her government rather better than they would have done beneath a more equable rule.

Now, with regard to the doctor's notion of leaving Hintock, he had advanced further towards completing the purchase of the Budmouth surgeon's goodwill than he had admitted to Mrs Charmond. The whole matter hung upon what he might do in the ensuing twenty-four hours. The evening after leaving her he went out into the lane, and walked and pondered between the high hedges, now greenish-white with wild clematis – here called 'old-man's-beard' from its aspect later in the year.

The letter of acceptance was to be written that night, after which his departure from Hintock would be irrevocable. But could he go away, remembering what had just passed? The trees, the hills, the leaves, the grass – each had been endowed and quickened with a subtle light since he had discovered the person and history, and, above all, the mood of their owner. There was every temporal reason for leaving: it would be entering again into a world which he had only quitted in a passion for isolation, induced by a fit of Achillean moodiness after an imagined slight. His wife herself saw the awkwardness of their position here, and cheerfully welcomed the purposed change, towards which every step had been taken but the last. But could he find it in his heart – as he found it clearly enough in his conscience – to go away? No.

He drew a troubled breath and went indoors. Here he rapidly penned a letter, wherein he withdrew, once for all, from the treaty for the Budmouth practice. As the postman had already left Little Hintock for that night he sent one of Melbury's men to intercept a mail-cart on another turnpike-road, and so got the letter off.

The man returned, met Fitzpiers in the lane, and told him the thing was done. Fitzpiers went back to his house musing. Why had he carried out this impulse – taken such wild trouble to effect a probable injury to his own and his young wife's prospects? His motive was fantastic, glowing, shapeless as the fiery scenery about the western sky. Mrs Charmond could overtly be nothing more to him than a patient, and to his wife, at the outside, a patron. Yet in the unattached bachelor days of his first sojourn here how highly proper an emotional reason for lingering on would have appeared to troublesome dubiousness. Matrimonial ambition is such an honourable thing!

'My father has told me that you have sent off one of the men with a late letter to Budmouth,' cried Grace, coming out vivaciously to meet him under the declining light of the sky, wherein hung, solitary, the folding star. 'I said at once that you had finally agreed to pay the premium they ask, and that the tedious question had been settled. When do we go, Edred?'

'I have changed my mind,' said he. 'They want too much – seven hundred and fifty is too large a sum, – and in short I had declined to go further. We must wait for another opportunity. I fear I am not a good business man.'

He spoke the last words with a momentary faltering at the great foolishness of his act; and as he looked in her fair and honourable face his heart reproached him for what he had done.

Her manner that evening showed her disappointment. Personally she liked the home of her childhood much, and she was not ambitious. But her husband had seemed so dissatisfied with the circumstances hereabout since their marriage that she had sincerely hoped to go for his sake.

It was two or three days before he visited Mrs Charmond again. The morning had been windy, and little showers had scattered themselves like grain against the walls and window-panes of the Hintock cottages. He went on foot across the wilder recesses of the park, where slimy streams of fresh moisture, exuding from decayed holes caused by old amputations, ran down the bark of the oaks and elms, the rind below being coated with a lichenous wash as green as emerald. They were stout-trunked trees, that never rocked their stems in the fiercest gale, responding to it only by crooking their limbs. Wrinkled like an old crone's face, and antlered with dead branches that rose above the foliage of their summits, they were nevertheless still green – though yellow had invaded the leaves of other trees.

She was in a little boudoir or writing-room on the first floor, and Fitzpiers was much surprised to find that the window curtains were closed and a red-shaded lamp and candles burning, though out of doors it was broad daylight. Moreover a large fire was burning in the grate, though it was not cold.

'What does it all mean?' he asked.

She sat in an easy-chair, her face being turned away.

'O,' she murmured, 'it is because the world is so dreary outside! Sorrow and bitterness in the sky, and floods of agonized tears beating against the panes. I lay awake last night, and I could hear the scrape of snails creeping up the window glass; it was so sad! My eyes were so heavy this morning that I could have wept my life away. I cannot bear you to see my face; I keep it away from you purposely. O! why were we given hungry hearts and wild desires if we have to live in a world like this? Why should Death alone lend what Life is compelled to borrow – rest? Answer that, Dr Fitzpiers.'

'You must eat of a second tree of knowledge before *you* can do it, Felice Charmond.'

'Then, when my emotions have exhausted themselves, I become full of fears, till I think I shall die for very fear. The terrible insistencies of society – how severe they are, and cold, and inexorable – ghastly towards those who are made of wax and not of stone. O, I am afraid of them; a stab for this error, and a stab for that – correctives and regulations pretendedly framed that society may tend to perfection – an end which I don't care for in the least. Yet for this all I do care for has to be stunted and starved.'

Fitzpiers had seated himself near her. 'What sets you in this mournful mood?' he asked gently. In reality he thought that it was the result of a loss of tone from staying indoors so much, but he did not say so.

'My reflections. Doctor, you must not come here any more. They begin to think it a farce already. I say you must come no more. There – don't be angry with me!' – and she jumped up, pressed his hand, and looked anxiously at him. 'It is necessary. It is best for both you and me.'

'But,' said Fitzpiers gloomily, 'what have we done?'

'Done – we have done nothing. Perhaps we have thought the more. However, it is all vexation. I am going away to Middleton Abbey, near Shottsford, where a relative of my late husband lives, who is confined to her bed. The engagement was made in London, and I can't get out of it. Perhaps it is for the best that I go there till all this is past. When are you going to enter on your new practice, and leave Hintock behind for ever, with your pretty wife on your arm?'

'I have refused the opportunity. I love this place too well to depart.'

'You *have*?' she said, regarding him with wild uncertainty. 'Why do you ruin yourself in that way? Great heaven, what have I done!'

'Nothing. Besides, you are going away.'

'O yes; but only to Middleton Abbey for a month or two. Yet perhaps I shall gain strength there – particularly strength of mind – I require it. And when I come back I shall be a new woman; and you can come and see me safely then, and bring your wife with you, and we'll be friends – she and I. O, how this shutting up of one's self does lead to indulgence in idle sentiments! I shall not wish to give your attendance to me after to-day. But I am glad that you are not going away – if your remaining does not injure your prospects at all.'

As soon as he had left the room the mild friendliness she had preserved in her tone at parting, the playful sadness with which she had conversed with him, equally departed from her. She became as heavy as lead – just as she had been before he arrived. Her whole being seemed to dissolve in a sad powerlessness to do anything, and sense of it made her lips tremulous and her closed eyes wet.

His footsteps again startled her, and she turned round.

'I return for a moment to tell you that the evening is going to be fine. The sun is shining, so do open your curtains and put out those lights. Shall I do it for you?'

'Please – if you don't mind.'

He drew back the window curtains, whereupon the red glow of the lamp and the two candle-flames became almost invisible under the flood of late autumn sunlight that poured in.

'Shall I come round to you?' he asked, her back being towards him.

'No,' she replied.

'Why not?'

'Because I am crying, and I don't want you to see my face in the full sun's rays.'

He stood a moment irresolute, and regretted that he had killed the rosy passionate lamplight by opening the curtains and letting in garish day.

'Then I am going,' he said.

'Very well,' she answered, stretching one hand round to him, and patting her eyes with a handkerchief held in the other.

'Shall I write a line to you at—?'

'No, no.' A gentle reasonableness came into her tone as she added, 'It must not be, you know. It won't do.'

'Very well. Good-bye.' The next moment he was gone.

In the evening with listless adroitness she encouraged the maid who dressed her for dinner to speak of Dr Fitzpiers's marriage.

'Mrs Fitzpiers was once supposed to favour Mr Winterborne,' said the young woman.

'But why didn't she marry him?' said Mrs Charmond.

'Because you see, ma'am, he lost his houses.'

'Lost his houses? How came he to do that?'

'The houses were held on lives, and the lives dropped, and your agent wouldn't renew them, though it is said that Mr Winterborne had a very good claim. That's as I've heard it, ma'am, and it was through it that the match was broke off.'

Being just then distracted by a dozen emotions, Mrs Charmond sank into a mood of dismal self-reproach. 'In refusing that poor man his reasonable request,' she said to herself, 'my agent foredoomed my revived girlhood's romance. Who would have thought such a business matter could have nettled my own heart like this! Now for a winter of regrets and agonies and useless wishes, till I forget him in the spring. O! I am glad I am going away!'

She left her chamber, and went down to dine with a sigh. On the stairs she stood opposite the large window for a moment, and looked out upon the lawn. It was not yet quite dark. Half-way up the steep green slope confronting her stood old Timothy Tangs, who was shortening his way homeward by clambering here where there was no road, and in opposition to express orders that no path was to be made there. Tangs had momentarily stopped to take a pinch of snuff, but observing Mrs Charmond gazing at him he hastened to get over the top out of hail. His precipitancy made him miss his footing, and he rolled like a barrel to the bottom, his snuff-box rolling in front of him.

Her indefinite idle impossible passion for Fitzpiers, her constitutional cloud of misery, the sorrowful drops that still hung upon her eyelashes, all made way for the impulse started by the spectacle. She burst into an immoderate fit of laughter; her very gloom of the previous hour seeming to render it the more uncontrollable. It had not died out of her when she reached the dining-room; and even here, before the servants, her shoulders suddenly shook as the scene returned upon her; and the tears of her risibility mingled with the remnants of those engendered by her grief.

She resolved to be sad no more. She drank two glasses of champagne, and a little more still after those; and amused herself in the evening with singing pretty amatory songs.

'I must do something for that poor man Winterborne, however,' she said.

CHAPTER TWENTY-EIGHT

A WEEK had passed, and Mrs Charmond had left Hintock House. Middleton Abbey, the place of her sojourn, was about a dozen miles distant by road, a little less by bridle-paths and footways.

Grace observed, for the first time, that her husband was restless, that at moments he even was disposed to avoid her. The scrupulous civility of mere acquaintanceship crept into his manner; yet when sitting at meals he seemed hardly to hear her remarks. Her little doings interested him no longer, whilst towards her father his bearing was not far from supercilious. It was plain that his mind was entirely outside her life, whereabouts outside it she could not tell; in some region of science possible, or of psychological literature. But her hope that he was again immersing himself in those lucubrations which before her marriage had made his light a landmark in Hintock, was founded simply on the slender fact that he often sat up late.

One day she discovered him leaning over a gate on High-Stoy Hill, some way from Little Hintock, which opened on the brink of a declivity, slanting down directly into White-Hart or Blackmoor Vale, extending beneath the eye at this point to a distance of many miles. His attention was fixed on the landscape far away eastward, and Grace's approach was so noiseless that he did not hear her. When she came close she could see his lips moving unconsciously, as on some impassioned visionary theme.

She spoke, and Fitzpiers started. 'What are you looking at?' she asked.

'O! I was contemplating my mother's people's old place of Sherton Abbas, in my idle way,' he said.

It had seemed to her that he was looking much to the right of that cradle and tomb of his ancestral dignity; but she made no further observation, and taking his arm walked home beside him almost in silence. She did not know that Middleton Abbey lay in the direction of his gaze.

'Are you going to have out Darling this afternoon?' she asked presently.

Darling, the aged light-grey mare which Winterborne had bought for Grace, Fitzpiers now constantly used, the animal having turned out a wonderful bargain in combining a perfect docility with an almost human intelligence; moreover, she was not too young. Fitzpiers was unfamiliar with horses, and he valued these qualities.

'Yes,' he replied, 'but not to drive. I am riding here. I practise crossing a horse as often as I can now, for I find that I can take much shorter cuts on horseback.'

He had, in fact, taken these riding exercises for about a week, only since Mrs Charmond's absence; his universal practice hitherto having been to drive.

Some few days later Fitzpiers started on the back of this horse to see a patient in the aforesaid Vale. It was about five o'clock in the evening when he went away, and at bedtime he had not reached home. There was nothing very singular in this, though she was not aware that he had any patient more than five or six miles distant in that direction. The clock had struck one before Fitzpiers entered the house, and he came to his room softly, as if anxious not to disturb her.

The next morning she was stirring considerably earlier than he. In the yard there was a conversation going on about the mare; the man who attended to the horses, Darling included, insisted that the latter was 'hag-rid'; for when he had arrived at the stable that morning she was in such a state as no horse could be in by honest riding. It was true that the doctor had stabled her himself when he got home, so that she was not looked after as she would have been if the speaker had groomed and fed her; but that did not account for the appearance she presented, if Mr Fitzpiers's journey had been only where he had stated. The unprecedented exhaustion of Darling, as thus related, was sufficient to develop a whole series of tales about equestrian witches and demons, the narration of which occupied a considerable time.

Grace returned indoors. In passing through the outer room she picked up her husband's overcoat which he had carelessly flung down across a chair. A turnpike ticket fell out of the breast-pocket, and she saw that it had been issued at Middleton Gate. He had therefore visited Middleton the previous night, a distance of at least four-and-twenty miles on horseback, there and back.

During the day she made some inquiries, and learnt for the first time that Mrs Charmond was staying at Middleton Abbey. She could not resist an inference – strange as that inference was.

A few days later he prepared to start again, at the same time and in the same direction. She knew that the state of the cottager who lived that way was a mere pretext; she was quite sure he was going to Mrs Charmond.

Grace was amazed at the mildness of the anger which the suspicion engendered in her. She was but little excited, and her jealousy was languid even to death. It told tales of the nature of her affection for him. In truth, her ante-nuptial regard for Fitzpiers had been rather of the quality of awe towards a superior being than of tender solicitude for a lover. It had been based upon mystery and strangeness – the mystery of his past, of his knowledge, of his professional skill, of his beliefs. When this structure of ideals was demolished by the intimacy of common life, and she found him as merely human as the Hintock people themselves, a new foundation was in demand for an enduring and staunch affection – a sympathetic interdependence, wherein mutual weaknesses are made the grounds of a defensive alliance. Fitzpiers had furnished nothing of that single-minded confidence and truth out of which alone such a second union could spring; hence it was with a controllable emotion that she now watched the mare brought round.

'I'll walk with you to the hill if you are not in a great hurry,' she said, rather loth, after all, to let him go.

'Do; there's plenty of time,' replied her husband.

Accordingly he led along the horse, and walked beside her, impatient enough nevertheless. Thus they proceeded to the turnpike road, and ascended towards the base of High-Stoy and Dogbury Hill, till they were just beneath the gate he had been leaning over when she surprised him ten days before. This was the end of her excursion. Fitzpiers bade her adieu with affection, even with tenderness, and she observed that he looked weary-eyed.

'Why do you go to-night?' she said. 'You have been called up two nights in succession already.'

'I must go,' he answered, almost gloomily. 'Don't wait up for me.' With these words he mounted his horse, turned into a branch road by the turnpike, and ambled down the incline to the valley.

She ascended the slope of High-Stoy and watched his descent, and then his journey onward. His way was east, the evening sun which stood behind her back beaming full upon him as soon as he got out from the shade of the hill. Notwithstanding this untoward proceeding she was determined to be loyal if he proved true; and the determination to love one's best will carry a heart a long way towards making that best an ever-growing thing.

The conspicuous coat of the active though blanching mare made horse and rider easy objects for the vision. Though Darling had been chosen with such pains by Winterborne for Grace, she had never ridden the sleek creature; but her husband had found the animal exceedingly convenient, particularly now that he had taken to the saddle, plenty of staying power being left in Darling yet for journeys of moderate length. Fitzpiers, like others of his character, while despising Melbury and his station, did not at all disdain to spend Melbury's money, or appropriate to his own use the horse which belonged to Melbury's daughter.

And so the infatuated surgeon went along through the gorgeous autumn landscape of White-Hart Vale, surrounded by orchards lustrous with the reds of apple-crops, berries, and foliage, the whole intensified by the gilding of the declining sun. The earth this year had been prodigally bountiful, and now was the supreme moment of her bounty. In the poorest spots the hedges were bowed with haws and blackberries; acorns cracked underfoot, and the burst husks of chestnuts lay exposing their auburn contents as if arranged by anxious sellers in a fruit-market. In all this proud show some kernels were unsound as her own situation, and she wondered if there were one world in the universe where the fruit had no worm, and marriage no sorrow.

Her Tannhäuser still moved on, his plodding steed rendering him distinctly visible yet. Could she have heard Fitzpiers's voice at that moment she would have found it murmuring –

> '–Towards the loadstar of my one desire
> I flitted, like a dizzy moth, whose flight
> Is as a dead leaf's in the owlet light.'

But he was a silent spectacle to her. Soon he rose out of the valley, and skirted a high plateau of the chalk formation on his right, which rested abruptly upon the fruity district of deep loam, the character and herbage of the two formations being so distinct that the calcareous upland appeared but as a deposit of a few years' antiquity upon the level vale.

He kept along the edge of this high, uninclosed country, and the sky behind him being deep violet she could still see white Darling in relief upon it – a mere speck now – a Wouvermans eccentricity reduced to microscopic dimensions. Upon this high ground he gradually disappeared.

Thus she had beheld the pet animal purchased for her own use, in pure love of her, by one who had always been true, impressed to convey her husband away from her to the side of a new-found idol. While she was musing on the vicissitudes of horses and wives she discerned shapes moving up the valley towards her, quite near at hand, though till now hidden by the hedges. Surely they were Giles Winterborne, with two horses and a cider-apparatus, conducted by Robert Creedle. Up, upward they crept, a stray beam of the sun alighting every now and then like a star on the blades of the pomace-shovels, which had been converted to steel mirrors by the action of the malic acid. She descended to the road when he came close, and the panting horses rested as they achieved the ascent.

'How do you do, Giles?' said she, under a sudden impulse to be familiar with him.

He replied with much more reserve. 'You are going for a walk, Mrs Fitzpiers?' he added. 'It is pleasant just now.'

'No, I am returning,' said she.

The vehicles passed on, and Creedle with them, and Winterborne walked by her side in the rear of the apple-mill.

He looked and smelt like Autumn's very brother, his face being sunburnt to wheat-colour, his eyes blue as corn-flowers, his sleeves and leggings dyed with fruit-stains, his hands clammy with the sweet juice of apples, his hat sprinkled with pips, and everywhere about him that atmosphere of cider which at its first return each season has such an indescribable fascination for those who have been born and bred among the orchards. Her heart rose from its late sadness like a released bough; her senses revelled in the sudden lapse back to Nature unadorned. The consciousness of having to be genteel because of her husband's profession, the veneer of artificiality which she had acquired at the fashionable schools, were thrown off, and she became the crude country girl of her latent early instincts.

Nature was bountiful, she thought. No sooner had she been cast aside by Edred Fitzpiers than another being, impersonating chivalrous and undiluted manliness, had arisen out of the earth ready to her hand. This, however, was an excursion of the imagination which she did not wish to encourage, and she said suddenly, to disguise the confused regard which had followed her thoughts, 'Did you meet my husband?'

Winterborne, with some hesitation: 'Yes.'

'Where did you meet him?'

'Near Reveller's Inn. I come from Middleton Abbey; I have been making there for the last week.'

'Haven't they a mill of their own?'

'Yes, but it's out of repair.'

'I think – I heard that Mrs Charmond had gone there to stay?'

'Yes, I have seen her at the windows once or twice.'

Grace waited an interval before she went on; 'Did Mr Fitzpiers take the way to Middleton?'

'Yes. . . . I met him on Darling.' As she did not reply, he added with a gentler inflection, 'You know why the mare was called that?'

'O yes – of course,' she answered quickly.

With their minds on these things they passed so far round the hill that the whole west sky was revealed. Between the broken clouds they could see far into the recesses of heaven as they mused and walked, the eye journeying on under a species of golden arcades, and past fiery obstructions, fancied cairns, logan-stones, stalactites and stalagmite of topaz. Deeper than this their gaze passed thin flakes of incandescence, till it plunged into a bottomless medium of soft green fire.

Her abandonment to the seductive hour and scene after her sense of ill-usage, her revolt for the nonce against social law, her passionate desire for primitive life may have showed in her face. Winterborne was looking at her, his eyes lingering on a flower that she wore in her bosom. Almost with the abstraction of a somnambulist he stretched out his hand and gently caressed the flower.

She drew back. 'What are you doing, Giles Winterborne?' she exclaimed, with severe surprise.

The evident absence of all premeditation from the act, however, speedily led her to think that it was not necessary to stand upon her dignity here and now. 'You must bear in mind, Giles,' she said kindly, 'that we are not as we were; and some people might have said that what you did was taking a liberty.'

It was more than she need have told him; his action of forgetfulness had made him so angry with himself that he flushed through his tan.

'I don't know what I am coming to!' he exclaimed savagely. 'Ah – I was not once like this!' Tears of vexation were in his eyes.

'No, now – it was nothing! I was too reproachful.'

'It would not have occurred to me if I had not seen something like it done elsewhere – at Middleton lately,' he said thoughtfully after a while.

'By whom?'

'Don't ask it.'

She scanned him narrowly. 'I know quite well enough,' she returned indifferently. 'It was by my husband, and the woman was Mrs Charmond. Association of ideas reminded you when you saw me. . . . Giles – tell me all you know about that – please do, Giles! But no – I won't hear it. Let the subject cease. And as you are my friend say nothing to my father.'

They had descended into the vale again to a place where their ways divided. Winterborne continued along the highway which kept outside the copse, and Grace opened a gate that entered it.

CHAPTER TWENTY-NINE

SHE walked up the soft grassy ride, screened on either hand by nut-bushes just now heavy with clusters of twos and threes and fours. A little way on the track she pursued was crossed by a similar one at right angles. Here Grace stopped; some few yards up the transverse ride the buxom Suke Damson was visible – her gown tucked up high through her pocket-hole, and no bonnet on her head – in the act of pulling down boughs from which she was gathering and eating nuts with great rapidity, her lover Tim Tangs standing near her engaged in the same pleasant meal.

Crack, crack, went Suke's jaws every second or two. By an automatic leap of thought Grace's mind reverted to the tooth-drawing scene described by her husband; and for the first time she wondered if that narrative were really true,

Susan's jaws being so obviously sound and strong. Grace turned up towards the nut-gatherers, and conquered her reluctance to speak to the girl, who was a little in advance of Tim. 'Good evening, Susan,' she said.

'Good evening, Miss Melbury' – (crack).

'Mrs Fitzpiers.'

'O yes, ma'am – Mrs Fitzpiers,' said Suke with a peculiar sniff and curtsey.

Grace, not to be daunted, continued, 'Take care of your teeth, Suke. That accounts for your toothache.'

'O, I don't know what an ache is, either in tooth, ear, or head, thank the Lord' – (crack).

'Nor the loss of one, either?'

'See for yourself, ma'am.' She parted her red lips and exhibited the whole double row, full up and unimpaired.

'You have never had one drawn?'

'Never.'

'So much the better for your stomach,' said Mrs Fitzpiers in an altered voice. And turning away quickly she went on thinking what gall she could drop into poor Tim Tangs's honey if she chose.

As her husband's character thus shaped itself under the touch of time, Grace was almost startled to find how little she suffered from that jealous excitement which is conventionally attributed to all wives in such circumstances. But though possessed by none of the feline wildness which it was her moral duty to experience, she did not fail to suspect that she had made a frightful mistake in her marriage. Acquiescence in her father's wishes had been degradation to herself. People are not given premonitions for nothing; she should have obeyed her impulse on that early morning when she peeped and saw the figure come from Fitzpiers's door, and have steadfastly refused her hand.

O that plausible tale which her then betrothed had told her about Suke – the dramatic account of her entreaties to him to draw the aching enemy, and the fine artistic finish he had given to the story by explaining that it was a lovely molar without a flaw!

She traced the remainder of the woodland track, dazed by the complications of her position. If his protestations to her before their marriage could be believed, her husband had felt affection of some sort for herself and this woman simultaneously; and was now again spreading the same conjoint emotion over Mrs Charmond and herself, his manner being still kind and fond at times. But surely, rather than that, he must have played the hypocrite towards her in each case with elaborate completeness; and the thought of this sickened her, for it involved the conjecture that if he had not loved her his only motive for making her his wife must have been her little fortune.

Yet here Grace made a mistake, for the love of men like Fitzpiers is unquestionably of such quality as to bear division and transference. He had indeed once declared, though not to her, that on one occasion he had noticed himself to be possessed by five distinct infatuations at the same time. If this were true, his differed from the highest affection as the lower orders of the animal world differ from advanced organisms, partition causing not death but a multiplied existence. He had loved her sincerely in his selfish way, and had by no means ceased to love her now. But such double and treble-barrelled hearts were naturally beyond her conception.

Of poor Suke Damson Grace thought no more. She had had her day.

'If he does not love me I will not love him!' said Grace proudly.

And though these were mere words it was a somewhat formidable thing for Fitzpiers that her heart was approximating to a state in which it might be possible to carry them out. That very absence of hot jealousy in her which made his courses so easy, and on which, indeed, he congratulated himself, meant, unknown to either wife or husband, more mischief than the inconvenient watchfulness of a jaundiced eye.

Her sleep that night was nervous. The wing allotted to her and her husband had never seemed so lonely. At last she got up, put on her dressing-gown, and went downstairs. Her father, who slept lightly, heard her descend, and came to the stair-head.

'Is that you, Grace? What's the matter?' he said.

'Nothing more than that I am restless. Edred is detained by a case in White-Hart Vale.'

'But how's that? I met the woman's husband going to Great Hintock just afore bedtime; and she was going on well, and the doctor gone then.'

'Then he's detained somewhere else,' said Grace. 'Never mind me; he will soon be home. I expect him about one.'

She went back to her room, and dozed and woke several times. One o'clock had been the hour of his return on the last occasion; but it had passed now by a long way, and still Fitzpiers did not come. Just before dawn she heard the men stirring in the yard, and the flashes of their lanterns spread every now and then through her window-blind. She remembered that her father had told her not to be disturbed if she noticed them, as they would be rising early to send off four loads of hurdles to a distant sheep-fair. Peeping out she saw them bustling about, the hollow-turner among the rest; he was loading his wares – wooden bowls, dishes, spigots, spoons, cheese-vats, funnels and so on – upon one of her father's waggons, who carried them to the fair for him every year out of neighbourly kindness.

The scene and the occasion would have enlivened her but that her husband was still absent, though it was now five o'clock. She could hardly suppose him, whatever his infatuation, to have prolonged to a later hour than ten an ostensibly professional call on Mrs Charmond at Middleton; and he could have ridden home in two hours. What then had become of him? That he had been out the greater part of the two preceding nights added to her uneasiness.

She dressed herself, descended, and went out, the weird twilight of advancing day chilling the rays from the lanterns, and making the men's faces wan. As soon as Melbury saw her he came round, showing his alarm.

'Edred is not come,' she said. 'And I have reason to know that he's not attending anybody. He has had no rest for two nights before this. I was going to the top of the hill to look for him.'

'I'll come with you,' said Melbury.

She begged him not to hinder himself; but he insisted, for he saw a peculiar and rigid gloom in her face over and above her uneasiness, and did not like the look of it. Telling the men he would be with them again soon he walked beside her into the turnpike road, and partly up the way whence she had watched Fitzpiers the night before as he skirted the Great Blackmoor or White-Hart Valley.

They halted beneath a half-dead oak, hollow and disfigured with white tumours, its roots spreading out like claws grasping the ground. A chilly wind circled round them, upon whose currents the seeds of a neighbouring lime-tree, supported parachute-wise by the wing attached, flew out of the boughs downward like fledglings from their nest. The vale was wrapped in a dim atmosphere of unnaturalness, and the east was like a livid curtain edged with pink. There was no sign nor sound of Fitzpiers.

'It is no use standing here,' said her father. 'He may come home fifty ways. . . . Why, look here – here be Darling's tracks – turned homeward and nearly blown dry and hard! He must have come in hours ago without your seeing him.'

'He has not done that,' said she.

They went back hastily. On entering their own gates they perceived that the men had left the waggons, and were standing round the door of the stable which had been appropriated to the doctor's use.

'Is there anything the matter?' cried Grace.

'O no, ma'am. All's well that ends well,' said old Timothy Tangs. 'I've heard of such things before – amongst workfolk, though not amongst your gentlepeople – that's true.'

They entered the stable, and saw the pale shape of Darling standing in the middle of her stall, with Fitzpiers on her back, sound asleep. Darling was munching hay as well as she could with the bit in her mouth, and the reins which had fallen from Fitzpiers's hand, hung upon her neck.

Grace went and touched his hand; shook it, before she could arouse him. He moved, started, opened his eyes, and exclaimed, 'Ah, Felice. . . . O, it's Grace. I could not see in the gloom. What – am I in the saddle!'

'Yes,' said she. 'How do you come here?'

He collected his thoughts, and in a few minutes stammered as he began dismounting: 'I was riding along homeward through the Vale, very, very sleepy, having been up so much of late. When I came opposite Lydden Spring the mare turned her head that way as if she wanted to drink. I let her go in, and she drank; I thought she would never finish. While she was drinking the clock of Newland Buckton church struck twelve. I distinctly remember counting the strokes. From that moment I positively recollect nothing till I saw you here by my side.'

'The Name! If it had been any other horse you'd have had a broken neck!' mumured Melbury.

' 'Tis wonderful, sure, how a quiet hoss will bring a man home at such times!' said John Upjohn. 'And – what's more wonderful than keeping your seat in a deep slumbering sleep – I've knowed men drowze off walking home from randies where the beer and other liquors have gone round well, and keep walking for more than a mile on end without waking. Well, doctor, 'tis a mercy you wasn't a-drownded, or a-splintered, or a-hanged up to a tree like Absalont – also a handsome gentleman like yerself, as the prophets say!'

'True,' murmured old Timothy piously, 'from the sole of his boots to the crown of his hat there was no blemish in him!'

'Or leastwise you might ha' been a-wounded into tatters a'most, and no brother-tradesman to jine your few limbs together within seven mile!'

Whilst this impressive address was proceeding Fitzpiers had dismounted, and taking Grace's arm walked stiffly indoors with her. Melbury stood staring at the horse, which, in addition to being very weary, was spattered with mud. Whilst they were rubbing down the mare Melbury's mind coupled with the mud, which was not local, the name he had heard unconsciously muttered by the surgeon when Grace took his hand – 'Felice'. Who was Felice? Why, Mrs Charmond; and she, as he knew, was staying at Middleton.

Melbury had indeed pounced upon the image that filled Fitzpiers's half-awakened soul – wherein there had been a retrospect of a recent interview on a starlit lawn with a capriciously passionate woman, who had begged him not to come there again in tones whose modulation incited him to disobey, 'What are you doing here? Why do you pursue me? Another belongs to you. If they were to see you getting over the fence they would seize you as a thief!' And she had turbulently admitted to his wringing questions that her visit to Middleton had been undertaken less because of the invalid relative than in shamefaced fear of her own weakness if she remained near his home. A triumph then it was to Fitzpiers, poor and hampered as he had become, to recognise his real conquest of this beauty, delayed so many years. His was the passion of Congreve's Millamant, whose delight lay in seeing 'the heart which others bled for, bleed for me'.

When the horse had been attended to Melbury stood uneasily here and there about his premises; he was rudely disturbed in the comfortable views which had lately possessed him on his domestic concerns. It is true that he had for some days discerned that Grace more and more sought his company, preferred supervising his kitchen and bakehouse with her step-mother to occupying herself with the lighter details of her own apartments. She seemed no longer able to find in her own hearth an adequate focus for her life, and hence, like a weak queen-bee after leading off to an independent home, had hovered again into the parent hive. But he had not construed these and other incidents of the kind till now.

Something was wrong in the homestead. A ghastly sense beset him that he alone would be responsible for whatever unhappiness should be brought upon her for whom he almost solely lived; whom to retain under his roof he had faced the numerous inconveniences involved in giving up the best part of his house to Fitzpiers. There was no room for doubt that, had he allowed events to take their natural course she would have accepted Winterborne, and realised his old dream of restitution to that young man's family.

That Fitzpiers would allow himself to look for a moment on any other creature than Grace filled Melbury with grief and astonishment. In the simple life he had led it had scarcely occurred to him that after marriage a man might be faithless. That he could sweep to the heights of Mrs Charmond's position, lift the veil of Isis, so to speak, would have amazed Melbury by its audacity if he had not suspected encouragement from that quarter. What could he and his simple Grace do to countervail the passions of those two sophisticated beings – versed in the world's ways, armed with every apparatus for victory? In such an encounter the homely timber-dealer felt as inferior as a savage with his bow and arrows to the precise weapons of modern warfare.

Grace came out of the house as the morning drew on. The village was silent, most of the folk having gone to the fair. Fitzpiers had retired to bed, and was sleeping off his fatigue. She went to the stable and looked at poor Darling: in all probability Giles Winterborne, by obtaining for her a horse of such intelligence and docility, had been the means of saving her husband's life. She paused over the strange thought; and then there appeared her father behind her.

She saw that he knew things were not as they ought to be, from the troubled dulness of his eye, and from his face, different points of which had motions, twitchings, and tremblings, unknown to himself and involuntary.

'He was detained, I suppose, last night?' said Melbury.

'O yes; a bad case in the Vale,' she replied calmly.

'Nevertheless he should have stayed at home.'

'But he couldn't, father.'

Her father turned away. He could hardly bear to see his whilom truthful girl brought to the humiliation of having to talk like that.

That night carking care sat beside Melbury's pillow, and his stiff limbs tossed at its presence.

'I can't lie here any longer,' he muttered. Striking a light he wandered about the room. 'What have I done, what have I done for her!' he said to his wife. 'I had long planned that she should marry the son of the man I wanted to make amends to; do ye mind how I told you all about it, Lucy, the night before she came home? Ah! but I was not content with doing right, I wanted to do more!'

'Don't raft yourself without good need, George,' she replied. 'I won't quite believe that things are so much amiss. I won't believe that Mrs Charmond has encouraged him. Even supposing she has encouraged a great many, she can have no motive to do it now. What so likely as that she is not yet quite well, and doesn't care to let another doctor come near her?'

He did not heed. 'Grace used to be so busy every day with fixing a curtain here and driving a tin-tack there; but she cares for no employment now!'

'Do you know anything of Mrs Charmond's past history? Perhaps that would throw some light upon things. Before she came here as the wife of old Charmond four or five years ago, not a soul seems to have heard aught of her. Why not make inquiries? And then do ye wait and see more; there'll be plenty of opportunity. Time enough to cry when you know 'tis a crying matter; 'tis bad to meet troubles half way.'

There was some good sense in the notion of seeing further. Melbury resolved to inquire and wait, hoping still, but oppressed between whiles with much fear.

CHAPTER THIRTY

Examine Grace as her father might, she would admit nothing. For the present, therefore, he simply watched.

The suspicion that his darling child was slighted wrought almost a miraculous change in Melbury's nature. No man so furtive for the time as the ingenuous countryman who finds that his ingenuousness has been abused. Melbury's heretofore confidential candour towards his gentlemanly son-in-law was displaced by a feline stealth that did injury to his every action, thought, and mood.

He knew that a woman once given to a man for life took, as a rule, her lot as it came, and made the best of it, without external interference; but for the first time he asked himself why this so generally should be done. Besides, this case was not, he argued, like ordinary cases. Leaving out the question of Grace being anything but an ordinary woman, her peculiar situation, as it were in mid-air between two storeys of society, together with the loneliness of Hintock, made a husband's neglect a far more tragical matter to her than it would be to one who had a large circle of friends to fall back upon. Wisely or unwisely, and whatever other fathers did, he resolved to fight his daughter's battle still.

Mrs Charmond had returned. But Hintock House scarcely gave forth signs of life, so quietly had she re-entered it. Autumn drew shiveringly to its end. One day something seemed to be gone from the gardens; the tenderer leaves of vegetables had shrunk under the first smart frost, and hung like faded linen rags; the forest leaves, which had been descending at leisure, descended in haste and in multitudes, and all the golden colours that had hung overhead were now crowded together in a degraded mass underfoot, where the fallen myriads got redder and hornier, and curled themselves up to rot. The only suspicious features in Mrs Charmond's existence at this season were two; the first, that she lived with no companion or relative about her, which considering her age and attractions was somewhat unusual conduct for a young widow in a lonely country house; the other, that she did not, as in previous years, start from Hintock to winter abroad. In Fitzpiers, the only change from his last autumn's habits lay in his abandonment of night study; his lamp never shone from his new dwelling as from his old.

If the suspected ones met it was by such adroit contrivances that even Melbury's vigilance could not encounter them together. A simple call at her house by the doctor had nothing irregular about it, and that he had paid two or three such calls was certain. What had passed at those interviews was known only to the parties themselves; but that Felice Charmond was under some one's influence Melbury soon had opportunity of perceiving.

Winter had come on. Owls began to be noisy in the mornings and evenings, and flocks of wood-pigeons made themselves prominent again. On a day in February, about six months after the marriage of Fitzpiers, Melbury was returning from Great Hintock on foot down to Little Hintock, when he saw before him the surgeon also walking. Melbury would have overtaken him, but at that moment Fitzpiers turned in through a gate to one of the rambling drives among the trees at this side of the wood, which led to nowhere in particular, and the beauty of whose serpentine curves was the only justification of their existence. Felice almost simultaneously trotted into the road ahead of the timber-dealer, in a little basket-carriage which she sometimes drove about the estate, unaccompanied by a servant. She turned in at the same gate without having seen either Melbury or, apparently, Fitzpiers.

Melbury was soon at the spot, despite his aches and his sixty years. Mrs Charmond had come up with the doctor, inside the gate, who was standing immediately behind the carriage. She had turned to him, her arm being thrown carelessly over the back of the seat.

They looked in each other's faces without uttering a word, an arch yet gloomy smile wreathing her lips. Fitzpiers clasped her hanging hand, and, while she still remained in the same listless attitude, looking volumes into his eyes, he stealthily unbuttoned her glove, and stripped her hand of it by rolling back the gauntlet over the fingers, so that it came off inside out. He then raised her hand to his mouth, she still reclining passively, watching him as she might have watched a fly upon her dress. At last she said, 'Well, sir, what excuse for this disobedience?'

'I make none.'

'Then go your way, and let me go mine.' She snatched away her hand, touched the pony with the whip, and left him standing there, holding the reversed glove.

Melbury had not been seen, and his first impulse was to reveal his presence to Fitzpiers, and upbraid him bitterly. But a moment's thought was sufficient to show him the futility of any such simple proceeding. There was not, after all, so much in what he had witnessed as in what that scene might be the surface and froth of – probably a state of mind which censure aggravates rather than cures. Moreover, he said to himself that the point of attack should be the woman, if either. He therefore kept out of sight, and musing sadly, even tearfully – for he was meek as a child in matters concerning his daughter – continued his way towards Hintock.

The insight which is bred of deep sympathy was never more finely exemplified than in this instance. Through her guarded manner, her dignified speech, her placid countenance, he discerned the interior of Grace's life only too truly, hidden as were its incidents from every outer eye.

These incidents had become painful enough. Fitzpiers had latterly developed an irritable discontent which vented itself in monologues when Grace was present to hear them. The early morning of this day had been dull, after a night of wind, and on looking out of the window in the grey grim dawn Fitzpiers had observed some of Melbury's men dragging away a large limb which had been snapped off a beech-tree. Everything was cold and colourless.

'My good God!' he said, as he stood in his dressing-gown. 'This is life!'

He did not know whether Grace was awake or not, and he would not turn his head to ascertain. 'Ah, Edred,' he went on to himself, 'to clip your own wings when you were free to soar! . . . But I could not rest till I had done it. Why do I never recognize an opportunity till I have missed it, nor the good or ill of a step till it is irrevocable? . . . I fell in love!'

Grace moved. He thought she had heard some part of his soliloquy. He was sorry – though he had not taken any precaution to prevent her.

He expected a scene at breakfast, but she only exhibited an extreme reserve. It was enough, however, to make him repent that he should have done anything to produce discomfort; for he attributed her manner entirely to what he had said. But Grace's manner had not its cause either in his sayings or in his doings. She had not heard a single word of his regrets. Something even nearer home than her husband's blighted prospects – if blighted they were – was the origin of her mood.

She had made a discovery – one which to a girl of her nature was almost appalling. She had looked into her heart, and found that her early interest in

Giles Winterborne had become revitalized into growth by her widening
perceptions of what was great and little in life. His homeliness no longer offended
her acquired tastes; his comparative want of so-called culture did not now jar on
her intellect; his country dress even pleased her eye; his exterior roughness
fascinated her. Having discovered by marriage how much that was humanly not
great could co-exist with attainments of an exceptional order, there was a
revulsion in her sentiments from all that she had formerly clung to in this kind.
Honesty, goodness, manliness, tenderness, devotion, for her only existed in their
purity now in the breasts of unvarnished men; and here was one who had
manifested such towards her from his youth up.

There was, further, that never-ceasing pity in her soul for Giles as a man whom
she had wronged – a man who had been unfortunate in his worldly transactions;
who notwithstanding these things, had, like Hamlet's friend, borne himself
throughout his scathing

> 'As one, in suffering all, that suffers nothing,'

investing himself thereby with a real touch of sublimity. It was these perceptions,
and no subtle catching of her husband's murmurs, that had bred the abstraction
visible in her.

When her father approached the house after witnessing the interview between
Fitzpiers and Mrs Charmond, Grace was looking out of her sitting-room
window, as if she had nothing to do, or think of, or care for. He stood still.

'Ah, Grace,' he said, regarding her fixedly.

'Yes, father,' she murmured.

'Waiting for your dear husband?' he inquired, speaking with the sarcasm of
pitiful affection.

'O no – not especially. He has a great many patients to see this afternoon.'

Melbury came quite close. 'Grace, what's the use of talking like that when you
know—? Here, come down and walk with me out in the garden, child.'

He unfastened the door in the ivy-laced wall, and waited. This apparent
indifference alarmed him. He would far rather that she had rushed in all the fire
of jealousy to Hintock House regardless of conventionality, confronted and
attacked Felice Charmond *unguibus et rostro*, and accused her even in
exaggerated shape of stealing away her husband. Such a storm might have
cleared the air.

She emerged in a minute or two, and they went into the garden together. 'You
know as well as I do,' he resumed, 'that there is something threatening mischief to
your life, yet you pretend you do not. Do you suppose I don't see the trouble in
your face every day? I am very sure that this quietude is wrong conduct in you.
You should look more into matters.'

'I am quiet because my sadness is not of a nature to stir me to action.'

Melbury wanted to ask her a dozen questions – did she not feel jealous? was
she not indignant? – but a natural delicacy restrained him. 'You are very tame
and let-alone, I am bound to say,' he remarked pointedly.

'I am what I feel, father,' she repeated.

He glanced at her, and there returned upon his mind the scene of her offering to
wed Winterborne instead of Fitzpiers in the last days before her marriage; and he
asked himself if it could be the fact that she loved Winterborne now that she had

lost him more than she had ever done when she was comparatively free to choose him.

'What would you have me do?' she asked in a low voice.

He recalled his mind from the retrospective pain to the practical matter before them. 'I would have you go to Mrs Charmond,' he said.

'Go to Mrs Charmond – what for?' said she.

'Well – if I must speak plain, dear Grace – to ask her, appeal to her in the name of your common womanhood, and your many like sentiments on things, not to make unhappiness between you and your husband. It lies with her entirely to do one or the other – that I can see.'

Grace's face had heated at her father's words, and the very rustle of her skirts upon the box-edging bespoke disdain. 'I shall not *think* of going to her, father – of course, I could not!' she answered.

'Why – don't 'ee want to be happier than you be at present?' said Melbury, more moved on her account than she was herself.

'I don't wish to be more humiliated. If I have anything to bear I can bear it in silence.'

'But, my dear maid, you are too young – you don't know what the present state of things may lead to. Just see the harm done a'ready! Your husband would have gone away to Budmouth to a bigger practice if it had not been for this. Although it has gone such a little way it is poisoning your future even now. Mrs Charmond is thoughtlessly bad, not bad by calculation; and just a word to her now might save 'ee a peck of woes.'

'Ah, I loved her once,' said Grace with a broken articulation, 'and she would not care for me then! Now I no longer love her. Let her do her worst; I don't care.'

'You ought to care. You have got into a very good position to start with. You have been well educated, well tended, and you have become the wife of a professional man of unusually good family. Surely you ought to make the best of your position.'

'I don't see that I ought. I wish I had never got into it. I wish you had never, never thought of educating me. I wish I worked in the woods like Marty South! I hate genteel life, and I want to be no better than she!'

'Why?' said her amazed father.

'Because cultivation has only brought me inconveniences and troubles. I say again, I wish you had never sent me to those fashionable schools you set your mind on. It all arose out of that, father. If I had stayed at home I should have married—'

She closed up her mouth suddenly and was silent; and he saw that she was not far from crying.

Melbury was much grieved. 'What, and would you like to have grown up as we be here in Hintock – knowing no more, and with no more chance of seeing good life than we have here?'

'Yes. I have never got any happiness outside Hintock that I know of, and I have suffered many a heartache at being sent away. O, the misery of those January days when I got back to school, and left you all here in the wood so happy! I used to wonder why I had to bear it. And I was always a little despised by the other girls at school, because they knew where I came from, and that my parents were not in so good a station as theirs.'

Her poor father was much hurt at what he thought her ingratitude and intractability. He had admitted to himself bitterly enough that he should have let young hearts have their way, or rather should have helped on her affection for Winterborne, and given her to him according to his original plan; but he was not prepared for her deprecating those attainments whose completion had been a labour of years and a severe tax upon his purse.

'Very well,' he said with much heaviness of spirit. 'If you don't like to go to her I don't wish to force you.'

And so the question remained for him still: How should he remedy this perilous state of things? For days he sat in a moody attitude over the fire, a pitcher of cider standing on the hearth beside him, and his drinking-horn inverted upon the top of it. He spent a week and more thus, composing a letter to the chief offender, which he would every now and then attempt to complete and suddenly crumple up in his hand.

CHAPTER THIRTY-ONE

As February merged in March, and lighter evenings broke the gloom of the woodmen's homeward journey, the Hintocks Great and Little began to have ears for a rumour of the events out of which had grown the timber-dealer's troubles.

It took the form of a wide sprinkling of conjecture, wherein no man knew the exact truth. Tantalizing phenomena, at once showing and concealing the real relationship of the persons concerned, caused a diffusion of excited surprise. Honest people as the woodlanders were, it was hardly to be expected that they could remain immersed in the study of their trees and gardens amid such circumstances, or sit with their backs turned like the good burghers of Coventry at the passage of the lady.

Rumour, for a wonder, exaggerated little. There threatened, in fact, in Grace's case as in thousands, the domestic disaster, old as the hills, which, with more or less variation, made a mourner of Ariadne, a by-word of Vashti, and a corpse of Amy Dudley. The incidents were rencounters accidental and contrived, stealthy correspondence, sudden misgivings on one side, sudden self-reproaches on the other. The inner state of the twain was one as of confused noise that would not allow the accents of politic reason to be heard. Determination to go in this direction, and headlong plunges in that; dignified safeguards, undignified collapses; not a single rash step by deliberate intention, and all against judgement.

It was all that Melbury had expected and feared. It was more, for he had overlooked the publicity that would be likely to result, as it now had done. What should he do? Appeal to Mrs Charmond himself, since Grace would not? He bethought himself of Winterborne, and resolved to consult him, feeling the strong need of some friend of his own sex to whom he might unburden his mind.

He had entirely lost faith in his own judgment. That judgment on which he had relied for so many years seemed recently, like a false companion unmasked, to have disclosed unexpected depths of hypocrisy and speciousness where all had seemed solidity. He felt almost afraid to form a conjecture on the weather, or the time, or the fruit-promise, so great was his self-mistrust.

He set out to look for Giles on a rimy evening when the woods seemed to be in a cold sweat; beads of perspiration hung from every bare twig; the sky had no colour, and the trees rose before him as haggard, grey phantoms whose days of substantiality were passed. Melbury seldom saw Winterborne now, but he believed him to be occupying a lonely hut just beyond the boundary of Mrs Charmond's estate, though still within the circuit of the woodland. The timber-merchant's thin legs stalked on through the pale damp scenery, his eyes declining on the dead leaves of last year; while every now and then a hasty 'ay!' escaped his lips in reply to some bitter mental proposition.

His notice was attracted by a thin blue haze of smoke, behind which arose sounds of voices and chopping; bending his steps that way he saw Winterborne just in front of him.

Though few knew of it, Giles had had a serious illness during the winter; but it just now happened that after being for a long time apathetic and unemployed on that account he had become one of the busiest men in the neighbourhood. It is often thus; fallen friends lost sight of we expect to find starving; we discover them going on fairly well. Without any solicitation or desire to profit on his part, he had been asked to execute a very large order for hurdles and other copse-ware, for which purpose he had been obliged to buy several acres of hazel brushwood standing. He was now engaged in the cutting and manufacture of the same, proceeding with the work daily like an automaton.

The hazel-tree did not belie its name to-day. The whole of the copse-wood where the mist had cleared returned purest tints of that hue, amid which Winterborne himself was in the act of making a hurdle, the stakes being driven firmly into the ground in a row, over which he bent and wove the twigs. Beside him was a square, compact pile like the altar of Cain, formed of hurdles already finished, which bristled on all sides with the sharp points of their stakes. At a little distance the men in his employ were assisting him to carry out his contract. Rows of brushwood lay on the ground as it had fallen under the axe; and a shelter had been constructed near at hand, in front of which burnt the fire whose smoke had attracted Melbury. The air was so dank that the smoke hung heavily, and crept away amid the bushes without rising from the ground.

After wistfully regarding the scene awhile Melbury drew nearer, and briefly inquired of Giles how he came to be so busily engaged, with an undertone of slight surprise that Winterborne could recommence thriving, even to this degree, after being deprived of Grace. Melbury was not without emotion at the meeting, for Grace's affairs had divided them, and ended their intimacy of old times.

Winterborne explained just as briefly, without raising his eyes from his occupation of chopping a bough that he held in front of him.

' 'Twill be up in April before you get it all cleared,' said Melbury.

'Yes, there or thereabouts,' said Winterborne, a chop of the bill-hook jerking the last word into two pieces.

There was another interval; Melbury still looked on, a chip from Winterborne's hook occasionally flying against the waistcoat or legs of his visitor, who took no heed.

'Ah, Giles, you should have been my partner. You should have been my son-in-law,' the old man said at last. 'It would have been far better for her and for me!'

Winterborne saw that something had gone wrong with his former friend, and throwing down the switch he was about to interweave he responded only too readily to the mood of the timber-dealer. 'Is she ill?' he said hurriedly.

'No, no.' Melbury stood without speaking for some minutes, and then, as though he could not bring himself to proceed, turned to go away.

Winterborne told one of his men to pack up the tools for the night, and walked after Melbury.

'Heaven forbid that I should seem too inquisitive, sir,' he said, 'especially since we don't stand as we used to stand to one another; but I hope it is well with them all over your way?'

'No,' said Melbury, 'no.'

He stopped, and struck the smooth trunk of a young ash-tree with the flat of his hand. 'I would that his ear had been where that rind is!' he exclaimed; 'I should have treated him to little compared wi' what he deserves.'

'Now,' said Winterborne, 'don't be in a hurry to go home. I've put some ale down to warm in my shelter here, and we'll sit and drink it and talk this over.'

Melbury turned unresistingly as Giles took his arm, and they went back to where the fire was, and sat down under the screen, the other woodmen having gone. He drew out the ale-cup from the ashes, and they drank together.

'Giles, you ought to have had her, as I said just now,' repeated Melbury. 'I'll tell you why for the first time.'

He thereupon told Winterborne, as with great relief, the story of how he won away Giles's father's chosen one – by nothing worse than a lover's cajoleries, it is true; but by means which, except in love, would certainly have been pronounced cruel and unfair. He explained how he had always intended to make reparation to Winterborne the father, by giving Grace to Winterborne the son; till the devil tempted him in the person of Fitzpiers, and he broke his virtuous vow.

'How highly I thought of that man to be sure! Who'd have supposed he'd have been so weak and wrong-headed as this! You ought to have had her, Giles, and there's an end on't.'

Winterborne knew how to preserve his calm under this unconsciously cruel tearing of a healing wound, to which Melbury's concentration on the more vital subject had blinded him. The young man endeavoured to make the best of the case for Grace's sake.

'She would hardly have been happy with me,' he said, in the dry, un-impassioned voice under which he hid his feelings. 'I was not well enough educated: too rough in short. I couldn't have surrounded her with the refinements she looked for, anyhow at all.'

'Nonsense – you are quite wrong there,' said the unwise old man doggedly. 'She told me only this day that she hates refinements and such like. All that my trouble and money bought for her in that way is thrown away upon her quite. She'd fain be like Marty South – think o' that! That's the top of her ambition! Perhaps she's right. Giles, she loved you – under the rind: and what's more she loves 'ee still – worse luck for the poor maid!'

If Melbury only had known what fires he was recklessly stirring up he might have held his peace. Winterborne was silent a long time. The darkness had closed

in round them, and the monotonous drip of the fog from the branches quickened
as it turned to fine rain.

'O, she never cared much for me,' Giles managed to say as he stirred the embers
with a brand.

'She did, and does, I tell ye,' said the other obstinately. 'However, all that's
vain talking now. What I come to ask you about is a more practical matter – how
to make the best of things as they are. I am thinking of a desperate step – of
calling on the woman Charmond. I am going to appeal to her since Grace will
not. 'Tis she who holds the balance in her hands – not he. While she's got the will
to lead him astray he will follow – poor unpractical lofty-notioned dreamer –
and how long she'll do it depends upon her whim. Did ye ever hear anything
about her character before she came to Hintock?'

'She's been a bit of a charmer in her time, I believe,' replied Giles, with the same
level quietude, as he regarded the red coals. 'A body who has smiled where she
has not loved, and loved where she has not married. Before Mr Charmond made
her his wife she was a play-actress a short while.'

'Hey? But how close you have kept all this, Giles! What besides?'

'Mr Charmond was a rich man engaged in the iron trade in the north – twenty
or thirty years older than she. He married her, and retired, and came down here
and bought this property.'

'Yes, yes – I know all about that. But the other I did not know. I fear it bodes
no good. For how can I go and appeal to the forbearance of a woman who made
cross-loves and crooked passions her study for years? I thank ye, Giles, for
finding it out; but it makes my plan the harder that she should have belonged to
that unstable tribe!'

Another pause ensued, and they looked gloomily at the smoke that beat about
the roof of hurdles through whose weavings a large drop of rain fell at intervals
and spat smartly into the fire. Mrs Charmond had been no friend to
Winterborne, but he was manly, and it was not in his heart to let her be
condemned without a trial.

'She is said to be generous,' he answered. 'You might not appeal to her in vain.'

'It shall be done,' said Melbury, rising. 'For good, or for evil, to Mrs
Charmond I'll go.'

CHAPTER THIRTY-TWO

At nine o'clock the next morning Melbury dressed himself up in shining
broadcloth, creased with folding and smelling of camphor, and started for
Hintock House. He was the more impelled to go at once by the absence of his son-
in-law in London for a few days, to attend really or ostensibly some professional
meetings.

He said nothing of his destination either to his wife or to Grace, fearing that
they might entreat him to abandon so risky a project; and went out unobserved.
He had chosen his time with a view, he supposed, of conveniently catching Mrs

Charmond when she had just finished her breakfast, before any other business people should be about, if any came. Plodding thoughtfully onward he crossed a glade lying between Little Hintock woods and the plantation which abutted on the park. The spot being open he was discerned there by Winterborne from the copse on the next hill, where he and his men were working. Knowing his mission the younger man hastened down from the copse and managed to intercept the timber-merchant.

'I have been thinking of this, sir,' he said, 'and I am of opinion that it would be best to put off your visit for the present.'

But Melbury would not even stop to hear him. His mind was fixed, the appeal was to be made; and Winterborne stood and watched him sadly till he entered the second plantation and disappeared.

Melbury rang at the tradesmen's door of the manor-house, and was at once informed that the lady was not yet visible, as indeed he might have guessed had he been anybody but the man he was. Melbury said he would wait, whereupon the young page informed him in a neighbourly way that, between themselves, she was in bed and asleep.

'Never mind,' said Melbury, retreating into the court, 'I'll stand about here.' Charged so fully with his mission he shrank from contact with anybody.

But he walked about the paved court till he was tired, and nobody came to him. He entered the house and sat down in a small waiting-room, from which he got glimpses of the kitchen-corridor, and of the white-capped maids flitting jauntily hither and thither. They had heard of his arrival, but had not seen him enter, and imagining him still in the court discussed freely the possible reason of his calling. They marvelled at his temerity; for though most of the tongues which had been let loose attributed the chief blame to Fitzpiers, these of her household preferred to regard their mistress as the deeper sinner.

Melbury sat with his hands resting on the familiar knobbed thorn walking-stick, whose growing he had seen before he enjoyed its use. The scene to him was not the material environment of his person, but a tragic vision that travelled with him like an envelope. Through this vision the incidents of the moment but gleamed confusedly here and there, as an outer landscape through the high-coloured scenes of a stained window.

He waited thus an hour, an hour and a half, two hours. He began to look pale and ill, whereupon the butler, who came in, asked him to have a glass of wine.

Melbury roused himself, and said, 'No, no. Is she almost ready?'

'She is just finishing breakfast, Mr Melbury,' said the butler. 'She will soon see you now. I am just going up to tell her you are here.'

'What, haven't you told her before?' said Melbury.

'O no,' said the other. 'You see you came so very early.'

At last the bell rang; Mrs Charmond could see him. She was not in her private sitting-room when he reached it, but in a minute he heard her coming from the front staircase, and she entered where he stood.

At this time of the morning Mrs Charmond looked her full age and more. She might almost have been taken for the typical *femme de trente ans*, though she was really not more than seven or eight and twenty. But the *édition définitive* of her beauty had been reached, even if it were not a little worn.

There being no fire in the room she came in with a shawl thrown loosely round her shoulders, and obviously without the least suspicion that Melbury had called upon any other errand than timber. Felice was, indeed, the only woman in the parish who had not heard the rumour of her own weaknesses; she was at this moment living in a fool's paradise in respect of that rumour, though not in respect of the weaknesses themselves, which, if the truth be told, caused her grave misgivings.

'Do sit down, Mr Melbury. You have felled all the trees that were to be purchased by you this season, except the oaks, I believe?'

'Yes, yes,' said Melbury, in a reverie.

He did not take a chair, and she also remained standing. Resting upon his stick he began: Mrs Charmond, I have called upon a more serious matter – at least to me – than tree-throwing. And whatever mistakes I make in my manner of speaking upon it to you, madam, do me the justice to set 'em down to my want of practice, and not to my want of care.'

Mrs Charmond looked ill at ease. She might have begun to guess his meaning; but apart from that she had such dread of contact with anything painful, harsh, or even earnest, that his preliminaries alone were enough to distress her.

'Yes, what is it?' she said quickly.

'I am an old man,' said Melbury, 'that, somewhat late in life, God thought fit to bless with one child, and she a daughter. Her mother was a very dear wife to me; but she was taken away from us when the child was young; and the child became precious as the apple of my eye to me, for she was all I had left to love. For her sake entirely I married as second wife a homespun woman who had been kind as a mother to her. In due time the question of her education came on; and I said, "I will educate the maid well if I live upon bread to do it." Of her possible marriage I could not bear to think, for it seemed like a death that she should cleave to another man, and grow to think his house her home rather than mine. But I saw it was the law of nature that this should be, and that it was for the maid's happiness that she should have a home when I was gone; and I made up my mind without a murmur to help it on for her sake. In my youth I had wronged my dead friend, and to make amends I determined to give her, my most precious prize, to my friend's son, seeing that they liked each other well. Things came about which made me doubt if it would be for my daughter's happiness to do this, inasmuch as the young man was poor, and she was delicately reared. Another man came and paid court to her – one her equal in breeding and accomplishments; in every way it seemed to me that he only could give her the home which her training had made a necessity a'most. I urged her on, and she married him. But, ma'am, a fatal mistake was at the root of my reckoning; I found that this well-born gentleman I had calculated on so surely was not staunch of heart, and that therein lay a danger of great sorrow for my daughter. Madam, he saw you, and you know the rest. . . . I have come to make no demands – to utter no threats; I have come simply as a father in great grief about his only child, and I beseech you to deal kindly with my daughter and to do nothing which can turn her husband's heart away from her for ever! Forbid him your presence, ma'am, and speak to him on his duty, as one with your power over him well can do: and I am hopeful that the rent between them may be patched up. For it is not as if you would lose by so doing; your course is far higher than the courses of a professional man; and the gratitude you would win from me and mine by your kindness is more than I can say!'

Mrs Charmond had first rushed into a mood of indignation, on comprehending Melbury's story: hot and cold by turns she had murmured, 'Leave me, leave me!' But, as he seemed to take no notice of this, his words began to influence her, and when he ceased speaking she said with hurried breath, 'What has led you to think this of me? Who says I have won your daughter's husband away from her? Some monstrous calumnies are afloat – of which I have known nothing until now!'

Melbury started, and looked at her simply: 'But surely, ma'am, you know the truth better than I?'

Her features became a little pinched, and the touches of powder on her handsome face for the first time showed themselves as an extrinsic film.

'Will you leave me to myself?' she said with a faintness which suggested a guilty conscience. 'This is so utterly unexpected – you obtain admission to my presence by misrepresentation—'

'As God's in heaven, ma'am, that's not true. I made no pretence; and I thought in reason you would know why I had come. This gossip—'

'I have heard nothing of it. Tell me the gist of it, pray!'

'Tell you, ma'am – not I. What the gossip is, no matter. What really is, you know. Set facts right, and the scandal will right itself. But pardon me – I speak rough; and I came to speak gentle, to coax you, beg you to be my daughter's friend. She loved you once, ma'am; you began by loving her. Then you dropped her without a reason, and it hurt her warm heart more than I can tell ye. But you were within your right as the superior, no doubt. But if you would consider her position now – surely, surely, you would do her no harm!'

'Certainly I would do her no harm – I—'

Melbury's eye met hers. It was curious, but the allusion to Grace's former love for her seemed to touch her more than all Melbury's other arguments. 'O, Melbury,' she burst out, 'you have made me so unhappy! How could you come to me like this! It is too dreadful! Now go away – go, go!'

'I will, and leave you to think,' he said, in a husky tone.

As soon as he was out of the room she went to a corner and there burst into tears, and writhed, under an emotion in which hurt pride and vexation mingled with better sentiments.

Mrs Charmond's mobile spirit was subject to these fierce periods of high tide and storm. She had never so clearly perceived till now that her soul was being slowly invaded by a delirium which had brought about all this; that she was losing judgment and dignity under it, becoming an animated impulse only, a passion incarnate. A fascination had led her on; it was as if she had been seized by a hand of velvet; and this was where she found herself – overshadowed with sudden night, as if a tornado had passed.

While she sat, or rather crouched, unhinged by the interview, lunch-time came and then the early afternoon, almost without her consciousness. Then 'a strange gentleman, who says it is not necessary to give his name,' was suddenly announced.

Felice knew who the strange gentleman was – that Continental follower on whom she had once smiled, among others too numerous to name. But to meet this lover now – the thought made her sick.

'I cannot see him, whoever he may be! I am not at home to anybody.'

She heard no more of her visitor: and shortly after, in an attempt to recover some mental serenity by violent physical exercise, she put on her hat and cloak and went out of doors, taking a path which led her up the slopes to the nearest spur of the wood. She disliked the woods, but they had the advantage of being a place in which she could walk comparatively unobserved.

CHAPTER THIRTY-THREE

T H E R E was agitation that day in the lives of all whom these matters concerned. It was not till the Hintock dinner-time – one o'clock – that Grace discovered her father's absence from the house after a departure in the morning under somewhat unusual conditions. By a little reasoning and inquiry she was able to divine his errand.

Her husband, too, was away, and her father did not return. He had, in truth, gone on to Sherton after the interview, in the hope of calming himself by business; but this Grace did not know. In an indefinite dread that something serious would arise out of Melbury's visit by reason of the inequalities of temper and nervous irritation to which he was subject, something possibly that would bring her much more misery than accompanied her present negative state of mind, she left the house about three o'clock, and took a loitering walk in the woodland track by which she imagined he would come home. This track under the bare trees and over the cracking sticks, screened and roofed in from the outer world of wind by a network of boughs, led her slowly on till in time she had left the larger trees behind her and swept round into the coppice where Winterborne and his men were clearing the undergrowth.

Had Giles's attention been concentrated on his hurdles he would not have seen her, but ever since Melbury's passage across the opposite glade in the morning he had been as uneasy and unsettled as Grace herself; and her advent now was the one appearance which, since her father's avowal, could arrest him more than Melbury's return with his tidings. Fearing that something might be the matter he hastened up to her.

She had not seen her old lover for a long time, and too conscious of the late pranks of her heart she could not behold him calmly. 'I am only looking for my father,' she said in an unnecessary tone of apology.

'I was looking for him too,' said Giles. 'I think he may perhaps have gone on further.'

'Then you knew he was going to the House, Giles?' she said, turning her large tender eyes anxiously upon him. 'Did he tell you what for?'

Winterborne glanced doubtingly at her, and softly hinted that her father had visited him the evening before, and that their old friendship was quite restored; on which she guessed the rest.

'O, I am glad indeed that you two are friends again!' she cried.

And then they stood facing each other, fearing each other, troubling each other's souls. Grace experienced acute regret at the sight of these wood-cutting scenes, because she had estranged herself from them; craving, even to its defects and inconveniences, that homely sylvan life of her father which in the best probable succession of events would shortly be denied her.

At a little distance, on the edge of the clearing, Marty South was shaping spargads to take home for manufacture during the evenings. Winterborne and Mrs Fitzpiers stood looking at her in their mutual embarrassment at each other's presence, and while doing so they beheld, approaching the girl, a lady in a dark fur mantle and black hat, having a white veil tied picturesquely round it. She spoke to Marty, who turned and curtsied, and the lady fell into conversation with her. It was Mrs Charmond.

After leaving her house Mrs Charmond had walked on, under the fret and fever of her mind, with more vigour than she was accustomed to show in her normal moods – a fever which the solace of a cigarette did not entirely allay. Reaching the coppice she had listlessly observed Marty at work, when she threw away her cigarette and drew near. Chop, chop, chop, went Marty's little billhook with never more assiduity, till Mrs Charmond spoke.

'Who is that young lady I see talking to the woodman yonder?' she asked.

'Mrs Fitzpiers, ma'am,' said Marty.

'O,' said Mrs Charmond, with something like a start; for she had not recognized Grace at that distance. 'And the man she is talking to?'

'That's Mr Winterborne.'

A redness stole into Marty's face as she mentioned Giles's name, which Mrs Charmond did not fail to notice. 'Are you engaged to him?' she asked softly.

'No, ma'am,' said Marty. '*She* was once; and I think—'

But Marty could not possibly explain the complications of her thought on this matter – a thought nothing less than one of extraordinary acuteness for a girl so young and inexperienced – namely, that she saw danger to two hearts, naturally honest, in Grace being thrown back into Winterborne's society by the neglect of her husband. Mrs Charmond, however, with the almost supersensory means to knowledge which women have on such occasions, quite understood what Marty had intended to convey; and the picture thus exhibited to her of lives drifting awry, involving the wreck of poor Marty's hopes, prompted her yet further in those generous resolves which Melbury's remonstrances had stimulated.

Full of such feelings she bade the girl good-afternoon, and went on over the stumps of hazel to where Grace and Winterborne were standing. They saw her approach, and Winterborne said, 'She is coming to you; it is a good omen. She dislikes me, so I'll go away.'

He accordingly retreated to where he had been working before Grace came, and Grace's formidable rival approached her, each woman taking the other's measure as she drew near.

'Dear – Mrs Fitzpiers!' said Felice Charmond, with some inward turmoil which stopped her speech. 'I have not seen you for a long time.'

She held out her hand tentatively, while Grace stood like a wild animal on first confronting a mirror or other puzzling product of civilization. Was it really Mrs Charmond speaking to her thus? If it was she could no longer form any guess as to what life signified.

'I want to talk to you,' said Mrs Charmond sensitively, for the gaze of the young woman had chilled her through. 'Can you walk on with me till we are quite alone?'

Sick with distaste Grace nevertheless complied as by clockwork, and they moved evenly side by side into the deeper recesses of the woods. They went further, much further than Mrs Charmond had meant to go; but mental indiscipline hindered her from beginning her conversation, and in default of it she kept walking.

'I have seen your father,' she at length observed. 'And – I am much troubled by what he told me.'

'What did he tell you? I have not been admitted to his confidence on anything he may have said to you.'

'Nevertheless, why should I repeat to you what you can easily divine?'

'True – true,' returned Grace mournfully. 'Why should you repeat what we both have in our minds already?'

'Mrs Fitzpiers, your husband—'

The moment that the speaker's tongue touched the dangerous subject a vivid look of self-consciousness flashed over her; in which her heart revealed, as by a lightning-gleam, what filled it to overflowing. So transitory was the expression that none but a quick-sensed woman, and she in Grace's position, would have had the power to catch its meaning. Upon her the phase was not lost.

'Then you *do* love him!' she exclaimed in a tone of much surprise.

'What do you mean, my young friend?'

'Why,' cried Grace, 'I thought till now that you had only been cruelly flirting with my husband to amuse your idle moments – a rich lady with a poor professional gentleman whom in her heart she despised not much less than her who belongs to him. But I guess from your manner that you love him desperately; and I don't hate you as I did before. . . . Yes, indeed,' continued Mrs Fitzpiers, with a trembling tongue, 'since it is not sport in your case at all but *real* – O, I do pity you, more than I despise you! For *you* will suffer most!'

Mrs Charmond was now as much agitated as Grace. 'I ought not to allow myself to argue about this!' she exclaimed. 'I demean myself by doing it. But I liked you once, and for the sake of that time I try to tell you how mistaken you are!'

Much of her confusion resulted from her wonder and alarm at finding herself, in a sense, dominated mentally and emotionally by this simple school-girl. 'I do not love him!' she went on with insistent untruth. 'It was a kindness – my making somewhat more of him than one usually does of one's doctor. I was lonely; I talked – well, I trifled with him. I am very sorry if such child's play, out of pure friendship, has been a serious matter to you. Who could have expected it? But the world is so simple here!'

'O, that's affectation,' said Grace, shaking her head. 'It is no use – you *love* him! I can see in your face that in this matter of my husband you have not let your acts belie your feelings. During these last four or six months you have been terribly indiscreet, but you have not been insincere; and that almost disarms me.'

'I *have* been insincere – if you will have the word – I mean I *have* coquetted, and do *not* love him!'

But Grace clung to her position like a limpet. 'You may have trifled with others; but him you love as you never loved another man!'

'O, well – I won't argue,' said Mrs Charmond, laughing faintly. 'And you come to reproach me for it, child?'

'No,' said Grace magnanimously. 'You may go on loving him if you like – I don't mind at all. You'll find it, let me tell you, a bitterer business for yourself than for me in the end. He'll get tired of you soon, as tired as can be – you don't know him so well as I! – and then you may wish you had never seen him!'

Mrs Charmond had grown quite pale and weak under this prophecy. It was extraordinary that Grace, whom almost every one would have characterized as a gentle girl, should be of tougher fibre than her interlocutor.

'You exaggerate – cruel, silly young woman,' she reiterated, writhing with little agonies. 'It is nothing but playful friendship – nothing! It will be proved by my future conduct. I shall at once refuse to see him more – since it will make no difference to my heart, and much to my name.'

'I question if you will refuse to see him again,' said Grace dryly, as she bent a sapling back. 'But I am not incensed against you as you are against me,' she added, abandoning the tree to its natural perpendicular. 'Before I came I had been despising you for wanton cruelty; now I only pity your weakness for its misplaced affection. When Edred has gone out of the house in hope of seeing you, at seasonable hours and unseasonable; when I have found him riding miles and miles across the country at midnight, and risking his life, and getting covered with mud, to get a glimpse of you, I have called him a foolish man – the plaything of a finished coquette. I thought that what was getting to be a tragedy to me was a comedy to you. But now I see that tragedy lies on your side of the situation no less than on mine, and more; that if I have felt trouble at my position you have felt anguish at yours; that if I have had disappointments you have had despairs. Philosophy may fortify *me* – God help *you!*'

'I cannot attempt to reply to your ravings,' returned the other, struggling to restore a dignity which had completely collapsed. 'My acts will be my proofs. In the world which you have seen nothing of, friendships between men and women are not unknown; and it would have been better both for you and your father if you had each judged me more respectfully, and left me alone. As it is, I wish never, never to see or speak to you, madam, any more!'

Grace bowed, and Mrs Charmond haughtily turned away. The two went apart in directly opposite courses, and were soon hidden from each other by their umbrageous surroundings and by the shadows of eve.

In the excitement of their long argument they had walked onward and zigzagged about without regarding direction or distance. All sound of the woodcutters had long since faded into remoteness, and even had not the interval been too great for hearing them they would have been silent and homeward bound at this twilight hour.

But Grace went on her course without any misgiving, though there was much underwood here with only the narrowest passages for walking, across which brambles hung. She had not, however, traversed this, the wildest, part of the wood since her childhood, and the transformation of outlines had been great; old trees which once were landmarks had been felled or blown down, and the bushes which then had been small and scrubby were now large and overhanging. She soon found that her ideas as to direction were vague – that she had indeed no ideas as to direction at all. If the evening had not been growing so dark, and the wind had not put on its night-moan so distinctly, Grace would not have minded; but she was rather frightened now, and began to strike across hither and thither in random courses.

Denser grew the darkness, more developed the wind-voices, and still no recognizable spot or outlet of any kind appeared, nor any sound of the Hintocks floated near, though she had wandered probably between one and two hours, and began to be weary. She was vexed at her foolishness, since the ground she had covered, if in a straight line, must inevitably have taken her out of the wood to some remote village or other; but she had wasted her forces in counter-marches; and now, in much alarm, wondered if she would have to pass the night here.

She stood still to meditate, and fancied that between the soughing of the wind she heard shuffling footsteps on the leaves heavier than those of rabbits or other startled 'beasts of beating heart' who lived there. Though fearing at first to meet anybody on the chance of his being a friend, she decided that her fellow-noctambulist, even if a poacher, would not injure her, and that he might possibly be some one sent to search for her. She accordingly shouted a rather timid 'Hoi!'

The cry was immediately returned by the other person; and Grace running at once in the direction whence it came beheld an indistinct figure hastening up to her as rapidly. They were almost in each other's arms before she recognized the outline and white veil of her whom she had parted from hours before – Mrs Charmond.

'I have lost my way, I have lost my way!' cried the latter. 'O – is it indeed you? I am so glad to meet you or anybody. I have been wandering up and down ever since we parted, and am nearly dead with terror and misery and fatigue!'

'So am I,' said Grace. 'What *shall* we – *shall* we do!'

'You won't go away from me?' asked her companion anxiously.

'No, indeed. Are you very tired?'

'I can scarcely move, and I am scratched dreadfully about the ankles.'

Grace reflected. 'Perhaps, as it is dry underfoot, the best thing for us to do would be to sit down for half-an-hour, and then start again when we have thoroughly rested. By walking straight we must come to a track leading somewhere, before the morning.'

They found a clump of bushy hollies which afforded a shelter from the wind, and sat down under it, some tufts of dead fern, crisp and dry, that remained from the previous season, forming a sort of nest for them. But it was cold, nevertheless, on this March night, particularly for Grace, who, with the sanguine prematureness of youth in matters of dress, had considered it spring-time, and hence was not so warmly clad as Mrs Charmond, who still wore her winter furs.

But after sitting awhile the latter lady shivered no less than Grace as the warmth imparted by her hasty walking began to go off; and they felt the cold air drawing through the holly leaves which scratched their backs and shoulders. Moreover they could hear some drops of rain falling on the trees, though none reached the nook in which they had ensconced themselves.

'If we were to cling close together,' said Mrs Charmond, 'we should keep each other warm. . . . But,' she added in an uneven voice, 'I suppose you won't come near me for the world!'

'Why not?'

'Because – well, you know.'

'Yes, I will – I don't hate you at all.'

They consequently crept up to one another, and being in the dark, lonely, and weary, did what neither had dreamed of doing beforehand – clasped each other closely. Mrs Charmond's furs consoled Grace's cold face; and each one's body, as she breathed, alternately heaved against that of her companion; while the funereal trees rocked and chanted dirges unceasingly.

When a few minutes had been spent thus Mrs Charmond said, 'I am so wretched!' in a heavy emotional whisper.

'You are frightened,' said Grace. 'But there is nothing to fear; I know these woods well.'

'I am not at all frightened at the wood; but I am at other things.'

Mrs Charmond embraced Grace more and more tightly, and put her face against that of her companion. The younger woman could feel her neighbour's breathings grow deeper and more spasmodic, as though uncontrollable feelings were germinating.

'After I had left you,' Felice went on, 'I regretted something I had said. I have to make a confession – I must make it!' she whispered brokenly, the instinct to indulge in warmth of sentiment which had led this woman of passions to respond to Fitzpiers in the first place, leading her now to find luxurious comfort in opening her heart to his wife. 'I said to you I could give him up without pain or deprivation – that he had only been my pastime. That was absolutely untrue – it was said to deceive you! I could not do it without much pain; and what is more dreadful I cannot give him up – even if I would – of myself alone.'

'Why? Because you love him, you mean.'

Felice Charmond denoted assent by a movement.

'I knew I was right!' said Grace exaltedly. 'But that should not deter you,' she presently added in a moral tone. 'O, do struggle against it, and you will conquer!'

'You are so simple, so simple!' cried Felice. 'You think, because you guessed my assumed indifference to him to be a sham, that you know the extremes that people are capable of going to! But a good deal more may have been going on than you have fathomed with all your insight. I *cannot* give him up until he chooses to give up me!'

'But surely you are the superior in station and in every way, and the cut must come from you.'

'Tchut! Must I tell verbatim, you simple child? O, I suppose I must! It will eat away my heart if I do not let out all, after meeting you like this and finding how guileless you are!'

She thereupon whispered a few words in the girl's ear, and burst into a violent fit of sobbing.

Grace started roughly away from the shelter of the furs, and sprang to her feet.

'O, my great God!' she exclaimed, thunderstruck at a revelation transcending her utmost suspicion. 'He's had you! Can it be – can it be!'

She turned as if to hasten away. But Felice Charmond's sobs came to her ear: deep darkness circled her about, the cold lips of the wind kissed her where Mrs Charmond's warm fur had been, and she did not know which way to go. After the moment of energy she felt mild again, and turned to the motionless woman at her feet.

'Are you rested?' she asked, in what seemed her own voice grown ten years older.

Without an answer Mrs Charmond slowly rose. 'You mean to betray me!' she asked out of the bitterest depths of her soul. 'O, fool, fool I!'

'No,' said Grace shortly. 'I mean no such thing. But let us be quick now. We have a serious undertaking before us. Think of nothing but going straight on.'

They walked on in profound silence, pulling back boughs now growing wet, and treading down woodbine, but still keeping a pretty straight course. Grace began to be thoroughly worn out, and her companion too, when, on a sudden, they broke into the deserted highway where the Sherton man had waited for Mrs Dollery's van. Grace recognized the spot as soon as she looked around her.

'How we have got here I cannot tell,' she said with cold civility. 'We have made a complete circuit of Little Hintock. The hazel copse is quite on the other side. Now we have only to follow the road.'

They dragged themselves onward, turned into the lane, passed the track to Little Hintock, and so reached the park.

'Here I turn back,' said Grace in the same passionless voice. 'You are quite near home.'

Mrs Charmond stood inert, seeming appalled by her late admission.

'I have told you something in a moment of irresistible desire to unburden my soul, which all but a fool would have kept silent as the grave,' she said. 'I cannot help it now. Is it to be a secret, or do you mean war?'

'A secret certainly,' said Grace mournfully. 'How can you expect war from such a helpless, wretched being as me?'

'And I'll do my best not to see him. I am his slave; but I'll try.'

Grace was naturally kind, but she could not help using a small dagger now.

'Pray don't distress yourself,' she said with fine scorn. 'You may see him as much as you like – for me.' Had she been wounded instead of mortified she could not have used the words; but Fitzpiers's hold upon her heart just now was slight.

They parted thus and there, kissing each other almost unintentionally, and Grace went moodily homeward. Passing Marty's cottage she observed through the window that the girl was writing instead of chopping as usual, and wondered what her correspondence could be. Directly afterwards she met people in search of her, and reached the house to find all in serious alarm. She soon explained that she had lost her way, and her general depression was attributed to exhaustion on that account.

Could she have known what Marty was writing she would have been surprised. The rumour which agitated the other folk of Hintock had reached the young girl, and she was penning a letter to Fitzpiers to tell him that Mrs Charmond's magnificent pile of hair was made up of the writer's more largely than of her own. It was poor Marty's only card, and she played it, knowing nothing of fashion, and thinking her revelation a fatal one for a lover.

CHAPTER THIRTY-FOUR

It was at the beginning of April, a few days after the meeting between Grace and Mrs Charmond in the wood, that Fitzpiers, just returned from London, was travelling from Sherton Abbas to Hintock in a hired carriage. In his eye there was a doubtful light, and the lines of his fastidious face showed a vague disquietude. He appeared like one of those whose aspect seems to say to a beholder that they have suffered a certain wrong in being born.

His position was in truth gloomy, and to his impressible mind it looked even gloomier than it was. His practice had been slowly dwindling of late, and now threatened to die out altogether, the undaunted old Dr Jones capturing patients up to Fitzpiers's very door. Fitzpiers knew only too well the latest and greatest cause of his unpopularity; and yet, so illogical is man, the second branch of his sadness grew out of a remedial measure proposed for the first — a letter from Felice Charmond imploring him not to see her again. To bring about their severance still more effectually, she added, she had decided upon almost immediate departure for the Continent.

The time was that dull interval in a woodlander's life which coincides with great activity in the life of the woodland itself — a period following the close of the winter tree-cutting and preceding the barking season, when the saps are just beginning to heave with the force of hydraulic lifts inside all the trunks of the forest.

Winterborne's contract was completed, and the plantations were deserted. It was dusk: there were no leaves as yet; the nightingales would not begin to sing for a fortnight; and the Mother of the Months was in her most attenuated phase — starved and bent to a mere bowed skeleton, which glided along behind the bare twigs in Fitzpiers's company.

When he reached home he went straight up to his wife's sitting-room. He found it deserted and without a fire. He had mentioned no day for his return; nevertheless he wondered why she was not there waiting to receive him.

On descending to the other wing of the house and inquiring of Mrs Melbury he learnt with much surprise that Grace had gone on a visit to an acquaintance at Shottsford-Forum three days earlier: that tidings had on this morning reached her father of her being very unwell there, in consequence of which he had ridden over to see her.

Fitzpiers went upstairs again, and the little drawing-room, now lighted by a solitary candle, was not rendered more cheerful by the entrance of Grammer Oliver with an apronful of wood which she threw on the hearth while she raked out the grate and rattled about the fire-irons with a view to making things comfortable. Fitzpiers, guessing nothing of the revelations in the wood, considered that Grace ought to have let him know her plans more accurately before leaving home in a freak like this. He went desultorily to the window, the blind of which had not been pulled down, and looked out at the thin, fast-sinking moon, and at the stalk of smoke rising from the top of Suke Damson's chimney, signifying that the young woman had just lit her fire to prepare supper.

He became conscious of a discussion in progress on the opposite side of the court. Somebody had looked over the wall to talk to the sawyers, and was telling them in a loud voice news in which the name of Mrs Charmond soon arrested his ears.

'Grammer, don't make so much noise with that grate,' said the surgeon; at which Grammer reared herself upon her knees and held the fuel suspended in her hand, while Fitzpiers half opened the window.

'She is off to foreign lands again at last – have made up her mind quite sudden-like – and it is thoughted she'll leave in a day or two. She's been all as if her mind were low for some days past – with a sort of fret in her face, as if she chid her own soul. She's the wrong sort of woman for Hintock – hardly knowing a beech from a woak. But I don't care who the man is, she's been a very kind friend to me.'

'Well – the day after to-morrow is the Sabbath day, and without charity we be but tinkling simples; but this I do say, that her going will be a blessed thing for a certain married couple who remain.'

The fire was lighted, and Fitzpiers sat down in front of it, restless as the last leaf upon a tree. 'A sort of fret in her face, as if she chid her own soul. Poor, poor Felice!'

How her frame must be pulsing under the conditions of which he had just heard the caricature; how her fair temples must ache; what a mood of wretchedness she must be in! But for this mixing up of his name with hers, and her determination to sunder their too close acquaintance on that account, she would probably have sent for him professionally. She was now sitting alone, suffering, perhaps wishing she had not forbidden him to come again.

Unable to remain in this lonely room any longer, or to wait for the meal which was in course of preparation, he made himself ready for riding, descended to the yard, stood by the stable-door while Darling was saddled, and rode off down the lane. He would have preferred walking, but was weary with his day's travel.

As he approached the door of Marty South's cottage, which it was necessary to pass on his way, she came from the porch as if she had been awaiting him, and met him in the middle of the road, holding up a letter. Fitzpiers took it without stopping, and asked over his shoulder from whom it came.

Marty hesitated. 'From me,' she said with noticeable firmness.

This letter contained, in fact, Marty's declaration that she was the original owner of Mrs Charmond's supplementary locks, and inclosed a sample from the native stock, which had grown considerably by this time. It was her long contemplated apple of discord, and much her hand trembled as she handed the document up to him.

But it was impossible, on account of the gloom, for Fitzpiers to read it then, while he had the curiosity to do so, and he put it in his pocket. His imagination having already centred itself on Hintock House, in his pocket the letter remained unopened and forgotten, all the while that Marty was hopefully picturing its excellent weaning effect upon him.

He was not long in reaching the precincts of the manor-house. He drew rein under a group of oaks commanding a view of the front, and reflected awhile. His entry would not be altogether unnatural in the circumstances of her possible indisposition; but upon the whole he thought it best to avoid riding up to the door. By silently approaching he could retreat unobserved in the event of her not being alone. He dismounted, hitched Darling to a stray bough hanging a little below the general browsing line of the trees, and proceeded to the door on foot.

In the meantime Melbury had returned from Shottsford-Forum. The great court or quadrangle of the timber-merchant's house, divided from the shady lane by an ivy-covered wall, was entered by two white gates, one standing near each extremity of the wall. It had so happened that at the moment when Fitzpiers was riding out at the lower gate on his way to the manor-house, Melbury was approaching the upper gate to enter it. Fitzpiers, being in front of Melbury, was seen by the latter, but the surgeon, never turning his head, did not observe his father-in-law ambling up slowly and silently under the trees, though his horse, too, was a grey one.

'How is Grace?' said his wife, as soon as he entered.

Melbury looked gloomy. 'She is not at all well,' he said. 'I don't like the looks of her at all. I couldn't bear the notion of her staying away in a strange place any longer, and I begged her to let me get her home. At last she agreed to it, but not till after much persuading. I was then sorry that I rode over instead of driving; but I have hired a nice comfortable carriage – the easiest-going I could get – and she'll be here in a couple of hours or less. I rode on ahead to tell you to get her room ready; but I see her husband has come back.'

'Yes,' said Mrs Melbury. She expressed her concern that her husband had hired a carriage all the way from Shottsford. 'What it will cost!' she said.

'I don't care what it costs!' he exclaimed testily. 'I was determined to get her home. Why she went away, I can't think! She acts in a way that is not at all likely to mend matters as far as I can see.'

Grace had not told her father of her interview with Mrs Charmond and the disclosure that had been whispered in her startled ear.

'Since Edred is come,' he continued, 'he might have waited in till I got back, to ask me how she was, if it was only for a compliment. I saw him go out; where is he gone?'

Mrs Melbury reminded her husband that there was not much doubt about the place of his first visit after an absence. She had, in fact, seen Fitzpiers take the direction of the manor-house.

Melbury said no more. It was exasperating to him that just at this moment, when there was every reason for Fitzpiers to stay indoors, or, at any rate, to ride along the Shottsford road to meet his ailing wife, he should be doing despite to her by going elsewhere. The old man went out of doors again; and, his horse being hardly unsaddled as yet, he told Upjohn to re-tighten the girths; again mounting he rode off at the heels of the surgeon.

By the time that Melbury reached the park he was prepared to go any lengths in combating this rank and reckless errantry of his daughter's husband. He would fetch home Edred Fitzpiers to-night by some means, rough or fair; in his view there could come of his interference nothing worse than what existed at present. And yet to every bad there is a worse.

He had entered by the bridle-gate which admitted to the park on this side, and cantered over the soft turf almost in the tracks of Fitzpiers's horse, till he reached the clump of trees under which his precursor had halted. The whitish object that was indistinctly visible here in the gloom of the boughs he found to be Darling, as left by Fitzpiers.

'Damn him! why did he not ride up to the house in an honest way?' said Melbury.

He profited by Fitzpiers's example; dismounting, he tied his horse under an adjoining tree, and went on to the house on foot, as the other had done. He was no longer disposed to stick at trifles in his investigation, and did not hesitate to gently open the front door without ringing.

The large square hall, with its oak floor, staircase, and wainscot, was lighted by a dim lamp hanging from a beam. Not a soul was visible. He went into the corridor and listened at a door which he knew to be that of the drawing-room; there was no sound, and on turning the handle he found the room empty. A fire burning low in the grate was the sole light of the apartment; its beams flashed mockingly on the somewhat showy Versaillese furniture and gilding here, in style as unlike that of the structural parts of the building as it was possible to be, and probably introduced by Felice to counter-act the fine old English gloom of the place. Disappointed in his hope of confronting his son-in-law at once, he went on to the dining-room, which was without light or fire, and pervaded by a cold atmosphere signifying that she had not dined there that day.

By this time Melbury's mood had a little mollified. Everything here was so pacific, so unaggressive in its repose, that he was no longer incited to provoke a collision with Fitzpiers or with anybody. The comparative stateliness of the apartments influenced him to an emotion, rather than to a belief, that where all was outwardly so good and proper there could not be quite that delinquency within which he had suspected. It occurred to him, too, that even if his suspicion were justified his abrupt, if not unwarrantable, entry into the house might end in confounding its inhabitant at the expense of his daughter's dignity and his own. Any ill result would be pretty sure to hit Grace hardest in the long run. He would, after all, adopt the more rational course and plead with Fitzpiers privately, as he had pleaded with Mrs Charmond.

He accordingly retreated as silently as he had come. Passing the door of the drawing-room anew he fancied that he heard a noise within which was not the crackling of the fire. Melbury gently reopened the door to a distance of a few inches and saw at the opposite window two figures in the act of stepping out – a man and a woman – in whom he recognized the lady of the house and his son-in-law. In a moment they had disappeared amid the gloom of the lawn.

He drew back into the hall and let himself out by the carriage-entrance door, coming round to the lawn-front in time to see the two figures parting at the railing which divided the precincts of the house from the open park.

Mrs Charmond turned to hasten back immediately that her lover had left her side; and Fitzpiers going onward was speedily absorbed into the duskiness of the trees.

Melbury waited till Mrs Charmond had re-entered the drawing-room window, and then followed after Fitzpiers. He would give that precious young man a piece of his mind to-night, even if he were not tempted to give him more.

On plunging however into the thick shade of the clump of oaks he could not discover Fitzpiers; neither could he perceive his horse Blossom anywhere; but feeling his way carefully along he by and by discerned Fitzpiers's mare Darling still standing as before under the tree adjoining that to which he had hitched Blossom. For a moment Melbury thought that his own horse, being young and strong, had broken away from her fastening; but on listening intently he could hear her ambling comfortably along a little way ahead, and a creaking of the saddle which showed that she had a rider. Walking on as far as the small gate in the corner of the park he met a labourer, who, in reply to Melbury's inquiry if he had seen any person on a grey horse, said that he had only met Dr Fitzpiers.

It was just what Melbury had begun to suspect; Fitzpiers had mounted the mare which did not belong to him in mistake for his own – an oversight easily explicable, in a man ever unwitting in horseflesh, by the gloom of the spot and the near similarity of the animals in appearance, though Melbury's was readily enough seen to be the darker horse by day.

He hastened back, and did what seemed best in the circumstances – got upon old Darling, and rode rapidly after Fitzpiers.

Melbury had just entered the wood, and was winding along the cart-way which led through it, channelled deep in the leaf-mould with large ruts that were formed by the timber-waggons in fetching the spoil of the plantations, when all at once he descried in front, at a point where the road took a turning round a large chestnut tree, the form of his own horse Blossom. Melbury quickened Darling's pace, thinking to come up with Fitzpiers.

Nearer view revealed that the horse had no rider. At Melbury's approach it galloped friskily away under the trees in a homeward direction. Thinking something was wrong the timber-merchant dismounted as soon as he reached the chestnut, and after feeling about for a minute or two discovered Fitzpiers lying on the ground.

'Here – help!' cried the latter as soon as he felt Melbury's touch: 'I have been thrown off. . . . But there's not much harm done, I think.'

Since Melbury could not now very well read the younger man the lecture he had intended, and as friendliness would be hypocrisy, his instinct was to speak not a single word to his son-in-law. He raised Fitzpiers into a sitting posture, and found that he was a little stunned and stupefied, but, as he had said, not otherwise hurt. How this fall had come about was readily conjecturable: Fitzpiers, imagining there was only old Darling under him, had been taken unawares by the younger horse, anxious for the stable.

Melbury was a traveller of the old-fashioned sort: having just come from Shottsford-Forum he still had in his pocket the pilgrim's flask of rum which he always carried on journeys exceeding a dozen miles, though he seldom drank much of it. He poured it down the surgeon's throat with such effect that he quickly revived. Melbury got him on his legs; but the question was what to do with him. He could not walk more than a few steps, and the other horse had gone away.

With great exertion Melbury contrived to get him astride Darling, mounting himself behind and holding Fitzpiers round his waist with one arm. Darling being broad, straight-backed, and high in the withers, was well able to carry double, at any rate the short distance to Hintock and at a gentle pace.

CHAPTER THIRTY-FIVE

The mare paced along with firm and cautious tread through the copse where Winterborne had worked, and into the heavier soil where the oaks grew: thence towards Marshcombe Bottom, intensely dark now with overgrowth, and popularly supposed to be haunted by spirits.

By this time Fitzpiers had quite recovered his physical strength. But he had eaten nothing since making a hasty breakfast in London that morning, his anxiety about Felice having hurried him away from home before dining; as a consequence the old rum administered by his father-in-law flew to the young man's head and loosened his tongue without his ever having recognized who it was that had lent him a kindly hand. He began to speak in desultory sentences, Melbury still supporting him.

'I've come all the way from London to-day,' said Fitzpiers. 'Ah, that's the place to meet your equals. I live at Hintock – worse, at Little Hintock! – and I am quite wasted there. There's not a man within ten miles of Hintock who can comprehend me. . . . I tell you, Farmer What's-your-name, that I'm a man of education. I know several languages: the poets and I are familiar friends: I used to read more in metaphysics than anybody within fifty miles; and since I gave that up there's nobody can match me in the whole county of South Wessex as a scientist. . . . Yet I am doomed to live with tradespeople in a miserable little hole like Hintock!'

'Indeed!' muttered Melbury.

Here Fitzpiers, with alcoholic energy, reared himself up suddenly from the bowed posture he had hitherto held, thrusting his shoulders so violently against Melbury's breast as to make it difficult for the old man to keep a hold on the reins.

'People don't appreciate me here!' the surgeon exclaimed; then, lowering his voice, he added softly and slowly, 'except one – except one! . . . A passionate soul, as warm as she is clever, as beautiful as she is warm, and as rich as she is beautiful. I say, old fellow, those claws of yours clutch me rather tight – rather like the eagle's, you know, that ate out the liver of Pro – Pre –, the man on Mount Caucasus. . . . People don't appreciate me, I say, except *her*! . . . Ah, God, I am an unlucky man! She would have been mine, she would have taken my name; but unfortunately it cannot be so! I stooped to mate beneath me; and now I rue it.'

The position was becoming a very trying one for Melbury, corporeally and mentally. He was obliged to steady Fitzpiers with his left arm, and he began to hate the contact. He hardly knew what to do. It was useless to remonstrate with Fitzpiers in his intellectual confusion from the rum and from the fall. He remained silent, his hold upon his companion, however, being stern rather than compassionate.

'You hurt me a little, farmer! – though I am much obliged to you for your kindness. . . . People don't appreciate me, I say. Between ourselves, I am losing my practice here; and why? Because I see matchless attraction where matchless attraction is, both in person and position. – I mention no names, so nobody will be the wiser. . . . But I have lost her, – in a legitimate sense, that is. If I were a free man now, things have come to such a pass between us that she could not refuse me; while with her fortune (which I don't covet for itself) I should have a chance of satisfying an honourable ambition – a chance I have not had yet! . . . and now never, never shall have probably!'

Melbury, his heart throbbing against the other's backbone, and his brain on fire with indignation, ventured to mutter huskily, 'Why?'

The horse ambled on some steps before Fitzpiers replied. 'Because I am tied and bound to another by law, as tightly as I am to you by your arm – not that I complain of your arm – I thank you for helping me. Well, where are we? Not nearly home yet? . . . Home, say I. It *is* a home! When I might have been at the other house over there.' In a stupefied way he flung his hand in the direction of the park. 'I was just two months too early in committing myself. Had I only seen the other first—'

Here the old man's arm gave Fitzpiers a convulsive shake.

'What are you doing?' continued the latter. 'Keep still, please, or put me down. . . . I was saying that I lost her by a mere little two months! There is no chance for me now in this world, and it makes me reckless – reckless! Unless, indeed, anything should happen to the other one. She is amiable enough; but if anything should happen to her – and I hear she is ill at this moment – well, if it *should*, I should be free – and my fame, my happiness, would be insured!'

These were the last words that Fitzpiers uttered in his seat in front of the timber-merchant. Unable longer to master himself Melbury whipped away his spare arm from Fitzpiers's waist, and seized him by the collar.

'You heartless villain – after all that we have done for 'ee!' he cried with a quivering lip. 'And the money of hers that you've had, and the roof we've provided to shelter 'ee! – It is to me, George Melbury, that you dare to talk like that!' The exclamation was accompanied by a powerful swing from the shoulder, which flung the young man headlong into the road.

Fitzpiers fell with a heavy thud upon the stumps of some brush-wood which had been cut during the winter preceding. Darling continued her walk for a few paces further and stopped.

'God forgive me!' Melbury murmured, repenting of what he had done. 'He tried me too sorely, and now perhaps I've murdered him!'

He turned round in the saddle and looked towards the spot on which Fitzpiers had fallen. To his great surprise he beheld the surgeon rise to his feet as if scarcely hurt, and walk away rapidly under the trees.

Melbury listened till the rustle of Fitzpiers's footsteps died away. 'It might have been a crime, but for the mercy of Providence in providing leaves for his fall,' he said to himself. And then his mind reverted to the words of Fitzpiers, and his indignation so mounted within him that he almost wished the fall had put an end to the surgeon there and then.

He had not ridden far when he discerned his own grey mare standing under some bushes. Leaving Darling for a moment, Melbury went forward and easily caught the younger animal, now disheartened at its freak. He made the pair of them fast to a tree, and turning back endeavoured to find some trace of Fitzpiers, feeling pitifully that, after all, he had gone further than he intended with the offender. But though he threaded the wood hither and thither, his toes ploughing layer after layer of the little horny scrolls that had once been leaves, he could not find him. He stood still, listening and looking round. The breeze was oozing through the network of boughs as through a strainer; the trunks and larger branches stood against the light of the sky in the forms of sentinels, gigantic candelabra, pikes, halberds, lances, and whatever else the fancy chose to make of them. Giving up the search Melbury came back to the horses, and walked slowly homeward leading one in each hand.

It happened that on the selfsame evening a boy had been returning through Hintock Park to Little Hintock about the time of Fitzpiers's passage home along that route. A horse-collar that had been left at the harness-mender's to be repaired was required for use at five o'clock next morning, and in consequence the boy had to fetch it overnight. He put his head through the collar, and the way of the park being a short cut he took it, whistling the one tune he knew as an antidote to fear.

The boy suddenly became aware of a horse brushing rather frisky along the track behind him. Not knowing whether to expect friend or foe, prudence suggested that he should cease his whistling and retreat among the trees till the horse and his rider had gone by, a course to which he was still more inclined when he found how noiselessly they approached, and saw that the horse looked pale, and remembered what he had read about Death in the Revelation. He therefore deposited the collar by a tree and hid himself behind it. The horseman came on, and the youth, whose eyes were as keen as telescopes, to his great relief recognized the doctor.

As Melbury surmised, Fitzpiers had in the darkness taken Blossom for Darling, and he had not discovered his mistake when he came up opposite the boy, though he was somewhat surprised at the liveliness of his usually placid mare. The only other pair of eyes on the spot whose vision was keen as the young carter's were those of the horse; and, with that strongly conservative objection to the unusual which animals show, Blossom, on eyeing the collar under the tree — quite invisible to Fitzpiers — exercised none of the patience of the older horse, but shied sufficiently to unseat so second-rate an equestrian as the surgeon.

He fell and did not move, lying as Melbury afterwards found him. The boy ran away, salving his conscience for the desertion by thinking how vigorously he would spread the alarm of the accident when he got to Hintock — which he uncompromisingly did, incrusting the skeleton event with a load of dramatic horrors.

Grace had returned, and the fly hired on her account, though not by her husband, at the Crown Hotel, Shottsford-Forum, had been paid for and dismissed. The long drive had somewhat revived her, her illness being a feverish intermittent nervousness which had more to do with mind than body, and she walked about her sitting-room in something of a hopeful mood. Mrs Melbury had told her as soon as she arrived that her husband had returned from London. He had gone out, she said, to see a patient as she supposed, and he must soon be back, since he had had no dinner or tea. Grace would not allow her mind to harbour any suspicion of his whereabouts, and her step-mother said nothing of Mrs Charmond's rumoured sorrows and plans of departure.

So the young wife sat by the fire, waiting silently. She had left Hintock in a turmoil of aversion from her husband, after the revelation of Mrs Charmond, and had intended not to be at home when he returned. But she had thought the matter over, and had allowed her father's influence to prevail and bring her back; and now somewhat regretted that Edred's arrival had preceded hers.

By and by Mrs Melbury came upstairs with a slight air of flurry and abruptness.

'I have something to tell – some bad news,' she said. 'But you must not be alarmed, as it is not so bad as it might have been. Edred has been thrown off his horse. We don't think he is hurt much. It happened in the wood the other side of Marshcombe Bottom.'

She went on to give a few of the particulars, but none of the invented horrors that had been communicated by the boy. 'I thought it better to tell you at once,' she added, 'in case he should not – be very well able to walk home, and somebody should bring him.'

Mrs Melbury really thought matters much worse than she represented, and Grace knew that she thought so. She sat down dazed for a few minutes, returning a negative to her stepmother's inquiry if she could do anything for her.

'Ah – yes – please go into the bedroom,' Grace said on second thoughts, 'and see if all is ready there – in case it is serious.' Mrs Melbury thereupon called Grammer, and they did as directed, supplying the room with everything they could think of for the accommodation of an injured man.

Nobody was left in the lower part of the house. Not many minutes had passed when Grace heard a knock at the door – a single knock, not loud enough to reach the ears of those in the bedroom.

She went to the top of the stairs and said faintly, 'Come up,' knowing that the door stood, as usual in such houses, wide open. Retreating into the gloom of the broad landing she saw rise up the stairs a woman whom at first she did not recognize, till her voice revealed her to be Suke Damson in great fright and sorrow. A streak of light from the partially closed door of Grace's room fell upon her face as she came forward, and it was drawn and pale.

'O, Miss Melbury – I would say Mrs Fitzpiers,' she said, wringing her hands. 'This terrible news – is he dead? Is he hurted very bad? Tell me; I couldn't help coming – please forgive me, Miss Melbury – Mrs Fitzpiers, I would say!'

Grace sank down on the oak chest which stood on the landing, and put her hands to her now flushed face and head. Ought she not to order Suke Damson downstairs and out of the house? Her husband might be brought in at any moment, and what would happen? But could she order this genuinely grieved woman away?

There was a dead silence of half a minute or so, till Suke said, 'Why don't ye speak? Is he here? Is he dead? If so, why can't I see him – would it be so very wrong?'

Before Grace had answered somebody else came to the door below – a footfall light as a roe's. There was a hurried tapping upon the panel, as if with the impatient tips of fingers whose owner thought not whether a knocker were there or no. Without a pause, and possibly guided by the stray beam of light on the landing, the new-comer ascended the staircase as the first had done. Grace started; it was a lady. Grace was sufficiently visible, and the lady came to her side.

'I could make nobody hear downstairs,' said Felice Charmond with lips whose dryness could almost be heard, and panting as she stood ready to sink on the floor with distress. 'What is – the matter – tell me the worst! Can he live?'

She looked at Grace imploringly, without perceiving poor Suke who, dismayed at such a presence, had shrunk away into the shade. Mrs Charmond's little feet were covered with mud: she was quite unconscious of her appearance now.

'I have heard such a dreadful report,' she went on: 'I came to ascertain the truth of it. Is he – killed?'

'She won't tell us – he's dying – he's in that room!' burst out Suke, regardless of consequences, as she heard the distant movements of Mrs Melbury and Grammer in the bedroom at the end of the passage.

'Where?' said Mrs Charmond; and on Suke pointing out the direction she made as if to go thither.

Grace barred the way.

'He is not there,' she said. 'I have not seen him any more than you. I have heard a report only – not so bad as you think. It must have been exaggerated to you.'

'Please do not conceal anything – let me know all!' said Felice doubtingly.

'You shall know all I know. Indeed, you have a perfect right to go into his bedroom; who can have a better than either of you?' said Grace with a delicate sting which was lost upon them now as, ceasing to obstruct the way, she led on to the chamber door, and flung it open. 'Wives all, let's enter together! . . . I repeat, I have only heard a less alarming account than you have heard; how much it means, and how little, I cannot say. I pray God that it means not much – in common humanity. You probably pray the same – *for other reasons*.'

Then she regarded them there in the dim light awhile, as, gathering with her round the empty bed of Fitzpiers, they stood dumb in their trouble, staring at it, and at his night-shirt lying on the pillow; not stinging back at her, not heeding her mood. A tenderness spread over Grace like a dew. It was well enough, conventionally, to address either one of them in the wife's regulation terms of virtuous sarcasm, as woman, creature, or thing. But life, what was it, after all? She had, like the singer of the Psalm of Asaph, been plagued and chastened all the day long; but could she, by retributive words, in order to please herself, the individual, 'offend against the generation', as that singer would not?

'He is dying, perhaps!' blubbered Suke Damson, putting her apron to her eyes.

In their gestures and faces there were anxieties, affection, agony of heart – all for a man who had wronged them – had never really behaved towards either of them anyhow but selfishly. Neither one but would have well-nigh sacrificed half her life to him, even now. The tears which his possible critical situation could not bring to her eyes surged over at the contemplation of these fellow-women whose relations with him were as close as her own without its conventionality. She went out to the balustrade, bent herself upon it, and wept.

Thereupon Felice following began to cry also, without using her handkerchief, letting the tears run down silently. While the three stood together thus, pitying another though most to be pitied themselves, the pacing of a horse or horses became audible in the court, and in a moment Melbury's voice was heard calling to his stableman.

Grace at once started up, ran down the stairs, and out into the quadrangle as her father crossed it towards the door. 'Father, what is the matter with him?' she cried.

'Who, Edred?' said Melbury abruptly. 'Matter? Nothing. What, my dear, and have you got home safe? Why, you are better already! But you ought not to be out in the air like this.'

'But he has been thrown off his horse!'

'I know; I know. I saw it. He got up again, and walked off as well as ever. A fall on the leaves didn't hurt a spry fellow like him. He did not come this way,' he added significantly. 'I suppose he went to look for his horse. I tried to find him, but could not. But after seeing him go away under the trees I found the horse, and have led it home for safety. So he must walk. Now, don't you stay out here in this night air.'

She returned to the house with her father. When she had again ascended to the landing and to her own rooms beyond, it was a great relief to her to find that both Petticoat the First and Petticoat the Second of her *Bien-aimé* had silently disappeared. They had in all probability heard the words of her father, and departed with their anxieties relieved.

Presently her parents came up to Grace, and busied themselves to see that she was comfortable. Perceiving soon that she would prefer to be left alone they went away.

Grace waited on. The clock raised its voice now and then, but her husband did not return. At her father's usual hour for retiring he again came in to see her. 'Do not stay up,' she said as soon as he entered. 'I am not at all tired. I will sit up for him.'

'I think it will be useless, Grace,' said Melbury slowly.

'Why?'

'I have had a bitter quarrel with him. And on that account I hardly think he will return to-night.'

'A quarrel? Was that after the fall seen by the boy?'

Melbury nodded an affirmative – without taking his eyes off the candle.

'Yes; it was as we were coming home together,' he said.

Something had been swelling up in Grace while her father was speaking. 'How could you want to quarrel with him?' she cried suddenly. 'Why could you not let him come home quietly, if he were inclined to? He is my husband; and now you have married me to him surely you need not provoke him unnecessarily? First you induce me to accept him, and then you do things that divide us more than we should naturally be divided!'

'How can you speak so unjustly to me, Grace?' said Melbury, with indignant sorrow. '*I* divide you from your husband, indeed! You little think—'

He was inclined to say more – to tell her the whole story of the encounter, and that the provocation he had received had lain entirely in hearing her despised. But it would have greatly distressed her, and he forbore.

'You had better lie down. You are tired,' he said soothingly. 'Good-night.'

The household went to bed, and a silence fell upon the dwelling, broken only by the occasional skirr of a halter in Melbury's stables. Despite her father's advice Grace still waited up. But nobody came.

It was a critical time in Grace's emotional life, that night. She thought of her husband a good deal, and for the nonce forgot Winterborne.

'How these unhappy women must have admired Edred!' she said to herself. 'How attractive he must be to everybody; and indeed, he is attractive.' The possibility is that, piqued by rivalry, these ideas might have been transmuted into their corresponding emotions by a show of the least reciprocity in Fitzpiers. There was, in truth, a lovebird yearning to fly from her heart; and it wanted a lodging badly.

But no husband came. The fact was that Melbury had been much mistaken about the condition of Fitzpiers. People do not fall headlong on stumps of underwood with impunity. Had the old man been able to watch Fitzpiers narrowly enough, he would have observed that, on rising and walking into the thicket, he dropped blood as he went; that he had not proceeded fifty yards before he showed signs of being dizzy, and, raising his hands to his head, reeled and fell.

CHAPTER THIRTY-SIX

GRACE was not the only one who watched and meditated in Hintock that night. Felice Charmond was in no mood to retire to rest at a customary hour; and over her drawing-room fire at the manor-house she sat as motionless and in as deep a reverie as Grace in her little chamber at the homestead.

Having caught ear of Melbury's intelligence while she had stood on the landing at his house, and been eased of much of her mental distress, her sense of personal decorum had returned upon her with a rush. She descended the stairs and left the door like a ghost, keeping close to the walls of the building till she got round to the gate of the quadrangle, through which she noiselessly passed almost before Grace and her father had finished their discourse. Suke Damson had thought it well to imitate her superior in this respect, and, descending the back stairs as Felice descended the front, went out at the side door and home to her cottage.

Once outside Melbury's gates Mrs Charmond ran with all her speed to the manor-house without stopping or turning her head. She entered her own dwelling as she had emerged from it – by the drawing-room window. Everything was just as she had left it: she had been gone about three-quarters of an hour by the clock, and nobody seemed to have discovered her absence. Tired in body but tense in mind she sat down, palpitating, round-eyed, bewildered at what she had done.

She had been betrayed by affrighted love into a visit which, now that the emotion instigating it had calmed down under her belief that Fitzpiers was in no danger, was the saddest surprise to her. This was how she had set about doing her best to escape her passionate bondage to him! Somehow, in declaring to Grace and to herself the unseemliness of her infatuation, she had grown a convert to its irresistibility.

If Heaven would only give her strength; but Heaven never did! One thing was indispensable: she must go away from Hintock if she meant to withstand further temptation. The struggle was too wearying, too hopeless, while she remained. It was but a continual capitulation of conscience to what she dared not name.

By degrees, as she sat on and on, Felice's mind – helped perhaps by the anticlimax of supposing that her lover was unharmed after all her fright about him – grew wondrously strong in wise resolve. For the moment she was in a mood, in the words of Mrs Elizabeth Montagu, 'to run mad with discretion'; and was so persuaded that discretion lay in departure that she wished to set about going that very minute. Jumping up from her seat she began to gather together some small personal knick-knacks scattered about the room, to feel that preparations were really in train.

While moving here and there she fancied that she heard a slight noise out of doors, and stood still. Surely it was a tapping at the window. A thought entered her mind, and burnt her cheek. He had come to that window before; yet was it possible that he should dare to do so now! All the servants were in bed, and in the ordinary course of affairs she would have retired also. Then she remembered that on stepping in by the casement and closing it she had not fastened the window-shutter, so that a streak of light from the interior of the room might have revealed her vigil to an observer on the lawn. How all things conspired against her keeping faith with Grace!

The tapping recommenced, light as from the bill of a little bird: her illegitimate hope overcame her discretion: she went and pulled back the shutter, determining however to shake her head at him, and keep the casement securely closed.

What she saw outside might have struck terror into a heart stouter than a helpless woman's at midnight. In the centre of the lowest pane of the window, close to the glass, was a human face which she barely recognized as the face of Fitzpiers. It was surrounded with the darkness of the night without, corpse-like in its pallor, and covered with blood. As disclosed in the square area of the pane it met her frightened eyes like a replica of the Sudarium of St Veronica.

He moved his lips and looked at her imploringly. Her rapid mind pieced together in an instant a possible concatenation of events which might have led to this tragical issue. She unlatched the casement with a terrified hand, and bending down to where he was crouching pressed her face to his with passionate solicitude. She assisted him into the room without a word, to do which it was almost necessary to lift him bodily.

Quickly closing the window and fastening the shutters she bent over him breathlessly.

'Are you hurt much, much?' she cried faintly. 'O, O, how is this!'

'Rather much – but don't be frightened,' he answered in a difficult whisper, and turning himself to obtain an easier position if possible. 'A little water, please.'

She ran across into the dining-room, and brought a bottle and glass, from which he eagerly drank. He could then speak much better, and with her help got upon the nearest couch.

'Are you dying, Edred?' she said. 'Do speak to me!'

'I am half dead,' gasped Fitzpiers. 'But perhaps I shall get over it. . . . It is chiefly loss of blood.'

'But I thought your fall did not hurt you?' said she. 'Who did this?'

'Felice – my father-in-law! . . . I have crawled to you more than a mile on my hands and knees – God, I thought I should never have got here! . . . I have come to you – because you are the only friend – I have in the world now. . . . I can never go back to Hintock – never – the roof of the Melburys! Not poppy nor mandragora will ever medicine this bitter feud. . . . If I were only well again—'

'Let me bind your head, now that you have rested.'

'Yes – but wait a moment – it stopped bleeding, fortunately, or I should be a dead man before now! While in the wood I managed to make a tourniquet of some halfpence and my handkerchief, as well as I could in the dark. . . . But listen, dear Felice! Can you hide me till I am well? Whatever comes, I can be seen in Hintock no more. My practice is nearly gone, you know – and after this I would not care to recover it if I could.'

By this time Felice's tears began to blind her. Where were now her discreet plans for sundering their lives for ever? To administer to him in his pain, and trouble, and poverty, was her single thought. The first step was to hide him, and she asked herself where. A place occurred to her mind.

She got him some wine from the dining-room, which strengthened him much. Then she managed to remove his boots, and, as he could now keep himself upright by leaning upon her on one side and a walking-stick on the other, they went thus in slow march out of the room and up the stairs. At the top she took him along a gallery, pausing whenever he required rest, and thence up a smaller staircase to the least used part of the house, where she unlocked a door. Within was a lumber-room, containing abandoned furniture of all descriptions, built up in piles which obscured the light of the windows, and formed between them nooks and lairs in which a person would not be discerned even should an eye gaze in at the door. The articles were mainly those that had belonged to the previous owner of the house, and had been bought in by the late Mr Charmond at the auction; but changing fashion, and the tastes of a young wife, had caused them to be relegated to this dungeon.

Here Fitzpiers sat on the floor against the wall till she had hauled out materials for a bed, which she spread on the floor in one of the aforesaid nooks. She obtained water and a basin, and washed the dried blood from his face and hands; and when he was comfortably reclining fetched food from the larder. While he ate her eyes lingered anxiously on his face, following its every movement with such lovingkindness as only a fond woman can show.

He was now in better condition, and discussed his position with her.

'What I fancy I said to Melbury must have been enough to enrage any man, if uttered in cold blood, and with knowledge of his presence. But I did not know him, and I was stupefied by what he had given me, so that I hardly was aware of what I said. Well – the veil of that temple is rent in twain! . . . As I am not going to be seen again in Hintock, my first efforts must be directed to allay any alarm that may be felt at my absence, before I am able to get clear away. Nobody must suspect that I have been hurt, or there will be a country talk about me. Felice, I must at once concoct a letter to check all search for me. I think if you can bring me a pen and paper I may be able to do it now. I could rest better if it were done. Poor thing! how I tire her with running up and down!'

She fetched writing materials and held up the blotting-book as a support to his hand, while he penned a brief note to his nominal wife.

'The animosity shown towards me by your father,' he wrote in this coldest of marital epistles, 'is such that I cannot return again to a roof which is his, even though it shelters you. A parting is unavoidable, as you are sure to be on his side in this division. I am starting on a journey which will take me a long way from Hintock, and you must not expect to see me there again for some time.'

He then gave Grace a few directions bearing upon his professional engagements and other practical matters, concluding without a hint of his destination, or a notion of when she would see him again. He offered to read the note to Felice before he closed it up; but she would not hear or see it: that side of his obligations distressed her beyond endurance. She turned away from Fitzpiers and sobbed bitterly.

'If you can get this posted at a place some miles away,' he whispered, exhausted by the effort of writing, 'at Sherton Abbas, or Port-Bredy, or still better, Budmouth, it will divert all suspicion from this house as the place of my refuge.'

'I will drive to one or other of the places myself—anything to keep it unknown!' she murmured, her voice weighted with vague foreboding now that the excitement of helping him had passed away.

Fitzpiers told her that there was yet one thing more to be done. 'In creeping over the fence on to the lawn,' he said, 'I made the rail bloody, and it shows rather too plainly on the white paint — I could see it in the dark. At all hazards it should be washed off. Could you do that also, Felice?'

What will not women do on such devoted occasions? Weary as she was she went —all the way down the rambling staircases to the ground floor, then to search for a lantern, which she lighted and hid under her cloak; then for a wet sponge, and next forth into the night. The white railing stared out in the darkness at her approach, and a ray from the enshrouded lantern fell upon the blood — just where he had told her it would be found. She shuddered. It was almost too much to bear in one day; but with a shaking hand she sponged the rail clean, and returned to the house.

The time occupied by these several proceedings was not much less than two hours. When all was done, and she had smoothed his extemporized bed, and kissed him, and placed everything within his reach that she could think of, she took her leave of him and locked him in.

CHAPTER THIRTY-SEVEN

W HEN her husband's letter reached Grace's hands, bearing upon it the postmark of a distant town, it never once crossed her mind that Fitzpiers was lying wounded within a mile or two of her still. She felt relieved that he did not write more bitterly of the quarrel with her father, whatever its nature might have been; but the general frigidity of his communication quenched in her the incipient spark that events had kindled so shortly before.

From this centre of information it was made known in Hintock that the doctor had gone away, and as none but the Melbury household was aware that he did not return on the night of his accident, no excitement manifested itself in the village.

Thus the early days of May passed by. None but the nocturnal birds and animals observed that late one evening, towards the middle of the month, a closely wrapped figure, with a crutch under one arm and a stick in his hand, crept out from Hintock House across the lawn to the shelter of the trees, taking thence a slow and laborious walk to the nearest point of the turnpike road.

The mysterious personage was so disguised that his own wife would hardly have known him. Felice Charmond was a practised hand at such work, as well she might be; and she had done her utmost in padding and painting Fitzpiers with the old materials of her art in recesses of that lumber-room.

In the highway he was met by a covered carriage which conveyed him to Sherton Abbas, whence he proceeded to the nearest port on the south coast, and immediately crossed the Channel.

But it was known to everybody that three days after this time Mrs Charmond executed her oft-deferred plan of setting out for a long term of travel and residence on the Continent. She went off one morning as unostentatiously as could be, and took no maid with her, having, she said, engaged one to meet her at a point further on in her route. After that, Hintock House, so frequently deserted, was to be let. Spring had not merged in summer when a clinching rumour, founded on the best of evidence, reached the parish and neighbourhood. Mrs Charmond and Fitzpiers had been seen together in Baden in relations which set at rest the question that had agitated the little community ever since the winter.

Melbury had entered the Valley of Humiliation even further than Grace. His spirit seemed broken.

But once a week he mechanically went to market as usual, and here, as he was passing by the conduit one day, his mental condition expressed largely by his gait, he heard his name spoken by a voice formerly familiar. He turned and saw a certain Fred Beaucock — once a promising lawyer's clerk and local dandy, who had been called the cleverest fellow in Sherton, without whose brains the firm of solicitors employing him would be nowhere. But later on Beaucock had fallen into the mire. He was invited out a good deal, sang songs at agricultural meetings and burgesses' dinners: in sum, victualled himself with spirits more frequently than was good for the clever brains or body either. He lost his post, and after an absence spent in trying his powers elsewhere came back to his native town, where, at the time of the foregoing events in Hintock, he gave legal advice for astonishingly small fees — mostly carrying on his profession in public-house settles, in whose recesses he might often have been overheard making country-people's wills for half-a-crown, calling with a learned voice for pen and ink and a halfpenny sheet of paper, on which he drew up the testament while resting it in a little space wiped with his hand on the table amid the liquid circles formed by the cups and glasses. An idea implanted early in life is difficult to uproot, and many elderly tradespeople still clung to the notion that Fred Beaucock knew a great deal of law.

It was he who had called Melbury by name.

'You look very down, Mr Melbury — very, if I may say as much,' he observed, when the timber-merchant turned. 'But I know — I know. A very sad case — very.

I was bred to the law, as you are aware, and am professionally no stranger to such matters. Well, Mrs Fitzpiers has her remedy.'

'How – what – a remedy?' said Melbury.

'Under the new law, sir. A new court was established last year, and under the new statute, twenty and twenty-one Vic., cap. eighty-five unmarrying is as easy as marrying. No more Acts of Parliament necessary: no longer one law for the rich and another for the poor. But come inside – I was just going to have a nipperkin of rum-hot – I'll explain it all to you.'

The intelligence amazed Melbury, who saw little of newspapers. And though he was a severely correct man in his habits, and had no taste for entering a tavern with Fred Beaucock – nay, would have been quite uninfluenced by such a character on any other matter in the world – such fascination lay in the idea of delivering his poor girl from bondage that it deprived him of the critical faculty. He could not resist the ex-lawyer's clerk, and entered the inn.

Here they sat down to the rum, which Melbury paid for as a matter of course, Beaucock leaning back on the settle with a legal gravity, that would hardly allow him to be conscious of the spirits before him; which nevertheless disappeared with mysterious quickness.

How much of the exaggerated information on the then new divorce laws imparted by Beaucock to his listener was the result of ignorance, and how much of dupery, was never ascertained. But he related such a plausible story of the ease with which Grace could become a free woman that her father was irradiated with the project; and though he scarcely wetted his lips Melbury never knew how he came out of the inn, or when or where he mounted his gig to pursue his way homeward.

But home he found himself, his brain having all the way seemed to ring sonorously as a gong in the intensity of its stir. Before he had seen Grace he was accidentally met by Winterborne, who found him as Stephen was beheld by the Council, with a face like the face of an angel.

He relinquished his horse and took Winterborne by the arm to a heap of rendlewood – as barked oak was here called – which lay under a privet hedge.

'Giles,' he said, when they had sat down upon the logs, 'there's a new law in the land! Grace can be free quite easily. I only knew it by the merest accident. I might not have found it out for the next ten years. She can get rid of him – d'ye hear – get rid of him. Think of that, my friend Giles!'

He related what he had learnt of the new legal remedy. A subdued tremulousness about the mouth was all the response that Winterborne made; and Melbury added, 'My boy, you shall have her yet – if you want her.' His feelings had gathered volume as he said this, and the articulate sound of the old idea drowned his sight in mist.

'Are you sure – about this new law?' asked Winterborne, so disquieted by a gigantic exultation which loomed alternately with fearful doubt that he evaded the full acceptance of Melbury's last statement.

Melbury said that he had no manner of doubt, for since his talk with Beaucock it had come into his mind that he had seen some time ago in the weekly paper an allusion to such a legal change; but, having no interest in those desperate remedies at the moment, he had passed it over.

'But I'm not going to let the matter rest doubtful for a single day,' he continued. 'I am going to London. Beaucock will go with me, and we shall get the best advice as soon as we possibly can. Beaucock is a thorough lawyer – nothing the matter with him but a fiery palate. I knew him as the stay and refuge of Sherton in knots of law at one time.'

Winterborne's replies were of the vaguest. The new possibility was almost unthinkable at the moment. He was what was called at Hintock 'a solid-going fellow'; he maintained his abeyant mood not from want of reciprocity, but from a taciturn hesitancy taught by life as he knew it.

'But,' continued the timber-merchant, a temporary crease or two of anxiety supplementing those already established in his forehead by time, 'Grace is not at all well. Nothing constitutional, you know; but she has been in a low nervous state ever since that night of fright. I don't doubt but that she will be all right soon. . . . I wonder how she is this evening?' He rose with the words as if he had too long forgotten her personality in the excitement of her previsioned career.

They had sat till evening was beginning to dye the garden brown, and now went towards Melbury's house, Giles a few steps in the rear of his old friend, who was stimulated by the enthusiasm of the moment to outstep the more ordinary pace of Winterborne. He felt shy of entering Grace's presence as her reconstituted lover – which was how her father's manner would be sure to present him – before definite information as to her future state was forthcoming: it seemed too nearly like the act of those who rush in where angels fear to tread.

A chill to counterbalance all the glowing promise of the day was prompt enough in coming. No sooner had he followed the timber-merchant in at the door than he heard Grammer inform him that Mrs Fitzpiers was still more unwell than she had been in the morning. Old Dr Jones being in the neighbourhood they had called him in, and he had instantly directed them to get her to bed. They were not, however, to consider her illness serious – a feverish, nervous attack, the result of recent events, was what she was suffering from – and she would doubtless be well in a few days.

Winterborne therefore did not remain, and his hope of seeing her that evening was disappointed.

Even this aggravation of her morning condition did not greatly depress Melbury. He knew, he said, that his daughter's constitution was sound enough. It was only these domestic troubles that were pulling her down. Once free she would be blooming again. Melbury diagnosed rightly, as parents usually do.

He set out for London the next morning, Jones having paid another visit and assured him that he might leave home without uneasiness, especially on an errand of that sort, which would the sooner put an end to her suspense.

The timber-merchant had been away only a day or two when it was told in Hintock that Mr Fitzpiers's hat had been found in the wood. Later on in the afternoon the hat was brought to Melbury's, and, by a piece of ill-fortune, into Grace's presence. It had doubtless lain in the wood ever since his fall from the horse; but it looked so clean and uninjured – the summer weather and leafy shelter having much favoured its preservation – that Grace could not believe it had remained so long concealed. A very little fact was enough to set her fevered fancy at work at this juncture – she thought him still in the neighbourhood, she feared his sudden appearance; and her nervous malady developed consequences so grave that Dr Jones began to look serious, and the household was alarmed.

It was the beginning of June, and the cuckoo at this time of the summer scarcely ceased his cry for more than a couple of hours during the night. The bird's note, so familiar to her ears from infancy, was now absolute torture to the poor girl. On the Friday following the Wednesday of Melbury's departure, and the day after the discovery of Fitzpiers's hat, the cuckoo began at two o'clock in the morning with a sudden cry from one of Melbury's apple-trees, not three yards from the window of Grace's room.

'O – he is coming!' she cried, and in her terror sprang clean out of the bed upon the floor.

These starts and frights continued till noon; and when the doctor had arrived and had seen her, and had talked with Mrs Melbury, he sat down and meditated. That ever-present terror it was indispensable to remove from her mind at all hazards; and he thought how this might be done.

Without saying a word to anybody in the house, or to the disquieted Winterborne waiting in the lane below, Dr Jones went home and wrote to Mr Melbury at the address in London he had obtained from his wife. The gist of his communication was that Mrs Fitzpiers should be assured as soon as possible that steps were taken to sever the bond which was becoming a torture to her; that she would soon be free; and was even then virtually so. 'If you can say it *at once* it may be the means of averting much harm,' he said. 'Write to herself; not to me.'

On Saturday he drove over to Hintock, and assured her with mysterious pacifications that in a day or two she might expect to receive some good news.

So it turned out. When Sunday morning came there was a letter for Grace from her father. It arrived at seven o'clock, the usual time at which the toddling postman passed by Hintock; at eight Grace awoke, having slept an hour or two for a wonder, and Mrs Melbury brought up the letter.

'Can you open it yourself?' said she.

'O yes, yes!' said Grace with feeble impatience. She tore the envelope, unfolded the sheet, and read; when a creeping blush tinctured her white neck and cheek.

Her father had exercised a bold discretion. He informed her that she need have no further concern about Fitzpiers's return; that she would shortly be a free woman; and therefore if she should desire to wed her old lover – which he trusted was the case, since it was his own deep wish – she would be in a position to do so. In this Melbury had not written beyond his belief. But he very much stretched the facts in adding that the legal formalities for dissolving her union were practically settled.

The truth was that on the arrival of the doctor's letter poor Melbury had been much agitated, and could with difficulty be prevented by Beaucock from returning to her bedside. What was the use of his rushing back to Hintock? Beaucock had asked him. The only thing that could do her any good was a breaking of the bond. Though he had not as yet had an interview with the eminent solicitor they were about to consult, he was on the point of seeing him; and the case was clear enough. Thus the simple Melbury, urged by his parental alarm at her danger, by the representations of his companion, and by the doctor's letter, had yielded, and sat down to tell her roundly that she was virtually free.

'And you'd better write also to the gentleman,' suggested Beaucock, who, scenting fame and the germ of a large practice in the case, wished to commit Melbury to it irretrievably: to effect which he knew that nothing would be so potent as awakening the passion of Grace for Winterborne, so that her father might not have the heart to withdraw from his attempt to make her love legitimate when he discovered that there were difficulties in the way.

The nervous, impatient Melbury was much pleased with the idea of 'starting them at once', as he called it. To put his long-delayed reparative scheme in train had become a passion with him now. He added to the letter addressed to his daughter a passage hinting that she ought to begin to encourage Winterborne, lest she should lose him altogether; and he wrote to Giles that the path was virtually open for him at last. Life was short, he declared; he, her father, was getting old; there were slips betwixt the cup and the lip; her interest in him should be reawakened at once, that all might be ready when the good time came for uniting them.

CHAPTER THIRTY-EIGHT

At these warm words Winterborne was much moved. The novelty of the avowal rendered what it carried with it inapprehensible by him all at once. Only a few short months ago completely estranged from this family – beholding Grace going to and fro in the distance, clothed with the alienating radiance of obvious superiority, the wife of the then popular and fashionable Fitzpiers, hopelessly outside his social boundary down to so recent a time that flowers then folded were hardly faded yet – he was now asked by that jealously-guarding father of hers to take courage; to get himself ready for the day when he should be able to claim her.

The old times came back to him in dim procession. How he had been snubbed; how Melbury had despised his Christmas party: how that sweet, coy Grace herself had looked down upon him and his household arrangements, and poor Creedle's contrivances!

Well, he could not believe it. Surely the adamantine barrier of marriage with another could not be pierced like this! It did violence to custom. Yet a new law might do anything. But was it at all within the bounds of probability that a woman who, over and above her own attainments, had been accustomed to those of a cultivated professional man, could ever be the wife of such as he? – that the ceorl Giles Winterborne would be able to make such a dainty girl happy now that she stood in a position further removed from his own than at first? He was full of doubt.

Nevertheless, it was not in him to show backwardness. To act so promptly as Melbury desired him to act seemed, indeed, scarcely wise, because of the uncertainty of events. Giles knew nothing of legal procedure; but he did know that for him to step up to Grace as a lover before the bond which bound her was actually dissolved was simply an extravagant dream of her father's overstrained mind. He pitied Melbury for his almost childish enthusiasm and saw that the ageing man must have suffered acutely to be weakened to this unreasoning desire.

Winterborne was far too magnanimous to harbour any cynical conjecture that the timber-merchant, in his intense affection for Grace, was courting him now because that young lady, when disunited, would be left in an anomalous position, to escape which a bad husband was better than none. He felt quite sure that his old friend was simply on tenterhooks of anxiety to repair the almost irreparable error of dividing two whom nature had striven to join together in earlier days, and that in his ardour to do this he was oblivious of formalities. The cautious supervision of his past years had overleapt itself at last. Hence Winterborne perceived that, in this new beginning, the necessary care not to compromise Grace by too early advances must be exercised by himself.

There is no such thing as a stationary love: men are either loving more or loving less; but Giles recognized no decline in his sense of her dearness. He had been labouring ever since his rejection and her marriage to reduce his former passion to a docile friendship, out of pure regard to its expediency; but hitherto he had experienced no great success in his attempt.

A week and more passed and there was no further news of Melbury. But the effect of the intelligence he had already transmitted upon the elastic-nerved daughter of the woods had been much as the old surgeon Jones had surmised. It had soothed her perturbed spirit better than all the opiates in the pharmacopœia. She had slept unbrokenly a whole night and a day. The 'new law' was to her a mysterious, beneficent, god-like entity, lately descended upon earth, that would make her as she once had been without trouble or annoyance. Her position fretted her, its abstract features rousing an aversion which was greater than her aversion to the personality of him who had caused it. It was mortifying, productive of slights, undignified. Him she could forget: her circumstances she had always with her.

She saw nothing of Winterborne during the days of her recovery; and perhaps on that account her fancy wove about him a more romantic tissue than it could have done if he had stood before her with all the specks and flaws inseparable from concrete humanity. He rose upon her memory as the fruit-god and the wood-god in alternation: sometimes leafy and smeared with green lichen, as she had seen him amongst the sappy boughs of the plantations: sometimes cider-stained and starred with apple-pips, as she had met him on his return from cider-making in Blackmoor Vale, with his vats and presses beside him. In her secret heart she approximated to her father's enthusiasm in wishing to show Giles once for all how she still regarded him.

The question whether the future would indeed bring them together for life was a standing wonder with her. She knew that it could not with any propriety do so just yet. But reverently believing in her father's sound judgement and knowledge, as good girls are wont to do, she remembered what he had written about her giving a hint to Winterborne lest there should be risk in delay, and her feelings were not averse to such a step, so far as it could be done without danger at this early stage of the proceedings.

From being but a frail phantom of her former self she returned in bounds to a condition of passable hopefulness. She bloomed again in the face in the course of a few days, and was well enough to go about as usual.

One day Mrs Melbury proposed that for change she should be driven in the gig to Sherton market, whither Melbury's man was going on other errands. Grace had no business whatever in Sherton; but it crossed her mind that Winterborne would probably be there, and this made the thought of such a drive interesting.

On the way she saw nothing of him; but when the horse was walking slowly through the obstructions of Sheep Street she discerned the young man on the pavement. She thought of that time when he had been standing under his apple-tree on her return from school, and of the tender opportunity then missed through her fastidiousness. Her heart rose in her throat. She abjured all fastidiouness now. Nor did she forget the last occasion on which she had beheld him in that town, making cider in the courtyard of the Earl of Wessex Hotel, while she was figuring as a fine lady in the balcony above.

Grace directed the man to set her down there in the midst, and immediately went up to her lover. Giles had not before observed her, and his eyes now suppressedly looked his pleasure, without, perhaps, quite so much embarrassment as had formerly marked him at such meetings.

When a few words had been spoken she said invitingly, 'I have nothing to do. Perhaps you are deeply engaged?'

'I? Not a bit. My business now at the best of times is small, I am sorry to say.'

'Well, then – I am going into the Abbey. Come along with me.'

The proposition had suggested itself as a quick escape from publicity, for many eyes were regarding her. She had hoped that sufficient time had elapsed for the extinction of curiosity; but it was quite otherwise. The people looked at her with tender interest as the deserted girl-wife – without obtrusiveness, and without vulgarity; but she was ill prepared for scrutiny in any shape.

They walked about the Abbey aisles, and presently sat down. Not a soul was in the building save themselves. She regarded a high marble tomb to the last representative of an extinct Earldom, without a thought that it was the family with which Fitzpiers was maternally connected; and with her head sideways tentatively asked her companion if he remembered the last time they were in that town alone.

He remembered it perfectly, and remarked, 'You were a proud damsel then, and as dainty as you were high. Perhaps you are now?'

Grace slowly shook her head. 'Affliction has taken all that out of me,' she answered impressively. 'Perhaps I am too far the other way now.' As there was something lurking in this that she could not explain, she added so quickly as not to allow him time to think of it, 'Has my father written to you at all?'

'Yes,' said Winterborne.

She glanced ponderingly up at him. 'Not about me?'

'Yes.'

She saw that he had been bidden to take the hint as to the future which she had been bidden to give, and the discovery sent a scarlet pulsation through her for the moment. However it was only Giles who sat there, of whom she had no fear; and her self-possession returned.

'He said I was to sound you with a view to – what you will understand, if you care to,' continued Winterborne in a low voice. Having been put on this track by herself he was not disposed to abandon it in a hurry.

They had been children together, and there was between them that familiarity as to personal affairs which only such acquaintanceship can give. 'You know, Giles,' she answered, speaking in a very practical tone, 'that that is all very well;

but I am in a very anomalous position at present, and I cannot say anything to the point about such things as those.'

'No?' he said, with a stray air as regarded the subject. He was looking at her with a curious consciousness of discovery.

He had not been imagining that their renewed intercourse would show her to him thus. For the first time he realized an unexpectedness in her, which after all should not have been unexpected. She before him was not the girl Grace Melbury, whom he had used to know. Of course, he might easily have prefigured as much; but it had never occurred to him. She was a woman who had been married; she had moved on; and without having lost her girlish modesty she had lost her girlish shyness. The inevitable change, though known to him, had not been heeded; and it struck him into a momentary fixity. The truth was that he had never come into close comradeship with her since her engagement to Fitzpiers, with the brief exception of the evening encounter under High-Stoy Hill, when she met him with his cider apparatus; and that interview had been of too cursory a kind for insight.

Winterborne had advanced, too. Shy though he was he could criticize her somewhat. Times had been when to criticize a single trait in Grace Melbury would have lain as far beyond his powers as to criticize a deity. And this thing was sure as the result of his criticism: it was a new woman in many ways whom he had come out to see: a creature of more ideas, more dignity, and, above all, more assurance, than the original Grace had been capable of. He could not at first decide whether he were pleased or displeased at this. But upon the whole the novelty attracted him.

She was so sweet and sensitive that she feared his silence betokened something in his brain of the nature of an enemy to her.

'What are you thinking of that makes those lines come in your forehead?' she asked. 'I did not mean to offend you by speaking of the time being premature.'

Touched by the genuine lovingkindness which had lain at the foundation of these words, and much moved, Winterborne turned his face aside as he took her by the hand. He was grieved that he had criticized her.

'You are very good, dear Grace,' he said in a low voice. 'You are better, much better, than you used to be.'

'How?'

He could not very well tell her how, and said with an evasive smile, 'You are prettier'; which was not what he really had meant. He then remained still holding her right hand in his own right, so that they faced in opposite ways; and, as he did not let go she ventured upon a tender remonstrance.

'I think we have gone as far as we ought to go at present – and far enough to satisfy my poor father that we are the same as ever. You see, Giles, my case is not settled yet, and if – O, suppose I *never* get free! – there should be any hitch or informality!'

She drew a catching breath and turned pale. The duologue had been affectionate comedy up to this point. The gloomy atmosphere of the past, and the still gloomy horizon of the present, had been for the interval forgotten. Now the whole environment came back; the due balance of shade among the light was restored.

'It is sure to be all right, I trust,' she resumed in uneasy accents. 'What did my father say the solicitor had told him?'

'O – that all is sure enough. The case is so clear – nothing can be clearer. But the legal part is not yet quite done and finished, as is natural.'

'O no, – of course not,' she said, sunk in meek thought. 'But father said it was *almost* – did he not? Do you know anything about the new law that makes these things so easy?'

'Nothing – except the general fact that it enables ill-assorted husbands and wives to part in a way they could not formerly do without an Act of Parliament.'

'Have you to sign a paper, or swear anything? Is it something like that?'

'Yes, I believe so.'

'How long has it been introduced?'

'About six months or a year, the lawyer said, I think.'

To hear these two Arcadian innocents talk of imperial law would have made a humane person weep who should have known what a dangerous structure they were building up on their supposed knowledge. They remained in thought, like children in the presence of the incomprehensible.

'Giles,' she said at last, 'it makes me quite weary when I think how serious my situation is, or has been. Shall we not go out from here now, as it may seem rather fast of me – our being so long together, I mean – if anybody were to see us? I am almost sure,' she added uncertainly, 'that I ought not to let you hold my hand yet, knowing that the documents – or whatever it may be – have not been signed; so that I am still as married as ever – or almost. My dear father has forgotten himself. Not that I feel morally bound to any one else after what has taken place – no woman of spirit could – now, too, that several months have passed. But I wish to keep the proprieties as well as I can.'

'Yes, yes. Still, your father reminds us that life is short. I myself feel that it is; that is why I wished to understand you in this that we have begun. At times, dear Grace, since receiving your father's letter, I am as uneasy and fearful as a child at what he said. If one of us were to die before the formal signing and sealing that is to release you have been done – if we should drop out of the world and never have made the most of this little, short, but real opportunity, I should think to myself as I sank down dying, "Would to my God that I had spoken out my whole heart – given her one poor little kiss when I had the chance to give it! But I never did, although she had promised to be mine some day; and now I never can." That's what I should think.'

She had begun by watching the words from his lips with a mournful regard, as though their passage were visible; but as he went on she dropped her glance.

'Yes,' she said, 'I have thought that, too. And, because I have thought it, I by no means meant, in speaking of the proprieties, to be reserved and cold to you who loved me so long ago, or to hurt your heart as I used to at that thoughtless time. O, not at all, indeed! But – ought I to allow you – O, it is too quick – sure!' Her eyes filled with tears of bewildered, alarmed emotion.

Winterborne was too straightforward to influence her further against her better judgment. 'Yes – I suppose it is,' he said repentantly. 'I'll wait till all is settled. What has your father said in his letters to you?'

He meant about his progress with the petition; but she, mistaking him, frankly spoke of the personal part. 'He says – what I have implied. Should I tell more plainly?'

'O no – don't, if it is a secret.'

'Not at all. I will tell every word, straight out, Giles, if you wish. He says I am to encourage you. There! But I cannot obey him further to-day. Come, let us go now.' She gently slid her hand from his and went in front of him out of the Abbey.

'I was thinking of getting some dinner,' said Winterborne, changing to the prosaic as they walked. 'And you, too, must require something. Do let me take you to a place I know.'

Grace was almost without a friend in the world outside her father's house; her life with Fitzpiers had brought her no society; had sometimes, indeed, brought her deeper solitude than any she had ever known before. Hence it was a treat to her to find herself again the object of thoughtful care. But she questioned if to go publicly to dine alone with Giles Winterborne were not a proposal due rather to his unsophistication than to his prudence. She said gently that she would much prefer his ordering her lunch at some place, and then coming to tell her it was ready, while she remained in the Abbey porch. Giles saw her secret reasoning, thought how hopelessly blind to propriety he was beside her, and went to do as she wished.

He was not absent more than ten minutes, and found Grace where he had left her.

'It will be quite ready by the time you get there,' he said, and told her the name of the inn at which the meal had been ordered, which was one that she had never heard of.

'I'll find it by inquiry,' said Grace, setting out.

'And shall I see you again?'

'O yes – come to me there. It will not be like going together. I shall want you to find my father's man and the gig for me.'

He waited on some ten minutes or a quarter of an hour, till he thought her lunch ended, and that he might fairly take advantage of her invitation to start her on her way home. He went straight to where he had sent her, an old commercial tavern, scrupulously clean, but humble and inexpensive. On his way he had an occasional misgiving as to whether the place had been elegant enough for her; and as soon as he entered it, and saw her ensconced there, he perceived that he had blundered.

Grace was seated in the only dining-room that the simple old hostelry could boast of, which was also a general parlour on market days: a long, low apartment, with a sanded floor herring-boned with a broom, a wide, red-curtained window to the street, and another to the garden. Grace had retreated to the end of the room looking out upon the latter, the front part being full of a mixed company of dairymen and butchers which had, to be just to him, dropped in since he was there.

She was in a mood of the greatest depression. On arriving and seeing what the tavern was like she had been taken by surprise; but having gone too far to retreat she had heroically entered and sat down on the well-scrubbed settle, opposite the narrow table with its knives and steel forks, tin pepper-boxes, blue salt-cellars, and posters advertising the sale of bullocks against the wall. The last time that she had taken any meal in a public place it had been with Fitzpiers at the dignified

Earl of Wessex Hotel in that town, after a two months' roaming and sojourning at the gigantic hotels of the Continent.

How could she have expected any other kind of accommodation in present circumstances than such as Giles had provided? And yet how unprepared she was for this change! The tastes that she had acquired from Fitzpiers had been imbibed so subtly that she hardly knew she possessed them till confronted by this contrast. The elegant Fitzpiers, in fact, at that very moment owed a long bill at the above-mentioned hotel for the luxurious style in which he used to put her up there whenever they drove to Sherton. But such is social sentiment that she had been quite comfortable under those debt-impending conditions, whilst she felt humiliated by her present situation, which Winterborne had paid for honestly on the nail.

He had noticed in a moment that she shrank from her position, and all his pleasure was gone. It was the same susceptibility over again which had spoiled his Christmas party long ago.

But he did not know that this recrudescence was only the casual result of Grace's apprenticeship to what she was determined to learn in spite of it – a consequence of one of those sudden surprises which confront everybody bent upon turning over a new leaf. She had finished her lunch, which he saw had been a very mincing performance; and he brought her out of the house as soon as he could.

'Now,' he said, with great sad eyes, 'you have not finished at all well, I know! Come round to the Earl of Wessex. I'll order a tea there. I did not remember that what was good enough for me was not good enough for you.'

Her face faded into an aspect of deep distress when she saw what had happened. 'O no, Giles!' she said with extreme earnestness; 'certainly not. Why do you – say that, when you know better? You *ever* will misunderstand me.'

'Indeed, that's not so, Mrs Fitzpiers. Can you deny that you felt out of place at that tavern?'

'I don't know! . . . Well, since you make me speak, I do not deny it.'

'And yet I have felt at home there these twenty years. Your husband used always to take you to the Earl of Wessex, did he not?'

'Yes,' she reluctantly admitted. How could she explain in the street of a market-town that it was her superficial and transitory taste which had been offended, and not her nature or her affection?

Fortunately, or unfortunately, at that moment they saw Melbury's man driving vacantly along the street in search of her, the hour having passed at which he had been told to take her up. Winterborne hailed him, and she was powerless then to prolong the discourse. She entered the vehicle sadly, and the horse trotted away.

CHAPTER THIRTY-NINE

ALL night did Winterborne think over that unsatisfactory ending of a pleasant time, forgetting the pleasant time itself. He feared anew that they could never be happy together, even should she be free to choose him. She was accomplished: he was unrefined. It was the original difficulty, which he was too thoughtful to recklessly ignore as some men would have done in his place.

He was one of those silent, unobtrusive beings who want little from others in the way of favour or condescension, and perhaps on that very account scrutinize those others' behaviour too closely. He was not versatile, but one in whom a hope or belief which had once had its rise, meridian, and decline, seldom again exactly recurred, as in the breasts of more sanguine mortals. He had once worshipped her, laid out his life to suit her, wooed her, and lost her. Though it was with almost the same zest it was with not quite the same hope that he had begun to tread the old tracks again, and had allowed himself to be so charmed with her that day.

Move another step towards her he would not. He would even repulse her – as a tribute to conscience. It would be sheer sin to let her prepare a pitfall for her happiness not much smaller than the first by inveigling her into a union with such as he. Her poor father was now blind to these subtleties, which he had formerly beheld as in noontide light. It was his own duty to declare them – for her dear sake.

Grace, too, had a very uncomfortable night, and her solicitous embarrassment was not lessened the next morning when another letter from her father was put into her hands. Its tenor was an intenser strain of the one that had preceded it.

After stating how extremely glad he was to hear that she was better, and able to get out of doors, he went on:

'This is a wearisome business, the solicitor we have come to see being out of town. I do not know when I shall get home. My great anxiety in this delay is still lest you should lose Giles Winterborne. I cannot rest at night for thinking that while our business is hanging fire he may become estranged, or in his shyness go away from the neighbourhood. I have set my heart upon seeing him your husband, if you ever have another. Do then, Grace, give him some temporary encouragement, even though it is over-early. For when I consider the past I do think God will forgive me and you for being a little forward. I have another reason for this, my dear. I feel myself going rapidly down hill, and late affairs have still further helped me that way. And until this thing is done I cannot rest in peace.'

He added a postscript:

'I have just heard that the solicitor is to be seen tomorrow. Possibly, therefore, I shall return in the evening after you get this.'

The paternal longing ran on all-fours with her own desire; and yet in forwarding it yesterday she had been on the brink of giving offence. While craving to be a country girl again, just as her father requested; to put off the old Eve, the fastidious miss – or rather madam – completely, her first attempt had been beaten by the unexpected vitality of that fastidiousness. Her father on returning and seeing the trifling coolness of Giles would be sure to say that the same perversity which had led her to make difficulties about marrying Fitzpiers was now prompting her to blow hot and cold with poor Winterborne.

If the latter had been the most subtle hand at touching the stops of her delicate soul instead of one who had just bound himself to let her be mute on all that appertained to his personality, he could not have acted more seductively than he did that day. He chanced to be superintending some temporary work in a field opposite her windows. She could not discover what he was doing, but she read his mood keenly and truly: she could see in his coming and going an air of determined abandonment of the whole prospect that lay in her direction.

O, how she longed to make it up with him! Her father coming in the evening – which meant, she supposed, that all formalities would be in train, her marriage virtually annulled, and she be free to be won again – how could she look him in the face if he should see them estranged thus?

It being a fair green afternoon in June she seated herself in the garden, in the rustic chair which stood under the laurel-bushes, made of peeled oak branches that came to Melbury's premises as refuse after barking-time. The mass of full-juiced leafage on the heights around her was just swayed into faint gestures by a nearly spent wind which, even in its enfeebled state, did not reach her shelter. She had expected Giles to call – to inquire how she had got home, or something or other; but he did not come. And he still tantalized her by going athwart and across that orchard opposite. She could see him as she sat.

A slight diversion was presently created by Creedle bringing him a letter. She knew from this that Creedle had just come from Sherton, and had called as usual at the post-office for anything that had arrived by the afternoon post, of which there was no delivery at Hintock. She pondered on what the letter might contain – particularly whether it were a second refresher for Winterborne from her father, like her own of the morning.

But it appeared to have no bearing upon herself whatever. Giles read its contents and almost immediately turned away to a gap in the hedge of the orchard – if that could be called a hedge which, owing to the drippings of the trees, was little more than a bank with a bush upon it here and there. He entered the plantation, and was no doubt going that way homeward to the mysterious hut he occupied on the other side of the woodland.

The sad sands were running swiftly through Time's glass; she had often felt it in these latter days; and, like Giles, she felt it doubly now after the solemn and pathetic reminder in her father's communication. Her freshness would pass, the long-suffering devotion of Giles might suddenly end – might end that very hour. Men were so strange. The thought took away from her all her former reticence and made her action bold. She started from her seat. If the little breach, quarrel, or whatever it might be called, of yesterday, was to be healed up it must be done by her on the instant. She crossed into the orchard and clambered through the gap after Giles, just as he was diminishing to a faun-like figure under the green canopy and over the brown floor.

Grace had been wrong – very far wrong – in assuming that the letter had no reference to herself because Giles had turned away into the wood after its perusal. It was, sad to say, because the missive had so much reference to herself that he had thus turned away. He feared that his grieved discomfiture might be observed.

The letter was from Beaucock, written a few hours later than Melbury's to his daughter. It announced failure.

Giles had once done that thriftless man a good turn, and now was the moment when Beaucock had chosen to remember it, in his own way. During his absence in town with Melbury the lawyer's clerk had naturally heard a great deal of the timber-merchant's family scheme of justice to Giles, and his communication was to inform Winterborne at the earliest possible moment that their attempt had failed, in order that the young man should not place himself in a false position towards Grace in the belief of its coming success. The news was, in sum, that Fitzpiers's conduct had not been sufficiently cruel to Grace to enable her to snap the bond. She was apparently doomed to be his wife till the end of the chapter.

Winterborne quite forgot his superficial differences with the poor girl under the warm rush of deep and distracting love for her which the almost tragical information engendered.

To renounce her for ever – that was then the end of it for him, after all. There was no longer any question about suitability, or room for tiffs on petty tastes. The curtain had fallen again between them. She could not be his. The cruelty of their late revived hope was now terrible. How could they all have been so simple as to suppose this thing could be done?

It was at this moment that, hearing some one coming behind him, he turned and saw her hastening on between the thickets. He perceived in an instant that she did not know the blighting news.

'Giles, why didn't you come across to me?' she asked with arch reproach. 'Didn't you see me sitting there ever so long?'

'O yes,' he said in unprepared, provisional tones, for her unexpected presence caught him without the slightest plan of behaviour in the conjuncture. His manner made her think that she had been too chiding in her speech; and a mild scarlet wave passed over her as she resolved to soften it.

'I have had another letter from my father,' she hastened to continue. 'He thinks he may come home this evening. And – in view of his hopes – it will grieve him if there is any little difference between us, Giles.'

'There is none,' he said, sadly regarding her from the face downwards as he pondered how to lay the cruel truth bare.

'Still – I fear you have not quite forgiven me about my being uncomfortable at the inn.'

'I have, I'm sure.'

'But you speak in quite an unhappy way,' she returned, coming up quite close to him with the most winning of the many pretty airs that appertained to her. 'Don't you think you will ever be happy, Giles?'

He did not reply for some instants. 'When the sun shines flat on the north front of Sherton Abbey – that's when my happiness will come to me!' said he, staring as it were into the earth.

'But – then that means that there is something more than my offending you in not liking the Sherton tavern? If it is because I – did not like to let you kiss me in the Abbey – well, you know, Giles, that it was not on account of my cold feelings, but because I did certainly, just then, think it was rather premature, in spite of my poor father. That was the true reason – the sole one. But I do not want to be hard – God knows I do not!' she said, her voice fluctuating. 'And perhaps – as I am on the verge of freedom – I am not right, after all, in thinking there is any harm in your kissing me.'

'O Heaven!' groaned Winterborne to himself. His head was turned askance as he still resolutely regarded the ground. For the last several minutes he had seen this great temptation approaching him in regular siege; and now it had come. The wrong, the social sin, of now taking advantage of the offer of her lips, had a magnitude in the eyes of one whose life had been so primitive, so ruled by household laws as Giles's, which can hardly be explained.

'Did you say anything?' she asked timidly.

'O no – only that—'

'You mean that it must *be already* settled, since my father is coming home?' she said gladly.

'Ah – yes.'

'Then why don't you do what you want to?' She was almost pouting at his hesitation.

Winterborne, though fighting valiantly against himself all this while – though he would have protected Grace's good repute as the apple of his eye, was a man; and, as Desdemona said, men are not gods. In face of the agonizing seductiveness shown by her, in her unenlightened school-girl simplicity about the laws and ordinances, he betrayed a man's weakness. Since it was so – since it had come to this, that Grace, deeming herself free to do it, was virtually asking him to demonstrate that he loved her – since he could demonstrate it only too truly – since life was short and love was strong – he gave way to the temptation, notwithstanding that he perfectly well knew her to be wedded irrevocably to Fitzpiers. Indeed, he cared for nothing past or future, simply accepting the present and what it brought, deciding once in his life to clasp in his arms her he had watched over and loved so long.

She looked up suddenly from his long embrace and passionate kiss, influenced by a sort of inspiration. 'O, I suppose,' she stammered, 'that I am really free? – that this is right? Is there *really* a new law? Father cannot have been too sanguine in saying—'

He did not answer, and a moment afterwards Grace burst into tears in spite of herself. 'O, why does not my father come home and explain!' she sobbed upon his breast, 'and let me know clearly what I am! It is too trying, this, to ask me to – and then to leave me so long in so vague a state that I do not know what to do, and perhaps do wrong!'

Winterborne felt like a very Cain, over and above his previous sorrow. How he had sinned against her in not telling her himself only knew. He lifted her up and turned aside: the feeling of his cruelty mounted higher and higher. How could he have dreamt of kissing her? He could hardly refrain from tears. Surely nothing more pitiable had ever been known than the condition of this poor young thing, now as heretofore the victim of her father's well-meant but blundering policy.

Even in the hour of Melbury's greatest assurance Winterborne had harboured a suspicion that no law, new or old, could undo Grace's marriage without her appearance in public; though he was not sufficiently sure of what might have been enacted to destroy by his own words her pleasing idea that a mere dash of the pen, on her father's testimony, was going to be sufficient. But he had never suspected the sad fact that the position was irremediable.

Poor Grace, perhaps feeling that she had indulged in too much fluster for a mere embrace, even though it had been prolonged an unconscionable time, calmed herself at finding how grave he was.

'I am glad we are friends again anyhow,' she said, smiling through her tears. 'Giles, if you had only shown half the boldness before I married that you show now, you would have carried me off for your own, first instead of second. If we do marry I hope you will never think badly of me for encouraging you a little, but my father is *so* impatient, you know, as his years and infirmities increase, that he will wish to see us a little advanced when he comes. That is my only excuse.'

To Winterborne all this was sadder than it was sweet. How could she so trust her father's conjectures! He did not know how to tell her the truth and shame himself. And yet he felt that it must be done.

To hasten the revelation, however, was beyond even him. The endearments that had been begun between them were repeated as they walked, and the afternoon was far advanced before he could actually set about opening her eyes.

'We may have been wrong,' he began almost fearfully, 'in supposing that it can all be carried out whilst we stay here at Hintock. I am not sure but that people may have to appear in a public court even under the new Act; and if there should be any difficulty and we cannot marry after all—'

Her cheeks became slowly bloodless. 'O Giles,' she said, grasping his arm, 'you have heard something! What—cannot my father conclude it there and now? Surely, he has done it? O Giles, Giles, don't deceive me! After letting you go on like this—what terrible position am I in?'

He could not tell her, try as he would. The sense of her implicit trust in his honour disabled him. 'I cannot inform you,' he murmured, his voice as husky as that of the leaves under foot. 'Your father will soon be here. Then we shall know. I will take you home.'

Inexpressibly dear as she was to him he offered her his arm with the most reserved air as he added correctly, 'I will take you at any rate into the drive.'

Thus they walked on together, Grace vibrating between happiness and misgiving. It was only a few minutes' walk to where the drive ran, and they had hardly descended into it when they heard a voice behind them cry, 'Take out that arm!'

For a moment they did not heed, and the voice repeated more loudly and hoarsely:

'Take out that arm!'

It was Melbury's. He had returned sooner than they expected, and now came up to them. Grace's hand had been withdrawn like lightning on her hearing the second command.

'I don't blame you, I don't blame you,' he said, in the weary cadence of one broken down with scourgings. 'But you two must walk together no more—I have been surprised—I have been cruelly deceived—Giles, don't say anything to me, but go away!'

He was evidently not aware that Winterborne had known the truth before he brought it; and Giles would not stay to discuss it with him then. When the younger man had gone Melbury took his daughter indoors to the room he used as his office. There he sat down and bent over the slope of the bureau, her bewildered gaze fixed upon him.

When Melbury had recovered a little he said, 'You are now as ever Fitzpiers's wife. I was deluded. He has not done you *enough* harm! You are still subject to his beck and call.'

'Then let it be, and never mind, father,' she said with dignified sorrow. 'I can bear it. It is your trouble that grieves me most!' She stooped over him and put her arm round his neck, which distressed Melbury still more.

'I don't mind at all what comes to me,' Grace continued; 'whose wife I am, or whose I am not! I do love Giles: I cannot help that; and I have gone further with him than I should have done if I had known exactly how things were. But I do not reproach you.'

'Then Giles did not tell you?' said Melbury.

'No,' said she. 'He could not have known it. His behaviour to me proved that he did not know.'

Her father said nothing more, and Grace went away to the solitude of her chamber.

Her heavy disquietude had many shapes; and for a time she put aside the dominant fact to think of her too free conduct towards Giles. His love-making had been brief as it was sweet; but would he on reflection contemn her for forwardness? How could she have been so simple as to suppose she was in a position to behave as she had done! Thus she mentally blamed her ignorance; and yet in the centre of her heart she blessed it a little for what it had momentarily brought her.

CHAPTER FORTY

LIFE among the people involved in these events seemed to be suppressed and hide-bound for a while. Grace seldom showed herself outside the house, never outside the garden; for she feared she might encounter Giles Winterborne; and that she could not bear.

This pensive intramural existence of the self-constituted nun appeared likely to continue for an indefinite time. She had learnt that there was one possibility in which her formerly imagined position might become real, and only one; that her husband's absence should continue long enough to amount to positive desertion. But she never allowed her mind to dwell much upon the thought; still less did she deliberately hope for such a result. Her regard for Winterborne had been rarefied by the shock which followed its avowal into an ethereal emotion that had little to do with living and doing.

As for Giles he was lying – or rather sitting – ill at his distant hut. A feverish indisposition which had been hanging about him for some time, the result of a chill caught the previous winter, seemed to acquire virulence with the prostration of his hopes. But not a soul knew of his languor, and he did not think the case serious enough to send for a medical man. After a few days he was better again, and crept about his home in a great-coat, attending to his simple wants as usual with his own hands.

So matters stood when the inertion of Grace's pool-like existence was disturbed as by a geyser. She received a letter from Fitzpiers.

A startling letter it was in its import, though couched in the gentlest language. In his absence Grace had grown to regard him with toleration, and her relation to him with equanimity, till she had almost forgotten how trying his presence would be. He wrote briefly and unaffectedly: he made no excuses, but informed her that he was living quite alone, and had been led to think that they ought to be together, if she would make up her mind to forgive him. He therefore purported to cross the Channel to Budmouth by the steamer on a day he named, which she found to be three days after the time of her present reading.

He said that he could not come to Hintock for obvious reasons, which her father would understand even better than herself. As the only alternative she was to be on the quay to meet the steamer when it arrived from the opposite coast, probably about half-an-hour before midnight, bringing with her any luggage she might require; join him there, and pass with him into the twin vessel, which left immediately the other entered the harbour: returning thus with him to his continental dwelling-place, which he did not name. He had no intention of showing himself on land at all.

The troubled Grace took the letter to her father, who now continued for long hours by the fireless summer chimney-corner as if he thought it were winter, the pitcher of cider standing beside him, mostly untasted, and coated with a film of dust. After reading it he looked up.

'You sha'n't go,' said he.

'I had felt I would not,' she answered. 'But I did not know what you would say.'

'If he comes and lives in England, not too near here, and in a respectable way, and wants you to come to him, I am not sure that I'll oppose him in wishing it,' muttered Melbury. 'I'd stint myself to keep you both in a genteel and seemly style. But go abroad you never shall with my consent.'

There the question rested that day. Grace was unable to reply to her husband in the absence of an address, and the morrow came, and next day, and the evening on which he had requested her to meet him. Throughout the whole of it she remained within the four walls of her room.

The sense of her harassment, carking doubt of what might be impending, hung like a cowl of blackness over the Melbury household. They spoke almost in whispers, and wondered what Fitzpiers would do next. It was the hope of everyone that, finding she did not arrive, he would return again to France; and as for Grace, she was willing to write to him on the most kindly terms if he would only keep away.

The night passed, Grace lying tense and wide awake, and her relatives in great part likewise. When they met the next morning they were pale and anxious, though neither speaking of the subject which occupied all their thoughts. The day passed as quietly as the previous ones, and she began to think that in the rank caprice of his moods he had abandoned the idea of getting her to join him as quickly as it was formed.

All on a sudden some person who had just come from Casterbridge entered the house with the news that Mr Fitzpiers was on his way home to Hintock. He had been seen hiring a carriage at the King's Arms Hotel.

Her father and Grace were both present when the intelligence was announced.

'Now,' said Melbury, 'we must make the best of what has been a very bad matter. The man is repenting: the partner of his folly, I hear, is gone away from him to Switzerland, so that chapter of his life is probably over. If he chooses to make a home for 'ee I think you should not say him nay, Grace. Certainly he cannot very well live at Hintock without a blow to his pride; but if he can bear that, and likes Hintock best, why, there's the empty wing of the house as it was before.'

'O father!' said Grace, turning white with dismay.

'Why not?' said he, a little of his former doggedness returning. He was, in truth, disposed to somewhat more leniency towards her husband just now than he had shown formerly, from a conviction that he had treated him over roughly in his anger.

'Surely it is the most respectable thing to do?' he continued. 'I don't like this state that you are in – neither married nor single. It hurts me, and it hurts you, and it will always be remembered against us in Hintock. There has never been any scandal like it in the Melbury family before.'

'He will be here in less than an hour,' murmured Grace.

The twilight of the room prevented her father seeing the despondent misery of her face. The one intolerable condition, the condition she had deprecated above all others, was that of Fitzpiers's reinstatement there. 'O, I won't, I won't see him!' she said, sinking down. She was almost hysterical.

'Try if you cannot,' he returned moodily.

'O yes, I will, I will!' she went on inconsequently: 'I'll try'; and jumping up suddenly she left the room.

In the darkness of the apartment to which she flew nothing could have been seen during the next half-hour; but from a corner a quick breathing was audible from this impressionable creature, who combined modern nerves with primitive feelings, and was doomed by such co-existence to be numbered among the distressed, and to take her scourgings to their exquisite extremity.

The window was open. On this quiet, late summer evening whatever sound arose in so secluded a district – the chirp of a bird, a call from a voice, the turning of a wheel – extended over bush and tree to unwonted distances. Very few sounds did arise. But as Grace invisibly breathed in the brown glooms of the chamber the small remote noise of light wheels came to her, accompanied by the trot of a horse on the turnpike road. There seemed to be a sudden hitch or pause in the progress of the vehicle, which was what first drew her attention to it. She knew the point whence the sound proceeded – the upper ground down which travellers came on their way hitherward from the south – the place at which she had emerged from the wood with Mrs Charmond. Grace slid along the floor and bent her head over the window-sill, listening with open lips. The carriage had stopped, and she heard a man use exclamatory words. Then another said, 'What the devil is the matter with the horse?' She recognized the voice as her husband's.

The accident, such as it had been, was soon remedied, and the carriage could be heard resuming its descent, soon to turn into the lane leading out of the highway and then into the 'drong' which led to the house where she was.

A spasm passed through Grace. A Daphnean instinct, exceptionally strong in her as a girl, had been revived by her widowed seclusion; and it was not lessened by her affronted sentiments towards the comer, and her regard for another man. She opened some little ivory tablets that lay on the dressing-table, scribbled in pencil on one of them, 'I am gone to visit one of my school-friends,' gathered a few toilet necessaries into a hand-bag, and, not three minutes after that voice had been heard, her slim form, hastily wrapped up from observation, might have been seen passing out of the back door of Melbury's house. Thence she skimmed up the garden-path, through the gap in the hedge, and into the mossy cart-track under the trees which led into the depths of the woods.

The leaves overhead were now in their latter green — so opaque, that it was darker at some of the densest spots than in winter time, scarce a crevice existing by which a ray could get down to the ground. But in open places she could see well enough. Summer was ending: in the daytime singing insects hung in every sunbeam: vegetation was heavy nightly with globes of dew; and after showers creeping damps and twilight chills came up from the hollows.

The plantations were always weird at this hour of eve — more spectral far than in the leafless season, when there were fewer masses and more minute lineality. The smooth surfaces of glossy plants came out like weak, lidless eyes: there were strange faces and figures from expiring lights that had somehow wandered into the canopied obscurity; while now and then low peeps of the sky between the trunks were like sheeted shapes, and on the tips of boughs sat faint cloven tongues.

But Grace's fear just now was not imaginative or spiritual; and she heeded these impressions but little. She went on as silently as she could, avoiding the hollows wherein leaves had accumulated, and stepping upon soundless moss and grass-tufts. She paused breathlessly once or twice, and fancied that she could hear, above the sound of her strumming pulse, the vehicle containing Fitzpiers turning in at the gate of her father's premises. She hastened on again.

The Hintock woods owned by Mrs Charmond were presently left behind, and those into which she next plunged were divided from the latter by a highway. It was with some caution that Grace now walked, though she was quite free from any of the commonplace timidities of her ordinary pilgrimages to such spots. She feared no lurking harms, but that her effort would be all in vain, and her return to the house rendered imperative.

She had walked three or four miles westward when that prescriptive comfort and relief to wanderers in woods — a distant light — broke at last upon her searching eyes. It was so very small as to be almost sinister to a stranger, but to her it was what she sought. She pushed forward, and the dim outline of a dwelling was disclosed. It was the place she sought.

The house was a square cot of one story only, sloping up on all sides to a chimney in the midst. It had formerly been the home of a charcoal-burner, in times when that fuel was still used in the county houses. Its only appurtenance was a paled inclosure, there being no garden, the shade of the trees preventing the growth of vegetables. She advanced to the window whence the rays of light proceeded, and the shutters being as yet unclosed she could survey the whole interior through the panes.

The room within was kitchen, parlour, and bed-chamber all in one: the natural sandstone floor was worn into hills and dales by long treading, so that none of the furniture stood level, and the table slanted like a desk. A fire burnt on the hearth, in front of which revolved the skinned carcase of a very small rabbit, suspended by a string from a nail. Leaning with one arm on the mantel-shelf stood Winterborne, his eyes on the roasting animal, his face so rapt that speculation could build nothing on it concerning his thoughts, more than that they were not with the scene before him. She thought his features had changed a little since she saw them last. The firelight did not enable her to perceive that they were positively haggard.

Grace's throat emitted a gasp of relief at finding the result so nearly as she had hoped. She went to the door and tapped lightly.

He seemed to be accustomed to the noises of woodpeckers, squirrels and such small creatures, for he took no notice of her tiny signal, and she knocked again. This time he came and opened the door.

When the light of the room fell upon her face he started; and, hardly knowing what he did, crossed the threshold to her, placing his hands upon her two arms, while surprise, joy, alarm, sadness, chased through him by turns. With Grace it was the same; even in this stress there was the fond fact that they had met again.

Thus they stood,

> 'Long tears upon their faces, waxen white
> With extreme sad delight,'

till he broke the silence by saying in a whisper, 'Come in.'

'No, no, Giles!' she answered hurriedly, stepping yet further back from the door. 'I am passing by – and I have called on you, I won't enter. Will you help me? I am afraid. I want to get by a round-about way to Ivell, and so to Exonbury. I have a school-fellow there – but I cannot get to Ivell alone. O, if you will only accompany me a little way! Don't condemn me, Giles, and be offended! I was obliged to come to you, because I have no other help here. Three months ago you were my lover; now you are only my friend. The law has stepped in and forbidden what we thought of. It must not be. But we can act honestly, and yet you can be my friend for one little hour! I have no other—'

She could get no further. Covering her eyes with one hand, by an effort of repression she wept silent tears without a sigh or sob. Winterborne took her other hand in both his.

'What has happened?' he said.

'He has come.'

There was a stillness as of death till Winterborne asked, 'You mean this, Grace – that I am to help you get away?'

'Yes,' said she. 'Appearance is no matter, when the reality is right. I have said to myself, I can trust you.'

Giles knew from this that she did not suspect his treachery – if it could be called such – earlier in the summer, when they met for the last time as lovers; and in the intensity of his contrition for that tender wrong he determined to deserve her faith now at least, and so wipe out that reproach from his conscience.

'I'll come at once,' he said. 'I'll light a lantern.'

He unhooked a dark lantern from a nail under the eaves, and she did not notice how his hand shook with the slight strain, or dream that in making this offer he was taxing a convalescence which could ill afford such self-sacrifice. The lantern was lit and they started.

CHAPTER FORTY-ONE

T HE first hundred yards of their course lay under motionless trees, whose upper foliage began to hiss with falling drops of rain. By the time that they emerged upon a glade it rained heavily.

'This is awkward!' said Grace, with a forced little laugh to hide her concern.

Winterborne stopped. 'Grace,' he said, preserving a strictly business manner which belied him; 'you cannot go to Ivell to-night.'

'But I must.'

'Why? It is seven or eight miles from here. It is almost an impossibility in this rain.'

'True – *why*,' she replied mournfully at the end of a silence. 'What is reputation to me?'

'Now hearken,' said Giles. 'You won't – go back to your—'

'No, no, no! Don't make me!' she cried piteously.

'Then let us turn.' They slowly retraced their steps, and again stood before his door. 'Now this house from this moment is yours, and not mine,' he said deliberately. 'I have a place near by where I can stay very well.'

Her face had dropped. 'O,' she murmured as she saw the dilemma. 'What have I done!'

There was a smell of something burning within, and he looked through the window. The young rabbit that he had been cooking to coax a weak appetite was beginning to char. 'Please go in and attend to it,' he said. 'Do what you like. Now I leave. You will find everything about the hut that is necessary.'

'But, Giles – your supper!' she exclaimed. 'An outhouse would do for me – anything – till to-morrow at daybreak!'

He signified a negative. 'I tell you to go in – you may catch agues out here in your weakly state. You can give me my supper through the window, if you feel well enough. I'll wait awhile.'

He gently urged her to pass the doorway, and was relieved when he saw her within sitting down on his bed. Without so much as crossing the threshold himself he closed the door upon her, and turned the key in the lock. Tapping at the window he signified that she should open the casement, and when she had done this he handed in the key to her.

'You are locked in,' he said; 'and your own mistress.'

Even in her trouble she could not refrain from a faint smile at his scrupulousness, as she took the door-key.

'Do you feel better?' he went on. 'If so, and you wish to give me some of your supper, please do. If not it is of no importance. I can get some elsewhere.'

The grateful sense of his kindness stirred her to action, though she only knew half what that kindness really was. At the end of some ten minutes she again came to the window, pushed it open, and said in a whisper 'Giles!' He at once emerged from the shade, and saw that she was preparing to hand him his share of the meal upon a plate.

'I don't like to treat you so hardly,' she murmured with deep regret in her words as she heard the rain pattering on the leaves. 'But – I suppose it is best to arrange like this?'

'O yes,' he said quickly.

'I feel that I could never have reached Ivell.'

'It was impossible.'

'Are you sure you have a snug place out there?' (With renewed misgiving.)

'Quite. Have you found everything you want? I am afraid it is rather rough accommodation.'

'Can I notice defects? I have long passed that stage, and you know it, Giles, or you ought to.'

His eyes contemplated her face as its responsiveness modulated through a crowd of expressions that showed only too clearly to what a pitch she was strung. If ever Winterborne's heart chafed his bosom it was at this sight of a perfectly defenceless creature conditioned by such harsh circumstances. He forgot his own agony in the satisfaction of having at least found her a shelter. He took his plate and cup from her hands, saying, 'Now I'll push the shutter to, and you will find an iron pin on the inside, which you must fix into the bolt. Do not stir in the morning till I come and call you.'

She expressed an alarmed hope that he would not go very far away.

'O no – I shall be quite within hail,' said Winterborne.

She bolted the window as directed, and he retreated. His 'snug place' without the hut proved to be a wretched little shelter of the roughest kind, formed of four hurdles thatched with brake-fern. Underneath were dry sacks, hay, and other litter of the sort, upon which he sat down; and there in the dark tried to eat his meal. But his appetite was quite gone. He pushed the plate aside, and shook up the hay and sacks, so as to form a rude couch, on which he flung himself down to sleep, for it was getting late.

But sleep he could not for many reasons, of which not the least was thought of his charge. He sat up, and looked towards the cot through the damp obscurity. With all its external features the same as usual, he could scarcely believe that it contained the dear friend – he would not use a warmer name – who had come to him so unexpectedly and, he could not help admitting, so rashly.

He had not ventured to ask her any particulars; but the position was pretty clear without them. Though social law had negatived for ever their opening paradise of the previous June, it was not without stoical pride that he accepted the present trying conjuncture. There was one man on earth in whom she believed absolutely, and he was that man. That this crisis could end in nothing but sorrow was a view for a moment effaced by his triumphant thought of her trust in him; and the purity of the affection with which he responded to that trust rendered him more than proof against any frailty that besieged him in relation to her.

The rain, which had never ceased, now drew his attention by beginning to drop through the meagre screen that covered him. He rose to attempt some remedy for his discomfort, but the trembling of his knees and the throbbing of his pulse told him that in his weakness he was unable to fence against the storm, and he lay down to bear it as best he might. He was angry with himself for his feebleness – he who had been so strong. It was imperative that she should know nothing of his present state, and to do that she must not see his face by daylight, for its thinness would inevitably betray him.

The next morning, accordingly, when it was hardly light, he rose and dragged his stiff limbs about the precincts, preparing for her everything she could require for getting breakfast within. On the bench outside the window-sill he placed water, wood, and other necessaries, writing with a piece of chalk beside them, 'It is best that I should not see you. Put my breakfast on the bench.'

At seven o'clock he tapped at her window as he had promised, retreating at once that she might not catch sight of him. But from his shelter under the boughs he could see her very well, when, in response to his signal, she opened the window and the light fell upon her face. The languid largeness of her eyes showed that her sleep had been little more than his own, and the pinkness of their lids that her waking hours had not been free from tears.

She read the writing, seemed, he thought, disappointed, but took up the materials he had provided, evidently thinking him some way off. Giles waited on, assured that a girl who, in spite of her culture, knew what country life was, would find no difficulty in the simple preparation of their food.

Within the cot it was all very much as he conjectured, though Grace had slept much longer than he. After the loneliness of the night she would have been glad to see him; but appreciating his feeling when she read the request she made no attempt to recall him. She found abundance of provisions laid in, his plan being to replenish his buttery weekly, and this being the day after the victualling-van had called from Ivell. When the meal was ready she put what he required outside, as she had done with the supper; and, notwithstanding her longing to see him, withdrew from the window promptly, and left him to himself.

It had been a leaden dawn, and the rain now steadily renewed its fall. As she heard no more of Winterborne she concluded that he had gone away to his daily work, and forgotten that he had promised to accompany her to Ivell; an erroneous conclusion, for he remained all day, by force of his condition, within fifty yards of where she was.

The morning wore on; and in her doubt when to start, and how to travel, she lingered yet; keeping the door carefully bolted lest an intruder should discover her. Locked in this place she was comparatively safe, at any rate, and doubted if she would be safe elsewhere.

The humid gloom of an ordinary wet day was doubled by the shade and drip of the leafage. Autumn, this year, was coming in with rains. Gazing in her enforced idleness from the one window of the single room, she could see various small members of the animal community that lived unmolested there – creatures of hair, fluff, and scale; the toothed kind and the billed kind; underground creatures jointed and ringed – circumambulating the hut under the impression that, Giles having gone away, nobody was there; and eyeing it inquisitively with a view to winter quarters. Watching these neighbours who knew neither law nor sin distracted her a little from her trouble; and she managed to while away some portion of the afternoon by putting Giles's home in order, and making little improvements which she deemed that he would value when she was gone.

Once or twice she fancied that she heard a faint noise amid the trees resembling a cough; but as it never came any nearer she concluded that it was a squirrel or a bird.

At last the daylight lessened and she made up a larger fire, for the evenings were chilly. As soon as it was too dark – which was comparatively early – to discern the human countenance in this place of shadows, there came to the window, to her great delight, a tapping which she knew from its method to be Giles's.

She opened the casement instantly, and put out her hand to him, though she could only just perceive his outline. He clasped her fingers, and she noticed the heat of his palm, and its shakiness.

'He has been walking fast in order to get here quickly,' she thought. How could she know that he had just crawled out from the straw of the shelter hard by: and that the heat of his hand was feverishness?

'My dear, good Giles!' she burst out impulsively.

'Anybody would have done it for you,' replied Winterborne, with as much matter-of-fact as he could summon.

'About my getting to Ivell and Exonbury?'

'I have been thinking,' responded Giles, with tender deference, 'that you had better stay where you are for the present, if you wish not to be caught. I need not tell you that the place is yours as long as you like; and perhaps in a day or two, finding you absent, he will go away. At any rate in two or three days I could do anything to assist – such as make inquiries, or go a great way towards Ivell with you; for the cider season will soon be coming on, and I want to run down that way to see how the crops are. But for a day or two I am busy here.' He was hoping that by the time mentioned he would be strong enough to engage himself actively on her behalf. 'I hope you do not feel over-much melancholy in being a prisoner?'

She declared that she did not mind it; but she sighed.

From long acquaintance they could read each other's heart-symptoms like books of large type. 'I fear you are sorry you came,' said Giles, 'and that you think I should have advised you more firmly than I did not to stay.'

'O no! dear, dear friend,' answered Grace with a heaving bosom. 'Don't think that that is what I regret. What I regret is my enforced treatment of you – dislodging you, excluding you from your own house. Why should I not speak out? You know what I feel for you – what I have felt for no other living man, what I shall never feel for a man again. But as I have vowed myself to somebody else than you, and cannot be released, I must behave as I do behave, and keep that vow. I am not bound to him by any divine law, after what he has done; but I have promised, and I will pay.'

The rest of the evening was passed in his handing her such things as she would require the next day, and casual remarks thereupon, an occupation which diverted her mind to some degree from pathetic views of her attitude towards him and of her life in general. The only infringement – if infringement it could be called – of his predetermined bearing towards her was an involuntary pressing of her hand to his lips when she put it through the casement to bid him good-night. He knew she was weeping, though he could not see her tears.

She again entreated his forgiveness for so selfishly appropriating the cottage. But it would only be for a day or two more, she thought, since go she must.

He yearningly replied: 'I – I don't like you to go away!'

'O Giles,' said she, 'I know – I know! But – I am a woman, and you are a man. I cannot speak more plainly. I yearn to let you in, but – you know what is in my mind, because you know me so well.'

'Yes, Gracie, yes. I do not at all mean that the question between us has not been settled by your marriage turning out hopelessly unalterable. I merely meant – well, a feeling – no more.'

'In a week, at the outside, I should be discovered if I stayed here; and I think that by law he could compel me to return to him.'

'Yes; perhaps you are right. Go when you wish, dear Grace.'

His last words that evening were a hopeful remark that all might be well with her yet: that Mr Fitzpiers would not intrude upon her life, if he found that his presence cost her so much pain. Then the window was closed, the shutters folded, and the rustle of his footsteps died away.

No sooner had she retired to rest that night than the wind began to rise, and after a few prefatory blasts to be accompanied by rain. The wind grew more violent, and as the storm went on it was difficult to believe that no opaque body, but only an invisible colourless thing, was trampling and climbing over the roof, making branches creak, springing out of the trees upon the chimney, popping its head into the flue, and shrieking and blaspheming at every corner of the walls. As in the grisly story, the assailant was a spectre which could be felt but not seen. She had never before been so struck with the devilry of a gusty night in a wood, because she had never been so entirely alone in spirit as she was now. She seemed almost to be apart from herself – a vacuous duplicate only. The recent self of physical animation and clear intentions was not there.

Sometimes a bough from an adjoining tree was swayed so low as to smite the roof in the manner of a gigantic hand smiting the mouth of an adversary, to be followed by a trickle of rain, as blood from the wound. To all this weather Giles must be more or less exposed; how much, she did not know.

At last Grace could hardly endure the idea of such a hardship in relation to him. Whatever he was suffering it was she who had caused it; he had vacated his single-roomed hut on account of her. She was not worth such self-sacrifice; she should not have accepted it of him. And then, as her anxiety increased with increasing thought, there returned upon her mind some incidents of her late intercourse with him, which she had heeded but little at the time. The look of his face – what had there been about his face which seemed different from its appearance of yore? Was it not thinner, less rich in hue, less like that of ripe Autumn's brother to whom she had formerly compared him? And his voice; she had distinctly noticed a change in tone. And his gait; surely it had been feebler, stiffer, more like the gait of a weary man. That slight occasional noise she had heard in the day, and attributed to squirrels; it might have been his cough after all.

Thus conviction took root in her perturbed mind that Winterborne was unwell, or had been so, and that he had carefully concealed his condition from her that she might have no scruples about accepting a hospitality which by the nature of the case expelled her entertainer.

'My own, own, true love – my dear kind friend!' she cried to herself. 'O, it shall not be – it shall not be!'

She hastily got out of bed, obtained a light, and partially dressed herself; and taking the key went at once to the door, which was close at hand, the cot possessing only one floor. Before turning the key in the lock she paused, her fingers still clutching it; and pressing her other hand to her forehead, she fell into agitating thought.

A tattoo on the window, caused by the tree-droppings blowing against it, brought her indecision to a close. She turned the key, and opened the door.

The darkness was intense, seeming to touch her pupils like a substance. She only now became aware how heavy the rainfall had been and was: the dripping of the eaves splashed like a fountain. She stood listening with parted lips, and holding the door in one hand, till her eyes growing accustomed to the obscurity she discerned the wild brandishing of their arms by the adjoining trees. At last she cried loudly with an effort: 'Giles! you must come in!'

There was no answer to her cry, and overpowered by her own temerity Grace retreated quickly, shut the door, and stood looking on the floor with flushed cheeks. Perhaps he was very well after all. But this mood was not for long. She again lifted the latch, and with far more determination than at first.

'Giles, Giles!' she cried, with the full strength of her voice, and without any of the shamefacedness that had characterized her first cry. 'O, come in – come in! Where are you? I have been wicked – I have thought too much of myself! Do you hear? I don't want to keep you out any longer. I cannot bear that you should suffer so. I want you here! Gi-i-iles!'

A reply? It was a reply! Through the darkness and wind a feeble voice reached her, floating upon the weather as though a part of it.

'Here I am – all right! Don't trouble about me.'

'Don't you want to come in? Are you not wet? *Come to me, dearest! I don't mind what they say or what they think of us any more.*'

'I am all right,' he repeated. 'It is not necessary for me to come. Good night! good night!'

Grace sighed, turned, and shut the door slowly. Could she have shocked him by her impulsive words? Perhaps, after all, she had perceived a change in him because she had not seen him for so long. Time sometimes did his ageing work in jerks, as she knew. Well, she had done all she could. He would not come in. She retired to rest again.

CHAPTER FORTY-TWO

T H E next morning Grace was at the window early. She felt determined to see him somehow that day, and prepared his breakfast eagerly. Eight o'clock struck, and she then remembered that he had not come to arouse her by a knocking as usual, her own anxiety having caused her to stir.

His breakfast was set in its place without. But he did not appear to take it; and she waited on. Nine o'clock arrived, and the breakfast was cold; and still there was no Giles. A thrush who had been repeating himself a good deal on an opposite bush for some time, came and took a morsel from the plate, bolted it, waited, looked around, and took another. At ten o'clock she drew in the tray and sat down to her own solitary meal. He must have been called away on business early, the rain having cleared off.

Yet she would have liked to assure herself, by thoroughly exploring the precincts of the hut, that he was nowhere in its vicinity; but as the day was comparatively fine the dread lest some stray passenger or woodman should encounter her in such a recormoitre paralyzed her wish. The solitude was further accentuated to-day by the stopping of the clock for want of winding, and the fall into the chimney-corner of flakes of soot loosened by the rains. At noon she heard a slight rustling outside the window, and found that it was caused by an eft which had crept out of the leaves to bask in the last sun-rays that would be worth having till the following May.

She continually peeped out through the lattice, but could see little. In front lay the brown leaves of last year, and upon them some yellowish green ones of this season that had been prematurely blown down by the gale. Above stretched an old beech, with vast arm-pits, and great pocket-holes in its sides where branches had been removed in past times; a black slug was trying to climb it. Dead boughs were scattered about like ichthyosauri in a museum, and beyond them were perishing woodbine stems resembling old ropes.

From the other window all she could see were more trees, in jackets of lichen and stockings of moss. At their roots were stemless yellow fungi like lemons and apricots, and tall fungi with more stem than stool. Next were more trees close together, wrestling for existence, their branches disfigured with wounds resulting from their mutual rubbings and blows. It was the struggle between these neighbours that she had heard in the night. Beneath them were the rotting stumps of those of the group that had been vanquished long ago, rising from their mossy setting like black teeth from green gums. Further on were other tufts of moss in islands divided by the shed leaves – variety upon variety, dark green and pale green; moss like little fir-trees, like plush, like malachite stars; like nothing on earth except moss.

The strain upon Grace's mind in various ways was so great on this the most desolate day she had passed there that she felt it would be well-nigh impossible to spend another in such circumstances. The evening came at last; the sun, when its chin was on the earth, found an opening through which to pierce the shade, and stretched irradiated gauzes across the damp atmosphere, making the wet trunks shine, and throwing splotches of such ruddiness on the leaves beneath the beech that they were turned to gory hues. When night at last arrived, and with it the time for his return, she was nearly broken down with suspense.

The simple evening meal, partly tea, partly supper, which Grace had prepared, stood waiting upon the hearth; and yet Giles did not come. It was now nearly twenty-four hours since she had seen him. As the room grew darker, and only the fire-light broke against the gloom of the walls, she was convinced that it would be beyond her staying power to pass the night without hearing from him or from somebody. Yet eight o'clock drew on, and his form at the window did not appear.

The meal remained untasted. Suddenly rising from before the hearth of smouldering embers, where she had been crouching with her hands clasped over her knees, she crossed the room, unlocked the door, and listened. Every breath of wind had ceased with the decline of day, but the rain had resumed the steady dripping of the night before. Grace might have stood there five minutes when she fancied she heard that old sound, a cough, at no great distance; and it was presently repeated. If it were Winterborne's he must be near her; why, then, had he not visited her?

A horrid misgiving that he could not visit her took possession of Grace, and she looked up anxiously for the lantern, which was hanging above her head. To light it and go in the direction of the sound would be the obvious way to solve the dread problem; but the conditions made her hesitate, and in a moment a cold sweat pervaded her at further sounds from the same quarter.

They were low mutterings; at first like persons in conversation, but gradually resolving themselves into varieties of one voice. It was an endless monologue, like that we sometimes hear from inanimate nature in deep secret places where water flows, or where ivy leaves flap against stones; but by degrees she was convinced that the voice was Winterborne's. Yet who could be his listener, so mute, and so patient? for though he argued rapidly and persistently nobody replied.

A dreadful enlightenment spread through the mind of Grace. 'O,' she cried in her anguish as she hastily prepared herself to go out; 'how selfishly correct I am always – too, too correct! Can it be that cruel propriety is killing the dearest heart that ever woman clasped to her own!'

While speaking thus to herself she had lit the lantern, and hastening out without further thought took the direction whence the mutterings had proceeded. The course was marked by a little path, which ended at a distance of about forty yards in a small erection of hurdles, not much larger than a shock of corn, such as were frequent in the woods and copses when the cutting season was going on. It was too slight even to be called a hovel, and was not high enough to stand upright in; appearing, in short, to be erected for the temporary shelter of fuel. The side towards Grace was open, and turning the light upon the interior she beheld what her prescient fear had pictured in snatches all the way thither.

Upon the hay within her lover lay in his clothes, just as she had seen him during the whole of her stay here except that his hat was off, and his hair matted and wild.

Both his clothes and the hay were saturated with rain. His arms were flung over his head; his face was flushed to an unnatural crimson. His eyes had a burning brightness, and, though they met her own, she perceived that he did not recognize her.

'O, my Giles,' she cried, 'what have I done to you!'

But she stopped no longer even to reproach herself. She saw that the first thing to be thought of was to get him indoors.

How Grace performed that labour she never could have exactly explained. But by dint of clasping her arms around him, rearing him into a sitting posture and straining her strength to the uttermost, she put him on one of the hurdles that was loose alongside, and taking the end of it in both her hands, dragged him along the path to the entrance of the hut, and, after a pause for breath, in at the doorway.

It was somewhat singular that Giles in his semi-conscious state acquiesced unresistingly in all that she did. But he never for a moment recognized her, continuing his rapid conversation to himself and seeming to look upon her as some angel or other supernatural creature of the visionary world in which he was mentally living. The undertaking occupied her more than ten minutes; but by that time, to her great thankfulness, he was in the hut lying in her bed, his damp clothing removed.

Then the unhappy Grace regarded him by the light of the candle. There was something in his look which agonized her, in the rush of his thoughts, accelerating their speed from minute to minute. His soul seemed to be passing through the universe of ideas like a comet; erratic, inapprehensible, untraceable.

Grace's distraction was almost as great as his. In a few moments she firmly believed he was dying. Unable to withstand her impulse she knelt down beside him, kissed his hands, and his face, and his hair, moaning in a low voice: 'How could I! How could I!'

Her timid morality had, indeed, underrated his chivalry till now, though she knew him so well. The purity of his nature, his freedom from the grosser passions, his scrupulous delicacy, had never been fully understood by Grace till this strange self-sacrifice in lonely juxtaposition to her own person was revealed. The perception of it added something that was little short of reverence to the deep affection for him of a woman who, herself, had more of Artemis than of Aphrodite in her constitution.

All that a tender nurse could do Grace did; and the power to express her solicitude in action, unconscious though the sufferer was, brought her mournful satisfaction. She bathed his hot head, clasped his twitching hands, moistened his lips, cooled his fiery eyelids, sponged his heated skin, and administered whatever she could find in the house that the imagination could conceive as likely to be in any way alleviating. That she might have been the cause, or partially the cause, of all this, interfused misery with her sorrow.

Six months before this date a scene, almost similar in its mechanical parts, had been enacted at Hintock House. It was between a pair of persons most intimately connected in their lives with these. Outwardly like as it had been, it was yet infinite in spiritual difference; though a woman's devotion had been common to both.

Grace rose from her attitude of affection and, bracing her energies, saw that something practical must immediately be done. Much as she would have liked, in the emotion of the moment, to keep him entirely to herself, medical assistance was necessary whilst there remained a possibility of preserving him alive. Such assistance was fatal to her own concealment; but even had the chance of benefiting him been less than it was she would have run the hazard for his sake. The question was, where should she get a medical man, competent and near?

There was one such man, and only one, within accessible distance: a man who, if it were possible to save Winterborne's life, had the brain most likely to do it. If human pressure could bring him that man ought to be brought to the sick Giles's side. Though completely stultifying her flight the attempt should be made.

Yet she dreaded to leave her patient, and the minutes raced past, and still she postponed her departure. At last, when it was after eleven o'clock, Winterborne fell into a fitful sleep, and it seemed to afford her an opportunity.

She hastily made him as comfortable as she could, put on her things, cut a new candle from the bunch hanging in the cupboard, and having set it up, and placed it so that the light did not fall upon his eyes, she closed the door and started, there being now no rain.

The spirit of Winterborne seemed to keep her company and banish all sense of darkness from her mind. The rains had imparted a phosphorescence to the pieces of touchwood and rotting leaves that lay about her path, which, as scattered by her feet, spread abroad like luminous milk. She would not run the hazard of losing her way by plunging into any short, unfrequented track through the woodland, but followed a more open course round by the highway. She went along with great speed, animated by a devoted purpose which had much about it that was stoical; and it was with scarcely any faltering of spirit that, after an hour's progress, she saw High-Stoy Hill and drew onwards towards that same Hintock and that same house out of which she had fled a few days before in irresistible alarm. But that had happened which, above all other things of chance and change, could make her deliberately frustrate her plan of flight, and sink all regard of personal consequences.

One speciality of Fitzpiers was respected by Grace as much as ever: his professional skill. In this she was right. Had his persistence equalled his insight instead of being the spasmodic and fitful thing it was, fame and fortune need never have remained a wish with him. His freedom from conventional errors and crusted prejudices had indeed been such as to retard rather than accelerate his advance in Hintock and its neighbourhood, where people could not believe that Nature herself effected cures, and that the doctor's business was only to smooth the way.

It was past midnight when Grace arrived opposite her father's house, now again temporarily occupied by her husband, unless he had already gone away. Ever since her emergence from the denser plantations about Winterborne's residence a pervasive lightness had hung in the damp autumn sky in spite of the vault of cloud, signifying that a moon of some age was shining above its arch. The two white gates were distinct, and the white balls on the pillars: and the puddles and damp ruts left by the recent rain had a cold corpse-eyed luminousness. She entered by the lower gate and crossed the quadrangle to the wing wherein the apartments that had been hers since her marriage were situate, till she stood under a window, which, if her husband were in the house, gave light to his bed-chamber.

She faltered, and paused with her hand on her heart, in spite of herself. Could she call to her presence the very cause of all her foregoing troubles? Alas! – old Jones was many miles off; Giles was possibly dying – what else could she do?

It was in a perspiration, wrought even more by consciousness than by exercise, that she picked up some gravel, threw it at the panes, and waited to see the result. The night-bell which had been fixed when Fitzpiers first took up his residence there still remained; but as it had fallen into disuse with the collapse of his practice, and his elopement, she did not venture to pull it now.

Whoever slept in the room had heard her signal, slight as it was. In half a minute the window was opened, and a voice said 'Yes?' inquiringly. Grace recognized her husband in the speaker at once. Her effort was now to disguise her own accents.

'Doctor,' she said, in as unusual a tone as she could command, 'a man is dangerously ill in One-Chimney Hut, by Delborough, and you must go to him at once – in all mercy!'

'I will, readily.'

The alacrity, surprise, and even pleasure, expressed in his reply, amazed her for a moment. But, in truth, they denoted the sudden relief of a man who, having got back in a mood of contrition from erratic abandonment to doubtful joys, found the soothing routine of professional practice unexpectedly opening anew to him. The highest desire of his soul just now was for a respectable life of painstaking. If this, his first summons since his return, had been to attend upon a cat or dog, he would scarcely have refused it in the circumstances.

'Do you know the way?' she asked.

'Yes, I think,' said he.

'One-Chimney Hut – in King's-Hintock Wood, by Delborough,' she repeated. 'And – immediately!'

'Yes, yes,' said Fitzpiers.

Grace remained no longer. She passed through the white gate without slamming it, and hastened on her way back. Her husband, then, had re-entered her father's house. How he had been able to effect a reconciliation with the old man, what were the terms of the treaty between them, she could not so much as conjecture. Some sort of truce must have been entered into, that was all she could say. But close as the question lay to her own life there was a more urgent one which banished it; and she traced her steps quickly along the meandering trackways.

Meanwhile Fitzpiers was preparing to leave the house. The state of his mind, over and above his professional zeal, was peculiar. At Grace's first remark he had not recognized or suspected her presence; but as she went on he was awakened to the great resemblance of the speaker's voice to his wife's. He had taken in such good faith the statement of the household on his arrival, that she had gone on a visit for a time because she could not at once bring her mind to be reconciled to him, that he could not quite believe this neighbour to be she. It was one of the features of Fitzpiers's repentant humour at this date that, on receiving the explanation of her absence, he had made no attempt to outrage her feelings by following her; though nobody had informed him how very shortly her departure had preceded his entry, and of all that might have been inferred from her precipitancy.

Melbury, after much alarm and consideration, had decided not to follow her either. He sympathized with her flight, much as he deplored it; moreover, the tragic colour of the antecedent events that he had been a great means of creating checked his instinct to interfere. He prayed and trusted that she had got into no danger on her way (as he supposed) to Ivell, and thence to Exonbury, if that were the place she had gone to, forbearing all inquiry which the strangeness of her departure would have made natural. A few months before this time a performance by Grace of one-tenth the magnitude of this would have aroused him to unwonted investigation.

It was in the same spirit that he had tacitly assented to Fitzpiers's domiciliation there. The two men had not met face to face, but Mrs Melbury had proposed herself as an intermediary who made the surgeon's re-entrance comparatively easy to him. Everything was provisional, and nobody asked questions. Fitzpiers had come in the performance of a plan of penitence which had originated in circumstances hereafter to be explained; his self-humiliation to the very bass-string was deliberate; and as soon as a voice reached him from the bedside of a dying man his desire was to set to work and do as much good as he could with the least possible fuss or show. He therefore refrained from calling up a stableman to get ready any horse or gig, and set out for One-Chimney Hut on foot as Grace had done.

CHAPTER FORTY-THREE

She re-entered the hut, flung off her bonnet and cloak, and approached the sufferer. He had begun anew those terrible mutterings, and his hands were cold. As soon as she saw him there returned to her that agony of mind which the stimulus of her journey had thrown off for a time.

Could he really be dying? She bathed him, kissed him, forgot all things but the fact that lying there before her was he who had loved her more than the mere lover would have loved; had immolated himself for her comfort, cared more for her self-respect than she had thought of caring. This mood continued till she heard quick, smart footsteps without; she knew whose footsteps they were.

Grace sat on the inside of the bed against the wall, holding her lover's hand, so that when her husband entered the patient lay between herself and him. He stood transfixed at first, noticing Grace only. Slowly he dropped his glance and discerned who the prostrate man was. Strangely enough, though Grace's distaste for her husband's company had amounted almost to dread, and culminated in actual flight, at this moment her last and least feeling was personal. Sensitive femininity was eclipsed by devoted purpose; and that it was a husband who stood there was forgotten. The first look that possessed her face was relief; satisfaction at the presence of the physician obliterated the thought of the man, which only returned in the form of a subconsciousness that did not interfere with her words.

'Is he dying – is there any hope?' she asked.

'Grace!' said Fitzpiers in an indescribable whisper – more than invocating – if not quite deprecatory.

He was arrested by the spectacle, not so much in its intrinsic character – though that was striking enough to a man who called himself the husband of the sufferer's friend and nurse – but in its character as the counterpart of one that had had its run many months before, in which he had figured as the patient, and the woman had been Felice Charmond.

'Is he in great danger – can you save him?' she asked again.

Fitzpiers aroused himself, came a little nearer, and examined Winterborne as he stood. His inspection was concluded in a mere glance. Before he spoke he looked at her contemplatively as to the effect of his coming words..

'He is dying,' he said with dry precision.

'What?' said she.

'Nothing can be done by me or any other man. It will soon be all over. The extremities are dead already.' His eye still remained fixed on her, the conclusion to which he had come seeming to end his interest, professional and otherwise, in Winterborne for ever.

'But it cannot be! He was well a week ago.'

'Not well, I suspect. This seems like what we call a sequel, which has followed some previous disorder – possibly typhoid – it may have been months ago, or recently.'

'Ah – he was ill last year – you are right. And he must have been ill when I came!'

There was nothing more to do or say. She crouched down at the side of the bed, and Fitzpiers took a seat. Thus they remained in silence, and long as it lasted she never turned her eyes, or apparently her thoughts, at all to her husband. He occasionally murmured, with automatic authority, some slight directions for alleviating the pain of the dying man, which she mechanically obeyed, bending over him during the intervals in silent tears.

Winterborne never recovered consciousness of what was passing; and that he was going became soon perceptible also to her. In less than an hour the delirium ceased; then there was an interval of somnolent painlessness and soft breathing, at the end of which Winterborne passed quietly away.

Then Fitzpiers broke the silence. 'Have you lived here long?' he said.

Grace was wild with sorrow – bitter with all that had befallen her – with the cruelties that had attacked her – with life – with Heaven. She answered at random. 'Yes. By what right do you ask?'

'Don't think I claim any right,' said Fitzpiers. ' It is for you to do and say what you choose. I admit, quite as much as you feel, that I am a vagabond – a brute – not worthy to possess the smallest fragment of you. But here I am, and I have happened to take sufficient interest in you to make that inquiry.'

'He is everything to me!' said Grace, hardly heeding her husband, and laying her hand reverently on the dead man's eyelids, where she kept it a long time, pressing down their lashes with gentle touches, as if she were stroking a little bird.

He watched her awhile, and then glanced round the chamber, where his eyes fell upon a few dressing necessaries that she had brought.

'Grace – if I may call you so,' he said, 'I have been already humiliated almost to the depths. I have come back – since you refused to join me elsewhere – I have entered your father's house – and borne all which that cost me without flinching, because I have felt I deserved humiliation. But is there a yet greater humiliation in store for me? You say you have been living here with him – that he was everything to you. Am I to draw from that the obvious, the extremest inference?'

Triumph at any price is sweet to men and women – especially the latter. It was her first and last opportunity of repaying him for the slights which she had borne at his hands so docilely.

'Yes,' she answered; 'the extremest inference'; and there was that in her subtly compounded nature which made her feel a thrill of pride as she did so.

Yet the moment after she had so mightily belied her conduct she half repented. Her husband had turned as white as the wall behind him. It seemed as if all that remained to him of hope and spirit had been abstracted at a stroke. Yet he did not move, and in his efforts at self-control closed his mouth together as a vice. His determination was fairly successful, though she saw how very much greater than she had expected her triumph had been. Presently he looked across at Winterborne.

'Would it startle you to hear,' he said, as if he hardly had breath to utter words, 'that she who was to me what he was to you is dead also?'

'Dead – *she* dead?' exclaimed Grace.

'Yes. Felice Charmond is where this young man is.'

'Never!' said Grace vehemently.

He went on without heeding the insinuation: 'And I came back to try to make it up with you; but—'

Fitzpiers rose and moved across the room to go away, looking downwards with the droop of a man whose hope was turned to apathy, if not despair. In going round the door his eye fell upon her once more. She was still bending over the body of Winterborne, her face close to his.

'Have you been kissing him during his illness?' asked her husband.

'Yes.'

'Since his fevered state set in?'

'Yes.'

'On his lips?'

'Yes, a hundred times!'

'Then you will do well to take a few drops of this in water as soon as possible.'

He drew a small phial from his pocket, and returned to offer it to her.

Grace shook her head.

'If you don't do as I tell you, you may soon be like him.'

'I don't care! I wish to die.'

'I'll put it here,' said Fitzpiers, placing the bottle on a ledge beside him. 'The sin of not having warned you will not be upon my head at any rate, amongst my other sins. I am now going, and I will send somebody to you. Your father does not know that you are here, so I suppose I shall be bound to tell him?'

'Certainly.'

Fitzpiers left the cot, and the stroke of his feet was soon immersed in the silence that pervaded the spot. Grace remained kneeling and weeping, she hardly knew how long, and then she sat up, covered Giles's fixed statuesque features, and went towards the door where her husband had stood. No sign of any other comer greeted her ear, the only perceptible sounds being the tiny cracklings of the dead leaves which, like a feather bed, had not yet done rising to their normal level where indented by the pressure of her husband's receding footsteps. It reminded her that she had been struck with the change in his aspect; the extremely intellectual look that had always been in his face was wrought to a finer phase by thinness, and a careworn dignity had been superadded. She returned to Winterborne's side, and during her meditations another tread drew near the door, entered the room, and halted at the foot of the bed.

'What – Marty!' said Grace.

'Yes. I have heard,' said Marty, whose demeanour had lost all its girlishness under the stroke that seemed almost literally to have bruised her.

'He died for me!' murmured Grace heavily.

Marty did not fully comprehend and she answered, 'He belongs to neither of us now, and your beauty is no more powerful with him than my plainness. I have come to help you, ma'am. He never cared for me, and he cared much for you; but he cares for us both alike now.'

'O don't, don't, Marty!'

Marty said no more, but knelt over Winterborne from the other side.

'Did you meet my hus— Mr Fitzpiers?'

'No.'

'Then what brought you here?'

'I come this way sometimes. I have got to go to the further side of the wood at this time o' year, and am obliged to get there before four o'clock in the morning, to begin heating the oven for the early baking. I have passed by here often at this time.'

Grace looked at her quickly. 'Then did you know I was here?'

'Yes, ma'am.'

'Did you tell anybody?'

'No. I knew you lived in the hut, that he had gi'ed it up to 'ee, and lodged out himself.'

'Did you know where he lodged?'

'No. That I couldn't find out. Was it at Delborough?'

'No. It was not there, Marty. Would it had been! It would have saved – saved—' To check her tears she turned, and seeing a book in the window-bench, took it up. 'Look, Marty, this is a Psalter. He was not an outwardly religious man; but he was pure and perfect in his heart. Shall we read a psalm over him?'

'O yes, we will; with all my heart!'

Grace opened the thin brown book, which poor Giles had kept at hand mainly for the convenience of whetting his penknife upon its leather covers. She began to read in that rich, devotional voice peculiar to women on such occasions. When it was over Marty said, 'I should like to pray for his soul.'

'So should I,' said her companion. 'But we must not.'

'Why? Nobody would know.'

Grace could not resist the argument, influenced as she was by the sense of making amends for having neglected him in the body; and their tender voices united and filled the narrow room with supplicatory murmurs that a Calvinist might have countenanced. They had hardly ended when new and more numerous footfalls were audible; also persons in conversation, one of whom Grace recognized as her father.

She rose and went to the outside of the hut, where there was only such light as beamed from the doorway. Melbury and Mrs Melbury were standing there.

'I don't reproach you, Grace,' said her father, with an estranged manner and in a voice not at all like his old voice. 'What has come upon you and us through you giving up yourself to him is beyond reproach, beyond weeping and beyond wailing. Perhaps I drove you to it. But I am hurt; I am scourged; I am astonished! In the face of this there is nothing to be said.'

Without replying Grace turned and glided back to the chamber. 'Marty,' she said quickly, 'I cannot look my father in the face until he knows the true circumstances of my life here. Go and tell him – what you have told me – what you saw – that he gave up his house to me.'

She sat down, her face buried in her hands, and Marty went, and after a short absence returned. Then Grace rose, and going out, asked her father if he had talked to Marty.

'Yes,' said Melbury.

'And you know all that has happened? I will let my husband think the utmost, but not you.'

'I do. Forgive me, Grace, for suspecting 'ee of worse than rashness – I ought to know 'ee better. Are you coming with me to what was once your home?'

'No. I stay here with him. Take no account of me any more.'

The tender, perplexing, agitating relations in which she had stood to Winterborne quite lately – brought about by Melbury's own contrivance – could not fail to soften the natural anger of a parent at her more recent doings. 'My daughter, things are bad,' he rejoined. 'But why do you persevere to make 'em worse? What good can you do to Giles by staying here with him? Mind, I ask no questions. I don't inquire why you decided to come here, or anything as to what your course would have been if he had not died, though I know there's no deliberate harm in 'ee. As for me, I have lost all claim upon you; and I make no complaint. But I do say that by coming back with me now you will show no less kindness to him, and escape any sound of shame.'

'But I don't wish to escape it.'

'If you don't on your own account, cannot you wish to on mine and hers? Nobody except our household knows that you have left home. Then why should you by a piece of perverseness bring down my hairs with sorrow to the grave?'

'If it were not for my husband—' she began, moved by his words. 'But how can I meet him there? How can any woman who is not a mere man's creature live with him after what has taken place?'

'He would go away again rather than keep you out of my house.'

'How do you know that, father?'

'We met him on our way here, and he told us so,' said Mrs Melbury. 'He had said something like it before. He seems very much upset altogether.'

'He declared to her when he came to our house that he would wait for time and devotion to bring about his forgiveness,' said Melbury. 'That was it, wasn't it, Lucy?'

'Yes. That he would not intrude upon you, Grace, till you gave him absolute permission,' Mrs Melbury added.

This antecedent considerateness in Fitzpiers was as welcome to Grace as it was unexpected; and though she did not desire his presence, she was sorry that by her retaliatory fiction she had given him a different reason for avoiding her. She made no further objections to accompanying her parents, taking them into the hut to give Winterborne a last look, and gathering up the two or three things that belonged to her. While she was doing this the two women came who had been called by Melbury, and at their heels poor Creedle.

'Forgive me, but I can't rule my mourning nohow as a man should, Mr Melbury,' he said. 'I ha'n't seen him since Thursday se'night, and have wondered for days and days where he's been keeping. There was I expecting him to come and tell me to wash out the cider-barrels against the making, and here was he. . . . Well, I've knowed him from table-high; I knowed his father – used to bide about upon two sticks in the sun afore he died! – and now I've seen the end of the family, which we can ill afford to lose, wi' such a scanty lot of good folk in Hintock as we've got. And now Robert Creedle will be nailed up in parish boards 'a b'lieve; and nobody will glutch down a sigh for he!'

They started for home, Marty and Creedle remaining behind. For a time Grace and her father walked side by side without speaking. It was just in the blue of the dawn, and the chilling tone of the sky was reflected in her cold, wet face. The whole wood seemed to be a house of death, pervaded by loss to its uttermost length and breadth. Winterborne was gone, and the copses seemed to show the want of him; those young trees, so many of which he had planted, and of which he had spoken so truly when he said that he should fall before they fell, were at that very moment sending out their roots in the direction that he had given them with his subtle hand.

'One thing made it tolerable to us that your husband should come back to the house,' said Melbury at last. 'The death of Mrs Charmond.'

'Ah, yes,' said Grace, arousing slightly to the recollection; 'he told me so.'

'Did he tell you how she died? It was no such death as Giles's. She was shot – by a disappointed lover. It occurred in Germany. The unfortunate man shot himself afterwards. He was that South Carolina gentleman of very passionate nature, who used to haunt this place to force her to favour him, and followed her about everywhere. So ends the brilliant Felice Charmond – once a good friend to me – but no friend to you.'

'I can forgive her,' said Grace absently. 'Did Edred tell you this?'

'No; but he put a London newspaper, giving an account of it, on the hall-table, folded in such a way that we should see it. It will be in the Sherton paper this week, no doubt. To make the event more solemn still to him he had just before had sharp words with her, and left her. He told Lucy this, as nothing about him appears in the newspaper. And the cause of the quarrel was, of all people, she we've left behind us.'

'Do you mean Marty?' Grace spoke the words but perfunctorily. For, pertinent and pointed as Melbury's story was, she had no care for it now.

'Yes. Marty South.' Melbury persisted in his narrative to divert her from her present grief if possible. 'Before he went away she wrote him a letter, which he kept in his pocket a long while before reading. He chanced to pull it out in Mrs Charmond's presence, and read it out loud. It contained something which teased her very much, and that led to the rupture. She was following him to make it up when she met with her terrible death.'

Melbury did not know enough to give the gist of the incident, which was that Marty South's letter had been concerning a certain personal adornment common to herself and Mrs Charmond. Her bullet reached its billet at last. The scene between Fitzpiers and Felice had been sharp, as only a scene can be which arises out of the mortification of one woman by another in the presence of a lover. True, Marty had not effected it by word of mouth; the charge about the locks of hair was made simply by Fitzpiers reading her letter to him aloud to Felice in the playfully ironical tones of one who had become a little weary of his situation, and was finding his friend, in the phrase of George Herbert, a 'flat delight'. He had stroked those false tresses with his hand many a time without knowing them to be transplanted, and it was impossible when the discovery was so abruptly made to avoid being finely satirical, despite his generous disposition.

That was how it had begun, and tragedy had been its end. On his abrupt departure she had followed him to the station, but the train was gone; and in travelling to Homburg in search of him she had met his rival, whose reproaches led to an altercation, and the death of both. Of that precipitate scene of passion and crime Fitzpiers had known nothing till he saw an account of it in the papers, where, fortunately for himself, no mention was made of his prior acquaintance with the unhappy lady; nor was there any allusion to him in the subsequent inquiry, the double death being attributed to some gambling losses, though in point of fact neither one of them had visited the tables.

Melbury and his daughter drew near their house, having seen but one living thing on their way, a squirrel, which did not run up its tree, but, dropping the sweet chestnut which it carried, cried chut-chut-chut and stamped with its hind-legs on the ground. When the roofs and chimneys of the homestead began to emerge from the screen of boughs Grace started, and checked herself in her abstracted advance.

'You clearly understand,' she said to her stepmother, some of her old misgiving returning, 'that I am coming back only on condition of his leaving as he promised? Will you let him know this, that there may be no mistake?'

Mrs Melbury, who had had some long private talks with Fitzpiers, assured Grace that she need have no doubts on that point, and that he would probably be gone by the evening. Grace then entered with them into Melbury's wing of the house, and sat down listlessly in the parlour while her stepmother went to Fitzpiers.

The prompt obedience to her wishes which the doctor showed did honour to him, if anything could. Before Mrs Melbury had returned to the room Grace, who was sitting on the parlour window-bench, saw her husband go from the door under the increasing light of morning, with a bag in his hand. While passing through the gate he turned his head. The firelight of the room she sat in threw her figure into dark relief against the window as she looked through the panes, and he must have seen her distinctly. In a moment he went on, the gate fell to, and he disappeared. At the hut she had declared that another had usurped his rights; now she had banished him.

CHAPTER FORTY-FOUR

FITZPIERS had hardly been gone an hour when Grace began to sicken. The next day she kept her room. Old Jones was called in: he murmured some statements in which the words 'feverish symptoms' occurred. Grace heard them, and guessed the means by which she had brought this visitation upon herself.

One day while she still lay there with her head throbbing, wondering if she were really going to join him who had gone before, Grammer Oliver came to her bedside. 'I don't know whe'r this is meant for you to take, ma'am,' she said. 'But I have found it on the table. It was left by Marty, I think, when she came this morning.'

Grace turned her hot eyes upon what Grammer held up. It was the phial left at the hut by her husband when he had begged her to take some drops of its contents, if she wished to preserve herself from falling a victim to the malady which had pulled down Winterborne. She examined it as well as she could. The liquid was of a brownish hue, and bore a label with an inscription in Italian. He had probably got it in his wanderings abroad. She knew but little Italian, but could understand that the cordial was a febrifuge of some sort. Her father, her mother, and all the household were anxious for her recovery, and she resolved to obey her husband's directions. Whatever the risk, if any, she was prepared to run it. A glass of water was brought, and the drops dropped in.

The effect, though not miraculous, was remarkable. In less than an hour she felt calmer, cooler, better able to reflect, less inclined to fret and chafe and wear herself away. She took a few drops more. From that time the fever retreated, and went out like a damped conflagration.

'How clever he is!' she said regretfully. 'Why could he not have had more principle, so as to turn his great talents to good account! Perhaps he has saved my useless life. But he doesn't know it, and doesn't care whether he has saved it or not; and on that account will never be told by me. Probably he only gave it to me in the arrogance of his skill, to show the greatness of his resources beside mine, as Elijah drew down fire from Heaven!'

As soon as she had quite recovered from this foiled attack upon her life Grace went to Marty South's cottage. The current of her being had again set towards the lost Giles Winterborne.

'Marty,' she said, 'we both loved him. We will go to his grave together.'

The church stood somewhat outside the village, and could be reached without passing through the street. In the dusk of the late September day they went thither by secret ways, walking mostly in silence side by side, each busied with her own thoughts. Grace had a trouble exceeding Marty's, that haunting sense of having put out the light of his life by her own hasty doings. She had tried to persuade herself that he might have died of his illness, even if she had not taken possession of his house. Sometimes she succeeded in her attempt; sometimes she did not.

They stood by the grave together, and though the sun had gone down they could get glimpses over the woodland for miles, and along the vale in which he had been accustomed to descend every year with his portable mill and press to make cider about this time.

Perhaps Grace's first grief, the discovery that if he had lived he could never have claimed her, had some power in softening this, the second. On Marty's part there was the same consideration; never would she have been his. As no anticipation of gratified affection had been in existence while he was with them there was none to be disappointed now that he had gone.

Grace was abased when, by degrees, she found that she had never understood Giles as Marty had done. Marty South alone, of all the women in Hintock and the world, had approximated to Winterborne's level of intelligent intercourse with Nature. In that respect she had formed his true complement in the other sex, had lived as his counterpart, had subjoined her thoughts to his as a corollary.

The casual glimpses which the ordinary population bestowed upon that wondrous world of sap and leaves called the Hintock woods had been with these two, Giles and Marty, a clear gaze. They had been possessed of its finer mysteries as of commonplace knowledge; had been able to read its hieroglyphs as ordinary writing; to them the sights and sounds of night, winter, wind, storm, amid those dense boughs, which had to Grace a touch of the uncanny, and even of the supernatural, were simple occurrences whose origin, continuance, and laws they foreknew. They had planted together, and together they had felled; together they had, with the run of the years, mentally collected those remoter signs and symbols which seen in few were of runic obscurity, but all together made an alphabet. From the light lashing of the twigs upon their faces when brushing through them in the dark either could pronounce upon the species of the tree whence they stretched; from the quality of the wind's murmur through a bough either could in like manner name its sort afar off. They knew by a glance at a trunk if its heart were sound, or tainted with incipient decay; and by the state of its upper twigs the stratum that had been reached by its roots. The artifices of the seasons were seen by them from the conjuror's own point of view, and not from that of the spectator.

'He ought to have married *you*, Marty, and nobody else in the world!' said Grace with conviction, after thinking in the above strain.

Marty shook her head. 'In all our outdoor days and years together, ma'am,' she replied, 'the one thing he never spoke of to me was love; nor I to him.'

'Yet you and he could speak in a tongue that nobody else knew – not even my father, though he came nearest knowing – the tongue of the trees and fruits and flowers themselves.'

She could indulge in mournful fancies like this to Marty; but the hard core to her grief – which Marty's had not – remained. Had she been sure that Giles's death resulted entirely from his exposure, it would have driven her well-nigh to insanity; but there was always the bare possibility that his exposure had only precipitated what was inevitable. She longed to believe that it had not done even this.

There was only one man whose opinion on the circumstances she would be at all disposed to trust. Her husband was that man. Yet to ask him it would be necessary to detail the true conditions in which she and Winterborne had lived during these three or four critical days that followed her flight; and in withdrawing her original defiant announcement on that point there seemed a weakness she did not care to show. She never doubted that Fitzpiers would believe her if she made a clean confession of the actual situation; but to volunteer the correction would seem like signalling for a truce, and that in her present frame of mind was what she did not feel the need of.

It will probably not appear a surprising statement, after what has been already declared of Fitzpiers, that the man whom Grace's matrimonial fidelity could not keep faithful was stung into passionate throbs of interest concerning her by her avowal of the contrary.

He declared to himself that he had never known her dangerously full compass if she were capable of such a reprisal; and, melancholy as it may be to admit the fact, his own humiliation and regret engendered a smouldering admiration of her.

He passed a month or two of nervous misery at some midland town – the place to which he had retired – quite as much misery indeed as Grace, could she have known of it, would have been inclined to inflict upon any living creature, how much soever he might have wronged her. Then a sudden hope dawned upon him; he wondered if her affirmation were true. He asked himself whether it were not the act of an innocent woman whose pique had for the moment blinded her to the contingencies of such an announcement. His wide experience of the sex had taught him that, in many cases, women who ventured on hazardous phrases did so because they lacked an imagination gross enough to feel their full force. In this light Grace's bold avowal might merely have denoted the desperation of one who was a child to the realities of faithlessness.

Fitzpiers's mental sufferings and suspense led him at last to take a melancholy journey to the neighbourhood of Little Hintock; and here he hovered for hours around the scene of the purest emotional experiences that he had ever known in his life. He walked about the woods that surrounded Melbury's house, keeping out of sight like a criminal. It was a fine evening, and on his way homeward he passed near Marty South's cottage. As usual she had lighted her candle without closing her shutters; he saw her within as he had seen her many times before.

She was polishing tools, and though he had not wished to show himself he could not resist speaking to her through the half-open door. 'What are you doing that for, Marty?'

'Because I want to clean them. They are not mine.' He could see indeed that they were not hers, for one was a spade, large and heavy, and another was a bill-hook which she could only have used with both hands. The spade, though not a new one, had been so completely burnished that it was bright as silver.

Fitzpiers somehow divined that they were Giles Winterborne's, and he put the question to her.

She replied in the affirmative. 'I am going to keep 'em,' she said, 'but I can't get his apple-mill and press. I wish I could; it is going to be sold, they say.'

'Then I will buy it for you,' said Fitzpiers. 'That will be making you a return for a kindness you did me.' His glance fell upon the girl's rare-coloured hair, which had grown again. 'O Marty, those locks of yours – and that letter! . . . But it was a kindness to send it, nevertheless,' he added musingly.

After this there was confidence between them – such confidence as there had never been before. Marty was shy, indeed, of speaking about the letter and her motives in writing it; but she thanked him warmly for his promise of the cider-press. She would travel with it in the autumn season as poor Giles had done, she said. She would be quite strong enough with old Creedle as an assistant.

'Ah! – there was one nearer to him than you,' said Fitzpiers, referring to Grace. 'One who lived where he lived, and was with him when he died.'

Then Marty, suspecting that he did not know the true circumstances, from the fact that Mrs Fitzpiers and himself were living apart, told him of Giles's generosity to Grace in giving up his house to her at the risk, and possibly the sacrifice, of his own life. When the surgeon heard it he almost envied Giles his chivalrous character. He expressed a wish to Marty that his visit to her should be kept secret, and went home thoughtful, feeling that in more than one sense his journey to Hintock had not been in vain.

He would have given much to win Grace's forgiveness then. But whatever he dared hope for in that kind from the future there was nothing to be done yet, while Giles Winterborne's memory was green. To wait was imperative. A little time might melt her frozen thoughts, and lead her to look on him with toleration, if not with love.

CHAPTER FORTY-FIVE

W EEKS and months of mourning for Winterborne had been passed by Grace in the soothing monotony of the memorial act to which she and Marty had devoted themselves. Twice a week the pair went in the dusk to Hintock Churchyard, and, like the two mourners in *Cymbeline*, sweetened his sad grave with their flowers and their tears.

Nothing ever had brought home to her with such force as this death how little acquirements and culture weigh beside sterling personal character. While her simple sorrow for his loss took a softer edge with the lapse of the autumn and winter seasons, her self-reproach at having had a possible hand in causing it knew slight abatement.

Little occurred at Hintock during these months of the fall and decay of the leaf. Discussion of the almost contemporaneous death of Mrs Charmond abroad had waxed and waned. There was a rumour that her death had resulted less from the shot than from the effect of fright upon her personal condition at the time; but this was never verified. Fitzpiers had had a fortunate escape from being dragged into the inquiry which followed the catastrophe, through the accident of having parted from his mistress just before it, under the influence of Marty South's letter – the tiny instrument of a cause deep in nature.

Her body was not brought home. It seemed to accord well with the fitful fever of that impassioned woman's life that she should not have found an English grave. She had enjoyed but a life-interest in the estate, which after her death passed to a relative of her husband's – one who knew not Felice, one whose purpose seemed to be to blot out every vestige of her.

On a certain day in February – the cheerful day of St Valentine – a letter reached Mrs Fitzpiers, which had been mentally promiséd her for that particular day a long time before.

Her husband announced that he was living at some midland town, where he had obtained a temporary practice as assistant to a local medical man, whose curative principles were all wrong, though he dared not set them right. He had thought fit to communicate with her on that day of tender traditions to inquire if, in the event of his obtaining a substantial practice that he had in view elsewhere, she could forget the past and bring herself to join him.

There the practical part ended: he then went on: –

My last year of experience has added ten years to my age, dear Grace, and dearest wife that ever erring man under-valued. You may be absolutely indifferent to what I say, but let me say it; I have never loved any woman alive or dead as I love, respect, and honour you at this present moment. What you told me in the pride and naughtiness of your heart I never believed [this, by the way, was not strictly true]; but even if I had believed it, it could never have estranged me from you. Is there any use in telling you – no, there is not – that I dream of your fresh lips more frequently than I say my prayers: that the old familiar rustle of your dress often returns upon my mind till it distracts me? If you could condescend even only to see me again you would be breathing life into a corpse. My pure, pure Grace, modest as a turtledove, how came I ever to possess you? For the sake of being present in your mind on this lovers' day, I think I would almost rather have you hate me a little than not think of me at all. You may call my fancies whimsical; but remember, sweet, lost one, that 'nature is fine in love, and where 'tis fine it sends some instance of itself'. — I will not intrude upon you further now. Make me a little bit happy by sending back one line to say that you will consent, at any rate, to a short interview. I will meet you and leave you as a mere acquaintance, if you will only afford me this slight means of making a few explanations, and of putting my position before you. Believe me, in spite of all you may do or feel, your lover always (once your husband),   E.F.

It was, oddly enough, the first occasion, or nearly the first, on which Grace had ever received a love-letter from him, his courtship having taken place under conditions which rendered letter-writing unnecessary. Its perusal, therefore, had a certain novelty for her. She thought that, upon the whole, he wrote love-letters very well. But the chief rational interest of the letter to the reflective Grace lay in the chance that such a meeting as he proposed would afford her of setting her doubts at rest one way or the other on her actual share in Winterborne's death. The relief of consulting a skilled mind, the one professional man who had seen Giles at that time, would be immense. As for that statement that she had uttered in her disdainful grief, which at the time she had regarded as her triumph, she was quite prepared to admit to him that his belief was the true one; for in wronging herself as she did when she made it she had done what to her was a far more serious thing, wronged Winterborne's memory.

Without consulting her father, or any one in the house or out of it, Grace replied to the letter. She agreed to meet Fitzpiers on two conditions, of which the first was that the place of meeting should be the top of High-Stoy Hill, the second that he would not object to Marty South accompanying her.

Whatever art, much or little, there may have been in Fitzpiers's so-called valentine to his wife, he felt a delight as of the bursting of spring when her brief reply came. It was one of the few pleasures that he had experienced of late years at all resembling those of his early youth. He promptly replied that he accepted the conditions, and named the day and hour at which he would be on the spot she mentioned.

A few minutes before three on the appointed day found him climbing the well-known hill, which had been the axis of so many critical movements in their lives during his residence at Hintock.

The sight of each homely and well-remembered object swelled the regret that seldom left him now. Whatever paths might lie open to his future the soothing shades of Hintock were forbidden him for ever as a permanent dwelling-place.

He longed for the society of Grace. But to lay offerings on her slighted altar was his first aim, and until her propitiation was complete he would constrain her in no way to return to him. The least reparation that he could make, in a case where he would gladly have made much, would be to let her feel herself absolutely free to choose between living with him and without him.

Moreover, a subtlist in emotions, he cultivated as under glasses strange and mournful pleasures that he would not willingly let die just at present. To show any forwardness in suggesting a *modus vivendi* to Grace would be to put an end to these exotics. To be the vassal of her sweet will for a time — he demanded no more, and found solace in the contemplation of the soft miseries she caused him.

Approaching the hill with a mind strung to these notions Fitzpiers discerned a gay procession of people coming down the way, and was not long in perceiving it to be a wedding-party. Though the wind was keen the women were in light attire, and the flowered waistcoats of the men had a pleasing vividness of pattern. Each of the gentler ones clung to the arm of her partner so tightly as to have with him one step, rise, swing, gait, almost one centre of gravity. In the buxom bride Fitzpiers recognized no other than Suke Damson, who in her light gown looked a giantess; the small husband beside her he saw to be Tim Tangs.

Fitzpiers could not escape, for they had seen him; though of all the beauties of the world whom he did not wish to meet Suke was the chief. But he put the best face on the matter that he could and came on, the approaching company evidently discussing him and his separation from Mrs Fitzpiers. As the couples closed upon him he expressed his congratulations.

'We be just walking round the parishes to show ourselves a bit,' said Tim. 'First we het across to Great Hintock, then back to here, and from here we go to Revellers Inn and Marshwood, and then round by the cross roads home. Home, says I, but it won't be that long. We be off in a couple of months.'

'Indeed. Where to?'

Tim informed him that they were going to New Zealand. Not but that he would have been contented with Hintock, but his wife was ambitious and wanted to leave; so he had given way.

'Then good-bye,' said Fitzpiers; 'I may not see you again.' He shook hands with Tim and turned to the bride. 'Good-bye, Suke,' he said, taking her hand also. 'I wish you and your husband prosperity in the country you have chosen.' With this he left them, and hastened on to his appointment.

The wedding-party re-formed and resumed march likewise. But in restoring his arm to Suke, Tim noticed that her full and blooming countenance had undergone a change. 'Hullo! me dear — what's the matter?' said Tim.

'Nothing to speak o',' said she. But to give the lie to her assertion she was seized with lachrymose twitches, that soon produced a dribbling face.

'How — what the devil's this about?' exclaimed the bridegroom.

'She's a little wee bit overcome, poor dear!' said the first bridesmaid, unfolding her handkerchief and wiping Suke's eyes.

'I never did like parting from people!' said Suke as soon as she could speak.

'Why him in particular?'

'Well — he's such a clever doctor, that 'tis a thousand pities we sha'n't see him any more! There'll be no such clever doctor as he in New Zealand, if I should be wanting one in a few months; and the thought o't got the better of my feelings!'

They walked on, but Tim's face had grown rigid and pale, for he recalled slight circumstances disregarded at the time of their occurrence. The former boisterous laughter of the wedding-party at the groomsman's jokes was heard rising between the hedges no more.

By this time Fitzpiers had advanced on his way to the hill, where he saw two figures emerging from the bank on the right hand. These were the expected ones, Grace and Marty South, who had evidently come there by a short and secret path through the wood. Grace was muffled up in her winter dress, and he thought that she had never looked so seductive as at this moment, in the noontide, bright, but heatless sun, and the keen wind, and the purplish-grey masses of brushwood around. Fitzpiers continued to regard the nearing picture, till at length their glances met for a moment, when she demurely sent off hers at a tangent and gave him the benefit of her three-quarter face, while with courteous completeness of conduct he lifted his hat in a large arc. Marty dropped behind; and when Fitzpiers held out his hand Grace touched it with her fingers.

'I have agreed to be here mostly because I wanted to ask you something important,' said Mrs Fitzpiers, her intonation modulating in a direction that she had not quite wished it to take.

'I am most attentive,' said her husband. 'Shall we take to the trees for privacy?'

Grace demurred, and Fitzpiers gave in, and they kept outside by the gate.

At any rate, she would take his arm? This also was gravely negatived, the refusal being audible to Marty.

'Why not?' he inquired.

'O, Mr Fitzpiers – how can you ask?'

'Right, right,' said he, his effusiveness shrivelled up.

As they walked on she returned to her inquiry. 'It is about a matter that may perhaps be unpleasant to you. But I think I need not consider that too carefully.'

'Not at all,' said Fitzpiers heroically.

She then took him back to the time of poor Winterborne's death, and related the precise circumstances amid which his fatal illness had come upon him, particularizing the dampness of the shelter to which he had betaken himself, his concealment from her of the hardships that he was undergoing, all that he had put up with, all that he had done for her in his scrupulous considerateness. The retrospect brought her to tears as she asked him if he thought that the sin of having driven him to his death was upon her.

Fitzpiers could hardly help showing his satisfaction at what her narrative indirectly revealed, the actual harmlessness of an escapade with her lover which had at first, by her own showing, looked so grave, and he did not care to inquire whether that harmlessness had been the result of aim or of accident. With regard to her question he declared that in his judgment no human being could answer it. He thought that upon the whole the balance of probabilities turned in her favour. Winterborne's apparent strength, during the last months of his life, must have been delusive. It had often occurred that after a first attack of that insidious disease a person's apparent recovery was a physiological mendacity.

The relief which came to Grace lay almost as much in sharing her knowledge of the particulars with an intelligent mind as in the assurances Fitzpiers gave her. 'Well, then, to put this case before you and obtain your professional opinion was chiefly why I consented to come here to-day,' said she, when he had reached the aforesaid conclusion.

'For no other reason at all?' he asked ruefully.

'It was nearly the whole.'

They stood and looked over a gate at twenty or thirty starlings feeding in the grass, and he started the talk again by saying in a low voice,' And yet I love you more than ever I loved you in my life.'

Grace did not move her eyes from the birds, and folded her delicate lips as if to keep them in subjection.

'It is a different kind of love altogether,' said he. 'Less passionate; more profound. It has nothing to do with the material conditions of the object at all;

much to do with her character and goodness, as revealed by closer observation. "Love talks with better knowledge, and knowledge with dearer love." '

'That's out of *Measure for Measure*, said she slily.

'O yes – I meant it as a citation,' blandly replied Fitzpiers. 'Well then, why not give me a very little bit of your heart again?'

The crash of a felled tree in the depths of the nearest wood recalled the past at that moment, and all the homely faithfulness of Winterborne. 'Don't ask it! My heart is in the grave with Giles,' she replied staunchly.

'Mine is with you – in no less deep a grave, I fear, according to that.'

'I am very sorry; but it cannot be helped.'

'How can you be sorry for me, when you wilfully keep open the grave?'

'O no – that's not so,' returned Grace quickly; and moved to go away from him.

'But dearest Grace!' said he. 'You have condescended to come; and I thought from it that perhaps when I had passed through a long state of probation you would be generous. But if there can be no hope of our getting completely reconciled, treat me gently – wretch though I am.'

'I did not say you were a wretch, nor have I ever said so.'

'But you have such a contemptuous way of looking at me that I fear you think so.'

Grace's heart struggled between the wish not to be harsh and the fear that she might mislead him. 'I cannot look contemptuous unless I feel contempt,' she said evasively, 'and all I feel is lovelessness.'

'I have been very bad I know,' he returned. 'But unless you can really love me again, Grace, I would rather go away from you for ever. I don't want you to receive me again for duty's sake, or anything of that sort. If I had not cared more for your affection and forgiveness than my own personal comfort I should never have come back here. I could have obtained a practice at a distance, and have lived my own life without coldness or reproach. But I have chosen to return to the one spot on earth where my name is tarnished – to enter the house of a man from whom I have had worse treatment than from any other man alive – all for you!'

This was undeniably true, and it had its weight with Grace, who began to look as if she thought she had been shockingly severe.

'Before you go,' he continued, 'I want to know your pleasure about me: what you wish me to do, or not to do.'

'You are independent of me, and it seems a mockery to ask that. Far be it from me to advise. But I will think it over. I rather need advice myself than stand in a position to give it.'

'*You* don't need advice, wisest, dearest woman that ever lived. If you did. . . .'

'Would you give it to me?'

'Would you act upon what I gave?'

'That's not a fair inquiry,' said she, smiling despite her gravity. 'I don't mind hearing it – what you do really think the most correct and proper course for me.'

'It is so easy for me to say, and yet I dare not, for it would be provoking you to remonstrances.'

Knowing, of course, what the advice would be, she did not press him further, and was about to beckon Marty forward and leave him, when he interrupted her with, 'O! one moment, dear Grace – you will meet me again?'

She eventually agreed to see him that day fortnight. Fitzpiers expostulated at the interval, but the half-alarmed earnestness with which she entreated him not to come sooner made him say hastily that he submitted to her will – that he would regard her as a friend only, anxious for his reform and well-being, till such time as she might allow him to exceed that privilege.

All this was to assure her; it was only too clear that he had not won her confidence yet. It amazed Fitzpiers, and overthrew all his deductions from previous experience, to find that this girl, though she had been married to him, could yet be so coy. Notwithstanding a certain fascination that it carried with it his reflections were sombre as he went homeward; he saw how deep had been his offence to produce so great a wariness in a gentle and once unsuspicious soul.

He was himself too fastidious to care to coerce her. To be an object of misgiving or dislike to a woman who shared his home was what he could not endure the thought of. Life as it stood was more tolerable.

When he was gone Marty joined Mrs Fitzpiers. She would fain have consulted Marty on the question of Platonic relations with her former husband, as she preferred to regard him. But Marty showed no great interest in their affairs, so Grace said nothing. They came onward and saw Melbury standing at the scene of the felling which had been audible to them, when, telling Marty that she wished her meeting with Mr Fitzpiers to be kept private, she left the girl to join her father. At any rate she would consult him on the expediency of occasionally seeing her husband.

Her father was cheerful, and walked by her side as he had done in earlier days. 'I was thinking of you when you came up,' he said. 'I have considered that what has happened is for the best. Since your husband is gone away, and seems not to wish to trouble you, why, let him go, and drop out of your life. Many women are worse off. You can live here comfortably enough, and he can emigrate, or do what he likes for his good. I wouldn't mind sending him the further sum of money he might naturally expect to come to him, so that you may not be bothered with him any more. He could hardly have gone on living here without speaking to me, or meeting me; and that would have been very unpleasant on both sides.'

These remarks checked her intentions. There was a sense of weakness in following them by saying that she had just met her husband by appointment. 'Then you would advise me not to communicate with him?' she observed.

'I shall never advise 'ee again. You are your own mistress – do as you like. But my opinion is that if you don't live with him you had better live without him, and not go shilly-shallying and playing bo-peep. You sent him away; and now he's gone. Very well; trouble him no more.'

Grace felt a guiltiness – she hardly knew why – and made no confession.

CHAPTER FORTY-SIX

THE woods were uninteresting, and Grace stayed indoors a great deal. She became quite a student, reading more than she had done since her marriage. But her seclusion was always broken for the periodical visit to Winterborne's grave with Marty, which was kept up with pious strictness for the purpose of putting snowdrops, primroses, and other vernal flowers thereon as they came.

One afternoon at sunset she was standing under the trees just at the back of her father's garden which, like the rest of the Hintock inclosures, abutted into the wood. A slight footpath led along here, forming a secret way to either of the houses by getting through its boundary hedge. Grace was about to adopt this mode of entry when a figure approached along the path, and held up his hand to detain her. It was her husband.

'I am delighted,' he said, coming up out of breath; and there seemed no reason to doubt his words. 'I saw you some way off – I was afraid you would go in before I could reach you.'

'It is a week before time,' said she reproachfully. 'I said a fortnight from the last meeting.'

'My dear, you don't suppose I could wait a fortnight without trying to get a glimpse of you, even though you had declined to meet me! Would it make you angry to know that I have been along this path at dusk three or four times since our last meeting? Well, how are you?'

She did not refuse her hand, but when he showed a wish to retain it a moment longer than mere formality required she made it smaller, so that it slipped away from him, with again that same alarmed look which always followed his attempts in this direction. He saw that she was not yet out of the elusive mood; not yet to be treated presumingly; and he was correspondingly careful to tranquillize her.

His assertion had seemed to impress her somewhat. 'I had no idea you came so often,' she said. 'How far do you come from?'

'From Sherton Abbas where I am temporarily staying. I always walk the distance here, for if I hire people will know that I come; and my success with you so far has not been great enough to justify such overtness. Now, my dear one – as I *must* call you – I put it to you: will you see me a little oftener as the spring advances?'

Grace lapsed into unwonted sedateness and avoiding the question, said: 'I wish you would concentrate on your profession, and give up those strange studies that used to distract you so much. I am sure you would get on.'

'It is the very thing I am doing. I was going to ask you to burn – or, at least get rid of – all my philosophical literature. It is in the bookcases in your rooms. The fact is I never cared much for abstruse studies.'

'I am so glad to hear you say that. And those other books – those piles of old plays – what good are they to a medical man?'

'None whatever!' he replied cheerfully. 'Sell them at Sherton for what they will fetch.'

'And those dreadful old French romances with their horrid spellings of "filz" and "ung" and "ilz" and "mary" and "ma foy"?'

'You haven't been reading them, Grace?'

'O no – I just looked into them, that was all.'

'Make a bonfire of 'em directly you get home. I meant to do it myself. I can't think what possessed me ever to collect them. I have only a few professional hand-books now, and am quite a practical man. I am in hopes of having some good news to tell you soon, and then do you think that you could – come to me again?'

'I would rather you did not press me on that just now,' she replied with some feeling. 'You have said you mean to lead a new, useful, effectual life; but I should like to see you put it in practice for a little while before you address that query to me. Besides – I could not live with you!'

'Why not?'

Grace was silent a few instants. 'I go with Marty to Giles's grave. I almost worship him. We swore we would show him that devotion. And I mean to keep it up.'

'Well, I wouldn't mind that at all. I have no right to expect anything else, and I will not wish you to keep away. I liked the man as well as any I ever knew. In short, I would accompany you a part of the way to the grave, and smoke a cigar on the stile while I waited till you came back.'

'Then you haven't given up smoking?'

'Well – ahem – no. I have thought of doing so, but—'

His extreme complaisance had rather disconcerted Grace, and the question about smoking had been to effect a diversion. Presently she said firmly, and with a moisture in her eye that he could not see, as her mind returned to poor Giles's 'frustrate ghost': 'I don't like you – to speak lightly on that subject, if you did speak lightly. To be frank with you – quite frank – I think of him as my betrothed lover still. I cannot help it. So that it would be wrong for me to join you.'

Fitzpiers was now uneasy. 'You say your betrothed lover still,' he rejoined. 'When, then, were you betrothed to him, or engaged, as we common people say?'

'When you were away.'

'How could that be?'

Grace would have avoided this; but her natural candour led her on. 'It was when I was under the impression that my marriage with you was about to be dissolved, and that he could then marry me. So I encouraged him to love me.'

Fitzpiers winced visibly; and yet, upon the whole, she was right in telling it. Indeed, his perception that she was right in her absolute sincerity kept up his affectionate admiration for her under the pain of the rebuff. Time had been when the avowal that Grace had deliberately taken steps to replace him would have brought him no sorrow. But she so far dominated him now that he could not bear to hear her words, although the object of her high regard was no more.

'It is rough upon me – that!' he said bitterly. 'O, Grace – I did not know you – tried to get rid of me! I suppose it is of no use, but I ask, cannot you hope to – find a little love in your heart for me again?'

'If I could I would oblige you; but I fear I cannot!' she replied, with illogical ruefulness. 'And I don't see why you should mind my having had one lover besides yourself in my life, when you have had so many.'

'But I can tell you honestly that I love you better than all of them put together, and that's what you will not tell me!'

'I am sorry, but I fear I cannot,' she said, sighing again.

'I wonder if you ever will?' He looked musingly into her indistinct face as if he would read the future there. 'Now have pity, and tell me: will you try?'

'To love you again?'

'Yes; if you can.'

'I don't know how to reply,' she answered, her embarrassment proving her truth. 'Will you promise to leave me quite free as to seeing you or not seeing you?'

'Certainly. Have I given any ground for you to doubt my first promise in that respect?'

She was obliged to admit that he had not.

'Then I think you might get your heart out of that grave,' said he with playful sadness. 'It has been there a long time.'

She faintly shook her head, but said: 'I'll try to think of you more – if I can.'

With this Fitzpiers was compelled to be satisfied, and he asked her when she would meet him again.

'As we arranged – in a fortnight.'

'If it must be a fortnight it must!'

'This time at least. I'll consider by the day I see you again if I can shorten the interval.'

'Well, be that as it may, I shall come at least twice a week to look at your window.'

'You must do as you like about that. Goodnight.'

'Say "husband".'

She seemed almost inclined to give him the word; but exclaiming, 'No, no; I cannot,' slipped through the garden hedge and disappeared.

Fitzpiers did not exaggerate when he told her that he should haunt the precincts of the dwelling. But his persistence in this course did not result in his seeing her much oftener than at the fortnightly interval which she had herself marked out as proper. At these times, however, she punctually appeared, and as the spring wore on the meetings were kept up, though their character changed but little with the increase in their number.

The small garden of the cottage occupied by the Tangs family – father, son, and now son's wife – aligned with the larger one of the timber-dealer at its upper end; and when young Tim, after leaving work at Melbury's, stood at dusk in the little bower at the corner of his inclosure to smoke a pipe, he frequently observed the surgeon pass along the outside track before-mentioned. Fitzpiers always walked loiteringly, pensively, looking with a sharp eye into the gardens one after another as he proceeded; for Fitzpiers did not wish to leave the now absorbing spot too quickly after travelling so far to reach it; hoping always for a glimpse of her whom he passionately desired to take to his arms anew.

Now Tim began to be struck with these loitering progresses along the garden boundaries in the gloaming, and wondered what they boded. It was naturally quite out of his power to divine the singular sentimental revival in Fitzpiers's heart: the fineness of tissue which could take a deep, emotional – almost also an artistic – pleasure in being the yearning *innamorato* of a woman he once had deserted would have seemed an absurdity to the young sawyer. Mr and Mrs Fitzpiers were separated; therefore the question of affection as between them was settled. But his Suke had, since that meeting on their marriage day, repentantly admitted, to the urgency of his questioning, a good deal concerning her past levities. Putting all things together he could hardly avoid connecting Fitzpiers's mysterious visits to this spot with Suke's residence under his roof. But he made himself fairly easy; the vessel in which they were about to emigrate sailed that month; and then Suke would be out of Fitzpiers's way for ever.

The interval at last expired, and the eve of their departure arrived. They were pausing in the room of the cottage allotted to them by Tim's father, after a busy day of preparation which left them weary. In a corner stood their boxes, crammed and corded, their large case for the hold having already been sent away. The firelight shone upon Suke's plump face and form as she stood looking into it, and upon the face of Tim seated in a corner, and upon the walls of his father's house, which he was beholding that night almost for the last time.

Tim Tangs was not happy. This scheme of emigration was dividing him from his father — for old Tangs would on no account leave Hintock — and had it not been for Suke's reputation and his own dignity Tim would at the last moment have abandoned the project. As he sat in the back part of the room he regarded her moodily, and the fire, and the boxes. One thing he had particularly noticed this evening — she was very restless, fitful in her actions, unable to remain seated, and in a marked degree depressed.

'Sorry that you be going, after all, Suke?' he said.

She sighed involuntarily. 'I don't know but that I be,' she answered. ''Tis natural, isn't it, when one is going away?'

'But you wasn't born here as I was.'

'No.'

'There's folk left behind that you'd fain have with 'ee, I reckon?'

'Why do you think that?'

'I've seen things, and I've heard things; and Suke, I say 'twill be a good move for me to get 'ee away. I don't mind his leavings abroad, but I do mind 'em at home.'

Suke's face was not changed from its aspect of listless indifference by the words. She answered nothing; and shortly after he went out for his customary pipe of tobacco at the top of the garden.

The restlessness of Suke had indeed owed its presence to the gentleman of Tim's suspicions, but in a different and — it must be added in justice to her — more innocent sense than he supposed, judging from former doings. She had accidentally discovered that Fitzpiers was in the habit of coming secretly once or twice a week to Hintock, and knew that this evening was a favourite one of the seven for his journey. As she was going next day to leave the country Suke thought there could be no great harm in giving way to a little sentimentality by obtaining a glimpse of him quite unknown to himself or to anybody, and thus taking a silent last farewell. Aware that Fitzpiers's time for passing was at hand she thus betrayed her feeling. No sooner, therefore, had Tim left the room than she let herself noiselessly out of the house and hastened to the corner of the garden, whence she could witness the surgeon's transit across the scene, if he had not already gone by.

Her light cotton dress was visible to Tim lounging in the arbour of the opposite corner, though he was hidden from her. He saw her stealthily climb into the hedge, and so ensconce herself there that nobody could have the least doubt her purpose was to watch unseen for a passer-by.

He went across to the spot and stood behind her. Suke started, having in her blundering way forgotten that he might be near. She at once descended from the hedge.

'So he's coming to-night,' ? said Tim laconically. 'And we always anxious to see our dears.'

'He *is* coming to-night,' she replied with defiance. 'And we *be* anxious for our dears!'

'Then will you step indoors, where your dear will soon jine 'ee? We've to mouster by half-past three to-morrow, and if we don't get to bed by eight at latest our faces will be as long as clock-cases all day.'

She hesitated for a minute but ultimately obeyed, going slowly down the garden to the house, where he heard the door-latch click behind her.

Tim was incensed beyond measure. His marriage had so far been a total failure, a source of bitter regret; and the only course for improving his case, that of leaving the country, was a sorry, and possibly might not be a very effectual one. Do what he would his domestic sky was likely to be overcast to the end of the day. Thus he brooded, and his resentment gathered force. He craved a means of striking one blow back at the cause of his cheerless plight while he was still on the scene of his discomfiture. For some minutes no method suggested itself, and then he had an idea.

Coming to a sudden resolution he hastened along the garden, and entered the one attached to the next cottage, which had formerly been the dwelling of a gamekeeper. Tim descended the path to the back of the house, where only an old woman lived at present, and reaching the wall he stopped. Owing to the slope of the ground the roof-eaves of the linhay were here within touch, and he thrust his arm up under them, feeling about in the space on the top of the wall plate.

'Ah, I thought my memory didn't deceive me!' he lipped silently.

With some exertion he drew down a cobwebbed object curiously framed in iron, which clanked as he moved it. It was about three feet in length and half as wide. Tim contemplated it as well as he could in the dying light of day, and raked off the cobwebs with his hand.

'That will spoil his pretty shins for'n, I reckon!' he said.

It was a man-trap.

CHAPTER FORTY-SEVEN

WERE the inventors of automatic machines to be ranged according to the excellence of their devices for producing sound artistic torture, the creator of the man-trap would occupy a very respectable, if not a very high, place.

It should rather, however, be said, the inventor of the particular form of man-trap of which this found in the keeper's outhouse was a specimen. For there were other shapes and other sizes, instruments which, if placed in a row beside one of the type disinterred by Tim, would have worn the subordinate aspect of the bears, wild boars, or wolves in a travelling menagerie as compared with the leading lion or tiger. In short, though many varieties had been in use during those centuries which we are accustomed to look back upon as the true and only period of merry England – in the rural districts more especially – and onward down to the third decade of the nineteenth century, this model had borne the palm, and had been most usually followed when the orchards and estates required new ones.

There had been the toothless variety used by the softer-hearted landlords — quite contemptible in their clemency. The jaws of these resembled the jaws of an old woman to whom time has left nothing but gums. There were also the intermediate or half-toothed sorts, probably devised by the middle-natured squires, or those under the influence of their wives: two inches of mercy, two inches of cruelty, two inches of mere nip, two inches of probe, and so on, through the whole extent of the jaws. There were also, as a class apart, the bruisers, which did not lacerate the flesh, but only crushed the bone.

The sight of one of these gins, when set, produced a vivid impression that it was endowed with life. It exhibited the combined aspects of a shark, a crocodile, and a scorpion. Each tooth was in the form of a tapering spine two and a quarter inches long, which, when the jaws were closed, stood in alternation from this side and from that. When they were open the two halves formed a complete circle between two and three feet in diameter, the plate or treading-place in the midst being about a foot square, while from beneath extended in opposite directions the soul of the apparatus, the pair of springs, each one having been in its prime of a stiffness to render necessary a lever or the whole weight of the body when forcing it down, though rust had weakened it somewhat now.

There were men at this time still living at Hintock who remembered when the gin and others like it were in use. Tim Tangs's great-uncle had endured a night of six hours in this very trap, which lamed him for life. Once a keeper of Hintock woods set it on the track of a poacher, and afterwards coming back that way forgetful of what he had done walked into it himself. The wound brought on lockjaw, of which he died. This event occurred during the thirties, and by the year 1840 the use of such implements was well-nigh discontinued in the neighbourhood. But being made entirely of iron they by no means disappeared, and in almost every village one could be found in some nook or corner as readily as this was found by Tim. It had indeed been a fearful amusement of Tim and other Hintock lads — especially those who had a dim sense of becoming renowned poachers when they reached their prime — to drag out this trap from its hiding, set it, and throw it with billets of wood, which were penetrated by the teeth to the depth of near an inch.

As soon as he had examined the trap and found that the hinges and springs were fairly perfect, he shouldered it without more ado and returned with his burden to his own garden, passing on through the hedge to the path immediately outside the boundary. Here by the help of a stout stake he set the trap, and laid it carefully behind a bush while he went forward to reconnoitre. As has been stated, nobody passed this way for days together sometimes; but there was just a possibility that some other pedestrian than the one in request might arrive, and it behoved Tim to be careful as to the identity of his victim.

Going about a hundred yards along the rising ground to the right he reached a ridge whereon a large and thick holly grew. Beyond this for some distance the wood was more open, and the course which Fitzpiers must pursue to reach the point, if he came to-night, was visible a long way forward.

For some time there was no sign of him or of anybody. Then there shaped itself a spot out of the dim mid-distance, between the masses of brushwood on each hand. It enlarged, and Tim could hear the brushing of feet over the tufts of sour grass. The airy gait revealed Fitzpiers even before his exact outline could be seen.

Tim Tangs turned about and ran down the opposite side of the hill till he was again at the head of his own garden. It was the work of a few moments to drag out the man-trap very gently — that the plate might not be disturbed sufficiently to throw it — to a space between a pair of young oaks which, rooted in contiguity, grew apart upward, forming a V-shaped opening between; and, being backed up by bushes, left this as the only course for a foot-passenger. In it he laid the trap with the same gentleness of handling, locked the chain round one of the trees, and finally slid back the guard which was placed to keep the gin from accidentally catching the arms of him who set it, or, to use the local and better word, 'toiled' it. Having completed these arrangements Tim sprang through the adjoining hedge of his father's garden, ran down the path, and softly entered the house.

Obedient to his order Suke had gone to bed; and as soon as he had bolted the door Tim unlaced and kicked off his boots at the foot of the stairs and retired likewise, without lighting a candle. His object seemed to be to undress as soon as possible. Before, however, he had completed the operation a long cry resounded without — penetrating, but indescribable.

'What's that?' said Suke, starting up in bed.

'Sounds as if somebody had caught a hare in his gin.'

'O no,' said she. 'It was not a hare, 'twas louder. Hark!'

'Do 'ee get to sleep,' said Tim. 'How be you going to wake at half-past three else?'

She lay down and was silent. Tim stealthily opened the window and listened. Above the low harmonies produced by the instrumentation of the various species of tree around the premises he could hear the twitching of a chain from the spot whereon he had set the man-trap. But further human sound there was none.

Tim was puzzled. In the haste of his project he had not calculated upon a cry; but if one, why not more? He soon ceased to essay an answer, for Hintock was dead to him already. In half-a-dozen hours he would be out of its precincts for life, on his way to the antipodes. He closed the window and lay down.

The hour which had brought these movements of Tim to birth had been operating actively elsewhere. Awaiting in her father's house the minute of her appointment with her husband, Grace Fitzpiers deliberated on many things. Should she inform her father before going out that the estrangement of herself and Edred was not so complete as he had imagined and deemed desirable for her happiness? If she did so she must in some measure become the apologist of her husband, and she was not prepared to go so far.

As for him, he kept her in a mood of considerate gravity. He certainly had changed. He had at his worst times always been gentle in his manner towards her. Could it be that she might make of him a true and worthy husband yet? She had married him; there was no getting over that; and ought she any longer to keep him at a distance? His suave deference to her lightest whim on the question of his comings and goings, when as her lawful husband he might show a little insistence, was a trait in his character as unexpected as it was engaging. If she had been his empress, and he her thrall, he could not have exhibited a more sensitive care to avoid intruding upon her against her will.

Impelled by a remembrance she took down a prayer-book and turned to the marriage-service. Reading it slowly through she became quite appalled at her recent off-handedness, when she rediscovered what awfully solemn promises she had made him at Hintock chancel steps not so very long ago. She became lost in long ponderings on how far a person's conscience might be bound by vows made without at the time a full recognition of their force. That particular sentence, beginning, 'Whom God hath joined together,' was a staggerer for a gentle woman of strong devotional sentiment. She wondered whether God really did join them together. Before she had done deliberating the time of her engagement drew near, and she went out of the house almost at the moment that Tim Tangs retired to his own.

The position of things at that critical juncture was as follows. Two hundred yards to the right of the upper end of Tangs's garden Fitzpiers was still advancing, having now nearly reached the summit of the wood-clothed ridge, the path being the actual one which further on passed between the two young oaks. Thus far it was according to Tim's conjecture. But about two hundred yards to the left, or rather less, was arising a condition which he had not divined, the emergence of Grace as aforesaid from the upper corner of her father's garden with the view of meeting Tim's intended victim. Midway between husband and wife was the diabolical trap, silent, open, ready.

Fitzpiers's walk that night had been cheerful, for he was convinced that the slow and gentle method he had adopted was promising success. The very restraint that he was obliged to exercise upon himself, so as not to kill the delicate bud of returning confidence, fed his flame. He walked so much more rapidly than Grace that if they continued advancing as they had begun, he would reach the trap a good half minute before she could reach the same spot. But here a new circumstance came in: to escape the unpleasantness of being watched or listened to by lurkers – naturally curious by reason of their strained relations – they had arranged that their meeting for to-night should be at the holm-tree on the ridge above-named. So soon, accordingly, as Fitzpiers reached the tree he stood still to await her.

He had not paused under the prickly foliage more than two minutes when he thought he heard a scream from the other side of the ridge. Fitzpiers wondered what it could mean; but such wind as there was just now blew in an adverse direction, and his mood was light. He set down the origin of the sound to one of the superstitious freaks or frolicsome scrimmages between sweethearts that still survived in Hintock from old-English times; and waited on where he stood till ten minutes had passed. Feeling then a little uneasy his mind reverted to the scream; and he went forward over the summit and down the embowered incline till he reached the pair of sister oaks with the narrow opening between them.

Fitzpiers stumbled and all but fell. Stretching down his hand to ascertain the obstruction it came in contact with a confused mass of silken drapery and ironwork that conveyed absolutely no explanatory idea to his mind at all. It was but the work of a moment to strike a match; and then he saw a sight which congealed his blood.

The man-trap was thrown; and between its jaws was part of a woman's clothing – a patterned silk skirt – gripped with such violence that the iron teeth had passed through it, skewering its tissue in a score of places. He immediately recognized the skirt as that of one of his wife's gowns – the gown that she had worn when she met him on the very last occasion.

Fitzpiers had often studied the effect of these instruments when examining the collection at Hintock House, and the conception instantly flashed through him that Grace had been caught, taken out mangled by some chance passer, and carried home, some of her clothes being left behind in the difficulty of getting her free. The shock of this conviction, striking into the very current of high hope, was so great that he cried out like one in corporal agony, and in his misery bowed himself down to the ground.

Of all the degrees and qualities of punishment that Fitzpiers had undergone since his sins against Grace first began, not any even approximated in intensity to this. 'O, my own – my darling! O, cruel Heaven – it is too much this!' he cried, writhing and rocking himself over the sorry accessories of her he deplored.

The voice of his distress was sufficiently loud to be audible to any one who might have been there to hear it; and one there was. Right and left of the narrow pass between the oaks were dense bushes; and now from behind these a female figure glided, whose appearance even in the gloom was, though graceful in outline, noticeably strange.

She was white up to the waist, and figured above. She was, in short, Grace, his wife, lacking the portion of her dress which the gin retained.

'Don't be grieved about me – don't, dear Edred!' she exclaimed, rushing up and bending over him. 'I am not hurt a bit! I was coming on to find you after I had released myself, but I heard footsteps; and I hid away because I was without some of my clothing, and I did not know who the person might be.'

Fitzpiers had sprung to his feet, and his next act was no less unpremeditated by him than it was irresistible by her, and would have been so by any woman not of Amazonian strength. He clasped his arms completely round her, pressed her to his breast and kissed her passionately.

'You are not dead! – you are not hurt! Thank God – thank God!' he said, almost sobbing in his delight and relief from the horror of his apprehension. 'Grace, my wife, my love, how is this – what has happened?'

'I was coming on to you,' she said as distinctly as she could in the half-smothered state of her face against his. 'I was trying to be as punctual as possible, and as I had started a minute late I ran along the path very swiftly – fortunately for myself. Just when I had passed between these trees I felt something clutch at my dress from behind with a noise, and the next moment I was pulled backwards by it, and fell to the ground. I screamed with terror, thinking it was a man lying down there to murder me, but the next moment I discovered it was iron, and that my clothes were caught in a trap. I pulled this way and that, but the thing would not let go, drag it as I would, and I did not know what to do. I did not want to alarm my father or anybody, as I wished nobody to know of these meetings with you, so I could think of no other plan than slipping off my skirt, meaning to run on and tell you what a strange accident had happened to me. But when I had just freed myself by leaving the dress behind I heard steps, and not being sure it was you I did not like to be seen in such a pickle, so I hid away.'

'It was only your speed that saved you! One or both of your legs would have been broken if you had come at ordinary walking pace.'

'Or yours, if you had got here first,' said she, beginning to realize the whole ghastliness of the possibility, or what seemed a possibility to them, though whether the old springs would have done quite so much mischief may be doubted. 'O, Edred, there has been an Eye watching over us to-night, and we should be thankful indeed!'

He continued to press his face to hers. 'You are mine – mine again now!'

She owned that she supposed she was. 'I heard what you said when you thought I was injured,' she went on shyly, 'and I know that a man who could suffer as you were suffering must have a tender regard for me. But how does this awful thing come here?'

'I suppose it has something to do with poachers.' Fitzpiers was still so shaken by the sense of her danger that he was obliged to sit awhile, and it was not until Grace said, 'If I could only get my skirt out nobody would know anything about it,' that he bestirred himself.

By their united efforts, each standing on one of the springs of the trap, they pressed them down sufficiently to insert across the jaws a billet which they dragged from a faggot near at hand, and it was then possible to extract the silk mouthful from the monster's bite, creased and pierced with small holes, but not torn. Fitzpiers assisted her to put it on again; and when her customary contours were thus restored they walked on together, Grace taking his arm till he effected an improvement by passing it round her waist.

The ice having been broken in this unexpected manner, she made no further attempt at reserve. 'I would ask you to come into the house,' she said, 'but my meetings with you have been kept secret from my father, and I should like to prepare him.'

'Never mind, dearest. I could not very well have accepted the invitation. I shall never live here again – as much for your sake as for mine. I have news to tell you on this very point, but my alarm had put it out of my head. I have bought a practice, or rather a partnership, in the Midlands, and I must go there in a week to take up permanent residence. My poor old great-aunt died about eight months ago, and left me enough to do this. I have taken a little furnished house for a time, till we can get one of our own.'

He described the place; and the surroundings, and the view from the windows; and Grace became much interested. 'But why are you not there now?' she said.

'Because I cannot tear myself away from here till I have your promise. Now, darling, you will accompany me there soon – will you not? To-night has settled that?'

Grace's tremblings had gone off, and she did not say nay. They went on together.

The adventure, and the emotions consequent upon the reunion which that event had forced on, combined to render Grace oblivious of the direction of their desultory ramble, till she noticed they were in an encircled glade in the densest part of the wood. The moon, that had imperceptibly added her rays to the scene, shone almost vertically. It was an exceptionally soft, balmy evening for the time of year, which was just that transient period in the May month when beech trees have suddenly unfolded large limp young leaves of the softness of butterflies' wings. Boughs bearing such leaves hung low around and completely inclosed them, so that it was as if they were in a great green vase, which had moss for its bottom and leaf sides. Here they sat down.

The clouds having been packed in the west that evening so as to retain the departing glare a long while, the hour had seemed much earlier than it was. But suddenly the question of time occurred to her.

'I must go back,' she said, springing up; and without further delay they set their faces towards Hintock. As they walked he examined his watch by the aid of the now strong moonlight.

'By the gods, I think I have lost my train!' said Fitzpiers.

'Dear me – whereabouts are we?' said she.

'Two miles in the direction of Sherton.'

'Then do you hasten on, Edred. I am not in the least afraid. I recognize now the part of the wood we are in, and I can find my way back quite easily. I'll tell my father that we have made it up. I wish I had not kept our meetings so private, for it may vex him a little to know I have been seeing you. He is getting old and irritable, that was why I did not. Good-bye.'

'But, as I must stay at the Earl of Wessex to-night, for I cannot possibly catch the train, I think it would be safer for you to let me take care of you.'

'But what will my father think has become of me! He does not know in the least where I am – he thinks I only went into the garden for a few minutes.'

'He will surely guess – somebody has seen me for certain. I'll go all the way back with you to-morrow.'

'But that newly-done-up place – the Earl of Wessex!'

'If you are so very particular about the publicity I will stay at a little quiet one.'

'O no – it is not that I am particular – but I haven't a brush or comb or anything!'

CHAPTER FORTY-EIGHT

ALL the evening Melbury had been coming to his door saying, 'I wonder where in the world that girl is! Never in all my born days did I know her bide out like this! She surely said she was going into the garden to get some parsley.'

Melbury searched the garden, the outbuildings, and the orchard, but could find no trace of her, and then he made inquiries at the cottages of such of his workmen as had not gone to bed, avoiding Tangs's because he knew the young people were to rise early to leave. In these inquiries one of the men's wives somewhat incautiously let out the fact that she had heard a scream in the wood, though from which direction she could not say.

This set Melbury's fears on end. He told the men to light lanterns, and headed by himself they started, Creedle following at the last moment with a bundle of grapnels and ropes which he could not be persuaded to leave behind, and the company being joined by the hollow-turner and Cawtree as they went along.

They explored the precincts of the village, and in a short time lighted upon the man-trap. Its discovery simply added an item of fact without helping their conjectures; but Melbury's indefinite alarm was greatly increased when, holding a candle to the ground, he saw in the teeth of the instrument some frayings from Grace's clothing. No intelligence of any kind was gained till they met a woodman of Delborough, who said that he had seen a lady answering to the description her father gave of Grace, walking through the wood on a gentleman's arm in the direction of Sherton.

'Was he supporting her?' said Melbury.

'Well – rather,' said the man.

'Did she walk lame?'

'Well, 'tis true her head hung over towards him a bit.'

Creedle groaned tragically.

Melbury, not suspecting the presence of Fitzpiers, coupled this account with the man-trap and the scream; he could not understand what it all meant, but the sinister event of the trap made him follow on. Accordingly, they bore away towards the town shouting as they went, and in due course emerged upon the highway.

Nearing Sherton Abbas the previous information was confirmed by other strollers, though the gentleman's supporting arm had disappeared from these later accounts. At last they were so near Sherton that Melbury informed his faithful followers that he did not wish to drag them further at so late an hour, since he could go on by himself and inquire if the woman who had been seen were really Grace. But they would not leave him alone in his anxiety, and trudged onward till the lamplight from the town began to illuminate their faces. At the entrance to the borough they got fresh scent of the pursued, but coupled with the new condition that the lady in the costume described had been going up the street alone.

'Faith – I believe she's mesmerized, or walking in her sleep!' said Melbury.

However, the identity of this woman with Grace was by no means certain; but they plodded along the street. Percomb the hairdresser, who had despoiled Marty of her tresses, was standing at his door, and they duly put inquiries to him.

'Ah – how's Little Hintock folk by now!' he cried before replying. 'Never have I been over there since one winter night some three year ago – and then I lost myself finding it. How can ye live in such a one-eyed place? Great Hintock is bad enough – but Little Hintock – the bats and owls would drive me melancholy-mad! It took two days to raise my sperrits to their true pitch again after that night I went there. Mr Melbury, sir, as a man that's put by money, why not retire and live here, and see something of the world?'

The responses at last given by him to their queries guided them to the building that offered the best accommodation in Sherton – having been rebuilt contemporaneously with the construction of the railway – namely, the Earl of Wessex Hotel.

Leaving the others without, Melbury made prompt inquiry here. His alarm was lessened, though his perplexity was increased, when he received a brief reply that such a lady was in the house.

'Do you know if it is my daughter?' asked Melbury.

The waiter did not.

'Do you know the lady's name?'

Of this, too, the household was ignorant, the hotel having been taken by brand-new people from a distance. They knew the gentleman very well by sight, and had not thought it necessary to ask him to enter his name.

'Oh, the gentleman appears again now,' said Melbury to himself. 'Well, I want to see the lady,' he declared.

A message was taken up, and after some delay the shape of Grace appeared descending round the bend of the staircase, looking as if she lived there, but in other respects rather guilty and frightened.

'Why – what the name—' began her father. 'I thought you went out to get parsley!'

'O yes – I did – but it is all right,' said Grace in a flurried whisper. 'I am not alone here. I am here with Edred. It is entirely owing to an accident, father.'

'Edred? An accident? How does he come here? I thought he was two hundred mile off.'

'Yes – so he is – I mean he has got a beautiful practice two hundred miles off: he has bought it with his own money, some that came to him. But he travelled here, and I was nearly caught in a man-trap, and that's how it is I am here. We were just thinking of sending a messenger to let you know.'

Melbury did not seem to be particularly enlightened by this explanation.

'You were caught in a man-trap?'

'Yes; my dress was. That's how it arose. Edred is upstairs in the sitting-room,' she went on. 'He would not mind seeing you, I am sure.'

'O faith, I don't want to see him! I have seen him too often a'ready. I'll see him another time, perhaps, if 'tis to oblige 'ee.'

'He came to see me; he wanted to consult me about this large partnership I speak of, as it is very promising.'

'Oh; I am glad to hear it,' said Melbury drily.

A pause ensued, during which the inquiring faces and whity-brown clothes of Melbury's companions appeared in the doorway.

'Then bain't you coming home with us?' he asked.

'I – I think not,' said Grace, blushing.

'H'm – very well – you are your own mistress,' he returned, in tones which seemed to assert otherwise. 'Good-night'; and Melbury retreated towards the door.

'Don't be angry, father,' she said, following him a few steps. 'I have done it for the best!'

'I am not angry, though it is true I have been a little misled in this! However, good-night. I must get home-along.'

He left the hotel, not without relief, for to be under the eyes of strangers while he conversed with his lost child had embarrassed him much. His search-party, too, had looked awkward there, having rushed to the task of investigation some in their shirt-sleeves, others in their leather aprons, and all much stained – just as they had come from their work of barking, and not in their Sherton marketing attire; while Creedle, with his ropes and grapnels and air of impending tragedy had added melancholy to gawkiness.

'Now, neighbours,' said Melbury, on joining them, 'as it is getting late we'll leg it home again as fast as we can. I ought to tell you that there has been some mistake – some arrangement entered into between Mr and Mrs Fitzpiers which I didn't quite understand – an important practice in the Midland counties has come to him, which made it necessary for her to join him to-night – so she says. That's all it was – and I'm sorry I dragged you out.'

'Well,' said the hollow-turner, 'here be we seven miles from home, and night-time, and not a hoss or four-footed creeping thing to our name. I say, we'll have a mossel and a drop o' summat to strengthen our nerves afore we vamp all the way back again! My throat's as dry as a kex. What d'ye say, so's?'

They all concurred on the need for sustenance, and proceeded to the antique back street in which the red curtain of the tavern to which Winterborne had taken Grace was the only radiant object. As soon as they had stumbled down into the room Melbury ordered them to be served, when they made themselves comfortable by the long table, and stretched out their legs upon the herring-boned sand of the floor. Melbury himself, restless as usual, walked to the door while he waited for them, and looked up and down the street.

'Well – he's her husband,' Melbury said to himself, 'and let her take him back to her bed if she will! . . . But let her bear in mind that the woman walks and laughs somewhere at this very moment whose neck he'll be coling next year as he does hers to-night; and as he did Felice Charmond's last year; and Suke Damson's the year afore! . . . It's a forlorn hope for her; and God knows how it will end!'

Inside the inn the talk was also of the reunited pair.

'I'd gie her a good shaking if she were my maid; pretending to go out in garden, and leading folk a dozen-mile traipse that have got to get up at five o'clock to-morrow,' said a bark-ripper; who, not working regularly for Melbury, could afford to indulge in strong opinions.

'I don't speak so warm as that,' said the hollow-turner, 'but if 'tis right for couples to make a country talk about their parting for ever, and excite the neighbours, and then make fools of 'em like this, why, I haven't stood upon one leg for five-and-twenty year.'

All his listeners knew that when he alluded to his foot-lathe in these enigmatic terms the speaker meant to be impressive; and Creedle chimed in with, 'Ah, young women do wax wanton in these days! Why couldn't she ha' bode with her father, and been faithful!' Poor Creedle was thinking of his old employer.

'But this deceiving of folks is nothing unusual in matrimony,' said Farmer Cawtree. 'I know'd a man and wife – faith, I don't mind owing, as there's no strangers here, that the pair were my own relations – they'd be at it that hot one hour that you'd hear the poker, and the tongs, and the bellows, and the warming-pan, flee across the house with the movements of their vengeance; and the next hour you'd hear 'em singing "The Spotted Cow" together, as peaceable as two holy twins; yes – and very good voices they had, and would strike in like street ballet-singers to one another's support in the high notes.'

' 'Tis so with couples: they do make up differences in all manner of queer ways,' said the bark-ripper. 'I knowed a woman; and the husband o' her went away for four-and-twenty year. And one night he came home when she was sitting by the fire, and thereupon he sat down himself on the other side of the chimney-corner. "Well," says she, "have ye got any news?" "Don't know as I have," says he; "have you?" "No," says she, "except that my daughter by the husband that succeeded 'ee was married last month, which was a year after I was made a widow by him." "Oh! Anything else?" he says. "No," says she. And there they sat, one on each side of that chimney-corner, and were found by the neighbours sound asleep in their chairs, not having known what to talk about at all.'

'Well, I don't care who the man is,' said Creedle, 'it took a good deal to interest 'em, and that's true. It won't be the same with these.'

'No. He is such a projick, you see. And she is a wonderful scholar too!'

'What women do know nowadays!' observed the hollow-turner. 'You can't deceive 'em as you could in my time.'

'What they knowed then was not small,' said John Upjohn. 'Always a good deal more than the men! Why, when I went courting my wife that is now, the skilfulness that she would show in keeping me on her pretty side as she walked was beyond all belief. Perhaps you've noticed that she's got a pretty side to her face as well as a plain one?'

'I can't say I've noticed it particular much,' said the hollow-turner blandly.

'Well,' continued Upjohn, not disconcerted, 'she has. All women under the sun be prettier one side than t'other. And, as I was saying, the pains she would take to make me walk on the pretty side were unending! I warrant that whether we were going with the sun or against the sun, uphill or downhill, in wind or in lewth, that wart of hers was always towards the hedge, and that dimple towards me. There was I, too simple to see her wheelings and turnings; and she so artful, though two years younger, that she could lead me with a cotton thread, like a blind ram; for that was in the third climate of our courtship. . . . No: I don't think the women have got cleverer, for they was never otherwise.'

'How many climates may there be in courtship, Mr Upjohn?' inquired a youth – the same who had assisted at Winterborne's Christmas party.

'Five – from the coolest to the hottest – leastwise there was five in mine.'

'Can ye give us the chronicle of 'em, Mr Upjohn?'

'Yes – I could. I could certainly. But 'tis quite unnecessary. They'll come to ye by nater, young man, too soon for your good.'

'At present Mrs Fitzpiers can lead the doctor as your mis'ess could lead you,' the hollow-turner remarked. 'She's got him quite tame. But how long 'twill last I can't say. I happened to be setting a wire on the top of my garden one night when he met her on the other side of the hedge; and the way she queened it, and fenced, and kept that poor feller at a distance was enough to freeze yer blood. I should never have supposed it of such a girl.'

Melbury now returned to the room, and the men having declared themselves refreshed they all started on the homeward journey, which was by no means cheerless under the rays of the high moon. Having to walk the whole distance they came by a footpath rather shorter than the highway, though difficult except to those who knew the country well. This brought them by way of the church: and passing the graveyard they observed as they talked a motionless figure standing by the gate.

'I think it was Marty South,' said the hollow-turner parenthetically.

'I think 'twas; 'a was always a lonely maid,' said Upjohn. And they passed on homeward, and thought of the matter no more.

It was Marty, as they had supposed. That evening had been the particular one of the week upon which Grace and herself had been accustomed to privately deposit flowers on Giles's grave, and this was the first occasion since his death eight months earlier on which Grace had failed to keep her appointment. Marty had waited in the road just outside Melbury's, where her fellow-pilgrim had been wont to join her, till she was weary; and at last, thinking that Grace had missed her, and gone on alone, she followed the way to the church, but saw no Grace in front of her. It got later, and Marty continued her walk till she reached the churchyard gate; but still no Grace. Yet her sense of comradeship would not allow her to go on to the grave alone, and still thinking the delay had been unavoidable she stood there with her little basket of flowers in her clasped hands, and her feet chilled by the damp ground, till more than two hours had passed. She then heard the footsteps of Melbury's men, who presently passed on their return from the search. In the silence of the night Marty could not help hearing fragments of their conversation, from which she acquired a general idea of what had occurred, and that Mrs Fitzpiers was by that time in the arms of another man than Giles.

Immediately they had dropped down the hill she entered the churchyard, going to a secluded corner behind the bushes where rose the unadorned stone that marked the last bed of Giles Winterborne. As this solitary and silent girl stood there in the moonlight, a straight slim figure, clothed in a plaitless gown, the contours of womanhood so undeveloped as to be scarcely perceptible in her, the marks of poverty and toil effaced by the misty hour, she touched sublimity at points, and looked almost like a being who had rejected with indifference the attribute of sex for the loftier quality of abstract humanism. She stooped down and cleared away the withered flowers that Grace and herself had laid there the previous week, and put her fresh ones in their place.

'Now, my own, own love,' she whispered, 'you are mine, and only mine; for she has forgot 'ee at last, although for her you died! But I —whenever I get up I'll think of 'ee, and whenever I lie down I'll think of 'ee again. Whenever I plant the young larches I'll think that none can plant as you planted; and whenever I split a gad, and whenever I turn the cider wring, I'll say none could do it like you. If ever I forget your name let me forget home and heaven! . . . But no, no, my love, I never can forget 'ee; for you was a good man, and did good things!'

WESSEX TALES

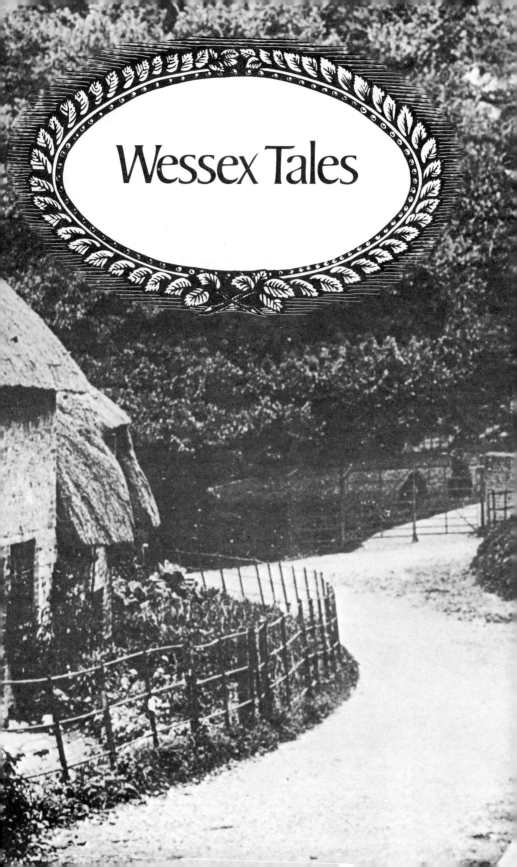

Wessex Tales

Contents

The Three Strangers

A MONG the few features of agricultural England which retain an appearance but little modified by the lapse of centuries, may be reckoned the long, grassy and furzy downs, coombs, or ewe-leases, as they are called according to their kind, that fill a large area of certain counties in the south and south-west. If any mark of human occupation is met with hereon, it usually takes the form of the solitary cottage of some shepherd.

Fifty years ago such a lonely cottage stood on such a down, and may possibly be standing there now. In spite of its loneliness, however, the spot, by actual measurement, was not three miles from a county-town. Yet that affected it little. Three miles of irregular upland, during the long inimical seasons, with their sleets, snows, rains, and mists, afford withdrawing space enough to isolate a Timon or a Nebuchadnezzar; much less, in fair weather, to please that less repellent tribe, the poets, philosophers, artists, and others who 'conceive and meditate of pleasant things'.

Some old earthen camp or barrow, some clump of trees, at least some starved fragment of ancient hedge is usually taken advantage of in the erection of these forlorn dwellings. But, in the present case, such a kind of shelter had been disregarded. Higher Crowstairs, as the house was called, stood quite detached and undefended. The only reason for its precise situation seemed to be the crossing of two footpaths at right angles hard by, which may have crossed there and thus for a good five hundred years. Hence the house was exposed to the elements on all sides. But, though the wind up here blew unmistakably when it did blow, and the rain hit hard whenever it fell, the various weathers of the winter season were not quite so formidable on the down as they were imagined to be by dwellers on low ground. The raw rimes were not so pernicious as in the hollows, and the frosts were scarcely so severe. When the shepherd and his family who tenanted the house were pitied for their sufferings from the exposure, they said that upon the whole they were less inconvenienced by 'wuzzes and flames' (hoarses and phlegms) than when they had lived by the stream of a snug neighbouring valley.

The night of March 28, 182–, was precisely one of the nights that were wont to call forth these expressions of commiseration. The level rainstorm smote walls, slopes, and hedges like the clothyard shafts of Senlac and Crecy. Such sheep and outdoor animals as had no shelter stood with their buttocks to the winds; while the tails of little birds trying to roost on some scraggy thorn were blown inside-out like umbrellas. The gable-end of the cottage was stained with wet, and the eavesdroppings flapped against the wall. Yet never was commiseration for the shepherd more misplaced. For that cheerful rustic was entertaining a large party in glorification of the christening of his second girl.

The guests had arrived before the rain began to fall, and they were all now assembled in the chief or living-room of the dwelling. A glance into the apartment at eight o'clock on this eventful evening would have resulted in the opinion that it was as cosy and comfortable a nook as could be wished for in boisterous weather. The calling of its inhabitant was proclaimed by a number of highly-polished sheep-crooks without stems that were hung ornamentally over the fireplace, the curl of each shining crook varying from the antiquated type engraved in the patriarchal pictures of old family Bibles to the most approved fashion of the last local sheep-fair. The room was lighted by half-a-dozen candles, having wicks only a trifle smaller than the grease which enveloped them, in candlesticks that were never used but at high-days, holy-days, and family feasts. The lights were scattered about the room, two of them standing on the chimney-piece. This position of candles was in itself significant. Candles on the chimney-piece always meant a party.

On the hearth, in front of a back-brand to give substance, blazed a fire of thorns, that crackled 'like the laughter of the fool'.

Nineteen persons were gathered here. Of these, five women, wearing gowns of various bright hues, sat in chairs along the wall; girls shy and not shy filled the window-bench; four men, including Charley Jake the hedge-carpenter, Elijah New the parish-clerk, and John Pitcher, a neighbouring dairyman, the shepherd's father-in-law, lolled in the settle; a young man and maid, who were blushing over tentative *pourparlers* on a life-companionship, sat beneath the corner-cupboard; and an elderly engaged man of fifty or upward moved restlessly about from spots where his betrothed was not to the spot where she was. Enjoyment was pretty general, and so much the more prevailed in being unhampered by conventional restrictions. Absolute confidence in each other's good opinion begat perfect ease, while the finishing stroke of manner, amounting to a truly princely serenity, was lent to the majority by the absence of any expression or trait denoting that they wished to get on in the world, enlarge their minds, or do any eclipsing thing whatever – which nowadays so generally nips the bloom and *bonhomie* of all except the two extremes of the social scale.

Shepherd Fennel had married well, his wife being a dairyman's daughter from a vale at a distance, who brought fifty guineas in her pocket – and kept them there, till they should be required for ministering to the needs of a coming family. This frugal woman had been somewhat exercised as to the character that should be given to the gathering. A sit-still party had its advantages; but an undisturbed position of ease in chairs and settles was apt to lead on the men to such an unconscionable deal of toping that they would sometimes fairly drink the house dry. A dancing-party was the alternative; but this, while avoiding the foregoing objection on the score of good drink, had a counterbalancing disadvantage in the matter of good victuals, the ravenous appetites engendered by the exercise causing immense havoc in the buttery. Shepherdess Fennel fell back upon the intermediate plan of mingling short dances with short periods of talk and singing, so as to hinder any ungovernable rage in either. But this scheme was entirely confined to her own gentle mind: the shepherd himself was in the mood to exhibit the most reckless phases of hospitality.

The fiddler was a boy of those parts, about twelve years of age, who had a wonderful dexterity in jigs and reels, though his fingers were so small and short as to necessitate a constant shifting for the high notes, from which he scrambled back to the first position with sounds not of unmixed purity of tone. At seven the shrill tweedle-dee of this youngster had begun, accompanied by a booming ground-bass from Elijah New, the parish-clerk, who had thoughtfully brought with him his favourite musical instrument, the serpent. Dancing was instantaneous, Mrs Fennel privately enjoining the players on no account to let the dance exceed the length of a quarter of an hour.

But Elijah and the boy in the excitement of their position quite forgot the injunction. Moreover, Oliver Giles, a man of seventeen, one of the dancers, who was enamoured of his partner, a fair girl of thirty-three rolling years, had recklessly handed a new crown-piece to the musicians, as a bribe to keep going as long as they had muscle and wind. Mrs Fennel, seeing the steam begin to generate on the countenances of her guests, crossed over and touched the fiddler's elbow and put her hand on the serpent's mouth. But they took no notice, and fearing she might lose her character of genial hostess if she were to interfere too markedly, she retired and sat down helpless. And so the dance whizzed on with cumulative fury, the performers moving in their planet-like courses, direct and retrograde, from apogee to perigee, till the hand of the well-kicked clock at the bottom of the room had travelled over the circumference of an hour.

While these cheerful events were in course of enactment within Fennel's pastoral dwelling an incident having considerable bearing on the party had occurred in the gloomy night without. Mrs Fennel's concern about the growing fierceness of the dance corresponded in point of time with the ascent of a human figure to the solitary hill of Higher Crowstairs from the direction of the distant town. This personage strode on through the rain without a pause, following the little-worn path which, further on in its course, skirted the shepherd's cottage.

It was nearly the time of full moon, and on this account, though the sky was lined with a uniform sheet of dripping cloud, ordinary objects out of doors were readily visible. The sad wan light revealed the lonely pedestrian to be a man of supple frame; his gait suggested that he had somewhat passed the period of perfect and instinctive agility, though not so far as to be otherwise than rapid of motion when occasion required. At a rough guess, he might have been about forty years of age. He appeared tall, but a recruiting sergeant, or other person accustomed to the judging of men's heights by the eye, would have discerned that this was chiefly owing to his gauntness, and that he was not more than five-feet-eight or nine.

Notwithstanding the regularity of his tread there was caution in it, as in that of one who mentally feels his way; and despite the fact that it was not a black coat nor a dark garment of any sort that he wore, there was something about him which suggested that he naturally belonged to the black-coated tribes of men. His clothes were of fustian, and his boots hobnailed, yet in his progress he showed not the mud-accustomed bearing of hobnailed and fustianed peasantry.

By the time that he had arrived abreast of the shepherd's premises the rain came down, or rather came along, with yet more determined violence. The outskirts of the little settlement partially broke the force of wind and rain, and this induced him to stand still. The most salient of the shepherd's domestic erections was an empty sty at the forward corner of his hedgeless garden, for in these latitudes the principle of masking the homelier features of your establishment by a conventional frontage was unknown. The traveller's eye was attracted to this small building by the pallid shine of the wet slates that covered it. He turned aside, and, finding it empty, stood under the pent-roof for shelter.

While he stood, the boom of the serpent within the adjacent house, and the lesser strains of the fiddler, reached the spot as an accompaniment to the surging hiss of the flying rain on the sod, its louder beating on the cabbage-leaves of the garden, on the straw hackles of eight or ten beehives just discernible by the path, and its dripping from the eaves into a row of buckets and pans that had been placed under the walls of the cottage. For at Higher Crowstairs, as at all such elevated domiciles, the grand difficulty of housekeeping was an insufficiency of water; and a casual rainfall was utilized by turning out, as catchers, every utensil that the house contained. Some queer stories might be told of the contrivances for economy in suds and dish-waters that are absolutely necessitated in upland habitations during the droughts of summer. But at this season there were no such exigencies; a mere acceptance of what the skies bestowed was sufficient for an abundant store.

At last the notes of the serpent ceased and the house was silent. This cessation of activity aroused the solitary pedestrian from the reverie into which he had lapsed, and, emerging from the shed, with an apparently new intention, he walked up the path to the house-door. Arrived here, his first act was to kneel down on a large stone beside the row of vessels, and to drink a copious draught from one of them. Having quenched his thirst he rose and lifted his hand to knock, but paused with his eye upon the panel. Since the dark surface of the wood revealed absolutely nothing, it was evident that he must be mentally looking through the door, as if he wished to measure thereby all the possibilities that a house of this sort might include, and how they might bear upon the question of his entry.

In his indecision he turned and surveyed the scene around. Not a soul was anywhere visible. The garden-path stretched downward from his feet, gleaming like the track of a snail; the roof of the little well (mostly dry), the well-cover, the top rail of the garden-gate, were varnished with the same dull liquid glaze; while, far away in the vale, a faint whiteness of more than usual extent showed that the rivers were high in the meads. Beyond all this winked a few bleared lamplights through the beating drops — lights that denoted the situation of the county-town from which he had appeared to come. The absence of all notes of life in that direction seemed to clinch his intentions, and he knocked at the door.

Within, a desultory chat had taken the place of movement and musical sound. The hedge-carpenter was suggesting a song to the company, which nobody just then was inclined to undertake, so that the knock afforded a not unwelcome diversion.

'Walk in!' said the shepherd promptly.

The latch clicked upward, and out of the night our pedestrian appeared upon the door-mat. The shepherd arose, snuffed two of the nearest candles, and turned to look at him.

Their light disclosed that the stranger was dark in complexion and not unprepossessing as to feature. His hat, which for a moment he did not remove, hung low over his eyes, without concealing that they were large, open, and determined, moving with a flash rather than a glance round the room. He seemed pleased with his survey, and, baring his shaggy head, said, in a rich deep voice, 'The rain is so heavy, friends, that I ask leave to come in and rest awhile.'

'To be sure, stranger,' said the shepherd. 'And faith, you've been lucky in choosing your time, for we are having a bit of a fling for a glad cause – though, to be sure, a man could hardly wish that glad cause to happen more than once a year.'

'Nor less,' spoke up a woman. 'For 'tis best to get your family over and done with, as soon as you can, so as to be all the earlier out of the fag o't.'

'And what may be this glad cause?' asked the stranger.

'A birth and christening,' said the shepherd.

The stranger hoped his host might not be made unhappy either by too many or too few of such episodes, and being invited by a gesture to a pull at the mug, he readily acquiesced. His manner, which, before entering, had been so dubious, was now altogether that of a careless and candid man.

'Late to be traipsing athwart this coomb – hey?' said the engaged man of fifty.

'Late it is, master, as you say. – I'll take a seat in the chimney-corner, if you have nothing to urge against it, ma'am; for I am a little moist on the side that was next the rain.'

Mrs Shepherd Fennel assented, and made room for the self-invited comer, who, having got completely inside the chimney-corner, stretched out his legs and his arms with the expansiveness of a person quite at home.

'Yes, I am rather cracked in the vamp,' he said freely, seeing that the eyes of the shepherd's wife fell upon his boots, 'and I am not well fitted either. I have had some rough times lately, and have been forced to pick up what I can get in the way of wearing, but I must find a suit better fit for working-days when I reach home.'

'One of hereabouts?' she inquired.

'Not quite that – further up the country.'

'I thought so. And so be I; and by your tongue you come from my neighbourhood.'

'But you would hardly have heard of me,' he said quickly. 'My time would be long before yours, ma'am, you see.'

This testimony to the youthfulness of his hostess had the effect of stopping her cross-examination.

'There is only one thing more wanted to make me happy,' continued the new-comer. 'And that is a little baccy, which I am sorry to say I am out of.'

'I'll fill your pipe,' said the shepherd.

'I must ask you to lend me a pipe likewise.'

'A smoker, and no pipe about 'ee?'

'I have dropped it somewhere on the road.'

The shepherd filled and handed him a new clay pipe, saying, as he did so, 'Hand me your baccy-box – I'll fill that too, now I am about it.'

The man went through the movement of searching his pockets.

'Lost that too?' said his entertainer, with some surprise.

'I am afraid so,' said the man with some confusion. 'Give it to me in a screw of paper.' Lighting his pipe at the candle with a suction that drew the whole flame into the bowl, he resettled himself in the corner and bent his looks upon the faint steam from his damp legs, as if he wished to say no more.

Meanwhile the general body of guests had been taking little notice of this

visitor by reason of an absorbing discussion in which they were engaged with the
band about a tune for the next dance. The matter being settled, they were about
to stand up when an interruption came in the shape of another knock at the door.

At sound of the same the man in the chimney-corner took up the poker and
began stirring the brands as if doing it thoroughly were the one aim of his
existence; and a second time the shepherd said, 'Walk in!' In a moment another
man stood upon the straw-woven door-mat. He too was a stranger.

This individual was one of a type radically different from the first. There was
more of the commonplace in his manner, and a certain jovial cosmopolitanism
sat upon his features. He was several years older than the first arrival, his hair
being slightly frosted, his eyebrows bristly, and his whiskers cut back from his
cheeks. His face was rather full and flabby, and yet it was not altogether a face
without power. A few grog-blossoms marked the neighbourhood of his nose. He
flung back his long drab greatcoat, revealing that beneath it he wore a suit of
cinder-gray shade throughout, large heavy seals, of some metal or other that
would take a polish, dangling from his fob as his only personal ornament.
Shaking the water-drops from his low-crowned glazed hat, he said, 'I must ask
for a few minutes' shelter, comrades, or I shall be wetted to my skin before I get to
Casterbridge.'

'Make yourself at home, master,' said the shepherd, perhaps a trifle less
heartily than on the first occasion. Not that Fennel had the least tinge of
niggardliness in his composition; but the room was far from large, spare chairs
were not numerous, and damp companions were not altogether desirable at close
quarters for the women and girls in their bright-coloured gowns.

However, the second comer, after taking off his greatcoat, and hanging his hat
on a nail in one of the ceiling-beams as if he had been specially invited to put it
there, advanced and sat down at the table. This had been pushed so closely into
the chimney-corner, to give all available room to the dancers, that its inner edge
grazed the elbow of the man who had ensconced himself by the fire; and thus the
two strangers were brought into close companionship. They nodded to each
other by way of breaking the ice of unacquaintance, and the first stranger handed
his neighbour the family mug — a huge vessel of brown ware, having its upper
edge worn away like a threshold by the rub of whole generations of thirsty lips
that had gone the way of all flesh, and bearing the following inscription burnt
upon its rotund side in yellow letters: —

THERE IS NO FUN
UNTILL i CUM

The other man, nothing loth, raised the mug to his lips, and drank on, and on,
and on — till a curious blueness overspread the countenance of the shepherd's
wife, who had regarded with no little surprise the first stranger's free offer to the
second of what did not belong to him to dispense.

'I knew it!' said the toper to the shepherd with much satisfaction. 'When I
walked up your garden before coming in, and saw the hives all of a row, I said to
myself, "Where there's bees there's honey, and where there's honey there's
mead." But mead of such a truly comfortable sort as this I really didn't expect to
meet in my older days.' He took yet another pull at the mug, till it assumed an
ominous elevation.

'Glad you enjoy it!' said the shepherd warmly.

'It is goodish mead,' assented Mrs Fennel, with an absence of enthusiasm which seemed to say that it was possible to buy praise for one's cellar at too heavy a price. 'It is trouble enough to make – and really I hardly think we shall make any more. For honey sells well, and we ourselves can make shift with a drop o' small mead and metheglin for common use from the comb-washings.'

'O, but you'll never have the heart!' reproachfully cried the stranger in cinder-gray, after taking up the mug a third time and setting it down empty. 'I love mead, when 'tis old like this, as I love to go to church o' Sundays or to relieve the needy any day of the week.'

'Ha, ha, ha!' said the man in the chimney-corner, who, in spite of the taciturnity induced by the pipe of tobacco, could not or would not refrain from this slight testimony to his comrade's humour.

Now the old mead of those days, brewed of the purest first-year or maiden honey, four pounds to the gallon – with its due complement of white of eggs, cinnamon, ginger, cloves, mace, rosemary, yeast, and processes of working, bottling, and cellaring – tasted remarkably strong; but it did not taste so strong as it actually was. Hence, presently, the stranger in cinder-gray at the table, moved by its creeping influence, unbuttoned his waistcoat, threw himself back in his chair, spread his legs, and made his presence felt in various ways.

'Well, well, as I say,' he resumed, 'I am going to Casterbridge, and to Casterbridge I must go. I should have been almost there by this time; but the rain drove me into your dwelling, and I'm not sorry for it.'

'You don't live in Casterbridge?' said the shepherd.

'Not as yet; though I shortly mean to move there.'

'Going to set up in trade, perhaps?'

'No, no,' said the shepherd's wife. 'It is easy to see that the gentleman is rich, and don't want to work at anything.'

The cinder-gray stranger paused, as if to consider whether he would accept that definition of himself. He presently rejected it by answering, 'Rich is not quite the word for me, dame. I do work, and I must work. And even if I only get to Casterbridge by midnight I must begin work there at eight to-morrow morning. Yes, het or wet, blow or snow, famine or sword, my day's work to-morrow must be done.'

'Poor man! Then, in spite o' seeming, you be worse off than we?' replied the shepherd's wife.

''Tis the nature of my trade, men and maidens. 'Tis the nature of my trade more than my poverty. . . . But really and truly I must up and off, or I shan't get a lodging in the town.' However, the speaker did not move, and directly added, 'There's time for one more draught of friendship before I go; and I'd perform it at once if the mug were not dry.'

'Here's a mug o' small,' said Mrs Fennel. 'Small, we call it, though to be sure 'tis only the first wash o' the combs.'

'No,' said the stranger disdainfully. 'I won't spoil your first kindness by partaking o' your second.'

'Certainly not,' broke in Fennel. 'We don't increase and multiply every day, and I'll fill the mug again.' He went away to the dark place under the stairs where the barrel stood. The shepherdess followed him.

'Why should you do this?' she said reproachfully, as soon as they were alone. 'He's emptied it once, though it held enough for ten people; and now he's not contented wi' the small, but must needs call for more o' the strong! And a stranger unbeknown to any of us. For my part, I don't like the look o' the man at all.'

'But he's in the house, my honey; and 'tis a wet night, and a christening. Daze it, what's a cup of mead more or less? There'll be plenty more next bee-burning.'

'Very well – this time, then,' she answered, looking wistfully at the barrel. 'But what is the man's calling, and where is he one of, that he should come in and join us like this?'

'I don't know. I'll ask him again.'

The catastrophe of having the mug drained dry at one pull by the stranger in cinder-gray was effectually guarded against this time by Mrs Fennel. She poured out his allowance in a small cup, keeping the large one at a discreet distance from him. When he had tossed off his portion the shepherd renewed his inquiry about the stranger's occupation.

The latter did not immediately reply, and the man in the chimney-corner, with sudden demonstrativeness, said, 'Anybody may know my trade – I'm a wheelwright.'

'A very good trade for these parts,' said the shepherd.

'And anybody may know mine – if they've the sense to find it out,' said the stranger in cinder-gray.

'You may generally tell what a man is by his claws,' observed the hedge-carpenter, looking at his own hands. 'My fingers be as full of thorns as an old pin-cushion is of pins.'

The hands of the man in the chimney-corner instinctively sought the shade, and he gazed into the fire as he resumed his pipe. The man at the table took up the hedge-carpenter's remark, and added smartly, 'True; but the oddity of my trade is that, instead of setting a mark upon me, it sets a mark upon my customers.'

No observation being offered by anybody in elucidation of this enigma the shepherd's wife once more called for a song. The same obstacles presented themselves as at the former time – one had no voice, another had forgotten the first verse. The stranger at the table, whose soul had now risen to a good working temperature, relieved the difficulty by exclaiming that, to start the company, he would sing himself. Thrusting one thumb into the arm-hole of his waistcoat, he waved the other hand in the air, and, with an extemporizing gaze at the shining sheep-crooks above the mantelpiece, began: –

> 'O my trade it is the rarest one,
>   Simple shepherds all –
>   My trade is a sight to see;
> For my customers I tie, and take them up on high,
>   And waft 'em to a far countree!'

The room was silent when he had finished the verse – with one exception, that of the man in the chimney-corner, who, at the singer's word, 'Chorus!' joined him in a deep bass voice of musical relish –

> 'And waft 'em to a far countree!'

Oliver Giles, John Pitcher the dairyman, the parish-clerk, the engaged man of fifty, the row of young women against the wall, seemed lost in thought not of the gayest kind. The shepherd looked meditatively on the ground, the shepherdess gazed keenly at the singer, and with some suspicion; she was doubting whether this stranger were merely singing an old song from recollection, or was composing one there and then for the occasion. All were as perplexed at the obscure revelation as the guests at Belshazzar's Feast, except the man in the chimney-corner, who quietly said, 'Second verse, stranger,' and smoked on.

The singer thoroughly moistened himself from his lips inwards, and went on with the next stanza as requested: –

> 'My tools are but common ones,
> Simple shepherds all –
> My tools are no sight to see:
> A little hempen string, and a post whereon to swing,
> Are implements enough for me!'

Shepherd Fennel glanced round. There was no longer any doubt that the stranger was answering his question rhythmically. The guests one and all started back with suppressed exclamations. The young woman engaged to the man of fifty fainted half-way, and would have proceeded, but finding him wanting in alacrity for catching her she sat down trembling.

'O, he's the ——!' whispered the people in the background, mentioning the name of an ominous public officer. 'He's come to do it! 'Tis to be at Casterbridge jail to-morrow – the man for sheep-stealing – the poor clockmaker we heard of, who used to live away at Shottsford and had no work to do – Timothy Summers, whose family were a-starving, and so he went out of Shottsford by the high-road, and took a sheep in open daylight, defying the farmer's wife and the farmer's lad, and every man jack among 'em. He' (and they nodded towards the stranger of the deadly trade) 'is come from up the country to do it because there's not enough to do in his own county-town, and he's got the place here now our own county man's dead; he's going to live in the same cottage under the prison wall.'

The stranger in cinder-gray took no notice of this whispered string of observations, but again wetted his lips. Seeing that his friend in the chimney-corner was the only one who reciprocated his joviality in any way, he held out his cup towards that appreciative comrade, who also held out his own. They clinked together, the eyes of the rest of the room hanging upon the singer's actions. He parted his lips for the third verse; but at that moment another knock was audible upon the door. This time the knock was faint and hesitating.

The company seemed scared; the shepherd looked with consternation towards the entrance, and it was with some effort that he resisted his alarmed wife's deprecatory glance, and uttered for the third time the welcoming words, 'Walk in!'

The door was gently opened, and another man stood upon the mat. He, like those who had preceded him, was a stranger. This time it was a short, small personage, of fair complexion, and dressed in a decent suit of dark clothes.

'Can you tell me the way to—?' he began: when, gazing round the room to observe the nature of the company amongst whom he had fallen, his eyes lighted on the stranger in cinder-gray. It was just at the instant when the latter, who had thrown his mind into his song with such a will that he scarcely heeded the interruption, silenced all whispers and inquiries by bursting into his third verse: —

> 'To-morrow is my working day,
>   Simple shepherds all —
>   To-morrow is a working day for me:
> For the farmer's sheep is slain, and the lad who did it ta'en,
>   And on his soul may God ha' merc-y!'

The stranger in the chimney-corner, waving cups with the singer so heartily that his mead splashed over on the hearth, repeated in his bass voice as before: —

> 'And on his soul may God ha' merc-y!'

All this time the third stranger had been standing in the doorway. Finding now that he did not come forward or go on speaking, the guests particularly regarded him. They noticed to their surprise that he stood before them the picture of abject terror — his knees trembling, his hand shaking so violently that the door-latch by which he supported himself rattled audibly: his white lips were parted, and his eyes fixed on the merry officer of justice in the middle of the room. A moment more and he had turned, closed the door, and fled.

'What a man can it be?' said the shepherd.

The rest, between the awfulness of their late discovery and the odd conduct of this third visitor, looked as if they knew not what to think, and said nothing. Instinctively they withdrew further and further from the grim gentleman in their midst, whom some of them seemed to take for the Prince of Darkness himself, till they formed a remote circle, an empty space of floor being left between them and him —

> '. . . . circulus, cujus centrum diabolus'.

The room was so silent — though there were more than twenty people in it — that nothing could be heard but the patter of the rain against the window-shutters, accompanied by the occasional hiss of a stray drop that fell down the chimney into the fire, and the steady puffing of the man in the corner, who had now resumed his pipe of long clay.

The stillness was unexpectedly broken. The distant sound of a gun reverberated through the air — apparently from the direction of the county-town.

'Be jiggered!' cried the stranger who had sung the song, jumping up.

'What does that mean?' asked several.

'A prisoner escaped from the jail — that's what it means.'

All listened. The sound was repeated, and none of them spoke but the man in the chimney-corner, who said quietly, 'I've often been told that in this county they fire a gun at such times; but I never heard it till now.'

'I wonder if it is *my* man?' murmured the personage in cinder-gray.

'Surely it is!' said the shepherd involuntarily. 'And surely we've zeed him! That little man who looked in at the door by now, and quivered like a leaf when he zeed ye and heard your song!'

'His teeth chattered, and the breath went out of his body,' said the dairyman.

'And his heart seemed to sink within him like a stone,' said Oliver Giles.

'And he bolted as if he'd been shot at,' said the hedge-carpenter.

'True – his teeth chattered, and his heart seemed to sink; and he bolted as if he'd been shot at,' slowly summed up the man in the chimney-corner.

'I didn't notice it,' remarked the hangman.

'We were all a-wondering what made him run off in such a fright,' faltered one of the women against the wall, 'and now 'tis explained!'

The firing of the alarm-gun went on at intervals, low and sullenly, and their suspicions became a certainty. The sinister gentleman in cinder-gray roused himself. 'Is there a constable here?' he asked, in thick tones. 'If so, let him step forward.'

The engaged man of fifty stepped quavering out from the wall, his betrothed beginning to sob on the back of the chair.

'You are a sworn constable?'

'I be, sir.'

'Then pursue the criminal at once, with assistance, and bring him back here. He can't have gone far.'

'I will, sir, I will – when I've got my staff. I'll go home and get it, and come sharp here, and start in a body.'

'Staff! – never mind your staff; the man'll be gone!'

'But I can't do nothing without my staff – can I, William, and John, and Charles Jake? No; for there's the king's royal crown a painted on en in yaller and gold, and the lion and the unicorn, so as when I raise en up and hit my prisoner, 'tis made a lawful blow thereby. I wouldn't 'tempt to take up a man without my staff – no, not I. If I hadn't the law to gie me courage, why, instead o' my taking up him he might take up me!'

'Now, I'm a king's man myself, and can give you authority enough for this,' said the formidable officer in gray. 'Now then, all of ye, be ready. Have ye any lanterns?'

'Yes – have ye any lanterns? – I demand it!' said the constable.

'And the rest of you able-bodied—'

'Able-bodied men – yes – the rest of ye!' said the constable.

'Have you some good stout staves and pitchforks—'

'Staves and pitchforks – in the name o' the law! And take 'em in yer hands and go in quest, and do as we in authority tell ye!'

Thus aroused, the men prepared to give chase. The evidence was, indeed, though circumstantial, so convincing, that but little argument was needed to show the shepherd's guests that after what they had seen it would look very much like connivance if they did not instantly pursue the unhappy third stranger, who could not as yet have gone more than a few hundred yards over such uneven country.

A shepherd is always well provided with lanterns; and, lighting these hastily, and with hurdle-staves in their hands, they poured out of the door, taking a direction along the crest of the hill, away from the town, the rain having fortunately a little abated.

Disturbed by the noise, or possibly by unpleasant dreams of her baptism, the child who had been christened began to cry heart-brokenly in the room overhead. These notes of grief came down through the chinks of the floor to the ears of the women below, who jumped up one by one, and seemed glad of the excuse to

ascend and comfort the baby, for the incidents of the last half-hour greatly
oppressed them. Thus in the space of two or three minutes the room on the
ground-floor was deserted quite.

But it was not for long. Hardly had the sound of footsteps died away when a
man returned round the corner of the house from the direction the pursuers had
taken. Peeping in at the door, and seeing nobody there, he entered leisurely. It
was the stranger of the chimney-corner, who had gone out with the rest. The
motive of his return was shown by his helping himself to a cut piece of skimmer-
cake that lay on a ledge beside where he had sat, and which he had apparently
forgotten to take with him. He also poured out half a cup more mead from the
quantity that remained, ravenously eating and drinking these as he stood. He had
not finished when another figure came in just as quietly – his friend in cinder-
gray.

'O – you here?' said the latter, smiling. 'I thought you had gone to help in the
capture.' And this speaker also revealed the object of his return by looking
solicitously round for the fascinating mug of old mead.

'And I thought you had gone,' said the other, continuing his skimmer-cake
with some effort.

'Well, on second thoughts, I felt there were enough without me,' said the first
confidentially, 'and such a night as it is, too. Besides, 'tis the business o' the
Government to take care of its criminals – not mine.'

'True; so it is. And I felt as you did, that there were enough without me.'

'I don't want to break my limbs running over the humps and hollows of this
wild country.'

'Nor I neither, between you and me.'

'These shepherd-people are used to it – simple-minded souls, you know,
stirred up to anything in a moment. They'll have him ready for me before the
morning, and no trouble to me at all.'

'They'll have him, and we shall have saved ourselves all labour in the matter.'

'True, true. Well, my way is to Casterbridge; and 'tis as much as my legs will do
to take me that far. Going the same way?'

'No, I am sorry to say! I have to get home over there' (he nodded indefinitely to
the right), 'and I feel as you do, that it is quite enough for my legs to do before
bedtime.'

The other had by this time finished the mead in the mug, after which, shaking
hands heartily at the door, and wishing each other well, they went their several
ways.

In the meantime the company of pursuers had reached the end of the hog's-
back elevation which dominated this part of the down. They had decided on no
particular plan of action; and, finding that the man of the baleful trade was no
longer in their company, they seemed quite unable to form any such plan now.
They descended in all directions down the hill, and straightway several of the
party fell into the snare set by Nature for all misguided midnight ramblers over
this part of the cretaceous formation. The 'lanchets', or flint slopes, which belted
the escarpment at intervals of a dozen yards, took the less cautious ones
unawares, and losing their footing on the rubbly steep they slid sharply
downwards, the lanterns rolling from their hands to the bottom, and there lying
on their sides till the horn was scorched through.

When they had again gathered themselves together the shepherd, as the man who knew the country best, took the lead, and guided them round these treacherous inclines. The lanterns, which seemed rather to dazzle their eyes and warn the fugitive than to assist them in the exploration, were extinguished, due silence was observed; and in this more rational order they plunged into the vale. It was a grassy, briery, moist defile, affording some shelter to any person who had sought it; but the party perambulated it in vain, and ascended on the other side. Here they wandered apart, and after an interval closed together again to report progress. At the second time of closing in they found themselves near a lonely ash, the single tree on this part of the coomb, probably sown there by a passing bird some fifty years before. And here, standing a little to one side of the trunk, as motionless as the trunk itself, appeared the man they were in quest of, his outline being well defined against the sky beyond. The band noiselessly drew up and faced him.

'Your money or your life!' said the constable sternly to the still figure.

'No, no,' whispered John Pitcher. ''Tisn't our side ought to say that. That's the doctrine of vagabonds like him, and we be on the side of the law.'

'Well, well,' replied the constable impatiently; 'I must say something, mustn't I? and if you had all the weight o' this undertaking upon your mind, perhaps you'd say the wrong thing too! – Prisoner at the bar, surrender, in the name of the Father – the Crown, I mane!'

The man under the tree seemed now to notice them for the first time, and, giving them no opportunity whatever for exhibiting their courage, he strolled slowly towards them. He was, indeed, the little man, the third stranger; but his trepidation had in a great measure gone.

'Well, travellers,' he said, 'did I hear ye speak to me?'

'You did: you've got to come and be our prisoner at once!' said the constable. 'We arrest 'ee on the charge of not biding in Casterbridge jail in a decent proper manner to be hung to-morrow morning. Neighbours, do your duty, and seize the culpet!'

On hearing the charge the man seemed enlightened, and, saying not another word, resigned himself with preternatural civility to the search-party, who, with their staves in their hands, surrounded him on all sides, and marched him back towards the shepherd's cottage.

It was eleven o'clock by the time they arrived. The light shining from the open door, a sound of men's voices within, proclaimed to them as they approached the house that some new events had arisen in their absence. On entering they discovered the shepherd's living-room to be invaded by two officers from Casterbridge jail, and a well-known magistrate who lived at the nearest country-seat, intelligence of the escape having become generally circulated.

'Gentlemen,' said the constable, 'I have brought back your man – not without risk and danger; but every one must do his duty! He is inside this circle of able-bodied persons, who have lent me useful aid, considering their ignorance of Crown work. Men, bring forward your prisoner!' And the third stranger was led to the light.

'Who is this?' said one of the officials.

'The man,' said the constable.

'Certainly not,' said the turnkey; and the first corroborated his statement.

'But how can it be otherwise?' asked the constable. 'Or why was he so terrified at sight o' the singing instrument of the law who sat there?' Here he related the strange behaviour of the third stranger on entering the house during the hangman's song.

'Can't understand it,' said the officer coolly. 'All I know is that it is not the condemned man. He's quite a different character from this one; a gauntish fellow, with dark hair and eyes, rather good-looking, and with a musical bass voice that if you heard it once you'd never mistake as long as you lived.'

'Why, souls — 'twas the man in the chimney-corner!'

'Hey — what?' said the magistrate, coming forward after inquiring particulars from the shepherd in the background. 'Haven't you got the man after all?'

'Well, sir,' said the constable, 'he's the man we were in search of, that's true; and yet he's not the man we were in search of. For the man we were in search of was not the man we wanted, sir, if you understand my every-day way; for 'twas the man in the chimney-corner!'

'A pretty kettle of fish altogether!' said the magistrate. 'You had better start for the other man at once.'

The prisoner now spoke for the first time. The mention of the man in the chimney-corner seemed to have moved him as nothing else could do. 'Sir,' he said, stepping forward to the magistrate, 'take no more trouble about me. The time is come when I may as well speak. I have done nothing; my crime is that the condemned man is my brother. Early this afternoon I left home at Shottsford to tramp it all the way to Casterbridge jail to bid him farewell. I was benighted, and called here to rest and ask the way. When I opened the door I saw before me the very man, my brother, that I thought to see in the condemned cell at Casterbridge. He was in this chimney-corner; and jammed close to him, so that he could not have got out if he had tried, was the executioner who'd come to take his life, singing a song about it and not knowing that it was his victim who was close by, joining in to save appearances. My brother threw a glance of agony at me, and I knew he meant, "Don't reveal what you see; my life depends on it." I was so terror-struck that I could hardly stand, and, not knowing what I did, I turned and hurried away.'

The narrator's manner and tone had the stamp of truth, and his story made a great impression on all around.

'And do you know where your brother is at the present time?' asked the magistrate.

'I do not. I have never seen him since I closed this door.'

'I can testify to that, for we've been between ye ever since,' said the constable.

'Where does he think to fly to? — what is his occupation?'

'He's a watch-and-clock-maker, sir.'

''A said 'a was a wheelwright — a wicked rogue,' said the constable.

'The wheels of clocks and watches he meant, no doubt,' said Shepherd Fennel. 'I thought his hands were palish for's trade.'

'Well, it appears to me that nothing can be gained by retaining this poor man in custody,' said the magistrate; 'your business lies with the other, unquestionably.'

And so the little man was released off-hand; but he looked nothing the less sad on that account, it being beyond the power of magistrate or constable to raze out the written troubles in his brain, for they concerned another whom he regarded with more solicitude than himself. When this was done, and the man had gone his way, the night was found to be so far advanced that it was deemed useless to renew the search before the next morning.

Next day, accordingly, the quest for the clever sheep-stealer became general and keen, to all appearance at least. But the intended punishment was cruelly disproportioned to the transgression, and the sympathy of a great many country-folk in that district was strongly on the side of the fugitive. Moreover, his marvellous coolness and daring in hob-and-nobbing with the hangman, under the unprecedented circumstances of the shepherd's party, won their admiration. So that it may be questioned if all those who ostensibly made themselves so busy in exploring woods and fields and lanes were quite so thorough when it came to the private examination of their own lofts and outhouses. Stories were afloat of a mysterious figure being occasionally seen in some old overgrown trackway or other, remote from turnpike roads; but when a search was instituted in any of these suspected quarters nobody was found. Thus the days and weeks passed without tidings.

In brief, the bass-voiced man of the chimney-corner was never recaptured. Some said that he went across the sea, others that he did not, but buried himself in the depths of a populous city. At any rate, the gentleman in cinder-gray never did his morning's work at Casterbridge, nor met anywhere at all, for business purposes, the genial comrade with whom he had passed an hour of relaxation in the lonely house on the slope of the coomb.

The grass has long been green on the graves of Shepherd Fennel and his frugal wife; the guests who made up the christening party have mainly followed their entertainers to the tomb; the baby in whose honour they all had met is a matron in the sere and yellow leaf. But the arrival of the three strangers at the shepherd's that night, and the details connected therewith, is a story as well known as ever in the country about Higher Crowstairs.

March 1883

A Tradition of Eighteen Hundred and Four

T HE widely discussed possibility of an invasion of England through a Channel tunnel has more than once recalled old Solomon Selby's story to my mind.

The occasion on which I numbered myself among his audience was one evening when he was sitting in the yawning chimney-corner of the inn-kitchen, with some others who had gathered there, and I entered for shelter from the rain. Withdrawing the stem of his pipe from the dental notch in which it habitually rested, he leaned back in the recess behind him and smiled into the fire. The smile was neither mirthful nor sad, not precisely humorous nor altogether thoughtful. We who knew him recognized it in a moment: it was his narrative smile. Breaking off our few desultory remarks we drew up closer, and he thus began: –

'My father, as you mid know, was a shepherd all his life, and lived out by the Cove four miles yonder, where I was born and lived likewise, till I moved here shortly afore I was married. The cottage that first knew me stood on the top of the down, near the sea; there was no house within a mile and a half of it; it was built o' purpose for the farm-shepherd, and had no other use. They tell me that it is now pulled down, but that you can see where it stood by the mounds of earth and a few broken bricks that are still lying about. It was a bleak and dreary place in winter-time, but in summer it was well enough, though the garden never came to much, because we could not get up a good shelter for the vegetables and currant bushes; and where there is much wind they don't thrive.

'Of all the years of my growing up the ones that bide clearest in my mind were eighteen hundred and three, four, and five. This was for two reasons: I had just then grown to an age when a child's eyes and ears take in and note down everything about him, and there was more at that date to bear in mind than there ever has been since with me. It was, as I need hardly tell ye, the time after the first peace, when Bonaparte was scheming his descent upon England. He had crossed the great Alp mountains, fought in Egypt, drubbed the Turks, the Austrians, and the Proossians, and now thought he'd have a slap at us. On the other side of the Channel, scarce out of sight and hail of a man standing on our English shore, the French army of a hundred and sixty thousand men and fifteen thousand horses had been brought together from all parts, and were drilling every day. Bonaparte had been three years a-making his preparations; and to ferry these soldiers and cannon and horses across he had contrived a couple of thousand flat-bottomed boats. These boats were small things, but wonderfully built. A good few of 'em were so made as to have a little stable on board each for the two horses that were to haul the cannon carried at the stern. To get in order all these, and other things required, he had assembled there five or six thousand fellows that worked at trades – carpenters, blacksmiths, wheelwrights, saddlers, and what not. O 'twas a curious time!

'Every morning Neighbour Boney would muster his multitude of soldiers on the beach, draw 'em up in line, practise 'em in the manœuvre of embarking, horses and all, till they could do it without a single hitch. My father drove a flock of ewes up into Sussex that year, and as he went along the drover's track over the high downs thereabout he could see this drilling actually going on – the accoutrements of the rank and file glittering in the sun like silver. It was thought and always said by my uncle Job, sergeant of foot (who used to know all about these matters), that Bonaparte meant to cross with oars on a calm night. The grand query with us, was, Where would my gentleman land? Many of the common people thought it would be at Dover; others, who knew how unlikely it was that any skilful general would make a business of landing just where he was expected, said he'd go either east into the River Thames, or west'ard to some convenient place, most likely one of the little bays inside the Isle of Portland, between the Beal and St Alban's Head – and for choice the three-quarter-round Cove screened from every mortal eye, that seemed made o' purpose, out by where we lived, and which I've climmed up with two tubs of brandy across my shoulders on scores o' dark nights in my younger days. Some had heard that a part o' the French fleet would sail right round Scotland, and come up the Channel to a suitable haven. However, there was much doubt upon the matter; and no wonder, for after-years proved that Bonaparte himself could hardly make up his mind upon that great and very particular point, where to land. His uncertainty came about in this wise, that he could get no news as to where and how our troops lay in waiting, and that his knowledge of possible places where flat-bottomed boats might be quietly run ashore, and the men they brought marshalled in order, was dim to the last degree. Being flat-bottomed, they didn't require a harbour for unshipping their cargo of men, but a good shelving beach away from sight, and with a fair open road toward London. How the question posed that great Corsican tyrant (as we used to call him), what pains he took to settle it, and, above all, what a risk he ran on one particular night in trying to do so, were known only to one man here and there; and certainly to no maker of newspapers or printer of books, or my account o't would not have had so many heads shaken over it as it has by gentry who only believe what they see in printed lines.

'The flocks my father had charge of fed all about the downs near our house, overlooking the sea and shore each way for miles. In winter and early spring father was up a deal at nights, watching and tending the lambing. Often he'd go to bed early, and turn out at twelve or one; and on the other hand, he'd sometimes stay up till twelve or one, and then turn in to bed. As soon as I was old enough I used to help him, mostly in the way of keeping an eye upon the ewes while he was gone home to rest. This is what I was doing in a particular month in either the year four or five – I can't certainly fix which, but it was long before I was took away from the sheepkeeping to be bound prentice to a trade. Every night at that time I was at the fold, about half a mile, or it may be a little more, from our cottage, and no living thing at all with me but the ewes and young lambs. Afeared? No; I was never afeared of being alone at these times; for I had been reared in such an out-step place that the lack o' human beings at night made me less fearful than the sight of 'em. Directly I saw a man's shape after dark in a lonely place I was frightened out of my senses.

'One day in that month we were surprised by a visit from my uncle Job, the sergeant in the Sixty-first foot, then in camp on the downs above King George's watering-place, several miles to the west yonder. Uncle Job dropped in about dusk, and went up with my father to the fold for an hour or two. Then he came home, had a drop to drink from the tub of sperrits that the smugglers kept us in for housing their liquor when they'd made a run, and for burning 'em off when there was danger. After that he stretched himself out on the settle to sleep. I went to bed: at one o'clock father came home, and waking me to go and take his place, according to custom, went to bed himself. On my way out of the house I passed Uncle Job on the settle. He opened his eyes, and upon my telling him where I was going he said it was a shame that such a youngster as I should go up there all alone; and when he had fastened up his stock and waist-belt he set off along with me, taking a drop from the sperrit-tub in a little flat bottle that stood in the corner-cupboard.

'By and by we drew up to the fold, saw that all was right, and then, to keep ourselves warm, curled up in a heap of straw that lay inside the thatched hurdles we had set up to break the stroke of the wind when there was any. To-night, however, there was none. It was one of those very still nights when, if you stand on the high hills anywhere within two or three miles of the sea, you can hear the rise and fall of the tide along the shore, coming and going every few moments like a sort of great snore of the sleeping world. Over the lower ground there was a bit of a mist, but on the hill where we lay the air was clear, and the moon, then in her last quarter, flung a fairly good light on the grass and scattered straw.

'While we lay there Uncle Job amused me by telling me strange stories of the wars he had served in and the wownds he had got. He had already fought the French in the Low Countries, and hoped to fight 'em again. His stories lasted so long that at last I was hardly sure that I was not a soldier myself, and had seen such service as he told of. The wonders of his tales quite bewildered my mind, till I fell asleep and dreamed of battle, smoke, and flying soldiers, all of a kind with the doings he had been bringing up to me.

'How long my nap lasted I am not prepared to say. But some faint sounds over and above the rustle of the ewes in the straw, the bleat of the lambs, and the tinkle of the sheep-bell brought me to my waking senses. Uncle Job was still beside me; but he too had fallen asleep. I looked out from the straw, and saw what it was that had aroused me. Two men, in boat-cloaks, cocked hats, and swords, stood by the hurdles about twenty yards off.

'I turned my ear thitherward to catch what they were saying, but though I heard every word o't, not one did I understand. They spoke in a tongue that was not ours – in French, as I afterward found. But if I could not gain the meaning of a word, I was shrewd boy enough to find out a deal of the talkers' business. By the light o' the moon I could see that one of 'em carried a roll of paper in his hand, while every moment he spoke quick to his comrade, and pointed right and left with the other hand to spots along the shore. There was no doubt that he was explaining to the second gentleman the shapes and features of the coast. What happened soon after made this still clearer to me.

'All this time I had not waked Uncle Job, but now I began to be afeared that they might light upon us, because uncle breathed so heavily through's nose. I put my mouth to his ear and whispered, "Uncle Job."

'"What is it, my boy?" he said, just as if he hadn't been asleep at all.

'"Hush!" says I. "Two French generals—"

'"French?" says he.

' "Yes," says I. "Come to see where to land their army!"

'I pointed 'em out; but I could say no more, for the pair were coming at that moment much nearer to where we lay. As soon as they got as near as eight or ten yards, the officer with a roll in his hand stooped down to a slanting hurdle, unfastened his roll upon it, and spread it out. Then suddenly he sprung a dark lantern open on the paper, and showed it to be a map.

' "What be they looking at?" I whispered to Uncle Job.

' "A chart of the Channel," says the sergeant (knowing about such things).

'The other French officer now stooped likewise, and over the map they had a long consultation, as they pointed here and there on the paper, and then hither and thither at places along the shore beneath us. I noticed that the manner of one officer was very respectful toward the other, who seemed much his superior, the second in rank calling him by a sort of title that I did not know the sense of. The head one, on the other hand, was quite familiar with his friend, and more than once clapped him on the shoulder.

'Uncle Job had watched as well as I, but though the map had been in the lantern-light, their faces had always been in shade. But when they rose from stooping over the chart the light flashed upward, and fell smart upon one of 'em's features. No sooner had this happened than Uncle Job gasped, and sank down as if he'd been in a fit.

' "What is it—what is it, Uncle Job?" said I.

' "O good God!" says he, under the straw.

' "What?" says I.

' "Boney!" he groaned out.

' "Who?" says I.

' "Bonaparty," he said. "The Corsican ogre. O that I had got but my new-flinted firelock, that there man should die! But I haven't got my new-flinted firelock, and that there man must live. So lie low, as you value your life!"

'I did lie low, as you mid suppose. But I couldn't help peeping. And then I too, lad as I was, knew that it was the face of Bonaparte. Not know Boney? I should think I did know Boney. I should have known him by half the light o' that lantern. If I had seen a picture of his features once, I had seen it a hundred times. There was his bullet head, his short neck, his round yaller cheeks and chin, his gloomy face, and his great glowing eyes. He took off his hat to blow himself a bit, and there was the forelock in the middle of his forehead, as in all the draughts of him. In moving, his cloak fell a little open, and I could see for a moment his white-fronted jacket and one of the epaulettes.

'But none of this lasted long. In a minute he and his general had rolled up the map, shut the lantern, and turned to go down toward the shore.

'Then Uncle Job came to himself a bit. "Slipped across in the night-time to see how to put his men ashore," he said. "The like o' that man's coolness eyes will never again see! Nephew, I must act in this, and immediate, or England's lost!"

'When they were over the brow, we crope out, and went some little way to look after them. Half-way down they were joined by two others, and six or seven minutes brought them to the shore. Then, from behind a rock, a boat came out into the weak moonlight of the Cove, and they jumped in; it put off instantly, and vanished in a few minutes between the two rocks that stand at the mouth of the Cove as we all know. We climmed back to where we had been before, and I could see, a short way out, a larger vessel, though still not very large. The little boat drew up alongside, was made fast at the stern as I suppose, for the largest sailed away, and we saw no more.

'My uncle Job told his officers as soon as he got back to camp; but what they thought of it I never heard — neither did he. Boney's army never came, and a good job for me; for the Cove below my father's house was where he meant to land, as this secret visit showed. We coast-folk should have been cut down one and all, and I should not have sat here to tell this tale.'

We who listened to old Selby that night have been familiar with his simple grave-stone for these ten years past. Thanks to the incredulity of the age his tale has been seldom repeated. But if anything short of the direct testimony of his own eyes could persuade an auditor that Bonaparte had examined these shores for himself with a view to a practicable landing-place, it would have been Solomon Selby's manner of narrating the adventure which befell him on the down.

Christmas, 1882

The Melancholy Hussar of the German Legion

I

H ERE stretch the downs, high and breezy and green, absolutely unchanged since those eventful days. A plough has never disturbed the turf, and the sod that was uppermost then is uppermost now. Here stood the camp; here are distinct traces of the banks thrown up for the horses of the cavalry, and spots where the midden-heaps lay are still to be observed. At night, when I walk across the lonely place, it is impossible to avoid hearing, amid the scourings of the wind over the grass-bents and thistles, the old trumpet and bugle calls, the rattle of the halters; to help seeing rows of spectral tents and the *impedimenta* of the soldiery. From within the canvases come guttural syllables of foreign tongues, and broken songs of the fatherland; for they were mainly regiments of the King's German Legion that slept round the tent-poles hereabout at that time.

It was nearly ninety years ago. The British uniform of the period, with its immense epaulettes, queer cocked-hat, breeches, gaiters, ponderous cartridge-box, buckled shoes, and what not, would look strange and barbarous now. Ideas have changed; invention has followed invention. Soldiers were monumental objects then. A divinity still hedged kings here and there; and war was considered a glorious thing.

Secluded old manor-houses and hamlets lie in the ravines and hollows among these hills, where a stranger had hardly ever been seen till the King chose to take the baths yearly at the sea-side watering-place a few miles to the south; as a consequence of which battalions descended in a cloud upon the open country around. Is it necessary to add that the echoes of many characteristic tales, dating from that picturesque time, still linger about here in more or less fragmentary form, to be caught by the attentive ear? Some of them I have repeated; most of them I have forgotten; one I have never repeated, and assuredly can never forget.

Phyllis told me the story with her own lips. She was then an old lady of seventy-five, and her auditor a lad of fifteen. She enjoined silence as to her share in the incident, till she should be 'dead, buried, and forgotten'. Her life was prolonged twelve years after the day of her narration, and she has now been dead nearly twenty. The oblivion which in her modesty and humility she courted for herself has only partially fallen on her, with the unfortunate result of inflicting an injustice upon her memory; since such fragments of her story as got abroad at the time, and have been kept alive ever since, are precisely those which are most unfavourable to her character.

It all began with the arrival of the York Hussars, one of the foreign regiments above alluded to. Before that day scarcely a soul had been seen near her father's house for weeks. When a noise like the brushing skirt of a visitor was heard on the doorstep, it proved to be a scudding leaf; when a carriage seemed to be nearing the door, it was her father grinding his sickle on the stone in the garden for his favourite relaxation of trimming the box-tree borders to the plots. A sound like luggage thrown down from the coach was a gun far away at sea; and what looked like a tall man by the gate at dusk was a yew bush cut into a quaint and attenuated shape. There is no such solitude in country places now as there was in those old days.

Yet all the while King George and his Court were at his favourite seaside resort, not more than five miles off.

The daughter's seclusion was great, but beyond the seclusion of the girl lay the seclusion of the father. If her social condition was twilight, his was darkness. Yet he enjoyed his darkness, while her twilight oppressed her. Dr Grove had been a professional man whose taste for lonely meditation over metaphysical questions had diminished his practice till it no longer paid him to keep it going; after which he had relinquished it and hired at a nominal rent the small, dilapidated, half farm, half manor-house of this obscure inland nook, to make a sufficiency of an income which in a town would have been inadequate for their maintenance. He stayed in his garden the greater part of the day, growing more and more irritable with the lapse of time, and the increasing perception that he had wasted his life in the pursuit of illusions. He saw his friends less and less frequently. Phyllis became so shy that if she met a stranger anywhere in her short rambles she felt ashamed at his gaze, walked awkwardly, and blushed to her shoulders.

Yet Phyllis was discovered even here by an admirer, and her hand most unexpectedly asked in marriage.

The King, as aforesaid, was at the neighbouring town, where he had taken up his abode at Gloucester Lodge; and his presence in the town naturally brought many county people thither. Among these idlers – many of whom professed to have connections and interests with the Court – was one Humphrey Gould, a bachelor; a personage neither young nor old; neither good-looking nor positively plain. Too steady-going to be 'a buck' (as fast and unmarried men were then called), he was an approximately fashionable man of a mild type. This bachelor of thirty found his way to the village on the down: beheld Phyllis; made her father's acquaintance in order to make hers; and by some means or other she sufficiently inflamed his heart to lead him in that direction almost daily; till he became engaged to marry her.

As he was of an old local family, some of whose members were held in respect in the county, Phyllis, in bringing him to her feet, had accomplished what was considered a brilliant move for one in her constrained position. How she had done it was not quite known to Phyllis herself. In those days unequal marriages were regarded rather as a violation of the laws of nature than as a mere infringement of convention, the more modern view, and hence when Phyllis, of the watering-place *bourgeoisie*, was chosen by such a gentlemanly fellow, it was as if she were going to be taken to heaven, though perhaps the uninformed would have seen no great difference in the respective positions of the pair, the said Gould being as poor as a crow.

This pecuniary condition was his excuse – probably a true one – for postponing their union, and as the winter drew nearer, and the King departed for the season, Mr Humphrey Gould set out for Bath, promising to return to Phyllis in a few weeks. The winter arrived, the date of his promise passed, yet Gould postponed his coming, on the ground that he could not very easily leave his father in the city of their sojourn, the elder having no other relative near him. Phyllis, though lonely in the extreme, was content. The man who had asked her in marriage was a desirable husband for her in many ways; her father highly approved of his suit; but this neglect of her was awkward, if not painful, for Phyllis. Love him in the true sense of the word she assured me she never did, but she had a genuine regard for him; admired a certain methodical and dogged way in which he sometimes took his pleasure; valued his knowledge of what the Court was doing, had done, or was about to do; and she was not without a feeling of pride that he had chosen her when he might have exercised a more ambitious choice.

But he did not come; and the spring developed. His letters were regular though formal; and it is not to be wondered that the uncertainty of her position, linked with the fact that there was not much passion in her thoughts of Humphrey, bred an indescribable dreariness in the heart of Phyllis Grove. The spring was soon summer, and the summer brought the King; but still no Humphrey Gould. All this while the engagement by letter was maintained intact.

At this point of time a golden radiance flashed in upon the lives of people here, and charged all youthful thought with emotional interest. This radiance was the aforesaid York Hussars.

II

The present generation has probably but a very dim notion of the celebrated York Hussars of ninety years ago. They were one of the regiments of the King's German Legion, and (though they somewhat degenerated later on) their brilliant uniform, their splendid horses, and above all, their foreign air and mustachios (rare appendages then), drew crowds of admirers of both sexes wherever they went. These with other regiments had come to encamp on the downs and pastures, because of the presence of the King in the neighbouring town.

The spot was high and airy, and the view extensive, commanding Portland – the Isle of Slingers – in front, and reaching to St Aldhelm's Head eastward, and almost to the Start on the west.

Phyllis, though not precisely a girl of the village, was as interested as any of them in this military investment. Her father's home stood somewhat apart, and on the highest point of ground to which the lane ascended, so that it was almost level with the top of the church tower in the lower part of the parish. Immediately from the outside of the garden-wall the grass spread away to a great distance, and it was crossed by a path which came close to the wall. Ever since her childhood it had been Phyllis's pleasure to clamber up this fence and sit on the top – a feat not so difficult as it may seem, the walls in this district being built of rubble, without mortar, so that there were plenty of crevices for small toes.

She was sitting up here one day, listlessly surveying the pasture without, when her attention was arrested by a solitary figure walking along the path. It was one of the renowned German Hussars, and he moved onward with his eyes on the ground, and with the manner of one who wished to escape company. His head would probably have been bent like his eyes but for his stiff neck-gear. On nearer view she perceived that his face was marked with deep sadness. Without observing her, he advanced by the footpath till it brought him almost immediately under the wall.

Phyllis was much surprised to see a fine, tall soldier in such a mood as this. Her theory of the military, and of the York Hussars in particular (derived entirely from hearsay, for she had never talked to a soldier in her life), was that their hearts were as gay as their accoutrements.

At this moment the Hussar lifted his eyes and noticed her on her perch, the white muslin neckerchief which covered her shoulders and neck where left bare by her low gown, and her white raiment in general, showing conspicuously in the bright sunlight of this summer day. He blushed a little at the suddenness of the encounter, and without halting a moment from his pace passed on.

All that day the foreigner's face haunted Phyllis; its aspect was so striking, so handsome, and his eyes were so blue, and sad, and abstracted. It was perhaps only natural that on some following day at the same hour she should look over that wall again, and wait till he had passed a second time. On this occasion he was reading a letter, and at the sight of her his manner was that of one who had half expected or hoped to discover her. He almost stopped, smiled, and made a courteous salute. The end of the meeting was that they exchanged a few words. She asked him what he was reading, and he readily informed her that he was re-perusing letters from his mother in Germany; he did not get them often, he said, and was forced to read the old ones a great many times. This was all that passed at the present interview, but others of the same kind followed.

Phyllis used to say that his English, though not good, was quite intelligible to her, so that their acquaintance was never hindered by difficulties of speech. Whenever the subject became too delicate, subtle, or tender, for such words of English as were at his command, the eyes no doubt helped out the tongue, and — though this was later on — the lips helped out the eyes. In short, this acquaintance, unguardedly made, and rash enough on her part, developed and ripened. Like Desdemona, she pitied him, and learnt his history.

His name was Matthäus Tina, and Saarbrück his native town, where his mother was still living. His age was twenty-two, and he had already risen to the grade of corporal, though he had not long been in the army. Phyllis used to assert that no such refined or well-educated young man could have been found in the ranks of the purely English regiments, some of these foreign soldiers having rather the graceful manner and presence of our native officers than of our rank and file.

She by degrees learnt from her foreign friend a circumstance about himself and his comrades which Phyllis would least have expected of the York Hussars. So far from being as gay as its uniform, the regiment was pervaded by a dreadful melancholy, a chronic home-sickness, which depressed many of the men to such an extent that they could hardly attend to their drill. The worst sufferers were the younger soldiers who had not been over here long. They hated England and English life; they took no interest whatever in King George and his island kingdom, and they only wished to be out of it and never to see it any more. Their bodies were here, but their hearts and minds were always far away in their dear fatherland, of which — brave men and stoical as they were in many ways — they would speak with tears in their eyes. One of the worst of the sufferers from this home-woe, as he called it in his own tongue, was Matthäus Tina, whose dreamy musing nature felt the gloom of exile still more intensely from the fact that he had left a lonely mother at home with nobody to cheer her.

Though Phyllis, touched by all this, and interested in his history, did not disdain her soldier's acquaintance, she declined (according to her own account, at least) to permit the young man to overstep the line of mere friendship for a long while – as long, indeed, as she considered herself likely to become the possession of another; though it is probable that she had lost her heart to Matthäus before she was herself aware. The stone wall of necessity made anything like intimacy difficult; and he had never ventured to come, or to ask to come, inside the garden, so that all their conversation had been overtly conducted across this boundary.

III

But news reached the village from a friend of Phyllis's father concerning Mr Humphrey Gould, her remarkably cool and patient betrothed. This gentleman had been heard to say in Bath that he considered his overtures to Miss Phyllis Grove to have reached only the stage of a half-understanding; and in view of his enforced absence on his father's account, who was too great an invalid now to attend to his affairs, he thought it best that there should be no definite promise as yet on either side. He was not sure, indeed, that he might not cast his eyes elsewhere.

This account – though only a piece of hearsay, and as such entitled to no absolute credit – tallied so well with the infrequency of his letters and their lack of warmth, that Phyllis did not doubt its truth for one moment; and from that hour she felt herself free to bestow her heart as she should choose. Not so her father; he declared the whole story to be a fabrication. He had known Mr Gould's family from his boyhood; and if there was one proverb which expressed the matrimonial aspect of that family well, it was 'Love me little, love me long.' Humphrey was an honourable man, who would not think of treating his engagement so lightly. 'Do you wait in patience,' he said; 'all will be right enough in time.'

From these words Phyllis at first imagined that her father was in correspondence with Mr Gould; and her heart sank within her; for in spite of her original intentions she had been relieved to hear that her engagement had come to nothing. But she presently learnt that her father had heard no more of Humphrey Gould than she herself had done; while he would not write and address her affianced directly on the subject, lest it should be deemed an imputation on that bachelor's honour.

'You want an excuse for encouraging one or other of those foreign fellows to flatter you with his unmeaning attentions,' her father exclaimed, his mood having of late been a very unkind one towards her. 'I see more than I say. Don't you ever set foot outside that garden-fence without my permission. If you want to see the camp I'll take you myself some Sunday afternoon.'

Phyllis had not the smallest intention of disobeying him in her actions, but she assumed herself to be independent with respect to her feelings. She no longer checked her fancy for the Hussar, though she was far from regarding him as her lover in the serious sense in which an Englishman might have been regarded as such. The young foreign soldier was almost an ideal being to her, with none of the appurtenances of an ordinary house-dweller; one who had descended she knew not whence, and would disappear she knew not whither; the subject of a fascinating dream – no more.

They met continually now – mostly at dusk – during the brief interval between the going down of the sun and the minute at which the last trumpet-call summoned him to his tent. Perhaps her manner had become less restrained latterly; at any rate that of the Hussar was so; he had grown more tender every day, and at parting after these hurried interviews she reached down her hand from the top of the wall that he might press it. One evening he held it such a while that she exclaimed, 'The wall is white, and somebody in the field may see your shape against it!'

He lingered so long that night that it was with the greatest difficulty that he could run across the intervening stretch of ground and enter the camp in time. On the next occasion of his awaiting her she did not appear in her usual place at the usual hour. His disappointment was unspeakably keen; he remained staring blankly at the spot, like a man in a trance. The trumpets and tattoo sounded, and still he did not go.

She had been delayed purely by an accident. When she arrived she was anxious because of the lateness of the hour, having heard as well as he the sounds denoting the closing of the camp. She implored him to leave immediately.

'No,' he said gloomily. 'I shall not go in yet – the moment you come – I have thought of your coming all day.'

'But you may be disgraced at being after time?'

'I don't mind that, I should have disappeared from the world some time ago if it had not been for two persons – my beloved, here, and my mother in Saarbrück. I hate the army. I care more for a minute of your company than for all the promotion in the world.'

Thus he stayed and talked to her, and told her interesting details of his native place, and incidents of his childhood, till she was in a simmer of distress at his recklessness in remaining. It was only because she insisted on bidding him goodnight, and leaving the wall, that he returned to his quarters.

The next time that she saw him he was without the stripes that had adorned his sleeve. He had been broken to the level of private for his lateness that night; and as Phyllis considered herself to be the cause of his disgrace her sorrow was great. But the position was now reversed; it was his turn to cheer her.

'Don't grieve, meine Liebliche!' he said. 'I have got a remedy for whatever comes. First, even supposing I regain my stripes, would your father allow you to marry a non-commissioned officer in the York Hussars?'

She flushed. This practical step had not been in her mind in relation to such an unrealistic person as he was; and a moment's reflection was enough for it. 'My father would not – certainly would not,' she answered unflinchingly. 'It cannot be thought of! My dear friend, please do forget me: I fear I am ruining you and your prospects!'

'Not at all!' said he. 'You are giving this country of yours just sufficient interest to me to make me care to keep alive in it. If my dear land were here also, and my old parent, with you, I could be happy as I am, and would do my best as a soldier. But it is not so. And now listen. This is my plan. That you go with me to my own country, and be my wife there, and live there with my mother and me. I am not a Hanoverian, as you know, though I entered the army as such; my country is by the Saar, and is at peace with France, and if I were once in it I should be free.'

'But how get there?' she asked. Phyllis had been rather amazed than shocked at his proposition. Her position in her father's house was growing irksome and painful in the extreme; his parental affection seemed to be quite dried up. She was not a native of the village, like all the joyous girls around her; and in some way Matthäus Tina had infected her with his own passionate longing for his country, and mother, and home.

'But how?' she repeated, finding that he did not answer. 'Will you buy your discharge?'

'Ah, no,' he said. 'That's impossible in these times. No; I came here against my will; why should I not escape? Now is the time, as we shall soon be striking camp, and I might see you no more. This is my scheme. I will ask you to meet me on the highway two miles off, on some calm night next week that may be appointed. There will be nothing unbecoming in it, or to cause you shame; you will not fly alone with me, for I will bring with me my devoted young friend, Christoph, an Alsatian, who has lately joined the regiment, and who has agreed to assist in this enterprise. We shall have come from yonder harbour, where we shall have examined the boats, and found one suited to our purpose. Christoph has already a chart of the Channel, and we will then go to the harbour, and at midnight cut the boat from her moorings, and row away round the point out of sight; and by the next morning we are on the coast of France, near Cherbourg. The rest is easy, for I have saved money for the land journey, and can get a change of clothes. I will write to my mother, who will meet us on the way.'

He added details in reply to her inquiries, which left no doubt in Phyllis's mind of the feasibility of the undertaking. But its magnitude almost appalled her; and it is questionable if she would ever have gone further in the wild adventure if, on entering the house that night, her father had not accosted her in the most significant terms.

'How about the York Hussars?' he said.

'They are still at the camp; but they are soon going away, I believe.'

'It is useless for you to attempt to cloak your actions in that way. You have been meeting one of those fellows; you have been seen walking with him — foreign barbarians, not much better than the French themselves! I have made up my mind — don't speak a word till I have done, please! — I have made up my mind that you shall stay here no longer while they are on the spot. You shall go to your aunt's.'

It was useless for her to protest that she had never taken a walk with any soldier or man under the sun except himself. Her protestations were feeble, too, for though he was not literally correct in his assertion, he was virtually only half in error.

The house of her father's sister was a prison to Phyllis. She had quite recently undergone experience of its gloom; and when her father went on to direct her to pack what would be necessary for her to take, her heart died within her. In after-years she never attempted to excuse her conduct during this week of agitation; but the result of her self-communing was that she decided to join in the scheme of her lover and his friend, and fly to the country which he had coloured with such lovely hues in her imagination. She always said that the one feature in his proposal which overcame her hesitation was the obvious purity and straightforwardness of his intentions. He showed himself to be so virtuous and kind; he treated her with a respect to which she had never before been accustomed; and she was braced to the obvious risks of the voyage by her confidence in him.

IV

It was on a soft, dark evening of the following week that they engaged in the adventure. Tina was to meet her at a point in the highway at which the lane to the village branched off. Christoph was to go ahead of them to the harbour where the boat lay, row it round the Nothe — or Look-out as it was called in those days — and pick them up on the other side of the promontory, which they were to reach by crossing the harbour-bridge on foot, and climbing over the Look-out hill.

As soon as her father had ascended to his room she left the house, and, bundle in hand, proceeded at a trot along the lane. At such an hour not a soul was afoot anywhere in the village, and she reached the junction of the lane with the highway unobserved. Here she took up her position in the obscurity formed by the angle of a fence, whence she could discern every one who approached along the turnpike-road, without being herself seen.

She had not remained thus waiting for her lover longer than a minute — though from the tension of her nerves the lapse of even that short time was trying — when, instead of the expected footsteps, the stage-coach could be heard descending the hill. She knew that Tina would not show himself till the road was clear, and waited impatiently for the coach to pass. Nearing the corner where she was it slackened speed, and, instead of going by as usual, drew up within a few yards of her. A passenger alighted, and she heard his voice. It was Humphrey Gould's.

He had brought a friend with him, and luggage. The luggage was deposited on the grass, and the coach went on its route to the royal watering-place.

'I wonder where that young man is with the horse and trap?' said her former admirer to his companion. 'I hope we shan't have to wait here long. I told him half-past nine o'clock precisely.'

'Have you got her present safe?'

'Phyllis's? O, yes. It is in this trunk. I hope it will please her.'

'Of course it will. What woman would not be pleased with such a handsome peace-offering?'

'Well — she deserves it. I've treated her rather badly. But she has been in my mind these last two days much more than I should care to confess to everybody. Ah, well; I'll say no more about that. It cannot be that she is so bad as they make out. I am quite sure that a girl of her good wit would know better than to get entangled with any of those Hanoverian soldiers. I won't believe it of her, and there's an end on't.'

More words in the same strain were casually dropped as the two men waited; words which revealed to her, as by a sudden illumination, the enormity of her conduct. The conversation was at length cut off by the arrival of the man with the vehicle. The luggage was placed in it, and they mounted, and were driven on in the direction from which she had just come.

Phyllis was so conscience-stricken that she was at first inclined to follow them; but a moment's reflection led her to feel that it would only be bare justice to Matthäus to wait till he arrived, and explain candidly that she had changed her mind – difficult as the struggle would be when she stood face to face with him. She bitterly reproached herself for having believed reports which represented Humphrey Gould as false to his engagement, when, from what she now heard from his own lips, she gathered that he had been living full of trust in her. But she knew well enough who had won her love. Without him her life seemed a dreary prospect, yet the more she looked at his proposal the more she feared to accept it – so wild as it was, so vague, so venturesome. She had promised Humphrey Gould, and it was only his assumed faithlessness which had led her to treat that promise as nought. His solicitude in bringing her these gifts touched her; her promise must be kept, and esteem must take the place of love. She would preserve her self-respect. She would stay at home, and marry him, and suffer.

Phyllis had thus braced herself to an exceptional fortitude when, a few minutes later, the outline of Matthäus Tina appeared behind a field-gate, over which he lightly leapt as she stepped forward. There was no evading it, he pressed her to his breast.

'It is the first and last time!' she wildly thought as she stood encircled by his arms.

How Phyllis got through the terrible ordeal of that night she could never clearly recollect. She always attributed her success in carrying out her resolve to her lover's honour, for as soon as she declared to him in feeble words that she had changed her mind, and felt that she could not, dared not, fly with him, he forbore to urge her, grieved as he was at her decision. Unscrupulous pressure on his part, seeing how romantically she had become attached to him, would no doubt have turned the balance in his favour. But he did nothing to tempt her unduly or unfairly.

On her side, fearing for his safety, she begged him to remain. This, he declared, could not be. 'I cannot break faith with my friend,' said he. Had he stood alone he would have abandoned his plan. But Christoph, with the boat and compass and chart, was waiting on the shore; the tide would soon turn; his mother had been warned of his coming; go he must.

Many precious minutes were lost while he tarried, unable to tear himself away. Phyllis held to her resolve, though it cost her many a bitter pang. At last they parted, and he went down the hill. Before his footsteps had quite died away she felt a desire to behold at least his outline once more, and running noiselessly after him regained view of his diminishing figure. For one moment she was sufficiently excited to be on the point of rushing forward and linking her fate with his. But she could not. The courage which at the critical instant failed Cleopatra of Egypt could scarcely be expected of Phyllis Grove.

A dark shape, similar to his own, joined him in the highway. It was Christoph, his friend. She could see no more; they had hastened on in the direction of the town and harbour, four miles ahead. With a feeling akin to despair she turned and slowly pursued her way homeward.

Tattoo sounded in the camp; but there was no camp for her now. It was as dead as the camp of the Assyrians after the passage of the Destroying Angel.

She noiselessly entered the house, seeing nobody, and went to bed. Grief, which kept her awake at first, ultimately wrapped her in a heavy sleep. The next morning her father met her at the foot of the stairs.

'Mr Gould is come!' he said triumphantly.

Humphrey was staying at the inn, and had already called to inquire for her. He had brought her a present of a very handsome looking-glass in a frame of *repoussé* silverwork, which her father held in his hand. He had promised to call again in the course of an hour, to ask Phyllis to walk with him.

Pretty mirrors were rarer in country-houses at that day than they are now, and the one before her won Phyllis's admiration. She looked into it, saw how heavy her eyes were, and endeavoured to brighten them. She was in that wretched state of mind which leads a woman to move mechanically onward in what she conceives to be her allotted path. Mr Humphrey had, in his undemonstrative way, been adhering all along to the old understanding; it was for her to do the same, and to say not a word of her own lapse. She put on her bonnet and tippet, and when he arrived at the hour named she was at the door awaiting him.

V

Phyllis thanked him for his beautiful gift; but the talking was soon entirely on Humphrey's side as they walked along. He told her of the latest movements of the world of fashion — a subject which she willingly discussed to the exclusion of anything more personal — and his measured language helped to still her disquieted heart and brain. Had not her own sadness been what it was she must have observed his embarrassment. At last he abruptly changed the subject.

'I am glad you are pleased with my little present,' he said. 'The truth is that I brought it to propitiate 'ee, and to get you to help me out of a mighty difficulty.'

It was inconceivable to Phyllis that this independent bachelor — whom she admired in some respects — could have a difficulty.

'Phyllis — I'll tell you my secret at once; for I have a monstrous secret to confide before I can ask your counsel. The case is, then, that I am married: yes, I have privately married a dear young belle; and if you knew her, and I hope you will, you would say everything in her praise. But she is not quite the one that my father would have chose for me — you know the paternal idea as well as I — and I have kept it secret. There will be a terrible noise, no doubt; but I think that with your help I may get over it. If you would only do me this good turn — when I have told my father, I mean — say that you never could have married me, you know, or something of that sort — 'pon my life it will help to smooth the way vastly. I am so anxious to win him round to my point of view, and not to cause any estrangement.'

What Phyllis replied she scarcely knew, or how she counselled him as to his unexpected situation. Yet the relief that his announcement brought her was perceptible. To have confided her trouble in return was what her aching heart longed to do; and had Humphey been a woman she would instantly have poured out her tale. But to him she feared to confess; and there was a real reason for silence, till a sufficient time had elapsed to allow her lover and his comrade to get out of harm's way.

As soon as she reached home again she sought a solitary place, and spent the time in half regretting that she had not gone away, and in dreaming over the meetings with Matthäus Tina from their beginning to their end. In his own country, amongst his own countrywomen, he would possibly soon forget her, even to her very name.

Her listlessness was such that she did not go out of the house for several days. There came a morning which broke in fog and mist, behind which the dawn could be discerned in greenish grey; and the outlines of the tents, and the rows of horses at the ropes. The smoke from the canteen fires drooped heavily.

The spot at the bottom of the garden where she had been accustomed to climb the wall to meet Matthäus was the only inch of English ground in which she took any interest; and in spite of the disagreeable haze prevailing she walked out there till she reached the well-known corner. Every blade of grass was weighted with little liquid globes, and slugs and snails had crept out upon the plots. She could hear the usual faint noises from the camp, and in the other direction the trot of farmers on the road to the town, for it was market-day. She observed that her frequent visits to this corner had quite trodden down the grass in the angle of the wall, and left marks of garden soil on the stepping-stones by which she had mounted to look over the top. Seldom having gone there till dusk, she had not considered that her traces might be visible by day. Perhaps it was these which had revealed her trysts to her father.

While she paused in melancholy regard, she fancied that the customary sounds from the tents were changing their character. Indifferent as Phyllis was to camp doings now, she mounted by the steps to the old place. What she beheld at first awed and perplexed her; then she stood rigid, her fingers hooked to the wall, her eyes staring out of her head, and her face as if hardened to stone.

On the open green stretching before her all the regiments in the camp were drawn up in line, in the mid-front of which two empty coffins lay on the ground. The unwonted sounds which she had noticed came from an advancing procession. It consisted of the band of the York Hussars playing a dead march; next two soldiers of that regiment in a mourning coach, guarded on each side, and accompanied by two priests. Behind came a crowd of rustics who had been attracted by the event. The melancholy procession marched along the front of the line, returned to the centre, and halted beside the coffins, where the two condemned men were blindfolded, and each placed kneeling on his coffin; a few minutes' pause was now given while they prayed.

A firing-party of twenty-four men stood ready with levelled carbines. The commanding officer, who had his sword drawn, waved it through some cuts of the sword-exercise till he reached the downward stroke, whereat the firing-party discharged their volley. The two victims fell, one upon his face across his coffin, the other backwards.

As the volley resounded there arose a shriek from the wall of Dr Grove's garden, and some one fell down inside; but nobody among the spectators without noticed it at the time. The two executed Hussars were Matthäus Tina and his friend Christoph. The soldiers on guard placed the bodies in the coffins almost instantly; but the colonel of the regiment, an Englishman, rode up and exclaimed in a stern voice: 'Turn them out — as an example to the men!'

The coffins were lifted endwise, and the dead Germans flung out upon their faces on the grass. Then all the regiments wheeled in sections, and marched past the spot in slow time. When the survey was over the corpses were again coffined, and borne away.

Meanwhile Dr Grove, attracted by the noise of the volley, had rushed out into his garden, where he saw his wretched daughter lying motionless against the wall. She was taken indoors, but it was long before she recovered consciousness; and for weeks they despaired of her reason.

It transpired that the luckless deserters from the York Hussars had cut the boat from her moorings in the adjacent harbour, according to their plan, and, with two other comrades who were smarting under ill-treatment from their colonel, had sailed in safety across the Channel. But mistaking their bearings they steered into Jersey, thinking that island the French coast. Here they were perceived to be deserters, and delivered up to the authorities. Matthäus and Christoph interceded for the other two at the court-martial, saying that it was entirely by the former's representations that these were induced to go. Their sentence was accordingly commuted to flogging, the death punishment being reserved for their leaders.

The visitor to the well-known old Georgian watering-place, who may care to ramble to the neighbouring village under the hills, and examine the register of burials, will there find two entries in these words: –

> 'Matth: Tina (Corpl) in His Majesty's Regmt of York Hussars, and Shot for Desertion, was Buried June 30th, 1801, aged 22 years. Born in the town of Sarrbruk, Germany.
> 'Christoph Bless, belonging to His Majesty's Regmt of York Hussars, who was Shot for Desertion, was Buried June 30th, 1801, aged 22 years. Born at Lothaargen, Alsatia.'

Their graves were dug at the back of the little church, near the wall. There is no memorial to mark the spot, but Phyllis pointed it out to me. While she lived she used to keep their mounds neat; but now they are overgrown with nettles, and sunk nearly flat. The older villagers, however, who know of the episode from their parents, still recollect the place where the soldiers lie. Phyllis lies near.

October 1889

The Withered Arm

IT was an eighty-cow dairy, and the troop of milkers, regular and super-numerary, were all at work; for, though the time of year was as yet but early April, the feed lay entirely in water-meadows, and the cows were 'in full pail'. The hour was about six in the evening, and three-fourths of the large, red, rectangular animals having been finished off, there was opportunity for a little conversation.

'He do bring home his bride to-morrow, I hear. They've come as far as Anglebury to-day.'

The voice seemed to proceed from the belly of the cow called Cherry, but the speaker was a milking-woman, whose face was buried in the flank of that motionless beast.

'Hav' anybody seen her?' said another.

There was a negative response from the first. 'Though they say she's a rosy-cheeked, tisty-tosty little body enough,' she added; and as the milkmaid spoke she turned her face so that she could glance past her cow's tail to the other side of the barton, where a thin, fading woman of thirty milked somewhat apart from the rest.

'Years younger than he, they say,' continued the second, with also a glance of reflectiveness in the same direction.

'How old do you call him, then?'

'Thirty or so.'

'More like forty,' broke in an old milkman near, in a long white pinafore or 'wropper', and with the brim of his hat tied down, so that he looked like a woman. ''A was born before our Great Weir was builded, and I hadn't man's wages when I laved water there.'

The discussion waxed so warm that the purr of the milk-streams became jerky, till a voice from another cow's belly cried with authority, 'Now then, what the Turk do it matter to us about Farmer Lodge's age, or Farmer Lodge's new mis'ess? I shall have to pay him nine pound a year for the rent of every one of these milchers, whatever his age or hers. Get on with your work, or 'twill be dark afore we have done. The evening is pinking in a'ready.' This speaker was the dairyman himself, by whom the milkmaids and men were employed.

Nothing more was said publicly about Farmer Lodge's wedding, but the first woman murmured under her cow to her next neighbour, ''Tis hard for *she*,' signifying the thin worn milkmaid aforesaid.

'O no,' said the second. 'He ha'n't spoke to Rhoda Brook for years.'

When the milking was done they washed their pails and hung them on a many-forked stand made as usual of the peeled limb of an oak-tree, set upright in the earth, and resembling a colossal antlered horn. The majority then dispersed in various directions homeward. The thin woman who had not spoken was joined by a boy of twelve or thereabout, and the twain went away up the field also.

Their course lay apart from that of the others, to a lonely spot high above the water-meads, and not far from the border of Egdon Heath, whose dark countenance was visible in the distance as they drew nigh to their home.

'They've just been saying down in barton that your father brings his young wife home from Anglebury to-morrow,' the woman observed. 'I shall want to send you for a few things to market, and you'll be pretty sure to meet 'em.'

'Yes, mother,' said the boy. 'Is father married then?'

'Yes. . . . You can give her a look, and tell me what she's like, if you do see her.'

'Yes, mother.'

'If she's dark or fair, and if she's tall — as tall as I. And if she seems like a woman who has ever worked for a living, or one that has been always well off, and has never done anything, and shows marks of the lady on her, as I expect she do.'

'Yes.'

They crept up the hill in the twilight and entered the cottage. It was built of mud-walls, the surface of which had been washed by many rains into channels and depressions that left none of the original flat face visible; while here and there in the thatch above a rafter showed like a bone protruding through the skin.

She was kneeling down in the chimney-corner, before two pieces of turf laid together with the heather inwards, blowing at the red-hot ashes with her breath till the turves flamed. The radiance lit her pale cheek, and made her dark eyes, that had once been handsome, seem handsome anew. 'Yes,' she resumed, 'see if she is dark or fair, and if you can, notice if her hands be white; if not, see if they look as though she had ever done housework, or are milker's hands like mine.'

The boy again promised, inattentively this time, his mother not observing that he was cutting a notch with his pocket-knife in the beech-backed chair.

II. THE YOUNG WIFE

The road from Anglebury to Holmstoke is in general level; but there is one place where a sharp ascent breaks its monotony. Farmers homeward-bound from the former market-town, who trot all the rest of the way, walk their horses up this short incline.

The next evening while the sun was yet bright a handsome new gig, with a lemon-coloured body and red wheels, was spinning west-ward along the level highway at the heels of a powerful mare. The driver was a yeoman in the prime of life, cleanly shaven like an actor, his face being toned to that bluish-vermilion hue which so often graces a thriving farmer's features when returning home after successful dealings in the town. Beside him sat a woman, many years his junior — almost, indeed, a girl. Her face too was fresh in colour, but it was of a totally different quality — soft and evanescent, like the light under a heap of rose-petals.

Few people travelled this way, for it was not a main road, and the long white riband of gravel that stretched before them was empty, save of one small scarce-moving speck, which presently resolved itself into the figure of a boy, who was creeping on at a snail's pace, and continually looking behind him — the heavy bundle he carried being some excuse for, if not the reason of, his dilatoriness. When the bouncing gig-party slowed at the bottom of the incline above mentioned, the pedestrian was only a few yards in front. Supporting the large bundle by putting one hand on his hip, he turned and looked straight at the farmer's wife as though he would read her through and through, pacing along abreast of the horse.

The low sun was full in her face, rendering every feature, shade, and contour distinct, from the curve of her little nostril to the colour of her eyes. The farmer, though he seemed annoyed at the boy's persistent presence, did not order him to get out of the way; and thus the lad preceded them, his hard gaze never leaving her, till they reached the top of the ascent, when the farmer trotted on with relief in his lineaments – having taken no outward notice of the boy whatever.

'How that poor lad stared at me!' said the young wife.

'Yes, dear; I saw that he did.'

'He is one of the village, I suppose?'

'One of the neighbourhood. I think he lives with his mother a mile or two off.'

'He knows who we are, no doubt?'

'O yes. You must expect to be stared at just at first, my pretty Gertrude.'

'I do, – though I think the poor boy may have looked at us in the hope we might relieve him of his heavy load, rather than from curiosity.'

'O no,' said her husband off-handedly. 'These country lads will carry a hundredweight once they get it on their backs; besides, his pack had more size than weight in it. Now, then, another mile and I shall be able to show you our house in the distance – if it is not too dark before we get there.' The wheels spun round, and particles flew from their periphery as before, till a white house of ample dimensions revealed itself, with farm-buildings and ricks at the back.

Meanwhile the boy had quickened his pace, and turning up a by-lane some mile and half short of the white farmstead, ascended towards the leaner pastures, and so on to the cottage of his mother.

She had reached home after her day's milking at the outlying dairy, and was washing cabbage at the doorway in the declining light. 'Hold up the net a moment,' she said, without preface, as the boy came up.

He flung down his bundle, held the edge of the cabbage-net, and as she filled its meshes with the dripping leaves she went on, 'Well, did you see her?'

'Yes; quite plain.'

'Is she ladylike?'

'Yes; and more. A lady complete.'

'Is she young?'

'Well, she's growed up, and her ways be quite a woman's.'

'Of course. What colour is her hair and face?'

'Her hair is lightish, and her face as comely as a live doll's.'

'Her eyes, then, are not dark like mine?'

'No – of a bluish turn, and her mouth is very nice and red; and when she smiles, her teeth show white.'

'Is she tall?' said the woman sharply.

'I couldn't see. She was sitting down.'

'Then do you go to Holmstoke church to-morrow morning: she's sure to be there. Go early and notice her walking in, and come home and tell me if she's taller than I.'

'Very well, mother. But why don't you go and see for yourself?'

'*I* go to see her! I wouldn't look up at her if she were to pass my window this instant. She was with Mr Lodge, of course. What did he say or do?'

'Just the same as usual.'

'Took no notice of you?'

'None.'

Next day the mother put a clean shirt on the boy, and started him off for Holmstoke church. He reached the ancient little pile when the door was just being opened and he was the first to enter. Taking his seat by the font, he watched all the parishioners file in. The well-to-do Farmer Lodge came nearly last, and his young wife, who accompanied him, walked up the aisle with the shyness natural to a modest woman who had appeared thus for the first time. As all other eyes were fixed upon her, the youth's stare was not noticed now.

When he reached home his mother said, 'Well?' before he had entered the room.

'She is not tall. She is rather short,' he replied.

'Ah!' said his mother, with satisfaction.

'But she's very pretty – very. In fact, she's lovely.' The youthful freshness of the yeoman's wife had evidently made an impression even on the somewhat hard nature of the boy.

'That's all I want to hear,' said his mother quickly. 'Now, spread the tablecloth. The hare you wired is very tender; but mind that nobody catches you. – You've never told me what sort of hands she had.'

'I have never seen 'em. She never took off her gloves.'

'What did she wear this morning?'

'A white bonnet and a silver-coloured gownd. It whewed and whistled so loud when it rubbed against the pews that the lady coloured up more than ever for very shame at the noise, and pulled it in to keep it from touching; but when she pushed into her seat, it whewed more than ever. Mr Lodge, he seemed pleased, and his waistcoat stuck out, and his great golden seals hung like a lord's; but she seemed to wish her noisy gownd anywhere but on her.'

'Not she! However, that will do now.'

These descriptions of the newly-married couple were continued from time to time by the boy at his mother's request, after any chance encounter he had had with them. But Rhoda Brook, though she might easily have seen young Mrs Lodge for herself by walking a couple of miles, would never attempt an excursion towards the quarter where the farmhouse lay. Neither did she, at the daily milking in the dairyman's yard on Lodge's outlying second farm, ever speak on the subject of the recent marriage. The dairyman, who rented the cows of Lodge, and knew perfectly the tall milkmaid's history, with manly kindliness always kept the gossip in the cow-barton from annoying Rhoda. But the atmosphere thereabout was full of the subject during the first days of Mrs Lodge's arrival, and from her boy's description and the casual words of the other milkers, Rhoda Brook could raise a mental image of the unconscious Mrs Lodge that was realistic as a photograph.

III. A VISION

One night, two or three weeks after the bridal return, when the boy was gone to bed, Rhoda sat a long time over the turf ashes that she had raked out in front of her to extinguish them. She contemplated so intently the new wife, as presented to her in her mind's eye over the embers, that she forgot the lapse of time. At last, wearied with her day's work, she too retired.

But the figure which had occupied her so much during this and the previous days was not to be banished at night. For the first time Gertrude Lodge visited the supplanted woman in her dreams. Rhoda Brook dreamed – since her assertion that she really saw, before falling asleep, was not to be believed – that the young wife, in the pale silk dress and white bonnet, but with features shockingly distorted, and wrinkled as by age, was sitting upon her chest as she lay. The pressure of Mrs Lodge's person grew heavier; the blue eyes peered cruelly into her face, and then the figure thrust forward its left hand mockingly, so as to make the wedding-ring it wore glitter in Rhoda's eyes. Maddened mentally, and nearly suffocated by pressure, the sleeper struggled; the incubus, still regarding her, withdrew to the foot of the bed, only, however, to come forward by degrees, resume her seat, and flash her left hand as before.

Gasping for breath, Rhoda, in a last desperate effort, swung out her right hand, seized the confronting spectre by its obtrusive left arm, and whirled it backward to the floor, starting up herself as she did so with a low cry.

'O, merciful heaven!' she cried, sitting on the edge of the bed in a cold sweat; 'that was not a dream – she was here!'

She could feel her antagonist's arm within her grasp even now – the very flesh and bone of it, as it seemed. She looked on the floor whither she had whirled the spectre, but there was nothing to be seen.

Rhoda Brook slept no more that night, and when she went milking at the next dawn they noticed how pale and haggard she looked. The milk that she drew quivered into the pail: her hand had not calmed even yet, and still retained the feel of the arm. She came home to breakfast as wearily as if it had been supper-time.

'What was that noise in your chimmer, mother, last night?' said her son. 'You fell off the bed, surely?'

'Did you hear anything fall? At what time?'

'Just when the clock struck two.'

She could not explain, and when the meal was done went silently about her household work, the boy assisting her, for he hated going afield on the farms, and she indulged his reluctance. Between eleven and twelve the garden-gate clicked, and she lifted her eyes to the window. At the bottom of the garden, within the gate, stood the woman of her vision. Rhoda seemed transfixed.

'Ah, she said she would come!' exclaimed the boy, also observing her.

'Said so – when? How does she know us?'

'I have seen and spoken to her. I talked to her yesterday.'

'I told you,' said the mother, flushing indignantly, 'never to speak to anybody in that house, or go near the place.'

'I did not speak to her till she spoke to me. And I did not go near the place. I met her in the road.'

'What did you tell her?'

'Nothing. She said, "Are you the poor boy who had to bring the heavy load from market?" And she looked at my boots, and said they would not keep my feet dry if it came on wet, because they were so cracked. I told her I lived with my mother, and we had enough to do to keep ourselves, and that's how it was; and she said then, "I'll come and bring you some better boots, and see your mother." She gives away things to other folks in the meads besides us.'

Mrs Lodge was by this time close to the door – not in her silk, as Rhoda had dreamt of in the bed-chamber, but in a morning hat, and gown of common light material, which became her better than silk. On her arm she carried a basket.

The impression remaining from the night's experience was still strong. Brook had almost expected to see the wrinkles, the scorn, and the cruelty on her visitor's face. She would have escaped an interview had escape been possible. There was, however, no backdoor to the cottage, and in an instant the boy had lifted the latch to Mrs Lodge's gentle knock.

'I see I have come to the right house,' said she, glancing at the lad, and smiling. 'But I was not sure till you opened the door.'

The figure and action were those of the phantom; but her voice was so indescribably sweet, her glance so winning, her smile so tender, so unlike that of Rhoda's midnight visitant, that the latter could hardly believe the evidence of her senses. She was truly glad that she had not hidden away in sheer aversion, as she had been inclined to do. In her basket Mrs Lodge brought the pair of boots that she had promised to the boy, and other useful articles.

At these proofs of a kindly feeling towards her and hers Rhoda's heart reproached her bitterly. This innocent young thing should have her blessing and not her curse. When she left them a light seemed gone from the dwelling. Two days later she came again to know if the boots fitted, and less than a fortnight after that paid Rhoda another call. On this occasion the boy was absent.

'I walk a good deal,' said Mrs Lodge, 'and your house is the nearest outside our own parish. I hope you are well. You don't look quite well.'

Rhoda said she was well enough, and, indeed, though the paler of the two, there was more of the strength that endures in her well-defined features and large frame than in the soft-cheeked young woman before her. The conversation became quite confidential as regarded their powers and weaknesses; and when Mrs Lodge was leaving, Rhoda said, 'I hope you will find this air agree with you, ma'am, and not suffer from the damp of the water-meads.'

The younger one replied that there was not much doubt of it, her general health being usually good. 'Though, now you remind me,' she added, 'I have one little ailment which puzzles me. It is nothing serious, but I cannot make it out.'

She uncovered her left hand and arm, and their outline confronted Rhoda's gaze as the exact original of the limb she had beheld and seized in her dream. Upon the pink round surface of the arm were faint marks of an unhealthy colour, as if produced by a rough grasp. Rhoda's eyes became riveted on the discolorations; she fancied that she discerned in them the shape of her own four fingers.

'How did it happen?' she said mechanically.

'I cannot tell,' replied Mrs Lodge, shaking her head. 'One night when I was sound asleep, dreaming I was away in some strange place, a pain suddenly shot into my arm there, and was so keen as to awaken me. I must have struck it in the daytime, I suppose, though I don't remember doing so.' She added, laughing, 'I tell my dear husband that it looks just as if he had flown into a rage and struck me there. O, I daresay it will soon disappear.'

'Ha, ha! Yes. . . . On what night did it come?'

Mrs Lodge considered, and said it would be a fortnight ago on the morrow. 'When I awoke I could not remember where I was,' she added, 'till the clock striking two reminded me.'

She had named the night and the hour of Rhoda's spectral encounter, and Brook felt like a guilty thing. The artless disclosure startled her; she did not reason on the freaks of coincidence, and all the scenery of that ghastly night returned with double vividness to her mind.

'O, can it be,' she said to herself, when her visitor had departed, 'that I exercise a malignant power over people against my own will?' She knew that she had been slily called a witch since her fall; but never having understood why that particular stigma had been attached to her, it had passed disregarded. Could this be the explanation, and had such things as this ever happened before?

IV. A SUGGESTION

The summer drew on, and Rhoda Brook almost dreaded to meet Mrs Lodge again, notwithstanding that her feeling for the young wife amounted wellnigh to affection. Something in her own individuality seemed to convict Rhoda of crime. Yet a fatality sometimes would direct the steps of the latter to the outskirts of Holmstoke whenever she left her house for any other purpose than her daily work, and hence it happened that their next encounter was out of doors. Rhoda could not avoid the subject which had so mystified her, and after the first few words she stammered, 'I hope your — arm is well again, ma'am?' She had perceived with consternation that Gertrude Lodge carried her left arm stiffly.

'No; it is not quite well. Indeed, it is no better at all; it is rather worse. It pains me dreadfully sometimes.'

'Perhaps you had better go to a doctor, ma'am.'

She replied that she had already seen a doctor. Her husband had insisted upon her going to one. But the surgeon had not seemed to understand the afflicted limb at all; he had told her to bathe it in hot water, and she had bathed it, but the treatment had done no good.

'Will you let me see it?' said the milkwoman.

Mrs Lodge pushed up her sleeve and disclosed the place, which was a few inches above the wrist. As soon as Rhoda Brook saw it, she could hardly preserve her composure. There was nothing of the nature of a wound, but the arm at that point had a shrivelled look, and the outline of the four fingers appeared more distinct than at the former time. Moreover, she fancied that they were imprinted in precisely the relative position of her clutch upon the arm in the trance: the first finger towards Gertrude's wrist, and the fourth towards her elbow.

What the impress resembled seemed to have struck Gertrude herself since their last meeting. 'It looks almost like finger-marks,' she said; adding with a faint laugh, 'My husband says it is as if some witch, or the devil himself, had taken hold of me there, and blasted the flesh.'

Rhoda shivered. 'That's fancy,' she said hurriedly. 'I wouldn't mind it, if I were you.'

'I shouldn't so much mind it,' said the younger, with hesitation, 'if – if I hadn't a notion that it makes my husband – dislike me – no, love me less. Men think so much of personal appearance.'

'Some do – he for one.'

'Yes; and he was very proud of mine, at first.'

'Keep your arm covered from his sight.'

'Ah – he knows the disfigurement is there!' She tried to hide the tears that filled her eyes.

'Well, ma'am, I earnestly hope it will go away soon.'

And so the milkwoman's mind was chained anew to the subject by a horrid sort of spell as she returned home. The sense of having been guilty of an act of malignity increased, affect as she might to ridicule her superstition. In her secret heart Rhoda did not altogether object to a slight diminution of her successor's beauty, by whatever means it had come about; but she did not wish to inflict upon her physical pain. For though this pretty young woman had rendered impossible any reparation which Lodge might have made Rhoda for his past conduct, everything like resentment at the unconscious usurpation had quite passed away from the elder's mind.

If the sweet and kindly Gertrude Lodge only knew of the dreamscene in the bed-chamber, what would she think? Not to inform her of it seemed treachery in the presence of her friendliness; but tell she could not of her own accord – neither could she devise a remedy.

She mused upon the matter the greater part of the night, and the next day, after the morning milking, set out to obtain another glimpse of Gertrude Lodge if she could, being held to her by a gruesome fascination. By watching the house from a distance the milkmaid was presently able to discern the farmer's wife in a ride she was taking alone – probably to join her husband in some distant field. Mrs Lodge perceived her, and cantered in her direction.

'Good morning, Rhoda!' Gertrude said, when she had come up. 'I was going to call.'

Rhoda noticed that Mrs Lodge held the reins with some difficulty.

'I hope – the bad arm,' said Rhoda.

'They tell me there is possibly one way by which I might be able to find out the cause, and so perhaps the cure, of it,' replied the other anxiously. 'It is by going to some clever man over in Egdon Heath. They did not know if he was still alive – and I cannot remember his name at this moment; but they said that you knew more of his movements than anybody else hereabout, and could tell me if he were still to be consulted. Dear me – what was his name? But you know.'

'Not Conjuror Trendle?' said her thin companion, turning pale.

'Trendle – yes. Is he alive?'

'I believe so,' said Rhoda, with reluctance.

'Why do you call him conjuror?'

'Well – they say – they used to say he was a – he had powers other folks have not.'

'O, how could my people be so superstitious as to recommend a man of that sort! I thought they meant some medical man. I shall think no more of him.'

Rhoda looked relieved, and Mrs Lodge rode on. The milkwoman had inwardly seen, from the moment she heard of her having been mentioned as a reference for this man, that there must exist a sarcastic feeling among the workfolk that a sorceress would know the whereabouts of the exorcist. They suspected her, then. A short time ago this would have given no concern to a woman of her common sense. But she had a haunting reason to be superstitious now; and she had been seized with sudden dread that this Conjuror Trendle might name her as the malignant influence which was blasting the fair person of Gertrude and so lead her friend to hate her for ever, and to treat her as some fiend in human shape.

But all was not over. Two days after, a shadow intruded into the window-pattern thrown on Rhoda Brook's floor by the afternoon sun. The woman opened the door at once, almost breathlessly.

'Are you alone?' said Gertrude. She seemed to be no less harassed and anxious than Brook herself.

'Yes,' said Rhoda.

'The place on my arm seems worse, and troubles me!' the young farmer's wife went on. 'It is so mysterious! I do hope it will not be an incurable wound. I have again been thinking of what they said about Conjuror Trendle. I don't really believe in such men, but I should not mind just visiting him, from curiosity – though on no account must my husband know. Is it far to where he lives?'

'Yes – five miles,' said Rhoda backwardly. 'In the heart of Egdon.'

'Well, I should have to walk. Could not you go with me to show me the way – say to-morrow afternoon?'

'O, not I – that is,' the milkwoman murmured, with a start of dismay. Again the dread seized her that something to do with her fierce act in the dream might be revealed, and her character in the eyes of the most useful friend she had ever had be ruined irretrievably.

Mrs Lodge urged, and Rhoda finally assented, though with much misgiving. Sad as the journey would be to her, she could not conscientiously stand in the way of a possible remedy for her patron's strange affliction. It was agreed that, to escape suspicion of their mystic intent, they should meet at the edge of the heath at the corner of a plantation which was visible from the spot where they now stood.

V. CONJUROR TRENDLE

By the next afternoon Rhoda would have done anything to escape this inquiry. But she had promised to go. Moreover, there was a horrid fascination at times in becoming instrumental in throwing such possible light on her own character as would reveal her to be something greater in the occult world than she had ever herself suspected.

She started just before the time of day mentioned between them, and half-an-hour's brisk walking brought her to the south-eastern extension of the Egdon tract of country, where the fir plantation was. A slight figure, cloaked and veiled, was already there. Rhoda recognized, almost with a shudder, that Mrs Lodge bore her left arm in a sling.

They hardly spoke to each other, and immediately set out on their climb into the interior of this solemn country, which stood high above the rich alluvial soil they had left half-an-hour before. It was a long walk; thick clouds made the atmosphere dark, though it was as yet only early afternoon; and the wind howled dismally over the slopes of the heath – not improbably the same heath which had witnessed the agony of the Wessex King Ina, presented to after-ages as Lear. Gertrude Lodge talked most, Rhoda replying with monosyllabic preoccupation. She had a strange dislike to walking on the side of her companion where hung the afflicted arm, moving round to the other when inadvertently near it. Much heather had been brushed by their feet when they descended upon a cart-track, beside which stood the house of the man they sought.

He did not profess his remedial practices openly, or care anything about their continuance, his direct interests being those of a dealer in furze, turf, 'sharp sand', and other local products. Indeed, he affected not to believe largely in his own powers, and when warts that had been shown him for cure miraculously disappeared – which it must be owned they infallibly did – he would say lightly, 'O, I only drink a glass of grog upon 'em at your expense – perhaps it's all chance,' and immediately turn the subject.

He was at home when they arrived, having in fact seen them descending into his valley. He was a grey-bearded man, with a reddish face, and he looked singularly at Rhoda the first moment he beheld her. Mrs Lodge told him her errand; and then with words of self-disparagement he examined her arm.

'Medicine can't cure it,' he said promptly. ''Tis the work of an enemy.'

Rhoda shrank into herself, and drew back.

'An enemy? What enemy?' asked Mrs Lodge.

He shook his head. 'That's best known to yourself,' he said. 'If you like, I can show the person to you, though I shall not myself know who it is. I can do no more; and don't wish to do that.'

She pressed him; on which he told Rhoda to wait outside where she stood, and took Mrs Lodge into the room. It opened immediately from the door; and, as the latter remained ajar, Rhoda Brook could see the proceedings without taking part in them. He brought a tumbler from the dresser, nearly filled it with water, and fetching an egg, prepared it in some private way; after which he broke it on the edge of the glass, so that the white went in and the yolk remained. As it was getting gloomy, he took the glass and its contents to the window, and told Gertrude to watch the mixture closely. They leant over the table together, and the milkwoman could see the opaline hue of the egg-fluid changing form as it sank in the water, but she was not near enough to define the shape that it assumed.

'Do you catch the likeness of any face or figure as you look?' demanded the conjuror of the young woman.

She murmured a reply, in tones so low as to be inaudible to Rhoda, and continued to gaze intently into the glass. Rhoda turned, and walked a few steps away.

When Mrs Lodge came out, and her face was met by the light, it appeared

exceedingly pale – as pale as Rhoda's – against the sad dun shades of the upland's garniture. Trendle shut the door behind her, and they at once started
homeward together. But Rhoda perceived that her companion had quite
changed.

'Did he charge much?' she asked tentatively.

'O no – nothing. He would not take a farthing,' said Gertrude.

'And what did you see?' inquired Rhoda.

'Nothing I – care to speak of.' The constraint in her manner was remarkable;
her face was so rigid as to wear an oldened aspect, faintly suggestive of the face in
Rhoda's bed-chamber.

'Was it you who first proposed coming here?' Mrs Lodge suddenly inquired,
after a long pause. 'How very odd, if you did!'

'No. But I am not sorry we have come, all things considered,' she replied. For
the first time a sense of triumph possessed her, and she did not altogether deplore
that the young thing at her side should learn that their lives had been antagonized
by other influences than their own.

The subject was no more alluded to during the long and dreary walk home. But
in some way or other a story was whispered about the many-dairied lowland that
winter that Mrs Lodge's gradual loss of the use of her left arm was owing to her
being 'overlooked' by Rhoda Brook. The latter kept her own counsel about the
incubus, but her face grew sadder and thinner; and in the spring she and her boy
disappeared from the neighbourhood of Holmstoke.

VI. A SECOND ATTEMPT

Half a dozen years passed away, and Mr and Mrs Lodge's married experience
sank into prosiness, and worse. The farmer was usually gloomy and silent; the
woman whom he had wooed for her grace and beauty was contorted and
disfigured in the left limb; moreover, she had brought him no child, which
rendered it likely that he would be the last of a family who had occupied that
valley for some two hundred years. He thought of Rhoda Brook and her son; and
feared this might be a judgment from heaven upon him.

The once blithe-hearted and enlightened Gertrude was changing into an
irritable, superstitious woman, whose whole time was given to experimenting
upon her ailment with every quack remedy she came across. She was honestly
attached to her husband, and was ever secretly hoping against hope to win back
his heart again by regaining some at least of her personal beauty. Hence it arose
that her closet was lined with bottles, packets, and ointment-pots of every
description – nay, bunches of mystic herbs, charms, and books of necromancy,
which in her schoolgirl time she would have ridiculed as folly.

'Damned if you won't poison yourself with these apothecary messes and witch
mixtures some time or other,' said her husband, when his eye chanced to fall
upon the multitudinous array.

She did not reply, but turned her sad, soft glance upon him in such heart-
swollen reproach that he looked sorry for his words, and added, 'I only meant it
for your good, you know, Gertrude.'

'I'll clear out the whole lot, and destroy them,' said she huskily, 'and try such remedies no more!'

'You want somebody to cheer you,' he observed. 'I once thought of adopting a boy; but he is too old now. And he is gone away I don't know where.'

She guessed to whom he alluded; for Rhoda Brook's story had in the course of years become known to her; though not a word had ever passed between her husband and herself on the subject. Neither had she ever spoken to him of her visit to Conjuror Trendle, and of what was revealed to her, or she thought was revealed to her, by that solitary heathman.

She was now five-and-twenty; but she seemed older. 'Six years of marriage, and only a few months of love,' she sometimes whispered to herself. And then she thought of the apparent cause, and said, with a tragic glance at her withering limb, 'If I could only again be as I was when he first saw me!'

She obediently destroyed her nostrums and charms; but there remained a hankering wish to try something else – some other sort of cure altogether. She had never revisited Trendle since she had been conducted to the house of the solitary by Rhoda against her will; but it now suddenly occurred to Gertrude that she would, in a last desperate effort at deliverance from this seeming curse, again seek out the man, if he yet lived. He was entitled to a certain credence, for the indistinct form he had raised in the glass had undoubtedly resembled the only woman in the world who – as she now knew, though not then – could have a reason for bearing her ill-will. The visit should be paid.

This time she went alone, though she nearly got lost on the heath, and roamed a considerable distance out of her way. Trendle's house was reached at last, however; he was not indoors, and instead of waiting at the cottage, she went to where his bent figure was pointed out to her at work a long way off. Trendle remembered her, and laying down the handful of furze-roots which he was gathering and throwing into a heap, he offered to accompany her in her homeward direction, as the distance was considerable and the days were short. So they walked together, his head bowed nearly to the earth, and his form of a colour with it.

'You can send away warts and other excrescences, I know,' she said; 'why can't you send away this?' And the arm was uncovered.

'You think too much of my powers!' said Trendle; 'and I am old and weak now, too. No, no; it is too much for me to attempt in my own person. What have ye tried?'

She named to him some of the hundred medicaments and counter-spells which she had adopted from time to time. He shook his head.

'Some were good enough,' he said approvingly; 'but not many of them for such as this. This is of the nature of a blight, not of the nature of a wound, and if you ever do throw it off, it will be all at once.'

'If I only could!'

'There is only one chance of doing it known to me. It has never failed in kindred afflictions – that I can declare. But it is hard to carry out, and especially for a woman.'

'Tell me!' said she.

'You must touch with the limb the neck of a man who's been hanged.'

She started a little at the image he had raised.

'Before he's cold—just after he's cut down,' continued the conjuror impassively.

'How can that do good?'

'It will turn the blood and change the constitution. But, as I say, to do it is hard. You must go to the jail when there's a hanging, and wait for him when he's brought off the gallows. Lots have done it, though perhaps not such pretty women as you. I used to send dozens for skin complaints. But that was in former times. The last I sent was in '13—near twelve years ago.'

He had no more to tell her, and, when he had put her into a straight track homeward, turned and left her, refusing all money as at first.

VII. A RIDE

The communication sank deep into Gertrude's mind. Her nature was rather a timid one; and probably of all remedies that the white wizard could have suggested there was not one which would have filled her with so much aversion as this, not to speak of the immense obstacles in the way of its adoption.

Casterbridge, the county-town, was a dozen or fifteen miles off; and though in those days, when men were executed for horse-stealing, arson, and burglary, an assize seldom passed without a hanging, it was not likely that she could get access to the body of the criminal unaided. And the fear of her husband's anger made her reluctant to breathe a word of Trendle's suggestion to him or to anybody about him.

She did nothing for months, and patiently bore her disfigurement as before. But her woman's nature, craving for renewed love, through the medium of renewed beauty (she was but twenty-five), was ever stimulating her to try what, at any rate, could hardly do her any harm. 'What came by a spell will go by a spell surely,' she would say. Whenever her imagination pictured the act she shrank in terror from the possibility of it; then the words of the conjuror, 'It will turn your blood,' were seen to be capable of a scientific no less than a ghastly interpretation; the mastering desire returned, and urged her on again.

There was at this time but one county paper, and that her husband only occasionally borrowed. But old-fashioned days had old-fashioned means, and news was extensively conveyed by word of mouth from market to market, or from fair to fair, so that, whenever such an event as an execution was about to take place, few within a radius of twenty miles were ignorant of the coming sight; and, so far as Holmstoke was concerned, some enthusiasts had been known to walk all the way to Casterbridge and back in one day, solely to witness the spectacle. The next assizes were in March; and when Gertrude Lodge heard that they had been held, she inquired stealthily at the inn as to the result, as soon as she could find opportunity.

She was, however, too late. The time at which the sentences were to be carried out had arrived, and to make the journey and obtain admission at such short notice required at least her husband's assistance. She dared not tell him, for she had found by delicate experiment that these smouldering village beliefs made him furious if mentioned, partly because he half entertained them himself. It was therefore necessary to wait for another opportunity.

Her determination received a fillip from learning that two epileptic children had attended from this very village of Holmstoke many years before with beneficial results, though the experiment had been strongly condemned by the neighbouring clergy. April, May, June passed; and it is no overstatement to say that by the end of the last-named month Gertrude wellnigh longed for the death of a fellow-creature. Instead of her formal prayers each night, her unconscious prayer was, 'O Lord, hang some guilty or innocent person soon!'

This time she made earlier inquiries, and was altogether more systematic in her proceedings. Moreover, the season was summer, between the haymaking and the harvest, and in the leisure thus afforded him her husband had been holiday-taking away from home.

The assizes were in July, and she went to the inn as before. There was to be one execution – only one – for arson.

Her greatest problem was not how to get to Casterbridge, but what means she should adopt for obtaining admission to the jail. Though access for such purposes had formerly never been denied, the custom had fallen into desuetude; and in contemplating her possible difficulties, she was again almost driven to fall back upon her husband. But, on sounding him about the assizes, he was so uncommunicative, so more than usually cold, that she did not proceed, and decided that whatever she did she would do alone.

Fortune, obdurate hitherto, showed her unexpected favour. On the Thursday before the Saturday fixed for the execution, Lodge remarked to her that he was going away from home for another day or two on business at a fair, and that he was sorry he could not take her with him.

She exhibited on this occasion so much readiness to stay at home that he looked at her in surprise. Time had been when she would have shown deep disappointment at the loss of such a jaunt. However, he lapsed into his usual taciturnity, and on the day named left Holmstoke.

It was now her turn. She at first had thought of driving, but on reflection held that driving would not do, since it would necessitate her keeping to the turnpike-road, and so increase by tenfold the risk of her ghastly errand being found out. She decided to ride, and avoid the beaten track, notwithstanding that in her husband's stables there was no animal just at present which by any stretch of imagination could be considered a lady's mount, in spite of his promise before marriage to always keep a mare for her. He had, however, many cart-horses, fine ones of their kind; and among the rest was a serviceable creature, an equine Amazon, with a back as broad as a sofa, on which Gertrude had occasionally taken an airing when unwell. This horse she chose.

On Friday afternoon one of the men brought it round. She was dressed, and before going down looked at her shrivelled arm. 'Ah!' she said to it, 'if it had not been for you this terrible ordeal would have been saved me!'

When strapping up the bundle in which she carried a few articles of clothing, she took occasion to say to the servant, 'I take these in case I should not get back to-night from the person I am going to visit. Don't be alarmed if I am not in by ten, and close up the house as usual. I shall be at home to-morrow for certain.' She meant then to tell her husband privately; the deed accomplished was not like the deed projected. He would almost certainly forgive her.

And then the pretty palpitating Gertrude Lodge went from her husband's homestead; but though her goal was Casterbridge she did not take the direct route thither through Stickleford. Her cunning course at first was in precisely the opposite direction. As soon as she was out of sight, however, she turned to the left, by a road which led into Egdon, and on entering the heath wheeled round, and set out in the true course, due westerly. A more private way down the county could not be imagined; and as to direction, she had merely to keep her horse's head to a point a little to the right of the sun. She knew that she would light upon a furze-cutter or cottager of some sort from time to time, from whom she might correct her bearing.

Though the date was comparatively recent, Egdon was much less fragmentary in character than now. The attempts — successful and otherwise — at cultivation on the lower slopes, which intrude and break up the original heath into small detached heaths, had not been carried far; Enclosure Acts had not taken effect, and the banks and fences which now exclude the cattle of those villagers who formerly enjoyed rights of commonage thereon, and the carts of those who had turbary privileges which kept them in firing all the year round, were not erected. Gertrude, therefore, rode along with no other obstacles than the prickly furze-bushes, the mats of heather, the white water-courses, and the natural steeps and declivities of the ground.

Her horse was sure, if heavy-footed and slow, and though a draught animal, was easy-paced; had it been otherwise, she was not a woman who could have ventured to ride over such a bit of country with a half-dead arm. It was therefore nearly eight o'clock when she drew rein to breathe her bearer on the last outlying high point of heath-land towards Casterbridge, previous to leaving Egdon for the cultivated valleys.

She halted before a pool called Rushy-pond, flanked by the ends of two hedges; a railing ran through the centre of the pond, dividing it in half. Over the railing she saw the low green country; over the green trees the roofs of the town; over the roofs a white flat façade, denoting the entrance to the county jail. On the roof of this front specks were moving about; they seemed to be workmen erecting something. Her flesh crept. She descended slowly, and was soon amid corn-fields and pastures. In another half-hour, when it was almost dusk, Gertrude reached the White Hart, the first inn of the town on that side.

Little surprise was excited by her arrival; farmers' wives rode on horseback then more than they do now; though, for that matter, Mrs Lodge was not imagined to be a wife at all; the innkeeper supposed her some harum-skarum young woman who had come to attend 'hang-fair' next day. Neither her husband nor herself ever dealt in Casterbridge market, so that she was unknown. While dismounting she beheld a crowd of boys standing at the door of a harness-maker's shop just above the inn, looking inside it with deep interest.

'What is going on there?' she asked of the ostler.

'Making the rope for to-morrow.'

She throbbed responsively, and contracted her arm.

''Tis sold by the inch afterwards,' the man continued. 'I could get you a bit, miss, for nothing, if you'd like?'

She hastily repudiated any such wish, all the more from a curious creeping feeling that the condemned wretch's destiny was becoming interwoven with her own; and having engaged a room for the night, sat down to think.

Up to this time she had formed but the vaguest notions about her means of obtaining access to the prison. The words of the cunning-man returned to her mind. He had implied that she should use her beauty, impaired though it was, as a pass-key. In her inexperience she knew little about jail functionaries; she had heard of a high-sheriff and an under-sheriff, but dimly only. She knew, however, that there must be a hangman, and to the hangman she determined to apply.

VIII. A WATER-SIDE HERMIT

At this date, and for several years after, there was a hangman to almost every jail. Gertrude found, on inquiry, that the Casterbridge official dwelt in a lonely cottage by a deep slow river flowing under the cliff on which the prison buildings were situate – the stream being the self-same one, though she did not know it, which watered the Stickleford and Holmstoke meads lower down in its course.

Having changed her dress, and before she had eaten or drunk – for she could not take her ease till she had ascertained some particulars – Gertrude pursued her way by a path along the water-side to the cottage indicated. Passing thus the outskirts of the jail, she discerned on the level roof over the gateway three rectangular lines against the sky, where the specks had been moving in her distant view; she recognized what the erection was, and passed quickly on. Another hundred yards brought her to the executioner's house, which a boy pointed out. It stood close to the same stream, and was hard by a weir, the waters of which emitted a steady roar.

While she stood hesitating the door opened, and an old man came forth, shading a candle with one hand. Locking the door on the outside, he turned to a flight of wooden steps fixed against the end of the cottage, and began to ascend them, this being evidently the staircase to his bedroom. Gertrude hastened forward, but by the time she reached the foot of the ladder he was at the top. She called to him loudly enough to be heard above the roar of the weir; he looked down and said, 'What d'ye want here?'

'To speak to you a minute.'

The candlelight, such as it was, fell upon her imploring, pale, upturned face, and Davies (as the hangman was called) backed down the ladder. 'I was just going to bed,' he said. ' "Early to bed and early to rise", but I don't mind stopping a minute for such a one as you. Come into house.' He reopened the door, and preceded her to the room within.

The implements of his daily work, which was that of a jobbing gardener, stood in a corner, and seeing probably that she looked rural, he said, 'If you want me to undertake country work I can't come, for I never leave Casterbridge for gentle nor simple – not I. My real calling is officer of justice,' he added formally.

'Yes, yes! That's it. To-morrow!'

'Ah! I thought so. Well, what's the matter about that? 'Tis no use to come here about the knot – folks do come continually, but I tell 'em one knot is as merciful as another if ye keep it under the ear. Is the unfortunate man a relation; or, I should say, perhaps' (looking at her dress) 'a person who's been in your employ?'

'No. What time is the execution?'

'The same as usual — twelve o'clock, or as soon after as the London mail-coach gets in. We always wait for that, in case of a reprieve.'

'O — a reprieve — I hope not!' she said involuntarily.

'Well, — hee, hee! — as a matter of business, so do I! But still, if ever a young fellow deserved to be let off, this one does; only just turned eighteen, and only present by chance when the rick was fired. Howsomever, there's not much risk of it, as they are obliged to make an example of him, there having been so much destruction of property that way lately.'

'I mean,' she explained, 'that I want to touch him for a charm, a cure of an affliction, by the advice of a man who has proved the virtue of the remedy.'

'O yes, miss! Now I understand. I've had such people come in past years. But it didn't strike me that you looked of a sort to require blood-turning. What's the complaint? The wrong kind for this, I'll be bound.'

'My arm.' She reluctantly showed the withered skin.

'Ah! — 'tis all a-scram!' said the hangman, examining it.

'Yes,' said she.

'Well,' he continued, with interest, 'that *is* the class o' subject, I'm bound to admit! I like the look of the wownd; it is truly as suitable for the cure as any I ever saw. 'Twas a knowing-man that sent 'ee, whoever he was.'

'You can contrive for me all that's necessary?' she said breathlessly.

'You should really have gone to the governor of the jail, and your doctor with 'ee, and given your name and address — that's how it used to be done, if I recollect. Still, perhaps, I can manage it for a trifling fee.'

'O, thank you! I would rather do it this way, as I should like it kept private.'

'Lover not to know, eh?'

'No — husband.'

'Aha! Very well. I'll get 'ee a touch of the corpse.'

'Where is it now?' she said, shuddering.

'It? — *he*, you mean; he's living yet. Just inside that little small winder up there in the glum.' He signified the jail on the cliff above.

She thought of her husband and her friends. 'Yes, of course,' she said; 'and how am I to proceed?'

He took her to the door. 'Now, do you be waiting at the little wicket in the wall, that you'll find up there in the lane, not later than one o'clock. I will open it from the inside, as I shan't come home to dinner till he's cut down. Good-night. Be punctual; and if you don't want anybody to know 'ee, wear a veil. Ah — once I had such a daughter as you!'

She went away, and climbed the path above, to assure herself that she would be able to find the wicket next day. Its outline was soon visible to her — a narrow opening in the outer wall of the prison precincts. The steep was so great that, having reached the wicket, she stopped a moment to breathe; and, looking back upon the water-side cot, saw the hangman again ascending his outdoor staircase. He entered the loft or chamber to which it led, and in a few minutes extinguished his light.

The town clock struck ten, and she returned to the White Hart as she had come.

IX. A RENCOUNTER

It was one o'clock on Saturday. Gertrude Lodge, having been admitted to the jail as above described, was sitting in a waiting-room within the second gate, which stood under a classic archway of ashlar, then comparatively modern, and bearing the inscription, 'COVNTY JAIL: 1793'. This had been the façade she saw from the heath the day before. Near at hand was a passage to the roof on which the gallows stood.

The town was thronged, and the market suspended; but Gertrude had seen scarcely a soul. Having kept her room till the hour of the appointment, she had proceeded to the spot by a way which avoided the open space below the cliff where the spectators had gathered; but she could, even now, hear the multitudinous babble of their voices, out of which rose at intervals the hoarse croak of a single voice uttering the words, 'Last dying speech and confession!' There had been no reprieve, and the execution was over; but the crowd still waited to see the body taken down.

Soon the persistent woman heard a trampling overhead, then a hand beckoned to her, and, following directions, she went out and crossed the inner paved court beyond the gatehouse, her knees trembling so that she could scarcely walk. One of her arms was out of its sleeve, and only covered by her shawl.

On the spot at which she had now arrived were two trestles, and before she could think of their purpose she heard heavy feet descending stairs somewhere at her back. Turn her head she would not, or could not, and, rigid in this position, she was conscious of a rough coffin passing her shoulder, borne by four men. It was open, and in it lay the body of a young man, wearing the smockfrock of a rustic, and fustian breeches. The corpse had been thrown into the coffin so hastily that the skirt of the smockfrock was hanging over. The burden was temporarily deposited on the trestles.

By this time the young woman's state was such that a gray mist seemed to float before her eyes, on account of which, and the veil she wore, she could scarcely discern anything: it was as though she had nearly died, but was held up by a sort of galvanism.

'Now!' said a voice close at hand, and she was just conscious that the word had been addressed to her.

By a last strenuous effort she advanced, at the same time hearing persons approaching behind her. She bared her poor curst arm; and Davies, uncovering the face of the corpse, took Gertrude's hand, and held it so that her arm lay across the dead man's neck, upon a line the colour of an unripe blackberry, which surrounded it.

Gertrude shrieked: 'the turn o' the blood', predicted by the conjuror, had taken place. But at that moment a second shriek rent the air of the enclosure: it was not Gertrude's, and its effect upon her was to make her start round.

Immediately behind her stood Rhoda Brook, her face drawn, and her eyes red with weeping. Behind Rhoda stood Gertrude's own husband; his countenance lined, his eyes dim, but without a tear.

'D—n you! what are you doing here?' he said hoarsely.

'Hussy — to come between us and our child now!' cried Rhoda. 'This is the meaning of what Satan showed me in the vision! You are like her at last!' And clutching the bare arm of the younger woman, she pulled her unresistingly back against the wall. Immediately Brook had loosened her hold the fragile young Gertrude slid down against the feet of her husband. When he lifted her up she was unconscious.

The mere sight of the twain had been enough to suggest to her that the dead young man was Rhoda's son. At that time the relatives of an executed convict had the privilege of claiming the body for burial, if they chose to do so; and it was for this purpose that Lodge was awaiting the inquest with Rhoda. He had been summoned by her as soon as the young man was taken in the crime, and at different times since; and he had attended in court during the trial. This was the 'holiday' he had been indulging in of late. The two wretched parents had wished to avoid exposure; and hence had come themselves for the body, a waggon and sheet for its conveyance and covering being in waiting outside.

Gertrude's case was so serious that it was deemed advisable to call to her the surgeon who was at hand. She was taken out of the jail into the town; but she never reached home alive. Her delicate vitality, sapped perhaps by the paralyzed arm, collapsed under the double shock that followed the severe strain, physical and mental, to which she had subjected herself during the previous twenty-four hours. Her blood had been 'turned' indeed — too far. Her death took place in the town three days after.

Her husband was never seen in Casterbridge again; once only in the old market-place at Anglebury, which he had so much frequented, and very seldom in public anywhere. Burdened at first with moodiness and remorse, he eventually changed for the better, and appeared as a chastened and thoughtful man. Soon after attending the funeral of his poor young wife he took steps towards giving up the farms in Holmstoke and the adjoining parish, and, having sold every head of his stock, he went away to Port-Bredy, at the other end of the county, living there in solitary lodgings till his death two years later of a painless decline. It was then found that he had bequeathed the whole of his not inconsiderable property to a reformatory for boys, subject to the payment of a small annuity to Rhoda Brook, if she could be found to claim it.

For some time she could not be found; but eventually she reappeared in her old parish, — absolutely refusing, however, to have anything to do with the provision made for her. Her monotonous milking at the dairy was resumed, and followed for many long years, till her form became bent, and her once abundant dark hair white and worn away at the forehead — perhaps by long pressure against the cows. Here, sometimes, those who knew her experiences would stand and observe her, and wonder what sombre thoughts were beating inside that impassive, wrinkled brow, to the rhythm of the alternating milk-streams.

'Blackwood's Magazine',
January 1888

Fellow-Townsmen

I

THE shepherd on the east hill could shout out lambing intelligence to the shepherd on the west hill, over the intervening town chimneys, without great inconvenience to his voice, so nearly did the steep pastures encroach upon the burghers' backyards. And at night it was possible to stand in the very midst of the town and hear from their native paddocks on the lower levels of greensward the mild lowing of the farmer's heifers, and the profound, warm blowings of breath in which those creatures indulge. But the community which had jammed itself in the valley thus flanked formed a veritable town, with a real mayor and corporation, and a staple manufacture.

During a certain damp evening five-and-thirty years ago, before the twilight was far advanced, a pedestrian of professional appearance, carrying a small bag in his hand and an elevated umbrella, was descending one of these hills by the turnpike road when he was overtaken by a phaeton.

'Hullo, Downe – is that you?' said the driver of the vehicle, a young man of pale and refined appearance. 'Jump up here with me, and ride down to your door.'

The other turned a plump, cheery, rather self-indulgent face over his shoulder towards the hailer.

'O, good evening, Mr Barnet – thanks,' he said, and mounted beside his acquaintance.

They were fellow-burgesses of the town which lay beneath them, but though old and very good friends they were differently circumstanced. Barnet was a richer man than the struggling young lawyer Downe, a fact which was to some extent perceptible in Downe's manner towards his companion, though nothing of it ever showed in Barnet's manner towards the solicitor. Barnet's position in the town was none of his own making; his father had been a very successful flax-merchant in the same place, where the trade was still carried on as briskly as the small capacities of its quarters would allow. Having acquired a fair fortune, old Mr Barnet had retired from business, bringing up his son as a gentleman-burgher, and, it must be added, as a well-educated, liberal-minded young man.

'How is Mrs Barnet?' asked Downe.

'Mrs Barnet was very well when I left home,' the other answered constrainedly, exchanging his meditative regard of the horse for one of self-consciousness.

Mr Downe seemed to regret his inquiry, and immediately took up another thread of conversation. He congratulated his friend on his election as a councilman; he had not seen him since that event took place; Mrs Downe had meant to call and congratulate Mrs Barnet, but he feared that she had failed to do so as yet.

Barnet seemed hampered in his replies. 'We should have been glad to see you. I – my wife would welcome Mrs Downe at any time, as you know. . . . Yes, I am

756

a member of the corporation – rather an inexperienced member, some of them say. It is quite true; and I should have declined the honour as premature – having other things on my hands just now, too – if it had not been pressed upon me so very heartily.'

'There is one thing you have on your hands which I can never quite see the necessity for,' said Downe, with good-humoured freedom. 'What the deuce do you want to build that new mansion for, when you have already got such an excellent house as the one you live in?'

Barnet's face acquired a warmer shade of colour; but as the question had been idly asked by the solicitor while regarding the surrounding flocks and fields, he answered after a moment with no apparent embarrassment –

'Well, we wanted to get out of the town, you know; the house I am living in is rather old and inconvenient.'

Mr Downe declared that he had chosen a pretty site for the new building. They would be able to see for miles and miles from the windows. Was he going to give it a name? He supposed so.

Barnet thought not. There was no other house near that was likely to be mistaken for it. And he did not care for a name.

'But I think it has a name!' Downe observed: 'I went past – when was it? – this morning; and I saw something, – "Château Ringdale", I think it was, stuck up on a board!'

'It was an idea she – we had for a short time,' said Barnet hastily. 'But we have decided finally to do without a name – at any rate such a name as that. It must have been a week ago that you saw it. It was taken down last Satur-day. . . . Upon that matter I am firm!' he added grimly.

Downe murmured in an unconvinced tone that he thought he had seen it yesterday.

Talking thus they drove into the town. The street was unusually still for the hour of seven in the evening; an increasing drizzle from the sea had prevailed since the afternoon, and now formed a gauze across the yellow lamps, and trickled with a gentle rattle down the heavy roofs of stone tile, that bent the house-ridges hollow-backed with its weight, and in some instances caused the walls to bulge outwards in the upper story. Their route took them past the little town-hall, the Black-Bull Hotel, and onward to the junction of a small street on the right, consisting of a row of those two-and-two windowed brick residences of no particular age, which are exactly alike wherever found, except in the people they contain.

'Wait – I'll drive you up to your door,' said Barnet, when Downe prepared to alight at the corner. He thereupon turned into the narrow street, when the faces of three little girls could be discerned close to the panes of a lighted window a few yards ahead, surmounted by that of a young matron, the gaze of all four being directed eagerly up the empty street. 'You are a fortunate fellow, Downe,' Barnet continued, as mother and children disappeared from the window to run to the door. 'You must be happy if any man is. I would give a hundred such houses as my new one to have a home like yours.'

'Well – yes, we get along pretty comfortably,' replied Downe complacently.

'That house Downe, is none of my ordering,' Barnet broke out, revealing a bitterness hitherto suppressed, and checking the horse a moment to finish his speech before delivering up his passenger. 'The house I have already is good enough for me, as you supposed. It is my own freehold; it was built by my grandfather, and is stout enough for a castle. My father was born there, lived there, and died there. I was born there, and have always lived there; yet I must needs build a new one.'

'Why do you?' said Downe.

'Why do I? To preserve peace in the household. I do anything for that; but I don't succeed. I was firm in resisting "Château Ringdale", however; not that I would not have put up with the absurdity of the name, but it was too much to have your house christened after Lord Ringdale, because your wife once had a fancy for him. If you only knew everything, you would think all attempt at reconciliation hopeless. In your happy home you have had no such experiences; and God forbid that you ever should. See, here they are all ready to receive you!'

'Of course! And so will your wife be waiting to receive you,' said Downe. 'Take my word for it she will! And with a dinner prepared for you far better than mine.'

'I hope so,' Barnet replied dubiously.

He moved on to Downe's door, which the solicitor's family had already opened. Downe descended, but being encumbered with his bag and umbrella, his foot slipped, and he fell upon his knees in the gutter.

'O, my dear Charles!' said his wife, running down the steps; and, quite ignoring the presence of Barnet, she seized hold of her husband, pulled him to his feet, and kissed him, exclaiming, 'I hope you are not hurt, darling!' The children crowded round, chiming in piteously, 'Poor papa!'

'He's all right,' said Barnet, perceiving that Downe was only a little muddy, and looking more at the wife than at the husband. Almost at any other time – certainly during his fastidious bachelor years – he would have thought her a too demonstrative woman; but those recent circumstances of his own life to which he had just alluded made Mrs Downe's solicitude so affecting that his eye grew damp as he witnessed it. Bidding the lawyer and his family good-night he left them, and drove slowly into the main street towards his own house.

The heart of Barnet was sufficiently impressionable to be influenced by Downe's parting prophecy that he might not be so unwelcome home as he imagined: the dreary night might, at least on this one occasion, make Downe's forecast true. Hence it was in a suspense that he could hardly have believed possible that he halted at his door. On entering his wife was nowhere to be seen, and he inquired for her. The servant informed him that her mistress had the dressmaker with her, and would be engaged for some time.

'Dressmaker at this time of day!'

'She dined early, sir, and hopes you will excuse her joining you this evening.'

'But she knew I was coming to-night?'

'O yes, sir.'

'Go up and tell her I am come.'

The servant did so; but the mistress of the house merely transmitted her former words.

Barnet said nothing more, and presently sat down to his lonely meal, which was eaten abstractedly, the domestic scene he had lately witnessed still impressing him by its contrast with the situation here. His mind fell back into past years upon a certain pleasing and gentle being whose face would loom out of their shades at such times as these. Barnet turned in his chair, and looked with unfocused eyes in a direction southward from where he sat, as if he saw not the room but a long way beyond. 'I wonder if she lives there still!' he said.

II

He rose with a sudden rebelliousness, put on his hat and coat, and went out of the house, pursuing his way along the glistening pavement while eight o'clock was striking from St Mary's tower, and the apprentices and shopmen were slamming up the shutters from end to end of the town. In two minutes only those shops which could boast of no attendant save the master or the mistress remained with open eyes. These were ever somewhat less prompt to exclude customers than the others: for their owners' ears the closing hour had scarcely the cheerfulness that it possessed for the hired servants of the rest. Yet the night being dreary the delay was not for long, and their windows, too, blinked together one by one.

During this time Barnet had proceeded with decided step in a direction at right angles to the broad main thoroughfare of the town, by a long street leading due southward. Here, though his family had no more to do with the flax manufacture, his own name occasionally greeted him on gates and warehouses, being used allusively by small rising tradesmen as a recommendation, in such words as 'Smith, from Barnet & Co.' – 'Robinson, late manager at Barnet's'. The sight led him to reflect upon his father's busy life, and he questioned if it had not been far happier than his own.

The houses along the road became fewer, and presently open ground appeared between them on either side, the track on the right hand rising to a higher level till it merged in a knoll. On the summit a row of builders' scaffold-poles probed the indistinct sky like spears, and at their bases could be discerned the lower courses of a building lately begun. Barnet slackened his pace and stood for a few moments without leaving the centre of the road, apparently not much interested in the sight, till suddenly his eye was caught by a post in the fore part of the ground bearing a white board at the top. He went to the rails, vaulted over, and walked in far enough to discern painted upon the board 'Château Ringdale'.

A dismal irony seemed to lie in the words, and its effect was to irritate him. Downe, then, had spoken truly. He stuck his umbrella into the sod, and seized the post with both hands, as if intending to loosen and throw it down. Then, like one bewildered by an opposition which would exist none the less though its manifestations were removed, he allowed his arms to sink to his side.

'Let it be,' he said to himself. 'I have declared there shall be peace – if possible.'

Taking up his umbrella, he quietly left the enclosure, and went on his way, still keeping his back to the town. He had advanced with more decision since passing the new building, and soon a hoarse murmur rose upon the gloom; it was the sound of the sea. The road led to the harbour, at a distance of a mile from the town, from which the trade of the district was fed. After seeing the obnoxious name-board Barnet had forgotten to open his umbrella, and the rain tapped smartly on his hat, and occasionally stroked his face as he went on.

Though the lamps were still continued at the roadside they stood at wider intervals than before, and the pavement had given place to rough gravel. Every time he came to a lamp an increasing shine made itself visible upon his shoulders, till at last they quite glistened with wet. The murmur from the shore grew stronger, but it was still some distance off when he paused before one of the smallest of the detached houses by the wayside, standing in its own garden, 'the latter being divided from the road by a row of wooden palings. Scrutinizing the spot to ensure that he was not mistaken, he opened the gate and gently knocked at the cottage door.

When he had patiently waited minutes enough to lead any man in ordinary cases to knock again, the door was heard to open, though it was impossible to see by whose hand, there being no light in the passage. Barnet said at random, 'Does Miss Savile live here?'

A youthful voice assured him that she did live there, and by a sudden afterthought asked him to come in. It would soon get a light, it said: but the night being wet, mother had not thought it worth while to trim the passage lamp.

'Don't trouble yourself to get a light for me,' said Barnet hastily; 'it is not necessary at all. Which is Miss Savile's sitting-room?'

The young person, whose white pinafore could just be discerned, signified a door in the side of the passage, and Barnet went forward at the same moment, so that no light should fall upon his face. On entering the room he closed the door behind him, pausing till he heard the retreating footsteps of the child.

He found himself in an apartment which was simply and neatly, though not poorly furnished; everything, from the miniature chiffonnier to the shining little daguerreotype which formed the central ornament of the mantelpiece, being in scrupulous order. The picture was enclosed by a frame of embroidered card-board – evidently the work of feminine hands – and it was the portrait of a thin-faced, elderly lieutenant in the navy. From behind the lamp on the table a female form now rose into view, that of a young girl, and a resemblance between her and the portrait was early discoverable. She had been so absorbed in some occupation on the other side of the lamp as to have barely found time to realize her visitor's presence.

They both remained standing for a few seconds without speaking. The face that confronted Barnet had a beautiful outline; the Raffaelesque oval of its contour was remarkable for an English countenance, and that countenance housed in a remote country-road to an unheard-of harbour. But her features did not do justice to this splendid beginning: Nature had recollected that she was not in Italy; and the young lady's lineaments, though not so inconsistent as to make her plain, would have been accepted rather as pleasing than as correct. The preoccupied expression which, like images on the retina, remained with her for a moment after the state that caused it had ceased, now changed into a reserved, half-proud, and slightly indignant look, in which the blood diffused itself quickly across her cheek, and additional brightness broke the shade of her rather heavy eyes.

'I know I have no business here,' he said, answering the look. 'But I had a great wish to see you, and inquire how you were. You can give your hand to me, seeing how often I have held it in past days?'

'I would rather forget than remember all that, Mr Barnet,' she answered, as she coldly complied with the request. 'When I think of the circumstances of our last meeting, I can hardly consider it kind of you to allude to such a thing as our past – or, indeed, to come here at all.'

'There was no harm in it surely? I don't trouble you often, Lucy.'

'I have not had the honour of a visit from you for a very long time, certainly, and I did not expect it now,' she said, with the same stiffness in her air. 'I hope Mrs Barnet is very well?'

'Yes, yes!' he impatiently returned. 'At least, I suppose so – though I only speak from inference!'

'But she is your wife, sir,' said the young girl tremulously.

The unwonted tones of a man's voice in that feminine chamber had startled a canary that was roosting in its cage by the window; the bird awoke hastily, and fluttered against the bars. She went and stilled it by laying her face against the cage and murmuring a coaxing sound. It might partly have been done to still herself.

'I didn't come to talk of Mrs Barnet,' he pursued; 'I came to talk of you, of yourself alone; to inquire how you are getting on since your great loss.' And he turned towards the portrait of her father.

'I am getting on fairly well, thank you.'

The force of her utterance was scarcely borne out by her look; but Barnet courteously reproached himself for not having guessed a thing so natural; and to dissipate all embarrassment added, as he bent over the table, 'What were you doing when I came? – painting flowers, and by candlelight?'

'O no,' she said, 'not painting them – only sketching the outlines. I do that at night to save time – I have to get three dozen done by the end of the month.'

Barnet looked as if he regretted it deeply. 'You will wear your poor eyes out,' he said, with more sentiment than he had hitherto shown. 'You ought not to do it. There was a time when I should have said you must not. Well – I almost wish I had never seen light with my own eyes when I think of that!'

'Is this a time or place for recalling such matters?' she asked, with dignity. 'You used to have a gentlemanly respect for me, and for yourself. Don't speak any more as you have spoken, and don't come again. I cannot think that this visit is serious, or was closely considered by you.'

'Considered: well, I came to see you as an old and good friend – not to mince matters, to visit a woman I loved. Don't be angry! I could not help doing it, so many things brought you into my mind. . . . This evening I fell in with an acquaintance, and when I saw how happy he was with his wife and family welcoming him home, though with only one-tenth of my income and chances, and thought what might have been in my case, it fairly broke down my discretion, and off I came here. Now I am here I feel that I am wrong to some extent. But the feeling that I should like to see you, and talk of those we used to know in common, was very strong.'

'Before that can be the case a little more time must pass,' said Miss Savile quietly; 'a time long enough for me to regard with some calmness what at present I remember far too impatiently – though it may be you almost forget it. Indeed you must have forgotten it long before you acted as you did.' Her voice grew stronger and more vivacious as she added: 'But I am doing my best to forget it too, and I know I shall succeed from the progress I have made already!'

She had remained standing till now, when she turned and sat down, facing half away from him.

Barnet watched her moodily. 'Yes, it is only what I deserve,' he said. 'Ambition pricked me on – no, it was not ambition, it was wrongheadedness! Had I but reflected. . . .' He broke out vehemently: 'But always remember this, Lucy: if you had written to me only one little line after that misunderstanding, I declare I should have come back to you. That ruined me!' He slowly walked as far as the little room would allow him to go, and remained with his eyes on the skirting.

'But, Mr Barnet, how could I write to you? There was no opening for my doing so.'

'Then there ought to have been,' said Barnet, turning. 'That was my fault!'

'Well, I don't know anything about that; but as there had been nothing said by me which required any explanation by letter, I did not send one. Everything was so indefinite, and feeling your position to be so much wealthier than mine, I fancied I might have mistaken your meaning. And when I heard of the other lady – a woman of whose family even you might be proud – I thought how foolish I had been, and said nothing.'

'Then I suppose it was destiny – accident – I don't know what, that separated us, dear Lucy. Anyhow, you were the woman I ought to have made my wife – and I let you slip, like the foolish man that I was!'

'O, Mr Barnet,' she said, almost in tears, 'don't revive the subject to me; I am the wrong one to console you – think, sir, – you should not be here – it would be so bad for me if it were known!'

'It would – it would, indeed,' he said hastily. 'I am not right in doing this, and I won't do it again.'

'It is a very common folly of human nature, you know, to think the course you did *not* adopt must have been the best,' she continued, with gentle solicitude, as she followed him to the door of the room. 'And you don't know that I should have accepted you, even if you had asked me to be your wife.' At this his eye met hers, and she dropped her gaze. She knew that her voice belied her. There was a silence till she looked up to add, in a voice of soothing playfulness, 'My family was so much poorer than yours, even before I lost my dear father, that – perhaps your companions would have made it unpleasant for us on account of my deficiencies.'

'Your disposition would soon have won them round,' said Barnet.

She archly expostulated: 'Now, never mind my disposition; try to make it up with your wife! Those are my commands to you. And now you are to leave me at once.'

'I will. I must make the best of it all, I suppose,' he replied, more cheerfully than he had as yet spoken. 'But I shall never again meet with such a dear girl as you!' And he suddenly opened the door and left her alone. When his glance again fell on the lamps that were sparsely ranged along the dreary level road, his eyes were in a state which showed straw-like motes of light radiating from each flame into the surrounding air.

On the other side of the way Barnet observed a man under an umbrella, walking parallel with himself. Presently this man left the footway, and gradually converged on Barnet's course. The latter then saw that it was Charlson, a surgeon of the town, who owed him money. Charlson was a man not without ability; yet he did not prosper. Sundry circumstances stood in his way as a medical practitioner: he was needy; he was not a coddle; he gossiped with men instead of with women; he had married a stranger instead of one of the town young ladies; and he was given to conversational buffoonery. Moreover, his look was quite erroneous. Those only proper features in the family doctor, the quiet eye, and the thin straight passionless lips which never curl in public either for laughter or for scorn, were not his; he had a full-curved mouth, and a bold black eye that made timid people nervous. His companions were what in old times would have been called boon companions – an expression which, though of irreproachable root, suggests fraternization carried to the point of unscrupulousness. All this was against him in the little town of his adoption.

Charlson had been in difficulties, and to oblige him Barnet had put his name to a bill; and, as he had expected, was called upon to meet it when it fell due. It had been only a matter of fifty pounds, which Barnet could well afford to lose, and he bore no ill-will to the thriftless surgeon on account of it. But Charlson had a little too much brazen indifferentism in his composition to be altogether a desirable acquaintance.

'I hope to be able to make that little bill-business right with you in the course of three weeks, Mr Barnet,' said Charlson with hail-fellow friendliness.

Barnet replied good-naturedly that there was no hurry.

This particular three weeks had moved on in advance of Charlson's present with the precision of a shadow for some considerable time.

'I've had a dream,' Charlson continued. Barnet knew from his tone that the surgeon was going to begin his characteristic nonsense, and did not encourage him. 'I've had a dream,' repeated Charlson, who required no encouragement. 'I dreamed that a gentleman, who has been very kind to me, married a haughty lady in haste, before he had quite forgotten a nice little girl he knew before, and that one wet evening, like the present, as I was walking up the harbour-road, I saw him come out of that dear little girl's present abode.'

Barnet glanced towards the speaker. The rays from a neighbouring lamp struck through the drizzle under Charlson's umbrella, so as just to illumine his face against the shade behind, and show that his eye was turned up under the outer corner of its lid, whence it leered with impish jocoseness as he thrust his tongue into his cheek.

'Come,' said Barnet gravely, 'we'll have no more of that.'

'No, no – of course not,' Charlson hastily answered, seeing that his humour had carried him too far, as it had done many times before. He was profuse in his apologies, but Barnet did not reply. Of one thing he was certain – that scandal was a plant of quick root, and that he was bound to obey Lucy's injunction for Lucy's own sake.

III

He did so, to the letter; and though, as the crocus followed the snow-drop and the daffodil the crocus in Lucy's garden, the harbour-road was a not unpleasant place to walk in, Barnet's feet never trod its stones, much less approached her door. He avoided a saunter that way as he would have avoided a dangerous dram, and took his airings a long distance northward, among severely square and brown ploughed fields, where no other townsman came. Sometimes he went round by the lower lanes of the borough, where the rope-walks stretched in which his family formerly had share, and looked at the rope-makers walking backwards, overhung by apple-trees and bushes, and intruded on by cows and calves, as if trade had established itself there at considerable inconvenience to Nature.

One morning, when the sun was so warm as to raise a steam from the south-eastern slopes of those flanking hills that looked so lovely above the old roofs, but made every low-chimneyed house in the town as smoky as Tophet, Barnet glanced from the windows of the town-council room for lack of interest in what was proceeding within. Several members of the corporation were present, but there was not much business doing, and in a few minutes Downe came leisurely across to him, saying that he seldom saw Barnet now.

Barnet owned that he was not often present.

Downe looked at the crimson curtain which hung down beside the panes, reflecting its hot hues into their faces, and then out of the window. At that moment there passed along the street a tall commanding lady, in whom the solicitor recognized Barnet's wife. Barnet had done the same thing, and turned away.

'It will be all right some day,' said Downe, with cheering sympathy.

'You have heard, then, of her last outbreak?'

Downe depressed his cheerfulness to its very reverse in a moment. 'No, I have not heard of anything serious,' he said, with as long a face as one naturally round could be turned into at short notice. 'I only hear vague reports of such things.'

'You may think it will be all right,' said Barnet drily. 'But I have a different opinion. . . . No, Downe, we must look the thing in the face. Not poppy nor mandragora – however, how are your wife and children?'

Downe said that they were all well, thanks; they were out that morning somewhere; he was just looking to see if they were walking that way. Ah, there they were, just coming down the street; and Downe pointed to the figures of two children with a nursemaid, and a lady walking behind them.

'You will come out and speak to her?' he asked.

'Not this morning. The fact is I don't care to speak to anybody just now.'

'You are too sensitive, Mr Barnet. At school I remember you used to get as red as a rose if anybody uttered a word that hurt your feelings.'

Barnet mused. 'Yes,' he admitted, 'there is a grain of truth in that. It is because of that I often try to make peace at home. Life would be tolerable then at any rate, even if not particularly bright.'

'I have thought more than once of proposing a little plan to you,' said Downe with some hesitation. 'I don't know whether it will meet your views, but take it or leave it, as you choose. In fact, it was my wife who suggested it: that she would be very glad to call on Mrs Barnet and get into her confidence. She seems to think that Mrs Barnet is rather alone in the town, and without advisers. Her impression is that your wife will listen to reason. Emily has a wonderful way of winning the hearts of people of her own sex.'

'And of the other sex too, I think. She is a charming woman, and you were a lucky fellow to find her.'

'Well, perhaps I was,' simpered Downe, trying to wear an aspect of being the last man in the world to feel pride. 'However, she will be likely to find out what ruffles Mrs Barnet. Perhaps it is some misunderstanding, you know — something that she is too proud to ask you to explain, or some little thing in your conduct that irritates her because she does not fully comprehend you. The truth is, Emily would have been more ready to make advances if she had been quite sure of her fitness for Mrs Barnet's society, who has of course been accustomed to London people of good position, which made Emily fearful of intruding.'

Barnet expressed his warmest thanks for the well-intentioned proposition. There was reason in Mrs Downe's fear — that he owned. 'But do let her call,' he said. 'There is no woman in England I would so soon trust on such an errand. I am afraid there will not be any brilliant result; still, I shall take it as the kindest and nicest thing if she will try it, and not be frightened at a repulse.'

When Barnet and Downe had parted, the former went to the Town Savings-Bank, of which he was a trustee, and endeavoured to forget his troubles in the contemplation of low sums of money, and figures in a network of red and blue lines. He sat and watched the working-people making their deposits, to which at intervals he signed his name. Before he left in the afternoon Downe put his head inside the door.

'Emily has seen Mrs Barnet,' he said in a low voice. 'She has got Mrs Barnet's promise to take her for a drive down to the shore to-morrow, if it is fine. Good afternoon!'

Barnet shook Downe by the hand without speaking, and Downe went away.

IV

The next day was as fine as the arrangement could possibly require. As the sun passed the meridian and declined westward, the tall shadows from the scaffold-poles of Barnet's rising residence streaked the ground as far as to the middle of the highway. Barnet himself was there inspecting the progress of the works for the first time during several weeks. A building in an old-fashioned town five-and-thirty years ago did not, as in the modern fashion, rise from the sod like a booth at a fair. The foundations and lower courses were put in and allowed to settle for many weeks before the superstructure was built up, and a whole summer of drying was hardly sufficient to do justice to the important issues involved. Barnet stood within a window-niche which had as yet received no frame, and thence looked down a slope into the road. The wheels of a chaise were heard, and then his handsome Xantippe, in the company of Mrs Downe, drove past on their way to the shore. They were driving slowly; there was a pleasing light in Mrs Downe's face, which seemed faintly to reflect itself upon the countenance of her companion — that *politesse du cœur* which was so natural to her having possibly begun already to work results. But whatever the situation, Barnet resolved not to interfere, or do anything to hazard the promise of the day. He might well afford to trust the issue to another when he could never direct it but to ill himself. His wife's clenched rein-hand in its lemon-coloured glove, her stiff erect figure, clad in velvet and lace, and her boldly-outlined face, passed on, exhibiting their owner as one fixed for ever above the level of her companion – socially by her early breeding, and materially by her higher cushion.

Barnet decided to allow them a proper time to themselves, and then stroll down to the shore and drive them home. After lingering on at the house for another hour he started with this intention. A few hundred yards below 'Château Ringdale' stood the cottage in which the late lieutenant's daughter had her lodging. Barnet had not been so far that way for a long time, and as he approached the forbidden ground a curious warmth passed into him, which led him to perceive that, unless he were careful, he might have to fight the battle with himself about Lucy over again. A tenth of his present excuse would, however, have justified him in travelling by that road to-day.

He came opposite the dwelling, and turned his eyes for a momentary glance into the little garden that stretched from the palings to the door. Lucy was in the enclosure; she was walking and stooping to gather some flowers, possibly for the purpose of painting them, for she moved about quickly, as if anxious to save time. She did not see him; he might have passed unnoticed; but a sensation which was not in strict unison with his previous sentiments that day led him to pause in his walk and watch her. She went nimbly round and round the beds of anemones, tulips, jonquils, polyanthuses, and other old-fashioned flowers, looking a very charming figure in her half-mourning bonnet, and with an incomplete nosegay in her left hand. Raising herself to pull down a lilac blossom she observed him.

'Mr Barnet!' she said, innocently smiling. 'Why, I have been thinking of you many times since Mrs Barnet went by in the pony-carriage, and now here you are!'

'Yes, Lucy,' he said.

Then she seemed to recall particulars of their last meeting, and he believed that she flushed, though it might have been only the fancy of his own super-sensitiveness.

'I am going to the harbour,' he added.

'Are you?' Lucy remarked simply. 'A great many people begin to go there now the summer is drawing on.'

Her face had come more into his view as she spoke, and he noticed how much thinner and paler it was than when he had seen it last. 'Lucy, how weary you look! tell me, can I help you?' he was going to cry out. – 'If I do,' he thought, 'it will be the ruin of us both!' He merely said that the afternoon was fine, and went on his way.

As he went a sudden blast of air came over the hill as if in contradiction to his words, and spoilt the previous quiet of the scene. The wind had already shifted violently, and now smelt of the sea.

The harbour-road soon began to justify its name. A gap appeared in the rampart of hills which shut out the sea, and on the left of the opening rose a vertical cliff, coloured a burning orange by the sunlight, the companion cliff on the right being livid in shade. Between these cliffs, like the Libyan bay which sheltered the shipwrecked Trojans, was a little haven, seemingly a beginning made by Nature herself of a perfect harbour, which appealed to the passer-by as only requiring a little human industry to finish it and make it famous, the ground on each side as far back as the daisied slopes that bounded the interior valley being a mere layer of blown sand. But the Port-Bredy burgesses a mile inland had, in the course of ten centuries, responded many times to that mute appeal, with the result that the tides had invariably choked up their works with sand and shingle as soon as completed. There were but few houses here: a rough pier, a few boats, some stores, an inn, a residence or two, a ketch unloading in the harbour, were the chief features of the settlement. On the open ground by the shore stood his wife's pony-carriage, empty, the boy in attendance holding the horse.

When Barnet drew nearer, he saw an indigo-coloured spot moving swiftly along beneath the radiant base of the eastern cliff, which proved to be a man in a jersey, running with all his might. He held up his hand to Barnet, as it seemed, and they approached each other. The man was local, but a stranger to him.

'What is it, my man?' said Barnet.

'A terrible calamity!' the boatman hastily explained. Two ladies had been capsized in a boat—they were Mrs Downe and Mrs Barnet of the old town; they had driven down there that afternoon—they had alighted, and it was so fine, that, after walking about a little while, they had been tempted to go out for a short sail round the cliff. Just as they were putting in to the shore, the wind shifted with a sudden gust, the boat listed over, and it was thought they were both drowned. How it could have happened was beyond his mind to fathom, for John Green knew how to sail a boat as well as any man there.

'Which is the way to the place?' said Barnet.

It was just round the cliff.

'Run to the carriage and tell the boy to bring it to the place as soon as you can. Then go to the Harbour Inn and tell them to ride to town for a doctor. Have they been got out of the water?'

'One lady has.'

'Which?'

'Mrs Barnet. Mrs Downe, it is feared, has fleeted out to sea.'

Barnet ran on to that part of the shore which the cliff had hitherto obscured from his view, and there discerned, a long way ahead, a group of fishermen standing. As soon as he came up one or two recognized him, and, not liking to meet his eye, turned aside with misgiving. He went amidst them and saw a small sailing-boat lying draggled at the water's edge; and, on the sloping shingle beside it, a soaked and sandy woman's form in the velvet dress and yellow gloves of his wife.

V

All had been done that could be done. Mrs Barnet was in her own house under medical hands, but the result was still uncertain. Barnet had acted as if devotion to his wife were the dominant passion of his existence. There had been much to decide—whether to attempt restoration of the apparently lifeless body as it lay on the shore—whether to carry her to the Harbour Inn—whether to drive with her at once to his own house. The first course, with no skilled help or appliances near at hand, had seemed hopeless. The second course would have occupied nearly as much time as a drive to the town, owing to the intervening ridges of shingle, and the necessity of crossing the harbour by boat to get to the house, added to which much time must have elapsed before a doctor could have arrived down there. By bringing her home in the carriage some precious moments had slipped by; but she had been laid in her own bed in seven minutes, a doctor called to her side, and every possible restorative brought to bear upon her.

At what a tearing pace he had driven up that road, through the yellow evening sunlight, the shadows flapping irksomely into his eyes as each wayside object rushed past between him and the west! Tired workmen with their baskets at their backs had turned on their homeward journey to wonder at his speed. Half-way between the shore and Port-Bredy town he had met Charlson, who had been the first surgeon to hear of the accident. He was accompanied by his assistant in a gig. Barnet had sent on the latter to the coast in case that Downe's poor wife should by that time have been reclaimed from the waves, and had brought Charlson back with him to the house.

Barnet's presence was not needed here, and he felt it to be his next duty to set off at once and find Downe, that no other than himself might break the news to him.

He was quite sure that no chance had been lost for Mrs Downe by his leaving the shore. By the time that Mrs Barnet had been laid in the carriage a much larger group had assembled to lend assistance in finding her friend, rendering his own help superfluous. But the duty of breaking the news was made doubly painful by the circumstance that the catastrophe which had befallen Mrs Downe was solely the result of her own and her husband's loving kindness towards himself.

He found Downe in his office. When the solicitor comprehended the intelligence he turned pale, stood up, and remained for a moment perfectly still, as if bereft of his faculties; then his shoulders heaved, he pulled out his handkerchief and began to cry like a child. His sobs might have been heard in the next room. He seemed to have no idea of going to the shore, or of doing anything; but when Barnet took him gently by the hand and proposed to start at once, he quietly acquiesced, neither uttering any further word nor making any effort to repress his tears.

Barnet accompanied him to the shore, where, finding that no trace had as yet been seen of Mrs Downe, and that his stay would be of no avail, he left Downe with his friends and the young doctor, and once more hastened back to his own house.

At the door he met Charlson. 'Well!' Barnet said.

'I have just come down,' said the doctor; 'we have done everything, but without result. I sympathize with you in your bereavement.'

Barnet did not much appreciate Charlson's sympathy, which sounded to his ears as something of a mockey from the lips of a man who knew what Charlson knew about his domestic relations. Indeed, there seemed an odd spark in Charlson's full black eye as he said the words; but that might have been imaginary.

'And, Mr Barnet,' Charlson resumed, 'that little matter between us – I hope to settle it finally in three weeks at least.'

'Never mind that now,' said Barnet abruptly. He directed the surgeon to go to the harbour in case his services might even now be necessary there: and himself entered the house.

The servants were coming from his wife's chamber, looking helplessly at each other and at him. He passed them by and entered the room, where he stood regarding the shape on the bed for a few minutes, after which he walked into his own dressing-room adjoining, and there paced up and down. In a minute or two he noticed what a strange and total silence had come over the upper part of the house; his own movements, muffled as they were by the carpet, seemed noisy, and his thoughts to disturb the air like articulate utterances. His eye glanced through the window. Far down the road to the harbour a roof detained his gaze: out of it rose a red chimney, and out of the red chimney a curl of smoke, as from a fire newly kindled. He had often seen such a sight before. In that house lived Lucy Savile; and the smoke was from the fire which was regularly lighted at this time to make her tea.

After that he went back to the bedroom, and stood there some time regarding his wife's silent form. She was a woman some years older than himself, but had not by any means overpassed the maturity of good looks and vigour. Her passionate features, well-defined, firm, and statuesque in life, were doubly so now: her mouth and brow, beneath her purplish-black hair, showed only too clearly that the turbulency of character which had made a bear-garden of his house had been no temporary phase of her existence. While he reflected, he suddenly said to himself, I wonder if all has been done?

The thought was led up to by his having fancied that his wife's features lacked in its completeness the expression which he had been accustomed to associate with the faces of those whose spirits have fled for ever. The effacement of life was not so marked but that, entering uninformed, he might have supposed her sleeping. Her complexion was that seen in the numerous faded portraits by Sir Joshua Reynolds; it was pallid in comparison with life, but there was visible on a close inspection the remnant of what had once been a flush; the keeping between the cheeks and the hollows of the face being thus preserved, although positive colour was gone. Long orange rays of evening sun stole in through chinks in the blind, striking on the large mirror, and being thence reflected upon the crimson hangings and woodwork of the heavy bedstead, so that the general tone of light was remarkably warm; and it was probable that something might be due to this circumstance. Still the fact impressed him as strange. Charlson had been gone more than a quarter of an hour: could it be possible that he had left too soon, and that his attempts to restore her had operated so sluggishly as only now to have made themselves felt? Barnet laid his hand upon her chest, and fancied that ever and anon a faint flutter of palpitation, gentle as that of a butterfly's wing, disturbed the stillness there — ceasing for a time, then struggling to go on, then breaking down in weakness and ceasing again.

Barnet's mother had been an active practitioner of the healing art among her poorer neighbours, and her inspirations had all been derived from an octavo volume of Domestic Medicine, which at this moment was lying, as it had lain for many years, on a shelf in Barnet's dressing-room. He hastily fetched it, and there read under the head 'Drowning': —

'Exertions for the recovery of any person who has not been immersed for a longer period that half-an-hour should be continued for at least four hours, as there have been many cases in which returning life has made itself visible even after a longer interval.

'Should, however, a weak action of any of the organs show itself when the case seems almost hopeless, our efforts must be redoubled; the feeble spark in this case requires to be solicited; it will certainly disappear under a relaxation of labour.'

Barnet looked at his watch; it was now barely two hours and a half from the time when he had first heard of the accident. He threw aside the book and turned quickly to reach a stimulant which had previously been used. Pulling up the blind for more light, his eye glanced out of the window. There he saw that red chimney still smoking cheerily, and that roof, and through the roof that somebody. His mechanical movements stopped, his hand remained on the blind-cord, and he seemed to become breathless, as if he had suddenly found himself treading a high rope.

While he stood a sparrow lighted on the window-sill, saw him, and flew away. Next a man and a dog walked over one of the green hills which bulged above the roofs of the town. But Barnet took no notice.

We may wonder what were the exact images that passed through his mind during those minutes of gazing upon Lucy Savile's house, the sparrow, the man and the dog, and Lucy Savile's house again. There are honest men who will not admit to their thoughts, even as idle hypotheses, views of the future that assume as done a deed which they would recoil from doing; and there are other honest men for whom morality ends at the surface of their own heads, who will deliberate what the first will not so much as suppose. Barnet had a wife whose presence distracted his home; she now lay as in death; by merely doing nothing – by letting the intelligence which had gone forth to the world lie undisturbed – he would effect such a deliverance for himself as he had never hoped for, and open up an opportunity of which till now he had never dreamed. Whether the conjuncture had arisen through any unscrupulous, ill-considered impulse of Charlson to help out of a strait the friend who was so kind as never to press him for what was due could not be told; there was nothing to prove it; and it was a question which could never be asked. The triangular situation – himself – his wife – Lucy Savile – was the one clear thing.

From Barnet's actions we may infer that he *supposed* such and such a result, for a moment, but did not deliberate. He withdrew his hazel eyes from the scene without, calmly turned, rang the bell for assistance, and vigorously exerted himself to learn if life still lingered in that motionless frame. In a short time another surgeon was in attendance; and then Barnet's surmise proved to be true. The slow life timidly heaved again; but much care and patience were needed to catch and retain it, and a considerable period elapsed before it could be said with certainty that Mrs Barnet lived. When this was the case, and there was no further room for doubt, Barnet left the chamber. The blue evening smoke from Lucy's chimney had died down to an imperceptible stream, and as he walked about downstairs he murmured to himself, 'My wife was dead, and she is alive again.'

It was not so with Downe. After three hours' immersion his wife's body had been recovered, life, of course, being quite extinct. Barnet, on descending, went straight to his friend's house, and there learned the result. Downe was helpless in his wild grief, occasionally even hysterical. Barnet said little, but finding that some guiding hand was necessary in the sorrow-stricken household, took upon him to supervise and manage till Downe should be in a state of mind to do so for himself.

VI

One September evening, four months later, when Mrs Barnet was in perfect health, and Mrs Downe but a weakening memory, an errand-boy paused to rest himself in front of Mr Barnet's old house, depositing his basket on one of the window-sills. The street was not yet lighted, but there were lights in the house, and at intervals a flitting shadow fell upon the blind at his elbow. Words also were audible from the same apartment, and they seemed to be those of persons in violent altercation. But the boy could not gather their purport, and he went on his way.

Ten minutes afterwards the door of Barnet's house opened, and a tall closely-veiled lady in a travelling-dress came out and descended the freestone steps. The servant stood in the doorway watching her as she went with a measured tread down the street. When she had been out of sight for some minutes Barnet appeared at the door from within.

'Did your mistress leave word where she was going?' he asked.

'No, sir.'

'Is the carriage ordered to meet her anywhere?'

'No, sir.'

'Did she take a latch-key?'

'No, sir.'

Barnet went in again, sat down in his chair, and leaned back. Then in solitude and silence he brooded over the bitter emotions that filled his heart. It was for this that he had gratuitously restored her to life, and made his union with another impossible! The evening drew on, and nobody came to disturb him. At bedtime he told the servants to retire, that he would sit up for Mrs Barnet himself; and when they were gone he leaned his head upon his hand and mused for hours.

The clock struck one, two; still his wife came not, and, with impatience added to depression, he went from room to room till another weary hour had passed. This was not altogether a new experience for Barnet; but she had never before so prolonged her absence. At last he sat down again and fell asleep.

He awoke at six o'clock to find that she had not returned. In searching about the rooms he discovered that she had taken a case of jewels which had been hers before her marriage. At eight a note was brought him; it was from his wife, in which she stated that she had gone by the coach to the house of a distant relative near London, and expressed a wish that certain boxes, articles of clothing, and so on, might be sent to her forthwith. The note was brought to him by a waiter at the Black-Bull Hotel, and had been written by Mrs Barnet immediately before she took her place in the stage.

By the evening this order was carried out, and Barnet, with a sense of relief, walked out into the town. A fair had been held during the day, and the large clear moon which rose over the most prominent hill flung its light upon the booths and standings that still remained in the street, mixing its rays curiously with those from the flaring naphtha lamps. The town was full of country-people who had come in to enjoy themselves, and on this account Barnet strolled through the streets unobserved. With a certain recklessness he made for the harbour-road, and presently found himself by the shore, where he walked on till he came to the spot near which his friend the kindly Mrs Downe had lost her life, and his own wife's life had been preserved. A tremulous pathway of bright moonshine now stretched over the water which had engulfed them, and not a living soul was near.

Here he ruminated on their characters, and next on the young girl in whom he now took a more sensitive interest than at the time when he had been free to marry her. Nothing, so far as he was aware, had ever appeared in his own conduct to show that such an interest existed. He had made it a point of the utmost strictness to hinder that feeling from influencing in the faintest degree his attitude towards his wife; and this was made all the more easy for him by the small demand Mrs Barnet made upon his attentions, for which she ever evinced the greatest contempt; thus unwittingly giving him the satisfaction of knowing that their severance owed nothing to jealousy, or, indeed, to any personal behaviour of his at all. Her concern was not with him or his feelings, as she frequently told him; but that she had, in a moment of weakness, thrown herself away upon a common burgher when she might have aimed at, and possibly brought down, a peer of the realm. Her frequent depreciation of Barnet in these terms had at times been so intense that he was sorely tempted to retaliate on her egotism by owning that he loved at the same low level on which he lived; but prudence had prevailed, for which he was now thankful.

Something seemed to sound upon the shingle behind him over and above the raking of the wave. He looked round, and a slight girlish shape appeared quite close to him. He could not see her face because it was in the direction of the moon.

'Mr Barnet?' the rambler said, in timid surprise. The voice was the voice of Lucy Savile.

'Yes,' said Barnet. 'How can I repay you for this pleasure?'

'I only came because the night was so clear. I am now on my way home.'

'I am glad we have met. I want to know if you will let me do something for you, to give me an occupation, as an idle man? I am sure I ought to help you, for I know you are almost without friends.'

She hesitated. 'Why should you tell me that?' she said.

'In the hope that you will be frank with me.'

'I am not altogether without friends here. But I am going to make a little change in my life – to go out as a teacher of freehand drawing and practical perspective, of course I mean on a comparatively humble scale, because I have not been specially educated for that profession. But I am sure I shall like it much.'

'You have an opening?'

'I have not exactly got it, but I have advertised for one.'

'Lucy, you must let me help you!'

'Not at all.'

'You need not think it would compromise you, or that I am indifferent to delicacy. I bear in mind how we stand. It is very unlikely that you will succeed as teacher of the class you mention, so let me do something of a different kind for you. Say what you would like, and it shall be done.'

'No; if I can't be a drawing-mistress or governess, or something of that sort, I shall go to India and join my brother.'

'I wish I could go abroad, anywhere, everywhere with you, Lucy, and leave this place and its associations for ever!'

She played with the end of her bonnet-string, and hastily turned aside. 'Don't ever touch upon that kind of topic again,' she said, with a quick severity not free from anger. 'It simply makes it impossible for me to see you, much less receive any guidance from you. No, thank you, Mr Barnet; you can do nothing for me at present; and as I suppose my uncertainty will end in my leaving for India, I fear you never will. If ever I think you *can* do anything, I will take the trouble to ask you. Till then, good-bye.'

The tone of her latter words was equivocal, and while he remained in doubt whether a gentle irony was or was not inwrought with their sound, she swept lightly round and left him alone. He saw her form get smaller and smaller along the damp belt of sea-sand between ebb and flood, and when she had vanished round the cliff into the harbour-road he himself followed in the same direction.

That her hopes from an advertisement should be the single thread which held Lucy Savile in England was too much for Barnet. On reaching the town he went straight to the residence of Downe, now a widower with four children. The young motherless brood had been sent to bed about a quarter of an hour earlier, and when Barnet entered he found Downe sitting alone. It was the same room as that from which the family had been looking out for Downe at the beginning of the year, when Downe had slipped into the gutter and his wife had been so enviably tender towards him. The old neatness had gone from the house; articles lay in places which could show no reason for their presence, as if momentarily deposited there some months ago, and forgotten ever since; there were no flowers; things were jumbled together on the furniture which should have been in cupboards; and the place in general had that stagnant, unrenovated air which usually pervades the maimed home of the widower.

Downe soon renewed his customary full-worded lament over his wife, and even when he had worked himself up to tears, went on volubly, as if a listener were a luxury to be enjoyed whenever he could be caught.

'She was a treasure beyond compare, Mr Barnet! I shall never see such another. Nobody now to nurse me – nobody to console me in those daily troubles, you know, Barnet, which make consolation so necessary to a nature like mine. It would be unbecoming to repine, for her spirit's home was elsewhere – the tender light in her eyes always showed it; but it is a long dreary time that I have before me, and nobody else can ever fill the void left in my heart by her loss – nobody – nobody!' And Downe wiped his eyes again.

'She was a good woman in the highest sense,' gravely answered Barnet, who, though Downe's words drew genuine compassion from his heart, could not help feeling that a tender reticence would have been a finer tribute to Mrs Downe's really sterling virtues than such a second-class lament as this.

'I have something to show you,' Downe resumed, producing from a drawer a sheet of paper on which was an elaborate design for a canopied tomb. 'This has been sent me by the architect, but it is not exactly what I want.'

'You have got Jones to do it, I see, the man who is carrying out my house,' said Barnet, as he glanced at the signature to the drawing.

'Yes, but it is not quite what I want. I want something more striking – more like a tomb I have seen in St Paul's Cathedral. Nothing less will do justice to my feelings, and how far short of them that will fall!'

Barnet privately thought the design a sufficiently imposing one as it stood, even extravagantly ornate; but, feeling that he had no right to criticize, he said gently, 'Downe, should you not live more in your children's lives at the present time, and soften the sharpness of regret for your own past by thinking of their future?'

'Yes, yes; but what can I do more?' asked Downe, wrinkling his forehead hopelessly.

It was with anxious slowness that Barnet produced his reply — the secret object of his visit to-night. 'Did you not say one day that you ought by right to get a governess for the children?'

Downe admitted that he had said so, but that he could not see his way to it. 'The kind of woman I should like to have,' he said, 'would be rather beyond my means. No; I think I shall send them to school in the town when they are old enough to go out alone.'

'Now, I know of something better than that. The late Lieutenant Savile's daughter, Lucy, wants to do something for herself in the way of teaching. She would be inexpensive, and would answer your purpose as well as anybody for six or twelve months. She would probably come daily if you were to ask her, and so your housekeeping arrangements would not be much affected.'

'I thought she had gone away,' said the solicitor, musing. 'Where does she live?'

Barnet told him, and added that, if Downe should think of her as suitable, he would do well to call as soon as possible, or she might be on the wing. 'If you do see her,' he said, 'it would be advisable not to mention my name. She is rather stiff in her ideas of me, and it might prejudice her against a course if she knew that I recommended it.'

Downe promised to give the subject his consideration, and nothing more was said about it just then. But when Barnet rose to go, which was not till nearly bedtime, he reminded Downe of the suggestion and went up the street to his own solitary home with a sense of satisfaction at his promising diplomacy in a charitable cause.

VII

The walls of his new house were carried up nearly to their full height. By a curious though not infrequent reaction, Barnet's feelings about that unnecessary structure had undergone a change; he took considerable interest in its progress as a long-neglected thing, his wife before her departure having grown quite weary of it as a hobby. Moreover, it was an excellent distraction for a man in the unhappy position of having to live in a provincial town with nothing to do. He was probably the first of his line who had ever passed a day without toil, and perhaps something like an inherited instinct disqualifies such men for a life of pleasant inaction, such as lies in the power of those whose leisure is not a personal accident, but a vast historical accretion which has become part of their natures.

Thus Barnet got into a way of spending many of his leisure hours on the site of the new building, and he might have been seen on most days at this time trying the temper of the mortar by punching the joints with his stick, looking at the grain of a floor-board, and meditating where it grew, or picturing under what circumstances the last fire would be kindled in the at present sootless chimneys. One day when thus occupied he saw three children pass by in the company of a fair young woman, whose sudden appearance caused him to flush perceptibly.

'Ah, she is there,' he thought. 'That's a blessed thing.'

Casting an interested glance over the rising building and the busy workmen, Lucy Savile and the little Downes passed by; and after that time it became a regular though almost unconscious custom of Barnet to stand in the half-completed house and look from the ungarnished windows at the governess as she tripped towards the sea-shore with her young charges, which she was in the habit of doing on most fine afternoons. It was on one of these occasions, when he had been loitering on the first-floor landing, near the hole left for the staircase, not yet erected, that there appeared above the edge of the floor a little hat, followed by a little head.

Barnet withdrew through a doorway, and the child came to the top of the ladder, stepping on to the floor and crying to her sisters and Miss Savile to follow. Another head rose above the floor, and another, and then Lucy herself came into view. The troop ran hither and thither through the empty, shaving-strewn rooms, and Barnet came forward.

Lucy uttered a small exclamation: she was very sorry that she had intruded; she had not the least idea that Mr Barnet was there: the children had come up, and she had followed.

Barnet replied that he was only too glad to see them there. 'And now, let me show you the rooms,' he said.

She passively assented, and he took her round. There was not much to show in such a bare skeleton of a house, but he made the most of it, and explained the different ornamental fittings that were soon to be fixed here and there. Lucy made but few remarks in reply, though she seemed pleased with her visit, and stole away down the ladder, followed by her companions.

After this the new residence became yet more of a hobby for Barnet. Downe's children did not forget their first visit, and when the windows were glazed, and the handsome staircase spread its broad low steps into the hall, they came again, prancing in unwearied succession through every room from ground-floor to attics, while Lucy stood waiting for them at the door. Barnet, who rarely missed a day in coming to inspect progress, stepped out from the drawing-room.

'I could not keep them out,' she said, with an apologetic blush. 'I tried to do so very much; but they are rather wilful, and we are directed to walk this way for the sea air.'

'Do let them make the house their regular playground, and you yours,' said Barnet. 'There is no better place for children to romp and take their exercise in than an empty house, particularly in muddy or damp weather such as we shall get a good deal of now; and this place will not be furnished for a long time – perhaps never. I am not at all decided about it.'

'O, but it must!' replied Lucy, looking round at the hall. 'The rooms are excellent, twice as high as ours, and the views from the windows are so lovely.'

'I daresay, I daresay,' he said absently.

'Will all the furniture be new?' she asked.

'All the furniture be new – that's a thing I have not thought of. In fact, I only come here and look on. My father's house would have been large enough for me, but another person had a voice in the matter, and it was settled that we should build. However, the place grows upon me; its recent associations are cheerful, and I am getting to like it fast.'

A certain uneasiness in Lucy's manner showed that the conversation was taking too personal a turn for her. 'Still, as modern tastes develop, people require more room to gratify them in,' she said, withdrawing to call the children; and serenely bidding him good-afternoon she went on her way.

Barnet's life at this period was singularly lonely, and yet he was happier than he could have expected. His wife's estrangement and absence, which promised to be permanent, left him free as a boy in his movements, and the solitary walks that he took gave him ample opportunity for chastened reflection on what might have been his lot if he had only shown wisdom enough to claim Lucy Savile when there was no bar between their lives, and she was to be had for the asking. He would occasionally call at the house of his friend Downe; but there was scarcely enough in common between their two natures to make them more than friends of that excellent sort whose personal knowledge of each other's history and character is always in excess of intimacy, whereby they are not so likely to be severed by a clash of sentiment as in cases where intimacy springs up in excess of knowledge. Lucy was never visible at these times, being either engaged in the school-room, or in taking an airing out of doors; but, knowing that she was now comfortable, and had given up the, to him, depressing idea of going off to the other side of the globe, he was quite content.

The new house had so far progressed that the gardeners were beginning to grass down the front. During an afternoon which he was passing in marking the curve for the carriage-drive, he beheld her coming in boldly towards him from the road. Hitherto Barnet had only caught her on the premises by stealth; and this advance seemed to show that at last her reserve had broken down.

A smile gained strength upon her face as she approached, and it was quite radiant when she came up, and said, without a trace of embarrassment, 'I find I owe you a hundred thanks—and it comes to me quite as a surprise! It was through your kindness that I was engaged by Mr Downe. Believe me, Mr Barnet, I did not know it until yesterday, or I should have thanked you long and long ago!'

'I had offended you—just a trifle—at the time, I think?' said Barnet, smiling, 'and it was best that you should not know.'

'Yes, yes,' she returned hastily. 'Don't allude to that; it is past and over, and we will let it be. The house is finished almost, is it not? How beautiful it will look when the evergreens are grown! Do you call the style Palladian, Mr Barnet?'

'I—really don't quite know what it is. Yes, it must be Palladian, certainly. But I'll ask Jones, the architect; for, to tell the truth, I had not thought much about the style: I had nothing to do with choosing it, I am sorry to say.'

She would not let him harp on this gloomy refrain, and talked on bright matters till she said, producing a small roll of paper which he had noticed in her hand all the while, 'Mr Downe wished me to bring you this revised drawing of the late Mrs Downe's tomb, which the architect has just sent him. He would like you to look it over.'

The children came up with their hoops, and she went off with them down the harbour-road as usual. Barnet had been glad to get those words of thanks; he had been thinking for many months that he would like her to know of his share in finding her a home such as it was; and what he could not do for himself, Downe had now kindly done for him. He returned to his desolate house with a lighter tread; though in reason he hardly knew why his tread should be light.

On examining the drawing, Barnet found that, instead of the vast altar-tomb and canopy Downe had determined on at their last meeting, it was to be a more modest memorial even than had been suggested by the architect; a coped tomb of good solid construction, with no useless elaboration at all. Barnet was truly glad to see that Downe had come to reason of his own accord; and he returned the drawing with a note of approval.

He followed up the house-work as before, and as he walked up and down the rooms, occasionally gazing from the windows over the bulging green hills and the quiet harbour that lay between them, he murmured words and fragments of words which, if listened to, would have revealed all the secrets of his existence. Whatever his reason in going there, Lucy did not call again: the walk to the shore seemed to be abandoned: he must have thought it as well for both that it should be so, for he did not go anywhere out of his accustomed ways to endeavour to discover her.

VIII

The winter and the spring had passed, and the house was complete. It was a fine morning in the early part of June, and Barnet, though not in the habit of rising early, had taken a long walk before breakfast; returning by way of the new building. A sufficiently exciting cause of his restlessness to-day might have been the intelligence which had reached him the night before, that Lucy Savile was going to India after all, and notwithstanding the representations of her friends that such a journey was unadvisable in many ways for an unpractised girl, unless some more definite advantage lay at the end of it than she could show to be the case. Barnet's walk up the slope to the building betrayed that he was in a dissatisfied mood. He hardly saw that the dewy time of day lent an unusual freshness to the bushes and trees which had so recently put on their summer habit of heavy leafage, and made his newly-laid lawn look as well established as an old manorial meadow. The house had been so adroitly placed between six tall elms which were growing on the site beforehand, that they seemed like real ancestral trees; and the rooks, young and old, cawed melodiously to their visitor.

The door was not locked, and he entered. No workmen appeared to be present, and he walked from sunny window to sunny window of the empty rooms, with a sense of seclusion which might have been very pleasant but for the antecedent knowledge that his almost paternal care of Lucy Savile was to be thrown away by her wilfulness. Footsteps echoed through an adjoining room; and bending his eyes in that direction, he perceived Mr Jones, the architect. He had come to look over the building before giving the contractor his final certificate. They walked over the house together. Everything was finished except the papering: there were the latest improvements of the period in bell-hanging, ventilating, smoke-jacks, fire-grates, and French windows. The business was soon ended, and Jones, having directed Barnet's attention to a book of wall-paper patterns which lay on a bench for his choice, was leaving to keep another engagement, when Barnet said, 'Is the tomb finished yet for Mrs Downe?'

'Well – yes: it is at last,' said the architect, coming back and speaking as if he were in a mood to make a confidence. 'I have had no end of trouble in the matter, and, to tell the truth, I am heartily glad it is over.'

Barnet expressed his surprise. 'I thought poor Downe had given up those extravagant notions of his? Then he has gone back to the altar and canopy after all? Well, he is to be excused, poor fellow!'

'O no – he has not at all gone back to them – quite the reverse,' Jones hastened to say. 'He has so reduced design after design that the whole thing has been nothing but waste labour for me; till in the end it has become a common headstone, which a mason put up in half a day.'

'A common headstone?' said Barnet.

'Yes. I held out for some time for the addition of a footstone at least. But he said, "O no – he couldn't afford it." '

'Ah, well – his family is growing up, poor fellow, and his expenses are getting serious.'

'Yes, exactly,' said Jones, as if the subject were none of his. And again directing Barnet's attention to the wall-papers, the bustling architect left him to keep some other engagement.

'A common headstone,' murmured Barnet, left again to himself. He mused a minute or two, and next began looking over and selecting from the patterns; but had not long been engaged in the work when he heard another footstep on the gravel without, and somebody enter the open porch.

Barnet went to the door – it was his manservant in search of him.

'I have been trying for some time to find you, sir,' he said. 'This letter has come by the post, and it is marked immediate. And there's this one from Mr Downe, who called just now wanting to see you.' He searched his pocket for the second.

Barnet took the first letter – it had a black border, and bore the London post-mark. It was not in his wife's handwriting, or in that of any person he knew; but conjecture soon ceased as he read the page, wherein he was briefly informed that Mrs Barnet had died suddenly on the previous day, at the furnished villa she had occupied near London.

Barnet looked vaguely round the empty hall, at the blank walls, out of the doorway. Drawing a long palpitating breath, and with eyes down-cast, he turned and climbed the stairs slowly, like a man who doubted their stability. The fact of his wife having, as it were, died once already, and lived on again, had entirely dislodged the possibility of her actual death from his conjecture. He went to the landing, leant over the balusters, and after a reverie, of whose duration he had but the faintest notion, turned to the window and stretched his gaze to the cottage further down the road, which was visible from his landing, and from which Lucy still walked to the solicitor's house by a cross path. The faint words that came from his moving lips were simply, 'At last!'

Then, almost involuntarily, Barnet fell down on his knees and murmured some incoherent words of thanksgiving. Surely his virtue in restoring his wife to life had been rewarded! But, as if the impulse struck uneasily on his conscience, he quickly rose, brushed the dust from his trousers, and set himself to think of his next movements. He could not start for London for some hours; and as he had no preparations to make that could not be made in half-an-hour, he mechanically descended and resumed his occupation of turning over the wall-papers. They had all got brighter for him, those papers. It was all changed – who would sit in the rooms that they were to line? He went on to muse upon Lucy's conduct in so frequently coming to the house with the children; her occasional blush in speaking to him; her evident interest in him. What woman can in the long run avoid being interested in a man whom she knows to be devoted to her? If human solicitation could ever effect anything, there should be no going to India for Lucy now. All the papers previously chosen seemed wrong in their shades, and he began from the beginning to choose again.

While entering on the task he heard a forced 'Ahem!' from without the porch, evidently uttered to attract his attention, and footsteps again advancing to the door. His man, whom he had quite forgotten in his mental turmoil, was still waiting there.

'I beg your pardon, sir,' the man said from round the doorway; 'but here's the note from Mr Downe that you didn't take. He called just after you went out, and as he couldn't wait, he wrote this on your study-table.'

He handed in the letter – no black-bordered one now, but a practical-looking note in the well-known writing of the solicitor.

'DEAR BARNET' – it ran – 'Perhaps you will be prepared for the information I am about to give – that Lucy Savile and myself are going to be married this morning. I have hitherto said nothing as to my intention to any of my friends, for reasons which I am sure you will fully appreciate. The crisis has been brought about by her expressing her intention to join her brother in India. I then discovered that I could not do without her.

'It is to be quite a private wedding; but it is my particular wish that you come down here quietly at ten, and go to church with us; it will add greatly to the pleasure I shall experience in the ceremony, and, I believe, to Lucy's also. I have called on you very early to make the request, in the belief that I should find you at home; but you are beforehand with me in your early rising. – Yours sincerely,

C. DOWNE'

'Need I wait, sir?' said the servant after a dead silence.

'That will do, William. No answer,' said Barnet calmly.

When the man had gone Barnet re-read the letter. Turning eventually to the wall-papers, which he had been at such pains to select, he deliberately tore them into halves and quarters, and threw them into the empty fireplace. Then he went out of the house, locked the door, and stood in the front awhile. Instead of returning into the town, he went down the harbour-road and thoughtfully lingered about by the sea, near the spot where the body of Downe's late wife had been found and brought ashore.

Barnet was a man with a rich capacity for misery, and there is no doubt that he exercised it to its fullest extent now. The events that had, as it were, dashed themselves together into one half-hour of this day showed that curious refinement of cruelty in their arrangement which often proceeds from the bosom of the whimsical god at other times known as blind Circumstance. That his few minutes of hope, between the reading of the first and second letters, had carried him to extraordinary heights of rapture was proved by the immensity of his suffering now. The sun blazing into his face would have shown a close watcher that a horizontal line, which had never been seen before, but which was never to be gone thereafter, was somehow gradually forming itself in the smooth of his forehead. His eyes, of a light hazel, had a curious look which can only be described by the word bruised; the sorrow that looked from them being largely mixed with the surprise of a man taken unawares.

The secondary particulars of his present position, too, were odd enough, though for some time they appeared to engage little of his attention. Not a soul in the town knew, as yet, of his wife's death; and he almost owed Downe the kindness of not publishing it till the day was over: the conjuncture, taken with that which had accompanied the death of Mrs Downe, being so singular as to be quite sufficient to darken the pleasure of the impressionable solicitor to a cruel extent, if made known to him. But as Barnet could not set out on his journey to London, where his wife lay, for some hours (there being at this date no railway within a distance of many miles), no great reason existed why he should leave the town.

Impulse in all its forms characterized Barnet, and when he heard the distant clock strike the hour of ten his feet began to carry him up the harbour-road with the manner of a man who must do something to bring himself to life. He passed Lucy Savile's old house, his own new one, and came in view of the church. Now he gave a perceptible start, and his mechanical condition went away. Before the church-gate were a couple of carriages, and Barnet then could perceive that the marriage between Downe and Lucy was at that moment being solemnized within. A feeling of sudden, proud self-confidence, an indocile wish to walk unmoved in spite of grim environments, plainly possessed him, and when he reached the wicket-gate he turned in without apparent effort. Pacing up the paved footway he entered the church and stood for awhile in the nave passage. A group of people was standing round the vestry door; Barnet advanced through these and stepped into the vestry.

There they were, busily signing their names. Seeing Downe about to look round Barnet averted his somewhat disturbed face for a second or two; when he turned again front to front he was calm and quite smiling; it was a creditable triumph over himself, and deserved to be remembered in his native town. He greeted Downe heartily, offering his congratulations.

It seemed as if Barnet expected a half-guilty look upon Lucy's face; but no; save the natural flush and flurry engendered by the service just performed, there was nothing whatever in her bearing which showed a disturbed mind: her gray-brown eyes carried in them now as at other times the well-known expression of common-sensed rectitude which never went so far as to touch on hardness. She shook hands with him, and Downe said warmly, 'I wish you could have come sooner: I called on purpose to ask you. You'll drive back with us now?'

'No, no,' said Barnet; 'I am not at all prepared; but I thought I would look in upon you for a moment, even though I had not time to go home and dress. I'll stand back and see you pass out, and observe the effect of the spectacle upon myself as one of the public.'

Then Lucy and her husband laughed, and Barnet laughed and retired; and the quiet little party went gliding down the nave and towards the porch, Lucy's new silk dress sweeping with a smart rustle round the base-mouldings of the ancient font, and Downe's little daughters following in a state of round-eyed interest in their position, and that of Lucy, their teacher and friend.

So Downe was comforted after his Emily's death, which had taken place twelve months, two weeks, and three days before that time.

When the two flys had driven off and the spectators had vanished, Barnet followed to the door, and went out into the sun. He took no more trouble to preserve a spruce exterior; his step was unequal, hesitating, almost convulsive; and the slight changes of colour which went on in his face seemed refracted from some inward flame. In the churchyard he became pale as a summer cloud, and finding it not easy to proceed he sat down on one of the tombstones and supported his head with his hand.

Hard by was a sexton filling up a grave which he had not found time to finish on the previous evening. Observing Barnet, he went up to him, and recognizing him, said, 'Shall I help you home, sir?'

'O no, thank you,' said Barnet, rousing himself and standing up. The sexton returned to his grave, followed by Barnet, who, after watching him awhile, stepped into the grave, now nearly filled, and helped to tread in the earth.

The sexton apparently thought his conduct a little singular, but he made no observation, and when the grave was full, Barnet suddenly stopped, looked far away, and with a decided step proceeded to the gate and vanished. The sexton rested on his shovel and looked after him for a few moments, and then began banking up the mound.

In those short minutes of treading in the dead man Barnet had formed a design, but what it was the inhabitants of that town did not for some long time imagine. He went home, wrote several letters of business, called on his lawyer, an old man of the same place who had been the legal adviser of Barnet's father before him, and during the evening overhauled a large quantity of letters and other documents in his possession. By eleven o'clock the heap of papers in and before Barnet's grate had reached formidable dimensions, and he began to burn them. This, owing to their quantity, it was not so easy to do as he had expected, and he sat long into the night to complete the task.

The next morning Barnet departed for London, leaving a note for Downe to inform him of Mrs Barnet's sudden death, and that he was gone to bury her; but when a thrice-sufficient time for that purpose had elapsed, he was not seen again in his accustomed walks, or in his new house, or in his old one. He was gone for good, nobody knew whither. It was soon discovered that he had empowered his lawyer to dispose of all his property, real and personal, in the borough, and pay in the proceeds to the account of an unknown person at one of the large London banks. The person was by some supposed to be himself under an assumed name; but few, if any, had certain knowledge of that fact.

The elegant new residence was sold with the rest of his possessions; and its purchaser was no other than Downe, now a thriving man in the borough, and one whose growing family and new wife required more roomy accommodation than was afforded by the little house up the narrow side street. Barnet's old habitation was bought by the trustees of the Congregational Baptist body in that town, who pulled down the time-honoured dwelling and built a new chapel on its site. By the time the last hour of that, to Barnet, eventful year had chimed, every vestige of him had disappeared from the precincts of his native place, and the name became extinct in the borough of Port-Bredy, after having been a living force therein for more than two hundred years.

IX

Twenty-one years and six months do not pass without setting a mark even upon durable stone and triple brass; upon humanity such a period works nothing less than transformation. In Barnet's old birthplace vivacious young children with bones like india-rubber had grown up to be stable men and women, men and women had dried in the skin, stiffened, withered, and sunk into decrepitude; while selections from every class had been consigned to the outlying cemetery. Of inorganic differences the greatest was that a railway had invaded the town, tying it on to a main line at a junction a dozen miles off. Barnet's house on the harbour-road, once so insistently new, had acquired a respectable mellowness, with ivy, Virginia creepers, lichens, damp patches, and even constitutional infirmities of its own like its elder fellows. Its architecture, once so very improved and modern, had already become stale in style, without having reached the dignity of being old-fashioned. Trees about the harbour-road had increased in circumference or disappeared under the saw; while the church had had such a tremendous practical joke played upon it by some facetious restorer or other as to be scarce recognizable by its dearest old friends.

During this long interval George Barnet had never once been seen or heard of in the town of his fathers.

It was the evening of a market-day, and some half-dozen middle-aged farmers and dairymen were lounging round the bar of the Black-Bull Hotel, occasionally dropping a remark to each other, and less frequently to the two barmaids who stood within the pewter-topped counter in a perfunctory attitude of attention, these latter sighing and making a private observation to one another at odd intervals, on more interesting experiences than the present.

'Days get shorter,' said one of the dairymen, as he looked towards the street, and noticed that the lamplighter was passing by.

The farmers merely acknowledged by their countenances the propriety of this remark, and finding that nobody else spoke, one of the barmaids said 'yes', in a tone of painful duty.

'Come fair-day we shall have to light up before we start for home-along.'

'That's true,' his neighbour conceded, with a gaze of blankness.

'And after that we shan't see much further difference all's winter.'

The rest were not unwilling to go even so far as this.

The barmaid sighed again, and raised one of her hands from the counter on which they rested to scratch the smallest surface of her face with the smallest of her fingers. She looked towards the door, and presently remarked, 'I think I hear the 'bus coming in from station.'

The eyes of the dairymen and farmers turned to the glass door dividing the hall from the porch, and in a minute or two the omnibus drew up outside. Then there was a lumbering down of luggage, and then a man came into the hall, followed by a porter with a portmanteau on his poll, which he deposited on a bench.

The stranger was an elderly person, with curly ashen-white hair, a deeply-creviced outer corner to each eyelid, and a countenance baked by innumerable suns to the colour of terra-cotta, its hue and that of his hair contrasting like heat and cold respectively. He walked meditatively and gently, like one who was fearful of disturbing his own mental equilibrium. But whatever lay at the bottom of his breast had evidently made him so accustomed to its situation there that it caused him little practical inconvenience.

He paused in silence while, with his dubious eyes fixed on the barmaids, he seemed to consider himself. In a moment or two he addressed them, and asked to be accommodated for the night. As he waited he looked curiously round the hall, but said nothing. As soon as invited he disappeared up the staircase, preceded by a chambermaid and candle, and followed by a lad with his trunk. Not a soul had recognized him.

A quarter of an hour later, when the farmers and dairymen had driven off to their homesteads in the country, he came downstairs, took a biscuit and one glass of wine, and walked out into the town, where the radiance from the shop-windows had grown so in volume of late years as to flood with cheerfulness every standing cart, barrow, stall, and idler that occupied the wayside, whether shabby or genteel. His chief interest at present seemed to lie in the names painted over the shop-fronts and on doorways, as far as they were visible; these now differed to an ominous extent from what they had been one-and-twenty years before.

The traveller passed on till he came to the bookseller's, where he looked in through the glass door. A fresh-faced young man was standing behind the counter, otherwise the shop was empty. The gray-haired observer entered, asked for some periodical by way of paying for admission, and with his elbow on the counter began to turn over the pages he had bought, though that he read nothing was obvious.

At length he said, 'Is old Mr Watkins still alive?' in a voice which had a curious youthful cadence in it even now.

'My father is dead, sir,' said the young man.

'Ah, I am sorry to hear it,' said the stranger. 'But it is so many years since I last visited this town that I could hardly expect it should be otherwise.' After a short silence he continued – 'And is the firm of Barnet, Browse and Company still in existence? – they used to be large flax-merchants and twine-spinners here?'

'The firm is still going on, sir, but they have dropped the name of Barnet. I believe that was a sort of fancy name – at least, I never knew of any living Barnet. 'Tis now Browse and Co.'

'And does Andrew Jones still keep on as architect?'

'He's dead, sir.'

'And the vicar of St Mary's – Mr Melrose?'

'He's been dead a great many years.'

'Dear me!' He paused yet longer, and cleared his voice. 'Is Mr Downe, the solicitor, still in practice?'

'No, sir, he's dead. He died about seven years ago.'

Here it was a longer silence still; and an attentive observer would have noticed that the paper in the stranger's hand increased its imperceptible tremor to a visible shake. That gray-haired gentleman noticed it himself, and rested the paper on the counter. 'Is *Mrs* Downe still alive?' he asked, closing his lips firmly as soon as the words were out of his mouth, and dropping his eyes.

'Yes, sir, she's alive and well. She's living at the old place.'

'In East Street?'

'O no; at Château Ringdale. I believe it has been in the family for some generations.'

'She lives with her children, perhaps?'

'No; she has no children of her own. There were some Miss Downes; I think they were Mr Downe's daughters by a former wife; but they are married and living in other parts of the town. Mrs Downe lives alone.'

'Quite alone?'

'Yes, sir; quite alone.'

The newly-arrived gentleman went back to the hotel and dined; after which he made some change in his dress, shaved back his beard to the fashion that had prevailed twenty years earlier, when he was young and interesting, and once more emerging, bent his steps in the direction of the harbour-road. Just before getting to the point where the pavement ceased and the houses isolated themselves, he overtook a shambling, stooping, unshaven man, who at first sight appeared like a professional tramp, his shoulders having a perceptible greasiness as they passed under the gaslight. Each pedestrian momentarily turned and regarded the other, and the tramp-like gentleman started back.

'Good – why – is that Mr Barnet? 'Tis Mr Barnet, surely!'

'Yes; and you are Charlson?'

'Yes – ah – you notice my appearance. The Fates have rather ill-used me. By-the-bye, that fifty pounds. I never paid it, did I? . . . But I was not ungrateful!' Here the stooping man laid one hand emphatically on the palm of the other. 'I gave you a chance, Mr George Barnet, which many men would have thought full value received – the chance to marry your Lucy. As far as the world was concerned, your wife was a *drowned woman*, hey?'

'Heaven forbid all that, Charlson!'

'Well, well, 'twas a wrong way of showing gratitude, I suppose. And now a drop of something to drink for old acquaintance' sake! And, Mr Barnet, she's again free – there's a chance now if you care for it – ha, ha!' And the speaker pushed his tongue into his hollow cheek and slanted his eye in the old fashion.

'I know all,' said Barnet quickly; and slipping a small present into the hands of the needy, saddening man, he stepped ahead and was soon in the outskirts of the town.

He reached the harbour-road, and paused before the entrance to a well-known house. It was so highly bosomed in trees and shrubs planted since the erection of the building that one would scarcely have recognized the spot as that which had been a mere neglected slope till chosen as a site for a dwelling. He opened the swing-gate, closed it noiselessly, and gently moved into the semicircular drive, which remained exactly as it had been marked out by Barnet on the morning when Lucy Savile ran in to thank him for procuring her the post of governess to Downe's children. But the growth of trees and bushes which revealed itself at every step was beyond all expectation; sun-proof and moon-proof bowers vaulted the walks, and the walls of the house were uniformly bearded with creeping plants as high as the first-floor windows.

After lingering for a few minutes in the dusk of the bending boughs, the visitor rang the door-bell, and on the servant appearing, he announced himself as 'an old friend of Mrs Downe's'.

The hall was lighted, but not brightly, the gas being turned low, as if visitors were rare. There was a stagnation in the dwelling; it seemed to be waiting. Could it really be waiting for him? The partitions which had been probed by Barnet's walking-stick when the mortar was green, were now quite brown with the antiquity of their varnish, and the ornamental woodwork of the staircase, which had glistened with a pale yellow newness when first erected, was now of a rich wine-colour. During the servant's absence the following colloquy could be dimly heard through the nearly-closed door of the drawing-room.

'He didn't give his name?'

'He only said "an old friend", ma'am.'

'What kind of gentleman is he?'

'A staidish gentleman, with gray hair.'

The voice of the second speaker seemed to affect the listener greatly. After a pause, the lady said, 'Very well, I will see him.'

And the stranger was shown in face to face with the Lucy who had once been Lucy Savile. The round cheek of that formerly young lady had, of course, alarmingly flattened its curve in her modern representative; a pervasive grayness overspread her once dark brown hair, like morning rime on heather. The parting down the middle was wide and jagged; once it had been a thin white line, a narrow crevice between two high banks of shade. But there was still enough left to form a handsome knob behind, and some curls beneath inwrought with a few hairs like silver wires were very becoming. In her eyes the only modification was that their originally mild rectitude of expression had become a little more stringent than heretofore. Yet she was still girlish – a girl who had been gratuitously weighted by destiny with a burden of five-and-forty years instead of her proper twenty.

'Lucy, don't you know me?' he said, when the servant had closed the door.

'I knew you the instant I saw you!' she returned cheerfully. 'I don't know why, but I always thought you would come back to your old town again.'

She gave him her hand, and then they sat down. 'They said you were dead,' continued Lucy, 'but I never thought so. We should have heard of it for certain if you had been.'

'It is a very long time since we met.'

'Yes; what you must have seen, Mr Barnet, in all these roving years, in comparison with what I have seen in this quiet place!' Her face grew more serious. 'You know my husband has been dead a long time? I am a lonely old woman now, considering what I have been; though Mr Downe's daughters – all married – manage to keep me pretty cheerful.'

'And I am a lonely old man, and have been any time these twenty years.'

'But where have you kept yourself? And why did you go off so mysteriously?'

'Well, Lucy, I have kept myself a little in America, and a little in Australia, a little in India, a little at the Cape, and so on; I have not stayed in any place for a long time, as it seems to me, and yet more than twenty years have flown. But when people get to my age two years go like one! – Your second question, why did I go away so mysteriously, is surely not necessary. You guessed why, didn't you?'

'No, I never once guessed,' she said simply; 'nor did Charles, nor did anybody as far as I know.'

'Well, indeed! Now think it over again, and then look at me, and say if you can't guess?'

She looked him in the face with an inquiring smile. 'Surely not because of me?' she said, pausing at the commencement of surprise.

Barnet nodded, and smiled again; but his smile was sadder than hers.

'Because I married Charles?' she asked.

'Yes; solely because you married him on the day I was free to ask you to marry me. My wife died four-and-twenty hours before you went to church with Downe. The fixing of my journey at that particular moment was because of her funeral; but once away I knew I should have no inducement to come back, and took my steps accordingly.'

Her face assumed an aspect of gentle reflection, and she looked up and down his form with great interest in her eyes. 'I never thought of it!' she said. 'I knew, of course, that you had once implied some warmth of feeling towards me, but I concluded that it passed off. And I have always been under the impression that your wife was alive at the time of my marriage. Was it not stupid of me! – But you will have some tea or something? I have never dined late, you know, since my husband's death. I have got into the way of making a regular meal of tea. You will have some tea with me, will you not?'

The travelled man assented quite readily, and tea was brought in. They sat and chatted over the tray, regardless of the flying hour. 'Well, well!' said Barnet presently, as for the first time he leisurely surveyed the room; 'how like it all is, and yet how different! Just where your piano stands was a board on a couple of trestles, bearing the patterns of wall-papers, when I was last here. I was choosing them – standing in this way, as it might be. Then my servant came in at the door, and handed me a note, so. It was from Downe, and announced that you were just going to be married to him. I chose no more wall-papers – tore up all those I had selected, and left the house. I never entered it again till now.'

'Ah, at last I understand it all,' she murmured.

They had both risen and gone to the fireplace. The mantel came almost on a level with her shoulder, which gently rested against it, and Barnet laid his hand upon the shelf close beside her shoulder. 'Lucy,' he said, 'better late than never. Will you marry me now?'

She started back, and the surprise which was so obvious in her wrought even greater surprise in him that it should be so. It was difficult to believe that she had been quite blind to the situation, and yet all reason and common sense went to prove that she was not acting.

'You take me quite unawares by such a question!' she said, with a forced laugh of uneasiness. It was the first time she had shown any embarrassment at all. 'Why,' she added, 'I couldn't marry you for the world.'

'Not after all this! Why not?'

'It is – I would – I really think I may say it – I would upon the whole rather marry you, Mr Barnet, than any other man I have ever met, if I ever dreamed of marriage again. But I don't dream of it – it is quite out of my thoughts; I have not the least intention of marrying again.'

'But – on my account – couldn't you alter your plans a little? Come!'

'Dear Mr Barnet,' she said with a little flutter, 'I would on your account if on anybody's in existence. But you don't know in the least what it is you are asking – such an impracticable thing – I won't say ridiculous, of course, because I see that you are really in earnest, and earnestness is never ridiculous to my mind.'

'Well, yes,' said Barnet more slowly, dropping her hand, which he had taken at the moment of pleading, 'I am in earnest. The resolve, two months ago, at the Cape, to come back once more was, it is true, rather sudden, and as I see now, not well considered. But I am in earnest in asking.'

'And I in declining. With all good feeling and all kindness, let me say that I am quite opposed to the idea of marrying a second time.'

'Well, no harm has been done,' he answered, with the same subdued and tender humorousness that he had shown on such occasions in early life. 'If you really won't accept me, I must put up with it, I suppose.' His eye fell on the clock as he spoke. 'Had you any notion that it was so late?' he asked. 'How absorbed I have been!'

She accompanied him to the hall, helped him to put on his overcoat, and let him out of the house herself.

'Good-night,' said Barnet, on the doorstep, as the lamp shone in his face. 'You are not offended with me?'

'Certainly not. Nor you with me?'

'I'll consider whether I am or not,' he pleasantly replied. 'Good-night.'

She watched him safely through the gate; and when his footsteps had died away upon the road, closed the door softly and returned to the room. Here the modest widow long pondered his speeches, with eyes dropped to an unusually low level. Barnet's urbanity under the blow of her refusal greatly impressed her. After having his long period of probation rendered useless by her decision, he had shown no anger, and had philosophically taken her words as if he deserved no better ones. It was very gentlemanly of him, certainly; it was more than gentlemanly: it was heroic and grand. The more she meditated, the more she questioned the virtue of her conduct in checking him so peremptorily; and went to her bedroom in a mood of dissatisfaction. On looking in the glass she was reminded that there was not so much remaining of her former beauty as to make his frank declaration an impulsive natural homage to her cheeks and eyes; it must undoubtedly have arisen from an old staunch feeling of his, deserving tenderest consideration. She recalled to her mind with much pleasure that he had told her he was staying at the Black-Bull Hotel; so that if, after waiting a day or two, he should not, in his modesty, call again, she might then send him a nice little note. To alter her views for the present was far from her intention; but she would allow herself to be induced to reconsider the case, as any generous woman ought to do.

The morrow came and passed, and Mr Barnet did not drop in. At every knock, light youthful hues flew across her cheek; and she was abstracted in the presence of her other visitors. In the evening she walked about the house, not knowing what to do with herself; the conditions of existence seemed totally different from those which ruled only four-and-twenty short hours ago. What had been at first a tantalizing, elusive sentiment was getting acclimatized within her as a definite hope, and her person was so informed by that emotion that she might almost have stood as its emblematical representative by the time the clock struck ten. In short, an interest in Barnet precisely resembling that of her early youth led her present heart to belie her yesterday's words to him, and she longed to see him again.

The next day she walked out early, thinking she might meet him in the street. The growing beauty of her romance absorbed her, and she went from the street to the fields, and from the fields to the shore, without any consciousness of distance, till reminded by her weariness that she could go no further. He had nowhere appeared. In the evening she took a step which under the circumstances seemed justifiable; she wrote a note to him at the hotel, inviting him to tea with her at six precisely, and signing her note 'Lucy'.

In a quarter of an hour the messenger came back. Mr Barnet had left the hotel early in the morning of the day before, but he had stated that he would probably return in the course of the week.

The note was sent back, to be given to him immediately on his arrival.

There was no sign from the inn that this desired event had occurred, either on the next day or the day following. On both nights she had been restless, and had scarcely slept half-an-hour.

On the Saturday, putting off all diffidence, Lucy went herself to the Black-Bull, and questioned the staff closely.

Mr Barnet had cursorily remarked when leaving that he might return on the Thursday or Friday, but they were directed not to reserve a room for him unless he should write.

He had left no address.

Lucy sorrowfully took back her note, went home, and resolved to wait.

She did wait – years and years – but Barnet never reappeared.

April 1880

Interlopers at the Knap

THE north road from Casterbridge is tedious and lonely, especially in winter-time. Along a part of its course it connects with Long-Ash Lane, a monotonous track without a village or hamlet for many miles, and with very seldom a turning. Unapprized wayfarers who are too old, or too young, or in other respects too weak for the distance to be traversed, but who, nevertheless, have to walk it, say, as they look wistfully ahead, 'Once at the top of that hill, and I must surely see the end of Long-Ash Lane!' But they reach the hilltop, and Long-Ash Lane stretches in front as mercilessly as before.

Some few years ago a certain farmer was riding through this lane in the gloom of a winter evening. The farmer's friend, a dairyman, was riding beside him. A few paces in the rear rode the farmer's man. All three were well horsed on strong, round-barrelled cobs; and to be well horsed was to be in better spirits about Long-Ash Lane than poor pedestrians could attain to during its passage.

But the farmer did not talk much to his friend as he rode along. The enterprise which had brought him there filled his mind; for in truth it was important. Not altogether so important was it, perhaps, when estimated by its value to society at large; but if the true measure of a deed be proportionate to the space it occupies in the heart of him who undertakes it, Farmer Charles Darton's business to-night could hold its own with the business of kings.

He was a large farmer. His turnover, as it is called, was probably thirty thousand pounds a year. He had a great many draught horses, a great many milch cows, and of sheep a multitude. This comfortable position was, however, none of his own making. It had been created by his father, a man of a very different stamp from the present representative of the line.

Darton, the father, had been a one-idea'd character, with a buttoned-up pocket and a chink-like eye brimming with commercial subtlety. In Darton the son, this trade subtlety had become transmuted into emotional, and the harshness had disappeared; he would have been called a sad man but for his constant care not to divide himself from lively friends by piping notes out of harmony with theirs. Contemplative, he allowed his mind to be a quiet meeting-place for memories and hopes. So that, naturally enough, since succeeding to the agricultural calling, and up to his present age of thirty-two, he had neither advanced nor receded as a capitalist — a stationary result which did not agitate one of his unambitious, unstrategic nature, since he had all that he desired. The motive of his expedition to-night showed the same absence of anxious regard for Number One.

The party rode on in the slow, safe trot proper to night-time and bad roads, Farmer Darton's head jigging rather unromantically up and down against the sky, and his motions being repeated with bolder emphasis by his friend Japheth

Johns; while those of the latter were travestied in jerks still less softened by art in the person of the lad who attended them. A pair of whitish objects hung one on each side of the latter, bumping against him at each step, and still further spoiling the grace of his seat. On close inspection they might have been perceived to be open rush baskets – one containing a turkey, and the other some bottles of wine.

'D'ye feel ye can meet your fate like a man, neighbour Darton?' asked Johns, breaking a silence which had lasted while five-and-twenty hedgerow trees had glided by.

Mr Darton with a half-laugh murmured, 'Ay – call it my fate! Hanging and wiving go by destiny.' And then they were silent again.

The darkness thickened rapidly, at intervals shutting down on the land in a perceptible flap, like the wave of a wing. The customary close of day was accelerated by a simultaneous blurring of the air. With the fall of night had come a mist just damp enough to incommode, but not sufficient to saturate them. Countrymen as they were – born, as may be said, with only an open door between them and the four seasons – they regarded the mist but as an added obscuration, and ignored its humid quality.

They were travelling in a direction that was enlivened by no modern current of traffic, the place of Darton's pilgrimage being an old-fashioned village – one of the Hintocks (several villages of that name, with a distinctive prefix or affix, lying thereabout) – where the people make the best cider and cider-wine in all Wessex, and where the dunghills smell of pomace instead of stable refuse as elsewhere. The lane was sometimes so narrow that the brambles of the hedge, which hung forward like anglers' rods over a stream, scratched their hats and hooked their whiskers as they passed. Yet this neglected lane had been a highway to Queen Elizabeth's subjects and the cavalcades of the past. Its days was over now, and its history as a national artery done for ever.

'Why I have decided to marry her,' resumed Darton (in a measured musical voice of confidence which revealed a good deal of his composition), as he glanced round to see that the lad was not too near, 'is not only that I like her, but that I can do no better, even from a fairly practical point of view. That I might ha' looked higher is possibly true, though it is really all nonsense. I have had experience enough in looking above me. "No more superior women for me," said I – you know when. Sally is a comely, independent, simple character, with no make-up about her, who'll think me as much a superior to her as I used to think – you know who I mean – was to me.'

'Ay,' said Johns. 'However, I shouldn't call Sally Hall simple. Primary, because no Sally is; secondary, because if some could be, this one wouldn't. 'Tis a wrong denomination to apply to a woman, Charles, and affects me, as your best man, like cold water. 'Tis like recommending a stage play by saying there's neither murder, villainy, nor harm of any sort in it, when that's what you've paid your half-crown to see.'

'Well; may your opinion do you good. Mine's a different one.' And turning the conversation from the philosophical to the practical, Darton expressed a hope that the said Sally had received what he'd sent on by the carrier that day.

Johns wanted to know what that was.

'It is a dress,' said Darton. 'Not exactly a wedding-dress; though she may use it as one if she likes. It is rather serviceable than showy – suitable for the winter weather.'

'Good,' said Johns. 'Serviceable is a wise word in a bridegroom. I commend 'ee, Charles.'

'For,' said Darton, 'why should a woman dress up like a rope-dancer because she's going to do the most solemn deed of her life except dying?'

'Faith, why? But she will, because she will, I suppose,' said Dairyman Johns.

'H'm,' said Darton.

The lane they followed had been nearly straight for several miles, but they now left it for a smaller one which after winding uncertainly for some distance forked into two. By night country roads are apt to reveal ungainly qualities which pass without observation during day; and though Darton had travelled this way before, he had not done so frequently, Sally having been wooed at the house of a relative near his own. He never remembered seeing at this spot a pair of alternative ways looking so equally probable as these two did now. Johns rode on a few steps.

'Don't be out of heart, sonny,' he cried. 'Here's a handpost. Ezra – come and climm this post, and tell us the way.'

The lad dismounted, and jumped into the hedge where the post stood under a tree.

'Unstrap the baskets, or you'll smash up that wine!' cried Darton, as the young man began spasmodically to climb the post, baskets and all.

'Was there ever less head in a brainless world?' said Johns. 'Here, simple Ezzy, I'll do it.' He leapt off, and with much puffing climbed the post, striking a match when he reached the top, and moving the light along the arm, the lad standing and gazing at the spectacle.

'I have faced tantalization these twenty years with a temper as mild as milk!' said Japheth; 'but such things as this don't come short of devilry!' And flinging the match away, he slipped down to the ground.

'What's the matter?' asked Darton.

'Not a letter, sacred or heathen – not so much as would tell us the way to the town of Smokeyhole – ever I should sin to say it! Either the moss and mildew have eat away the words, or we have arrived in a land where the natyves have lost the art o' writing, and should ha' brought our compass like Christopher Columbus.'

'Let us take the straightest road,' said Darton placidly; 'I shan't be sorry to get there – 'tis a tiresome ride. I would have driven if I had known.'

'Nor I neither, sir,' said Ezra. 'These straps plough my shoulder like a zull. If 'tis much further to your lady's home, Maister Darton, I shall ask to be let carry half of these good things in my innerds – hee, hee!'

'Don't you be such a reforming radical, Ezra,' said Johns sternly. 'Here, I'll take the turkey.'

This being done, they went forward by the right-hand lane, which ascended a hill, the left winding away under a plantation. The pit-a-pit of their horses' hoofs lessened up the slope; and the ironical directing-post stood in solitude as before, holding out its blank arms to the raw breeze, which brought a snore from the wood as if Skrymir the Giant were sleeping there.

II

Three miles to the left of the travellers, along the road they had not followed, rose an old house with mullioned windows of Ham-hill stone, and chimneys of lavish solidity. It stood at the top of a slope beside King's-Hintock village-street, only a mile or two from King's-Hintock Court, yet quite shut away from that mansion and its precincts. Immediately in front of it grew a large sycamore tree, whose bared roots formed a convenient staircase from the road below to the front door of the dwelling. Its situation gave the house what little distinctive name it possessed, namely, 'The Knap'. Some forty yards off a brook dribbled past, which, for its size, made a great deal of noise. At the back was a dairy barton, accessible for vehicles and live-stock by a side 'drong'. Thus much only of the character of the homestead could be divined out of doors at this shady evening-time.

But within there was plenty of light to see by, as plenty was construed at Hintock. Beside a Tudor fireplace, whose moulded four-centred arch was nearly hidden by a figured blue-cloth blower, were seated two women – mother and daughter – Mrs Hall, and Sarah, or Sally; for this was a part of the world where the latter modification had not as yet been effaced as a vulgarity by the march of intellect. The owner of the name was the young woman by whose means Mr Darton proposed to put an end to his bachelor condition on the approaching day.

The mother's bereavement had been so long ago as not to leave much mark of its occurrence upon her now, either in face or clothes. She had resumed the mob-cap of her early married life, enlivening its whiteness by a few rose-du-Barry ribbons. Sally required no such aids to pinkness. Roseate good-nature lit up her gaze; her features showed curves of decision and judgment; and she might have been regarded without much mistake as a warm-hearted, quick-spirited, handsome girl.

She did most of the talking, her mother listening with a half-absent air, as she picked up fragments of red-hot wood ember with the tongs, and piled them upon the brands. But the number of speeches that passed was very small in proportion to the meanings exchanged. Long experience together often enabled them to see the course of thought in each other's minds without a word being spoken. Behind them, in the centre of the room, the table was spread for supper, certain whiffs of air laden with fat vapours, which ever and anon entered from the kitchen, denoting its preparation there.

'The new gown he was going to send you stays about on the way like himself,' Sally's mother was saying.

'Yes, not finished, I daresay,' cried Sally independently. 'Lord, I shouldn't be amazed if it didn't come at all! Young men make such kind promises when they are near you, and forget 'em when they go away. But he doesn't intend it as a wedding-gown – he gives it to me merely as a gown to wear when I like – a travelling-dress is what it would be called by some. Come rathe or come late it don't much matter, as I have a dress of my own to fall back upon. But what time is it?'

She went to the family clock and opened the glass, for the hour was not otherwise discernible by night, and indeed at all times was rather a thing to be investigated than beheld, so much more wall than window was there in the apartment. 'It is nearly eight,' said she.

'Eight o'clock, and neither dress nor man,' said Mrs Hall.

'Mother, if you think to tantalize me by talking like that, you are much mistaken! Let him be as late as he will – or stay away altogether – I don't care,' said Sally. But a tender minute quaver in the negation showed that there was something forced in that statement.

Mrs Hall perceived it, and drily observed that she was not so sure about Sally not caring. 'But perhaps you don't care so much as I do, after all,' she said. 'For I see what you don't, that it is a good and flourishing match for you; a very honourable offer in Mr Darton. And I think I see a kind husband in him. So pray God 'twill go smooth, and wind up well.'

Sally would not listen to misgivings. Of course it would go smoothly, she asserted. 'How you are up and down, mother!' she went on. 'At this moment, whatever hinders him, we are not so anxious to see him as he is to be here, and his thought runs on before him, and settles down upon us like the star in the east. Hark!' she exclaimed, with a breath of relief, her eyes sparkling. 'I heard something. Yes – here they are!'

The next moment her mother's slower ear also distinguished the familiar reverberation occasioned by footsteps clambering up the roots of the sycamore.

'Yes, it sounds like them at last,' she said. 'Well, it is not so very late after all, considering the distance.'

The footfall ceased, and they arose, expecting a knock. They began to think it might have been, after all, some neighbouring villager under Bacchic influence, giving the centre of the road a wide berth, when their doubts were dispelled by the new-comer's entry into the passage. The door of the room was gently opened, and there appeared, not the pair of travellers with whom we have already made acquaintance, but a pale-faced man in the garb of extreme poverty – almost in rags.

'O, it's a tramp – gracious me!' said Sally, starting back.

His cheeks and eye-orbits were deep concaves – rather, it might be, from natural weakness of constitution than irregular living, though there were indications that he had led no careful life. He gazed at the two women fixedly for a moment: then with an abashed, humiliated demeanour, dropped his glance to the floor, and sank into a chair without uttering a word.

Sally was in advance of her mother, who had remained standing by the fire. She now tried to discern the visitor across the candles.

'Why – mother,' said Sally faintly, turning back to Mrs Hall. 'It is Phil, from Australia!'

Mrs Hall started, and grew pale, and a fit of coughing seized the man with the ragged clothes. 'To come home like this!' she said. 'O, Philip – are you ill?'

'No, no, mother,' replied he impatiently, as soon as he could speak.

'But for God's sake how do you come here – and just now, too?'

'Well, I am here,' said the man. 'How it is I hardly know. I've come home, mother, because I was driven to it. Things were against me out there, and went from bad to worse.'

'Then why didn't you let us know? – you've not writ a line for the last two or three years.'

The son admitted sadly that he had not. He said that he had hoped and thought he might fetch up again, and be able to send good news. Then he had been obliged to abandon that hope, and had finally come home from sheer necessity – previously to making a new start. 'Yes, things are very bad with me,' he repeated, perceiving their commiserating glances at his clothes.

They brought him nearer the fire, took his hat from his thin hand, which was so small and smooth as to show that his attempts to fetch up again had not been in a manual direction. His mother resumed her inquiries, and dubiously asked if he had chosen to come that particular night for any special reason.

For no reason, he told her. His arrival had been quite at random. Then Philip Hall looked round the room, and saw for the first time that the table was laid somewhat luxuriously, and for a larger number than themselves; and that an air of festivity pervaded their dress. He asked quickly what was going on.

'Sally is going to be married in a day or two,' replied the mother; and she explained how Mr Darton, Sally's intended husband, was coming there that night with the groomsman, Mr Johns, and other details. 'We thought it must be their step when we heard you,' said Mrs Hall.

The needy wanderer looked again on the floor. 'I see – I see,' he murmured. 'Why, indeed, should I have come to-night? Such folk as I are not wanted here at these times, naturally. And I have no business here – spoiling other people's happiness.'

'Phil,' said his mother, with a tear in her eye, but with a thinness of lip and severity of manner which were presumably not more than past events justified; 'since you speak like that to me, I'll speak honestly to you. For these three years you have taken no thought for us. You left home with a good supply of money, and strength and education, and you ought to have made good use of it all. But you come back like a beggar; and that you come in a very awkward time for us cannot be denied. Your return to-night may do us much harm. But mind – you are welcome to this home as long as it is mine. I don't wish to turn you adrift. We will make the best of a bad job; and I hope you are not seriously ill?'

'O no, I have only his infernal cough.'

She looked at him anxiously. 'I think you had better go to bed at once,' she said.

'Well – I shall be out of the way there,' said the son wearily. 'Having ruined myself, don't let me ruin you by being seen in these togs, for Heaven's sake. Who do you say Sally is going to be married to – a Farmer Darton?'

'Yes – a gentleman-farmer – quite a wealthy man. Far better in station than she could have expected. It is a good thing, altogether.'

'Well done, little Sal!' said her brother, brightening and looking up at her with a smile. 'I ought to have written; but perhaps I have thought of you all the more. But let me get out of sight. I would rather go and jump into the river than be seen here. But have you anything I can drink? I am confoundedly thirsty with my long tramp.'

'Yes, yes, we will bring something upstairs to you,' said Sally, with grief in her face.

'Ay, that will do nicely. But, Sally and mother—' He stopped, and they waited.

'Mother, I have not told you all,' he resumed slowly, still looking on the floor between his knees. 'Sad as what you see of me is, there's worse behind.'

His mother gazed upon him in grieved suspense, and Sally went and leant upon the bureau, listening for every sound, and sighing. Suddenly she turned round, saying, 'Let them come, I don't care! Philip, tell the worst, and take your time.'

'Well, then,' said the unhappy Phil, 'I am not the only one in this mess. Would to Heaven I were! But—'

'O, Phil!'

'I have a wife as destitute as I.'

'A wife?' said his mother.

'Unhappily!'

'A wife! Yes, that is the way with sons!'

'And besides—' said he.

'Besides! O, Philip, surely—'

'I have two little children.'

'Wife and children!' whispered Mrs Hall, sinking down confounded.

'Poor little things!' said Sally involuntarily.

His mother turned again to him. 'I suppose these helpless beings are left in Australia?'

'No. They are in England.'

'Well, I can only hope you've left them in a respectable place.'

'I have not left them at all. They are here – within a few yards of us. In short, they are in the stable.'

'Where?'

'In the stable. I did not like to bring them indoors till I had seen you, mother, and broken the bad news a bit to you. They were very tired, and are resting out there on some straw.'

Mrs Hall's fortitude visibly broke down. She had been brought up not without refinement, and was even more moved by such a collapse of genteel aims as this than a substantial dairyman's widow would in ordinary have been moved. 'Well, it must be borne,' she said, in a low voice, with her hands tightly joined. 'A starving son, a starving wife, starving children! Let it be. But why is this come to us now, to-day, to-night? Could no other misfortune happen to helpless women than this, which will quite upset my poor girl's chance of a happy life? Why have you done us this wrong, Philip? What respectable man will come here, and marry open-eyed into a family of vagabonds?'

'Nonsense, mother!' said Sally vehemently, while her face flushed. 'Charley isn't the man to desert me. But if he should be, and won't marry me because Phil's come, let him go and marry elsewhere. I won't be ashamed of my own flesh and blood for any man in England – not I!' And then Sally turned away and burst into tears.

'Wait till you are twenty years older and you will tell a different tale,' replied her mother.

The son stood up. 'Mother,' he said bitterly, 'as I have come, so I will go. All I ask of you is that you will allow me and mine to lie in your stable to-night. I give you my word that we'll be gone by break of day, and trouble you no further!'

Mrs Hall, the mother, changed at that. 'O no,' she answered hastily; 'never shall it be said that I sent any of my own family from my door. Bring 'em in, Philip, or take me out to them.'

'We will put 'em all into the large bedroom,' said Sally, brightening, 'and make up a large fire. Let's go and help them in, and call Rebekah.' (Rebekah was the woman who assisted at the dairy and housework; she lived in a cottage hard by with her husband, who attended to the cows.)

Sally went to fetch a lantern from the back-kitchen, but her brother said, 'You won't want a light. I lit the lantern that was hanging there.'

'What must we call your wife?' asked Mrs Hall.

'Helena,' said Philip.

With shawls over their heads they proceeded towards the back door.

'One minute before you go,' interrupted Philip. 'I – I haven't confessed all.'

'Then Heaven help us!' said Mrs Hall, pushing to the door and clasping her hands in calm despair.

'We passed through Evershead as we came,' he continued, 'and I just looked in at the "Sow-and-Acorn" to see if old Mike still kept on there as usual. The carrier had come in from Sherton Abbas at that moment, and guessing that I was bound for this place – for I think he knew me – he asked me to bring on a dressmaker's parcel for Sally that was marked "immediate". My wife had walked on with the children. 'Twas a flimsy parcel, and the paper was torn, and I found on looking at it that it was a thick warm gown. I didn't wish you to see poor Helena in a shabby state. I was ashamed that you should – 'twas not what she was born to. I untied the parcel in the road, took it on to her where she was waiting in the Lower Barn, and told her I had managed to get it for her, and that she was to ask no question. She, poor thing, must have supposed I obtained it on trust, through having reached a place where I was known, for she put it on gladly enough. She has it on now. Sally has other gowns, I daresay.'

Sally looked at her mother, speechless.

'You have others, I daresay!' repeated Phil, with a sick man's impatience. 'I thought to myself, "Better Sally cry than Helena freeze." Well, is the dress of great consequence? 'Twas nothing very ornamental, as far as I could see.'

'No – no; not of consequence,' returned Sally sadly, adding in a gentle voice, 'You will not mind if I lend her another instead of that one, will you?'

Philip's agitation at the confession had brought on another attack of the cough, which seemed to shake him to pieces. He was so obviously unfit to sit in a chair that they helped him upstairs at once; and having hastily given him a cordial and kindled the bedroom fire, they descended to fetch their unhappy new relations.

III

It was with strange feelings that the girl and her mother, lately so cheerful, passed out of the back door into the open air of the barton, laden with hay scents and the herby breath of cows. A fine sleet had begun to fall, and they trotted across the yard quickly. The stable-door was open; a light shone from it – from the lantern which always hung there, and which Philip had lighted, as he said. Softly nearing the door, Mrs Hall pronounced the name 'Helena!'

There was no answer for the moment. Looking in she was taken by surprise. Two people appeared before her. For one, instead of the drabbish woman she had expected, Mrs Hall saw a pale, dark-eyed, ladylike creature, whose personality ruled her attire rather than was ruled by it. She was in a new and handsome gown, Sally's own, and an old bonnet. She was standing up, agitated; her hand was held by her companion – none else than Sally's affianced, Farmer Charles Darton, upon whose fine figure the pale stranger's eyes were fixed, as his were fixed upon her. His other hand held the rein of his horse, which was standing saddled as if just led in.

At sight of Mrs Hall they both turned, looking at her in a way neither quite conscious nor unconscious, and without seeming to recollect that words were necessary as a solution to the scene. In another moment Sally entered also, when Mr Darton dropped his companion's hand, led the horse aside, and came to greet his betrothed and Mrs Hall.

'Ah!' he said, smiling – with something like forced composure – 'this is a roundabout way of arriving, you will say, my dear Mrs Hall. But we lost our way, which made us late. I saw a light here, and led in my horse at once – my friend Johns and my man have gone onward to the little inn with theirs, not to crowd you too much. No sooner had I entered than I saw that this lady had taken temporary shelter here – and found I was intruding.'

'She is my daughter-in-law,' said Mrs Hall calmly. 'My son, too, is in the house, but he has gone to bed unwell.'

Sally had stood staring wonderingly at the scene until this moment, hardly recognizing Darton's shake of the hand. The spell that bound her was broken by her perceiving the two little children seated on a heap of hay. She suddenly went forward, spoke to them, and took one on her arm and the other in her hand.

'And two children?' said Mr Darton, showing thus that he had not been there long enough as yet to understand the situation.

'My grandchildren,' said Mrs Hall, with as much affected ease as before.

Philip Hall's wife, in spite of this interruption to her first rencounter, seemed scarcely so much affected by it as to feel anyone's presence in addition to Mr Darton's. However, arousing herself by a quick reflection, she threw a sudden critical glance of her sad eyes upon Mrs Hall, and, apparently finding her satisfactory, advanced to her in a meek initiative. Then Sally and the stranger spoke some friendly words to each other, and Sally went on with the children into the house. Mrs Hall and Helena followed, and Mr Darton followed these, looking at Helena's dress and outline, and listening to her voice like a man in a dream.

By the time the others reached the house Sally had already gone upstairs with the tired children. She rapped against the wall for Rebekah to come in and help to attend to them, Rebekah's house being a little 'spit-and-daub' cabin leaning against the substantial stonework of Mrs Hall's taller erection. When she came a bed was made up for the little ones, and some supper given to them. On descending the stairs after seeing this done Sally went to the sitting-room. Young Mrs Hall entered it just in advance of her, having in the interim retired with her mother-in-law to take off her bonnet, and otherwise make herself presentable. Hence it was evident that no further communication could have passed between her and Mr Darton since their brief interview in the stable.

Mr Japheth Johns now opportunely arrived, and broke up the restraint of the company, after a few orthodox meteorological commentaries had passed between him and Mrs Hall by way of introduction. They at once sat down to supper, the present of wine and turkey not being produced for consumption to-night, lest the premature display of those gifts should seem to throw doubt on Mrs Hall's capacities as a provider.

'Drink hearty, Mr Johns – drink hearty,' said that matron magnanimously. 'Such as it is there's plenty of. But perhaps cider-wine is not to your taste? – though there's body in it.'

'Quite the contrairy, ma'am – quite the contrairy,' said the dairyman. 'For though I inherit the malt-liquor principle from my father, I am a cider-drinker on my mother's side. She came from these parts, you know. And there's this to be said for't – 'tis a more peaceful liquor, and don't lie about a man like your hotter drinks. With care, one may live on it a twelve-month without knocking down a neighbour, or getting a black eye from an old acquaintance.'

The general conversation thus begun was continued briskly, though it was in the main restricted to Mrs Hall and Japheth, who in truth required but little help from anybody. There being slight call upon Sally's tongue, she had ample leisure to do what her heart most desired, namely, watch her intended husband and her sister-in-law with a view of elucidating the strange momentary scene in which her mother and herself had surprised them in the stable. If that scene meant anything, it meant, at least, that they had met before. That there had been no time for explanations Sally could see, for their manner was still one of suppressed amazement at each other's presence there. Darton's eyes, too, fell continually on the gown worn by Helena as if this were an added riddle to his perplexity; though to Sally it was the one feature in the case which was no mystery. He seemed to feel that fate had impishly changed his *vis-à-vis* in the lover's jig he was about to foot; that while the gown had been expected to enclose a Sally, a Helena's face looked out from the bodice; that some long-lost hand met his own from the sleeves.

Sally could see that whatever Helena might know of Darton, she knew nothing of how the dress entered into his embarrassment. And at moments the young girl would have persuaded herself that Darton's looks at her sister-in-law were entirely the fruit of the clothes query. But surely at other times a more extensive range of speculation and sentiment was expressed by her lover's eye than that which the changed dress would account for.

Sally's independence made her one of the least jealous of women. But there was something in the relations of these two visitors which ought to be explained.

Japheth Johns continued to converse in his well-known style, interspersing his talk with some private reflections on the position of Darton and Sally, which, though the sparkle in his eye showed them to be highly entertaining to himself, were apparently not quite communicable to the company. At last he withdrew for the night, going off to the roadside inn half-a-mile ahead, whither Darton promised to follow him in a few minutes.

Half-an-hour passed, and then Mr Darton also rose to leave, Sally and her sister-in-law simultaneously wishing him good-night as they retired upstairs to their rooms. But on his arriving at the front door with Mrs Hall a sharp shower of rain began to come down, when the widow suggested that he should return to the fireside till the storm ceased.

Darton accepted her proposal, but insisted that, as it was getting late, and she was obviously tired, she should not sit up on his account, since he could let himself out of the house, and would quite enjoy smoking a pipe by the hearth alone. Mrs Hall assented; and Darton was left by himself. He spread his knees to the brands, lit up his tobacco as he had said, and sat gazing into the fire, and at the notches of the chimney-crook which hung above.

An occasional drop of rain rolled down the chimney with a hiss, and still he smoked on; but not like a man whose mind was at rest. In the long run, however, despite his meditations, early hours afield and a long ride in the open air produced their natural result. He began to doze.

How long he remained in this half-unconscious state he did not know. He suddenly opened his eyes. The back-brand had burnt itself in two, and ceased to flame; the light which he had placed on the mantelpiece had nearly gone out. But in spite of these deficiencies there was a light in the apartment, and it came from elsewhere. Turning his head he saw Philip Hall's wife standing at the entrance of the room with a bed-candle in one hand, a small brass tea-kettle in the other, and *his* gown, as it certainly seemed, still upon her.

'Helena!' said Darton, starting up.

Her countenance expressed dismay, and her first words were an apology. 'I – did not know you were here, Mr Darton,' she said, while a blush flashed to her cheek. 'I thought every one had retired – I was coming to make a little water boil; my husband seems to be worse. But perhaps the kitchen fire can be lighted up again.'

'Don't go on my account. By all means put it on here as you intended,' said Darton. 'Allow me to help you.' He went forward to take the kettle from her hand, but she did not allow him, and placed it on the fire herself.

They stood some way apart, one on each side of the fireplace, waiting till the water should boil, the candle on the mantel between them, and Helena with her eyes on the kettle. Darton was the first to break the silence. 'Shall I call Sally?' he said.

'O no,' she quickly returned. 'We have given trouble enough already. We have no right here. But we are the sport of fate, and were obliged to come.'

'No right here!' said he in surprise.

'None. I can't explain it now,' answered Helena. 'This kettle is very slow.'

There was another pause; the proverbial dilatoriness of watched pots was never more clearly exemplified.

Helena's face was of that sort which seems to ask for assistance without the owner's knowledge – the very antipodes of Sally's, which was self-reliance expressed. Darton's eyes travelled from the kettle to Helena's face, then back to the kettle, then to the face for rather a longer time. 'So I am not to know anything of the mystery that has distracted me all the evening?' he said. 'How is it that a woman, who refused me because (as I supposed) my position was not good enough for her taste, is found to be the wife of a man who certainly seems to be worse off than I?'

'He had the prior claim,' said she.

'What! you knew him at that time?'

'Yes, yes! And he went to Australia, and sent for me, and I joined him out there!'

'Ah – that was the mystery!'

'Please say no more,' she implored. 'Whatever my errors, I have paid for them during the last five years!'

The heart of Darton was subject to sudden overflowings. He was kind to a fault. 'I am sorry from my soul,' he said, involuntarily approaching her. Helena withdrew a step or two, at which he became conscious of his movement, and quickly took his former place. Here he stood without speaking, and the little kettle began to sing.

'Well, you might have been my wife if you had chosen,' he said at last. 'But that's all past and gone. However, if you are in any trouble or poverty I shall be glad to be of service, and as your relation by marriage I shall have a right to be. Does your uncle know of your distress?'

'My uncle is dead. He left me without a farthing. And now we have two children to maintain.'

'What, left you nothing? How could he be so cruel as that?'

'I disgraced myself in his eyes.'

'Now,' said Darton earnestly, 'let me take care of the children, at least while you are so unsettled. *You* belong to another, so I cannot take care of you.'

'Yes, you can,' said a voice; and suddenly a third figure stood beside them. It was Sally. 'You can, since you seem to wish to,' she repeated. 'She no longer belongs to another. . . . My poor brother is dead!'

Her face was red, her eyes sparkled, and all the woman came to the front. 'I have heard it!' she went on to him passionately. 'You can protect her now as well as the children!' She turned then to her agitated sister-in-law. 'I heard something,' said Sally (in a gentle murmur, differing much from her previous passionate words), 'and I went into his room. It must have been the moment you left. He went off so quickly, and weakly, and it was so unexpected, that I couldn't leave even to call you.'

Darton was just able to gather from the confused discourse which followed that, during his sleep by the fire, Sally's brother whom he had never seen had become worse; and that during Helena's absence for water the end had unexpectedly come. The two young women hastened upstairs, and he was again left alone.

After standing there a short time he went to the front door and looked out; till, softly closing it behind him, he advanced and stood under the large sycamore-tree. The stars were flickering coldly, and the dampness which had just descended upon the earth in rain now sent up a chill from it. Darton was in a strange position, and he felt it. The unexpected appearance, in deep poverty, of Helena – a young lady, daughter of a deceased naval officer, who had been brought up by her uncle, a solicitor, and had refused Darton in marriage years ago – the passionate, almost angry demeanour of Sally at discovering them, the abrupt announcement that Helena was a widow; all this coming together was a conjuncture difficult to cope with in a moment, and made him question whether he ought to leave the house or offer assistance. But for Sally's manner he would unhesitatingly have done the latter.

He was still standing under the tree when the door in front of him opened, and Mrs Hall came out. She went round to the garden-gate at the side without seeing him. Darton followed her, intending to speak. Pausing outside, as if in thought, she proceeded to a spot where the sun came earliest in spring-time, and where the north wind never blew; it was where the row of beehives stood under the wall. Discerning her object, he waited till she had accomplished it.

It was the universal custom thereabout to wake the bees by tapping at their hives whenever a death occurred in the household, under the belief that if this were not done the bees themselves would pine away and perish during the ensuing year. As soon as an interior buzzing responded to her tap at the first hive Mrs Hall went on to the second, and thus passed down the row. As soon as she came back he met her.

'What can I do in this trouble, Mrs Hall?' he said.

'O – nothing, thank you, nothing,' she said in a tearful voice, now just perceiving him. 'We have called Rebekah and her husband, and they will do everything necessary.' She told him in a few words the particulars of her son's arrival, broken in health – indeed, at death's very door, though they did not suspect it – and suggested, as the result of a conversation between her and her daughter, that the wedding should be postponed.

'Yes, of course,' said Darton. 'I think now to go straight to the inn and tell Johns what has happened.' It was not till after he had shaken hands with her that he turned hesitatingly and added, 'Will you tell the mother of his children that, as they are now left fatherless, I shall be glad to take the eldest of them, if it would be any convenience to her and to you?'

Mrs Hall promised that her son's widow should be told of the offer, and they parted. He retired down the rooty slope and disappeared in the direction of the inn, where he informed Johns of the circumstances. Meanwhile Mrs Hall had entered the house. Sally was downstairs in the sitting-room alone, and her mother explained to her that Darton had readily assented to the postponement.

'No doubt he has,' said Sally, with sad emphasis. 'It is not put off for a week, or a month, or a year. I shall never marry him, and she will!'

IV

Time passed, and the household on the Knap became again serene under the composing influences of daily routine. A desultory, very desultory, correspondence dragged on between Sally Hall and Darton, who, not quite knowing how to take her petulant words on the night of her brother's death, had continued passive thus long. Helena and her children remained at the dairy-house, almost of necessity, and Darton therefore deemed it advisable to stay away.

One day, seven months later on, when Mr Darton was as usual at his farm, twenty miles from King's-Hintock, a note reached him from Helena. She thanked him for his kind offer about her children, which her mother-in-law had duly communicated, and stated that she would be glad to accept it as regarded the eldest, the boy. Helena had, in truth, good need to do so, for her uncle had left her penniless, and all application to some relatives in the north had failed. There was, besides, as she said, no good school near Hintock to which she could send the child.

On a fine summer day the boy came. He was accompanied half-way by Sally and his mother – to the 'White Horse', the fine old Elizabethan inn at Chalk Newton,[1] where he was handed over to Darton's bailiff in a shining spring-cart, who met them there.

He was entered as a day-scholar at a popular school at Casterbridge, three or four miles from Darton's, having first been taught by Darton to ride a forest-pony, on which he cantered to and from the aforesaid fount of knowledge, and (as Darton hoped) brought away a promising headful of the same at each diurnal expedition. The thoughtful taciturnity into which Darton had latterly fallen was quite dissipated by the presence of this boy.

When the Christmas holidays came it was arranged that he should spend them with his mother. The journey was, for some reason or other, performed in two stages, as at his coming, except that Darton in person took the place of the bailiff, and that the boy and himself rode on horseback.

Reaching the renowned 'White Horse', Darton inquired if Miss and young Mrs Hall were there to meet little Philip (as they had agreed to be). He was answered by the appearance of Helena alone at the door.

'At the last moment Sally would not come,' she faltered.

That meeting practically settled the point towards which these long-severed persons were converging. But nothing was broached about it for some time yet. Sally Hall had, in fact, imparted the first decisive motion to events by refusing to accompany Helena. She soon gave them a second move by writing the following note: –

'[*Private.*]
'DEAR CHARLES, – Living here so long and intimately with Helena, I have naturally learnt her history, especially that of it which refers to you. I am sure she would accept you as a husband at the proper time, and I think you ought to give her the opportunity. You inquire in an old note if I am sorry that I showed temper (which it *wasn't*) that night when I heard you talking to her. No, Charles, I am not sorry at all for what I said then. – Yours sincerely,

SALLY HALL'

Thus set in train, the transfer of Darton's heart back to its original quarters proceeded by mere lapse of time. In the following July, Darton went to his friend Japheth to ask him at last to fulfil the bridal office which had been in abeyance since the previous January twelvemonths.

'With all my heart, man o' constancy!' said Dairyman Johns warmly. 'I've lost most of my genteel fair complexion haymaking this hot weather, 'tis true, but I'll do your business as well as them that look better. There be scents and good hair-oil in the world yet, thank God, and they'll take off the roughest o' my edge. I'll compliment her. "Better late than never, Sally Hall," I'll say.'

'It is not Sally,' said Darton hurriedly. 'It is young Mrs Hall.'

Japheth's face, as soon as he really comprehended, became a picture of reproachful dismay. 'Not Sally?' he said. 'Why not Sally? I can't believe it! Young Mrs Hall! Well, well – where's your wisdom?'

Darton shortly explained particulars; but Johns would not be reconciled. 'She was a woman worth having if ever woman was,' he cried. 'And now to let her go!'

---

[1] It is now pulled down, and its site occupied by a modern one in red brick (1912).

'But I suppose I can marry where I like,' said Darton.

'H'm,' replied the dairyman, lifting his eyebrows expressively. 'This don't become you, Charles – it really do not. If I had done such a thing you would have sworn I was a curst no'thern fool to be drawn off the scent by such a red-herring doll-oll-oll.'

Farmer Darton responded in such sharp terms to this laconic opinion that the two friends finally parted in a way they had never parted before. Johns was to be no groomsman to Darton after all. He had flatly declined. Darton went off sorry, and even unhappy, particularly as Japheth was about to leave that side of the county, so that the words which had divided them were not likely to be explained away or softened down.

A short time after the interview Darton was united to Helena at a simple matter-of-fact wedding, and she and her little girl joined the boy who had already grown to look on Darton's house as home.

For some months the farmer experienced an unprecedented happiness and satisfaction. There had been a flaw in his life, and it was as neatly mended as was humanly possible. But after a season the stream of events followed less clearly, and there were shades in his reveries. Helena was a fragile woman, of little staying-power, physically or morally, and since the time that he had originally known her – eight or ten years before – she had been severely tried. She had loved herself out, in short, and was now occasionally given to moping. Sometimes she spoke regretfully of the gentilities of her early life, and instead of comparing her present state with her condition as the wife of the unlucky Hall, she mused rather on what it had been before she took the first fatal step of clandestinely marrying him. She did not care to please such people as those with whom she was thrown as a thriving farmer's wife. She allowed the pretty trifles of agricultural domesticity to glide by her as sorry details, and had it not been for the children Darton's house would have seemed but little brighter than it had been before.

This led to occasional unpleasantness, until Darton sometimes declared to himself that such endeavours as his to rectify early deviations of the heart by harking back to the old point mostly failed of success. 'Perhaps Johns was right,' he would say. 'I should have gone on with Sally. Better go with the tide and make the best of its course than stem it at the risk of a capsize.' But he kept these unmelodious thoughts to himself, and was outwardly considerate and kind.

This somewhat barren tract of his life had extended to less than a year and a half when his ponderings were cut short by the loss of the woman they concerned. When she was in her grave he thought better of her than when she had been alive; the farm was a worse place without her than with her, after all. No woman short of divine could have gone through such an experience as hers with her first husband without becoming a little soured. Her stagnant sympathies, her sometimes unreasonable manner, had covered a heart frank and well-meaning, and originally hopeful and warm. She left him a tiny red infant in white wrappings. To make life as easy as possible to this touching object became at once his care.

As this child learnt to walk and talk Darton learnt to see feasibility in a scheme which pleased him. Revolving the experiment which he had hitherto made upon life, he fancied he had gained wisdom from his mistakes and caution from his miscarriages.

What the scheme was needs no penetration to discover. Once more he had opportunity to recast and rectify his ill-wrought situations by returning to Sally Hall, who still lived quietly on under her mother's roof at Hintock. Helena had been a woman to lend pathos and refinement to a home; Sally was the woman to brighten it. She would not, as Helena did, despise the rural simplicities of a farmer's fireside. Moreover, she had a pre-eminent qualification for Darton's household; no other woman could make so desirable a mother to her brother's two children and Darton's one as Sally — while Darton, now that Helena had gone, was a more promising husband for Sally than he had ever been when liable to reminders from an uncured sentimental wound.

Darton was not a man to act rapidly, and the working out of his reparative designs might have been delayed for some time. But there came a winter evening precisely like the one which had darkened over that former ride to Hintock, and he asked himself why he should postpone longer, when the very landscape called for a repetition of that attempt.

He told his man to saddle the mare, booted and spurred himself with a younger horseman's nicety, kissed the two youngest children, and rode off. To make the journey a complete parallel to the first, he would fain have had his old acquaintance Japheth Johns with him. But Johns, alas! was missing. His removal to the other side of the county had left unrepaired the breach which had arisen between him and Darton; and though Darton had forgiven him a hundred times, as Johns had probably forgiven Darton, the effort of reunion in present circumstances was one not likely to be made.

He screwed himself up to as cheerful a pitch as he could without his former crony, and became content with his own thoughts as he rode, instead of the words of a companion. The sun went down; the boughs appeared scratched in like an etching against the sky; old crooked men with faggots at their backs said 'Good-night, sir,' and Darton replied 'Good-night' right heartily.

By the time he reached the forking roads it was getting as dark as it had been on the occasion when Johns climbed the directing-post. Darton made no mistake this time. 'Nor shall I be able to mistake, thank Heaven, when I arrive,' he murmured. It gave him peculiar satisfaction to think that the proposed marriage, like his first, was of the nature of setting in order things long awry, and not a momentary freak of fancy.

Nothing hindered the smoothness of his journey, which seemed not half its former length. Though dark, it was only between five and six o'clock when the bulky chimneys of Mrs Hall's residence appeared in view behind the sycamore tree. On second thoughts he retreated and put up at the ale-house as in former time; and when he had plumed himself before the inn mirror, called for something to drink, and smoothed out the incipient wrinkles of care, he walked on to the Knap with a quick step.

v

That evening Sally was making 'pinners' for the milkers, who were now increased by two, for her mother and herself no longer joined in milking the cows themselves. But upon the whole there was little change in the household economy, and not much in its appearance, beyond such minor particulars as that the crack over the window, which had been a hundred years coming, was a trifle wider; that the beams were a shade blacker; that the influence of modernism had supplanted the open chimney-corner by a grate; that Rebekah, who had worn a cap when she had plenty of hair, had left it off now she had scarce any, because it was reported that caps were not fashionable; and that Sally's face had naturally assumed a more womanly and experienced cast.

Mrs Hall was actually lifting coals with the tongs, as she had used to do.

'Five years ago this very night, if I am not mistaken—' she said, laying on an ember.

'Not this very night – though 'twas one night this week,' said the correct Sally.

'Well, 'tis near enough. Five years ago Mr Darton came to marry you, and my poor boy Phil came home to die.' She sighed. 'Ah, Sally,' she presently said, 'if you had managed well Mr Darton would have had you, Helena or none.'

'Don't be sentimental about that, mother,' begged Sally. 'I didn't care to manage well in such a case. Though I liked him, I wasn't so anxious. I would never have married the man in the midst of such a hitch as that was,' she added with decision; 'and I don't think I would if he were to ask me now.'

'I am not sure about that, unless you have another in your eye.'

'I wouldn't; and I'll tell you why. I could hardly marry him for love at this time o' day. And as we've quite enough to live on if we give up the dairy to-morrow, I should have no need to marry for any meaner reason. . . . I am quite happy enough as I am, and there's an end of it.'

Now it was not long after his dialogue that there came a mild rap at the door, and in a moment there entered Rebekah, looking as though a ghost had arrived. The fact was that that accomplished skimmer and churner (now a resident in the house) had overheard the desultory observations between mother and daughter, and on opening the door to Mr Darton thought the coincidence must have a grisly meaning in it. Mrs Hall welcomed the farmer with warm surprise, as did Sally, and for a moment they rather wanted words.

'Can you push up the chimney-crook for me, Mr Darton? – the notches hitch,' said the matron. He did it, and the homely little act bridged over the awkward consciousness that he had been a stranger for four years.

Mrs Hall soon saw what he had come for, and left the principals together while she went to prepare him a late tea, smiling at Sally's recent hasty assertions of indifference, when she saw how civil Sally was. When tea was ready she joined them. She fancied that Darton did not look so confident as when he had arrived; but Sally was quite light-hearted, and the meal passed pleasantly.

About seven he took his leave of them. Mrs Hall went as far as the door to light him down the slope. On the doorstep he said frankly –

'I came to ask your daughter to marry me; chose the night and everything, with an eye to a favourable answer. But she won't.'

'Then she's a very ungrateful girl!' emphatically said Mrs Hall.

Darton paused to shape his sentence, and asked, 'I – I suppose there's nobody else more favoured?'

'I can't say that there is, or that there isn't,' answered Mrs Hall. 'She's private in some things. I'm on your side, however, Mr Darton, and I'll talk to her.'

'Thank 'ee, thank 'ee!' said the farmer in a gayer accent; and with this assurance the not very satisfactory visit came to an end. Darton descended the roots of the sycamore, the light was withdrawn, and the door closed. At the bottom of the slope he nearly ran against a man about to ascend.

'Can a jack-o'-lent believe his few senses on such a dark night, or can't he?' exclaimed one whose utterance Darton recognized in a moment, despite its unexpectedness. 'I dare not swear he can, though I fain would!' The speaker was Johns.

Darton said he was glad of this opportunity, bad as it was, of putting an end to the silence of years, and asked the dairyman what he was travelling that way for.

Japheth showed the old jovial confidence in a moment. 'I'm going to see your – relations – as they always seem to me,' he said – 'Mrs Hall and Sally. Well, Charles, the fact is I find the natural barbarousness of man is much increased by a bachelor life, and, as your leavings were always good enough for me, I'm trying civilization here.' He nodded towards the house.

'Not with Sally – to marry her?' said Darton, feeling something like a rill of ice water between his shoulders.

'Yes, by the help of Providence and my personal charms. And I think I shall get her. I am this road every week – my present dairy is only four miles off, you know, and I see her through the window. 'Tis rather odd that I was going to speak practical to-night to her for the first time. You've just called?'

'Yes, for a short while. But she didn't say a word about you.'

'A good sign, a good sign. Now that decides me. I'll swing the mallet and get her answer this very night as I planned.'

A few more remarks, and Darton, wishing his friend joy of Sally in a slightly hollow tone of jocularity, bade him good-bye. Johns promised to write particulars, and ascended, and was lost in the shade of the house and tree. A rectangle of light appeared when Johns was admitted, and all was dark again.

'Happy Japheth!' said Darton. 'This then is the explanation!'

He determined to return home that night. In a quarter of an hour he passed out of the village, and the next day went about his swede-lifting and storing as if nothing had occurred.

He waited and waited to hear from Johns whether the wedding-day was fixed: but no letter came. He learnt not a single particular till, meeting Johns one day at a horse-auction, Darton exclaimed genially – rather more genially than he felt – 'When is the joyful day to be?'

To his great surprise a reciprocity of gladness was not conspicuous in Johns. 'Not at all,' he said, in a very subdued tone. ' 'Tis a bad job; she won't have me.'

Darton held his breath till he said with treacherous solicitude, 'Try again – 'tis coyness.'

'O no,' said Johns decisively. 'There's been none of that. We talked it over dozens of times in the most fair and square way. She tells me plainly, I don't suit her. 'Twould be simply annoying her to ask her again. Ah, Charles, you threw a prize away when you let her slip five years ago.'

'I did – I did,' said Darton.

He returned from that auction with a new set of feelings in play. He had certainly made a surprising mistake in thinking Johns his successful rival. It really seemed as if he might hope for Sally after all.

This time, being rather pressed by business, Darton had recourse to pen-and-ink, and wrote her as manly and straightforward a proposal as any woman could wish to receive. The reply came promptly: —

'DEAR MR DARTON, — I am as sensible as any woman can be of the goodness that leads you to make me this offer a second time. Better women than I would be proud of the honour, for when I read your nice long speeches on mangold-wurzel, and such-like topics, at the Casterbridge Farmers' Club, I do feel it an honour, I assure you. But my answer is just the same as before. I will not try to explain what, in truth, I cannot explain — my reasons; I will simply say that I must decline to be married to you. With good wishes as in former times, I am, your faithful friend,

SALLY HALL'

Darton dropped the letter hopelessly. Beyond the negative, there was just a possibility of sarcasm in it — 'nice long speeches on mangold-wurzel' had a suspicious sound. However, sarcasm or none, there was the answer, and he had to be content.

He proceeded to seek relief in a business which at this time engrossed much of his attention — that of clearing up a curious mistake just current in the county, that he had been nearly ruined by the recent failure of a local bank. A farmer named Darton had lost heavily, and the similarity of name had probably led to the error. Belief in it was so persistent that it demanded several days of letter-writing to set matters straight, and persuade the world that he was as solvent as ever he had been in his life. He had hardly concluded this worrying task when, to his delight, another letter arrived in the handwriting of Sally.

Darton tore it open; it was very short.

'DEAR MR DARTON, — We have been so alarmed these last few days by the report that you were ruined by the stoppage of——'s Bank, that, now it is contradicted, I hasten, by my mother's wish, to say how truly glad we are to find there is no foundation for the report. After your kindness to my poor brother's children, I can do no less than write at such a moment. We had a letter from each of them a few days ago. — Your faithful friend,

SALLY HALL'

'Mercenary little woman!' said Darton to himself with a smile. 'Then that was the secret of her refusal this time — she thought I was ruined.'

Now, such was Darton, that as hours went on he could not help feeling too generously towards Sally to condemn her in this. What did he want in a wife? he asked himself. Love and integrity. What next? Worldly wisdom. And was there really more than worldly wisdom in her refusal to go aboard a sinking ship? She now knew it was otherwise. 'Begad,' he said, 'I'll try her again.'

The fact was he had so set his heart upon Sally, and Sally alone, that nothing was to be allowed to baulk him, and his reasoning was purely formal.

Anniversaries having been unpropitious, he waited on till a bright day late in May — a day when all animate nature was fancying, in its trusting, foolish way, that it was going to bask under blue sky for evermore. As he rode through Long-Ash Lane it was scarce recognizable as the track of his two winter journeys. No mistake could be made now, even with his eyes shut. The cuckoo's note was as its best, between April tentativeness and midsummer decrepitude, and the reptiles in the sun behaved as winningly as kittens on a hearth. Though afternoon, and about the same time as on the last occasion, it was broad day and sunshine when he entered Hintock, and the details of the Knap dairy-house were visible far up the road. He saw Sally in the garden, and was set vibrating. He had first intended to go on to the inn; but 'No,' he said; 'I'll tie my horse to the garden-gate. If all goes well it can soon be taken round; if not, I mount and ride away.'

The tall shade of the horseman darkened the room in which Mrs Hall sat, and made her start, for he had ridden by a side path to the top of the slope, where riders seldom came. In a few seconds he was in the garden with Sally.

Five – ay, three minutes – did the business at the back of that row of bees. Though spring had come and heavenly blue consecrated the scene, Darton succeeded not. 'No,' said Sally firmly. 'I will never, never marry you, Mr Darton. I would have done it once; but now I never can.'

'But—!' implored Mr Darton. And with a burst of real eloquence he went on to declare all sorts of things that he would do for her. He would drive her to see her mother every week – take her to London – settle so much money upon her – Heaven knows what he did not promise, suggest, and tempt her with. But it availed nothing. She interposed with a stout negative which closed the course of his argument like an iron gate across a highway. Darton paused.

'Then,' said he simply, 'you hadn't heard of my supposed failure when you declined last time?'

'I had not,' she said. 'That you believed me capable of refusing you for such a reason does not help your cause.'

'And 'tis not because of any soreness from my slighting you years ago?'

'No. That soreness is long past.'

'Ah – then you despise me, Sally!'

'No,' she slowly answered. 'I don't altogether despise you. I don't think you quite such a hero as I once did – that's all. The truth is, I am happy enough as I am, and I don't mean to marry at all. Now, may *I* ask a favour, sir?' She spoke with an ineffable charm, which, whenever he thought of it, made him curse his loss of her as long as he lived.

'To any extent.'

'Please do not put this question to me any more. Friends as long as you like, but lovers and married never.'

'I never will,' said Darton. 'Not if I live a hundred years.'

And he never did. That he had worn out his welcome in her heart was only too plain.

When his step-children had grown up and were placed out in life all communication between Darton and the Hall family ceased. It was only by chance that, years after, he learnt that Sally, notwithstanding the solicitations her attractions drew down upon her, had refused several offers of marriage, and steadily adhered to her purpose of leading a single life.

May 1884

The Distracted Preacher

SOMETHING delayed the arrival of the Wesleyan minister, and a young man
came temporarily in his stead. It was on the thirteenth of January 183— that Mr
Stockdale, the young man in question, made his humble entry into the village,
unknown, and almost unseen. But when those of the inhabitants who styled
themselves of his connection became acquainted with him, they were rather
pleased with the substitute than otherwise, though he had scarcely as yet acquired
ballast of character sufficient to steady the consciences of the hundred-and-forty
Methodists of pure blood who, at this time, lived in Nether-Moynton, and to give
in addition supplementary support to the mixed race which went to church in
the morning and chapel in the evening, or when there was a tea — as many as a
hundred-and-ten people more, all told, and including the parish-clerk in the
winter-time, when it was too dark for the vicar to observe who passed up the
street at seven o'clock — which, to be just to him, he was never anxious to do.

It was owing to this overlapping of creeds that the celebrated population-
puzzle arose among the denser gentry of the district around Nether-Moynton:
how could it be that a parish containing fifteen score of strong full-grown
Episcopalians, and nearly thirteen score of well-matured Dissenters, numbered
barely two-and-twenty score adults in all?

The young man being personally interesting, those with whom he came in
contact were content to waive for a while the graver question of his sufficiency. It
is said that at this time of his life his eyes were affectionate, though without a ray
of levity; that his hair was curly, and his figure tall; that he was, in short, a very
lovable youth, who won upon his female hearers as soon as they saw and heard
him, and caused them to say, 'Why didn't we know of this before he came, that we
might have gi'ed him a warmer welcome!'

The fact was that, knowing him to be only provisionally selected, and
expecting nothing remarkable in his person or doctrine, they and the rest of his
flock in Nether-Moynton had felt almost as indifferent about his advent as if they
had been the soundest church-going parishioners in the country, and he their true
and appointed parson. Thus when Stockdale set foot in the place nobody had
secured a lodging for him, and though his journey had given him a bad cold in the
head he was forced to attend to that business himself. On inquiry he learnt that
the only possible accommodation in the village would be found at the house of
one Mrs Lizzy Newberry, at the upper end of the street.

It was a youth who gave this information, and Stockdale asked him who Mrs
Newberry might be.

The boy said that she was a widow-woman, who had got no husband, because
he was dead. Mr Newberry, he added, had been a well-to-do man enough, as the
saying was, and a farmer; but he had gone off in a decline. As regarded Mrs

Newberry's serious side, Stockdale gathered that she was one of the trimmers who went to church and chapel both.

'I'll go there,' said Stockdale, feeling that, in the absence of purely sectarian lodgings, he could do no better.

'She's a little particular, and won't hae gover'ment folks, or curates, or the pa'son's friends, or such like,' said the lad dubiously.

'Ah, that may be a promising sign: I'll call. Or no; just you go up and ask first if she can find room for me. I have to see one or two persons on another matter. You will find me down at the carrier's.'

In a quarter of an hour the lad came back, and said that Mrs Newberry would have no objection to accommodate him, whereupon Stockdale called at the house. It stood within a garden-hedge, and seemed to be roomy and comfortable. He saw an elderly woman, with whom he made arrangements to come the same night, since there was no inn in the place, and he wished to house himself as soon as possible; the village being a local centre from which he was to radiate at once to the different small chapels in the neighbourhood. He forthwith sent his luggage to Mrs Newberry's from the carrier's, where he had taken shelter, and in the evening walked up to his temporary home.

As he now lived there, Stockdale felt it unnecessary to knock at the door, and entering quietly he had the pleasure of hearing footsteps scudding away like mice into the back quarters. He advanced to the parlour, as the front room was called, though its stone floor was scarcely disguised by the carpet, which only overlaid the trodden areas, leaving sandy deserts under the furniture. But the room looked snug and cheerful. The firelight shone out brightly, trembling on the bulging mouldings of the table-legs, playing with brass knobs and handles, and lurking in great strength on the under surface of the chimney-piece. A deep armchair, covered with horsehair, and studded with a countless throng of brass nails, was pulled up on one side of the fireplace. The tea-things were on the table, the teapot cover was open, and a little handbell had been laid at that precise point towards which a person seated in the great chair might be expected instinctively to stretch his hand.

Stockdale sat down, not objecting to his experience of the room thus far, and began his residence by tinkling the bell. A little girl crept in at the summons, and made tea for him. Her name, she said, was Marther Sarer, and she lived out there, nodding towards the road and village generally. Before Stockdale had got far with his meal a tap sounded on the door behind him, and on his telling the inquirer to come in, a rustle of garments caused him to turn his head. He saw before him a fine and extremely well-made young woman, with dark hair, a wide, sensible, beautiful forehead, eyes that warmed him before he knew it, and a mouth that was in itself a picture to all appreciative souls.

'Can I get you anything else for tea?' she said, coming forward a step or two, an expression of liveliness on her features, and her hand waving the door by its edge.

'Nothing, thank you,' said Stockdale, thinking less of what he replied than of what might be her relation to the household.

'You are quite sure?' said the young woman, apparently aware that he had not considered his answer.

He conscientiously examined the tea-things, and found them all there. 'Quite sure, Miss Newberry,' he said.

'It is Mrs Newberry,' she said. 'Lizzy Newberry. I used to be Lizzy Simp-kins.'

'O, I beg your pardon, Mrs Newberry.' And before he had occasion to say more she left the room.

Stockdale remained in some doubt till Martha Sarah came to clear the table. 'Whose house is this, my little woman?' said he.

'Mrs Lizzy Newberry's, sir.'

'Then Mrs Newberry is not the old lady I saw this afternoon?'

'No. That's Mrs Newberry's mother. It was Mrs Newberry who comed in to you just by now, because she wanted to see if you was good-looking.'

Later in the evening, when Stockdale was about to begin supper, she came again. 'I have come myself, Mr Stockdale,' she said. The minister stood up in acknowledgment of the honour. 'I am afraid little Marther might not make you understand. What will you have for supper? – there's cold rabbit, and there's a ham uncut.'

Stockdale said he could get on nicely with those viands, and supper was laid. He had no more than cut a slice when tap-tap came to the door again. The minister had already learnt that this particular rhythm in taps denoted the fingers of his enkindling landlady, and the doomed young fellow buried his first mouthful under a look of receptive blandness.

'We have a chicken in the house, Mr Stockdale – I quite forgot to mention it just now. Perhaps you would like Marther Sarer to bring it up?'

Stockdale had advanced far enough in the art of being a young man to say that he did not want the chicken, unless she brought it up herself; but when it was uttered he blushed at the daring gallantry of the speech, perhaps a shade too strong for a serious man and a minister. In three minutes the chicken appeared, but, to his great surprise, only in the hands of Martha Sarah. Stockdale was disappointed, which perhaps it was intended that he should be.

He had finished supper, and was not in the least anticipating Mrs Newberry again that night, when she tapped and entered as before. Stockdale's gratified look told that she had lost nothing by not appearing when expected. It happened that the cold in the head from which the young man suffered had increased with the approach of night, and before she had spoken he was seized with a violent fit of sneezing which he could not anyhow repress.

Mrs Newberry looked full of pity. 'Your cold is very bad to-night, Mr Stockdale.'

Stockdale replied that it was rather troublesome.

'And I've a good mind—' she added archly, looking at the cheerless glass of water on the table, which the abstemious minister was going to drink.

'Yes, Mrs Newberry?'

'I've a good mind that you should have something more likely to cure it than that cold stuff.'

'Well,' said Stockdale, looking down at the glass, 'as there is no inn here, and nothing better to be got in the village, of course it will do.'

To this she replied, 'There is something better, not far off, though not in the house. I really think you must try it, or you may be ill. Yes, Mr Stockdale, you shall.' She held up her finger, seeing that he was about to speak. 'Don't ask what it is; wait, and you shall see.'

Lizzy went away, and Stockdale waited in a pleasant mood. Presently she returned with her bonnet and cloak on, saying, 'I am so sorry, but you must help me to get it. Mother has gone to bed. Will you wrap yourself up, and come this way, and please bring that cup with you?'

Stockdale, a lonely young fellow, who had for weeks felt a great craving for somebody on whom to throw away superfluous interest, and even tenderness, was not sorry to join her, and followed his guide through the back door across the garden, to the bottom, where the boundary was a wall. This wall was low, and beyond it Stockdale discerned in the night shades several grey headstones, and the outlines of the church roof and tower.

'It is easy to get up this way,' she said, stepping upon a bank which abutted on the wall; then putting her foot on the top of the stonework, and descending by a spring inside, where the ground was much higher, as is the manner of graveyards to be. Stockdale did the same, and followed her in the dusk across the irregular ground till they came to the tower door, which, when they had entered, she softly closed behind them.

'You can keep a secret?' she said, in a musical voice.

'Like an iron chest!' said he fervently.

Then from under her cloak she produced a small lighted lantern, which the minister had not noticed that she carried at all. The light showed them to be close to the singing-gallery stairs, under which lay a heap of lumber of all sorts, but consisting mostly of decayed framework, pews, panels, and pieces of flooring, that from time to time had been removed from their original fixings in the body of the edifice and replaced by new.

'Perhaps you will drag some of those boards aside?' she said, holding the lantern over her head to light him better. 'Or will you take the lantern while I move them?'

'I can manage it,' said the young man, and acting as she ordered, he uncovered, to his surprise, a row of little barrels bound with wood hoops, each barrel being about as large as the nave of a heavy waggon-wheel. When they were laid open Lizzy fixed her eyes on him, as if she wondered what he would say.

'You know what they are?' she asked, finding that he did not speak.

'Yes, barrels,' said Stockdale simply. He was an inland man, the son of highly respectable parents, and brought up with a single eye to the ministry, and the sight suggested nothing beyond the fact that such articles were there.

'You are quite right, they are barrels,' she said, in an emphatic tone of candour that was not without a touch of irony.

Stockdale looked at her with an eye of sudden misgiving. 'Not smugglers' liquor?' he said.

'Yes,' said she. 'They are tubs of spirit that have accidentally floated over in the dark from France.'

In Nether-Moynton and its vicinity at this date people always smiled at the sort of sin called in the outside world illicit trading; and these little kegs of gin and brandy were as well known to the inhabitants as turnips. So that Stockdale's innocent ignorance, and his look of alarm when he guessed the sinister mystery, seemed to strike Lizzy first as ludicrous, and then as very awkward for the good impression that she wished to produce upon him.

'Smuggling is carried on here by some of the people,' she said in a gentle, apologetic voice. 'It has been their practice for generations, and they think it no harm. Now, will you roll out one of the tubs?'

'What to do with it?' said the minister.

'To draw a little from it to cure your cold,' she answered. 'It is so 'nation strong that it drives away that sort of thing in a jiffy. O, it is all right about our taking it. I may have what I like; the owner of the tubs says so. I ought to have had some in the house, and then I shouldn't ha' been put to this trouble; but I drink none myself, and so I often forget to keep it indoors.'

'You are allowed to help yourself, I suppose, that you may not inform where their hiding-place is?'

'Well, no; not that particularly; but I may take any if I want it. So help yourself.'

'I will, to oblige you, since you have a right to it,' murmured the minister; and though he was not quite satisfied with his part in the performance, he rolled one of the 'tubs' out from the corner into the middle of the tower floor. 'How do you wish me to get it out — with a gimlet, I suppose?'

'No, I'll show you,' said his interesting companion; and she held up with her other hand a shoemaker's awl and a hammer. 'You must never do these things with a gimlet, because the wood-dust gets in; and when the buyers pour out the brandy that would tell them that the tub had been broached. An awl makes no dust, and the hole nearly closes up again. Now tap one of the hoops forward.'

Stockdale took the hammer and did so.

'Now make the hole in the part that was covered by the hoop.'

He made the hole as directed. 'It won't run out,' he said.

'O yes it will,' said she. 'Take the tub between your knees, and squeeze the heads; and I'll hold the cup.'

Stockdale obeyed; and the pressure taking effect upon the tub, which seemed to be thin, the spirit spirted out in a stream. When the cup was full he ceased pressing, and the flow immediately stopped. 'Now we must fill up the keg with water,' said Lizzy, 'or it will cluck like forty hens when it is handled, and show that 'tis not full.'

'But they tell you you may take it?'

'Yes, the *smugglers*; but the *buyers* must not know that the smugglers have been kind to me at their expense.'

'I see,' said Stockdale doubtfully. 'I much question the honesty of this proceeding.'

By her direction he held the tub with the hole upwards, and while he went through the process of alternately pressing and ceasing to press, she produced a bottle of water, from which she took mouthfuls, conveying each to the keg by putting her pretty lips to the hole, where it was sucked in at each recovery of the cask from pressure. When it was again full he plugged the hole, knocked the hoop down to its place, and buried the tub in the lumber as before.

'Aren't the smugglers afraid that you will tell?' he asked, as they recrossed the churchyard.

'O no; they are not afraid of that. I couldn't do such a thing.'

'They have put you into a very awkward corner,' said Stockdale emphatically. 'You must, of course, as an honest person, sometimes feel that it is your duty to inform — really you must.'

'Well, I have never particularly felt it as a duty; and, besides, my first husband—' She stopped, and there was some confusion in her voice. Stockdale was so honest and unsophisticated that he did not at once discern why she paused: but at last he did perceive that the words were a slip, and that no woman would have uttered 'first husband' by accident unless she had thought pretty frequently of a second. He felt for her confusion, and allowed her time to recover and proceed. 'My husband,' she said, in a self-corrected tone, 'used to know of their doings, and so did my father, and kept the secret. I cannot inform, in fact, against anybody.'

'I see the hardness of it,' he continued, like a man who looked far into the moral of things. 'And it is very cruel that you should be tossed and tantalized between your memories and your conscience. I do hope, Mrs Newberry, that you will soon see your way out of this unpleasant position.'

'Well, I don't just now,' she murmured.

By this time they had passed over the wall and entered the house, where she brought him a glass and hot water, and left him to his own reflections. He looked after her vanishing form, asking himself whether he, as a respectable man, and a minister, and a shining light, even though as yet only of the halfpenny-candle sort, were quite justified in doing this thing. A sneeze settled the question; and he found that when the fiery liquid was lowered by the addition of twice or thrice the quantity of water, it was one of the prettiest cures for a cold in the head that he had ever known, particularly at this chilly time of the year.

Stockdale sat in the deep chair about twenty minutes sipping and meditating, till he at length took warmer views of things, and longed for the morrow, when he would see Mrs Newberry again. He then felt that, though chronologically at a short distance, it would in an emotional sense be very long before to-morrow came, and walked restlessly round the room. His eye was attracted by a framed and glazed sampler in which a running ornament of fir-trees and peacocks surrounded the following pretty bit of sentiment: —

> 'Rose-leaves smell when roses thrive,
> Here's my work while I'm alive;
> Rose-leaves smell when shrunk and shed,
> Here's my work when I am dead.

> 'Lizzy Simpkins. Fear God. Honour the King.
> Aged 11 years.'

''Tis hers,' he said to himself. 'Heavens, how I like that name!'

Before he had done thinking that no other name from Abigail to Zenobia would have suited his young landlady so well, tap-tap came again upon the door; and the minister started as her face appeared yet another time, looking so disinterested that the most ingenious would have refrained from asserting that she had come to affect his feelings by her seductive eyes.

'Would you like a fire in your room, Mr Stockdale, on account of your cold?'

The minister, being still a little pricked in the conscience for countenancing her in watering the spirits, saw here a way to self-chastisement. 'No, I thank you,' he said firmly; 'it is not necessary. I have never been used to one in my life, and it would be giving way to luxury too far.'

'Then I won't insist,' she said, and disconcerted him by vanishing instantly.

Wondering if she was vexed by his refusal, he wished that he had chosen to have a fire, even though it should have scorched him out of bed and endangered his self-discipline for a dozen days. However, he consoled himself with what was in truth a rare consolation for a budding lover, that he was under the same roof with Lizzy; her guest, in fact, to take a poetical view of the term lodger; and that he would certainly see her on the morrow.

The morrow came, and Stockdale rose early, his cold quite gone. He had never in his life so longed for the breakfast-hour as he did that day, and punctually at eight o'clock, after a short walk to reconnoitre the premises, he re-entered the door of his dwelling. Breakfast passed, and Martha Sarah attended, but nobody came voluntarily as on the night before to inquire if there were other wants which he had not mentioned, and which she would attempt to gratify. He was disappointed, and went out, hoping to see her at dinner. Dinner-time came; he sat down to the meal, finished it, lingered on for a whole hour, although two new teachers were at that moment waiting at the chapel-door to speak to him by appointment. It was useless to wait longer, and he slowly went his way down the lane, cheered by the thought that, after all, he would see her in the evening, and perhaps engage again in the delightful tub-broaching in the neighbouring church tower, which proceeding he resolved to render more moral by steadfastly insisting that no water should be introduced to fill up, though the tub should cluck like all the hens in Christendom. But nothing could disguise the fact that it was a queer business; and his countenance fell when he thought how much more his mind was interested in that matter than in his serious duties.

However, compunction vanished with the decline of day. Night came, and his tea and supper; but no Lizzy Newberry, and no sweet temptations. At last the minister could bear it no longer, and said to his quaint little attendant, 'Where is Mrs Newberry to-day?' judiciously handing a penny as he spoke.

'She's busy,' said Martha.

'Anything serious happened?' he asked, handing another penny, and revealing yet additional pennies in the background.

'O no—nothing at all!' said she, with breathless confidence. 'Nothing ever happens to her. She's only biding upstairs in bed because 'tis her way sometimes.'

Being a young man of some honour he would not question further, and assuming that Lizzy must have a bad headache, or other slight ailment, in spite of what the girl had said, he went to bed dissatisfied, not even setting eyes on old Mrs Simpkins. 'I said last night that I should see her to-morrow,' he reflected; 'but that was not to be!'

Next day he had better fortune, or worse, meeting her at the foot of the stairs in the morning, and being favoured by a visit or two from her during the day—once for the purpose of making kindly inquiries about his comfort, as on the first evening, and at another time to place a bunch of winter-violets on his table, with a promise to renew them when they drooped. On these occasions there was something in her smile which showed how conscious she was of the effect she produced, though it must be said that it was rather a humorous than a designing consciousness, and savoured more of pride than of vanity.

As for Stockdale, he clearly perceived that he possessed unlimited capacity for backsliding, and wished that tutelary saints were not denied to Dissenters. He set a watch upon his tongue and eyes for the space of one hour and a half, after which he found it was useless to struggle further, and gave himself up to the situation. 'The other minister will be here in a month,' he said to himself when sitting over the fire. 'Then I shall be off, and she will distract my mind no more! . . . And then, shall I go on living by myself for ever? No; when my two years of probation are finished, I shall have a furnished house to live in, with a varnished door and a brass knocker; and I'll march straight back to her, and ask her flat, as soon as the last plate is on the dresser!'

Thus a titillating fortnight was passed by young Stockdale, during which time things proceeded much as such matters have done ever since the beginning of history. He saw the object of attachment several times one day, did not see her at all the next, met her when he least expected to do so, missed her when hints and signs as to where she should be at a given hour almost amounted to an appointment. This mild coquetry was perhaps fair enough under the circumstances of their being so closely lodged, and Stockdale put up with it as philosophically as he was able. Being in her own house she could, after vexing him or disappointing him of her presence, easily win him back by suddenly surrounding him with those little attentions which her position as his landlady put it in her power to bestow. When he had waited indoors half the day to see her, and on finding that she would not be seen, had gone off in a huff to the dreariest and dampest walk he could discover, she would restore equilibrium in the evening with 'Mr Stockdale, I have fancied you must feel draught o' nights from your bedroom window, and so I have been putting up thicker curtains this afternoon while you were out'; or, 'I noticed that you sneezed twice again this morning, Mr Stockdale. Depend upon it that cold is hanging about you yet; I am sure it is − I have thought of it continually; and you must let me make a posset for you.'

Sometimes in coming home he found his sitting-room rearranged, chairs placed where the table had stood, and the table ornamented with the few fresh flowers and leaves that could be obtained at this season, so as to add a novelty to the room. At times she would be standing on a chair outside the house, trying to nail up a branch of the monthly rose which the winter wind had blown down; and of course he stepped forward to assist her, when their hands got mixed in passing the shreds and nails. Thus they became friends again after a disagreement. She would utter on these occasions some pretty and deprecatory remark on the necessity of her troubling him anew; and he would straightway say that he would do a hundred times as much for her if she should so require.

II. HOW HE SAW TWO OTHER MEN

Matters being in this advancing state, Stockdale was rather surprised one cloudy evening, while sitting in his room, at hearing her speak in low tones of expostulation to some one at the door. It was nearly dark, but the shutters were not yet closed, nor the candles lighted; and Stockdale was tempted to stretch his head towards the window. He saw outside the door a young man in clothes of a whitish colour, and upon reflection judged their wearer to be the well-built and rather handsome miller who lived below. The miller's voice was alternately low and firm, and sometimes it reached the level of positive entreaty; but what the words were Stockdale could in no way hear.

Before the colloquy had ended, the minister's attention was attracted by a second incident. Opposite Lizzy's home grew a clump of laurels, forming a thick and permanent shade. One of the laurel boughs now quivered against the light background of sky, and in a moment the head of a man peered out, and remained still. He seemed to be also much interested in the conversation at the door, and was plainly lingering there to watch and listen. Had Stockdale stood in any other relation to Lizzy than that of a lover, he might have gone out and investigated the meaning of this: but being as yet but an unprivileged ally, he did nothing more than stand up and show himself against the firelight, whereupon the listener disappeared, and Lizzy and the miller spoke in lower tones.

Stockdale was made so uneasy by the circumstance, that as soon as the miller was gone, he said, 'Mrs Newberry, are you aware that you were watched just now, and your conversation heard?'

'When?' she said.

'When you were talking to that miller. A man was looking from the laurel-tree as jealously as if he could have eaten you.'

She showed more concern than the trifling event seemed to demand, and he added, 'Perhaps you were talking of things you did not wish to be overheard?'

'I was talking only on business,' she said.

'Lizzy, be frank!' said the young man. 'If it was only on business, why should anybody wish to listen to you?'

She looked curiously at him. 'What else do you think it could be, then?'

'Well – the only talk between a young woman and man that is likely to amuse an eavesdropper.'

'Ah yes,' she said, smiling in spite of her preoccupation. 'Well, my cousin Owlett has spoken to me about matrimony, every now and then, that's true; but he was not speaking of it then. I wish he had been speaking of it, with all my heart. It would have been much less serious for me.'

'O Mrs Newberry!'

'It would. Not that I should ha' chimed in with him, of course. I wish it for other reasons. I am glad, Mr Stockdale, that you have told me of that listener. It is a timely warning, and I must see my cousin again.'

'But don't go away till I have spoken,' said the minister. 'I'll out with it at once, and make no more ado. Let it be Yes or No between us, Lizzy; please do!' And he held out his hand, in which she freely allowed her own to rest, but without speaking.

'You mean Yes by that?' he asked, after waiting a while.

'You may be my sweetheart, if you will.'

'Why not say at once you will wait for me until I have a house and can come back to marry you.'

'Because I am thinking – thinking of something else,' she said with embarrassment. 'It all comes upon me at once, and I must settle one thing at a time.'

'At any rate, dear Lizzy, you can assure me that the miller shall not be allowed to speak to you except on business? You have never directly encouraged him?'

She parried the question by saying, 'You see, he and his party have been in the habit of leaving things on my premises sometimes, and as I have not denied him, it makes him rather forward.'

'Things – what things?'

'Tubs – they are called Things here.'

'But why don't you deny him, my dear Lizzy?'

'I cannot well.'

'You are too timid. It is unfair of him to impose so upon you, and get your good name into danger by his smuggling tricks. Promise me that the next time he wants to leave his tubs here you will let me roll them into the street?'

She shook her head. 'I would not venture to offend the neighbours so much as that,' said she, 'or do anything that would be so likely to put poor Owlett into the hands of the Customs-men.'

Stockdale sighed, and said that he thought hers a mistaken generosity when it extended to assisting those who cheated the king of his dues. 'At any rate, you will let me make him keep his distance as your lover, and tell him flatly that you are not for him?'

'Please not, at present,' she said. 'I don't wish to offend my old neighbours. It is not only Mr Owlett who is concerned.'

'This is too bad,' said Stockdale impatiently.

'On my honour, I won't encourage him as my lover,' Lizzy answered earnestly. 'A reasonable man will be satisfied with that.'

'Well, so I am,' said Stockdale, his countenance clearing.

III. THE MYSTERIOUS GREATCOAT

Stockdale now began to notice more particularly a feature in the life of his fair landlady, which he had casually observed but scarcely ever thought of before. It was that she was markedly irregular in her hours of rising. For a week or two she would be tolerably punctual, reaching the ground-floor within a few minutes of half-past seven. Then suddenly she would not be visible till twelve at noon, perhaps for three or four days in succession; and twice he had certain proof that she did not leave her room till half-past three in the afternoon. The second time that this extreme lateness came under his notice was on a day when he had particularly wished to consult with her about his future movements; and he concluded, as he always had done, that she had a cold, headache, or other ailment, unless she had kept herself invisible to avoid meeting and talking to him, which he could hardly believe. The former supposition was disproved, however, by her innocently saying, some days later, when they were speaking on a question of health, that she had never had a moment's heaviness, headache, or illness of any kind since the previous January twelvemonth.

'I am glad to hear it,' said he. 'I thought quite otherwise.'

'What, do I look sickly?' she asked, turning up her face to show the impossibility of his gazing on it and holding such a belief for a moment.

'Not at all; I merely thought so from your being sometimes obliged to keep your room through the best part of the day.'

'O, as for that – it means nothing,' she murmured, with a look which some might have called cold, and which was the worst look that he liked to see upon her. 'It is pure sleepiness, Mr Stockdale.'

'Never!'

'It is, I tell you. When I stay in my room till half-past three in the afternoon, you may always be sure that I slept soundly till three, or I shouldn't have stayed there.'

'It is dreadful,' said Stockdale, thinking of the disastrous effects of such indulgence upon the household of a minister, should it become a habit of everyday occurrence.

'But then,' she said, divining his good and prescient thoughts, 'it only happens when I stay awake all night. I don't go to sleep till five or six in the morning sometimes.'

'Ah, that's another matter,' said Stockdale. 'Sleeplessness to such an alarming extent is real illness. Have you spoken to a doctor?'

'O no – there is no need for doing that – it is all natural to me.' And she went away without further remark.

Stockdale might have waited a long time to know the real cause of her sleeplessness, had it not happened that one dark night he was sitting in his bedroom jotting down notes for a sermon, which occupied him perfunctorily for a considerable time after the other members of the household had retired. He did not get to bed till one o'clock. Before he had fallen asleep he heard a knocking at the front door, first rather timidly performed, and then louder. Nobody answered it, and the person knocked again. As the house still remained undisturbed, Stockdale got out of bed, went to his window, which overlooked the door, and opening it, asked who was there.

A young woman's voice replied that Susan Wallis was there, and that she had come to ask if Mrs Newberry could give her some mustard to make a plaster with, as her father was taken very ill on the chest.

The minister, having neither bell nor servant, was compelled to act in person. 'I will call Mrs Newberry,' he said. Partly dressing himself, he went along the passage and tapped at Lizzy's door. She did not answer, and, thinking of her erratic habits in the matter of sleep, he thumped the door persistently, when he discovered, by its moving ajar under his knocking, that it had only been gently pushed to. As there was now a sufficient entry for the voice, he knocked no longer, but said in firm tones, 'Mrs Newberry, you are wanted.'

The room was quite silent; not a breathing, not a rustle, came from any part of it. Stockdale now sent a positive shout through the open space of the door: 'Mrs Newberry!' – still no answer, or movement of any kind within. Then he heard sounds from the opposite room, that of Lizzy's mother, as if she had been aroused by his uproar though Lizzy had not, and was dressing herself hastily. Stockdale softly closed the younger woman's door and went on to the other, which was opened by Mrs Simpkins before he could reach it. She was in her ordinary clothes, and had a light in her hand.

'What's the person calling about?' she said in alarm.

Stockdale told the girl's errand, adding seriously, 'I cannot wake Mrs Newberry.'

'It is no matter,' said her mother. 'I can let the girl have what she wants as well as my daughter.' And she came out of the room and went downstairs.

Stockdale retired towards his own apartment, saying, however, to Mrs Simpkins from the landing, as if on second thoughts, 'I suppose there is nothing the matter with Mrs Newberry, that I could not wake her?'

'O no,' said the old lady hastily. 'Nothing at all.'

Still the minister was not satisfied. 'Will you go in and see?' he said. 'I should be much more at ease.'

Mrs Simpkins returned up the staircase, went to her daughter's room, and came out again almost instantly. 'There is nothing at all the matter with Lizzy,' she said; and descended again to attend to the applicant, who, having seen the light, had remained quiet during this interval.

Stockdale went into his room and lay down as before. He heard Lizzy's mother open the front door, admit the girl, and then the murmured discourse of both as they went to the store-cupboard for the medicament required. The girl departed, the door was fastened, Mrs Simpkins came upstairs, and the house was again in silence. Still the minister did not fall asleep. He could not get rid of a singular suspicion, which was all the more harassing in being, if true, the most unaccountable thing within his experience. That Lizzy Newberry was in her bedroom when he made such a clamour at the door he could not possibly convince himself, notwithstanding that he had heard her come upstairs at the usual time, go into her chamber, and shut herself up in the usual way. Yet all reason was so much against her being elsewhere, that he was constrained to go back again to the unlikely theory of a heavy sleep, though he had heard neither breath nor movement during a shouting and knocking loud enough to rouse the Seven Sleepers.

Before coming to any positive conclusion he fell asleep himself, and did not awake till day. He saw nothing of Mrs Newberry in the morning, before he went out to meet the rising sun, as he liked to do when the weather was fine; but as this was by no means unusual, he took no notice of it. At breakfast-time he knew that she was not far off by hearing her in the kitchen, and though he saw nothing of her person, that back apartment being rigorously closed against his eyes, she seemed to be talking, ordering, and bustling about among the pots and skimmers in so ordinary a manner, that there was no reason for his wasting more time in fruitless surmise.

The minister suffered from these distractions, and his extemporized sermons were not improved thereby. Already he often said Romans for Corinthians in the pulpit, and gave out hymns in strange cramped metres, that hitherto had always been skipped, because the congregation could not raise a tune to fit them. He fully resolved that as soon as his few weeks of stay approached their end he would cut the matter short, and commit himself by proposing a definite engagement, repenting at leisure if necessary.

With this end in view, he suggested to her on the evening after her mysterious sleep that they should take a walk together just before dark, the latter part of the proposition being introduced that they might return home unseen. She consented to go; and away they went over a stile, to a shrouded footpath suited for the occasion. But, in spite of attempts on both sides, they were unable to infuse much spirit into the ramble. She looked rather paler than usual, and sometimes turned her head away.

'Lizzy,' said Stockdale reproachfully, when they had walked in silence a long distance.

'Yes,' said she.

'You yawned — much my company is to you!' He put it in that way, but he was really wondering whether her yawn could possibly have more to do with physical weariness from the night before than mental weariness of that present moment. Lizzy apologized, and owned that she was rather tired, which gave him an opening for a direct question on the point; but his modesty would not allow him to put it to her; and he uncomfortably resolved to wait.

The month of February passed with alternations of mud and frost, rain and sleet, east winds and north-westerly gales. The hollow places in the ploughed fields showed themselves as pools of water, which had settled there from the higher levels, and had not yet found time to soak away. The birds began to get lively, and a single thrush came just before sunset each evening, and sang hopefully on the large elm-tree which stood nearest to Mrs Newberry's house. Cold blasts and brittle earth had given place to an oozing dampness more unpleasant in itself than frost; but it suggested coming spring, and its unpleasantness was of a bearable kind.

Stockdale had been going to bring about a practical understanding with Lizzy at least half a dozen times; but, what with the mystery of her apparent absence on the night of the neighbour's call, and her curious way of lying in bed at unaccountable times, he felt a check within him whenever he wanted to speak out. Thus they still lived on as indefinitely affianced lovers, each of whom hardly acknowledged the other's claim to the name of chosen one. Stockdale persuaded himself that his hesitation was owing to the postponement of the ordained minister's arrival, and the consequent delay in his own departure, which did away with all necessity for haste in his courtship; but perhaps it was only that his discretion was reasserting itself, and telling him that he had better get clearer ideas of Lizzy before arranging for the grand contract of his life with her. She, on her part, always seemed ready to be urged further on that question than he had hitherto attempted to go; but she was none the less independent, and to a degree which would have kept from flagging the passion of a far more mutable man.

On the evening of the first of March he went casually into his bedroom about dusk, and noticed lying on a chair a greatcoat, hat, and breeches. Having no recollection of leaving any clothes of his own in that spot, he went and examined them as well as he could in the twilight, and found that they did not belong to him. He paused for a moment to consider how they might have got there. He was the only man living in the house; and yet these were not his garments, unless he had made a mistake. No, they were not his. He called up Martha Sarah.

'How did these things come in my room?' he said, flinging the objectionable articles to the floor.

Martha said that Mrs Newberry had given them to her to brush, and that she had brought them up there thinking they must be Mr Stockdale's, as there was no other gentleman a-lodging there.

'Of course you did,' said Stockdale. 'Now take them down to your mis'ess, and say they are some clothes I have found here and know nothing about.'

As the door was left open he heard the conversation downstairs. 'How stupid!' said Mrs Newberry, in a tone of confusion. 'Why, Marther Sarer, I did not tell you to take 'em to Mr Stockdale's room!'

'I thought they must be his as they was so muddy,' said Martha humbly.

'You should have left 'em on the clothes-horse,' said the young mistress severely; and she came upstairs with the garments on her arm, quickly passed

Stockdale's room, and threw them forcibly into a closet at the end of a passage. With this the incident ended, and the house was silent again.

There would have been nothing remarkable in finding such clothes in a widow's house had they been clean; or moth-eaten, or creased, or mouldy from long lying by; but that they should be splashed with recent mud bothered Stockdale a good deal. When a young pastor is in the aspen stage of attachment, and open to agitation at the merest trifles, a really substantial incongruity of this complexion is a disturbing thing. However, nothing further occurred at that time; but he became watchful, and given to conjecture, and was unable to forget the circumstance.

One morning, on looking from his window, he saw Mrs Newberry herself brushing the tails of a long drab greatcoat, which, if he mistook not, was the very same garment as the one that had adorned the chair of his room. It was densely splashed up to the hollow of the back with neighbouring Nether-Moynton mud, to judge by its colour, the spots being distinctly visible to him in the sunlight. The previous day or two having been wet, the inference was irresistible that the wearer had quite recently been walking some considerable distance about the lanes and fields. Stockdale opened the window and looked out, and Mrs Newberry turned her head. Her face became slowly red; she never had looked prettier, or more incomprehensible. He waved his hand affectionately, and said good-morning; she answered with embarrassment, having ceased her occupation on the instant that she saw him, and rolled up the coat half-cleaned.

Stockdale shut the window. Some simple explanation of her proceeding was doubtless within the bounds of possibility; but he himself could not think of one; and he wished that she had placed the matter beyond conjecture by voluntarily saying something about it there and then.

But, though Lizzy had not offered an explanation at the moment, the subject was brought forward by her at the next time of their meeting. She was chatting to him concerning some other event, and remarked that it happened about the time when she was dusting some old clothes that had belonged to her poor husband.

'You keep them clean out of respect to his memory?' said Stockdale tentatively.

'I air and dust them sometimes,' she said, with the most charming innocence in the world.

'Do dead men come out of their graves and walk in mud?' murmured the minister, in a cold sweat at the deception that she was practising.

'What did you say?' asked Lizzy.

'Nothing, nothing,' said he mournfully. 'Mere words – a phrase that will do for my sermon next Sunday.' It was too plain that Lizzy was unaware that he had seen fresh pedestrian splashes upon the skirts of the tell-tale overcoat, and that she imagined him to believe it had come direct from some chest or drawer.

The aspect of the case was now considerably darker. Stockdale was so much depressed by it that he did not challenge her explanation, or threaten to go off as a missionary to benighted islanders, or reproach her in any way whatever. He simply parted from her when she had done talking, and lived on in perplexity, till by degrees his natural manner became sad and constrained.

IV. AT THE TIME OF THE NEW MOON

The following Thursday was changeable, damp, and gloomy; and the night threatened to be windy and unpleasant. Stockdale had gone away to Knollsea in the morning, to be present at some commemoration service there, and on his return he was met by the attractive Lizzy in the passage. Whether influenced by the tide of cheerfulness which had attended him that day, or by the drive through the open air, or whether from a natural disposition to let bygones alone, he allowed himself to be fascinated into forgetfulness of the greatcoat incident, and upon the whole passed a pleasant evening; not so much in her society as within sound of her voice, as she sat talking in the back parlour to her mother, till the latter went to bed. Shortly after this Mrs Newberry retired, and then Stockdale prepared to go upstairs himself. But before he left the room he remained standing by the dying embers a while, thinking long of one thing and another; and was only aroused by the flickering of his candle in the socket as it suddenly declined and went out. Knowing that there were a tinder-box, matches, and another candle in his bedroom, he felt his way upstairs without a light. On reaching his chamber he laid his hand on every possible ledge and corner for the tinder-box, but for a long time in vain. Discovering it at length, Stockdale produced a spark, and was kindling the brimstone, when he fancied that he heard a movement in the passage. He blew harder at the lint, the match flared up, and looking by aid of the blue light through the door, which had been standing open all this time, he was surprised to see a male figure vanishing round the top of the staircase with the evident intention of escaping unobserved. The personage wore the clothes which Lizzy had been brushing, and something in the outline and gait suggested to the minister that the wearer was Lizzy herself.

But he was not sure of this; and, greatly excited, Stockdale determined to investigate the mystery, and to adopt his own way for doing it. He blew out the match without lighting the candle, went into the passage, and proceeded on tiptoe towards Lizzy's room. A faint gray square of light in the direction of the chamber-window as he approached told him that the door was open, and at once suggested that the occupant was gone. He turned and brought down his fist upon the handrail of the staircase: 'It was she; in her late husband's coat and hat!'

Somewhat relieved to find that there was no intruder in the case, yet none the less surprised, the minister crept down the stairs, softly put on his boots, overcoat, and hat, and tried the front door. It was fastened as usual; he went to the back door, found this unlocked, and emerged into the garden. The night was mild and moonless, and rain had lately been falling, though for the present it had ceased. There was a sudden dropping from the trees and bushes every now and then, as each passing wind shook their boughs. Among these sounds Stockdale heard the faint fall of feet upon the road outside, and he guessed from the step that it was Lizzy's. He followed the sound, and, helped by the circumstance of the wind blowing from the direction in which the pedestrian moved, he got nearly close to her, and kept there, without risk of being overheard. While he thus followed her up the street or lane, as it might indifferently be called, there being more hedge than houses on either side, a figure came forward to her from one of the cottage doors. Lizzy stopped; the minister stepped upon the grass and stopped also.

'Is that Mrs Newberry?' said the man who had come out, whose voice Stockdale recognized as that of one of the most devout members of his congregation.

'It is,' said Lizzy.

'I be quite ready – I've been here this quarter-hour.'

'Ah, John,' said she, 'I have bad news; there is danger to-night for our venture.'

'And d'ye tell o't! I dreamed there might be.'

'Yes,' she said hurriedly; 'and you must go at once round to where the chaps are waiting, and tell them they will not be wanted till to-morrow night at the same time. I go to burn the lugger off.'

'I will,' he said; and instantly went off through a gate, Lizzy continuing her way.

On she tripped at a quickening pace till the lane turned into the turnpike-road, which she crossed, and got into the track for Ringsworth. Here she ascended the hill without the least hesitation, passed the lonely hamlet of Holworth, and went down the vale on the other side. Stockdale had never taken any extensive walks in this direction, but he was aware that if she persisted in her course much longer she would draw near to the coast, which was here between two and three miles distant from Nether-Moynton; and as it had been about a quarter-past eleven o'clock when they set out, her intention seemed to be to reach the shore about midnight.

Lizzy soon ascended a small mound, which Stockdale at the same time adroitly skirted on the left; and a dull monotonous roar burst upon his ear. The hillock was about fifty yards from the top of the cliffs, and by day it apparently commanded a full view of the bay. There was light enough in the sky to show her disguised figure against it when she reached the top, where she paused, and afterwards sat down. Stockdale, not wishing on any account to alarm her at this moment, yet desirous of being near her, sank upon his hands and knees, crept a little higher up, and there stayed still.

The wind was chilly, the ground damp, and his position one in which he did not care to remain long. However, before he had decided to leave it, the young man heard voices behind him. What they signified he did not know; but, fearing that Lizzy was in danger, he was about to run forward and warn her that she might be seen, when she crept to the shelter of a little bush which maintained a precarious existence in that exposed spot; and her form was absorbed in its dark and stunted outline as if she had become part of it. She had evidently heard the men as well as he. They passed near him, talking in loud and careless tones, which could be heard above the uninterrupted washings of the sea, and which suggested that they were not engaged in any business at their own risk. This proved to be the fact; some of their words floated across to him, and caused him to forget at once the coldness of his situation.

'What's the vessel?'

'A lugger, about fifty tons.'

'From Cherbourg, I suppose?'

'Yes, 'a b'lieve.'

'But it don't all belong to Owlett?'

'O no. He's only got a share. There's another or two in it — a farmer and such like, but the names I don't know.'

The voices died away, and the heads and shoulders of the men diminished towards the cliff, and dropped out of sight.

'My darling has been tempted to buy a share by that unbeliever Owlett,' groaned the minister, his honest affection for Lizzy having quickened to its intensest point during these moments of risk to her person and name. 'That's why she's here,' he said to himself. 'O, it will be the ruin of her!'

His perturbation was interrupted by the sudden bursting out of a bright and increasing light from the spot where Lizzy was in hiding. A few seconds later, and before it had reached the height of a blaze, he heard her rush past him down the hollow like a stone from a sling, in the direction of home. The light now flared high and wide, and showed its position clearly. She had kindled a bough of furze and stuck it into the bush under which she had been crouching; the wind fanned the flame, which crackled fiercely, and threatened to consume the bush as well as the bough. Stockdale paused just long enough to notice thus much, and then followed rapidly the route taken by the young woman. His intention was to overtake her, and reveal himself as a friend; but run as he would he could see nothing of her. Thus he flew across the open country about Holworth, twisting his legs and ankles in unexpected fissures and descents, till, on coming to the gate between the downs and the road, he was forced to pause to get breath. There was no audible movement either in front or behind him, and he now concluded that she had not outrun him, but that, hearing him at her heels, and believing him one of the excise party, she had hidden herself somewhere on the way, and let him pass by.

He went on at a more leisurely pace towards the village. On reaching the house he found his surmise to be correct, for the gate was on the latch, and the door unfastened, just as he had left them. Stockdale closed the door behind him, and waited silently in the passage. In about ten minutes he heard the same light footstep that he had heard in going out; it paused at the gate, which opened and shut softly, and then the door-latch was lifted, and Lizzy came in.

Stockdale went forward and said at once, 'Lizzy, don't be frightened. I have been waiting up for you.'

She started, though she had recognized the voice. 'It is Mr Stockdale, isn't it?' she said.

'Yes,' he answered, becoming angry now that she was safe indoors, and not alarmed. 'And a nice game I've found you out in to-night. You are in man's clothes, and I am ashamed of you!'

Lizzy could hardly find a voice to answer this unexpected reproach.

'I am only partly in man's clothes,' she faltered, shrinking back to the wall. 'It is only his greatcoat and hat and breeches that I've got on, which is no harm, as he was my own husband; and I do it only because a cloak blows about so, and you can't use your arms. I have got my own dress under just the same — it is only tucked in! Will you go away upstairs and let me pass? I didn't want you to see me at such a time as this!'

'But I have a right to see you! How do you think there can be anything between us now?' Lizzy was silent. 'You are a smuggler,' he continued sadly.

'I have only a share in the run,' she said.

'That makes no difference. Whatever did you engage in such a trade as that for, and keep it such a secret from me all this time?'

'I don't do it always. I only do it in winter-time when 'tis new moon.'

'Well, I suppose that's because it can't be done anywhen else. . . . You have regularly upset me, Lizzy.'

'I am sorry for that,' Lizzy meekly replied.

'Well now,' said he more tenderly, 'no harm is done as yet. Won't you for the sake of me give up this blameable and dangerous practice altogether?'

'I must do my best to save this run,' said she, getting rather husky in the throat. 'I don't want to give you up – you know that; but I don't want to lose my venture. I don't know what to do now! Why I have kept it so secret from you is that I was afraid you would be angry if you knew.'

'I should think so! I suppose if I had married you without finding this out you'd have gone on with it just the same?'

'I don't know. I did not think so far ahead. I only went to-night to burn the folks off, because we found that the Preventive-men knew where the tubs were to be landed.'

'It is a pretty mess to be in altogether, is this,' said the distracted young minister. 'Well, what will you do now?'

Lizzy slowly murmured the particulars of their plan, the chief of which were that they meant to try their luck at some other point of the shore the next night; that three landing-places were always agreed upon before the run was attempted, with the understanding that, if the vessel was 'burnt off' from the first point, which was Ringsworth, as it had been by her to-night, the crew should attempt to make the second, which was Lulwind Cove, on the second night; and if there, too, danger threatened, they should on the third night try the third place, which was behind a headland further west.

'Suppose the officers hinder them landing there, too?' he said, his attention to this interesting programme displacing for a moment his concern at her share in it.

'Then we shan't try anywhere else all this dark – that's what we call the time between moon and moon – and perhaps they'll string the tubs to a stray-line, and sink 'em a little-ways from shore, and take the bearings; and then when they have a chance they'll go to creep for 'em.'

'What's that?'

'O, they'll go out in a boat and drag a creeper – that's a grapnel – along the bottom till it catch hold of the stray-line.'

The minister stood thinking; and there was no sound within doors but the tick of the clock on the stairs, and the quick breathing of Lizzy, partly from her walk and partly from agitation, as she stood close to the wall, not in such complete darkness but that he could discern against its whitewashed surface the greatcoat, breeches, and broad hat which covered her.

'Lizzy, all this is very wrong,' he said. 'Don't you remember the lesson of the tribute-money? "Render unto Cæsar the things that are Cæsar's." Surely you have heard that read times enough in your growing up?'

'He's dead,' she pouted.

'But the spirit of the text is in force just the same.'

'My father did it, and so did my grandfather, and almost everybody in Nether-

Moynton lives by it, and life would be so dull if it wasn't for that, that I should not care to live at all.'

'I am nothing to live for, of course,' he replied bitterly. 'You would not think it worth while to give up this wild business and live for me alone?'

'I have never looked at it like that.'

'And you won't promise and wait till I am ready?'

'I cannot give you my word to-night.' And, looking thoughtfully down, she gradually moved and moved away, going into the adjoining room, and closing the door between them. She remained there in the dark till he was tired of waiting, and had gone up to his own chamber.

Poor Stockdale was dreadfully depressed all the next day by the discoveries of the night before. Lizzy was unmistakably a fascinating young woman, but as a minister's wife she was hardly to be contemplated. 'If I had only stuck to father's little grocery business, instead of going in for the ministry, she would have suited me beautifully!' he said sadly, until he remembered that in that case he would never have come from his distant home to Nether-Moynton, and never have known her.

The estrangement between them was not complete, but it was sufficient to keep them out of each other's company. Once during the day he met her in the garden-path, and said, turning a reproachful eye upon her, 'Do you promise, Lizzy?' But she did not reply. The evening drew on, and he knew well enough that Lizzy would repeat her excursion at night – her half-offended manner had shown that she had not the slightest intention of altering her plans at present. He did not wish to repeat his own share of the adventure; but, act as he would, his uneasiness on her account increased with the decline of day. Supposing that an accident should befall her, he would never forgive himself for not being there to help, much as he disliked the idea of seeming to countenance such unlawful escapades.

V. HOW THEY WENT TO LULWIND COVE

As he had expected, she left the house at the same hour at night, this time passing his door without stealth, as if she knew very well that he would be watching, and were resolved to brave his displeasure. He was quite ready, opened the door quickly, and reached the back door almost as soon as she.

'Then you will go, Lizzy?' he said as he stood on the step beside her, who now again appeared as a little man with a face altogether unsuited to his clothes.

'I must,' she said, repressed by his stern manner.

'Then I shall go, too,' said he.

'And I am sure you will enjoy it!' she exclaimed in more buoyant tones. 'Everybody does who tries it.'

'God forbid that I should!' he said. 'But I must look after you.'

They opened the wicket and went up the road abreast of each other, but at some distance apart, scarcely a word passing between them. The evening was rather less favourable to smuggling enterprise than the last had been, the wind being lower, and the sky somewhat clear towards the north.

'It is rather lighter,' said Stockdale.

' 'Tis, unfortunately,' said she. 'But it is only from those few stars over there.

The moon was new to-day at four o'ciock, and I expected clouds. I hope we shall be able to do it this dark, for when we have to sink 'em for long it makes the stuff taste bleachy, and folks don't like it so well.'

Her course was different from that of the preceding night, branching off to the left over Lord's Barrow as soon as they had got out of the lane and crossed the highway. By the time they reached Chaldon Down, Stockdale, who had been in perplexed thought as to what he should say to her, decided that he would not attempt expostulation now, while she was excited by the adventure, but wait till it was over, and endeavour to keep her from such practices in future. It occurred to him once or twice, as they rambled on, that should they be surprised by the Preventive-guard, his situation would be more awkward than hers, for it would be difficult to prove his true motive in coming to the spot; but the risk was a slight consideration beside his wish to be with her.

They now arrived at a ravine which lay on the outskirts of Chaldon, a village two miles on their way towards the point of the shore they sought. Lizzy broke the silence this time: 'I have to wait here to meet the carriers. I don't know if they have come yet. As I told you, we go to Lulwind Cove to-night, and it is two miles further than Ringsworth.'

It turned out that the men had already come; for while she spoke two or three dozen heads broke the line of the slope, and a company of them at once descended from the bushes where they had been lying in wait. These carriers were men whom Lizzy and other proprietors regularly employed to bring the tubs from the boat to a hiding-place inland. They were all young fellows of Nether-Moynton, Chaldon, and the neighbourhood, quiet and inoffensive persons, even though some held heavy sticks, who simply engaged to carry the cargo for Lizzy and her cousin Owlett, as they would have engaged in any other labour for which they were fairly well paid.

At a word from her they closed in together. 'You had better take it now,' she said to them; and handed to each a packet. It contained six shillings, their remuneration for the night's undertaking, which was paid beforehand without reference to success or failure; but, besides this, they had the privilege of selling as agents when the run was successfully made. As soon as it was done, she said to them, 'The place is the old one, Dagger's Grave, near Lulwind Cove'; the men till that moment not having been told whither they were bound, for obvious reasons. 'Mr Owlett will meet you there,' added Lizzy. 'I shall follow behind, to see that we are not watched.'

The carriers went on, and Stockdale and Mrs Newberry followed at a distance of a stone's throw. 'What do these men do by day?' he said.

'Twelve or fourteen of them are labouring men. Some are brickmakers, some carpenters, some shoemakers, some thatchers. They are all known to me very well. Nine of 'em are of your own congregation.'

'I can't help that,' said Stockdale.

'O, I know you can't. I only told you. The others are more church-inclined, because they supply the pa'son with all the spirits he requires, and they don't wish to show unfriendliness to a customer.'

'How do you choose 'em?' said Stockdale.

'We choose 'em for their closeness, and because they are strong and surefooted, and able to carry a heavy load a long way without being tired.'

Stockdale sighed as she enumerated each particular, for it proved how far involved in the business a woman must be who was so well acquainted with its conditions and needs. And yet he felt more tenderly towards her at this moment than he had felt all the foregoing day. Perhaps it was that her experienced manner and bold indifference stirred his admiration in spite of himself.

'Take my arm, Lizzy,' he murmured.

'I don't want it,' she said. 'Besides, we may never be to each other again what we once have been.'

'That depends upon you,' said he, and they went on again as before.

The hired carriers paced along over Chaldon Down with as little hesitation as if it had been day, avoiding the cartway, and leaving the village of East Chaldon on the left, so as to reach the crest of the hill at a lonely trackless place not far from the ancient earthwork called Round Pound. A quarter-hour more of brisk walking brought them within sound of the sea, to the place called Dagger's Grave, not many hundred yards from Lulwind Cove. Here they paused, and Lizzy and Stockdale came up with them, when they went on together to the verge of the cliff. One of the men now produced an iron bar, which he drove firmly into the soil a yard from the edge, and attached to it a rope that he had uncoiled from his body. They all began to descend, partly stepping, partly sliding down the incline, as the rope slipped through their hands.

'You will not go to the bottom, Lizzy?' said Stockdale anxiously.

'No. I stay here to watch,' she said. 'Mr Owlett is down there.'

The men remained quite silent when they reached the shore; and the next thing audible to the two at the top was the dip of heavy oars, and the dashing of waves against a boat's bow. In a moment the keel gently touched the shingle, and Stockdale heard the footsteps of the thirty-six carriers running forwards over the pebbles towards the point of landing.

There was a sousing in the water as of a brood of ducks plunging in, showing that the men had not been particular about keeping their legs, or even their waists, dry from the brine: but it was impossible to see what they were doing, and in a few minutes the shingle was trampled again. The iron bar sustaining the rope, on which Stockdale's hand rested, began to swerve a little, and the carriers one by one appeared climbing up the sloping cliff, dripping audibly as they came, and sustaining themselves by the guide-rope. Each man on reaching the top was seen to be carrying a pair of tubs, one on his back and one on his chest, the two being slung together by cords passing round the chine hoops, and resting on the carrier's shoulders. Some of the stronger men carried three by putting an extra one on the top behind, but the customary load was a pair, these being quite weighty enough to give their bearer the sensation of having chest and backbone in contact after a walk of four or five miles.

'Where is Mr Owlett?' said Lizzy to one of them.

'He will not come up this way,' said the carrier. 'He's to bide on shore till we be safe off.' Then, without waiting for the rest, the foremost men plunged across the down, and, when the last had ascended, Lizzy pulled up the rope, wound it round her arm, wriggled the bar from the sod, and turned to follow the carriers.

'You are very anxious about Owlett's safety,' said the minister.

'Was there ever such a man!' said Lizzy. 'Why, isn't he my cousin?'

'Yes. Well, it is a bad night's work,' said Stockdale heavily. 'But I'll carry the bar and rope for you.'

'Thank God, the tubs have got so far all right,' said she.

Stockdale shook his head, and, taking the bar, walked by her side towards the downs; and the moan of the sea was heard no more.

'Is this what you meant the other day when you spoke of having business with Owlett?' the young man asked.

'This is it,' she replied. 'I never see him on any other matter.'

'A partnership of that kind with a young man is very odd.'

'It was begun by my father and his, who were brother-laws.'

Her companion could not blind himself to the fact that where tastes and pursuits were so akin as Lizzy's and Owlett's, and where risks were shared, as with them, in every undertaking, there would be a peculiar appropriateness in her answering Owlett's standing question on matrimony in the affirmative. This did not soothe Stockdale, its tendency being rather to stimulate in him an effort to make the pair as inappropriate as possible, and win her away from this nocturnal crew to correctness of conduct and a minister's parlour in some far-removed inland county.

They had been walking near enough to the file of carriers for Stockdale to perceive that, when they got into the road to the village, they split up into two companies of unequal size, each of which made off in a direction of its own. One company, the smaller of the two, went towards the church, and by the time that Lizzy and Stockdale reached their own house these men had scaled the churchyard wall, and were proceeding noiselessly over the grass within.

'I see that Mr Owlett has arranged for one batch to be put in the church again,' observed Lizzy. 'Do you remember my taking you there the first night you came?'

'Yes, of course,' said Stockdale. 'No wonder you had permission to broach the tubs – they were his, I suppose?'

'No, they were not – they were mine; I had permission from myself. The day after that they went several miles inland in a waggon-load of manure, and sold very well.'

At this moment the group of men who had made off to the left some time before began leaping one by one from the hedge opposite Lizzy's house, and the first man, who had no tubs upon his shoulders, came forward.

'Mrs Newberry, isn't it?' he said hastily.

'Yes, Jim,' said she. 'What's the matter?'

'I find that we can't put any in Badger's Clump to-night, Lizzy,' said Owlett. 'The place is watched. We must sling the apple-tree in the orchet if there's time. We can't put any more under the church lumber than I have sent on there, and my mixen hev already more in en than is safe.'

'Very well,' she said. 'Be quick about it – that's all. What can I do?'

'Nothing at all, please. Ah, it is the minister! – you two that can't do anything had better get indoors and not be zeed.'

While Owlett thus conversed, in a tone so full of contraband anxiety and so free from lover's jealousy, the men who followed him had been descending one by one from the hedge; and it unfortunately happened that when the hindmost took his leap, the cord slipped which sustained his tubs; the result was that both the kegs fell into the road, one of them being stove in by the blow.

''Od drown it all!' said Owlett, rushing back.

'It is worth a good deal, I suppose?' said Stockdale.

'O no – about two guineas and half to us now,' said Lizzy excitedly. 'It isn't that – it is the smell! It is so blazing strong before it has been lowered by water, that it smells dreadfully when spilt in the road like that! I do hope Latimer won't pass by till it is gone off.'

Owlett and one or two others picked up the burst tub and began to scrape and trample over the spot, to disperse the liquor as much as possible; and then they all entered the gate of Owlett's orchard, which adjoined Lizzy's garden on the right. Stockdale did not care to follow them, for several on recognizing him had looked wonderingly at his presence, though they said nothing. Lizzy left his side and went to the bottom of the garden, looking over the hedge into the orchard, where the men could be dimly seen bustling about, and apparently hiding the tubs. All was done noiselessly, and without a light; and when it was over they dispersed in different directions, those who had taken their cargoes to the church having already gone off to their homes.

Lizzy returned to the garden-gate, over which Stockdale was still abstractedly leaning. 'It is all finished: I am going indoors now,' she said gently. 'I will leave the door ajar for you.'

'O no – you needn't,' said Stockdale; 'I am coming too.'

But before either of them had moved, the faint clatter of horses' hoofs broke upon the ear, and it seemed to come from the point where the track across the down joined the hard road.

'They are just too late!' cried Lizzy exultingly.

'Who?' said Stockdale.

'Latimer, the riding-officer, and some assistant of his. We had better go indoors.'

They entered the house, and Lizzy bolted the door. 'Please don't get a light, Mr Stockdale,' she said.

'Of course I will not,' said he.

'I thought you might be on the side of the king,' said Lizzy, with faintest sarcasm.

'I am,' said Stockdale. 'But, Lizzy Newberry, I love you, and you know it perfectly well, and you ought to know, if you do not, what I have suffered in my conscience on your account these last few days!'

'I guess very well,' she said hurriedly. 'Yet I don't see why. Ah, you are better than I!'

The trotting of the horses seemed to have again died away, and the pair of listeners touched each other's fingers in the cold 'Good-night' of those whom something seriously divided. They were on the landing, but before they had taken three steps apart, the tramp of the horsemen suddenly revived, almost close to the house. Lizzy turned to the staircase window, opened the casement about an inch, and put her face close to the aperture. 'Yes, one of 'em is Latimer,' she whispered. 'He always rides a white horse. One would think it was the last colour for a man in that line.'

Stockdale looked, and saw the white shape of the animal as it passed by; but before the riders had gone another ten yards Latimer reined in his horse, and said something to his companion which neither Stockdale nor Lizzy could hear. Its drift was, however, soon made evident, for the other man stopped also; and sharply turning the horses' heads they cautiously retraced their steps. When they were again opposite Mrs Newberry's garden, Latimer dismounted, and the man on the dark horse did the same.

Lizzy and Stockdale, intently listening and observing the proceedings, naturally put their heads as close as possible to the slit formed by the slightly opened casement; and thus it occurred that at last their cheeks came positively into contact. They went on listening, as if they did not know of the singular incident which had happened to their faces, and the pressure of each to each rather increased than lessened with the lapse of time.

They could hear the Customs-men sniffing the air like hounds as they paced slowly along. When they reached the spot where the tub had burst, both stopped on the instant.

'Ay, ay, 'tis quite strong here,' said the second officer. 'Shall we knock at the door?'

'Well, no,' said Latimer. 'Maybe this is only a trick to put us off the scent. They wouldn't kick up this stink anywhere near their hiding-place. I have known such things before.'

'Anyhow, the things, or some of 'em, must have been brought this way,' said the other.

'Yes,' said Latimer musingly. 'Unless 'tis all done to tole us the wrong way. I have a mind that we go home for to-night without saying a word, and come the first thing in the morning with more hands. I know they have storages about here, but we can do nothing by this owl's light. We will look round the parish and see if everybody is in bed, John; and if all is quiet, we will do as I say.'

They went on, and the two inside the window could hear them passing leisurely through the whole village, the street of which curved round at the bottom and entered the turnpike road at another junction. This way the officers followed, and the amble of their horses died quite away.

'What will you do?' said Stockdale, withdrawing from his position.

She knew that he alluded to the coming search by the officers to divert her attention from their own tender incident by the casement, which he wished to be passed over as a thing rather dreamt of than done. 'O, nothing,' she replied, with as much coolness as she could command under her disappointment at his manner. 'We often have such storms as this. You would not be frightened if you knew what fools they are. Fancy riding o' horseback through the place; of course they will hear and see nobody while they make that noise; but they are always afraid to get off, in case some of our fellows should burst out upon 'em, and tie them up to the gate-post, as they have done before now. Good-night, Mr Stockdale.'

She closed the window and went to her room, where a tear fell from her eyes; and that not because of the alertness of the riding-officers.

VI. THE GREAT SEARCH AT NETHER-MOYNTON

Stockdale was so excited by the events of the evening, and the dilemma that he was placed in between conscience and love, that he did not sleep, or even doze, but remained as broadly awake as at noonday. As soon as the gray light began to touch ever so faintly the whiter objects in his bedroom he arose, dressed himself, and went downstairs into the road.

The village was already astir. Several of the carriers had heard the well-known canter of Latimer's horse while they were undressing in the dark that night, and had already communicated with each other and Owlett on the subject. The only doubt seemed to be about the safety of those tubs which had been left under the church gallery-stairs, and after a short discussion at the corner of the mill, it was agreed that these should be removed before it got lighter, and hidden in the middle of a double hedge bordering the adjoining field. However, before anything could be carried into effect, the footsteps of many men were heard coming down the lane from the highway.

'Damn it, here they be,' said Owlett, who, having already drawn the hatch and started his mill for the day, stood stolidly at the mill-door covered with flour, as if the interest of his whole soul was bound up in the shaking walls around him.

The two or three with whom he had been talking dispersed to their usual work, and when the Customs-officers, and the formidable body of men they had hired, reached the village cross, between the mill and Mrs Newberry's house, the village wore the natural aspect of a place beginning its morning labours.

'Now,' said Latimer to his associates, who numbered thirteen men in all, 'what I know is that the things are somewhere in this here place. We have got the day before us, and 'tis hard if we can't light upon 'em and get 'em to Budmouth Custom-house before night. First we will try the fuel-houses, and then we'll work our way into the chimmers, and then to the ricks and stables, and so creep round. You have nothing but your noses to guide ye, mind, so use 'em to-day if you never did in your lives before.'

Then the search began. Owlett, during the early part, watched from his mill-window, Lizzy from the door of her house, with the greatest self-possession. A farmer down below, who also had a share in the run, rode about with one eye on his fields and the other on Latimer and his myrmidons, prepared to put them off the scent if he should be asked a question. Stockdale, who was no smuggler at all, felt more anxiety than the worst of them, and went about his studies with a heavy heart, coming frequently to the door to ask Lizzy some question or other on the consequences to her of the tubs being found.

'The consequences,' she said quietly, ' are simply that I shall lose 'em. As I have none in the house or garden, they can't touch me personally.'

'But you have some in the orchard?'

'Mr Owlett rents that of me, and he lends it to others. So it will be hard to say who put any tubs there if they should be found.'

There was never such a tremendous sniffing known as that which took place in Nether-Moynton parish and its vicinity this day. All was done methodically, and mostly on hands and knees. At different hours of the day they had different plans. From daybreak to breakfast-time the officers used their sense of smell in a direct and straightforward manner only, pausing nowhere but at such places as the tubs might be supposed to be secreted in at that very moment, pending their removal on the following night. Among the places tested and examined were: —

Hollow trees	Cupboards	Culverts
Potato-graves	Clock-cases	Hedgerows
Fuel-houses	Chimney-flues	Faggot-ricks
Bedrooms	Rainwater-butts	Haystacks
Apple-lofts	Pigsties	Coppers and ovens

After breakfast they recommenced with renewed vigour, taking a new line; that is to say, directing their attention to clothes that might be supposed to have come in contact with the tubs in their removal from the shore, such garments being usually tainted with the spirit, owing to its oozing between the staves. They now sniffed at —

Smock-frocks	Smiths' and shoemakers' aprons
Old shirts and waistcoats	Knee-naps and hedging-gloves
Coats and hats	Tarpaulins
Breeches and leggings	Market-cloaks
Women's shawls and gowns	Scarecrows

And as soon as the midday meal was over, they pushed their search into places where the spirits might have been thrown away in alarm: —

Horse-ponds	Mixens	Sinks in yards
Stable-drains	Wet ditches	Road-scrapings, and
Cinder-heaps	Cesspools	Back-door gutters

But still these indefatigable Custom-house men discovered nothing more than the original tell-tale smell in the road opposite Lizzy's house, which even yet had not passed off.

'I'll tell ye what it is, men,' said Latimer, about three o'clock in the afternoon, 'we must begin over again. Find them tubs I will.'

The men, who had been hired for the day, looked at their hands and knees, muddy with creeping on all fours so frequently, and rubbed their noses, as if they had almost had enough of it; for the quantity of bad air which had passed into each one's nostril had rendered it nearly as insensible as a flue. However, after a moment's hesitation, they prepared to start anew, except three, whose power of smell had quite succumbed under the excessive wear and tear of the day.

By this time not a male villager was to be seen in the parish. Owlett was not at his mill, the farmers were not in their fields, the parson was not in his garden, the smith had left his forge, and the wheelwright's shop was silent.

'Where the divil are the folk gone?' said Latimer, waking up to the fact of their absence, and looking round. 'I'll have 'em up for this! Why don't they come and help us? There's not a man about the place but the Methodist parson, and he's an old woman. I demand assistance in the king's name!'

'We must find the jineral public afore we can demand that,' said his lieutenant.

'Well, well, we shall do better without 'em,' said Latimer, who changed his moods at a moment's notice. 'But there's great cause of suspicion in this silence and this keeping out of sight, and I'll bear it in mind. Now we will go across to Owlett's orchard and see what we can find there.'

Stockdale, who heard this discussion from the garden-gate, over which he had been leaning, was rather alarmed, and thought it a mistake of the villagers to keep so completely out of the way. He himself, like the Preventives, had been wondering for the last half-hour what could have become of them. Some labourers were of necessity engaged in distant fields, but the master-workmen should have been at home; though one and all, after just showing themselves at their shops, had apparently gone off for the day. He went in to Lizzy, who sat at a back window sewing, and said, 'Lizzy, where are the men?'

Lizzy laughed. 'Where they mostly are when they're run so hard as this.' She cast her eyes to heaven. 'Up there,' she said.

Stockdale looked up. 'What – on the top of the church tower?' he asked, seeing the direction of her glance.

'Yes.'

'Well, I expect they will soon have to come down,' said he gravely. 'I have been listening to the officers, and they are going to search the orchard over again, and then every nook in the church.'

Lizzy looked alarmed for the first time. 'Will you go and tell our folk?' she said. 'They ought to be let know.' Seeing his conscience struggling within him like a boiling pot, she added, 'No, never mind, I'll go myself.'

She went out, descended the garden, and climbed over the churchyard wall at the same time that the Preventive-men were ascending the road to the orchard. Stockdale could do no less than follow her. By the time that she reached the tower entrance he was at her side, and they entered together.

Nether-Moynton church-tower was, as in many villages, without a turret, and the only way to the top was by going up to the singers' gallery, and thence ascending by a ladder to a square trap-door in the floor of the bell-loft, above which a permanent ladder was fixed, passing through the bells to a hole in the roof. When Lizzy and Stockdale reached the gallery and looked up, nothing but the trap-door and the five holes for the bell-ropes appeared. The ladder was gone.

'There's no getting up,' said Stockdale.

'O yes, there is,' said she. 'There's an eye looking at us at this moment through a knot-hole in that trap-door.'

And as she spoke the trap opened, and the dark line of the ladder was seen descending against the whitewashed wall. When it touched the bottom Lizzy dragged it to its place, and said, 'If you'll go up, I'll follow.'

The young man ascended, and presently found himself among consecrated bells for the first time in his life, nonconformity having been in the Stockdale blood for some generations. He eyed them uneasily, and looked round for Lizzy. Owlett stood here, holding the top of the ladder.

'What, be you really one of us?' said the miller.

'It seems so,' said Stockdale sadly.

'He's not,' said Lizzy, who overheard. 'He's neither for nor against us. He'll do us no harm.'

She stepped up beside them, and then they went on to the next stage, which, when they had clambered over the dusty bell-carriages, was of easy ascent, leading towards the hole through which the pale sky appeared, and into the open air. Owlett remained behind for a moment, to pull up the lower ladder.

'Keep down your heads,' said a voice, as soon as they set foot on the flat.

Stockdale here beheld all the missing parishioners, lying on their stomachs on the tower roof, except a few who, elevated on their hands and knees, were peeping through the embrasures of the parapet. Stockdale did the same, and saw the village lying like a map below him, over which moved the figures of the Customs-men, each foreshortened to a crablike object, the crown of his hat forming a circular disc in the centre of him. Some of the men had turned their heads when the young preacher's figure arose among them.

'What, Mr Stockdale?' said Matt Grey, in a tone of surprise.

'I'd as lief that it hadn't been,' said Jim Clarke. 'If the pa'son should see him a-trespassing here in his tower, 'twould be none the better for we, seeing how 'a do hate chapel-members. He'd never buy a tub of us again, and he's as good a customer as we have got this side o' Warm'll.'

'Where is the pa'son?' said Lizzy.

'In his house, to be sure, that he mid see nothing of what's going on — where all good folks ought to be, and this young man likewise.'

'Well, he has brought some news,' said Lizzy. 'They are going to search the orchard and church; can we do anything if they should find?'

'Yes,' said her cousin Owlett. 'That's what we've been talking o', and we have settled our line. Well, be dazed!'

The exclamation was caused by his perceiving that some of the searchers, having got into the orchard, and begun stooping and creeping hither and thither, were pausing in the middle, where a tree smaller than the rest was growing. They drew closer, and bent lower than ever upon the ground.

'O, my tubs!' said Lizzy faintly, as she peered through the parapet at them.

'They have got 'em, 'a b'lieve,' said Owlett.

The interest in the movements of the officers was so keen that not a single eye was looking in any other direction; but at that moment a shout from the church beneath them attracted the attention of the smugglers, as it did also of the party in the orchard, who sprang to their feet and went towards the churchyard wall. At the same time those of the Government men who had entered the church unperceived by the smugglers cried aloud, 'Here be some of 'em at last.'

The smugglers remained in a blank silence, uncertain whether 'some of 'em' meant tubs or men; but again peeping cautiously over the edge of the tower they learnt that tubs were the things descried; and soon these fated articles were brought one by one into the middle of the churchyard from their hiding-place under the gallery-stairs.

'They are going to put 'em on Hinton's vault till they find the rest!' said Lizzy hopelessly. The Customs-men had, in fact, begun to pile up the tubs on a large stone slab which was fixed there; and when all were brought out from the tower, two or three of the men were left standing by them, the rest of the party again proceeding to the orchard.

The interest of the smugglers in the next manœuvres of their enemies became painfully intense. Only about thirty tubs had been secreted in the lumber of the tower, but seventy were hidden in the orchard, making up all that they had brought ashore as yet, the remainder of the cargo having been tied to a sinker and dropped overboard for another night's operations. The Preventives, having re-entered the orchard, acted as if they were positive that here lay hidden the rest of the tubs, which they were determined to find before nightfall. They spread themselves out round the field, and advancing on all fours as before, went anew round every apple-tree in the enclosure. The young tree in the middle again led them to pause, and at length the whole company gathered there in a way which signified that a second chain of reasoning had led to the same results as the first.

When they had examined the sod hereabouts for some minutes, one of the men rose, ran to a disused part of the church where tools were kept, and returned with the sexton's pickaxe and shovel, with which they set to work.

'Are they really buried there?' said the minister, for the grass was so green and uninjured that it was difficult to believe it had been disturbed. The smugglers were too interested to reply, and presently they saw, to their chagrin, the officers stand several on each side of the tree; and, stooping and applying their hands to the soil, they bodily lifted the tree and the turf around it. The apple-tree now showed itself to be growing in a shallow box, with handles for lifting at each of the four sides. Under the site of the tree a square hole was revealed, and an officer went and looked down.

'It is all up now,' said Owlett quietly. 'And now all of ye get down before they notice we are here; and be ready for our next move. I had better bide here till dark, or they may take me on suspicion, as 'tis on my ground. I'll be with ye as soon as daylight begins to pink in.'

'And I!' said Lizzy.

'You please look to the linch-pins and screws; then go indoors and know nothing at all. The chaps will do the rest.'

The ladder was replaced, and all but Owlett descended, the men passing off one by one at the back of the church, and vanishing on their respective errands. Lizzy walked boldly along the street, followed closely by the minister.

'You are going indoors, Mrs Newberry?' he said.

She knew from the words 'Mrs Newberry' that the division between them had widened yet another degree.

'I am not going home,' she said. 'I have a little thing to do before I go in. Martha Sarah will get your tea.'

'O, I don't mean on that account,' said Stockdale. 'What *can* you have to do further in this unhallowed affair?'

'Only a little,' she said.

'What is that? I'll go with you.'

'No, I shall go by myself. Will you please go indoors? I shall be there in less than an hour.'

'You are not going to run any danger, Lizzy?' said the young man, his tenderness reasserting itself.

'None whatever — worth mentioning,' answered she, and went down towards the Cross.

Stockdale entered the garden-gate, and stood behind it looking on. The Preventive-men were still busy in the orchard, and at last he was tempted to enter and watch their proceedings. When he came closer he found that the secret cellar, of whose existence he had been totally unaware, was formed by timbers placed across from side to side about a foot under the ground, and grassed over.

The officers looked up at Stockdale's fair and downy countenance, and evidently thinking him above suspicion, went on with their work again. As soon as all the tubs were taken out they began tearing up the turf, pulling out the timbers, and breaking in the sides, till the cellar was wholly dismantled and shapeless, the apple-tree lying with its roots high to the air. But the hole which had in its time held so much contraband merchandize was never completely filled up, either then or afterwards, a depression in the greensward marking the spot to this day.

VII. THE WALK TO WARM'ELL CROSS, AND AFTERWARDS

As the goods had all to be carried to Budmouth that night, the next object of the Custom-house officers was to find horses and carts for the journey, and they went about the village for that purpose. Latimer strode hither and thither with a lump of chalk in his hand, marking broad-arrows so vigorously on every vehicle and set of harness that he came across, that it seemed as if he would chalk broad-arrows on the very hedges and roads. The owner of every conveyance so marked was bound to give it up for Government purposes. Stockdale, who had had enough of the scene, turned indoors thoughtful and depressed. Lizzy was already there, having come in at the back, though she had not yet taken off her bonnet. She looked tired, and her mood was not much brighter than his own. They had but little to say to each other; and the minister went away and attempted to read; but at this he could not succeed, and he shook the little bell for tea.

Lizzy herself brought in the tray, the girl having run off into the village during the afternoon, too full of excitement at the proceedings to remember her state of life. However, almost before the sad lovers had said anything to each other, Martha came in in a steaming state.

'O, there's such a stoor, Mrs Newberry and Mr Stockdale! The king's officer can't get the carts ready nohow at all! They pulled Thomas Artnell's, and William Rogers's, and Stephen Sprake's carts into the road, and off came the wheels, and down fell the carts; and they found there was no linch-pins in the arms; and then they tried Samuel Shane's waggon, and found that the screws were gone from he, and at last they looked at the dairyman's cart, and he's got none neither! They have gone now to the blacksmith's to get some made, but he's nowhere to be found!'

Stockdale looked at Lizzy, who blushed very slightly, and went out of the room, followed by Martha Sarah. But before they had got through the passage there was a rap at the front door, and Stockdale recognized Latimer's voice addressing Mrs Newberry, who had turned back.

'For God's sake, Mrs Newberry, have you seen Hardman the blacksmith up this way? If we could get hold of him, we'd e'en a'most drag him by the hair of his head to his anvil, where he ought to be.'

'He's an idle man, Mr Latimer,' said Lizzy archly. 'What do you want him for?'

'Why, there isn't a horse in the place that has got more than three shoes on, and some have only two. The waggon-wheels be without strakes, and there's no linch-pins to the carts. What with that, and the bother about every set of harness being out of order, we shan't be off before nightfall – upon my soul we shan't. 'Tis a rough lot, Mrs Newberry, that you've got about you here; but they'll play at this game once too often, mark my words they will! There's not a man in the parish that don't deserve to be whipped.'

It happened that Hardman was at that moment a little further up the lane, smoking his pipe behind a holly-bush. When Latimer had done speaking he went on in this direction, and Hardman, hearing the riding-officer's steps, found curiosity too strong for prudence. He peeped out from the bush at the very moment that Latimer's glance was on it. There was nothing left for him to do but to come forward with unconcern.

'I've been looking for you for the last hour!' said Latimer with a glare in his eye.

'Sorry to hear that,' said Hardman. 'I've been out for a stroll, to look for more hid tubs, to deliver 'em up to Gover'ment.'

'O yes, Hardman, we know it,' said Latimer, with withering sarcasm. 'We know that you'll deliver 'em up to Gover'ment. We know that all the parish is helping us, and have been all day! Now you please walk along with me down to your shop, and kindly let me hire ye in the king's name.'

They went down the lane together, and presently there resounded from the smithy the ring of a hammer not very briskly swung. However, the carts and horses were got into some sort of travelling condition, but it was not until after the clock had struck six, when the muddy roads were glistening under the horizontal light of the fading day. The smuggled tubs were soon packed into the vehicles, and Latimer, with three of his assistants, drove slowly out of the village in the direction of the port of Budmouth, some considerable number of miles distant, the other men of the Preventive-guard being left to watch for the remainder of the cargo, which they knew to have been sunk somewhere between Ringsworth and Lulwind Cove, and to unearth Owlett, the only person clearly implicated by the discovery of the cave.

Women and children stood at the doors as the carts, each chalked with the Government pitchfork, passed in the increasing twilight; and as they stood they looked at the confiscated property with a melancholy expression that told only too plainly the relation which they bore to the trade.

'Well, Lizzy,' said Stockdale, when the crackle of the wheels had nearly died away. 'This is a fit finish to your adventure. I am truly thankful that you have got off without suspicion, and the loss only of the liquor. Will you sit down and let me talk to you?'

'By and by,' she said. 'But I must go out now.'

'Not to that horrid shore again?' he said blankly.

'No, not there. I am only going to see the end of this day's business.'

He did not answer to this, and she moved towards the door slowly, as if waiting for him to say something more.

'You don't offer to come with me,' she added at last. 'I suppose that's because you hate me after all this!'

'Can you say it, Lizzy, when you know I only want to save you from such practices? Come with you! – of course I will, if it is only to take care of you. But why will you go out again?'

'Because I cannot rest indoors. Something is happening, and I must know what. Now, come!' And they went into the dusk together.

When they reached the turnpike-road she turned to the right, and he soon perceived that they were following the direction of the Preventive-men and their load. He had given her his arm, and every now and then she suddenly pulled it back, to signify that he was to halt a moment and listen. They had walked rather quickly along the first quarter of a mile, and on the second or third time of standing still she said, 'I hear them ahead – don't you?'

'Yes,' he said; 'I hear the wheels. But what of that?'

'I only want to know if they get clear away from the neighbourhood.'

'Ah,' said he, a light breaking upon him. 'Something desperate is to be attempted! – and now I remember there was not a man about the village when we left.'

'Hark!' she murmured. The noise of the cart-wheels had stopped, and given place to another sort of sound.

''Tis a scuffle!' said Stockdale. 'There'll be murder! Lizzy, let go my arm; I am going on. On my conscience, I must not stay here and do nothing!'

'There'll be no murder, and not even a broken head,' she said. 'Our men are thirty to four of them: no harm will be done at all.'

'Then there *is* an attack!' exclaimed Stockdale; 'and you knew it was to be. Why should you side with men who break the laws like this?'

'Why should you side with men who take from country traders what they have honestly bought wi' their own money in France?' said she firmly.

'They are not honestly bought,' said he.

'They are,' she contradicted. 'I and Mr Owlett and the others paid thirty shillings for every one of the tubs before they were put on board at Cherbourg, and if a king who is nothing to us sends his people to steal our property we have a right to steal it back again.'

Stockdale did not stop to argue the matter but went quickly in the direction of the noise, Lizzy keeping at his side. 'Don't you interfere, will you, dear Richard?' she said anxiously, as they drew near. 'Don't let us go any closer: 'tis at Warm'ell Cross where they are seizing 'em. You can do no good, and you may meet with a hard blow!'

'Let us see first what is going on,' he said. But before they had got much further the noise of the cart-wheels began again; and Stockdale soon found that they were coming towards him. In another minute the three carts came up, and Stockdale and Lizzy stood in the ditch to let them pass.

Instead of being conducted by four men, as had happened when they went out of the village, the horses and carts were now accompanied by a body of from twenty to thirty, all of whom, as Stockdale perceived to his astonishment, had blackened faces. Among them walked six or eight huge female figures, whom, from their wide strides, Stockdale guessed to be men in disguise. As soon as the party discerned Lizzy and her companion four or five fell back, and when the carts had passed, came close to the pair.

'There is no walking up this way for the present,' said one of the gaunt women, who wore curls a foot long, dangling down the sides of her face, in the fashion of the time. Stockdale recognized this lady's voice as Owlett's.

'Why not?' said Stockdale. 'This is the public highway.'

'Now look here, youngster,' said Owlett. 'O, 'tis the Methodist parson! – what, and Mrs Newberry! Well, you'd better not go up that way, Lizzy. They've all run off, and folks have got their own again.'

The miller then hastened on and joined his comrades. Stockdale and Lizzy also turned back. 'I wish all this hadn't been forced upon us,' she said regretfully. 'But if those Coast-men had got off with the tubs, half the people in the parish would have been in want for the next month or two.'

Stockdale was not paying much attention to her words, and he said, 'I don't think I can go back like this. Those four poor Preventives may be murdered for all I know.'

'Murdered!' said Lizzy impatiently. 'We don't do murder here.'

'Well, I shall go as far as Warm'ell Cross to see,' said Stockdale decisively; and, without wishing her safe home or anything else, the minister turned back. Lizzy stood looking at him till his form was absorbed in the shades; and then, with sadness, she went in the direction of Nether-Moynton.

The road was lonely, and after nightfall at this time of the year there was often not a passer for hours. Stockdale pursued his way without hearing a sound beyond that of his own footsteps; and in due time he passed beneath the trees of the plantation which surrounded the Warm'ell Cross-road. Before he had reached the point of intersection he heard voices from the thicket.

'Hoi-hoi-hoi! Help, help!'

The voices were not at all feeble or despairing, but they were unmistakably anxious. Stockdale had no weapon, and before plunging into the pitchy darkness of the plantation he pulled a stake from the hedge, to use in case of need. When he got among the trees he shouted—'What's the matter—where are you?'

'Here,' answered the voices; and, pushing through the brambles in that direction, he came near the objects of his search.

'Why don't you come forward?' said Stockdale.

'We be tied to the trees!'

'Who are you?'

'Poor Will Latimer the Customs-officer!' said one plaintively. 'Just come and cut these cords, there's a good man. We were afraid nobody would pass by to-night.'

Stockdale soon loosened them, upon which they stretched their limbs and stood at their ease.

'The rascals!' said Latimer, getting now into a rage, though he had seemed quite meek when Stockdale first came up. ''Tis the same set of fellows. I know they were Moynton chaps to a man.'

'But we can't swear to 'em,' said another. 'Not one of 'em spoke.'

'What are you going to do?' said Stockdale.

'I'd fain go back to Moynton, and have at 'em again!' said Latimer.

'So would we!' said his comrades.

'Fight till we die!' said Latimer.

'We will, we will!' said his men.

'But,' said Latimer, more frigidly, as they came out of the plantation, 'we don't *know* that these chaps with black faces were Moynton men? And proof is a hard thing.'

'So it is,' said the rest.

'And therefore we won't do nothing at all,' said Latimer, with complete dispassionateness. 'For my part, I'd sooner be them than we. The clitches of my arms are burning like fire from the cords those two strapping women tied round 'em. My opinion is, now I have had time to think o't, that you may serve your

Gover'ment at too high a price. For these two nights and days I have not had an hour's res.; and, please God, here's for home-along.'

The other officers agreed heartily to this course; and, thanking Stockdale for his timely assistance, they parted from him at the Cross, taking themselves the western road, and Stockdale going back to Nether-Moynton.

During that walk the minister was lost in reverie of the most painful kind. As soon as he got into the house, and before entering his own rooms, he advanced to the door of the little back parlour in which Lizzy usually sat with her mother. He found her there alone. Stockdale went forward, and, like a man in a dream, looked down upon the table that stood between him and the young woman, who had her bonnet and cloak still on. As he did not speak, she looked up from her chair at him, with misgiving in her eye.

'Where are they gone?' he then said listlessly.

'Who? – I don't know. I have seen nothing of them since. I came straight in here.'

'If your men can manage to get off with those tubs, it will be a great profit to you, I suppose?'

'A share will be mine, a share my cousin Owlett's, a share to each of the two farmers, and a share divided amongst the men who helped us.'

'And you still think,' he went on slowly, 'that you will not give this business up?'

Lizzy rose, and put her hand upon his shoulder. 'Don't ask that,' she whispered. 'You don't know what you are asking. I must tell you, though I meant not to do it. What I make by that trade is all I have to keep my mother and myself with.'

He was astonished. 'I did not dream of such a thing,' he said. 'I would rather have scraped the roads, had I been you. What is money compared with a clear conscience?'

'My conscience is clear. I know my mother, but the king I have never seen. His dues are nothing to me. But it is a great deal to me that my mother and I should live.'

'Marry me, and promise to give it up. I will keep your mother.'

'It is good of you,' she said, moved a little. 'Let me think of it by myself. I would rather not answer now.'

She reserved her answer till the next day, and came into his room with a solemn face. 'I cannot do what you wished!' she said passionately. 'It is too much to ask. My whole life ha' been passed in this way.' Her words and manner showed that before entering she had been struggling with herself in private, and that the contention had been strong.

Stockdale turned pale, but he spoke quietly. 'Then, Lizzy, we must part. I cannot go against my principles in this matter, and I cannot make my profession a mockery. You know how I love you, and what I would do for you; but this one thing I cannot do.'

'But why should you belong to that profession?' she burst out. 'I have got this large house; why can't you marry me, and live here with us, and not be a Methodist preacher any more? I assure you, Richard, it is no harm, and I wish you could only see it as I do! We only carry it on in winter: in summer it is never done at all. It stirs up one's dull life at this time o' the year, and gives excitement, which I have got so used to now that I should hardly know how to do 'ithout it. At nights, when the wind blows, instead of being dull and stupid, and not noticing whether it do blow or not, your mind is afield, even if you are not afield yourself; and you are wondering how the chaps are getting on; and you walk up and down the room, and look out o' window, and then you go out yourself, and know your way about as well by night as by day, and have hair-breadth escapes from old Latimer and his fellows, who are too stupid ever to really frighten us, and only make us a bit nimble.'

'He frightened you a little last night, anyhow: and I would advise you to drop it before it is worse.'

She shook her head. 'No, I must go on as I have begun. I was born to it. It is in my blood, and I can't be cured. O, Richard, you cannot think what a hard thing you have asked, and how sharp you try me when you put me between this and my love for 'ee!'

Stockdale was leaning with his elbow on the mantelpiece, his hands over his eyes. 'We ought never to have met, Lizzy,' he said. 'It was an ill day for us! I little thought there was anything so hopeless and impossible in our engagement as this. Well, it is too late now to regret consequences in this way. I have had the happiness of seeing you and knowing you at least.'

'You dissent from Church, and I dissent from State,' she said. 'And I don't see why we are not well matched.'

He smiled sadly, while Lizzy remained looking down, her eyes beginning to overflow.

That was an unhappy evening for both of them, and the days that followed were unhappy days. Both she and he went mechanically about their employments, and his depression was marked in the village by more than one of his denomination with whom he came in contact. But Lizzy, who passed her days indoors, was unsuspected of being the cause: for it was generally understood that a quiet engagement to marry existed between her and her cousin Owlett, and had existed for some time.

Thus uncertainly the week passed on; till one morning Stockdale said to her: 'I have had a letter, Lizzy. I must call you that till I am gone.'

'Gone?' said she blankly.

'Yes,' he said. 'I am going from this place. I felt it would be better for us both that I should not stay after what has happened. In fact, I couldn't stay here, and look on you from day to day, without becoming weak and faltering in my course. I have just heard of an arrangement by which the other minister can arrive here in about a week; and let me go elsewhere.'

That he had all this time continued so firmly fixed in his resolution came upon her as a grievous surprise. 'You never loved me!' she said bitterly.

'I might say the same,' he returned; 'but I will not. Grant me one favour. Come and hear my last sermon on the day before I go.'

Lizzy, who was a church-goer on Sunday mornings, frequently attended Stockdale's chapel in the evening with the rest of the double-minded; and she promised.

It became known that Stockdale was going to leave, and a good many people outside his own sect were sorry to hear it. The intervening days flew rapidly away, and on the evening of the Sunday which preceded the morning of his departure Lizzy sat in the chapel to hear him for the last time. The little building was full to overflowing, and he took up the subject which all had expected, that of the contraband trade so extensively practised among them. His hearers, in laying his words to their own hearts, did not perceive that they were most particularly directed against Lizzy, till the sermon waxed warm, and Stockdale nearly broke down with emotion. In truth his own earnestness, and her sad eyes looking up at him, were too much for the young man's equanimity. He hardly knew how he ended. He saw Lizzy, as through a mist, turn and go away with the rest of the congregation; and shortly afterwards followed her home.

She invited him to supper, and they sat down alone, her mother having, as was usual with her on Sunday nights, gone to bed early.

'We will part friends, won't we?' said Lizzy, with forced gaiety, and never alluding to the sermon: a reticence which rather disappointed him.

'We will,' he said, with a forced smile on his part; and they sat down.

It was the first meal that they had ever shared together in their lives, and probably the last that they would so share. When it was over, and the indifferent conversation could no longer be continued, he arose and took her hand. 'Lizzy,' he said, 'do you say we must part – do you?'

'You do,' she said solemnly. 'I can say no more.'

'Nor I,' said he. 'If that is your answer, good-bye!'

Stockdale bent over her and kissed her, and she involuntarily returned his kiss. 'I shall go early,' he said hurriedly. 'I shall not see you again.'

And he did leave early. He fancied, when stepping forth into the gray morning light, to mount the van which was to carry him away, that he saw a face between the parted curtains of Lizzy's window, but the light was faint, and the panes glistened with wet; so he could not be sure. Stockdale mounted the vehicle, and was gone; and on the following Sunday the new minister preached in the chapel of the Moynton Wesleyans.

One day, two years after the parting, Stockdale, now settled in a midland town, came into Nether-Moynton by carrier in the original way. Jogging along in the van that afternoon he had put questions to the driver, and the answers that he received interested the minister deeply. The result of them was that he went without the least hesitation to the door of his former lodging. It was about six o'clock in the evening, and the same time of year as when he had left; now, too, the ground was damp and glistening, the west was bright, and Lizzy's snowdrops were raising their heads in the border under the wall.

Lizzy must have caught sight of him from the window, for by the time that he reached the door she was there holding it open: and then, as if she had not sufficiently considered her act of coming out, she drew herself back, saying with some constraint, 'Mr Stockdale!'

'You knew it was,' said Stockdale, taking her hand. 'I wrote to say I should call.'

'Yes, but you did not say when,' she answered.

'I did not. I was not quite sure when my business would lead me to these parts.'

'You only came because business brought you near?'

'Well, that is the fact; but I have often thought I should like to come on purpose to see you. . . . . But what's all this that has happened? I told you how it would be, Lizzy, and you would not listen to me.'

'I would not,' she said sadly. 'But I had been brought up to that life; and it was second nature to me. However, it is all over now. The officers have blood-money for taking a man dead or alive, and the trade is going to nothing. We were hunted down like rats.'

'Owlett is quite gone, I hear.'

'Yes. He is in America. We had a dreadful struggle that last time, when they tried to take him. It is a perfect miracle that he lived through it; and it is a wonder that I was not killed. I was shot in the hand. It was not by aim; the shot was really meant for my cousin; but I was behind, looking on as usual, and the bullet came to me. It bled terribly, but I got home without fainting;and it healed after a time. You know how he suffered?'

'No,' said Stockdale. 'I only heard that he just escaped with his life.'

'He was shot in the back; but a rib turned the ball. He was badly hurt. We would not let him be took. The men carried him all night across the meads to Kingsbere, and hid him in a barn, dressing his wound as well as they could, till he was so far recovered as to be able to get about. Then he was caught, and tried with the others at the assizes; but they all got off. He had given up his mill for some time; and at last he went to Bristol, and took a passage to America, where he's settled.'

'What do you think of smuggling now?' said the minister gravely.

'I own that we were wrong,' said she. 'But I have suffered for it. I am very poor now, and my mother has been dead these twelve months. . . . But won't you come in, Mr Stockdale?'

Stockdale went in; and it is to be supposed that they came to an understanding; for a fortnight later there was a sale of Lizzy's furniture, and after that a wedding at a chapel in a neighbouring town.

He took her away from her old haunts to the home that he had made for himself in his native county, where she studied her duties as a minister's wife with praiseworthy assiduity. It is said that in after years she wrote an excellent tract called *Render unto Cæsar; or, The Repentant Villagers*, in which her own experience was anonymously used as the introductory story. Stockdale got it printed, after making some corrections, and putting in a few powerful sentences of his own; and many hundreds of copies were distributed by the couple in the course of their married life.

April 1879

NOTE. — The ending of this story with the marriage of Lizzy and the minister was almost *de rigueur* in an English magazine at the time of writing. But at this late date, thirty years after, it may not be amiss to give the ending that would have been preferred by the writer to the convention used above. Moreover it corresponds more closely with the true incidents of which the tale is a vague and flickering shadow. Lizzy did not, in fact, marry the minister, but — much to her credit in the author's opinion — stuck to Jim the smuggler, and emigrated with him after their marriage, an expatrial step rather forced upon him by his adventurous antecedents. They both died in Wisconsin between 1850 and 1860. (*May 1912*)

TESS OF THE D'URBERVILLES

Tess of the
d'Urbervilles

Contents

The Maiden

CHAPTER ONE

ON an evening in the latter part of May a middle-aged man was walking homeward from Shaston to the village of Marlott, in the adjoining Vale of Blakemore or Blackmoor. The pair of legs that carried him were rickety, and there was a bias in his gait which inclined him somewhat to the left of a straight line. He occasionally gave a smart nod, as if in confirmation of some opinion, though he was not thinking of anything in particular. An empty egg-basket was slung upon his arm, the nap of his hat was ruffled, a patch being quite worn away at its brim where his thumb came in taking it off. Presently he was met by an elderly parson astride on a gray mare, who, as he rode, hummed a wandering tune.

'Good night t'ee,' said the man with the basket.

'Good night, Sir John,' said the parson.

The pedestrian, after another pace or two, halted, and turned round.

'Now, sir, begging your pardon; we met last market-day on this road about this time, and I zaid "Good night", and you made reply "*Good night, Sir John*", as now.'

'I did,' said the parson.

'And once before that – near a month ago.'

'I may have.'

'Then what might your meaning be in calling me "Sir John" these different times, when I be plain Jack Durbeyfield, the haggler?'

The parson rode a step or two nearer.

'It was only my whim,' he said; and, after a moment's hesitation: 'It was on account of a discovery I made some little time ago, whilst I was hunting up pedigrees for the new county history. I am Parson Tringham, the antiquary, of Stagfoot Lane. Don't you really know, Durbeyfield, that you are the lineal representative of the ancient and knightly family of the d'Urbervilles, who derive their descent from Sir Pagan d'Urberville, that renowned knight who came from Normandy with William the Conqueror, as appears by Battle Abbey Roll?'

'Never heard it before, sir!'

'Well it's true. Throw up your chin a moment, so that I may catch the profile of your face better. Yes, that's the d'Urberville nose and chin – a little debased. Your ancestor was one of the twelve knights who assisted the Lord of Estremavilla in Normandy in his conquest of Glamorganshire. Branches of your

family held manors over all this part of England; their names appear in the Pipe
Rolls in the time of King Stephen. In the reign of King John one of them was rich
enough to give a manor to the Knights Hospitallers; and in Edward the Second's
time your forefather Brian was summoned to Westminster to attend the great
Council there. You declined a little in Oliver Cromwell's time, but to no serious
extent, and in Charles the Second's reign you were made Knights of the Royal
Oak for your loyalty. Aye, there have been generations of Sir Johns among you,
and if knighthood were hereditary, like a baronetcy, as it practically was in old
times, when men were knighted from father to son, you would be Sir John now.'

'Ye don't say so!'

'In short,' concluded the parson, decisively smacking his leg with his switch,
'there's hardly such another family in England.'

'Daze my eyes, and isn't there?' said Durbeyfield. 'And here have I been
knocking about, year after year, from pillar to post, as if I was no more than the
commonest feller in the parish. . . . And how long hev this news about me been
knowed, Pa'son Tringham?'

The clergyman explained that, as far as he was aware, it had quite died out of
knowledge, and could hardly be said to be known at all. His own investigations
had begun on a day in the preceding spring when, having been engaged in tracing
the vicissitudes of the d'Urberville family, he had observed Durbeyfield's name
on his waggon, and had thereupon been led to make inquiries about his father
and grandfather till he had no doubt on the subject.

'At first I resolved not to disturb you with such a useless piece of information,'
said he. 'However, our impulses are too strong for our judgment sometimes. I
thought you might perhaps know something of it all the while.'

'Well, I have heard once or twice, 'tis true, that my family had seen better days
afore they came to Blackmoor. But I took no notice o't, thinking it to mean that
we had once kept two horses where we now keep only one. I've got a wold silver
spoon, and a wold graven seal at home, too; but, Lord, what's a spoon and
seal? . . . And to think that I and these noble d'Urbervilles were one flesh all the
time. 'Twas said that my gr't-grandfer had secrets, and didn't care to talk of
where he came from. . . . And where do we raise our smoke, now, parson, if I
may make so bold; I mean, where do we d'Urbervilles live?'

'You don't live anywhere. You are extinct – as a county family.'

'That's bad.'

'Yes – what the mendacious family chronicles call extinct in the male line –
that is, gone down – gone under.'

'Then where do we lie?'

'At Kingsbere-sub-Greenhill: rows and rows of you in your vaults, with your
effigies under Purbeck-marble canopies.'

'And where be our family mansions and estates?'

'You haven't any.'

'Oh? No lands neither?'

'None; though you once had 'em in abundance, as I said, for your family
consisted of numerous branches. In this county there was a seat of yours at
Kingsbere, and another at Sherton, and another at Millpond, and another at
Lullstead, and another at Wellbridge.'

'And shall we ever come into our own again?'

'Ah – that I can't tell!'

'And what had I better do about it, sir?' asked Durbeyfield, after a pause.

'Oh – nothing, nothing; except chasten yourself with the thought of "how are the mighty fallen". It is a fact of some interest to the local historian and genealogist, nothing more. There are several families among the cottagers of this county of almost equal lustre. Good night.'

'But you'll turn back and have a quart of beer wi' me on the strength o't, Pa'son Tringham? There's a very pretty brew in tap at The Pure Drop – though, to be sure, not so good as at Rolliver's.'

'No, thank you – not this evening, Durbeyfield. You've had enough already.' Concluding thus the parson rode on his way, with doubts as to his discretion in retailing this curious bit of lore.

When he was gone Durbeyfield walked a few steps in a profound reverie, and then sat down upon the grassy bank by the roadside, depositing his basket before him. In a few minutes a youth appeared in the distance, walking in the same direction as that which had been pursued by Durbeyfield. The latter, on seeing him, held up his hand, and the lad quickened his pace and came near.

'Boy, take up that basket! I want 'ee to go on an errand for me.'

The lath-like stripling frowned. 'Who be you, then, John Durbeyfield, to order me about and call me "boy"? You know my name as well as I know yours!'

'Do you, do you? That's the secret – that's the secret! Now obey my orders, and take the message I'm going to charge 'ee wi'. . . . Well, Fred, I don't mind telling you that the secret is that I'm one of a noble race – it has been just found out by me this present afternoon, p.m.' And as he made the announcement, Durbeyfield, declining from his sitting position, luxuriously stretched himself out upon the bank among the daisies.

The lad stood before Durbeyfield, and contemplated his length from crown to toe.

'Sir John d'Urberville – that's who I am,' continued the prostrate man. 'That is if knights were baronets – which they be. 'Tis recorded in history all about me. Dost know of such a place, lad, as Kingsbere-sub-Greenhill?'

'Ees. I've been there to Greenhill Fair.'

'Well, under the church of that city there lie—'

''Tisn't a city, the place I mean; leastwise 'twaddn' when I was there – 'twas a little one-eyed, blinking sort o' place.'

'Never you mind the place, boy, that's not the question before us. Under the church of that there parish lie my ancestors – hundreds of 'em – in coats of mail and jewels, in gr't lead coffins weighing tons and tons. There's not a man in the county o' South Wessex that's got grander and nobler skillentons in his family than I.'

'Oh?'

'Now take up that basket, and goo on to Marlott, and when you've come to The Pure Drop Inn, tell 'em to send a horse and carriage to me immed'ately, to carry me hwome. And in the bottom o' the carriage they be to put a noggin o' rum in a small bottle, and chalk it up to my account. And when you've done that goo on to my house with the basket, and tell my wife to put away that washing, because she needn't finish it, and wait till I come hwome, as I've news to tell her.'

As the lad stood in a dubious attitude, Durbeyfield put his hand in his pocket, and produced a shilling, one of the chronically few that he possessed.

'Here's for your labour, lad.'

This made a difference in the young man's estimate of the position.

'Yes, Sir John. Thank 'ee. Anything else I can do for 'ee, Sir John?'

'Tell 'em at hwome that I should like for supper, — well, lamb's fry if they can get it; and if they can't, black-pot; and if they can't get that, well, chitterlings will do.'

'Yes, Sir John.'

The boy took up the basket, and as he set out the notes of a brass band were heard from the direction of the village.

'What's that?' said Durbeyfield. 'Not on account o' I?'

''Tis the women's club-walking, Sir John. Why, your da'ter is one o' the members.'

'To be sure — I'd quite forgot it in my thoughts of greater things! Well, vamp on to Marlott, will ye, and order that carriage, and maybe I'll drive round and inspect the club.'

The lad departed, and Durbeyfield lay waiting on the grass and daisies in the evening sun. Not a soul passed that way for a long while, and the faint notes of the band were the only human sounds audible within the rim of blue hills.

CHAPTER TWO

THE village of Marlott lay amid the north-eastern undulations of the beautiful Vale of Blakemore or Blackmoor aforesaid, an engirdled and secluded region, for the most part untrodden as yet by tourist or landscape-painter, though within a four hours' journey from London.

It is a vale whose acquaintance is best made by viewing it from the summits of the hills that surround it — except perhaps during the droughts of summer. An unguided ramble into its recesses in bad weather is apt to engender dissatisfaction with its narrow, tortuous, and miry ways.

This fertile and sheltered tract of country, in which the fields are never brown and the springs never dry, is bounded on the south by the bold chalk ridge that embraces the prominences of Hambledon Hill, Bulbarrow, Nettlecombe-Tout, Dogbury, High Stoy, and Bubb Down. The traveller from the coast, who, after plodding northward for a score of miles over calcareous downs and corn-lands, suddenly reaches the verge of one of these escarpments, is surprised and delighted to behold, extended like a map beneath him, a country differing absolutely from that which he has passed through. Behind him the hills are open, the sun blazes down upon fields so large as to give an unenclosed character to the landscape, the lanes are white, the hedges low and plashed, the atmosphere colourless. Here, in the valley, the world seems to be constructed upon a smaller and more delicate scale; the fields are mere paddocks, so reduced that from this height their hedgerows appear a network of dark green threads overspreading the paler green of the grass. The atmosphere beneath is languorous, and is so tinged with azure that what artists call the middle distance partakes also of that hue, while the horizon beyond is of the deepest ultramarine. Arable lands are few and limited; with but slight exceptions the prospect is a broad rich mass of grass and trees, mantling minor hills and dales within the major. Such is the Vale of Blackmoor.

The district is of historic, no less than of topographical interest. The Vale was known in former times as the Forest of White Hart, from a curious legend of King Henry III's reign, in which the killing by a certain Thomas de la Lynd of a beautiful white hart which the king had run down and spared, was made the occasion of a heavy fine. In those days, and till comparatively recent times, the country was densely wooded. Even now, traces of its earlier condition are to be found in the old oak copses and irregular belts of timber that yet survive upon its slopes, and the hollow-trunked trees that shade so many of its pastures.

The forests have departed, but some old customs of their shades remain. Many, however, linger only in a metamorphosed or disguised form. The May-Day dance, for instance, was to be discerned on the afternoon under notice, in the guise of the club revel, or 'club-walking', as it was there called.

It was an interesting event to the younger inhabitants of Marlott, though its real interest was not observed by the participators in the ceremony. Its singularity lay less in the retention of a custom of walking in procession and dancing on each anniversary than in the members being solely women. In men's clubs such celebrations were, though expiring, less uncommon; but either the natural shyness of the softer sex, or a sarcastic attitude on the part of male relatives, had denuded such women's clubs as remained (if any other did) of this their glory and consummation. The club of Marlott alone lived to uphold the local Cerealia. It had walked for hundreds of years, if not as benefit-club, as votive sisterhood of some sort; and it walked still.

The banded ones were all dressed in white gowns – a gay survival from Old Style days, when cheerfulness and May-time were synonyms – days before the habit of taking long views had reduced emotions to a monotonous average. Their first exhibition of themselves was in a processional march of two and two round the parish. Ideal and real clashed slightly as the sun lit up their figures against the green hedges and creeper-laced house-fronts; for, though the whole troop wore white garments, no two whites were alike among them. Some approached pure blanching; some had a bluish pallor; some worn by the older characters (which had possibly lain by folded for many a year) inclined to a cadaverous tint, and to a Georgian style.

In addition to the distinction of a white frock, every woman and girl carried in her right hand a peeled willow wand, and in her left a bunch of white flowers. The peeling of the former, and the selection of the latter, had been an operation of personal care.

There were a few middle-aged and even elderly women in the train, their silver-wiry hair and wrinkled faces, scourged by time and trouble, having almost a grotesque, certainly a pathetic, appearance in such a jaunty situation. In a true view, perhaps, there was more to be gathered and told of each anxious and experienced one, to whom the years were drawing nigh when she should say, 'I have no pleasure in them,' than of her juvenile comrades. But let the elder be passed over here for those under whose bodices the life throbbed quick and warm.

The young girls formed, indeed, the majority of the band, and their heads of luxuriant hair reflected in the sunshine every tone of gold, and black, and brown. Some had beautiful eyes, others a beautiful nose, others a beautiful mouth and figure: few, if any, had all. A difficulty of arranging their lips in this crude exposure to public scrutiny, an inability to balance their heads, and to dissociate self-consciousness from their features, was apparent in them, and showed that they were genuine country girls, unaccustomed to many eyes.

And as each and all of them were warmed without by the sun, so each had a private little sun for her soul to bask in; some dream, some affection, some hobby, at least some remote and distant hope which, though perhaps starving to nothing, still lived on, as hopes will. Thus they were all cheerful, and many of them merry.

They came round by The Pure Drop Inn, and were turning out of the high road to pass through a wicket-gate into the meadows, when one of the women said —

'The Lord-a-Lord! Why, Tess Durbeyfield, if there isn't thy father riding hwome in a carriage!'

A young member of the band turned her head at the exclamation. She was a fine and handsome girl — not handsomer than some others, possibly — but her mobile peony mouth and large innocent eyes added eloquence to colour and shape. She wore a red ribbon in her hair, and was the only one of the white company who could boast of such a pronounced adornment. As she looked round Durbeyfield was seen moving along the road in a chaise belonging to The Pure Drop, driven by a frizzle-headed brawny damsel with her gown-sleeves rolled above her elbows. This was the cheerful servant of that establishment, who, in her part of factotum, turned groom and ostler at times. Durbeyfield, leaning back, and with his eyes closed luxuriously, was waving his hand above his head, and singing in a slow recitative —

'I've-got-a-gr't-family-vault-at-Kingsbere — and knighted-fore-fathers-in-lead-coffins-there!'

The clubbists tittered, except the girl called Tess — in whom a slow heat seemed to rise at the sense that her father was making himself foolish in their eyes.

'He's tired, that's all,' she said hastily, 'and he has got a lift home, because our own horse has to rest to-day.'

'Bless thy simplicity, Tess,' said her companions. 'He's got his market-nitch. Haw-haw!'

'Look here; I won't walk another inch with you, if you say any jokes about him!' Tess cried, and the colour upon her cheeks spread over her face and neck. In a moment her eyes grew moist, and her glance drooped to the ground. Perceiving that they had really pained her they said no more, and order again prevailed. Tess's pride would not allow her to turn her head again, to learn what her father's meaning was, if he had any; and thus she moved on with the whole body to the enclosure where there was to be dancing on the green. By the time the spot was reached she had recovered her equanimity, and tapped her neighbour with her wand and talked as usual.

Tess Durbeyfield at this time of her life was a mere vessel of emotion untinctured by experience. The dialect was on her tongue to some extent, despite the village school: the characteristic intonation of that dialect for this district being the voicing approximately rendered by the syllable UR, probably as rich an utterance as any to be found in human speech. The pouted-up deep red mouth to which this syllable was native had hardly as yet settled into its definite shape, and her lower lip had a way of thrusting the middle of her top one upward, when they closed together after a word.

Phases of her childhood lurked in her aspect still. As she walked along to-day, for all her bouncing handsome womanliness, you could sometimes see her twelfth year in her cheeks, or her ninth sparkling from her eyes; and even her fifth would flit over the curves of her mouth now and then.

Yet few knew, and still fewer considered this. A small minority, mainly strangers, would look long at her in casually passing by, and grow momentarily fascinated by her freshness, and wonder if they would ever see her again: but to almost everybody she was a fine and picturesque country girl, and no more.

Nothing was seen or heard of Durbeyfield in his triumphal chariot under the conduct of the ostleress, and the club having entered the allotted space, dancing began. As there were no men in the company the girls danced at first with each other, but when the hour for the close of labour drew on, the masculine inhabitants of the village, together with other idlers and pedestrians, gathered round the spot, and appeared inclined to negotiate for a partner.

Among these on-lookers were three young men of a superior class, carrying small knapsacks strapped to their shoulders, and stout sticks in their hands. Their general likeness to each other, and their consecutive ages, would almost have suggested that they might be, what in fact they were, brothers. The eldest wore the white tie, high waistcoat, and thin-brimmed hat of the regulation curate; the second was the normal undergraduate; the appearance of the third and youngest would hardly have been sufficient to characterize him; there was an uncribbed, uncabined aspect in his eyes and attire, implying that he had hardly as yet found the entrance to his professional groove. That he was a desultory tentative student of something and everything might only have been predicted of him.

These three brethren told casual acquaintance that they were spending their Whitsun holidays in a walking tour through the Vale of Blackmoor, their course being south-westerly from the town of Shaston on the north-east.

They leant over the gate by the highway, and inquired as to the meaning of the dance and the white-frocked maids. The two elder of the brothers were plainly not intending to linger more than a moment, but the spectacle of a bevy of girls dancing without male partners seemed to amuse the third, and make him in no hurry to move on. He unstrapped his knapsack, put it, with his stick, on the hedge-bank, and opened the gate.

'What are you going to do, Angel?' asked the eldest.

'I am inclined to go and have a fling with them. Why not all of us — just for a minute or two — it will not detain us long?'

'No — no; nonsense!' said the first. 'Dancing in public with a troop of country hoydens — suppose we should be seen! Come along, or it will be dark before we get to Stourcastle, and there's no place we can sleep at nearer than that; besides, we must get through another chapter of *A Counterblast to Agnosticism* before we turn in, now I have taken the trouble to bring the book.'

'All right – I'll overtake you and Cuthbert in five minutes; don't stop; I give my word that I will, Felix.'

The two elder reluctantly left him and walked on, taking their brother's knapsack to relieve him in following, and the youngest entered the field.

'This is a thousand pities,' he said gallantly, to two or three of the girls nearest him, as soon as there was a pause in the dance. 'Where are your partners, my dears?'

'They've not left off work yet,' answered one of the boldest. 'They'll be here by and by. Till then, will you be one, sir?'

'Certainly. But what's one among so many!'

'Better than none. 'Tis melancholy work facing and footing it to one of your own sort, and no clipsing and colling at all. Now, pick and choose.'

''Ssh – don't be so for'ard!' said a shyer girl.

The young man, thus invited, glanced them over, and attempted some discrimination; but, as the group were all so new to him, he could not very well exercise it. He took almost the first that came to hand, which was not the speaker, as she had expected; nor did it happen to be Tess Durbeyfield. Pedigree, ancestral skeletons, monumental record, the d'Urberville lineaments, did not help Tess in her life's battle as yet, even to the extent of attracting to her a dancing-partner over the heads of the commonest peasantry. So much for Norman blood unaided by Victorian lucre.

The name of the eclipsing girl, whatever it was, has not been handed down; but she was envied by all as the first who enjoyed the luxury of a masculine partner that evening. Yet such was the force of example that the village young men, who had not hastened to enter the gate while no intruder was in the way, now dropped in quickly, and soon the couples became leavened with rustic youth to a marked extent, till at length the plainest woman in the club was no longer compelled to foot it on the masculine side of the figure.

The church clock struck, when suddenly the student said that he must leave – he had been forgetting himself – he had to join his companions. As he fell out of the dance his eyes lighted on Tess Durbeyfield, whose own large orbs wore, to tell the truth, the faintest aspect of reproach that he had not chosen her. He, too, was sorry then that, owing to her backwardness, he had not observed her; and with that in his mind he left the pasture.

On account of his long delay he started in a flying-run down the lane westward, and had soon passed the hollow and mounted the next rise. He had not yet overtaken his brothers, but he paused to get breath, and looked back. He could see the white figures of the girls in the green enclosure whirling about as they had whirled when he was among them. They seemed to have quite forgotten him already.

All of them, except, perhaps, one. This white shape stood apart by the hedge alone. From her position he knew it to be the pretty maiden with whom he had not danced. Trifling as the matter was, he yet instinctively felt that she was hurt by his oversight. He wished that he had asked her; he wished that he had inquired her name. She was so modest, so expressive, she had looked so soft in her thin white gown that he felt he had acted stupidly.

However, it could not be helped, and turning, and bending himself to a rapid walk, he dismissed the subject from his mind.

CHAPTER THREE

As for Tess Durbeyfield, she did not so easily dislodge the incident from her consideration. She had no spirit to dance again for a long time, though she might have had plenty of partners; but, ah! they did not speak so nicely as the strange young man had done. It was not till the rays of the sun had absorbed the young stranger's retreating figure on the hill that she shook off her temporary sadness and answered her would-be partner in the affirmative.

She remained with her comrades till dusk, and participated with a certain zest in the dancing; though, being heart-whole as yet, she enjoyed treading a measure purely for its own sake; little divining when she saw 'the soft torments, the bitter sweets, the pleasing pains, and the agreeable distresses' of those girls who had been wooed and won, what she herself was capable of in that kind. The struggles and wrangles of the lads for her in a jig were an amusement to her — no more; and when they became fierce she rebuked them.

She might have stayed even later, but the incident of her father's odd appearance and manner returned upon the girl's mind to make her anxious, and wondering what had become of him she dropped away from the dancers and bent her steps towards the end of the village at which the parental cottage lay.

While yet many score yards off, other rhythmic sounds than those she had quitted became audible to her; sounds that she knew well — so well. They were a regular series of thumpings from the interior of the house, occasioned by the violent rocking of a cradle upon a stone floor, to which movement a feminine voice kept time by singing, in a vigorous gallopade, the favourite ditty of 'The Spotted Cow' —

> I saw her lie do'—own in yon'—der green gro'—ove;
> Come, love!' and I'll tell' you where!'

The cradle-rocking and the song would cease simultaneously for a moment, and an exclamation at highest vocal pitch would take the place of the melody.

'God bless thy diment eyes! And thy waxen cheeks! And thy cherry mouth! And thy Cubit's thighs! And every bit o' thy blessed body!'

After this invocation the rocking and the singing would recommence, and the 'Spotted Cow' proceed as before. So matters stood when Tess opened the door, and paused upon the mat within it surveying the scene.

The interior, in spite of the melody, struck upon the girl's senses with an unspeakable dreariness. From the holiday gaieties of the field — the white gowns, the nosegays, the willow-wands, the whirling movements on the green, the flash of gentle sentiment towards the stranger — to the yellow melancholy of this one-candled spectacle, what a step! Besides the jar of contrast there came to her a chill self-reproach that she had not returned sooner, to help her mother in these domesticities, instead of indulging herself out-of-doors.

There stood her mother amid the group of children, as Tess had left her, hanging over the Monday washing-tub, which had now, as always, lingered on to the end of the week. Out of that tub had come the day before – Tess felt it with a dreadful sting of remorse – the very white frock upon her back which she had so carelessly greened about the skirt on the damping grass – which had been wrung up and ironed by her mother's own hands.

As usual, Mrs Durbeyfield was balanced on one foot beside the tub, the other being engaged in the aforesaid business of rocking her youngest child. The cradle-rockers had done hard duty for so many years, under the weight of so many children, on that flagstone floor, that they were worn nearly flat, in consequence of which a huge jerk accompanied each swing of the cot, flinging the baby from side to side like a weaver's shuttle, as Mrs Durbeyfield, excited by her song, trod the rocker with all the spring that was left in her after a long day's seething in the suds.

Nick-knock, nick-knock, went the cradle; the candle-flame stretched itself tall, and began jigging up and down; the water dribbled from the matron's elbows, and the song galloped on to the end of the verse, Mrs Durbeyfield regarding her daughter the while. Even now, when burdened with a young family, Joan Durbeyfield was a passionate lover of tune. No ditty floated into Blackmoor Vale from the outer world but Tess's mother caught up its notation in a week..

There still faintly beamed from the woman's features something of the freshness, and even the prettiness, of her youth; rendering it probable that the personal charms which Tess could boast of were in main part her mother's gift, and therefore unknightly, unhistorical.

'I'll rock the cradle for 'ee, mother,' said the daughter gently. 'Or I'll take off my best frock and help you wring up? I thought you had finished long ago.'

Her mother bore Tess no ill-will for leaving the house-work to her single-handed efforts for so long; indeed, Joan seldom upbraided her thereon at any time, feeling but slightly the lack of Tess's assistance whilst her instinctive plan for relieving herself of her labours lay in postponing them. To-night, however, she was even in a blither mood than usual. There was a dreaminess, a preoccupation, an exaltation, in the maternal look which the girl could not understand.

'Well, I'm glad you've come,' her mother said, as soon as the last note had passed out of her. 'I want to go and fetch your father; but what's more'n that, I want to tell 'ee what have happened. Y'll be fess enough, my poppet, when th'st know!' (Mrs Durbeyfield habitually spoke the dialect; her daughter, who had passed the Sixth Standard in the National School under a London-trained mistress, spoke two languages; the dialect at home, more or less; ordinary English abroad and to persons of quality.)

'Since I've been away?' Tess asked.

'Ay!'

'Had it anything to do with father's making such a mommet of himself in thik carriage this afternoon? Why did 'er? I felt inclined to sink into the ground with shame!'

'That wer all a part of the larry! We've been found to be the greatest gentlefolk in the whole county – reaching all back long before Oliver Grumble's time – to the days of the Pagan Turks – with monuments, and vaults, and crests, and 'scutcheons, and the Lord knows what all. In Saint Charles's days we was made

Knights o' the Royal Oak, our real name being d'Urberville! . . . Don't that make your bosom plim? 'Twas on this account that your father rode home in the vlee; not because he'd been drinking, as people supposed.'

'I'm glad of that. Will it do us any good, mother?'

'O yes! 'Tis thoughted that great things may come o't. No doubt a mampus of volk of our own rank will be down here in their carriages as soon as 'tis known. Your father learnt it on his way hwome from Shaston, and he has been telling me the whole pedigree of the matter.'

'Where is father now?' asked Tess suddenly.

Her mother gave irrelevant information by way of answer: 'He called to see the doctor to-day in Shaston. It is not consumption at all, it seems. It is fat round his heart, 'a says. There, it is like this.' Joan Durbeyfield, as she spoke, curved a sodden thumb and forefinger to the shape of the letter C, and used the other forefinger as a pointer. ' "At the present moment," he says to your father, "your heart is enclosed all round there, and all round there; this space is still open," ' a says. "As soon as it do meet, so," ' – Mrs Durbeyfield closed her fingers into a circle complete –' "off you will go like a shadder, Mr Durbeyfield," ' a says. "You mid last ten years; you mid go off in ten months or ten days." '

Tess looked alarmed. Her father possibly to go behind the eternal cloud so soon, notwithstanding this sudden greatness!

'But where *is* father?' she asked again.

Her mother put on a deprecating look. 'Now don't you be bursting out angry! The poor man – he felt so rafted after this uplifting by the pa'son's news – that he went up to Rolliver's half an hour ago. He do want to get up his strength for his journey to-morrow with that load of beehives, which must be delivered, family or no. He'll have to start shortly after twelve to-night, as the distance is so long.'

'Get up his strength!' said Tess impetuously, the tears welling to her eyes. 'O my God! Go to a public-house to get up his strength! And you as well agreed as he, mother!'

Her rebuke and her mood seemed to fill the whole room, and to impart a cowed look to the furniture, and candle, and children playing about, and to her mother's face.

'No.' said the latter touchily, 'I be not agreed. I have been waiting for 'ee to bide and keep house while I go to fetch him.'

'I'll go.'

'O no, Tess. You see, it would be no use.'

Tess did not expostulate. She knew what her mother's objection meant. Mrs Durbeyfield's jacket and bonnet were already hanging slily upon a chair by her side, in readiness for this contemplated jaunt, the reason for which the matron deplored more than its necessity.

'And take the *Compleat Fortune-Teller* to the outhouse,' Joan continued, rapidly wiping her hands, and donning the garments.

The *Compleat Fortune-Teller* was an old thick volume, which lay on a table at her elbow, so worn by pocketing that the margins had reached the edge of the type. Tess took it up, and her mother started.

This going to hunt up her shiftless husband at the inn was one of the Mrs Durbeyfield's still extant enjoyments in the muck and muddle of rearing children. To discover him at Rolliver's, to sit there for an hour or two by his side and dismiss all thought and care of the children during the interval, made her happy. A sort of halo, an occidental glow, came over life then. Troubles and other realities took on themselves a metaphysical impalpability, sinking to mere mental phenomena for serene contemplation, and no longer stood as pressing concretions which chafed body and soul. The youngsters, not immediately within sight, seemed rather bright and desirable appurtenances than otherwise; the incidents of daily life were not without humorousness and jollity in their aspect there. She felt a little as she had used to feel when she sat by her now wedded husband in the same spot during wooing, shutting her eyes to his defects of character, and regarding him only in his ideal presentation as lover.

Tess, being left alone with the younger children, went first to the outhouse with the fortune-telling book, and stuffed it into the thatch. A curious fetichistic fear of this grimy volume on the part of her mother prevented her ever allowing it to stay in the house all night, and hither it was brought back whenever it had been consulted. Between the mother, with her fast-perishing lumber of superstitions, folk-lore, dialect, and orally transmitted ballads, and the daughter, with her trained National teachings and Standard knowledge under an infinitely Revised Code, there was a gap of two hundred years as ordinarily understood. When they were together the Jacobean and the Victorian ages were juxtaposed.

Returning along the garden path Tess mused on what the mother could have wished to ascertain from the book on this particular day. She guessed the recent ancestral discovery to bear upon it, but did not divine that it solely concerned herself. Dismissing this, however, she busied herself with sprinkling the linen dried during the day-time, in company with her nine-year-old brother Abraham, and her sister Eliza-Louisa of twelve and a half, called "Liza-Lu', the youngest ones being put to bed. There was an interval of four years and more between Tess and the next of the family, the two who had filled the gap having died in their infancy, and this left her a deputy-maternal attitude when she was alone with her juniors. Next in juvenility to Abraham came two more girls, Hope and Modesty; then a boy of three, and then the baby, who had just completed his first year.

All these young souls were passengers in the Durbeyfield ship — entirely dependent on the judgment of the two Durbeyfield adults for their pleasures, their necessities, their health, even their existence. If the heads of the Durbeyfield household chose to sail into difficulty, disaster, starvation, disease, degradation, death, thither were these half-dozen little captives under hatches compelled to sail with them — six helpless creatures, who had never been asked if they wished for life on any terms, much less if they wished for it on such hard conditions as were involved in being of the shiftless house of Durbeyfield. Some people would like to know whence the poet whose philosophy is in these days deemed as profound and trustworthy as his song is breezy and pure, gets his authority for speaking of 'Nature's holy plan'.

It grew later, and neither father nor mother reappeared. Tess looked out of the door, and took a mental journey through Marlott. The village was shutting its eyes. Candles and lamps were being put out everywhere: she could inwardly behold the extinguisher and the extended hand.

Her mother's fetching simply meant one more to fetch. Tess began to perceive that a man in indifferent health, who proposed to start on a journey before one in the morning, ought not to be at an inn at this late hour celebrating his ancient blood.

'Abraham,' she said to her little brother, 'do you put on your hat — you bain't afraid? — and go up to Rolliver's, and see what has gone wi' father and mother.'

The boy jumped promptly from his seat, and opened the door, and the night swallowed him up. Half an hour passed yet again; neither man, woman, nor child returned. Abraham, like his parents, seemed to have been limed and caught by the ensnaring inn.

'I must go myself,' she said.

'Liza-Lu then went to bed, and Tess, locking them all in, started on her way up the dark and crooked lane or street not made for hasty progress; a street laid out before inches of land had value, and when one-handed clocks sufficiently subdivided the day.

CHAPTER FOUR

R OLLIVER'S inn, the single alehouse at this end of the long and broken village, could only boast of an off-license; hence, as nobody could drink on the premises, the amount of overt accommodation for consumers was strictly limited to a little board about six inches wide and two yards long, fixed to the garden palings by pieces of wire, so as to form a ledge. On this board thirsty strangers deposited their cups as they stood in the road and drank, and threw the dregs on the dusty ground to the pattern of Polynesia, and wished they could have a restful seat inside.

Thus the strangers. But there were also local customers who felt the same wish; and where there's a will there's a way.

In a large bedroom upstairs, the window of which was thickly curtained with a great woollen shawl lately discarded by the landlady Mrs Rolliver, were gathered on this evening nearly a dozen persons, all seeking beatitude; all old inhabitants of the nearer end of Marlott, and frequenters of this retreat. Not only did the distance to The Pure Drop, the fully-licensed tavern at the further part of the dispersed village, render its accommodation practically unavailable for dwellers at this end; but the far more serious question, the quality of the liquor, confirmed the prevalent opinion that it was better to drink with Rolliver in a corner of the housetop than with the other landlord in a wide house.

A gaunt four-post bedstead which stood in the room afforded sitting-space for several persons gathered round three of its sides; a couple more men had elevated themselves on a chest of drawers; another rested on the oak-carved 'cwoffer'; two on the wash-stand; another on the stool; and thus all were, somehow, seated at their ease. The stage of mental comfort to which they had arrived at this hour was one wherein their souls expanded beyond their skins, and spread their personalities warmly through the room. In this process the chamber and its furniture grew more and more dignified and luxurious; the shawl hanging at the window took upon itself the richness of tapestry; the brass handles of the chest of drawers were as golden knockers; and the carved bed-posts seemed to have some kinship with the magnificent pillars of Solomon's temple.

Mrs Durbeyfield, having quickly walked hitherward after parting from Tess, opened the front door, crossed the downstairs room, which was in deep gloom, and then unfastened the stair-door like one whose fingers knew the tricks of the latches well. Her ascent of the crooked staircase was a slower process, and her face, as it rose into the light above the last stair, encountered the gaze of all the party assembled in the bedroom.

' – Being a few private friends I've asked in to keep up club-walking at my own expense,' the landlady exclaimed at the sound of footsteps, as glibly as a child repeating the Catechism, while she peered over the stairs. 'Oh, 'tis you, Mrs Durbeyfield – Lard – how you frightened me! – I thought it might be some gaffer sent by Gover'ment.'

Mrs Durbeyfield was welcomed with glances and nods by the remainder of the conclave, and turned to where her husband sat. He was humming absently to himself, in a low tone: 'I be as good as some folks here and there! I've got a great family vault at Kingsbere-sub-Greenhill, and finer skillentons than any man in Wessex!'

'I've something to tell 'ee that's come into my head about that – a grand projick!' whispered his cheerful wife. 'Here, John, don't 'ee see me?' She nudged him, while he, looking through her as through a window-pane, went on with his recitative.

'Hush! Don't 'ee sing so loud, my good man,' said the landlady; 'in case any member of the Gover'ment should be passing, and take away my licends.'

'He's told 'ee what's happened to us, I suppose?' asked Mrs Durbeyfield.

'Yes – in a way. D'ye think there's any money hanging by it?'

'Ah, that's the secret,' said Joan Durbeyfield sagely. 'However, 'tis well to be kin to a coach, even if you don't ride in 'en.' She dropped her public voice, and continued in a low tone to her husband: 'I've been thinking since you brought the news that there's a great rich lady out by Trantridge, on the edge o' The Chase, of the name of d'Urberville.'

'Hey – what's that?' said Sir John.

She repeated the information. 'That lady must be our relation,' she said. 'And my projick is to send Tess to claim kin.'

'There *is* a lady of the name, now you mention it,' said Durbeyfield. 'Pa'son Tringham didn't think of that. But she's nothing beside we – a junior branch of us, no doubt, hailing long since King Norman's day.'

While this question was being discussed neither of the pair noticed, in their preoccupation, that little Abraham had crept into the room and was awaiting an opportunity of asking them to return.

'She is rich, and she'd be sure to take notice o' the maid,' continued Mrs Durbeyfield; 'and 'twill be a very good thing. I don't see why two branches o' one family should not be on visiting terms.'

'Yes; and we'll all claim kin!' said Abraham brightly from under the bedstead. 'And we'll all go and see her when Tess has gone to live with her; and we'll ride in her coach and wear black clothes!'

'How do you come here, child? What nonsense be ye talking! Go away, and play on the stairs till father and mother be ready! . . . Well, Tess ought to go to this other member of our family. She'd be sure to win the lady – Tess would; and likely enough 'twould lead to some noble gentleman marrying her. In short, I know it.'

'How?'

'I tried her fate in the *Fortune-Teller*, and it brought out that very thing! . . . You should ha' seen how pretty she looked to-day; her skin is as sumple as a duchess's.'

'What says the maid herself to going?'

'I've not asked her. She don't know there is any such lady-relation yet. But it would certainly put her in the way of a grand marriage, and she won't say nay to going.'

'Tess is queer.'

'But she's tractable at bottom. Leave her to me.'

Though this conversation had been private, sufficient of its import reached the understandings of those around to suggest to them that the Durbeyfields had weightier concerns to talk of now than common folks had, and that Tess, their pretty eldest daughter, had fine prospects in store.

'Tess is a fine figure o' fun, as I said to myself to-day when I zeed her vamping round parish with the rest,' observed one of the elderly boozers in an undertone. 'But Joan Durbeyfield must mind that she don't get green malt in floor.' It was a local phrase which had a peculiar meaning, and there was no reply.

The conversation became inclusive, and presently other footsteps were heard crossing the room below.

' – Being a few private friends asked in to-night to keep up club-walking at my own expense.' The landlady had rapidly re-used the formula she kept on hand for intruders before she recognized that the newcomer was Tess.

Even to her mother's gaze the girl's young features looked sadly out of place amid the alcoholic vapours which floated here as no unsuitable medium for wrinkled middle-age; and hardly was a reproachful flash from Tess's dark eyes needed to make her father and mother rise from their seats, hastily finish their ale, and descend the stairs behind her, Mrs Rolliver's caution following their footsteps.

'No noise, please, if ye'll be so good, my dears; or I mid lose my licends, and be summons'd, and I don't know what all! 'Night t'ye!'

They went home together, Tess holding one arm of her father, and Mrs Durbeyfield the other. He had, in truth, drunk very little – not a fourth of the quantity which a systematic tippler could carry to church on a Sunday afternoon without a hitch in his eastings or genuflections; but the weakness of Sir John's constitution made mountains of his petty sins in this kind. On reaching the fresh air he was sufficiently unsteady to incline the row of three at one moment as if they were marching to London, and at another as if they were marching to Bath – which produced a comical effect, frequent enough in families on nocturnal homegoings; and, like most comical effects, not quite so comic after all. The two women valiantly disguised these forced excursions and counter-marches as well as they could from Durbeyfield their cause, and from Abraham, and from themselves; and so they approached by degrees their own door, the head of the family bursting suddenly into his former refrain as he drew near, as if to fortify his soul at sight of the smallness of his present residence –

'I've got a fam—ily vault at Kingsbere!'

'Hush — don't be so silly, Jacky,' said his wife. 'Yours is not the only family that was of 'count in wold days. Look at the Anktells, and Horseys, and the Tringhams themselves — gone to seed a'most as much as you — though you was bigger folks than they, that's true. Thank God, I was never of no family, and have nothing to be ashamed of in that way!'

'Don't you be so sure o' that. From your nater 'tis my belief you've disgraced yourselves more than any o' us, and was kings and queens outright at one time.'

Tess turned the subject by saying what was far more prominent in her own mind at the moment than thoughts of her ancestry —

'I am afraid father won't be able to take the journey with the beehives to-morrow so early.'

'I? I shall be all right in an hour or two,' said Durbeyfield.

It was eleven o'clock before the family were all in bed, and two o'clock next morning was the latest hour for starting with the beehives if they were to be delivered to the retailers in Casterbridge before the Saturday market began, the way thither lying by bad roads over a distance of between twenty and thirty miles, and the horse and waggon being of the slowest. At half-past one Mrs Durbeyfield came into the large bedroom where Tess and all her little brothers and sisters slept.

'The poor man can't go,' she said to her eldest daughter, whose great eyes had opened the moment her mother's hand touched the door.

Tess sat up in bed, lost in a vague interspace between a dream and this information.

'But somebody must go,' she replied. 'It is late for the hives already. Swarming will soon be over for the year; and if we put off taking 'em till next week's market the call for 'em will be past, and they'll be thrown on our hands.'

Mrs Durbeyfield looked unequal to the emergency. 'Some young feller, perhaps, would go? One of them who were so much after dancing with 'ee yesterday,' she presently suggested.

'O no — I wouldn't have it for the world!' declared Tess proudly. 'And letting everybody know the reason — such a thing to be ashamed of! I think *I* could go if Abraham could go with me to kip me company.'

Her mother at length agreed to this arrangement. Little Abraham was aroused from his deep sleep in a corner of the same apartment, and made to put on his clothes while still mentally in the other world. Meanwhile Tess had hastily dressed herself; and the twain, lighting a lantern, went out to the stable. The rickety little waggon was already laden, and the girl led out the horse Prince, only a degree less rickety than the vehicle.

The poor creature looked wonderingly round at the night, at the lantern, at their two figures, as if he could not believe that at that hour, when every living thing was intended to be in shelter and at rest, he was called upon to go out and labour. They put a stock of candle-ends into the lantern, hung the latter to the off-side of the load, and directed the horse onward, walking at his shoulder at first during the uphill parts of the way, in order not to overload an animal of so little vigour. To cheer themselves as well as they could, they made an artificial morning with the lantern, some bread and butter, and their own conversation, the real morning being far from come. Abraham, as he more fully awoke (for he had moved in a sort of trance so far), began to talk of the strange shapes assumed by the various dark objects against the sky; of this tree that looked like a raging tiger springing from a lair; of that which resembled a giant's head.

When they had passed the little town of Stourcastle, dumbly somnolent under its thick brown thatch, they reached higher ground. Still higher, on their left, the elevation called Bulbarrow or Bealbarrow, well-nigh the highest in South Wessex, swelled into the sky, engirdled by its earthen trenches. From hereabout the long road was fairly level for some distance onward. They mounted in front of the waggon, and Abraham grew reflective.

'Tess!' he said in a preparatory tone, after a silence.

'Yes, Abraham.'

'Bain't you glad that we've become gentlefolk?'

'Not particular glad.'

'But you be glad that you 'm going to marry a gentleman?'

'What?' said Tess, lifting her face.

'That our great relation will help 'ee to marry a gentleman.'

'I? Our great relation? We have no such relation. What has put that into your head?'

'I heard 'em talking about it up at Rolliver's when I went to find father. There's a rich lady of our family out at Trantridge, and mother said that if you claimed kin with the lady, she'd put 'ee in the way of marrying a gentleman.'

His sister became abruptly still, and lapsed into a pondering silence. Abraham talked on, rather for the pleasure of utterance than for audition, so that his sister's abstraction was of no account. He leant back against the hives, and with upturned face made observations on the stars, whose cold pulses were beating amid the black hollows above, in serene dissociation from those two wisps of human life. He asked how far away those twinklers were, and whether God was on the other side of them. But ever and anon his childish prattle recurred to what impressed his imagination even more deeply than the wonders of creation. If Tess were made rich by marrying a gentleman, would she have money enough to buy a spy-glass so large that it would draw the stars as near to her as Nettlecombe-Tout?

The renewed subject, which seemed to have impregnated the whole family, filled Tess with impatience.

'Never mind that now!' she exclaimed.

'Did you say the stars were worlds, Tess?'

'Yes.'

'All like ours?'

'I don't know; but I think so. They sometimes seem to be like the apples on our stubbard-tree. Most of them splendid and sound —a few blighted.'

'Which do we live on —a splendid one or a blighted one?'

'A blighted one.'

''Tis very unlucky that we didn't pitch on a sound one, when there were so many more of 'em!'

'Yes.'

'Is it like that *really*, Tess?' said Abraham, turning to her much impressed, on reconsideration of this rare information. 'How would it have been if we had pitched on a sound one?'

'Well, father wouldn't have coughed and creeped about as he does, and wouldn't have got too tipsy to go this journey; and mother wouldn't have been always washing, and never getting finished.'

'And you would have been a rich lady ready-made, and not have had to be made rich by marrying a gentleman?'

'O Aby, don't – don't talk of that any more!'

Left to his reflections Abraham soon grew drowsy. Tess was not skilful in the management of a horse, but she thought that she could take upon herself the entire conduct of the load for the present, and allow Abraham to go to sleep if he wished to do so. She made him a sort of nest in front of the hives, in such a manner that he could not fall, and, taking the reins into her own hands, jogged on as before.

Prince required but slight attention, lacking energy for superfluous movements of any sort. With no longer a companion to distract her, Tess fell more deeply into reverie than ever, her back leaning against the hives. The mute procession past her shoulders of trees and hedges became attached to fantastic scenes outside reality, and the occasional heave of the wind became the sigh of some immense sad soul, conterminous with the universe in space, and with history in time.

Then, examining the mesh of events in her own life, she seemed to see the vanity of her father's pride; the gentlemanly suitor awaiting herself in her mother's fancy; to see him as a grimacing personage, laughing at her poverty, and her shrouded knightly ancestry. Everything grew more and more extravagant, and she no longer knew how time passed. A sudden jerk shook her in her seat, and Tess awoke from the sleep into which she, too, had fallen.

They were a long way further on than when she had lost consciousness, and the waggon had stopped. A hollow groan, unlike anything she had ever heard in her life, came from the front, followed by a shout of 'Hoi there!'

The lantern hanging at her waggon had gone out, but another was shining in her face – much brighter than her own had been. Something terrible had happened. The harness was entangled with an object which blocked the way.

In consternation Tess jumped down, and discovered the dreadful truth. The groan had proceeded from her father's poor horse Prince. The morning mail-cart, with its two noiseless wheels, speeding along these lanes like an arrow, as it always did, had driven into her slow and unlighted equipage. The pointed shaft of the cart had entered the breast of the unhappy Prince like a sword, and from the wound his life's blood was spouting in a stream, and falling with a hiss into the road.

In her despair Tess sprang forward and put her hand upon the hole, with the only result that she became splashed from face to skirt with the crimson drops. Then she stood helplessly looking on. Prince also stood firm and motionless as long as he could; till he suddenly sank down in a heap.

By this time the mail-cart man had joined her, and began dragging and unharnessing the hot form of Prince. But he was already dead, and, seeing that nothing more could be done immediately, the mail-cart man returned to his own animal, which was uninjured.

'You was on the wrong side,' he said. 'I am bound to go on with the mail-bags, so that the best thing for you to do is to bide here with your load. I'll send somebody to help you as soon as I can. It is getting daylight, and you have nothing to fear.'

He mounted and sped on his way; while Tess stood and waited. The atmosphere turned pale, the birds shook themselves in the hedges, arose, and twittered; the lane showed all its white features, and Tess showed hers, still whiter. The huge pool of blood in front of her was already assuming the iridescence of coagulation; and when the sun rose a hundred prismatic hues were reflected from it. Prince lay alongside still and stark; his eyes half open, the hole in his chest looking scarcely large enough to have let out all that had animated him.

''Tis all my doing — all mine!' the girl cried, gazing at the spectacle. 'No excuse for me — none. What will mother and father live on now? Aby, Aby!' She shook the child, who had slept soundly through the whole disaster. 'We can't go on with our load — Prince is killed!'

When Abraham realized all, the furrows of fifty years were extemporized on his young face.

'Why, I danced and laughed only yesterday!' she went on to herself. 'To think that I was such a fool!'

''Tis because we be on a blighted star, and not a sound one, isn't it, Tess?' murmured Abraham through his tears.

In silence they waited through an interval which seemed endless. At length a sound, and an approaching object, proved to them that the driver of the mail-cart had been as good as his word. A farmer's man from near Stourcastle came up, leading a strong cob. He was harnessed to the waggon of beehives in the place of Prince, and the load taken on towards Casterbridge.

The evening of the same day saw the empty waggon reach again the spot of the accident. Prince had lain there in the ditch since the morning; but the place of the blood-pool was still visible in the middle of the road, though scratched and scraped over by passing vehicles. All that was left of Prince was now hoisted into the waggon he had formerly hauled, and with his hoofs in the air, and his shoes shining in the setting sunlight, he retraced the eight or nine miles to Marlott.

Tess had gone back earlier. How to break the news was more than she could think. It was a relief to her tongue to find from the faces of her parents that they already knew of their loss, though this did not lessen the self-reproach which she continued to heap upon herself for her negligence.

But the very shiftlessness of the household rendered the misfortune a less terrifying one to them than it would have been to a striving family, though in the present case it meant ruin, and in the other it would only have meant inconvenience. In the Durbeyfield countenances there was nothing of the red wrath that would have burnt upon the girl from parents more ambitious for her welfare. Nobody blamed Tess as she blamed herself.

When it was discovered that the knacker and tanner would give only a very few shillings for Prince's carcase because of his decrepitude, Durbeyfield rose to the occasion.

'No,' said he stoically, 'I won't sell his old body. When we d'Urbervilles was knights in the land, we didn't sell our chargers for cat's meat. Let 'em keep their shillings! He've served me well in his lifetime, and I won't part from him now.'

He worked harder the next day in digging a grave for Prince in the garden than he had worked for months to grow a crop for his family. When the hole was ready, Durbeyfield and his wife tied a rope round the horse and dragged him up the path towards it, the children following in funeral train. Abraham and 'Liza-Lu sobbed, Hope and Modesty discharged their griefs in loud blares which echoed from the walls; and when Prince was tumbled in they gathered round the grave. The bread-winner had been taken away from them; what would they do?

'Is he gone to heaven?' asked Abraham, between the sobs.

Then Durbeyfield began to shovel in the earth, and the children cried anew. All except Tess. Her face was dry and pale, as though she regarded herself in the light of a murderess.

CHAPTER FIVE

The haggling business, which had mainly depended on the horse, became disorganized forthwith. Distress, if not penury, loomed in the distance. Durbeyfield was what was locally called a slack-twisted fellow; he had good strength to work at times; but the times could not be relied on to coincide with the hours of requirement; and, having been unaccustomed to the regular toil of the day-labourer, he was not particularly persistent when they did so coincide.

Tess, meanwhile, as the one who had dragged her parents into this quagmire, was silently wondering what she could do to help them out of it; and then her mother broached her scheme.

'We must take the ups wi' the downs, Tess,' said she; 'and never could your high blood have been found out at a more called-for moment. You must try your friends. Do ye know that there is a very rich Mrs d'Urberville living on the outskirts o' The Chase, who must be our relation? You must go to her and claim kin, and ask for some help in our trouble.'

'I shouldn't care to do that,' says Tess. 'If there is such a lady, 'twould be enough for us if she were friendly – not to expect her to give us help.'

'You could win her round to do anything, my dear. Besides, perhaps there's more in it than you know of. I've heard what I've heard, good-now.'

The oppressive sense of the harm she had done led Tess to be more deferential than she might otherwise have been to the maternal wish; but she could not understand why her mother should find such satisfaction in contemplating an enterprise of, to her, such doubtful profit. Her mother might have made inquiries, and have discovered that this Mrs d'Urberville was a lady of unequalled virtues and charity. But Tess's pride made the part of poor relation one of particular distaste to her.

'I'd rather try to get work,' she murmured.

'Durbeyfield, you can settle it,' said his wife, turning to where he sat in the background. 'If you say she ought to go, she will go.'

'I don't like my children going and making themselves beholden to strange kin,' murmured he. 'I'm the head of the noblest branch o' the family, and I ought to live up to it.'

His reasons for staying away were worse to Tess than her own objection to going. 'Well, as I killed the horse, mother,' she said mournfully, 'I suppose I ought to do something. I don't mind going and seeing her, but you must leave it to me about asking for help. And don't go thinking about her making a match for me – it is silly.'

'Very well said, Tess!' observed her father setentiously.

'Who said I had such a thought?' asked Joan.

'I fancy it is in your mind, mother. But I'll go.'

Rising early next day she walked to the hill-town called Shaston, and there took advantage of a van which twice in the week ran from Shaston eastward to Chaseborough, passing near Trantridge, the parish in which the vague and mysterious Mrs d'Urberville had her residence.

Tess Durbeyfield's route on this memorable morning lay amid the north-eastern undulations of the Vale in which she had been born, and in which her life had unfolded. The Vale of Blackmoor was to her the world, and its inhabitants the races thereof. From the gates and stiles of Marlott she had looked down its length in the wondering days of infancy, and what had been mystery to her then was not much less than mystery to her now. She had seen daily from her chamber-window towers, villages, faint white mansions; above all the town of Shaston standing majestically on its height; its windows shining like lamps in the evening sun. She had hardly ever visited the place, only a small tract even of the Vale and its environs being known to her by close inspection. Much less had she been far outsde the valley. Every contour of the surrounding hills was as personal to her as that of her relatives' faces; but for what lay beyond her judgment was dependent on the teaching of the village school, wher she had held a leading place at the time of her leaving, a year or two before this date.

In those early days she had been much loved by others of her own sex and age, and had used to be seen about the village as one of three – all nearly of the same year – walking home from school side by side; Tess the middle one – in a pink print pinafore, of finely reticulated pattern, worn over a stuff frock that had lost its original colour for a nondescript tertiary – marching on upon long stalky legs, in tight stockings which had little ladder-like holes at the knees, torn by kneeling in the roads and banks in search of vegetable and mineral treasures; her then earth-coloured hair hanging like pot-hooks; the arms of the two outside girls resting round the waist of Tess; her arms on the shoulders of the two supporters.

As Tess grew older, and began to see how matters stood, she felt quite a Malthusian towards her mother for thoughtlessly giving her so many little sisters and brothers, when it was such a trouble to nurse and provide for them. Her mother's intelligence was that of a happy child: Joan Durbeyfield was simply an additional one, and that not the eldest, to her own long family of waiters on Providence.

However, Tess became humanely beneficent towards the small ones, and to help them as much as possible she used, as soon as she left school, to lend a hand at haymaking or harvesting on neighbouring farms; or, by preference, at milking or butter-making processes, which she had learnt when her father had owned cows; and being deft-fingered it was a kind of work in which she excelled.

Everyday seemed to throw upon her young shoulders more of the family burdens, and that Tess should be the representative of the Durbeyfields at the d'Urberville mansion came as a thing of course. In this instance it must be admitted that the Durbeyfields were putting their fairest side outward.

She alighted from the van at Trantridge Cross, and ascended on foot a hill in the direction of the district known as The Chase, on the borders of which, as she had been informed, Mrs d'Urberville's seat, The Slopes, would be found. It was not a manorial home in the ordinary sense, with fields, and pastures, and a grumbling farmer, out of whom the owner had to squeeze an income for himself and his family by hook or by crook. It was more, far more; a country-house built for enjoyment pure and simple, with not an acre of troublesome land attached to it beyond what was required for residential purposes, and for a little fancy farm kept in hand by the owner, and tended by a bailiff.

The crimson brick lodge came first in sight, up to its eaves in dense evergreens. Tess thought this was the mansion itself till, passing through the side wicket with some trepidation, and onward to a point at which the drive took a turn, the house proper stood in full view. It was of recent erection — indeed almost new — and of the same rich red colour that formed such a contrast with the evergreens of the lodge. Far behind the corner of the house — which rose like a geranium bloom against the subdued colours around — stretched the soft azure landscape of The Chase — a truly venerable tract of forest land, one of the few remaining woodlands in England of undoubted primæval date, wherein Druidical mistletoe was still found on aged oaks, and where enormous yew-trees, not planted by the hand of man, grew as they had grown when they were pollarded for bows. All this sylvan antiquity, however, though visible from The Slopes, was outside the immediate boundaries of the estate.

Everything on this snug property was bright, thriving, and well kept; acres of glass-houses stretched down the inclines to the copses at their feet. Everything looked like money — like the last coin issued from the Mint. The stables, partly screened by Austrian pines and evergreen oaks, and fitted with every late appliance, were as dignified as Chapels-of-Ease. On the extensive lawn stood an ornamental tent, its door being towards her.

Simple Tess Durbeyfield stood at gaze, in a half-alarmed attitude, on the edge of the gravel sweep. Her feet had brought her onward to this point before she had quite realized where she was; and now all was contrary to her expectation.

'I thought we were an old family; but this is all new!' she said, in her artlessness. She wished that she had not fallen in so readily with her mother's plans for 'claiming kin', and had endeavoured to gain assistance nearer home.

The d'Urbervilles — or Stoke-d'Urbervilles, as they at first called themselves — who owned all this, were a somewhat unusual family to find in such an old-fashioned part of the country. Parson Tringham had spoken truly when he said that our shambling John Durbeyfield was the only really lineal representative of the old d'Urberville family existing in the county, or near it; he might have added, what he knew very well, that the Stoke-d'Urbervilles were no more d'Urbervilles of the true tree than he was himself. Yet it must be admitted that this family formed a very good stock whereon to regraft a name which sadly wanted such renovation.

When old Mr Simon Stoke, latterly deceased, had made his fortune as an honest merchant (some said money-lender) in the North, he decided to settle as a county man in the South of England, out of hail of his business district; and in doing this he felt the necessity of recommencing with a name that would not too readily identify him with the smart tradesman of the past, and that would be less commonplace than the original bald stark words. Conning for an hour in the British Museum the pages of works devoted to extinct, half-extinct, obscured, and ruined families appertaining to the quarter of England in which he proposed to settle, he considered that *d'Urberville* looked and sounded as well as any of them: and d'Urberville accordingly was annexed to his own name for himself and his heirs eternally. Yet he was not an extravagant-minded man in this, and in constructing his family tree on the new basis was duly reasonable in framing his intermarriages and aristocratic links, never inserting a single title above a rank of strict moderation.

Of this work of imagination poor Tess and her parents were naturally in ignorance – much to their discomfiture; indeed, the very possibility of such annexations was unknown to them; who supposed that, though to be well-favoured might be the gift of fortune, a family name came by nature.

Tess still stood hesitating like a bather about to make his plunge, hardly knowing whether to retreat or to persevere, when a figure came forth from the dark triangular door of the tent. It was that of a tall young man, smoking.

He had an almost swarthy complexion, with full lips, badly moulded, though red and smooth, above which was a well-groomed black moustache with curled points, though his age could not be more than three- or four-and-twenty. Despite the touches of barbarism in his contours, there was a singular force in the gentleman's face, and in his bold rolling eye.

'Well, my Beauty, what can I do for you?' said he, coming forward. And perceiving that she stood quite confounded: 'Never mind me. I am Mr d'Urberville. Have you come to see me or my mother?'

This embodiment of a d'Urberville and a namesake differed even more from what Tess had expected than the house and grounds had differed. She had dreamed of an aged and dignified face, the sublimation of all the d'Urberville lineaments, furrowed with incarnate memories representing in hieroglyphic the centuries of her family's and England's history. But she screwed herself up to the work in hand, since she could not get out of it, and answered –

'I came to see your mother, sir.'

'I am afraid you cannot see her – she is an invalid,' replied the present representative of the spurious house; for this was Mr Alec, the only son of the lately deceased gentleman. 'Cannot I answer your purpose? What is the business you wish to see her about?'

'It isn't business – it is – I can hardly say what!'

'Pleasure?'

'Oh no. Why, sir, if I tell you, it will seem—'

Tess's sense of a certain ludicrousness in her errand was now so strong that, notwithstanding her awe of him, and her general discomfort at being here, her rosy lips curved towards a smile, much to the attraction of the swarthy Alexander.

'It is so very foolish,' she stammered; 'I fear I can't tell you!'

'Never mind; I like foolish things. Try again, my dear,' said he kindly.

'Mother asked me to come,' Tess continued; 'and, indeed, I was in the mind to do so myself likewise. But I did not think it would be like this. I came, sir to tell you that we are of the same family as you.'

'Ho! Poor relations?'

'Yes.'

'Stokes?'

'No; d'Urbervilles.'

'Ay, ay; I mean d'Urbervilles.'

'Our names are worn away to Durbeyfield; but we have several proofs that we are d'Urbervilles. Antiquarians hold we are, – and – and we have an old seal, marked with a ramping lion on a shield, and a castle over him. And we have a very old silver spoon, round in the bowl like a little ladle, and marked with the same castle. But it is so worn that mother uses it to stir the peasoup.'

'A castle argent is certainly my crest,' said he blandly. 'And my arms a lion rampant.'

'And so mother said we ought to make ourselves beknown to you – as we've lost our horse by a bad accident, and are the oldest branch o' the family.'

'Very kind of your mother, I'm sure. And I, for one, don't regret her step.' Alec looked at Tess as he spoke, in a way that made her blush a little. 'And so, my pretty girl, you've come on a friendly visit to us, as relations?'

'I suppose I have,' faltered Tess, looking uncomfortable again.

'Well – there's no harm in it. Where do you live? What are you?'

She gave him brief particulars; and responding to further inquiries told him that she was intending to go back by the same carrier who had brought her.

'It is a long while before he returns past Trantridge Cross. Supposing we walk round the grounds to pass the time, my pretty Coz?'

Tess wished to abridge her visit as much as possible; but the young man was pressing, and she consented to accompany him. He conducted her about the lawns, and flower-beds, and conservatories; and thence to the fruit-garden and greenhouses, where he asked her if she liked strawberries.

'Yes,' said Tess, 'when they come.'

'They are already here.' D'Urberville began gathering specimens of the fruit for her, handing them back to her as he stooped; and, presently, selecting a specially fine product of the 'British Queen' variety, he stood up and held it by the stem to her mouth.

'No – no!' she said quickly, putting her fingers between his hand and her lips. 'I would rather take it in my own hand.'

'Nonsense!' he insisted; and in a slight distress she parted her lips and took it in.

They had spent some time wandering desultorily thus, Tess eating in a half-pleased, half-reluctant state whatever d'Urberville offered her. When she could consume no more of the strawberries he filled her little basket with them; and then the two passed round to the rose trees, whence he gathered blossoms and gave her to put in her bosom. She obeyed like one in a dream, and when she could affix no more he himself tucked a bud or two into her hat, and heaped her basket with others in the prodigality of his bounty. At last, looking at his watch, he said, 'Now by the time you have had something to eat, it will be time for you to leave, if you want to catch the carrier to Shaston. Come here, and I'll see what grub I can find.'

Stoke-d'Urberville took her back to the lawn and into the tent, where he left her, soon reappearing with a basket of light luncheon, which he put before her himself. It was evidently the gentleman's wish not to be disturbed in this pleasant *tête-à-tête* by the servantry.

'Do you mind my smoking?' he asked.

'Oh, not at all, sir.'

He watched her pretty and unconscious munching through the skeins of smoke that pervaded the tent, and Tess Durbeyfield did not divine, as she innocently looked down at the roses in her bosom, that there behind the blue narcotic haze was potentially the 'tragic mischief' of her drama – one who stood fair to be the blood-red ray in the spectrum of her young life. She had an attribute which amounted to a disadvantage just now; and it was this that caused Alec d'Urberville's eyes to rivet themselves upon her. It was a luxuriance of aspect, a fulness of growth, which made her appear more of a woman than she really was. She had inherited the feature from her mother without the quality it denoted. It had troubled her mind occasionally, till her companions had said that it was a fault which time would cure.

She soon had finished her lunch. 'Now I am going home, sir,' she said, rising.

'And what do they call you?' he asked, as he accompanied her along the drive till they were out of sight of the house.

'Tess Durbeyfield, down at Marlott.'

'And you say your people have lost their horse?'

'I – killed him!' she answered, her eyes filling with tears as she gave particulars of Prince's death. 'And I don't know what to do for father on account of it!'

'I must think if I cannot do something. My mother must find a berth for you. But, Tess, no nonsense about "d'Urberville"; – "Durbeyfield" only, you know – quite another name.'

'I wish for no better, sir,' said she with something of dignity.

For a moment – only for a moment – when they were in the turning of the drive, between the tall rhododendrons and conifers, before the lodge became visible, he inclined his face towards her as if – but, no: he thought better of it, and let her go.

Thus the thing began. Had she perceived this meeting's import she might have asked why she was doomed to be seen and coveted that day by the wrong man, and not by some other man, the right and desired one in all respects – as nearly as humanity can supply the right and desired; yet to him who amongst her acquaintance might have approximated to this kind, she was but a transient impression, half forgotten.

In all ill-judged execution of the well-judged plan of things the call seldom produces the comer, the man to love rarely coincides with the hour for loving. Nature does not often say 'See!' to her poor creature at a time when seeing can lead to happy doing; or reply 'Here!' to a body's cry of 'Where?' till the hide-and-seek has become an irksome, outworn game. We may wonder whether at the acme and summit of the human progress these anachronisms will be corrected by a finer intuition, a closer interaction of the social machinery than that which now jolts us round and along; but such completeness is not to be prophesied, or even conceived as possible. Enough that in the present case, as in millions, it was not the two halves of a perfect whole that confronted each other at the perfect moment; a missing counterpart wandered independently about the earth waiting in crass obtuseness till the late time came. Out of which maladroit delay sprang anxieties, disappointments, shocks, catastrophes, and passing-strange destinies.

When d'Urberville got back to the tent he sat down astride on a chair reflecting, with a pleased gleam in his face. Then he broke into a loud laugh.

'Well, I'm damned! What a funny thing! Ha-ha-ha! And what a crumby girl!'

CHAPTER SIX

TESS went down the hill to Trantridge Cross, and inattentively waited to take her seat in the van returning from Chaseborough to Shaston. She did not know what the other occupants said to her as she entered, though she answered them; and when they had started anew she rode along with an inward and not an outward eye.

One among her fellow-travellers addressed her more pointedly than any had spoken before: 'Why, you be quite a posy! And such roses in early June!'

Then she became aware of the spectacle she presented to their surprised vision: roses at her breast; roses in her hat; roses and strawberries in her basket to the brim. She blushed, and said confusedly that the flowers had been given to her. When the passengers were not looking she stealthily removed the more prominent blooms from her hat and placed them in the basket, where she covered them with her handkerchief. Then she fell to reflecting again, and in looking downwards a thorn of the rose remaining in her breast accidentally pricked her chin. Like all the cottagers in Blackmoor Vale, Tess was steeped in fancies and prefigurative superstitions; she thought this an ill omen – the first she had noticed that day.

The van travelled only so far as Shaston, and there were several miles of pedestrian descent from that mountain-town into the vale to Marlott. Her mother had advised her to stay here for the night, at the house of a cottage-woman they knew, if she should feel too tired to come on; and this Tess did, not descending to her home till the following afternoon.

When she entered the house she perceived in a moment from her mother's triumphant manner that something had occurred in the interim.

'O yes; I know all about it! I told 'ee it would be all right, and now 'tis proved!'

'Since I've been away? What has?' said Tess rather wearily.

Her mother surveyed the girl up and down with arch approval, and went on banteringly: 'So you've brought 'em round!'

'How do you know, mother?'

'I've had a letter.'

Tess then remembered that there would have been time for this.

'They say – Mrs d'Urberville says – that she wants you to look after a little fowl-farm which is her hobby. But this is only her artful way of getting 'ee there without raising your hopes. She's going to own 'ee as kin – that's the meaning o't.'

'But I didn't see her.'

'You zid somebody, I suppose?'

'I saw her son.'

'And did he own 'ee?'

'Well – he called me Coz.'

'An' I knew it! Jacky – he called her Coz!' cried Joan to her husband. 'Well, he spoke to his mother, of course, and she do want 'ee there.'

'But I don't know that I am apt at tending fowls,' said the dubious Tess.

'Then I don't know who is apt. You've be'n born in the business, and brought up in it. They that be born in a business always know more about it than any 'prentice. Besides, that's only just a show of something for you to do, that you midn't feel beholden.'

'I don't altogether think I ought to go,' said Tess thoughtfully. 'Who wrote the letter? Will you let me look at it?'

'Mrs d'Urberville wrote it. Here it is.'

The letter was in the third person, and briefly informed Mrs Durbeyfield that her daughter's services would be useful to that lady in the management of her poultry-farm, that a comfortable room would be provided for her if she could come, and that the wages would be on a liberal scale if they liked her.

'Oh – that's all!' said Tess.

'You couldn't expect her to throw her arms round 'ee, an' to kiss and coll 'ee all at once.'

Tess looked out of the window.

'I would rather stay here with father and you,' she said.

'But why?'

'I'd rather not tell you why, mother; indeed, I don't quite know why.'

A week afterwards she came in one evening from an unavailing search for some light occupation in the immediate neighbourhood. Her idea had been to get together sufficient money during the summer to purchase another horse. Hardly had she crossed the threshold before one of the children danced across the room, saying, 'The gentleman's been here!'

Her mother hastened to explain, smiles breaking from every inch of her person. Mrs d'Urberville's son had called on horseback, having been riding by chance in the direction of Marlott. He had wished to know, finally, in the name of his mother, if Tess could really come to manage the old lady's fowl-farm or not; the lad who had hitherto superintended the birds having proved untrustworthy. 'Mr d'Urberville says you must be a good girl if you are at all as you appear; he knows you must be worth your weight in gold. He is very much interested in 'ee – truth to tell.'

Tess seemed for the moment really pleased to hear that she had won such high opinion from a stranger when, in her own esteem, she had sunk so low.

'It is very good of him to think that,' she murmured; 'and If I was quite sure how it would be living there, I would go any-when.'

'He is a mighty handsome man!'

'I don't think so,' said Tess coldly.

'Well, there's your chance, whether or no; and I'm sure he wears a beautiful diamond ring!'

'Yes,' said little Abraham, brightly, from the window-bench; 'and I seed it! and it did twinkle when he put his hand up to his mistarshers. Mother, why did our grand relation keep on putting his hand up to his mistarshers?'

'Hark at that child!' cried Mrs Durbeyfield, with parenthetic admiration.

'Perhaps to show his diamond ring,' murmured Sir John, dreamily, from his chair.

'I'll think it over,' said Tess, leaving the room.

'Well, she's made a conquest o' the younger branch of us, straight off,' continued the matron to her husband, 'and she's a fool if she don't follow it up.'

'I don't quite like my children going away from home,' said the haggler. 'As the head of the family, the rest ought to come to me.'

'But do let her go, Jacky,' coaxed his poor witless wife. 'He's struck wi' her — you can see that. He called her Coz! He'll marry her, most likely, and make a lady of her; and then she'll be what her forefathers was.'

John Durbeyfield had more conceit than energy or health, and this supposition was pleasant to him.

'Well, perhaps, that's what young Mr d'Urberville means,' he admitted; 'and sure enough he mid have serious thoughts about improving his blood by linking on to the old line. Tess, the little rogue! And have she really paid 'em a visit to such an end as this?'

Meanwhile Tess was walking thoughtfully among the gooseberry-bushes in the garden, and over Prince's grave. When she came in her mother pursued her advantage.

'Well, what be you going to do? she asked.

'I wish I had seen Mrs d'Urberville,' said Tess.

'I think you mid as well settle it. Then you'll see her soon enough.'

Her father coughed in his chair.

'I don't know what to say!' answered the girl restlessly. 'It is for you to decide. I killed the old horse, and I suppose I ought to do something to get ye a new one. But — but — I don't quite like Mr d'Urberville being there!'

The children, who had made use of this idea of Tess being taken up by their wealthy kinsfolk (which they imagined the other family to be) as a species of dolorifuge after the death of the horse, began to cry at Tess's reluctance, and teased and reproached her for hesitating.

'Tess won't go—o—o and be made a la—a—dy of! — no, she says she wo—o—on't!' they wailed, with square mouths. 'And we shan't have a nice new horse, and lots o' golden money to buy fairlings! And Tess won't look pretty in her best cloze no mo—o—ore!'

Her mother chimed in to the same tune: a certain way she had of making the labours in the house seem heavier than they were by prolonging them indefinitely, also weighed in the argument. Her father alone preserved an attitude of neutrality.

'I will go,' said Tess at last.

Her mother could not repress her consciousness of the nuptial Vision conjured up by the girl's consent.

'That's right! For such a pretty maid as 'tis, this is a fine chance!'

'I hope it is a chance for earning money. It is no other kind of chance. You had better say nothing of that silly sort about parish.'

Mrs Durbeyfield did not promise. She was not quite sure that she did not feel proud enough, after the visitor's remarks, to say a good deal.

Thus it was arranged; and the young girl wrote, agreeing to be ready to set out on any day on which she might be required. She was duly informed that Mrs d'Urberville was glad of her decision, and that a spring-cart should be sent to meet her and her luggage at the top of the Vale on the day after the morrow, when she must hold herself prepared to start. Mrs d'Urberville's handwriting seemed rather masculine.

'A cart?' murmured Joan Durbeyfield doubtingly. 'It might have been a carriage for her own kin!'

Having at last taken her course Tess was less restless and abstracted, going about her business with some self-assurance in the thought of acquiring another horse for her father by an occupation which would not be onerous. She had hoped to be a teacher at the school, but the fates seemed to decide otherwise. Being mentally older than her mother she did not regard Mrs Durbeyfield's matrimonial hopes for her in a serious aspect for a moment. The light-minded woman had been discovering good matches for her daughter almost from the year of her birth.

CHAPTER SEVEN

O N the morning appointed for her departure Tess was awake before dawn – at the marginal minute of the dark when the grove is still mute, save for one prophetic bird who sings with a clear-voiced conviction that he at least knows the correct time of day, the rest preserving silence as if equally convinced that he is mistaken. She remained upstairs packing till breakfast-time, and then came down in her ordinary weekday clothes, her Sunday apparel being carefully folded in her box.

Her mother expostulated. 'You will never set out to see your folks without dressing up more the dand than that?'

'But I am going to work!' said Tess.

'Well, yes,' said Mrs Durbeyfield; and in a private tone, 'at first there mid be a little pretence o't. . . . But I think it will be wiser of 'ee to put your best side outward,' she added.

'Very well; I suppose you know best,' replied Tess with calm abandonment.

And to please her parent the girl put herself quite in Joan's hands, saying serenely – 'Do what you like with me, mother.'

Mrs Durbeyfield was only too delighted at this tractability. First she fetched a great basin, and washed Tess's hair with such thoroughness that when dried and brushed it looked twice as much as at other times. She tied it with a broader pink ribbon than usual. Then she put upon her the white frock that Tess had worn at the club-walking, the airy fulness of which, supplementing her enlarged *coiffure*, imparted to her developing figure an amplitude which belied her age, and might cause her to be estimated as a woman when she was not much more than a child.

'I declare there's a hole in my stocking-heel!' said Tess.

'Never mind holes in your stockings – they don't speak! When I was a maid, so long as I had a pretty bonnet the devil might ha' found me in heels.'

Her mother's pride in the girl's appearance led her to step back, like a painter from his easel, and survey her work as a whole.

'You must zee yourself!' she cried. 'It is much better than you was t'other day.'

As the looking-glass was only large enough to reflect a very small portion of Tess's person at one time, Mrs Durbeyfield hung a black cloak outside the casement, and so made a large reflector of the panes, as it is the wont of bedecking cottagers to do. After this she went downstairs to her husband, who was sitting in the lower room.

'I'll tell 'ee what 'tis, Durbeyfield,' said she exultingly; 'he'll never have the heart not to love her. But whatever you do, don't zay too much to Tess of his fancy for her, and this chance she has got. She is such an odd maid that it mid zet her against him, or against going there, even now. If all goes well, I shall certainly be for making some return to that pa'son at Stagfoot Lane for telling us – dear, good man!'

However, as the moment for the girl's setting out drew nigh, when the first excitement of the dressing had passed off, a slight misgiving found place in Joan Durbeyfield's mind. It prompted the matron to say that she would walk a little way – as far as to the point where the acclivity from the valley began its first steep ascent to the outer world. At the top Tess was going to be met with the spring-cart sent by the Stoke-d'Urbervilles, and her box had already been wheeled ahead towards this summit by a lad with trucks, to be in readiness.

Seeing their mother put on her bonnet the younger children clamoured to go with her.

'I do want to walk a little-ways wi' Sissy, now she's going to marry our gentleman-cousin, and wear fine cloze!'

'Now,' said Tess, flushing and turning quickly, 'I'll hear no more o' that! Mother, how could you ever put such stuff into their heads?'

'Going to work, my dears, for our rich relation, and help get enough money for a new horse,' said Mrs Durbeyfield pacifically.

'Good-bye, father,' said Tess, with a lumpy throat.

'Good-bye, my maid,' said Sir John, raising his head from his breast as he suspended his nap, induced by a slight excess this morning in honour of the occasion. 'Well, I hope my young friend will like such a comely sample of his own blood. And tell'n, Tess, that being sunk, quite, from our former grandeur, I'll sell him the title – yes, sell it – and at no onreasonable figure.'

'Not for less than a thousand pound!' cried Lady Durbeyfield.

'Tell'n – I'll take a thousand pound. Well, I'll take less, when I come to think o't. He'll adorn it better than a poor lammicken feller like myself can. Tell'n he shall hae it for a hundred. But I won't stand upon trifles – tell'n he shall hae it for fifty – for twenty pound! Yes, twenty pound–that's the lowest. Dammy, family honour is family honour, and I won't take a penny less!'

Tess's eyes were too full and her voice too choked to utter the sentiments that were in her. She turned quickly, and went out.

So the girls and their mother all walked together, a child on each side of Tess, holding her hand, and looking at her meditatively from time to time, as at one who was about to do great things; her mother just behind with the smallest; the group forming a picture of honest beauty flanked by innocence, and backed by simple-souled vanity. They followed the way till they reached the beginning of the ascent, on the crest of which the vehicle from Trantridge was to receive her, this limit having been fixed to save the horse the labour of the last slope. Far away behind the first hills the cliff-like dwellings of Shaston broke the lines of the ridge. Nobody was visible in the elevated road which skirted the ascent save the lad whom they had sent on before them, sitting on the handle of the barrow that contained all Tess's worldly possessions.

'Bide here a bit, and the cart will soon come, no doubt,' said Mrs Durbeyfield. 'Yes, I see it yonder!'

It had come – appearing suddenly from behind the forehead of the nearest upland, and stopping beside the boy with the barrow. Her mother and the children thereupon decided to go no farther, and bidding them a hasty good-bye Tess bent her steps up the hill.

They saw her white shape draw near to the spring-cart, on which her box was already placed. But before she had quite reached it another vehicle shot out from a clump of trees on the summit, came round the bend of the road there, passed the luggage-cart, and halted beside Tess, who looked up as if in great surprise.

Her mother perceived, for the first time that the second vehicle was not a humble conveyance like the first, but a spick-and-span gig or dog-cart, highly varnished and equipped. The driver was a young man of three- or four-and-twenty, with a cigar between his teeth; wearing a dandy cap, drab jacket, breeches of the same hue, white neckcloth, stick-up collar, and brown driving-gloves – in short, he was the handsome, horsey young buck who had visited Joan a week or two before to get her answer about Tess.

Mrs Durbeyfield clapped her hands like a child. Then she looked down, then stared again. Could she be deceived as to the meaning of this?

'Is dat the gentleman-kinsman who'll make Sissy a lady?' asked the youngest child.

Meanwhile the muslined form of Tess could be seen standing still, undecided, beside this turn-out, whose owner was talking to her. Her seeming indecision was, in fact, more than indecision: it was misgiving. She would have preferred the humble cart. The young man dismounted and appeared to urge her to ascend. She turned her face down the hill to her relatives, and regarded the little group. Something seemed to quicken her to a determination; possibly the thought that she had killed Prince. She suddenly stepped up; he mounted beside her, and immediately whipped on the horse. In a moment they had passed the slow cart with the box, and disappeared behind the shoulder of the hill.

Directly Tess was out of sight, and the interest of the matter as a drama was at an end, the little ones' eyes filled with tears. The youngest child said, 'I wish poor, poor Tess wasn't gone away to be a lady!' and, lowering the corners of his lips, burst out crying. The new point of view was infectious, and the next child did likewise, and then the next, till the whole three of them wailed loud.

There were tears also in Joan Durbeyfield's eyes as she turned to go home. But by the time she had got back to the village she was passively trusting to the favour of accident. However, in bed that night she sighed, and her husband asked her what was the matter.

'Oh, I don't know exactly,' she said. 'I was thinking that perhaps it would ha' been better if Tess had not gone.'

'Oughtn't ye to have thought of that before?'

'Well, 'tis a chance for the maid—Still, if 'twere the doing again, I wouldn't let her go till I had found out whether the gentleman is really a good-hearted young man and choice over her as his kinswoman.'

'Yes, you ought, perhaps, to ha' done that,' snored Sir John.

Joan Durbeyfield always managed to find consolation somewhere: 'Well, as one of the genuine stock, she ought to make her way with 'en, if she plays her trump card aright. And if he don't marry her afore he will after. For that he's all afire wi' love for her any eye can see.'

'What's her trump card? Her d'Urberville blood, you mean?'

'No, stupid; her face – as 'twas mine.'

CHAPTER EIGHT

HAVING mounted beside her, Alec d'Urberville drove rapidly along the crest of the first hill, chatting compliments to Tess as they went, the cart with her box being left far beind. Rising still, an immense landscape stretched around them on every side; behind, the green valley of her birth, before, a gray country of which she knew nothing except from her first brief visit to Trantridge. Thus they reached the verge of an incline down which the road stretched in a long straight descent of nearly a mile.

Ever since the accident with her father's horse Tess Durbeyfield, courageous as she naturally was, had been exceedingly timid on wheels; the least irregularity of motion startled her. She began to get uneasy at a certain recklessness in her conductor's driving.

'You will go down slow, sir, I suppose?' she said with attempted unconcern.

D'Urberville looked round upon her, nipped his cigar with the tips of his large white centre-teeth, and allowed his lips to smile slowly of themselves.

'Why, Tess,' he answered, after another whiff or two, 'it isn't a brave bouncing girl like you who asks that? Why, I always go down at full gallop. There's nothing like it for raising your spirits.'

'But perhaps you need not now?'

'Ah,' he said, shaking his head, 'there are two to be reckoned with. It is not me alone. Tib has to be considered, and she has a very queer temper.'

'Who?'

'Why, this mare. I fancy she looked round at me in a very grim way just then. Didn't you notice it?'

'Don't try to frighten me, sir,' said Tess stiffly.

'Well, I don't. If any living man can manage this horse I can: – I won't say any living man can do it–but if such has the power, I am he.'

'Why do you have such a horse?'

'Ah, well may you ask it! It was my fate, I suppose. Tib has killed one chap; and just after I bought her she nearly killed me. And then, take my word for it, I nearly killed he⌐ But she's touchy still, very touchy; and one's life is hardly safe behind her sometimes.'

They were just beginning to descend; and it was evident that the horse, whether of her own will or of his (the latter being the more likely), knew so well the reckless performance expected of her that she hardly required a hint from behind.

Down, down, they sped, the wheels humming like a top, the dog-cart rocking right and left, its axis acquiring a slightly oblique set in relation to the line of progress; the figure of the horse rising and falling in undulations before them. Sometimes a wheel was off the ground, it seemed, for many yards; sometimes a stone was sent spinning over the hedge, and flinty sparks from the horse's hoofs outshone the daylight. The aspect of the straight road enlarged with their advance, the two banks dividing like a splitting stick; one rushing past at each shoulder.

The wind blew through Tess's white muslin to her very skin, and her washed hair flew out behind. She was determined to show no open fear, but she clutched d'Urberville's rein-arm.

'Don't touch my arm! We shall be thrown out if you do! Hold on round my waist!'

She grasped his waist, and so they reached the bottom.

'Safe, thank God, in spite of your fooling!' said she, her face on fire.

'Tess – fie! that's temper!' said d'Urberville.

''Tis truth.'

'Well, you need not let go your hold of me so thanklessly the moment you feel yourself out of danger.'

She had not considered what she had been doing; whether he were man or woman, stick or stone, in her involuntary hold on him. Recovering her reserve she sat without replying, and thus they reached the summit of another declivity.

'Now then, again!' said d'Urberville.

'No, no!' said Tess. 'Show more sense, do, please.'

'But when people find themselves on one of the highest points in the county, they must get down again,' he retorted.

He loosened rein, and away they went a second time. D'Urberville turned his face to her as they rocked, and said, in playful raillery: 'Now then, put your arms round my waist again, as you did before, my Beauty.'

'Never!' said Tess independently, holding on as well as she could without touching him.

'Let me put one little kiss on those holmberry lips, Tess, or even on that warmed cheek, and I'll stop – on my honour, I will'

Tess surprised beyond measure, slid farther back still on her seat, at which he urged the horse anew, and rocked her the more.

'Will nothing else do?' she cried at length, in desperation, her large eyes staring at him like those of a wild animal. This dressing her up so prettily by her mother had apparently been to lamentable purpose.

'Nothing, dear Tess,' he replied.

'Oh, I don't know – very well; I don't mind!' she panted miserably.

He drew rein, and as they slowed he was on the point of imprinting the desired salute, when as if hardly yet aware of her own modesty, she dodged aside. His arms being occupied with the reins there was left him no power to prevent her manœuvre.

'Now, damn it – I'll break both our necks!' swore her capriciously passionate companion. 'So you can go from your word like that, you young witch, can you?'

'Very well,' said Tess, 'I'll not move since you be so determined! But I – thought you would be kind to me, and protect me, as my kinsman!'

'Kinsman be hanged! Now!'

'But I don't want anybody to kiss me, sir!' she implored, a big tear beginning to roll down her face, and the corners of her mouth trembling in her attempts not to cry. 'And I wouldn't ha' come if I had known!'

He was inexorable, and she sat still, and d'Urberville gave the kiss of mastery. No sooner had he done so than she flushed with shame, took out her handkerchief, and wiped the spot on her cheek that had been touched by his lips. His ardour was nettled at the sight, for the act on her part had been unconsciously done.

'You are mighty sensitive for a cottage girl!' said the young man.

Tess made no reply to this remark, of which, indeed, she did not quite comprehend the drift, unheeding the snub she had administered by her instinctive rub upon her cheek. She had, in fact, undone the kiss, as far as such a thing was physically possible. With a dim sense that he was vexed she looked steadily ahead as they trotted on near Melbury Down and Wingreen, till she saw, to her consternation, that there was yet another descent to be undergone.

'You shall be made sorry for that!' he resumed, his injured tone still remaining, as he flourished the whip anew. 'Unless, that is, you agree willingly to let me do it again, and no handkerchief.'

She sighed. 'Very well, sir!' she said. 'Oh – let me get my hat!'

At that moment of speaking her hat had blown off into the road, their present speed on the upland being by no means slow. D'Urberville pulled up, and said he would get it for her, but Tess was down on the other side.

She turned back and picked up the article.

'You look prettier with it off, upon my soul, if that's possible,' he said, contemplating her over the back of the vehicle. 'Now then, up again! What's the matter?'

The hat was in place and tied, but Tess had not stepped forward.

'No, sir,' she said, revealing the red and ivory of her mouth as her eye lit in defiant triumph; 'not again, if I know it!'

'What – you won't get up beside me?'

'No; I shall walk.'

''Tis five or six miles yet to Trantridge.'

'I don't care if 'tis dozens. Besides, the cart is behind.'

'You artful hussy! Now, tell me – didn't you make that hat blow off on purpose? I'll swear you did!'

Her strategic silence confirmed his suspicion.

Then d'Urberville cursed and swore at her, and called her everything he could think of for the trick. Turning the horse suddenly he tried to drive back upon her, and so hem her in between the gig and the hedge. But he could not do this short of injuring her.

'You ought to be ashamed of yourself for using such wicked words!' cried Tess
with spirit, from the top of the hedge into which she had scrambled. 'I don't
like 'ee at all! I hate and detest you! I'll go back to mother, I will!'

D'Urberville's bad temper cleared up at sight of hers; and he laughed heartily.
'Well, I like you all the better,' he said. 'Come, let there be peace. I'll never do it
any more against your will. My life upon it now!'

Still Tess could not be induced to remount. She did not, however, object to his
keeping his gig alongside her; and in this manner, at a slow pace, they advanced
towards the village of Trantridge. From time to time d'Urberville exhibited a sort
of fierce distress at the sight of the tramping he had driven her to undertake by his
misdemeanour. She might in truth have safely trusted him now; but he had
forfeited her confidence for the time, and she kept on the ground, progressing
thoughtfully, as if wondering whether it would be wiser to return home. Her
resolve, however, had been taken, and it seemed vacillating even to childishness
to abandon it now, unless for graver reasons. How could she face her parents, get
back her box, and disconcert the whole scheme for the rehabilitation of her
family on such sentimental grounds?

A few minutes later the chimneys of The Slopes appeared in view, and in a snug
nook to the right the poultry-farm and cottage of Tess's destination.

CHAPTER NINE

THE community of fowls to which Tess had been appointed as supervisor,
purveyor, nurse, surgeon, and friend, made its head-quarters in an old thatched
cottage standing in an enclosure that had once been a garden, but was now a
trampled and sanded square. The house was overrun with ivy, its chimney being
enlarged by the boughs of the parasite to the aspect of a ruined tower. The lower
rooms were entirely given over to the birds, who walked about them with a
proprietary air, as though the place had been built by themselves, and not by
certain dusty copyholders who now lay east and west in the churchyard. The
descendants of these bygone owners felt it almost as a slight to their family when
the house which had so much of their affection, had cost so much of their
forefathers' money, and had been in their possession for several generations
before the d'Urbervilles came and built here, was indifferently turned into a fowl-
house by Mrs Stoke-d'Urberville as soon as the property fell into hand
according to law. ' 'Twas good enough for Christians in grandfather's time,' they
said.

The rooms wherein dozens of infants had wailed at their nursing now
resounded with the tapping of nascent chicks. Distracted hens in coops occupied
spots where formerly stood chairs supporting sedate agriculturists. The chimney-
corner and once blazing hearth was now filled with inverted beehives, in which
the hens laid their eggs; while out of doors the plots that each succeeding
householder had carefully shaped with his spade were torn by the cocks in wildest
fashion.

The garden in which the cottage stood was surrounded by a wall, and could only be entered through a door.

When Tess had occupied herself about an hour the next morning in altering and improving the arrangements, according to her skilled ideas as the daughter of a professed poulterer, the door in the wall opened and a servant in white cap and apron entered. She had come from the manor-house.

'Mrs d'Urberville wants the fowls as usual,' she said; but perceiving that Tess did not quite understand, she explained, 'Mis'ess is a old lady, and blind.'

'Blind!' said Tess.

Almost before her misgiving at the news could find time to shape itself she took, under her companion's direction, two of the most beautiful of the Hamburghs in her arms, and followed the maid-servant, who had likewise taken two, to the adjacent mansion, which, though ornate and imposing, showed traces everywhere on this side that some occupant of its chambers could bend to the love of dumb creatures – feathers floating within view of the front, and hencoops standing on the grass.

In a sitting-room on the ground-floor, ensconced in an armchair with her back to the light, was the owner and mistress of the estate, a white-haired woman of not more than sixty, or even less, wearing a large cap. She had the mobile face frequent in those whose sight had decayed by stages, has been laboriously striven after, and reluctantly let go, rather than the stagnant mien apparent in persons long sightless or born blind. Tess walked up to this lady with her feathered charges – one sitting on each arm.

'Ah, you are the young woman come to look after my birds?' said Mrs d'Urberville, recognizing a new footstep. 'I hope you will be kind to them. My bailiff tells me you are quite the proper person. Well, where are they? Ah, this is Strut! But he is hardly so lively to-day, is he? He is alarmed at being handled by a stranger, I suppose. And Phena too – yes, they are a little frightened – aren't you, dears? But they will soon get used to you.'

While the old lady had been speaking Tess and the other maid, in obedience to her gestures, had placed the fowls severally in her lap, and she had felt them over from head to tail, examining their beaks, their combs, the manes of the cocks, their wings, and their claws. Her touch enabled her to recognize them in a moment, and to discover if a single feather were crippled or draggled. She handled their crops, and knew what they had eaten, and if too little or too much; her face enacting a vivid pantomime of the criticisms passing in her mind.

The birds that the two girls had brought in were duly returned to the yard, and the process was repeated till all the pet cocks and hens had been submitted to the old woman – Hamburghs, Bantams, Cochins, Brahmas, Dorkings, and such other sorts as were in fashion just then – her perception of each visitor being seldom at fault as she received the bird upon her knees.

It reminded Tess of a Confirmation, in which Mrs d'Urberville was the bishop, the fowls the young people presented, and herself and the maid-servant the parson and curate of the parish bringing them up. At the end of the ceremony Mrs d'Urberville abruptly asked Tess, wrinkling and twitching her face into undulations, 'Can you whistle?'

'Whistle, Ma'am?'

'Yes, whistle tunes.'

Tess could whistle like most other country girls, though the accomplishment was one which she did not care to profess in genteel company. However, she blandly admitted that such was the fact.

'Then you will have to practise it every day. I had a lad who did it very well, but he has left. I want you to whistle to my bullfinches; as I cannot see them I like to hear them, and we teach 'em airs that way. Tell her where the cages are, Elizabeth. You must begin to-morrow, or they will go back in their piping. They have been neglected these several days.'

'Mr d'Urberville whistled to 'em this morning, ma'am,' said Elizabeth.

'He! Pooh!'

The old lady's face creased into furrows of repugnance, and she made no further reply.

Thus the reception of Tess by her fancied kinswoman terminated, and the birds were taken back to their quarters. The girl's surprise at Mrs d'Urberville's manner was not great; for since seeing the size o the house she had expected no more. But she was far from being aware that the old lady had never heard a word of the so-called kinship. She gathered that no great affection flowed between the blind woman and her son. But in that, too, she was mistaken. Mrs d'Urberville was not the first mother compelled to love her off-spring resentfully, and to be bitterly fond.

In spite of the unpleasant initiation of the day before, Tess inclined to the freedom and novelty of her new position in the morning when the sun shone, now that she was once installed there; and she was curious to test her powers in the unexpected direction asked of her, so as to ascertain her chance of retaining her post. As soon as she was alone within the walled garden she sat herself down on a coop, and seriously screwed up her mouth for the long-neglected practice. She found her former ability to have degenerated to the production of a hollow rush of wind through the lips, and no clear note at all.

She remained fruitlessly blowing and blowing, wondering how she could have so grown out of the art which had come by nature, till she became aware of a movement among the ivy-boughs which cloaked the garden-wall ro less than the cottage. Looking that way she beheld a form springing from the coping to the plot. It was Alec d'Urberville, whom she had not set eyes on since he had conducted her the day before to the door of the gardener's cottage where she had lodgings.

'Upon my honour!' cried he, 'there was never before such a beautiful thing in Nature or Art as you look "Cousin" Tess ["Cousin" had a faint ring of mockery]. I have been watching you from over the wall – sitting like *Im*-patience on a monument, and pouting up that pretty red mouth to whistling shape, and whooping and whooing, and privately swearing, and never being able to produce a note. Why, you are quite cross because you can't do it.'

'I may be cross, but I didn't swear.'

'Ah! I understand why you are trying – those bullies! My mother wants you to carry on their musical education. How selfish of her! As if attending to these curst cocks and hens here were not enough work for any girl. I would flatly refuse, if I were you.'

'But she wants me particularly to do it, and to be ready by to-morrow morning.'

'Does she? Well then – I'll give you a lesson or two.'

'Oh no, you won't!' said Tess, withdrawing towards the door.

'Nonsense; I don't want to touch you. See – I'll stand on this side of the wire-netting, and you can keep on the other; so you may feel quite safe. Now, look here; you screw up your lips too harshly. There 'tis – so.'

He suited the action to the word, and whistled a line of 'Take, O take those lips away'. But the allusion was lost upon Tess.

'Now try,' said d'Urberville.

She attempted to look reserved; her face put on a sculptural severity. But he persisted in his demand, and at last, to get rid of him, she did put up her lips as directed for producing a clear note; laughing distressfully, however, and then blushing with vexation that she had laughed.

He encouraged her with 'Try again!'

Tess was quite serious, painfully serious by this time; and she tried – ultimately and unexpectedly emitting a real round sound. The momentary pleasure of success got the better of her; her eyes enlarged, and she involuntarily smiled in his face.

'That's it! Now I have started you – you'll go on beautifully. There – I said I would not come near you; and, in spite of such temptation as never before fell to mortal man, I'll keep my word. . . . Tess, do you think my mother a queer old soul?'

'I don't know much of her yet, sir.'

'You'll find her so; she must be, to make you learn to whistle to her bullfinches. I am rather out of her books just now, but you will be quite in favour if you treat her live-stock well. Good morning. If you meet with any difficulties and want help here, don't go to the bailiff, come to me.'

It was in the economy of this *régime* that Tess Durbeyfield had undertaken to fill a place. Her first day's experiences were fairly typical of those which followed through many succeeding days. A familiarity with Alec d'Urberville's presence – which that young man carefully cultivated in her by playful dialogue, and by jestingly calling her his cousin when they were alone – removed much of her original shyness of him, without, however, implanting any feeling which could engender shyness of a new and tenderer kind. But she was more pliable under his hands than a mere companionship would have made her, owing to her unavoidable dependence upon his mother, and, through that lady's comparative helplessness, upon him.

She soon found that whistling to the bullfinches in Mrs d'Urberville's room was no such onerous business when she had regained the art, for she had caught from her musical mother numerous airs that suited those songsters admirably. A far more satisfactory time than when she practised in the garden was this whistling by the cages each morning. Unrestrained by the young man's presence she threw up her mouth, put her lips near the bars, and piped away in easeful grace to the attentive listeners.

Mrs d'Urberville slept in a large four-post bedstead hung with heavy damask curtains, and the bullfinches occupied the same apartment, where they flitted about freely at certain hours, and made little white spots on the furniture and upholstery. Once while Tess was at the window where the cages were ranged, giving her lesson as usual, she thought she heard a rustling behind the bed. The old lady was not present, and turning round the girl had an impression that the toes of a pair of boots were visible below the fringe of the curtains. Thereupon her whistling became so disjointed that the listener, if such there were, must have discovered her suspicion of his presence. She searched the curtains every morning after that, but never found anybody within them. Alec d'Urberville had evidently thought better of his freak to terrify her by an ambush of that kind.

CHAPTER TEN

E VERY village has its idiosyncrasy, its constitution, often its own code of morality. The levity of some of the younger women in and about Trantridge was marked, and was perhaps symptomatic of the choice spirit who ruled The Slopes in that vicinity. The place had also a more abiding defect; it drank hard. The staple conversation on the farms around was on the uselessness of saving money; and smockfrocked arithmeticians, leaning on their ploughs or hoes, would enter into calculations of great nicety to prove that parish relief was a fuller provision for a man in his old age than any which could result from savings out of their wages during a whole lifetime.

The chief pleasure of these philosophers lay in going every Saturday night, when work was done, to Chaseborough, a decayed market-town two or three miles distant; and, returning in the small hours of the next morning, to spend Sunday in sleeping off the dyspeptic effects of the curious compounds sold to them as beer by the monopolizers of the once independent inns.

For a long time Tess did not join in the weekly pilgrimages. But under pressure from matrons not much older than herself – for a field-man's wages being as high at twenty-one as at forty, marriage was early here – Tess at length consented to go. Her first experience of the journey afforded her more enjoyment than she had expected, the hilariousness of the others being quite contagious after her monotonous attention to the poultry-farm all the week. She went again and again. Being graceful and interesting, standing moreover on the momentary threshold of womanhood, her appearance drew down upon her some sly regards from loungers in the streets of Chaseborough; hence, though sometimes her journey to the town was made independently, she always searched for her fellows at nightfall, to have the protection of their companionship homeward.

This had gone on for a month or two when there came a Saturday in September, on which a fair and a market coincided; and the pilgrims from Trantridge sought double delights at the inns on that account. Tess's occupations made her late in setting out, so that her comrades reached the town long before her. It was a fine September evening, just before sunset, when yellow lights struggle with blue shades in hair-like lines, and the atmosphere itself forms a prospect without aid from more solid objects, except the innumerable winged insects that dance in it. Through this low-lit mistiness Tess walked leisurely along.

She did not discover the coincidence of the market with the fair till she had reached the place, by which time it was close upon dusk. Her limited marketing was soon completed; and then as usual she began to look about for some of the Trantridge cottagers.

At first she could not find them, and she was informed that most of them had gone to what they called a private little jig at the house of a hay-trusser and peat-dealer who had transactions with their farm. He lived in an out-of-the-way nook of the townlet, and in trying to find her course thither her eyes fell upon Mr d'Urberville standing at a street corner.

'What – my Beauty? You here so late?' he said.

She told him that she was simply waiting for company homeward.

'I'll see you again,' said he over her shoulder as she went on down the back lane.

Approaching the hay-trussers she could hear the fiddled notes of a reel proceeding from some building in the rear; but no sound of dancing was audible – an exceptional state of things for these parts, where as a rule the stamping drowned the music. The front door being open she could see straight through the house into the garden at the back as far as the shades of night would allow; and nobody appearing to her knock she traversed the dwelling and went up the path to the outhouse whence the sound had attracted her.

It was a windowless erection used for storage, and from the open door there floated into the obscurity a mist of yellow radiance, which at first Tess thought to be illuminated smoke. But on drawing nearer she perceived that it was a cloud of dust, lit by candles within the outhouse, whose beams upon the haze carried forward the outline of the doorway into the wide night of the garden.

When she came close and looked in she beheld indistinct forms racing up and down to the figure of the dance, the silence of their footfalls arising from their being overshoe in 'scroff' – that is to say, the powdery residuum from the storage of peat and other products, the stirring of which by their turbulent feet created the nebulosity that involved the scene. Through this floating, fusty *débris* of peat and hay, mixed with the perspirations and warmth of the dancers, and forming together a sort of vegeto-human pollen, the muted fiddles feebly pushed their notes, in marked contrast to the spirit with which the measure was trodden out. They coughed as they danced, and laughed as they coughed. Of the rushing couples there could barely be discerned more than the high lights – the indistinctness shaping them to satyrs clasping nymphs – a multiplicity of Pans whirling a multiplicity of Syrinxes; Lotis attempting to elude Priapus, and always failing.

At intervals a couple would approach the doorway for air, and the haze no longer veiling their features, the demigods resolved themselves into the homely personalities of her own next-door neighbours. Could Trantridge in two or three short hours have metamorphosed itself thus madly!

Some Sileni of the throng sat on benches and hay-trusses by the wall; and one of them recognized her.

'The maids don't think it respectable to dance at "The Flower-de-Luce",' he explained. 'They don't like to let everybody see which be their fancy-men.

Besides, the house sometimes shuts up just when their jints begin to get greased. So we come here and send out for liquor.'

'But when be any of you going home?' asked Tess with some anxiety.

'Now — a'most directly. This is all but the last jig.'

She waited. The reel drew to a close, and some of the party were in the mind for starting. But others would not, and another dance was formed. This surely would end it, thought Tess. But it merged in yet another. She became restless and uneasy; yet, having waited so long, it was necessary to wait longer; on account of the fair the roads were dotted with roving characters of possibly ill intent; and, though not fearful of measurable dangers, she feared the unknown. Had she been near Marlott she would have had less dread.

'Don't ye be nervous, my dear good soul,' expostulated, between his coughs, a young man with a wet face, and his straw hat so far back upon his head that the brim encircled it like the nimbus of a saint. 'What's yer hurry? To-morrow is Sunday, thank God, and we can sleep it off in church-time. Now, have a turn with me?'

She did not abhor dancing, but she was not going to dance here. The movement grew more passionate: the fiddlers behind the luminous pillar of cloud now and then varied the aid by playing on the wrong side of the bridge or with the back of the bow. But it did not matter; the panting shapes spun on-wards.

They did not vary their partners if their inclination were to stick to previous ones. Changing partners simply meant that a satisfactory choice had not as yet been arrived at by one or other of the pair, and by this time every couple had been suitably matched. It was then that the ecstasy and the dream began, in which emotion was the matter of the universe, and matter but an adventitious intrusion likely to hinder you from spinning where you wanted to spin.

Suddenly there was a dull thump on the ground: a couple had fallen, and lay in a mixed heap. The next couple, unable to check its progress, came toppling over the obstacle. An inner cloud of dust rose around the prostrate figures amid the general one of the room, in which a twitching entanglement of arms and legs was discernible.

'You shall catch it for this, my gentleman, when you get home!' burst in female accents from the human heap — those of the unhappy partner of the man whose clumsiness had caused the mishap; she happened also to be his recently married wife, in which assortment there was nothing unusual at Trantridge as long as any affection remained between wedded couples; and, indeed, it was not un-customary in their later lives, to avoid making odd lots of the single people between whom there might be a warm understanding.

A loud laugh from behind Tess's back, in the shade of the garden, united with the titter within the room. She looked round, and saw the red coal of a cigar: Alec d'Urberville was standing there alone. He beckoned to her, and she reluctantly retreated towards him.

'Well, my Beauty, what are you doing here?'

She was so tired after her long day and her walk that she confided her trouble to him — that she had been waiting ever since he saw her to have their company home, because the road at night was strange to her. 'But it seems they will never leave off, and I really think I will wait no longer.'

'Certainly do not. I have only a saddle-horse here to-day; but come to "The Flower-de-Luce", and I'll hire a trap, and drive you home with me.'

Tess, though flattered, had never quite got over her original mistrust of him, and, despite their tardiness, she preferred to walk home with the work-folk. So she answered that she was much obliged to him, but would not trouble him. 'I have said that I will wait for 'em, and they will expect me to now.'

'Very well, Miss Independence. Please yourself. . . . Then I shall not hurry. . . . My good Lord, what a kick-up they are having there!'

He had not put himself forward into the light, but some of them had perceived him, and his presence led to a slight pause and a consideration of how the time was flying. As soon as he had re-lit a cigar and walked away the Trantridge people began to collect themselves from amid those who had come in from other farms, and prepared to leave in a body. Their bundles and baskets were gathered up, and half an hour later, when the clock-chime sounded a quarter past eleven, they were straggling along the lane which led up the hill towards their homes.

It was a three-mile walk, along a dry white road, made whiter to-night by the light of the moon.

Tess soon perceived as she walked in the flock, sometimes with this one, sometimes with that, that the fresh night air was producing staggerings and serpentine courses among the men who had partaken too freely; some of the more careless women also were wandering in their gait – to wit, a dark virago, Car Darch, dubbed Queen of Spades, till lately a favourite of d'Urberville's; Nancy, her sister, nicknamed the Queen of Diamonds; and the young married woman who had already tumbled down. Yet however terrestrial and lumpy their appearance just now to the mean unglamoured eye, to themselves the case was different. They followed the road with a sensation that they were soaring along in a supporting medium, possessed of original and profound thoughts, themselves and surrounding nature forming an organism of which all the parts harmoniously and joyously interpenetrated each other. They were as sublime as the moon and stars above them, and the moon and stars were as ardent as they.

Tess, however, had undergone such painful experiences of this kind in her father's house, that the discovery of their condition spoilt the pleasure she was beginning to feel in the moonlight journey. Yet she stuck to the party, for reasons above given.

In the open highway they had progressed in scattered order; but now their route was through a field-gate, and the foremost finding a difficulty in opening it they closed up together.

This leading pedestrian was Car the Queen of Spades, who carried a wicker-basket containing her mother's groceries, her own draperies, and other purchases for the week. The basket being large and heavy, Car had placed it for convenience of porterage on the top of her head, where it rode on in jeopardized balance as she walked with arms akimbo.

'Well – whatever is that a-creeping down thy back, Car Darch?' said one of the group suddenly.

All looked at Car. Her gown was a light cotton print, and from the back of her head a kind of rope could be seen descending to some distance below her waist, like a Chinaman's queue.

' 'Tis her hair falling down,' said another.

No; it was not her hair: it was a black stream of something oozing from her basket, and it glistened like a slimy snake in the cold still rays of the moon.

' 'Tis treacle,' said an observant matron.

Treacle it was. Car's poor old grandmother had a weakness for the sweet stuff. Honey she had in plenty out of her own hives, but treacle was what her soul desired, and Car had been about to give her a treat of surprise. Hastily lowering the basket the dark girl found that the vessel containing the syrup had been smashed within.

By this time there had arisen a shout of laughter at the extraordinary appearance of Car's back, which irritated the dark queen into getting rid of the disfigurement by the first sudden means available, and independently of the help of the scoffers. She rushed excitedly into the field they were about to cross, and flinging herself flat on her back upon the grass, began to wipe her gown as well as she could by spinning horizontally on the herbage and dragging herself over it upon her elbows.

The laughter rang louder; they clung to the gate, to the posts, rested on their staves, in the weakness engendered by their convulsions at the spectacle of Car. Our heroine, who had hitherto held her peace, at this wild moment could not help joining in with the rest.

It was a misfortune — in more ways than one. No sooner did the dark queen hear the soberer richer note of Tess among those of the other work-people than a long smouldering sense of rivalry inflamed her to madness. She sprang to her feet and closely faced the object of her dislike.

'How darest th' laugh at me, hussy!' she cried.

'I couldn't really help it when t'others did,' apologized Tess, still tittering.

'Ah, th'st think th' beest everybody, dostn't, because th' beest first favourite with He just now! But stop a bit, my lady, stop a bit! I'm as good as two of such! Look here — here's at 'ee!'

To Tess's horror the dark queen began stripping off the bodice of her gown — which for the added reason of its ridiculed condition she was only too glad to be free of — till she had bared her plump neck, shoulders, and arms to the moonshine, under which they looked as luminous and beautiful as some Praxitelean creation, in their possession of the faultless rotundities of a lusty country girl. She closed her fists and squared up at Tess.

'Indeed, then, I shall not fight!' said the latter majestically; 'and if I had known you was of that sort, I wouldn't have so let myself down as to come with such a whorage as this is!'

The rather too inclusive speech brought down a torrent of vituperation from other quarters upon fair Tess's unlucky head, particularly from the Queen of Diamonds, who having stood in the relations to d'Urberville that Car had also been suspected of, united with the latter against the common enemy. Several other women also chimed in, with an animus which none of them would have been so fatuous as to show but for the rollicking evening they had passed. Thereupon, finding Tess unfairly browbeaten, the husbands and lovers tried to make peace by defending her; but the result of that attempt was directly to increase the war.

Tess was indignant and ashamed. She no longer minded the loneliness of the way and the lateness of the hour; her one object was to get away from the whole crew as soon as possible. She knew well enough that the better among them would repent of their passion next day. They were all now inside the field, and she was edging back to rush off alone when a horseman emerged almost silently from the corner of the hedge that screened the road, and Alec d'Urberville looked round upon them.

'What the devil is all this row about, work-folk?' he asked.

The explanation was not readily forthcoming; and, in truth, he did not require any. Having heard their voices while yet some way off he had ridden creepingly forward, and learnt enough to satisfy himself.

Tess was standing apart from the rest, near the gate. He bent over towards her. 'Jump up behind me,' he whispered, 'and we'll get shot of the screaming cats in a jiffy!'

She felt almost ready to faint, so vivid was her sense of the crisis. At almost any other moment of her life she would have refused such proffered aid and company, as she had refused them several times before; and now the loneliness would not of itself have forced her to do otherwise. But coming as the invitation did at the particular juncture when fear and indignation at these adversaries could be transformed by a spring of the foot into a triumph over them, she abandoned herself to her impulse, climbed the gate, put her toe upon his instep, and scrambled into the saddle behind him. The pair were speeding away into the distant gray by the time that the contentious revellers became aware of what had happened.

The Queen of Spades forgot the stain on her bodice, and stood beside the Queen of Diamonds and the new-married, staggering young woman — all with a gaze of fixity in the direction in which the horse's tramp was diminishing into silence on the road.

'What be ye looking at?' asked a man who had not observed the incident.

'Ho-ho-ho!' laughed dark Car.

'Hee-hee-hee!' laughed the tippling bride, as she steadied herself on the arm of her fond husband.

'Heu-heu-heu!' laughed dark Car's mother, stroking her moustache as she explained laconically: 'Out of the frying-pan into the fire!'

Then these children of the open air, whom even excess of alcohol could scarce injure permanently, betook themselves to the field-path; and as they went there moved onward with them, around the shadow of each one's hand, a circle of opalized light, formed by the moon's rays upon the glistening sheet of dew. Each pedestrian could see no halo but his or her own, which never deserted the head-shadow, whatever its vulgar unsteadiness might be; but adhered to it, and persistently beautified it; till the erratic motions seemed an inherent part of the irradiation, and the fumes of their breathing a component of the night's mist; and the spirit of the scene, and of the moonlight, and of Nature, seemed harmoniously to mingle with the spirit of wine.

CHAPTER ELEVEN

THE twain cantered along for some time without speech, Tess as she clung to him still panting in her triumph, yet in other respects dubious. She had perceived that the horse was not the spirited one he sometimes rode, and felt no alarm on that score, though her seat was precarious enough despite her tight hold of him. She begged him to slow the animal to a walk, which Alec accordingly did.

'Neatly done, was it not, dear Tess?' he said by and by.

'Yes!' said she. 'I am sure I ought to be much obliged to you.'

'And are you?'

She did not reply.

'Tess, why do you always dislike my kissing you?'

'I suppose — because I don't love you.'

'You are quite sure?'

'I am angry with you sometimes!'

'Ah, I half feared as much.' Nevertheless, Alec did not object to that confession. He knew that anything was better than frigidity. 'Why haven't you told me when I have made you angry?'

'You know very well why. Because I cannot help myself here.'

'I haven't offended you often by love-making?'

'You have sometimes.'

'How many times?'

'You know as well as I — too many times.'

'Every time I have tried?'

She was silent, and the horse ambled along for a considerable distance, till a faint luminous fog, which had hung in the hollows all the evening, became general and enveloped them. It seemed to hold the moonlight in suspension, rendering it more pervasive than in clear air. Whether on this account, or from absent-mindedness, or from sleepiness, she did not perceive that they had long ago passed the point at which the lane to Trantridge branched from the highway, and that her conductor had not taken the Trantridge track.

She was inexpressibly weary. She had risen at five o'clock every morning of that week, had been on foot the whole of each day, and on this evening had in addition walked the three miles to Chaseborough, waited three hours for her neighbours without eating or drinking, her impatience to start them preventing either; she had then walked a mile of the way home, and had undergone the excitement of the quarrel, till, with the slow progress of their steed, it was now nearly one o'clock. Only once, however, was she overcome by actual drowsiness. In that moment of oblivion her head sank gently against him.

D'Urberville stopped the horse, withdrew his feet from the stirrups, turned sideways on the saddle, and enclosed her waist with his arm to support her.

This immediately put her on the defensive, and with one of those sudden impulses of reprisal to which she was liable she gave him a little push from her. In his ticklish position he nearly lost his balance and only just avoided rolling over into the road, the horse, though a powerful one, being fortunately the quietest he rode.

'That is devilish unkind!' he said. 'I mean no harm – only to keep you from falling.'

She pondered suspiciously; till, thinking that this might after all be true, she relented, and said quite humbly, 'I beg your pardon, sir.'

'I won't pardon you unless you show some confidence in me. Good God!' he burst out, 'what am I, to be repulsed so by a mere chit like you? For near three mortal months have you trifled with my feelings, eluded me, and snubbed me; and I won't stand it!'

'I'll leave you to-morrow, sir.'

'No, you will not leave me to-morrow! Will you, I ask once more, show your belief in me by letting me clasp you with my arm? Come, between us two and nobody else, now. We know each other well; and you know that I love you, and think you the prettiest girl in the world, which you are. Mayn't I treat you as a lover?'

She drew a quick pettish breath of objection, writhing uneasily on her seat, looked far ahead, and murmured, 'I don't know – I wish – how can I say yes or no when—'

He settled the matter by clasping his arm round her as he desired, and Tess expressed no further negative. Thus they sidled slowly onward till it struck her they had been advancing for an unconscionable time – far longer than was usually occupied by the short journey from Chaseborough, even at this walking pace, and that they were no longer on hard road, but in a mere track-way.

'Why, where be we?' she exclaimed.

'Passing by a wood.'

'A wood – what wood? Surely we are quite out of the road?'

'A bit of The Chase – the oldest wood in England. It is a lovely night, and why should we not prolong our ride a little?'

'How could you be so treacherous!' said Tess, between archness and real dismay, and getting rid of his arm by pulling open his fingers one by one, though at the risk of slipping off herself 'Just when I've been putting such trust in you, and obliging you to please you, because I thought I had wronged you by that push! Please set me down, and let me walk home.'

'You cannot walk home, darling, even if the air were clear. We are miles away from Trantridge, if I must tell you, and in this growing fog you might wander for hours among these trees.'

'Never mind that,' she coaxed. 'Put me down, I beg you. I don't mind where it is; only let me get down, sir, please!'

'Very well, then, I will – on one condition. Having brought you here to this out-of-the-way place, I feel myself responsible for your safe-conduct home, whatever you may yourself feel about it. As to your getting to Trantridge without assistance, it is quite impossible; for, to tell the truth, dear, owing to this fog, which so disguises everything, I don't quite know where we are myself. Now, if you will promise to wait beside the horse while I walk through the bushes till I come to some road or house, and ascertain exactly our whereabouts, I'll deposit you here willingly. When I come back I'll give you full directions, and if you insist upon walking you may; or you may ride – at your pleasure.'

She accepted these terms, and slid off on the near side, though not till he had stolen a cursory kiss. He sprang down on the other side.

'I suppose I must hold the horse?' said she.

'Oh no; it's not necessary,' replied Alec, patting the panting creature. 'He's had enough of it for to-night.'

He turned the horse's head into the bushes, hitched him on to a bough, and made a sort of couch or nest for her in the deep mass of dead leaves.

'Now, you sit there,' he said. 'The leaves have not got damp as yet. Just give an eye to the horse – it will be quite sufficient.'

He took a few steps away from her, but, returning, said, 'By the bye, Tess, your father has a new cob to-day. Somebody gave it to him.'

'Somebody? You!'

D'Urberville nodded.

'O how very good of you that is!' she exclaimed, with a painful sense of the awkwardness of having to thank him just then.

'And the children have some toys.'

'I didn't know – you ever sent them anything!' she murmured, much moved. 'I almost wish you had not – yes, I almost wish it!'

'Why, dear?'

'It – hampers me so.'

'Tessy – don't you love me ever so little now?'

'I'm grateful,' she reluctantly admitted. 'But I fear I do not—' The sudden vision of his passion for herself as a factor in this result so distressed her that, beginning with one slow tear, and then following with another, she wept outright.

'Don't cry, dear, dear one! Now sit down here, and wait till I come.' She passively sat down amid the leaves he had heaped, and shivered slightly. 'Are you cold?' he asked.

'Not very – a little.'

He touched her with his fingers, which sank into her as into down. 'You have only that puffy muslin dress on – how's that?'

'It's my best summer one. 'Twas very warm when I started, and I didn't know I was going to ride, and that it would be night.'

'Nights grow chilly in September. Let me see.' He pulled off a light overcoat that he had worn, and put it round her tenderly. 'That's it – now you'll feel warmer,' he continued. 'Now, my pretty, rest there; I shall soon be back again.'

Having buttoned the overcoat round her shoulders he plunged into the webs of vapour which by this time formed veils between the trees. She could hear the rustling of the branches as he ascended the adjoining slope, till his movements were no louder than the hopping of a bird, and finally died away. With the setting of the moon the pale light lessened, and Tess became invisible as she fell into reverie upon the leaves where he had left her.

In the meantime Alec d'Urberville had pushed on up the slope to clear his genuine doubt as to the quarter of The Chase they were in. He had, in fact, ridden quite at random for over an hour, taking any turning that came to hand in order to prolong companionship with her, and giving far more attention to Tess's moonlit person than to any wayside object. A little rest for the jaded animal being desirable, he did not hasten his search for landmarks. A clamber over the hill into the adjoining vale brought him to the fence of a highway whose contours he recognized, which settled the question of their whereabouts. D'Urberville thereupon turned back; but by this time the moon had quite gone down, and partly on account of the fog The Chase was wrapped in thick darkness, although morning was not far off. He was obliged to advance with outstretched hands to avoid contact with the boughs, and discovered that to hit the exact spot from which he had started was at first entirely beyond him. Roaming up and down, round and round, he at length heard a slight movement of the horse close at hand; and the sleeve of his overcoat unexpectedly caught his foot.

'Tess!' said d'Urberville.

There was no answer. The obscurity was now so great that he could see absolutely nothing but a pale nebulousness at his feet, which represented the white muslin figure he had left upon the dead leaves. Everything else was blackness alike. D'Urberville stooped; and heard a gentle regular breathing. He knelt and bent lower, till her breath warmed his face, and in a moment his cheek was in contact with hers. She was sleeping soundly, and upon her eyelashes there lingered tears.

Darkness and silence ruled everywhere around. Above them rose the primeval yews and oaks of The Chase, in which were poised gentle roosting birds in their last nap; and about them stole the hopping rabbits and hares. But, might some say, where was Tess's guardian angel? where was the providence of her simple faith? Perhaps, like that other god of whom the ironical Tishbite spoke, he was talking, or he was pursuing, or he was in a journey, or he was sleeping and not to be awaked.

Why it was that upon this beautiful feminine tissue, sensitive as gossamer, and practically blank as snow as yet, there should have been traced such a coarse pattern as it was doomed to receive; why so often the coarse appropriates the finer thus, the wrong man the woman, the wrong woman the man, many thousand years of analytical philosophy have failed to explain to our sense of order. One may, indeed, admit the possibility of a retribution lurking in the present catastrophe. Doubtless some of Tess d'Urberville's mailed ancestors rollicking home from a fray had dealt the same measure even more ruthlessly towards peasant girls of their time. But though to visit the sins of the fathers upon the children may be a morality good enough for divinities, it is scorned by average human nature; and it therefore does not mend the matter.

As Tess's own people down in those retreats are never tired of saying among each other in their fatalistic way: 'It was to be.' There lay the pity of it. An immeasurable social chasm was to divide our heroine's personality thereafter from that previous self of hers who stepped from her mother's door to try her fortune at Trantridge poultry-farm.

Maiden no More

CHAPTER TWELVE

T HE basket was heavy and the bundle was large, but she lugged them along like a person who did not find her especial burden in material things. Occasionally she stopped to rest in a mechanical way by some gate or post; and then, giving the baggage another hitch upon her full round arm, went steadily on again.

It was a Sunday morning in late October, about four months after Tess Durbeyfield's arrival at Trantridge, and some few weeks subsequent to the night ride in The Chase. The time was not long past daybreak, and the yellow luminosity upon the horizon behind her back lighted the ridge towards which her face was set – the barrier of the vale wherein she had of late been a stranger – which she would have to climb over to reach her birthplace. The ascent was gradual on this side, and the soil and scenery differed much from those within Blakemore Vale. Even the character and accent of the two peoples had shades of difference, despite the amalgamating effects of a roundabout railway; so that, though less than twenty miles from the place of her sojourn at Trantridge, her native village had seemed a far-away spot. The field-folk shut in there traded northward and westward, travelled, courted, and married northward and westward, thought northward and westward; those on this side mainly directed their energies and attention to the east and south.

The incline was the same down which d'Urberville had driven with her so wildly on that day in June. Tess went up the remainder of its length without stopping, and on reaching the edge of the escarpment gazed over the familiar green world beyond, now half-veiled in mist. It was always beautiful from here; it was terribly beautiful to Tess to-day, for since her eyes last fell upon it she had learnt that the serpent hisses where the sweet birds sing, and her views of life had been totally changed for her by the lesson. Verily another girl than the simple one she had been at home was she who, bowed by thought, stood still here, and turned to look behind her. She could not bear to look forward into the Vale.

Ascending by the long white road that Tess herself had just laboured up, she saw a two-wheeled vehicle, beside which walked a man, who held up his hand to attract her attention.

She obeyed the signal to wait for him with unspeculative repose, and in a few minutes man and horse stopped beside her.

'Why did you slip away by stealth like this?' said d'Urberville, with upbraiding breathlessness; 'on a Sunday morning, too, when people were all in bed! I only discovered it by accident, and I have been driving like the deuce to overtake you. Just look at the mare. Why go off like this? You know that nobody wished to hinder your going. And how unnecessary it has been for you to toil along on foot, and encumber yourself with this heavy load! I have followed like a madman, simply to drive you the rest of the distance, if you won't come back.'

'I shan't come back,' said she.

'I thought you wouldn't – I said so! Well, then, put up your baskets, and let me help you on.'

She listlessly placed her basket and bundle within the dog-cart, and stepped up, and they sat side by side. She had no fear of him now, and in the cause of her confidence her sorrow lay.

D'Urberville mechanically lit a cigar, and the journey was continued with broken unemotional conversation on the commonplace objects by the wayside. He had quite forgotten his struggle to kiss her when, in the early summer, they had driven in the opposite direction along the same road. But she had not, and she sat now, like a puppet, replying to his remarks in monosyllables. After some miles they came in view of the clump of trees beyond which the village of Marlott stood. It was only then that her still face showed the least emotion, a tear or two beginning to trickle down.

'What are you crying for?' he coldly asked.

'I was only thinking that I was born over there,' murmured Tess.

'Well – we must all be born somewhere.'

'I wish I had never been born – there or anywhere else!'

'Pooh! Well, if you didn't wish to come to Trantridge why did you come?' She did not reply.

'You didn't come for love of me, that I'll swear.'

' 'Tis quite true. If I had gone for love o' you, if I had ever sincerely loved you, if I loved you still, I should not so loathe and hate myself for my weakness as I do now! . . . My eyes were dazed by you for a little, and that was all.'

He shrugged his shoulders. She resumed –

'I didn't understand your meaning till it was too late.'

'That's what every woman says.'

'How can you dare to use such words!' she cried, turning impetuously upon him, her eyes flashing as the latent spirit (of which he was to see more some day) awoke in her. 'My God! I could knock you out of the gig! Did it never strike your mind that what every woman says some women may feel?'

'Very well,' he said, laughing; 'I am sorry to wound you. I did wrong – I admit it.' He dropped into some little bitterness as he continued: 'Only you needn't be so everlastingly flinging it in my face. I am ready to pay to the uttermost farthing. You know you need not work in the fields or the dairies again. You know you may clothe yourself with the best, instead of in the bald plain way you have lately affected, as if you couldn't get a ribbon more than you earn.'

Her lip lifted slightly, though there was little scorn, as a rule, in her large and impulsive nature.

'I have said I will not take anything more from you, and I will not – I cannot! I *should* be your creature to go on doing that, and I won't!'

'One would think you were a princess from your manner, in addition to a true and original d'Urberville – ha! ha! Well, Tess, dear, I can say no more. I suppose

I am a bad fellow – a damn bad fellow. I was born bad, and I have lived bad, and I shall die bad in all probability. But, upon my lost soul, I won't be bad towards you again, Tess. And if certain circumstances should arise – you understand – in which you are in the least need, the least difficulty, send me one line, and you shall have by return whatever you require. I may not be at Trantridge – I am going to London for a time – I can't stand the old woman. But all letters will be forwarded.'

She said that she did not wish him to drive her further, and they stopped just under the clump of trees. D'Urberville alighted, and lifted her down bodily in his arms, afterwards placing her articles on the ground beside her. She bowed to him slightly, her eye just lingering in his; and then she turned to take the parcels for departure.

Alec d'Urberville removed his cigar, bent towards her, and said –

'You are not going to turn away like that, dear? Come!'

'If you wish,' she answered indifferently. 'See how you've mastered me!'

She thereupon turned round and lifted her face to his, and remained like a marble term while he imprinted a kiss upon her cheek – half perfunctorily, half as if zest had not yet quite died out. Her eyes vaguely rested upon the remotest trees in the lane while the kiss was given, as though she were nearly unconscious of what he did.

'Now the other side, for old acquaintance' sake.'

She turned her head in the same passive way, as one might turn at the request of a sketcher or hairdresser, and he kissed the other side, his lips touching cheeks that were damp and smoothly chill as the skin of the mushrooms in the fields around.

'You don't give me your mouth and kiss me back. You never willingly do that – you'll never love me, I fear.'

'I have said so, often. It is true. I have never really and truly loved you, and I think I never can.' She added mournfully, 'Perhaps, of all things, a lie on this thing would do the most good to me now; but I have honour enough left, little as 'tis, not to tell that lie. If I did love you I may have the best o' causes for letting you know it. But I don't.'

He emitted a laboured breath, as if the scene were getting rather oppressive to his heart, or to his conscience, or to his gentility.

'Well, you are absurdly melancholy, Tess. I have no reason for flattering you now, and I can say plainly that you need not be so sad. You can hold your own for beauty against any woman of these parts, gentle or simple; I say it to you as a practical man and well-wisher. If you are wise you will show it to the world more than you do before it fades. . . . And yet, Tess, will you come back to me? Upon soul I don't like to let you go like this!'

Never, never! I made up my mind as soon as I saw – what I ought to have seen sooner; and I won't come.'

'Then good morning, my four months' cousin – good-bye!'

He leapt up lightly, arranged the reins, and was gone between the tall red-berried hedges.

Tess did not look after him, but slowly wound along the crooked lane. It was still early, and though the sun's lower limb was just free of the hill, his rays, ungenial and peering, addressed the eye rather than the touch as yet. There was not a human soul near. Sad October and her sadder self seemed the only two existences haunting that lane.

As she walked, however, some footsteps approached behind her, the footsteps of a man; and owing to the briskness of his advance he was close at her heels and had said 'Good morning' before she had been long aware of his propinquity. He appeared to be an artisan of some sort, and carried a tin pot of red paint in his hand. He asked in a business-like manner if he should take her basket, which she permitted him to do, walking beside him.

'It is early to be astir this Sabbath morn!' he said cheerfully.

'Yes,' said Tess.

'When most people are at rest from their week's work.'

She also assented to this.

'Though I do more real work to-day than all the week besides.'

'Do you?'

'All the week I work for the glory of man, and on Sunday for the glory of God. That's more real than the other – hey? I have a little to do here at this stile.' The man turned as he spoke to an opening at the roadside leading into a pasture. 'If you'll wait a moment,' he added, 'I shall not be long.'

As he had her basket she could not well do otherwise; and she waited, observing him. He set down her basket and the tin pot, and stirring the paint with the brush that was in it began painting large square letters on the middle board of the three composing the stile, placing a comma after each word, as if to give pause while that word was driven well home to the reader's heart –

THY, DAMNATION, SLUMBERETH, NOT

2 Pet. ii 3

Against the peaceful landscape, the pale, decaying tints of the copses, the blue air of the horizon, and the lichened stile-boards, these staring vermilion words shone forth. They seemed to shout themselves out and made the atmosphere ring. Some people might have cried 'Alas, poor Theology!' at the hideous defacement – the last grotesque phase of a creed which had served mankind well in its time. But the words entered Tess with accusatory horror. It was as if this man had known her recent history; yet he was a total stranger.

Having finished his text he picked up her basket, and she mechanically resumed her walk beside him.

'Do you believe what you paint?' she asked in low tones.

'Believe that tex? Do I believe in my own existence!'

'But,' said she tremulously, 'suppose your sin was not of your own seeking?'

He shook his head.

'I cannot split hairs on that burning query,' he said. 'I have walked hundreds of miles this past summer, painting these texes on every wall, gate, and stile in the length and breadth of this district. I leave their application to the hearts of the people who read 'em.'

'I think they are horrible,. said Tess. 'Crushing! killing!'

'That's what they are meant to be!' he replied in a trade voice. 'But you should read my hottest ones – them I kips for slums and seaports. They'd make ye wriggle! Not but what this is a very good tex for rural districts. . . . Ah – there's a nice bit of blank wall up by that barn standing to waste. I must put one there –

one that it will be good for dangerous young females like yerself to heed. Will ye wait, missy?'

'No,' said she; and taking her basket Tess trudged on. A little way forward she turned her head. The old gray wall began to advertise a similar fiery lettering to the first, with a strange and unwonted mien, as if distressed at duties it had never before been called upon to perform. It was with a sudden flush that she read and realized what was to be the inscription he was now half-way through —

THOU, SHALT, NOT, COMMIT—

Her cheerful friend saw her looking, stopped his brush, and shouted —

'If you want to ask for edification on these things of moment, there's a very earnest good man going to preach a charity-sermon to-day in the parish you are going to — Mr Clare of Emminster. I'm not of his persuasion now, but he's a good man, and he'll expound as well as any parson I know. 'Twas he began the work in me.'

But Tess did not answer; she throbbingly resumed her walk, her eyes fixed on the ground. 'Pooh — I don't believe God said such things!' she murmured contemptuously when her flush had died away.

A plume of smoke soared up suddenly from her father's chimney, the sight of which made her heart ache. The aspect of the interior, when she reached it, made her heart ache more. Her mother, who had just come down stairs, turned to greet her from the fireplace, where she was kindling barked-oak twigs under the breakfast kettle. The young children were still above, as was also her father, it being Sunday morning, when he felt justified in lying an additional half-hour.

'Well — my dear Tess!' exclaimed her surprised mother, jumping up and kissing the girl. 'How be ye? I didn't see you till you was in upon me! Have you come home to be married?'

'No, I have not come for that, mother.'

'Then for a holiday?'

'Yes — for a holiday; for a long holiday,' said Tess.

'What, isn't your cousin going to do the handsome thing?'

'He's not my cousin, and he's not going to marry me.'

Her mother eyed her narrowly.

'Come, you have not told me all,' she said.

Then Tess went up to her mother, put her face upon Joan's neck, and told.

'And yet th'st not got him to marry 'ee!' reiterated her mother. 'Any woman would have done it but you, after that!'

'Perhaps any woman would except me.'

'It would have been something like a story to come back with, if you had!' continued Mrs Durbeyfield, ready to burst into tears of vexation. 'After all the talk about you and him which has reached us here, who would have expected it to end like this! Why didn't ye think of doing some good for your family instead o' thinking only of yourself? See how I've got to teave and slave, and your poor weak father with his heart clogged like a dripping-pan. I did hope for something to come out o' this! To see what a pretty pair you and he made that day when you drove away together four months ago! See what he has given us — all, as we thought, because we were his kin. But if he's not, it must have been done because of his love for 'ee. And yet you've not got him to marry!'

Get Alec d'Urberville in the mind to marry her! He marry *her*! On matrimony he had never once said a word. And what if he had? How a convulsive snatching at social salvation might have impelled her to answer him she could not say. But her poor foolish mother little knew her present feeling towards this man. Perhaps it was unusual in the circumstances, unlucky, unaccountable; but there it was; and this, as she had said, was what made her detest herself. She had never wholly cared for him, she did not at all care for him now. She had dreaded him, winced before him, succumbed to adroit advantages he took of her helplessness; then, temporarily blinded by his ardent manners, had been stirred to confused surrender awhile: had suddenly despised and disliked him, and had run away. That was all. Hate him she did not quite; but he was dust and ashes to her, and even for her name's sake she scarcely wished to marry him.

'You ought to have been more careful if you didn't mean to get him to make you his wife!'

'O mother, my mother!' cried the agonized girl, turning passionately upon her parent as if her poor heart would break. 'How could I be expected to know? I was a child when I left this house four months ago. Why didn't you tell me there was danger in men-folk? Why didn't you warn me? Ladies know what to fend hands against, because they read novels that tell them of these tricks; but I never had the chance o' learning in that way, and you did not help me!'

Her mother was subdued.

'I thought if I spoke of his fond feelings and what they might lead to, you would be hontish wi' him and lose your chance,' she murmured, wiping her eyes with her apron. 'Well, we must make the best of it, I suppose. 'Tis nater, after all, and what do please God!'

CHAPTER THIRTEEN

T HE event of Tess Durbeyfield's return from the manor of her bogus kinsfolk was rumoured abroad, if rumour be not too large a word for a space of a square mile. In the afternoon several young girls of Marlott, former schoolfellows and acquaintances of Tess, called to see her, arriving dressed in their best starched and ironed, as became visitors to a person who had made a transcendent conquest (as they supposed), and sat round the room looking at her with great curiosity. For the fact that it was this said thirty-first cousin, Mr d'Urberville, who had fallen in love with her, a gentleman not altogether local, whose reputation as a reckless gallant and heartbreaker was beginning to spread beyond the immediate boundaries of Trantridge, lent Tess's supposed position, by its fearsomeness, a far higher fascination than it would have exercised if unhazardous.

Their interest was so deep that the younger ones whispered when her back was turned —

'How pretty she is; and how that best frock do set her off! I believe it cost an immense deal, and that it was a gift from him.'

Tess, who was reaching up to get the tea-things from the corner-cupboard, did not hear these commentaries. If she had heard them, she might soon have set her friends right on the matter. But her mother heard, and Joan's simple vanity, having been denied the hope of a dashing marriage, fed itself as well as it could upon the sensation of a dashing flirtation. Upon the whole she felt gratified, even though such a limited and evanescent triumph should involve her daughter's reputation; it might end in marriage yet, and in the warmth of her responsiveness to their admiration she invited her visitors to stay to tea.

Their chatter, their laughter, their good-humoured innuendoes, above all, their flashes and flickerings of envy, revived Tess's spirits also; and, as the evening wore on, she caught the infection of their excitement, and grew almost gay. The marble hardness left her face, she moved with something of her old bounding step, and flushed in all her young beauty.

At moments, in spite of thought, she would reply to their inquiries with a manner of superiority, as if recognizing that her experiences in the field of courtship had, indeed, been slightly enviable. But so far was she from being, in the words of Robert South, 'in love with her own ruin', that the illusion was transient as lightning; cold reason came back to mock her spasmodic weakness; the ghastliness of her momentary pride would convict her, and recall her to reserved listlessness again.

And the despondency of the next morning's dawn, when it was no longer Sunday, but Monday; and no best clothes; and the laughing visitors were gone, and she awoke alone in her old bed, the innocent younger children breathing softly around her. In place of the excitement of her return, and the interest it had inspired, she saw before her a long and stony highway which she had to tread, without aid, and with little sympathy. Her depression was then terrible, and she could have hidden herself in a tomb.

In the course of a few weeks Tess revived sufficiently to show herself so far as was necessary to get to church one Sunday morning. She liked to hear the chanting – such as it was – and the old Psalms, and to join in the Morning Hymn. That innate love of melody, which she had inherited from her ballad-singing mother, gave the simplest music a power over her which could well-nigh drag her heart out of her bosom at times.

To be as much out of observation as possible for reasons of her own, and to escape the gallantries of the young men, she set out before the chiming began, and took a back seat under the gallery, close to the lumber, where only old men and women came, and where the bier stood on end among the churchyard tools.

Parishioners dropped in by twos and threes, deposited themselves in rows before her, rested three-quarters of a minute on their foreheads as if they were praying, though they were not; then sat up, and looked around. When the chants came on one of her favourites happened to be chosen among the rest – the old double chant 'Langdon' – but she did not know what it was called, though she would much have liked to know. She thought, without exactly wording the thought, how strange and godlike was a composer's power, who from the grave could lead through sequences of emotion, which he alone had felt at first, a girl like her who had never heard of his name, and never would have a clue to his personality.

The people who had turned their heads turned them again as the service proceeded; and at last observing her they whispered to each other. She knew what their whispers were about, grew sick at heart, and felt that she could come to church no more.

The bedroom which she shared with some of the children formed her retreat more continually than ever. Here, under her few square yards of thatch, she watched winds, and snows, and rains, gorgeous sunsets, and successive moons at their full. So close kept she that at length almost everybody thought she had gone away.

The only exercise that Tess took at this time was after dark; and it was then, when out in the woods, that she seemed least solitary. She knew how to hit to a hair's-breadth that moment of evening when the light and the darkness are so evenly balanced that the constraint of day and the suspense of night neutralize each other, leaving absolute mental liberty. It is then that the plight of being alive becomes attenuated to its least possible dimensions. She had no fear of the shadows; her sole idea seemed to be to shun mankind — or rather that cold accretion called the world, which, so terrible in the mass, is so unformidable, even pitiable, in its units.

On these lonely hills and dales her quiescent glide was of a piece with the element she moved in. Her flexuous and stealthy figure became an integral part of the scene. At times her whimsical fancy would intensify natural processes around her till they seemed a part of her own story. Rather they became a part of it; for the world is only a psychological phenomenon, and what they seemed they were. The midnight airs and gusts, moaning amongst the tightly-wrapped buds and bark of the winter twigs, were formulae of bitter reproach. A wet day was the expression of irremediable grief at her weakness in the mind of some vague ethical being whom she could not class definitely as the God of her childhood, and could not comprehend as any other.

But this encompassment of her own characterization, based on shreds of convention, peopled by phantoms and voices antipathetic to her, was a sorry and mistaken creation of Tess's fancy — a cloud of moral hobgoblins by which she was terrified without reason. It was they that were out of harmony with the actual world, not she. Walking among the sleeping birds in the hedges, watching the skipping rabbits on a moonlit warren, or standing under a pheasant-laden bough, she looked upon herself as a figure of Guilt intruding into the haunts of Innocence. But all the while she was making a distinction where there was no difference. Feeling herself in antagonism she was quite in accord. She had been made to break an accepted social law, but no law known to the environment in which she fancied herself such an anomaly.

CHAPTER FOURTEEN

I T was a hazy sunrise in August. The denser nocturnal vapours, attacked by the warm beams, were dividing and shrinking into isolated fleeces within hollows and coverts, where they waited till they should be dried away to nothing.

The sun, on account of the mist, had a curious sentient, personal look, demanding the masculine pronoun for its adequate expression. His present aspect, coupled with the lack of all human forms in the scene, explained the old-time heliolatries in a moment. One could feel that a saner religion had never prevailed under the sky. The luminary was a golden-haired, beaming, mild-eyed, God-like creature, gazing down in the vigour and intentness of youth upon an earth that was brimming with interest for him.

His light, a little later, broke through chinks of cottage shutters, throwing stripes like red-hot pokers upon cupboards, chests of drawers, and other furniture within; and awakening harvesters who were not already astir.

But of all ruddy things that morning the brightest were two broad arms of painted wood, which rose from the margin of a yellow cornfield hard by Marlott village. They, with two others below, formed the revolving Maltese cross of the reaping-machine, which had been brought to the field on the previous evening to be ready for operations this day. The paint with which they were smeared, intensified in hue by the sunlight, imparted to them a look of having been dipped in liquid fire.

The field had already been 'opened'; that is to say, a lane a few feet wide had been hand-cut through the wheat along the whole circumference of the field, for the first passage of the horses and machine.

Two groups, one of men and lads, the other of women, had come down the lane just at the hour when the shadows of the eastern hedge-top struck the west hedge midway, so that the heads of the groups were enjoying sunrise while their feet were still in the dawn. They disappeared from the lane between the two stone posts which flanked the nearest field-gate.

Presently there arose from within a ticking like the love-making of the grasshopper. The machine had begun, and a moving concatenation of three horses and the aforesaid long rickety machine was visible over the gate, a driver sitting upon one of the hauling horses, and an attendant on the seat of the implement. Along one side of the field the whole wain went, the arms of the mechanical reaper revolving slowly, till it passed down the hill quite out of sight. In a minute it came up on the other side of the field at the same equable pace; the glistening brass star in the forehead of the fore horse first catching the eye as it rose into view over the stubble, then the bright arms, and then the whole machine.

The narrow lane of stubble encompassing the field grew wider with each circuit, and the standing corn was reduced to smaller area as the morning wore on. Rabbits, hares, snakes, rats, mice, retreated inwards as into a fastness, unaware of the ephemeral nature of their refuge, and of the doom that awaited them later in the day when, their covert shrinking to a more and more horrible narrowness, they were huddled together, friends and foes, till the last few hundred yards of upright wheat fell also under the teeth of the unerring reaper, and they were every one put to death by the sticks and stones of the harvesters.

The reaping-machine left the fallen corn behind it in little heaps, each heap being of the quantity for a sheaf; and upon these the active binders in the rear laid their hands — mainly women, but some of them men in print shirts, and trousers supported round their waists by leather straps, rendering useless the two buttons behind, which twinkled and bristled with sunbeams at every movement of each wearer, as if they were a pair of eyes in the small of his back.

But those of the other sex were the most interesting of this company of binders, by reason of the charm which is acquired by woman when she becomes part and parcel of outdoor nature, and is not merely an object set down therein as at ordinary times. A field-man is a personality afield; a field-woman is a portion of the field; she has somehow lost her own margin, imbibed the essence of her surrounding, and assimilated herself with it.

The women – or rather girls, for they were mostly young – wore drawn cotton bonnets with great flapping curtains to keep off the sun, and gloves to prevent their hands being wounded by the stubble. There was one wearing a pale pink jacket, another in a cream-coloured tight-sleeved gown, another in a petticoat as red as the arms of the reaping-machine; and others, older, in the brown-rough 'wrapper' or over-all – the old-established and most appropriate dress of the field-woman, which the young ones were abandoning. This morning the eye returns involuntarily to the girl in the pink cotton jacket, she being the most flexuous and finely-drawn figure of them all. But her bonnet is pulled so far over her brow that none of her face is disclosed while she binds, though her complexion may be guessed from a stray twine or two of dark brown hair which extends below the curtain of her bonnet. Perhaps one reason why she seduces casual attention is that she never courts it, though the other women often gaze around them.

Her binding proceeds with clock-like monotony. From the sheaf last finished she draws a handful of ears, patting their tips with her left palm to bring them even. Then stooping low she moves forward, gathering the corn with both hands against her knees, and pushing her left gloved hand under the bundle to meet the right on the other side, holding the corn in an embrace like that of a lover. She brings the ends of the bond together, and kneels on the sheaf while she ties it, beating back her skirts now and then when lifted by the breeze. A bit of her naked arm is visible between the buff leather of the gauntlet and the sleeve of her gown; and as the day wears on its feminine smoothness becomes scarified by the stubble, and bleeds.

At intervals she stands up to rest, and to retie her disarranged apron, or to pull her bonnet straight. Then one can see the oval face of a handsome young woman with deep eyes and long heavy clinging tresses, which seem to clasp in a beseeching way anything they fall against. The cheeks are paler, the teeth more regular, the red lips thinner than is usual in a country-bred girl.

It is Tess Durbeyfield, otherwise d'Urberville, somewhat changed – the same, but not the same; at the present stage of her existence living as a stranger and an alien here, though it was no strange land that she was in. After a long seclusion she had come to a resolve to undertake outdoor work in her native village, the busiest season of the year in the agricultural world having arrived, and nothing that she could do within the house being so remunerative for the time as harvesting in the fields.

The movements of the other women were more or less similar to Tess's, the whole bevy of them drawing together like dancers in a quadrille at the completion of a sheaf by each, every one placing her sheaf on end against those of the rest, till a shock, or 'stitch' as it was here called, of ten or a dozen was formed.

They went to breakfast, and came again, and the work proceeded as before. As the hour of eleven drew near a person watching her might have noticed that every now and then Tess's glance flitted wistfully to the brow of the hill, though she did not pause in her sheafing. On the verge of the hour the heads of a group of children, of ages ranging from six to fourteen, rose above the stubbly convexity of the hill.

The face of Tess flushed slightly, but still she did not pause.

The eldest of the comers, a girl who wore a triangular shawl, its corner draggling on the stubble, carried in her arms what at first sight seemed to be a doll, but proved to be an infant in long clothes. Another brought some lunch. The harvesters ceased working, took their provisions, and sat down against one of the shocks. Here they fell to, the men plying a stone jar freely, and passing round a cup.

Tess Durbeyfield had been one of the last to suspend her labours. She sat down at the end of the shock, her face turned somewhat away from her companions. When she had deposited herself a man in a rabbit-skin cap and with a red handkerchief tucked into his belt, held the cup of ale over the top of the shock for her to drink. But she did not accept his offer. As soon as her lunch was spread she called up the big girl her sister, and took the baby of her, who, glad to be relieved of the burden, went away to the next shock and joined the other children playing there. Tess, with a curiously stealthy yet courageous movement, and with a still rising colour, unfastened her frock and began suckling the child.

The men who sat nearest considerately turned their faces towards the other end of the field, some of them beginning to smoke; one, with absent-minded fondness, regretfully stroking the jar that would no longer yield a stream. All the women but Tess fell into animated talk, and adjusted the disarranged knots of their hair.

When the infant had taken its fill the young mother sat it upright in her lap, and looking into the far distance dandled it with a gloomy indifference that was almost dislike; then all of a sudden she fell to violently kissing it some dozens of times, as if she could never leave off, the child crying at the vehemence of an onset which strangely combined passionateness with contempt.

'She's fond of that there child, though she mid pretend to hate en, and say she wishes the baby and her too were in the churchyard,' observed the woman in the red petticoat.

'She'll soon leave off saying that,' replied the one in buff. 'Lord, 'tis wonderful what a body can get used to o' that sort in time!'

'A little more than persuading had to do wi' the coming o't, I reckon. There were they that heard a sobbing one night last year in The Chase; and it mid ha' gone hard wi' a certain party if folks had come along.'

'Well, a little more, or a little less, 'twas a thousand pities that it should have happened to she, of all others. But 'tis always the comeliest! The plain ones be as safe as churches – hey, Jenny?' The speaker turned to one of the group who certainly was not ill-defined as plain.

It was a thousand pities, indeed; it was impossible for even an enemy to feel otherwise on looking at Tess as she sat there, with her flower-like mouth and large tender eyes, neither black nor blue nor gray nor violet; rather all those shades together, and a hundred others, which could be seen if one looked into their irises – shade behind shade – tint beyond tint – around pupils that had no bottom; an almost standard woman, but for the slight incautiousness of character inherited from her race.

A resolution which had surprised herself had brought her into the fields this week for the first time during many months. After wearing and wasting her palpitating heart with every engine of regret that lonely inexperience could devise, common-sense had illumined her. She felt that she would do well to be useful again – to taste anew sweet independence at any price. The past was past; whatever it had been it was no more at hand. Whatever its consequences, time would close over them; they would all in a few years be as if they had never been, and she herself grassed down and forgotten. Meanwhile the trees were just as green as before; the birds sang and the sun shone as clearly now as ever. The familiar surroundings had not darkened because of her grief, nor sickened because of her pain.

She might have seen that what had bowed her head so profoundly – the thought of the world's concern at her situation – was founded on an illusion. She was not an existence, an experience, a passion, a structure of sensations, to anybody but herself. To all humankind besides Tess was only a passing thought. Even to friends she was no more than a frequently passing thought. If she made herself miserable the livelong night and day it was only this much to them – 'Ah, she makes herself unhappy.' If she tried to be cheerful, to dismiss all care, to take pleasure in the daylight, the flowers, the baby, she could only be this idea to them – 'Ah, she bears it very well.' Moreover, alone in a desert island would she have been wretched at what had happened to her? Not greatly. If she could have been but just created, to discover herself as a spouseless mother, with no experience of life except as the parent of a nameless child, would the position have caused her to despair? No, she would have taken it calmly, and found pleasures therein. Most of the misery had been generated by her conventional aspect, and not be her innate sensations.

Whatever Tess's reasoning, some spirit had induced her to dress herself up neatly as she had formerly done, and come out into the fields, harvest-hands being greatly in demand just then. This was why she had borne herself with dignity, and had looked people calmly in the face at times, even when holding the baby in her arms.

The harvest-men rose from the shock of corn, and stretched their limbs, and extinguished their pipes. The horses, which had been unharnessed and fed, were again attached to the scarlet machine. Tess, having quickly eaten her own meal, beckoned to her eldest sister to come and take away the baby, fastened her dress, put on the buff gloves again, and stooped anew to draw a bond from the last completed sheaf for the tying of the next.

In the afternoon and evening the proceedings of the morning were continued, Tess staying on till dusk with the body of harvesters. Then they all rode home in one of the largest wagons, in the company of a broad tarnished moon that had risen from the ground to the eastwards, its face resembling the outworn gold-leaf halo of some worm-eaten Tuscan saint. Tess's female companions sang songs, and showed themselves very sympathetic and glad at her reappearance out of doors, though they could not refrain from mischievously throwing in a few verses of the ballad about the maid who went to the merry green wood and came back a changed state. There are counterpoises and compensations in life; and the event which had made of her a social warning had also for the moment made her the most interesting personage in the village to many. Their friendliness won her still farther away from herself, their lively spirits were contagious, and she became almost gay.

But now that her moral sorrows were passing away a fresh one arose on the natural side of her which knew no social law. When she reached home it was to learn to her grief that the baby had been suddenly taken ill since the afternoon. Some such collapse had been probable, so tender and puny was its frame; but the event came as a shock nevertheless.

The baby's offence against society in coming into the world was forgotten by the girl-mother; her soul's desire was to continue that offence by preserving the life of the child. However, it soon grew clear that the hour of emancipation for that little prisoner of the flesh was to arrive earlier than her worst misgivings had conjectured. And when she had discovered this she was plunged into a misery which transcended that of the child's simple loss. Her baby had not been baptized.

Tess had drifted into a frame of mind which accepted passively the consideration that if she should have to burn for what she had done, burn she must, and there was an end of it. Like all village girls she was well grounded in the Holy Scriptures, and had dutifully studied the histories of Aholah and Aholibah, and knew the inferences to be drawn therefrom. But when the same question arose with regard to the baby, it had a very different colour. Her darling was about to die, and no salvation.

It was nearly bedtime, but she rushed downstairs and asked if she might send for the parson. The moment happened to be one at which her father's sense of the antique nobility of his family was highest, and his sensitiveness to the smudge which Tess had set upon that nobility most pronounced, for he had just returned from his weekly booze at Rolliver's Inn. No parson should come inside his door, he declared, prying into his affairs, just then, when by her shame, it had become more necessary than ever to hide them. He locked the door and put the key in his pocket.

The household went to bed, and, distressed beyond measure, Tess retired also. She was continually waking as she lay, and in the middle of the night found that the baby was still worse. It was obviously dying – quietly and painlessly, but none the less surely.

In her misery she rocked herself upon the bed. The clock struck the solemn hour of one, that hour when fancy stalks outside reason, and malignant possibilities stand rock-firm as facts. She thought of the child consigned to the nethermost corner of hell, as its double doom for lack of baptism and lack of legitimacy; saw the arch-fiend tossing it with his three-pronged fork, like the one they used for heating the oven on baking days; to which picture she added many other quaint and curious details of torment sometimes taught the young in this Christian country. The lurid presentment so powerfully affected her imagination in the silence of the sleeping house that her nightgown became damp with perspiration, and the bedstead shook with each throb of her heart.

The infant's breathing grew more difficult, and the mother's mental tension increased. It was useless to devour the little thing with kisses; she could stay in bed no longer, and walked feverishly about the room.

'O merciful God, have pity; have pity upon my poor baby!' she cried. 'Heap as much anger as you want to upon me, and welcome; but pity the child!'

She leant against the chest of drawers, and murmured incoherent supplications for a long while, till she suddenly started up.

'Ah! perhaps baby can be saved! Perhaps it will be just the same!'

She spoke so brightly that it seemed as though her face might have shone in the gloom surrounding her.

She lit a candle, and went to a second and a third bed under the wall, where she awoke her young sisters and brothers, all of whom occupied the same room. Pulling out the washing-stand so that she could get behind it, she poured some water from a jug, and made them kneel around, putting their hands together with fingers exactly vertical. While the children, scarcely awake, awe-stricken at her manner, their eyes growing larger and larger, remained in this position, she took the baby from her bed – a child's child – so immature as scarce to seem a sufficient personality to endow its producer with the maternal title. Tess then stood erect with the infant on her arm beside the basin, the next sister held the Prayer-Book open before her, as the clerk at church held it before the parson; and thus the girl set about baptizing her child.

Her figure looked singularly tall and imposing as she stood in her long white nightgown, a thick cable of twisted dark hair hanging straight down her back to her waist. The kindly dimness of the weak candle abstracted from her form and features the little blemishes which sunlight might have revealed – the stubble scratches upon her wrists, and the weariness of her eyes – her high enthusiasm having a transfiguring effect upon the face which had been her undoing, showing it as a thing of immaculate beauty, with a touch of dignity which was almost regal. The little ones kneeling round, their sleepy eyes blinking and red, awaited her preparations full of a suspended wonder which their physical heaviness at that hour would not allow to become active.

The most impressed of them said:

'Be you really going to christen him, Tess?'

The girl-mother replied in a grave affirmative.

'What's his name going to be?'

She had not thought of that, but a name suggested by a phrase in the book of Genesis came into her head as she proceeded with the baptismal service, and now she pronounced it:

'Sorrow, I baptize thee in the name of the Father, and of the Son, and of the Holy Ghost.'

She sprinkled the water, and there was silence.

'Say "Amen", children.'

The tiny voices piped in obedient response 'Amen!'

Tess went on:

'We receive this child' – and so forth – 'and do sign him with the sign of the Cross.'

Here she dipped her hand into the basin, and fervently drew an immense cross upon the baby with her forefinger, continuing with the customary sentences as to his manfully fighting against sin, the world, and the devil, and being a faithful soldier and servant unto his life's end. She duly went on with the Lord's Prayer, the children lisping it after her in a thin gnat-like wail, till at the conclusion, raising their voices to clerk's pitch, they again piped into the silence, 'Amen!'

Then their sister, with much augmented confidence in the efficacy of this sacrament, poured forth from the bottom of her heart the thanksgiving that follows, uttering it boldly and triumphantly in the stopt-diapason note which her voice acquired when her heart was in her speech, and which will never be forgotten by those who knew her. The ecstasy of faith almost apotheosized her; it set upon her face a glowing irradiation, and brought a red spot into the middle of each cheek; while the miniature candle-flame inverted in her eye-pupils shone like a diamond. The children gazed up at her with more and more reverence, and no longer had a will for questioning. She did not look like Sissy to them now, but as a being large, towering, and awful – a divine personage with whom they had nothing in common.

Poor Sorrow's campaign against sin, the world, and the devil was doomed to be of limited brilliancy – luckily perhaps for himself, considering his beginnings. In the blue of the morning that fragile soldier and servant breathed his last, and when the other children awoke they cried bitterly, and begged Sissy to have another pretty baby.

The calmness which had possessed Tess since the christening remained with her in the infant's loss. In the daylight, indeed, she felt her terrors about his soul to have been somewhat exaggerated; whether well founded or not she had no uneasiness now, reasoning that if Providence would not ratify such an act of approximation she, for one, did not value the kind of heaven lost by the irregularity – either for herself or for her child.

So passed away Sorrow the Undesired – that intrusive creature, that bastard gift of shameless Nature who respects not the social law; a waif to whom eternal Time had been a matter of days merely, who knew not that such things as years and centuries ever were; to whom the cottage interior was the universe, the week's weather climate, new-born babyhood human existence, and the instinct to suck human knowledge.

Tess, who mused on the christening a good deal, wondered if it were doctrinally sufficient to secure a Christian burial for the child. Nobody could tell this but the parson of the parish, and he was a new-comer, and did not know her. She went to his house after dusk, and stood by the gate, but could not summon courage to go in. The enterprise would have been abandoned if she had not by accident met him coming homeward as she turned away. In the gloom she did not mind speaking freely.

'I should like to ask you something, sir.'

He expressed his willingness to listen, and she told the story of the baby's illness and the extemporized ordinance.

'And now, sir,' she added earnestly, 'can you tell me this – will it be just the same for him as if you had baptized him?'

Having the natural feelings of a tradesman at finding that a job he should have been called in for had been unskilfully botched by his customers among themselves, he was disposed to say no. Yet the dignity of the girl, the strange tenderness in her voice, combined to affect his nobler impulses – or rather those that he had left in him after ten years of endeavour to graft technical belief on

actual scepticism. The man and the ecclesiastic fought within him, and the
victory fell to the man.

'My dear girl,' he said, 'it will be just the same.'

'Then will you give him a Christian burial?' she asked quickly.

The Vicar felt himself cornered. Hearing of the baby's illness, he had
conscientiously gone to the house after nightfall to perform the rite, and,
unaware that the refusal to admit him had come from Tess's father and not from
Tess, he could not allow the plea of necessity for its irregular administration.

'Ah – that's another matter,' he said.

'Another matter – why?' asked Tess, rather warmly.

'Well – I would willingly do so if only we two were concerned. But I must not –
for certain reasons.'

'Just for once, sir!'

'Really I must not.'

'O sir!' She seized his hand as she spoke.

He withdrew it, shaking his head.

'Then I don't like you!' she burst out, 'and I'll never come to your church no
more!'

'Don't talk so rashly.'

'Perhaps it will be just the same to him if you don't? . . . Will it be just the
same? Don't for God's sake speak as saint to sinner, but as you yourself to me
myself – poor me!'

How the Vicar reconciled his answer with the strict notions he supposed
himself to hold on these subjects it is beyond a layman's power to tell, though not
to excuse. Somewhat moved, he said in this case also –

'It will be just the same.'

So the baby was carried in a small deal box, under an ancient woman's shawl,
to the churchyard that night, and buried by lantern-light, at the cost of a shilling
and a pint of beer to the sexton, in that shabby corner of God's allotment where
He lets the nettles grow, and where all unbaptized infants, notorious drunkards,
suicides, and others of the conjecturally damned are laid. In spite of the untoward
surroundings, however, Tess bravely made a little cross of two laths and a piece
of string, and having bound it with flowers, she stuck it up at the head of the grave
one evening when she could enter the churchyard without being seen, putting at
the foot also a bunch of the same flowers in a little jar of water to keep them alive.
What matter was it that on the outside of the jar the eye of mere observation
noted the words 'Keelwell's Marmalade'? The eye of maternal affection did not
see them in its vision of higher things.

CHAPTER FIFTEEN

'BY experience,' says Roger Ascham, 'we find out a short way by a long
wandering.' Not seldom that long wandering unfits us for further travel, and of
what use is our experience to us then? Tess Durbeyfield's experience was of this

incapacitating kind. At last she had learned what to do; but who would now accept her doing?

If before going to the d'Urbervilles' she had vigorously moved under the guidance of sundry gnomic texts and phrases known to her and to the world in general, no doubt she would never have been imposed on. But it had not been in Tess's power – nor is it in anybody's power – to feel the whole truth of golden opinions while it is possible to profit by them. She – and how many more – might have ironically said to God with Saint Augustine: 'Thou hast counselled a better course than Thou hast permitted.'

She remained in her father's house during the winter months, plucking fowls, or cramming turkeys and geese, or making clothes for her sisters and brothers out of some finery which d'Urberville had given her, and she had put by with contempt. Apply to him she would not. But she would often clasp her hands behind her head and muse when she was supposed to be working hard.

She philosophically noted dates as they came past in the revolution of the year; the disastrous night of her undoing at Trantridge with its dark background of The Chase; also the dates of the baby's birth and death; also her own birthday; and every other day individualized by incidents in which she had taken some share. She suddenly thought one afternoon, when looking in the glass at her fairness, that there was yet another date, of greater importance to her than those; that of her own death, when all these charms would have disappeared; a day which lay sly and unseen among all the other days of the year, giving no sign or sound when she annually passed over it; but not the less surely there. When was it? Why did she not feel the chill of each yearly encounter with such a cold relation? She had Jeremy Taylor's thought that some time in the future those who had known her would say: 'It is the —th, the day that poor Tess Durbeyfield died'; and there would be nothing singular to their minds in the statement. Of that day, doomed to be her terminus in time through all the ages, she did not know the place in month, week, season, or year.

Almost at a leap Tess thus changed from simple girl to complex woman. Symbols of reflectiveness passed into her face, and a note of tragedy at times into her voice. Her eyes grew larger and more eloquent. She became what would have been called a fine creature; her aspect was fair and arresting; her soul that of a woman whom the turbulent experiences of the last year or two had quite failed to demoralize. But for the world's opinion those experiences would have been simply a liberal education.

She had held so aloof of late that her trouble, never generally known, was nearly forgotten in Marlott. But it became evident to her that she could never be really comfortable again in a place which had seen the collapse of her family's attempt to 'claim kin' – and, through her, even closer union – with the rich d'Urbervilles. At least she could not be comfortable there till long years should have obliterated her keen consciousness of it. Yet even now Tess felt the pulse of hopeful life still warm within her; she might be happy in some nook which had no memories. To escape the past and all that appertained thereto was to annihilate it, and to do that she would have to get away.

Was once lost always lost really true of chastity? she would ask herself. She might prove it false if she would veil bygones. The recuperative power which pervaded organic nature was surely not denied to maidenhood alone.

She waited a long time without finding opportunity for a new departure. A particularly fine spring came round, and the stir of germination was almost audible in the buds; it moved her, as it moved the wild animals, and made her passionate to go. At last, one day in early May, a letter reached her from a former friend of her mother's, to whom she had addressed inquiries long before – a person whom she had never seen – that a skilful milkmaid was required at a dairy-house many miles to the southward, and that the dairyman would be glad to have her for the summer months.

It was not quite so far off as could have been wished; but it was probably far enough, her radius of movement and repute having been so small. To persons of limited spheres, miles are as geographical degrees, parishes as counties, counties as provinces and kingdoms.

On one point she was resolved: there should be no more d'Urberville air-castles in the dreams and deeds of her new life. She would be the dairymaid Tess, and nothing more. Her mother knew Tess's feeling on this point so well, though no words had passed between them on the subject, that she never alluded to the knightly ancestry now.

Yet such is human inconsistency that one of the interests of the new place to her was the accidental virtue of its lying near her forefathers' country (for they were not Blakemore men, though her mother was Blakemore to the bone). The dairy called Talbothays, for which she was bound, stood not remotely from some of the former estates of the d'Urbervilles, near the great family vaults of her granddames and their powerful husbands. She would be able to look at them, and think not only that d'Urberville, like Babylon, had fallen, but that the individual innocence of a humble descendant could lapse as silently. All the while she wondered if any strange good thing might come of her being in her ancestral land; and some spirit within her rose automatically as the sap in the twigs. It was unexpended youth, surging up anew after its temporary check, and bringing with it hope, and the invincible instinct towards self-delight.

The Rally

CHAPTER SIXTEEN

O N a thyme-scented, bird-hatching morning in May, between two and three years after the return from Trantridge – silent reconstructive years for Tess Durbeyfield – she left her home for the second time.

Having packed up her luggage so that it could be sent to her later, she started in a hired trap for the little town of Stourcastle, through which it was necessary to pass on her journey, now in a direction almost opposite to that of her first adventuring. On the curve of the nearest hill she looked back regretfully at Marlott and her father's house, although she had been so anxious to get away.

Her kindred dwelling there would probably continue their daily lives as heretofore, with no great diminution of pleasure in their consciousness, although she would be far off, and they deprived of her smile. In a few days the children would engage in their games as merrily as ever without the sense of any gap left by her departure. This leaving of the younger children she had decided to be for the best; were she to remain they would probably gain less good by her precepts than harm by her example.

She went through Stourcastle without pausing, and onward to a junction of highways, where she could await a carrier's van that ran to the south-west; for the railways which engirdled this interior tract of country had never yet struck across it. While waiting, however, there came along a farmer in his spring cart, driving approximately in the direction that she wished to pursue. Though he was a stranger to her she accepted his offer of a seat beside him, ignoring that its motive was a mere tribute to her countenance. He was going to Weatherbury, and by accompanying him thither she could walk the remainder of the distance instead of travelling in the van by way of Casterbridge.

Tess did not stop at Weatherbury, after this long drive, further than to make a slight nondescript meal at noon at a cottage to which the farmer recommended her. Thence she started on foot, basket in hand, to reach the wide upland of heath dividing this district from the low-lying meads of a further valley in which the dairy stood that was the aim and end of her day's pilgrimage.

Tess had never before visited this part of the country, and yet she felt akin to the landscape. Not so very far to the left of her she could discern a dark patch in the scenery, which inquiry confirmed her in supposing to be trees marking the environs of Kingsbere – in the church of which parish the bones of her ancestors – her useless ancestors – lay entombed.

She had no admiration for them now; she almost hated them for the dance they had led her; not a thing of all that had been theirs did she retain but the old seal and spoon. 'Pooh – I have as much of mother as father in me!' she said. 'All my prettiness comes from her, and she was only a dairymaid.'

The journey over the intervening uplands and lowlands of Egdon, when she reached them, was a more troublesome walk than she had anticipated, the distance being actually but a few miles. It was two hours, owing to sundry wrong turnings, ere she found herself on a summit commanding the long-sought-for vale, the Valley of the Great Dairies, the valley in which milk and butter grew to rankness, and were produced more profusely, if less delicately, than at her home – the verdant plain so well watered by the river Var or Froom.

It was intrinsically different from the Vale of Little Dairies, Blackmoor Vale, which, save during her disastrous sojourn at Trantridge, she had exclusively known till now. The world was drawn to a larger pattern here. The enclosures numbered fifty acres instead of ten, the farmsteads were more extended, the groups of cattle formed tribes hereabout; there only families. These myriads of cows stretching under her eyes from the far east to the far west outnumbered any she had ever seen at one glance before. The green lea was speckled as thickly with them as a canvas by Van Alsloot or Sallaert with burghers. The ripe hues of the red and dun kine absorbed the evening sunlight, which the white-coated animals returned to the eye in rays almost dazzling, even at the distant elevation on which she stood.

The bird's-eye perspective before her was not so luxuriantly beautiful, perhaps, as that other one which she knew so well; yet it was more cheering. It lacked the intensely blue atmosphere of the rival vale, and its heavy soils and scents; the new air was clear, bracing, ethereal. The river itself, which nourished the grass and cows of these renowned dairies, flowed not like the streams in Blackmoor. Those were slow, silent, often turbid; flowing over beds of mud into which the incautious wader might sink and vanish unawares. The Froom waters were clear as the pure River of Life shown to the Evangelist, rapid as the shadow of a cloud, with pebbly shallows that prattled to the sky all day long. There the water-flower was the lily; the crowfoot here.

Either the change in the quality of the air from heavy to light, or the sense of being amid new scenes where there were no invidious eyes upon her, sent up her spirits wonderfully. Her hopes mingled with the sunshine in an ideal photosphere which surrounded her as she bounded along against the soft south wind. She heard a pleasant voice in every breeze, and in every bird's note seemed to lurk a joy.

Her face had latterly changed with changing states of mind, continually fluctuating between beauty and ordinariness, according as the thoughts were gay or grave. One day she was pink and flawless; another pale and tragical. When she was pink she was feeling less than when pale; her more perfect beauty accorded with her less elevated mood; her more intense mood with her less perfect beauty. It was her best face physically that was now set against the south wind.

The irresistible, universal, automatic tendency to find sweet pleasure some-where, which pervades all life, from the meanest to the highest, had at length mastered Tess. Being even now only a young woman of twenty, one who mentally and sentimentally had not finished growing, it was impossible that any event should have left upon her an impression that was not in time capable of transmutation.

And thus her spirits, and her thankfulness, and her hopes, rose higher and higher. She tried several ballads, but found them inadequate; till, recollecting the psalter that her eyes had so often wandered over of a Sunday morning before she had eaten of the tree of knowledge, she chanted: 'O ye Sun and Moon . . . O ye Stars . . . ye Green Things upon the Earth . . . ye Fowls of the Air . . . Beasts and Cattle . . . Children of Men . . . bless ye the Lord, praise Him and magnify Him for ever!'

She suddenly stopped and murmured: 'But perhaps I don't quite know the Lord as yet.'

And probably the half-unconscious rhapsody was a Fetichistic utterance in a Monotheistic setting; women whose chief companions are the forms and forces of outdoor Nature retain in their souls far more of the Pagan fantasy of their remote forefathers than of the systematized religion taught their race at later date. However, Tess found at least approximate expression for her feelings in the old *Benedicite* that she had lisped from infancy; and it was enough. Such high contentment with such a slight initial performance as that of having started towards a means of independent living was a part of the Durbeyfield temperament. Tess really wished to walk uprightly, while her father did nothing of the kind; but she resembled him in being content with immediate and small achievements, and in having no mind for laborious effort towards such petty social advancement as could alone be effected by a family so heavily handicapped as the once powerful d'Urbervilles were now.

There was, it might be said, the energy of her mother's unexpended family, as well as the natural energy of Tess's years, rekindled after the experience which had so overwhelmed her for the time. Let the truth be told — women do as a rule live through such humiliations, and regain their spirits, and again look about them with an interested eye. While there's life there's hope is a conviction not so entirely unknown to the 'betrayed' as some amiable theorists would have us believe.

Tess Durbeyfield, then, in good heart, and full of zest for life, descended the Egdon slopes lower and lower towards the dairy of her pilgrimage.

The marked difference, in the final particular, between the rival vales now showed itself. The secret of Blackmoor was best discovered from the heights around; to read aright the valley before her it was necessary to descend into its midst. When Tess had accomplished this feat she found herself to be standing on a carpeted level, which stretched to the east and west as far as the eye could reach.

The river had stolen from the higher tracts and brought in particles to the vale all this horizontal land; and now, exhausted, aged, and attenuated, lay serpentining along through the midst of its former spoils.

Not quite sure of her direction Tess stood still upon the hemmed expanse of verdant flatness, like a fly on a billiard-table of indefinite length, and of no more consequence to the surroundings than that fly. The sole effect of her presence upon the placid valley so far had been to excite the mind of a solitary heron, which, after descending to the ground not far from her path, stood with neck erect, looking at her.

Suddenly there arose from all parts of the lowland a prolonged and repeated call –

'Waow! waow! waow!'

From the furthest east to the furthest west the cries spread as if by contagion, accompanied in some cases by the barking of a dog. It was not the expression of the valley's consciousness that beautiful Tess had arrived, but the ordinary announcement of milking-time – half-past four o'clock, when the dairymen set about getting in the cows.

The red and white herd nearest at hand, which had been phlegmatically waiting for the call, now trooped towads the steading in the background, their great bags of milk swinging under them as they walked. Tess followed slowly in their rear, and entered the barton by the open gate through which they had entered before her. Long thatched sheds stretched round the enclosure, their slopes encrusted with vivid green moss, and their eaves supported by wooden posts rubbed to a glossy smoothness by the flanks of infinite cows and calves of bygone years, now passed to an oblivion almost inconceivable in its profundity. Between the posts were ranged the milchers, each exhibiting herself at the present moment to a whimsical eye in the rear as a circle on two stalks, down the centre of which a switch moved pendulum-wise; while the sun, lowering itself behind this patient row, threw their shadows accurately inwards upon the wall. Thus it threw shadows of these obscure and homely figures every evening with as much care over each contour as if it had been the profile of a Court beauty on a palace wall; copied them as diligently as it had copied Olympian shapes on marble *façades* long ago, or the outline of Alexander, Cæsar, and the Pharaohs.

They were the less restful cows that were stalled. These that would stand still of their own will were milked in the middle of the yard, where many of such better behaved ones stood waiting now – all prime milchers, such as were seldom seen out of this valley, and not always within it; nourished by the succulent feed which the water-meads supplied at this prime season of the year. Those of them that were spotted with white reflected the sunshine in dazzling brilliancy, and the polished brass knobs on their horns glittered with something of military display. Their large-veined udders hung ponderous as sandbags, the teats sticking out like the legs of a gipsy's cock; and as each animal lingered for her turn to arrive the milk oozed forth and fell in drops to the ground.

CHAPTER SEVENTEEN

T HE dairymaids and men had flocked down from their cottages and out of the dairy-house with the arrival of the cows from the meads; the maids walking in pattens, not on account of the weather, but to keep their shoes above the mulch of the barton. Each girl sat down on her three-legged stool, her face sideways, her right cheek resting against the cow; and looked musingly along the animal's flank at Tess as she approached. The male milkers, with hat-brims turned down, resting flat on their foreheads and gazing on the ground did not observe her.

One of these was a sturdy middle-aged man – whose long white 'pinner' was somewhat finer and cleaner than the wraps of the others, and whose jacket underneath had a presentable marketing aspect – the master-dairyman, of whom she was in quest, his double character as a working milker and butter-maker here during six days, and on the seventh as a man in shining broad-cloth in his family pew at church, being so marked as to have inspired a rhyme –

> Dairyman Dick
> All the week: –
> On Sundays Mister Richard Crick.

Seeing Tess standing at gaze he went across to her.

The majority of dairymen have a cross manner at milking-time, but it happened that Mr Crick was glad to get a new hand – for the days were busy ones now – and he received her warmly; inquiring for her mother and the rest of the family – (though this as a matter of form merely, for in reality he had not been aware of Mrs Durbeyfield's existence till apprised of the fact by a brief business-letter about Tess).

'Oh – ay, as a lad I knowed your part o' the country very well,' he said terminatively. 'Though I've never been there since. And a aged woman of ninety that used to live nigh here, but is dead and gone long ago, told me that a family of some such name as yours in Blackmoor Vale came originally from these parts, and that 'twere a old ancient race that had all but perished off the earth – though the new generations didn't know it. But, Lord, I took no notice of the old woman's ramblings, not I.'

'Oh no – it is nothing,' said Tess.

Then the talk was of business only.

'You can milk 'em clean, my maidy? I don't want my cows going azew at this time o' year.'

She reassured him on that point, and he surveyed her up and down. She had been staying indoors a good deal, and her complexion had grown delicate.

'Quite sure you can stand it? 'Tis comfortable enough here for rough folk; but we don't live in a cowcumber frame.'

She declared that she could stand it, and her zest and willingness seemed to win him over.

'Well, I suppose you'll want a dish o' tay, or victuals of some sort, hey? Not yet? Well, do as ye like about it. But faith, if 'twas I, I should be as dry as a kex wi' travelling so far.'

'I'll begin milking now, to get my hand in,' said Tess.

She drank a little milk as temporary refreshment – to the surprise – indeed, slight contempt – of Dairyman Crick, to whose mind it had apparently never occurred that milk was good as a beverage.

'Oh, if ye can swaller that, be it so,' he said indifferently, while one held up the pail that she sipped from. ''Tis what I hain't touched for years – not I. Rot the stuff; it would lie in my innerds like lead. You can try your hand upon she,' he pursued, nodding to the nearest cow. 'Not but what she do milk rather hard. We've hard ones and we've easy ones, like other folks. However, you'll find out that soon enough.'

When Tess had changed her bonnet for a hood, and was really on her stool under the cow, and the milk was squirting from her fists into the pail, she appeared to feel that she really had laid a new foundation for her future. The conviction bred serenity, her pulse slowed, and she was able to look about her.

The milkers formed quite a little battalion of men and maids, the men operating on the hard-teated animals, the maids on the kindlier natures. It was a large dairy. There were nearly a hundred milchers under Crick's management, all told; and of the herd the master-dairyman milked six or eight with his own hands, unless away from home. These were the cows that milked hardest of all; for his journey-milkmen being more or less casually hired, he would not entrust this half-dozen to their treatment, lest, from indifference, they should not milk them fully; nor to the maids, lest they should fail in the same way for lack of finger-grip; with the result that in course of time the cows would 'go azew' – that is, dry up. It was not the loss for the moment that made slack milking so serious, but that with the decline of demand there came decline, and ultimately cessation, of supply.

After Tess had settled down to her cow there was for a time no talk in the barton, and not a sound interfered with the purr of the milk-jets into the numerous pails, except a momentary exclamation to one or other of the beasts requesting her to turn round or stand still. The only movements were those of the milkers' hands up and down, and the swing of the cows' tails. Thus they all worked on, encompassed by the vast flat mead which extended to either slope of the valley – a level landscape compounded of old landscapes long forgotten, and, no doubt, differing in character very greatly from the landscape they composed now.

'To my thinking,' said the dairyman, rising suddenly from a cow he had just finished off, snatching up his three-legged stool in one hand and the pail in the other, and moving on to the next hard-yielder in his vicinity; 'to my thinking, the cows don't gie down their milk to'day as usual. Upon my life, if Winker do begin keeping back like this, she'll not be worth going under by midsummer.'

''Tis because there's a new hand come among us,' said Jonathan Kail. 'I've noticed such things afore.'

'To be sure. It may be so. I didn't think o't.'

'I've been told that it goes up into their horns at such times,' said a dairymaid.

'Well, as to going up into their horns,' replied Dairyman Crick dubiously, as though even witchcraft might be limited by anatomical possibilities, 'I couldn't say; I certainly could not. But as nott cows will keep it back as well as the horned ones, I don't quite agree to it. Do ye know that riddle about the nott cows, Jonathan? Why do nott cows give less milk in a year than horned?'

'I don't!' interposed the milkmaid. 'Why do they?'

'Because there bain't so many of 'em,' said the dairyman. 'Howsomever, these gam'sters do certainly keep back their milk to-day. Folks, we must lift up a stave or two – that's the only cure for't.'

Songs were often resorted to in dairies hereabout as an enticement to the cows when they showed signs of withholding their usual yield; and the band of milkers at this request burst into melody – in purely business-like tones, it is true, and with no great spontaneity; the result, according to their own belief, being a decided improvement during the song's continuance. When they had gone through fourteen or fifteen verses of a cheerful ballad about a murderer who was afraid to go to bed in the dark because he saw certain brimstone flames around him, one of the male milkers said –

'I wish singing on the stoop didn't use up so much of a man's wind! You should get your harp, sir; not but what a fiddle is best.'

Tess, who had given ear to this, thought the words were addressed to the dairyman, but she was wrong. A reply, in the shape of 'Why?' came as it were out of the belly of a dun cow in the stalls; it had been spoken by a milker behind the animal, whom she had not hitherto perceived.

'Oh yes; there's nothing like a fiddle,'said the dairyman. 'Though I think that bulls are more moved by a tune than cows – at least that's my experience. Once there was a old aged man over at Mellstock – William Dewy by name – one of the family that used to do a good deal of business as tranters over there, Jonathan, do ye mind? – I knowed the man by sight as well as I know my own brother, in a manner of speaking. Well, this man was a-coming home-along from a wedding where he had been playing his fiddle, one fine moonlight night, and for shortness' sake he took a cut across Forty-acres, a field lying that way, where a bull was out to grass. The bull seed William, and took after him, horns aground, begad; and though William runned his best, and hadn't *much* drink in him (considering 'twas a wedding, and the folks well off), he found he'd never reach the fence and get over in time to save himself. Well, as a last thought, he pulled out his fiddle as he runned, and struck up a jig, turning to the bull, and backing towards the corner. The bull softened down, and stood still, looking hard at William Dewy, who fiddled on and on; till a sort of a smile stole over the bull's face. But no sooner did William stop his playing and turn to get over hedge than the bull would stop his smiling and lower his horns towards the seat of William's breeches. Well, William had to turn about and play on, willy-nilly; and 'twas only three o'clock in the world, and 'a knowed that nobody would come that way for hours, and he so leery and tired that 'a didn't know what to do. When he had scraped till about four o'clock he felt that he verily would have to give over soon, and he said to himself, "There's only this last tune between me and eternal welfare! Heaven save me, or I'm a done man." Well,then he called to mind how he'd seen the cattle kneel o' Christmas Eves in the dead o' night. It was not Christmas Eve then, but it came into his head to play a trick upon the bull. So he broke into the 'Tivity Hymn, just as at Christmas carol-singing; when, lo and behold, down went the bull on his bended knees, in his ignorance, just as if 'twere the true 'Tivity night and hour. As soon as his horned friend were down, William turned, clinked off like a long-dog, and jumped safe over hedge, before the praying bull had got on his feet again to take after him. William used to say that he'd seen a man look a fool a good many times, but never such a fool as that bull looked when he found his pious feelings had been played upon, and 'twas not Christmas Eve . . . . Yes, William Dewy, that was the man's name; and I can tell you to a foot where's he a-lying in Mellstock Churchyard at this very moment – just between the second yew-tree and the north aisle.'

'It's a curious story; it carries us back to mediæval times, when faith was a living thing!'

The remark, singular for a dairy-yard, was murmured by the voice behind the dun cow; but as nobody understood the reference no notice was taken, except that the narrator seemed to think it might imply scepticism as to his tale.

'Well, 'tis quite true, sir, whether or no. I knowed the man well.'

'Oh yes; I have no doubt of it,' said the person behind the dun cow.

Tess's attention was thus attracted to the dairyman's interlocutor, of whom she could see but the merest patch, owing to his burying his head so persistently in the flank of the milcher. She could not understand why he should be addressed as 'sir' even by the dairyman himself. But no explanation was discernible; he remained under the cow long enough to have milked three, uttering a private ejaculation now and then, as if he could not get on.

'Take it gentle, sir; take it gentle,' said the dairyman. ''Tis knack, not strength that does it.'

'So I find,' said the other, standing up at last and stretching his arms. 'I think I have finished her, however, though she made my fingers ache.'

Tess could then see him at full length. He wore the ordinary white pinner and leather leggings of a dairy-farmer when milking, and his boots were clogged with the mulch of the yard; but this was all his local livery. Beneath it was something educated, reserved, subtle, sad, differing.

But the details of his aspect were temporarily thrust aside by the discovery that he was one whom she had seen before. Such vicissitudes had Tess passed through since that time that for a moment she could not remember where she had met him; and then it flashed upon her that he was the pedestrian who had joined in the club dance at Marlott – the passing stranger who had come she knew not whence, had danced with others but not with her, had slightingly left her, and gone on his way with his friends.

The flood of memories brought back by this revival of an incident anterior to her troubles produced a momentary dismay lest, recognizing her also, he should by some means discover her story. But it passed away when she found no sign of remembrance in him. She saw by degrees that since their first and only encounter his mobile face had grown more thoughtful, and had acquired a young man's shapely moustache and beard – the latter of the palest straw colour where it began upon his cheeks, and deepening to a warm brown farther from its root. Under his linen milking-pinner he wore a dark velveteen jacket, cord breeches and gaiters, and a starched white shirt. Without the milking-gear nobody could have guessed what he was. He might with equal probability have been an eccentric land-owner or a gentlemanly ploughman. That he was but a novice at dairy-work she had realized in a moment, from the time he had spent upon the milking of one cow.

Meanwhile many of the milkmaids had said to one another of the new-comer, 'How pretty she is!' with something of real generosity and admiration, though with a half hope that the auditors would qualify the assertion – which, strictly speaking, they might have done, prettiness being an inexact definition of what struck the eye in Tess. When the milking was finished for the evening they straggled indoors, where Mrs Crick, the dairyman's wife – who was too respectable to go out milking herself, and wore a hot stuff gown in warm weather because the dairymaids wore prints – was giving an eye to the leads and things.

Only two or three of the maids, Tess learnt, slept in the dairy-house besides herself; most of the helpers going to their homes. She saw nothing at supper-time of the superior milker who had commented on the story, and asked no questions about him, the remainder of the evening being occupied in arranging her place in the bed-chamber. It was a large room over the milk-house, some thirty feet long; the sleeping-cots of the other three indoor milk-maids being in the same apartment. They were blooming young women, and, except one, rather older than herself. By bedtime Tess was thoroughly tired, and fell asleep immediately.

But one of the girls who occupied an adjoining bed was more wakeful than Tess, and would insist upon relating to the latter various particulars of the homestead into which she had just entered. The girls whispered words mingled with the shades, and, to Tess's drowsy mind, they seemed to be generated by the darkness in which they floated.

'Mr Angel Clare – he that is learning milking, and that plays the harp – never says much to us. He is a pa'son's son, and is too much taken up wi' his own thoughts to notice girls. He is the dairyman's pupil – learning farming in all its branches. He has learnt sheep-farming at another place, and he's now mastering dairy-work. . . . Yes, he is quite the gentleman-born. His father is the Reverent Mr Clare at Emminster – a good many miles from here.'

'Oh – I have heard of him,' said her companion, now awake. 'A very earnest clergyman, is he not?'

'Yes – that he is – the earnestest man in all Wessex, they say – the last of the old Low Church sort, they tell me – for all about here be what they call High. All his sons, except our Mr Clare, be made pa'sons too.'

Tess had not at this hour the curiosity to ask why the present Mr Clare was not made a parson like his brethren, and gradually fell asleep again, the words of her informant coming to her along with the smell of the cheeses in the adjoining cheese-loft, and the measured dripping of the whey from the wrings downstairs.

CHAPTER EIGHTEEN

A NGEL C LARE rises out of the past not altogether as a distinct figure, but as an appreciative voice, a long regard of fixed, abstracted eyes, and a mobility of mouth somewhat too small and delicately lined for a man's though with an unexpectedly firm close of the lower lip now and then; enough to do away with any inference of indecision. Nevertheless, something nebulous, preoccupied, vague, in his bearing and regard, marked him as one who probably had no very definite aim or concern about his material future. Yet as a lad people had said of him that he was one who might do anything if tried.

He was the youngest son of his father, a poor parson at the other end of the county, and had arrived at Talbothays Dairy as a six months' pupil, after going the round of some other farms, his object being to acquire a practical skill in the various processes of farming, with a view either to the Colonies, or the tenure of a home-farm, as circumstances might decide.

His entry into the ranks of the agriculturists and breeders was a step in the young man's career which had been anticipated neither by himself nor by others.

Mr Clare the elder, whose first wife had died and left him a daughter, married a second late in life. This lady had somewhat unexpectedly brought him three sons, so that between Angel, the youngest, and his father the vicar there seemed to be almost a missing generation. Of these boys the aforesaid Angel, the child of his old age, was the only son who had not taken a University degree, though he was the single one of them whose early promise might have done full justice to an academical training.

Some two or three years before Angel's appearance at the Marlott dance, on a day when he had left school and was pursuing his studies at home, a parcel came to the vicarage from the local bookseller's, directed to the Reverend James Clare. The vicar having opened it and found it to contain a book, read a few pages; whereupon he jumped up from his seat and went straight to the shop with the book under his arm.

'Why has this been sent to my house?' he asked peremptorily, holding up the volume.

'It was ordered, sir.'

'Not by me, or any one belonging to me, I am happy to say.'

The shopkeeper looked into his order-book.

'Oh, it has been misdirected, sir,' he said. 'It was ordered by Mr Angel Clare, and should have been sent to him.'

Mr Clare winced as if he had been struck. He went home pale and dejected, and called Angel into his study.

'Look into this book, my boy,' he said. 'What do you know about it?'

'I ordered it,' said Angel simply.

'What for?'

'To read.'

'How can you think of reading it?'

'How can I? Why – it is a system of philosophy. There is no more moral, or even religious, work published.'

'Yes – moral enough; I don't deny that. But religious! – and for *you,* who intend to be a minister of the Gospel!'

'Since you have alluded to the matter, father,' said the son, with anxious thought upon his face, 'I should like to say, once for all, that I should prefer not to take Orders. I fear I could not conscientiously do so. I love the Church as one loves a parent. I shall always have the warmest affection for her. There is no institution for whose history I have a deeper admiration; but I cannot honestly be ordained her minister, as my brothers are, while she refuses to liberate her mind from an untenable redemptive theolatry.'

It had never occurred to the straightforward and simple-minded Vicar that one of his own flesh and blood could come to this! He was stultified, shocked, paralyzed. And if Angel were not going to enter the Church, what was the use of sending him to Cambridge? The University as a step to anything but ordination seemed, to this man of fixed ideas, a preface without a volume. He was a man not merely religious, but devout; a firm believer – not as the phrase is now elusively construed by theological thimble-riggers in the Church and out of it, but in the old and ardent sense of the Evangelical school: one who could

> Indeed opine
> That the Eternal and Divine
> Did, eighteen centuries ago
> In very truth. . . .

Angel's father tried argument, persuasion, entreaty.

'No, father; I cannot underwrite Article Four (leave alone the rest), taking it "in the literal and grammatical sense" as required by the Declaration; and, therefore, I can't be a parson in the present state of affairs,' said Angel. 'My whole instinct in matters of religion is towards reconstruction; to quote your favorite Epistle to the Hebrews, "*the removing of those things that are shaken, as of things that are made, that those things which cannot be shaken may remain*" .'

His father grieved so deeply that it made Angel quite ill to see him.

'What is the good of your mother and me economizing and stinting ourselves to give you a University education, if it is not to be used for the honour and glory of God?' his father repeated.

'Why, that it may be used for the honour and glory of man, father.'

Perhaps if Angel had persevered he might have gone to Cambridge like his brothers. But the Vicar's view of that seat of learning as a stepping-stone to Orders alone was quite a family tradition; and so rooted was the idea in his mind that perseverance began to appear to the sensitive son akin to an intent to misappropriate a trust, and wrong the pious heads of the household, who had been and were, as his father had hinted, compelled to exercise much thrift to carry out this uniform plan of education for the three young men.

'I will do without Cambridge,' said Angel at last. 'I feel that I have no right to go there in the circumstances.'

The effects of this decisive debate were not long in showing themselves. He spent years and years in desultory studies, undertakings, and meditations; he began to evince considerable indifference to social forms and observances. The material distinctions of rank and wealth he increasingly despised. Even the 'good old family' (to use a favourite phrase of a late local worthy) had no aroma for him unless there were good new resolutions in its representatives. As a balance to these austerities, when he went to live in London to see what the world was like, and with a view to practising a profession or business there, he was carried off his head, and nearly entrapped by a woman much older than himself, though luckily he escaped not greatly the worse for the experience.

Early association with country solitudes had bred in him an unconquerable, and almost unreasonable, aversion to modern town life, and shut him out from such success as he might have aspired to by following a mundane calling in the impracticability of the spiritual one. But something had to be done; he had wasted many valuable years; and having an acquaintance who was starting on a thriving life as a Colonial farmer, it occurred to Angel that this might be a lead in the right direction. Farming, either in the Colonies, America, or at home – farming, at any rate, after becoming well qualified for the business by a careful apprenticeship – that was a vocation which would probably afford an independence without the sacrifice of what he valued even more than a competency – intellectual liberty.

So we find Angel Clare at six-and-twenty here at Talbothays as a student of kine, and, as there were no houses near at hand in which he could get comfortable lodging, a boarder at the dairyman's.

His room was an immense attic which ran the whole length of the dairy-house. It could only be reached by a ladder from the cheese-loft, and had been closed up for a long time till he arrived and selected it as his retreat. Here Clare had plenty of space, and could often be heard by the dairy-folk pacing up and down when the household had gone to rest. A portion was divided off at one end by a curtain, behind which was his bed, the outer part being furnished as a homely sitting-room.

At first he lived up above entirely, reading a good deal, and strumming upon an old harp which he had bought at a sale, saying when in a bitter humour that he might have to get his living by it in the streets some day. But he soon preferred to read human nature by taking his meals downstairs in the general dining-kitchen, with the dairyman and his wife, and the maids and men, who all together formed a lively assembly; for though but few milking hands slept in the house, several joined the family at meals. The longer Clare resided here the less objection had he to his company, and the more did he like to share quarters with them in common.

Much to his surprise he took, indeed, a real delight in their companionship. The conventional farm-folk of his imagination personified in the newspaper-press by the pitiable dummy known as Hodge – were obliterated after a few days' residence. At close quarters no Hodge was to be seen. At first, it is true, when Clare's intelligence was fresh from a contrasting society, these friends with whom he now hobnobbed seemed a little strange. Sitting down as a level member of the dairyman's household seemed at the outset an undignified proceeding. The ideas, the modes, the surroundings, appeared retrogressive and unmeaning. But with living on there, day after day, the acute sojourner because conscious of a new aspect in the spectacle. Without any obective change whatever, variety had taken the place of monotonousness. His host and his host's house-hold, his men and his maids, as they became intimately known to Clare, began to differentiate themselves as in a chemical process. The thought of Pascal's was brought home to him: 'A mesure qu'on a plus d'esprit, on trouve qu'il y a plus d'hommes originaux. Les gens du commun ne trouvent pas de différence entre les hommes.' The typical and unvarying Hodge ceased to exist. He had been disintegrated into a number of varied fellow-creatures – beings of many minds, beings infinite in difference; some happy, many serene, a few depressed, one here and there bright even to genius, some stupid, others wanton, others austere; some mutely Miltonic, some potentially Cromwellian; into men who had private views of each other, as he had of his friends; who could applaud or condemn each other, amuse or sadden themselves by the contemplation of each other's foibles or vices; men every one of whom walked in his own individual way the road to dusty death.

Unexpectedly he began to like the outdoor life for its own sake, and for what it brought, apart from its bearing on his own proposed career. Considering his position he became wonderfully free from the chronic melancholy which is taking hold of the civilized races with the decline of belief in a beneficent Power. For the first time of late years he could read as his musing inclined him, without any eye to cramming for a profession. since the few farming handbooks which he deemed it desirable to master occupied him but little time.

He grew away from old associations, and saw something new in life and humanity. Secondarily, he made close acquaintance with phenomena which he had before known but darkly – the seasons in their moods, morning and evening, night and noon, winds in their different tempers, trees, waters and mists, shades and silences, and the voices of inanimate things.

The early mornings were still sufficiently cool to render a fire acceptable in the large room wherein they breakfasted; and, by Mrs Crick's orders, who held that he was too genteel to mess at their table, it was Angel Clare's custom to sit in the yawning chimney-corner durying the meal, his cup-and-saucer and plate being placed on a hinged flap at his elbow. The light from the long, wide, mullioned window opposite shone in upon his nook, and, assisted by a secondary light of cold blue quality which shone down the chimney, enabled him to read there easily whenever disposed to do so. Between Clare and the window was the table at which his companions sat, their munching profiles rising sharp against the panes; while to the side was the milk-house door, through which were visible the rectangular leads in rows, full to the brim with the morning's milk. At the further end the great churn could be seen revolving, and its slip-slopping heard—the moving power being discernible through the window in the form of a spiritless horse walking in a circle and driven by a boy.

For several days after Tess's arrival Clare, sitting abstractedly reading from some book, periodical, or piece of music just come by post, hardly noticed that she was present at table. She talked so little, and the other maids talked so much, that the babble did not strike him as possessing a new note, and he was ever in the habit of neglecting the particulars of an outward scene for the general impression. One day, however, when he had been conning one of his music-scores, and by force of imagination was hearing the tune in his head, he lapsed into listlessness, and the music-sheet rolled to the hearth. He looked at the fire of logs, with its one flame pirouetting on the top in a dying dance after the breakfast-cooking and boiling, and it seemed to jig to his inward tune; also at the two chimney crooks dangling down from the cotterel or cross-bar, plumed with soot which quivered to the same melody; also at the half-empty kettle whining an accompaniment. The conversation at the table mixed in with his phantasmal orchestra till he thought: 'What a fluty voice one of those milkmaids has! I suppose it is the new one.'

Clare looked round upon her, seated with the others.

She was not looking towards him. Indeed, owing to his long silence, his presence in the room was almost forgotten.

'I don't know about ghosts,' she was saying; 'but I do know that our souls can be made to go outside our bodies when we are alive.'

The dairyman turned to her with his mouth full, his eyes charged with serious inquiry, and his great knife and fork (breakfasts were breakfasts here) planted erect on the table, like the beginning of a gallows.

'What—really now? And is it so, maidy?' he said.

'A very easy way to feel 'em go,' continued Tess, 'is to lie on the grass at night and look straight up at some big bright star; and, by fixing your mind upon it, you will soon find that you are hundreds and hundreds o' miles away from your body, which you don't seem to want at all.'

The dairyman removed his hard gaze from Tess, and fixed it on his wife.

'Now that's a rum thing, Christianner—hey? To think o' the miles I've vamped o' starlight nights these last thirty year, courting, or trading, or for doctor, or for nurse, and yet never had the least notion o' that till now, or felt my soul rise so much as an inch above my shirt-collar.'

The general attention being drawn to her, including that of the dairyman's pupil, Tess flushed, and remarking evasively that it was only a fancy, resumed her breakfast.

Clare continued to observe her. She soon finished her eating, and having a consciousness that Clare was regarding her, began to trace imaginary patterns on the tablecloth with her forefinger with the constraint of a domestic animal that perceives itself to be watched.

'What a fresh and virginal daughter of Nature that milkmaid is!' he said to himself.

And then he seemed to discern in her something that was familiar, something which carried him back into a joyous and unforeseeing past, before the necessity of taking thought had made the heavens gray. He concluded that he had beheld her before; where he could not tell. A casual encounter during some country ramble it certainly had been, and he was not greatly curious about it. But the circumstance was sufficient to lead him to select Tess in preference to the other pretty milkmaids when he wished to contemplate contiguous womankind.

CHAPTER NINETEEN

I N general the cows were milked as they presented themselves, without fancy or choice. But certain cows will show a fondness for a particular pair of hands, sometimes carrying this predilection so far as to refuse to stand at all except to their favourite, the pail of a stranger being unceremoniously kicked over.

It was Dairyman Crick's rule to insist on breaking down these partialities and aversions by constant interchange, since otherwise, in the event of a milkman or maid going away from the dairy, he was placed in a difficulty. The maids' private aims, however, were the reverse of the dairyman's rule, the daily selection by each damsel of the eight or ten cows to which she had grown accustomed rendering the operation on their willing udders surprisingly easy and effortless.

Tess, like her compeers, soon discovered which of the cows had a preference for her style of manipulation, and her fingers having become delicate from the long domiciliary imprisonments to which she had subjected herself at intervals during the last two or three years, she would have been glad to meet the milchers' views in this respect. Out of the whole ninety-five there were eight in particular — Dumpling, Fancy, Lofty, Mist, Old Pretty, Young Pretty, Tidy, and Loud — who, though the teats of one or two were as hard as carrots, gave down to her with a readiness that made her work on them a mere touch of the fingers. Knowing, however, the dairyman's wish, she endeavoured conscientiously to take the animals just as they came, excepting the very hard yielders which she could not yet manage.

But she soon found a curious correspondence between the ostensibly chance position of the cows and her wishes in this matter, till she felt that their order could not be the result of accident. The dairyman's pupil had lent a hand in getting the cows together of late, and at the fifth or sixth time she turned her eyes, as she rested against the cow, full of sly inquiry upon him.

'Mr Clare, you have ranged the cows!' she said, blushing; and in making the accusation symptoms of a smile gently lifted her upper lip in spite of her, so as to show the tips of her teeth, the lower lip remaining severely still.

'Well, it makes no difference,' said he. 'You will always be here to milk them.'

'Do you think so? I *hope* I shall! But I don't *know*.'

She was angry with herself afterwards, thinking that he, unaware of her grave reasons for liking this seclusion, might have mistaken her meaning. She had spoken so earnestly to him, as if his presence were somehow a factor in her wish. Her misgiving was such that at dusk, when the milking was over, she walked in the garden alone, to continue her regrets that she had disclosed to him her discovery of his considerateness.

It was a typical summer evening in June, the atmosphere being in such delicate equilibrium and so transmissive that inanimate objects seemed endowed with two or three senses, if not five. There was no distinction between the near and the far, and an auditor felt close to everything within the horizon. The soundlessness impressed her as a positive entity rather than as the mere negation of noise. It was broken by the strumming of strings.

Tess had heard those notes in the attic above her head. Dim, flattened, constrained by their confinement, they had never appealed to her as now, when they wandered in the still air with a stark quality like that of nudity. To speak absolutely, both instrument and execution were poor; but the relative is all, and as she listened Tess, like a fascinated bird, could not leave the spot. Far from leaving she drew up towards the performer, keeping behind the hedge that he might not guess her presence.

The outskirt of the garden in which Tess found herself had been left uncultivated for some years, and was now damp and rank with juicy grass which sent up mists of pollen at a touch; and with tall blooming weeds emitting offensive smells—weeds whose red and yellow and purple hues formed a polychrome as dazzling as that of cultivated flowers. She went stealthily as a cat through this profusion of growth, gathering cuckoo-spittle on her skirts, cracking snails that were underfoot, staining her hands with thistle-milk and slug-slime, and rubbing off upon her naked arms sticky blights which, though snow-white on the apple-tree trunks, made madder stains on her skin; thus she drew quite near to Clare, still unobserved of him.

Tess was conscious of neither time nor space. The exaltation which she had described as being producible at will by gazing at a star, came now without any determination of hers; she undulated upon the thin notes of the second-hand harp, and their harmonies passed like breezes through her, bringing tears into her eyes. The floating pollen seemed to be his notes made visible, and the dampness of the garden the weeping of the garden's sensibility. Though near nightfall, the rank-smelling weed-flowers glowed as if they would not close for intentness, and the waves of colour mixed with the waves of sound.

The light which still shone was derived mainly from a large hole in the western bank of cloud; it was like a piece of day left behind by accident, dusk having closed in elsewhere. He concluded his plaintive melody, a very simple performance, demanding no great skill; and she waited, thinking another might be begun. But, tired of playing, he had desultorily come round the fence, and was rambling up behind her. Tess, her cheeks on fire, moved away furtively, as if hardly moving at all.

Angel, however, saw her light summer gown, and he spoke; his low tones reaching her, though he was some distance off.

'What makes you draw off in that way, Tess?' said he. 'Are you afraid?'

'Oh no, sir . . . not of outdoor things; especially just now when the apple-blooth is falling, and everything so green.'

'But you have your indoor fears — eh?'

'Well — yes, sir.'

'What of?'

'I couldn't quite say.'

'The milk turning sour?'

'No.'

'Life in general?'

'Yes, sir.'

'Ah — so have I, very often. This hobble of being alive is rather serious, don't you think so?'

'It is — now you put it that way.'

'All the same, I shouldn't have expected a young girl like you to see it so just yet. How is it you do?'

She maintained a hesitating silence.

'Come, Tess, tell me in confidence.'

She thought that he meant what were the aspects of things to her, and replied shyly —

'The trees have inquisitive eyes, haven't they? — that is, seem as if they had. And the river says, — "Why do ye trouble me with your looks?" And you seem to see numbers of to-morrows just all in a line, the first of them the biggest and clearest, the others getting smaller and smaller as they stand farther away; but they all seem very fierce and cruel and as if they said, "I'm coming! Beware of me! Beware of me!" . . . But *you*, sir, can raise up dreams with your music, and drive all such horrid fancies away!'

He was surprised to find this young woman — who though but a milkmaid had just that touch of rarity about her which might make her the envied of her housemates — shaping such sad imaginings. She was expressing her own native phrases — assisted a little by her Sixth Standard training — feelings which might almost have been called those of the age — the ache of modernism. The perception arrested him less when he reflected that what are called advanced ideas are really in great part but the latest fashion in definition — a more accurate expression, by words in *logy* and *ism*, of sensations which men and women have vaguely grasped for centuries.

Still, it was strange that they should have come to her while yet so young; more than strange; it was impressive, interesting, pathetic. Not guessing the cause, there was nothing to remind him that experience is as to intensity, and not as to duration. Tess's passing corporeal blight had been her mental harvest.

Tess, on her part, could not understand why a man of clerical family and good education, and abve physical want, should look upon it as a mishap to be alive. For the unhappy pilgrim herself there was very good reason. But how could this admirable and poetic man ever have descended into the Valley of Humiliation, have felt the man of Uz – as she herself had felt two or three years ago – 'My soul chooseth strangling and death rather than my life. I loathe it; I would not live alway.'

It was true that he was at present out of his class. But she knew that was only because, like Peter the Great in a shipwright's yard, he was studying what he wanted to know. He did not milk cows because he was obliged to milk cows, but because he was learning how to be a rich and prosperous dairyman, landowner, agriculturist, and breeder of cattle. He would become an American or Australian Abraham, commanding like a monarch his flocks and his herds, his spotted and his ring-straked, his men-servants and his maids. At times, nevertheless, it did seem unaccountable to her that a decidedly bookish, musical, thinking young man should have chosen deliberately to be a farmer, and not a clergyman, like his father and brothers.

Thus, neither having the clue to the other's secret, they were respectively puzzled at what each revealed, and awaited new knowledge of each other's character and moods without attempting to pry into each other's history.

Every day, every hour, brought to him one more little stroke of her nature, and to her one more of his. Tess was trying to lead a repressed life, but she little divined the strength of her own vitality.

At first Tess seemed to regard Angel Clare as an intelligence rather than as a man. As such she compared him with herself; and at every discovery of the abundance of his illuminations of the distance between her own modest mental standpoint and the unmeasurable, Andean altitude of his, she became quite dejected, disheartened from all further effort on her own part whatever.

He observed her dejection one day, when he had casually mentioned something to her about pastoral life in ancient Greece. She was gathering the buds called 'lords and ladies' from the bank while he spoke.

'Why do you look so woebegone all of a sudden?' he asked.

'Oh, 'tis only – about my own self,' she said, with a frail laugh of sadness, fitfully beginning to peel 'a lady' meanwhile. 'Just a sense of what might have been with me! My life looks as if it had been wasted for want of chances! When I see what you know, what you have read, and seen, and thought, I feel what a nothing I am! I'm like the poor Queen of Sheba who lived in the Bible. There is no more spirit in me.'

'Bless my soul, don't go troubling about that! Why,' he said with some enthusiasm, 'I should be only too glad, my dear Tess, to help you to anything in the way of history, or any line of reading you would like to take up –'

'It is a lady again,' interrupted she, holding out the bud she had peeled.

'What?'

'I meant that there are always more ladies than lords when you come to peel them.'

'Never mind about the lords and ladies. Would you like to take up any course of study – history, for example?'

'Sometimes I feel I don't want to know anything more about it than I know already.'

'Why not?'

'Because what's the use of learning that I am one of a long row only – finding

out that there is set down in some old book somebody just like me, and to know
that I shall only act her part; making me sad, that's all. The best is not to
remember that your nature and your past doings have been just like thousands'
and thousands', and that your coming life and doings 'll be like thousands' and
thousands'.'

'What, really, then, you don't want to learn anything?'

'I shouldn't mind learning why – why the sun do shine on the just and the
unjust alike,' she answered, with a slight quaver in her voice. 'But that's what
books will not tell me.'

'Tess, fie for such bitterness!' Of course he spoke with a conventional sense of
duty only, for that sort of wondering had not been unknown to himself in bygone
days. And as he looked at the unpractised mouth and lips, he thought that such a
daughter of the soil could only have caught up the sentiment by rote. She went on
peeling the lords and ladies till Clare, regarding for a moment the wave-like curl
of her lashes as they drooped with her bent gaze on her soft cheek, lingeringly
went away. When he was gone she stood awhile, thoughtfully peeling the last
bud; and then, awakening from her reverie, flung it and all the crowd of floral
nobility impatiently on the ground, in an ebullition of displeasure with herself for
her *niaiseries*, and with a quickening warmth in her heart of hearts.

How stupid he must think her! In an access of hunger for his good opinion she
bethought herself of what she had latterly endeavoured to forget, so unpleasant
had been its issues – the identity of her family with that of the knightly
d'Urbervilles. Barren attribute as it was, disastrous as its discovery had been in
many ways to her, perhaps Mr Clare, as a gentleman and a student of history,
would respect her sufficiently to forget her childish conduct with the lords and
ladies if he knew that those Purbeck-marble and alabaster people in Kingsbere
Church really represented her own lineal forefathers; that she was no spurious
d'Urberville, compounded of money and ambition like those at Trantridge, but
true d'Urberville to the bone.

But, before venturing to make the revelation, dubious Tess indirectly sounded
the dairyman as to its possible effect upon Mr Clare, by asking the former if Mr
Clare had any great respect for old county families when they had lost all their
money and land.

'Mr Clare,' said the dairyman emphatically, 'is one of the most rebellest
rozums you ever knowed – not a bit like the rest of his family; and if there's one
thing that he do hate more than another 'tis the notion of what's called a' old
family. He says that it stands to reason that old families have done their spurt of
work in past days, and can't have anything left in 'em now. There's the Billetts
and the Drenkhards and the Greys and the St Quintins and the Hardys and the
Goulds, who used to own the lands for miles down this valley; you could buy 'em
all up now for an old song a'most. Why, our little Retty Priddle here, you know,
is one of the Paridelles – the old family that used to own lots o' the lands out by
King's-Hintock now owned by the Earl o' Wessex, afore even he or his was heard
of. Well, Mr Clare found this out, and spoke quite scornful to the poor girl for
days. "Ah!" he says to her, "you'll never make a good dairymaid! All your skill
was used up ages ago in Palestine, and you must lie fallow for a thousand years to
git strength for more deeds!" A boy came here t'other day asking for a job, and
said his name was Matt, and when we asked him his surname he said he'd never

heard that 'a had any surname, and when we asked why, he said he supposed his folks hadn't been 'stablished long enough. "Ah! you're the very boy I want!" says Mr Clare, jumping up and shaking hands wi'en; "I've great hopes of you"; and gave him half-a-crown. O no! he can't stomach old families!'

After hearing this caricature of Clare's opinions poor Tess was glad that she had not said a word in a weak moment about her family —even though it was so unusually old as almost to have gone round the circle and become a new one. Besides, another dairy-girl was as good as she, it seemed, in that respect. She held her tongue about the d'Urberville vault, and the Knight of the Conqueror whose name she bore. The insight afoforded into Clare's character suggested to her that it was largely owing to her supposed untraditional newness that she had won interest in his eyes.

CHAPTER TWENTY

T HE season developed and matured. Another year's instalment of flowers, leaves, nightingales, thrushes, finches, and such ephemeral creatures, took up their positions where only a year ago others had stood in their place when these were nothing more than germs and inorganic particles. Rays from the sunrise drew forth the buds and stretched them into long stalks, lifted up sap in noiseless streams, opened petals, and sucked out scents in invisible jets and breathings.

Dairyman Crick's household of maids and men lived on comfortably, placidly, even merrily. Their position was perhaps the happiest of all positions in the social scale, being above the line at which neediness ends, and below the line at which the *convenances* begin to cramp natural feeling, and the stress of threadbare modishness makes too little of enough.

Thus passed the leafy time when arborescence seems to be the one thing aimed at out of doors. Tess and Clare unconsciously studied each other, ever balanced on the edge of a passion, yet apparently keeping out of it. All the while they were converging, under an irresistible law, as surely as two streams in one vale.

Tess had never in her recent life been so happy as she was now, possibly never would be so happy again. She was, for one thing, physically and mentally suited among these new surroundings. The sapling which had rooted down to a poisonous stratum on the spot of its sowing had been transplanted to a deeper soil. Moreover she, and Clare also, stood as yet on the debatable land between predilection and love; where no profundities have been reached; no reflections have set in, awkwardly inquiring, 'Whither does this new current tend to carry me? What does it mean to my future? How does it stand towards my past?'

Tess was the merest stray phenomenon to Angel Clare as yet —a rosy warming apparition which had only just acquired the attribute of persistence in his consciousness. So he allowed his mind to be occupied with her, deeming his preoccupation to be no more than a philosopher's regard of an exceedingly novel, fresh, and interesting specimen of womankind.

They met continually; they could not help it. They met daily in that strange and solemn interval, the twilight of the morning, in the violet or pink dawn; for it was necessary to rise early, so very early, here. Milking was done betimes; and before the milking came the skimming, which began at a little past three. It usually fell to the lot of some one or other of them to wake the rest, the first being aroused by an alarm-clock; and, as Tess was the latest arrival, and they soon discovered that she could be depended upon not to sleep through the alarm as the others did, this task was thrust most frequently upon her. No sooner had the hour of three struck and whizzled, than she left her room and ran to the dairyman's door; then up the ladder to Angel's, calling him in a loud whisper; then woke her fellow-milkmaids. By the time that Tess was dressed Clare was downstairs and out in the humid air. The remaining maids and the dairyman usually gave themselves another turn on the pillow, and did not appear till a quarter of an hour later.

The gray half-tones of daybreak are not the gray half-tones of the day's close, though the degree of their shade may be the same. In the twilight of the morning light seems active, darkness passive; in the twilight of evening it is the darkness which is active and crescent, and the light which is the drowsy reverse.

Being so often – possibly not always by chance – the first two persons to get up at the dairy-house, they seemed to themselves the first persons up of all the world. In these early days of her residence here Tess did not skim, but went out of doors at once after rising, where he was generally awaiting her. The spectral, half-compounded, aqueous light which pervaded the open mead, impressed them with a feeling of isolation, as if they were Adam and Eve. At this dim inceptive stage of the day Tess seemed to Clare to exhibit a dignified largeness both of disposition and physique, an almost regnant power, possibly because he knew that at that preternatural time hardly any woman so well endowed in person as she was likely to be walking in the open air within the boundairies of his horizon; very few in all England. Fair women are usually asleep at midsummer dawns. She was close at hand, and the rest were nowhere.

The mixed, singular, luminous gloom in which they walked along together to the spot where the cows lay, often made him think of the Resurrection hour. He little thought that the Magdalen might be at his side. Whilst all the landscape was in neutral shade his companion's face, which was the focus of his eyes, rising above the mist stratum, seemed to have a sort of phosphorescence upon it. She looked ghostly, as if she were merely a soul at large. In reality her face, without appearing to do so, had caught the cold gleam of day from the north-east; his own face, though he did not think of it, wore the same aspect to her.

It was then, as has been said, that she impressed him most deeply. She was no longer the milkmaid, but a visionary essence of woman – a whole sex condensed into one typical form. He called her Artemis, Demeter, and other fanciful names half teasingly, which she did not like because she did not understand them.

'Call me Tess,' she would say askance; and he did.

Then it would grow lighter, and her features would become simply feminine; they had changed from those of a divinity who could confer bliss to those of a being who craved it.

At these non-human hours they could get quite close to the waterfowl. Herons came, with a great bold noise as of opening doors and shutters, out of the boughs of a plantation which they frequented at the side of the mead; or, if already on the spot, hardly maintained their standing in the water as the pair walked by, watching them by moving their heads round in a slow, horizontal, passionless wheel, like the turn of puppets by clockwork.

They could then see the faint summer fogs in layers, woolly, level, and apparently no thicker than counterpanes, spread about the meadows in detached remnants of small extent. On the gray moisture of the grass were marks where the cows had lain through the night – dark-green islands of dry herbage the size of their carcases, in the general sea of dew. From each island proceeded a serpentine trail, by which the cow had rambled away to feed after getting up, at the end of which trail they found her; the snoring puff from her nostrils, when she recognized them, making an intenser little fog of her own amid the prevailing one. Then they drove the animals back to the barton, or sat down to milk them on the spot, as the case might require.

Or perhaps the summer fog was more general, and the meadows lay like a white sea, out of which the scattered trees rose like dangerous rocks. Birds would soar through it into the upper radiance, and hang on the wing sunning themselves, or alight on the wet rails subdividing the mead, which now shone like glass rods. Minute diamnds of moisture from the mist hung, too, upon Tess's eyelashes, and drops upon her hair, like seed pearls. When the day grew quite strong and commonplace these dried off her; moreover, Tess then lost her strange and ethereal beauty; her teeth, lips, and eyes scintillated in the sunbeams, and she was again the dazzlingly fair dairymaid only, who had to hold her own against the other women of the world.

About this time they would hear Dairyman Crick's voice, lecturing the non-resident milkers for arriving late, and speaking sharply to old Deborah Fyander for not washing her hands.

'For Heaven's sake, pop thy hands under the pump, Deb! Upon my soul, if the London folk only knowed of thee and thy slovenly ways, they'd swaller their milk and butter more mincing than they do a'ready; and that's saying a good deal.'

The milking progressed, till towards the end Tess and Clare, in common with the rest, could hear the heavy breakfast table dragged out from the wall in the kitchen by Mrs Crick, this being the invariable preliminary to each meal; the same horrible scrape accompanying its return journey when the table had been cleared.

CHAPTER TWENTY-ONE

THERE was a great stir in the milk-house just after breakfast. The churn revolved as usual, but the butter would not come. Whenever this happened the dairy was paralyzed. Squish, squash, echoed the milk in the great cylinder, but never arose the sound they waited for.

Dairyman Crick and his wife, the milkmaids Tess, Marian, Retty Priddle, Izz Huett, and the married ones from the cottages; also Mr Clare, Jonathan Kail, old Deborah, and the rest, stood gazing hopelessly at the churn; and the boy who kept the horse going outside put on moon-like eyes to show his sense of the situation. Even the melancholy horse himself seemed to look in at the window in inquiring despair at each walk round.

''Tis years since I went to Conjuror Trendle's son in Egdon — years!' said the dairyman bitterly. 'And he was nothing to what his father had been. I have said fifty times, if I have said once, that I don't believe in en; though he do cast folks' waters very true. But I shall have to go to 'n if he's alive. O yes, I shall have to go to 'n, if this sort of thing continnys!'

Even Mr Clare began to feel tragical at the dairyman's desperation.

'Conjuror Fall, t'other side of Casterbridge, that they used to call "Wide-O", was a very good man when I was a boy,' said Jonathan Kail. 'But he's rotten as touchwood by now.'

'My grandfather used to go to Conjuror Mynterne, out at Owlscombe, and a clever man a' were, so I've heard grandf'er say,' continued Mr Crick. 'But there's no such genuine folk about nowadays!'

Mrs Crick's mind kept nearer to the matter in hand.

'Perhaps somebody in the house is in love,' she said tentatively. 'I've heard tell in my younger days that that will cause it. Why, Crick — that maid we had years ago, do ye mind, and how the butter didn't come then—'

'Ah yes, yes! — but that isn't the rights o't. It had nothing to do with the love-making. I can mind all about it — 'twas the damage to the churn.'

He turned to Clare.

'Jack Dollop, a 'hore's-bird of a fellow we had here as milker at one time, sir, courted a young woman over at Mellstock, and deceived her as he had deceived many afore. But he had another sort o' woman to reckon wi' this time, and it was not the girl herself. One Holy Thursday, of all days in the almanack, we was here as we mid be now, only there was no churning in hand, when we zid the girl's mother coming up to the door, wi' a great brass-mounted umbrella in her hand that would ha' felled an ox, and saying "Do Jack Dollop work here? — because I want him! I have a big bone to pick with he, I can assure 'n!" And some way behind her mother walked Jack's young woman, crying bitterly into her handkercher. "O Lard, here's a time!" said Jack, looking out o' winder at 'em. "She'll murder me! Where shall I get — where shall I—? Don't tell her where I be!" And with that he scrambled into the churn through the trap-door, and shut himself inside, just as the young woman's mother busted into the milk-house. "The villain — where is he?" says she, "I'll claw his face for'n, let me only catch him!" Well, she hunted about everywhere, ballyragging Jack by side and by seam, Jack lying a'most stifled inside the churn, and the poor maid — or young woman rather — standing at the door crying her eyes out. I shall never forget it, never! 'Twould have melted a marble stone! But she couldn't find him nowhere at all.'

The dairyman paused, and one or two words of comment came from the listeners.

Dairyman Crick's stories often seemed to be ended when they were not really so, and strangers were betrayed into premature interjections of finality; though old friends knew better. The narrator went on —

'Well, how the old woman should have had the wit to guess it I could never tell, but she found out that he was inside that there churn. Without saying a word she took hold of the winch (it was turned by handpower then), and round she swung him, and Jack began to flop about inside. "O Lard! stop the churn! let me out!" says he, popping out his head, "I shall be churned into a pummy!" (he was a cowardly chap in his heart, as such men mostly be). "Not till ye make amends for ravaging her virgin innocence!" says the old woman. "Stop the churn, you old witch!" screams he. "You call me old witch, do ye, you deceiver!" says she, "when ye ought to ha' been calling me mother-law these last five months!" And on went the churn, and Jack's bones rattled round again. Well, none of us ventured to interfere; and at last 'a promised to make it right wi' her. "Yes – I'll be as good as my word!" he said. And so it ended that day.'

While the listeners were smiling their comments there was a quick movement behind their backs, and they looked round. Tess, pale-faced, had gone to the door.

'How warm 'tis to-day!' she said, almost inaudibly.

It was warm, and none of them connected her withdrawal with the reminiscences of the dairyman. He went forward, and opened the door for her, saying with tender raillery –

'Why, maidy' (he frequently, with unconscious irony, gave her this pet name), 'the prettiest milker I've got in my dairy; you mustn't get so fagged as this at the first breath of summer weather, or we shall be finely put to for want of 'ee by dog-days, shan't we, Mr Clare?'

'I was faint – and – I think I am better out o' doors,' she said mechanically; and disappeared outside.

Fortunately for her the milk in the revolving churn at that moment changed its squashing for a decided flick-flack.

''Tis coming!' cried Mrs Crick, and the attention of all was called off from Tess.

That fair sufferer soon recovered herself externally; but she remained much depressed all the afternoon. When the evening milking was done she did not care to be with the rest of them, and went out of doors wandering along she knew not whither. She was wretched – O so wretched – at the perception that to her companions the dairyman's story had been rather a humorous narration than otherwise; none of them but herself seemed to see the sorrow of it; to a certainty, not one knew how cruelly it touched the tender place in her experience. The evening sun was now ugly to her, like a great inflamed wound in the sky. Only a solitary cracked-voiced reed-sparrow greeted her from the bushes by the river, in a sad, machine-made tone, resembling that of a past friend whose friendship she had outworn.

In these long June days the milkmaids, and, indeed, most of the household, went to bed at sunset or sooner, the morning work before milking being so early and heavy at a time of full pails. Tess usually accompanied her fellows upstairs. To-night, however, she was the first to go to their common chamber; and she had dozed when the other girls came in. She saw them undressing in the orange light of the vanished sun, which flushed their forms with its colour; she dozed again, but she was reawakened by their voices, and quietly turned her eyes towards them.

Neither of her three chamber-companions had got into bed. They were standing in a group, in their nightgowns, barefooted, at the window, the last red rays of the west still warming their faces and necks, and the walls around them.

All were watching somebody in the garden with deep interest, their three faces close together: a jovial and round one, a pale one with dark hair, and a fair one whose tresses were auburn.

'Don't push! You can see as well as I,' said Retty, the auburn-haired and youngest girl, without removing her eyes from the window.

''Tis no use for you to be in love with him any more than me, Retty Priddle,' said jolly-faced Marian, the eldest, slily. 'His thoughts be of other cheeks than thine!'

Retty Priddle still looked, and the others looked again.

'There he is again!' cried Izz Huett, the pale girl with dark damp hair and keenly cut lips.

'You needn't say anything, Izz,' answered Retty. 'For I zid you kissing his shade.'

'*What* did you see her doing?' asked Marian.

'Why – he was standing over the whey-tub to let off the whey, and the shade of his face came upon the wall behind, close to Izz, who was standing there filling a vat. She put her mouth against the wall and kissed the shade of his mouth; I zid her, though he didn't.'

'O Izz Huett!' said Marian.

A rosy spot came into the middle of Izz Huett's cheek.

'Well, there was no harm in it,' she declared, with attempted coolness. 'And if I be in love wi'en, so is Retty, too; and so be you, Marian, come to that.'

Marian's full face could not blush past its chronic pinkness.

'I!' she said. 'What a tale! Ah, there he is again! Dear eyes – dear face – dear Mr Clare!'

'There – you've owned it!'

'So have you – so have we all,' said Marian, with the dry frankness of complete indifference to opinion. 'It is silly to pretend otherwise amongst ourselves, though we need not own it to other folks. I would just marry 'n to-morrow!'

'So would I – and more,' murmured Izz Huett.

'And I too,' whispered the more timid Retty.

The listener grew warm.

'We can't all marry him,' said Izz.

'We shan't, either of us; which is worse still,' said the eldest. 'There he is again!'

They all three blew him a silent kiss.

'Why?' asked Retty quickly.

'Because he likes Tess Durbeyfield best,' said Marian, lowering her voice. 'I have watched him every day, and have found it out.'

There was a reflective silence.

'But she don't care anything for 'n?' at length breathed Retty.

'Well – I sometimes think that too.'

'But how silly all this is!' said Izz Huett impatiently. 'Of course he won't marry any one of us, or Tess either – a gentleman's son, who's going to be a great landowner and farmer abroad! More likely to ask us to come wi'en as farm-hands at so much a year!'

One sighed, and another sighed, and Marian's plump figure sighed biggest of all. Somebody in bed hard by sighed too. Tears came into the eyes of Retty Priddle, the pretty red-haired youngest – the last bud of the Paridelles, so important in the county annals. They watched silently a little longer, their three faces still close together as before, and the triple hues of their hair mingling. But the unconscious Mr Clare had gone indoors, and they saw him no more; and, the shades beginning to deepen, they crept into their beds. In a few minutes they heard him ascend the ladder to his own room. Marian was soon snoring, but Izz did not drop into forgetfulness for a long time. Retty Priddle cried herself to sleep.

The deeper-passioned Tess was very far from sleeping even then. This conversation was another of the bitter pills she had been obliged to swallow that day. Scarce the least feeling of jealousy arose in her breast. For that matter she knew herself to have the preference. Being more finely formed, better educated, and, though the youngest except Retty, more woman than either, she perceived that only the slightest ordinary care was necessary for holding her own in Angel Clare's heart against these her candid friends. But the grave question was, ought she to do this? There was, to be sure, hardly a ghost of a chance for either of them, in a serious sense; but there was, or had been, a chance of one or the other inspiring him with a passing fancy for her, and enjoying the pleasure of his attentions while he stayed here. Such unequal attachments had led to marriage; and she had heard from Mrs Crick that Mr Clare had one day asked, in a laughing way, what would be the use of his marrying a fine lady, and all the while ten thousand acres of Colonial pasture to feed, and cattle to rear, and corn to reap. A farm-woman would be the only sensible kind of wife for him. But whether Mr Clare had spoken seriously or not, why should she, who could never conscientiously allow any man to marry her now, and who had religiously determined that she never would be tempted to do so, draw off Mr Clare's attention from other women, for the brief happiness of sunning herself in his eyes while he remained at Talbothays?

CHAPTER TWENTY-TWO

THEY came downstairs yawning next morning; but skimming and milking were proceeded with as usual, and they went indoors to breakfast. Dairyman Crick was discovered stamping about the house. He had received a letter, in which a customer had complained that the butter had a twang.

'And begad, so 't have!' said the dairyman, who held in his left hand a wooden slice on which a lump of butter was stuck. 'Yes — taste for yourself!'

Several of them gathered round him; and Mr Clare tasted, Tess tasted, also the other indoor milkmaids, one or two of the milking-men, and last of all Mrs Crick, who came out from the waiting breakfast-table. There certainly was a twang.

The dairyman, who had thrown himself into abstraction to better realize the taste, and so divine the particular species of noxious weed to which it appertained, suddenly exclaimed —

''Tis garlic! and I thought there wasn't a blade left in that mead!'

Then all the old hands remembered that a certain dry mead, into which a few of the cows had been admitted of late, had, in years gone by, spoilt the butter in the same way. The dairyman had not recognized the taste at that time, and thought the butter bewitched.

'We must overhaul that mead,' he resumed; 'this mustn't continny!'

All having armed themselves with old pointed knives they went out together. As the inimical plant could only be present in very microscopic dimensions to have escaped ordinary observation, to find it seemed rather a hopeless attempt in the stretch of rich grass before them. However, they formed themselves into line, all assisting, owing to the importance of the search; the dairyman at the upper end with Mr Clare, who had volunteered to help; then Tess, Marian, Izz Huett, and Retty; then Bill Lewell, Jonathan, and the married dairywomen – Beck Knibbs, with her woolly black hair and rolling eyes; and flaxen Frances, consumptive from the winter damps of the water-meads – who lived in their respective cottages.

With eyes fixed upon the ground they crept slowly across a strip of the field, returning a little further down in such a manner that, when they should have finished, not a single inch of the pasture but would have fallen under the eye of some one of them. It was a most tedious business, not more than half a dozen shoots of garlic being discoverable in the whole field; yet such was the herb's pungency that probably one bite of it by one cow had been sufficient to season the whole dairy's produce for the day.

Differing one from another in natures and moods so greatly as they did, they yet formed, bending, a curiously uniform row – automatic, noiseless; and an alien observer passing down the neighouring lane might well have been excused for massing them as 'Hodge'. As they crept along, stooping low to discern the plant, a soft yellow gleam was reflected from the buttercups into their shaded faces, giving them an elfish, moonlit aspect, though the sun was pouring upon their backs in all the strength of noon.

Angel Clare, who communistically stuck to his rule of taking part with the rest in everything, glanced up now and then. It was not, of course, by accident that he walked next to Tess.

'Well, how are you?' he murmured.

'Very well, thank you, sir,' she replied demurely.

As they had been discussing a score of personal matters only half-an-hour before, the introductory style seemed a little superfluous. But they got no further in speech just then. They crept and crept, the hem of her petticoat just touching his gaiter, and his elbow sometimes brushing hers. At last the dairyman, who came next, could stand it no longer.

'Upon my soul and body, this here stooping do fairly make my back open and shut!' he exclaimed, straightening himself slowly with an excruciated look till quite upright. 'And you, maidy Tess, you wasn't well a day or two ago – this will make your head ache finely! Don't do any more, if you feel fainty; leave the rest to finish it.'

Dairyman Crick withdrew, and Tess dropped behind. Mr Clare also stepped out of line, and began privateering about for the weed. When she found him near her, her very tension at what she had heard the night before made her the first to speak.

'Don't they look pretty?' she said.

'Who?'

'Izzy Huett and Retty.'

Tess had moodily decided that either of these maidens would make a good farmer's wife, and that she ought to recommend them, and obscure her own wretched charms.

'Pretty? Well, yes — they are pretty girls — fresh looking. I have often thought so.'

'Though, poor dears, prettiness won't last long!'

'O no, unfortunately.'

'They are excellent dairywomen.'

'Yes: though not better than you.'

'They skim better than I.'

'Do they?'

Clare remained observing them — not without their observing him.

'She is colouring up,' continued Tess heroically.

'Who?'

'Retty Priddle.'

'Oh! Why is that?'

'Because you are looking at her.'

Self-sacrificing as her mood might be Tess could not well go further and cry, 'Marry one of them, if you really do want a dairywoman and not a lady; and don't think of marrying me!' She followed Dairyman Crick, and had the mournful satisfaction of seeing that Clare remained behind.

From this day she forced herself to take pains to avoid him — never allowing herself, as formerly, to remain long in his company, even if their juxtaposition were purely accidental. She gave the other three every chance.

Tess was woman enough to realize from their avowals to herself that Angel Clare had the honour of all the dairymaids in his keeping, and her perception of his care to avoid compromising the happiness of either in the least degree bred a tender respect in Tess for what she deemed, rightly or wrongly, the self-controlling sense of duty shown by him, a quality which she had never expected to find in one of the opposite sex, and in the absence of which more than one of the simple hearts who were his housemates might have gone weeping on her pilgrimage.

CHAPTER TWENTY-THREE

THE hot weather of July had crept upon them unawares, and the atmosphere of the flat vale hung heavy as an opiate over the dairy-folk, the cows, and the trees. Hot steaming rains fell frequently, making the grass where the cows fed yet more rank, and hindering the late haymaking in the other meads.

It was Sunday morning; the milking was done; the outdoor milkers had gone home. Tess and the other three were dressing themselves rapidly, the whole bevy having agreed to go together to Mellstock Church, which lay some three or four miles distant from the dairy-house. She had now been two months at Talbothays, and this was her first excursion.

All the preceding afternoon and night heavy thunderstorms had hissed down upon the meads, and washed some of the hay into the river; but this morning the sun shone out all the more brilliantly for the deluge, and the air was balmy and clear.

The crooked lane leading from their own parish to Mellstock ran along the lowest levels in a portion of its length, and when the girls reached the most depressed spot they found that the result of the rain had been to flood the lane over-shoe to a distance of some fifty yards. This would have been no serious hindrance on a week-day; they would have clicked through it in their high pattens and boots quite unconcerned; but on this day of vanity, this Sun's-day, when flesh went forth to coquet with flesh while hypocritically affecting business with spiritual things; on this occasion for wearing their white stockings and thin shoes, and their pink, white, and lilac gowns, on which every mud spot would be visible, the pool was an awkward impediment. They could hear the church-bell calling — as yet nearly a mile off.

'Who would have expected such a rise in the river in summertime!' said Marian, from the top of the roadside-bank on which they had climbed, and were maintaining a precarious footing in the hope of creeping along its slope till they were past the pool.

'We can't get there anyhow, without walking right through it, or else going round the Turnpike way; and that would make us so very late!' said Retty, pausing hopelessly.

'And I do colour up so hot, walking into church late, and all the people staring round,' said Marian, 'that I hardly cool down again till we get into the That-it-may-please-Thees.'

While they stood clinging to the bank they heard a splashing round the bend of the road, and presently appeared Angel Clare, advancing along the lane towards them through the water.

Four hearts gave a big throb simultaneously.

His aspect was probably as un-Sabbatarian a one as a dogmatic parson's son often presented; his attire being his dairy clothes, long wading boots, a cabbage-leaf inside his hat to keep his head cool, with a thistle-spud to finish him off.

'He's not going to church,' said Marian.

'No — I wish he was!' murmured Tess.

Angel, in fact, rightly or wrongly (to adopt the safe phrase of evasive controversialists), preferred sermons in stones to sermons in churches and chapels on fine summer days. This morning, moreover, he had gone out to see if the damage to the hay by the flood was considerable or not. On his walk he observed the girls from a long distance, though they had been so occupied with their difficulties of passage as not to notice him. He knew that the water had risen at that spot, and that it would quite check their progress. So he had hastened on, with a dim idea of how he could help them — one of them in particular.

The rosy-cheeked, bright-eyed quartet looked so charming in their light summer attire, clinging to the roadside bank like pigeons on a roof-slope, that he stopped a moment to regard them before coming close. Their gauzy skirts had burshed up from the grass innumerable flies and butterflies which, unable to escape, remained caged in the transparent tissue as in an aviary. Angel's eye at last fell upon Tess, the hindmost of the four; she, being full of suppressed laughter at their dilemma, could not help meeting his glance radiantly.

He came beneath them in the water, which did not rise over his long boots; and stood looking at the entrapped flies and butterflies.

'Are you trying to get to church?' he said to Marian, who was in front, including the next two in his remark, but avoiding Tess.

'Yes, sir; and 'tis getting late; and my colour do come up so—'

'I'll carry you through the pool—every Jill of you.'

The whole four flushed as if one heart beat through them.

'I think you can't, sir,' said Marian.

'It is the only way for you to get past. Stand still. Nonsense—you are not too heavy! I'd carry you all four together. Now, Marian, attend,' he continued, 'and put your arms round my shoulders, so. Now! Hold on. That's well done.'

Marian had lowered herself upon his arm and shoulder as directed, and Angel strode off with her, his slim figure, as viewed from behind, looking like the mere stem to the great nosegay suggested by hers. They disappeared round the curve of the road, and only his sousing footsteps and the top ribbon of Marian's bonnet told where they were. In a few minutes he reappeared. Izz Huett was the next in order upon the bank.

'Here he comes,' she murmured, and they could hear that her lips were dry with emotion. 'And I have to put my arms round his neck and look into his face as Marian did.'

'There's nothing in that,' said Tess quickly.

'There's a time for everything,' continued Izz, unheeding. 'A time to embrace, and a time to refrain from embracing; the first is now going to be mine.'

'Fie—it is Scripture, Izz!'

'Yes,' said Izz, 'I've always a' ear at church for pretty verses.'

Angel Clare, to whom three-quarters of this performance was a commonplace act of kindness, now approached Izz. She quietly and dreamily lowered herself into his arms, and Angel methodically marched off with her. When he was heard returning for the third time Retty's throbbing heart could be almost seen to shake her. He went up to the red-haired girl, and while he was seizing her he glanced at Tess. His lips could not have pronounced more plainly, 'It will soon be you and I.' Her comprehension appeared in her face; she could not help it. There was an understanding between them.

Poor little Retty, though by far the lightest weight, was the most troublesome of Clare's burdens. Marian had been like a sack of meal, a dead weight of plumpness under which he had literally staggered. Izz had ridden sensibly and calmly. Retty was a bunch of hysterics.

However, he got through with the disquieted creature, deposited her, and returned. Tess could see over the hedge the distant three in a group, standing as he had placed them on the next rising ground. It was now her turn. She was embarrassed to discover that excitement at the proximity of Mr Clare's breath and eyes, which she had contemned in her companions, was intensified in herself; and as if fearful of betraying her secret she paltered with him at the last moment.

'I may be able to clim' along the bank perhaps—I can clim' better than they. You must be so tired, Mr Clare!'

'No, no, Tess,' said he quickly. And almost before she was aware she was seated in his arms and resting against his shoulder.

'Three Leahs to get one Rachel,' he whispered.

'They are better women than I,' she replied, magnanimously sticking to her resolve.

'Not to me,' said Angel.

He saw her grow warm at this; and they went some steps in silence.

'I hope I am not too heavy?' she said timidly.

'O no. You should lift Marian! Such a lump. You are like an undulating billow warmed by the sun. And all this fluff of muslin about you is the froth.'

'It is very pretty – if I seem like that to you.'

'Do you know that I have undergone three-quarters of this labour entirely for the sake of the fourth quarter?'

'No.'

'I did not expect such an event to-day.'

'Nor I. . . . The water came up so sudden.'

That the rise in the water was what she understood him to refer to, the state of her breathing belied. Clare stood still and inclined his face towards hers.

'O Tessy!' he exclaimed.

The girl's cheeks burned to the breeze, and she could not look into his eyes for her emotion. It reminded Angel that he was somewhat unfairly taking advantage of an accidental position; and he went no further with it. No definite words of love had crossed their lips as yet, and suspension at this point was desirable now. However, he walked slowly, to make the remainder of the distance as long as possible; but at last they came to the bend, and the rest of their progress was in full view of the other three. The dry land was reached, and he set her down.

Her friends were looking with round thoughtful eyes at her and him, and she could see that they had been talking of her. He hastily bade them farewell, and splashed back along the stretch of submerged road.

The four moved on together as before, till Marian broke the silence by saying –

'No – in all truth; we have no chance against her!' She looked joylessly at Tess.

'What do you mean?' asked the latter.

'He likes 'ee best – the very best! We could see it as he brought 'ee. He would have kissed 'ee, if you had encouraged him to do it, ever so little.'

'No, no,' said she.

The gaiety with which they had set out had somehow vanished; and yet there was no enmity or malice between them. They were generous young souls; they had been reared in the lonely country nooks where fatalism is a strong sentiment, and they did not blame her. Such supplanting was to be.

Tess's heart ached. There was no concealing from herself the fact that she loved Angel Clare, perhaps all the more passionately from knowing that the others had also lost their hearts to him. There is contagion in this sentiment, especially among women. And yet that same hungry heart of hers compassionated her friends. Tess's honest nature had fought against this, but too feebly, and the natural result had followed.

'I will never stand in your way, nor in the way of either of you!' she declared to Retty that night in the bedroom (her tears running down). 'I can't help this, my dear! I don't think marrying is in his mind at all; but if he were even to ask me I should refuse him, as I should refuse any man.'

'Oh! would you? Why?' said wondering Retty.

'It cannot be! But I will be plain. Putting myself quite on one side, I don't think he will choose either of you.'

'I have never expected it – thought of it!' moaned Retty. 'But O! I wish I was dead!'

The poor child, torn by a feeling which she hardly understood, turned to the other two girls who came upstairs just then.

'We be friends with her again,' she said to them. 'She thinks no more of his choosing her than we do.'

So the reserve went off, and they were confiding and warm.

'I don't seem to care what I do now,' said Marian, whose mood was tuned to its lowest bass. 'I was going to marry a dairyman at Stickleford, who's asked me twice; but – my soul – I would put an end to myself rather'n be his wife now! Why don't ye speak, Izz?'

'To confess, then,' murmured Izz, 'I made sure to-day that he was going to kiss me as he held me; and I lay still against his breast, hoping and hoping, and never moved at all. But he did not. I don't like biding here at Talbothays any longer! I shall go hwome.'

The air of the sleeping-chamber seemed to palpitate with the hopeless passion of the girls. They writhed feverishly under the oppressiveness of an emotion thrust on them by cruel Nature's law – an emotion which they had neither expected nor desired. The incident of the day had fanned the flame that was burning the inside of their hearts out, and the torture was almost more than they could endure. The differences which distinguished them as individuals were abstracted by this passion, and each was but portion of one organism called sex. There was so much frankness and so little jealousy because there was no hope. Each one was a girl of fair common sense, and she did not delude herself with any vain conceits, or deny her love, or give herself airs, in the idea of outshining the others. The full recognition of the futility of their infatuation, from a social point of view; its purposeless beginning; its self-founded outlook; its lack of everything to justify its existence in the eye of civilization (while lacking nothing in the eye of Nature); the one fact that it did exist, ecstasizing them to a killing joy; all this imparted to them a resignation, a dignity, which a practical and sordid expectation of winning him as a husband would have destroyed.

They tossed and turned on their little beds, and the cheese-wring dripped monotonously downstairs.

'B' you awake, Tess?' whispered one, half-an-hour later.

It was Izz Huett's voice.

Tess replied in the affirmative, whereupon also Retty and Marian suddenly flung the bedclothes off them, and sighed –

'So be we!'

'I wonder what she is like – the lady they say his family have looked out for him!'

'I wonder,' said Izz.

'Some lady looked out for him?' gasped Tess, starting. 'I have never heard o' that!'

'O yes — 'tis whispered; a young lady of his own rank, chosen by his family; a Doctor of Divinity's daughter near his father's parish of Emminster; he don't much care for her, they say. But he is sure to marry her.'

They had heard so very little of this; yet it was enough to build up wretched dolorous dreams upon, there in the shade of the night. They pictured all the details of his being won round to consent, of the wedding preparations, of the bride's happiness, of her dress and veil, of her blissful home with him, when oblivion would have fallen upon themselves as far as he and their love were concerned. Thus they talked, and ached, and wept till sleep charmed their sorrow away.

After this disclosure Tess nourished no further foolish thought that there lurked any grave and deliberate import in Clare's attentions to her. It was a passing summer love of her face, for love's own temporary sake — nothing more. And the thorny crown of this sad conception was that she whom he really did prefer in a cursory way to the rest, she who knew herself to be more impassioned in nature, cleverer, more beautiful than they, was in the eyes of propriety far less worthy of him than the homelier ones whom he ignored.

CHAPTER TWENTY-FOUR

A MID the oozing fatness and warm ferments of the Froom Vale, at a season when the rush of juices could almost be heard below the hiss of fertilization, it was impossible that the most fanciful love should not grow passionate. The ready bosoms existing there were impregnated by their surroundings.

July passed over their heads, and the Thermidorean weather which came in its wake seemed an effort on the part of Nature to match the state of hearts at Talbothays Dairy. The air of the place, so fresh in the spring and early summer, was stagnant and enervating now. Its heavy scents weighed upon them, and at mid-day the landscape seemed lying in a swoon. Ethiopic scorchings browned the upper slopes of the pastures, but there was still bright green herbage here where the watercourses purled. And as Clare was oppressed by the outward heats, so was he burdened inwardly by waxing fervour of passion for the soft and silent Tess.

The rains having passed the uplands were dry. The wheels of the dairyman's spring cart, as he sped home from market, licked up the pulverized surface of the highway, and were followed by white ribands of dust, as if they had set a thin powder-train on fire. The cows jumped wildly over the five-barred barton-gate, maddened by the gad-fly; Dairyman Crick kept his shirt-sleeves permanently rolled up from Monday to Saturday: open windows had no effect in ventilation without open doors, and in the dairy-garden the black-birds and thrushes crept about under the currant-bushes, rather in the manner of quadrupeds than of winged creatures. The flies in the kitched were lazy, teasing, and familiar, crawling about in unwonted places, on the floor, into drawers, and over the backs of the milk-maids' hands. Conversations were concerning sunstroke; while butter-making, and still more butter-keeping, was a despair.

They milked entirely in the meads for coolness and convenience, without driving in the cows. During the day the animals obsequiously followed the shadow of the smallest tree as it moved round the stem with the diurnal roll; and when the milkers came they could hardly stand still for the flies.

On one of these afternoons four or five unmilked cows chanced to stand apart from the general herd, behind the corner of a hedge, among them being Dumpling and Old Pretty, who loved Tess's hands above those of any other maid. When she rose from her stool under a finished cow Angel Clare, who had been observing her for some time, asked her if she would take the aforesaid creatures next. She silently assented, and with her stool at arm's length, and the pail against her knee, went round to where they stood. Soon the sound of Old Pretty's milk fizzing into the pail came through the hedge, and then Angel felt inclined to go round the corner also, to finish off a hard-yielding milcher who had strayed there, he being now as capable of this as the dairyman himself.

All the men, and some of the women, when milking, dug their foreheads into the cow and gazed into the pail. But a few — mainly the younger ones — rested their heads sideways. This was Tess Durbeyfield's habit, her temple pressing the milcher's flank, her eyes fixed on the far end of the meadow with the quiet of one lost in meditation. She was milking Old Pretty thus, and the sun chancing to be on the milking-side it shone flat upon her pink-gowned form and her white curtain-bonnet, and upon her profile, rendering it keen as a cameo cut from the dun background of the cow.

She did not know that Clare had followed her round, and that he sat under his cow watching her. The stillness of her head and features was remarkable: she might have been in a trance, her eyes open, yet unseeing. Nothing in the picture moved but Old Pretty's tail and Tess's pink hands, the latter so gently as to be a rhythmic pulsation only, as if they were obeying a reflex stimulus, like a beating heart.

How very lovable her face was to him. Yet there was nothing ethereal about it; all was real vitality, real warmth, real incarnation. And it was in her mouth that this culminated. Eyes almost as deep and speaking he had seen before, and cheeks perhaps as fair; brows as arched, a chin and throat almost as shapely; her mouth he had seen nothing to equal on the face of the earth. To a young man with the least fire in him that little upward lift in the middle of her red top lip was distracting, infatuating, maddening. He had never before seen a woman's lips and teeth which forced upon his mind with such persistent iteration the old Elizabethan simile of roses filled with snow. Perfect, he, as a lover, might have called them off-hand. But no — they were not perfect. And it was the touch of the imperfect upon the would-be perfect that gave the sweetness, because it was that which gave the humanity.

Clare had studied the curves of those lips so many times that he could reproduce them mentally with ease: and now, as they again confronted him, clothed with colour and life, they sent an *aura* over his flesh, a breeze through his nerves, which wellnigh produced a qualm; and actually produced, by some mysterious physiological process, a prosaic sneeze.

She then became conscious that he was observing her; but she would not show it by any change of position, though the curious dream-like fixity disappeared, and a close eye might easily have discerned that the rosiness of her face deepened, and then faded till only a tinge of it was left.

The influence that had passed into Clare like an excitation from the sky did not die down. Resolutions, reticences, prudences, fears, fell back like a defeated battalion. He jumped up from his seat, and leaving his pail to be kicked over if the milcher had such a mind, went quickly towards the desire of his eyes, and, kneeling down beside her, clasped her in his arms.

Tess was taken completely by surprise, and she yielded to his embrace with unreflecting inevitableness. Having seen that it was really her lover who had advanced, and no one else, her lips parted, and she sank upon him in her momentary joy, with something very like an ecstatic cry.

He had been on the point of kissing that too tempting mouth, but he checked himself, for tender conscience' sake.

'Forgive me, Tess dear!' he whispered. 'I ought to have asked. I – did not know what I was doing. I do not mean it as a liberty. I am devoted to you, Tessy, dearest, in all sincerity!'

Old Pretty by this time had looked round, puzzled; and seeing two people crouching under her where, by immemorial custom, there should have been only one, lifted her hind leg crossly.

'She is angry – she doesn't know what we mean – she'll kick over the milk!' exclaimed Tess, gently striving to free herself, her eyes concerned with the quadruped's actions, her heart more deeply concerned with herself and Clare.

She slipped up from her seat, and they stood together, his arm still encircling her. Tess's eyes, fixed on distance, began to fill.

'Why do you cry, my darling?' he said.

'O – I don't know!' she murmured.

As she saw and felt more clearly the position she was in she became agitated and tried to withdraw.

'Well, I have betrayed my feeling, Tess, at last,' said he, with a curious sigh of desperation, signifying unconsciously that his heart had outrun his judgment. 'That I – love you dearly and truly I need not say. But I – it shall go no further now – it distresses you – I am as surprised as you are. You will not think I have presumed pon your defencelessness – been too quick and unreflecting, will you?'

'N' – I can't tell.'

He had allowed her to free herself; and in a minute or two the milking of each was resumed. Nobody had beheld the gravitation of the two into one; and when the dairyman came round by that screened nook a few minutes later there was not a sign to reveal that the markedly sundered pair were more to each other than mere acquaintance. Yet in the interval since Crick's last view of them something had occurred which changed the pivot of the universe for their two natures; something which, had he known its quality, the dairyman would have despised, as a practical man; yet which was based upon a more stubborn and resistless tendency than a whole heap of so-called practicalities. A veil had been whisked aside; the tract of each one's outlook was to have a new horizon thenceforward – for a short time or for a long.

PHASE THE FOURTH

The Consequence

CHAPTER TWENTY-FIVE

CLARE, restless, went out into the dusk when evening drew on, she who had won him having retired to her chamber.

The night was as sultry as the day. There was no coolness after dark unless on the grass. Roads, garden-paths, the house-fronts, the barton-walls were warm as hearths, and reflected the noontide temperature into the noctambulist's face.

He sat on the east gate of the dairy-yard, and knew not what to think of himself. Feeling had indeed smothered judgment that day.

Since the sudden embrace, three hours before, the twain had kept apart. She seemed stilled, almost alarmed, at what had occurred, while the novelty, unpremeditation, mastery of circumstance disquieted him – palpitating, contemplative being that he was. He could hardly realize their true relations to each other as yet, and what their mutual bearing should be before third parties thenceforward.

Angel had come as pupil to this dairy in the idea that his temporary existence here was to be the merest episode in his life, soon passed through and early forgotten; he had come as to a place from which as from a screened alcove he could calmly view the absorbing world without, and, apostrophizing it with Walt Whitman –

> Crowds of men and women attired in the usual costumes,
> How curious you are to me! –

resolve upon a plan for plunging into that world anew. But, behold, the absorbing scene had been imported hither. What had been the engrossing world had dissolved into an uninteresting outer dumbshow; while here, in this apparently dim and unimpassioned place, novelty had volcanically started up, as it had never, for him, started up elsewhere.

Every window of the house being open Clare could hear across the yard each trivial sound of the retiring household. That dairy-house, so humble, so insignificant, so purely to him a place of constrained sojourn that he had never hitherto deemed it of sufficient importance to be reconnoitred as an object of any quality whatever in the landscape; what was it now? The aged and lichened brick gables breathed forth 'Stay!' The windows smiled, the door coaxed and beckoned, the creeper blushed confederacy. A personality within it was so far-reaching in her influence as to spread into and make the bricks, mortar, and whole overhanging sky throb with a burning sensibility. Whose was this mighty personality? A milkmaid's.

It was amazing, indeed, to find how great a matter the life of the obscure dairy had become to him. And though new love was to be held partly responsible for this it was not solely so. Many besides Angel have learnt that the magnitude of lives is not as to their external displacements, but as to their subjective experiences. The impressionable peasant leads a larger, fuller, more dramatic life than the pachydermatous king. Looking at it thus he found that life was to be seen of the same magnitude here as elsewhere.

Despite his heterodoxy, faults, and weaknesses, Clare was a man with a conscience. Tess was no insignificant creature to toy with and dismiss; but a woman living her precious life – a life which, to herself who endured or enjoyed it, possessed as great a dimension as the life of the mightiest to himself. Upon her sensations the whole world depended to Tess; through her existence all her fellow-creatures existed, to her. The universe itself only came into being for Tess on the particular day in the particular year in which she was born.

This consciousness upon which he had intruded was the single opportunity of existence ever vouchsafed to Tess by an unsympathetic First Cause – her all; her every and only chance. How then should he look upon her as of less consequence than himself; as a pretty trifle to caress and grow weary of; and not deal in the greatest seriousness with the affection which he knew that he had awakened in her – so fervid and so impressionable as she was under her reserve; in order that it might not agonize and wreck her?

To encounter her daily in the accustomed manner would be to develop what had begun. Living in such close relations, to meet meant to fall into endearment; flesh and blood could not resist it; and, having arrived at no conclusion as to the issue of such a tendency, he decided to hold aloof for the present from occupations in which they would be mutually engaged. As yet the harm done was small.

But it was not easy to carry out the resolution never to approach her. He was driven towards her by every heave of his pulse.

He thought he would go and see his friends. It might be possible to sound them upon this. In less than five months his term here would have ended, and after a few additional months spent upon other farms he would be fully equipped in agricultural knowledge, and in a position to start on his own account. Would not a farmer want a wife, and should a farmer's wife be a drawing-room wax-figure, or a woman who understood farming? Notwithstanding the pleasing answer returned to him by the silence he resolved to go his journey.

One morning when they sat down to breakfast at Talbothays Dairy some maid observed that she had not seen anything of Mr Clare that day.

'O no,' said Dairyman Crick. 'Mr Clare has gone hwome to Emminster to spend a few days wi' his kinsfolk.'

For four impassioned ones around that table the sunshine of the morning went out at a stroke, and the birds muffled their song. But neither girl by word or gesture revealed her blankness.

'He's getting on towards the end of his time wi' me,' added the dairyman, with a phlegm which unconsciously was brutal; 'and so I suppose he is beginning to see about his plans elsewhere.'

'How much longer is he to bide here?' asked Izz Huett, the only one of the gloom-stricken bevy who could trust her voice with the question.

The others waited for the dairyman's answer as if their lives hung upon it; Retty, with parted lips, gazing on the table-cloth, Marian with heat added to her redness, Tess throbbing and looking out at the meads.

'Well, I can't mind the exact day without looking at my memorandum-book,' replied Crick, with the same intolerable unconcern. 'And even that may be altered a bit. He'll bide to get a little practice in the calving out at the straw-yard, for certain. He'll hang on till the end of the year I should say.'

Four months or so of torturing ecstasy in his society – of 'pleasure girdled about with pain'. After that the blackness of unutterable night.

At this moment of the morning Angel Clare was riding along a narrow lane ten miles distant from the breakfasters, in the direction of his father's vicarage at Emminster, carrying, as well as he could, a little basket which contained some black-puddings and a bottle of mead, sent by Mrs Crick, with her kind respects, to his parents. The white lane stretched before him, and his eyes were upon it; but they were staring into next year, and not at the lane. He loved her; ought he to marry her? Dared he to marry her? What would his mother and his brothers say? What would he himself say a couple of years after the event? That would depend upon whether the germs of staunch comradeship underlay the temporary emotion, or whether it were a sensuous joy in her form only, with no substratum of everlastingness.

His father's hill-surrounded little town, the Tudor church-tower of red stone, the clump of trees near the vicarage, came at last into view beneath him, and he rode down towards the well-known gate. Casting a glance in the direction of the church before entering his home, he beheld standing by the vestry-door a group of girls, of ages between twelve and sixteen, apparently awaiting the arrival of some other one, who in a moment became visible; a figure somewhat older than the school-girls, wearing a broad-brimmed hat and highly-starched cambric morning-gown, with a couple of books in her hand.

Clare knew her well. He could not be sure that she observed him; he hoped she did not, so as to render it unnecessary that he should go and speak to her, blameless creature that she was. An over-powering reluctance to greet her made him decide that she had not seen him. The young lady was Miss Mercy Chant, the only daughter of his father's neighbour and friend, whom it was his parents' quiet hope that he might wed some day. She was great at Antinomianism and Bible-classes, and was plainly going to hold a class now. Clare's mind flew to the impassioned, summer-steeped heathens in the Var Vale, their rosy faces court-patched with cow-droppings; and to one the most impassioned of them all.

It was on the impulse of the moment that he had resolved to trot over to Emminster, and hence had not written to apprise his mother and father, aiming, however, to arrive about the breakfast hour, before they should have gone out to their parish duties. He was a little late, and they had already sat down to the morning meal. The group at table jumped up to welcome him as soon as he entered. They were his father and mother, his brother the Reverend Felix – curate at a town in the adjoining county, home for the inside of a fortnight – and his other brother, the Reverend Cuthbert, the classical scholar, and Fellow and

Dean of his College, down from Cambridge for the long vacation. His mother appeared in a cap and silver spectacles, and his father looked what in fact he was – an earnest, God-fearing man, somewhat gaunt, in years about sixty-five, his pale face lined with thought and purpose. Over their heads hung the picture of Angel's sister, the eldest of the family, sixteen years his senior, who had married a missionary and gone out to Africa.

Old Mr Clare was a clergyman of a type which, within the last twenty years, has wellnigh dropped out of contemporary life. A spiritual descendant in the direct line from Wycliff, Huss, Luther, Calvin; an Evangelical of the Evangelicals, a Conversionist, a man of Apostolic simplicity in life and thought, he had in his raw youth made up his mind once for all on the deeper questions of existence, and admitted no further reasoning on them thenceforward. He was regarded even by those of his own date and school of thinking as extreme; while, on the other hand, those totally opposed to him were unwillingly won to admiration for his thoroughness, and for the remarkable power he showed in dismissing all question as to principles in his energy for applying them. He loved Paul of Tarsus, liked St John, hated St James as much as he dared, and regarded with mixed feelings Timothy, Titus, and Philemon. The New Testament was less a Christiad than a Pauliad to his intelligence – less an argument than an intoxication. His creed of determinism was such that it almost amounted to a vice, and quite amounted, on its negative side, to a renunciative philosophy which had cousinship with that of Schopenhauer and Leopardi. He despised the Canons and Rubric, swore by the Articles, and deemed himself consistent through the whole category – which in a way he might have been. One thing he certainly was – sincere.

To the æsthetic, sensuous, pagan pleasure in natural life and lush womanhood which his son Angel had lately been experiencing in Var Vale, his temper would have been antipathetic in a high degree, had he either by inquiry or imagination been able to apprehend it. Once upon a time Angel had been so unlucky as to say to his father, in a moment of irritation, that it might have resulted far better for mankind if Greece had been the source of the religion of modern civilization, and not Palestine; and his father's grief was of that blank description which could not realize that there might lurk a thousandth part of a truth, much less a half truth or a whole truth, in such a proposition. He had simply preached austerely at Angel for some time after. But the kindness of his heart was such that he never resented anything for long, and welcomed his son to-day with a smile which was as candidly sweet as a child's.

Angel sat down, and the place felt like home; yet he did not so much as formerly feel himself one of the family gathered there. Every time that he returned hither he was conscious of this divergence, and since he had last shared in the Vicarage life it had grown even more distinctly foreign to his own than usual. Its transcendental aspirations – still unconsciously based on the geocentric view of things, a zenithal paradise, a nadiral hell – were as foreign to his own as if they had been the dreams of people on another planet. Latterly he had seen only Life, felt only the great passionate pulse of existence, unwarped, uncontorted, untrammelled by those creeds which futilely attempt to check what wisdom would be content to regulate.

On their part they saw a great difference in him, a growing divergence from the

Angel Clare of former times. It was chiefly a difference in his manner that they noticed just now, particularly his brothers. He was getting to behave like a farmer; he flung his legs about; the muscles of his face had grown more expressive; his eyes looked as much information as his tongue spoke, and more. The manner of the scholar had nearly disappeared; still more the manner of the drawing-room young man. A prig would have said that he had lost culture, and a prude that he had become coarse. Such was the contagion of domiciliary fellowship with the Talbothays nymphs and swains.

After breakfast he walked with his two brothers, non-evangelical, well-educated, hall-marked young men, correct to their remotest fibre; such unimpeachable models as are turned out yearly by the lathe of a systematic tuition. They were both somewhat short-sighted, and when it was the custom to wear a single eyeglass and string they wore a single eyeglass and string; when it was the custom to wear a double glass they wore a double glass; when it was the custom to wear spectacles they wore spectacles straightway, all without reference to the particular variety of defect in their own vision. When Wordsworth was enthroned they carried pocket copies; and when Shelley was belittled they allowed him to grow dusty on their shelves. When Correggio's Holy Families were admired, they admired Correggio's Holy Families; when he was decried in favour of Velasquez, they sedulously followed suit without any personal objection.

If these two noticed Angel's growing social ineptness, he noticed their growing mental limitations. Felix seemed to him all Church; Cuthbert all College. His Diocesan Synod and Visitations were the mainsprings of the world to the one; Cambridge to the other. Each brother candidly recognized that there were a few unimportant scores of millions of outsiders in civilized society, persons who were neither University men nor churchmen; but they were to be tolerated rather than reckoned with and respected.

They were both dutiful and attentive sons, and were regular in their visits to their parents. Felix, though an offshoot from a far more recent point in the devolution of theology than his father, was less self-sacrificing and disinterested. More tolerant than his father of a contradictory opinion, in its aspect as a danger to its holder, he was less ready than his father to pardon it as a slight to his own teaching. Cuthbert was, upon the whole, the more liberal-minded, though, with greater subtlety, he had not so much heart.

As they walked along the hillside Angel's former feeling revived in him – that whatever their advantages by comparison with himself, neither saw or set forth life as it really was lived. Perhaps, as with many men, their opportunities of observation were not so good as their opportunities of expression. Neither had an adequate conception of the complicated forces at work outside the smooth and gentle current in which they and their associates floated. Neither saw the difference between local truth and universal truth; that what the inner world said in their clerical and academic hearing was quite a different thing from what the outer world was thinking.

'I suppose it is farming or nothing for you now, my dear fellow,' Felix was saying, among other things, to his youngest brother, as he looked through his spectacles at the distant fields with sad austerity. 'And, therefore, we must make the best of it. But I do entreat you to endeavour to keep as much as possible in touch with moral ideals. Farming, of course, means roughing it externally; but high thinking may go with plain living, nevertheless.'

'Of course it may,' said Angel. 'Was it not proved nineteen hundred years ago – if I may trespass upon your domain a little? Why should you think, Felix, that I am likely to drop my high thinking and my moral ideals?'

'Well, I fancied, from the tone of your letters and our conversation – it may be fancy only – that you were somehow losing intellectual grasp. Hasn't it struck you, Cuthbert?'

'Now, Felix,' said Angel drily, 'we are very good friends, you know; each of us treading our allotted circles; but if it comes to intellectual grasp, I think you, as a contented dogmatist, had better leave mine alone, and inquire what has become of yours.'

They returned down the hill to dinner, which was fixed at any time at which their father's and mother's morning work in the parish usually concluded. Convenience as regarded afternoon callers was the last thing to enter into the consideration of unselfish Mr and Mrs Clare; though the three sons were sufficiently in unison on this matter to wish that their parents would conform a little to modern notions.

The walk had made them hungry, Angel in particular, who was now an outdoor man, accustomed to the profuse *dapes inemptæ* of the dairyman's somewhat coarsely-laden table. But neither of the old people had arrived, and it was not till the sons were almost tired of waiting that their parents entered. The self-denying pair had been occupied in coaxing the appetites of some of their sick parishioners, whom they, somewhat inconsistently, tried to keep imprisoned in the flesh, their own appetites being quite forgotten.

The family sat down to table, and a frugal meal of cold viands was deposited before them. Angel looked round for Mrs Crick's black-puddings, which he had directed to be nicely grilled, as they did them at the dairy, and of which he wished his father and mother to appreciate the marvellous herbal savours as highly as he did himself.

'Ah! you are looking for the black-puddings, my dear boy,' observed Clare's mother. 'But I am sure you will not mind doing without them, as I am sure your father and I shall not, when you know the reason. I suggested to him that we should take Mrs Crick's kind present to the children of the man who can earn nothing just now because of his attacks of delirium tremens; and he agreed that it would be a great pleasure to them; so we did.'

'Of course,' said Angel cheerfully, looking round for the mead.

'I found the mead so extremely alcoholic,' continued his mother, 'that it was quite unfit for use as a beverage, but as valuable as rum or brandy in an emergency; so I have put it in my medicine-closet.'

'We never drink spirits at this table, on principle,' added his father.

'But what shall I tell the dairyman's wife?' said Angel.

'The truth, of course,' said his father.

'I rather wanted to say we enjoyed the mead and the black-puddings very much. She is a kind, jolly sort of body, and is sure to ask me directly I return.'

'You cannot, if we did not,' Mr Clare answered lucidly.

'Ah – no; though that mead was a drop of pretty tipple.'

'A what?' said Cuthbert and Felix both.

'Oh — 'tis an expression they use down at Talbothays,' replied Angel, blushing. He felt that his parents were right in their practice if wrong in their want of sentiment, and said no more.

CHAPTER TWENTY-SIX

I t was not till the evening, after family prayers, that Angel found opportunity of broaching to his father one or two subjects near his heart. He had strung himself up to the purpose while kneeling behind his brothers on the carpet, studying the little nails in the heels of their walking boots. When the service was over they went out of the room with their mother, and Mr Clare and himself were left alone.

The young man first discussed with the elder his plans for the attainment of his position as a farmer on an extensive scale — either in England or in the Colonies. His father then told him that, as he had not been put to the expense of sending Angel up to Cambridge, he had felt it his duty to set by a sum of money every year towards the purchase or lease of land for him some day, that he might not feel himself unduly slighted.

'As far as worldly wealth goes,' continued his father, 'you will no doubt stand far superior to your brothers in a few years.'

This considerateness on old Mr Clare's part led Angel onward to the other and dearer subject. He observed to his father that he was then six-and-twenty, and that when he should start in the farming business he would require eyes in the back of his head to see to all matters — some one would be necessary to superintend the domestic labours of his establishment whilst he was afield. Would it not be well, therefore, for him to marry?

His father seemed to think this idea not unreasonable; and then Angel put the question —

'What kind of wife do you think would be best for me as a thrifty hard-working farmer?'

'A truly Christian woman, who will be a help and a comfort to you in your goings-out and your comings-in. Beyond that, it really matters little. Such an one can be found; indeed, my earnest-minded friend and neighbour, Dr Chant—'

'But ought she not primarily to be able to milk cows, churn good butter, make immense cheeses; know how to sit hens and turkeys, and rear chickens, to direct a field of labourers in an emergency, and estimate the value of sheep and calves?'

'Yes; a farmer's wife; yes, certainly. It would be desirable.' Mr Clare, the elder, had plainly never thought of these points before. 'I was going to add,' he said, 'that for a pure and saintly woman you will not find one more to your true advantage, and certainly not more to your mother's mind and my own, than your friend Mercy, whom you used to show a certain interest in. It is true that my neighbour Chant's daughter has lately caught up the fashion of the younger clergy round about us for decorating the Communion-table — altar, as I was shocked to hear her call it one day — with flowers and other stuff on festival occasions. But her father, who is quite as opposed to such flummery as I, says that can be cured. It is a mere girlish outbreak which, I am sure, will not be permanent.'

'Yes, yes; Mercy is good and devout, I know. But, father, don't you think that a young woman equally pure and virtuous as Miss Chant, but one who, in place of that lady's ecclesiastical accomplishments, understands the duties of farm life as well as a farmer himself, would suit me infinitely better?'

His father persisted in his conviction that a knowledge of a farmer's wife's duties came second to a Pauline view of humanity; and the impulsive Angel, wishing to honour his father's feelings and to advance the cause of his heart at the same time, grew specious. He said that fate or Providence had thrown in his way a woman who possessed every qualification to be the helpmate of an agriculturist, and was decidedly of a serious turn of mind. He would not say whether or not she had attached herself to the sound Low Church School of his father; but she would probably be open to conviction on that point; she was a regular church-goer of simple faith; honest-hearted, receptive, intelligent, graceful to a degree, chaste as a vestal, and, in personal appearance, exceptionally beautiful.

'Is she of a family such as you would care to marry into – a lady, in short?' asked his startled mother, who had come softly into the study during the conversation.

'She is not what in common parlance is called a lady,' said Angel, unflinchingly, 'for she is a cottager's daughter, as I am proud to say. But she *is* a lady, nevertheless – in feeling and nature.'

'Mercy Chant is of a very good family.'

'Pooh! – what's the advantage of that, mother?' said Angel quickly. 'How is family to avail the wife of a man who has to rough it as I have, and shall have to do?'

'Mercy is accomplished. And accomplishments have their charm,' returned his mother, looking at him through her silver spectacles.

'As to external accomplishments, what will be the use of them in the life I am going to lead? – while as to her reading, I can take that in hand. She'll be apt pupil enough, as you would say if you knew her. She's brim full of poetry – actualized poetry, if I may use the expression. She *lives* what paper-poets only write. . . . And she is an unimpeachable Christian, I am sure; perhaps of the very tribe, genus, and species you desire to propagate.'

'O Angel, you are mocking!'

'Mother, I beg pardon. But as she really does attend Church almost every Sunday morning, and is a good Christian girl, I am sure you will tolerate any social shortcomings for the sake of that quality, and feel that I may do worse than choose her.' Angel waxed quite earnest on that rather automatic orthodoxy in his beloved Tess which (never dreaming that it might stand him in such good stead) he had been prone to slight when observing it practised by her and the other milkmaids, because of its obvious unreality amid beliefs essentially naturalistic.

In their sad doubts as to whether their son had himself any right whatever to the title he claimed for the unknown young woman, Mr and Mrs Clare began to feel it as an advantage not to be overlooked that she at least was sound in her views; especially as the conjunction of the pair must have arisen by an act of Providence; for Angel never would have made orthodoxy a condition of his choice. They said finally that it was better not to act in a hurry, but that they would not object to see her.

Angel therefore refrained from declaring more particulars now. He felt that, single-minded and self-sacrificing as his parents were, there yet existed certain latent prejudices of theirs, as middle-class people, which it would require some tact to overcome. For though legally at liberty to do as he chose, and though their daughter-in-law's qualifications could make no practical difference to their lives, in the probability of her living far away from them, he wished for affection's sake not to wound their sentiment in the most important decision of his life.

He observed his own inconsistencies in dwelling upon accidents in Tess's life as if they were vital features. It was for herself that he loved Tess; her soul, her heart, her substance – not for her skill in the dairy, her aptness as his scholar, and certainly not for her simple formal faith-professions. Her unsophisticated open-air existence required no varnish of conventionality to make it palatable to him. He held that education had as yet but little affected the beats of emotion and impulse on which domestic happiness depends. It was probable that, in the lapse of ages, improved systems of moral and intellectual training would appreciably, perhaps considerably, elevate the involuntary and even the unconscious instincts of human nature; but up to the present day culture, as far as he could see, might be said to have affected only the mental epiderm of those lives which had been brought under its influence. This belief was confirmed by his experience of women, which, having latterly been extended from the cultivated middle-class into the rural community, had taught him how much less was the intrinsic difference between the good and wise woman of one social stratum and the good and wise woman of another social stratum, than between the good and bad, the wise and the foolish, of the same stratum or class.

It was the morning of his departure. His brothers had already left the vicarage to proceed on a walking tour in the north, whence one was to return to his college, and the other to his curacy. Angel might have accompanied them, but preferred to rejoin his sweetheart at Talbothays. He would have been an awkward member of the party; for, though the most appreciative humanist, the most ideal religionist, even the best-versed Christologist of the three, there was alienation in the standing consciousness that his squareness would not fit the round hole that had been prepared for him. To neither Felix nor Cuthbert had he ventured to mention Tess.

His mother made him sandwiches, and his father accompanied him, on his own mare, a little way along the road. Having fairly well advanced his own affairs Angel listened in a willing silence, as they jogged on together through the shady lanes, to his father's account of his parish difficulties, and the coldness of brother clergymen whom he loved, because of his strict interpretations of the New Testament by the light of what they deemed a pernicious Calvinistic doctrine.

'Pernicious!' said Mr Clare, with genial scorn; and he proceeded to recount experiences which would show the absurdity of that idea. He told of wondrous conversions of evil livers of which he had been the instrument, not only amongst the poor, but amongst the rich and well-to-do; and he also candidly admitted many failures.

As an instance of the latter, he mentioned the case of a young upstart squire

named d'Urberville, living some forty miles off, in the neighbourhood of
Trantridge.

'Not one of the ancient d'Urbervilles of Kingsbere and other places?' asked his
son. 'That curiously historic worn-out family with its ghostly legend of the coach-
and-four?'

'O no. The original d'Urbervilles decayed and disappeared sixty or eighty
years ago – at least, I believe so. This seems to be a new family which has taken
the name; for the credit of the former knightly line I hope they are spurious, I'm
sure. But it is odd to hear you express interest in old families. I thought you set
less store by them even than I.'

'You misapprehended me, father; you often do,' said Angel with a little
impatience. 'Politically I am sceptical as to the virtue of their being old. Some of
the wise even among themselves "exclaim against their own succession", as
Hamlet puts it; but lyrically, dramatically, and even historically, I am tenderly
attached to them.'

This distraction, though by no means a subtle one, was yet too subtle for Mr
Clare the elder, and he went on with the story he had been about to relate; which
was that after the death of the senior so-called d'Urberville the young man
developed the most culpable passions, though he had a blind mother, whose
condition should have made him know better. A knowledge of his career having
come to the ears of Mr Clare, when he was in that part of the country preaching
missionary sermons, he boldly took occasion to speak to the delinquent on his
spiritual state. Though he was a stranger, occupying another's pulpit, he had felt
this to be his duty, and took for his text the words from St Luke: 'Thou fool, this
night thy soul shall be required of thee!' The young man much resented this
directness of attack, and in the war of words which followed when they met he did
not scruple publicly to insult Mr Clare, without respect for his gray hairs.

Angel flushed with distress.

'Dear father,' he said sadly, 'I wish you would not expose yourself to such
gratuitous pain from scoundrels!'

'Pain?' said his father, his rugged face shining in the ardour of self-abnegation.
'The only pain to me was pain on his account, poor, foolish young man. Do you
suppose his incensed words could give me any pain, or even his blows? "Being
reviled we bless; being persecuted we suffer it; being defamed we entreat; we are
made as the filth of the world, and as the offscouring of all things unto this day."
Those ancient and noble words to the Corinthians are strictly true at this present
hour.'

'Not blows, father? He did not proceed to blows?'

'No, he did not. Though I have borne blows from men in a mad state of
intoxication.'

'No!'

'A dozen times, my boy. What then? I have saved them from the guilt of
murdering their own flesh and blood thereby; and they have lived to thank me,
and praise God.'

'May this young man do the same!' said Angel fervently. 'But I fear otherwise,
from what you say.'

'We'll hope, nevertheless,' said Mr Clare. 'And I continue to pray for him,
though on this side of the grave we shall probably never meet again. But, after all,

one of those poor words of mine may spring up in his heart as a good seed some day.'

Now, as always, Clare's father was sanguine as a child; and though the younger could not accept his parent's narrow dogma he revered his practice, and recognized the hero under the pietist. Perhaps he revered his father's practice even more now than ever, seeing that, in the question of making Tessy his wife, his father had not once thought of inquiring whether she were well provided or penniless. The same unworldliness was what had necessitated Angel's getting a living as a farmer, and would probably keep his brothers in the position of poor parsons for the term of their activities; yet Angel admired it none the less. Indeed, despite his own heterodoxy, Angel often felt that he was nearer to his father on the human side than was either of his brethren.

CHAPTER TWENTY-SEVEN

A N up-hill and down-dale ride of twenty-odd miles through a garish mid-day atmosphere brought him in the afternoon to a detached knoll a mile or two west of Talbothays, whence he again looked into that green trough of sappiness and humidity, the valley of the Var or Froom. Immediately he began to descend from the upland to the fat alluvial soil below, the atmosphere grew heavier; the languid perfume of the summer fruits, the mists, the hay, the flowers, formed therein a vast pool of odour which at this hour seemed to make the animals, the very bees and butterflies, drowsy. Clare was now so familiar with the spot that he knew the individual cows by their names when, a long distance off, he saw them dotted about the meads. It was with a sense of luxury that he recognized his power of viewing life here from its inner side, in a way that had been quite foreign to him in his student-days; and, much as he loved his parents, he could not help being aware that to come here, as now, after an experience of home-life, affected him like throwing off splints and bandages; even the one customary curb on the humours of English rural societies being absent in this place, Talbothays having no resident landlord.

Not a human being was out of doors at the dairy. The denizens were all enjoying the usual afternoon nap of an hour or so which the exceedingly early hours kept in summer-time rendered a necessity. At the door the wood-hooped pails sodden and bleached by infinite scrubbings, hung like hats on a stand upon the forked and peeled limb of an oak fixed there for that purpose; all of them ready and dry for the evening milking. Angel entered, and went through the silent passages of the house to the back quarters, where he listened for a moment. Sustained snores came from the cart-house, where some of the men were lying down; the grunt and squeal of sweltering pigs arose from the still further distance. The large-leaved rhubarb and cabbage plants slept too, their broad limp surfaces hanging in the sun like half-closed umbrellas.

He unbridled and fed his horse, and as he re-entered the house the clock struck three. Three was the afternoon skimming-hour; and, with the stroke, Clare heard the creaking of the floor-boards above, and then the touch of a descending foot on the stairs. It was Tess's, who in another moment came down before his eyes.

She had not heard him enter, and hardly realized his presence there. She was yawning, and he saw the red interior of her mouth as if it had been a snake's. She had stretched one arm so high above her coiled-up cable of hair that he could see its satin delicacy above the sunburn; her face was flushed with sleep, and her eyelids hung heavy over their pupils. The brim-fulness of her nature breathed from her. It was a moment when a woman's soul is more incarnate than at any other time; when the most spiritual beauty bespeaks itself flesh; and sex takes the outside place in the presentation.

Then those eyes flashed brightly through their filmy heaviness, before the remainder of her face was well awake. With an oddly compounded look of gladness, shyness, and surprise, she exclaimed –

'O Mr Clare! How you frightened me – I—'

There had not at first been time for her to think of the changed relations which his declaration had introduced; but the full sense of the matter rose up in her face when she encountered Clare's tender look as he stepped forward to the bottom stair.

'Dear, darling Tessy!' he whispered, putting his arm round her, and his face to her flushed cheek. 'Don't, for Heaven's sake, Mister me any more. I have hastened back so soon because of you!'

Tess's excitable heart beat against his by way of reply; and there they stood upon the red-brick floor of the entry, the sun slanting in by the window upon his back, as he held her tightly to his breast; upon her inclining face, upon the blue veins of her temple, upon her naked arm, and her neck, and into the depths of her hair. Having been lying down in her clothes she was warm as a sunned cat. At first she would not look straight up at him, but her eyes soon lifted, and his plumbed the deepness of the ever-varying pupils, with their radiating fibrils of blue, and black, and gray, and violet, while she regarded him as Eve at her second waking might have regarded Adam.

'I've got to go a-skimming,' she pleaded, 'and I have on'y old Deb to help me to-day. Mrs Crick is gone to market with Mr Crick, and Retty is not well, and the others are gone out somewhere, and won't be home till milking.'

As they retreated to the milk-house Deborah Fyander appeared on the stairs.

'I have come back, Deborah,' said Mr Clare, upwards. 'So I can help Tess with the skimming; and, as you are very tired, I am sure, you needn't come down till milking-time.'

Possibly the Talbothays milk was not very thoroughly skimmed that afternoon. Tess was in a dream wherein familiar objects appeared as having light and shade and position, but no particular outline. Every time she held the skimmer under the pump to cool it for the work her hand trembled, the ardour of his affection being so palpable that she seemed to flinch under it like a plant in too burning a sun.

Then he pressed her again to his side, and when she had done running her forefinger round the leads to cut off the cream-edge, he cleaned it in nature's way; for the unconstrained manners of Talbothays dairy came convenient now.

'I may as well say it now as later, dearest,' he resumed gently. 'I wish to ask you something of a very practical nature, which I have been thinking of ever since that day last week in the meads. I shall soon want to marry, and, being a farmer, you see I shall require for my wife a woman who knows all about the management of farms. Will you be that woman, Tessy?'

He put it in that way that she might not think he had yielded to an impulse of which his head would disapprove.

She turned quite careworn. She had bowed to the inevitable result of proximity, the necessity of loving him; but she had not calculated upon this sudden corollary, which, indeed, Clare had put before her without quite meaning himself to do it so soon. With pain that was like the bitterness of dissolution she murmured the words of her indispensable and sworn answer as an honourable woman.

'O Mr Clare – I cannot be your wife – I cannot be!'

The sound of her own decision seemed to break Tess's very heart, and she bowed her face in her grief.

But, Tess!' he said, amazed at her reply, and holding her still more greedily close. 'Do you say no? Surely you love me?'

'O yes, yes! And I would rather be yours than anybody's in the world,' returned the sweet and honest voice of the distressed girl. 'But I *cannot* marry you!'

'Tess,' he said, holding her at arm's length, 'you are engaged to marry some one else!'

'No, no!'

'Then why do you refuse me?'

'I don't want to marry! I have not thought of doing it. I cannot! I only want to love you.'

'But why?'

Driven to subterfuge, she stammered –

'Your father is a parson, and your mother wouldn' like you to marry such as me. She will want you to marry a lady.'

'Nonsense – I have spoken to them both. That was partly why I went home.'

'I feel I cannot – never, never!' she echoed.

'Is it too sudden to be asked thus, my Pretty?'

'Yes – I did not expect it.'

'If you will let it pass, please, Tessy, I will give you time,' he said. 'It was very abrupt to come home and speak to you all at once. I'll not allude to it again for a while.'

She again took up the shining skimmer, held it beneath the pump, and began anew. But she could not, as at other times, hit the exact under-surface of the cream with the delicate dexterity required, try as she might: sometimes she was cutting down into the milk, sometimes in the air. She could hardly see, her eyes having filled with two blurring tears drawn forth by a grief which, to this her best friend and dear advocate, she could never explain.

'I can't skim – I can't!' she said, turning away from him.

Not to agitate and hinder her longer the considerate Clare began talking in a more general way:

'You quite misapprehend my parents. They are the most simple-mannered people alive, and quite unambitious. They are two of the few remaining Evanglical school. Tessy, are you an Evangelical?'

'I don't know.'

'You go to church very regularly, and our parson here is not very High, they tell me.'

Tess's ideas on the views of the parish clergyman, whom she heard every week, seemed to be rather more vague than Clare's, who had never heard him at all.

'I wish I could fix my mind on what I hear there more firmly than I do,' she remarked as a safe generality. 'It is often a great sorrow to me.'

She spoke so unaffectedly that Angel was sure in his heart that his father could not object to her on religious grounds, even though she did not know whether her principles were High, Low, or Broad. He himself knew that, in reality, the confused beliefs which she held, apparently imbibed in childhood, were, if anything, Tractarian as to phraseology, and Pantheistic as to essence. Confused or otherwise, to disturb them was his last desire:

> Leave thou thy sister, when she prays,
> Her early Heaven, her happy views;
> Nor thou with shadow'd hint confuse
> A life that leads melodious days.

He had occasionally thought the counsel less honest than musical; but he gladly conformed to it now.

He spoke further of the incidents of his visit, of his father's mode of life, of his zeal for his principles; she grew serener, and the undulations disappeared from her skimming; as she finished one lead after another he followed her, and drew the plugs for letting down the milk.

'I fancied you looked a little downcast when you came in,' she ventured to observe, anxious to keep away from the subject of herself.

'Yes—well, my father has been talking a good deal to me of his troubles and difficulties, and the subject always tends to depress me. He is so zealous that he gets many snubs and buffetings from people of a different way of thinking from himself, and I don't like to hear of such humiliations to a man of his age, the more particularly as I don't think earnestness does any good when carried so far. He has been telling me of a very unpleasant scene in which he took part quite recently. He went as the deputy of some missionary society to preach in the neighbourhood of Trantridge, a place forty miles from here, and made it his business to expostulate with a lax young cynic he met with somewhere about there—son of some landowner up that way—and who has a mother afflicted with blindness. My father addressed himself to the gentleman point-blank, and there was quite a disturbance. It was very foolish of my father, I must say, to intrude his conversation upon a stranger when the probabilities were so obvious that it would be useless. But whatever he thinks to be his duty, that he'll do, in season or out of season; and, of course, he makes many enemies, not only among the absolutely vicious, but among the easy-going, who hate being bothered. He says he glories in what happened, and that good may be done indirectly; but I wish he would not so wear himself out now he is getting old, and would leave such pigs to their wallowing.'

Tess's look had grown hard and worn, and her ripe mouth tragical; but she no longer showed any tremulousness. Clare's revived thoughts of his father prevented his noticing her particularly; and so they went on down the white row of liquid rectangles till they had finished and drained them off, when the other

maids returned, and took their pails, and Deb came to scald out the leads for the new milk. As Tess withdrew to go afield to the cows he said to her softly –
'And my question, Tessy?'
'O no – no!' replied she with grave hopelessness, as one who had heard anew the turmoil of her own past in the allusion to Alec d'Urberville. 'It *can't* be!'
She went out towards the mead, joining the other milkmaids with a bound, as if trying to make the open air drive away her sad constraint. All the girls drew onward to the spot where the cows were grazing in the farther mead, the bevy advancing with the bold grace of wild animals – the reckless unchastened motion of women accustomed to unlimited space – in which they abandoned themselves to the air as a swimmer to the wave. It seemed natural enough to him now that Tess was again in sight to choose a mate from unconstrained Nature, and not from the abodes of Art.

CHAPTER TWENTY-EIGHT

HER refusal, though unexpected, did not permanently daunt Clare. His experience of women was great enough for him to be aware that the negative often meant nothing more than the preface to the affirmative; and it was little enough for him not to know that in the manner of the present negative there lay a great exception to the dallyings of coyness. That she had already permitted him to make love to her he read as an additional assurance, not fully trowing that in the fields and pastures to 'sigh gratis' is by no means deemed waste; love-making being here more often accepted inconsiderately and for its own sweet sake than in the carking anxious homes of the ambitious, where a girl's craving for an establishment paralyzes her healthy thought of a passion as an end.
'Tess, why did you say "no" in such a positive way?' he asked her in the course of a few days.
She started.
'Don't ask me. I told you why – partly. I am not good enough – not worthy enough.'
'How? Not fine lady enough?'
'Yes – something like that,' murmured she. 'Your friends would scorn me.'
'Indeed, you mistake them – my father and mother. As for my brothers, I don't care—' He clasped his fingers behind her back to keep her from slipping away. 'Now – you did not mean it, sweet? – I am sure you did not! You have made me so restless that I cannot read, or play, or do anything. I am in no hurry, Tess, but I want to know – to hear from your own warm lips – that you will some day be mine – any time you may choose; but some day?'
She could only shake her head and look away from him.
Clare regarded her attentively, conned the characters of her face as if they had been hieroglyphics. The denial seemed real.
'Then I ought not to hold you in this way – ought I? I have no right to you – no right to seek out where you are, or to walk with you! Honestly, Tess, do you love any other man?'

'How can you ask?' she said, with continued self-suppression.

'I almost know that you do not. But then, why do you repulse me?'

'I don't repulse you. I like you to – tell me you love me; and you may always tell me so as you go about with me – and never offend me.'

'But you will not accept me as a husband?'

'Ah – that's different – it is for your good, indeed my dearest! O, believe me, it is only for your sake! I don't like to give myself the great happiness o' promising to be yours in that way – because – because I am *sure* I ought not to do it.'

'But you will make me happy!'

'Ah – you think so, but you don't know!'

At such times as this, apprehending the grounds of her refusal to be her modest sense of incompetence in matters social and polite, he would say that she was wonderfully well-informed and versatile – which was certainly true, her natural quickness, and her admiration for him, having led her to pick up his vocabulary, his accent, and fragments of his knowledge, to a surprising extent. After these tender contests and her victory she would go away by herself under the remotest cow, if at milking-time, or into the sedge, or into her room, if at a leisure interval, and mourn silently, not a minute after an apparently phlegmatic negative.

The struggle was so fearful; her own heart was so strongly on the side of his – two ardent hearts against one poor little conscience – that she tried to fortify her resolution by every means in her power. She had come to Talbothays with a made-up mind. On no account could she agree to a step which might afterwards cause bitter rueing to her husband for his blindness in wedding her. And she held that what her conscience had decided for her when her mind was unbiassed ought not to be overruled now.

'Why don't somebody tell him all about me?' she said. 'It was only forty miles off – why hasn't it reached here? Somebody must know!'

Yet nobody seemed to know; nobody told him.

For two or three days no more was said. She guessed from the sad countenances of her chamber companions that they regarded her not only as the favourite, but as the chosen; but they could see for themselves that she did not put herself in his way.

Tess had never before known a time in which the thread of her life was so distinctly twisted of two strands, positive pleasure and positive pain. At the next cheese-making the pair were again left alone together. The dairyman himself had been lending a hand; but Mr Crick, as well as his wife, seemed latterly to have acquired a suspicion of mutual interest between these two; though they walked so circumspectly that suspicion was but of the faintest. Anyhow, the dairyman left them to themselves.

They were breaking up the masses of curd before putting them into the vats. The operation resembled the act of crumbling bread on a large scale; and amid the immaculate whiteness of the curds Tess Durbeyfield's hands showed themselves of the pinkness of the rose. Angel, who was filling the vats with his handfuls, suddenly ceased, and laid his hands flat upon hers. Her sleeves were rolled far above the elbow, and bending lower he kissed the inside vein of her soft arm.

Although the early September weather was sultry, her arm, from her dabbling in the curds, was as cold and damp to his mouth as a new-gathered mushroom, and tasted of the whey. But she was such a sheaf of susceptibilities that her pulse was accelerated by the touch, her blood driven to her finger-ends, and the cool arms flushed hot. Then, as though her heart had said, 'Is coyness longer necessary? Truth is truth between man and woman, as between man and man,' she lifted her eyes, and they beamed devotedly into his, as her lip rose in a tender half-smile.

'Do you know why I did that, Tess?' he said.

'Because you love me very much!'

'Yes, and as a preliminary to a new entreaty.'

'Not *again*!'

She looked a sudden fear that her resistance might break down under her own desire.

'O, Tessy!' he went on, 'I *cannot* think why you are so tantalizing. Why do you disappoint me so? You seem almost like a coquette, upon my life you do —a coquette of the first urban water! They blow hot and blow cold, just as you do; and it is the very last sort of thing to expect to find in a retreat like Talbothays. . . . And yet, dearest,' he quickly added, observing how the remark had cut her, 'I know you to be the most honest, spotless creature that ever lived. So how can I suppose you a flirt? Tess, why don't you like the idea of being my wife, if you love me as you seem to do?'

'I have never said I don't like the idea, and I never could say it; because —it isn't true!'

The stress now getting beyond endurance her lip quivered, and she was obliged to go away. Clare was so pained and perplexed that he ran after and caught her in the passage.

'Tell me, tell me!' he said, passionately clasping her, in forgetfulness of his curdy hands: 'do tell me that you won't belong to anybody but me!'

'I will, I will tell you!' she exclaimed. 'And I will give you a complete answer, if you will let me go now. I will tell you my experiences —all about myself —all!'

'Your experiences, dear; yes, certainly; any number.' He expressed assent in loving satire, looking into her face. 'My Tess has, no doubt, almost as many experiences as that wild convolvulus out there on the garden hedge, that opened itself this morning for the first time. Tell me anything, but don't use that wretched expression any more about not being worthy of me.'

'I will try —not! And I'll give you my reasons to-morrow —next week.'

'Say on Sunday?'

'Yes, on Sunday.'

At last she got away, and did not stop in her retreat till she was in the thicket of pollard willows at the lower side of the barton, where she could be quite unseen. Here Tess flung herself down upon the rustling undergrowth of spear-grass, as upon a bed, and remained crouching in palpitating misery broken by momentary shoots of joy, which her fears about the ending could not altogether suppress.

In reality, she was drifting into acquiescence. Every see-saw of her breath, every wave of her blood, every pulse singing in her ears, was a voice that joined with nature in revolt against her scrupulousness. Reckless, inconsiderate acceptance of him; to close with him at the altar, revealing nothing, and chancing discovery; to snatch ripe pleasure before the iron teeth of pain could have time to shut upon her: that was what love counselled; and in almost a terror of ecstasy

Tess divined that, despite her many months of lonely self-chastisement, wrestlings, communings, schemes to lead a future of austere isolation, love's counsel would prevail.

The afternoon advanced, and still she remained among the willows. She heard the rattle of taking down the pails from the forked stands; the 'waow-waow!' which accompanied the getting together of the cows. But she did not go to the milking. They would see her agitation; and the dairyman, thinking the cause to be love alone, would good-naturedly tease her; and that harassment could not be borne.

Her lover must have guessed her overwrought state, and invented some excuse for her non-appearance, for no inquiries were made or calls given. At half-past six the sun settled down upon the levels, with the aspect of a great forge in the heavens, and presently a monstrous pumpkin-like moon arose on the other hand. The pollard willows, tortured out of their natural shape by incessant choppings, became spiny-haired monsters as they stood up against it. She went in, and upstairs without a light.

It was now Wednesday. Thursday came, and Angel looked thoughtfully at her from a distance, but intruded in no way upon her. The indoor milkmaids, Marian and the rest, seemed to guess that something definite was afoot, for they did not force any remarks upon her in the bedchamber. Friday passed; Saturday. To-morrow was the day.

'I shall give way — I shall say yes — I shall let myself marry him — I cannot help it!' she jealously panted, with her hot face to the pillow that night, on hearing one of the other girls sigh his name in her sleep. 'I can't bear to let anybody have him but me! Yet it is a wrong to him, and may kill him when he knows! O my heart — O – O – O!'

CHAPTER TWENTY-NINE

'Now, who mid ye think I've heard news o' this morning?' said Dairyman Crick, as he sat down to breakfast next day, with a riddling gaze round upon the munching men and maids. 'Now, just who mid ye think?'

One guessed, and another guessed. Mrs Crick did not guess, because she knew already.

'Well,' said the dairyman, ''tis that slack-twisted 'hore's-bird of a feller, Jack Dollop. He's lately got married to a widow-woman.'

'Not Jack Dollop? A villain — to think o' that!' said a milker.

The name entered quickly into Tess Durbeyfield's consciousness, for it was the name of the lover who had wronged his sweetheart, and had afterwards been so roughly used by the young woman's mother in the butter-churn.

'And has he married the valiant matron's daughter, as he promised?' asked Angel Clare absently, as he turned over the newspaper he was reading at the little table to which he was always banished by Mrs Crick, in her sense of his gentility.

'Not he, sir. Never meant to,' replied the dairyman. 'As I say, 'tis a widow-woman, and she had money, it seems – fifty poun' a year or so; and that was all he was after. They were married in a great hurry; and then she told him that by marrying she had lost her fifty poun' a year. Just fancy the state o' my gentleman's mind at that news! Never such a cat-and-dog life as they've been leading ever since! Serves him well beright. But onluckily the poor woman gets the worst o't.'

'Well, the silly body should have told en sooner that the ghost of her first man would trouble him,' said Mrs Crick.

'Ay; ay,' responded the dairyman indecisively. 'Still, you can see exactly how 'twas. She wanted a home, and didn't like to run the risk of losing him. Don't ye think that was something like it, maidens?'

He glanced towards the row of girls.

'She ought to ha' told him just before they went to church, when he could hardly have backed out,' exclaimed Marian.

'Yes, she ought,' agreed Izz.

'She must have seen what he was after, and should ha' refused him,' cried Retty spasmodically.

'And what do you say, my dear?' asked the dairyman of Tess.

'I think she ought – to have told him the true state of things – or else refused him – I don't know,' replied Tess, the bread-and-butter choking her.

'Be cust if I'd have done either o't,' said Beck Knibbs, a married helper from one of the cottages. 'All's fair in love and war. I'd ha' married en just as she did, and if he'd said two words to me about not telling him beforehand anything whatsomdever about my first chap that I hadn't chose to tell, I'd ha' knocked him down wi' the rolling-pin – a scram little feller like he! Any woman could do it.'

The laughter which followed this sally was supplemented only by a sorry smile, for form's sake, from Tess. What was comedy to them was tragedy to her; and she could hardly bear their mirth. She soon rose from table, and, with an impression that Clare would follow her, went along a little wriggling path, now stepping to one side of the irrigating channels, and now to the other, till she stood by the main stream of the Var. Men had been cutting the water-weeds higher up the river, and masses of them were floating past her – moving islands of green crowfoot, whereon she might almost have ridden; long locks of which weed had lodged against the piles driven to keep the cows from crossing.

Yes, there was the pain of it. This question of a woman telling her story – the heaviest of crosses to herself – seemed but amusement to others. It was as if people should laugh at martyrdom.

'Tessy!' came from behind her, and Clare sprang across the gully, alighting beside her feet. 'My wife – soon!'

'No, no; I cannot. For your sake, O Mr Clare; for your sake, I say no!'

'Tess!'

'Still I say no!' she repeated.

Not expecting this he had put his arm lightly round her waist the moment after speaking, beneath her hanging tail of hair. (The younger dairymaids, including Tess, breakfasted with their hair loose on Sunday mornings before building it up extra high for attending church, a style they could not adopt when milking with their heads against the cows.) If she had said 'Yes' instead of 'No' he would have kissed her; it had evidently been his intention; but her determined negative deterred his scrupulous heart. Their condition of domiciliary comradeship put her, as the woman, to such disadvantage by its enforced intercourse, that he felt it unfair to her to exercise any pressure of blandishment which he might have honestly employed had she been better able to avoid him. He released her momentarily-imprisoned waist, and withheld the kiss.

It all turned on that release. What had given her strength to refuse him this time was solely the tale of the widow told by the dairyman; and that would have been overcome in another moment. But Angel said no more; his face was perplexed; he went away.

Day after day they met – somewhat less constantly than before; and thus two or three weeks went by. The end of September drew near, and she could see in his eye that he might ask her again.

His plan of procedure was different now – as though he had made up his mind that her negatives were, after all, only coyness and youth startled by the novelty of the proposal. The fitful evasiveness of her manner when the subject was under discussion countenanced the idea. So he played a more coaxing game; and while never going beyond words, or attempting the renewal of caresses, he did his utmost orally.

In this way Clare persistently wooed her in undertones like that of the purling milk – at the cow's side, at skimmings, at butter-makings, at cheese-makings, among broody poultry, and among farrowing pigs – as no milkmaid was ever wooed before by such a man.

Tess knew that she must break down. Neither a religious sense of a certain moral validity in the previous union nor a conscientious wish for candour could hold out against it much longer. She loved him so passionately, and he was so godlike in her eyes; and being, though untrained, instinctively refined, her nature cried for his tutelary guidance. And thus, though Tess kept repeating to herself, 'I can never be his wife,' the words were vain. A proof of her weakness lay in the very utterance of what calm strength would not have taken the trouble to formulate. Every sound of his voice beginning on the old subject stirred her with a terrifying bliss, and she coveted the recantation she feared.

His manner was – what man's is not? – so much that of one who would love and cherish and defend her under any conditions, changes, charges, or revelations, that her gloom lessened as she basked in it. The season meanwhile was drawing onward to the equinox, and though it was still fine, the days were much shorter. The dairy had again worked by morning candle-light for a long time; and a fresh renewal of Clare's pleading occurred one morning between three and four.

She had run up in her bedgown to his door to call him as usual; then had gone back to dress and call the others; and in ten minutes was walking to the head of the stairs with the candle in her hand. At the same moment he came down his steps from above in his shirt-sleeves and put his arm across the stairway.

'Now, Miss Flirt, before you go down,' he said peremptorily. 'It is a fortnight since I spoke, and this won't do any longer. You *must* tell me what you mean, or I shall have to leave this house. My door was ajar just now, and I saw you. For your own safety I must go. You don't know. Well? Is it to be yes at last?'

'I am only just up, Mr Clare, and it is too early to take me to task!' she pouted. 'You need not call me Flirt. 'Tis cruel and untrue. Wait till by and by. Please wait till by and by! I will really think seriously about it between now and then. Let me go downstairs!'

She looked a little like what he said she was as, holding the candle sideways, she tried to smile away the seriousness of her words.

'Call me Angel, then, and not Mr Clare.'

'Angel.'

'Angel dearest – why not?'

''Twould mean that I agree, wouldn't it?'

'It would only mean that you love me, even if you cannot marry me; and you were so good as to own that long ago.'

'Very well, then, "Angel dearest", if I *must*,' she murmured, looking at her candle, a roguish curl coming upon her mouth, notwithstanding her suspense.

Clare had resolved never to kiss her until he had obtained her promise; but somehow, as Tess stood there in her prettily tucked-up milking gown, her hair carelessly heaped upon her head till there should be leisure to arrange it when skimming and milking were done, he broke his resolve, and brought his lips to her cheek for one moment. She passed downstairs very quickly, never looking back at him or saying another word. The other maids were already down, and the subject was not pursued. Except Marian they all looked wistfully and suspiciously at the pair, in the sad yellow rays which the morning candles emitted in contrast with the first cold signals of the dawn without.

When skimming was done – which, as the milk diminished with the approach of autumn, was a lessening process day by day – Retty and the rest went out. The lovers followed them.

'Our tremulous lives are so different from theirs, are they not?' he musingly observed to her, as he regarded the three figures tripping before him through the frigid pallor of opening day.

'Not so very different, I think,' she said.

'Why do you think that?'

'There are very few women's lives that are not – tremulous,' Tess replied, pausing over the new word as if it impressed her. 'There's more in those three than you think.'

'What is in them?'

'Almost either of 'em,' she began, 'would make – perhaps would make – a properer wife than I. And perhaps they love you as well as I – almost.'

'O, Tessy!'

There were signs that it was an exquisite relief to her to hear the impatient exclamation, though she had resolved so intrepidly to let generosity make one bid against herself. That was now done, and she had not the power to attempt self-immolation a second time then. They were joined by a milker from one of the cottages, and no more was said on that which concerned them so deeply. But Tess knew that this day would decide it.

In the afternoon several of the dairyman's household and assistants went down to the meads as usual, a long way from the dairy, where many of the cows were milked without being driven home. The supply was getting less as the animals advanced in calf, and the supernumerary milkers of the lush green season had been dismissed.

The work progressed leisurely. Each pailful was poured into tall cans that stood in a large spring-waggon which had been brought upon the scene; and when they were milked the cows trailed away.

Dairyman Crick, who was there with the rest, his wrapper gleaming miraculously white against a leaden evening sky, suddenly looked at his heavy watch.

'Why, 'tis later than I thought,' he said. 'Begad! We shan't be soon enough with this milk at the station, if we don't mind. There's no time to-day to take it home and mix it with the bulk afore sending off. It must go to station straight from here. Who'll drive it across?'

Mr Clare volunteered to do so, though it was none of his business, asking Tess to accompany him. The evening, though sunless, had been warm and muggy for the season, and Tess had come out with her milking-hood only, naked-armed and jacketless; certainly not dressed for a drive. She therefore replied by glancing over her scant habiliments; but Clare gently urged her. She assented by relinquishing her pail and stool to the dairyman to take home; and mounted the spring-waggon beside Clare.

CHAPTER THIRTY

I N the diminishing daylight they went along the level roadway through the meads, which stretched away into gray miles, and were backed in the extreme edge of distance by the swarthy and abrupt slopes of Egdon Heath. On its summit stood clumps and stretches of fir-trees, whose notched tips appeared like battlemented towers crowning black-fronted castles of enchantment.

They were so absorbed in the sense of being close to each other that they did not begin talking for a long while, the silence being broken only by the clucking of the milk in the tall cans behind them. The lane they followed was so solitary that the hazel nuts had remained on the boughs till they slipped from their shells, and the blackberries hung in heavy clusters. Every now and then Angel would fling the lash of his whip round one of these, pluck it off, and give it to his companion.

The dull sky soon began to tell its meaning by sending down herald-drops of rain, and the stagnant air of the day changed into a fitful breeze which played about their faces. The quicksilvery glaze on the rivers and pools vanished; from broad mirrors of light they changed to lustreless sheets of lead, with a surface like a rasp. But that spectacle did not affect her preoccupation. Her countenance, a natural carnation slightly embrowned by the season, had deepened its tinge with the beating of the rain-drops; and her hair, which the pressure of the cows' flanks had, as usual, caused to tumble down from its fastenings and stray beyond the curtain of her calico bonnet, was made clammy by the moisture, till it hardly was better than seaweed.

'I ought not to have come, I suppose,' she murmured, looking at the sky.

'I am sorry for the rain,' said he. 'But how glad I am to have you here!'

Remote Egdon disappeared by degrees behind the liquid gauze. The evening grew darker, and the roads being crossed by gates it was not safe to drive faster than at a walking pace. The air was rather chill.

'I am so afraid you will get cold, with nothing upon your arms and shoulders,' he said. 'Creep close to me, and perhaps the drizzle won't hurt you much. I should be sorrier still if I did not think that the rain might be helping me.'

She imperceptibly crept closer, and he wrapped round them both a large piece of sail-cloth, which was sometimes used to keep the sun off the milk-cans. Tess held it from slipping off him as well as herself, Clare's hands being occupied.

'Now we are all right again. Ah — no we are not! It runs down into my neck a little, and it must still more into yours. That's better. Your arms are like wet marble, Tess. Wipe them in the cloth. Now, if you stay quiet, you will not get another drop. Well, dear — about that question of mine — that long-standing question?'

The only reply that he could hear for a little while was the smack of the horse's hoofs on the moistening road, and the cluck of the milk in the cans behind them.

'Do you remember what you said?'

'I do,' she replied.

'Before we get home, mind.'

'I'll try.'

He said no more then. As they drove on the fragment of an old manor house of Caroline date rose against the sky, and was in due course passed and left behind.

'That,' he observed, to entertain her, 'is an interesting old place — one of the several seats which belonged to an ancient Norman family formerly of great influence in this county, the d'Urbervilles. I never pass one of their residences without thinking of them. There is something very sad in the extinction of a family of renown, even if it was fierce, domineering, feudal renown.'

'Yes,' said Tess.

They crept along towards a point in the expanse of shade just at hand at which a feeble light was beginning to assert its presence, a spot where, by day, a fitful white streak of steam at intervals upon the dark green background denoted intermittent moments of contact between their secluded world and modern life. Modern life stretched out its steam feeler to this point three or four times a day, touched the native existences, and quickly withdrew its feeler again, as if what it touched had been uncongenial.

They reached the feeble light, which came from the smoky lamp of a little railway station; a poor enough terrestrial star, yet in one sense of more importance to Talbothays Dairy and mankind than the celestial ones to which it stood in such humiliating contrast. The cans of new milk were unladen in the rain, Tess getting a little shelter from a neighbouring holly tree.

Then there was the hissing of a train, which drew up almost silently upon the wet rails, and the milk was rapidly swung can by can into the truck. The light of the engine flashed for a second upon Tess Durbeyfield's figure, motionless under the great holly tree. No object could have looked more foreign to the gleaming cranks and wheels than this unsophisticated girl, with the round bare arms, the rainy face and hair, the suspended attitude of a friendly leopard at pause, the print gown of no date or fashion, and the cotton bonnet drooping on her brow.

She mounted again beside her lover, with a mute obedience characteristic of impassioned natures at times, and when they had wrapped themselves up over head and ears in the sail-cloth again, they plunged back into the now thick night. Tess was so receptive that the few minutes of contact with the whirl of material progress lingered in her thought.

'Londoners will drink it at their breakfasts to-morrow, won't they!' she asked. 'Strange people that we have never seen.'

'Yes – I suppose they will. Though not as we send it. When its strength has been lowered, so that it may not get up into their heads.'

'Noble men and noble women, ambassadors and centurions, ladies and tradeswomen, and babies who have never seen a cow.'

'Well, yes; perhaps; particularly centurions.'

'Who don't know anything of us, and where it comes from; or think how we two drove miles across the moor to-night in the rain that it might reach 'em in time?'

'We did not drive entirely on account of these precious Londoners; we drove a little on our own – on account of that anxious matter which you will, I am sure, set at rest, dear Tess. Now, permit me to put it in this way. You belong to me already, you know; your heart, I mean. Does it not?'

'You know as well as I. O yes – yes!'

'Then, if your heart does, why not your hand?'

'My only reason was on account of you – on account of a question. I have something to tell you—'

'But suppose it to be entirely for my happiness, and my worldly convenience also?'

'O yes; if it is for your happiness and worldly convenience. But my life before I came here – I want—'

'Well, it is for my convenience as well as my happiness. If I have a very large farm, either English or colonial, you will be invaluable as a wife to me; better than a woman out of the largest mansion in the country. So please – please, dear Tessy, disabuse your mind of the feeling that you will stand in my way.'

'But my history. I want you to know it – you must let me tell you – you will not like me so well!'

'Tell it if you wish to, dearest. This precious history then. Yes, I was born at so and so, Anno Domini—'

'I was born at Marlott,' she said, catching at his words as a help, lightly as they were spoken. 'And I grew up there. And I was in the Sixth Standard when I left school, and they said I had great aptness, and should make a good teacher, so it was settled that I should be one. But there was trouble in my family; father was not very industrious, and he drank a little.'

'Yes, yes. Poor child! Nothing new.' He pressed her more closely to his side.

'And then – there is something very unusual about it – about me. I – I was—' Tess's breath quickened.

'Yes, dearest. Never mind.'

'I – I – am not a Durbeyfield, but a d'Urberville – a descendant of the same family as those that owned the old house we passed. And – we are all gone to nothing!'

'A d'Urberville! – Indeed! And is that all the trouble, dear Tess?'

'Yes,' she answered faintly.

'Well – why should I love you less after knowing this?'

'I was told by the dairyman that you hated old families.'

He laughed.

'Well, it is true, in one sense. I do hate the aristocratic principle of blood before everything, and do think that as reasoners the only pedigrees we ought to respect are those spiritual ones of the wise and virtuous, without regard to corporeal paternity. But I am extremely interested in this news – you can have no idea how interested I am! Are not you interested yourself in being one of that well-known line?'

'No. I have thought it sad – especially since coming here, and knowing that many of the hills and fields I see once belonged to my father's people. But other hills and fields belonged to Retty's people, and perhaps others to Marian's, so that I don't value it particularly.'

'Yes – it is surprising how many of the present tillers of the soil were once owners of it, and I sometimes wonder that a certain school of politicians don't make capital of the circumstance; but they don't seem to know it. . . . I wonder that I did not see the resemblance of your name to d'Urberville, and trace the manifest corruption. And this was the carking secret!'

She had not told. At the last moment her courage had failed her, she feared his blame for not telling him sooner; and her instinct of self-preservation was stronger than her candour.

'Of course,' continued the unwitting Clare, 'I should have been glad to know you to be descended exclusively from the long-suffering, dumb, unrecorded rank and file of the English nation, and not from the self-seeking few who made themselves powerful at the expense of the rest. But I am corrupted away from that by my affection for you, Tess [he laughed as he spoke], and made selfish likewise. For your own sake I rejoice in your descent. Society is hopelessly snobbish, and this fact of your extraction may make an appreciable difference to its acceptance of you as my wife, after I have made you the well-read woman that I mean to make you. My mother too, poor soul, will think so much better of you on account of it. Tess, you must spell your name correctly – d'Urberville – from this very day.'

'I like the other way rather best.'

'But you *must*, dearest! Good heavens, why dozens of mushroom millionaires would jump at such a possession! By the bye, there's one of that kidney who has taken the name – where have I heard of him? – Up in the neighbourhood of The Chase, I think. Why, he is the very man who had that rumpus with my father I told you of. What an odd coincidence!'

'Angel, I think I would rather not take the name! It is unlucky, perhaps!'

She was agitated.

'Now then, Mistress Teresa d'Urberville, I have you. Take my name, and so you will escape yours! The secret is out, so why should you any longer refuse me?'

'If it is *sure* to make you happy to have me as your wife, and you feel that you do wish to marry me, *very, very* much—'

'I do, dearest, of course!'

'I mean, that it is only your wanting me very much, and being hardly able to keep alive without me, whatever my offences, that would make me feel I ought to say I will.'

'You will – you do say it, I know! You will be mine for ever and ever.'

He clasped her close and kissed her.

'Yes!'

She had no sooner said it than she burst into a dry hard sobbing, so violent that it seemed to rend her. Tess was not a hysterical girl by any means, and he was surprised.

'Why do you cry, dearest?'

'I can't tell – quite! – I am so glad to think – of being yours, and making you happy!'

'But this does not seem very much like gladness, my Tessy!'

'I mean – I cry because I have broken down in my vow! I said I would die unmarried!'

'But, if you love me you would like me to be your husband?'

'Yes, yes, yes! But O, I sometimes wish I had never been born!'

'Now, my dear Tess, if I did not know that you are very much excited, and very inexperienced, I should say that remark was not very complimentary. How came you to wish that if you care for me? Do you care for me? I wish you would prove it in some way.'

'How can I prove it more than I have done?' she cried, in a distraction of tenderness. 'Will this prove it more?'

She clasped his neck, and for the first time Clare learnt what an impassioned woman's kisses were like upon the lips of one whom she loved with all her heart and soul, as Tess loved him.

'There – now do you believe?' she asked, flushed, and wiping her eyes.

'Yes. I never really doubted – never, never!'

So they drove on through the gloom, forming one bundle inside the sail-cloth, the horse going as he would, and the rain driving against them. She had consented. She might as well have agreed at first. The 'appetite for joy' which pervades all creation, that tremendous force which sways humanity to its purpose, as the tide sways the helpless weed, was not to be controlled by vague lucubrations over the social rubric.

'I must write to my mother,' she said. 'You don't mind my doing that?'

'Of course not, dear child. You are a child to me, Tess, not to know how very proper it is to write to your mother at such a time, and how wrong it would be in me to object. Where does she live?'

'At the same place – Marlott. On the further side of Blackmoor Vale.'

'Ah, then I *have* seen you before this summer—'

'Yes; at that dance on the green; but you would not dance with me. O, I hope that is of no ill-omen for us now!'

CHAPTER THIRTY-ONE

TESS wrote a most touching and urgent letter to her mother the very next day, and by the end of the week a respose to her communication arrived in Joan Durbeyfield's wandering last-century hand.

DEAR TESS, — J write these few lines Hoping they will find you well, as they leave me at Present, thank God for it. Dear Tess, we are all glad to Hear that you are going really to be married soon. But with respect to your question, Tess, J say between ourselves, quite private but very strong, that on no account do you say a word of your Bygone Trouble to him. J did not tell everything to your Father, he being so Proud on account of his Respectability, which, perhaps, your Intended is the same. Many a woman — some of the Highest in the Land — have had a Trouble in their time; and why should you Trumpet yours when others don't Trumpet theirs? No girl would be such a Fool, specially as it is so long ago, and not your Fault at all. J shall answer the same if you ask me fifty times. Besides, you must bear in mind that, knowing it to be your Childish Nature to tell all that's in your heart — so simple! — J made you promise me never to let it out by Word or Deed, having your Welfare in my Mind; and you most solemnly did promise it going from this Door. J have not named either that Question or your coming marriage to your Father, as he would blab it everywhere, poor Simple Man.

Dear Tess, keep up your Spirits, and we mean to send you a Hogshead of Cyder for your Wedding knowing there is not much in your parts, and thin Sour Stuff what there is. So no more at present, and with kind love to your Young Man. — From your affectte. Mother,
J. DURBEYFIELD

'O mother, mother!' murmured Tess.

She was recognizing how light was the touch of events the most oppressive upon Mrs Durbeyfield's elastic spirit. Her mother did not see life as Tess saw it. That haunting episode of bygone days was to her mother but a passing accident. But perhaps her mother was right as to the course to be followed, whatever she might be in her reasons. Silence seemed, on the face of it, best for her adored one's happiness: silence it should be.

Thus steadied by a command from the only person in the world who had any shadow of right to control her action, Tess grew calmer. The responsibility was shifted, and her heart was lighter than it had been for weeks. The days of declining autumn which followed her assent, beginning with the month of October, formed a season through which she lived in spiritual altitudes more nearly approaching ecstasy than any other period of her life.

There was hardly a touch of earth in her love for Clare. To her sublime trustfulness he was all that goodness could be — knew all that a guide, philosopher, and friend should know. She thought every line in the contour of his person the perfection of masculine beauty, his soul the soul of a saint, his intellect that of a seer. The wisdom of her love for him, as love, sustained her dignity; she seemed to be wearing a crown. The compassion of his love for her, as she saw it, made her lift up her heart to him in devotion. He would sometimes catch her large, worshipful eyes, that had no bottom to them, looking at him from their depths, as if she saw something immortal before her.

She dismissed the past — trod upon it and put it out, as one treads on a coal that is smouldering and dangerous.

She had not known that men could be so disinterested, chivalrous, protective, in their love for women as he. Angel Clare was far from all that she thought him in this respect; absurdly far, indeed; but he was, in truth, more spiritual than animal; he had himself well in hand, and was singularly free from grossness. Though not cold-natured, he was rather bright than hot — less Byronic than Shelleyan; could love desperately, but with a love more especially inclined to the imaginative and ethereal; it was a fastidious emotion which could jealously guard the loved one against his very self. This amazed and enraptured Tess, whose slight experiences had been so infelicitous till now; and in her reaction from indignation against the male sex she swerved to excess of honour for Clare.

They unaffectedly sought each other's company; in her honest faith she did not disguise her desire to be with him. The sum of her instincts on this matter, if clearly stated, would have been that the elusive quality in her sex which attracts men in general might be distasteful to so perfect a man after an avowal of love, since it must in its very nature carry with it a suspicion of art.

The country custom of unreserved comradeship out of doors during betrothal was the only custom she knew, and to her it had no strangeness; though it seemed oddly anticipative to Clare till he saw how normal a thing she, in common with all the other dairy-folk, regarded it. Thus, during this October month of wonderful afternoons they roved along the meads by creeping paths which followed the brinks of trickling tributary brooks, hopping across by little wooden bridges to the other side, and back again. They were never out of the sound of some purling weir, whose buzz accompanied their own murmuring, while the beams of the sun, almost as horizontal as the mead itself, formed a pollen of radiance over the landscape. They saw tiny blue fogs in the shadows of trees and hedges, all the time that there was bright sunshine elsewhere. The sun was so near the ground, and the sward so flat, that the shadows of Clare and Tess would stretch a quarter of a mile ahead of them, like two long fingers pointing afar to where the green alluvial reaches abutted against the sloping sides of the vale.

Men were at work here and there – for it was the season for 'taking up' the meadows, or digging the little waterways clear for the winter irrigation, and mending their banks where trodden down by the cows. The shovelfuls of loam, black as jet, brought there by the river when it was as wide as the whole valley, were an essence of soils, pounded champaigns of the past, steeped, refined, and subtilized to extraordinary richness, out of which came all the fertility of the mead, and of the cattle grazing there.

Clare hardily kept his arm round her waist in sight of these water-men, with the air of a man who was accustomed to public dalliance, though actually as shy as she who, with lips parted and eyes askance on the labourers, wore the look of a wary animal the while.

'You are not ashamed of owning me as yours before them!' she said gladly.

'Oh no!'

'But if it should reach the ears of your friends at Emminster that you are walking about like this with me, a milkmaid—'

'The most bewitching milkmaid ever seen.'

'They might feel it a hurt to their dignity.'

'My dear girl – a d'Urberville hurt the dignity of a Clare! It is a grand card to play – that of your belonging to such a family, and I am reserving it for a grand effect when we are married, and have the proofs of your descent from Parson Tringham. Apart from that, my future is to be totally foreign to my family – it will not affect even the surface of their lives. We shall leave this part of England – perhaps England itself – and what does it matter how people regard us here? You will like going, will you not?'

She could answer no more than a bare affirmative, so great was the emotion aroused in her at the thought of going through the world with him as his own familiar friend. Her feelings almost filled her ears like a babble of waves, and

surged up to her eyes. .
where the reflected sun g..
metallic glow that dazzled t..
bridge. They stood still, whereup his, and thus they went on, to a place
from the smooth surface of the wat..ver, under a bridge, with a molten-
had paused, and not passed by, they a.he sun itself was hidden by the
they lingered till the fog began to close round feathered heads popped up
evening at this time of the year — settling on the .at the disturbing presences
like crystals, and on his brows and hair. .in. Upon this river-brink
                                           .ch was very early in the
They walked later on Sundays, when it was quite eyes, where it rested
people, who were also out of doors on the first Sund.. .e of the dairy-
engagement, heard her impulsive speeches, ecstasized to fragi..ng after their
were too far off to hear the words discoursed; noted the spasmo.hough they
remarks, broken into syllables by the leapings of her heart, as she wa..ch in her
on his arm; her contented pauses, the occasional little laugh upon which i..aning
seemed to ride — the laugh of a woman in company with the man she loves a..oul
has won from all other women — unlike anything else in nature. They marked the
buoyancy of her tread, like the skim of a bird which has not quite alighted.

Her affection for him was now the breath and life of Tess's being; it enveloped
her as a photosphere, irradiated her into forgetfulness of her past sorrows,
keeping back the gloomy spectres that would persist in their attempts to touch
her — doubt, fear, moodiness, care, shame. She knew that they were waiting like
wolves just outside the circumscribing light, but she had long spells of power to
keep them in hungry subjection there.

A spiritual forgetfulness co-existed with an intellectual remembrance. She
walked in brightness, but she knew that in the background those shapes of
darkness were always spread. They might be receding, or they might be
approaching, one or the other, a little every day.

One evening Tess and Clare were obliged to sit indoors keeping house, all the
other occupants of the domicile being away. As they talked she looked
thoughtfully up at him, and met his two appreciative eyes.

'I am not worthy of you — no, I am not!' she burst out, jumping up from her
low stool as though appalled at his homage, and the fulness of her own joy
thereat.

Clare, deeming the whole basis of her excitement to be that which was only the
smaller part of it, said —

'I won't have you speak like it, dear Tess! Distinction does not consist in the
facile use of a contemptible set of conventions, but in being numbered among
those who are true, and honest, and just, and pure, and lovely, and of good
report — as you are, my Tess.'

She struggled with the sob in her throat. How often had that string of
excellences made her young heart ache in church of late years, and how strange
that he should have cited them now.

'Why didn't you stay and love me when I — was sixteen; living with my little
sisters and brothers, and you danced on the green? O, why didn't you, why didn't
you!' she said, impetuously clasping her hands.

Angel began to comfort and reassure her, thinking to himself, truly enough,

areful he would have to be of her
.ely on him.
. is just what I feel. If I had only known!
regret — why should you be?'
'Ah — why didn't I stay... de she diverged hastily —
But you must not be so... more of your heart than I can ever have now.
With the woman's ...d my time as I have done — I should have had so
'I should have ha...
Then I should no...an with a long dark vista of intrigue behind her who was
much longer ha... a girl of simple life, not yet one-and-twenty, who had been
It was no m... days of immaturity like a bird in a springe. To calm herself the
tormented ... caught du...ly she rose from her little stool and left the room, overturning the
more con...er skirts as she went.
stool ...on by the cheerful firelight thrown from a bundle of green ash-sticks laid
...ss the dogs; the sticks snapped pleasantly, and hissed out bubbles of sap from
... heir ends. When she came back she was herself again.

'Do you not think you are just a wee bit capricious, fitful, Tess?' he said, good humouredly, as he spread a cushion for her on the stool, and seated himself in the settle beside her. 'I wanted to ask you something, and just then you ran away.'

'Yes, perhaps I am capricious,' she murmured. She suddenly approached him, and put a hand upon each of his arms. 'No, Angel, I am not really so — by nature, I mean!' The more particularly to assure him that she was not, she placed herself close to him in the settle, and allowed her head to find a resting-place against Clare's shoulder. 'What did you want to ask me — I am sure I will answer it,' she continued humbly.

'Well, you love me, and have agreed to marry me, and hence there follows a thirdly, "When shall the day be?"'

'I like living like this.'

'But I must think of starting in business on my own hook with the new year, or a little later. And before I get involved in the multifarious details of my new position, I should like to have secured my partner.'

'But,' she timidly answered, 'to talk quite practically, wouldn't it be best not to marry till after all that? — Though I can't bear the thought o' your going away and leaving me here!'

'Of course you cannot — and it is not best in this case. I want you to help me in many ways in making my start. When shall it be? Why not a fortnight from now?'

'No,' she said, becoming grave; 'I have so many things to think of first.'

'But—'

He drew her gently nearer to him.

The reality of marriage was startling when it loomed so near. Before discussion of the question had proceeded further there walked round the corner of the settle into the full firelight of the apartment Mr Dairyman Crick, Mrs Crick, and two of the milkmaids.

Tess sprang like an elastic ball from his side to her feet, while her face flushed and her eyes shone in the firelight.

'I knew how it would be if I sat so close to him!' she cried, with vexation. 'I said to myself, they are sure to come and catch us! But I wasn't really sitting on his knee, though it might ha' seemed as if I was almost!'

'Well – if so be you hadn't told us, I am sure we shouldn't ha' noticed that ye had been sitting anywhere at all in this light,' replied the dairyman. He continued to his wife, with the stolid mien of a man who understood nothing of the emotions relating to matrimony – Now, Christianer, that shows that folks should never fancy other folks be supposing things when they bain't. O no, I should never ha' thought a word of where she was a sitting to, if she hadn't told me – not I.'

'We are going to be married soon,' said Clare, with improvised phlegm.

'Ah – and be ye! Well, I am truly glad to hear it, sir. I've thought you mid do such a thing for some time. She's too good for a dairymaid – I said so the very first day I zid her – and a prize for any man; and what's more, a wonderful woman for a gentleman-farmer's wife; he won't be at the mercy of his baily wi' her at his side.'

Somehow Tess disappeared. She had been even more struck with the look of the girls who followed Crick than abashed by Crick's blunt praise.

After supper, when she reached her bedroom, they were all present. A light was burning, and each damsel was sitting up whitely in her bed, awaiting Tess, the whole like a row of avenging ghosts.

But she saw in a few moments that there was no malice in their mood. They could scarcely feel as a loss what they had never expected to have. Their condition was objective, contemplative.

'He's going to marry her!' murmured Retty, never taking eyes off Tess. 'How her face do show it!'

'You *be* going to marry him?' asked Marian.

'Yes,' said Tess.

'When?'

'Some day.'

They thought that this was evasiveness only.

'*Yes* – going to *marry* him – a gentleman!' repeated Izz Huett.

And by a sort of fascination the three girls, one after another, crept out of their beds, and came and stood barefooted round Tess. Retty put her hands upon Tess's shoulders, as if to realize her friend's corporeality after such a miracle, and the other two laid their arms round her waist, all looking into her face.

'How it do seem! Almost more than I can think of!' said Izz Huett.

Marian kissed Tess. 'Yes,' she murmured as she withdrew her lips.

'Was that because of love for her, or because other lips have touched there by now?' continued Izz drily to Marian.

'I wasn't thinking o' that,' said Marian simply. 'I was on'y feeling all the strangeness o't – that she is to be his wife, and nobody else. I don't say nay to it, nor either of us, because we did not think of it – only loved him. Still, nobody else is to marry'n in the world – no fine lady, nobody in silks and satins; but she who do live like we.'

'Are you sure you don't dislike me for it?' said Tess in a low voice.

They hung about her in their white neightgowns before replying, as if they considered their answer might lie in her look.

'I don't know – I don't know,' murmured Retty Priddle. 'I want to hate 'ee; but I cannot!'

'That's how I feel,' echoed Izz and Marian. 'I can't hate her. Somehow she hinders me!'

'He ought to marry one of you,' murmured Tess.

'Why?'

'You are all better than I.'

'We better than you?' said the girls in a low, slow whisper. 'No, no, dear Tess!'

'You are!' she contradicted impetuously. And suddenly tearing away from their clinging arms she burst into a hysterical fit of tears, bowing herself on the chest of drawers and repeating incessantly, 'O yes, yes, yes!'

Having once given way she could not stop her weeping.

'He ought to have had one of you!' she cried. 'I think I ought to make him even now! You would be better for him than – I don't know what I'm saying! O! O!'

They went up to her and clasped her round, but still her sobs tore her.

'Get some water,' said Marian. 'She's upset by us, poor thing, poor thing!'

They gently led her back to the side of her bed, where they kissed her warmly.

'You are best for'n,' said Marian. 'More ladylike, and a better scholar than we, especially since he has taught 'ee so much. But even you ought to be proud. You *be* proud, I'm sure!'

'Yes, I am,' she said; 'and I am ashamed at so breaking down!'

When they were all in bed, and the light was out, Marian whispered across to her –

'You will think of us when you be his wife, Tess, and of how we told 'ee that we loved him, and how we tried not to hate you, and did not hate you, and could not hate you, because you were his choice, and we never hoped to be chose by him.'

They were not aware that, at these words, salt, stinging tears trickled down upon Tess's pillow anew, and how she resolved, with a bursting heart, to tell all her history to Angel Clare, despite her mother's command – to let him for whom she lived and breathed despise her if he would, and her mother regard her as a fool, rather than preserve a silence which might be deemed a treachery to him, and which somehow seemed a wrong to these.

CHAPTER THIRTY-TWO

T his penitential mood kept her from naming the wedding-day. The beginning of November found its date still in abeyance, though he asked her at the most tempting times. But Tess's desire seemed to be for a perpetual betrothal in which everything should remain as it was then.

The meads were changing now; but it was still warm enough in early afternoons before milking to idle there awhile, and the state of dairy-work at this time of year allowed a spare hour for idling. Looking over the damp sod in the direction of the sun, a glistening ripple of gossamer webs was visible to their eyes under the luminary, like the track of moonlight on the sea. Gnats, knowing nothing of their brief glorification, wandered across the shimmer of this pathway, irradiated as if they bore fire within them, then passed out of its line, and were quite extinct. In the presence of these things he would remind her that the date was still the question.

Or he would ask her at night, when he accompanied her on some mission invented by Mrs Crick to give him the opportunity. This was mostly a journey to the farmhouse on the slopes above the vale, to inquire how the advanced cows were getting on in the straw-barton to which they were relegated. For it was a time of the year that brought great changes to the world of kine. Batches of the animals were sent away daily to this lying-in hospital, where they lived on straw till their calves were born, after which event, and as soon as the calf could walk, mother and offspring were driven back to the dairy. In the interval which elapsed before the calves were sold there was, of course, little milking to be done, but as soon as the calf had been taken away the milkmaids would have to set to work as usual.

Returning from one of these dark walks they reached a great gravel-cliff immediately over the levels, where they stood still and listened. The water was now high in the streams, squirting through the weirs, and tinkling under culverts; the smallest gullies were all full; there was no taking short cuts anywhere, and foot-passengers were compelled to follow the permanent ways. From the whole extent of the invisible vale came a multitudinous intonation; it forced upon their fancy that a great city lay below them, and that the murmur was the vociferation of its populace.

'It seems like tens of thousands of them,' said Tess; 'holding public-meetings in their market-places, arguing, preaching, quarrelling, sobbing, groaning, praying, and cursing.'

Clare was not particularly heeding.

'Did Crick speak to you to-day, dear, about his not wanting much assistance during the winter months?'

'No.'

'The cows are going dry rapidly.'

'Yes. Six or seven went to the straw-barton yesterday, and three the day before, making nearly twenty in the straw already. Ah — is it that the farmer don't want my help for the calving? O, I am not wanted here any more! And I have tried so hard to—'

'Crick didn't exactly say that he would no longer require you. But, knowing what our relations were, he said in the most good-natured and respectful manner possible that he supposed on my leaving at Christmas I should take you with me, and on my asking what he would do without you he merely observed that, as a matter of fact, it was a time of year when he could do with a very little female help. I am afraid I was sinner enough to feel rather glad that he was in this way forcing your hand.'

'I don't think you ought to have felt glad, Angel. Because 'tis always mournful not to be wanted, even if at the same time 'tis convenient.'

'Well, it is convenient — you have admitted that.' He put his finger upon her cheek. 'Ah!' he said.

'What?'

'I feel the red rising up at her having been caught! But why should I trifle so! We will not trifle — life is too serious.'

'It is. Perhaps I saw that before you did.'

She was seeing it then. To decline to marry him after all – in obedience to her emotion of last night – and leave the dairy, meant to go to some strange place, not a dairy; for milkmaids were not in request now calving-time was coming on; to go to some arable farm where no divine being like Angel Clare was. She hated the thought, and she hated more the thought of going home.

'So that, seriously, dearest Tess,' he continued, 'since you will probably have to leave at Christmas, it is in every way desirable and convenient that I should carry you off then as my property. Besides, if you were not the most uncalculating girl in the world you would know that we could not go on like this for ever.'

'I wish we could. That it would always be summer and autumn, and you always courting me, and always thinking as much of me as you have done through the past summer-time!'

'I always shall.'

'O, I know you will!' she cried, with a sudden fervour of faith in him. 'Angel, I will fix the day when I will become yours for always!'

Thus at last it was arranged between them, during that dark walk home, amid the myriads of liquid voices on the right and left.

When they reached the dairy Mr and Mrs Crick were promptly told – with injunctions to secrecy; for each of the lovers was desirous that the marriage should be kept as private as possible. The dairyman, though he had thought of dismissing her soon, now made a great concern about losing her. What should he do about his skimming? Who would make the ornamental butter-pats for the Anglebury and Sandbourne ladies? Mrs Crick congratulated Tess on the shilly-shallying having at last come to an end, and said that directly she set eyes on Tess she divined that she was to be the chosen one of somebody who was no common outdoor man; Tess had looked so superior as she walked across the barton on that afternoon of her arrival; that she was of a good family she could have sworn. In point of fact Mrs Crick did remember thinking that Tess was graceful and good-looking as she approached; but the superiority might have been a growth of the imagination aided by subsequent knowledge.

Tess was now carried along upon the wings of the hours, without the sense of a will. The word had been given; the number of the day written down. Her naturally bright intelligence had begun to admit the fatalistic convictions common to field-folk and those who associate more extensively with natural phenomena than with their fellow-creatures; and she accordingly drifted into that passive responsiveness to all things her lover suggested, characteristic of the frame of mind.

But she wrote anew to her mother, ostensibly to notify the wedding-day; really to again implore her advice. It was a gentleman who had chosen her, which perhaps her mother had not sufficiently considered. A post-nuptial explanation, which might be accepted with a light heart by a rougher man, might not be received with the same feeling by him. But this communication brought no reply from Mrs Durbeyfield.

Despite Angel Clare's plausible representations to himself and to Tess of the practical need for their immediate marriage, there was in truth an element of precipitancy in the step, as became apparent at a later date. He loved her dearly, though perhaps rather ideally and fancifully than with the impassioned thoroughness of her feeling for him. He had entertained no notion, when doomed as he had thought to an unintellectual bucolic life, that such charms as he beheld in this idyllic creature would be found behind the scenes. Unsophistication was a thing to talk of; but he had not known how it really struck one until he came here. Yet he was very far from seeing his future track clearly, and it might be a year or two before he would be able to consider himself fairly started in life. The secret lay in the tinge of recklessness imparted to his career and character by the sense that he had been made to miss his true destiny through the prejudices of his family.

'Don't you think 'twould have been better for us to wait till you were quite settled in your midland farm?' she once asked timidly. (A midland farm was the idea just then.)

'To tell the truth, my Tess, I don't like you to be left anywhere away from my protection and sympathy.'

The reason was a good one, so far as it went. His influence over her had been so marked that she had caught his manner and habits, his speech and phrases, his likings and his aversions. And to leave her in farmland would be to let her slip back again out of accord with him. He wished to have her under his charge for another reason. His parents had naturally desired to see her once at least before he carried her off to a distant settlement, English or colonial; and as no opinion of theirs was to be allowed to change his intention, he judged that a couple of months' life with him in lodgings whilst seeking for an advantageous opening would be of some social assistance to her at what she might feel to be a trying ordeal – her presentation to his mother at the Vicarage.

Next, he wished to see a little of the working of a flour-mill, having an idea that he might combine the use of one with corn-growing. The proprietor of a large old water-mill at Wellbridge – once the mill of an Abbey – had offered him the inspection of his time-honoured mode of procedure, and a hand in the operations for a few days, whenever he should choose to come. Clare paid a visit to the place, some few miles distant, one day at this time, to inquire particulars, and returned to Talbothays in the evening. She found him determined to spend a short time at the Wellbridge flour-mills. And what had determined him? Less the opportunity of an insight into grinding and bolting than the casual fact that lodgings were to be obtained in that very farmhouse which, before its mutilation, had been the mansion of a branch of the d'Urberville family. This was always how Clare settled practical questions; by a sentiment which had nothing to do with them. They decided to go immediately after the wedding, and remain for a fortnight, instead of journeying to towns and inns.

'Then we will start off to examine some farms on the other side of London that I have heard of,' he said, 'and by March or April we will pay a visit to my father and mother.'

Questions of procedure such as these arose and passed, and the day, the incredible day, on which she was to become his, loomed large in the near future. The thirty-first of December, New Year's Eve, was the date. His wife, she said to herself. Could it ever be? Their two selves together, nothing to divide them, every incident shared by them; why not? And yet why?

One Sunday morning Izz Huett returned from church, and spoke privately to Tess.

'You was not called home[1] this morning.'

'What?'

'It should ha' been the first time of asking to-day,' she answered, looking quietly at Tess. 'You meant to be married New Year's Eve, deary?'

The other returned a quick affirmative.

'And there must be three times of asking. And now there be only two Sundays left between.'

Tess felt her cheek paling; Izz was right; of course there must be three. Perhaps he had forgotten! If so, there must be a week's postponement, and that was unlucky. How could she remind her lover? She who had been so backward was suddenly fired with impatience and alarm lest she should lose her dear prize.

A natural incident relieved her anxiety. Izz mentioned the omission of the banns to Mrs Crick, and Mrs Crick assumed a matron's privilege of speaking to Angel on the point.

'Have ye forgot 'em, Mr Clare? The banns, I mean.'

'No, I have not forgot 'em,' says Clare.

As soon as he caught Tess alone he assured her:

'Don't let them tease you about the banns. A licence will be quieter for us, and I have decided on a licence without consulting you. So if you go to church on Sunday morning you will not hear your own name, if you wished to.'

'I didn't wish to hear it, dearest,' she said proudly.

But to know that things were in train was an immense relief to Tess notwithstanding, who had wellnigh feared that somebody would stand up and forbid the banns on the ground of her history. How events were favouring her!

'I don't quite feel easy,' she said to herself. 'All this good fortune may be scourged out of me afterwards by a lot of ill. That's how Heaven mostly does. I wish I could have had common banns!'

But everything went smoothly. She wondered whether he would like her to be married in her present best white frock, or if she ought to buy a new one. The question was set at rest by his forethought, disclosed by the arrival of some large packages addressed to her. Inside them she found a whole stock of clothing, from bonnet to shoes, including a perfect morning costume, such as would well suit the simple wedding they planned. He entered the house shortly after the arrival of the packages, and heard her upstairs undoing them.

A minute later she came down with a flush on her face and tears in her eyes.

'How thoughtful you've been!' she murmured, her cheek upon his shoulder. 'Even to the gloves and handkerchief! My own love – how good, how kind!'

'No, no, Tess; just an order to a tradeswoman in London – nothing more.'

And to divert her from thinking too highly of him he told her to go upstairs, and take her time, and see if it all fitted; and, if not, to get the village sempstress to make a few alterations.

She did return upstairs, and put on the gown. Alone, she stood for a moment

---

[1] 'Called home' – local phrase for publication of banns.

before the glass looking at the effect of her silk attire; and then there came into her head her mother's ballad of the mystic robe —

> That never would become that wife
> That had once done amiss,

which Mrs Durbeyfield had used to sing to her as a child, so blithely and so archly, her foot on the cradle, which she rocked to the tune. Suppose this robe should betray her by changing colour, as her robe had betrayed Queen Guénever. Since she had been at the dairy she had not once thought of the lines till now.

CHAPTER THIRTY-THREE

A NGEL felt that he would like to spend a day with her before the wedding, somewhere away from the dairy, as a last jaunt in her company while they were yet mere lover and mistress; a romantic day, in circumstances that would never be repeated; with that other and greater day beaming close ahead of them. During the preceding week, therefore, he suggested making a few purchases in the nearest town, and they started together.

Clare's life at the dairy had been that of a recluse in respect to the world of his own class. For months he had never gone near a town, and, requiring no vehicle, had never kept one, hiring the dairyman's cob or gig if he rode or drove. They went in the gig that day.

And then for the first time in their lives they shopped as partners in one concern. It was Christmas Eve, with its loads of holly and mistleoe, and the town was very full of strangers who had come in from all parts of the country on account of the day. Tess paid the penalty of walking about with happiness superadded to beauty on her countenance by being much stared at as she moved amid them on his arm.

In the evening they returned to the inn at which they had put up, and Tess waited in the entry while Angel went to see the horse and gig brought to the door. The general sitting-room was full of guests, who were continually going in and out. As the door opened and shut each time for the passage of these, the light within the parlour fell full upon Tess's face. Two men came out and passed by her among the rest. One of them had stared her up and down in surprise, and she fancied he was a Trantridge man, though that village lay so many miles off that Trantridge folk were rarities here.

'A comely maid that,' said the other.

'True, comely enough. But unless I make a great mistake—' And he negatived the remainder of the definition forthwith.

Clare had just returned from the stable-yard, and, confronting the man on the threshold, heard the words, and saw the shrinking of Tess. The insult to her stung him to the quick, and before he had considered anything at all he struck the man on the chin with the full force of his fist, sending him staggering backwards into the passage.

The man recovered himself, and seemed inclined to come on, and Clare, stepping outside the door, put himself in a posture of defence. But his opponent began to think better of the matter. He looked anew at Tess as he passed her, and said to Clare –

'I beg pardon, sir; 'twas a complete mistake. I thought she was another woman, forty miles from here.'

Clare, feeling then that he had been too hasty, and that he was, moreover, to blame for leaving her standing in an inn-passage, did what he usually did in such cases, gave the man five shillings to plaster the blow; and thus they parted, bidding each other a pacific good-night. As soon as Clare had taken the reins from the ostler, and the young couple had driven off, the two men went in the other direction.

'And was it a mistake?' said the second one.

'Not a bit of it. But I didn't want to hurt the gentleman's feelings – not I.'

In the meatime the lovers were driving onward.

'Could we put off our wedding till a little later?' Tess asked in a dry dull voice.'I mean if we wished?'

'No, my love. Calm yourself. Do you mean that the fellow may have time to summon me for assault?' he asked good-humouredly.

'No – I only meant – if it should have to be put off.'

What she meant was not very clear, and he directed her to dismiss such fancies from her mind, which she obediently did as well as she could. But she was grave, very grave, all the way home; till she thought, 'We shall go away, a very long distance, hundreds of miles from these parts, and such as this can never happen again, and no ghosts of the past reach there.'

They parted tenderly that night on the landing, and Clare ascended to his attic. Tess sat up getting on with some little requisites, lest the few remaining days should not afford sufficient time. While she sat she heard a noise in Angel's room overhead, a sound of thumping and struggling. Everybody else in the house was asleep, and in her anxiety lest Clare should be ill she ran up and knocked at his door, and asked him what was the matter.

'Oh, nothing, dear,' he said from within. 'I am so sorry I disturbed you! But the reason is rather an amusing one: I fell asleep and dreamt that I was fighting that fellow again who insulted you and the noise you heard was my pummelling away with my fists at my portmanteau, which I pulled out to-day for packing. I am occasionally liable to these freaks in my sleep. Go to bed and think of it no more.'

This was the last drachm required to turn the scale of her indecision. Declare the past to him by word of mouth she could not; but there was another way. She sat down and wrote on the four pages of a note-sheet a succinct narrative of those events of three or four years ago, put it into an envelope, and directed it to Clare. Then, lest the flesh should again be weak, she crept upstairs without any shoes and slipped the note under his door.

Her night was a broken one, as it well might be, and she listened for the first faint noise overhead. It came, as usual; he descended, as usual. She descended. He met her at the bottom of the stairs and kissed her. Surely it was as warmly as ever!

He looked a little disturbed and worn, she thought. But he said not a word to her about her revelation, even when they were alone. Could he have had it? Unless he began the subject she felt that she could say nothing. So the day passed, and it was evident that whatever he thought he meant to keep to himself. Yet he was frank and affectionate as before. Could it be that her doubts were childish? that he forgave her; that he loved her for what she was, just as she was, and smiled at her disquiet as at a foolish nightmare? Had he really received her note? She glanced into his room, and could see nothing of it. It might be that he forgave her. But even if he had not received it she had a sudden enthusiastic trust that he surely would forgive her.

Every morning and night he was the same, and thus New Year's Eve broke – the wedding-day.

The lovers did not rise at milking-time, having through the whole of this last week of their sojourn at the dairy been accorded something of the position of guests, Tess being honoured with a room of her own. When they arrived downstairs at breakfast-time they were surprised to see what effects had been produced in the large kitchen for their glory since they had last beheld it. At some unnatural hour of the morning the dairyman had caused the yawning chimney-corner to be whitened, and the brick hearth reddened, and a blazing yellow damask blower to be hung across the arch in place of the old grimy blue cotton one with a black strip pattern which had formerly done duty here. This renovated aspect of what was the focus indeed of the room on a dull winter morning, threw a smiling demeanour over the whole apartment.

'I was determined to do summat in honour o't,' said the dairyman. 'And as you wouldn't hear of my gieing a rattling good randy wi' fiddles and bass-viols complete, as we should ha' done in old times, this was all I could think o' as a noiseless thing.'

Tess's friends lived so far off that none could conveniently have been present at the ceremony, even had any been asked; but as a fact nobody was invited from Marlott. As for Angel's family, he had written and duly informed them of the time, and assured them that he would be glad to see one at least of them there for the day if he would like to come. His brothers had not replied at all, seeming to be indignant with him; while his father and mother had written a rather sad letter, deploring his precipitancy in rushing into marriage, but making the best of the matter by saying that, though a dairywoman was the last daughter-in-law they could have expected, their son had arrived at an age at which he might be supposed to be the best judge.

This coolness in his relations distressed Clare less than it would have done had he been without the grand card with which he meant to surprise them ere long. To produce Tess, fresh from the dairy, as a d'Urberville and a lady, he had felt to be temerarious and risky; hence he had concealed her lineage till such time as, familiarized with worldly ways by a few months' travel and reading with him, he could take her on a visit to his parents, and impart the knowledge while triumphantly producing her as worthy of such an ancient line. It was a pretty lover's dream, if no more. Perhaps Tess's lineage had more value for himself than for anybody in the world besides.

Her perception that Angel's bearing towards her still remained in no whit altered by her own communication rendered Tess guiltily doubtful if he could have received it. She rose from breakfast before he had finished, and hastened upstairs. It had occurred to her to look once more into the queer gaunt room which had been Clare's den, or rather eyrie, for so long, and climbing the ladder she stood at the open door of the apartment, regarding and pondering. She stooped to the threshold of the doorway, where she had pushed in the note two or three days earlier in such excitement. The carpet reached close to the sill, and under the edge of the carpet she discerned the faint white margin of the envelope containing her letter to him, which he obviously had never seen, owing to her having in her haste thrust it beneath the carpet as well as beneath the door.

With a feeling of faintness she withdrew the letter. There it was – sealed up, just as it had left her hands. The mountain had not yet been removed. She could not let him read it now, the house being in full bustle of preparation; and descending to her own room she destroyed the letter there.

She was so pale when he saw her again that he felt quite anxious. The incident of the misplaced letter she had jumped at as if it prevented a confession; but she knew in her conscience that it need not; there was still time. Yet everything was in a stir; there was coming and going; all had to dress, the dairyman and Mrs Crick having been asked to accompany them as witnesses; and reflection or deliberate talk was wellnigh impossible. The only minute Tess could get to be alone with Clare was when they met upon the landing.

'I am so anxious to talk to you – I want to confess all my faults and blunders!' she said with attempted lightness.

'No, no – we can't have faults talked of – you must be deemed perfect to-day at least, my Sweet!' he cried. 'We shall have plenty of time, hereafter, I hope, to talk over our failings. I will confess mine at the same time.'

'But it would be better for me to do it now, I think, so that you could not say—'

'Well, my quixotic one, you shall tell me anything – say, as soon as we are settled in our lodging; not now. I, too, will tell you my faults then. But do not let us spoil the day with them; they will be excellent matter for a dull time.'

'Then you don't wish me to, dearest?'

'I do not, Tessy, really.'

The hurry of dressing and starting left no time for more than this. Those words of his seemed to reassure her on further reflection. She was whirled onward through the next couple of critical hours by the mastering tide of her devotion to him, which closed up further meditation. Her one desire, so long resisted, to make herself his, to call him her lord, her own – then, if necessary, to die – had at last lifted her up from her plodding reflective pathway. In dressing, she moved about in a mental cloud of many-coloured idealities, which eclipsed all sinister contingencies by its brightness.

The church was a long way off, and they were obliged to drive, particularly as it was winter. A close carriage was ordered from a roadside inn, a vehicle which had been kept there ever since the old days of post-chaise travelling. It had stout wheel-spokes, and heavy felloes, a great curved bed, immense straps and springs, and a pole like a battering-ram. The postilion was a venerable 'boy' of sixty – a martyr to rheumatic gout, the result of excessive exposure in youth, counteracted by strong liquors – who had stood at inn-doors doing nothing for the whole five-and-twenty years that had elapsed since he had no longer been required to ride professionally, as if expecting the old times to come back again. He had a permanent running wound on the outside of his right leg, originated by the constant bruisings of aristocratic carriage-poles during the many years that he had been in regular employ at the King's Arms, Casterbridge.

Inside this cumbrous and creaking structure, and behind this decayed conductor, the *partie carrée* took their seats – the bride and bridegroom and Mr and Mrs Crick. Angel would have liked one at least of his brothers to be present as groomsman, but their silence after his gentle hint to that effect by letter had signified that they did not care to come. They disapproved of the marriage, and could not be expected to countenance it. Perhaps it was as well that they could not be present. They were not worldly young fellows, but fraternizing with dairy-folk would have struck unpleasantly upon their biassed niceness, apart from their views of the match.

Upheld by the momentum of the time Tess knew nothing of this; did not see anything; did not know the road they were taking to the church. She knew that Angel was close to her; all the rest was a luminous mist. She was a sort of celestial person, who owed her being to poetry – one of those classical divinities Clare was accustomed to talk to her about when they took their walks together.

The marriage being by licence there were only a dozen or so of people in the church; had there been a thousand they would have produced no more effect upon her. They were at stellar distances from her present world. In the ecstatic solemnity with which she swore her faith to him the ordinary sensibilities of sex seemed a flippancy. At a pause in the service, while they were kneeling together, she unconsciously inclined herself towards him, so that her shoulder touched his arm; she had been frightened by a passing thought, and the movement had been automatic, to assure herself that he was really there, and to fortify her belief that his fidelity would be proof against all things.

Clare knew that she loved him – every curve of her form showed that – but he did not know at that time the full depth of her devotion, its single-mindedness, its meekness; what long-suffering it guaranteed, what honesty, what endurance, what good faith.

As they came out of church the ringers swung the bells off their rests, and a modest peal of three notes broke forth – that limited amount of expression having been deemed sufficient by the church builders for the joys of such a small parish. Passing by the tower with her husband on the path to the gate she could feel the vibrant air humming round them from the louvred belfry in a circle of sound, and it matched the highly-charged mental atmosphere in which she was living.

This condition of mind, wherein she felt glorified by an irradiation not her own, like the angel whom St John saw in the sun, lasted till the sounds of the church bells had died away, and the emotions of the wedding-service had calmed down. Her eyes could dwell upon details more clearly now, and Mr and Mrs Crick having directed their own gig to be sent for them, to leave the carriage to the young couple, she observed the build and character of that conveyance for the first time. Sitting in silence she regarded it long.

'I fancy you seem oppressed, Tessy,' said Clare.

'Yes,' she answered, putting her hand to her brow. 'I tremble at many things. It is all so serious, Angel. Among other things I seem to have seen this carriage before, to be very well acquainted with it. It is very odd – I must have seen it in a dream.'

'Oh – you have heard the legend of the d'Urberville Coach – that well-known superstition of this county about your family when they were very popular here; and this lumbering old thing reminds you of it.'

'I have never heard of it to my knowledge,' said she. 'What is the legend – may I know it?'

'Well – I would rather not tell it in detail just now. A certain d'Urberville of the sixteenth or seventeenth century committed a dreadful crime in his family coach; and since that time members of the family see or hear the old coach whenever— But I'll tell you another day – it is rather gloomy. Evidently some dim knowledge of it has been brought back to your mind by the sight of this venerable caravan.'

'I don't remember hearing it before,' she murmured. 'Is it when we are going to die, Angel, that members of my family see it, or is it when we have committed a crime?'

'Now, Tess!'

He silenced her by a kiss.

By the time they reached home she was contrite and spiritless. She was Mrs Angel Clare, indeed, but had she any moral right to the name? Was she not more truly Mrs Alexander d'Urberville? Could intensity of love justify what might be conidered in upright souls as culpable reticence? She knew not what was expected of women in such cases; and she had no counsellor.

However, when she found herself alone in her room for a few minutes – the last day this on which she was ever to enter it – she knelt down and prayed. She tried to pray to God, but it was her husband who really had her supplication. Her idolatry of this man was such that she herself almost feared it to be ill-omened. She was conscious of the notion expressed by Friar Laurence: 'These violent delights have violent ends.' It might be too desperate for human conditions – too rank, too wild, too deadly.

'O my love, my love, why do I love you so!' she whispered there alone; 'for she you love is not my real self, but one in my image; the one I might have been!'

Afternoon came, and with it the hour for departure. They had decided to fulfil the plan of going for a few days to the lodgings in the old farmhouse near Wellbridge Mill, at which he meant to reside during his investigation of flour processes. At two o'clock there was nothing left to do but to start. All the servantry of the dairy were standing in the red-brick entry to see them go out, the dairyman and his wife following to the door. Tess saw her three chamber-mates in a row against the wall, pensively inclining their heads. She had much questioned if they would appear at the parting moment; but there they were, stoical and staunch to the last. She knew why the delicate Retty looked so fragile, and Izz so tragically sorrowful, and Marian so blank; and she forgot her own dogging shadow for a moment in contemplating theirs.

She impulsively whispered to him –

'Will you kiss 'em all, once, poor things, for the first and last time?'

Clare had not the least objection to such a farewell formality – which was all that it was to him – and as he passed them he kissed them in succession where they stood, saying 'Good-bye' to each as he did so. When they reached the door Tess femininely glanced back to discern the effect of that kiss of charity; there was no triumph in her glance, as there might have been. If there had it would have disappeared when she saw how moved the girls all were. The kiss had obviously done harm by awakening feelings they were trying to subdue.

Of all this Clare was unconscious. Passing on to the wicket-gate he shook hands with the dairyman and his wife, and expressed his last thanks to them for their attentions; after which there was a moment of silence before they had moved off. It was interrupted by the crowing of a cock. The white one with the rose comb had come and settled on the palings in front of the house, within a few yards of them, and his notes thrilled their ears through, dwindling away like echoes down a valley of rocks.

'Oh?' said Mrs Crick. 'An afternoon crow!'

Two men were standing by the yard gate, holding it open.

'That's bad,' one murmured to the other, not thinking that the words could be heard by the group at the door-wicket.

The cock crew again – straight towards Clare.

'Well!' said the dairyman.

'I don't like to hear him!' said Tess to her husband. 'Tell the man to drive on. Good-bye, good-bye!'

The cock crew again.

'Hoosh! Just you be off, sir, or I'll twist your neck!' said the dairyman with some irritation, turning to the bird and driving him away. And to his wife as they went indoors: 'Now, to think o' that just to-day! I've not heard his crow of an afternoon all the year afore.'

'It only means a change in the weather,' said she; 'not what you think: 'tis impossible!'

CHAPTER THIRTY-FOUR

THEY drove by the level road along the valley to a distance of a few miles, and, reaching Wellbridge, turned away from the village to the left, and over the great Elizabethan bridge which gives the place half its name. Immediately behind it stood the house wherein they had engaged lodgings, whose exterior features are so well known to all travellers through the Froom Valley; once portion of a fine manorial residence, and the property and seat of a d'Urbervlle, but since its partial demolition a farm-house.

'Welcome to one of your ancestral mansions!' sad Clare as he handed her down. But he regretted the pleasantry; it was too near a satire.

On entering they found that, though they had only engaged a couple of rooms, the farmer had taken advantage of their proposed presence during the coming days to pay a New Year's visit to some friends, leaving a woman from a neighbouring cottage to minister to their few wants. The absoluteness of possession pleased them, and they realized it as the first moment of their experience under their own exclusive roof-tree.

But he found that the mouldy old habitation somewhat depressed his bride.

When the carriage was gone they ascended the stairs to wash their hands, the charwoman showing the way. On the landing Tess stopped and started.

'What's the matter?' said he.

'Those horrid women!' she answered, with a smile. 'How they frightened me.'

He looked up, and perceived two life-size portraits on panels built into masonry. As all visitors to the mansion are aware, these paintings represent women of middle age, of a date some two hundred years ago, whose lineaments once seen can never be forgotten. The long pointed features, narrow eye, and smirk of the one, so suggestive of merciless treachery; the bill-hook nose, large teeth, and bold eye of the other, suggesting arrogance to the point of ferocity, haunt the beholder afterwards in his dreams.

'Whose portraits are those?' asked Clare of the charwoman.

'I have been told by old folk that they were ladies of the d'Urberville family, the ancient lords of this manor,' she said. 'Owing to their being builded into the wall they can't be moved away.'

The unpleasantness of the matter was that, in addition to their effect upon Tess, her fine features were unquestionably traceable in these exaggerated forms. He said nothing of this, however, and, regretting that he had gone out of his way to choose the house for their bridal time, went on into the adjoining room. The place having been rather hastily prepared for them they washed their hands in one basin. Clare touched hers under the water.

'Which are my fingers and which are yours?' he said, looking up. 'They are very much mixed.'

'They are all yours,' said she, very prettily, and endeavoured to be gayer than she was. He had not been displeased with her thoughtfulness on such an occasion; it was what every sensible woman would show: but Tess knew that she had been thoughtful to excess, and struggled against it.

The sun was so low on that short last afternoon of the year that it shone in through a small opening and formed a golden staff which stretched across to her skirt, where it made a spot like a paint-mark set upon her. They went into the ancient parlour to tea, and here they shared their first common meal alone. Such was their childishness, or rather his, that he found it interesting to use the same bread-and-butter plate as herself, and to brush crumbs from her lips with his own. He wondered a little that she did not enter into these frivolities with his own zest.

Looking at her silently for a long time; 'She is a dear dear Tess,' he thought to himself, as one deciding on the true construction of a difficult passage. 'Do I realize solemnly enough how utterly and irretrievably this little womanly thing is the creature of my good or bad faith and fortune? I think not. I think I could not, unless I were a woman myself. What I am in worldly estate, she is. What I become, she must become. What I cannot be, she cannot be. And shall I ever neglect her, or hurt her, or even forget to consider her? God forbid such a crime!'

They sat on over the tea-table waiting for their luggage, which the dairyman had promised to send before it grew dark. But evening began to close in, and the luggage did not arrive, and they had brought nothing more than they stood in. With the departure of the sun the calm mood of the winter day changed. Out of doors there began noises as of silk smartly rubbed; the restful dead leaves of the preceding autumn were stirred to irritated resurrection, and whirled about unwillingly, and tapped against the shutters. It soon began to rain.

'That cock knew the weather was going to change,' said Clare.

The woman who had attended upon them had gone home for the night, but she had placed candles upon the table, and now they lit them. Each candle-flame drew towards the fireplace.

'These old houses are so draughty,' continued Angel, looking at the flames, and at the grease guttering down the sides. 'I wonder where that luggage is. We haven't even a brush and comb.'

'I don't know,' she answered, absent-minded.

'Tess, you are not a bit cheerful this evening – not at all as you used to be. Those harridans on the panels upstairs have unsettled you. I am sorry I brought you here. I wonder if you really love me, after all?'

He knew that she did, and the words had no serious intent; but she was surcharged with emotion, and winced like a wounded animal. Though she tried not to shed tears she could not help showing one or two.

'I did not mean it!' said he, sorry. 'You are worried at not having your things, I know. I cannot think why old Jonathan has not come with them. Why, it is seven o'clock? Ah, there he is!'

A knock had come to the door, and, there being nobody else to answer it Clare went out. He returned to the room with a small package in his hand.

'It is not Jonathan, after all,' he said.

'How vexing!' said Tess.

The packet had been brought by a special messenger, who had arrived at Talbothays from Emminster Vicarage immediately after the departure of the married couple, and had followed them hither, being under injunction to deliver it into nobody's hands but theirs. Clare brought it to the light. It was less than a foot long, sewed up in canvas, sealed in red wax with his father's seal, and directed in his father's hand to 'Mrs Angel Clare'.

'It is a little wedding-present for you, Tess,' said he, handing it to her. 'How thoughtful they are!'

Tess looked a little flustered as she took it.

'I think I would rather have you open it, dearest,' said she, turning over the parcel. 'I don't like to break those great seals; they look so serious. Please open it for me!'

He undid the parcel. Inside was a case of morocco leather, on the top of which lay a note and a key.

The note was for Clare, in the following words:

MY DEAR SON, – Possibly you have forgotten that on the death of your godmother, Mrs Pitney, when you were a lad, she – vain kind woman that she was – left to me a portion of the contents of her jewel-case in trust for your wife, if you should ever have one, as a mark of her affection for you and whomsoever you should choose. This trust I have fulfilled, and the diamonds have been locked up at my banker's ever since. Though I feel it to be a somewhat incongruous act in the circumstances, I am, as you will, see, bound to hand over the articles to the woman to whom the use of them for her lifetime will now rightly belong, and they are therefore promptly sent. They become, I believe, heirlooms, strictly speaking, according to the terms of your godmother's will. The precise words of the clause that refers to this matter are enclosed.

'I do remember,' said Clare; 'but I had quite forgotten.'

Unlocking the case, they found it to contain a necklace, with pendant, bracelets, and ear-rings; and also some other small ornaments.

Tess seemed afraid to touch them at first, but her eyes sparkled for a moment as much as the stones when Clare spread out the set.

'Are they mine?' she asked incredulously.

'They are, certainly,' said he.

He looked into the fire. He remembered how, when he was a lad of fifteen, his godmother, the Squire's wife — the only rich person with whom he had ever come in contact — had pinned her faith to his success; had prophesied a wondrous career for him. There had seemed nothing at all out of keeping with such a conjectured career in the storing up of these showy ornaments for his wife and the wives of her descendants. They gleamed somewhat ironically now. 'Yet why?' he asked himself. It was but a question of vanity throughout; and if that were admitted into one side of the equation it should be admitted into the other. His wife was a d'Urberville: whom could they become better than her?

Suddenly he said with enthusiasm —

'Tess, put them on — put them on!' And he turned from the fire to help her.

But as if by magic she had already donned them — necklace, earings, bracelets, and all.

'But the gown isn't right, Tess,' said Clare. 'It ought to be a low one for a set of brilliants like that.'

'Ought it?' said Tess.

'Yes,' said he.

He suggested to her how to tuck in the upper edge of her bodice, so as to make it roughly approximate to the cut for evening wear; and when she had done this, and the pendant to the necklace hung isolated amid the whiteness of her throat, as it was designed to do, he stepped back to survey her.

'My heavens,' said Clare, 'how beautiful you are!'

As everybody knows, fine feathers make fine birds; a peasant girl but very moderately prepossessing to the casual observer in her simple condition and attire, will bloom as an amazing beauty if clothed as a woman of fashion with the aids that Art can render; while the beauty of the midnight crush would often cut but a sorry figure if placed inside the field-woman's wrapper upon a monotonous acreage of turnips on a dull day. He had never till now estimated the artistic excellence of Tess's limbs and features.

'If you were only to appear in a ball-room!' he said. 'But no — no, dearest; I think I love you best in the wing-bonnet and cotton-frock — yes, better than in this, well as you support these dignities.'

Tess's sense of her striking appearance had given her a flush of excitement, which was yet not happiness.

'I'll take them off,' she said, 'in case Jonathan should see me. They are not fit for me, are they? They must be sold, I suppose?'

'Let them stay a few minutes longer. Sell them? Never. It would be a breach of faith.'

Influenced by a second thought she readily obeyed. She had something to tell, and there might be help in these. She sat down with the jewels upon her; and they again indulged in conjectures as to where Jonathan could possibly be with their baggage. The ale they had poured out for his consumption when he came had gone flat with long standing.

Shortly after this they began supper, which was already laid on a side-table. Ere they had finished there was a jerk in the fire-smoke, the rising skein of which bulged out into the room, as if some giant had laid his hand on the chimney-top for a moment. It had been caused by the opening of the outer door. A heavy step was now heard in the passage, and Angel went out.

'I couldn' make nobody hear at all by knocking,' apologized Jonathan Kail, for it was he at last; 'and as't was raining out I opened the door. I've brought the things, sir.'

'I am very glad to see them. But you are very late.'

'Well, yes, sir.'

There was something subdued in Jonathan Kail's tone which had not been there in the day, and lines of concern were ploughed upon his forehead in addition to the lines of years. He continued –

'We've all been gallied at the dairy at what might ha' been a most terrible affliction since you and your Mis'ess – so to name her now – left us this a'ternoon. Perhaps you ha'nt forgot the cock's afternoon crow?'

'Dear me; – what—'

'Well, some says it do mane one thing, and some another; but what's happened is that poor little Retty Priddle hev tried to drown herself.'

'No! Really! Why, she bade us good-bye with the rest—'

'Yes. Well, sir, when you and your Mis'ess – so to name what she lawful is – when you two drove away, as I say, Retty and Marian put on their bonnets and went out; and as there is not much doing now, being New Year's Eve, and folks mops and brooms from what's inside 'em, nobody took much notice. They went on to Lew-Everard, where they had summut to drink, and then on they vamped to Dree-armed Cross, and there they seemed to have parted, Retty striking across the water-meads as if for home, and Marian going on to the next village, where there's another public-house. Nothing more was zeed or heard o' Retty till the waterman, on his way home, noticed something by the Great Pool; 'twas her bonnet and shawl packed up. In the water he found her. He and another man brought her home, thinking 'a was dead; but she fetched round by degrees.'

Angel, suddenly recollecting that Tess was overhearing this gloomy tale, went to shut the door between the passage and the ante-room to the inner parlour where she was; but his wife, flinging a shawl round her, had come tthe outer room and was listening to the man's narrative, her eyes resting absently on the luggage and the drops of rain glistening upon it.

'And, more than this, there's Marian; she's been found dead drunk by the withy-bed – a girl who hev never been known to touch anything before except shilling ale; though, to be sure, 'a was always a good trencher-woman, as her face showed. It seems as if the maids had all gone out o' their minds!'

'And Izz?' asked Tess.

'Izz is about house as usual; but 'a do say 'a can guess how it happened; and she seems to be very low in mind about it, poor maid, as well she mid be. And so you see, sir, as all this happened just when we was packing your few traps and your Mis'ess's night-rail and dressing things into the cart, why, it belated me.'

'Yes. Well, Jonathan, will you get the trunks upstairs, and drink a cup of ale, and hasten back as soon as you can, in case you should be wanted?'

Tess had gone back to the inner parlour, and sat down by the fire, looking wistfully into it. She heard Jonathan Kail's heavy footsteps up and down the stairs till he had done placing the luggage, and heard him express his thanks for the ale her husband took out to him, and for the gratuity he received. Jonathan's footsteps then died from the door, and his cart creaked away.

Angel slid forward the massive oak bar which secured the door, and coming in to where she sat over the hearth, pressed her cheeks between his hands from behind. He expected her to jump up gaily and unpack the toilet-gear that she had been so anxious about, but as she did not rise he sat down with her in the firelight, the candles on the supper-table being too thin and glimmering to interfere with its glow.

'I am so sorry you should have heard this sad story about the girls,' he said. 'Still, don't let it depress you. Retty was naturally morbid, you know.'

'Without the least cause,' said Tess. 'While they who have cause to be, hide it, and pretend they are not.'

This incident had turned the scale for her. They were simple and innocent girls on whom the unhappiness of unrequited love had fallen; they had deserved better at the hands of Fate. She had deserved worse — yet she was the chosen one. It was wicked of her to take all without paying. She would pay to the uttermost farthing; she would tell, there and then. This final determination she came to when she looked into the fire, he holding her hand.

A steady glare from the now flameless embers painted the sides and back of the fireplace with its colour, and the well-polished andirons, and the old brass tongs that would not meet. The underside of the mantel-shelf was flushed with the high-coloured light, and the legs of the table nearest the fire. Tess's face and neck reflected the same warmth, which each gem turned into an Aldebaran or a Sirius — a constellation of white, red, and green flashes, that interchanged their hues with her every pulsation.

'Do you remember what we said to each other this morning about telling our faults?' he asked abruptly, finding that she still remained immovable. 'We spoke lightly perhaps, and you may well have done so. But for me it was no light promise. I want to make a confession to you, Love.'

This, from him, so unexpectedly apposite, had the effect upon her of a Providential interposition.

'You have to confess something?' she said quickly, and even with gladness and relief.

'You did not expect it? Ah — you thought too highly of me. Now listen. Put your head there, because I want you to forgive me, and not be indignant with me for not telling you before, as perhaps I ought to have done.'

How strange it was! He seemed to be her double. She did not speak, and Clare went on —

'I did not mention it because I was afraid of endangering my chance of you, darling, the great prize of my life — my Fellowship I call you. My brother's Fellowship was won at his college, mine at Talbothays Dairy. Well, I would not risk it. I was going to tell you a month ago — at the time you agreed to be mine, but I could not; I thought it might frighten you away from me. I put it off; then I thought I would tell you yesterday, to give you a chance at least of escaping me. But I did not. And I did not this morning, when you proposed our confessing our faults on the landing – the sinner that I was! But I must, now I see you sitting there so solemnly. I wonder if you will forgive me?'

'O yes! I am sure that—'

'Well, I hope so. But wait a minute. You don't know. To begin at the beginning. Though I imagine my poor father fears that I am one of the eternally lost for my doctrines, I am of course, a believer in good morals, Tess, as much as you. I used to wish to be a teacher of men, and it was a great disappointment to me when I found I could not enter the Church. I admired spotlessness, even though I could lay no claim to it, and hated impurity, as I hope I do now. Whatever one may think of plenary inspiration, one must heartily subscribe to these words of Paul: "Be thou an example – in word, in conversation, in charity, in spirit, in faith, in purity." It is the only safeguard for us poor human beings. "Integer vitae," says a Roman poet, who is strange company for St Paul –

> The man of upright life, from frailties free,
> Stands not in need of Moorish spear or bow.

Well, a certain place is paved with good intentions, and having felt all that so strongly, you will see what a terrible remorse it bred in me when, in the midst of my fine aims for other people, I myself fell.'

He then told her of that time of his life to which allusion has been made when, tossed about by doubts and difficulties in London, like a cork on the waves, he plunged into eight-and-forty hours' dissipation with a stranger.

'Happily I awoke almost immediately to a sense of my folly,' he continued. 'I would have no more to say to her, and I came home. I have never repeated the offence. But I felt I should like to treat you with perfect frankness and honour, and I could not do so without telling this. Do you forgive me?'

She pressed his hand tightly for an answer.

'Then we will dismiss it at once and for ever! – too painful as it is for the occasion – and talk of something lighter.'

'O, Angel – I am almost glad – because now *you* can forgive *me*! I have not made my confession. I have a confession, too – remember, I said so.'

'Ah, to be sure! Now then for it, wicked little one.'

'Perhaps, although you smile, it is as serious as yours, or more so.'

'It can hardly be more serious, dearest.'

'It cannot – O no, it cannot!' She jumped up joyfully at the hope. 'No, it cannot be more serious, certainly,' she cried, 'because 'tis just the same! I will tell you now.'

She sat down again.

Their hands were still joined. The ashes under the grate were lit by the fire vertically, like a torrid waste. Imagination might have beheld a Last Day luridness in this red-coaled glow, which fell on his face and hand, and on hers, peering into the loose hair about her brow, and firing the delicate skin underneath. A large shadow of her shape rose upon the wall and ceiling. She bent forward, at which each diamond on her neck gave a sinister wink like a toad's;

and pressing her forehead against his temple she entered on her story of her acquaintance with Alec d'Urberville and its results, murmuring the words without flinching, and with her eyelids drooping down.

The Woman Pays

CHAPTER THIRTY-FIVE

H ER narrative ended; even its re-assertions and secondary explanations were done. Tess's voice throughout had hardly risen higher than its opening tone; there had been no exculpatory phrase of any kind, and she had not wept.

But the complexion even of external things seemed to suffer transmutation as her announcement progressed. The fire in the grate looked impish — demoniacally funny, as if it did not care in the least about her strait. The fender grinned idly, as if it too did not care. The light from the water-bottle was merely engaged in a chromatic problem. All material objects around announced their irresponsibility with terrible iteration. And yet nothing had changed since the moments when he had been kissing her; or rather, nothing in the substance of things. But the essence of things had changed.

When she ceased the auricular impressions from their previous endearments seemed to hustle away into the corners of their brains, repeating themselves as echoes from a time of supremely purblind foolishness.

Clare performed the irrelevant act of stirring the fire; the intelligence had not even yet got to the bottom of him. After stirring the embers he rose to his feet; all the force of her disclosure had imparted itself now. His face had withered. In the strenuousness of his concentration he treadled fitfully on the floor. He could not, by any contrivance, think closely enough; that was the meaning of his vague movement. When he spoke it was in the most inadequate, commonplace voice of the many varied tones she had heard from him.

'Tess!'

'Yes, dearest.'

'Am I to believe this? From your manner I am to take it as true. O you cannot be out of your mind! You ought to be! Yet you are not. . . . My wife, my Tess — nothing in you warrants such a supposition as that?'

'I am not out of my mind,' she said.

'And yet—' He looked vacantly at her, to resume with dazed senses: 'Why didn't you tell me before? Ah, yes, you would have told me, in a way — but I hindered you, I remember!'

These and other of his words were nothing but the perfunctory babble of the surface while the depths remained paralyzed. He turned away, and bent over a chair. Tess followed him to the middle of the room where he was, and stood there staring at him with eyes that did not weep. Presently she slid down upon her knees beside his foot, and from this position she crouched in a heap.

'In the name of our love, forgive me!' she whispered with a dry mouth. 'I have forgiven you for the same!'

And, as he did not answer, she said again –

'Forgive me as you are forgiven! *I* forgive *you*, Angel.'

'You – yes, you do.'

'But you do not forgive me?'

'O Tess, forgiveness does not apply to the case! You were one person; now you are another. My God – how can forgiveness meet such a grotesque – prestidigitation as that!'

He paused, contemplating this definition; then suddenly broke into horrible laughter – as unnatural and ghastly as a laugh in hell.

'Don't – don't! It kills me quite, that!' she shrieked. 'O have mercy upon me – have mercy!'

He did not answer; and, sickly white, she jumped up.

'Angel, Angel! what do you mean by that laugh?' she cried out. 'Do you know what this is to me?'

He shook his head.

'I have been hoping, longing, praying, to make you happy! I have thought what joy it will be to do it, what an unworthy wife I shall be if I do not! That's what I have felt, Angel!'

'I know that.'

'I thought, Angel, that you loved me – me, my very self! If it is I you do love, O how can it be that you look and speak so? It frightens me! Having begun to love you, I love you for ever – in all changes, in all disgraces, because you are yourself. I ask no more. Then how can you, O my own husband, stop loving me?'

'I repeat, the woman I have been loving is not you.'

'But who?'

'Another woman in your shape.'

She perceived in his words the realization of her own apprehensive foreboding in former times. He looked upon her as a species of impostor; a guilty woman in the guise of an innocent one. Terror was upon her white face as she saw it; her cheek was flaccid, and her mouth had almost the aspect of a round little hole. The horrible sense of his view of her so deadened her that she staggered; and he stepped forward, thinking she was going to fall.

'Sit down, sit down,' he said gently. 'You are ill; and it is natural that you should be.'

She did sit down, without knowing where she was, that strained look still upon her face, and her eyes such as to make his flesh creep.

'I don't belong to you any more, then; do I, Angel?' she asked helplessly. 'It is not me, but another woman like me that he loved, he says.'

The image raised caused her to take pity upon herself as one who was ill-used. Her eyes filled as she regarded her position further; she turned round and burst into a flood of self-sympathetic tears.

Clare was relieved at this change, for the effect on her of what had happened was beginning to be a trouble to him only less than the woe of the disclosure itself. He waited patiently, apathetically, till the violence of her grief had worn itself out, and her rush of weeping had lessened to a catching gasp at intervals.

'Angel,' she said suddenly, in her natural tones, the insane, dry voice of terror having left her now. 'Angel, am I too wicked for you and me to live together?'

'I have not been able to think what we can do.'

'I shan't ask you to let me live with you, Angel, because I have no right to! I shall not write to mother and sisters to say we be married, as I said I would do; and I shan't finish the good-hussif I cut out and meant to make while we were in lodgings.'

'Shan't you?'

'No, I shan't do anything, unless you order me to; and if you go away from me I shall not follow 'ee; and if you never speak to me any more I shall not ask why, unless you tell me I may.'

'And if I do order you to do anything?'

'I will obey you like your wretched slave, even if it is to lie down and die.'

'You are very good. But it strikes me that there is a want of harmony between your present mood of self-sacrifice and your past mood of self-preservation.'

These were the first words of antagonism. To fling elaborate sarcasms at Tess, however, was much like flinging them at a dog or cat. The charms of their subtlety passed by her unappreciated, and she only received them as inimical sounds which meant that anger ruled. She remained mute, not knowing that he was smothering his affection for her. She hardly observed that a tear descended slowly upon his cheek, a tear so large that it magnified the pores of the skin over which it rolled, like the object lens of a microscope. Meanwhile reillumination as to the terrible and total change that her confession had wrought in his life, in his universe, returned to him, and he tried desperately to advance among the new conditions in which he stood. Some consequent action was necessary; yet what?

'Tess,' he said, as gently as he could speak, 'I cannot stay — in this room — just now. I will walk out a little way.'

He quietly left the room, and the two glasses of wine that he had poured out for their supper — one for her, one for him — remained on the table untasted. This was what their *Agape* had come to. At tea, two or three hours earlier, they had, in the freakishness of affection, drunk from one cup.

The closing of the door behind him, gently as it had been pulled to, roused Tess from her stupor. He was gone; she could not stay. Hastily flinging her cloak around her she opened the door and followed, putting out the candles as if she were never coming back. The rain was over and the night was now clear.

She was soon close at his heels, for Clare walked slowly and without purpose. His form beside her light gray figure looked black, sinister, and forbidding, and she felt as sarcasm the touch of the jewels of which she had been momentarily so proud. Clare turned at hearing her footsteps, but his recognition of her presence seemed to make no difference in him, and he went on over the five yawning arches of the great bridge in front of the house.

The cow and horse tracks in the road were full of water, the rain having been enough to charge them, but not enough to wash them away. Across these minute pools the reflected stars flitted in a quick transit as she passed; she would not have known they were shining overhead if she had not seen them there — the vastest things of the universe imaged in objects so mean.

The place to which they had travelled to-day was in the same valley as

Talbothays, but some miles lower down the river; and the surroundings being open she kept easily in sight of him. Away from the house the road wound through the meads, and along these she followed Clare without any attempt to come up with him or to attract him, but with dumb and vacant fidelity.

At last, however, her listless walk brought her up alongside him, and still he said nothing. The cruelty of fooled honesty is often great after enlightenment, and it was mighty in Clare now. The outdoor air had apparently taken away from him all tendency to act on impulse; she knew that he saw her without irradiation – in all her bareness; that Time was chanting his satiric psalm at her then –

> Behold, when thy face is made bare, he that loved thee shall hate;
> Thy face shall be no more fair at the fall of thy fate.
> For thy life shall fall as a leaf and be shed as the rain;
> And the veil of thine head shall be grief, and the crown shall be pain.

He was still intently thinking, and her companionship had now insufficient power to break or divert the strain of thought. What a weak thing her presence must have become to him! She could not help addressing Clare.

'What have I done – what *have* I done! I have not told of anything that interferes with or belies my love for you. You don't think I planned it, do you? It is in your own mind what you are angry at, Angel; it is not in me. O, it is not in me, and I am not that deceitful woman you think me!'

'H'm – well. Not deceitful, my wife; but not the same. No, not the same. But do not make me reproach you. I have sworn that I will not; and I will do everything to avoid it.'

But she went on pleading in her distraction; and perhaps said things that would have been better left to silence.

'Angel! – Angel! I was a child – a child when it happened! I knew nothing of men.'

'You were more sinned against than sinning, that I admit.'

'Then will you not forgive me?'

'I do forgive you, but forgiveness is not all.'

'And love me?'

To this question he did not answer.

'O Angel – my mother says that it sometimes happens so! – she knows several cases where they were worse than I, and the husband has not minded it much – has got over it at least. And yet the woman has not loved him as I do you!'

'Don't, Tess; don't argue. Different societies, different manners. You almost make me say you are an unapprehending peasant woman, who have never been initiated into the proportions of social things. You don't know what you say.'

'I am only a peasant by position, not by nature!'

She spoke with an impulse to anger, but it went as it came.

'So much the worse for you. I think that parson who unearthed your pedigree would have done better if he had held his tongue. I cannot help associating your decline as a family with this other fact – of your want of firmness. Decrepit families imply decrepit wills, decrepit conduct. Heaven, why did you give me a handle for despising you more by informing me of your descent! Here was I thinking you a new-sprung child of nature; there were you, the belated seedling of an effete aristocracy!'

'Lots of families are as bad as mine in that! Retty's family were once large landowners, and so were Dairyman Billet's. And the Debbyhouses, who now are carters, were once the De Bayeux family. You find such as I everywhere; 'tis a feature of our county, and I can't help it.'

'So much the worse for the county.'

She took these reproaches in their bulk simply, not in their particulars; he did not love her as he had loved her hitherto, and to all else she was indifferent.

They wandered on again in silence. It was said afterwards that a cottager of Wellbridge, who went out late that night for a doctor, met two lovers in the pastures, walking very slowly, without converse, one behind the other, as in a funeral procession, and the glimpse that he obtained of their faces seemed to denote that they were anxious and sad. Returning later, he passed them again in the same field, progressing just as slowly, and as regardless of the hour and of the cheerless night as before. It was only on account of his preoccupation with his own affairs, and the illness in his house, that he did not bear in mind the curious incident, which, however, he recalled a long while after.

During the interval of the cottager's going and coming, she had said to her husband –

'I don't see how I can help being the cause of much misery to you all your life. The river is down there. I can put an end to myself in it. I am not afraid.'

'I don't wish to add murder to my other follies,' he said.

'I will leave something to show that I did it myself – on account of my shame. They will not blame you then.'

'Don't speak so absurdly – I wish not to hear it. It is nonsense to have such thoughts in this kind of case, which is rather one for satirical laughter than for tragedy. You don't in the least understand the quality of the mishap. It would be viewed in the light of a joke by nine-tenths of the world if it were known. Please oblige me by returning to the house, and going to bed.'

'I will,' said she dutifully.

They had rambled round by a road which led to the well-known ruins of the Cistercian abbey behind the mill, the latter having, in centuries past, been attached to the monastic establishment. The mill still worked on, food being a perennial necessity; the abbey had perished, creeds being transient. One continually sees the ministration of the temporary outlasting the ministration of the eternal. Their walk having been circuitous they were still not far from the house, and in obeying his direction she only had to reach the large stone bridge across the main river, and follow the road for a few yards. When she got back everything remained as she had left it, the fire being still burning. She did not stay downstairs for more than a minute, but proceeded to her chamber, whither the luggage had been taken. Here she sat down on the edge of the bed, looking blankly around, and presently began to undress. In removing the light towards the bedstead its rays fell upon the tester of white dimity; something was hanging beneath it, and she lifted the candle to see what it was. A bough of mistletoe. Angel had put it there; she knew that in an instant. This was the explanation of that mysterious parcel which it had been so difficult to pack and bring; whose contents he would not explain to her, saying that time would soon show her the purpose thereof. In his zest and his gaiety he had hung it there. How foolish and inopportune that mistletoe looked now.

Having nothing more to fear, having scarce anything to hope, for that he would relent there seemed no promise whatever, she lay down dully. When sorrow ceases to be speculative sleep sees her opportunity. Among so many happier moods which forbid repose this was a mood which welcomed it, and in a few minutes the lonely Tess forgot existence, surrounded by the aromatic stillness of the chamber that had once, possibly, been the bride-chamber of her own ancestry.

Later that night Clare also retraced his steps to the house. Entering softly to the sitting-room he obtained a light, and with the manner of one who had considered his course he spread his rugs upon the old horse-hair sofa which stood there, and roughly shaped it to a sleeping-couch. Before lying down he crept shoeless upstairs, and listened at the door of her apartment. Her measured breathing told that she was sleeping profoundly.

'Thank God!' murmured Clare; and yet he was conscious of a pang of bitterness at the thought – approximately true, though not wholly so – that having shifted the burden of her life to his shoulders she was now reposing without care.

He turned away to descend; then, irresolute, faced round to her door again. In the act he caught sight of one of the d'Urberville dames, whose portrait was immediately over the entrance to Tess's bedchamber. In the candlelight the painting was more than unpleasant. Sinister design lurked in the woman's features, a concentrated purpose of revenge on the other sex – so it seemed to him then. The Caroline bodice of the portrait was low – precisely as Tess's had been when he tucked it in to show the necklace; and again he experienced the distressing sensation of a resemblance between them.

The check was sufficient. He resumed his retreat and descended.

His air remained calm and cold, his small compressed mouth indexing his powers of self-control; his face wearing still that terribly sterile expression which had spread thereon since her disclosure. It was the face of a man who was no longer passion's slave, yet who found no advantage in his enfranchisement. He was simply regarding the harrowing contingencies of human experience, the unexpectedness of things. Nothing so pure, so sweet, so virginal as Tess had seemed possible all the long while that he had adored her, up to an hour ago; but

The little less, and what worlds away!

He argued erroneously when he said to himself that her heart was not indexed in the honest freshness of her face; but Tess had no advocate to set him right. Could it be possible, he continued, that eyes which as they gazed never expressed any divergence from what the tongue was telling, were yet ever seeing another world behind her ostensible one, discordant and contrasting?

He reclined on his couch in the sitting-room, and extinguished the light. The night came in, and took up its place there, unconcerned and indifferent; the night which had already swallowed up his happiness, and was now digesting it listlessly; and was ready to swallow up the happiness of a thousand other people with as little disturbance or change of mien.

CHAPTER THIRTY-SIX

CLARE arose in the light of a dawn that was ashy and furtive, as though associated with crime. The fireplace confronted him with its extinct embers; the spread supper-table, whereon stood the two full glasses of untasted wine, now flat and filmy; her vacated seat and his own; the other articles of furniture, with their eternal look of not being able to help it, their intolerable inquiry what was to be done? From above there was no sound; but in a few minutes there came a knock at the door. He remembered that it would be the neighbouring cottager's wife, who was to minister to their wants while they remained here.

The presence of a third person in the house would be extremely awkward just now, and, being already dressed, he opened the window and informed her that they could manage to shift for themselves that morning. She had a milk-can in her hand, which he told her to leave at the door. When the dame had gone away he searched in the back quarters of the house for fuel, and speedily lit a fire. There was plenty of eggs, butter, bread, and so on in the larder, and Clare soon had breakfast laid, his experiences at the dairy having rendered him facile in domestic preparations. The smoke of the kindled wood rose from the chimney without like a lotus-headed column; local people who were passing by saw it, and thought of the newly-married couple, and envied their happiness.

Angel cast a final glance round, and then going to the foot of the stairs, called in a conventional voice –

'Breakfast is ready!'

He opened the front door, and took a few steps in the morning air. When, after a short space, he came back she was already in the sitting-room, mechanically readjusting the breakfast things. As she was fully attired, and the interval since his calling her had been but two or three minutes, she must have been dressed or nearly so before he went to summon her. Her hair was twisted up in a large round mass at the back of her head, and she had put on one of the new frocks – a pale blue woollen garment with neck-frillings of white. Her hands and face appeared to be cold, and she had possibly been sitting dressed in the bedroom a long time without any fire. The marked civility of Clare's tone in calling her seemed to have inspired her, for the moment, with a new glimmer of hope. But it soon died when she looked at him.

The pair were, in truth, but the ashes of their former fires. To the hot sorrow of the previous night had succeeded heaviness; it seemed as if nothing could kindle either of them to fervour of sensation any more.

He spoke gently to her, and she replied with a like undemonstrativeness. At last she came up to him, looking in his sharply-defined face as one who had no consciousness that her own formed a visible object also.

'Angel!' she said, and paused, touching him with her fingers lightly as a breeze, as though she could hardly believe to be there in the flesh the man who was once her lover. Her eyes were bright, her pale cheek still showed its wonted roundness, though half-dried tears had left glistening traces thereon; and the usually ripe red mouth was almost as pale as her cheek. Throbbingly alive as she was still, under the stress of her mental grief the life beat so brokenly, that a little further pull upon it would cause real illness, dull her characteristic eyes, and make her mouth thin.

She looked absolutely pure. Nature, in her fantastic trickery, had set such a seal of maidenhood upon Tess's countenance that he gazed at her with a stupefied air.

'Tess! Say it is not true! No, it is not true!'

'It is true.'

'Every word?'

'Every word.'

He looked at her imploringly, as if he would willingly have taken a lie from her lips, knowing it to be one, and have made of it, by some sort of sophistry, a valid denial. However, she only repeated –

'It is true.'

'Is he living?' Angel then asked.

'The baby died.'

'But the man?'

'He is alive.'

A last despair passed over Clare's face.

'Is he in England?'

'Yes.'

He took a few vague steps.

'My position – is this,' he said abruptly. 'I thought – any man would have thought – that by giving up all ambition to win a wife with social standing, with fortune, with knowledge of the world, I should secure rustic innocence as surely as I should secure pink cheeks; but—However, I am no man to reproach you, and I will not.'

Tess felt his position so entirely that the remainder had not been needed. Therein lay just the distress of it; she saw that he had lost all round.

'Angel – I should not have let it go on to marriage with you if I had not known that, after all, there was a last way out of it for you; though I hoped you would never—'

Her voice grew husky.

'A last way?'

'I mean, to get rid of me. You *can* get rid of me.'

'How?'

'By divorcing me.'

'Good heavens – how can you be so simple! How can I divorce you?'

'Can't you – now I have told you? I thought my confession would give you grounds for that.'

'O Tess – you are too, too – childish – unformed – crude, I suppose! I don't know what you are. You don't understand the law – you don't understand!'

'What – you cannot?'

'Indeed I cannot.'

A quick shame mixed with the misery upon her listener's face.

'I thought – I thought,' she whispered. 'O, now I see how wicked I seem to you!

Believe me – believe me, on my soul, I never thought but that you could! I hoped you would not; yet I believed, without a doubt, that you could cast me off if you were determined, and didn't love me at – at – all!'

'You were mistaken,' he said.

'O, then I ought to have done it, to have done it last night! But I hadn't the courage. That's just like me!'

'The courage to do what?'

As she did not answer he took her by the hand.

'What were you thinking of doing?' he inquired.

'Of putting an end to myself.'

'When?'

She writhed under this inquisitorial manner of his. 'Last night,' she answered.

'Where?'

'Under your mistletoe.'

'My good—! How?' he asked sternly.

'I'll tell you, if you won't be angry with me!' she said, shrinking. 'It was with the cord of my box. But I could not – do the last thing! I was afraid that it might cause a scandal to your name.'

The unexpected quality of this confession, wrung from her, and not volunteered, shook him perceptibly. But he still held her, and, letting his glance fall from her face downwards, he said,

'Now, listen to this. You must not dare to think of such a horrible thing! How could you! You will promise me as your husband to attempt that no more.'

'I am ready to promise. I saw how wicked it was.'

'Wicked! The idea was unworthy of you beyond description.'

'But, Angel,' she pleaded, enlarging her eyes in calm unconcern upon him, 'it was thought of entirely on your account – to set you free without the scandal of the divorce that I thought you would have to get. I should never have dreamt of doing it on mine. However, to do it with my own hand is too good for me, after all. It is you, my ruined husband, who ought to strike the blow. I think I should love you more, if that were possible, if you could bring yourself to do it, since there's no other way of escape for 'ee. I feel I am so utterly worthless! So very greatly in the way!'

'Ssh!'

'Well, since you say no, I won't. I have no wish opposed to yours.'

He knew this to be true enough. Since the desperation of the night her activities had dropped to zero, and there was no further rashness to be feared.

Tess tried to busy herself again over the breakfast-table with more or less success, and they sat down both on the same side, so that their glances did not meet. There was at first something awkward in hearing each other eat and drink, but this could not be escaped; moreover, the amount of eating done was small on both sides. Breakfast over he rose, and telling her the hour at which he might be expected to dinner, went off to the miller's in a mechanical pursuance of the plan of studying that business, which had been his only practical reason for coming here.

When he was gone Tess stood at the window, and presently saw his form crossing the great stone bridge which conducted to the mill premises. He sank behind it, crossed the railway beyond, and disappeared. Then, without a sigh, she turned her attention to the room, and began clearing the table and setting it in order.

The charwoman soon came. Her presence was at first a strain upon Tess, but afterwards an alleviation. At half-past twelve she left her assistant alone in the kitchen, and, returning to the sitting room, waited for the reappearance of Angel's form behind the bridge.

About one he showed himself. Her face flushed, although he was a quarter of a mile off. She ran to the kitchen to get the dinner served by the time he should enter. He went first to the room where they had washed their hands together the day before, and as he entered the sitting-room the dish-covers rose from the dishes as if by his own motion.

'How punctual!' he said.

'Yes. I saw you coming over the bridge,' said she.

The meal was passed in commonplace talk of what he had been doing during the morning at the Abbey Mill, of the methods of bolting and the old-fashioned machinery, which he feared would not enlighten him greatly on modern improved methods, some of it seeming to have been in use ever since the days it ground for the monks in the adjoining conventual buildings — now a heap of ruins. He left the house again in the course of an hour, coming home at dusk, and occupying himself through the evening with his papers. She feared she was in the way, and, when the old woman was gone, retired to the kitchen, where she made herself busy as well as she could for more than an hour.

Clare's shape appeared at the door.

'You must not work like this,' he said. 'You are not my servant; you are my wife.'

She raised her eyes, and brightened somewhat. 'I may think myself that — indeed?' she murmured, in piteous raillery. 'You mean in name! Well, I don't want to be anything more.'

'You *may* think so, Tess! You are. What do you mean?'

'I don't know,' she said hastily, with tears in her accents. 'I thought I — because I am not respectable, I mean. I told you I thought I was not respectable enough long ago — and on that account I didn't want to marry you, only — only you urged me!'

She broke into sobs, and turned her back to him. It would almost have won round any man but Angel Clare. Within the remote depths of his constitution, so gentle and affectionate as he was in general, there lay hidden a hard logical deposit, like a vein of metal in a soft loam, which turned the edge of everything that attempted to traverse it. It had blocked his acceptance of the Church; it blocked his acceptance of Tess. Moreover, his affection itself was less fire than radiance, and, with regard to the other sex, when he ceased to believe he ceased to follow: contrasting in this with many impressionable natures, who remain sensuously infatuated with what they intellectually despise. He waited till her sobbing ceased.

'I wish half the women in England were as respectable as you,' he said, in an ebullition of bitterness against womankind in general. 'It isn't a question of respectability, but one of principle!'

He spoke such things as these and more of a kindred sort to her, being still swayed by the antipathetic wave which warps direct souls with such persistence when once their vision finds itself mocked by appearances. There was, it is true, underneath, a back current of sympathy through which a woman of the world might have conquered him. But Tess did not think of this; she took everything as her deserts, and hardly opened her mouth. The firmness of her devotion to him was indeed almost pitiful; quick-tempered as she naturally was, nothing that he could say made her unseemly; she sought not her own; was not provoked; thought no evil of his treatment of her. She might just now have been Apostolic Charity herself returned to a self-seeking modern world.

This evening, night, and morning were passed precisely as the preceding ones had been passed. On one, and only one, occasion did she – the formerly free and independent Tess – venture to make any advances. It was on the third occasion of his starting after a meal to go out to the flour-mill. As he was leaving the table he said 'Good-bye', and she replied in the same words, at the same time inclining her mouth in the way of his. He did not avail himself of the invitation, saying, as he turned hastily aside –

'I shall be home punctually.'

Tess shrank into herself as if she had been struck. Often enough had he tried to reach those lips against her consent – often had he said gaily that her mouth and breath tasted of the butter and eggs and milk and honey on which she mainly lived, that he drew sustenance from them, and other follies of that sort. But he did not care for them now. He observed her sudden shrinking, and said gently –

'You know, I have to think of a course. It was imperative that we should stay together a little while, to avoid the scandal to you that would have resulted from our immediate parting. But you must see it is only for form's sake.'

'Yes,' said Tess absently.

He went out, and on his way to the mill stood still, and wished for a moment that he had responded yet more kindly, and kissed her once at least.

Thus they lived through this despairing day or two; in the same house, truly; but more widely apart than before they were lovers. It was evident to her that he was, as he had said, living with paralyzed activities, in his endeavour to think of a plan of procedure. She was awe-stricken to discover such determination under such apparent flexibility. His consistency was, indeed, too cruel. She no longer expected forgiveness now. More than once she thought of going away from him during his absence at the mill; but she feared that this, instead of benefiting him, might be the means of hampering and humiliating him yet more if it should become known.

Meanwhile Clare was meditating, verily. His thought had been unsuspended; he was becoming ill with thinking; eaten out with thinking, withered by thinking; scourged out of all his former pulsating flexuous domesticity. He walked about saying to himself, 'What's to be done – what's to be done?' and by chance she overheard him. It caused her to break the reserve about their future which had hitherto prevailed.

'I suppose – you are not going to live with me – long, are you, Angel?' she asked, the sunk corners of her mouth betraying how purely mechanical were the means by which she retained that expression of chastened calm upon her face.

'I cannot,' he said, 'without despising myself, and what is worse, perhaps, despising you. I mean, of course, cannot live with you in the ordinary sense. At present, whatever I feel, I do not despise you. And, let me speak plainly, or you may not see all my difficulties. How can we live together while that man lives? — he being your husband in nature, and not I. If he were dead it might be different. . . . Besides, that's not all the difficulty; it lies in another consideration — one bearing upon the future of other people than ourselves. Think of years to come, and children being born to us, and this past matter getting known — for it must get known. There is not an uttermost part of the earth but somebody comes from it or goes to it from elsewhere. Well, think of wretches of our flesh and blood growing up under a taunt which they will gradually get to feel the full force of with their expanding years. What an awakening for them! What a prospect! Can you honestly say Remain, after contemplating this contingency? Don't you think we had better endure the ills we have than fly to others?'

Her eyelids, weighted with trouble, continued drooping as before.

'I cannot say Remain,' she answered. 'I cannot; I had not thought so far.'

Tess's feminine hope — shall we confess it? — had been so obstinately re-cuperative as to revive in her surreptitious visions of a domiciliary intimacy continued long enough to break down his coldness even against his judgment. Though unsophisticated in the usual sense, she was not incomplete; and it would have denoted deficiency of womanhood if she had not instinctively known what an argument lies in propinquity. Nothing else would serve her, she knew, if this failed. It was wrong to hope in what was of the nature of strategy, she said to herself: yet that sort of hope she could not extinguish. His last representation had now been made, and it was, as she said, a new view. She had truly never thought so far as that, and his lucid picture of possible offspring who would scorn her was one that brought deadly conviction to an honest heart which was humanitarian to its centre. Sheer experience had already taught her that, in some circum-stances, there was one thing better than to lead a good life, and that was to be saved from leading any life whatever. Like all who have been previsioned by suffering, she could, in the words of M. Sully-Prudhomme, hear a penal sentence in the fiat, 'You shall be born', particularly if addressed to potential issue of hers.

Yet such is the vulpine slyness of Dame Nature, that, till now, Tess had been hoodwinked by her love for Clare into forgetting it might result in vitalizations that would inflict upon others what she had bewailed as a misfortune to herself.

She therefore could not withstand his argument. But with the self-combating proclivity of the super-sensitive, an answer thereto arose in Clare's own mind, and he almost feared it. It was based on her exceptional physical nature; and she might have used it promisingly. She might have added besides: 'On an Australian upland or Texan plain, who is to know or care about my misfortunes, or to reproach me or you?' Yet, like the majority of women, she accepted the momentary presentment as if it were the inevitable. And she may have been right. The intuitive heart of woman knoweth not only its own bitterness, but its husband's, and even if these assumed reproaches were not likely to be addressed to him or to his by strangers, they might have reached his ears from his own fastidious brain.

It was the third day of the estrangement. Some might risk the odd paradox that with more animalism he would have been the nobler man. We do not say. Yet Clare's love was doubtless ethereal to a fault, imaginative to impracticability. With these natures, corporeal presence is sometimes less appealing than corporeal absence; the latter creating an ideal presence that conveniently drops the defects of the real. She found that her personality did not plead her cause so forcibly as she had anticipated. The figurative phrase was true: she was another woman than the one who had excited his desire.

'I have thought over what you say,' she remarked to him, moving her forefinger over the tablecloth, her other hand, which bore the ring that mocked them both, supporting her forehead. 'It is quite true all of it; it must be. You must go away from me.'

'But what can you do?'

'I can go home.'

Clare had not thought of that.

'Are you sure?' he inquired.

'Quite sure. We ought to part, and we may as well get it past and done. You once said that I was apt to win men against their better judgment; and if I am constantly before your eyes I may cause you to change your plans in opposition to your reason and wish; and afterwards your repentance and my sorrow will be terrible.'

'And you would like to go home?' he asked.

'I want to leave you, and go home.'

'Then it shall be so.'

Though she did not look up at him, she started. There was a difference between the proposition and the covenant, which she had felt only too quickly.

'I feared it would come to this,' she murmured, her countenance meekly fixed. 'I don't complain, Angel. I – I think it best. What you said has quite convinced me. Yes, though nobody else should reproach me if we should stay together, yet somewhen, years hence, you might get angry with me for any ordinary matter, and knowing what you do of my bygones you yourself might be tempted to say words, and they might be overheard, perhaps by my own children. O, what only hurts me now would torture and kill me then! I will go – to-morrow.'

'And I shall not stay here. Though I didn't like to initiate it, I have seen that it was advisable we should part – at least for a while, till I can better see the shape that things have taken, and can write to you.'

Tess stole a glance at her husband. He was pale, even tremulous; but, as before, she was appalled by the determination revealed in the depths of this gentle being she had married – the will to subdue the grosser to the subtler emotion, the substance to the conception, the flesh to the spirit. Propensities, tendencies, habits, were as dead leaves upon the tyrannous wind of his imaginative ascendency.

He may have observed her look, for he explained –

'I think of people more kindly when I am away from them', adding cynically, 'God knows; perhaps we shall shake down together some day, for weariness; thousands have done it!'

That day he began to pack up, and she went upstairs and began to pack also. Both knew that it was in their two minds that they might part the next morning for ever, despite the gloss of assuaging conjectures thrown over their proceeding because they were of the sort to whom any parting which has an air of finality is a torture. He knew, and she knew, that, though the fascination which each had exercised over the other – on her part independently of accomplishments – would probably in the first days of their separation be even more potent than

ever, time must attenuate that effect; the practical arguments against accepting
her as a housemate might pronounce themselves more strongly in the boreal light
of a remoter view. Moreover, when two people are once parted – have
abandoned a common domicile and a common environment – new growths
insensibly bud upward to fill each vacated place; unforeseen accidents hinder
intentions, and old plans are forgotten.

CHAPTER THIRTY-SEVEN

MIDNIGHT came and passed silently, for there was nothing to announce it in the
Valley of the Froom.

Not long after one o'clock there was a slight creak in the darkened farmhouse
once the mansion of the d'Urbervilles. Tess, who used the upper chamber, heard
it and awoke. It had come from the corner step of the staircase, which, as usual,
was loosely nailed. She saw the door of her bedroom open, and the figure of her
husband crossed the stream of moonlight with a curiously careful tread. He was
in his shirt and trousers only, and her first flush of joy died when she perceived
that his eyes were fixed in an unnatural stare on vacancy. When he reached the
middle of the room he stood still and murmured, in tones of indescribable
sadness –

'Dead! dead! dead!'

Under the influence of any strongly-disturbing force Clare would occasionally
walk in his sleep, and even perform strange feats, such as he had done on the night
of their return from market just before their marriage, when he re-enacted in his
bedroom his combat with the man who had insulted her. Tess saw that continued
mental distress had wrought him into that somnambulistic state now.

Her loyal confidence in him lay so deep down in her heart that, awake or
asleep, he inspired her with no sort of personal fear. If he had entered with a pistol
in his hand he would scarcely have disturbed her trust in his protectiveness.

Clare came close, and bent over her. 'Dead, dead, dead!' he murmured.

After fixedly regarding her for some moments with the same gaze of
unmeasurable woe he bent lower, enclosed her in his arms, and rolled her in the
sheet as in a shroud. Then lifting her from the bed with as much respect as one
would show to a dead body, he carried her across the room, murmuring –

'My poor, poor Tess – my dearest, darling Tess! So sweet, so good, so true!'

The words of endearment, withheld so severely in his waking hours, were
inexpressibly sweet to her forlorn and hungry heart. If it had been to save her
weary life she would not, by moving or struggling, have put an end to the position
she found herself in. Thus she lay in absolute stillness, scarcely venturing to
breathe, and, wondering what he was going to do with her, suffered herself to be
borne out upon the landing.

'My wife – dead, dead!' he said.

He paused in his labours for a moment to lean with her against the banister.
Was he going to throw her down? Self-solicitude was near extinction in her, and

in the knowledge that he had planned to depart on the morrow, possibly for always, she lay in his arms in this precarious position with a sense rather of luxury than of terror. If they could only fall together, and both be dashed to pieces, how fit, how desirable.

However, he did not let her fall, but took advantage of the support of the handrail to imprint a kiss upon her lips — lips in the daytime scorned. Then he clasped her with a renewed firmness of hold, and descended the staircase. The creak of the loose stair did not awaken him, and they reached the ground-floor safely. Freeing one of his hands from his grasp of her for a moment, he slid back the door-bar and passed out, slightly striking his stockinged toe against the edge of the door. But this he seemed not to mind, and, having room for extension in the open air, he lifted her against his shoulder, so that he could carry her with ease, the absence of clothes taking much from his burden. Thus he bore her off the premises in the direction of the river a few yards distant.

His ultimate intention, if he had any, she had not yet divined; and she found herself conjecturing on the matter as a third person might have done. So easefully had she delivered her whole being up to him that it pleased her to think he was regarding her as his absolute possession, to dispose of as he should choose. It was consoling, under the hovering terror of to-morrow's separation, to feel that he really recognized her now as his wife Tess, and did not cast her off, even if in that recognition he went so far as to arrogate to himself the right of harming her.

Ah! now she knew what he was dreaming of — that Sunday morning when he had borne her along through the water with the other dairymaids, who had loved him nearly as much as she, if that were possible, which Tess could hardly admit. Clare did not cross the bridge with her, but proceeding several paces on the same side towards the adjoining mill, at length stood still on the brink of the river.

Its waters, in creeping down these miles of meadow-land, frequently divided, serpentining in purposeless curves, looping themselves around little islands that had no name, returning and reembodying themselves as a broad main stream further on. Opposite the spot to which he had brought her was such a general confluence, and the river was proportionately voluminous and deep. Across it was a narrow foot-bridge; but now the autumn flood had washed the handrail away, leaving the bare plank only, which, lying a few inches above the speeding current, formed a giddy pathway for even steady heads; and Tess had noticed from the window of the house in the daytime young men walking across upon it as a feat in balancing. Her husband had possibly observed the same performance; anyhow, he now mounted the plank, and, sliding one foot forward, advanced along it.

Was he going to drown her? Probably he was. The spot was lonely, the river deep and wide enough to make such a purpose easy of accomplishment. He might drown her if he would; it would be better than parting to-morrow to lead severed lives.

The swift stream raced and gyrated under them, tossing, distorting, and splitting the moon's reflected face. Spots of froth travelled past, and intercepted weeds waved behind the piles. If they could both fall together into the current now, their arms would be so tightly clasped together that they could not be saved; they would go out of the world almost painlessly, and there would be no more reproach to her, or to him for marrying her. His last half-hour with her would have been a loving one, while if they lived till he awoke his daytime aversion would return, and this hour would remain to be contemplated only as a transient dream.

The impulse stirred in her, yet she dared not indulge it, to make a movement that would have precipitated them both into the gulf. How she valued her own life had been proved; but his — she had no right to tamper with it. He reached the other side with her in safety.

Here they were within a plantation which formed the Abbey grounds, and taking a new hold of her he went onward a few steps till they reached the ruined choir of the Abbey-church. Against the north wall was the empty stone coffin of an abbot, in which every tourist with a turn for grim humour was accustomed to stretch himself. In this Clare carefully laid Tess. Having kissed her lips a second time he breathed deeply, as if a greatly desired end were attained. Clare then lay down on the ground alongside, when he immediately fell into the deep dead slumber of exhaustion, and remained motionless as a log. The spurt of mental excitement which had produced the effort was now over.

Tess sat up in the coffin. The night, though dry and mild for the season, was more than sufficiently cold to make it dangerous for him to remain here long, in his half-clothed state. If he were left to himself he would in all probability stay there till the morning, and be chilled to certain death. She had heard of such deaths after sleep-walking. But how could she dare to awaken him, and let him know what he had been doing, when it would mortify him to discover his folly in respect of her? Tess, however, stepping out of her stone confine, shook him slightly, but was unable to arouse him without being violent. It was indispensable to do something, for she was beginning to shiver, the sheet being but a poor protection. Her excitement had in a measure kept her warm during the few minutes' adventure; but that beatific interval was over.

It suddenly occurred to her to try persuasion; and accordingly she whispered in his ear, with as much firmness and decision as she could summon —

'Let us walk on, darling,' at the same time taking him suggestively by the arm. To her relief, he unresistingly acquiesced; her words had apparently thrown him back into his dream, which thenceforward seemed to enter on a new phase, wherein he fancied she had risen as a spirit, and was leading him to Heaven. Thus she conducted him by the arm to the stone bridge in front of their residence, crossing which they stood at the manor-house door. Tess's feet were quite bare, and the stones hurt her, and chilled her to the bone; but Clare was in his woollen stockings, and appeared to feel no discomfort.

There was no further difficulty. She induced him to lie down on his own sofa bed, and covered him up warmly, lighting a temporary fire of wood, to dry any dampness out of him. The noise of these attentions she thought might awaken him, and secretly wished that they might. But the exhaustion of his mind and body was such that he remained undisturbed.

As soon as they met the next morning Tess divined that Angel knew little or nothing of how far she had been concerned in the night's excursion, though, as regarded himself, he may have been aware that he had not lain still. In truth, he had awakened that morning from a sleep deep as annihilation; and during those first few moments in which the brain, like a Samson shaking himself, is trying its strength, he had some dim notion of an unusual nocturnal proceeding. But the realities of his situation soon displaced conjecture on the other subject.

He waited in expectancy to discern some mental pointing; he knew that if any intention of his, concluded over-night, did not vanish in the light of morning, it stood on a basis approximating to one of pure reason, even if initiated by impulse of feeling; that it was so far, therefore, to be trusted. He thus beheld in the pale morning light the resolve to separate from her; not as a hot and indignant instinct, but denuded of the passionateness which had made it scorch and burn; standing in its bones; nothing but a skeleton, but none the less there. Clare no longer hesitated.

At breakfast, and while they were packing the few remaining articles, he showed his weariness from the night's effort so unmistakably that Tess was on the point of revealing all that had happened; but the reflection that it would anger him, grieve him, stultify him, to know that he had instinctively manifested a fondness for her of which his common-sense did not approve; that his inclination had compromised his dignity when reason slept, again deterred her. It was too much like laughing at a man when sober for his erratic deeds during intoxication.

It just crossed her mind, too, that he might have a faint recollection of his tender vagary, and was disinclined to allude to it from a conviction that she would take amatory advantage of the opportunity it gave her of appealing to him anew not to go.

He had ordered by letter a vehicle from the nearest town, and soon after breakfast it arrived. She saw in it the beginning of the end – the temporary end, at least, for the revelation of his tenderness by the incident of the night raised dreams of a possible future with him. The luggage was put on the top, and the man drove them off, the miller and the old waiting-woman expressing some surprise at their precipitate departure, which Clare attributed to his discovery that the mill-work was not of the modern kind which he wished to investigate, a statement that was true so far as it went. Beyond this there was nothing in the manner of their leaving to suggest a *fiasco*, or that they were not going together to visit friends.

Their route lay near the dairy from which they had started with such solemn joy in each other a few days back, and, as Clare wished to wind up his business with Mr Crick, Tess could hardly avoid paying Mrs Crick a call at the same time, unless she would excite suspicion of their unhappy state.

To make the call as unobtrusive as possible they left the carriage by the wicket leading down from the high road to the dairy-house, and descended the track on foot, side by side. The withy-bed had been cut, and they could see over the stumps the spot to which Clare had followed her when he pressed her to be his wife; to the left the enclosure in which she had been fascinated by his harp; and far away behind the cowstalls the mead which had been the scene of their first embrace. The gold of the summer picture was now gray, the colours mean, the rich soil mud, and the river cold.

Over the barton-gate the dairyman saw them, and came forward, throwing into his face the kind of jocularity deemed appropriate in Talbothays and its vicinity on the re-appearance of the newly-married. Then Mrs Crick emerged from the house, and several others of their old acquaintance, though Marian and Retty did not seem to be there.

Tess valiantly bore their sly attacks and friendly humours, which affected her far otherwise than they supposed. In the tacit agreement of husband and wife to keep their estrangement a secret they behaved as would have been ordinary. And then, although she would rather there had been no word spoken on the subject, Tess had to hear in detail the story of Marian and Retty. The latter had gone home to her father's, and Marian had left to look for employment elsewhere. They feared she would come to no good.

To dissipate the sadness of this recital Tess went and bade all her favourite cows good-bye, touching each of them with her hand, and as she and Clare stood side by side at leaving, as if united body and soul, there would have been something peculiarly sorry in their aspect to one who should have seen it truly; two limbs of one life, as they outwardly were, his arm touching hers, her skirts touching him, facing one way, as against all the dairy facing the other, speaking in their adieux as 'we', and yet sundered like the poles. Perhaps something unusually stiff and embarrassed in their attitude, some awkwardness in acting up to their profession of unity, different from the natural shyness of young couples, may have been apparent, for when they were gone Mrs Crick said to her husband —

'How onnatural the brightness of her eyes did seem, and how they stood like waxen images and talked as if they were in a dream! Didn't it strike 'ee that 'twas so? Tess had always sommat strange in her, and she's not now quite like the proud young bride of a well-be-doing man.'

They re-entered the vehicle, and were driven along the roads towards Weatherbury and Stagfoot Lane, till they reached the Lane inn, where Clare dismissed the fly and man. They rested here a while, and entering the Vale were next driven onward towards her home by a stranger who did not know their relations. At a midway point, when Nuttlebury had been passed, and where there were cross-roads, Clare stopped the conveyance and said to Tess that if she meant to return to her mother's house it was here that he would leave her. As they could not talk with freedom in the driver's presence he asked her to accompany him for a few steps on foot along one of the branch roads; she assented, and directing the man to wait a few minutes they strolled away.

'Now, let us understand each other,' he said gently. 'There is no anger between us, though there is that which I cannot endure at present. I will try to bring myself to endure it. I will let you know where I go to as soon as I know myself. And if I can bring myself to bear it — if it is desirable, possible — I will come to you. But until I come to you it will be better that you should not try to come to me.'

The severity of the decree seemed deadly to Tess; she saw his view of her clearly enough; he could regard her in no other light than that of one who had practised gross deceit upon him. Yet could a woman who had done even what she had done deserve all this? But she could contest the point with him no further. She simply repeated after him his own words.

'Until you come to me I must not try to come to you?'

'Just so.'

'May I write to you?'

'O yes — if you are ill, or want anything at all. I hope that will not be the case; so that it may happen that I write first to you.'

'I agree to the conditions, Angel; because you know best what my punishment ought to be; only – only – don't make it more than I can bear!'

That was all she said on the matter. If Tess had been artful, had she made a scene, fainted, wept hysterically, in that lonely lane, notwithstanding the fury of fastidiousness with which he was possessed, he would probably not have withstood her. But her mood of long-suffering made his way easy for him, and she herself was his best advocate. Pride, too, entered into her submission – which perhaps was a symptom of that reckless acquiescence in chance too apparent in the whole d'Urberville family – and the many effective chords which she could have stirred by an appeal were left untouched.

The remainder of their discourse was on practical matters only. He now handed her a packet containing a fairly good sum of money, which he had obtained from his bankers for the purpose. The brilliants, the interest in which seemed to be Tess's for her life only (if he understood the wording of the will), he advised her to let him send to a bank for safety; and to this she readily agreed.

These things arranged he walked with Tess back to the carriage, and handed her in. The coachman was paid and told where to drive her. Taking next his own bag and umbrella – the sole articles he had brought with him hitherwards – he bade her good-bye; and they parted there and then.

The fly moved creepingly up a hill, and Clare watched it go with an unpremeditated hope that Tess would look out of the window for one moment. But that she never thought of doing, would not have ventured to do, lying in a half-dead faint inside. Thus he beheld her recede, and in the anguish of his heart quoted a line from a poet, with peculiar emendations of his own –

God's *not* in his heaven: all's *wrong* with the world!

When Tess had passed over the crest of the hill he turned to go his own way, and hardly knew that he loved her still.

CHAPTER THIRTY-EIGHT

As she drove on through Blackmoor Vale, and the landscape of her youth began to open around her, Tess aroused herself from her stupor. Her first thought was how would she be able to face her parents?

She reached a turnpike-gate which stood upon the highway to the village. It was thrown open by a stranger, not by the old man who had kept it for many years, and to whom she had been known; he had probably left on New Year's Day, the date when such changes were made. Having received no intelligence lately from her home, she asked the turnpike-keeper for news.

'Oh – nothing, miss,' he answered. 'Marlott is Marlott still. Folks have died and that. John Durbeyfield, too, hev had a daughter married this week to a gentleman-farmer; not from John's own house, you know; they was married elsewhere; the gentleman being of that high standing that John's own folk was not considered well-be-doing enough to have any part in it, the bridegroom seeming not to know how't have been discovered that John is a old and ancient nobleman himself by blood, with family skillentons in their own vaults to this day, but done out of his property in the time o' the Romans. However, Sir John, as we call'n now, kept up the wedding-day as well as he could, and stood treat to everybody in the parish; and John's wife sung songs at The Pure Drop till past eleven o'clock.'

Hearing this, Tess felt so sick at heart that she could not decide to go home publicly in the fly with her luggage and belongings. She asked the turnpike-keeper if she might deposit her things at his house for a while, and, on his offering no objection, she dismissed her carriage, and went on to the village alone by a back lane.

At sight of her father's chimney she asked herself how she could possibly enter the house? Inside that cottage her relations were calmly supposing her far away on a wedding-tour with a comparatively rich man, who was to conduct her to bouncing prosperity; while here she was, friendless, creeping up to the old door quite by herself, with no better place to go to in the world.

She did not reach the house unobserved. Just by the garden-hedge she was met by a girl who knew her – one of the two or three with whom she had been intimate at school. After making a few inquiries as to how Tess came there, her friend, unheeding her tragic look, interrupted with –

'But where's thy gentleman, Tess?'

Tess hastily explained that he had been called away on business, and, leaving her interlocutor, clambered over the garden-hedge, and thus made her way to the house.

As she went up the garden-path she heard her mother singing by the back door, coming in sight of which she perceived Mrs Durbeyfield on the doorstep in the act of wringing a sheet. Having performed this without observing Tess, she went indoors, and her daughter followed her.

The washing-tub stood in the same old place on the same old quarter-hogshead, and her mother, having thrown the sheet aside, was about to plunge her arms in anew.

'Why – Tess – my chil' – I thought you was married! – married really and truly this time – we sent the cider—'

'Yes, mother; so I am.'

'Going to be?'

'No – I am married.'

'Married! Then where's thy husband?'

'Oh, he's gone away for a time.'

'Gone away! When was you married, then? The day you said?'

'Yes, Tuesday, mother.'

'And now 'tis on'y Saturday, and gone away?'

'Yes; he's gone.'

'What's the meaning o' that? 'Nation seize such husbands as you seem to get, say I!'

'Mother!' Tess went across to Joan Durbeyfield, laid her face upon the matron's bosom, and burst into sobs. 'I don't know how to tell 'ee, mother! You said to me, and wrote to me, that I was not to tell him. But I did tell him – I couldn't help it – and he went away!'

'O you little fool – you little fool!' burst out Mrs Durbetfield, splashing Tess and herself in her agitation. 'My good God! that ever I should ha' lived to say it, but I say it again, you little fool!'

Tess was convulsed with weeping, the tension of so many days having relaxed at last.

'I know it – I know – I know!' she gasped through her sobs. 'But, O my mother, I could not help it! He was so good – and I felt the wickedness of trying to blind him as to what had happened! If – if – it were to be done again – I should do the same. I could not – I dared not – so sin – against him!'

'But you sinned enough to marry him first!'

'Yes, yes; that's where my misery do lie! But I thought he could get rid o' me by law if he were determined not to overlook it. And O, if you knew – if you could only half know how I loved him – how anxious I was to have him – and how wrung I was between caring so much for him and my wish to be fair to him!'

Tess was so shaken that she could get no further, and sank a helpless thing into a chair.

'Well, well; what's done can't be undone! I'm sure I don't know why children o'my bringing forth should all be bigger simpletons than other people's – not to know better than to blab such a thing as that, when he couldn't ha' found it out till too late!' Here Mrs Durbeyfield began shedding tears on her own account as a mother to be pitied. 'What your father will say I don't know,' she continued; 'for he's been talking about the wedding up at Rolliver's and The Pure Drop every day since, and about his family getting back to their rightful position through you – poor silly man! – and now you've made this mess of it! The Lord-a-Lord!'

As if to bring matters to a focus, Tess's father was heard approaching at that moment. He did not, however, enter immediately, and Mrs Durbeyfield said that she would break the bad news to him herself, Tess keeping out of sight for the present. After her first burst of disappointment Joan began to take the mishap as she had taken Tess's original trouble, as she would have taken a wet holiday or failure in the potato-crop; as a thing which had come upon them irrespective of desert or folly; a chance external impingement to be borne with; not a lesson.

Tess retreated upstairs, and beheld casually that the beds had been shifted, and new arrangements made. Her old bed had been adapted for two younger children. There was no place here for her now.

The room below being unceiled she could hear most of what went on there. Presently her father entered, apparently carrying a live hen. He was a foot-haggler now, having been obliged to sell his second horse, and he travelled with his basket on his arm. The hen had been carried about this morning as it was often carried, to show people that he was in his work, though it had lain, with its legs tied, under the table at Rolliver's for more than an hour.

'We've just had up a story about—' Durbeyfield began, and thereupon related in detail to his wife a discussion which had arisen at the inn about the clergy, originated by the fact of his daughter having married into a clerical family. 'They was formerly styled "sir", like my own ancestry,' he said, 'though nowadays their true style, strictly speaking, is "clerk" only.' As Tess had wished that no great publicity should be given to the event, he had mentioned no particulars. He hoped she would remove that prohibition soon. He proposed that the couple should take Tess's own name, d'Urberville, as uncorrupted. It was better than her husband's. He asked if any letter had come from her that day.

Then Mrs Durbeyfiled informed him that no letter had come, but Tess unfortunately had come herself.

When at length the collapse was explained to him a sullen mortification, not usual with Durbeyfield, overpowered the influence of the cheering glass. Yet the intrinsic quality of the event moved his touchy sensitiveness less than its conjectured effect upon the minds of others.

'To think, now, that this was to be the end o't!' said Sir John. 'And I with a family vault under that there church of Kingsbere as big as Squire Jollard's ale-cellar, and my folk lying there in sixes and sevens, as genuine county bones and marrow as any recorded in history. And now to be sure what they fellers at Rolliver's and The Pure Drop will say to me! How they'll squint and glane, and say, "This is yer mighty match is it; this is yer getting back to the true level of yer forefathers in King Norman's time!" I feel this is too much, Joan; I shall put an end to myself, title and all – I can bear it no longer! . . . But she can make him keep her if he's married her?'

'Why, yes. But she won't think o'doing that.'

'D'ye think he really have married her? – or is it like the first—'

Poor Tess, who had heard as far as this, could not bear to hear more. The perception that her word could be doubted even here, in her own parental house, set her mind against the spot as nothing else could have done. How unexpected were the attacks of destiny! And if her father doubted her a little, would not neighbours and acquaintance doubt her much? O, she could not live long at home!

A few days, accordingly, were all that she allowed herself here, at the end of which time she received a short note from Clare, informing her that he had gone to the North of England to look at a farm. In her craving for the lustre of her true position as his wife, and to hide from her parents the vast extent of the division between them, she made use of this letter as her reason for again departing, leaving them under the impression that she was setting out to join him. Still further to screen her husband from any imputation of unkindness to her, she took twenty-five of the fifty pounds Clare had given her, and handed the sum over to her mother, as if the wife of a man like Angel Clare could well afford it, saying that it was a slight return for the trouble and humiliation she had brought upon them in years past. With this assertion of her dignity she bade them farewell; and after that there were lively doings in the Durbeyfield household for some time on the strength of Tess's bounty, her mother saying, and, indeed, believing, that the rupture which had arisen between the young husband and wife had adjusted itself under their strong feeling that they could not live apart from each other.

CHAPTER THIRTY-NINE

I T was three weeks after the marriage that Clare found himself descending the hill which led to the well-known parsonage of his father. With his downward course the tower of the church rose into the evening sky in a manner of inquiry as to why he had come; and no living person in the twilighted town seemed to notice him, still less to expect him. He was arriving like a ghost, and the sound of his own footsteps was almost an encumbrance to be got rid of.

The picture of life had changed for him. Before this time he had known it but speculatively; now he thought he knew it as a practical man; though perhaps he did not, even yet. Nevertheless humanity stood before him no longer in the pensive sweetness of Italian art, but in the staring and ghastly attitudes of a Wiertz Museum, and with the leer of a study by Van Beers.

His conduct during these first weeks had been desultory beyond description. After mechanically attempting to pursue his agricultural plans as though nothing unusual had happened, in the manner recommended by the great and wise men of all ages, he concluded that very few of those great and wise men had ever gone so far outside themselves as to test the feasibility of their counsel. 'This is the chief thing: be not perturbed,' said the Pagan moralist. That was just Clare's own opinion. But he was perturbed. 'Let not your heart be troubled, neither let it be afraid,' said the Nazarene. Clare chimed in cordially; but his heart was troubled all the same. How he would have liked to confront those two great thinkers, and earnestly appeal to them as fellow-man to fellow-men, and ask them to tell him their method!

His mood transmuted itself into a dogged indifference till at length he fancied he was looking on his own existence with the passive interest of an outsider.

He was embittered by the conviction that all this desolation had been brought about by the accident of her being a d'Urberville. When he found that Tess came of that exhausted ancient line, and was not of the new tribes from below, as he had fondly dreamed, why had he not stoically abandoned her, in fidelity to his principles? This was what he had got by apostasy, and his punishment was deserved.

Then he became weary and anxious, and his anxiety increased. He wondered if he had treated her unfairly. He ate without knowing that he ate, and drank without tasting. As the hours dropped past, as the motive of each act in the long series of bygone days presented itself to his view, he perceived how intimately the notion of having Tess as a dear possession was mixed up with all his schemes and words and ways.

In going hither and thither he observed in the outskirts of a small town a red-and-blue placard setting forth the great advantages of the Empire of Brazil as a field for the emigrating agriculturist. Land was offered there on exceptionally advantageous terms. Brazil somewhat attracted him as a new idea. Tess could eventually join him there, and perhaps in that country of contrasting scenes and notions and habits the conventions would not be so operative which made life with her seem impracticable to him here. In brief he was strongly inclined to try Brazil, especially as the season for going thither was just at hand.

With this view he was returning to Emminster to disclose his plan to his parents, and to make the best explanation he could make of arriving without Tess, short of revealing what had actually separated them. As he reached the door the new moon shone upon his face, just as the old one had done in the small hours of that morning when he had carried his wife in his arms across the river to the graveyard of the monks; but his face was thinner now.

Clare had given his parents no warning of his visit, and his arrival stirred the atmosphere of the Vicarage as the dive of the kingfisher stirs a quiet pool. His father and mother were both in the drawing-room, but neither of his brothers was now at home. Angel entered, and closed the door quietly behind him.

'But – where's your wife, dear Angel?' cried his mother. 'How you surprise us!'

'She is at her mother's – temporarily. I have come home rather in a hurry because I've decided to go to Brazil.'

'Brazil! Why they are all Roman Catholics there surely!'

'Are they? I hadn't thought of that.'

But even the novelty and painfulness of his going to a Papistical land could not displace for long Mr and Mrs Clare's natural interest in their son's marriage.

'We had your brief note three weeks ago announcing that it had taken place,' said Mrs Clare, 'and your father sent your godmother's gift to her, as you know. Of course it was best that none of us should be present, especially as you preferred to marry her from the dairy, and not at her home, wherever that may be. It would have embarrassed you, and given us no pleasure. Your brothers felt that very strongly. Now it is done we do not complain, particularly if she suits you for the business you have chosen to follow instead of the ministry of the Gospel. . . . Yet I wish I could have seen her first, Angel, or have known a little more about her. We sent her no present of our own, not knowing what would best give her pleasure, but you must suppose it only delayed. Angel, there is no irritation in my mind or your father's against you for this marriage; but we have thought it much better to reserve our liking for your wife till we could see her. And now you have not brought her. It seems strange. What has happened?'

He replied that it had been thought best by them that she should go to her parents' home for the present, whilst he came there.

'I don't mind telling you, dear mother,' he said, 'that I always meant to keep her away from this house till I should feel she could come with credit to you. But this idea of Brazil is quite a recent one. If I do go it will be unadvisable for me to take her on this my first journey. She will remain at her mother's till I come back.'

'And I shall not see her before you start?'

He was afraid they would not. His original plan had been, as he had said, to refrain from bringing her there for some little while – not to wound their prejudices – feelings – in any way; and for other reasons he had adhered to it. He would have to visit home in the course of a year, if he went out at once; and it would be possible for them to see her before he started a second time – with her.

A hastily prepared supper was brouht in, and Clare made further exposition of his plans. His mother's disappointment at not seeing the bride still remained with her. Clare's late enthusiasm for Tess had infected her through her maternal sympathies, till she had almost fancied that a good thing could come out of Nazareth — a charming woman out of Talbothays Dairy. She watched her son as he ate.

'Cannot you describe her? I am sure she is very pretty, Angel.'

'Of that there can be no question!' he said, with a zest which covered its bitterness.

'And that she is pure and virtuous goes without question?'

'Pure and virtuous, of course, she is.'

'I can see her quite distinctly. You said the other day that she was fine in figure; roundly built; had deep red lips like Cupid's bow; dark eyelashes and brows, an immense rope of hair like a ship's cable; and large eyes violety-bluey-blackish.'

'I did, mother.'

'I quite see her. And living in such seclusion she naturally had scarce ever seen any young man from the world without till she saw you.'

'Scarcely.'

'You were her first love?'

'Of course.'

'There are worse wives than these simple, rosy-mouthed, robust girls of the farm. Certainly I could have wished — well, since my son is to be an agriculturist, it is perhaps but proper that his wife should have been accustomed to an outdoor life.'

His father was less inquisitive; but when the time came for the chapter from the Bible which was always read before evening prayers, the Vicar observed to Mrs Clare —

'I think, since Angel has come, that it will be more appropriate to read the thirty-first of Proverbs than the chapter which we should have had in the usual course of our reading?'

'Yes, certainly,' said Mrs Clare. 'The words of King Lemuel' (she could cite chapter and verse as well as her husband). 'My dear son, your father has decided to read us the chapter in Proverbs in praise of a virtuous wife. We shall not need to be reminded to apply the words to the absent one. May Heaven shield her in all her ways!'

A lump rose in Clare's throat. The portable lectern was taken out from the corner and set in the middle of the fireplace, the two old servants came in, and Angel's father began to read at the tenth verse of the aforesaid chapter —

' " Who can find a virtuous woman? for her price is far above rubies. She riseth while it is yet night, and giveth meat to her household. She girdeth her loins with strength and strengtheneth her arms. She perceiveth that her merchandise is good; her candle goeth not out by night. She looketh well to the ways of her household, and eateth not the bread of idleness. Her children arise up and call her blessed; her husband also, and he praiseth her. Many daughters have done virtuously, but thou excellest them all." '

When prayers were over, his mother said —

'I could not help thinking how very aptly that chapter your dear father read applied, in some of its particulars, to the woman you have chosen. The perfect woman, you see, was a working woman; not an idler; not a fine lady; but one who used her hands and her head and her heart for the good of others. "Her children arise up and call her blessed; her husband also, and he praiseth her. Many daughters have done virtuously, but she excelleth them all." Well, I wish I could have seen her, Angel. Since she is pure and chaste she would have been refined enough for me.'

Clare could bear this no longer. His eyes were full of tears, which seemed like drops of molten lead. He bade a quick good-night to these sincere and simple souls whom he loved so well; who knew neither the world, the flesh, nor the devil in their own hearts; only as something vague and external to themselves. He went to his own chamber.

His mother followed him, and tapped at his door. Clare opened it to discover her standing without, with anxious eyes.

'Angel,' she asked, 'is there something wrong that you go away so soon? I am quite sure you are not yourself.'

'I am not, quite, mother,' said he.

'About her? Now, my son, I know it is that — I know it is about her! Have you quarrelled in these three weeks?'

'We have not exactly quarrelled,' he said. 'But we have had a difference —'

'Angel — is she a young woman whose history will bear investigation?'

With a mother's instinct Mrs Clare had put her finger on the kind of trouble that would cause such a disquiet as seemed to agitate her son.

'She is spotless!' he replied; and felt that if it had sent him to eternal hell there and then he would have told that lie.

'Then never mind the rest. After all, there are few purer things in nature than an unsullied country maid. Any crudeness of manner which may offend your more educated sense at first, will, I am sure, disappear under the influence of your companionship and tuition.'

Such terrible sarcasm of blind magnanimity brought home to Clare the secondary perception that he had utterly wrecked his career by this marriage, which had not been among his early thoughts after the disclosure. True, on his own account he cared very little about his career; but he had wished to make it at least a respectable one on account of his parents and brothers. And now as he looked into the candle its flame dumbly expressed to him that it was made to shine on sensible people, and that it abhorred lighting the face of a dupe and a failure.

When his agitation had cooled he would be at moments incensed with his poor wife for causing a situation in which he was obliged to practise deception on his parents. He almost talked to her in his anger, as if she had been in the room. And then her cooing voice, plaintive in expostulation, disturbed the darkness, the velvet touch of her lips passed over his brow, and he could distinguish in the air the warmth of her breath.

This night the woman of his belittling deprecations was thinking how great and good her husband was. But over them both there hung a deeper shade than the shade which Angel Clare perceived, namely, the shade of his own limitations. With all his attempted independence of judgment this advanced and well-meaning young man, a sample product of the last five-and-twenty years, was yet the slave to custom and conventionality when surprised back into his early teachings. No prophet had told him, and he was not prophet enough to tell himself, that essentially this young wife of his was as deserving of the praise of King Lemuel as any other woman endowed with the same dislike of evil, her moral value having to be reckoned not by achievement but by tendency. Moreover, the figure near at hand suffers on such occasions, because it shows up its sorriness without shade; while vague figures afar off are honoured, in that their distance makes artistic virtues of their stains. In considering what Tess was not, he overlooked what she was, and forgot that the defective can be more than the entire.

CHAPTER FORTY

A T breakfast Brazil was the topic, and all endeavoured to take a hopeful view of Clare's proposed experiment with that country's soil, notwithstanding the discouraging reports of some farm-labourers who had emigrated thither and returned home within the twelve months. After breakfast Clare went into the little town to wind up such trifling matters as he was concerned with there, and to get from the local bank all the money he possessed. On his way back he encountered Miss Mercy Chant by the church, from whose walls she seemed to be a sort of emanation. She was carrying an armful of Bibles for her class, and such was her view of life that events which produced heartache in others wrought beatific smiles upon her – an enviable result, although, in the opinion of Angel, it was obtained by a curiously unnatural sacrifice of humanity to mysticism.

She had learnt that he was about to leave England, and observed what an excellent and promising scheme it seemed to be.

'Yes; it is a likely scheme enough in a commercial sense, no doubt,' he replied. 'But, my dear Mercy, it snaps the continuity of existence. Perhaps a cloister would be preferable.'

'A cloister! O, Angel Clare!'

'Well?'

'Why, you wicked man, a cloister implies a monk, and a monk Roman Catholicism.'

'And Roman Catholicism sin, and sin damnation. Thou art in a parlous state, Angel Clare.'

'*I* glory in my Protestantism!' she said severely.

Then Clare, thrown by sheer misery into one of the demoniacal moods in which a man does despite to his true principles, called her close to him, and fiendishly whispered in her ear the most heterodox ideas he could think of. His momentary laughter at the horror which appeared on her fair face ceased when it merged in pain and anxiety for his welfare.

'Dear Mercy,' he said, 'you must forgive me. I think I am going crazy!'

She thought that he was; and thus the interview ended, and Clare re-entered the Vicarage. With the local banker he deposited the jewels till happier days should arise. He also paid into the bank thirty pounds – to be sent to Tess in a few months, as she might require; and wrote to her at her parents' home in Blackmoor Vale to inform her of what he had done. This amount, with the sum he had already placed in her hands – about fifty pounds – he hoped would be amply sufficient for her wants just at present, particularly as in an emergency she had been directed to apply to his father.

He deemed it best not to put his parents into communication with her by informing them of her address; and, being unaware of what had really happened to estrange the two, neither his father nor his mother suggested that he should do so. During the day he left the parsonage, for what he had to complete he wished to get done quickly.

As the last duty before leaving this part of England it was necessary for him to call at the Welbridge farmhouse, in which he had spent with Tess the first three days of their marriage, the trifle of rent having to be paid, the key given up of the rooms they had occupied, and two or three small articles fetched away that they had left behind. It was under this roof that the deepest shadow ever thrown upon his life had stretched its gloom over him. Yet when he had unlocked the door of the sitting-room and looked into it, the memory which returned first upon him was that of their happy arrival on a similar afternoon, the first fresh sense of sharing a habitation conjointly, the first meal together, the chatting by the fire with joined hands.

The farmer and his wife were in the field at the moment of his visit, and Clare was in the rooms alone for some time. Inwardly swollen with a renewal of sentiments that he had not quite reckoned with, he went upstairs to her chamber, which had never been his. The bed was smooth as she had made it with her own hands on the morning of leaving. The mistletoe hung under the tester just as he had placed it. Having been there three or four weeks it was turning colour, and the leaves and berries were wrinkled. Angel took it down and crushed it into the grate. Standing there he for the first time doubted whether his course in this conjuncture had been a wise, much less a generous, one. But had he not been cruelly blinded? In the incoherent multitude of his emotions he knelt down at the bedside wet-eyed. 'O Tess! If you had only told me sooner, I would have forgiven you!' he mourned.

Hearing a footstep below he rose and went to the top of the stairs. At the bottom of the flight he saw a woman standing, and on her turning up her face recognised the pale, dark-eyed Izz Huett.

'Mr Clare,' she said, 'I've called to see you and Mrs Clare, and to inquire if ye be well. I thought you might be back here again.'

This was a girl whose secret he had guessed, but who had not yet guessed his; an honest girl who loved him – one who would have made as good, or nearly as good, a practical farmer's wife as Tess.

'I am here alone,' he said; 'we are not living here now.' Explaining why he had come, he asked, 'Which way are you going home, Izz?'

'I have no home at Talbothays Dairy now, sir,' she said.

'Why is that?'

Izz looked down.

'It was so dismal there that I left! I am staying out this way.' She pointed in a contrary direction, the direction in which he was journeying.

'Well – are you going there now? I can take you if you wish for a lift.'

Her olive complexion grew richer in hue.

'Thank 'ee, Mr Clare,' she said.

He soon found the farmer, and settled the account for his rent and the few other items which had to be considered by reason of the sudden abandonment of the lodgings. On Clare's return to his horse and gig Izz jumped up beside him.

'I am going to leave England, Izz,' he said, as they drove on. 'Going to Brazil.'

'And do Mrs Clare like the notion of such a journey?' she asked.

'She is not going at present – say for a year or so. I am going out to reconnoitre – to see what life there is like.'

They sped along eastward for some considerable distance, Izz making no observation.

'How are the others?' he inquired. 'How is Retty?'

'She was in a sort of nervous state when I zid her last; and so thin and hollow-cheeked that 'a do seem in a decline. Nobody will ever fall in love wi' her any more,' said Izz absently.

'And Marian?'

Izz lowered her voice.

'Marian drinks.'

'Indeed!'

'Yes. The dairyman has got rid of her.'

'And you!'

'I don't drink, and bain't in a decline. But – I am no great things at singing afore breakfast now!'

'How is that? Do you remember how neatly you used to turn "'Twas down in Cupid's Gardens" and "The Tailor's Breeches" at morning milking?'

'Ah, yes! When you first came, sir, that was. Not when you had been there a bit.'

'Why was that falling-off?'

Her black eyes flashed up to his face for one moment by way of answer.

'Izz! – how weak of you – for such as I!' he said, and fell into reverie. 'Then – suppose I had asked *you* to marry me?'

'If you had I should have said "Yes", and you would have married a woman who loved 'ee!'

'Really!'

'Down to the ground!' she whispered vehemently. 'O my God! did you never guess it till now!'

By-and-by they reached a branch road to a village.

'I must get down. I live out there,' said Izz abruptly, never having spoken since her avowal.

Clare slowed the horse. He was incensed against his fate, bitterly disposed towards social ordinances; for they had cooped him up in a corner, out of which there was no legitimate pathway. Why not be revenged on society by shaping his future domesticities loosely, instead of kissing the pedagogic rod of convention in this ensnaring manner?

'I am going to Brazil alone, Izz,' said he. 'I have separated from my wife for personal, not voyaging, reasons. I may never live with her again. I may not be able to love you; but – will you go with me instead of her?'

'You truly wish me to go?'

'I do. I have been badly used enough to wish for relief. And you at least love me disinterestedly.'

'Yes – I will go,' said Izz, after a pause.

'You will? You know what it means, Izz?'

'It means that I shall live with you for the time you are over there – that's good enough for me.'

'Remember, you are not to trust me in morals now. But I ought to remind you that it will be wrong-doing in the eyes of civilization – Western civilization, that is to say.'

'I don't mind that; no woman do when it comes to agony-point, and there's no other way!'

'Then don't get down, but sit where you are.'

He drove past the cross-roads, one mile, two miles, without showing any signs of affection.

'You love me very, very much, Izz?' he suddenly asked.

'I do – I have said I do! I loved you all the time we was at the dairy together!'

'More than Tess?'

She shook her head.

'No,' she murmured, 'not more than she.'

'How's that?'

'Because nobody could love 'ee more than Tess did! . . . She would have laid down her life for 'ee. I could do no more.'

Like the prophet on the top of Peor Izz Huett would fain have spoken perversely at such a moment, but the fascination exercised over her rougher nature by Tess's character compelled her to grace.

Clare was silent; his heart had risen at these straightforward words from such an unexpected unimpeachable quarter. In his throat was something as if a sob had solidified there. His ears repeated, '*She would have laid down her life for 'ee. I could do no more!*'

'Forget our idle talk, Izz,' he said, turning the horse's head suddenly. 'I don't know what I've been saying! I will now drive you back to where your lane branches off.'

'So much for honesty towards 'ee! O – how can I bear it – how can I – how can I!'

Izz Huett burst into wild tears, and beat her forehead as she saw what she had done.

'Do you regret that poor little act of justice to an absent one? O, Izz, don't spoil it by regret!'

She stilled herself by degrees.

'Very well, sir. Perhaps I didn't know what I was saying, either, wh – when I agreed to go! I wish – what cannot be!'

'Because I have a loving wife already.'

'Yes, yes! You have.'

They reached the corner of the lane which they had passed half an hour earlier, and she hopped down.

'Izz – please, please forget my momentary levity!' he cried. 'It was so ill-considered, so ill-advised!'

'Forget it? Never! O, it was no levity to me!'

He felt how richly he deserved the reproach that the wounded cry conveyed, and, in a sorrow that was inexpressible, leapt down and took her hand.

'Well, but, Izz, we'll part friends, anyhow? You don't know what I've had to bear!'

She was a really generous girl, and allowed no further bitterness to mar their adieux.

'I forgive 'ee, sir!' she said.

'Now, Izz,' he said, while she stood beside him there, forcing himself to the mentor's part he was far from feeling; 'I want you to tell Marian when you see her that she is to be a good woman, and not to give way to folly. Promise that, and tell Retty that there are more worthy men than I in the world, that for my sake she is to act wisely and well — remember the words — wisely and well — for my sake. I send this message to them as a dying man to the dying; for I shall never see them again. And you, Izzy, you have saved me by your honest words about my wife from an incredible impulse towards folly and treachery. Women may be bad, but they are not so bad as men in these things! On that one account I can never forget you. Be always the good and sincere girl you have hitherto been; and think of me as a worthless lover, but a faithful friend. Promise.'

She gave the promise.

'Heaven bless and keep you, sir. Good-bye!'

He drove on; but no sooner had Izz turned into the lane, and Clare was out of sight, than she flung herself down on the bank in a fit of racking anguish; and it was with a strained unnatural face that she entered her mother's cottage late that night. Nobody ever was told how Izz spent the dark hours that intervened between Angel Clare's parting from her and her arrival home.

Clare, too, after bidding the girl farewell, was wrought to aching thoughts and quivering lips. But his sorrow was not for Izz. That evening he was within a feather-weight's turn of abandoning his road to the nearest station, and driving across that elevated dorsal line of South Wessex which divided him from his Tess's home. It was neither a contempt for her nature, nor the probable state of her heart, which deterred him.

No; it was a sense that, despite her love, as corroborated by Izz's admission, the facts had not changed. If he was right at first, he was right now. And the momentum of the course on which he had embarked tended to keep him going in it, unless diverted by a stronger, more sustained force than had played upon him this afternoon. He could soon come back to her. He took the train that night for London, and five days after shook hands in farewell of his brothers at the port of embarkation.

CHAPTER FORTY-ONE

From the foregoing events of the winter-time let us press on to an October day, more than eight months subsequent to the parting of Clare and Tess. We discover the latter in changed conditions; instead of a bride with boxes and trunks which others bore, we see her a lonely woman with a basket and a bundle in her own porterage, as at an earlier time when she was no bride; instead of the ample means that were projected by her husband for her comfort through this probationary period, she can produce only a flattened purse.

After again leaving Marlott, her home, she had got through the spring and summer without any great stress upon her physical powers, the time being mainly spent in rendering light irregular service at dairy-work near Port Bredy to the west of the Blackmoor Valley, equally remote from her native place and from Talbothays. She preferred this to living on his allowance. Mentally she remained in utter stagnation, a condition which the mechanical occupation rather fostered than checked. Her consciousness was at that other dairy, at that other season, in the presence of the tender lover who had confronted her there – he who, the moment she had grasped him to keep for her own, had disappeared like a shape in a vision.

The dairy-work lasted only till the milk began to lessen, for she had not met with a second regular engagement as at Talbothays, but had done duty as a supernumerary only. However, as harvest was now beginning, she had simply to remove from the pasture to the stubble to find plenty of further occupation, and this continued till harvest was done.

Of the five-and-twenty pounds which had remained to her of Clare's allowance, after deducting the other half of the fifty as a contribution to her parents for the trouble and expense to which she had put them, she had as yet spent but little. But there now followed an unfortunate interval of wet weather, during which she was obliged to fall back upon her sovereigns.

She could not bear to let them go. Angel had put them into her hand, had obtained them bright and new from his bank for her; his touch had consecrated them to souvenirs of himself – they appeared to have had as yet no other history than such as was created by his and her own experiences – and to disperse them was like giving away relics. But she had to do it, and one by one they left her hands.

She had been compelled to send her mother her address from time to time, but she concealed her circumstances. When her money had almost gone a letter from her mother reached her. Joan stated that they were in dreadful difficulty; the autumn rains had gone through the thatch of the house, which required entire renewal; but this could not be done because the previous thatching had never been paid for. New rafters and a new ceiling upstairs also were required, which, with the previous bill, would amount to a sum of twenty pounds. As her husband was a man of means, and had doubtless returned by this time, could she not send them the money?

Tess had thirty pounds coming to her almost immediately from Angel's bankers, and, the case being so deplorable, as soon as the sum was received she sent the twenty as requested. Part of the remainder she was obliged to expend in winter clothing, leaving only a nominal sum for the whole inclement season at hand. When the last pound had gone, a remark of Angel's that whenever she required further resources she was to apply to his father, remained to be considered.

But the more Tess thought of the step the more reluctant was she to take it. The same delicacy, pride, false shame, whatever it may be called, on Clare's account, which had led her to hide from her own parents the prolongation of the estrangement, hindered her in owning to his that she was in want after the fair allowance he had left her. They probably despised her already; how much more they would despise her in the character of a mendicant! The consequence was that by no effort could the parson's daughter-in-law bring herself to let him know her state.

Her reluctance to communicate with her husband's parents might, she thought, lessen with the lapse of time; but with her own the reverse obtained. On her leaving their house after the short visit subsequent to her marriage they were under the impression that she was ultimately going to join her husband; and from that time to the present she had done nothing to disturb their belief that she was awaiting his return in comfort, hoping against hope that his journey to Brazil would result in a short stay only, after which he would come to fetch her, or that he would write for her to join him; in any case that they would soon present a united front to their families and the world. This hope she still fostered. To let her parents know that she was a deserted wife, dependent, now that she had relieved their necessities, on her own hands for a living, after the *éclat* of a marriage which was to nullify the collapse of the first attempt, would be too much indeed.

The set of brilliants returned to her mind. Where Clare had deposited them she did not know, and it mattered little, if it were true that she could only use and not sell them. Even were they absolutely hers it would be passing mean to enrich herself by a legal title to them which was not essentially hers at all.

Meanwhile her husband's days had been by no means free from trial. At this moment he was lying ill of fever in the clay lands near Curitiba in Brazil, having been drenched with thunder-storms and persecuted by other hardships, in common with all the English farmers and farm-labourers who, just at this time, were deluded into going thither by the promises of the Brazilian Government, and by the baseless assumption that those frames which, ploughing and sowing on English uplands, had resisted all the weathers to whose moods they had been born, could resist equally well all the weathers by which they were surprised on Brazilian plains.

To return. Thus it happened that when the last of Tess's sovereigns had been spent she was unprovided with others to take their place, while on account of the season she found it increasingly difficult to get employment. Not being aware of the rarity of intelligence, energy, health, and willingness in any sphere of life, she refrained from seeking an indoor occupation; fearing towns, large houses, people of means and social sophistication, and of manners other than rural. From that direction of gentility Black Care had come. Society might be better than she supposed from her slight experience of it. But she had no proof of this, and her instinct in the circumstances was to avoid its purlieus.

The small dairies to the west, beyond Port-Bredy, in which she had served as supernumerary milkmaid during the spring and summer required no further aid. Room would probably have been made for her at Talbothays, if only out of sheer compassion; but comfortable as her life had been there she could not go back. The anti-climax would be too intolerable; and her return might bring reproach upon her idolized husband. She could not have borne their pity, and their whispered remarks to one another upon her strange situation; though she would almost have faced a knowledge of her circumstances by every individual there, so long as her story had remained isolated in the mind of each. It was the interchange of ideas about her that made her sensitiveness wince. Tess could not account for this distinction; she simply knew that she felt it.

She was now on her way to an upland farm in the centre of the county, to which she had been recommended by a wandering letter which had reached her from Marian. Marian had somehow heard that Tess was separated from her husband – probably through Izz Huett – and the good-natured and now tippling girl, deeming Tess in trouble, had hastened to notify to her former friend that she herself had gone to this upland spot after leaving the dairy, and would like to see her there, where there was room for other hands it if was really true that she worked again as of old.

With the shortening of the days all hope of obtaining her husband's forgiveness began to leave her: and there was something of the habitude of the wild animal in the unreflecting instinct with which she rambled on – disconnecting herself by littles from her eventful past at every step, obliterating her identity, giving no thought to accidents or contingencies which might make a quick discovery of her whereabouts by others of importance to her own happiness, if not to theirs.

Among the difficulties of her lonely position not the least was the attention she excited by her appearance, a certain bearing of distinction, which she had caught from Clare, being superadded to her natural attractiveness. Whilst the clothes lasted which had been prepared for her marriage, these casual glances of interest caused her no inconvenience, but as soon as she was compelled to don the wrapper of a fieldwoman, rude words were addressed to her more than once; but nothing occurred to cause her bodily fear till a particular November afternoon

She had preferred the country west of the River Brit to the upland farm for which she was now bound, because, for one thing, it was nearer to the home of her husband's father; and to hover about that region unrecognized, with the notion that she might decide to call at the Vicarage some day, gave her pleasure. But having once decided to try the higher and drier levels, she pressed back eastward, marching afoot towards the village of Chalk-Newton, where she meant to pass the night.

The lane was long and unvaried, and, owing to the rapid shortening of the days, dusk came upon her before she was aware. She had reached the top of a hill down which the lane stretched its serpentine length in glimpses, when she heard footsteps behind her back, and in a few moments she was overtaken by a man. He stepped up alongside Tess and said –

'Good-night, my pretty maid'; to which she civilly replied.

The light still remaining in the sky lit up her face, though the landscape was nearly dark. The man turned and stared hard at her.

'Why, surely, it is the young wench who was at Trantridge awhile – young Squire d'Urberville's friend? I was there at that time, though I don't live there now.'

She recognized in him the well-to-do boor whom Angel had knocked down at the inn for addressing her coarsely. A spasm of anguish shot through her, and she returned him no answer.

'Be honest enough to own it, and that what I said in the town was true, though your fancy-man was so up about it – hey, my sly one? You ought to beg my pardon for that blow of his, considering.'

Still no answer came from Tess. There seemed only one escape for her hunted soul. She suddenly took to her heels with the speed of the wind, and, without looking behind her, ran along the road till she came to a gate which opened directly into a plantation. Into this she plunged, and did not pause till she was deep enough in its shade to be safe against any possibility of discovery.

Under foot the leaves were dry, and the foliage of some holly bushes which grew among the deciduous trees was dense enough to keep off draughts. She scraped together the dead leaves till she had formed them into a large heap, making a sort of nest in the middle. Into this Tess crept.

Such sleep as she got was naturally fitful; she fancied she heard strange noises, but persuaded herself that they were caused by the breeze. She thought of her husband in some vague warm clime on the other side of the globe, while she was here in the cold. Was there another such a wretched being as she in the world? Tess asked herself; and, thinking of her wasted life, said 'All is vanity.' She repeated the words mechanically, till she reflected that this was a most inadequate thought for modern days. Solomon had thought as far as that more than two thousand years ago; she herself, though not in the van of thinkers, had got much further. If all were only vanity, who would mind it? All was, alas, worse than vanity – injustice, punishment, exaction, death. The wife of Angel Clare put her hand to her brow, and felt its curve, and the edges of her eye-sockets perceptible under the soft skin, and thought as she did so that a time would come when that bone would be bare. 'I wish it were now,' she said.

In the midst of these whimsical fancies she heard a new strange sound among the leaves. It might be the wind; yet there was scarcely any wind. Sometimes it was a palpitation, sometimes a flutter; sometimes it was a sort of gasp or gurgle. Soon she was certain that the noises came from wild creatures of some kind, the more so when, originating in the boughs overhead, they were followed by the fall of a heavy body upon the ground. Had she been ensconced here under other more pleasant conditions she would have become alarmed; but, outside humanity, she had at present no fear.

Day at length broke in the sky. When it had been day aloft for some little while it became day in the wood.

Directly the assuring and prosaic light of the world's active hours had grown strong she crept from under her hillock of leaves, and looked around boldly. Then she perceived what had been going on to disturb her. The plantation wherein she had taken shelter ran down at this spot into a peak, which ended it hitherward, outside the hedge being arable ground. Under the trees several pheasants lay about, their rich plumage dabbled with blood; some were dead, some feebly twitching a wing, some staring up at the sky, some pulsating quickly, some contorted, some stretched out – all of them writhing in agony, except the fortunate ones whose tortures had ended during the night by the inability of nature to bear more.

Tess guessed at once the meaning of this. The birds had been driven down into this corner the day before by some shooting-party; and while those that had dropped dead under the shot, or had died before nightfall had been searched for and carried off, many badly wounded birds had escaped and hidden themselves away, or risen among the thick boughs, where they had maintained their position till they grew weaker with loss of blood in the night-time, when they had fallen one by one as she had heard them.

She had occasionally caught glimpses of these men in girlhood, looking over hedges, or peering through bushes, and pointing their guns, strangely accoutred, a bloodthirsty light in their eyes. She had been told that, rough and brutal as they seemed just then, they were not like this all the year round, but were, in fact, quite civil persons save during certain weeks of autumn and winter, when, like the inhabitants of the Malay Peninsula, they ran amuck, and made it their purpose to destroy life – in this case harmless feathered creatures, brought into being by artificial means solely to gratify these propensities – at once so unmannerly and so unchivalrous towards their weaker fellows in Nature's teeming family.

With the impulse of a soul who could feel for kindred sufferers as much as for herself, Tess's first thought was to put the still living birds out of their torture, and to this end with her own hands she broke the necks of as many as she could find, leaving them to lie where she had found them till the gamekeepers should come – as they probably would come – to look for them a second time.

'Poor darlings – to suppose myself the most miserable being on earth in the sight o' such misery as yours!' she exclaimed, her tears running down as she killed the birds tenderly. 'And not a twinge of bodily pain about me! I be not mangled, and I be not bleeding, and I have two hands to feed and clothe me.' She was ashamed of herself for her gloom of the night, based on nothing more tangible than a sense of condemnation under an arbitrary law of society which had no foundation in Nature.

CHAPTER FORTY-TWO

I T was now broad day, and she started again, emerging cautiously upon the highway. But there was no need for caution; not a soul was at hand, and Tess went onward with fortitude, her recollection of the birds' silent endurance of their night of agony impressing upon her the relativity of sorrows and the tolerable nature of her own, if she could once rise high enough to despise opinion. But that she could not do so long as it was held by Clare.

She reached Chalk-Newton, and breakfasted at an inn, where several young men were troublesomely complimentary to her good looks. Somehow she felt hopeful, for was it not possible that her husband also might say these same things to her even yet? She was bound to take care of herself on the chance of it, and keep off these casual lovers. To this end Tess resolved to run no further risks from her appearance. As soon as she got out of the village she entered a thicket and took from her basket one of the oldest field-gowns, which she had never put on even at the dairy – never since she had worked among the stubble at Marlott. She also, by a felicitous thought, took a handkerchief from her bundle and tied it round her face under her bonnet, covering her chin and half her cheeks and temples, as if she were suffering from toothache. Then with her little scissors, by the aid of a pocket looking-glass, she mercilessly nipped her eyebrows off, and thus insured against aggressive admiration she went on her uneven way.

'What a mommet of a maid!' said the next man who met her to a companion. Tears came into her eyes for very pity of herself as she heard him.

'But I don't care!' she said. 'O no – I don't care! I'll always be ugly now, because Angel is not here, and I have nobody to take care of me. My husband that was is gone away, and never will love me any more; but I love him just the same, and hate all other men, and like to make 'em think scornfully of me!'

Thus Tess walks on; a figure which is part of the landscape; a fieldwoman pure and simple, in winter guise; a gray serge cape, a red woollen cravat, a stuff skirt covered by a whitey-brown rough wrapper, and buff-leather gloves. Every thread of that old attire has become faded and thin under the stroke of raindrops, the burn of sunbeams, and the stress of winds. There is no sign of young passion in her now –

> The maiden's mouth is cold
> .   .   .
>
> Fold over simple fold
> Binding her head.

Inside this exterior, over which the eye might have roved as over a thing scarcely percipient, almost inorganic, there was the record of a pulsing life which had learnt too well, for its years, of the dust and ashes of things, of the cruelty of lust and the fragility of love.

Next day the weather was bad, but she trudged on, the honesty, directness, and impartiality of elemental enmity disconcerting her but little. Her object being a winter's occupation and a winter's home, there was no time to lose. Her experience of short hirings had been such that she was determined to accept no more.

Thus she went forward from farm to farm in the direction of the place whence Marian had written to her, which she determined to make use of as a last shift only, its rumoured stringencies being the reverse of tempting. First she inquired for the lighter kinds of employment, and, as acceptance in any variety of these grew hopeless, applied next for the less light, till, beginning with the dairy and poultry tendance that she liked best, she ended with the heavy and coarse pursuits which she liked least – work on arable land: work of such roughness, indeed, as she would never have deliberately volunteered for.

Towards the second evening she reached the irregular chalk tableland or plateau, bosomed with semi-globular tumuli – as if Cybele the Many-breasted were supinely extended there – which stretched between the valley of her birth and the valley of her love.

Here the air was dry and cold, and the long cart-roads were blown white and dusty within a few hours after rain. There were few trees, or none, those that would have grown in the hedges being mercilessly plashed down with the quickset by the tenant-farmers, the natural enemies of tree, bush, and brake. In the middle distance ahead of her she could see the summits of Bulbarrow and of Nettlecombe-Tout, and they seemed friendly. They had a low and unassuming aspect from this upland, though as approached on the other side from Blackmoor in her childhood they were as lofty bastions against the sky.

Southerly, at many miles' distance, and over the hills and ridges coastward, she could discern a surface like polished steel: it was the English Channel at a point far out towards France.

Before her, in a slight depression, were the remains of a village. She had, in fact, reached Flintcomb-Ash, the place of Marian's sojourn. There seemed to be no help for it; hither she was doomed to come. The stubborn soil around her showed plainly enough that the kind of labour in demand here was of the roughest kind; but it was time to rest from searching, and she resolved to stay, particularly as it began to rain. At the entrance to the village was a cottage whose gable jutted into the road, and before applying for a lodging she stood under its shelter, and watched the evening close in.

'Who would think I was Mrs Angel Clare!' she said.

The wall felt warm to her back and shoulders, and she found that immediately within the gable was the cottage fireplace, the heat of which came through the bricks. She warmed her hands upon them, and also put her cheek – red and moist with the drizzle – against their comforting surface. The wall seemed to be the only friend she had. She had so little wish to leave it that she could have stayed there all night.

Tess could hear the occupants of the cottage – gathered together after their day's labour – talking to each other within, and the rattle of their supper-plates was also audible. But in the village-street she had seen no soul yet. The solitude was at last broken by the approach of one feminine figure, who, though the evening was cold, wore the print gown and the tilt-bonnet of summer time. Tess instinctively thought it might be Marian, and when she came near enough to be distinguishable in the gloom surely enough it was she. Marian was even stouter and redder in the face than formerly, and decidedly shabbier in attire. At any previous period of her existence Tess would hardly have cared to renew the acquaintance in such conditions; but her loneliness was excessive, and she responded readily to Marian's greeting.

Marian was quite respectful in her inquiries, but seemed much moved by the fact that Tess should still continue in no better condition than at first; though she had dimly heard of the separation.

'Tess – Mrs Clare – the dear wife of dear he! And is it really so bad as this, my child? Why is your cwomely face tied up in such a way? Anybody been beating 'ee? Not *he*?'

'No, no, no! I merely did it not to be clipsed or colled, Marian.'

She pulled off in disgust a bandage which could suggest such wild thoughts.

'And you've no collar on' (Tess had been accustomed to wear a little white collar at the dairy).

'I know it, Marian.'

'You've lost it travelling.'

'I've not lost it. The truth is, I don't care anything about my looks; and so I didn't put it on.'

'And you don't wear your wedding-ring?'

'Yes, I do; but not in public. I wear it round my neck on a ribbon. I don't wish people to think who I am by marriage, or that I am married at all; it would be so awkward while I lead my present life.'

Marian paused.

'But you *be* a gentleman's wife; and it seems hardly fair that you should live like this!'

'O yes it is, quite fair; though I am very unhappy.'

'Well, well. *He* married you – and you can be unhappy!'

'Wives are unhappy sometimes; from no fault of their husbands – from their own.'

'You've no faults, deary; that I'm sure of. And he's none. So it must be something outside ye both.'

'Marian, dear Marian, will you do me a good turn without asking questions? My husband has gone abroad, and somehow I have overrun my allowance, so that I have to fall back upon my old work for a time. Do not call me Mrs Clare, but Tess, as before. Do they want a hand here?'

'O yes; they'll take one always, because few care to come. 'Tis a starve-acre place. Corn and swedes are all they grow. Though I be here myself, I feel 'tis a pity for such as you to come.'

'But you used to be as good a dairywoman as I.'

'Yes; but I've got out o' that since I took to drink. Lord, that's the only comfort I've got now! If you engage, you'll be set swede-hacking. That's what I be doing; but you won't like it.'

'O – anything! Will you speak for me?'

'You will do better by speaking for yourself.'

'Very well. Now, Marian, remember – nothing about *him*, if I get the place. I don't wish to bring his name down to the dirt.'

Marian, who was really a trustworthy girl though of coarser grain than Tess, promised anything she asked.

'This is pay-night,' she said, 'and if you were to come with me you would know at once. I be real sorry that you are not happy; but 'tis because he's away, I know. You couldn't be unhappy if he were here, even if he gie'd ye no money – even if he used you like a drudge.'

'That's true; I could not!'

They walked on together, and soon reached the farmhouse, which was almost sublime in its dreariness. There was not a tree within sight; there was not, at this season, a green pasture – nothing but fallow and turnips everywhere; in large fields divided by hedges plashed to unrelieved levels.

Tess waited outside the door of the farmhouse till the group of workfolk had received their wages, and then Marian introduced her. The farmer himself, it appeared, was not at home, but his wife, who represented him this evening, made no objection to hiring Tess, on her agreeing to remain till Old Lady-Day. Female field-labour was seldom offered now, and its cheapness made it profitable for tasks which women could perform as readily as men.

Having signed the agreement, there was nothing more for Tess to do at present than to get a lodging, and she found one in the house at whose gable-wall she had warmed herself. It was a poor subsistence that she had ensured, but it would afford a shelter for the winter at any rate.

That night she wrote to inform her parents of her new address, in case a letter should arrive at Marlott from her husband. But she did not tell them of the sorriness of her situation: it might have brought reproach upon him.

CHAPTER FORTY-THREE

T H E R E was no exaggeration in Marian's definition of Flintcomb-Ash farm as a starve-acre place. The single fat thing on the soil was Marian herself; and she was an importation. Of the three classes of village, the village cared for by its lord, the village cared for by itself, and the village uncared for either by itself or by its lord (in other words, the village of a resident squire's tenantry, the village of free or copy-holders, and the absentee-owner's village, farmed with the land) this place, Flintcomb-Ash, was the third.

But Tess set to work. Patience, that blending of moral courage with physical timidity, was now no longer a minor feature in Mrs Angel Clare; and it sustained her.

The swede-field in which she and her companion were set hacking was a stretch of a hundred odd acres, in one patch, on the highest ground of the farm, rising above stony lanchets or lynchets – the outcrop of siliceous veins in the chalk formation, composed of myriads of loose white flints in bulbous, cusped, and phallic shapes. The upper half of each turnip had been eaten off by the live-stock, and it was the business of the two women to grub up the lower or earthy half of the root with a hooked fork called a hacker, that it might be eaten also. Every leaf of the vegetable having already been consumed, the whole field was in colour a desolate drab; it was a complexion without features, as if a face, from chin to brow, should be only an expanse of skin. The sky wore, in another colour, the same likeness; a white vacuity of countenance with the lineaments gone. So these two upper and nether visages confronted each other all day long, the white face looking down on the brown face, and the brown face looking up at the white face, without anything standing between them but the two girls crawling over the surface of the former like flies.

Nobody came near them, and their movements showed a mechanical regularity; their forms standing enshrouded in Hessian 'wroppers' – sleeved brown pinafores, tied behind to the bottom, to keep their gowns from blowing about – scant skirts revealing boots that reached high up the ankles, and yellow sheepskin gloves with gauntlets. The pensive character which the curtained hood lent to their bent heads would have reminded the observer of some early Italian conception of the two Marys.

They worked on hour after hour, unconscious of the forlorn aspect they bore in the landscape, not thinking of the justice or injustice of their lot. Even in such a position as theirs it was possible to exist in a dream. In the afternoon the rain came on again, and Marian said that they need not work any more. But if they did not work they would not be paid; so they worked on. It was so high a situation, this field, that the rain had no occasion to fall, but raced along horizontally upon the yelling wind, sticking into them like glass splinters till they were wet through. Tess had not known till now what was really meant by that. There are degrees of dampness, and a very little is called being wet through in common talk. But to stand working slowly in a field, and feel the creep of rain-water, first in legs and shoulders, then on hips and head, then at back, front, and sides, and yet to work on till the leaden light diminishes and marks that the sun is down, demands a distinct modicum of stoicism, even of valour.

Yet they did not feel the wetness so much as might be supposed. They were both young, and they were talking of the time when they lived and loved together at Talbothays Dairy, that happy green tract of land where summer had been liberal in her gifts; in substance to all, emotionally to these. Tess would fain not have conversed with Marian of the man who was legally, if not actually, her husband; but the irresistible fascination of the subject betrayed her into reciprocating Marian's remarks. And thus, as has been said, though the damp curtains of their bonnets flapped smartly into their faces, and their wrappers clung about them to wearisomeness, they lived all this afternoon in memories of green, sunny, romantic Talbothays.

'You can see a gleam of a hill within a few miles o' Froom Valley from here when 'tis fine,' said Marian.

'Ah! Can you?' said Tess, awake to the new value of this locality.

So the two forces were at work here as everywhere, the inherent will to enjoy, and the circumstantial will against enjoyment. Marian's will had a method of assisting itself by taking from her pocket as the afternoon wore on a pint bottle corked with white rag, from which she invited Tess to drink. Tess's unassisted power of dreaming, however, being enough for her sublimation at present, she declined except the merest sip, and then Marian took a pull herself from the spirits.

'I've got used to it,' she said, 'and can't leave it off now. 'Tis my only comfort — You see I lost him: you didn't; and you can do without it perhaps.'

Tess thought her loss as great as Marian's, but upheld by the dignity of being Angel's wife, in the letter at least, she accepted Marian's differentiation.

Amid this scene Tess slaved in the morning frosts and in the afternoon rains. When it was not swede-grubbing it was swede-trimming, in which process they sliced off the earth and the fibres with a bill-hook before storing the roots for future use. At this occupation they could shelter themselves by a thatched hurdle if it rained; but if it was frosty even their thick leather gloves could not prevent the frozen masses they handled from biting their fingers. Still Tess hoped. She had a conviction that sooner or later the magnanimity which she persisted in reckoning as a chief ingredient of Clare's character would lead him to rejoin her.

Marian, primed to a humorous mood, would discover the queer-shaped flints aforesaid, and shriek with laughter, Tess remaining severely obtuse. They often looked across the country to where the Var or Froom was known to stretch, even though they might not be able to see it; and, fixing their eyes on the cloaking gray mist, imagined the old times they had spent out there.

'Ah,' said Marian, 'how I should like another or two of our old set to come here! Then we could bring up Talbothays every day here afield, and talk of he, and of what nice times we had there, and o' the old things we used to know, and make it all come back again a'most, in seeming!' Marian's eyes softened, and her voice grew vague as the visions returned. 'I'll write to Izz Huett,' she said. 'She's biding at home doing nothing now, I know, and I'll tell her we be here, and ask her to come; and perhaps Retty is well enough now.'

Tess had nothing to say against the proposal, and the next she heard of this plan for importing old Talbothays' joys was two or three days later, when Marian informed her that Izz had replied to her inquiry, and had promised to come if she could.

There had not been such a winter for years. It came on in stealthy and measured glides, like the moves of a chess-player. One morning the few lonely trees and the thorns of the hedgerows appeared as if they had put off a vegetable for an animal integument. Every twig was covered with a white nap as of fur grown from the rind during the night, giving it four times its usual stoutness; the whole bush or tree forming a staring sketch in white lines on the mournful gray of the sky and horizon. Cobwebs revealed their presence on sheds and walls where none had ever been observed till brought out into visibility by the crystallizing atmosphere, hanging like loops of white worsted from salient points of the out-houses, posts, and gates.

After this season of congealed dampness came a spell of dry frost, when strange birds from behind the North Pole began to arrive silently on the upland of Flintcomb-Ash; gaunt spectral creatures with tragical eyes —eyes which had witnessed scenes of cataclysmal horror in inaccessible polar regions of a magnitude such as no human being had ever conceived, in curdling temperatures that no man could endure; which had beheld the crash of icebergs and the slide of snow-hills by the shooting light of the Aurora; been half blinded by the whirl of colossal storms and terraqueous distortions; and retained the expression of feature that such scenes had engendered. These nameless birds came quite near to Tess and Marian, but of all they had seen which humanity would never see, they brought no account. The traveller's ambition to tell was not theirs, and, with dumb impassivity, they dismissed experiences which they did not value for the immediate incidents of this homely upland — the trivial movements of the two girls in disturbing the clods with their hackers so as to uncover something or other that these visitants relished as food.

Then one day a peculiar quality invaded the air of this open country. There came a moisture which was not of rain, and a cold which was not of frost. It chilled the eyeballs of the twain, made their brows ache, penetrated to their skeletons, affecting the surface of the body less than its core. They knew that it meant snow, and in the night the snow came. Tess, who continued to live at the cottage with the warm gable that cheered any lonely pedestrian who paused beside it, awoke in the night, and heard above that thatch noises which seemed to signify that the roof had turned itself into a gymnasium of all the winds. When she lit her lamp to get up in the morning she found that the snow had blown through a chink in the casement, forming a white cone of the finest powder against the inside, and had also come down the chimney, so that it lay sole-deep upon the floor, on which her shoes left tracks when she moved about. Without, the storm drove so fast as to create a snow-mist in the kitchen; but as yet it was too dark out-of-doors to see anything.

Tess knew that it was impossible to go on with the swedes; and by the time she had finished breakfast beside the solitary little lamp, Marian arrived to tell her that they were to join the rest of the women at reed-drawing in the barn till the weather changed. As soon, therefore, as the uniform cloak of darkness without began to turn to a disordered medley of grays, they blew out the lamp, wrapped themselves up in their thickest pinners, tied their woollen cravats round their necks and across their chests, and started for the barn. The snow had followed the birds from the polar basin as a white pillar of a cloud, and individual flakes could not be seen. The blast smelt of icebergs, arctic seas, whales, and white bears, carrying the snow so that it licked the land but did not deepen on it. They trudged onwards with slanted bodies through the flossy fields, keeping as well as they could in the shelter of hedges, which, however, acted as strainers rather than screens. The air, afflicted to pallor with the hoary multitudes that infested it, twisted and spun them eccentrically, suggesting an achromatic chaos of things. But both the young women were fairly cheerful; such weather on a dry upland is not in itself dispiriting.

'Ha-ha! the cunning northern birds knew this was coming,' said Marian. 'Depend upon't, they keep just in front o't all the way from the North Star. Your husband, my dear, is, I make no doubt, having scorching weather all this time. Lord, if he could only see his pretty wife now! Not that this weather hurts your beauty at all – in fact, it rather does it good.'

'You mustn't talk about him to me, Marian,' said Tess severely.

'Well, but – surely you care for 'n! Do you?'

Instead of answering, Tess, with tears in her eyes, impulsively faced in the direction in which she imagined South America to lie, and, putting up her lips, blew out a passionate kiss upon the snowy wind.

'Well, well, I know you do. But 'pon my body, it is a rum life for a married couple! There – I won't say another word! Well, as for the weather, it won't hurt us in the wheat-barn; but reed-drawing is fearful hard work – worse than swede-hacking. I can stand it because I'm stout; but you be slimmer than I. I can't think why maister should have set 'ee at it.'

They reached the wheat-barn and entered it. One end of the long structure was full of corn; the middle was where the reed-drawing was carried on, and there had already been placed in the reed-press the evening before as many sheaves of wheat as would be sufficient for the women to draw from during the day.

'Why, here's Izz!' said Marian.

Izz it was, and she came forward. She had walked all the way from her mother's home on the previous afternoon, and, not deeming the distance so great, had been belated, arriving, however, just before the snow began, and sleeping at the ale-house. The farmer had agreed with her mother at market to take her on if she came to-day, and she had been afraid to disappoint him by delay.

In addition to Tess, Marian, and Izz, there were two women from a neighbouring village; two Amazonian sisters, whom Tess with a start re-membered as Dark Car the Queen of Spades and her junior the Queen of Diamonds – those who had tried to fight with her in the midnight quarrel at Trantridge. They showed no recognition of her, and possibly had none, for they had been under the influence of liquor on that occasion, and were only temporary sojourners there as here. They did all kinds of men's work by preference, including well-sinking, hedging, ditching, and excavating, without any sense of fatigue. Noted reed-drawers were they too, and looked round upon the other three with some superciliousness.

Putting on their gloves all set to work in a row in front of the press, an erection formed of two posts connected by a cross-beam, under which the sheaves to be drawn from were laid ears outward, the beam being pegged down by pins in the uprights, and lowered as the sheaves diminished.

The day hardened in colour, the light coming in at the barn-doors upwards from the snow instead of downwards from the sky. The girls pulled handful after handful from the press; but by reason of the presence of the strange women, who were recounting scandals, Marian and Izz could not at first talk of old times as they wished to do. Presently they heard the muffled tread of a horse, and the farmer rode up to the barn-door. When he had dismounted he came close to Tess, and remained looking musingly at the side of her face. She had not turned at first, but his fixed attitude led her to look round, when she perceived that her employer was the native of Trantridge from whom she had taken flight on the high-road because of his allusion to her history.

He waited till she had carried the drawn bundles to the pile outside, when he said, 'So you be the young woman who took my civility in such ill part? Be drowned if I didn't think you might be as soon as I heard of your being hired! Well, you thought you had got the better of me the first time at the inn with your fancy-man, and the second time on the road, when you bolted; but now I think I've got the better of you,' He concluded with a hard laugh.

Tess, between the Amazons and the farmer like a bird caught in a clap-net, returned no answer, continuing to pull the straw. She could read character sufficiently well to know by this time that she had nothing to fear from her employer's gallantry; it was rather the tyranny induced by his mortification at Clare's treatment of him. Upon the whole she preferred that sentiment in man and felt brave enough to endure it.

'You thought I was in love with 'ee I suppose? Some women are such fools, to take every look as serious earnest. But there's nothing like a winter afield for taking that nonsense out o' young wenches' heads; and you've signed and agreed till Lady-Day. Now, are you going to beg my pardon?'

'I think you ought to beg mine.'

'Very well – as you like. But we'll see which is master here. Be they all the sheaves you've done to-day?'

'Yes, sir.'

''Tis a very poor show. Just see what they've done over there' (pointing to the two stalwart women). 'The rest, too, have done better than you.'

'They've all practised it before, and I have not. And I thought it made no difference to you as it is task work, and we are only paid for what we do.'

'Oh, but it does. I want the barn cleared.'

'I am going to work all the afternoon instead of leaving at two as the others will do.'

He looked sullenly at her and went away. Tess felt that she could not have come to a much worse place; but anything was better than gallantry. When two o'clock arrived the professional reed-drawers tossed off the last half-pint in their flagon, put down their hooks, tied their last sheaves, and went away. Marian and Izz would have done likewise, but on hearing that Tess meant to stay, to make up by longer hours for her lack of skill, they would not leave her. Looking out at the snow, which still fell, Marian exclaimed, 'Now, we've got it all to ourselves.' And so at last the conversation turned to their old experiences at the dairy; and, of course, the incidents of their affection for Angel Clare.

'Izz and Marian,' said Mrs Angel Clare, with a dignity which was extremely touching, seeing how very little of a wife she was: 'I can't join in talk with you now, as I used to do, about Mr Clare; you will see that I cannot; because, although he is gone away from me for the present, he is my husband.'

Izz was by nature the sauciest and most caustic of all the four girls who had loved Clare. 'He was a very splendid lover, no doubt,' she said; 'but I don't think he is a too fond husband to go away from you so soon.'

'He had to go – he was obliged to go, to see about the land over there!' pleaded Tess.

'He might have tided 'ee over the winter.'

'Ah – that's owing to an accident – a misunderstanding; and we won't argue it,' Tess answered, with tearfulness in her words. 'Perhaps there's a good deal to be said for him! He did not go away, like some husbands, without telling me; and I can always find out where he is.'

After this they continued for some long time in a reverie, as they went on seizing the ears of corn, drawing out the straw, gathering it under their arms, and cutting off the ears with their bill-hooks, nothing sounding in the barn but the swish of the straw and the crunch of the hook. Then Tess suddenly flagged, and sank down upon the heap of wheat-ears at her feet.

'I knew you wouldn't be able to stand it!' cried Marian. 'It wants harder flesh than yours for this work.'

Just then the farmer entered. 'Oh, that's how you get on when I am away,' he said to her.

'But it is my own loss,' she pleaded. 'Not yours.'

'I want it finished,' he said doggedly, as he crossed the barn and went out at the other door.

'Don't 'ee mind him, there's a dear,' said Marian. 'I've worked here before. Now you go and lie down there, and Izz and I will make up your number.'

'I don't like to let you do that. I'm taller than you, too.'

However, she was so overcome that she consented to lie down awhile, and reclined on a heap of pull-tails – the refuse after the straight straw had been drawn – thrown up at the further side of the barn. Her succumbing had been as largely owing to agitation at reopening the subject of her separation from her husband as to the hard work. She lay in a state of percipience without volition, and the rustle of the straw and the cutting of the ears by the others had the weight of bodily touches.

She could hear from her corner, in addition to these noises, the murmur of their voices. She felt certain that they were continuing the subject already broached, but their voices were so low that she could not catch the words. At last Tess grew more and more anxious to know what they were saying, and, persuading herself that she felt better, she got up and resumed work.

Then Izz Huett broke down. She had walked more than a dozen miles the previous evening, had gone to bed at midnight, and had risen again at five o'clock. Marian alone, thanks to her bottle of liquor and her stoutness of build, stood the strain upon back and arms without suffering. Tess urged Izz to leave off, agreeing, as she felt better, to finish the day without her, and make equal division of the number of sheaves.

Izz accepted the offer gratefully, and disappeared through the great door into the snowy track to her lodging. Marian, as was the case every afternoon at this time on account of the bottle, began to feel in a romantic vein.

'I should not have thought it of him — never!' she said in a dreamy tone. 'And I loved him so! I didn't mind his having *you*. But this about Izz is too bad!'

Tess, in her start at the words, narrowly missed cutting off a finger with the bill-hook.

'Is it about my husband?' she stammered.

'Well, yes. Izz said. "Don't 'ee tell her", but I am sure I can't help it! It was what he wanted Izz to do. He wanted her to go off to Brazil with him.'

Tess's face faded as white as the scene without, and its curves straightened. 'And did Izz refuse to go?' she asked.

'I don't know. Anyhow he changed his mind.'

'Pooh — then he didn't mean it! 'Twas just a man's jest!'

'Yes he did; for he drove her good-ways towards the station.'

'He didn't take her!'

They pulled on in silence till Tess, without any premonitory symptoms, burst out crying.

'There!' said Marian. 'Now I wish I hadn't told 'ee!'

'No. It is a very good thing that you have done! I have been living on in a thirtover, lackaday way, and have not seen what it may lead to! I ought to have sent him a letter oftener. He said I could not go to him, but he didn't say I was not to write as often as I liked. I won't dally like this any longer! I have been very wrong and neglectful in leaving everything to be done by him!'

The dim light in the barn grew dimmer, and they could see to work no longer. When Tess had reached home that evening, and had entered into the privacy of her little white-washed chamber, she began impetuously writing a letter to Clare. But falling into doubt she could not finish it. Afterwards she took the ring from the ribbon on which she wore it next her heart, and retained it on her finger all night, as if to fortify herself in the sensation that she was really the wife of this elusive lover of hers, who could propose that Izz should go with him abroad, so shortly after he had left her. Knowing that, how could she write entreaties to him, or show that she cared for him any more?

CHAPTER FORTY-FOUR

B Y the disclosure in the barn her thoughts were led anew in the direction which they had taken more than once of late — to the distant Emminster Vicarage. It was through her husband's parents that she had been charged to send a letter to Clare if she desired; and to write to them direct if in difficulty. But that sense of her having morally no claim upon him had always led Tess to suspend her impulse to send these notes; and to the family at the Vicarage, therefore, as to her own parents since her marriage, she was virtually non-existent. This self-effacement in both directions had been quite in consonance with her independent character of desiring nothing by way of favour or pity to which she was not entitled on a fair consideration of her deserts. She had set herself to stand or fall by her qualities, and to waive such merely technical claims upon a strange family as had been established for her by the flimsy fact of a member of that family, in a season of impulse, writing his name in a church-book beside hers.

But now that she was stung to a fever by Izz's tale there was a limit to her powers of renunciation. Why had her husband not written to her? He had distinctly implied that he would at least let her know of the locality to which he had journeyed; but he had not sent a line to notify his address. Was he really indifferent? But was he ill? Was it for her to make some advance? Surely she might summon the courage of solicitude, call at the Vicarage for intelligence, and express her grief at his silence. If Angel's father were the good man she had heard him represented to be, he would be able to enter into her heart-starved situation. Her social hardships she could conceal.

To leave the farm on a week-day was not in her power; Sunday was the only possible opportunity. Flintcombe-Ash being in the middle of the cretaceous tableland over which no railway had climbed as yet, it would be necessary to walk. And the distance being fifteen miles each way she would have to allow herself a long day for the undertaking by rising early.

A fortnight later, when the snow had gone, and had been followed by a hard black frost, she took advantage of the state of the roads to try the experiment. At four o'clock that Sunday morning she came downstairs and stepped out into the starlight. The weather was still favourable, the ground ringing under her feet like an anvil.

Marian and Izz were much interested in her excursion, knowing that the journey concerned her husband. Their lodgings were in a cottage a little further along the lane, but they came and assisted Tess in her departure, and argued that she should dress up in her very prettiest guise to captivate the hearts of her parents-in-law; though she, knowing of the austere and Calvinistic tenets of old Mr Clare, was indifferent, and even doubtful. A year had now elapsed since her sad marriage, but she had preserved sufficient draperies from the wreck of her then full wardrobe to clothe her very charmingly as a simple country girl with no pretensions to recent fashion; a soft gray woollen gown, with white crape quilling against the pink skin of her face and neck, and a black velvet jacket and hat.

''Tis a thousand pities your husband can't see 'ee now — you do look a real beauty!' said Izz Huett, regarding Tess as she stood on the threshold between the steely starlight without and the yellow candlelight within. Izz spoke with a magnanimous abandonment of herself to the situation; she could not be — no woman with a heart bigger than a hazel-nut could be — antagonistic to Tess in her presence, the influence which she exercised over those of her own sex being of a warmth and strength quite unusual, curiously overpowering the less worthy feminine feelings of spite and rivalry.

With a final tug and touch here, and a slight brush there, they let her go; and she was absorbed into the pearly air of the fore-dawn. They heard her footsteps tap along the hard road as she stepped out to her full pace. Even Izz hoped she would win, and, though without any particular respect for her own virtue, felt glad that she had been prevented wronging her friend when momentarily tempted by Clare.

It was a year ago, all but a day, that Clare had married Tess, and only a few days less than a year that he had been absent from her. Still, to start on a brisk walk, and on such an errand as hers, on a dry clear wintry morning, through the rarefied air of these chalky hogs'-backs, was not depressing; and there is no doubt that her dream at starting was to win the heart of her mother-in-law, tell her whole history to that lady, enlist her on her side, and so gain back the truant.

In time she reached the edge of the vast escarpment below which stretched the loamy Vale of Blackmoor, now lying misty and still in the dawn. Instead of the colourless air of the uplands the atmosphere down there was a deep blue. Instead of the great enclosures of a hundred acres in which she was now accustomed to toil there were little fields below her of less than half-a-dozen acres, so numerous that they looked from this height like the meshes of a net. Here the landscape was whitey-brown; down there, as in Froom Valley, it was always green. Yet it was in that vale that her sorrow had taken shape, and she did not love it as formerly. Beauty to her, as to all who have felt, lay not in the thing, but in what the thing symbolized.

Keeping the Vale on her right she steered steadily westward; passing above the Hintocks, crossing at right-angles the high-road from Sherton-Abbas to Casterbridge, and skirting Dogbury Hill and High-Stoy, with the dell between them called 'The Devil's Kitchen'. Still following the elevated way she reached Cross-in-Hand, where the stone pillar stands desolate and silent, to mark the site of a miracle, or murder, or both. Three miles further she cut across the straight and deserted Roman road called Long-Ash Lane; leaving which as soon as she reached it she dipped down a hill by a transverse lane into the small town or village of Evershead, being now about half-way over the distance. She made a halt here, and breakfasted a second time, heartily enough – not at the Sow-and-Acorn, for she avoided inns, but at a cottage by the church.

The second half of her journey was through a more gentle country, by way of Benvill Lane. But as the mileage lessened between her and the spot of her pilgrimage, so did Tess's confidence decrease, and her enterprise loom out more formidably. She saw her purpose in such staring lines, and the landscape so faintly, that she was sometimes in danger of losing her way. However, about noon she paused by a gate on the edge of the basin in which Emminster and its Vicarage lay.

The square tower, beneath which she knew that at that moment the Vicar and his congregation were gathered, had a severe look in her eyes. She wished that she had somehow contrived to come on a weekday. Such a good man might be prejudiced against a woman who had chosen Sunday, never realizing the necessities of her case. But it was incumbent upon her to go on now. She took off the thick boots in which she had walked thus far, put on her pretty thin ones of patent leather, and, stuffing the former into the hedge by the gate-post where she might readily find them again, descended the hill; the freshness of colour she had derived from the keen air thinning away in spite of her as she drew near the parsonage.

Tess hoped for some accident that might favour her, but nothing favoured her. The shrubs on the Vicarage lawn rustled uncomfortably in the frosty breeze; she could not feel by any stretch of imagination, dressd to her highest as she was, that the house was the residence of near relations; and yet nothing essential, in nature or emotion, divided her from them: in pains, pleasures, thoughts, birth, death, and after-death, they were the same.

She nerved herself by an effort, entered the swing-gate, and rang the door-bell. The thing was done; there could be no retreat. No; the thing was not done. Nobody answered to her ringing. The effort had to be risen to and made again. She rang a second time, and the agitation of the act, coupled with her weariness after the fifteen miles' walk, led her to support herself while she waited by resting her hand on her hip, and her elbow against the wall of the porch. The wind was so nipping that the ivy-leaves had become wizened and gray, each tapping incessantly upon its neighbour with a disquieting stir of her nerves. A piece of blood-stained paper, caught up from some meat-buyer's dust-heap, beat up and down the road without the gate; too flimsy to rest, too heavy to fly away; and a few straws kept it company.

The second peal had been louder, and still nobody came. Then she walked out of the porch, opened the gate, and passed through. And though she looked dubiously at the house-front as if inclined to return, it was with a breath of relief that she closed the gate. A feeling haunted her that she might have been recognized (though how she could not tell), and orders been given not to admit her.

Tess went as far as the corner. She had done all she could do; but determined not to escape present trepidation at the expense of future distress, she walked back again past the house, looking up at all the windows.

Ah – the explanation was that they were all at church, every one. She remembered her husband saying that his father always insisted upon the household, servants included, going to morning-service, and, as a consequence, eating cold food when they came home. It was, therefore, only necessary to wait till the service was over. She would not make herself conspicuous by waiting on the spot, and she started to get past the church into the lane. But as she reached the churchyard-gate the people began pouring out, and Tess found herself in the midst of them.

The Emminster congregation looked at her as only a congregation of small country-townsfolk walking home at its leisure can look at a woman out of the common whom it perceives to be a stranger. She quickened her pace, and ascended the road by which she had come, to find a retreat between its hedges till the Vicar's family should have lunched, and it might be convenient for them to receive her. She soon distanced the churchgoers, except two youngish men, who linked arm-in-arm, were beating up behind her at a quick step.

As they drew nearer she could hear their voices engaged in earnest discourse, and, with the natural quickness of a woman in her situation, did not fail to recognize in those voices the quality of her husband's tones. The pedestrians were his two brothers. Forgetting all her plans, Tess's one dread was lest they should overtake her now, in her disorganized condition, before she was prepared to confront them; for though she felt that they could not identify her she instinctively dreaded their scrutiny. The more briskly they walked the more briskly walked she. They were plainly bent upon taking a short quick stroll before going indoors to lunch or dinner, to restore warmth to limbs chilled with sitting through a long service.

Only one person had preceded Tess up the hill – a ladylike young woman, somewhat interesting, though, perhaps, a trifle *guindée* and prudish. Tess had nearly overtaken her when the speed of her brothers-in-law brought them so nearly behind her back that she could hear every word of their conversation. They said nothing, however, which particularly interested her till, observing the young lady still further in front, one of them remarked, 'There is Mercy Chant. Let us overtake her.'

Tess knew the name. It was the woman who had been destined for Angel's life-companion by his and her parents, and whom he probably would have married but for her intrusive self. She would have known as much without previous information if she had waited a moment, for one of the brothers proceeded to say: 'Ah! poor Angel, poor Angel! I never see that nice girl without more and more regretting his precipitancy in throwing himself away upon a dairy-maid, or whatever she may be. It is a queer business, apparently. Whether she has joined him yet or not I don't know; but she had not done so some months ago when I heard from him.'

'I can't say. He never tells me anything nowadays. His illconsidered marriage seems to have completed that estrangement from me which was begun by his extraordinary opinions.'

Tess beat up the long hill still faster; but she could not outwalk them without exciting notice. At last they outsped her altogether, and passed her by. The young lady still further ahead heard their footsteps and turned. Then there was a greeting and a shaking of hands, and the three went on together.

They soon reached the summit of the hill, and, evidently intending this point to be the limit of their promenade, slackened pace and turned all three aside to the gate whereat Tess had paused an hour before that time to reconnoitre the town before descending into it. During their discourse one of the clerical brothers probed the hedge carefully with his umbrella, and dragged something to light.

'Here's a pair of old boots,' he said. 'Thrown away, I suppose, by some tramp or other.'

'Some impostor who wished to come into the town barefoot, perhaps, and so excite our sympathies,' said Miss Chant. 'Yes, it must have been, for they are excellent walking-boots – by no means worn out. What a wicked thing to do! I'll carry them home for some poor person.'

Cuthbert Clare, who had been the one to find them, picked them up for her with the crook of his stick; and Tess's boots were appropriated.

She, who had heard this, walked past under the screen of her woollen veil, till, presently looking back, she perceived that the church party had left the gate with her boots and retreated down the hill.

Thereupon our heroine resumed her walk. Tears, blinding tears, were running down her face. She knew that it was all sentiment, all baseless impressibility, which had caused her to read the scene as her own condemnation; nevertheless she could not get over it; she could not contravene in her own defenceless person all these untoward omens. It was impossible to think of returning to the Vicarage. Angel's wife felt almost as if she had been hounded up that hill like a scorned thing by those – to her – super-fine clerics. Innocently as the slight had been inflicted, it was somewhat unfortunate that she had encountered the sons and not the father, who, despite his narrowness, was far less starched and ironed than they, and had to the full the gift of charity. As she again thought of her dusty boots she almost pitied those habiliments for the quizzing to which they had been subjected, and felt how hopeless life was for their owner.

'Ah!' she said, still sighing in pity of herself, '*they* didn't know that I wore those over the roughest part of the road to save these pretty ones *he* bought for me – no – they did not know it! And they didn't think that *he* chose the colour o' my pretty frock – no – how could they? If they had known perhaps they would not have cared, for they don't care much for him, poor thing!'

Then she grieved for the beloved man whose conventional standard of judgment had caused her all these latter sorrows; and she went her way without knowing that the greatest misfortune of her life was ths feminine loss of courage at the last and critical moment through her estimating her father-in-law by his sons. Her present condition was precisely one which would have enlisted the sympathies of old Mr and Mrs Clare. Their hearts went out of them at a bound towards extreme cases, when the subtle mental troubles of the less desperate among mankind failed to win their interest or regard. In jumping at Publicans and Sinners they would forget that a word might be said for the worries of Scribes and Pharisees; and this defect of limitation might have recommended their own daughter-in-law to them at this moment as a fairly choice sort of lost person for their love.

Thereupon she began to plod back along the road by which she had come not altogether full of hope, but full of a conviction that a crisis in her life was approaching. No crisis, apparently, had supervened; and there was nothing left for her to do but to continue upon that starve-acre farm till she could again summon courage to face the vicarage. She did, indeed, take sufficient interest in herself to throw up her veil on this return journey, as if to let the world see that she could at least exhibit a face such as Mercy Chant could not show. But it was done with a sorry shake of the head. 'It is nothing – it is nothing!' she said. 'Nobody loves it; nobody sees it. Who cares about the looks of a castaway like me!'

Her journey back was rather a meander than a march. It had no sprightliness, no purpose; only a tendency. Along the tedious length of Benvill Lane she began to grow tired, and she leant upon gates and paused by milestones.

She did not enter any house till, at the seventh or eighth mile, she descended the steep long hill below which lay the village or townlet of Evershead, where in the morning she had breakfasted with such contrasting expectations. The cottage by the church, in which she again sat down, was almost the first at that end of the village, and while the woman fetched her some milk from the pantry, Tess, looking down the street, perceived that the place seemed quite deserted.

'The people are gone to afternoon service, I suppose?' she said.

'No, my dear,' said the old woman. ''Tis too soon for that; the bells hain't strook out yet. They be all gone to hear the preaching in yonder barn. A ranter preaches there between the services – an excellent, fiery, Christian man, they say. But, Lord, I don't go to hear'n! What comes in the regular way over the pulpit is hot enough for I.'

Tess soon went onward into the village, her footsteps echoing against the houses as though it were a place of the dead. Nearing the central part her echoes were intruded on by other sounds; and seeing the barn not far off the road, she guessed these to be the utterances of the preacher.

His voice became so distinct in the still clear air that she could soon catch his sentences, though she was on the closed side of the barn. The sermon, as might be expected, was of the extremest anti-nomian type; on justification by faith, as expounded in the theology of St Paul. This fixed idea of the rhapsodist was delivered with animated enthusiasm, in a manner entirely declamatory, for he had plainly no skill as a dialectician. Although Tess had not heard the beginning of the address, she learnt what the text had been from its constant iteration –

'*O foolish Galatians, who hath bewitched you, that ye should not obey the truth, before whose eyes Jesus Christ hath been evidently set forth, crucified among you?*'

Tess was all the more interested, as she stood listening behind, in finding that the preacher's doctrine was a vehement form of the views of Angel's father, and her interest intensified when the speaker began to detail his own spiritual experiences of how he had come by those views. He had, he said, been the greatest of sinners. He had scoffed; he had wantonly associated with the reckless and the lewd. But a day of awakening had come, and, in a human sense, it had been brought about mainly by the influence of a certain clergyman, whom he had at first grossly insulted; but whose parting words had sunk into his heart, and had remained there, till by the grace of Heaven they had worked this change in him, and made him what they saw him.

But more startling to Tess than the doctrine had been the voice, which, impossible as it seemed, was precisely that of Alec d'Urberville. Her face fixed in painful suspense she came round to the front of the barn, and passed before it. The low winter sun beamed directly upon the great double-doored entrance on this side; one of the doors being open, so that the rays stretched far in over the threshing-floor to the preacher and his audience, all snugly sheltered from the northern breeze. The listeners were entirely villagers, among them being the man whom she had seen carrying the red paint-pot on a former memorable occasion. But her attention was given to the central figure, who stood upon some sacks of corn, facing the people and the door. The three o'clock sun shone full upon him, and the strange enervating conviction that her seducer confronted her, which had been gaining ground in Tess ever since she had heard his words distinctly, was at last established as a faςt indeed.

The Convert

CHAPTER FORTY-FIVE

Till this moment she had never seen or heard from d'Urberville since her departure from Trantridge.

The rencounter came at a heavy moment, one of all moments calculated to permit its impact with the least emotional shock. But such was unreasoning memory that, though he stood there openly and palpably a converted man, who was sorrowing for his past irregularities, a fear overcame her, paralyzing her movement so that she neither retreated nor advanced.

To think of what emanated from that countenance when she saw it last, and to behold it now! . . . There was the same handsome unpleasantness of mien, but now he wore neatly trimmed, old-fashioned whiskers, the sable moustache having disappeared; and his dress was half-clerical, a modification which had changed his expession sufficiently to abstract the dandyism from his features, and to hinder for a second her belief in his identity.

To Tess's sense there was, just at first, a ghastly *bizarrerie*, a grim incongruity, in the march of these solemn words of Scripture out of such a mouth. This too familiar intonation, less than four years earlier, had brought to her ears expressions of such divergent purpose that her heart became quite sick at the irony of the contrast.

It was less a reform than a transfiguration. The former curves of sensuousness were now modulated to lines of devotional passion. The lip-shapes that had meant seductiveness were now made to express supplication; the glow on the cheek that yesterday could be translated as riotousness was evangelized to-day into the splendour of pious rhetoric; animalism had become fanaticism; Paganism Paulinism; the bold rolling eye that had flashed upon her form in the old time with such mastery now beamed with the rude energy of a theolatry that was almost ferocious. Those black angularities which his face had used to put on when his wishes were thwarted now did duty in picturing the incorrigible backslider who would insist upon turning again to his wallowing in the mire.

The lineaments, as such, seemed to complain. They had been diverted from their hereditary connotation to signify impressions for which Nature did not intend them. Strange that their very elevation was a misapplication, that to raise seemed to falsify.

Yet could it be so? She would admit the ungenerous sentiment no longer. D'Urberville was not the first wicked man who had turned away from his wickedness to save his soul alive, and why should she deem it unnatural in him? It was but the usage of thought which had been jarred in her at hearing good new words in bad old notes. The greater the sinner the greater the saint; it was not necessary to dive far into Christian history to discover that.

Such impressions as these moved her vaguely, and without strict definiteness. As soon as the nerveless pause of her surprise would allow her to stir, her impulse was to pass on out of his sight. He had obviously not discerned her yet in her position against the sun.

But the moment that she moved again he recognized her. The effect upon her old lover was electric, far stronger than the effect of his presence upon her. His fire, the tumultuous ring of his eloquence, seemed to go out of him. His lip struggled and trembled under the words that lay upon it; but deliver them it could not as long as she faced him. His eyes, after their first glance upon her face, hung confusedly in every other direction but hers, but came back in a desperate leap every few seconds. This paralysis lasted, however, but a short time; for Tess's energies returned with the atrophy of his, and she walked as fast as she was able past the barn and onward.

As soon as she could reflect it appalled her, this change in their relative platforms. He who had wrought her undoing was now on the side of the Spirit, while she remained unregenerate. And, as in the legend, it had resulted that her Cyprian image had suddenly appeared upon his altar, whereby the fire of the priest had been wellnigh extinguished.

She went on without turning her head. Her back seemed to be endowed with a sensitiveness to ocular beams — even her clothing — so alive was she to a fancied gaze which might be resting upon her from the outside of that barn. All the way along to this point her heart had been heavy with an inactive sorrow; now there was a change in the quality of its trouble. That hunger for affection too long withheld was for the time displaced by an almost physical sense of an implacable past which still engirdled her. It intensified her consciousness of error to a practical despair; the break of continuity between her earlier and present existence, which she had hoped for, had not, after all, taken place. Bygones would never be complete bygones till she was a bygone herself.

Thus absorbed she recrossed the northern part of Long-Ash Lane at right angles, and presently saw before her the road ascending whitely to the upland along whose margin the remainder of her journey lay. Its dry pale surface stretched severely onward, unbroken by a single figure, vehicle, or mark, save some occasional brown horse-droppings which dotted its cold aridity here and there. While slowly breasting this ascent Tess became conscious of footsteps behind her, and turning she saw approaching that well-known form — so strangely accoutred as the Methodist — the one personage in all the world she wished not to encounter alone on this side of the grave.

There was not much time, however, for thought or elusion, and she yielded as calmly as she could to the necessity of letting him overtake her. She saw that he was excited, less by the speed of his walk than by the feelings within him.

'Tess!' he said.

She slackened speed without looking round.

'Tess!' he repeated. 'It is I — Alec d'Urberville.'

She then looked back at him, and he came up.

'I see it is,' she answered coldly.

'Well – is that all? Yet I deserve no more! Of course,' he added, with a slight laugh, 'there is something of the ridiculous to your eyes in seeing me like this. But – I must put up with that. . . . I heard you had gone away, nobody knew where. Tess, you wonder why I have followed you?'

'I do, rather; and I would that you had not, with all my heart!'

'Yes – you may well say it,' he returned grimly, as they moved onward together she with unwilling tread. 'But don't mistake me; I beg this because you may have been led to do so in noticing – if you did notice it – how your sudden appearance unnerved me down there. It was but a momentary faltering; and considering what you had been to me, it was natural enough. But will helped me through it – though perhpas you think me a humbug for saying it – and immediately afterwards I felt that, of all persons in the world whom it was my duty and desire to save from the wrath to come – sneer if you like – the woman whom I had so grievously wronged was that person. I have come with that sole purpose in view – nothing more.'

There was the smallest vein of scorn in her words of rejoinder: 'Have you saved yourself? Charity begins at home, they say.'

'*I* have done nothing!' said he indifferently. 'Heaven, as I have been telling my hearers, has done all. No amount of contempt that you can pour upon me, Tess, will equal what I have poured upon myself – the old Adam of my former years! Well, it is a strange story; believe it or not; but I can tell you the means by which my conversion was brought about, and I hope you will be interested enough at least to listen. Have you ever heard the name of the parson of Emminster – you must have done so? – old Mr Clare; one of the most earnest of his school; one of the few intense men left in the Church; not so intense as the extreme wing of Christian believers with which I have thrown in my lot, but quite an exception among the Established clergy, the younger of whom are gradually attenuating the true doctrines by their sophistries, till they are but the shadow of what they were. I only differ from him on the question of Church and State – the interpretation of the text, "Come out from among them and be ye separate, saith the Lord" – that's all. He is one who, I firmly believe, has been the humble means of saving more souls in this country than any other man you can name. You have heard of him?'

'I have,' she said.

'He came to Trantridge two or three years ago to preach on behalf of some missionary society; and I, wretched fellow that I was, insulted him when, in his disinterestedness, he tried to reason with me and show me the way. He did not resent my conduct, he simply said that some day I should receive the first-fruits of the Spirit – that those who came to scoff sometimes remained to pray. There was a strange magic in his words. They sank into my mind. But the loss of my mother hit me most; and by degrees I was brought to see daylight. Since then my one desire has been to hand on the true view to others, and that is what I was trying to do to-day; though it is only lately that I have preached hereabout. The first months of my ministry have been spent in the North of England among strangers, where I preferred to make my earliest clumsy attempts, so as to acquire courage before undergoing that severest of all tests of one's sincerity, addressing those who have known one, and have been one's companions in the days of darkness. If you could only know, Tess, the pleasure of having a good slap at yourself, I am sure—'

'Don't go on with it!' she cried passionately, as she turned away from him to a stile by the wayside, on which she bent herself. 'I can't believe in such sudden things! I feel indignant with you for talking to me like this, when you know — when you know what harm you've done me! You, and those like you, take your fill of pleasure on earth by making the life of such as me bitter and black with sorrow; and then it is a fine thing, when you have had enough of that, to think of securing your pleasure in heaven by becoming converted! Out upon such — I don't believe in you — I hate it!'

'Tess,' he insisted; 'don't speak so! It came to me like a jolly new idea! And you don't believe me? What don't you believe?'

'Your conversion. Your scheme of religion.'

'Why?'

She dropped her voice. 'Because a better man than you does not believe in such.'

'What a woman's reason! Who is this better man?'

'I cannot tell you.'

'Well,' he declared, a resentment beneath his words seeming ready to spring out at a moment's notice, 'God forbid that I should say I am a good man — and you know I don't say any such thing. I am new to goodness, truly; but new comers see furthest sometimes.'

'Yes,' she replied sadly. 'But I cannot believe in your conversion to a new spirit. Such flashes as you feel, Alec, I fear don't last!'

Thus speaking she turned from the stile over which she had been leaning, and faced him; whereupon his eyes, falling casually upon the familiar countenance and form, remained contemplating her. The inferior man was quite in him now; but it was surely not extracted, nor even entirely subdued.

'Don't look at me like that!' he said abruptly.

Tess, who had been quite unconscious of her action and mien, instantly withdrew the large dark gaze of her eyes, stammering with a flush, 'I beg your pardon!' And there was revived in her the wretched sentiment which had often come to her before, that in inhabiting the fleshly tabernacle with which Nature had endowed her she was somehow doing wrong.

'No, no! Don't beg my pardon. But since you wear a veil to hide your good looks, why don't you keep it down?'

She pulled down the veil, saying hastily, 'It was mostly to keep off the wind.'

'It may seem harsh of me to dictate like this,' he went on; 'but it is better that I should not look too often on you. It might be dangerous.'

'Ssh!' said Tess.

'Well, women's faces have had too much power over me already for me not to fear them! An evangelist has nothing to do with such as they; and it reminds me of the old times that I would forget!'

After this their conversation dwindled to a casual remark now and then as they rambled onward, Tess inwardly wondering how far he was going with her, and not liking to send him back by positive mandate. Frequently when they came to a gate or stile they found painted thereon in red or blue letters some text of Scripture, and she asked him if he knew who had been at the pains to blazon these announcements. He told her that the man was employed by himself and others who were working with him in that district, to paint these reminders that no means might be left untried which might move the hearts of a wicked generation.

At length the road touched the spot called 'Cross-in-Hand'. Of all spots on the bleached and desolate upland this was the most forlorn. It was so far removed from the charm which is sought in landscape by artists and view-lovers as to reach a new kind of beauty, a negative beauty of tragic tone. The place took its name from a stone pillar which stood there, a strange rude monolith, from a stratum unknown in any local quarry, on which was roughly carved a human hand. Differing accounts were given of its history and purport. Some authorities stated that a devotional cross had once formed the complete erection thereon, of which the present relic was but the stump; others that the stone as it stood was entire, and that it had been fixed there to mark a boundary or place of meeting. Anyhow, whatever the origin of the relic, there was and is something sinister, or solemn, according to mood, in the scene amid which it stands; something tending to impress the most phlegmatic passer-by.

'I think I must leave you now,' he remarked, as they drew near to this spot. 'I have to preach at Abbot's-Cernel at six this evening, and my way lies across to the right from here. And you upset me somewhat too, Tessy – I cannot, will not, say why. I must go away and get strength. . . . How is it that you speak so fluently now? Who has taught you such good English?'

'I have learnt things in my troubles,' she said evasively.

'What troubles have you had?'

She told him of the first one – the only one that related to him.

D'Urberville was struck mute. 'I knew nothing of this till now!' he next murmured. 'Why didn't you write to me when you felt your trouble coming on?'

She did not reply; and he broke the silence by adding: 'Well – you will see me again.'

'No,' she answered. 'Do not again come near me!'

'I will think. But before we part come here.' He stepped up to the pillar. 'This was once a Holy Cross. Relics are not in my creed; but I fear you at moments – far more than you need fear me at present; and to lessen my fear, put your hand upon that stone hand, and swear that you will never tempt me – by your charms or ways.'

'Good God – how can you ask what is so unnecessary! All that is furthest from my thought!'

'Yes – but swear it.'

Tess, half frightened, gave way to his importunity; placed her hand upon the stone and swore.

'I am sorry you are not a believer,' he continued; 'that some unbelievers should have got hold of you and unsettled your mind. But no more now. At home at least I can pray for you; and I will; and who knows what may not happen? I'm off. Good-bye!'

He turned to a hunting-gate in the hedge, and without letting his eyes again rest upon her leapt over, and struck out across the down in the direction of Abbot's-Cernel. As he walked his pace showed perturbation, and by-and-by, as if instigated by a former thought, he drew from his pocket a small book, between the leaves of which was folded a letter, worn and soiled, as from much re-reading.

D'Urberville opened the letter. It was dated several months before this time, and was signed by Parson Clare.

The letter began by expressing the writer's unfeigned joy at d'Urberville's conversion, and thanked him for his kindness in communicating with the parson on the subject. It expressed Mr Clare's warm assurance of forgiveness for d'Urberville's former conduct, and his interest in the young man's plans for the future. He, Mr Clare, would much have liked to see d'Urberville in the Church to whose ministry he had devoted so many years of his own life, and would have helped him to enter a theological college to that end; but since his correspondent had possibly not cared to do this on account of the delay it would have entailed, he was not the man to insist upon its paramount importance. Every man must work as he could best work, and in the method towards which he felt impelled by the Spirit.

D'Urberville read and re-read this letter, and seemed to quiz himself cynically. He also read some passages from memoranda as he walked till his face assumed a calm, and apparently the image of Tess no longer troubled his mind.

She meanwhile had kept along the edge of the hill by which lay her nearest way home. Within the distance of a mile she met a solitary shepherd

'What is the meaning of that old stone I have passed?' she asked of him. 'Was it ever a Holy Cross?'

'Cross — no; 'twer not a cross! 'Tis a thing of ill-omen, Miss. It was put up in wuld times by the relations of a malefactor who was tortured there by nailing his hand to a post and afterwards hung. The bones lie underneath. They say he sold his soul to the devil, and that he walks at times.'

She felt the *petite mort* at this unexpectedly gruesome information, and left the solitary man behind her. It was dusk when she drew near to Flintcomb-Ash, and in the lane at the entrance to the hamlet she approached a girl and her lover without their observing her. They were talking no secrets, and the clear unconcerned voice of the young woman, in response to the warmer accents of the man, spread into the chilly air as the one soothing thing within the dusky horizon, full of a stagnant obscurity upon which nothing else intruded. For a moment the voices cheered the heart of Tess, till she reasoned that this interview had its origin, on one side or the other, in the same attraction which had been the prelude to her own tribulation. When she came close the girl turned serenely and recognized her, the young man walking off in embarrassment. The woman was Izz Huett, whose interest in Tess's excursion immediately superseded her own proceedings. Tess did not explain very clearly its results and Izz, who was a girl of tact, began to speak of her own little affair, a phase of which Tess had just witnessed.

'He is Amby Seedling, the chap who used to sometimes come and help at Talbothays,' she explained indifferently. 'He actually inquired and found out that I had come here, and has followed me. He says he's been in love wi' me these two years. But I've hardly answered him.'

CHAPTER FORTY-SIX

SEVERAL days had passed since her futile journey, and Tess was afield. The dry winter wind still blew, but a screen of thatched hurdles erected in the eye of the blast kept its force away from her. On the sheltered side was a turnip-slicing machine, whose bright blue hue of new paint seemed almost vocal in the otherwise subdued scene. Opposite its front was a long mound or 'grave', in which the roots had been preserved since early winter. Tess was standing at the uncovered end, chopping off with a bill-hook the fibres and earth from each root, and throwing it after the operation into the slicer. A man was turning the handle of the machine, and from its trough came the newly-cut swedes, the fresh smell of whose yellow chips was accompanied by the sounds of the snuffling wind, the smart swish of the slicing-blades, and the choppings of the hook in Tess's leather-gloved hand.

The wide acreage of blank agricultural brownness, apparent where the swedes had been pulled, was beginning to striped in wales of darker brown, gradually broadening to ribands. Along the edge of each of these something crept upon ten legs, moving without haste and without rest up and down the whole length of the field; it was two horses and a man, the plough going between them, turning up the cleared ground for a spring sowing.

For hours nothing relieved the joyless monotony of things. Then, far beyond the ploughing-teams, a black speck was seen. It had come from the corner of a fence, where there was a gap, and its tendency was up the incline, towards the swede cutters. From the proportions of a mere point it advanced to the shape of a ninepin, and was soon perceived to be a man in black, arriving from the direction of Flintcomb-Ash. The man at the slicer, having nothing else to do with his eyes, continually observed the comer, but Tess, who was occupied, did not perceive him till her companion directed her attention to his approach.

It was not her hard taskmaster, Farmer Groby; it was one in semi-clerical costume, who now represented what had once been the free-and-easy Alec d'Urberville. Not being hot at his preaching there was less enthusiasm about him now, and the presence of the grinder seemed to embarrass him. A pale distres was already on Tess's face, and she pulled her curtained hood further over it.

D'Urberville came up and said quietly –

'I want to speak to you, Tess.'

'You have refused my last request, not to come near me!' said she.

'Yes, but I have a good reason.'

'Well, tell it.'

'It is more serious than you may think.'

He glanced round to see if he were overheard. They were at some distance from the man who turned the slicer, and the movement of the machine, too, sufficiently prevented Alec's words reaching other ears. D'Urberville placed himself so as to screen Tess from the labourer, turning his back to the latter.

'It is this,' he continued, with capricious compunction. 'In thinking of your soul and mine when we last met, I neglected to inquire as to your worldly condition. You were well dressed, and I did not think of it. But I see now that it is hard – harder than it used to be when I – knew you – harder than you deserve. Perhaps a good deal of it is owing to me!'

She did not answer, and he watched her inquiringly, as, with bent head, her face completely screened by the hood, she resumed her trimming of the swedes. By going on with her work she felt better able to keep him outside her emotions.

'Tess,' he added, with a sigh of discontent, – 'yours was the very worst case I ever was concerned in! I had no idea of what had resulted till you told me. Scamp that I was to foul that innocent life! The whole blame was mine – the whole unconventional business of our time at Trantridge. You, too, the real blood of which I am but the base imitation, what a blind young thing you were as to possibilities! I say in all earnestness that it is a shame for parents to bring up their girls in such dangerous ignorance of the gins and nets that the wicked may set for them, whether their motive be a good one or the result of simple indifference.'

Tess still did no more than listen, throwing down one globular root and taking up another with automatic regularity, the pensive contour of the mere fieldwoman alone marking her.

'But it is not that I came to say,' d'Urberville went on. 'My circumstances are these. I have lost my mother since you were at Trantridge, and the place is my own. But I intend to sell it, and devote myself to missionary work in Africa. A devil of a poor hand I shall make at the trade, no doubt. Howeve, what I want to ask you is will you put it in my power to do my duty – to make the only reparation I can make for the trick played you: that is, will you be my wife, and go with me? . . . I have already obtained this precious document. It was my old mother's dying wish.'

He drew a piece of parchment from his pocket, with a slight fumbling of embarrassment.

'What is it?' said she.

'A marriage licence.'

'O no, sir – no!' she said quickly, starting back.

'You will not? Why is that?'

And as he asked the question a disappointment which was not entirely the disappointment of thwarted duty crossed d'Urberville's face. It was unmistakably a symptom that something of his old passion for her had been revived; duty and desire ran hand-in-hand.

'Surely,' he began again, in more impetuous tones, and then looked round at the labourer who turned the slicer.

Tess, too, felt that the argument could not be ended there. Informing the man that a gentleman had come to see her, with whom she wished to walk a little way, she moved off with d'Urberville across the zebra-striped field. When they reached the first newly-ploughed section he held out his hand to help her over it; but she stepped forward on the summits of the earth-rolls as if she did not see him.

'You will not marry me, Tess, and make me a self-respecting man?' he repeated, as soon as they were over the furrows.

'I cannot.'

'But why?'

'You know I have no affection for you.'

'But you would get to feel that in time, perhaps – as soon as you really could forgive me?'

'Never!'

'Why so positive?'

'I love somebody else.'

The words seemed to astonish him.

'You do?' he cried. 'Somebody else? But has not a sense of what is morally right and proper any weight with you?'

'No, no, no – don't say that!'

'Anyhow, then, your love for this other man may be only a passing feeling which you will overcome—'

'No – no.'

'Yes, yes! Why not?'

'I cannot tell you.'

'You must in honour!'

'Well then . . . I have married him.'

'Ah!' he exclaimed; and he stopped dead and gazed at her.

'I did not wish to tell – I did not mean to!' she pleaded. 'It is a secret here, or at any rate but dimly known. So will you, *please* will you, keep from questioning me? You must remember that we are now strangers.'

'Strangers – are we? Strangers!'

For a moment a flash of his old irony marked his face; but he determinedly chastened it down.

'Is that man your husband?' he asked mechanically, denoting by a sign the labourer who turned the machine.

'That man!' she said proudly. 'I should think not!'

'Who, then?'

'Do not ask what I do not wish to tell!' she begged, and flashed her appeal to him from her upturned face and lash-shadowed eyes.

D'Urberville was disturbed.

'But I only asked for your sake!' he retorted hotly. 'Angels of heaven! – God forgive me for such an expression – I came here, I swear, as I thought for your good. Tess – don't look at me so – I cannot stand your looks! There never were such eyes, surely, before Christianity or since! There – I won't lose my head; I dare not. I own that the sight of you has waked up my love for you, which, I believed, was extinguished with all such feelings. But I thought that our marriage might be a sanctification for us both. "The unbelieving husband is sanctified by the wife, and the unbelieving wife is sanctified by the husband," I said to myself. But my plan is dashed from me; and I must bear the disappointment!'

He moodily reflected with his eyes on the ground.

'Married. Married! . . . Well, that being so,' he added, quite calmly, tearing the licence slowly into halves and putting them in his pocket; 'that being prevented, I should like to do some good to you and your husband, whoever he may be. There are many questions that I am tempted to ask, but I will not do so, of course, in opposition to your wishes. Though, if I could know your husband, I might more easily benefit him and you. Is he on this farm?'

'No,' she murmured. 'He is far away.'

'Far away? From *you*? What sort of husband can he be?'

'O, do not speak against him! It was through you! He found out—'

'Ah, is it so! . . . That's sad, Tess!'

'Yes.'

'But to stay away from you—to leave you to work like this!'

'He does not leave me to work!' she cried, springing to the defence of the absent one with all her fervour. 'He don't know it! It is by my own arrangement.'

'Then, does he write?'

'I—I cannot tell you. There are things which are private to ourselves.'

'Of course that means that he does not. You are a deserted wife, my fair Tess!'

In an impulse he turned suddenly to take her hand; the buff-glove was on it, and he seized only the rough leather fingers which did not express the life or shape of those within.

'You must not—you must not!' she cried fearfully, slipping her hand from the glove as from a pocket, and leaving it in his grasp. 'O, will you go away—for the sake of me and my husband—go, in the name of your own Christianity!'

'Yes, yes; I will,' he said abruptly, and thrusting the glove back to her turned to leave. Facing round, however, he said, 'Tess, as God is my judge, I meant no humbug in taking your hand!'

A pattering of hoofs on the soil of the field, which they had not noticed in their pre-occupation ceased close behind them; and a voice reached her ear:

'What the devil are you doing away from your work at this time o'day?'

Farmer Groby had espied the two figures from the distance, and had inquisitively ridden across, to learn what was their business in his field.

'Don't speak like that to her!' said d'Urberville, his face blackening with something that was not Christianity.

'Indeed, Mister! And what mid Methodist pa'sons have to do with she?'

'Who is the fellow?' asked d'Urberville, turning to Tess.

She went close up to him.

'Go—I do beg you!' she said.

'What! And leave you to that tyrant? I can see in his face what a churl he is.'

'He won't hurt me. *He's* not in love with me. I can leave at Lady-Day.'

'Well, I have no right but to obey, I suppose. But—well, good-bye!'

Her defender, whom she dreaded more than her assailant, having reluctantly disappeared, the farmer continued his reprimand, which Tess took with the greatest coolness, that sort of attack being independent of sex. To have as a master this man of stone, who would have cuffed her if he had dared, was almost a relief after her former experiences. She silently walked back towards the summit of the field that was the scene of her labour, so absorbed in the interview which had just taken place that she was hardly aware that the nose of Groby's horse almost touched her shoulders.

'If so be you make an agreement to work for me till Lady-Day, I'll see that you carry it out,' he growled. ''Od rot the women—now 'tis one thing, and then 'tis another. But I'll put up with it no longer!'

Knowing very well that he did not harass the other women of the farm as he harassed her out of spite for the flooring he had once received, she did for one moment picture what might have been the result if she had been free to accept the offer just made her of being the monied Alec's wife. It would have lifted her completely out of subjection, not only to her present oppressive employer, but to a whole world who seemed to despise her. 'But no, no!' she said breathlessly; 'I could not have married him now! He is so unpleasant to me.'

That very night she began an appealing letter to Clare, concealing from him her hardships, and assuring him of her undying affection. Any one who had been in a position to read between the lines would have seen that at the back of her great loves was some monstrous fear – almost a desperation – as to some secret contingencies which were not disclosed. But again she did not finish her effusion; he had asked Izz to go with him, and perhaps he did not care for her at all. She put the letter in her box, and wondered if it would ever reach Angel's hands.

After this her daily tasks were gone through heavily enough, and brought on the day which was of great import to agriculturists – the day of the Candlemas Fair. It was at this fair that new engagements were entered into for the twelve months following the ensuing Lady-Day, and those of the farming population who thought of changing their places duly attended at the county-town where the fair was held. Nearly all the labourers on Flintcomb-Ash Farm intended flight, and early in the morning there was a general exodus in the direction of the town, which lay at a distance of from ten to a dozen miles over hilly country. Though Tess also meant to leave at the quarter-day she was one of the few who did not go to the fair, having a vaguely-shaped hope that something would happen to render another outdoor engagement unnecessary.

It was a peaceful February day, of wonderful softness for the time, and one would almost have thought that winter was over. She had hardly finished her dinner when d'Urberville's figure darkened the window of the cottage wherein she was a lodger, which she had all to herself to-day.

Tess jumped up, but her visitor had knocked at the door, and she could hardly in reason run away. D'Urberville's knock, his walk up to the door, had some indescribable quality of difference from his air when she last saw him. They seemed to be acts of which the doer was ashamed. She thought that she would not open the door; but, as there was no sense in that either, she arose, and having lifted the latch stepped back quickly. He came in, saw her, and flung himself down into a chair before speaking.

'Tess – I couldn't help it!' he began desperately, as he wiped his heated face, which had also a superimposed flush of excitement. 'I felt that I must call at least to ask how you are. I assure you I had not been thinking of you at all till I saw you that Sunday; now I cannot get rid of your image, try how I may! It is hard that a good woman should do harm to a bad man; yet so it is. If you would only pray for me, Tess!'

The suppressed discontent of his manner was almost pitiable, and yet Tess did not pity him.

'How can I pray for you,' she said, 'when I am forbidden to believe that the great Power who moves the world would alter His plans on my account?'

'You really think that?'

'Yes. I have been cured of the presumption of thinking otherwise.'

'Cured? By whom?'

'By my husband, if I must tell.'

'Ah – your husband – your husband! How strange it seems! I remember you hinted something of the sort the other day. What do you really believe in these matters, Tess?' he asked. 'You seem to have no religion – perhaps owing to me.'

'But I have. Though I don't believe in anything supernatural.'

D'Urberville looked at her with misgiving.

'Then do you think that the line I take is all wrong?'

'A good deal of it.'

'H'm – and yet I've felt so sure about it,' he said uneasily.

'I believe in the *spirit* of the Sermon on the Mount, and so did my dear husband. . . . But I don't believe—'

Here she gave her negations.

'The fact is,' said d'Urberville drily, 'whatever your dear husband believed you accept, and whatever he rejected you reject, without the least inquiry or reasoning on your own part. That's just like you women. Your mind is enslaved to his.'

'Ah, because he knew everything!' said she, with a triumphant simplicity of faith in Angel Clare that the most perfect man could hardly have deserved, much less her husband.

'Yes, but you should not take negative opinions wholesale from another person like that. A pretty fellow he must be to teach you such scepticism!'

'He never forced my judgment! He would never argue on the subject with me! But I looked at it in this way; what he believed, after inquiring deep into doctrines, was much more likely to be right than what I might believe, who hadn't looked into doctrines at all.'

'What used he to say? He must have said something?'

She reflected; and with her acute memory for the letter of Angel Clare's remarks, even when she did not comprehend their spirit, she recalled a merciless polemical syllogism that she had heard him use when, as it occasionally happened, he indulged in a species of thinking aloud with her at his side. In delivering it she gave also Clare's accent and manner with reverential faithfulness.

'Say that again,' asked d'Urberville, who had listened with the greatest attention.

She repeated the argument, and d'Urberville thoughtfully murmured the words after her.

'Anything else?' he presently asked.

'He said at another time something like this', and she gave another, which might possibly have been paralleled in many a work of the pedigree ranging from the *Dictionnaire Philosophique* to Huxley's *Essays*.

'Ah – ha! How do you remember them?'

'I wanted to believe what he believed, though he didn't wish me to; and I managed to coax him to tell me a few of his thoughts. I can't say I quite understand that one; but I know it is right.'

'H'm. Fancy your being able to teach me what you don't know yourself!'

He fell into thought.

'And so I threw in my spiritual lot with his,' she resumed. 'I didn't wish it to be different. What's good enough for him is good enough for me.'

'Does he know that you are as big an infidel as he?'

'No – I never told him – if I am an infidel.'

'Well – you are better off to-day than I am, Tess, after all! You don't believe that you ought to preach my doctrine, and, therefore, do no despite to your conscience in abstaining. I do believe I ought to preach it, but like the devils I believe and tremble, for I suddenly leave off preaching it, and give way to my passion for you.'

'How?'

'Why,' he said aridly; 'I have come all the way here to see you to-day! But I started from home to go to Casterbridge Fair, where I have undertaken to preach the Word from a waggon at half-past two this afternoon, and where all the brethren are expecting me this minute. Here's the announcement.'

He drew from his breast-pocket a poster whereon was printed the day, hour, and place of meeting, at which he, d'Urberville, would preach the Gospel as aforesaid.

'But how can you get there?' said Tess, looking at the clock.

'I cannot get there! I have come here.'

'What, you have really arranged to preach, and—'

'I have arranged to preach, and I shall not be there – by reason of my burning desire to see a woman whom I once despised! – No, by my word and truth, I never despised you; if I had I should not love you now! Why I did not despise you was on account of your being unsmirched in spite of all; you withdrew yourself from me so quickly and resolutely when you saw the situation; you did not remain at my pleasure; so there was one petticoat in the world for whom I had no contempt, and you are she. But you may well despise me now! I thought I worshipped on the mountains, but I find I still serve in the groves! Ha! ha!'

'O Alec d'Urberville! what does this mean? What have I done!'

'Done?' he said, with a soulless sneer in the word. 'Nothing intentionally. But you have been the means – the innocent means – of my backsliding, as they call it. I ask myself, am I, indeed, one of those "servants of corruption" who, "after they have escaped the pollutions of the world, are again entangled therein and overcome" – whose latter end is worse than their beginning?' He laid his hand on her shoulder. 'Tess, my girl, I was on the way to, at least, social salvation till I saw you again!' he said freakishly shaking her, as if she were a child. 'And why then have you tempted me? I was firm as a man could be till I saw those eyes and that mouth again – surely there never was such a maddening mouth since Eve's!' His voice sank, and a hot archness shot from his own black eyes. 'You temptress, Tess; you dear damned witch of Babylon – I could not resist you as soon as I met you again!'

'I couldn't help your seeing me again!' said Tess, recoiling.

'I know it – I repeat that I do not blame you. But the fact remains. When I saw you ill-used on the farm that day I was nearly mad to think that I had no legal right to protect you – that I could not have it; whilst he who has it seems to neglect you utterly!'

'Don't speak against him – he is absent!' she cried in much excitement. 'Treat him honourably – he has never wronged you! O leave his wife before any scandal spreads that may do harm to his honest name!'

'I will – I will,' he said, like a man awakening from a luring dream. 'I have broken my engagement to preach to those poor drunken boobies at the fair – it is the first time I have played such a practical joke. A month ago I should have been horrified at such a possibility. I'll go away – to swear – and – ah, can I! to keep away.' Then, suddenly: 'One clasp, Tessy – one! Only for old friendship—'

'I am without defence, Alec! A good man's honour is in my keeping – think – be ashamed!'

'Pooh! Well, yes – yes!'

He clenched his lips, mortified with himself for his weakness. His eyes were equally barren of worldly and religious faith. The corpses of those old fitful passions which had lain inanimate amid the lines of his face ever since his reformation seemed to wake and come together as in a resurrection. He went out indeterminately.

Though d'Urberville had declared that this breach of his engagement to-day was the simple backsliding of a believer, Tess's words, as echoed from Angel Clare, had made a deep impression upon him, and continued to do so after he had left her. He moved on in silence, as if his energies were benumbed by the hitherto undreamt-of possibility that his position was untenable. Reason had had nothing to do with his whimsical conversion, which was perhaps the mere freak of a careless man in search of a new sensation, and temporarily impressed by his mother's death.

The drops of logic Tess had let fall into the sea of his enthusiasm served to chill its effervescence to stagnation. He said to himself, as he pondered again and again over the crystallized phrases that she had handed on to him, 'That clever fellow little thought that, by telling her those things, he might be paving my way back to her!'

CHAPTER FORTY-SEVEN

IT is the threshing of the last wheat-rick at Flintcomb-Ash Farm. The dawn of the March morning is singularly inexpressive, and there is nothing to show where the eastern horizon lies. Against the twilight rises the trapezoidal top of the stack, which has stood forlornly here through the washing and bleaching of the wintry weather.

When Izz Huett and Tess arrived at the scene of operations only a rustling denoted that others had preceded them; to which, as the light increased, there were presently added the silhouettes of two men on the summit. They were busily 'unhaling' the rick, that is, stripping off the thatch before beginning to throw down the sheaves; and while this was in progress Izz and Tess, with the other women-workers, in their whitey-brown pinners, stood waiting and shivering, Farmer Groby having insisted upon their being on the spot thus early to get the job over if possible by the end of the day. Close under the eaves of the stack, and as yet barely visible, was the red tyrant that the women had come to serve – a timber-framed construction, with straps and wheels appertaining – the threshing-machine which, whilst it was going, kept up a despotic demand upon the endurance of their muscles and nerves.

A little way off there was another indistinct figure; this one black, with a sustained hiss that spoke of strength very much in reserve. The long chimney running up beside an ash-tree, and the warmth which radiated from the spot, explained without the necessity of much daylight that here was the engine which was to act as the *primum mobile* of this little world. By the engine stood a dark motionless being, a sooty and grimy embodiment of tallness, in a sort of trance, with a heap of coals by his side: it was the engineman. The isolation of his manner and colour lent him the appearance of a creature from Tophet, who had strayed into the pellucid smokelessness of this region of yellow grain and pale soil, with which he had nothing in common, to amaze and to discompose its aborigines.

What he looked he felt. He was in the agricultural world, but not of it. He served fire and smoke; these denizens of the fields served vegetation, weather, frost, and sun. He travelled with his engine from farm to farm, from county to county, for as yet the steam threshing-machine was itinerant in this part of Wessex. He spoke in a strange northern accent; his thoughts being turned inwards upon himself, his eye on his iron charge, hardly perceiving the scenes around him, and caring for them not at all: holding only strictly necessary intercourse with the natives, as if some ancient doom compelled him to wander here against his will in the service of his Plutonic master. The long strap which ran from the driving-wheel of his engine to the red thresher under the rick was the sole tie-line between agriculture and him.

While they uncovered the sheaves he stood apathetic beside his portable repository of force, round whose hot blackness the morning air quivered. He had nothing to do with the preparatory labour. His fire was waiting incandescent, his steam was at high pressure, in a few seconds he could make the long strap move at an invisible velocity. Beyond its extent the environment might be corn, straw, or chaos; it was all the same to him. If any of the autochthonous idlers asked him what he called himself, he replied shortly, 'an engineer.'

The rick was unhaled by full daylight; the men then took their places, the women mounted, and the work began. Farmer Groby – or, as they called him, 'he' – had arrived ere this, and by his orders Tess was placed on the platform of the machine, close to the man who fed it, her business being to untie every sheaf of corn handed on to her by Izz Huett, who stood next, but on the rick; so that the feeder could seize it and spread it over the revolving drum, which whisked out every grain in one moment.

They were soon in full progress, after a preparatory hitch or two, which rejoiced the hearts of those who hated machinery. The work sped on till breakfast-time, when the thresher was stopped for half an hour; and on starting again after the meal the whole supplementary strength of the farm was thrown into the labour of constructing the straw-rick, which began to grow beside the stack of corn. A hasty lunch was eaten as they stood, without leaving their positions, and then another couple of hours brought them near to dinner-time; the inexorable wheels continuing to spin, and the penetrating hum of the thresher to thrill to the very marrow all who were near the revolving wire-cage.

The old men on the rising straw-rick talked of the past days when they had been accustomed to thresh with flails on the oaken barn-floor; when everything, even to winnowing, was effected by hand-labour, which, to their thinking, though slow, produced better results. Those, too, on the corn-rick talked a little; but the perspiring ones at the machine, including Tess, could not lighten their duties by the exchange of many words. It was the ceaselessness of the work which tried her so severely, and began to make her wish that she had never come to Flintcomb-Ash. The women on the corn-rick — Marian, who was one of them, in particular — could stop to drink ale or cold tea from the flagon now and then, or to exchange a few gossiping remarks while they wiped their faces or cleared the fragments of straw and husk from their clothing; but for Tess there was no respite; for, as the drum never stopped, the man who fed it could not stop, and she, who had to supply the man with untied sheaves, could not stop either, unless Marian changed places with her, which she sometimes did for half an hour in spite of Groby's objection that she was too slow-handed for a feeder.

For some probably economical reason it was usually a woman who was chosen for this particular duty, and Groby gave as his motive in selecting Tess that she was one of those who best combined strength with quickness in untying, and both with staying power, and this may have been true. The hum of the thresher, which prevented speech, increased to a raving whenever the supply of corn fell short of the regular quantity. As Tess and the man who fed could never turn their heads she did not know that just before the dinner-hour a person had come silently into the field by the gate, and had been standing under a second rick watching the scene, and Tess in particular. He was dressed in a tweed suit of fashionable pattern, and he twirled a gay walking-cane.

'Who is that?' said Izz Huett to Marian. She had at first addressed the inquiry to Tess, but the latter could not hear it.

'Somebody's fancy-man, I s'pose,' said Marian laconically.

'I'll lay a guinea he's after Tess.'

'O no. 'Tis a ranter pa'son who's been sniffing after her lately; not a dandy like this.'

'Well — this is the same man.'

'The same man as the preacher? But he's quite different!'

'He hev left off his black coat and white neckercher, and hev cut off his whiskers; but he's the same man for all that.'

'D'ye really think so? Then I'll tell her,' said Marian.

'Don't. She'll see him soon enough, good-now.'

'Well, I don't think it at all right for him to join his preaching to courting a married woman, even though her husband mid be abroad, and she, in a sense, a widow.'

'Oh — he can do her no harm,' said Izz drily. 'Her mind can no more be heaved from that one place where it do bide than a stooded waggon from the hole he's in. Lord love 'ee, neither court-paying, nor preaching, nor the seven thunders themselves, can wean a woman when 'twould be better for her that she should be weaned.'

Dinner-time came, and the whirling ceased; whereupon Tess left her post, her knees trembling so wretchedly with the shaking of the machine that she could scarcely walk.

'You ought to het a quart o'drink into 'ee, as I've done,' said Marian. 'You wouldn't look so white then. Why, souls above us, your face is as if you'd been hagrode!'

It occurred to the good-natured Marian that, as Tess was so tired, her discovery of her visitor's presence might have the bad effect of taking away her appetite; and Marian was thinking of inducing Tess to descend by a ladder on the further side of the stack when the gentleman came forward and looked up.

Tess uttered a short little 'Oh!' And a moment after she said, quickly, 'I shall eat my dinner here – right on the rick.'

Sometimes, when they were so far from their cottages, they all did this; but as there was rather a keen wind going to-day, Marian and the rest descended, and sat under the straw-stack.

The new-comer, was indeed, Alec d'Urberville, the late Evangelist, despite his changed attire and aspect. It was obvious at a glance that the original *Weltlust* had come back; that he had restored himself, as nearly as a man could do who had grown three or four years older, to the old jaunty, slap-dash guise under which Tess had first known her admirer, and cousin so-called. Having decided to remain where she was, Tess sat down among the bundles, out of sight of the ground, and began her meal; till, by-and-by, she heard footsteps on the ladder, and immediately after Alec appeared upon the stack – now an oblong and level platform of sheaves. He strode across them, and sat down opposite to her without a word.

Tess continued to eat her modest dinner, a slice of thick pancake which she had brought with her. The other workfolk were by this time all gathered under the rick, where the loose straw formed a comfortable retreat.

'I am here again, as you see,' said d'Urberville.

'Why do you trouble me so!' she cried, reproach flashing from her very finger-ends.

'*I* trouble *you?* I think I may ask, why do you trouble me?'

'Sure, I don't trouble you any-when!'

'You say you don't? But you do! You haunt me. Those very eyes that you turned upon me with such a bitter flash a moment ago, they come to me just as you showed them then, in the night and in the day! Tess, ever since you told me of that child of ours, it is just as if my feelings, which have been flowing in a strong puritanical stream, had suddenly found a way open in the direction of you, and had all at once gushed through. The religious channel is left dry forthwith; and it is you who have done it!'

She gazed in silence.

'What – you have given up your preaching entirely?' she asked.

She had gathered from Angel sufficient of the incredulity of modern thought to despise flash enthusiasms; but, as a woman, she was somewhat appalled.

In affected severity d'Urberville continued –

'Entirely. I have broken every engagement since that afternoon I was to address the drunkards at Casterbridge Fair. The deuce only knows what I am thought of by the brethren. Ah-ha! The brethren! No doubt they pray for me – weep for me; for they are kind people in their way. But what do I care? How could I go on with the thing when I had lost my faith in it? – it would have been hypocrisy of the basest kind! Among them I should have stood like Hymenæus and Alexander, who were delivered over to Satan that they might learn not to blaspheme. What a grand revenge you have taken! I saw you innocent, and I deceived you. Four years after, you find me a Christian enthusiast; you then work upon me, perhaps to my complete perdition! But Tess, my coz, as I used to call you, this is only my way of talking, and you must not look so horribly concerned.

Of course you have done nothing except retain your pretty face and shapely figure. I saw it on the rick before you saw me – that tight pinafore-thing sets it off, and that wing-bonnet – you field-girls should never wear those bonnets if you wish to keep out of danger.' He regarded her silently for a few moments, and with a short cynical laugh resumed: 'I believe that if the bachelor-apostle, whose deputy I thought I was, had been tempted by such a pretty face, he would have let go the plough for her sake as I do!'

Tess attempted to expostulate, but at this juncture all her fluency failed her, and without heeding he added:

'Well, this paradise that you supply is perhaps as good as any other, after all. But to speak seriously, Tess.' D'Urberville rose and came nearer, reclining sideways amid the sheaves, and resting upon his elbow. 'Since I last saw you, I have been thinking of what you said that *he* said. I have come to the conclusion that there does seem rather a want of commonsense in these threadbare old propositions; how I could have been so fired by poor Parson Clare's enthusiasm, and have gone so madly to work, transcending even him, I cannot make out! As for what you said last time, on the strength of your wonderful husband's intelligence – whose name you have never told me – about having what they call an ethical system without any dogma, I don't see my way to that at all.'

'Why, you can have the religion of loving-kindness and purity at least, if you can't have – what do you call it – dogma.'

'O no! I'm a different sort of fellow from that! If there's nobody to say, "Do this, and it will be a good thing for you after you are dead; do that, and it will be a bad thing for you," I can't warm up. Hang it, I am not going to feel responsible for my deeds and passions if there's nobody to be responsible to; and if I were you, my dear, I wouldn't either!'

She tried to argue, and tell him that he had mixed in his dull brain two matters, theology and morals, which in the primitive days of mankind had been quite distinct. But owing to Angel Clare's reticence, to her absolute want of training, and to her being a vessel of emotions rather than reasons, she could not get on.

'Well, never mind,' he resumed. 'Here I am, my love, as in the old times!'

'Not as then – never as then – 'tis different!' she entreated. 'And there was never warmth with me! O why didn't you keep your faith, if the loss of it has brought you to speak to me like this!'

'Because you've knocked it out of me; so the evil be upon your sweet head! Your husband little thought how his teaching would recoil upon him! Ha-ha – I'm awfully glad you have made an apostate of me all the same! Tess, I am more taken with you than ever, and I pity you too. For all your closeness, I see you are in a bad way – neglected by one who ought to cherish you.'

She could not get her morsels of food down her throat; her lips were dry, and she was ready to choke. The voices and laughs of the workfolk eating and drinking under the rick came to her as if they were a quarter of a mile off.

'It is cruelty to me!' she said. 'How – how can you treat me to this talk, if you care ever so little for me?'

'True, true,' he said, wincing a little. 'I did not come to reproach you for my deeds. I came, Tess, to say that I don't like you to be working like this, and I have come on purpose for you. You say you have a husband who is not I. Well, perhaps you have; but I've never seen him, and you've not told me his name; and altogether he seems rather a mythological personage. However, even if you have one, I think I am nearer to you than he is. I, at any rate, try to help you out of trouble, but he does not, bless his invisible face! The words of the stern prophet Hosea that I used to read come back to me. Don't you know them, Tess? – "And she shall follow after her lover, but she shall not overtake him; and she shall seek him, but shall not find him; then shall she say, I will go and return to my first husband; for then was it better with me than now!" . . . Tess, my trap is waiting just under the hill, and – darling mine, not his! – you know the rest.'

Her face had been rising to a dull crimson fire while he spoke; but she did not answer.

'You have been the cause of my backsliding,' he continued, stretching his arm towards her waist; 'you should be willing to share it, and leave that mule you call husband for ever.'

One of her leather gloves, which she had taken off to eat her skimmer-cake, lay in her lap, and without the slightest warning she passionately swung the glove by the gauntlet directly in his face. It was heavy and thick as a warrior's, and it struck him flat on the mouth. Fancy might have regarded the act as the recrudescence of a trick in which her armed progenitors were not unpractised. Alec fiercely started up from his reclining position. A scarlet oozing appeared where her blow had alighted, and in a moment the blood began dropping from his mouth upon the straw. But he soon controlled himself, calmly drew his handkerchief from his pocket, and mopped his bleeding lips.

She too had sprung up, but she sank down again.

'Now, punish me!' she said, turning up her eyes to him with the hopeless defiance of the sparrow's gaze before its captor twists its neck. 'Whip me, crush me; you need not mind those people under the rick! I shall not cry out. Once victim, always victim – that's the law!'

'O no, no, Tess,' he said blandly. 'I can make full allowance for this. Yet you most unjustly forget one thing, that I would have married you if you had not put it out of my power to do so. Did I not ask you flatly to be my wife – hey? Answer me.'

'You did.'

'And you cannot be. But remember one thing!' His voice hardened as his temper got the better of him with the recollection of his sincerity in asking her and her present ingratitude, and he stepped across to her side and held her by the shoulders, so that she shook under his grasp. 'Remember, my lady, I was your master once! I will be your master again. If you are any man's wife you are mine!'

The threshers now began to stir below.

'So much for our quarrel,' he said, letting her go. 'Now I shall leave you, and shall come again for your answer during the afternoon. You don't know me yet! But I know you.'

She had not spoken again, remaining as if stunned. D'Urberville retreated over the sheaves, and descended the ladder, while the workers below rose and stretched their arms, and shook down the beer they had drunk. Then the threshing-machine started afresh; and amid the renewed rustle of the straw Tess resumed her position by the buzzing drum as one in a dream, untying sheaf after sheaf in endless succession.

CHAPTER FORTY-EIGHT

In the afternoon the farmer made it known that the rick was to be finished that night, since there was a moon by which they could see to work, and the man with the engine was engaged for another farm on the morrow. Hence the twanging and humming and rustling proceeded with even less intermission than usual.

It was not till 'nammet'-time, about three o'clock, that Tess raised her eyes and gave a momentary glance round. She felt but little surprise at seeing that Alec d'Urberville had come back, and was standing under the hedge by the gate. He had seen her lift her eyes, and waved his hand urbanely to her, while he blew her a kiss. It meant that their quarrel was over. Tess looked down again, and carefully abstained from gazing in that direction.

Thus the afternoon dragged on. The wheat-rick shrank lower, and the straw-rick grew higher, and the corn-sacks were carted away. At six o'clock the wheat-rick was about shoulder-high from the ground. But the unthreshed sheaves remaining untouched seemed countless still, notwithstanding the enormous numbers that had been gulped down by the insatiable swallower, fed by the man and Tess, through whose two young hands the greater part of them had passed. And the immense stack of straw where in the morning there had been nothing, appeared as the *faeces* of the same buzzing red glutton. From the west sky a wrathful shine — all that wild March could afford in the way of sunset — had burst forth after the cloudy day, flooding the tired and sticky faces of the threshers, and dyeing them with a coppery light, as also the flapping garments of the women, which clung to them like dull flames.

A panting ache ran through the rick. The man who fed was weary, and Tess could see that the red nape of his neck was encrusted with dirt and husks. She still stood at her post, her flushed and perspiring face coated with the corn-dust, and her white bonnet embrowned by it. She was the only woman whose place was upon the machine so as to be shaken bodily by its spinning, and the decrease of the stack now separated her from Marian and Izz, and prevented their changing duties with her as they had done. The incessant quivering, in which every fibre of her frame participated, had thrown her into a stupefied reverie in which her arms worked on independently of her consciousness. She hardly knew where she was, and did not hear Izz Huett tell her from below that her hair was tumbling down.

By degrees the freshest among them began to grow cadaverous and saucer-eyed. Whenever Tess lifted her head she beheld always the great upgrown straw-stack, with the men in shirt-sleeves upon it, against the gray north sky; in front of it the long red elevator like a Jacob's ladder, on which a perpetual stream of threshed straw ascended, a yellow river running up-hill, and spouting out on the top of the rick.

She knew that Alec d'Urberville was still on the scene, observing her from some point or other, though she could not say where. There was an excuse for his remaining, for when the threshed rick drew near its final sheaves a little ratting was always done, and men unconnected with the threshing sometimes dropped in for that performance — sporting characters of all descriptions, gents with terriers and facetious pipes, roughs with sticks and stones.

But there was another hour's work before the layer of live rats at the base of the stack would be reached; and as the evening light in the direction of the Giant's Hill by Abbot's-Cernel dissolved away, the white-faced moon of the season arose from the horizon that lay towards Middleton Abbey and Shottsford on the other side. For the last hour or two Marian had felt uneasy about Tess, whom she could not get near enough to speak to, the other women having kept up their strength by drinking ale, and Tess having done without it through traditionary dread, owing to its results at her home in childhood. But Tess still kept going: if she could not fill her part she would have to leave; and this contingency, which she would have regarded with equanimity and even with relief a month or two earlier, had become a terror since d'Urberville had begun to hover round her.

The sheaf-pitchers and feeders had now worked the rick so low that people on the ground could talk to them. To Tess's surprise Farmer Groby came up on the machine to her, and said that if she desired to join her friend he did not wish her to keep on any longer, and would send somebody else to take her place. The 'friend' was d'Urberville, she knew, and also that this concession had been granted in obedience to the request of that friend, or enemy. She shook her head and toiled on.

The time for the rat-catching arrived at last, and the hunt began. The creatures had crept downwards with the subsidence of the rick till they were all together at the bottom, and being now uncovered from their last refuge they ran across the open ground in all directions, a loud shriek from the by-this-time half-tipsy Marian informing her companions that one of the rats had invaded her person — a terror which the rest of the women had guarded against by various schemes of skirt-tucking and self-elevation. The rat was at last dislodged, and, amid the barking of dogs, masculine shouts, feminine screams, oaths, stampings, and confusion as of Pandemonium, Tess united her last sheaf; the drum slowed, the whizzing ceased, and she stepped from the machine to the ground.

Her lover, who had only looked on at the rat-catching, was promptly at her side.

'What — after all — my insulting slap, too!' said she in an underbreath. She was so utterly exhausted that she had not strength to speak louder.

'I should indeed be foolish to feel offended at anything you say or do,' he answered, in the seductive voice of the Trantridge time. 'How the little limbs tremble! You are as weak as a bled calf, you know you are; and yet you need have done nothing since I arrived. How could you be so obstinate? However, I have told the farmer that he has no right to employ women at steam-threshing. It is not proper work for them; and on all the better class of farms it has been given up, as he knows very well. I will walk with you as far as your home.'

'O yes,' she answered with a jaded gait. 'Walk wi' me if you will! I do bear in mind that you came to marry me before you knew o' my state. Perhaps — perhaps you are a little better and kinder than I have been thinking you were. Whatever is meant as kindness I am grateful for; whatever is meant in any other way I am angered at. I cannot sense your meaning sometimes.'

'If I cannot legitimize our former relations at least I can assist you. And I will do it with much more regard for your feelings than I formerly showed. My religious mania, or whatever it was, is over. But I retain a little good nature; I hope I do. Now, Tess, by all that's tender and strong between man and woman, trust me! I have enough and more than enough to put you out of anxiety, both for yourself and your parents and sisters. I can make them all comfortable if you will only show confidence in me.'

'Have you seen 'em lately?' she quickly inquired.

'Yes. They didn't know where you were. It was only by chance that I found you here.'

The cold moon looked aslant upon Tess's fagged face between the twigs of the garden-hedge as she paused outside the cottage which was her temporary home, d'Urberville pausing beside her.

'Don't mention my little brothers and sisters — don't make me break down quite!' she said. 'If you want to help them — God knows they need it — do it without telling me. But, no, no!' she cried. 'I will take nothing from you, either for them or for me!'

He did not accompany her further, since, as she lived with the household, all was public indoors. No sooner had she herself entered, laved herself in a washing-tub, and shared supper with the family than she fell into thought, and withdrawing to the table under the wall, by the light of her own little lamp wrote in a passionate mood —

My Own Husband, — Let me call you so — I must — even if it makes you angry to think of such an unworthy wife as I. I must cry to you in my trouble — I have no one else! I am so exposed to temptation, Angel. I fear to say who it is, and I do not like to write about it at all. But I cling to you in a way you cannot think! Can you not come to me now, at once, before anything terrible happens? O, I know you cannot, because you are so far away! I think I must die if you do not come soon, or tell me to come to you. The punishment you have measured out to me is deserved — I do know that — well deserved — and you are right and just to be angry with me. But, Angel, please, please, not to be just — only a little kind to me, even if I do not deserve it, and come to me! If you would come, I could die in your arms! I would be well content to do that if so be you had forgiven me!

Angel, I live entirely for you. I love you too much to blame you for going away, and I know it was necessary you should find a farm. Do not think I shall say a word of sting or bitterness. Only come back to me. I am desolate without you, my darling, O, so desolate! I do not mind having to work: but if you will send me one little line, and say, '*I am coming soon*,' I will bide on, Angel! — O, so cheerfully!

It has been so much my religion ever since we were married to be faithful to you in every thought and look, that even when a man speaks a compliment to me before I am aware, it seems wronging you. Have you never felt one little bit of what you used to feel when we were at the dairy? If you have, how can you keep away from me? I am the same woman, Angel, as you fell in love with; yes, the very same! — not the one you disliked but never saw. What was the past to me as soon as I met you? It was a dead thing altogether. I became another woman, filled full of new life from you. How could I be the early one? Why do you not see this? Dear, if you would only be a little more conceited, and believe in yourself so far as to see that you were strong enough to work this change in me, you would perhaps be in a mind to come to me, your poor wife.

How silly I was in my happiness when I thought I could trust you always to love me! I ought to have known that such as that was not for poor me. But I am sick at heart, not only for old times, but for the present. Think — think how it do hurt my heart not to see you ever — ever! Ah, if I could only make your dear heart ache one little minute of each day as mine does every day and all day long, it might lead you to show pity to your poor lonely one.

People still say that I am rather pretty, Angel (handsome is the word they use, since I wish to be truthful). Perhaps I am what they say. But I do not value my good looks; I only like to have them because they belong to you, my dear, and that there may be at least one thing about me worth your having. So much have I felt this, that when I met with annoyance on account of the same I tied up my face in a bandage as long as people would believe in it. O Angel, I tell you all this not from vanity — you will certainly know I do not — but only that you may come to me!

If you really cannot come to me will you let me come to you! I am, as I say, worried, pressed to do what I will not do. It cannot be that I shall yield one inch, yet I am in terror as to what an accident might lead to, and I so defenceless on account of my first error. I cannot say more about this — it makes me too miserable. But if I break down by falling into some fearful snare, my last state will be worse than my first. O God, I cannot think of it! Let me come at once, or at once come to me!

I would be content, ay, glad, to live with you as your servant, if I may not as your wife; so that I could only be near you, and get glimpses of you, and think of you as mine.

The daylight has nothing to show me, since you are not here, and I don't like to see the rooks and starlings in the fields, because I grieve and grieve to miss you who used to see them with me. I long for only one thing in heaven or earth or under the earth, to meet you, my own dear! Come to me — come to me, and save me from what threatens me! — Your faithful heartbroken

TESS

CHAPTER FORTY-NINE

THE appeal duly found its way to the breakfast-table of the quiet Vicarage to the westward, in that valley where the air is so soft and the soil so rich that the effort of growth requires but superficial aid by comparison with the tillage at Flintcomb-Ash, and where to Tess the human world seemed so different (though it was much the same). It was purely for security that she had been requested by Angel to send her communications through his father, whom he kept pretty well informed of his changing addresses in the country he had gone to exploit for himself with a heavy heart.

'Now,' said old Mr Clare to his wife, when he had read the envelope, 'if Angel proposes leaving Rio for a visit home at the end of next month, as he told us that he hoped to do, I think this may hasten his plans; for I believe it to be from his wife.' He breathed deeply at the thought of her; and the letter was redirected to be promptly sent on to Angel.

'Dear fellow, I hope he will get home safely,' murmured Mrs Clare. 'To my dying day I shall feel that he has been ill-used. You should have sent him to Cambridge in spite of his want of faith, and given him the same chance as the other boys had. He would have grown out of it under proper influence, and perhaps would have taken Orders after all. Church or no Church, it would have been fairer to him.'

This was the only wail with which Mrs Clare ever disturbed her husband's peace in respect of their sons. And she did not vent this often; for she was as considerate as she was devout, and knew that his mind too was troubled by doubts as to his justice in this matter. Only too often had she heard him lying awake at night, stifling sighs for Angel with prayers. But the uncompromising Evangelical did not even now hold that he would have been justified in giving his son, an unbeliever, the same academic advantages that he had given to the two others, when it was possible, if not probable, that those very advantages might have been used to decry the doctrines which he had made it his life's mission and desire to propagate, and the mission of his ordained sons likewise. To put with one hand a pedestal under the feet of the two faithful ones, and with the other to exalt the unfaithful by the same artificial means, he deemed to be alike inconsistent with his convictions, his position, and his hopes. Nevertheless, he loved his misnamed Angel, and in secret mourned over this treatment of him as Abraham might have mourned over the doomed Isaac while they went up the hill together. His silent self-generated regrets were far bitterer than the reproaches which his wife rendered audible.

They blamed themselves for this unlucky marriage. If Angel had never been destined for a farmer he would never have been thrown with agricultural girls. They did not distinctly know what had separated him and his wife, nor the date on which the separation had taken place. At first they had supposed it must be something of the nature of a serious aversion. But in his later letters he occasionally alluded to the intention of coming home to fetch her; from which expressions they hoped the division might not owe its origin to anything so hopelessly permanent as that. He had told them that she was with her relatives, and in their doubts they had decided not to intrude into a situation which they knew no way of bettering.

The eyes for which Tess's letter was intended were gazing at this time on a limitless expanse of country from the back of a mule which was bearing him from the interior of the South-American Continent towards the coast. His experiences of this strange land had been sad. The severe illness from which he had suffered shortly after his arrival had never wholly left him, and he had by degrees almost decided to relinquish his hope of farming here, though, as long as the bare possibility existed of his remaining, he kept this change of view a secret from his parents.

The crowds of agricultural labourers who had come out to the country in his wake, dazzled by representations of easy independence, had suffered, died, and wasted away. He would see mothers from English farms trudging along with their infants in their arms, when the child would be stricken with fever and would die; the mother would pause to dig a hole in the loose earth with her bare hands, would bury the babe therein with the same natural grave-tools, shed one tear, and again trudge on.

Angel's original intention had not been emigration to Brazil, but a northern or eastern farm in his own country. He had come to this place in a fit of desperation, the Brazil movement among the English agriculturists having by chance coincided with his desire to escape from his past existence.

During this time of absence he had mentally aged a dozen years. What arrested him now as of value in life was less its beauty than its pathos. Having long discredited the old systems of mysticism, he now began to discredit the old appraisements of morality. He thought they wanted readjusting. Who was the moral man? Still more pertinently, who was the moral woman? The beauty or ugliness of a character lay not only in its achievements, but in its aims and impulses; its true history lay, not among things done, but among things willed.

How, then, about Tess?

Viewing her in these lights, a regret for his hasty judgment began to oppress him. Did he reject her eternally, or did he not? He could no longer say that he would always reject her, and not to say that was in spirit to accept her now.

This growing fondness for her memory coincided in point of time with her residence at Flintcomb-Ash, but it was before she had felt herself at liberty to trouble him with a word about her circumstances or her feelings. He was greatly perplexed; and in his perplexity as to her motives in withholding intelligence he did not inquire. Thus her silence of docility was misinterpreted. How much it really said if he had understood! – that she adhered with literal exactness to orders which he had given and forgotten; that despite her natural fearlessness she asserted no rights, admitted his judgment to be in every respect the true one, and bent her head dumbly thereto.

In the before-mentioned journey by mules through the interior of the country, another man rode beside him. Angel's companion was also an Englishman, bent on the same errand, though he came from another part of the island. They were both in a state of mental depression, and they spoke of home affairs. Confidence begat confidence. With that curious tendency evinced by men, more especially when in distant lands, to entrust to strangers details of their lives which they would on no account mention to friends, Angel admitted to this man as they rode along the sorrowful facts of his marriage.

The stranger had sojourned in many more lands and among many more peoples than Angel; to his cosmopolitan mind such deviations from the social norm, so immense to domesticity, were no more than are the irregularities of vale and mountain-chain to the whole terrestrial curve. He viewed the matter in quite a different light from Angel; thought that what Tess had been was of no importance beside what she would be, and plainly told Clare that he was wrong in coming away from her.

The next day they were drenched in a thunder-storm. Angel's companion was struck down with fever, and died by the week's end. Clare waited a few hours to bury him, and then went on his way.

The cursory remarks of the large-minded stranger, of whom he knew absolutely nothing beyond a commonplace name, were sublimed by his death, and influenced Clare more than all the reasoned ethics of the philosophers. His own parochialism made him ashamed by its contrast. His inconsistencies rushed upon him in a flood. He had persistently elevated Hellenic Paganism at the expense of Christianity; yet in that civilization an illegal surrender was not certain dis-esteem. Surely then he might have regarded that abhorrence of the un-intact state, which he had inherited with the creed of mysticism, as at least open to correction when the result was due to treachery. A remorse struck into him. The words of Izz Huett, never quite stilled in his memory, came back to him. He had asked Izz if she loved him, and she had replied in the affirmative. Did she love him more than Tess did? No, she had replied; Tess would lay down her life for him, and she herself could do no more.

He thought of Tess as she had appeared on the day of the wedding. How her eyes had lingered upon him; how she had hung upon his words as if they were a god's! And during the terrible evening over the hearth, when her simple soul uncovered itself to his, how pitiful her face had looked by the rays of the fire, in her inability to realize that his love and protection could possibly be withdrawn.

Thus from being her critic he grew to be her advocate. Cynical things he had uttered to himself about her; but no man can be always a cynic and live; and he withdrew them. The mistake of expressing them had arisen from his allowing himself to be influenced by general principles to the disregard of the particular instance.

But the reasoning is somewhat musty; lovers and husbands have gone over the ground before to-day. Clare had been harsh towards her; there is no doubt of it. Men are too often harsh with women they love or have loved; women with men. And yet these harshnesses are tenderness itself when compared with the universal harshness out of which they grow; the harshness of the position towards the temperament, of the means towards the aims, of to-day towards yesterday, of hereafter towards to-day.

The historic interest of her family — that masterful line of d'Urbervilles — whom he had despised as a spent force, touched his sentiments now. Why had he not known the difference between the political value and the imaginative value of these things? In the latter aspect her d'Urberville descent was a fact of great dimensions; worthless to economics, it was a most useful ingredient to the dreamer, to the moralizer on declines and falls. It was a fact that would soon be forgotten — that bit of distinction in poor Tess's blood and name, and oblivion would fall upon her hereditary link with the marble monuments and leaded skeletons at Kingsbere. So does Time ruthlessly destroy his own romances. In recalling her face again and again, he thought now that he could see therein a flash of the dignity which must have graced her grand-dames; and the vision sent that *aura* through his veins which he had formerly felt, and which left behind it a sense of sickness.

Despite her not inviolate past, what still abode in such a woman as Tess outvalued the freshness of her fellows. Was not the gleaning of the grapes of Ephraim better than the vintage of Abi-ezer?

So spoke love renascent, preparing the way for Tess's devoted outpouring, which was then just being forwarded to him by his father; though owing to his distance inland it was to be a long time in reaching him.

Meanwhile the writer's expectation that Angel would come in response to the entreaty was alternately great and small. What lessened it was that the facts of her life which had led to the parting had not changed — could never change; and that, if her presence had not attenuated them, her absence could not. Nevertheless she addressed her mind to the tender question of what she could do to please him best if he should arrive. Sighs were expended on the wish that she had taken more notice of the tunes he played on his harp, that she had inquired more curiously of him which were his favourite ballads among those the country-girls sang. She indirectly inquired of Amby Seedling, who had followed Izz from Talbothays, and by chance Amby remembered that, amongst the snatches of melody in which they had indulged at the dairyman's, to induce the cows to let down their milk, Clare had seemed to like 'Cupid's Gardens', 'I have parks, I have hounds', and

'The break o' the day'; and had seemed not to care for 'The Tailor's Breeches',
and 'Such a beauty I did grow', excellent ditties as they were.

To perfect the ballads was now her whimsical desire. She practised them
privately at odd moments, especially 'The break o' the day':

> Arise, arise, arise!
> And pick your love a posy,
> All o' the sweetest flowers
> That in the garden grow.
> The turtle doves and sma' birds
> In every bough a-building,
> So early in the May-time
> At the break o' the day!

It would have melted the heart of a stone to hear her singing these ditties,
whenever she worked apart from the rest of the girls in this cold dry time; the
tears running down her cheeks all the while at the thought that perhaps he would
not, after all, come to hear her, and the simple silly words of the songs resounding
in painful mockery of the aching heart of the singer.

Tess was so wrapt up in this fanciful dream that she seemed not to know how
the season was advancing; that the days had lengthened, that Lady-Day was at
hand, and would soon be followed by Old Lady-Day, the end of her term here.

But before the quarter-day had quite come something happened which made
Tess think of far different matters. She was at her lodging as usual one evening,
sitting in the downstairs room with the rest of the family, when somebody
knocked at the door and inquired for Tess. Through the doorway she saw against
the declining light a figure with the height of a woman and the breadth of a child,
a tall, thin, girlish creature whom she did not recognize in the twilight till the girl
said 'Tess!'

'What – is it 'Liza-Lu?' asked Tess, in startled accents. Her sister, whom a little
over a year ago she had left at home as a child, had sprung up by a sudden shoot
to a form of this presentation, of which as yet Lu seemed herself scarce able to
understand the meaning. Her thin legs, visible below her once long frock, now
short by her growing, and her uncomfortable hands and arms, revealed her youth
and inexperience.

'Yes, I have been traipsing about all day, Tess,' said Lu, with unemotional
gravity, 'a-trying to find 'ee; and I'm very tired.'

'What is the matter at home?'

'Mother is took very bad, and the doctor says she's dying, and as father is not
very well neither, and says 'tis wrong for a man of such a high family as his to
slave and drave at common labouring work, we don't know what to do.'

Tess stood in reverie a long time before she thought of asking 'Liza-Lu to come
in and sit down. When she had done so, and 'Liza-Lu was having some tea, she
came to a decision. It was imperative that she should go home. Her agreement did
not end till Old Lady-Day, the sixth of April, but as the interval thereto was not a
long one she resolved to run the risk of starting at once.

To go that night would be a gain of twelve hours; but her sister was too tired to
undertake such a distance till the morrow. Tess ran down to where Marian and
Izz lived, informed them of what had happened, and begged them to make the
best of her case to the farmer. Returning, she got Lu a supper, and after that,

having tucked the younger into her own bed, packed up as many of her belongings as would go into a withy basket, and started, directing Lu to follow her next morning.

CHAPTER FIFTY

SHE plunged into the chilly equinoctial darkness as the clock struck ten, for her fifteen miles' walk under the steely stars. In lonely districts night is a protection rather than a danger to a noiseless pedestrian, and knowing this Tess pursued the nearest course along by-lanes that she would almost have feared in the daytime; but marauders were wanting now, and spectral fears were driven out of her mind by thoughts of her mother. Thus she proceeded mile after mile, ascending and descending till she came to Bulbarrow, and about midnight looked from that height into the abyss of chaotic shade which was all that revealed itself of the vale on whose further side she was born. Having already traversed about five miles on the upland she had now some ten or eleven in the lowland before her journey would be finished. The winding road downwards became just visible to her under the wan starlight as she followed it, and soon she paced a soil so contrasting with that above it that the difference was perceptible to the tread and to the smell. It was the heavy clay land of Blackmoor Vale, and a part of the Vale to which turnpike-roads had never penetrated. Superstitions linger longest on these heavy soils. Having once been forest, at this shadowy time it seemed to assert something of its old character, the far and the near being blended, and every tree and tall hedge making the most of its presence. The harts that had been hunted here, the witches that had been pricked and ducked, the green-spangled fairies that 'whickered' at you as you passed; — the place teemed with beliefs in them still, and they formed an impish multitude now.

At Nuttlebury she passed the village inn, whose sign creaked in response to the greeting of her footsteps, which not a human soul heard but herself. Under the thatched roofs her mind's eye beheld relaxed tendons and flaccid muscles, spread out in the darkness beneath coverlets made of little purple patchwork squares, and undergoing a bracing process at the hands of sleep for renewed labour on the morrow, as soon as a hint of pink nebulosity appeared on Hambledon Hill.

At three she turned the last corner of the maze of lanes she had threaded, and entered Marlott, passing the field in which, as a club-girl, she had first seen Angel Clare, when he had not danced with her; the sense of disappointment remained with her yet. In the direction of her mother's house she saw a light. It came from the bedroom window, and a branch waved in front of it and made it wink at her. As soon as she could discern the outline of the house — newly thatched with her money — it had all its old effect upon Tess's imagination. Part of her body and life it ever seemed to be; the slope of its dormers, the finish of its gables, the broken courses of brick which topped the chimney, all had something in common with her personal character. A stupefaction had come into these features, to her regard; it meant the illness of her mother.

She opened the door so softly as to disturb nobody; the lower room was vacant, but the neighbour who was sitting up with her mother came to the top of the stairs, and whispered that Mrs Durbeyfield was no better, though she was sleeping just then. Tess prepared herself a breakfast, and then took her place as nurse in her mother's chamber.

In the morning, when she contemplated the children, they had all a curiously elongated look; although she had been away little more than a year their growth was astounding; and the necessity of applying herself heart and soul to their needs took her out of her own cares.

Her father's ill-health was of the same indefinite kind, and he sat in his chair as usual. But the day after her arrival he was unusually bright. He had a rational scheme for living, and Tess asked him what it was.

'I'm thinking of sending round to all the old antiqueerians in this part of England,' he said, 'asking them to subscribe to a fund to maintain me. I'm sure they'd see it as a romantical, artistical, and proper thing to do. They spend lots o' money in keeping up old ruins, and finding the bones o' things, and such like; and living remains must be more interesting to 'em still, if they only knowed of me. Would that somebody would go round and tell 'em what there is living among 'em, and they thinking nothing of him! If Pa'son Tringham, who discovered me, had lived, he'd ha' done it, I'm sure.'

Tess postponed her arguments on this high project till she had grappled with pressing matters in hand, which seemed little improved by her remittances. When indoor necessities had been eased she turned her attention to external things. It was now the season for planting and sowing; many gardens and allotments of the villagers had already received their spring tillage; but the garden and the allotment of the Durbeyfields were behindhand. She found, to her dismay, that this was owing to their having eaten all the seed potatoes, – that last lapse of the improvident. At the earliest moment she obtained what others she could procure, and in a few days her father was well enough to see to the garden, under Tess's persuasive efforts: while she herself undertook the allotment-plot which they rented in a field a couple of hundred yards out of the village.

She liked doing it after the confinement of the sick chamber, where she was not now required by reason of her mother's improvement. Violent motion relieved thought. The plot of ground was in a high, dry, open enclosure, where there were forty or fifty such pieces, and where labour was at its briskest when the hired labour of the day had ended. Digging began usually at six o'clock, and extended indefinitely into the dusk or moonlight. Just now heaps of dead weeds and refuse were burning on many of the plots, the dry weather favouring their combustion.

One fine day Tess and 'Liza-Lu worked on here with their neighbours till the last rays of the sun smote flat upon the white pegs that divided the plots. As soon as twilight succeeded to sunset the flare of the couch-grass and cabbage-stalk fires began to light up the allotments fitfully, their outlines appearing and disappearing under the dense smoke as wafted by the wind. When a fire glowed, banks of smoke, blown level along the ground, would themselves become illuminated to an opaque lustre, screening the workpeople from one another; and the meaning of the 'pillar of a cloud', which was a wall by day and a light by night, could be understood.

As evening thickened some of the gardening men and women gave over for the night, but the greater number remained to get their planting done, Tess being among them, though she sent her sister home. It was on one of the couch-burning plots that she laboured with her fork, its four shining prongs resounding against the stones and dry clods in little clicks. Sometimes she was completely involved in the smoke of her fire; then it would leave her figure free, irradiated by the brassy glare from the heap. She was oddly dressed to-night, and presented a somewhat staring aspect, her attire being a gown bleached by many washings, with a short black jacket over it, the effect of the whole being that of a wedding and funeral guest in one. The women further back wore white aprons, which, with their pale faces, were all that could be seen of them in the gloom, except when at moments they caught a flash from the flames.

Westward, the wiry boughs of the bare thorn hedge which formed the boundary of the field rose against the pale opalescence of the lower sky. Above, Jupiter hung like a full-blown jonquil, so bright as almost to throw a shade. A few small nondescript stars were appearing elsewhere. In the distance a dog barked, and wheels occasionally rattled along the dry road.

Still the prongs continued to click assiduously, for it was not late; and though the air was fresh and keen there was a whisper of spring in it that cheered the workers on. Something in the place, the hour, the crackling fires, the fantastic mysteries of light and shade, made others as well as Tess enjoy being there. Nightfall, which in the frost of winter comes as a fiend and in the warmth of summer as a lover, came as a tranquillizer on this March day.

Nobody looked at his or her companions. The eyes of all were on the soil as its turned surface was revealed by the fires. Hence as Tess stirred the clods, and sang her foolish little songs with scarce now a hope that Clare would ever hear them, she did not for a long time notice the person who worked nearest to her — a man in a long smockfrock who, she found, was forking the same plot as herself, and whom she supposed her father had sent there to advance the work. She became more conscious of him when the direction of his digging brought him closer. Sometimes the smoke divided them; then it swerved, and the two were visible to each other but divided from all the rest.

Tess did not speak to her fellow-worker, nor did he speak to her. Nor did she think of him further than to recollect that he had not been there when it was broad daylight, and that she did not know him as any one of the Marlott labourers, which was no wonder, her absences having been so long and frequent of late years. By-and-by he dug so close to her that the fire-beams were reflected as distinctly from the steel prongs of his fork as from her own. On going up to the fire to throw a pitch of dead weeds upon it, she found that he did the same on the other side. The fire flared up, and she beheld the face of d'Urberville.

The unexpectedness of his presence, the grotesqueness of his appearance in a gathered smockfrock, such as was now worn only by the most old-fashioned of the labourers, had a ghastly comicality that chilled her as to its bearing. D'Urberville emitted a low long laugh.

'If I were inclined to joke I should say, How much this seems like Paradise!' he remarked whimsically, looking at her with an inclined head.

'What do you say?' she weakly asked.

'A jester might say this is just like Paradise. You are Eve, and I am the old Other One come to tempt you in the disguise of an inferior animal. I used to be quite up in that scene of Milton's when I was theological. Some of it goes –

> "Empress, the way is ready, and not long,
> Beyond a row of myrtles. . . .
> . . . If thou accept
> My conduct, I can bring thee thither soon."
> "Lead then," said Eve.

And so on. My dear, dear Tess, I am only putting this to you as a thing that you might have supposed or said quite untruly, because you think so badly of me.'

'I never said you were Satan, or thought it. I don't think of you in that way at all. My thoughts of you are quite cold, except when you affront me. What, did you come digging here entirely because of me?'

'Entirely. To see you; nothing more. The smockfrock, which I saw hanging for sale as I came along, was an after-thought, that I mightn't be noticed. I come to protest against your working like this.'

'But I like doing it – it is for my father.'

'Your engagement at the other place is ended?'

'Yes.'

'Where are you going to next? To join your dear husband?'

She could not bear the humiliating reminder.

'O – I don't know!' she said bitterly. 'I have no husband!'

'It is quite true – in the sense you mean. But you have a friend, and I have determined that you shall be comfortable in spite of yourself. When you get down to your house you will see what I have sent there for you.'

'O, Alec, I wish you wouldn't give me anything at all! I cannot take it from you! I don't like – it is not right!'

'It *is* right!' he cried lightly. 'I am not going to see a woman whom I feel so tenderly for as I do for you, in trouble without trying to help her.'

'But I am very well off! I am only in trouble about – about – not about living at all!'

She turned, and desperately resumed her digging, tears dripping upon the fork-handle and upon the clods.

'About the children – your brothers and sisters,' he resumed. 'I've been thinking of them.'

Tess's heart quivered – he was touching her in a weak place. He had divined her chief anxiety. Since returning home her soul had gone out to those children with an affection that was passionate.

'If your mother does not recover, somebody ought to do something for them; since your father will not be able to do much, I suppose?'

'He can with my assistance. He must!'

'And with mine.'

'No, sir!'

'How damned foolish this is!' burst out d'Urberville. 'Why, he thinks we are the same family; and will be quite satisfied!'

'He don't. I've undeceived him.'

'The more fool you!'

D'Urberville in anger retreated from her to the hedge, where he pulled off the long smockfrock which had disguised him; and rolling it up and pushing it into the couch-fire, went away.

Tess could not get on with her digging after this; she felt restless; she wondered if he had gone back to her father's house; and taking the fork in her hand proceeded homewards.

Some twenty yards from the house she was met by one of her sisters.

'O, Tessy — what do you think! 'Liza-Lu is a-crying, and there's a lot of folk in the house, and mother is a good deal better, but they think father is dead!'

The child realized the grandeur of the news; but not as yet its sadness; and stood looking at Tess with round-eyed importance, till, beholding the effect produced upon her, she said —

'What, Tess, shan't we talk to father never no more?'

'But father was only a little bit ill!' exclaimed Tess distractedly.

'Liza-Lu came up.

'He dropped down just now, and the doctor who was there for mother said there was no chance for him, because his heart was growed in.'

Yes; the Durbeyfield couple had changed places; the dying one was out of danger, and the indisposed one was dead. The news meant even more than it sounded. Her father's life had a value apart from his personal achievements, or perhaps it would not have had much. It was the last of the three lives for whose duration the house and premises were held under a lease; and it had long been coveted by the tenant-farmer for his regular labourers, who were stinted in cottage accommodation. Moreover, 'liviers' were disapproved of in villages almost as much as little freeholders, because of their independence of manner, and when a lease determined it was never renewed.

Thus the Durbeyfields, once d'Urbervilles, saw descending upon them the destiny which, no doubt, when they were among the Olympians of the county, they had caused to descend many a time, and severely enough, upon the heads of such landless ones as they themselves were now. So do flux and reflux — the rhythm of change — alternate and persist in everything under the sky.

CHAPTER FIFTY-ONE

AT length it was the eve of Old Lady-Day, and the agricultural world was in a fever of mobility such as only occurs at that particular date of the year. It is a day of fulfilment; agreements for outdoor service during the ensuing year, entered into at Candlemas, are to be now carried out. The labourers — or 'work-folk', as they used to call themselves immemorially till the other word was introduced from without — who wish to remain no longer in old places are removing to the new farms.

These annual migrations from farm to farm were on the increase here. When Tess's mother was a child the majority of the field-folk about Marlott had remained all their lives on one farm, which had been the home also of their fathers and grandfathers; but latterly the desire for yearly removal had risen to a high pitch. With the younger families it was a pleasant excitement which might possibly be an advantage. The Egypt of one family was the Land of Promise to the family who saw it from a distance, till by residence there it became in turn their Egypt also; and so they changed and changed.

However, all the mutations so increasingly discernible in village life did not originate entirely in the agricultural unrest. A depopulation was also going on. The village had formerly contained, side by side with the agricultural labourers, an interesting and better-informed class, ranking distinctly above the former – the class to which Tess's father and mother had belonged – and including the carpenter, the smith, the shoemaker, the huckster, together with nondescript workers other than farm-labourers; a set of people who owed a certain stability of aim and conduct to the fact of their being life-holders like Tess's father, or copyholders, or, occasionally, small freeholders. But as the long holdings fell in they were seldom again let to similar tenants, and were mostly pulled down, if not absolutely required by the farmer for his hands. Cottagers who were not directly employed on the land were looked upon with disfavour, and the banishment of some starved the trade of others, who were thus obliged to follow. These families, who had formed the backbone of the village life in the past, who were the depositaries of the village traditions, had to seek refuge in the large centres; the process, humorously designated by statisticians as 'the tendency of the rural population towards the large towns', being really the tendency of water to flow uphill when forced by machinery.

The cottage accommodation at Marlott having been in this manner considerably curtailed by demolitions, every house which remained standing was required by the agriculturist for his work-people. Ever since the occurrence of the event which had cast such a shadow over Tess's life, the Durbeyfield family (whose descent was not credited) had been tacitly looked on as one which would have to go when their lease ended, if only in the interests of morality. It was, indeed, quite true that the household had not been shining examples either of temperance, soberness, or chastity. The father, and even the mother, had got drunk at times, the younger children seldom had gone to church, and the eldest daughter had made queer unions. By some means the village had to be kept pure. So on this, the first Lady-Day on which the Durbeyfields were expellable, the house, being roomy, was required for a carter with a large family; and Widow Joan, her daughters Tess and 'Liza-Lu, the boy Abraham and the younger children, had to go elsewhere.

On the evening preceding their removal it was getting dark betimes by reason of a drizzling rain which blurred the sky. As it was the last night they would spend in the village which had been their home and birthplace, Mrs Durbeyfield, 'Liza-Lu, and Abraham had gone out to bid some friends good-bye, and Tess was keeping house till they should return.

She was kneeling in the window-bench, her face close to the casement, where an outer pane of rainwater was sliding down the inner pane of glass. Her eyes rested on the web of a spider, probably starved long ago, which had been mistakenly placed in a corner where no flies ever came, and shivered in the slight draught through the casement. Tess was reflecting on the position of the household, in which she perceived her own evil influence. Had she not come home her mother and the children might probably have been allowed to stay on as weekly tenants. But she had been observed almost immediately on her return by some people of scrupulous character and great influence: they had seen her idling in the churchyard, restoring as well as she could with a little trowel a baby's obliterated grave. By this means they had found that she was living here again; her mother was scolded for 'harbouring' her; sharp retorts had ensued from Joan, who had independently offered to leave at once; she had been taken at her word; and here was the result.

'I ought never to have come home,' said Tess to herself, bitterly.

She was so intent upon these thoughts that she hardly at first took note of a man in a white mackintosh whom she saw riding down the street. Possibly it was owing to her face being near to the pane that he saw her so quickly, and directed his horse so close to the cottage-front that his hoofs were almost upon the narrow border for plants growing under the wall. It was not till he touched the window with his riding-crop that she observed him. The rain had nearly ceased, and she opened the casement in obedience to his gesture.

'Didn't you see me?' asked d'Urberville.

'I was not attending,' she said. 'I heard you, I believe, though I fancied it was a carriage and horses. I was in a sort of dream.'

'Ah! you heard the d'Urberville Coach, perhaps. You know the legend, I suppose?'

'No. My – somebody was going to tell it me once, but didn't.'

'If you are a genuine d'Urberville I ought not to tell you either, I suppose. As for me, I'm a sham one, so it doesn't matter. It is rather dismal. It is that this sound of a non-existent coach can only be heard by one of d'Urberville blood, and it is held to be of ill-omen to the one who hears it. It has to do with a murder, committed by one of the family, centuries ago.'

'Now you have begun it, finish it.'

'Very well. One of the family is said to have abducted some beautiful woman, who tried to escape from the coach in which he was carrying her off, and in the struggle he killed her – or she killed him – I forget which. Such is one version of the tale. . . . I see that your tubs and buckets are packed. Going away, aren't you?'

'Yes, to-morrow – Old Lady-Day.'

'I heard you were, but could hardly believe it; it seems so sudden. Why is it?'

'Father's was the last life on the property, and when that dropped we had no further right to stay. Though we might, perhaps, have stayed as weekly tenants – if it had not been for me.'

'What about you?'

'I am not a – proper woman.'

D'Urberville's face flushed.

'What a blasted shame! Miserable snobs! May their dirty souls be burnt to cinders!' he exclaimed in tones of ironic resentment. 'That's why you are going, is it? Turned out?'

'We are not turned out exactly; but as they said we should have to go soon, it was best to go now everybody was moving, because there are better chances.'

'Where are you going to?'

'Kingsbere. We have taken rooms there. Mother is so foolish about father's people that she will go there.'

'But your mother's family are not fit for lodgings, and in a little hole of a town like that. Now why not come to my garden-house at Trantridge? There are hardly any poultry now, since my mother's death; but there's the house, as you know it, and the garden. It can be whitewashed in a day, and your mother can live there quite comfortably; and I will put the children to a good school. Really I ought to do something for you!'

'But we have already taken the rooms at Kingsbere!' she declared. 'And we can wait there—'

'Wait—what for? For that nice husband, no doubt. Now look here, Tess, I know what men are, and, bearing in mind the *grounds* of your separation, I am quite positive he will never make it up with you. Now, though I have been your enemy, I am your friend, even if you won't believe it. Come to this cottage of mine. We'll get up a regular colony of fowls, and your mother can attend to them excellently; and the children can go to school.'

Tess breathed more and more quickly, and at length she said—

'How do I know that you would do all this? Your views may change—and then—we should be—my mother would be—homeless again.'

'O no—no. I would guarantee you against such as that in writing, if necessary. Think it over.'

Tess shook her head. But d'Urberville persisted; she had seldom seen him so determined; he would not take a negative.

'Please just tell your mother,' he said, in emphatic tones. 'It is her business to judge—not yours. I shall get the house swept out and whitened to-morrow morning, and fires lit; and it will be dry by the evening, so that you can come straight there. Now mind, I shall expect you.'

Tess again shook her head; her throat swelling with complicated emotion. She could not look up at d'Urberville.

'I owe you something for the past, you know,' he resumed. 'And you cured me, too, of that craze; so I am glad—'

'I would rather you had kept the craze, so that you had kept the practice which went with it!'

'I am glad of this opportunity of repaying you a little. To-morrow I shall expect to hear your mother's goods unloading. . . . Give me your hand on it now—dear, beautiful Tess!'

With the last sentence he had dropped his voice to a murmur, and put his hand in at the half-open casement. With stormy eyes she pulled the stay-bar quickly, and, in doing so, caught his arm between the casement and the stone mullion.

'Damnation—you are very cruel!' he said, snatching out his arm. 'No, no!—I know you didn't do it on purpose. Well, I shall expect you, or your mother and the children at least.'

'I shall not come—I have plenty of money!' she cried.

'Where?'

'At my father-in-law's, if I ask for it.'

'*If* you ask for it. But you won't, Tess; I know you; you'll never ask for it—you'll starve first!'

With these words he rode off. Just at the corner of the street he met the man with the paint-pot, who asked him if he had deserted the brethren.

'You go to the devil!' said d'Urberville.

Tess remained where she was a long while, till a sudden rebellious sense of injustice caused the region of her eyes to swell with the rush of hot tears thither.

Her husband, Angel Clare himself, had, like others, dealt out hard measure to her, surely he had! She had never before admitted such a thought; but he had surely! Never in her life — she could swear it from the bottom of her soul — had she ever intended to do wrong; yet these hard judgments had come. Whatever her sins, they were not sins of intention, but of inadvertence, and why should she have been punished so persistently?

She passionately seized the first piece of paper that came to hand, and scribbled the following lines:

O why have you treated me so monstrously, Angel! I do not deserve it. I have thought it all over carefully, and I can never, never forgive you! You know that I did not intend to wrong you — why have you so wronged me? You are cruel, cruel indeed! I will try to forget you. It is all injustice I have received at your hands!

                                                                                    T.

She watched till the postman passed by, ran out to him with her epistle, and then again took her listless place inside the window panes.

It was just as well to write like that as to write tenderly. How could he give way to entreaty? The facts had not changed: there was no new event to alter his opinion.

It grew darker, the fire-light shining over the room. The two biggest of the younger children had gone out with their mother; the four smallest, their ages ranging from three-and-a-half years to eleven, all in black frocks, were gathered round the hearth babbling their own little subjects. Tess at length joined them, without lighting a candle.

'This is the last night that we shall sleep here, dears, in the house where we were born,' she said quickly. 'We ought to think of it, oughtn't we?'

They all became silent; with the impressibility of their age they were ready to burst into tears at the picture of finality she had conjured up, though all the day hitherto they had been rejoicing in the idea of a new place. Tess changed the subject.

'Sing to me, dears,' she said.

'What shall we sing?'

'Anything you know; I don't mind.'

There was a momentary pause; it was broken, first, by one little tentative note; then a second voice strengthened it, and a third and a fourth chimed in in unison, with words they had learnt at the Sunday-school —

> Here we suffer grief and pain,
> Here we meet to part again;
> In Heaven we part no more.

The four sang on with the phlegmatic passivity of persons who had long ago settled the question, and there being no mistake about it, felt that further thought was not required. With features strained hard to enunciate the syllables they continued to regard the centre of the flickering fire, the notes of the youngest straying over into the pauses of the rest.

Tess turned from them, and went to the window again. Darkness had now fallen without, but she put her face to the pane as though to peer into the gloom. It was really to hide her tears. If she could only believe what the children were singing; if she were only sure how different all would now be; how confidently she would leave them to Providence and their future kingdom! But, in default of that, it behoved her to do something; to be their Providence; for to Tess, as to not a few millions of others, there was ghastly satire in the poet's lines –

Not in utter nakedness
But trailing clouds of glory do we come.

To her and her like, birth itself was an ordeal of degrading personal compulsion, whose gratuitousness nothing in the result seemed to justify, and at best could only palliate.

In the shades of the wet road she soon discerned her mother with tall 'Liza-Lu and Abraham. Mrs Durbeyfield's pattens clicked up to the door, and Tess opened it.

'I see the tracks of a horse outside the window,' said Joan. 'Hev somebody called?'

'No,' said Tess.

The children by the fire looked gravely at her, and one murmured –

'Why, Tess, the gentleman a-horseback!'

'He didn't call,' said Tess. 'He spoke to me in passing.'

'Who was the gentleman?' asked her mother. 'Your husband?'

'No. He'll never, never come,' answered Tess in stony hopelessness.

'Then who was it?'

'Oh, you needn't ask. You've seen him before, and so have I.'

'Ah! What did he say?' said Joan curiously.

'I will tell you when we are settled in our lodgings at Kingsbere to-morrow – every word.'

It was not her husband, she had said. Yet a consciousness that in a physical sense this man alone was her husband seemed to weigh on her more and more.

CHAPTER FIFTY-TWO

DURING the small hours of the next morning, while it was still dark, dwellers near the highways were conscious of a disturbance of their night's rest by rumbling noises, intermittently continuing till daylight – noises as certain to recur in this particular first week of the month as the voice of the cuckoo in the third week of the same. They were the preliminaries of the general removal, the passing of the empty waggons and teams to fetch the goods of the migrating families; for it was always by the vehicle of the farmer who required his services that the hired man was conveyed to his destination. That this might be accomplished within the day was the explanation of the reverberation occurring so soon after midnight, the aim of the carters being to reach the door of the outgoing households by six o'clock, when the loading of their movables at once began.

But to Tess and her mother's household no such anxious farmer sent him team. They were only women; they were not regular labourers; they were not particularly required anywhere; hence they had to hire a waggon at their own expense, and got nothing sent gratuitously.

It was a relief to Tess, when she looked out of the window that morning, to find that though the weather was windy and louring, it did not rain, and that the waggon had come. A wet Lady-Day was a spectre which removing families never forgot; damp furniture, damp bedding, damp clothing accompanied it, and left a train of ills.

Her mother, 'Liza-Lu, and Abraham were also awake, but the younger children were let sleep on. The four breakfasted by the thin light, and the 'house-ridding' was taken in hand.

It proceeded with some cheerfulness, a friendly neighbour or two assisting. When the large articles of furniture had been packed in position a circular nest was made of the beds and bedding, in which Joan Durbeyfield and the young children were to sit through the journey. After loading there was a long delay before the horses were brought, these having been unharnessed during the ridding; but at length, about two o'clock, the whole was under way, the cooking-pot swinging from the axle of the waggon, Mrs Durbeyfield and family at the top, the matron having in her lap, to prevent injury to its works, the head of the clock, which, at any exceptional lurch of the waggon, struck one, or one-and-a-half, in hurt tones. Tess and the next eldest girl walked alongside till they were out of the village.

They had called on a few neighbours that morning and the previous evening, and some came to see them off, all wishing them well, though, in their secret hearts, hardly expecting welfare possible to such a family, harmless as the Durbeyfields were to all except themselves. Soon the equipage began to ascend to higher ground, and the wind grew keener with the change of level and soil.

The day being the sixth of April, the Durbeyfield waggon met many other waggons with families on the summit of the load, which was built on a wellnigh unvarying principle, as peculiar, probably, to the rural labourer as the hexagon to the bee. The groundwork of the arrangement was the family dresser, which, with its shining handles, and finger-marks, and domestic evidences thick upon it, stood importantly in front, over the tails of the shaft-horses, in its erect and natural position, like some Ark of the Covenant that they were bound to carry reverently.

Some of the households were lively, some mournful; some were stopping at the doors of wayside inns; where, in due time, the Durbeyfield menagerie also drew up to bait horses and refresh the travellers.

During the halt Tess's eyes fell upon a three-pint blue mug, which was ascending and descending through the air to and from the feminine section of a household, sitting on the summit of a load that had also drawn up at a little distance from the same inn. She followed one of the mug's journeys upward, and perceived it to be clasped by hands whose owner she well knew. Tess went towards the waggon.

'Marian and Izz!' she cried to the girls, for it was they, sitting with the moving family at whose house they had lodged. 'Are you house-ridding to-day, like everybody else?'

They were, they said. It had been too rough a life for them at Flintcomb-Ash, and they had come away, almost without notice, leaving Groby to prosecute them if he chose. They told Tess their destination, and Tess told them hers.

Marian leant over the load, and lowered her voice. 'Do you know that the gentleman who follows 'ee – you'll guess who I mean – came to ask for 'ee at Flintcomb after you had gone? We didn't tell'n where you was, knowing you wouldn't wish to see him.'

'Ah – but I did see him!' Tess murmured. 'He found me.'

'And do he know where you be going?'

'I think so.'

'Husband come back?'

'No.'

She bade her acquaintance good-bye – for the respective carters had now come out from the inn – and the two waggons resumed their journey in opposite directions; the vehicle whereon sat Marian, Izz, and the ploughman's family with whom they had thrown in their lot, being brightly painted, and drawn by three powerful horses with shining brass ornaments on their harness; while the waggon on which Mrs Durbeyfield and her family rode was a creaking erection that would scarcely bear the weight of the superincumbent load; one which had known no paint since it was made, and drawn by two horses only. The contrast well marked the difference between being fetched by a thriving farmer and conveying oneself whither no hirer waited one's coming.

The distance was great – too great for a day's journey – and it was with the utmost difficulty that the horses performed it. Though they had started so early it was quite late in the afternoon when they turned the flank of an eminence which formed part of the upland called Greenhill. While the horses stood to stale and breathe themselves Tess looked around. Under the hill, and just ahead of them, was the half-dead townlet of their pilgrimage, Kingsbere, where lay those ancestors of whom her father had spoken and sung to painfulness: Kingsbere, the spot of all spots in the world which could be considered the d'Urbervilles' home, since they had resided there for full five hundred years.

A man could be seen advancing from the outskirts towards them, and when he beheld the nature of their waggon-load he quickened his steps.

'You be the woman they call Mrs Durbeyfield, I reckon?' he said to Tess's mother, who had descended to walk the remainder of the way.

She nodded. 'Though widow of the late Sir John d'Urberville, poor nobleman, if I cared for my rights; and returning to the domain of his forefathers.'

'Oh? Well, I know nothing about that; but if you be Mrs Durbeyfield, I am sent to tell 'ee that the rooms you wanted be let. We didn't know you was coming till we got your letter this morning – when 'twas too late. But no doubt you can get other lodgings somewhere.'

The man had noticed the face of Tess, which had become ash-pale at his intelligence. Her mother looked hopelessly at fault. 'What shall we do now, Tess?' she said bitterly. 'Here's a welcome to your ancestors' lands! However, let's try further.'

They moved on into the town, and tried with all their might, Tess remaining with the waggon to take care of the children whilst her mother and 'Liza-Lu made inquiries. At the last return of Joan to the vehicle, an hour later, when her search for accommodation had still been fruitless, the driver of the waggon said the goods must be unloaded, as the horses were half-dead, and he was bound to return part of the way at least that night.

'Very well – unload it here,' said Joan recklessly. 'I'll get shelter somewhere.'

The waggon had drawn up under the churchyard wall, in a spot screened from view, and the driver, nothing loth, soon hauled down the poor heap of household goods. This done she paid him, reducing herself to almost her last shilling thereby, and he moved off and left them, only too glad to get out of further dealings with such a family. It was a dry night, and he guessed that they would come to no harm.

Tess gazed desperately at the pile of furniture. The cold sunlight of this spring evening peered invidiously upon the crocks and kettles, upon the bunches of dried herbs shivering in the breeze, upon the brass handles of the dresser, upon the wicker-cradle they had all been rocked in, and upon the well-rubbed clock-case, all of which gave out the reproachful gleam of indoor articles abandoned to the vicissitudes of a roofless exposure for which they were never made. Round about were deparked hills and slopes – now cut up into little paddocks – and the green foundations that showed where the d'Urberville mansion once had stood; also an outlying stretch of Egdon Heath that had always belonged to the estate. Hard by, the aisle of the church called the d'Urberville Aisle looked on imperturbably.

'Isn't your family vault your own freehold?' said Tess's mother, as she returned from a reconnoitre of the church and graveyard. 'Why, of course 'tis, and that's where we will camp, girls, till the place of your ancestors finds us a roof! Now, Tess and 'Liza and Abraham, you help me. We'll make a nest for these children, and then we'll have another look round.'

Tess listlessly lent a hand, and in a quarter of an hour the old four-post bedstead wad dissociated from the heap of goods, and erected under the south wall of the church, the part of the building known as the d'Urberville Aisle, beneath which the huge vaults lay. Over the tester of the bedstead was a beautifully traceried window, of many lights, its date being the fifteenth century. It was called the d'Urberville Window, and in the upper part could be discerned heraldic emblems like those on Durbeyfield's old seal and spoon.

Joan drew the curtains round the bed so as to make an excelleot tent of it, and put the smaller children inside. 'If it comes to the worst we can sleep there too, for one night,' she said. 'But let us try further on, and get something for the dears to eat! O, Tess, what's the use of your playing at marrying gentlemen, if it leaves us like this!'

Accompanied by 'Liza-Lu and the boy she again ascended the little lane which secluded the church from the townlet. As soon as they got into the street they beheld a man on horseback gazing up and down. 'Ah – I am looking for you!' he said, riding up to them. 'This is indeed a family gathering on the historic spot!'

It was Alec d'Urberville. 'Where is Tess?' he asked.

Personally Joan had no liking for Alec. She cursorily signified the direction of the church, and went on, d'Urberville saying that he would see them again, in case they should be still unsuccessful in their search for shelter, of which he had just heard. When they had gone d'Urberville rode to the inn, and shortly after came out on foot.

In the interim Tess, left with the children inside the bedstead, remained talking with them awhile, till, seeing that no more could be done to make them comfortable just then, she walked about the churchyard, now beginning to be embrowned by the shades of nightfall. The door of the church was unfastened, and she entered it for the first time in her life.

Within the window under which the bedstead stood were the tombs of the family, covering in their dates several centuries. They were canopied, altar-shaped, and plain; their carvings being defaced and broken; their brasses torn from the matrices, the rivet-holes remaining like martin-holes in a sand-cliff. Of all the reminders that she had ever received that her people were socially extinct there was none so forcible as this spoliation.

She drew near to a dark stone on which was inscribed:

𝕺stium sepulchri antiquae familiae d'𝖀rberv𝖎lle.

Tess did not read Church-Latin like a Cardinal, but she knew that this was the door of her ancestral sepulchre, and that the tall knights of whom her father had chanted in his cups lay inside.

She musingly turned to withdraw, passing near an altar-tomb, the oldest of them all, on which was a recumbent figure. In the dusk she had not noticed it before, and would hardly have noticed it now but for an odd fancy that the effigy moved. As soon as she drew close to it she discovered all in a moment that the figure was a living person; and the shock to her sense of not having been alone was so violent that she was quite overcome, and sank down nigh to fainting, not however till she had recognized Alec d'Urberville in the form.

He leapt off the slab and supported her.

'I saw you come in,' he said smiling, 'and got up there not to interrupt your meditations. A family gathering, is it not, with these old fellows under us here? Listen.'

He stamped with his heel heavily on the floor; whereupon there arose a hollow echo from below.

'That shook them a bit, I'll warrant!' he continued. 'And you thought I was the mere stone reproduction of one of them. But no. The old order changeth. The little finger of the sham d'Urberville can do more for you than the whole dynasty of the real underneath. . . . Now command me. What shall I do?'

'Go away!' she murmured.

'I will – I'll look for your mother,' said he blandly. But in passing her he whispered: 'Mind this; you'll be civil yet!'

When he was gone she bent down upon the entrance to the vaults, and said –

'Why am I on the wrong side of this door!'

In the meantime Marian and Izz Huett had journeyed onward with the chattels of the ploughman in the direction of their land of Canaan – the Egypt of some other family who had left it only that morning. But the girls did not for a long time think of where they were going. Their talk was of Angel Clare and Tess, and Tess's persistent lover, whose connection with her previous history they had partly heard and partly guessed ere this.

''Tisn't as though she had never known him afore,' said Marian. 'His having won her once makes all the difference in the world. 'Twould be a thousand pities if he were to tole her away again. Mr Clare can never be anything to us, Izz; and why should we grudge him to her, and not try to mend this quarrel? If he could on'y know what straits she's put to, and what's hovering round, he might come to take care of his own.'

'Could we let him know?'

They thought of this all the way to their destination; but the bustle of re-establishment in their new place took up all their attention then. But when they were settled, a month later, they heard of Clare's approaching return, though they had learnt nothing more of Tess. Upon that, agitated anew by their attachment to him, yet honourably disposed to her, Marian uncorked the penny ink bottle they shared, and a few lines were concocted between the two girls.

H onour'd S ir – Look to your Wife if you do love her as much as she do love you. For she is sore put to by an Enemy in the shape of a Friend. Sir, there is one near her who ought to be away. A woman should not be try'd beyond her Strength, and continual dropping will wear away a Stone – ay, more – a Diamond.

F rom T wo W ell-W ishers

This they addressed to Angel Clare at the only place they had ever heard him to be connected with, Emminster Vicarage; after which they continued in a mood of emotional exaltation at their own generosity, which made them sing in hysterical snatches and weep at the same time.

Fulfilment

CHAPTER FIFTY-THREE

I T was evening at Emminster Vicarage. The two customary candles were burning under their green shades in the Vicar's study, but he had not been sitting there. Occasionally he came in, stirred the small fire which sufficed for the increasing mildness of the spring, and went out again; sometimes pausing at the front door, going on to the drawing-room, then returning again to the front door.

It faced westward, and though gloom prevailed inside, there was still light enough without to see with distinctness. Mrs Clare, who had been sitting in the drawing-room, followed him hither.

'Plenty of time yet,' said the Vicar. 'He doesn't reach Chalk-Newton till six, even if the train should be punctual, and ten miles of country-road, five of them in Crimmercrock Lane, are not jogged over in a hurry by our old horse.'

'But he has done it in an hour with us, my dear.'

'Years ago.'

Thus they passed the minutes, each well knowing that this was only waste of breath, the one essential being simply to wait.

At length there was a slight noise in the lane, and the old pony-chaise appeared indeed outside the railings. They saw alight therefrom a form which they affected to recognize, but would actually have passed by in the street without identifying had he not got out of their carriage at the particular moment when a particular person was due.

Mrs Clare rushed through the dark passage to the door, and her husband came more slowly after her.

The new arrival, who was just about to enter, saw their anxious faces in the doorway and the gleam of the west in their spectacles because they confronted the last rays of day; but they could only see his shape against the light.

'O, my boy, my boy – home again at last!' cried Mrs Clare, who cared no more at that moment for the stains of heterodoxy which had caused all this separation than for the dust upon his clothes. What woman, indeed, among the most faithful adherents of the truth, believes the promises and threats of the Word in the sense in which she believes in her own children, or would not throw her theology to the wind if weighed against their happiness? As soon as they reached the room where the candles were lighted she looked at his face.

'O, it is not Angel – not my son – the Angel who went away!' she cried in all the irony of sorrow, as she turned herself aside.

His father, too, was shocked to see him, so reduced was that figure from its former contours by worry and the bad season that Clare had experienced, in the climate to which he had so rashly hurried in his first aversion to the mockery of events at home. You could see the skeleton behind the man, and almost the ghost behind the skeleton. He matched Crivelli's dead *Christus*. His sunken eye-pits were of morbid hue, and the light in his eyes had waned. The angular hollows and lines of his aged ancestors had succeeded to their reign in his face twenty years before their time.

'I was ill over there, you know,' he said. 'I am all right now.'

As if, however, to falsify this assertion, his legs seemed to give way, and he suddenly sat down to save himself from falling. It was only a slight attack of faintness, resulting from the tedious day's journey, and the excitement of arrival.

'Has any letter come for me lately?' he asked. 'I received the last you sent on by the merest chance, and after considerable delay through being inland; or I might have come sooner.'

'It was from your wife, we supposed?'

'It was.'

Only one other had recently come. They had not sent it on to him, knowing he would start for home so soon.

He hastily opened the letter produced, and was much disturbed to read in Tess's handwriting the sentiments expressed in her last hurried scrawl to him.

O why have you treated me so monstrously, Angel! I do not deserve it. I have thought it all over carefully, and I can never, never forgive you! You know that I did not intend to wrong you – why have you so wronged me? You are cruel, cruel indeed! I will try to forget you. It is all injustice I have received at your hands.

T.

'It is quite true!' said Angel, throwing down the letter. 'Perhaps she will never be reconciled to me!'

'Don't, Angel, be so anxious about a mere child of the soil!' said his mother.

'Child of the soil! Well, we all are children of the soil. I wish she were so in the sense you mean; but let me now explain to you what I have never explained before, that her father is a descendant in the male line of one of the oldest Norman houses, like a good many others who lead obscure agricultural lives in our villages, and are dubbed "sons of the soil".'

He soon retired to bed; and the next morning, feeling exceedingly unwell, he remained in his room pondering. The circumstances amid which he had left Tess were such that though, while on the south of the Equator and just in receipt of her loving epistle, it had seemed the easiest thing in the world to rush back into her arms the moment he chose to forgive her, now that he had arrived it was not so easy as it had seemed. She was passionate, and her present letter, showing that her estimate of him had changed under his delay – too justly changed, he sadly owned, – made him ask himself if it would be wise to confront her unannounced in the presence of her parents. Supposing that her love had indeed turned to dislike during the last weeks of separation, a sudden meeting might lead to bitter words.

Clare therefore thought it would be best to prepare Tess and her family by sending a line to Marlott announcing his return, and his hope that she was still living with them there, as he had arranged for her to do when he left England. He despatched the inquiry that very day, and before the week was out there came a short reply from Mrs Durbeyfield which did not remove his embarrassment, for it bore no address, though to his surprise it was not written from Marlott.

SIR – J write these few lines to say that my Daughter is away from me at present, and J am not sure when she will return, but J will let you know as Soon as she do. J do not feel at liberty to tell you Where she is temperly biding. J should say that me and my Family have left Marlott for some Time. – Yours,

J. DURBEYFIELD

It was such a relief to Clare to learn that Tess was at least apparently well that her mother's stiff reticence as to her whereabouts did not long distress him. They were all angry with him, evidently. He would wait till Mrs Durbeyfield could inform him of Tess's return, which her letter implied to be soon. He deserved no more. His had been a love 'which alters when it alteration finds'. He had undergone some strange experiences in his absence; he had seen the virtual Faustina in the literal Cornelia, a spiritual Lucretia in a corporeal Phryne; he had thought of the woman taken and set in the midst as one deserving to be stoned, and of the wife of Uriah being made a queen; and he had asked himself why he had not judged Tess constructively rather than biographically, by the will rather than by the deed?

A day or two passed while he waited at his father's house for the promised second note from Joan Durbeyfield, and indirectly to recover a little more strength. The strength showed signs of coming back, but there was no sign of Joan's letter. Then he hunted up the old letter sent on to him in Brazil, which Tess had written from Flintcomb-Ash, and re-read it. The sentences touched him now as much as when he had first perused them.

I must cry to you in my trouble – I have no one else. . . . I think I must die if you do not come soon, or tell me to come to you. . . . Please, please not to be just; only a little kind to me! . . . If you would come, I could die in your arms! I would be well content to do that if so be you had forgiven me! . . . If you will send me one little line and say, '*I am coming soon,*' I will bide on, Angel, O so cheerfully! . . . Think how it do hurt my heart not to see you ever – ever! Ah, if I could only make your dear heart ache one little minute of each day as mine does every day and all day long, it might lead you to show pity to your poor lonely one. . . . I would be content, ay, glad, to live with you as your servant, if I may not as your wife; so that I could only be near you, and get glimpses of you, and think of you as mine. . . . I long for only one thing in heaven, or earth, or under the earth, to meet you, my own dear! Come to me – come to me, and save me from what threatens me.

Clare determined that he would no longer believe in her more recent and severer regard of him; but would go and find her immediately. He asked his father if she had applied for any money during his absence. His father returned a negative, and then for the first time it occurred to Angel that her pride had stood in her way, and that she had suffered privation. From his remarks his parents now gathered the real reason of the separation; and their Christianity was such that, reprobates being their especial care, the tenderness towards Tess which her blood, her simplicity, even her poverty, had not engendered, was instantly excited by her sin.

Whilst he was hastily packing together a few articles for his journey he glanced over a poor plain missive also lately come to hand – the one from Marian and Izz Huett, beginning –

'HONOUR'D SIR – Look to your wife if you do love her as much as she do love you,' and signed, 'FROM TWO WELL-WISHERS'.

CHAPTER FIFTY-FOUR

IN a quarter of an hour Clare was leaving the house, whence his mother watched his thin figure as it disappeared into the street. He had declined to borrow his father's old mare, well knowing of its necessity to the household. He went to the inn, where he hired a trap, and could hardly wait during the harnessing. In a very few minutes after he was driving up the hill out of the town which, three or four months earlier in the year, Tess had descended with such hopes and ascended with such shattered purposes.

Benvill Lane soon stretched before him, its hedges and trees purple with buds; but he was looking at other things, and only recalled himself to the scene sufficiently to enable him to keep the way. In something less than an hour-and-a-half he had skirted the south of the King's Hintock estates and ascended to the untoward solitude of Cross-in-Hand, the unholy stone whereon Tess had been compelled by Alec d'Urberville, in his whim of reformation, to swear the strange oath that she would never wilfully tempt him again. The pale and blasted nettle-stems of the preceding year even now lingered nakedly in the banks, young green nettles of the present spring growing from their roots.

Thence he went along the verge of the upland overhanging the other Hintocks, and, turning to the right, plunged into the bracing calcareous region of Flintcomb-Ash, the address from which she had written to him in one of the letters, and which he supposed to be the place of sojourn referred to by her mother. Here, of course, he did not find her; and what added to his depression was the discovery that no 'Mrs Clare' had ever been heard of by the cottagers or by the farmer himself, though Tess was remembered well enough by her Christian name. His name she had obviously never used during their separation, and her dignified sense of their total severance was shown not much less by this abstention than by the hardships she had chosen to undergo (of which he now learnt for the first time) rather than apply to his father for more funds.

From this place they told him Tess Durbeyfield had gone, without due notice, to the home of her parents on the other side of Blackmoor, and it therefore became necessary to find Mrs Durbeyfield. She had told him she was not now at Marlott, but had been curiously reticent as to her actual address, and the only course was to go to Marlott and inquire for it. The farmer who had been so churlish with Tess was quite smooth-tongued to Clare, and lent him a horse and man to drive him towards Marlott, the gig he had arrived in being sent back to Emminster; for the limit of a day's journey with that horse was reached.

Clare would not accept the loan of the farmer's vehicle for a further distance than to the outskirts of the Vale, and, sending it back with the man who had driven him, he put up at an inn, and next day entered on foot the region wherein was the spot of his dear Tess's birth. It was as yet too early in the year for much colour to appear in the gardens and foliage; the so-called spring was but winter overlaid with a thin coat of greenness, and it was of a parcel with his expectations.

The house in which Tess had passed the years of her childhood was now inhabited by another family who had never known her. The new residents were in the garden, taking as much interest in their own doings as if the homestead had never passed its primal time in conjunction with the histories of others, beside which the histories of these were but as a tale told by an idiot. They walked about the garden paths with thoughts of their own concerns entirely uppermost, bringing their actions at every moment into jarring collision with the dim ghosts behind them, talking as though the time when Tess lived there were not one whit intenser in story than now. Even the spring birds sang over their heads as if they thought there was nobody missing in particular.

On inquiry of these precious innocents, to whom even the name of their predecessors was a failing memory, Clare learned that John Durbeyfield was dead; that his widow and children had left Marlott, declaring that they were going to live at Kingsbere, but instead of doing so had gone on to another place they mentioned. By this time Clare abhorred the house for ceasing to contain Tess, and hastened away from its hated presence without once looking back.

His way was by the field in which he had first beheld her at the dance. It was as bad as the house – even worse. He passed on through the churchyard, where, amongst the new headstones, he saw one of a somewhat superior design to the rest. The inscription ran thus:

In memory of John Durbeyfield, rightly d'Urberville, of the once powerful family of that Name, and Direct Descendant through an Illustrious Line from Sir Pagan d'Urberville, one of the Knights of the Conqueror. Died March 10th, 18—

HOW ARE THE MIGHTY FALLEN

Some man apparently the sexton, had observed Clare standing there, and drew nigh. 'Ah, sir, now that's a man who didn't want to lie here, but wished to be carried to Kingsbere, where his ancestors be.'

'And why didn't they respect his wish?'

'Oh – no money. Bless your soul, sir, why – there, I wouldn't wish to say it everywhere, but – even this headstone, for all the flourish wrote upon en, is not paid for.'

'Ah, who put it up?'

The man told the name of a mason in the village, and, on leaving the churchyard, Clare called at the mason's house. He found that the statement was true, and paid the bill. This done he turned in the direction of the migrants.

The distance was too long for a walk, but Clare felt such a strong desire for isolation that at first he would neither hire a conveyance nor go to a circuitous line of railway by which he might eventually reach the place. At Shaston, however, he found he must hire; but the way was such that he did not enter Joan's place till about seven o'clock in the evening, having traversed a distance of over twenty miles since leaving Marlott.

The village being small he had little difficulty in finding Mrs Durbeyfield's tenement, which was a house in a walled garden, remote from the main road, where she had stowed away her clumsy old furniture as best she could. It was plain that for some reason or other she had not wished him to visit her, and he felt his call to be somewhat of an intrusion. She came to the door herself, and the light from the evening sky fell upon her face.

This was the first time that Clare had ever met her, but he was too preoccupied to observe more than that she was still a handsome woman, in the garb of a respectable widow. He was obliged to explain that he was Tess's husband, and his object in coming there, and he did it awkwardly enough. 'I want to see her at once,' he added. 'You said you would write to me again, but you have not done so.'

'Because she've not come home,' said Joan.

'Do you know if she is well?'

'I don't. But you ought to, sir,' said she.

'I admit it. Where is she staying?'

From the beginning of the interview Joan had disclosed her embarrassment by keeping her hand to the side of her cheek.

'I – don't know exactly where she is staying,' she answered. 'She was – but –'

'Where was she?'

'Well, she is not there now.'

In her evasiveness she paused again, and the younger children had by this time crept to the door, where, pulling at his mother's skirts, the youngest murmured –

'Is this the gentleman who is going to marry Tess?'

'He has married her,' Joan whispered. 'Go inside.'

Clare saw her efforts for reticence, and asked –

'Do you think Tess would wish me to try and find her? If not, of course—'

'I don't think she would.'

'Are you sure?'

'I am sure she wouldn't.'

He was turning away; and then he thought of Tess's tender letter.

'I am sure she would!' he retorted passionately. 'I know her better than you do.'

'That's very likely, sir; for I have never really known her.'

'Please tell me her address, Mrs Durbeyfield, in kindness to a lonely wretched man!'

Tess's mother again restlessly swept her cheek with her vertical hand, and seeing that he suffered, she at last said, in a low voice –

'She is at Sandbourne.'

'Ah – where there? Sandbourne has become a large place, they say.'

'I don't know more particularly than I have said – Sandbourne. For myself, I was never there.'

It was apparent that Joan spoke the truth in this, and he pressed her no further.

'Are you in want of anything?' he said gently.

'No, sir,' she replied. 'We are fairly well provided for.'

Without entering the house Clare turned away. There was a station three miles ahead, and paying off his coachman, he walked thither. The last train to Sandbourne left shortly after, and it bore Clare on its wheels.

CHAPTER FIFTY-FIVE

At eleven o'clock that night, having secured a bed at one of the hotels and telegraphed his address to his father immediately on his arrival, he walked out into the streets of Sandbourne. It was too late to call on or inquire for any one, and he reluctantly postponed his purpose till the morning. But he could not retire to rest just yet.

This fashionable watering-place, with its eastern and its western stations, its piers, its groves of pines, its promenades, and its covered gardens, was, to Angel Clare, like a fairy place suddenly created by the stroke of a wand, and allowed to get a little dusty. An out-lying eastern tract of the enormous Egdon Waste was close at hand, yet on the very verge of that tawny piece of antiquity such a glittering novelty as this pleasure city had chosen to spring up. Within the space of a mile from its outskirts every irregularity of the soil was prehistoric, every channel an undisturbed British trackway; not a sod having been turned there since the days of the Cæsars. Yet the exotic had grown here, suddenly as the prophet's gourd; and had drawn hither Tess.

By the midnight lamps he went up and down the winding ways of this new world in an old one, and could discern between the trees and against the stars the lofty roofs, chimneys, gazebos, and towers of the numerous fanciful residences of which the place was composed. It was a city of detached mansions; a Mediterranean lounging-place on the English Channel; and as seen now by night it seemed even more imposing than it was.

The sea was near at hand, but not intrusive: it murmured, and he thought it was the pines; the pines murmured in precisely the same tones, and he thought they were the sea.

Where could Tess possibly be, a cottage-girl, his young wife, amidst all this wealth and fashion? The more he pondered the more was he puzzled. Were there any cows to milk here? There certainly were no fields to till. She was most probably engaged to do something in one of these large houses; and he sauntered along, looking at the chamber-windows and their lights going out one by one; and wondered which of them might be hers.

Conjecture was useless, and just after twelve o'clock he entered and went to bed. Before putting out his light he re-read Tess's impassioned letter. Sleep, however, he could not — so near her, yet so far from her — and he continually lifted the window-blind and regarded the backs of the opposite houses, and wondered behind which of the sashes she reposed at that moment.

He might almost as well have sat up all night. In the morning he arose at seven, and shortly after went out, taking the direction of the chief post-office. At the door he met an intelligent postman coming out with letters for the morning delivery.

'Do you know the address of a Mrs Clare?' asked Angel.

The postman shook his head.

Then, remembering that she would have been likely to continue the use of her maiden name, Clare said –

'Or a Miss Durbeyfield?'

'Durbeyfield?'

This also was strange to the postman addressed.

'There's visitors coming and going every day, as you know, sir,' he said; 'and without the name of the house 'tis impossible to find 'em'

One of his comrades hastening out at that moment, the name was repeated to him.

'I know no name of Durbeyfield; but there is the name of d'Urberville at The Herons,' said the second.

'That's it!' cried Clare, pleased to think that she had reverted to the real pronunciation. 'What place is The Herons?'

'A stylish lodging-house. 'Tis all lodging-houses here, bless 'ee.'

Clare received directions how to find the house, and hastened thither, arriving with the milkman. The Herons, though an ordinary villa, stood in its own grounds, and was certainly the last place in which one would have expected to find lodgings, so private was its appearance. If poor Tess was a servant here, as he feared, she would go to the back-door to that milkman, and he was inclined to go thither also. However, in his doubts he turned to the front, and rang.

The hour being early the landlady herself opened the door. Clare inquired for Teresa d'Urberville or Durbeyfield.

'Mrs d'Urberville?'

'Yes.'

Tess, then, passed as a married woman, and he felt glad, even though she had not adopted his name.

'Will you kindly tell her that a relative is anxious to see her?'

'It is rather early. What name shall I give, sir?'

'Angel.'

'Mr Angel?'

'No; Angel. It is my Christian name. She'll understand.'

'I'll see if she is awake.'

He was shown into the front room – the dining-room – and looked out through the spring curtains at the little lawn, and the rhododendrons and other shrubs upon it. Obviously her position was by no means so bad as he had feared, and it crossed his mind that she must somehow have claimed and sold the jewels to attain it. He did not blame her for one moment. Soon his sharpened ear detected footsteps upon the stairs, at which his heart thumped so painfully that he could hardly stand firm. 'Dear me! what will she think of me, so altered as I am!' he said to himself; and the door opened.

Tess appeared on the threshold – not at all as he had expected to see her – bewilderingly otherwise, indeed. Her great natural beauty was, if not heightened, rendered more obvious by her attire. She was loosely wrapped in a cashmere dressing-gown of gray-white, embroidered in half-mourning tints, and she wore slippers of the same hue. Her neck rose out of a frill of down, and her well-remembered cable of dark-brown hair was partially coiled up in a mass at the back of her head and partly hanging on her shoulder – the evident result of haste.

He had held out his arms, but they had fallen again to his side; for she had not come forward, remaining still in the opening of the doorway. Mere yellow skeleton that he was now he felt the contrast between them, and thought his appearance distasteful to her.

'Tess!' he said huskily, 'can you forgive me for going away? Can't you – come to me? How do you get to be – like this?'

'It is too late,' said she, her voice sounding hard through the room, her eyes shining unnaturally.

'I did not think rightly of you – I did not see you as you were!' he continued to plead. 'I have learnt to since, dearest Tessy mine!'

'Too late, too late!' she cried, waving her hand in the impatience of a person whose tortures cause every instant to seem an hour. 'Don't come close to me, Angel! No – you must not. Keep away.'

'But don't you love me, my dear wife, because I have been so pulled down by illness? You are not so fickle – I am come on purpose for you – my mother and father will welcome you now!'

'Yes – O, yes, yes! But I say, I say it is too late.'

She seemed to feel like a fugitive in a dream, who tries to move away, but cannot. 'Don't you know all – don't you know it? Yet how do you come here if you do not know?'

'I inquired here and there, and I found the way.'

'I waited and waited for you,' she went on, her tones suddenly resuming their old fluty pathos. 'But you did not come! And I wrote to you, and you did not come! He kept on saying you would never come any more, and that I was a foolish woman. He was very kind to me, and to mother, and to all of us after father's death. He—'

'I don't understand.'

'He has won me back to him.'

Clare looked at her keenly, then, gathering her meaning, flagged like one plague-stricken, and his glance sank; it fell on her hands, which, once rosy, were now white and more delicate.

She continued –

'He is upstairs. I hate him now, because he told me a lie – that you would not come again; and you *have* come! These clothes are what he's put upon me: I didn't care what he did wi' me! But – will you go away, Angel, please, and never come any more?'

They stood fixed, their baffled hearts looking out of their eyes with a joylessness pitiful to see. Both seemed to implore something to shelter them from reality.

'Ah – it is my fault!' said Clare.

But he could not get on. Speech was as inexpressive as silence. But he had a vague consciousness of one thing, though it was not clear to him till later; that his original Tess had spiritually ceased to recognize the body before him as hers – allowing it to drift, like a corpse upon the current, in a direction dissociated from its living will.

A few instants passed, and he found that Tess was gone. His face grew colder and more shrunken as he stood concentrated on the moment, and a minute or two after he found himself in the street, walking along he did not know whither.

CHAPTER FIFTY-SIX

MRS BROOKS, the lady who was the householder at The Herons, and owner of all the handsome furniture, was not a person of an unusually curious turn of mind. She was too deeply materialized, poor woman, by her long and enforced bondage to that arithmetical demon Profit-and-Loss, to retain much curiosity for its own sake, and apart from possible lodgers' pockets. Nevertheless, the visit of Angel Clare to her well-paying tenants, Mr and Mrs d'Urberville, as she deemed them, was sufficiently exceptional in point of time and manner to reinvigorate the feminine proclivity which had been stifled down as useless save in its bearings on the letting trade.

Tess had spoken to her husband from the doorway, without entering the dining-room, and Mrs Brooks, who stood within the partly-closed door of her own sitting-room at the back of the passage, could hear fragments of the conversation – if conversation it could be called – between those two wretched souls. She heard Tess re-ascend the stairs to the first floor, and the departure of Clare, and the closing of the front door behind him. Then the door of the room above was shut, and Mrs Brooks knew that Tess had re-entered her apartment. As the young lady was not fully dressed Mrs Brooks knew that she would not emerge again for some time.

She accordingly ascended the stairs softly, and stood at the door of the front room – a drawing-room, connected with the room immediately behind it (which was a bedroom) by folding-doors in the common manner. This first floor, containing Mrs Brooks's best apartments, had been taken by the week by the d'Urbervilles. The back room was now in silence; but from the drawing-room there came sounds.

All that she could at first distinguish of them was one syllable, continually repeated in a low note of moaning, as if it came from a soul bound to some Ixionian wheel –

'O – O – O!'

Then a silence, then a heavy sigh, and again –

'O – O – O!'

The landlady looked through the keyhole. Only a small space of the room inside was visible, but within that space came a corner of the breakfast table, which was already spread for the meal, and also a chair beside. Over the seat of the chair Tess's face was bowed, her posture being a kneeling one in front of it; her hands were clasped over her head, the skirts of her dressing-gown and the embroidery of her night-gown flowed upon the floor behind her, and her stockingless feet, from which the slippers had fallen, protruded upon the carpet. It was from her lips that came the murmur of unspeakable despair.

Then a man's voice from the adjoining bedroom –

'What's the matter?'

She did not answer, but went on, in a tone which was a soliloquy rather than an exclamation, and a dirge rather than a soliloquy. Mrs Brooks could only catch a portion:

'And then my dear, dear husband came home to me . . . and I did not know it! . . . And you had used your cruel persuasion upon me . . . you did not stop using it – no – you did not stop! My little sisters and brothers and my mother's needs – they were the things you moved me by . . . and you said my husband would never come back – never; and you taunted me, and said what a simpleton I was to expect him! . . . And at last I believed you and gave way! . . . And then he came back! Now he is gone. Gone a second time, and I have lost him now for ever . . . and he will not love me the littlest bit ever any more – only hate me! . . . O yes, I have lost him now – again because of – you!' In writhing, with her head on the chair, she turned her face towards the door, and Mrs Brooks could see the pain upon it; and that her lips were bleeding from the clench of her teeth upon them, and that the long lashes of her closed eyes stuck in wet tags to her cheeks. She continued: 'And he is dying – he looks as if he is dying! . . . And my sin will kill him and not kill me! . . . O, you have torn my life all to pieces . . . made me be what I prayed you in pity not to make me be again! . . . My own true husband will never, never – O God – I can't bear this! – I cannot!'

There were more and sharper words from the man; then a sudden rustle; and she had sprung to her feet. Mrs Brooks, thinking that the speaker was coming to rush out of the door, hastily retreated down the stairs.

She need not have done so, however, for the door of the sitting-room was not opened. But Mrs Brooks felt it unsafe to watch on the landing again, and entered her own parlour below.

She could hear nothing through the floor, although she listened intently, and thereupon went to the kitchen to finish her interrupted breakfast. Coming up presently to the front room on the ground floor she took up some sewing, waiting for her lodgers to ring that she might take away the breakfast, which she meant to do herself, to discover what was the matter if possible. Overhead, as she sat, she could now hear the floorboards slightly creak, as if some one were walking about, and presently the movement was explained by the rustle of garments against the banisters, the opening and the closing of the front door, and the form of Tess passing to the gate on her way into the street. She was fully dressed now in the walking costume of a well-to-do young lady in which she had arrived, with the sole addition that over her hat and black feathers a veil was drawn.

Mrs Brooks had not been able to catch any word of farewell, temporary or otherwise, between her tenants at the door above. They might have quarrelled, or Mr d'Urberville might still be asleep, for he was not an early riser.

She went into the back room which was more especially her own apartment, and continued her sewing there. The lady lodger did not return, nor did the gentleman ring his bell. Mrs Brooks pondered on the delay, and on what probable relation the visitor who had called so early bore to the couple upstairs. In reflecting she leant back in her chair.

As she did so her eyes glanced casually over the ceiling till they were arrested by a spot in the middle of its white surface which she had never noticed there before. It was about the size of a wafer when she first observed it, but it speedily grew as large as the palm of her hand, and then she could perceive that it was red. The oblong white ceiling, with this scarlet blot in the midst, had the appearance of a gigantic ace of hearts.

Mrs Brooks had strange qualms of misgiving. She got upon the table, and touched the spot in the ceiling with her fingers. It was damp, and she fancied that it was a blood stain.

Descending from the table, she left the parlour, and went upstairs, intending to enter the room overhead, which was the bed-chamber at the back of the drawing-room. But, nerveless woman as she had now become, she could not bring herself to attempt the handle. She listened. The dead silence within was broken only by a regular beat.

Drip, drip, drip.

Mrs Brooks hastened downstairs, opened the front door, and ran into the street. A man she knew, one of the workmen employed at an adjoining villa, was passing by, and she begged him to come in and go upstairs with her; she feared something had happened to one of her lodgers. The workman assented, and followed her to the landing.

She opened the door of the drawing-room, and stood back for him to pass in, entering herself behind him. The room was empty; the breakfast – a substantial repast of coffee, eggs, and a cold ham – lay spread upon the table untouched, as when she had taken it up, excepting that the carving knife was missing. She asked the man to go through the folding-doors into the adjoining room.

He opened the doors, entered a step or two, and came back almost instantly with a rigid face. 'My good God, the gentleman in bed is dead! I think he has been hurt with a knife – a lot of blood has run down upon the floor!'

The alarm was soon given, and the house which had lately been so quiet resounded with the tramp of many footsteps, a surgeon among the rest. The wound was small, but the point of the blade had touched the heart of the victim, who lay on his back, pale, fixed, dead, as if he had scarcely moved after the infliction of the blow. In a quarter of an hour the news that a gentleman who was a temporary visitor to the town had been stabbed in his bed, spread through every street and villa of the popular watering-place.

CHAPTER FIFTY-SEVEN

MEANWHILE Angel Clare had walked automatically along the way by which he had come, and entering his hotel, sat down over the breakfast, staring at nothingness. He went on eating and drinking unconsciously till on a sudden he demanded his bill; having paid which he took his dressing-bag in his hand, the only luggage he had brought with him, and went out.

At the moment of his departure a telegram was handed to him – a few words from his mother, stating that they were glad to know his address, and informing him that his brother Cuthbert had proposed to and been accepted by Mercy Chant.

Clare crumpled up the paper, and followed the route to the station; reaching it, he found that there would be no train leaving for an hour or more. He sat down to wait, and having waited a quarter of an hour felt that he could wait there no longer. Broken in heart and numbed, he had nothing to hurry for; but he wished to get out of a town which had been the scene of such an experience, and turned to walk to the first station onward, and let the train pick him up there.

The highway that he followed was open, and at a little distance dipped into a valley, across which it could be seen running from edge to edge. He had traversed the greater part of this depression, and was climbing the western acclivity, when, pausing for breath, he unconsciously looked back. Why he did so he could not say, but something seemed to impel him to the act. The tape-like surface of the road diminished in his rear as far as he could see, and as he gazed a moving spot intruded on the white vacuity of its perspective.

It was a human figure running. Clare waited, with a dim sense that somebody was trying to overtake him.

The form descending the incline was a woman's, yet so entirely was his mind blinded to the idea of his wife's following him that even when she came nearer he did not recognize her under the totally changed attire in which he now beheld her. It was not till she was quite close that he could believe her to be Tess.

'I saw you – turn away from the station – just before I got there – and I have been following you all this way!'

She was so pale, so breathless, so quivering in every muscle, that he did not ask her a single question, but seizing her hand, and pulling it within his arm, he led her along. To avoid meeting any possible wayfarers he left the high road, and took a footpath under some fir-trees. When they were deep among the moaning boughs he stopped and looked at her inquiringly.

'Angel,' she said, as if waiting for this, 'do you know what I have been running after you for? To tell you that I have killed him!' A pitiful white smile lit her face as she spoke.

'What!' said he, thinking from the strangeness of her manner that she was in some delirium.

I have done it – I don't know how,' she continued. 'Still, I owed it to you, and to myself, Angel. I feared long ago, when I struck him on the mouth with my glove, that I might do it someday for the trap he set for me in my simple youth, and his wrong to you through me. He has come between us and ruined us, and now he can never do it any more. I never loved him at all, Angel, as I loved you. You know it, don't you? You believe it? You didn't come back to me, and I was obliged to go back to him. Why did you go away – why did you – when I loved you so? I can't think why you did it. But I don't blame you; only, Angel, will you forgive me my sin against you, now I have killed him? I thought as I ran along that you would be sure to forgive me now I have done that. It came to me as a shining light that I should get you back that way. I could not bear the loss of you any longer – you don't know how entirely I was unable to bear your not loving me! Say you do now, dear, dear husband; say you do, now I have killed him!'

'I do love you, Tess – O, I do – it is all come back!' he said, tightening his arms round her with fervid pressure. 'But how do you mean – you have killed him?'

'I mean that I have,' she murmured in a reverie.

'What, bodily? Is he dead?'

'Yes. He heard me crying about you, and he bitterly taunted me; and called you by a foul name; and then I did it. My heart could not bear it. He had nagged me about you before. And then I dressed myself and came away to find you.'

By degrees he was inclined to believe that she had faintly attempted, at least, what she said she had done; and his horror at her impulse was mixed with amazement at the strength of her affection for himself, and at the strangeness of its quality, which had apparently extinguished her moral sense altogether. Unable to realize the gravity of her conduct she seemed at last content; and he looked at her as she lay upon his shoulder, weeping with happiness, and wondered what obscure strain in the d'Urberville blood had led to this aberration – if it were an aberration. There momentarily flashed through his mind that the family tradition of the coach and murder might have arisen because the d'Urbervilles had been known to do these things. As well as his confused and excited ideas could reason, he supposed that in the moment of mad grief of which she spoke her mind had lost its balance, and plunged her into this abyss.

It was very terrible if true; if a temporary hallucination, sad. But, anyhow, here was this deserted wife of his, this passionately-fond woman, clinging to him without a suspicion that he would be anything to her but a protector. He saw that for him to be otherwise was not, in her mind, within the region of the possible. Tenderness was absolutely dominant in Clare at last. He kissed her endlessly with his white lips, and held her hand, and said –

'I will not desert you! I will protect you by every means in my power, dearest love, whatever you may have done or not have done!'

They then walked on under the trees, Tess turning her head every now and then to look at him. Worn and unhandsome as he had become, it was plain that she did not discern the least fault in his appearance. To her he was, as of old, all that was perfection, personally and mentally. He was still her Antinous, her Apollo even; his sickly face was beautiful as the morning to her affectionate regard on this day no less than when she first beheld him; for was it not the face of the one man on earth who had loved her purely, and who had believed in her as pure.

With an instinct as to possibilities he did not now, as he had intended, make for the first station beyond the town, but plunged still farther under the firs, which here abounded for miles. Each clasping the other round the waist they promenaded over the dry bed of fir-needles, thrown into a vague intoxicating atmosphere at the consciousness of being together at last, with no living soul between them; ignoring that there was a corpse. Thus they proceeded for several miles till Tess, arousing herself, looked about her, and said, timidly –

'Are we going anywhere in particular?'

'I don't know, dearest. Why?'

'I don't know.'

'Well, we might walk a few miles further, and when it is evening find lodgings somewhere or other – in a lonely cottage, perhaps. Can you walk well, Tessy?'

'O yes! I could walk for ever and ever with your arm round me!'

Upon the whole it seemed a good thing to do. Thereupon they quickened their pace, avoiding high roads, and following obscure paths tending more or less northward. But there was an unpractical vagueness in their movements throughout the day; neither one of them seemed to consider any question of effectual escape, disguise, or long concealment. Their every idea was temporary and unforfending, like the plans of two children.

At mid-day they drew near to a roadside inn, and Tess would have entered it with him to get something to eat, but he persuaded her to remain among the trees and bushes of this half-woodland, half-moorland part of the country, till he should come back. Her clothes were of recent fashion; even the ivory handled parasol that she carried was of a shape unknown in the retired spot to which they had now wandered; and the cut of such articles would have attracted attention in the settle of a tavern. He soon returned, with food enough for half-a-dozen people and two bottles of wine – enough to last them for a day or more, should any emergency arise.

They sat down upon some dead boughs and shared their meal. Between one and two o'clock they packed up the remainder and went on again.

'I feel strong enough to walk any distance,' said she.

'I think we may as well steer in a general way towards the interior of the country, where we can hide for a time, and are less likely to be looked for than anywhere near the coast,' Clare remarked. 'Later on, when they have forgotten us, we can make for some port.'

She made no reply to this beyond that of grasping him more tightly, and straight inland they went. Though the season was an English May the weather was serenely bright, and during the afternoon it was quite warm. Through the latter miles of their walk their footpath had taken them into the depths of the New Forest, and towards evening, turning the corner of a lane, they perceived behind a brook and bridge a large board on which was painted in white letters, 'This desirable Mansion to be Let Furnished'; particulars following, with directions to apply to some London agents. Passing through the gate they could see the house, an old brick building of regular design and large accommodation.

'I know it,' said Clare. 'It is Bramshurst Court. You can see that it is shut up, and grass is growing on the drive.'

'Some of the windows are open,' said Tess.

'Just to air the rooms, I suppose.'

'All these rooms empty, and we without a roof to our heads!'

'You are getting tired, my Tess!' he said. 'We'll stop soon.' And kissing her sad mouth he again led her onwards.

He was growing weary likewise, for they had wandered a dozen or fifteen miles, and it became necessary to consider what they should do for rest. They looked from afar at isolated cottages and little inns, and were inclined to approach one of the latter, when their hearts failed them, and they sheered off. At length their gait dragged, and they stood still.

'Could we sleep under the trees?' she asked.

He thought the season insufficiently advanced.

'I have been thinking of that empty mansion we passed,' he said. 'Let us go back towards it again.'

They retraced their steps, but it was half an hour before they stood without the entrance-gate as earlier. He then requested her to stay where she was, whilst he went to see who was within.

She sat down among the bushes within the gate, and Clare crept towards the house. His absence lasted some considerable time, and when he returned Tess was wildly anxious, not for herself, but for him. He had found out from a boy that there was only an old woman in charge as caretaker, and she only came there on fine days, from the hamlet near, to open and shut the windows. She would come to shut them at sunset. 'Now, we can get in through one of the lower windows, and rest there,' said he.

Under his escort she went tardily forward to the main front, whose shuttered windows, like sightless eyeballs, excluded the possibility of watchers. The door was reached a few steps further, and one of the windows beside it was open. Clare clambered in, and pulled Tess in after him.

Except the hall the rooms were all in darkness, and they ascended the staircase. Up here also the shutters were tightly closed, the ventilation being perfunctorily done, for this day at least, by opening the hall-window in front and an upper window behind. Clare unlatched the door of a large chamber, felt his way across it, and parted the shutters to the width of two or three inches. A shaft of dazzling sunlight glanced into the room, revealing heavy, old fashioned furniture, crimson damask hangings, and an enormous four-post bedstead, along the head of which were carved running figures, apparently Atalanta's race.

'Rest at last!' said he, setting down his bag and the parcel of viands.

They remained in great quietness till the caretaker should have come to shut the windows: as a precaution, putting themselves in total darkness by barring the shutters as before, lest the woman should open the door of their chamber for any casual reason. Between six and seven o'clock she came, but did not approach the wing they were in. They heard her close the windows, fasten them, lock the door, and go away. Then Clare again stole a chink of light from the window, and they shared another meal, till by-and-by they were enveloped in the shades of night which they had no candle to disperse.

CHAPTER FIFTY-EIGHT

THE night was strangely solemn and still. In the small hours she whispered to him the whole story of how he had walked in his sleep with her in his arms across the Froom stream, at the imminent risk of both their lives, and laid her down in the stone coffin at the ruined abbey. He had never known of that till now.

'Why didn't you tell me the next day?' he said. 'It might have prevented much misunderstanding and woe.'

'Don't think of what's past!' said she. 'I am not going to think outside of now. Why should we! Who knows what to-morrow has in store?'

But it apparently had no sorrow. The morning was wet and foggy, and Clare, rightly informed that the caretaker only opened the windows on fine days, ventured to creep out of their chamber, and explore the house, leaving Tess asleep. There was no food on the premises, but there was water, and he took advantage of the fog to emerge from the mansion, and fetch tea, bread, and butter from a shop in a little place two miles beyond, as also a small tin kettle and spirit-lamp, that they might get fire without smoke. His re-entry awoke her; and they breakfasted on what he had brought.

They were indisposed to stir abroad, and the day passed, and the night following, and the next, and next; till, almost without their being aware, five days had slipped by in absolute seclusion, not a sight or sound of a human being disturbing their peacefulness, such as it was. The changes of the weather were their only events, the birds of the New Forest their only company. By tacit consent they hardly once spoke of any incident of the past subsequent to their wedding-day. The gloomy intervening time seemed to sink into chaos, over which the present and prior times closed as if it never had been. Whenever he suggested that they should leave their shelter, and go forwards towards Southampton or London, she showed a strange unwillingness to move.

'Why should we put an end to all that's sweet and lovely!' she deprecated. 'What must come will come.' And, looking through the shutter-chink: 'All is trouble outside there; inside here content.'

He peeped out also. It was quite true; within was affection, union, error forgiven: outside was the inexorable.

'And – and,' she said, pressing her cheek against his; 'I fear that what you think of me now may not last. I do not wish to outlive your present feeling for me. I would rather not. I would rather be dead and buried when the time comes for you to despise me, so that it may never be known to me that you despised me.'

'I cannot ever despise you.'

'I also hope that. But considering what my life has been I cannot see why any man should, sooner or later, be able to help despising me. . . . How wickedly mad I was! Yet formerly I never could bear to hurt a fly or a worm, and the sight of a bird in a cage used often to make me cry.'

They remained yet another day. In the night the dull sky cleared, and the result was that the old caretaker at the cottage awoke early. The brilliant sunrise made her unusually brisk; she decided to open the contiguous mansion immediately, and to air it thoroughly on such a day. Thus it occurred that, having arrived and opened the lower rooms before six o'clock, she ascended to the bedchambers, and was about to turn the handle of the one wherein they lay. At that moment she fancied she could hear the breathing of persons within. Her slippers and her antiquity had rendered her progress a noiseless one so far, and she made for instant retreat; then, deeming that her hearing might have deceived her, she turned anew to the door and softly tried the handle. The lock was out of order, but a piece of furniture had been moved forward on the inside, which prevented her opening the door more than an inch or two. A stream of morning light through the shutter-chink fell upon the faces of the pair, wrapped in profound slumber, Tess's lips being parted like a half-opened flower near his cheek. The caretaker was so struck with their innocent appearance, and with the elegance of Tess's gown hanging across a chair, her silk stockings beside it, the pretty parasol, and the other habits in which she had arrived because she had none else, that her first indignation at the effrontery of tramps and vagabonds gave way to a momentary sentimentality over this genteel elopement, as it seemed. She closed the door, and withdrew as softly as she had come, to go and consult with her neighbours on the odd discovery.

Not more than a minute had elapsed after her withdrawal when Tess woke, and then Clare. Both had a sense that something had disturbed them, though they could not say what; and the uneasy feeling which it engendered grew stronger. As soon as he was dressed he narrowly scanned the lawn through the two or three inches of shutter-chink.

'I think we will leave at once,' said he. 'It is a fine day. And I cannot help fancying somebody is about the house. At any rate, the woman will be sure to come to-day.'

She passively assented, and putting the room in order they took up the few articles that belonged to them, and departed noiselessly. When they had got into the Forest she turned to take a last look at the house.

'Ah, happy house – good-bye!' she said. 'My life can only be a question of a few weeks. Why should we not have stayed there?'

'Don't say it, Tess! We shall soon get out of this district altogether. We'll continue our course as we've begun it, and keep straight north. Nobody will think of looking for us there. We shall be looked for at the Wessex ports if we are sought at all. When we are in the north we will get to a port and away.'

Having thus persuaded her the plan was pursued, and they kept a bee line northward. Their long repose at the manor-house lent them walking power now; and towards mid-day they found that they were approaching the steepled city of Melchester, which lay directly in their way. He decided to rest her in a clump of trees during the afternoon, and push onward under cover of darkness. At dusk Clare purchased food as usual, and their night march began, the boundary between Upper and Mid-Wessex being crossed about eight o'clock.

To walk across country without much regard to roads was not new to Tess, and she showed her old agility in the performance. The intercepting city, ancient Melchester, they were obliged to pass through in order to take advantage of the town bridge for crossing a large river that obstructed them. It was about midnight when they went along the deserted streets, lighted fitfully by the few lamps, keeping off the pavement that it might not echo their footsteps. The graceful pile of cathedral architecture rose dimly on their left hand, but it was lost upon them now. Once out of the town they followed the turnpike-road, which after a few miles plunged across an open plain.

Though the sky was dense with cloud a diffused light from some fragment of a moon had hitherto helped them a little. But the moon had now sunk, the clouds seemed to settle almost on their heads, and the night grew as dark as a cave. However, they found their way along, keeping as much on the turf as possible that their tread might not resound, which it was easy to do, there being no hedge or fence of any kind. All around was open loneliness and black solitude, over which a stiff breeze blew.

They had proceeded thus gropingly two or three miles further when on a sudden Clare became conscious of some vast erection close in his front, rising sheer from the grass. They had almost struck themselves against it.

'What monstrous place is this?' said Angel.

'It hums,' said she. 'Hearken!'

He listened. The wind, playing upon the edifice, produced a booming tune, like the note of some gigantic one-stringed harp. No other sound came from it, and lifting his hand and advancing a step or two, Clare felt the vertical surface of the structure. It seemed to be of solid stone, without joint or moulding. Carrying his fingers onward he found that what he had come in contact with was a colossal rectangular pillar; by stretching out his left hand he could feel a similar one adjoining. At an indefinite height overhead something made the black sky blacker, which had the semblance of a vast architrave uniting the pillars horizontally. They carefully entered beneath and between; the surfaces echoed their soft rustle; but they seemed to be still out of doors. The place was roofless. Tess drew her breath fearfully, and Angel, perplexed, said –

'What can it be?'

Feeling sideways they encountered another tower-like pillar, square and uncompromising as the first; beyond it another and another. The place was all doors and pillars, some connected above by continuous architraves.

'A very Temple of the Winds,' he said.

The next pillar was isolated; others composed a trilithon; others were prostrate, their flanks forming a causeway wide enough for a carriage; and it was soon obvious that they made up a forest of monoliths grouped upon the grassy expanse of the plain. The couple advanced further into this pavilion of the night till they stood in its midst.

'It is Stonehenge!' said Clare.

'The heathen temple, you mean?'

'Yes. Older than the centuries; older than the d'Urbervilles! Well, what shall we do, darling? We may find shelter further on.'

But Tess, really tired by this time, flung herself upon an oblong slab that lay close at hand, and was sheltered from the wind by a pillar. Owing to the action of the sun during the preceding day the stone was warm and dry, in comforting contrast to the rough and chill grass around, which had damped her skirts and shoes.

'I don't want to go any further, Angel,' she said stretching out her hand for his. 'Can't we bide here?'

'I fear not. This spot is visible for miles by day, although it does not seem so now.'

'One of my mother's people was a shepherd hereabouts, now I think of it. And you used to say at Talbothays that I was a heathen. So now I am at home.'

He knelt down beside her outstretched form, and put his lips upon hers.

'Sleepy are you, dear? I think you are lying on an altar.'

'I like very much to be here,' she murmured. 'It is so solemn and lonely –after my great happiness –with nothing but the sky above my face. It seems as if there were no folk in the world but we two; and I wish there were not –except 'Liza-Lu.'

Clare thought she might as well rest here till it should get a little lighter, and he flung his overcoat upon her, and sat down by her side.

'Angel, if anything happens to me, will you watch over 'Liza-Lu for my sake?' she asked, when they had listened a long time to the wind among the pillars.

'I will.'

'She is so good and simple and pure. O, Angel – I wish you would marry her if you lose me, as you will do shortly. O, if you would!'

'If I lose you I lose all! And she is my sister-in-law.'

'That's nothing, dearest. People marry sister-laws continually about Marlott; and 'Liza-Lu is so gentle and sweet, and she is growing so beautiful. O I could share you with her willingly when we are spirits! If you would train her and teach her, Angel, and bring her up for your own self! . . . She has all the best of me without the bad of me; and if she were to become yours it would almost seem as if death had not divided us. . . . Well, I have said it. I won't mention it again.'

She ceased, and he fell into thought. In the far north-east sky he could see between the pillars a level streak of light. The uniform concavity of black cloud was lifting bodily like the lid of a pot, letting in at the earth's edge the coming day, against which the towering monoliths and trilithons began to be blackly defined.

'Did they sacrifice to God here?' asked she.

'No,' said he.

'Who to?'

'I believe to the sun. That lofty stone set away by itself is in the direction of the sun, which will presently rise behind it.'

'This reminds me, dear,' she said. 'You remember you never would interfere with any belief of mine before we were married? But I knew your mind all the same, and I thought as you thought—not from any reasons of my own, but because you thought so. Tell me now, Angel, do you think we shall meet again after we are dead? I want to know.'

He kissed her to avoid a reply at such a time.

'O, Angel—I fear that means no!' said she, with a suppressed sob. 'And I wanted so to see you again—so much, so much! What—not even you and I, Angel, who love each other so well?'

Like a greater than himself, to the critical question at the critical time he did not answer; and they were again silent. In a minute or two her breathing became more regular, her clasp of his hand relaxed, and she fell asleep. The band of silver paleness along the east horizon made even the distant parts of the Great Plain appear dark and near; and the whole enormous landscape bore that impress of reserve, taciturnity, and hesitation which is usual just before day. The eastward pillars and their architraves stood up blackly against the light, and the great flame-shaped Sun-stone beyond them; and the Stone of Sacrifice midway. Presently the night wind died out, and the quivering little pools in the cup-like hollows of the stones lay still. At the same time something seemed to move on the verge of the dip eastward—a mere dot. It was the head of a man approaching them from the hollow beyond the Sun-stone. Clare wished they had gone onward, but in the circumstnaces decided to remain quiet. The figure came straight towards the circle of the pillars in which they were.

He heard something behind him, the brush of feet. Turning, he saw over the prostrate columns another figure; then before he was aware, another was at hand on the right, under a trilithon, and another on the left. The dawn shone full on the front of the man westward, and Clare could discern from this that he was tall, and walked as if trained. They all closed in with evident purpose. Her story then was true! Springing to his feet, he looked around for a weapon, loose stone, means of escape, anything. By this time the nearest man was upon him.

'It is no use, sir,' he said. 'There are sixteen of us on the Plain, and the whole country is reared.'

'Let her finish her sleep!' he implored in a whisper of the men as they gathered round.

When they saw where she lay, which they had not done till then, they showed no objection, and stood watching her, as still as the pillars around. He went to the stone and bent over her, holding one poor little hand; her breathing now was quick and small, like that of a lesser creature than a woman. All waited in the growing light, their faces and hands as if they were silvered, the remainder of their figures dark, the stones glistening green-gray, the Plain still a mass of shade. Soon the light was strong, and a ray shone upon her unconscious form, peering under her eyelids and waking her.

'What is it, Angel?' she said, starting up. 'Have they come for me?'

'Yes, dearest,' he said. 'They have come.'

'It is as it should be,' she murmured. 'Angel, I am almost glad – yes, glad! This happiness could not have lasted. It was too much. I have had enough; and now I shall not live for you to despise me!'

She stood up, shook herself, and went forward, neither of the men having moved.

'I am ready,' she said quietly.

CHAPTER FIFTY-NINE

THE city of Wintoncester, that fine old city, aforetime capital of Wessex, lay amidst its convex and concave downlands in all the brightness and warmth of a July morning. The gabled brick, tile, and freestone houses had almost dried off for the season their integument of lichen, the streams in the meadows were low, and in the sloping High Street, from the West Gateway to the mediæval cross, and from the mediæval cross to the bridge, that leisurely dusting and sweeping was in progress which usually ushers in an old-fashioned market-day.

From the western gate aforesaid the highway, as every Wintoncestrian knows, ascends a long and regular incline of the exact length of a measured mile, leaving the houses gradually behind. Up this road from the precincts of the city two persons were walking rapidly, as if unconscious of the trying ascent – unconscious through preoccupation and not through buoyancy. They had emerged upon this road through a narrow barred wicket in a high wall a little lower down. They seemed anxious to get out of the sight of the houses and of their kind, and this road appeared to offer the quickest means of doing so. Though they were young they walked with bowed heads, which gait of grief the sun's rays smiled on pitilessly.

One of the pair was Angel Clare, the other a tall budding creature – half girl, half woman – a spiritualized image of Tess, slighter than she, but with the same beautiful eyes – Clare's sister-in-law, 'Liza-Lu. Their pale faces seemed to have shrunk to half their natural size. They moved on hand in hand, and never spoke a word, the drooping of their heads being that of Giotto's 'Two Apostles'.

When they had nearly reached the top of the great West Hill the clocks in the town struck eight. Each gave a start at the notes, and, walking onward yet a few steps, they reached the first milestone, standing whitely on the green margin of the grass, and backed by the down, which here was open to the road. They entered upon the turf, and, impelled by a force that seemed to overrule their will, suddenly stood still, turned, and waited in paralyzed suspense beside the stone.

The prospect from this summit was almost unlimited. In the valley beneath lay the city they had just left, its more prominent buildings showing as in an isometric drawing – among them the broad cathedral tower, with its Norman windows and immense length of aisle and nave, the spires of St Thomas's, the pinnacled tower of the College, and, more to the right, the tower and gables of the ancient hospice, where to this day the pilgrim may receive his dole of bread and ale. Behind the city swept the rotund upland of St Catherine's Hill; further off, landscape beyond landscape, till the horizon was lost in the radiance of the sun hanging above it.

Against these far stretches of country rose, in front of the other city edifices, a large red-brick building, with level gray roofs, and rows of short barred windows bespeaking captivity, the whole contrasting greatly by its formalism with the quaint irregularities of the Gothic erections. It was somewhat disguised from the road in passing it by yews and evergreen oaks, but it was visible enough up here. The wicket from which the pair had lately emerged was in the wall of this structure. From the middle of the building an ugly flat-topped octagonal tower ascended against the east horizon, and viewed from this spot, on its shady side and against the light, it seemed the one blot on the city's beauty. Yet it was with this blot, and not with the beauty, that the two gazers were concerned.

Upon the cornice of the tower a tall staff was fixed. Their eyes were riveted on it. A few minutes after the hour had struck something moved slowly up the staff, and extended itself upon the breeze. It was a black flag.

'Justice' was done, and the President of the Immortals, in Æschylean phrase, had ended his sport with Tess. And the d'Urberville knights and dames slept on in their tombs unknowing. The two speechless gazers bent themselves down to the earth, as if in prayer, and remained thus a long time, absolutely motionless: the flag continued to wave silently. As soon as they had strength they arose, joined hands again, and went on.